Pro Linux System Administration

Learn to Build Systems for Your Business
Using Free and Open Source Software

Second Edition

Dennis Matotek
James Turnbull
Peter Lieverdink

Apress®

Pro Linux System Administration: Learn to Build Systems for Your Business Using Free and Open Source Software

Dennis Matotek
Footscray, Victoria,
Australia

James Turnbull
Brooklyn, New York,
United States

Peter Lieverdink
North Melbourne, Victoria,
Australia

ISBN 978-1-4842-2007-8 (pbk)
DOI 10.1007/978-1-4842-2008-5

ISBN 978-1-4842-2008-5 (eBook)

Library of Congress Control Number: 2017935471

Managing Director: Welmoed Spahr
Editorial Director: Todd Green
Acquisitions Editor: Louise Corrigan
Development Editor: James Markham
Technical Reviewer: Sander van Vugt
Coordinating Editor: Nancy Chen
Copy Editors: Lori Jacobs and Kim Wimpsett
Compositor: SPi Global
Indexer: SPi Global
Artist: SPi Global

Distributed to the book trade worldwide by Springer Science+Business Media New York, 233 Spring Street, 6th Floor, New York, NY 10013. Phone 1-800-SPRINGER, fax (201) 348-4505, e-mail orders-ny@springer-sbm.com, or visit www.springeronline.com. Apress Media, LLC is a California LLC and the sole member (owner) is Springer Science + Business Media Finance Inc (SSBM Finance Inc). SSBM Finance Inc is a **Delaware** corporation.

For information on translations, please e-mail rights@apress.com, or visit www.apress.com/rights-permissions.

Apress titles may be purchased in bulk for academic, corporate, or promotional use. eBook versions and licenses are also available for most titles. For more information, reference our Print and eBook Bulk Sales web page at www.apress.com/bulk-sales.

Any source code or other supplementary material referenced by the author in this book is available to readers on GitHub via the book's product page, located at www.apress.com/9781484220078. For more detailed information, please visit www.apress.com/source-code.

Printed on acid-free paper

To Bianca, Ziggy, Anika, Othello, plus the cute little chickens.

And special thanks to Sander whose knowledge and advice were invaluable on this book.

—Dennis

Contents at a Glance

Contents

About the Authors

Dennis Matotek lives and works in Melbourne, Australia—possibly the birthplace of great coffee and the home to several exemplary coffeehouses and many, many average ones too.

He works as a senior development operations engineer at Envato, an online digital marketplace where a community of creatives can help bring ideas to life. There he helps a team of engineers deploy code, build infrastructure, and monitor performance for varying systems, mostly written in Rails. He usually works with AWS rather than bare metal and appreciates not having to change failed disks.

With two young children, Ziggy and Anika, he happily lives with his partner Bianca and a number of pets—one dog and six chickens.

James Turnbull is the CTO at Empatico, co-chair of O'Reilly's Velocity conference, an advisor at AccessNow and Docker Inc.

Previously CTO at Kickstarter, VP of Engineering at Venmo and was an early employee and executive at Docker and Puppet Labs.

He is a contributor to a number of open source projects and regularly speaks on topics related to writing, systems administration, and open source technologies. He is the author of several books: *https://terraformbook.com/*, *https://www.artofmonitoring.com/*, *https://www.dockerbook.com/*, *https://www.logstashbook.com/*, *Pro Puppet (Apress, 2011)*, *Pulling Strings with Puppet: Systems Administration Made Easy* (Apress, 2008), *Hardening Linux* (Apress, 2008), and *Pro Nagios 2.0* (Apress, 2006).

Peter Lieverdink was born in a small Dutch country town. He owns a pair of clogs but has never eaten tulips or lived in a windmill. On his 22nd birthday, Peter moved to Australia and briefly worked in an office cubicle. He now runs his own business, Creative Contingencies Pty, Ltd. The business depends on open source software for infrastructure and development as well as daily office tasks.

Peter specializes in web application development and helping other businesses implement open source solutions using Linux on both desktops and servers.

About the Technical Reviewer

Sander van Vugt is a best-selling author and technical trainer, living in the Netherlands. In his professional life, Sander focuses on enterprise Linux distributions and has authored several books and video courses about them. For more information, visit his web site, `www.sandervanvugt.com`.

PART I

■ ■ ■

The Beginning

CHAPTER 1

■ ■ ■

Introducing Linux

By James Turnbull, Peter Lieverdink, and Dennis Matotek

You've decided to learn more about System Administration or run your business on free and open source (FOSS) infrastructure? Congratulations and welcome to the world of Linux and open source software! This chapter will take you through the first steps into implementing that infrastructure. We cover choosing a platform or distribution, choosing appropriate and supported hardware, and finding the software you need. We also provide you with the location of some resources to help you support your Linux environment. Then, in Chapter 2, we'll show you how to install your first Linux hosts.

Linux Distributions

What is a Linux distribution? Well, in simple terms it is a collection of applications, packages, management, and features that run on top of the Linux kernel. The kernel is what all distributions have in common (it is sometimes customized by the distribution maintainers), but at their core they all run Linux.

■ **Note**   So what's a kernel, you ask? Don't panic, we'll fill you in. The *kernel* is the core of all computer operating systems and is usually the layer that allows the operating system to interact with the hardware in your computer. The kernel contains software that allows you to make use of your hard disk drives, network cards, RAM, and other hardware components. In the Linux world, the kernel is based on code originally developed by the founder of Linux, Finnish developer Linus Torvalds. The kernel is now maintained by a community of open source developers, and changes go through a software life-cycle process. Your distribution will come with a version of that kernel, and like Windows or other operating systems it can be updated and upgraded to provide new features or fix bugs.

The world of Linux distributions may at first seem a little confusing. You are probably thinking, "If they are all 'Linux,' why are there so many different names, and which do I choose?" You may have heard names like Red Hat, Fedora, Debian, and the more oddly titled Ubuntu (it's a Zulu word that loosely translates as "humanity toward others"!). In this section, we'll explain what a distribution is, describe the ways in which distributions differ, and suggest some strategies for selecting the right distribution for you.

© Dennis Matotek, James Turnbull and Peter Lieverdink 2017
D. Matotek et al., *Pro Linux System Administration*, DOI 10.1007/978-1-4842-2008-5_1

Distributions differ in several ways, and three of the most important are

- Purpose

- Configuration and packaging

- Support model

First, different distributions are often designed for different purposes and provide different user experiences. Some distributions are designed as servers and others as desktops, and some are designed to perform particular functions, for example, as embedded systems. The majority of Linux installations still tend to be servers. While more Linux desktops are appearing, the numbers do not yet challenge Windows and Apple OS X dominance of the desktop market.

The second major difference between distributions is in their configuration. While some distributions keep all their configuration settings and files in the same locations, others vary their locations. Additionally, the process of installing and updating applications (which are usually installed by a *package*) is not consistent across distributions. Many distributions use different application installation and management tools (generally called *package management tools*). This can be confusing and can make administration difficult if you have an environment with differing distributions. In Chapter 19, we'll look closely at configuration management tools and how to overcome these sorts of issues.

The third difference is that distributions also have differing support models. Some, like Debian, CentOS, and Fedora, are maintained by a community of volunteers. Others, like Red Hat Enterprise Linux and Ubuntu, are maintained and supported by a commercial vendor. The software is still open source, but you can pay for support and maintenance. Most commercial Linux vendors support themselves through the sale of maintenance and support services.

Let's look at some of the available choices; this won't be a comprehensive list, but we'll cover most of the major popular distributions and then present some reasons for selecting particular platforms. We'll also group together some of the like distributions, particularly focusing on distributions derived from two major distributions: CentOS (derived from the Red Hat distribution) and Ubuntu (itself a derivation from the Debian distribution).

■ **Note** So how can one distribution be "derived" from another distribution? Well, open source software means that the source code is available to developers. Developers can pick and choose the features they want in a distribution and potentially create their own distribution. Many of the major distributions appeared because a developer or group of developers decided to create their own version of another distribution. These new derivations often have their own branding and features. Some remain close to the parent distribution, and others follow their own path.

Red Hat Enterprise Linux

Red Hat Enterprise Linux (www.redhat.com/rhel/) is a popular commercially supported Linux platform. It comes in a number of versions, the two most common being Red Hat Enterprise Linux (also known as RHEL) and Red Hat Enterprise Linux Advanced Platform (RHELAP). The major difference between the versions is the number of CPUs (central processing units) supported, with RHEL supporting up to two CPUs and RHELAP supporting an unlimited number.

Red Hat platforms are commonly used by corporate organizations as server platforms due to the dedicated support and service levels available from the vendor. Red Hat, and most distributions based on it, make use of the Red Hat Package Management (RPM) packaging system.

At the time of writing, RHEL costs start at approximately $350 a year for basic support and range up to $1,500 for premium support. Its more advanced cousin, RHELAP, ranges in cost from $1,500 to $2,500+ per year depending on the hardware architecture and level of support desired. These costs provide you with technical support and any needed patches or updates to the distribution.

Red Hat used to be run by a community of volunteers too until the distribution became so important to the technical infrastructure of commercial organizations that people were happy to pay for guaranteed support. Their original volunteer community still lives on as the Fedora Project.

CentOS

CentOS (www.centos.org/) is a derivation of the Red Hat Enterprise Linux platform. Based on the same source code, it is available at no charge (and without Red Hat's support). People who wish to make use of the Red Hat platform and its stability without paying for additional support commonly use it. It employs the same packaging system, RPM, and many of the same administration tools as the Red Hat product. It is one of the distributions we will be using in this edition of the book.

The Fedora Project

The Fedora Project (http://fedoraproject.org/) is a distribution jointly run by the community and Red Hat. It is a derivative of Red Hat Enterprise Linux and provides a forward development platform for the product. Sponsored by Red Hat, Fedora is a testing ground for many of Red Hat's new features. As a result, it is occasionally considered by some to be too edgy for commercial use. Many of the features introduced in Fedora often make their way into the new RHEL releases. Fedora also makes use of RPM packages and many of the same administration tools used by RHEL.

Debian Linux

The Debian Linux distribution (www.debian.org) is a free community-developed and community-managed distribution with a diverse and active group of developers and users. It was started in 1993 and built around a social contract (www.debian.org/social_contract). The Debian distribution strives toward freedom, openness, and maintaining a focus on delivering what users want.

The Debian distribution is well known for the *dpkg* packaging system and the availability of nearly 23,000 applications and tools for the distribution.

Ubuntu

Initiated by South African technologist and entrepreneur Mark Shuttleworth, the Ubuntu operating system (www.ubuntu.com/) is free and based on the Debian Linux platform. It is community developed, and upgrades are released on a six-month cycle. Commercial support is also available from its coordinating organization, Canonical, as well as third-party support providers. It comes in different flavors to be used as desktops or servers. Some pundits believe the ubiquitous nature and stability of Ubuntu heralds the increased use of Linux as a desktop platform. Many people consider Ubuntu one of the easiest Linux platforms to use and understand, and much of its development is aimed at ease of use and good user experience. Ubuntu makes use of Debian's packaging system and a number of its administration tools.

Gentoo

The Gentoo distribution (www.gentoo.org/) is another community-developed platform. It is notable because it provides the option to compile the entire distribution from source code on your hardware. This allows you to customize every option to suit your particular hardware combination but can take a considerable time to complete. Gentoo can also be installed in a precompiled form for those with less technical skill who don't wish to compile everything. Gentoo is also well known for its frequent use as a platform for MythTV, an open source media center application similar to Microsoft Media Center. Gentoo makes use of a packaging system unique to the platform called Portage.

■ **Tip**   You can learn about the myriad of distributions available in the Linux world at DistroWatch (http://distrowatch.com/).

So Which Distribution Should You Choose?

Selecting a particular distribution should be based on your organization's budget, skills, and requirements. Our broad recommendation, though, is that you choose either a Red Hat–derived distribution or Ubuntu (a Debian-based distribution) or Debian. All of these are well supported by the organizations and communities that maintain them.

■ **Tip**   Online you'll find a useful unscientific automated quiz for selecting an appropriate Linux distribution available at www.proprofs.com/quiz-school/story.php?title=which-linux-distribution-are-you-1 and an article on the topic at http://lifehacker.com/5889950/how-to-find-the-perfect-linux-distribution-for-you.

With the exception of Red Hat Enterprise Linux, which requires a support contract to receive updates and patches, all of the distributions we've discussed are available free of charge. You can download and install them without having to pay a license fee.

■ **Note**   You can get the Red Hat Enterprise Linux software for free and install it without having to pay a license—the only trouble is that you will not be able to get any updates without a support agreement, which can leave you with a buggy and insecure host.

Several of the distributions we've discussed have commercial support, and if your technical skills are not strong, it is worth considering such a distribution, such as Red Hat Enterprise Linux or Ubuntu (with support provided by Canonical, their coordinating company). You should also remember that technical support may be available from a local provider. For example, a number of information technology (IT) companies and systems integrators provide Linux support, and there are frequently small-to-medium companies in the IT support business that could also provide relevant support services.

If you don't wish to pay for the third-party or vendor-provided commercial technical support, you might want to choose from a number of distributions that are noted for their large active communities where you can find support and assistance. Ubuntu support resources in particular have grown in recent years due to the many newcomers to Linux who have adopted that distribution.

Finally, don't discount your own personal experience. Explore the distributions yourself. Try out LiveCDs, install a few of the distributions, and get a feel for the various administration tools and interfaces. Your own feelings about which distribution suits you and is the easiest for you to work with shouldn't be underestimated.

So Which Distributions Does This Book Cover?

As we have discussed, two popular choices are Red Hat, or derivatives like CentOS and Fedora, and Ubuntu and other related distributions. We've chosen to cover a Red Hat–derived distribution and Ubuntu, a Debian-derived distribution. We've chosen these because they represent good examples of the two major families of distributions. They also allow us to demonstrate the major configuration options and styles, package management tools, and associated administrative techniques used by a broad swathe of the available Linux distributions.

Specifically, this book covers the material needed to implement applications and tools on

- Red Hat Enterprise Linux or a Red Hat–based distribution like CentOS or Fedora
- Ubuntu or other Debian-based distributions

When providing specific examples, we've chosen to demonstrate using CentOS 7 and Ubuntu LTS XenialXerus (16.04).

■ **Note** LTS is an abbreviation for "long-term support." The Ubuntu project updates its server and desktop releases every six months. The Ubuntu project guarantees that an LTS release will be supported (e.g., bugs fixed and security issues patched) for a period of five years after its release. Red Hat also has a similar release cycle where Red Hat tries to maintain binary compatibility for the life of the release (meaning it doesn't change major packages for life of the release). Red Hat also has an ELS (extended life-cycle support). For further information, see https://wiki.ubuntu.com/LTS and https://access.redhat.com/support/policy/updates/errata

---

Each chapter will provide examples of configuration for each distribution and document any differences between the distributions such as the location of configuration files or the names of packages.

Picking Hardware

Detailed analysis on choosing appropriate hardware is beyond the scope of this book. We generally recommend you purchase hardware with sufficient reliability and support to meet your organization's requirements. If you need to rely on your infrastructure 24/7/365 and require high levels of availability, you should purchase hardware with redundant features, such as backup power supplies. You should also purchase appropriate support capabilities such as spare parts and onsite, phone, or online support.

Of course buying your own hardware may not be a cost-effective way of implementing your services. Cloud providers may be your better option depending on your requirements. You can purchase a dedicated or virtual server from providers like Rackspace (www.rackspace.com) or Linode (www.linode.com). And if you want fully virtualized servers you can also look at Amazon Cloud Services (https://aws.amazon.com) or Google Compute Engine (https://cloud.google.com/compute) and even simple services like DigitalOcean (www.digitalocean.com)

■ **Note**   The decision to go to the Cloud or buy your own hardware comes down to various factors. Is there any real reason for the server to be in your office or data center? Do you have enough Internet bandwidth and stability to put your services into the Cloud. You can always settle on a combination of in house hardware and PaaS (Platform as a Service) depending on your requirements.

Supported Hardware

In addition to purchasing the right hardware, you should take into account some important selection and performance considerations. The most important consideration is that not all hardware is supported by the Linux operating system. While rare, some hardware components (e.g., some wireless network cards) lack drivers and support on some or all Linux platforms.

You should confirm that whatever hardware you purchase is supported by the distribution you have selected. Most distributions have Hardware Compatibility Lists (HCLs) you can use to verify your hardware is supported. Here are some of the currently maintained HCL sites:

- `https://access.redhat.com/ecosystem` (relevant for Red Hat, CentOS, and Fedora)

- `www.ubuntu.com/certification` (Ubuntu)

- `http://kmuto.jp/debian/hcl/wiki/` (Debian, but also relevant for Ubuntu)

- `www.linuxquestions.org/hcl/index.php` (generic listing)

There are also many large-scale hardware vendors that provide systems with OEM (Original Equipment Manufacturer) Linux software. You can choose from companies such as Dell, HP, and IBM to provide hardware guaranteed to work with a specified list of supported Linux distributions.

■ **Note**   We'll discuss a variety of specific performance issues in later chapters when we look at particular applications and tools.

Getting the Software

Where do you start with installing your first host? First, you need to get a copy of the software you require. There are a number of ways to acquire the base operating system software. Some distributions sell CD-ROMs and DVDs, and others offer ISO images to download (and some do both!). Other distributions also offer installation via network or the Internet.

■ **Note**   We'll look at processes for automated, network-based provisioning of servers in Chapter 19.

Following is a list of some of the sites where you can get CD-ROMs and DVDs:

- `www.ubuntu.com/download`

- `www.debian.org/distrib/`

- https://wiki.centos.org/Download

- www.gentoo.org/downloads/

- https://access.redhat.com/downloads/

- getfedora.org/

Once you have downloaded the required software, you can burn an ISO to CDs, DVD, or USB. Following are links to some software and instructions on how to do that:

- http://unetbootin.github.io/

- http://pcsupport.about.com/od/toolsofthetrade/ht/burnisofile.htm

- https://help.ubuntu.com/community/BurningIsoHowto

- www.ubuntu.com/download/desktop/create-a-usb-stick-on-windows

Or if you already have media available, you can just get started with your installation in Chapter 2.

Getting Support

Finding help and support for your Linux distribution varies greatly depending on the distribution. If you've chosen a commercial distribution, you can contact your vendor to get the support you need. For non-commercial distributions, you can log tickets or review documentation at your distribution's site.

Additionally, never underestimate the power of search engines to find solutions to your problems. Many people worldwide use Linux and may have experienced the same issue you have, and posted or written about solutions.

For specific distributions, the following sites are most useful:

- *Red Hat: www.redhat.com/en/services/support*

- *CentOS*: http://bugs.centos.org/main_page.php

- *Fedora*: https://fedoraproject.org/wiki/Communicating_and_getting_help

- *Debian*: www.debian.org/support

- *Ubuntu*: www.ubuntu.com/support

- *Gentoo*: www.gentoo.org/support

Check the sites of other distributions for their support mechanisms. Other useful sites include

- *ServerFault:* http://serverfault.com

- *AskUbuntu:* http://askubuntu.com

- *Unix & Linux: unix.stackexchange.com*

- *Linux Forums: www.linuxforums.org/forum*

Summary

In this chapter, we've introduced you to some varieties of Linux, including the two distributions this book focuses on:

- CentOS

- Ubuntu

We've also discussed some of the reasons to choose a particular distribution, how to choose some appropriate hardware, and where to get some basic support for your choice of distribution. In the next chapter, we'll show you how to install both of the distributions that this book covers.

CHAPTER 2

Installing Linux

By James Turnbull, Peter Lieverdink, and Dennis Matotek

In this chapter, we're going to take you through the process of installing a host with CentOS and a host with Ubuntu Server. We'll show each distribution's installation process using the graphical installation tools and detail the options available during installation. We're going to perform the base installation and also install the packages needed to run a basic web, mail, and DNS (Domain Name System) server. Don't worry if you don't know what these functions are at the moment—we explain DNS in Chapter 10, web servers in Chapter 11 and mail servers in Chapter 12.

■ **Tip**   We recommend you read the whole chapter, including the sections covering the CentOS and Ubuntu installation processes, to gain the best understanding of installing Linux hosts.

We'll start by installing a Red Hat–based distribution in the section "CentOS Server Installation." While the screenshots in this section are specific to CentOS, the installation processes for Red Hat Enterprise Linux (RHEL) and Fedora operate in a very similar fashion (CentOS and RHEL are derived from Fedora). So if you've chosen either of these distributions, you should be able to easily recognize the installation process of these distributions from our explanation. You'll find this is true of most configuration and management of Red Hat–derived distributions.

If you have chosen Ubuntu, you will find a full explanation of the Ubuntu installation process in the section "Ubuntu Installation." Ubuntu is derived from Debian, but it has a different installation process. The configuration and options are closely aligned, though, and by following the Ubuntu installation process you should be able to recognize the installation process for Debian and other Debian-derived distributions.

■ **Note**   If you want use the CD/DVD/USB-based installation process and the graphical installers provided, then you will need to install on a host with a monitor, a keyboard, and preferably a mouse. These peripherals will allow you to interact with the installation tool effectively. We'll describe how to do an *unattended* or *headless* (without a monitor) installation in Chapter 19.

We will also expand on the potential installation options in Chapter 8, when we look at installing software on Linux, and in Chapter 19, when we examine methods of automating installations and builds.

© Dennis Matotek, James Turnbull and Peter Lieverdink 2017
D. Matotek et al., *Pro Linux System Administration*, DOI 10.1007/978-1-4842-2008-5_2

■ **Caution**   Distributions change, and installation screens and options change with them. Don't panic if the screenshots presented in this chapter don't exactly match the ones you see during installation. Generally, most installation options and steps remain similar between releases.

LiveCDs and Virtual Machines

Before we begin our first installation, we'll cover two other options for getting to know Linux on a host that may be useful to try before committing to build a physical server: LiveCDs and virtual machines. These methods allow you to explore a Linux distribution and how to use it with a minimal investment of time and infrastructure.

LiveCDs

LiveCDs are versions of distributions that you can run on your computer from a CD or DVD. They load themselves into memory without the need to install any software on your computer. This means you can try a distribution on your computer and then remove the CD and reboot to return to your existing operating system, making it very easy to explore and test Linux distributions and software without changing anything on your computer. You can find out more about LiveCDs at http://en.wikipedia.org/wiki/Live_CD.

You can find popular distributions such as the following in LiveCD format:

- Ubuntu: https://help.ubuntu.com/community/LiveCD

- Fedora: http://fedoraproject.org/wiki/FedoraLiveCD

- Debian: http://debian-live.alioth.debian.org/

You can also find a full list of the many LiveCDs available at www.livecdlist.com/.

Virtual Machines

You can also run your Linux distribution on a virtual machine. *Virtual machines* are software implementations of hosts that run just like physical hosts. You can run multiple virtual hosts on a single physical host. Examples of virtualization applications and servers include VMware (www.vmware.com/), VirtualBox (www.virtualbox.org/), and open source alternatives like Xen (www.xen.org/), among others. You can also purchase virtual hosts from hosting companies.

■ **Note**   In Chapter 3, we demonstrate how to install VirtualBox. The following instructions apply to "*bare metal*" or virtual hosts. The differences between bare metal installs and virtual installs are relatively minor. One of the differences with virtual hosts is that you can install your host directly from an ISO image, rather than having to burn an ISO image to CD/DVD/USB first and load it into the CD/DVD drive or load it in the USB drive. Virtual host installations also make building and rebuilding your host easier, and you can perform functions like creating point-in-time backups of different kinds of hosts. When first exploring Linux a virtual host is the perfect way to learn.

You may also wish to take advantage of premade *virtual appliances,* which are virtual images of Linux distributions that you load with your virtualization software. They are already installed and configured, and the appliances are usually created with a particular purpose in mind, like a VoIP server, file server, or mail server. You can view the lists of appliances available at the following sites:

- `https://solutionexchange.vmware.com/store/category_groups/virtual-appliances/`: Virtual appliances for VMware

- `http://stacklet.com/`: Virtual appliances for Xen

CentOS Server Installation

Let's start by installing a CentOS host. We will make a few assumptions here:

- You are using a CentOS ISO from the CentOS web site (`www.centos.org/download/` and you have burned it onto a CD/DVD/USB.

- You are building just a basic mail, DNS (Domain Name System), and web server.

- You are installing on a fresh server without any previous operating system.

First, put your installation media (usually a CD, DVD, or USB) into your host and power it on.

■ **Note**   If you were building a virtual machine, you'd build instead from the raw ISO. A virtual machine usually includes a "virtual DVD," where you would mount the installation ISO to boot from. We show you this in the next chapter.

After loading your installation media and starting your host, you'll see the CentOS installation splash screen shown in Figure 2-1.

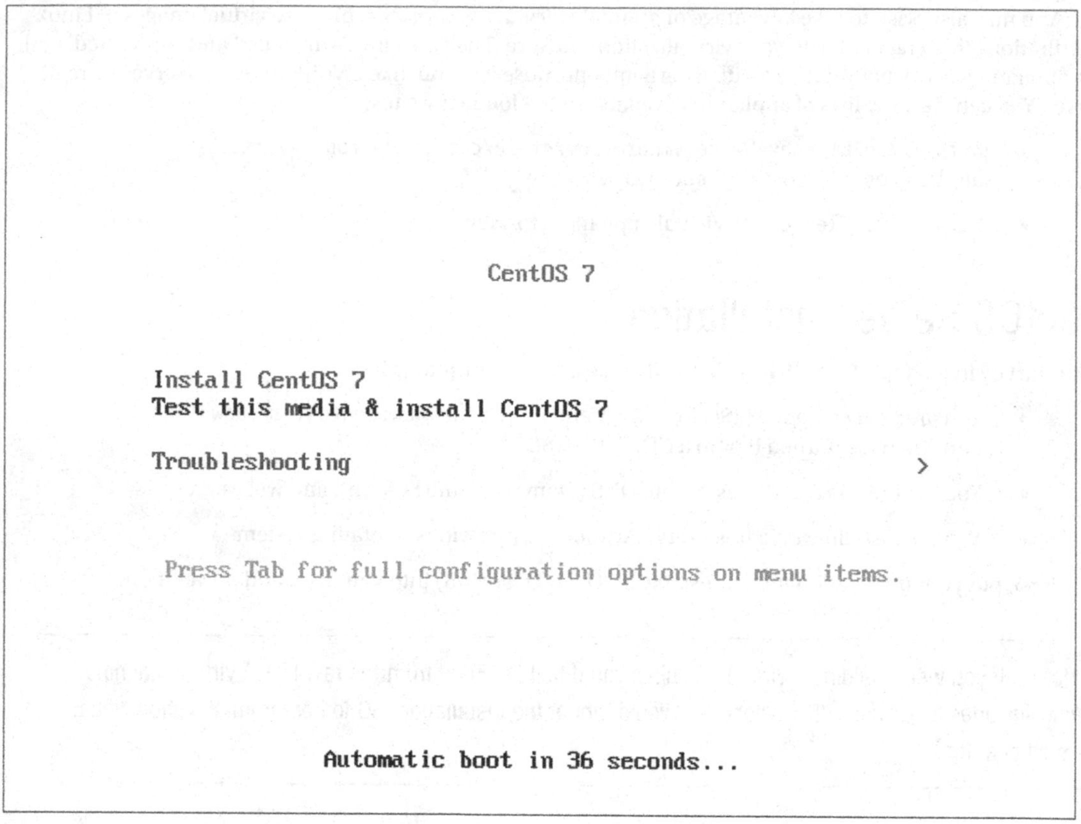

```
                              CentOS 7


      Install CentOS 7
      Test this media & install CentOS 7

      Troubleshooting                                    >


      Press Tab for full configuration options on menu items.




                   Automatic boot in 36 seconds...
```

Figure 2-1. *The CentOS 7 installation splash screen*

From the splash screen you can initiate the installation via a graphical interface. If we don't select anything the automatic boot will begin the install process. Just press Enter here to begin the install.

Pressing the *Tab* key will give you access to the boot command line. Here you could add other boot options that you feel appropriate to pass to the kernel you are about to boot, like a network kickstart file or other options. Later in the book we will show these options in action.

Finally, entering the section "Troubleshooting" gives further options like a *Rescue a CentOS system, Memory test,* and, *Boot from local drive.* Rescue mode assumes you already have Linux loaded, and it allows you to boot and potentially repair or rescue a broken Linux installation. You will boot into a rescue prompt that allows you to mount disks, edit configuration files, and access other useful utilities. For now, though, just press Enter to move on to the next stage of the installation.

In Figure 2-2, the "anaconda" installer process that will install the host has been started. The anaconda application is the software that installs CentOS, and it runs in the X Window System—also known as simply X. X is the graphical user interface used commonly on Linux; we'll talk a bit more about it in Chapter 4. There is a text-based installer mode that allows you to make the following selections as well. Systems with very low amounts of memory may have to run in this mode to install CentOS. This can also be via a process known as Kickstart, which is a way to automate the installation selections. We talk about Kickstart in Chapter 19.

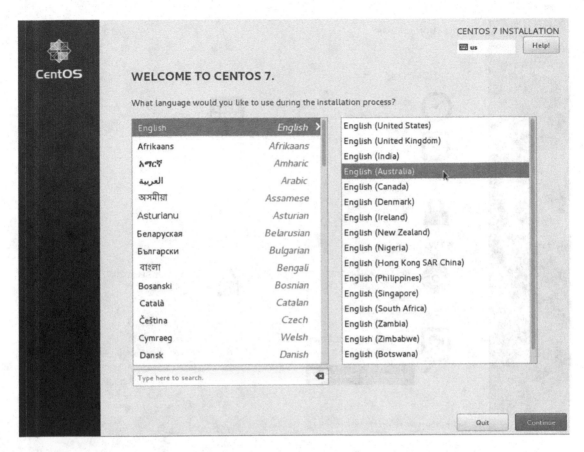

Figure 2-2. *The CentOS graphical installer*

In Figure 2-2 we select the language we wish to use. Here we are localizing English to the Australian version, mate. Select Continue to move to the next screen.

■ **Tip**   The Release Notes tell you what has changed between this version and the last version. If you were upgrading your host, it would be a good idea to read and understand the implications of any changes documented in the Release Notes. Release Note for CentOS 7 can be found here: https://wiki.centos.org/ Manuals/ReleaseNotes/CentOS7

Next in Figure 2-3 we have the main Installation Summary screen.

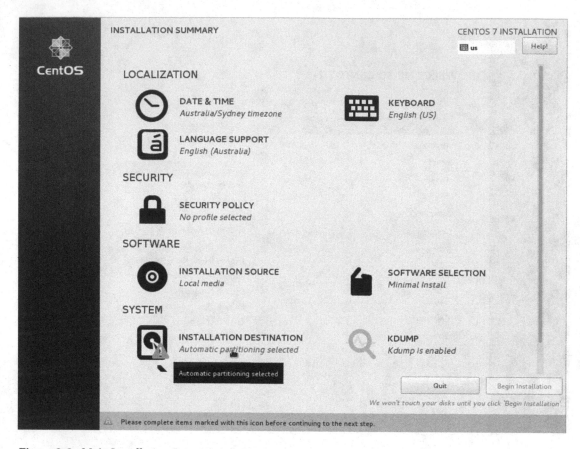

Figure 2-3. *Main Installation Summary screen*

Here we can access the main configuration items. They are broken up into sections: Localization, Security, Software, and System. Hovering your mouse over one of the items shows the link to the associated screen.

■ **Note**   It is not immediately obvious that some of the advanced configuration settings sometimes require the network settings to be configured first (like settings for NTP servers in the Date & Time settings). To configure the network settings, you must first have completed Installation Destination. Therefore, instead of starting at the top of Figure 2-3 we are going to start at the Installation Destination, then configure the network before we move on to the other steps.

As noted, instead of starting at the top of the list and working progressively down, we are going to start at the bottom and work our way up! Let's start with selecting Installation Destination first to set up where we are going to install our operating system.

■ **Caution**   The next few steps can be dangerous. If you are installing on a host that has an existing operating system or important data, you can lose all existing data and the operating system may become unusable. Please proceed with appropriate caution and a necessary backup regime if needed. For those that are just starting out in Linux, in Chapter 3 we will introduce you to VirtualBox which is a virtualization application that can allow you to install a Linux server inside your current operating system. Using virtualization software like VirtualBox will not destroy your current operating system when performing the following steps.

After selecting the Installation Destination screen as in in Figure 2-3 we are present with our current disk layout. Now we need to partition our disk.

Partitioning a disk is like slicing a cake: you can choose how big each "slice" of cake should be, depending on the appetite of those eating the cake. For example, if your system has a web site and that web site has pretty extensive logging, you may choose to divide the disk so that you have more room in the partition that holds your web data and logging files. If you are running a file server instead, you will reserve more of the disk for user data rather than web data or logging. The reason we use partitioning instead of lumping all the data into the one partition is that you can fill that partition completely without disrupting other partitions around it. In the foregoing scenario, if we fill the logging partition with data to 100%, our system partition and web data partitions will not be consumed by logging data.

In Figure 2-4 we have a simple disk layout from our VirtualBox installation. Depending on your system, you may have many more disks.

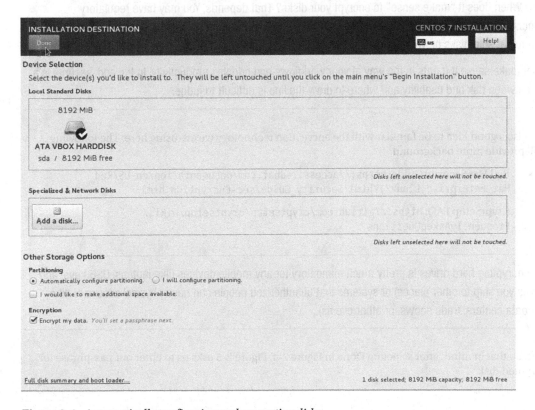

Figure 2-4. *Automatically configuring and encrypting disks*

17

In Figure 2-4 we have selected ATA VBOX HARDDISK and Encrypt my data. We have also selected Automatically configure partitioning. The installer will configure a sensible default disk partitioning layout for you. If you choose I will configure partitioning you will manually have to create the disk layout.

■ **Note**   We'll explain a lot more about partitions and how to customize and change your disks and storage in Chapter 9.

It is advisable to encrypt your data when it makes sense to do so, but it has some drawbacks you should be aware of. Whenever your system boots you will need to enter the password on the console as the system boots up. That means that unattended reboots are not possible and that you will need console access (physical or virtual) to enter it. One other problem is that the automation of installs is more difficult as the passphrase has to be passed at install time and that passphrase could be intercepted. Also this is only encryption at rest, effective when the system is not powered on or the passphrase has not been entered. Assuming you have only one disk, we could not take that disk and mount that disk on another system and read its contents. However, if we have access to the powered-on host where the encryption passphrase has been entered we can read and possibly copy off contents of the hard drives. It is also only as secure as your passphrase. Simple passphrases can defeat your encryption with dictionary-based attacks. Therefore, long and strong passphrases are highly recommended.

■ **Note**   When does it "make sense" to encrypt your disks? That depends. You may have regulatory requirements to have your data encrypted. You may have systems that don't reboot often and have sensitive data. You might ship disks between offices.

It may not make sense if it gets in the way of your workflows and cripples productivity. In the end, security is a balance between risk and usability and where to draw the line is difficult to judge.

It is also a good idea to be familiar with the encryption technology we are using here. The following links will provide more background.

- Red Hat Security Guide: `https://access.redhat.com/documentation/en-US/Red_Hat_Enterprise_Linux/7/html/Security_Guide/sec-Encryption.html`

- CryptSetup FAQ: `https://gitlab.com/cryptsetup/cryptsetup/wikis/FrequentlyAskedQuestions`

■ **Tip**   Encrypting hard drives is pretty much mandatory for any mobile devices (like laptops, USB keys, and hard drives you ship to other places) or systems that unauthorized people can have physical access to (like insecure data centers, trade shows, or other events).

With all that in mind, after selecting Done in Figure 2-4, Figure 2-5 asks us to enter our passphrase for the encrypted disk.

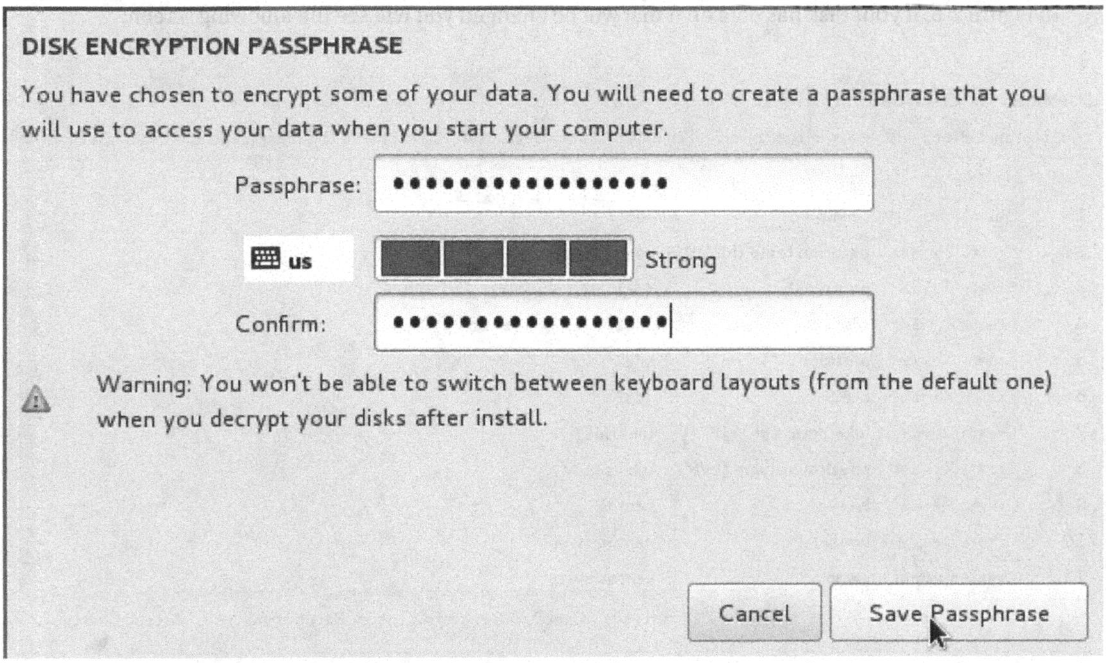

DISK ENCRYPTION PASSPHRASE

You have chosen to encrypt some of your data. You will need to create a passphrase that you will use to access your data when you start your computer.

Passphrase: ●●●●●●●●●●●●●●●●●

⌨ us [▮▮▮▮] Strong

Confirm: ●●●●●●●●●●●●●●●●●|

⚠ Warning: You won't be able to switch between keyboard layouts (from the default one) when you decrypt your disks after install.

Cancel   Save Passphrase

Figure 2-5. *Entering a strong passphrase*

Enter a strong passphrase and securely store that in an encrypted password manager.

■ **Tip** You can use a reputable browser-based encrypted password manager like 1Password, LastPass, or DashLane. Some of these have group or team support to allow you to share passwords among team members in an authorized way. Believe me, this is actually a hard problem. You will need to share passwords at some point among your teams and shared accounts and long-lived passwords can then become a massive problem for you. However, there may be some passwords that require stricter access and very limited sharing. Software like http://keepass.info or GPG encrypted password files stored securely may be your best solution.

In Figure 2-6, if your disk has data on it that will be changed you will see the following screen:

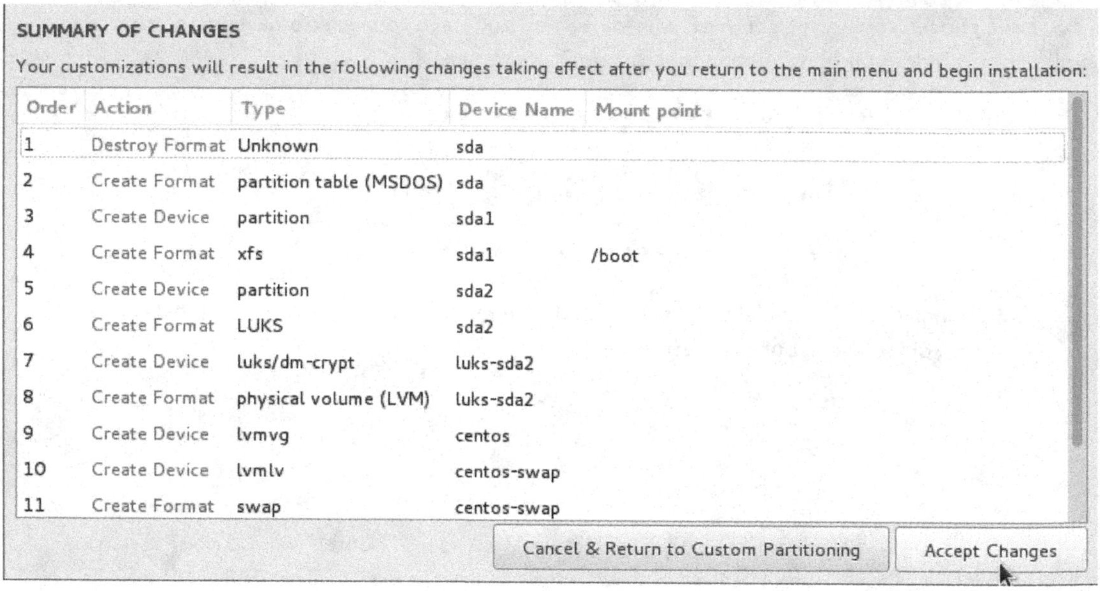

SUMMARY OF CHANGES

Your customizations will result in the following changes taking effect after you return to the main menu and begin installation:

Order	Action	Type	Device Name	Mount point
1	Destroy Format	Unknown	sda	
2	Create Format	partition table (MSDOS)	sda	
3	Create Device	partition	sda1	
4	Create Format	xfs	sda1	/boot
5	Create Device	partition	sda2	
6	Create Format	LUKS	sda2	
7	Create Device	luks/dm-crypt	luks-sda2	
8	Create Format	physical volume (LVM)	luks-sda2	
9	Create Device	lvmvg	centos	
10	Create Device	lvmlv	centos-swap	
11	Create Format	swap	centos-swap	

Cancel & Return to Custom Partitioning   Accept Changes

Figure 2-6. Destroying and recreating disk layout

At this point, depending on what you see, you may choose to proceed. But remember, this is an irreversible operation and data can be lost. If you have doubts Cancel & Return to Custom Partitioning.

If there are no changes to existing data you will see Figure 2-8. However, we want to show you a little behind the curtain here in Figure 2-7. To get here we selected I will configure partitions and then selected Click here to create them automatically. It now presents to us how it has automatically sliced up our disk.

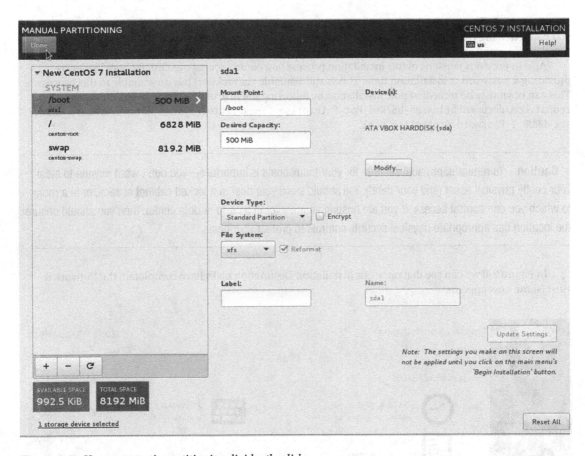

Figure 2-7. *How automatic partitioning divides the disks*

In Figure 2-7 that we have our disk divided up into three slices. A /boot partition, a / or root volume, and a swap volume. The /boot partition is where our kernel images and boot configuration files reside and so is set to "Standard Partition" and an xfs file system. The root volume / is a LVM (logical volume management) volume and has the most space allocated to it as a percentage of the disk size of the LVM. The main operating system programs are in /. Finally, swap is a slice of disk for writing out pages of memory to free up system RAM.

■ **Note**   LVM allows you to manage disk volumes and extend, shrink, and change the size of your disk partitions on the fly. The LVM software allows the administrator to change the disk layout, add new disk storage, or remove and repurpose disk storage to another part of the system without having to rebuild the system and reformat the underlying disks. Btrfs is also available and is a new-ish CoW (Copy-on-Write) filesystem. Like LVM it allows you to group your storage in a flexible way. But a Btrfs "subvolume" is not the same as a logical volume in LVM and has features and limitations that LVM does not. We'll talk about LVM and Btrfs in more detail in Chapter 9.

If you had any special requirements, you could alter this default structure and create new partitions, or you could delete everything and start again using the installer's partition manager. We will go into greater detail in Chapter 9 about how to carve up one or several drives for various purposes.

Also in previous versions of this installation process you could secure your GRUB2 boot loader by providing a password at installation time. This is still available via Kickstart but unavailable in this process. This can obviously be remedied post installation by following the instructions here: `https://access.redhat.com/documentation/en-US/Red_Hat_Enterprise_Linux/7/html/System_Administrators_Guide/sec-GRUB_2_Password_Protection.html`.

■ **Caution** To reiterate, physical security for your Linux hosts is important—you don't want anyone to steal your costly physical asset (and your data!). You should store your host in a locked cabinet or rack, or in a room to which you can control access. If you are hosting your server in a co-lo or data center, then you should ensure the location has appropriate physical security controls to protect your hosts.

In Figure 2-8 we can see that once our Installation Destination tasks have completed, the Network & Host Name now appears.

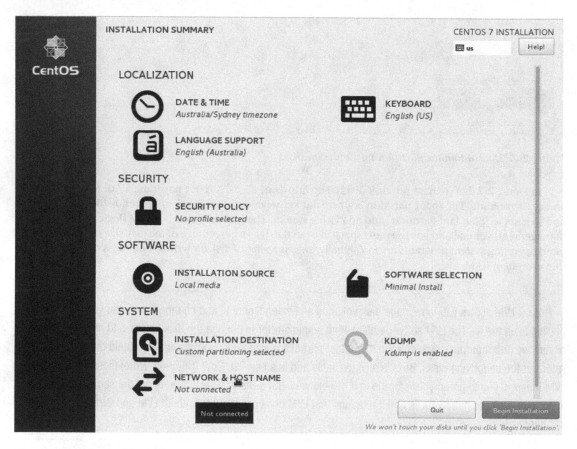

Figure 2-8. *Selecting Network & Host Name*

The most important configuration item here is your IP (Internet Protocol) address, which is the network address of your host that allows other hosts to find and communicate with it.

■ **Tip** You can read about IP addresses and addressing at `http://en.wikipedia.org/wiki/IP_address` and `http://computer.howstuffworks.com/internet/basics/question549.htm`.

Depending on your network setup the next steps can go two ways. You may have in your network a DHCP (Dynamic Host Configuration Protocol) server already. A DHCP server is a service that assigns IP addresses to MAC addresses (the special and unique address on your network card). Most offices and homes now have DHCP servers in their firewall or routers on their network. If you are following along with VirtualBox, VirtualBox has its own DHCP server that assigns addresses to its own internal network. In Figure 2-9 we rely on DHCP to provide us an IP address and we manually assign our host a name.

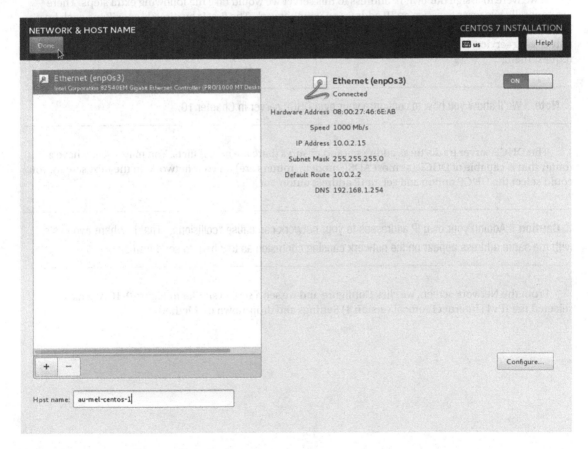

Figure 2-9. DHCP and manually assigning a hostname

In Figure 2-9 we allowed DHCP to assign the IP address of 10.0.2.15 by toggling the OFF button to ON in the top right corner.

In the Host name section in the lower left we have entered a hostname of *au-mel-centos-1*. In small startups and home networks it is common to name hosts after favorite TV characters, bands, or mythical creatures. While this is fun, it soon becomes annoying when you have multiple hosts in multiple geographical locations doing particular jobs. Plus you have used all your favorite characters first and it becomes really hard when you have to kill off your "pet" server. Our hostname is *au-mel-centos-1*, as we prefer the descriptive naming standard *region-city-OS type-number*. As another example of a descriptive naming format, if you have a file server in the United States with an IP address ending in 155, you could choose us-ny-fileserver-155. The main thing is to be descriptive rather than naming your host "Katy" or "Thor."

■ **Note** You can choose any naming standard you like that suits your environment. Our preference is for a descriptive naming convention.

If we were to assign our own IP address to this server we would take the following extra steps. There are generally two ways to assign an IP address on your network. The first is by directly specifying each host's IP address during configuration. These are called *static addresses*. The second method uses the DHCP networking service. DHCP uses a server located on your network to assign IP addresses to hosts when they request them.

■ **Note** We'll show you how to configure your own DHCP server in Chapter 10.

The DHCP server tracks these addresses and ensures there are no conflicts. You may already have a router that is capable of DHCP (as most ADSL modem/routers are) on your network. In the next screen, you could select the DHCP option and get an IP address automatically.

■ **Caution** Adding your own IP addresses to your network can cause "collisions." That is where two hosts with the same address appear on the network causing confusion as to where to send traffic.

From the Network screen, we click Configure and we see a screen similar to Figure 2-10. We have selected the IPv4 (Internet Protocol version 4) Settings and drop-down on Method.

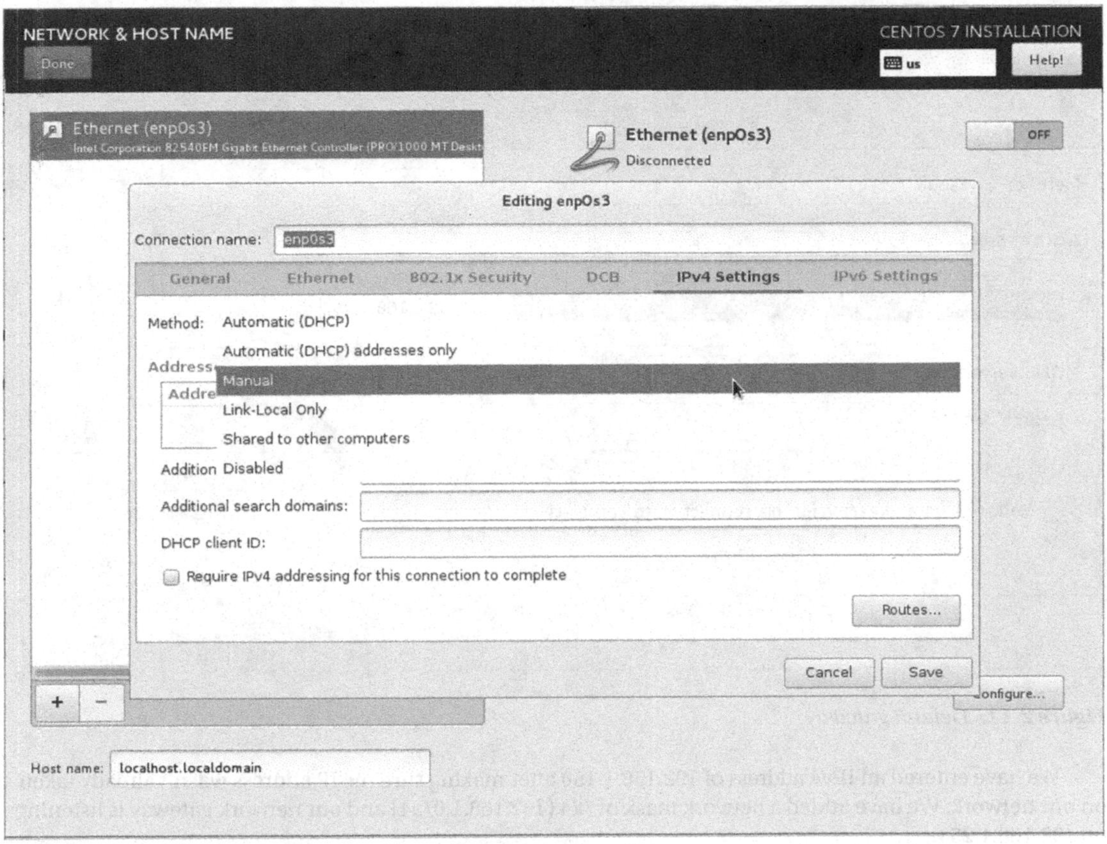

NETWORK & HOST NAME CENTOS 7 INSTALLATION

Done ⌨ us Help!

Ethernet (enpOs3) Ethernet (enpOs3) OFF
Intel Corporation 82540EM Gigabit Ethernet Controller (PRO/1000 MT Deskt) Disconnected

Editing enpOs3

Connection name: enpOs3

General   Ethernet   802.1x Security   DCB   **IPv4 Settings**   IPv6 Settings

Method: Automatic (DHCP)
           Automatic (DHCP) addresses only
Address
    Addre Manual
           Link-Local Only
           Shared to other computers
Addition Disabled

Additional search domains:

DHCP client ID:

☐ Require IPv4 addressing for this connection to complete

Routes...

Cancel   Save

+ − Configure...

Host name: localhost.localdomain

Figure 2-10. Setting IPv4 settings

The Connection name is the device we are configuring and that it automatically created from the system as it has booted. Yours may be different depending on your device. The drop-down allows us to select the different options for our network interface. DHCP we have already discussed, Link-Local Only is only useful for communicating to hosts in the local segment (not normally used) as is Shared to other computers. Selecting these two options for your network interface will mean you will not be assigned an IP address that can route through to the Internet. We wish to select Manual and assign our own IP address by clicking Add on the right-hand side.

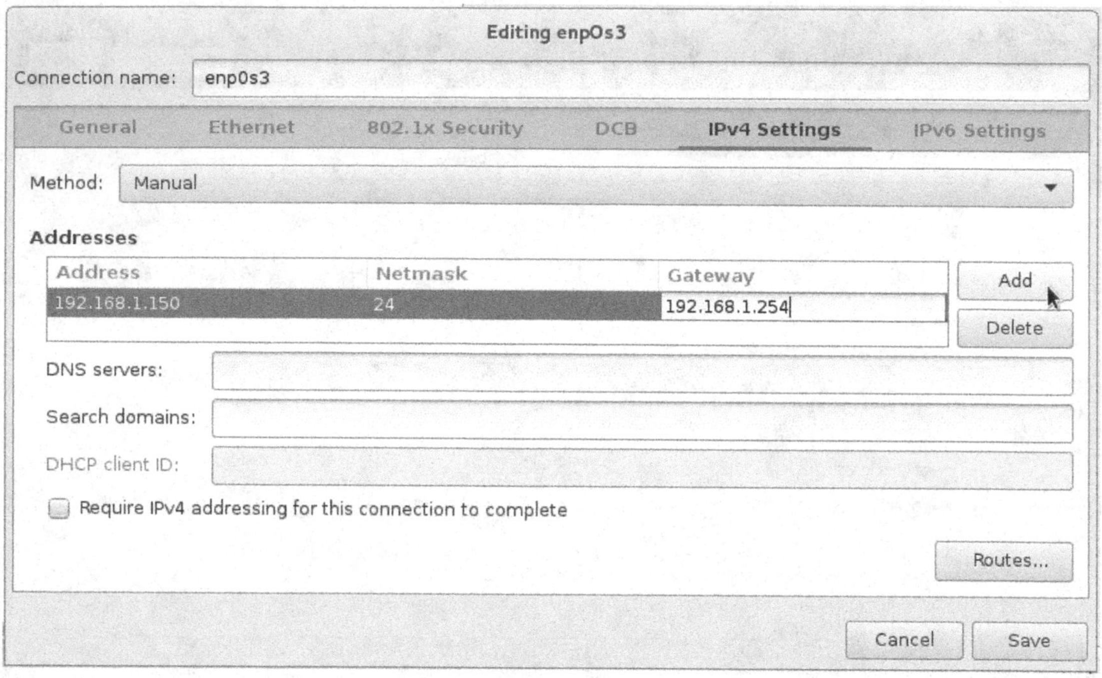

Figure 2-11. *Default gateway*

We have entered an IPv4 address of 192.168.1.150 after making sure the IP address wasn't already taken on our network. We have added a network mask of /24 (192.168.1.0/24) and our network gateway is listening on 192.168.1.254.

■ **Note** If you issue the command ping 192.168.1.150 on your local network and get a response back, then the address is already taken and you should choose a different address here. Also, the address space 192.168.1.0/24 may not be suitable for your network. We talk more about networking in Chapter 7. When in doubt, try DHCP.

Next we add our DNS details as in Figure 2-12.

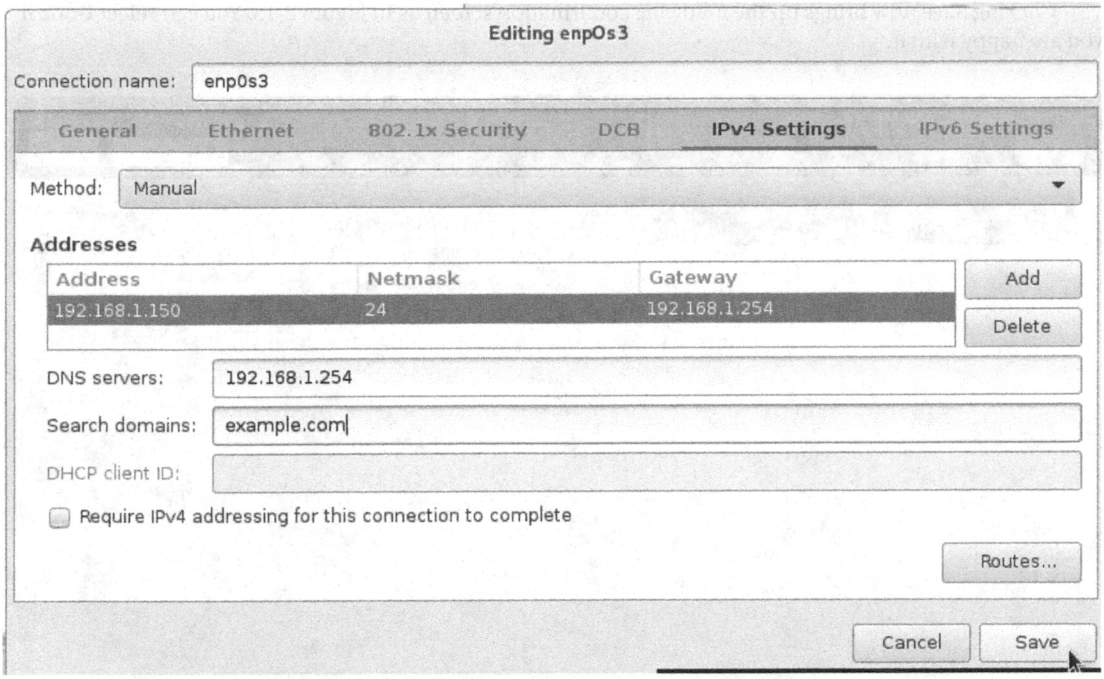

Figure 2-12. *DNS details*

In our case our DNS server is also our gateway address. You may have one or more DNS servers on your network and you can add them here, separated by a comma. Search domains are again DNS settings that allow you to append a domain name to your DNS search queries. For example, when you query for the IP address of au-mel-centos-2, your networking layer will know to add the domain au-mel-centos-2.example.com to the query for you. Again you can have multiple domains here separated by commas or you can leave this blank. We are going to set ours to *example.com* to match our pretend network.

The default gateway is the route all traffic passes along before leaving your network. It will be either a modem/ADSL gateway or a physical router that connects your network to the Internet or other private networks. The primary and secondary DNS name servers are special servers that resolve IP addresses to fully qualified domain names. A fully qualified domain name is *au-mel-centos-1.example.com* for example.

■ **Tip** Specifying a primary and a secondary DNS server adds redundancy to your network. If one server doesn't respond, your host will try the other server.

Every time your host goes to a web site, it uses both the default gateway and DNS server to find out how to get there. For example, if you type www.google.com in your browser's address bar, your host will first find the DNS server, which may or may not be on your network. If it is not on your network, your host will use the default gateway to reach it. Your host then will ask the DNS server for the IP address of www.google.com, and the DNS server will answer with something like 74.125.19.104. Your host will then again use your default gateway to leave your network and fetch the web page provided by www.google.com. In general terms, your DNS server is a map for IP addresses to hostnames, and your default gateway is the first link you traverse between networks.

Clicking Save now brings up the following confirmation screen as in Figure 2-13. You can select Done if you are happy with it.

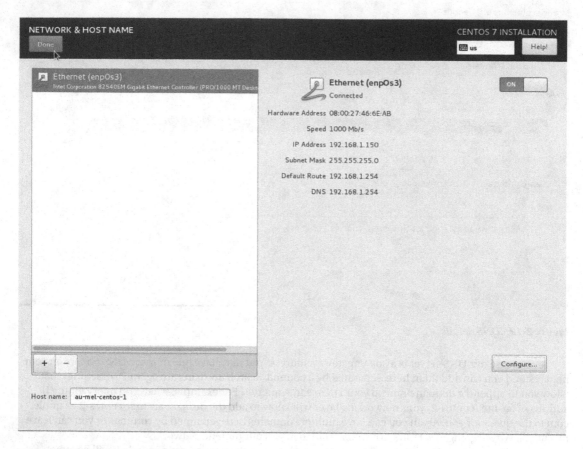

Figure 2-13. *Network confirmation screen*

■ **Note** We have shown you here how to configure an IPv4 IP address. There is also another kind that can be configured, an IPv6 address. If you have IPv6 your address can be configured using the IPv6 Settings tab. You go about configuring IPv6 the same way as IPv4. The DNS servers you set will also need to be IPv6 addresses.

IPV4 AND IPV6

The Internet works by computers being able to send each other messages. To be able to do this there needs to be a set of unique addresses all along the path between each other. IPv4 was the first release of this protocol that made this possible.

The unique addresses in IPv4 are based on a 32-bit address space. That means that there are a possible 4,294,967,296 unique addresses. This address space is too small for today's Internet and so IPv6 has been released to solve this problem.

IPv6 is based on a 128-bit address space and has 2^{128} unique addresses which is about 7.9×10^{28} more addresses than IPv4. Some networks have already migrated to this new address space.

However, there is no need to panic if you do not have an IPv6 address. Many ISPs offer a "dual-stack," offering IPv4 and IPv6 to their customers, while they themselves connect to other networks via IPv6. Your local network is most likely an IPv4 network too, and you most likely will be assigned a dynamic IPv4 address by your DHCP server. We talk more about networking in Chapter 7.

For a good info graphic on the differences between IPv4 and IPv6 see here: `www.networkworld.com/article/2692482/ipv6/infographic-ipv4-vs-ipv6.html`.

You can also refer to this entry here: `http://en.wikipedia.org/wiki/IPv6`.

With our network configured we can proceed to some of the other settings, like Date & Time. By selecting as we have in Figure 2-14 we are going to localize our Data & Time.

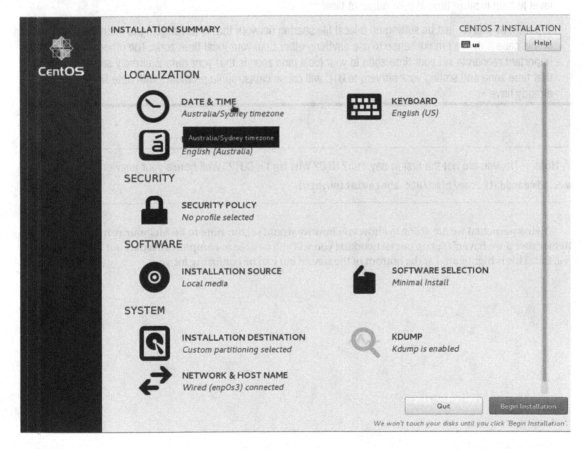

Figure 2-14. *Setting Date & Time*

Setting the correct time zone is very important for servers as it affects things like the timestamp in logs and the create and update records in databases. The Linux kernel uses Coordinated Universal Time (UTC) as its clock source but you can set your appropriate time zone here. You might also consider setting all your servers to UTC rather than a local time zone.

WHY SET ALL YOUR SERVERS TO UTC?

Consider you are building the infrastructure for a brand-new application. Most people don't think about a globalized world when they start designing their services. Your systems might start off in your local time zone but as you grow you might find your systems are in completely different time zones. This can lead to problems when you read a timestamp and wonder, "Yeah, but is that 4 am their time, our time or UTC?"

You can still get localized time information. You can use standard UTC zone offsets at the application level to help localize time in your different time zones.

You may, of course, just be setting up a local file sharing network that is never going to span the globe. In this case it doesn't make sense to use anything other than your local time zone. The other very important reason to set your time zone to your local time zone is that your data is already set with that time zone and setting your servers to UTC will cause catastrophic problems with date fields you already have.

■ **Note**　No, you are not the first to say, "uh? UTC? Why isn't it CUT?" Well here's your answer: www.timeanddate.com/time/utc-abbreviation.html.

Being parochial we are going to show you how we would set our time to be Melbourne in Figure 2-15. Remember if we haven't set up our networking you will still be able to complete this part but the next part will fail. This is highlighted at the bottom of the screen but can be confusing for you.

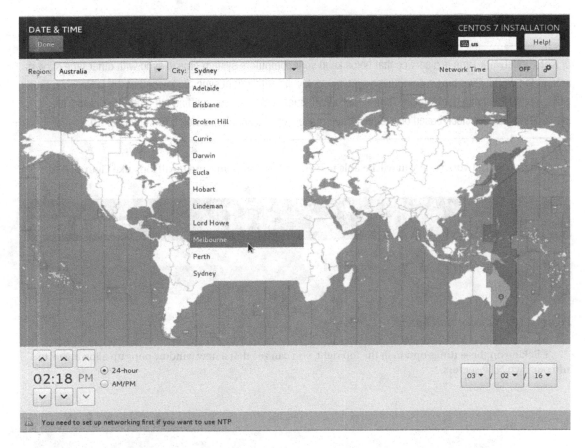

Figure 2-15. *Setting time zone and localizing to Melbourne*

But we really should set this to UTC, shouldn't we. So in Figure 2-16, that is what we will do.

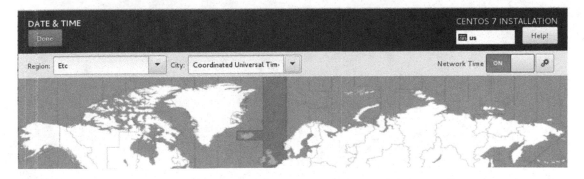

Figure 2-16. *Setting to UTC*

Once this is done we can move to the next step which is setting up our Network Time servers.

■ **Note**   Network Time is a service that helps keep your computers system time in sync with other time servers around the world. Over time a computer's system clock will "drift" out of sync. So to combat this a Network Time service or NTP service (for Network Time Protocol) will query time servers and find out what their clocks are. It then adjusts its own clock based on the best three responses. We speak more on NTP in chapter 10.

When your network is set you will be able to turn on Network Time and it will look like Figure 2-17.

Figure 2-17. *Network Time settings*

Clicking on the settings option in the top right, you can see that a new window pops up allowing us to add our own NTP servers.

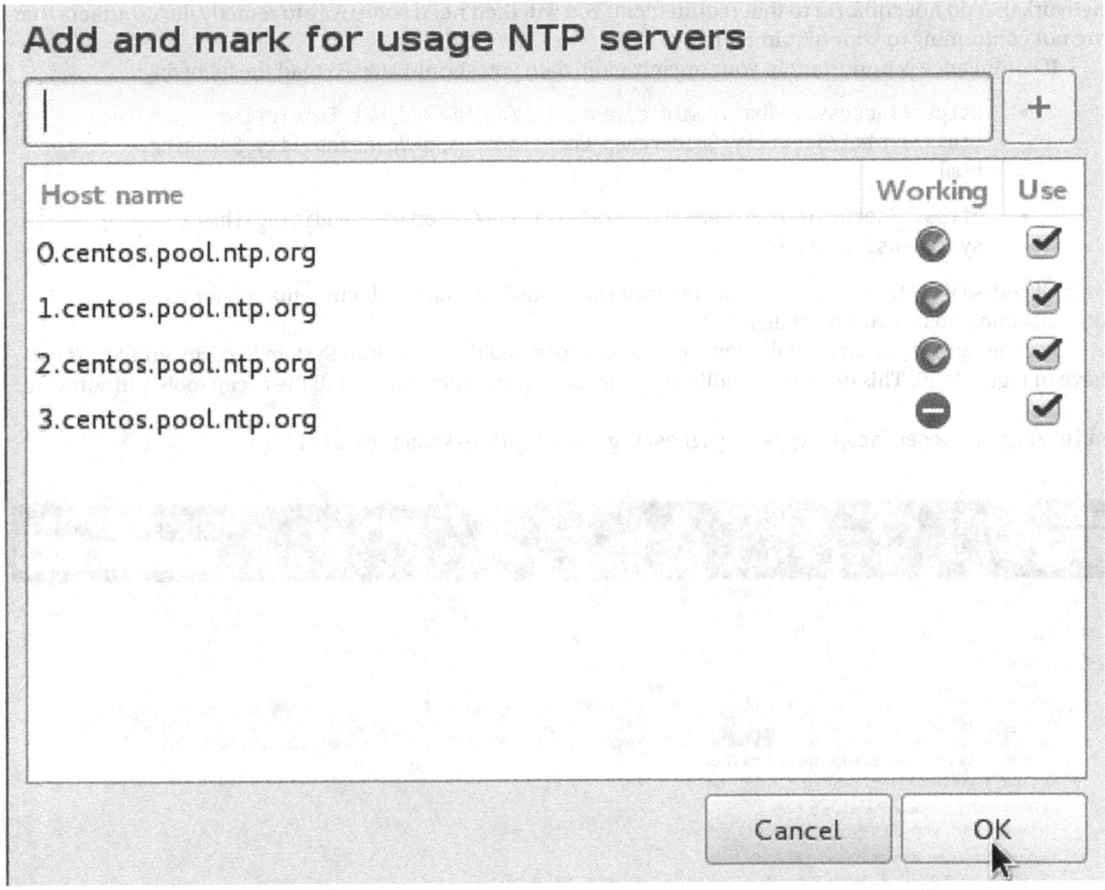

Add and mark for usage NTP servers

Host name	Working	Use
0.centos.pool.ntp.org	●	☑
1.centos.pool.ntp.org	●	☑
2.centos.pool.ntp.org	●	☑
3.centos.pool.ntp.org	⊖	☑

Cancel   OK

Figure 2-18. Network Time Servers

Here you can add a local time server or choose your favorite. The "closer" you are to the time server the better as distance and latency can skew your clock results. The NTP servers with the green tick are reachable and working. The red time server is unreachable. It is best to have at least three working time servers. You can add your own NTP server by clicking the + and adding your server to the list. To get back to the main screen select OK and Done.

Working our way down the summary screen we can see the Security Policy settings. If you select the Security Policy, you can add a security policy to your host. It is not mandatory that you implement a security policy but you may be required to by either government regulation or by individual security requirements. What this section does is install tools that perform Security Content Automation Protocol (SCAP) scans and integrity check against your system according to a predefined security policy.

Which should you choose? On their own they don't make your system any more secure but they can help you identify, report, and remedy any vulnerability. For example, when you are managing thousands of servers you want to make sure that all hosts conform to the same security profile and be able to prove that to external auditors.

For instance, thinking of a very simple example, if you are required by legislation to have all your hosts conform to a particular security standard which stipulates you must have a minimum password length of 8 characters (2 uppercase, 2 symbols), by running these scans you can ascertain there are no hosts on your

33

network that do not conform to that requirement. You will then need some way to remedy those outliers that are not conforming to your requirements.

If compliance is important to your organization, then you should at least read the following:

- `https://access.redhat.com/documentation/en-US/Red_Hat_Enterprise_`
  `Linux/7/html/Security_Guide/chap-Compliance_and_Vulnerability_Scanning.`
  `html`

- `https://securityblog.redhat.com/2013/11/13/automated-auditing-the-`
  `system-using-scap-2/`

Of course you should also read any relevant standards compliance documentation for your organization and take appropriate action.

For the purpose of this installation we are going to install the "Standard System Security Profile," as we have in Figure 2-19. This gives us the following bare minimum rules and install the oscap tools and software:

`http://static.open-scap.org/ssg-guides/ssg-rhel7-guide-standard.html`

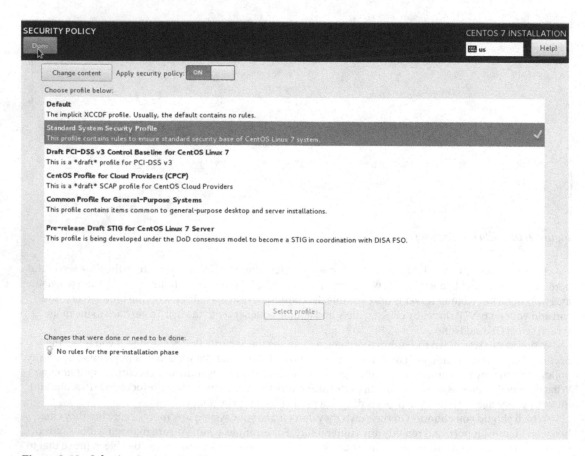

Figure 2-19. *Selecting Security Profile*

Once we have finished the system install we will be able to run a compliance test and get an idea of how our system looks compared to the DISA STIG for Red Hat Enterprise Linux 7 baseline.

■ **Note**   DISA stands for Defence Information Systems Agency and it is part of the US Department of Defense and runs information systems for US agencies. The STIG is the Standard Technical Implementation Guide. The role of the open-oscap is a way to run and collect these compliance reports. You can check out the source code here: https://github.com/OpenSCAP.

On selecting Done we are taken back to the Installation Summary screen. Next we are going to choose the software we will install. From the Installation Summary select the Software Selection screen.

We are going to select to install a DNS server and to make it easier, the Gnome Desktop. This is optional if you are comfortable with the Linux command line. Feel free to install other software that is of interest to you.

First we select Infrastructure Server and select DNS Name server as we have done in Figure 2-20

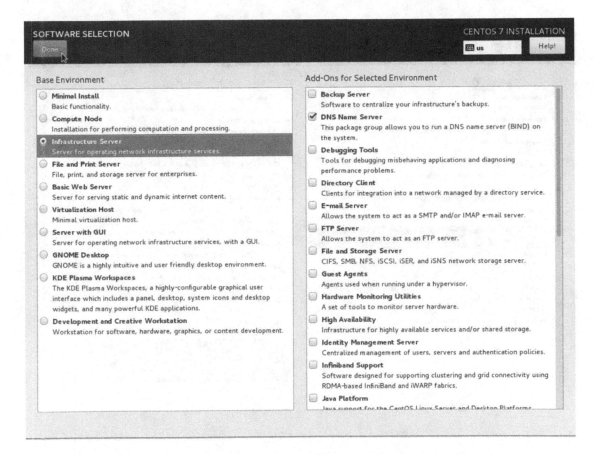

Figure 2-20. Selecting DNS Name server

We have spoken previously about DNS Name servers and what they do. They help computers map IP addresses to hostnames. We are going to select that from the Infrastructure Server list. As you can see there are others in that list like, E-mail Server, FTP server, and File and Storage Server. This will install only the barest of requirements you need for a DNS Name Server and will not install a GUI (graphical user interface).

Depending on what you are used to, this might feel a little uncomfortable for you as if we go ahead with this you will only be able to use the command line, not a nice GUI to get around.

■ **Tip** As you become more familiar with Linux you may find you rarely use a GUI to configure and use Linux. Practically everything can be run from the command line. Only if you are using desktop applications like graphical editors or integrated development environments (IDEs) do you really need to use a desktop GUI.

In Figure 2-21 we are going to install the desktop. CentOS provides two standard Linux desktops for you to choose from, Gnome being one, and KDE being the other. Both have their fans and it is up to your own personal preferences which you may prefer. You can install both and switch between them before you log in so that you can choose the one that feels best for you.

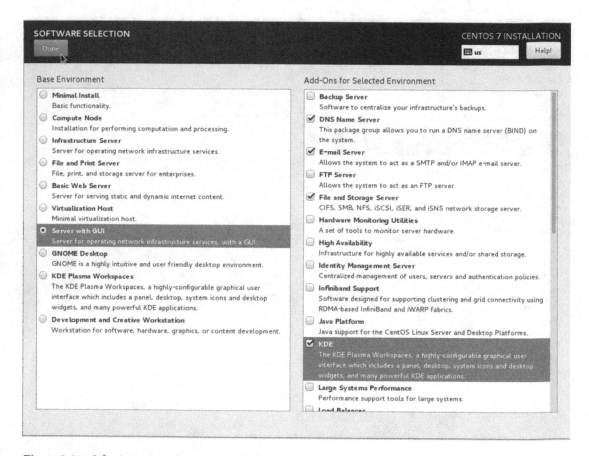

Figure 2-21. *Selecting to install a server with a GUI*

Select Done and we will now have a list of packages to install on our new server.

■ **Note** Packages are the bundles of files that are required by a software application. They can be binary files or configuration files. In Chapter 8 we explain more about packages and how to use them.

We will now quickly go over the last item, Installation Source. If we wanted to choose a different installation source to the current media (CD/DVD/USB), then we could add it here. You can install Linux from a network httpd server or run your installation via a proxy server. Once again you will need to have set up the Installation Destination and Networking before you will be able to configure anything that requires a network.

In Figure 2-22 you can see that we have added another installation source from the `builder.example.com` host which is somewhere on our network. This host would be serving via `http://` a copy of the ISO image. This means you don't need to have all the physical media physically attached to your host. You might choose to have a minimal install disk to get to this screen and then access the larger media over the network—when you are doing more than one server this can be very beneficial.

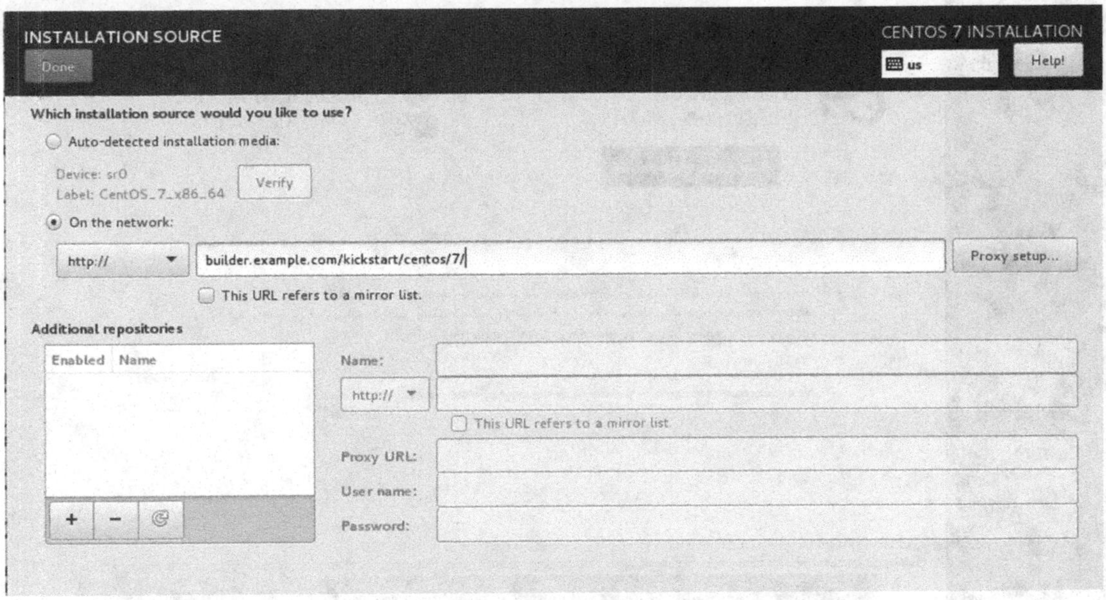

Figure 2-22. Adding a network installation source

You can also configure any proxy server settings that you may need to access to either access remote repository. Also, you can add additional repositories. Repositories are collections of packages and are normally serviced via `http://` servers either locally or on the Internet.

We are not going to add anything to this screen, we are just going to exit via Done and now we can begin our install.

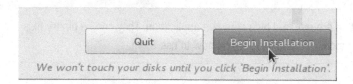

Figure 2-23. *Selecting Begin Installation*

After selecting Begin Installation you presented with a screen that shows your installation progress and also gives you the opportunity to create a "root" password and a "user" password. In Linux the root user is a superuser who has access to the whole system, much like the Windows Administrator in the Windows OS. In Figure 2-24 you can see again that we use our mouse to click *ROOT PASSWORD*.

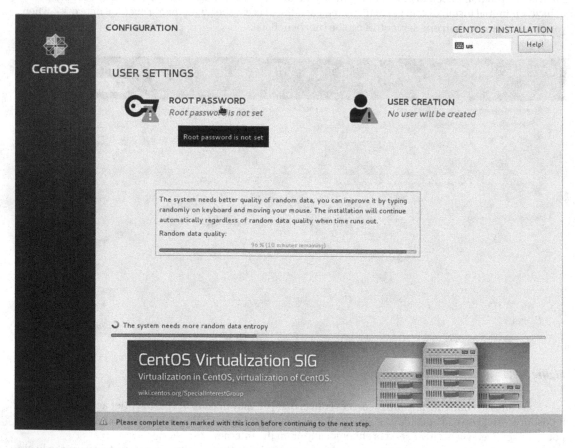

Figure 2-24. *Selecting to create the root user*

■ **Tip** We will discuss the root user in more detail in Chapters 5 and 6.

As we have discussed earlier, passwords should be complex and consist of a combination of upper- and lowercase characters, numbers, and special punctuation keys like the following: @!%#*. They should also be minimum of eight characters long. Remember to store this securely like you have the disk encryption password.

Here in Figure 2-25 you are again given an indicator of how strong your password is as you enter it. It also won't accept your password unless your confirmation matches. When you are finished select Done.

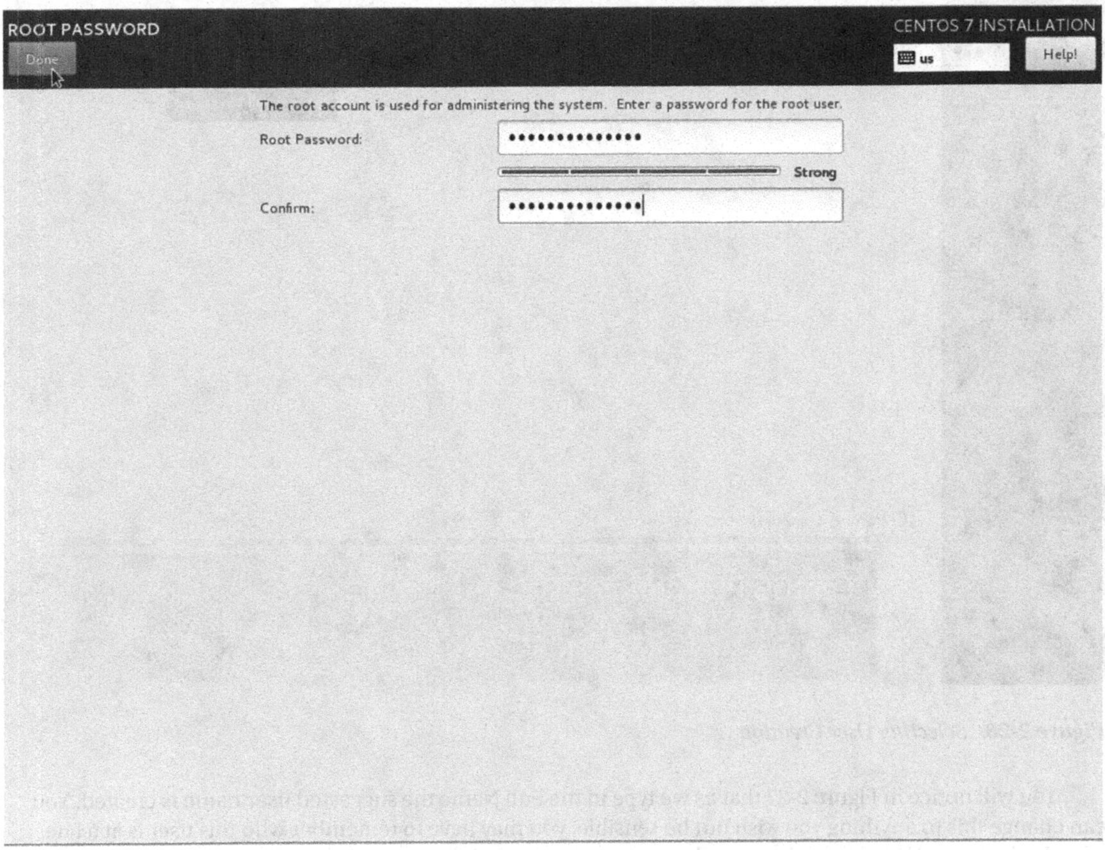

Figure 2-25. *Entering the root password*

■ **Tip** You can read about the characteristics of a good password at `http://en.wikipedia.org/wiki/Password_strength`.

It is optional to set up a user account on your host, but it is recommended you have one. In Ubuntu, which we will see later on, you don't get to access the root account directly. The root account being a very powerful account is one you don't use lightly. We are going to create a user on our system for our initial access.

In Figure 2-26 we are going to create a user called JSmith by first selecting User Creation.

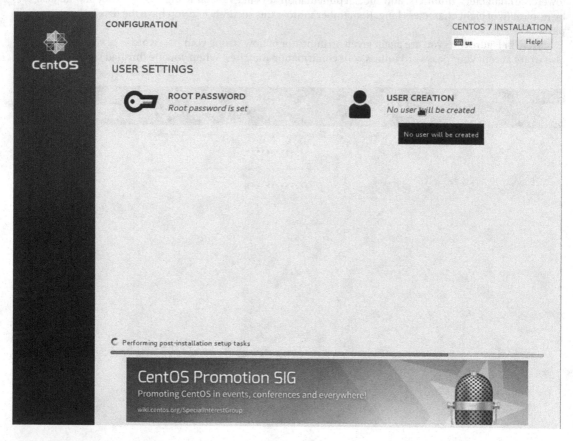

Figure 2-26. *Selecting User Creation*

You will notice in Figure 2-27 that as we type in the Full Name the suggested user name is created. You can change this to anything you wish but be sensible, you may have to remember who this user is at a later date. In this example we are going to make this person an administrator. That means the person will have similar abilities as the root user but will need to confirm his or her password before executing any root level commands.

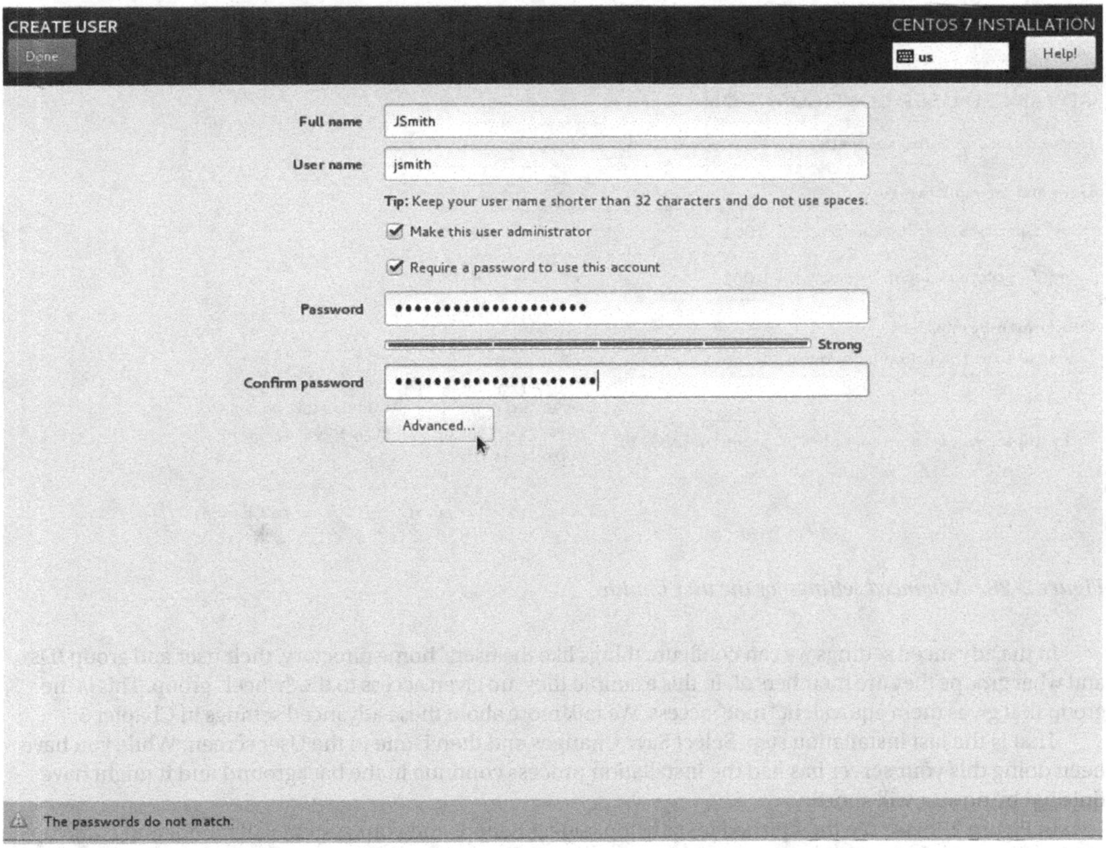

Figure 2-27. Creating new user JSmith

In Figure 2-27 also select the option that this user requires a password; some accounts are created where you don't expect the user to ever access the host or run commands that require passwords—like the user that runs the web server, for example. You will also notice that we will need to have correctly matched passwords before we can create this user. You can also have system or service users on your hosts. These system or service users do not have to have passwords (as they would never sign into the host but maybe execute a program like a database server). We talk more about users in Chapters 4 and 5.

After fixing the passwords, we are going to click Advanced and go on to Figure 2-28.

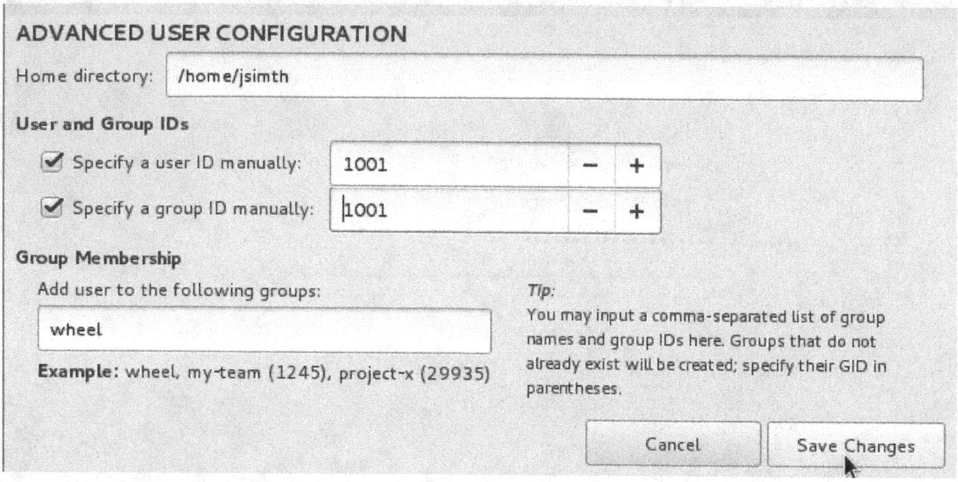

ADVANCED USER CONFIGURATION

Home directory: /home/jsimth

User and Group IDs

☑ Specify a user ID manually: 1001 − +

☑ Specify a group ID manually: 1001 − +

Group Membership

Add user to the following groups:

wheel

Tip:
You may input a comma-separated list of group names and group IDs here. Groups that do not already exist will be created; specify their GID in parentheses.

Example: wheel, my-team (1245), project-x (29935)

Cancel   Save Changes

Figure 2-28. *Advanced settings for the user JSmith*

In the advanced settings we can configure things like the users' home directory, their user and group IDs, and what groups they are members of. In this example they are given access to the "wheel" group. This is the group that gives them equivalent "root" access. We talk more about these advanced settings in Chapter 5.

That is the last installation step. Select Save Changes and then Done in the User screen. While you have been doing this your server has had the installation process continue in the background and it might have finished by now or will shortly.

In Figure 2-29 we see the finished installation. Select Reboot and your system will reboot and come up ready for your use.

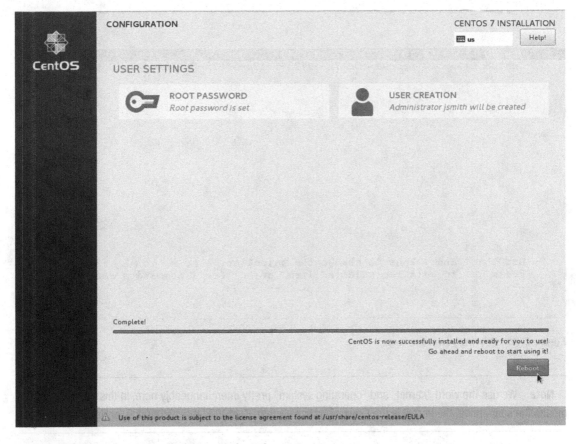

Figure 2-29. *Completed installation ready for Reboot*

Your system will begin to restart and present to you the GRUB2 (GRand Unified Bootloader) boot loader. The boot loader is the small bit of code that actually loads your operating system. This allows you to choose the operating system to boot into or boot into other operating systems you might have installed. If you press any key during this countdown process, loading will be interrupted.

Following the instructions on the screen in Figure 2-30, you can choose the kernel image you wish to boot into or change the way it loads (pressing e). You can access the GRUB2 shell by pressing c. We talk a lot more about the boot loader process in Chapter 6. If you press Enter on the highlighted CentOS Linux above you will be booted into that kernel.

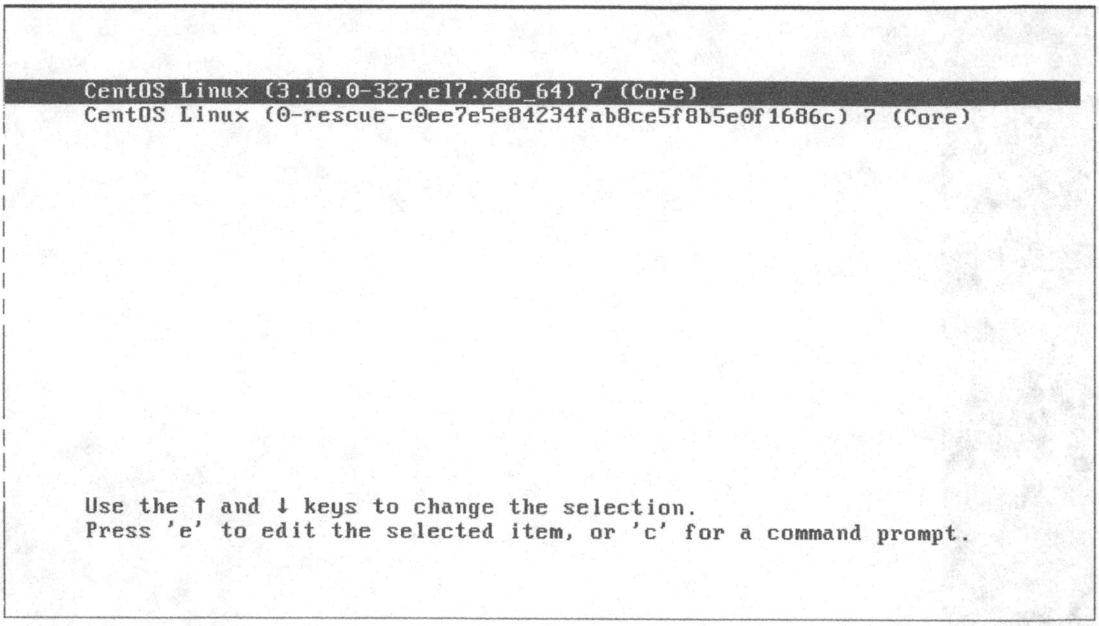

```
    CentOS Linux (3.10.0-327.el7.x86_64) 7 (Core)
    CentOS Linux (0-rescue-c0ee7e5e84234fab8ce5f8b5e0f1686c) 7 (Core)










    Use the ↑ and ↓ keys to change the selection.
    Press 'e' to edit the selected item, or 'c' for a command prompt.
```

Figure 2-30. *Booting your new host*

■ **Note**   We use the word "kernel" and "operating system" pretty interchangeably here. In this respect it means the same thing, the kernel is the Linux operating system. CentOS is the distribution, or flavor, of Linux.

When the system passes the boot loader we are required to put in the disk encryption password as in in Figure 2-31.

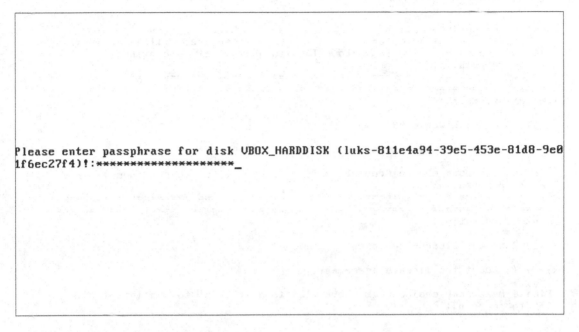

```
Please enter passphrase for disk VBOX_HARDDISK (luks-811e4a94-39e5-453e-81d8-9e0
1f6ec27f4)!:********************_
```

Figure 2-31. *Disk encryption password*

We cannot go further than here if we do not know the password, and if you have forgotten it you will have to start again. After successfully entering our password our system now starts to load information off our disks and our system continues to boot.

Now again, depending if you picked the Gnome package during your installation, you will see a EULA (End User License Agreement) appear. This to be honest is a little confusing and it is part of the gnome-initial-setup package. Here is the sequence you should try to get through it.

```
1) [!] License information          2) [ ] User creation
       (License not accepted)               (No user will be created)
 Please make your choice from above ['q' to quit ¦ 'c' to continue ¦
 'r' to refresh]: 1
============================================================================
============================================================================
License information

   1) Read the License Agreement

[ ] 2) I accept the license agreement.

 Please make your choice from above ['q' to quit ¦ 'c' to continue ¦
 'r' to refresh]: 2
============================================================================
============================================================================
License information

   1) Read the License Agreement

[x] 2) I accept the license agreement.

 Please make your choice from above ['q' to quit ¦ 'c' to continue ¦
 'r' to refresh]: c_
```

Figure 2-32. *Gnome Desktop EULA*

That is "1," "2," and "c" for the record. If you didn't install the desktop you will be spared all that and can continue on. Assuming you installed the desktop, you will now see the desktop login screen.

Here in Figure 2-33, are entering our password for the JSmith user. On entering your password you will be presented with the following desktop setup screens.

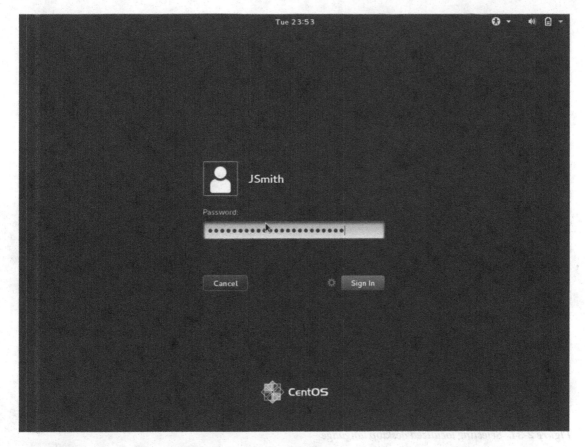

Figure 2-33. *Installation is complete and the system is ready to use*

In Figure 2-34 we are selecting our localized desktop language and selecting Next in the top right.

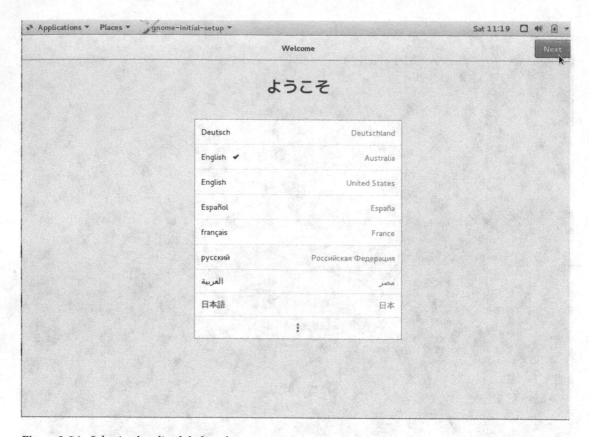

Figure 2-34. *Selecting localized desktop language*

Now we select keyboard layout in Figure 2-35. We are using the US-style keyboard.

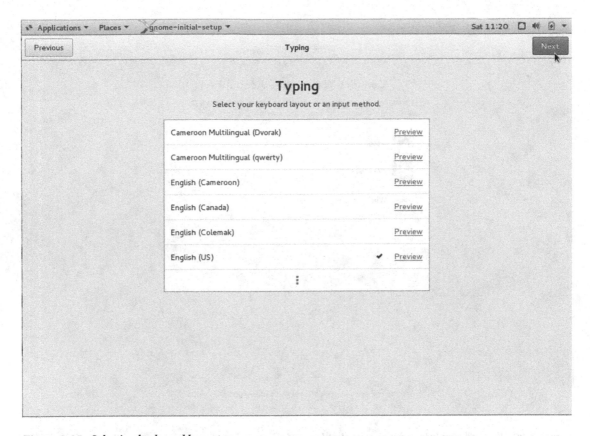

Figure 2-35. Selecting keyboard layout

In Figure 2-36 we are able to sign into Google to get access to the Google Apps and storage or ownCloud or even Windows Live. This is only really useful if you are running a desktop or allowing access to these cloud storage services via this server. Unless you are going to use these services you should skip.

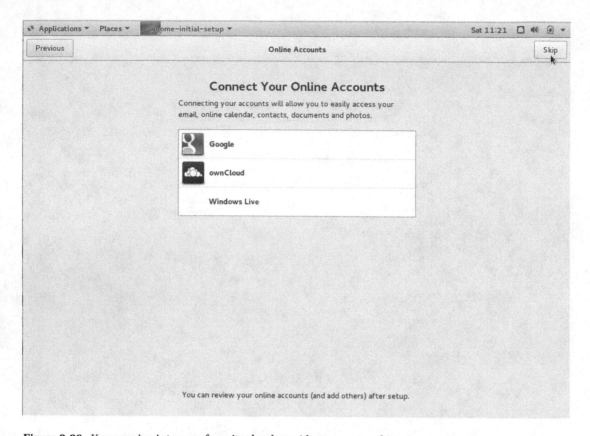

Figure 2-36. *You can sign into your favorite cloud provider or you can skip*

In Figure 2-37 you see an example of the Google sign in, but you do not have to sign up to any of them if you do not wish.

Figure 2-37. *An example of Google sign in*

Figure 2-38 brings us to the end of the desktop configuration part. Next we will show you quickly how to access a terminal console.

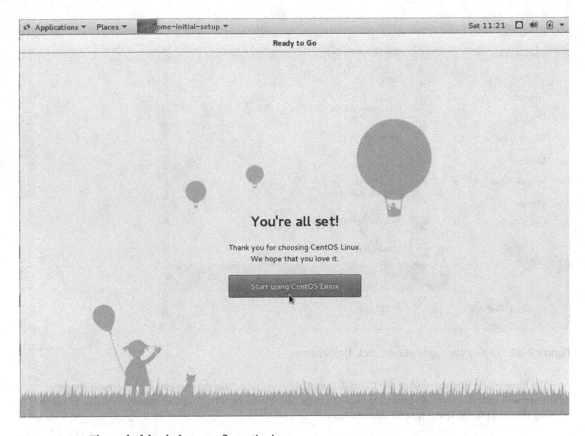

Figure 2-38. *The end of the desktop configuration!*

It is simple enough to find the applications, and the terminal application we are after as in Figure 2-39. Click *Applications, Utilities* and then scroll down to *Terminal*.

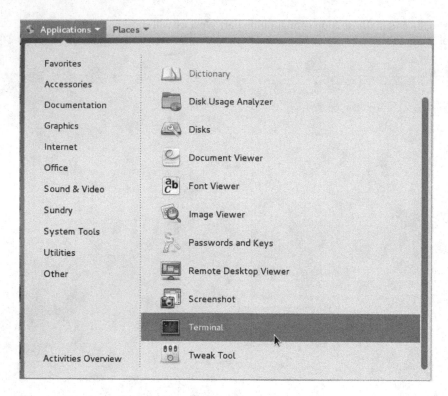

Figure 2-39. *To find the applications, click Applications*

We have made it to the end of the CentOS installation section. You can move on to the next chapter, where we will introduce you to Linux and how to start using your new host. Alternatively, you can continue reading this chapter to learn how to install Ubuntu.

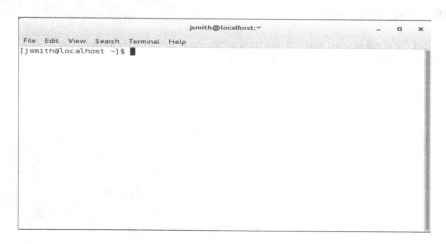

Figure 2-40. *Your first terminal session*

Ubuntu Installation

Ubuntu comes in two flavors: desktop and server. In this section, we'll demonstrate how to install the server version. Installing Ubuntu Server is a very similar process to installing a CentOS server. The main concepts are the same: choose the language and keyboard layout, choose the way you want to partition your disk, and then select the packages you want to install.

To install Ubuntu, we're going to download an ISO file from the Ubuntu website that contains much of the data we need to complete the installation. In this exercise we'll use the full-size ISO from `www.ubuntu.com/download/server`.

■ **Note**   Ubuntu and Debian make good use of net installers, providing installation flexibility. A *net installer* is a small version of the operating system usually provided as an ISO file that you can burn to a CD/USB drive and boot from. It contains a simple kernel and the distribution's installer. The net installer provides your host with the basics it needs to boot and start the installation process, and any additional software or applications are then downloaded from online repositories. This means you need to be connected to the Internet to install a new host. It can also mean that installing a complete 4GB operating system may take a long time on a slow Internet connection, but using a net installer can be a great way to load a smaller system. We will explore net installs further in Chapter 19, when we look at ways to provision multiple systems.

We will make a few assumptions here:

- You are using an Ubuntu 16.04 LTS Server Edition ISO from the Ubuntu web site (`www.ubuntu.com/download/server`), and you have burned it to a CD/DVD or a USB. You can find out more about burning ISO files to CD/DVD here: `https://help.ubuntu.com/community/BurningIsoHowto` and here: `https://help.ubuntu.com/community/Installation/FromUSBStick`

- You are building just a basic mail, DNS, and web server

- You are installing on a fresh server without any previous operating system.

After you place the CD in the CD drive or insert the USB and power on the host, the first screen you will see allows you to choose the language of the installation process (Figure 2-41).

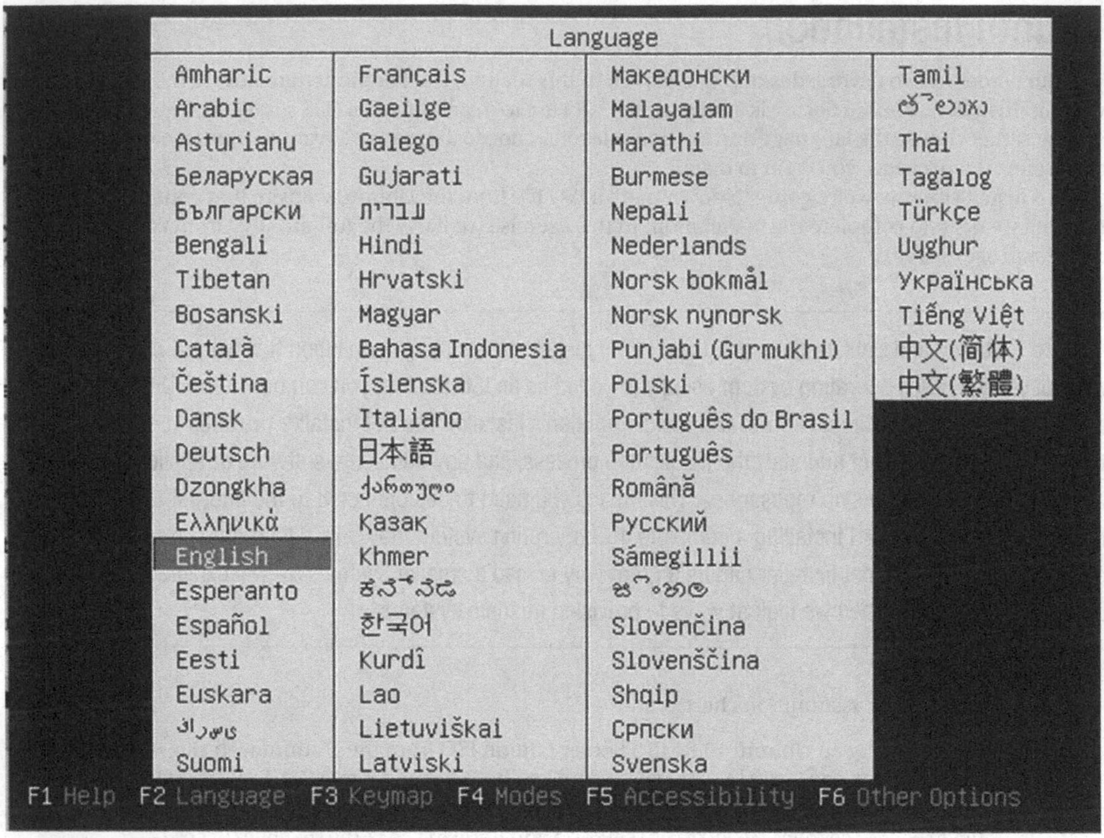

Figure 2-41. *Choose the installer language*

Then you are presented with a splash screen (see Figure 2-42) that gives several options. We are going to choose Install Ubuntu Server but you will also see some other new options. Ubuntu has a product called MAAS—or Metal As A Service. This is a a "zero-touch" deployment service for data center scale installations. Instead of installing just one server, MAAS can install thousands as soon as you plug the power in. We are going to discuss this sort of provisioning in Chapter 19. You can also see that we can run some system checks or boot into a rescue mode. In Chapter 9 we talk more about system recovery.

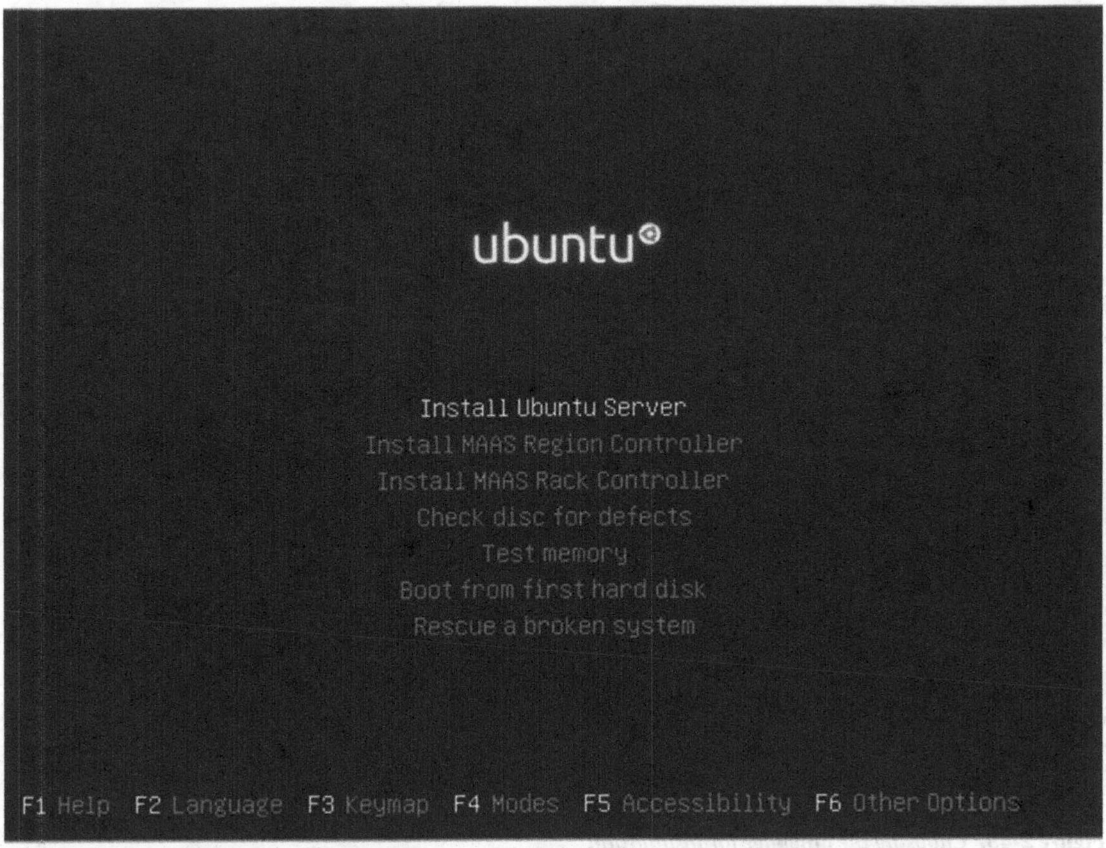

Figure 2-42. *First installation splash screen*

After selecting Install Ubuntu Server we are shown Figure 2-43, language selection for your installation. You should select the appropriate language for you.

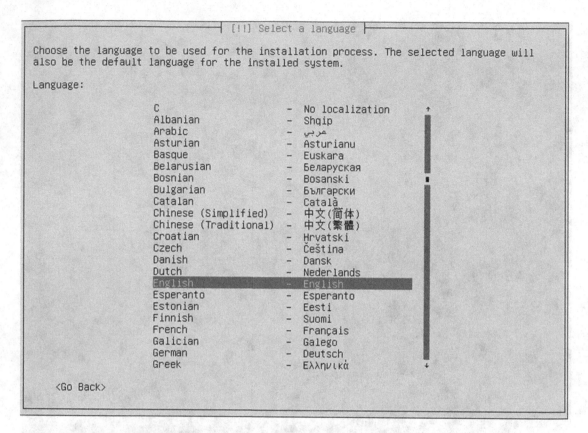

Figure 2-43. Choosing the language for installation

As shown in Figure 2-43, we chose English. This will also be the default language for the final system.

You are then asked to select your region. This is the geographical location in which the server you are installing is located. In Figure 2-44 we've selected Australia. This helps the installer also choose the closest Ubuntu archive repository to fetch extra packages from later.

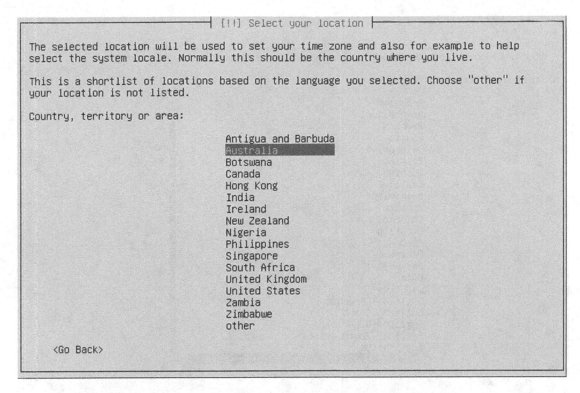

Figure 2-44. Selecting your region

Next, you select the keyboard and keyboard layout preference. As mentioned earlier, the keyboard layout is the keyboard mapping you are using. Different regions will have different mappings, so choose the one that best fits your area and language. Choosing Yes here, as shown in Figure 2-45, leads to a further series of questions and answers through which Ubuntu attempts to work out what type of keyboard you are using by having you press different keys.

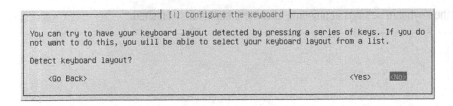

Figure 2-45. Ubuntu attempts to detect your keyboard

Select No to save time and directly tell the installation what kind of keyboard you are using. The default here will work for most installations, but feel free to select the one most appropriate to your area. Figure 2-45 begins a series of screenshots that show the keyboard selection.

After selecting No, the screen in Figure 2-46 appears, where you select the origin of the keyboard. We will pick US and continue on.

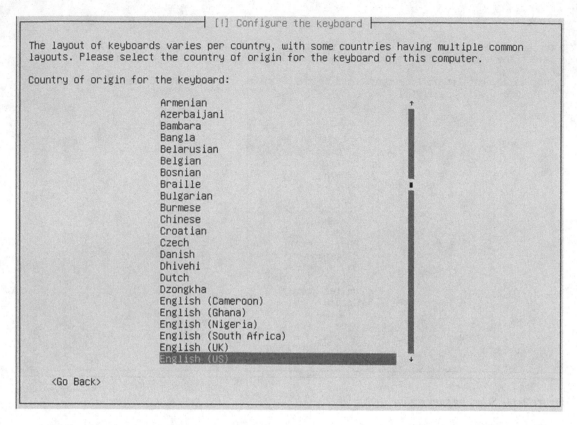

Figure 2-46. Selecting the origin of your keyboard

In Figure 2-47, we select the keyboard layout for US that will give us the standard key mapping for Australian computers.

■ **Tip** You can change the keyboard settings at any time after the installation is finished.

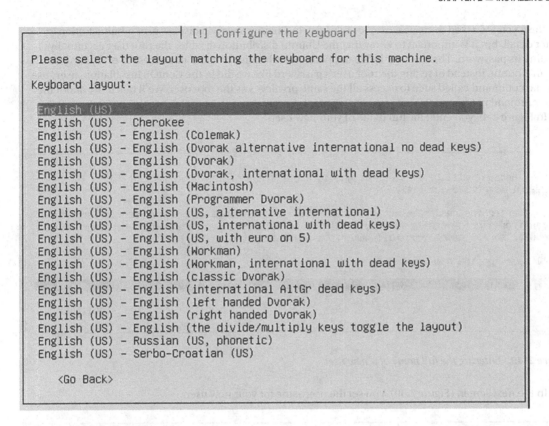

Figure 2-47. Selecting keyboard layout

The Ubuntu installation now takes a break to explore your hardware and discover more information about the target host. After this process is completed, you will be prompted for the hostname of your new host. As shown in Figure 2-48, we entered au-mel-ubuntu-1 here as it ties in with the naming standard discussed in the CentOS installation section.

```
┤ [!] Configure the network ├

Please enter the hostname for this system.

The hostname is a single word that identifies your system to the network. If you don't
know what your hostname should be, consult your network administrator. If you are setting
up your own home network, you can make something up here.

Hostname:

au-mel-ubuntu-1

    <Go Back>                                                        <Continue>
```

Figure 2-48. Setting the hostname

Next, you are asked to create a user for this host. In Chapter 5 we will discuss user administration in greater detail, but it is important to know that the Ubuntu distribution disables the root user account by disabling its password. The root user is like the Windows Administrator and has access to everything on the host. In Ubuntu, instead of setting the root user's password like we did in the CentOS installation, users use a special command called sudo to access all the same privileges as the root user. We'll talk more about the sudo command in Chapter 5.

In Figure 2-49 you enter the full name of your new user.

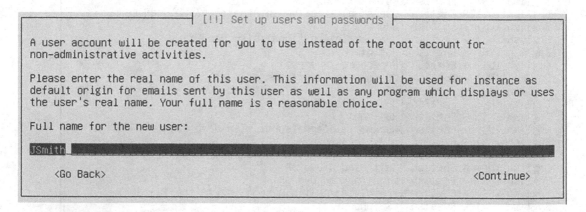

Figure 2-49. *Entering the full name of a new user*

In the next screen (Figure 2-50), you set the username for your new user.

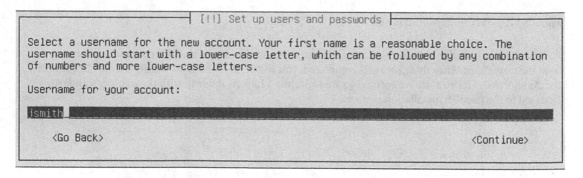

Figure 2-50. *Entering the username*

Finally, you set the password for your user, as shown in Figure 2-51. Again, as we discussed in the CentOS installation section, we recommend implementing a strong and complex password. You will be asked to verify that password.

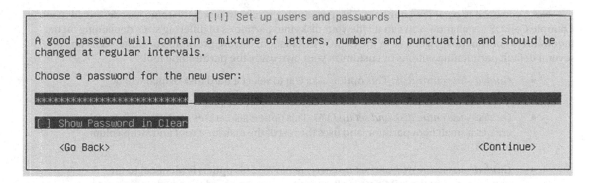

Figure 2-51. Entering the password for the new user

We are next asked if we wish to encrypt the home directory for that user. This has the same implications as disk encryption in CentOS. We are going to choose No here in Figure 2-52 in favor of doing a full disk encryption in a few steps time.

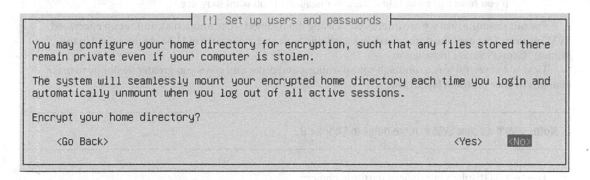

Figure 2-52. Choosing not to encrypt the home directory

We are now asked to confirm our time zone. Here we are using local time zone.

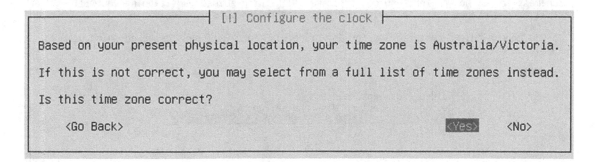

Figure 2-53. Confirming time zone

Next, you need to partition your host. This partitioning occurs in much the same way described in our example CentOS installation. You can divide your disks into partitions of differing sizes depending on the requirements of your host. Again, as in the CentOS installation, you are prompted to either select one of several default partitioning options or customize your own using the partitioning tool.

- *Guided—use entire disk*: This option asks you to select a hard disk, which will be completely erased. The system then creates a root partition and a swap partition.

- *Guided—use entire disk and set up LVM*: This option also erases all data. It then creates a small boot partition and uses the rest of the disk for a root and swap volume in LVM.

- *Guided—use entire disk and set up encrypted LVM*: This option is identical to the previous, except the LVM data is all encrypted. You are asked to provide a password. Note that you need to input this password at boot time, so this option is not suitable for a remote or headless server. If you lose the encryption password, you will not be able to retrieve your data.

- *Manual*: This option opens the partition editor and allows you to manually configure partitions, software raid, encryption, and LVM. This is the option you should choose if you have a pre-existing Windows installation you want to resize.

For our example host we are interested in using the "Guided—use entire disk and set up encrypted LVM" option. This uses the entire hard disk available to us and makes use of LVM. As described in the section "CentOS Server Installation,

LVM is a powerful way to manage your partitions and disks, and gives you greater flexibility to make changes to your partition layout later.

■ **Note** We'll discuss LVM in more detail in Chapter 9.

Figure 2-54 displays our default partition choices.

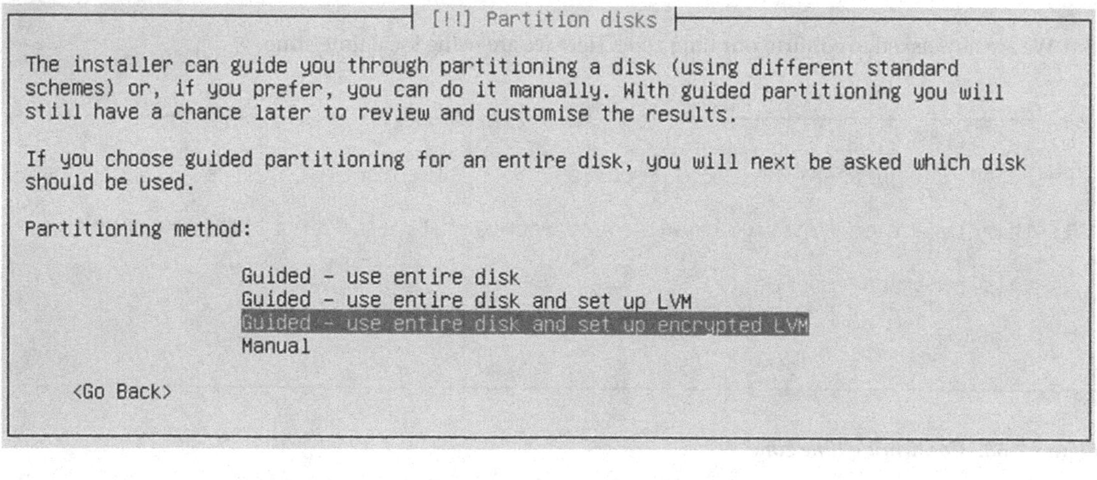

Figure 2-54. Choosing encrypted LVM to partition disks

Next, select the drive you wish to perform this partitioning on. We are given only one disk to select, as you can see in Figure 2-55.

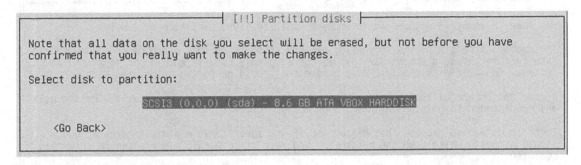

Figure 2-55. *Choosing the disk to partition*

■ **Caution** If the disk already contains partitions, you will be prompted to overwrite them. If you are confident that you want to do this, then specify Yes and continue. Selecting Yes here will destroy any existing data you may have if you are installing over a previous system. If you are not confident, then specify No. Alternatives to this include repartitioning your host using a tool like GParted from one of the LiveCD installations, installing on a hard disk that doesn't already have data on it, or installing on a virtual machine.

The next screen (see Figure 2-56) lets you confirm that you wish to write the partition information to the selected disk. The partition information needs to be written to disk before LVM can be configured. Select Yes and go to the next screen.

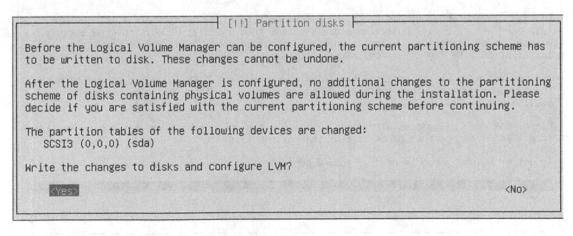

Figure 2-56. *Writing partition information to disk*

We now need to add a passphrase to secure the encrypted data. Again, make sure the password is long, complex, and stored securely.

You will also be asked for the password verification after Figure 2-57.

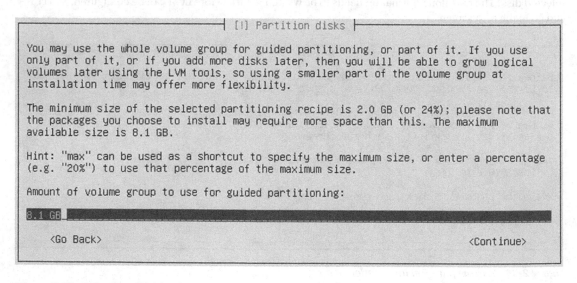

```
                          ┤ [!!] Partition disks ├

You need to choose a passphrase to encrypt SCSI3 (0,0,0), partition #5 (sda).

The overall strength of the encryption depends strongly on this passphrase, so you should
take care to choose a passphrase that is not easy to guess. It should not be a word or
sentence found in dictionaries, or a phrase that could be easily associated with you.

A good passphrase will contain a mixture of letters, numbers and punctuation. Passphrases
are recommended to have a length of 20 or more characters.

There is no way to recover this passphrase if you lose it. To avoid losing data, you
should normally write down the passphrase and keep it in a safe place separate from this
computer.

Encryption passphrase:

*****************************

[ ] Show Password in Clear

     <Go Back>                                                           <Continue>
```

Figure 2-57. *Providing the disk encryption password*

Next we are asked how much of the Volume Group we want to use in our LVM partitioning. In Figure 2-58 the default is all of the available LVM partition, or 8.1G.

```
                          ┤ [!] Partition disks ├

You may use the whole volume group for guided partitioning, or part of it. If you use
only part of it, or if you add more disks later, then you will be able to grow logical
volumes later using the LVM tools, so using a smaller part of the volume group at
installation time may offer more flexibility.

The minimum size of the selected partitioning recipe is 2.0 GB (or 24%); please note that
the packages you choose to install may require more space than this. The maximum
available size is 8.1 GB.

Hint: "max" can be used as a shortcut to specify the maximum size, or enter a percentage
(e.g. "20%") to use that percentage of the maximum size.

Amount of volume group to use for guided partitioning:

8.1 GB

     <Go Back>                                                           <Continue>
```

Figure 2-58. *LV group partitioning*

We will explain LVM better in Chapter 9, but just as partitioning a disk is slicing a disk up into parts, LVM groups are a further extension of the this concept. LVM volumes come from a bucket of shared storage called a group. We can slice this group up for our volumes and also use fancy disk magic to extend and shrink volumes after we have created them.

In Figure 2-58 we are asked how much of the Volume Group we want to use for this partitioning, and we will choose the default to use all of it, or 8.1 GB.

You will now be shown the LVM partition layout, which will show a small amount for swap space and the rest for the root or / partition. When we confirm this layout by selecting Yes, the LVM partitions shown in Figure 2-59 are created and formatted.

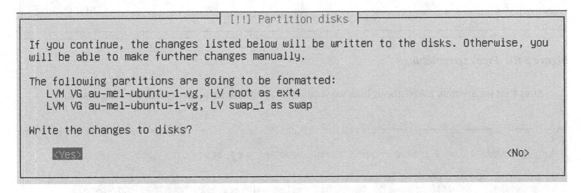

Figure 2-59. . *Writing LVM partition changes to disk*

■ **Note**   Swap space is additional storage on your hard disk drive that is used for "overflow" data from RAM. If you find your host frequently using all of your swap space or frequently swapping, then you probably need to tune your host and most often add more RAM. We'll talk about swap space in more detail in Chapters 9 and 17.

At this stage of the installation, Ubuntu will start installing the base package requirements needed to get the rest of the operating system installed. If you are using a net install, this may take some time depending on your Internet connection. You will be presented with a progress bar similar to the one shown in Figure 2-60.

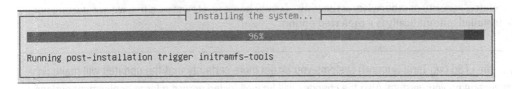

Figure 2-60. *Installing base system requirements*

Once that is complete, we are asked if we require the use of a proxy server to download the packages required for the complete installation. You can provide the URL including the username and password if you have one. We are going to leave it blank as in Figure 2-61.

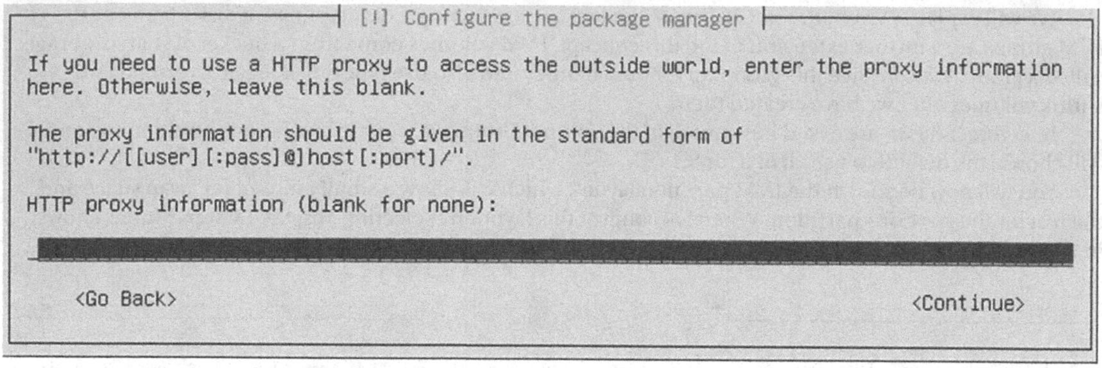

```
┤ [!] Configure the package manager ├

If you need to use a HTTP proxy to access the outside world, enter the proxy information
here. Otherwise, leave this blank.

The proxy information should be given in the standard form of
"http://[[user][:pass]@]host[:port]/".

HTTP proxy information (blank for none):

_____

    <Go Back>                                              <Continue>
```

Figure 2-61. *Proxy server settings*

After that we are now asked about how we would like to handle software updates on our system.

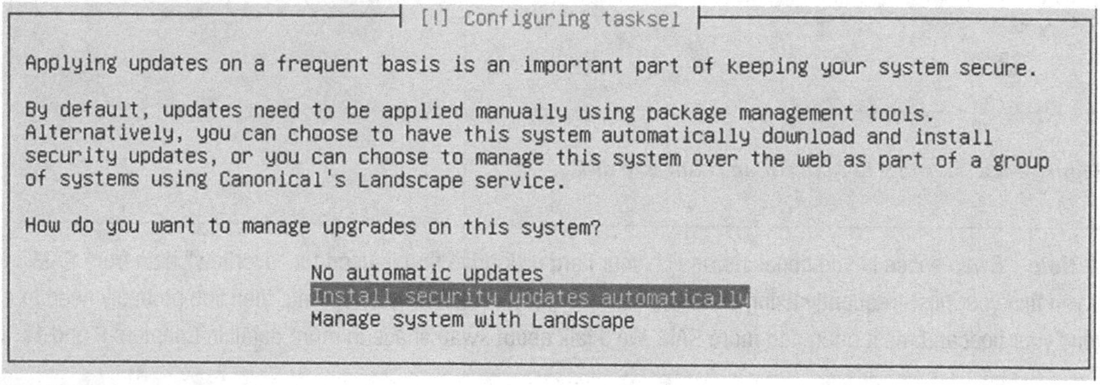

```
┤ [!] Configuring tasksel ├

Applying updates on a frequent basis is an important part of keeping your system secure.

By default, updates need to be applied manually using package management tools.
Alternatively, you can choose to have this system automatically download and install
security updates, or you can choose to manage this system over the web as part of a group
of systems using Canonical's Landscape service.

How do you want to manage upgrades on this system?

              No automatic updates
              Install security updates automatically
              Manage system with Landscape
```

Figure 2-62. *Automatically install system updates*

This can be a controversial issue. Some people don't like their systems being updated without their knowledge as it can cause unexpected results. Ideally you should know the state of your systems at all times and deploy updates, security or otherwise, at the time of your choosing. However, since we are starting out, having these installed automatically is a preferred option.

■ **Note** With the LTS(Long Term Support) systems you *do* get more certainty that the updates will make only the minimum change on your system. Also the changes will be well tested across a large deployment surface area. With bleeding-edge systems, you don't always get that same certainty.

You are then asked what applications you would like to install on your host via the selection of application groups. We chose DNS, LAMP server (Linux, Apache, MySQL, and PHP), mail (Postfix), and OpenSSH, as you can see in Figure 2-63. When you are ready, select Continue.

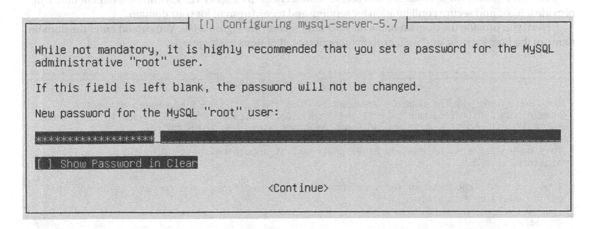

```
┤ [!] Software selection ├

At the moment, only the core of the system is installed. To tune the system to your
needs, you can choose to install one or more of the following predefined collections of
software.

Choose software to install:

              [ ] Manual package selection
              [*] DNS server
              [*] LAMP server
              [*] Mail server
              [ ] PostgreSQL database
              [ ] Samba file server
              [*] standard system utilities
              [ ] Virtual Machine host
              [*] OpenSSH server

                          <Continue>
```

Figure 2-63. *Selecting applications for your host*

In this particular installation, because of the applications you have chosen to install, you are asked
a series of questions to help Ubuntu configure or secure your chosen applications. Every time you install
new applications on Ubuntu that require input to be configured, you will be prompted to answer similar
questions.

As you can see in Figure 2-64, you are first asked to provide a password for the MySQL database root
user. This is the master password for your MySQL installation and you should enter a secure and complex
password. You will be asked to confirm this password by entering it again.

```
┤ [!] Configuring mysql-server-5.7 ├

While not mandatory, it is highly recommended that you set a password for the MySQL
administrative "root" user.

If this field is left blank, the password will not be changed.

New password for the MySQL "root" user:

*************************

[ ] Show Password in Clear

                          <Continue>
```

Figure 2-64. *Setting the MySQL root password*

Once you have provided this password, you are then asked to describe your mail server configuration.
The screen in Figure 2-65 shows the configuration options, with each option briefly described. We will just
choose the default, Internet Site.

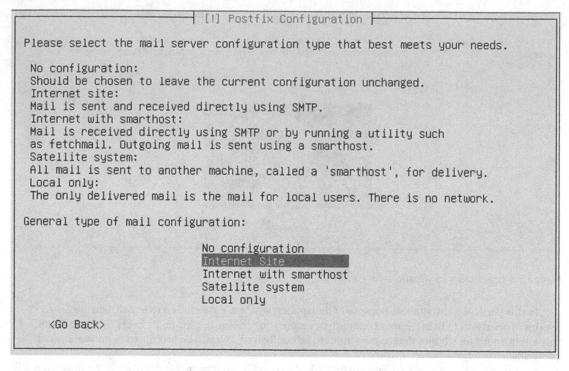

Figure 2-65. *Configuring the mail server*

We will explain how to configure and secure mail services in Chapter 12. Selecting the default here will provide a basic and secure configuration for sending and receiving mail for your domain.

Next, you provide the domain name for your mail server (see Figure 2-66). You should enter the domain name of the host for now, and we'll explain other potential options in Chapter 12.

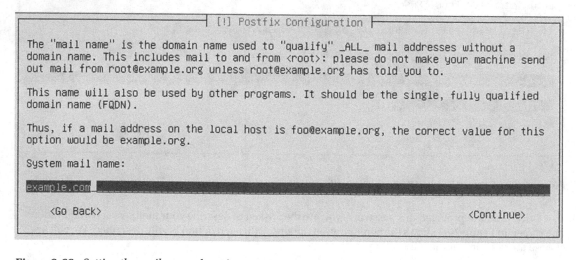

Figure 2-66. *Setting the mail server domain name*

Moving on, we have spoken about GRUB in the CentOS installation guide and talked about how it is the software that loads your operating system. In this screen we are asked to install it into the MBR, or Master Boot Record. The MBR is small bit of space on your hard drive that describes your partition layout to your system. It also has a small space where the GRUB boot loader is installed into.

■ **Note**   You may not see the GRUB installation screen (Figure 2-67). Systems running UEFI (Unified Extensible Firmware Interface) do not show this next screen. We talk about the differences between BIOS (Basic Input/Output System) and UEFI later on in Chapter 6.

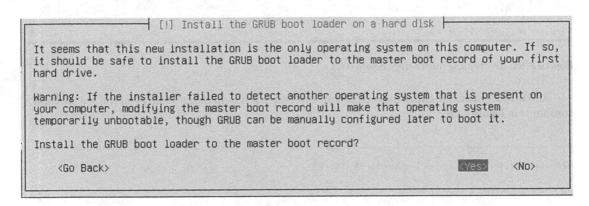

Figure 2-67. Installing the GRUB into the boot loader

In Figure 2-67 we are selecting Yes to install the boot loader into the MBR. And now your installation is complete and Ubuntu will notify you of this, as you can see in Figure 2-68.

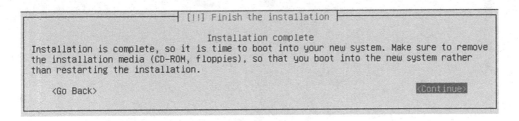

Figure 2-68. Installation complete

If you were using a CD or DVD, it should eject automatically. If you used a USB thumb drive, remove that and select Continue. Your system will now reboot and you will be presented with a password prompt (see Figure 2-69) to decrypt your hard drives.

```
[    5.626946]    avx        : 20240.000 MB/sec
[    5.629165] async_tx: api initialized (async)
[    5.639720] md: raid6 personality registered for level 6
[    5.640089] md: raid5 personality registered for level 5
[    5.640439] md: raid4 personality registered for level 4
[    5.645612] md: raid10 personality registered for level 10
done.
Begin: Running /scripts/init-premount ... done.
Begin: Mounting root file system ... Begin: Running /scripts/local-top ...    lvm
etad is not active yet, using direct activation during sysinit
  Volume group "au-mel-ubuntu-1-vg" not found
  Cannot process volume group au-mel-ubuntu-1-vg
  lvmetad is not active yet, using direct activation during sysinit
  Volume group "au-mel-ubuntu-1-vg" not found
  Cannot process volume group au-mel-ubuntu-1-vg
Please unlock disk sda5_crypt: _
```

Figure 2-69. *Decrypting hard drives before boot*

And now we are at the end of the installation. The system is now booting. Shortly you will see the login console as in Figure 2-70.

```
Ubuntu 16.04 LTS au-mel-ubuntu-1 tty1

au-mel-ubuntu-1 login: _
```

Figure 2-70. *Booting to the console screen*

You will notice that Ubuntu does not boot to a GUI but to a console screen. This is because the default Ubuntu Server installation does not install a GUI. We'll talk more about using the command line versus a GUI in Chapter 4.

You now have a usable mail, DNS, and web server running the Ubuntu distribution that is ready for you to customize further for your environment.

Troubleshooting

Every now and then an installation will fail for some reason. Most commonly this happens due to defective installation media; less often it happens due to unsupported or defective hardware.

If there is a problem with the installation media, you may see read errors being logged or the installer may display an error stating it was unable to read a file. You should check the installation CD or DVD for scratches. If you created the CD or DVD from an ISO file, it might be worth writing a new disc at a lower speed. Media problems usually recur at the same step in the installation process.

Network installations can also fail if the connection is interrupted, so check that cables are plugged in and your Internet connection is working.

The less common type of failure is caused by hardware not being supported. For example, if an installation kernel does not support the disk controller, the installer will be unable to access hard disks. If this happens, check which kernel version is included on the installation disc and verify that it in fact supports your hardware. A newer version of your distribution, with support for more and newer hardware, might be available. This is much less common now that major manufacturers have started to support Linux more and more and actively contribute drivers to the kernel.

Non-reproducible crashes at random points in the installation usually indicate a hardware problem, and the most common problems are bad RAM or overheating. You can run a RAM tester like memtest86 (www.memtest.org/), and you should verify that the CPU and case fans are working properly.

Diagnostic Information

If you need additional diagnostic information while you are installing, you can access a limited shell and some logging information from the installation process. You can use these to further diagnose any problems you might have. These are called virtual consoles (also known as a tty) and we talk about them again in Chapter 4.

On Ubuntu, Alt+F2 and Alt+F3 each give access to a limited shell. Alt+F4 provides verbose installation progress and logs for the installer. The Alt+F1 combination switches back to the installer interface.

OnCentOS, the graphical installation runs on Ctrl-Alt-F1. There is a shell prompt on Ctrl-Alt-F2, installation messages go to Ctrl-Alt-F3 with system messages going to Ctrl-Alt-F4 and other messages appear in Ctrl-Alt-F5.

You can use these terminals to gather information about your installation or see any error messages that might prove helpful if your installation doesn't go as planned.

Restarting Your Installation

After a problem, you should normally restart the installation from the beginning. Because files from the previous installation attempt might still be present on disk, it's best to have the installer re-initialize the partitions and start from scratch.

Troubleshooting Resources

Don't be afraid to make use of the communities that exist around most Linux distributions if you run into trouble. Chances are someone else has experienced the same problem you have and has documented the resolution. Here are some resources to try:

- Red Hat: www.redhat.com/en/services/support/

- Fedora: http://forums.fedoraforum.org/forumdisplay.php?f=6

- Ubuntu: http://ubuntuforums.org/forumdisplay.php?f=333

Summary

In this chapter, we stepped through the process of installing two of the popular Linux distribution choices:

- CentOS Server

- Ubuntu Server

We also explained what you might do if something goes wrong during installation. In the next chapter, we are going to give you an introduction to some of the tools we use to help quickly prototype our installations. We will use these tools more throughout the rest of the book.

CHAPTER 3

■ ■ ■

Introducing VirtualBox, Git, and Vagrant

By Dennis Matotek

In Chapter 2 we showed you how to install Linux on a physical server from an ISO image. However, there are many other options to deploying a Linux server—including network provisioning, deploying virtualized machine images, or launching a Linux instance in the "cloud." There is also a greater ability now to share virtualized machines with others locally or all over the world. We are going to show one way that might be helpful for you in following this book.

Some people find it hard to just get started with Linux, as there are many install options and choices—having all those options we regard as a great thing! Luckily there are tools that make investigating and exploring Linux somewhat easier. We want to take this opportunity to introduce some tools to you that we will be using later in this book, or you can use them now to follow along with us, as we take you through the different examples in the chapters to come. For you it means that you can follow along on your desktop, whatever that happens to be, and if you make a horrible mistake, you can recover quickly and safely. As a bonus, along the way you will get familiar with some of the tools we use.

One combination of tools we use daily in our prototyping and testing is VirtualBox, Vagrant and Git (to track changes to our configurations as we trial and test). Being able to prototype full systems without having to pollute your local host or another server is a real benefit. Being able to trial different types of operating systems and being able to run quick and effective testing to validate your work should be the aim of all administrators.

One way to cheaply and quickly build out a server is to use virtualization. Virtualization comes in many different forms, like KVM, Xen, and LXC containers for starters. What we would like to do in this chapter is show you the tools we use daily to prototype and test on the desktop—be that a Linux server, Mac, or Windows host. One such virtualization technology you can use on both Windows machines, Mac, and Linux is VirtualBox. VirtualBox, for this reason, makes a good entry-level virtualization platform to begin with and prototype on—it is not a platform you would use for performance, however. But it does allow you to further explore LXC container software like Docker if you are coming from the Windows and Mac world, which requires the Linux kernel to run.

VirtualBox also allows you to run up many different operating systems on your desktop. This saves you the time and trouble of dual booting different operating systems (which means you have to shut down one operating system to start another). It also allows you to share the resources, like the filesystem between your guest operating systems and your desktop.

© Dennis Matotek, James Turnbull and Peter Lieverdink 2017
D. Matotek et al., *Pro Linux System Administration*, DOI 10.1007/978-1-4842-2008-5_3

Git is a version source control technology for computer software. It is great at tracking changes to text-based files, like configuration files. Combined with resources like GitLab, GitHub, or BitBucket it is an empowering way to manage change in your organization in an open and collaborative way. With Git, your configuration changes can be compared to the current configuration, and you can give other administrators the ability to agree to those changes. You can also use Git for building testing pipelines that test changes to your systems prior to deploying to production.

And while you can use the VirtualBox GUI or VirtualBox CLI to create, install, and manage your VirtualBox machines, we will introduce to you the Vagrant tool. Vagrant is a "wrapper" for the VirtualBox CLI commands, but it is also much more than that. It has text-based configuration files that are suitable for tracking changes in Git. This helps you prototype and develop host builds or applications. It allows for integration with many of the configuration management tools like Puppet, Ansible, or SaltStack. But one of the major benefits is that you can share images, or "boxes" and build instructions with other developers. This helps your teams develop on a consistent set of images that run on desktop commodity hardware and that are easily created, recreated, developed, and produced.

System administrators find this kind of quick prototyping very useful. In the past to see what a new package did, or what the new update to the operating system would do, you might have to find some spare server and run up the new software. With VirtualBox and Vagrant you can do this much more quickly and without poisoning your local desktop. Later in the book we will be using Puppet and Ansible, the configuration management tools, to deploy our server configurations and we will be using the combination of VirtualBox, Vagrant, and Git to achieve and track this.

The ability to share and download Vagrant boxes, or shared VirtualBox machines, means that you quickly integrate or trial different technology. For example, you might have the need for a memcached service in your application. As far as your application is concerned, to test memcached with your application you just need the IP (Internet Protocol) address and a port to reach it. Instead of building out another server for this, you can download a Vagrant box with a fully configured memcached service created by somebody else in your team or a publicly available box from the online Vagrant box repository. From a development point view, this makes for much faster prototyping and building. If your application works well with memcached, you can, at a later stage, develop, test, and deploy a proper memcached service for your application.

For general information on virtualization technologies, please see the following:

- https://gendersec.tacticaltech.org/wiki/index.php/Linux_virtualisation

- https://en.wikipedia.org/wiki/Comparison_of_platform_virtualization_software

VirtualBox Installation

VirtualBox is very easy to install. There are self-installing packages for Windows, Mac, Linux, and even Solaris (which is a Unix operating system for those who don't know). Simply go to www.virtualbox.org/wiki/Downloads and choose the appropriate download for your operating system. You should be able to install VirtualBox easily. If you get into trouble you may find Chapter 2 of the following PDF helpful: http://download.virtualbox.org/virtualbox/5.0.14/UserManual.pdf.

Licensing

VirtualBox is an open source virtualization platform owned by Oracle. It has been released under the GNU General Public License (GPL) Version 2 license. Full details of that license can be found at www.gnu.org/licenses/old-licenses/gpl-2.0.html.

If you wish to also use the VirtualBox Oracle VM VirtualBox Extension Pack you are required to agree to the terms of the VirtualBox Personal Use and Evaluation License (see `www.virtualbox.org/wiki/VirtualBox_PUEL`). This license allows for personal or product evaluation or academic use only. If you intend to use this product in a commercial sense please abide by these licenses.

Creating a New VirtualBox Machine

Before we start our new VirtualBox machine, first make sure you have downloaded the appropriate ISO image file for CentOS 7. You can go to `www.CentOS.org/download` to fetch it. There are three options presented to you for download. The DVD ISO and Full ISO will take longer to download but will contain everything you will need for a desktop environment. If you choose the Minimal ISO your download will be quicker but you will have to download any extra packages (applications) from the Internet when you need them.

In this example we are installing CentOS from the following download link: `http://isoredirect.CentOS.org/CentOS/7/isos/x86_64/CentOS-7-x86_64-Minimal-1511.iso`.

The VirtualBox application runs like any other application on desktop. Find the application and start it. You will be presented with a screen similar to this one.

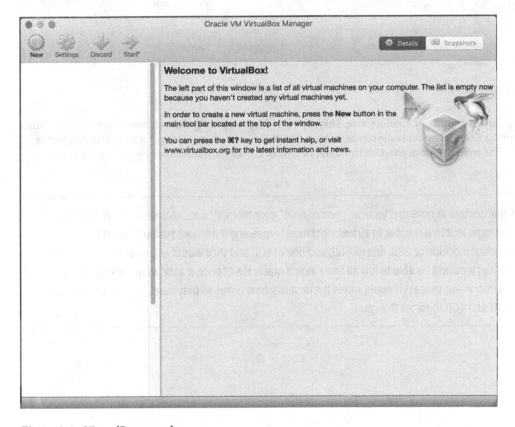

Figure 3-1. *VirtualBox console*

A new installation will not have any virtual machines installed. To create our own CentOS installation, we select the New button. In the window that comes up we will give the machine a name, Centos7 and we will select the Type and the Version of Linux and Red Hat (64 bit).

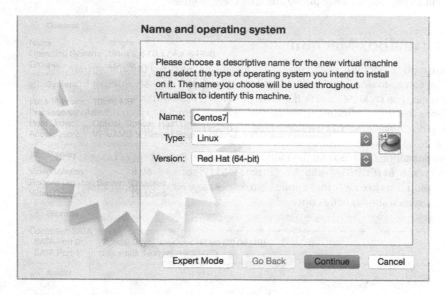

Figure 3-2. Naming and setting VirtualBox type

Next we can configure our memory size. This can be as large as your system allows. In general, 1024Mb is appropriate, or 512Mb for smaller systems without things like a graphic desktop. You can also adjust this after the install to match your needs. Use the slider or type in the amount of memory you need for your system.

■ **Note**   It is important to note that you can "overcommit" your memory (i.e., allocate more than your host system has available to it to a number of virtual machines)—meaning if my host system has 8GB RAM, we can have one virtual machine of 2GB, one of 4GB, and one of 6GB and they would all be able to run fine at the same time. We just wouldn't be able to run all three virtual machines at once if they were each to use their full allocation of memory—or at least it would make the host machine crawl. In that case, we may be able to run the hosts of 2GB and 4GB together though.

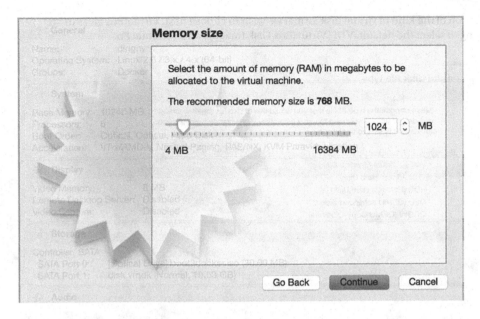

Figure 3-3. Memory allocation

We are now asked if we wish to create a *Hard disk*. Here you can make a selection to use an existing disk or choose not to have a disk at all. We are going to click Create a virtual hard disk now and click Continue.

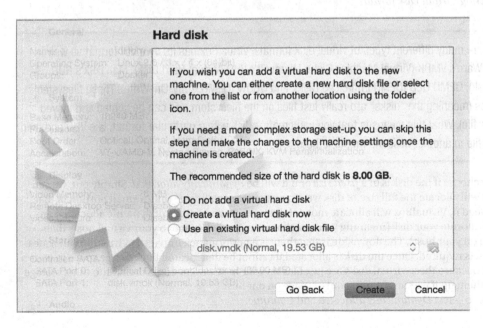

Figure 3-4. Choosing disk

There is a selection of the kind of virtual disk format we wish to choose next. VirtualBox gives us six options. We are going to select the default, VDI (VirtualBox Disk Image) , and continue on.

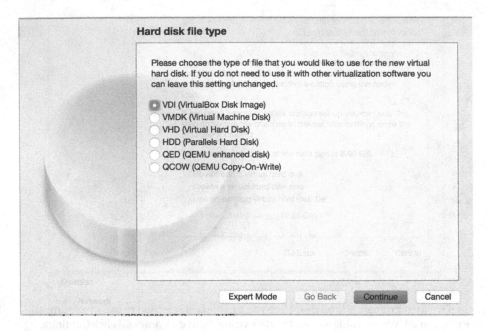

Figure 3-5. *Selecting Virtual Disk format*

■ **Note** There are many different types of virtual disk formats. VirtualBox has its own VDI format as well as supporting VMWare's VMDK (Virtual Machine Disk), Microsoft's VHD (Virtual Hard Disk), Mac OSX's HDD (Parallels Hard Disk), QEMU QED (QEMU Enhanced Disk), and QCOW (QEMU Copy-On-Write). These filesystems are all on disk files (meaning the "disks" are really just files on the filesystem and can be copied and moved just like any other file). What this means is that you can create a disk with a particular format, like VHD and then move that image file to another host and mount it there.

We can now choose if the disk is of a *fixed size* or if it will be *dynamically allocated*. Simply put, we can create a disk that will allocate the full size of disk we request or we can allocate only a small portion of that now, and as we need it, VirtualBox will allocate more of that space. The benefits of dynamic allocation are that you can overallocate your disk (meaning you can allocate more disk space to your virtual hosts than you actually have on your host). The downside is that there is a performance impact as VirtualBox allocates that space when it is required. Once the disk is allocated it cannot be deallocated back to free space in your virtual hosts. But because these virtual disks are just files on your host we can move them onto other storage devices or clean them up if we start running out of space on our host.

We are going to select *Dynamically allocated* and *Continue*.

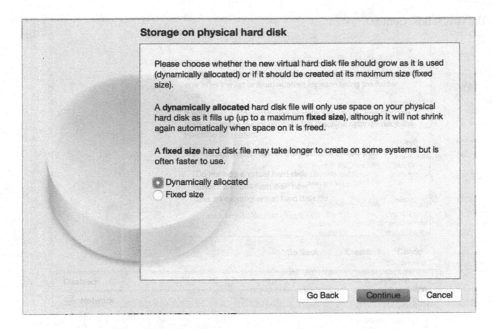

Figure 3-6. Dynamically allocating disk

The default disk size is 8GB. We are going to select this and you can use the slider or type in the amount of disk you wish for your virtual host. Here you can also change the name and the location of the disk if you wished by selecting the little folder icon.

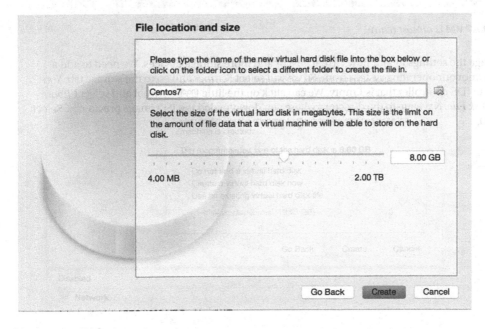

Figure 3-7. Disk amount

That creates the virtual host Centos7.

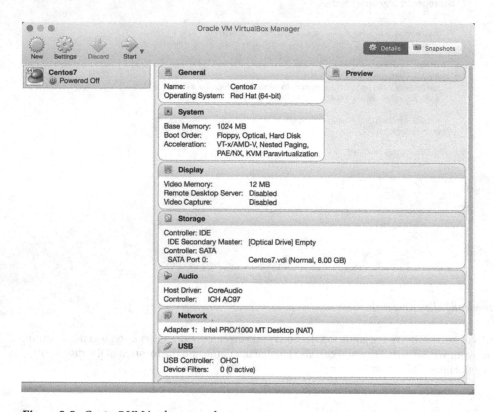

Figure 3-8. *Centos7 VM is almost ready*

We can change the settings for our new virtual host or add more storage devices. We need to add a storage device to boot our operating system from. So we will select *Settings* and go to the storage tab. You can see we have an IDE controller that is Empty. We can click on the little DVD symbol and select *Choose Optical Virtual Disk File*. Navigate to the directory where you downloaded the ISO image previously. Select the CentOS-7 ISO.

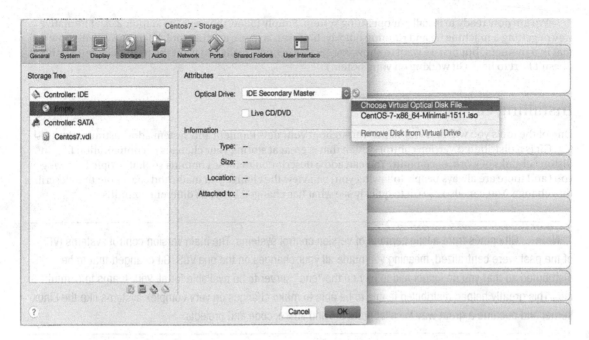

Figure 3-9. Selecting image

The disk should now appear attached to the IDE controller.

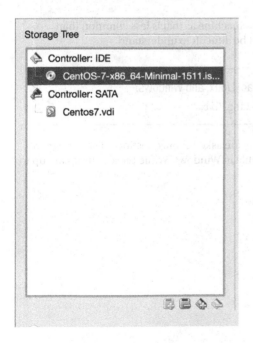

Figure 3-10. Selected CentOS ISO is ready

We are now ready to install our operating system. Simply follow the steps in Chapter 2. An alternative way of getting a machine up and running quickly, however, is to use another tool, Vagrant. We will show you that in a moment, but first we want to show you Git (we actually really just want the terminal emulator but it doesn't hurt to have Git working on your system).

Installing Git

One of the tools you will find very handy throughout your development and system administration tasks is Git. Git is a distributed version control system that is great at storing your changes to configuration files in distinct chunks of work, or commits. You can add a description to these commits so that people following you (and there are always people following you) can view the change you made and see a note that describes that change. You can also use Git to quickly see what has changed between different commits.

■ **Note**   Git comes from a long heritage of version control systems. The main version control systems (VCS) of the past were centralized, meaning you made all your changes on the one VCS. Git changed that to be distributed so that you no longer had to rely on the "one" server to be available for all your teams to commit into. This greatly helped distributed teams to be able to make changes on very complex systems like the Linux kernel and became a great way to collaborate on, and share, code and projects.

Downloading Git is very painless. You will either have it available to you as a standard package in most (if not all) Linux distributions or you can go to

`http://git-scm.com/download.`

We are going to demonstrate the installation on a Windows machine as that is less common than installing Git on Mac or Linux and has some options that might be difficult to understand.

■ **Tip**   The Git site here also has installation instructions for Mac, Linux, and Windows:
`https://git-scm.com/book/en/v1/Getting-Started-Installing-Git.`

Starting off, after downloading and opening the installer we are asked some questions. These might be new to some people. One of those is setting of the %PATH% variable in Windows. While these settings are up to you, we suggest the following:

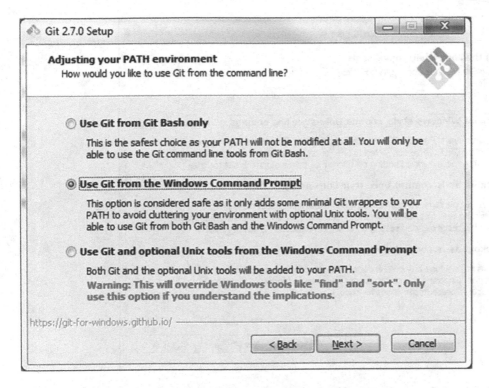

Figure 3-11. *Allow Git commands from the windows command line*

In Figure 3-11 we are choosing the setting that allows us to use Git from the Windows Command Prompt and the Git Bash prompt. This gives us a bit of flexibility when working with our files.

The next step may take a bit of thinking as well. Now to confuse things, Windows and Linux systems (and even Macs) have different ways of telling a computer where the end of a line is in a file. In Linux the end of a line in a file is called LF (line feed) and in Windows it is called CRLF (carriage return line feed). So when you are making changes to files, the operating system will add the appropriate line end to the end of each line in the file. When you open this file on another operating system you get strange formatting in your editor. What we are doing here is taking control of what Git does when you commit this change. Git can control what these invisible line endings should be.

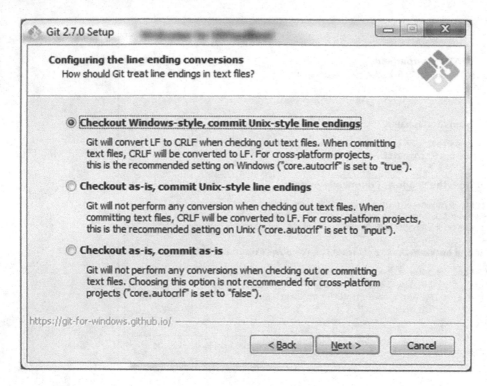

Figure 3-12. *Allow Git to change LF to CRLF on checkout and CRLF to LF on commits*

In Figure 3-12 we are allowing Git to convert LF to CRLF for Windows editing, but when we commit files we convert CRLF to LF again. With this option you should be able to interact with Git-controlled files without effort.

Next we configure which terminal emulator to use with Git. Git Bash is a good way to learn and to interact with Git. It has many Linux commands available to it as well as the Git commands. Of course, if you feel more comfortable with the Windows console feel free to select that.

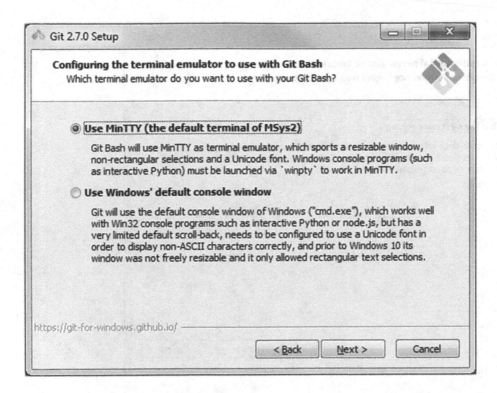

Figure 3-13. *Selecting the terminal*

The next screen is not very important right now. You can add some experimental performance tweaks by selecting the check box you see in Figure 3-14. We are not going to select it but if you're feeling adventurous you can.

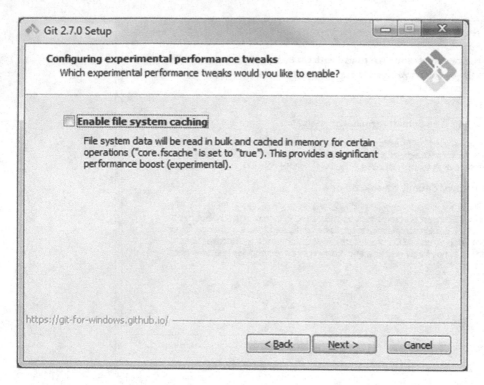

Figure 3-14. *Experimental performance options*

Git Basics

Let's quickly go through the common Git command you will need to know. The way that Git differs from centralized version control software is that it is decentralized! What that means is that each clone of the Git repository is equivalent to a "master" copy of the repository—including the history. This is the equivalent of each developer's local copy also being a distributed backup of the repository. However most people use a centrally hosted Git repository service like GitLab, GitHub, or BitBucket and one of the first actions is to clone the repository:

```
$ git clone git@<githost.com>:<username>/git-repository.git
```

The foregoing command will log into the githost.com server using the SSH protocol (you can also use HTTPS, Git, or a local protocol). You gain access to the repository using your SSH public key for authentication on the githost.com server. Git will then make a copy of the git-repository.git repository on your local filesystem in a directory of the same name.

Once you have a copy of the repository you can begin to make your changes. One of the first steps is to create a branch. A branch is a set of discrete commits that all relate to a particular change. There is a main branch that is considered the main line or master branch (usually called master). Changes in branches are usually merged into the master branch. To make a new branch from the master branch you do this following command:

```
$ git branch my_change
```

You do this so that you can make contained and discrete branches of work in a named branch—and branches are cheap with Git (it is one of the selling points!).

You have now cloned, created a branch, and you have edited some files. You can use the following command to view the changes you have made to those files:

```
$ git diff
```

This command will show all the changes in the repository, you can add the directory or filename to the command line if you wish to narrow the scope of the diff. But let's say you are happy with your diff and you are now ready to commit those changes.

```
$ git commit -v path/to/file/or/directory
```

You will be shown the diff of your changes again and you will be able to add a commit message to the commit so that people know what the change is. Good commit messages give some idea of what you did - preferably what was done and why it was done. Bad commit messages are "updated file." You now have a commit in your branch and you might wish to merge that back into the master branch (you might not want to do this directly if you are working on a shared project—you may instead want to "push" your branch to the remote repository you cloned from and get others review it first). To merge back to master, issue the following commands:

```
$ git checkout master
$ git pull origin master
$ git merge my_change
```

What we are doing above is that we are first leaving our my_change branch and checking out the master branch—the master branch is normally the branch from which production code is taken from. We first do a "pull" on the origin (or the githost.com master repository) to pull in any other changes that have been checked in already. Then you merge your changes into the master repository and take care of any conflicts this causes. Once you are happy with the state of the repository you can "push" back to the origin (githost. com repository).

```
$ git push origin master
```

Your change is now able to be shared with anybody using that githost.com copy of the repository. This, of course, is a very simplified and potentially bad example. A workflow like above will no doubt lead to breaking things and you should have a way of testing code prior to merging to master. GitHub provides a good document on git workflows here: https://guides.github.com/introduction/flow/

■ **Note**   For more information on Git please see https://git-scm.com/book/en/v2.

For Windows users, now that you have Git installed you can use *Git Bash* to access useful Linux utilities like *less, vi, grep,* and *tail*. We will show you how we use Git Bash in the next section.

Introducing Vagrant

Vagrant is a way of sharing and distributing development environments between developers quickly and easily. In this sense a "development environment" is a set of virtual machines and a configuration for running those machines. Originally it was designed to manage VirtualBox machines via a combination of configuration files and command-line tools, but it has since expanded to be much more and supports other virtualization technologies. It was developed by Mitchell Hashimoto who then founded HashiCorp on the popularity of the product. It is written in Ruby and can run on any operating system that supports Ruby. Currently you can download and run it for Linux, Mac OSX, and Windows.

Installing Vagrant

You first can download it here for your operating system:

`www.vagrantup.com/downloads.html`.

Vagrant is meant to be driven by the command line; it provides no graphical user interface (GUI). With Macs you can drive it all from a terminal window. On Windows machines you can run commands from the `cmd.exe` program, from PowerShell, or from Git Bash like we just installed.

■ **Tip** There are some things that you cannot natively do in the Windows command or PowerShell console. One of the them is SSH. SSH is a secure way to access consoles over a network. By installing Git Bash we get access to an SSH client. If you can't get SSH to work you should check that the path to your SSH executable is in your console environment's path. Common place in Windows is `C:\Program Files\Git\usr\bin`. Add it to your current PowerShell environment with `$env:path =+'; C:\Program Files\Git\usr\bin'`. For the Windows command prompt, `set PATH=%PATH%;C:\Program Files\Git\usr\bin`. You will need to set this permanently as it only lasts as long as your current console session. We will leave you to your own investigation for how to do that.

Licensing

Vagrant is distributed under the MIT License. Meaning that you can use this software in practically any way you wish. You can view the license at

`https://raw.githubusercontent.com/mitchellh/vagrant/master/LICENSE`

Vagrant Concepts

The problem space that Vagrant tried to solve when it was originally developed was the sharing of virtualized machines and their configurations run under VirtualBox. Since that time it has expanded its support for virtualization technologies but its core tenant remains the same. It does this in two ways. It provides a mechanism for distributing and downloading other VirtualBox virtual machines as well as tools to manage the configuration and running of them.

Primarily Vagrant works with *boxes*. Boxes are just compressed files of pre-built VirtualBox virtual machines that have a few special things configured. They have a "vagrant" user that has access to root privileges and OpenSSH has been installed and is running. Vagrant uses VirtualBox commands (or VBoxManage commands) to create, configure, start, and stop these boxes—it does this with a combination of the VirtualBox CLI and SSH access via the vagrant user. You can download boxes from HashiCorp's other service called Atlas or you can build your own. You can store, distribute, and publish boxes via Atlas too. Atlas has private and corporate offerings and integrations with other HashiCorp services.

■ **Note** There is a bit involved in building your own Vagrant box, but it is an exercise you should try when you get more familiar with Linux. When you are ready, check out here for details `www.vagrantup.com/docs/boxes/base.html`.

You are not limited to using just VirtualBox machines either. You can run Amazon AWS or Openstack instances, LXC containers, and of course Docker containers. In this exercise we are going to show you how to work with a VirtualBox virtual machine. You are free to explore others at your leisure.

HOW VAGRANT INTEGRATES WITH VIRTUALBOX

What we are going to do through this exercise is initialize a Vagrant configuration file, make some edits to that file, then use the Vagrant CLI to start that VirtualBox virtual machine. But how does that all work?

Well, when you download a Vagrant box, it is basically a compressed tarball (similiar to a zipped file) of VirtualBox virtual machine including the virtual disk images. The vagrant command will store these boxes in the appropriate .vagrant.d/boxes directory in your HOME directory.

```
virtualbox/
total 1029016
drwxr-xr-x  6  dennismatotek  staff            204 12 Dec 16:44 .
drwxr-xr-x  3  dennismatotek  staff            102 12 Dec 16:44 ..
-rw-r--r--  1  dennismatotek  staff            505 12 Dec 16:44 Vagrantfile
-rw-------  1  dennismatotek  staff      526833152 12 Dec 16:44 box-disk1.vmdk
-rw-------  1  dennismatotek  staff          10589 12 Dec 16:44 box.ovf
-rw-r--r--  1  dennismatotek  staff             25 12 Dec 16:44 metadata.json
```

When you issue the *vagrant up* command the first time, as we will do shortly, vagrant will download the specified box, store in a similarly named directory, then import that downloaded VirtualBox machine (box.ovf) into VirtualBox itself using the VBoxManage import command.

VirtualBox will then assign that virtual machine a UUID (universal unique identifier) which vagrant can then use to issue the *VBoxManage startvm <uuid>—headless* command. Similarly, Vagrant will use the *VBoxManage controlvm <uuid> poweroff* command to stop the virtual machine when a *vagrant halt* is called.

Vagrant will also do things like set up up network port forwards (for SSH access and other network services if configured to) and mount your file system inside the virtualbox virtual machine (unless you configure it not to).

These examples are specific to VirtualBox virtual machines—but Vagrant supports other virtualization and cloud-based instances by issuing the required commands or API (application programming interface) calls to manage them. This means we can use the same *vagrant up* command to start a VirtualBox virtual machine or an AWS instance—but with appropriate configuration file (Vagrantfile) changes of course.

Getting Started with Vagrant

After installing, the first thing you will need to do is either open a terminal or get to a command prompt via cmd.exe, PowerShell prompt, or Git Bash prompt. Go to your favorite workspace and create a new directory or folder called *first*. Use the cd command to enter that new directory.

The output of the commands will be the same no matter which operating system you have. Issue the following command:

Listing 3-1. Vagrant Options

```
> vagrant
Usage: vagrant [options] <command> [<args>]

    -v, --version                    Print the version and exit.
    -h, --help                       Print this help.

Common commands:
     box             manages boxes: installation, removal, etc.
     connect         connect to a remotely shared Vagrant environment
     destroy         stops and deletes all traces of the vagrant machine
     global-status   outputs status Vagrant environments for this user
     halt            stops the vagrant machine
     help            shows the help for a subcommand
     init            initializes a new Vagrant environment by creating a Vagrantfile
     login           log in to HashiCorp's Atlas
     package         packages a running vagrant environment into a box
     plugin          manages plugins: install, uninstall, update, etc.
     port            displays information about guest port mappings
     powershell      connects to machine via powershell remoting
     provision       provisions the vagrant machine
     push            deploys code in this environment to a configured destination
     rdp             connects to machine via RDP
     reload          restarts vagrant machine, loads new Vagrantfile configuration
     resume          resume a suspended vagrant machine
     share           share your Vagrant environment with anyone in the world
     snapshot        manages snapshots: saving, restoring, etc.
     ssh             connects to machine via SSH
     ssh-config      outputs OpenSSH valid configuration to connect to the machine
     status          outputs status of the vagrant machine
     suspend         suspends the machine
     up              starts and provisions the vagrant environment
     vbguest
     version         prints current and latest Vagrant version

For help on any individual command run `vagrant COMMAND -h`

Additional subcommands are available, but are either more advanced
or not commonly used. To see all subcommands, run the command
`vagrant list-commands`.
```

This shows you the full list of available subcommands to Vagrant. We are going to only show you four to get you started. The tasks we are planning to show you are

- initialize our *first* directory

- update the configuration file for Vagrant

- start our Vagrant Box

- check the status
- finally, SSH into the console

The first task we need to do is initialize our *first* directory. Issue the following command, `vagrant init` as shown in Listing 3-2.

Listing 3-2. Vagrant init

```
> vagrant init
A `Vagrantfile` has been placed in this directory. You are now
ready to `vagrant up` your first virtual environment! Please read
the comments in the Vagrantfile as well as documentation on
`vagrantup.com` for more information on using Vagrant.
```

The *vagrant init* command has simply placed a file inside your directory. This is the file that we use to configure our *first* Vagrant image. If we use the `ls` command to list the contents of our directory we will see the following (you may need to issue `dir` for Windows `cmd.exe`).

Listing 3-3. Showing the Vagrantfile

```
> ls
Vagrantfile
```

In Figure 3-3 we have one file called *Vagrantfile* and this file contains the configuration information used by the vagrant command to create our Vagrant hosts. If we look at the contents of that file it looks very much like Ruby code. That is because it is. This file uses Ruby code and Vagrant parses and loads this file when executing Vagrant commands. That means that you can use the Ruby language in the file to create lists, arrays, hashes, and so on. That becomes useful later on when working with more than one image in your Vagrantfile. Now open up the Vagrantfile with your editor. If you are using the Git Bash you can use the *vi* program. We explain a lot more about *vi* in Chapter 4.

The contents of the *Vagrantfile* looks similar to this shortened version shown in Listing 3-4.

Listing 3-4. Vagrantfile

```
Vagrant.configure(2) do |config|
 config.vm.box = "base"

 # config.vm.network "forwarded_port", guest: 80, host: 8080

 # config.vm.network "private_network", ip: "192.168.33.10"

 # config.vm.synced_folder "../data", "/vagrant_data"

 # config.vm.provider "virtualbox" do |vb|
 #   # Display the VirtualBox GUI when booting the machine
 #   vb.gui = true
 #
 #   # Customize the amount of memory on the VM:
 #   vb.memory = "1024"
 # end
end
```

In Listing 3-4 we have removed a lot of the comments and suggested settings. Without going too deep into the Ruby language here you may be able to see that we can write blocks of code between *do* and *end* statements. We pass the result of `Vagrant.configure(2)` to the *config* variable object. We can then use that to assign our Vagrant configuration. In Figure 3-4 we are setting `config.vm.box` to equal "base."

■ **Tip**   Ruby is a great flexible programming language. It is similar to the Python language, another very popular powerful language. I encourage you to go to `http://tryruby.org/` and check it out.

So let's create a basic configuration for our *first* Vagrant image. First we can head over to the following link and see all the available boxes:

`https://atlas.hashicorp.com/boxes/search`

■ **Note**   Remember a Vagrant "box" is a self-contained Linux virtual machine that can run inside your VirtualBox virtualization software. The boxes hosted by HashiCorp on Atlas are created by community members or organizations and vary widely in design and purpose.

The Ubuntu team regularly pushes an official Vagrant box for public download. We shall use that as our Vagrant box. These Vagrant boxes are *"base"* images. You download them and use them as the basis for your own boxes. There are many available for you to explore.

In Listing 3-5 we are adding the ubuntu/xenial64 box. Vagrant will automatically download this from Atlas when we start our Vagrant host.

Listing 3-5. Vagrantfile—Adding aBox

```
Vagrant.configure(2) do |config|
  config.vm.box = "ubuntu/xenial64"
end
```

In Listing 3-5 we are setting the `config.vm.box` to `ubuntu/xenial64`.

■ **Note**   The box listed here is a 64-bit operating system release (`ubuntu/xenial64`). Depending on the system you are working on, you might only have a 32-bit operating system. If that is the case, you can use the 32-bit version by replacing the above box with `ubuntu/xenial32`. If your system doesn't support a 64-bit operating system a message will pop up: *Vt-x/AMD-V hardware acceleration is not available on your system.* This indicates that your processor doesn't have the appropriate hardware virtualization extensions enabled or virtualization is not supported by your processor. You may be able to enable these extensions and you can check out the following FAQ post, `https://forums.virtualbox.org/viewtopic.php?f=1&t=62339`, for possible solutions.

Next we are going to show you how to configure a *forwarded_port*. A forwarded port allows a port connection from your host to the Vagrant host running inside VirtualBox. In this example we are connecting port 8080 on our host's *localhost* address to the guest Vagrant host's port of *80*. This means if we are running a web server in our Vagrant guest machine, we can open our browser and point it to `http://localhost:8080` and have a web server listening on port *80 on our vagrant host* respond.

Listing 3-6. Vagrantfile—Adding Forwarded Ports

```
Vagrant.configure(2) do |config|
  config.vm.box = "ubuntu/xenial64"
  config.vm.network "forwarded_port", guest: 80, host: 8080
end
```

In Listing 3-6 you can see we are adding the forwarded port by setting the config.vm.network. We can also synchronize folders from our host to our guest hosts. This is invaluable when developing. By default, Vagrant will mount the current directory into the guest's /vagrant directory. For the interest of this exercise, let's mount the ./temp directory into the Vagrant user's home directory on the guest.

Listing 3-7. Vagrantfile—Adding Synced Folder

```
Vagrant.configure(2) do |config|
  config.vm.box = "ubuntu/xenial64"
  config.vm.network "forwarded_port", guest: 80, host: 8080
  config.vm.synced_folder "./temp", "/home/vagrant/temp"
end
```

Finally, we can configure the following. In this code group we are acting on the *virtualbox* provider. That is, the underlying virtualization platform that is running our box. At times it is useful to boot up your host and see what is happening on the console as it boots, especially when learning and debugging. The follow will enable the VirtualBox GUI and sets the memory for the guest to 1024Mb.

Listing 3-8. Vagrantfile—Adding Synced Folder

```
Vagrant.configure(2) do |config|
  config.vm.box = "ubuntu/xenial64"
  config.vm.network "forwarded_port", guest: 80, host: 8080
  config.vm.synced_folder "./temp", "/home/vagrant/temp"
  config.vm.provider "virtualbox" do |vb|
    vb.gui = true
    vb.memory = "1024"
  end
end
```

Let's save all that into our Vagrantfile and bring up our first Vagrant host. Issue the following command shown in Listing 3-9.

Listing 3-9. Issuing vagrant up

```
> vagrant up
vagrant up
Bringing machine 'default' up with 'virtualbox' provider...
There are errors in the configuration of this machine. Please fix
the following errors and try again:

vm:
* The host path of the shared folder is missing: ./temp
```

Oh look. In Listing 3-9 we have an error. Vagrant is here telling us that something went wrong with the *"vm:* The host path of the shared folder is missing: ./temp"*. Of course, we did not create the temp folder. Vagrant will parse the Vagrantfile and make sure everything in is in place before we start our machine. Go ahead and create the temp directory in the *first* directory and try the command again (mkdir temp).

Listing 3-10. Issuing Vagrant up

```
> vagrant up
```

During your first "up" you will see things as shown in Listing 3-11:

Listing 3-11. Vagrant up Output

```
==> default: Importing base box 'ubuntu/xenial64'...
==> default: Setting the name of the VM: first_default_1455714694375_15606
==> default: Clearing any previously set forwarded ports...
==> default: Fixed port collision for 22 => 2222. Now on port 2203.
==> default: Clearing any previously set network interfaces...
==> default: Preparing network interfaces based on configuration...
    default: Adapter 1: nat
==> default: Forwarding ports...
    default: 80 (guest) => 8080 (host) (adapter 1)
    default: 22 (guest) => 2203 (host) (adapter 1)
==> default: Running 'pre-boot' VM customizations...
==> default: Booting VM...
==> default: Waiting for machine to boot. This may take a few minutes...
    default: SSH address: 127.0.0.1:2203
    default: SSH username: vagrant
    default: SSH auth method: private key
    default:
    default: Vagrant insecure key detected. Vagrant will automatically replace
    default: this with a newly generated keypair for better security.
    default:
    default: Inserting generated public key within guest...
    default: Removing insecure key from the guest if it's present...
    default: Key inserted! Disconnecting and reconnecting using new SSH key...
==> default: Machine booted and ready!
```

In Listing 3-11 we can see we are importing a base box (this one has already been downloaded, you might see the downloading step too). The name of the VM will be in the form of *directory_box name_random numbers*. You will be able to view this in your VirtualBox console (and change the settings just like any other VirtualBox). We can see the network is being set up including the ports we will use for SSH (22 => 2222). There is automatic port collision detection so instead of using port 2222, Vagrant chooses port 2203. The port forwarding for 80 => 8080 is next and then we wait for the machine to boot. When it does we create a set of SSH keys that we use to sign into the host. The public key of this key pair is injected into the machine. Finally we get the machine is booted and ready.

Listing 3-12. Final Steps of the vagrant up

```
==> default: Checking for guest additions in VM...
==> default: Mounting shared folders...
    default: /vagrant => /Users/dennismatotek/workspace/source/book/first
    default: /home/vagrant/temp => /Users/dennismatotek/workspace/source/book/first/temp
```

Once the machine is up we can then mount our directories. We have a default mount that mounts our first directory into `/vagrant` and we have our temp directory that we have mounted into `/home/vagrant/temp`.

Okay, now that our host is booted and ready let's check its status with the command shown in Listing 3-13.

Listing 3-13. Vagrant Status

```
> vagrant status
Current machine states:

default                 running (virtualbox)
```

By default, our host name is *default*. You can name our machines different names in your Vagrantfile. In Listing 3-13 we can see ours is in the state of running.

Next let's see if we can log into our Vagrant machine. To do that we issue the command shown in Listing 3-14.

Listing 3-14. SSH to the Vagrant Host

```
> vagrant ssh
Welcome to Ubuntu 14.04.1 LTS (GNU/Linux 3.13.0-35-generic x86_64)

 * Documentation:  https://help.ubuntu.com/

  System information as of Wed Feb 17 13:11:35 UTC 2016

  System load:  0.77            Processes:             80
  Usage of /:   2.7% of 39.34GB Users logged in:       0
  Memory usage: 12%             IP address for eth0: 10.0.2.15
  Swap usage:   0%

  Graph this data and manage this system at:
    https://landscape.canonical.com/

  Get cloud support with Ubuntu Advantage Cloud Guest:
    http://www.ubuntu.com/business/services/cloud

0 packages can be updated.
0 updates are security updates.

vagrant@vagrant-ubuntu-xenial-64:~$
```

There at vagrant@vagrant-ubuntu-xenial-64:~$ we have our command prompt of our Linux Ubuntu host. As you can see, it is a very simple way to build and run Linux servers. When you want to stop your Vagrant host, simply type exit to log out of the terminal session and then issue *vagrant halt*.

In Figure 3-15 we show the steps and output from our Git Bash terminal running on our Windows host.

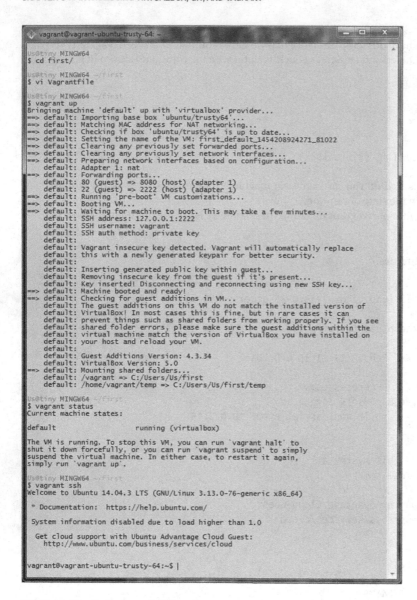

Figure 3-15. Summary of actions

Summary

This Chapter has introduced you to some handy virtualization software which will help you quickly and safely experiment and play with Linux. We have also shown you some of the tools that we use to develop and test our server configuration code. This also makes it easier to share your development environments with others.

In recapping we have shown the following:

- how to install VirtualBox

- how to create a virtual host

- how to install Git (on Windows)

- how to install Vagrant

- how to bring up a virtual host using Vagrant and VirtualBox

In the next chapter we are going to show you around a Linux host. In that chapter we will cover some of the basics concepts like logging in, navigating around, and some basic Linux commands.

CHAPTER 4

Linux Basics

By James Turnbull and Dennis Matotek

In Chapter 1, we talked a little about what Linux is and where it came from, and in Chapter 2 we installed our first Linux host. In this chapter, we're going to introduce you to some basic Linux concepts and skills. Some people find Linux intimidating because of what looks like arcane commands with strange switches and mysterious options. We'll decode some of the arcane commands you'll need to know and demonstrate these commands and their functions.

This chapter focuses on getting started, logging in, logging in locally and remotely, and working with and navigating the command line and the filesystem. We're also going to introduce some basic Linux concepts: users, groups, packages, services. We then will delve deeper into the filesystem and how to work with files and directories, including file types, how to set permissions, and then reading, editing, and managing them. In the chapters that follow, we'll expand on these concepts and introduce you to the key activities you'll need to know in order to operate and administer your Linux hosts.

In this chapter, we'll mostly talk about commands running on the command line. This gives you an introduction to using the command line and will help get you comfortable with operating on it. This is not to say that there isn't a broad array of graphical administration tools available for Linux. If you're more comfortable in a graphical, Windows-like environment, you can still easily and effectively find mechanisms to administer your Linux hosts. For most command-line tools we're going to show you, there is a graphical equivalent. However, you should find the Linux shell easier and faster to operate on one or several Linux systems at once.

■ **Note** This chapter is a broad introduction to Linux. It won't make you an expert. Rather, it'll prepare you to take the first steps to deploy your Linux infrastructure.

Getting Started

If you haven't already installed a Linux host, the easiest way to try out Linux commands prior to tackling a Linux install is to try a LiveCD. *LiveCDs* are Linux distributions on a CD, DVD, or USB. To use a LiveCD, you need to download an image, in the form of an ISO file. You can choose any LiveCD and burn that image to a CD, DVD, or USB. Following are some URLs that describe how to burn ISO files onto CDs, DVDs, or USBs:

- http://pcsupport.about.com/od/toolsofthetrade/ht/burnisofile.htm

- www.petri.co.il/how_to_write_iso_files_to_cd.htm

- https://help.ubuntu.com/community/BurningIsoHowto

- www.ubuntu.com/download/desktop/create-a-usb-stick-on-windows

© Dennis Matotek, James Turnbull and Peter Lieverdink 2017
D. Matotek et al., *Pro Linux System Administration*, DOI 10.1007/978-1-4842-2008-5_4

Once you have burned your LiveCD, you can then insert the disc or USB into your computer and reboot. Most computers will automatically detect the LiveCD and offer you the option of booting from it.

■ **Note**   If your host doesn't offer you the option to boot from CD/DVD, you may need to adjust your BIOS (Basic Input/Output System) settings to change your boot order so the CD, DVD, or USB is booted before your hard drive.

The LiveCD will load and present you with a working Linux distribution that you can experiment with. By default, this does not install anything to your host, and your original desktop configuration will be available when you remove the CD/DVD and reboot your computer.

LiveCDs are available for a variety of distributions. Some good distributions to try using their LiveCDs include the following:

- *Ubuntu*: You can find LiveCDs, called Desktop CDs, for Ubuntu at `www.ubuntu.com/download/desktop`.

- *Fedora*: You can find a LiveCD for Fedora (called Fedora Desktop Live Media) at `https://getfedora.org/`.

- *CentOS*: Available for the latest CentOS 7 release is a LiveCD from one of the mirror sites listed at `https://wiki.centos.org/Download`.

■ **Tip**   There is a comparison list of some of the available Linux LiveCDs available at `http://en.wikipedia.org/wiki/Comparison_of_Linux_LiveDistros`.

You can also consider using Vagrant, as we showed you in Chapter 3. Using Vagrant is a great way to explore and learn Linux without the need to install a physical server, and it runs inside the VirtualBox virtualization environment.

Logging In

After your Linux host or LiveCD boots, you will be presented with a login prompt: either a command-line or GUI (graphical user interface) login prompt.

In Figure 4-1, you can see a typical command-line login prompt for an Ubuntu Linux host, and in Figure 4-2, you can see the graphical login for a CentOS host.

■ **Note**   Don't panic if your initial screens differ slightly from these, as some minor changes do appear between versions.

```
Ubuntu 16.04 LTS au-mel-ubuntu-1 tty1

au-mel-ubuntu-1 login: _
```

Figure 4-1. *Command-line login prompt*

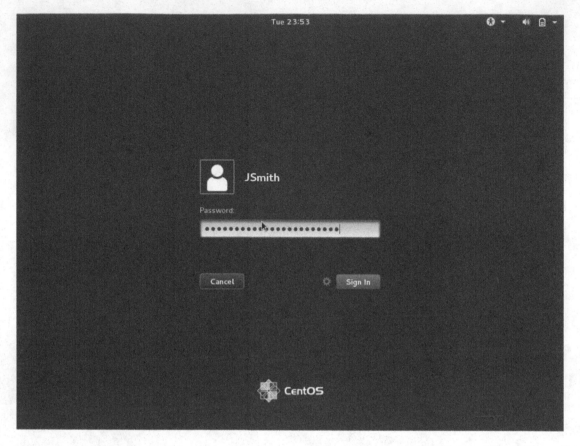

Figure 4-2. *Graphical login prompt*

At either login prompt you need to supply your username and a password or similar form of authentication. (Like Windows, Linux can also use smartcards or tokens or other mechanisms to authenticate users.)

If you just installed a Linux host, you'll have been prompted to create a user, and you can make use of that user to log in now. If you're testing Linux with a LiveCD, you may see a default username and password that you will be prompted to log in with, or you may even be automatically logged in. For example, the Ubuntu LiveCD has a default username of ubuntu with a password of ubuntu, and it usually automatically logs you in. If you don't see a default username and password, you may need to check the LiveCD's online documentation, or you may be prompted to create a username and a password.

Once your host has verified your access, then you'll be logged in and, depending on your configuration, your host will either display a command-line or a GUI desktop environment.

Linux vs. Microsoft Windows

The title of this section might sound a bit like we're about to present a pro wrestling match. However, it's more about the similarities between Linux and Microsoft Windows (hereafter just Windows) than their differences. Windows and Linux are both operating systems, and while different in many technical aspects, they share a lot of the same concepts. As a result, we're going to examine these similarities to help you leverage some of your existing knowledge about Windows as a means of understanding related concepts in Linux.

In this book, we're going to look at how to interface with your Linux host. There are two principal interfaces: the GUI desktop and the command line. We'll explore both of these interfaces in this book.

The GUI Desktop

Both Linux and Windows can have GUIs. Unlike recent Windows releases, Linux has always been able boot to either a GUI or the command line. Once you're booted up, you can also switch between these two modes, and we'll discuss how to do that in the section "Shells" later in this chapter and in some more detail in Chapter 5.

On Linux the GUI is a combination of several applications. The basic application is called the X Window System (you'll also see it called X11 or simply X). The X application provides an underlying "windowing" environment.

■ **Note**   You won't need to worry about installing or managing X. Your distribution will generally install this for you if you install a GUI desktop. If you don't install a GUI desktop, for example, if you are installing a server, X will not be installed, and you'll generally interact with Linux through the command-line interface. An example of a distribution that doesn't load a GUI by default is the Ubuntu Server distribution we installed in Chapter 2.

On top of X you then add a desktop environment to provide the "look and feel" and desktop functionality such as toolbars, icons, buttons, and the like. There are two major desktop environments popular on Linux: Gnome and KDE. Most distributions have one of these desktop environments as their default; for example, Gnome is the default desktop environment on the Debian, CentOS, Red Hat, and Fedora distributions, and KDE is the default on Ubuntu derivative Kubuntu and on SUSE, while Ubuntu uses Unity, which is a Gnome shell (based on Gnome).

■ **Tip**   In keeping with the flexibility of Linux, you can change the default desktop environment on all of these distributions. Unity, Gnome, and KDE are not the only desktops to choose either. For a discussion on the current desktops available check `www.techradar.com/au/news/software/operating-systems/best-linux-desktop-which-is-ideal-for-you--1194516`.

In Figure 4-3, you can see the default Gnome desktop on an Ubuntu distribution.

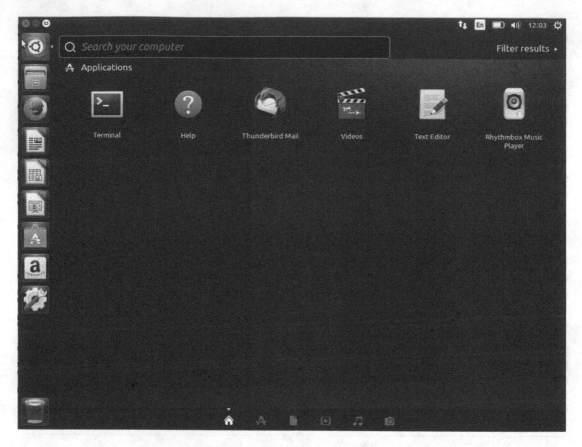

Figure 4-3. Ubuntu Unity desktop on the Xenial Xerus release

The Unity desktop has many of the underlying Gnome tools available to it. In this book we will talk primarily about the Gnome desktop in our examples and these examples will also apply to the Unity desktop.

The Command Line

In the Linux world, the command line is one of the most powerful tools available to you. The command line can be referred to as the "console," "terminal," or "shell"; each has a slightly different context, but in the end it is the place where you type Linux commands in. In this book, a lot of focus is going to be on the command line. This is where at least some of your administration tasks are going to occur, and it's important to be able to understand and make use of the command line. Indeed, in some cases you will not have a GUI environment available. If your GUI environment is not functional, you will need to be able to administer your hosts using the command line. The command line also offers some powerful tools that can make your administration tasks faster and more effective.

■ **Note**   This is not to say we're going to ignore the GUI. We'll also show you how to administer your Linux host using GUI tools.

Let's take a look at the Linux command line. You can access the command line in one of several ways. If your host has booted to a command-line prompt, as you can see in Figure 4-1, you can simply log in and use the prompt.

From inside the Gnome or KDE GUI, you have two options. The first is to use a virtual console—a kind of Linux management console that runs by default on most Linux distributions. Or you can launch a terminal emulator application like the Gnome Terminal or Konsole. In Figure 4-3 you can see how we would access the Terminal emulator in the Unity desktop.

■ **Note**   A *terminal emulator* is a tool that emulates a text terminal inside another application. For example, when you start a *command prompt*, or *command-line shell*, in Windows, you've started a Windows terminal emulator.

To launch a virtual console from inside a Gnome or KDE GUI, use the key combination Ctrl+Alt and one of the F1 through F7 keys. Each of the windows that can be opened is a new virtual console. Six virtual consoles are available. You can cycle through consoles using the Crtl+Alt+F1 to F7 keys. Each terminal is independent and separate. Ubuntu and CentOS have the GUI on different consoles. You use Ctrl+Alt+F7 to access the Ubuntu GUI and Ctrl+Alt+F1 for CentOS.

■ **Tip**   If you are not running a GUI interface, the virtual consoles are still available to you, and you can use the Alt+F1 to F6 keys and the Alt+left arrow and Alt+right arrow keys to navigate them.

You can also launch a terminal emulator. In Gnome, for example, you click the Applications menu, open the Accessories tab, and select the Terminal application. This will launch the Gnome Terminal application, as you can see in Figure 4-4.

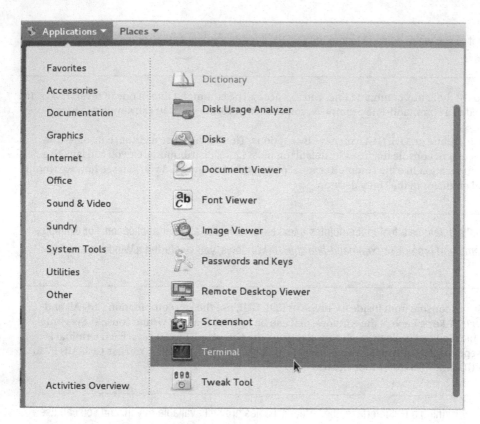

Figure 4-4. *Launching the Gnome Terminal application*

On KDE, things are slightly different. On earlier versions of KDE, you could launch the Konsole application by clicking Applications, opening System Tools, and selecting the Konsole application. On KDE version 4 and later, you launch Konsole by clicking Applications and then System, and selecting the Konsole application. And in Figure 4-3 we were able to see that we needed to bring up the search in Unity by selecting the Ubuntu symbol and typing Terminal. In Figure 4-3 we can see that it has already appeared without our searching for Terminal because it is a recently used application.

Shells

What command line is presented to you depends on what shell is running for your user. *Shells* are interfaces to the operating system and kernel of your host. For example, the command line on a Windows host is also a shell. Each shell contains a collection of built-in commands that allow you to interact with your host (these are supplemented by additional tools installed by your distribution).

A variety of shells are available, with the most common being the Bash (or Bourne-again) shell that is used by default on many distributions, including the popular Red Hat, Ubuntu, and Debian distributions.

■ **Note** We talked more about some specific distributions in Chapters 1 and 2.

We're going to use the Bash shell for all of our examples in this chapter, because it is most likely the shell you'll find by default.

Command-Line Prompt

After you have logged in to your Linux host, you should see a prompt that looks something like the following:

```
jsmith@au-mel-centos-1 ~$
```

So what does this mean? Well let's break it down.

user@host directory$

On most Linux distributions, the basic prompt is constructed from the username you're logged in as, the name of the host, the current directory, and the $ symbol, which indicates what sort of user you are logged in as.

■ **Tip**   You can customize your prompt to include additional information, add or change colors, or implement a variety of other options. Find more information at `http://tldp.org/HOWTO/Bash-Prompt-HOWTO/`.

In our case, jsmith is the name of the user we are logged in as; the @ symbol comes next and is followed by the name of the host we are logged into, i.e., `jsmith` at au-mel-centos-1.

■ **Note**   This part of the prompt looks like an e-mail address, for a good reason. This is how e-mail began— people with login accounts on connected Unix machines sending each other messages. The @ symbol was first used for this purpose in 1971! You can read about it at `http://openmap.bbn.com/~tomlinso/ray/` `firstemailframe.html`.

Next you see a ~ symbol, which is an abbreviated method of referring to your home directory. On a Linux host, most users have a special directory, called a *home directory*, which is created when the user is created. Like a Microsoft Window's user profile, the user's preferences and configuration files and data are stored in this directory. Any time you see the ~ symbol used, it indicates a shortcut that means home directory. We talked about home directories earlier, and they roughly equate to a combination of the Windows concept of the Documents and Settings profile and the My Documents folder. You would usually find home directories under a directory called /home.

■ **Note**   Linux is a multiuser operating system where multiple users can log on multiple times and work simultaneously. Like Windows, users can have their own environment, storage, access controls, and permissions.

Finally, you see the $ symbol. This symbol tells you what type of user you are; by default all normal users on the host will have $ as their prompt. There is a special user, called root, whose prompt uses the # symbol:

```
root@au-mel-centos-1 ~#
```

The root user is the superuser. On Windows, we'd call this user the Administrator. Like the Administrator user on Windows, the root user can control and configure everything. So if you see the # symbol, you know you are logged in as the root user.

In some distributions, you can log in as the root user, and you'll usually be prompted to specify a password for the root user during installation. Other distributions, most notably the Ubuntu distribution, disable the root user's password. On Ubuntu, you are assumed to never use the root user, but rather a special command called sudo. The sudo command allows you to run commands with the privileges of the root user without logging in as that user. We'll talk about the sudo command in Chapter 5. To use the sudo command, you simply type **sudo** and the command you wish to run. You will usually be prompted for your password, and if you enter the correct password, the command will be executed.

```
$ sudo passwd root
```

This command would change the password of the root user, which is one method of enabling the root user on Ubuntu.

The root user is all-powerful and can do anything on your host. As a result, it can be easy to accidentally make a mistake that could delete data or disrupt your applications and services when logged in as the root user. Thus, for security and safety reasons, you should never log in as the root user. We'll discuss other ways to administer your host without using the root user later in Chapter 5.

■ **Note**   In recent years, other security controls have been introduced that help reduce the reliance on the root user and provide more granular security controls. These controls include tools like SELinux and AppArmor, which we briefly discussed in Chapter 2.

Typing Your First Command

Now it's time to try entering a command. A command could be a binary executable (like a Windows executable or EXE file), or the command might be provided as part of the shell. Let's type a command called whoami and execute it by pressing the Enter key:

```
$ whoami
jsmith
```

The whoami command returns the name of the user you are logged in as. You can see our host has returned jsmith. This tells us we're logged in to our host as the user jsmith.

Each shell contains a series of built-in commands and functions to help you make use of the command line. Let's try one of these now. We start by running the whoami command again. This time, though, we make a spelling error and type the wrong command name:

```
$ whoamii
```

■ **Note**   Throughout this book, we're going to abbreviate the shell prompt to just the final prompt character, either $ or #.

We then press the Enter key to run the command and find that Bash has returned the following response:

```
-bash: whoamii: command not found
```

So what happened? Well, Bash is telling us that no command called whoami exists on the host. We can fix that. Let's start by correcting the command. We can bring back a previously typed command by using the up arrow key. Do that now, and you can see that the previous command has returned to the command line:

```
$ whoamii
```

Bash usefully has what is called *command history*, which keeps track of a number of the previous commands typed. Bash allows you to navigate through these commands by using the up and down arrow keys.

■ **Tip** The amount of history kept is user-configurable and can be manipulated using the history command. Enter the command history now to see your command history. If you've just signed on, you might find this history empty. In that case, use a few commands and try again. You will see a list of numbered lines showing previous commands you've typed. You can retrieve any of these commands by entering the number next to the command, prefixed by the ! symbol. For example, !12 would retrieve and execute command number 12 in your history. If you type !! you re-run the last command you entered.

You can also move the cursor along the command line to edit commands using the left and right arrow keys. Move to the end of the command using the arrow keys and delete the extra i, leaving you with

```
$ whoami
```

Now press the Enter key, and you will see the result on the command line:

```
jsmith
```

This time the corrected command, whoami, has again returned the name of the user who is logged in.

■ **Tip** Another useful Bash feature is autocompletion. Start typing a command and then press the Tab key, and Bash will search your path to try to find the command you're trying to issue. Type more characters, and the Tab key will further narrow the search.

THE PATH

When Linux informs you it can't find a binary or command, it may be that you have misspelled the name of the command, or it could be that it can't find that particular command. Like Windows, when executing commands, Linux searches a list of directories to try to find that particular command. By default, most distributions set a default path, usually containing the typical locations that contain executable binaries. Most of the time you won't need to set your path; the default path will be suitable. If you want to change the path, you'll need to update an environmental variable called $PATH. You can see what it is currently set to by typing $ echo $PATH. We'll talk about environmental variables in Chapter 5.

Remote Access

In the last two sections, we've talked about the GUI desktop and the command line. In both cases, we've assumed that you are logged on to your host locally (i.e., sitting in front of a screen and keyboard typing commands directly into the host). But in a lot of cases, people access Linux hosts remotely. This is particularly true for Linux hosts running as servers that might be hosted in a data center or in another geographical location, or stored in a rack or cabinet. In many cases, these hosts don't even have screens or keyboards attached and are only accessible via a network.

With Linux, it is very easy to remotely connect to these hosts so you can administer and manage them. You can use a number of different methods to do this remote connection. These include a desktop sharing protocol like Virtual Network Computing (commonly called VNC), Remote Desktop Protocol (RDP), which is often used to provide remote access to Windows hosts, and the extensively used Secure Shell (SSH).

Using SSH

We're quickly going to look at using SSH to provide remote command-line access to a Linux host. You can also access your GUI desktops with SSH, but we'll talk about that in Chapter 10.

SSH is both an application and a secure protocol used for a number of purposes but primarily for remote administration of hosts. On Linux hosts, SSH is provided by an open source version of the application called OpenSSH (see www.openssh.com/).

SSH connects over TCP/IP (Transmittion Control Protocol/Internet Protocol) networks in a client-server model. Your connecting host is the client. For example, if you are connecting to a remote host from your laptop, your laptop is the client. The host you are connecting to is called the server and receives and manages your connection.

Remote connections using SSH are encrypted and require authentication, either a password or public key cryptography. To make an SSH connection, you need to know the IP address or hostname of the remote host. A connection is then initiated on the client and connects to the server via TCP on port 22 (you can change this port, and we'll talk about how to do that in Chapter 10).

■ **Note**   You have probably encountered IP addresses and hostnames before, but you might not have come across ports. *Ports* are communications end points used by services like SSH. Port numbers range from 0 to 65535 with some commonly known ports being 80 for HTTP, 25 for SMTP, and 21 for FTP. Ports between 1 and 1023 are generally reserved for system services, while ports 1024 and higher (also called *ephemeral ports*) are more arbitrarily assigned. We'll go into more detail on this in Chapter 7.

After the initial connection, the client is then prompted by the server for a username and authentication credentials like a password. If the user exists on the server and the correct credentials are provided, the client is allowed to connect to the server.

On most distributions, SSH is installed as one of the default applications, and a server is started by default. This SSH server or SSH daemon (servers are also called *daemons* in the Linux world) allows remote connections to be made to the command line or GUI of your host.

You can use SSH via the command line or from one of a number of clients. Via the command line, client connections are made using a command called ssh. Most Linux and Unix-like operating systems (Mac OS X, for example) have SSH installed and have the ssh command available. To use the ssh command, you specify your username and the host you'd like to connect to separated with the @ symbol, as you can see in Listing 4-1.

Listing 4-1. SSH Connections

```
$ ssh  jsmith@us-ny-server-1.example.com
Password:
```

In Listing 4-1, we've connected to a host called `us-ny-server-1.example.com` as the user `jsmith`. We've then been prompted to input our password. If we have entered the correct password, we will be logged in to the command line of the remote host.

■ **Caution**   In reality, if you run this exact command, it won't work, as the host `us-ny-server-1.example.com` doesn't exist. If you want to test this, you'll need to specify an actual live host.

There are also a variety of SSH clients or terminal emulators available, for example, the popular and free PuTTY client (available from `www.chiark.greenend.org.uk/~sgtatham/putty/`), which runs on Windows (and also on Linux). You can also use the one that comes with Git Bash, which we installed in Chapter 3, which of course, runs on Windows.

SSH clients allow you to run text terminals to the command lines of your Unix or Linux hosts from your GUI. You can see the PuTTY client's configuration screen in Figure 4-5.

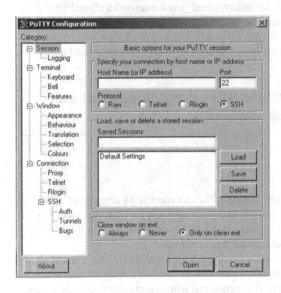

Figure 4-5. *The PuTTY client*

Using a GUI client like PuTTY is very simple. As with the command line, you need to specify the hostname (or IP address) and port of the host to which you wish to connect. With a client like PuTTY, you can also do useful things like save connections so you don't need to input your hostname again.

With Git Bash we can access ssh from the Bash terminal. We showed you how to install Git Bash in Chapter 3. Take a look at Figure 4-6, where we are making a connection to `us-ny-server-1.example.com`.

Figure 4-6. *Using Git Bash to make an ssh connection*

AS in Listing 4-1 we are making a connection to the US server. Here you will note that when we first connect to a host we have never connected to before, we are asked to accept the RSA key fingerprint. This is from the SSH server you are connecting to. After you accept this key, it is stored against the server name in a file called known_hosts. Every subsequent SSH connection to this host will check the fingerprint to see if it is changed. If it has you will be asked to clean the key before reconnecting. This gives you the opportunity to verify if the host or your communication has been tampered with. Again, we will talk more about this in Chapter 10.

In Figure 4-6 we accept the fingerprint after ideally first checking that we are connecting to the host we think we are connecting to (this is harder to do in an online world where you might connect to hosts outside your domains). Once this is done, we store the fingerprint and are then prompted for our password.

If you intend to manage Linux servers from Windows, we recommend you download a client like PuTTY if you prefer a GUI; otherwise you can install and use the Git Bash terminal, like we showed you in Chapter 3. Either will effectively allow you to remotely connect to and administer your Linux hosts from an environment that you're comfortable in. Mac OS, being Unix based, comes with an SSH client built in.

■ **Tip**   SSH clients also exist for operating systems like Windows Mobile, Android, Symbian, and the Apple iPhone, allowing road warriors to connect to their Linux hosts while on the go!

Getting Help

So how do you get help on your Linux host? You're probably thinking, "I can't use the F1 key, right?" Well, actually you can. In both Gnome's and KDE's GUI, the F1 key will bring up help text for that interface. But on the command line, there are also a wide variety of tools designed to tell you how things work, help you find the command you want, and then explain the options available for that command.

The easiest way is to check the command or application's man page (short for manual page). A man page tells you what the command can do, what options are available, and a variety of other information about it. You can access the man page by typing **man** and the name of the command whose man page you wish to view, as you can see in Listing 4-2.

Listing 4-2. The man Command

```
$ man ls
```

The man command will return a document that describes the ls (or list) command and its various options.

■ Note   The `ls` or list command lists the files and directories on your host. We're going to show you quite a bit more about files with the `ls` command later in this chapter, so stay tuned.

If you are struggling with a command, its man page is the first place you should look for help. Not all commands have man pages, and you'll get an error message if the man page of a particular command does not exist. In this case, it is often useful to try adding the `--help` switch to a command, as you can see in Listing 4-3.

■ Note   Switches are command-line options you can add to particular commands. They are specified using a dash (-) or two dashes (--) and the single-letter abbreviation or name of the switch, for example, -1 or --name. You can use either the abbreviated or longer version. The longer version is sometime more helpful when writing scripts and can be less ambiguous. Like making sure people know that you mean --version when using –v, and not --verbose.

Listing 4-3. The `--help` Switch

```
$ ls --help
```

■ Tip   Also available via the man command is a good introduction to Linux in general. To view this introduction, use the command `man intro`.

You can search for relevant man pages that match words in their short description.

```
$ man -k user
adduser (8)                          - create a new user or update default new user information
applygnupgdefaults (8) - Run gpgconf - apply-defaults for all users.
arpd (8)                             - userspace arp daemon.
```

Or you can also search *all* of the man pages on a host for a keyword using the -K option.

```
$ man -K user
```

This would search all man pages for the keyword user and return a list of all man pages containing the term. You will then be prompted to view each page that is returned, skip a page and go to the next page, or quit the search.

This search can be a little slow because your host usually has a lot of man pages, so there are two simpler search commands available that may offer a shortcut to what you are looking for: `whatis` and `apropos`. The `whatis` command searches a summary database of commands that is available on most Linux distributions for a complete word match as follows:

```
$ whatis useradd
useradd(8) - create a new user or update default new user information
```

The `whatis` search has returned the `useradd` command and included a brief description of what the command does.

The apropos command also searches the whatis database but searches for strings rather than complete words.

```
$ apropos whoam
ldapwhoami(1) - LDAP who am i? tool
whoami(1) - print effective userid
```

The apropos search has searched the whatis database for all references to the string whoami and returned a number of commands and functions that contain this string.

There are also some additional useful commands that can tell you about commands on your host. The info command, for example, sometimes provides a more verbose explanation of a command's function and options; try info ls to read about the ls command in more detail.

■ **Note**　The info interface is not very intuitive. It, and man pages, came about before the Internet (or good UX design) was everywhere. They are designed to have as much information as possible on the local system, in case you can't connected to Internet, but it is not meant to be pretty.

Users and Groups

Linux is multiuser operating system. This means it allows multiple users to connect simultaneously via multiple command-line or GUI sessions. Linux controls access to the host and its resources via user and group accounts. Users are also created for particular systems components and used to run services; for example, if you install a mail server, a user called mail might also be created that is used with this service, or a user called lp (for line printer) may exist to control printer resources.

Linux also relies on *groups*, which are collections of like users. Users can be members of one or more groups and are usually placed in a group so they can access some kind of resource. For example, all the users who need to access the Accounts Payable system might be added to a group called accounts.

■ **Tip**　Your user and group information is primarily contained in two files: /etc/passwd holds your user information, and /etc/group holds your group information. We'll talk more about these files in Chapter 6.

Users and groups are important, and we're going to explain how they work and how to create them in Chapter 6. Conceptually, users and groups operate in much the same way as they do on a Windows host. Each user has an account that is usually secured with a password. When most general users are created, a home directory analogous to a Windows profile is also created. This home directory provides users with a place to store their data and is also the default location for many applications to store their user-specific configuration. Users also belong to groups, as they do on Windows, which provide them with access to additional resources or services.

Services and Processes

On a Windows host, a lot of background activities and server applications run as *services*. Services can be started and stopped and often have to be restarted when an application is reconfigured. These services are usually controlled via the Services manager available in the Control Panel. On Linux hosts, the concept of services also exists. Services, also called daemons, run many of the key functions on your host.

▪ Note The term "Daemon" is the Greek spelling of demon and based on the imaginary being that sorted molecules in Maxwell's Demon thought experiment on the second law of thermodynamics. For more information, see `https://en.wikipedia.org/wiki/Daemon_(computing)`

Like on a Windows host, each service or daemon is one or more processes running on your host. These processes have names; for example, the Secure Shell daemon we discussed earlier usually runs as a process called sshd. Other common daemons include `master` (the Postfix mail server), `httpd` (the Apache web server), and `mysqld` (the MySQL database server). Some of these processes may be running by default on your host together with a number of other processes that perform a variety of system and application functions. Most daemon processes usually have a name ending in "d" for daemon.

In Listing 4-4, we've used the ps command with the -A flag (for all) to list all the processes currently running on our host.

Listing 4-4. The `ps` Command

```
$ ps -A
  PID TTY          TIME CMD
    1 ?        00:00:00 systemd
    2 ?        00:00:00 kthreadd
    3 ?        00:00:00 ksoftirqd/0
    4 ?        00:00:00 kworker/0:0
    5 ?        00:00:00 kworker/0:0H
    6 ?        00:00:00 kworker/u4:0
...<snip>...
  445 ?     00:00:00 crond
 1571 ?  00:00:00 sshd
```

In Listing 4-4, you can see a truncated list of the processes running on our host. This list was generated using the ps command with the -A (or list all processes) option. Each process running on the host is listed in order of its Process ID (PID), represented in Listing 4-4 by the left-hand column. PIDs are used to control processes, and we'll use them when we look at starting and stopping processes in Chapter 6. The most important process on your host is called systemd. The systemd process is the base process on Linux hosts that spawns all other processes on a host. This master process always uses PID 1 and must be running for your host to be functional.

▪ Note Depending on the operating system you have chosen you might notice that you don't have a `systemd` process but an `init` process instead at PID 1. Systemd is a recent addition to mainstream Linux OS's, having been accepted in OSs like Fedora and Debian Unstable for some time. On systems that are older you will see `init`. We help explain the difference between the two in Chapter 6.

Many of the processes whose name starts with "k" are not real processes, but kernel threads. These threads are a special kind of service that performs management tasks in the core of the operating system, the kernel. These "light weight processes" allow the kernel process to different tasks in the background, like handle what happens when someone plugs in a USB drive. The listing <thread>/0 indicates the name of the thread and the /0 is the processor it is running on.

Processes 445 and 1571 in Listing 4-4 are examples of daemon processes running on your system. We see the crond and sshd daemons, crond being a job scheduling service and sshd being the OpenSSH daemon for handling connections from ssh clients.

There is another useful command that can tell you which processes are running on your host and which are consuming the most CPU and memory. This command is called top, and we run it in Listing 4-5.

Listing 4-5. The top Command

```
$ top
```

The top command starts an interactive monitoring tool that updates every few seconds with the top running processes on your host. You can see a snapshot of the top command's output in Figure 4-7.

```
top - 04:22:59 up 13 min,  1 user,  load average: 0.00, 0.00, 0.00
Tasks: 107 total,   1 running, 106 sleeping,   0 stopped,   0 zombie
%Cpu(s):  0.0 us,  0.2 sy,  0.0 ni, 99.8 id,  0.0 wa,  0.0 hi,  0.0 si,  0.0 st
KiB Mem :   758232 total,   644996 free,    28080 used,    85156 buff/cache
KiB Swap:   783356 total,   783356 free,        0 used.   701816 avail Mem
```

PID	USER	PR	NI	VIRT	RES	SHR	S	%CPU	%MEM	TIME+	COMMAND
1	root	20	0	37720	5856	4032	S	0.0	0.8	0:00.62	systemd
2	root	20	0	0	0	0	S	0.0	0.0	0:00.00	kthreadd
3	root	20	0	0	0	0	S	0.0	0.0	0:00.01	ksoftirqd/0
5	root	0	-20	0	0	0	S	0.0	0.0	0:00.00	kworker/0:0H
6	root	20	0	0	0	0	S	0.0	0.0	0:00.09	kworker/u4:0
7	root	20	0	0	0	0	S	0.0	0.0	0:00.02	rcu_sched
8	root	20	0	0	0	0	S	0.0	0.0	0:00.00	rcu_bh
9	root	rt	0	0	0	0	S	0.0	0.0	0:00.00	migration/0
10	root	rt	0	0	0	0	S	0.0	0.0	0:00.00	watchdog/0
11	root	rt	0	0	0	0	S	0.0	0.0	0:00.00	watchdog/1
12	root	rt	0	0	0	0	S	0.0	0.0	0:00.00	migration/1
13	root	20	0	0	0	0	S	0.0	0.0	0:00.00	ksoftirqd/1
15	root	0	-20	0	0	0	S	0.0	0.0	0:00.00	kworker/1:0H
16	root	20	0	0	0	0	S	0.0	0.0	0:00.00	kdevtmpfs
17	root	0	-20	0	0	0	S	0.0	0.0	0:00.00	netns
18	root	0	-20	0	0	0	S	0.0	0.0	0:00.00	perf
19	root	20	0	0	0	0	S	0.0	0.0	0:00.00	khungtaskd

Figure 4-7. *The top process-monitoring command*

This is the output of a very quiet system. Top shows a lot of detail including system uptime, system load averages, CPU usage and memory utilization. Top refreshes every three minutes by default and processes will drift in and out of the listing as they consume resources. Processes that are heavy consumers of resources, like CPU, will always be listed at the top of the list, but you can also list by other resources like memory usage.

Packages

Applications in the Microsoft Windows world are usually installed by running a binary application and following an installation process. Some applications also come with uninstallers that remove them if you no longer require them. In some cases, you may instead use the Add or Remove Programs tool in the Control Panel to add or remove applications.

In the Linux world, *package managers* are the equivalent of the Add or Remove Programs tool. A package manager contains a collection of pre-packaged applications, for example, the Apache web server or the LibreOffice suite. These pre-packaged applications are, not surprisingly, called *packages*. Applications bundled as packages contain the required binaries, supporting files, and often configuration files as well, and they are ready to be run straight after being installed.

In Chapter 8, we're going to extensively cover two of the commonly used package management systems: RPM and Deb. These are used by distributions based on the Red Hat and Debian distributions, respectively. So Red Hat Enterprise Linux, CentOS, the Fedora Project, and even SUSE (a non-Red Hat based distribution) are distributions that all use RPM. Distributions that use Deb include Ubuntu, Debian, and a number of others.

Files and Filesystems

In Unix, there is a phrase that says, "Everything in UNIX is either a file or a process." Linux also adheres to this statement. There are several types of files, but we are going to start with files and directories. In Linux directories are just files containing the names of other files. Let's take a closer look at Linux files and the filesystem.

We're going to start by using a command called pwd, or print working directory.

```
$ pwd
/home/jsmith
```

The pwd command allows you to orient yourself in the filesystem by identifying our working or current directory. From here you can navigate the filesystem; start by changing the directory to the root directory using the cd, or change directory, command, as you can see in Listing 4-6.

Listing 4-6. Changing Directories

```
user@host:~$ cd /
user@host:/$
```

If you can ignore the user@host for a moment in Listing 4-6, you can see we've moved from our current directory to /, which is called the *root directory*. You can tell that by ~$ changing to '/$. The *root directory* is the base of the directory tree. The Linux filesystem is a single directory. This means that, unlike Windows, Linux has a single hierarchal directory structure. Instead of multiple drives, for example, C:\ and D:\, with separate directory trees beneath them, all drives, partitions, and storage are located off the root, or /, directory.

How does this work? Linux drives and devices are *mounted* (this can occur automatically when you boot, or you can do it manually). These mounted drives and devices appear in the filesystem as subdirectories under the '/' root directory. We explain how the '/' directory is initially mounted in Chapter 6.

■ **Note** We'll also discuss more about storage and mounting devices in Chapter 9.

With the cd command, you can traverse to other directories and subdirectories. Linux calls the steps you take to traverse the filesystem a *path*. There are two types of paths—absolute and relative. The absolute path always starts with a slash symbol (/) representing the root directory and specifies the definitive location of the place you are describing; for example, /home/jsmith/ is an absolute path.

Relative paths allow you to specify a location relative to your current location or starting point. For example, the command

```
$ cd foobar
```

attempts to change from the current directory to a directory called foobar. If no such directory is present, the cd command fails.

There are also a couple of symbols that are often used with relative paths:

```
$ cd ..
```

The .. indicates that we wish to traverse up one level on the directory tree (if we're already at the top, we won't go anywhere at all).

We can also traverse in other ways through the directory tree using this mechanism, as you can see on the following line:

```
$ cd ../foo/bar
```

In this instance we have

1. Traversed up one directory level as indicated by the .. notation

2. Changed into a directory called foo in the next level up

3. Then changed into a directory called bar under the foo directory

Let's illustrate this in Figure 4-8.

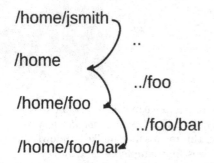

Figure 4-8. *Directory traversal to ../foo/bar*

■ **Note** If you're used to the Microsoft Windows command line, you may notice that the slash separating directories is a forward slash, or /, rather than a backslash, or \. This does take a little getting used to, but you'll soon be acclimatized!

We can also refer to relative objects in a directory using the following construct:

```
$ ./make
```

The addition of the ./ in front of the command executes the make command in our current directory.

Which directories you can traverse to depends on their permissions. Many directories only allow access to specific users and groups (the root user can go anywhere). If you try to change to a directory to which you don't have suitable permissions, you will get an error message:

```
$ cd /root
-bash: cd: /root: Permission denied
```

■ **Note** We will talk about permissions in the section "Permissions," later in this chapter.

So now you know how to move around in your directory tree. But where is everything located on your host? Most Linux distributions adhere to a very similar directory structure. This is not to say all distributions are identical, but generally speaking, files and directories are located in a logical and consistent model. You can see the typical directory structure under the root directory in Table 4-1. Each entry has a brief description of each directory.

***Table 4-1.** Linux Directory Structure*

Directory	Description
/bin/	User commands and binaries.
/boot/	Files used by the boot loader. (We talk about boot loaders in Chapter 6.)
/dev/	Device files.
/etc/	System configuration files.
/home/	User's home directories.
/lib/	Shared libraries and kernel modules.
/media/	Removable media is usually mounted here (see Chapter 8).
/mnt/	Temporary mounted filesystems are usually mounted here (see Chapter 8).
/opt/	Add-on application software packages.
/proc/	Kernel and process status data is stored in here in text-file format.
/root/	The root user's home directory.
/run/	A directory where applications can store data they require to operate.
/sbin/	System binaries.
/srv/	Data for services provided by this host.
/sys	Virtual filesystem that contains information and access to the Linux kernel subsystems.
/tmp/	Directory for temporary files.
/usr/	User utilities, libraries, and applications.
/var/	Variable or transient files and data, for example, logs, mail queues, and print jobs.

119

■ **Note** Not every distribution will have every one of these directories (and others might have additional directories), but generally this list is accurate.

Let's look at some of the key directories under the root (/) directory that are listed in Table 4-1. The first, and one of the most important, is /etc/. The /etc/ directory, named for etcetera, is where most of the important configuration files on your host are located. You'll be frequently working with files located in this directory as you add applications and services to your hosts.

Next, the /home/ directory contains all of the home directories for users (except the root user—whose home directory is usually /root/). The /tmp directory is where you'll commonly find temporary files. In a similar vein is the /var directory, in which transitory data such as logs are stored. You'll often look at log files contained in the /var/log/ directory that have been created by applications or via the host's syslog (or system logger) daemon. These log files contain a wide variety of information about the status of your applications, daemons, and services.

Let's take a closer look at files and directories and how to work with them. Start by changing to the root, or /, directory:

```
$ cd /
```

Now you're at the root directory, and you want to see what is contained in that directory. To do this, you use the ls, or list directory, command, as you can see in Listing 4-7.

Listing 4-7. Listing the Contents of a Directory

```
$ ls
bin dev etc lib lost+found mnt proc root sys usr
boot home  lib64  media opt sbin srv tmp var
```

In Listing 4-7, you can see the ls command has returned a list of files and directories that are in the root directory. You'll see it looks pretty close to the list in Table 4-1.

By default, ls lists all files in a directory, but you can limit it to displaying a single file name or several file names by listing that file on the command line as follows:

```
$ ls foobar
```

This command would display any file or directory called foobar. We could also use the wildcard or asterisk symbol to select files.

```
$ ls foo*
```

This would return any file called foo plus any files that started with foo, such as foobar, as well as the contents of any directories whose name starts with foo. Specifying the asterisk symbol alone lists all files and all directories and their contents.

■ **Tip** You'll see a lot more of the * symbol, as it is used on Linux much as it is on Windows. It indicates a wildcard that is used to substitute for one or more characters; for example, you've just seen foo*, which means anything starting with foo. A single character is matched using the ? symbol; for example, specifying ?at would match cat, mat, bat, etc. Collectively, this activity is called *globbing*, and you can read about its use in Linux shells at www.faqs.org/docs/abs/HTML/globbingref.html.

You can also list files in other directories by specifying the directory name:

```
$ ls /usr/local/bin
```

This would list all the files in the /usr/local/bin directory.

You don't see a lot of details about these files and directories in Listing 4-7, though. It only shows a list of names. To find out some more information about this list, you can add switches to the ls command, as you can see in Listing 4-8, to reveal more information.

Listing 4-8. Getting More Information from ls

```
$ ls -la
total 192
drwxr-xr-x     25  root  root           4096  2016-07-22 12:47  .
drwxr-xr x     25  root  root           4096  2016-07-22 12:47  ..
-rw-r--r--      1  root  root              0  2016-07-15 20:47  .autofsck
drwxr-xr-x      2  root  root           4096  2016-05-18 04:11  bin
drwxr-xr-x      6  root  root           3072  2016-05-25 21:57  boot
drwxr-xr-x     14  root  root           4100  2016-07-19 12:26  dev
drwxr-xr-x    116  root  root          12288  2016-07-22 12:47  etc
drwxr-xr-x      7  smtpd smtpd          4096  2016-05-02 12:00  home
drwxr-xr-x     12  root  root           4096  2016-05-17 18:14  lib
drwxr-xr-x      8  root  root           4096  2016-06-06 10:19  lib64
drwx------      2  root  root          16384  2016-06-11 16:01  lost+found
drwxr-xr-x      2  root  root           4096  2016-06-11 16:14  media
drwxr-xr-x      4  root  root           4096  2016-06-12 11:28  mnt
...
```

In Listing 4-8, the l and a switches have been added to the ls command. The l switch, which is an abbreviation of long, uses a long listing format, which as you can see shows a lot more information. The a switch tells ls to list all files and directories, even "hidden" ones, otherwise known as "dot" files.

■ **Tip**   In Linux (and Unix) "hidden" or "dot" files are prefixed with a full stop or period (e.g., the .autofsck file in Listing 4-8) and are often used to hold configuration and history information or as temporary files. They are normal files but some utilities, like ls, do not show them by default. They can also surprise you when you are looking for files in the directory that are using a lot of space. A ls -lh will show you the normal files in human-readable sizes (-h), were a ls -lah will show file sizes including the dot files. We talk more about this a little later.

You can see a full list of the available switches for the ls command by reading the command's man page—just enter man ls.

So what does the long listing format tell you about your files and directories? In Listing 4-8, each item has a small collection of information returned about it. In Listing 4-9, you can see a subset of that listing showing one file and one directory, which we're going to examine in more detail.

Listing 4-9. File Listing Subset

```
-rw-r--r--    1 root  root       0  2016-07-15 20:47  .autofsck
drwxr-xr-x  2 root  root   4096  2016-05-18 04:11  bin
```

Each line of the listing contains seven pieces of information about each object:

- Unix file type
- Permissions
- Number of hard links
- User and group ownership
- Size
- Date and time
- Name

Some of the information contained in the listing also introduces some key Linux concepts, such as permissions and users, groups, and ownership. We're going to take advantage of this introduction to not only explain each item but also explore some of the broader concepts they represent.

File Types and Permissions

The file type and permissions are contained in the first ten characters, the section resembling `-rw-r--r--`. This potentially intimidating collection of characters is actually quite simple to decipher: the first character describes the type of file, and the next nine characters describe the permissions of the file.

File Types

Almost everything on the Linux file system can be generally described as a file. The first character of the listing tells us exactly what sort of file. A dash (-) here indicates a regular file that might contain data or text, or be a binary executable. A d indicates a directory, which is essentially a file that lists other files. An l indicates a symbolic link. Symbolic links allow you to make files and directories visible in multiple locations in the filesystem. They are much like the shortcuts used in Microsoft Windows.

Table 4-2 lists the file types available.

Table 4-2. File Types

Type	Description
-	File
d	Directory
l	Link
c	Character devices
b	Block devices
s	Socket
p	Named pipe

We'll cover the other types here briefly. You won't regularly need most of the types, but they will appear occasionally in later chapters. The b and c file types are used for different types of input and output devices (if you look in the /dev directory, you will see examples of these device files). Devices allow the operating system to interact with particular hardware devices; for example, many distributions will have a device called /dev/usb that represents a USB drive attached to the host.

■ **Tip** You'll learn more about devices in Chapter 9 when we show you how to load a USB on your host.

Finally, sockets and named pipes are files that allow interprocess communications of varying types. They allow processes to communicate with each other. You'll see some sockets and named pipes later in the book.

Permissions

The next nine characters detail the access permissions assigned to the file or directory. On Linux, permissions are used to determine what access users and groups have to a file. Controlling your permissions and access to files and applications is critical for security on your Linux host, and frequently in this book we'll use permissions to provide the appropriate access to files. Thus it is important that you understand how permissions work and how to change them.

There are three commonly assigned types of permissions for files:

- Read, indicated by the letter r

- Write, indicated by the letter w

- Execute, indicated by the letter x

■ **Note** There are two other types of permissions, sticky and setuid/setgid permissions, represented by t or s characters, respectively. We discuss these in the sidebar "Setuid, Setgid, and Sticky Permissions" later in this chapter.

Read permissions allow a file to be read or viewed but not edited. If it is set on a directory, the names of the files in the directory can be read, but other details, like their permissions and size, are not visible. Write permissions allow you to make changes or write to a file. If the write permission is set on a directory, you are able to create, delete, and rename files in that directory. Execute permissions allow you to run a file; for example, all binary files and commands (binary files are similar to Windows executables) must be marked executable to allow you to run them. If this permission is set on a directory, you are able to traverse the directory, for example, by using the cd command to access a subdirectory. The combination of the read and execute permissions set on a directory thus allows you to both traverse the directory and view the details of its contents.

Each file on your host has three classes of permissions:

- User

- Group

- Other (everyone else)

Each class represents a different category of access to the file. The User class describes the permissions of the user who owns the file. These are the first three characters in our listing. The Group class describes the permissions of the group that owns the file. These are the second set of three characters in our listing.

■ **Note** Groups in Linux are collections of users. Groups allow like users to be collected together for the purpose of allowing access to applications and services; for example, all the users in the Accounting department can belong to the same group to allow them access to your Accounts Payable application. We'll talk about groups in Chapter 6.

Finally, the Other class describes the permissions that all others have to the file. These are the final set of three characters in the listing.

Figure 4-9 describes these classes and their positions.

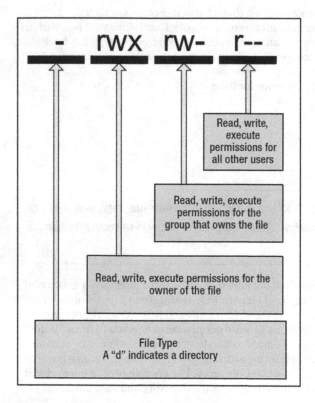

Figure 4-9. *File permission breakdown*

■ **Note** A dash in any position means that particular permission is not set at all.

You can see a single file in Listing 4-10 whose permissions we're going to examine in more detail, and then you'll learn how to make some changes to those permissions.

Listing 4-10. Permissions

```
-rw-r--r--   1 root  root      0 2016-07-15 20:47 myfile
```

In Listing 4-10, we have a file, as indicated by the dash (-) at the beginning of the listing. The file is owned by the `root` user and `root` group. The first three permissions are `rw-`, which indicates the `root` user can read and write the file, but the dash means execute permissions are not set, and the file can't be executed by the user. The next three permissions, `r--`, indicate that anyone who belongs to the `root` group can read the file but can do nothing else to it. Finally, we have `r--` for the last three permissions, which tell us what permissions the Other class has. In this case, others can read the file but cannot write to it or execute it.

Now you've seen what permissions look like, but how do you go about changing them? Permissions are changed using the `chmod` (change file mode bits) command. The key to changing permissions is that only the user who owns the file or the `root` user can change a file's permissions. So, in Listing 4-10, only the `root` user could change the permissions of the `myfile` file.

The `chmod` command has a simple syntax. In Listing 4-11, you can see some permissions being changed.

Listing 4-11. Changing Permissions

```
# chmod u+x myfile
# chmod u-x,og+w myfile
# chmod 654 myfile
```

In Listing 4-11, we've changed the `myfile` file's permissions three times. Permission changes are performed by specifying the class, the action you want to perform, the permission itself, and then the file you want to change. In our first example, you can see `u+x`. This translates to adding the execute permission to the User class.

■ **Note**   The execute permission is usually set only on files that are executable in nature such as scripts and binaries (a.k.a. applications or programs) and on directories. On directories x means traverse, meaning that you can list directories in the parent directory but you can't go any further.

After our update, the permissions on our file would now look as follows:

```
-rwxr--r--   1 root  root      0  2016-07-15 20:47 myfile
```

You can see the addition of the x to the User class. So how did `chmod` know to do that? Well, the u in our change represents the User class. With `chmod`, each class is abbreviated to a single letter:

- u: User
- g: Group
- o: Other or everyone
- a: All

After the class, you specify the action you'd like to take on the class. In the first line in Listing 4-11, the + sign represents adding a permission. You can specify the - sign to remove permissions from a class or the = sign to set absolute permissions on the class. Finally, you specify the permission to the action, in this case x.

You can also specify multiple permission changes in a single command, as you can see in the second line of Listing 4-11. In this second line, we have the change u-x,go+w. This would remove the x, or execute, permission from the User class and add the w, or write, permission to both the Group and Other classes. You can see we've separated each permission change with a comma and that we can list multiple classes to act upon. (You can also list multiple permissions; for example, u+rw would add the read and write permissions to the User class.)

Thus the second line in Listing 4-11 would leave our file permissions as

```
-rw-rw-rw-  1 root  root      0  2016-07-15 20:47 myfile
```

With chmod, you can also use the a class abbreviation, which indicates an action should be applied to all classes; for example, a+r would add read permissions to all classes: User, Group, and Other.

We can also apply the permissions of one class to another class by using the = symbol.

```
# chmod u=g myfile
```

On the previous line, we've set the User class permissions to be the same as the Group class permissions.

You can also set permissions for multiple files by listing each file separated by space as follows:

```
# chmod u+r file1 file2 file3
```

As with the ls command, you can also reference files in other locations as follows:

```
# chmod u+x /usr/local/bin/foobar
```

The previous line adds the execute permission to the User class for the foobar file located in the /usr/local/bin directory.

You can also use the asterisk symbol to specify all files and add the -R switch to recurse into lower directories as follows:

```
# chmod -R u+x /usr/local/bin/*
```

The chmod command on the previous line would add the execute permission to the User class to every file in the /usr/local/bin directory.

The last line in Listing 4-11 is a little different. Instead of classes and permissions, we've specified a number, 654. This number is called *octal notation*. Each digit represents one of the three classes: User, Group, and Other. Additionally, each digit is the sum of the permissions assigned to that class. In Table 4-3, you can see the values assigned to each permission type.

Table 4-3. *Octal Permission Values*

Permission	Value	Description
r	4	Read
w	2	Write
x	1	Execute

Each permission value is added together, resulting in a number ranging from 1 and 7 for each class. So the value of 654 in Listing 4-11 would represent the following permissions:

```
-rw-r-xr-- 1 root root 0  2016-08- 14 22:37 myfile
```

The first value, 6, equates to assigning the User class the read permission with a value of 4 plus the write permission with a value of 2. The second value, 5, assigns the Group class the read permission with a value of 4 and the execute permission with a value of 1. The last value, 4, assigns only the read permission to the Other class. To make this clearer, you can see a list of the possible values from 0 to 7 in Table 4-4.

Table 4-4. *The Octal Values*

Octal	permissions	Description
0	---	None
1	--x	Execute
2	-w-	Write
3	-wx	Write and execute
4	r--	Read
5	r-x	Read and execute
6	rw-	Read and write
7	rwx	Read, write, and execute

In Table 4-5, you can see some commonly used octal numbers and the corresponding permissions they represent.

Table 4-5. *Octal Permissions*

Octal Numbers	permissions
600	rw-r--r--
644	rw-r--r--
664	rw-rw-r--
666	rw-rw-rw-
755	rwxr-xr-x
777	rwxrwxrwx

■ **Tip** The chmod command has some additional syntax for changing permissions, and you can read about them in the command's man page.

Finally, there is an important concept called *umask* that you need to also understand to fully comprehend how permissions work. The umask dictates the default set of permissions assigned to a file when it is created. By default, without a umask set, files are created with permissions of 0666 (or read and write permissions for the owner, group, and others are all set), and directories are created with permissions of 0777 (or read, write, and execute for the owner, group, and others). You can use the umask command to modify these default permissions. Let's look at an example.

```
# umask 0022
```

Here we've specified a umask of 0022. This looks familiar, doesn't it? Yes, it's a type of octal notation; in this case, it indicates what's not being granted. So here we would take the default permissions for a file, 0666, and subtract the 0022 value, leaving us with permissions of 0644. With a umask of 0022, a new file would be created with read and write permissions for the owner of the file and read permissions for the group and others. Newly created directories (default permissions of 0777) would now have permissions of 0755 with a umask of 0022. Another commonly used umask is 0002, which results in default permissions of 0664 for files and 0775 for directories. This allows write access for the group also, and this umask is often used for files located in shared directories or file shares.

On most hosts, your umask is set automatically by a setting in your shell. For Bash shells, you can usually find the global umask in the /etc/bashrc file, but you can also override it on a per-user basis using the umask command or using the pam_umask module (we will give you more information about what PAM is in Chapter 5).

■ **Tip** The umask command can also set umasks using alternative syntax. We've just described the simplest and easiest. You can find more details in the umask man page.

SETUID, SETGID, AND STICKY PERMISSIONS

There are two additional types of permissions, setuid/setgid and sticky, that are also important to understand.

The setuid and setgid permissions allow a user to run a command as if he were the user or group that owned the command. So, why might this be needed? Well, this allows users to execute specific tasks that they would normally be restricted from doing or allows users to share resources, like accessing shared files on a fileserver with the same group id.

A good example of this is the passwd command. The passwd command allows a user to change her password. To do this, the command needs to write to the password file, a file that has restricted access. By adding the setuid permission, a user can execute the passwd command and run it as if she were the root user, hence allowing her to change her password.

You can recognize setuid and setgid permissions by the use of an s or S in the listing of permissions. For example, the permissions of the passwd command are

```
-rwsr-xr-x 1 root root 25708  2016-09- 25 17:32 /usr/bin/passwd
```

You can see the s in the execute position of the User class, which indicates that the passwd command has the setuid permission set. Take a look now at the following directory listing.

```
-rwSrwSr-- 1 jsmith jsmith    0 Jun  5 09:55 adirectory
```

This also shows that the setuid and setgid for the "adirectory" directory have been set but designated by "S" this time. What this means is that the directory does not have "execute" permissions associated with the user and group. In other words, the permissions for that directory (and a file would be the same) would have been set with 'u+rws,g+rws,o+r'.

On most distributions, setuid/setgid permissions are used sparely to allow this sort of access. They are used sparingly because you generally don't want one user be able to run applications as another user or to have particular elevated privileges (another way to do this is through the su and sudo commands, which we're going to describe further in Chapter 6). As they could also potentially be abused and represent a security exposure, they should not be used indiscriminately. In this book, you may see one or two applications that use setuid/setgid permissions.

Sticky permissions are slightly different and are used on directories (they have no effect on files). When the sticky bit is set on a directory, files in that directory can be deleted only by the user who owns them, the owner of the directory, or the root user, irrespective of any other permissions set on the directory. This allows the creation of public directories where every user can create files but only delete their own files. You can recognize a directory with sticky permissions from the t in the execute position of the Other class. Most frequently it is set on the /tmp directory:

```
drwxrwxrwt 4 root root 4096 2016-08-15 03:10 tmp
```

In octal notation, setuid/setgid and sticky permissions are represented by a fourth digit at the front of the notation, for example, 6755. Like other permissions, each special permission also has a numeric value: 4 for setuid, 2 for setgid, and 1 for sticky. So to set the sticky bit on a directory, you'd use an octal notation like 1755. If no setuid/setgid or sticky permissions are being set, this prefixed digit is 0 like so:

```
# chmod 0644 /etc/grub.conf
```

Links

Let's take another look at the example from Listing 4-9:

```
-rw-r--r--    1 root  root      0  2016-07-15 20:47  .autofsck
drwxr-xr-x    2 root  root   4096  2016-05-18 04:11  bin
```

In our listing, after our file type and permissions is the number of hard links to the file. *Hard links* are references that connect your file to the physical data on a storage volume. There can be multiple links to a particular piece of data. However, hard links are different from the symbolic links we introduced earlier (indicated by a file type of l), although both linkages are created with the same command, ln. We'll talk about the ln command later in this chapter in the section "Linking Files."

Users, Groups, and Ownership

Next in our listing is the ownership of the file. Each object is owned by a user and a group; in Listing 4-9, the root user and root group own the objects. We briefly discussed user and group ownership when we looked at permissions. We explained that only the user who owns a file could change its permissions, and that groups were collections of users. Groups are generally used to allow access to resources; for example, all users who need to access a printer or a file share might belong to groups that provide access to these resources. As we discussed earlier in this chapter, on Linux hosts a user must belong to at least one group, known as the *primary group*, but can also belong to one or more additional groups, called *supplementary groups*.

You can change the user and group ownership of a file using the chown command. Only the root user has authority to change the user ownership of a file (although you can assume this authority using the sudo command we discussed earlier in the chapter and will cover in more detail in Chapter 6).

In Listing 4-12 we show some examples of how to use the chown command to change user and group ownership.

Listing 4-12. Changing Ownership

```
# chown jsmith myfile
# chown jsmith:admin myfile
# chown -R jsmith:admin /home/jsmith/*
```

In Listing 4-12, we've got three chown commands. The first command changes the user who owns the myfile file to jsmith. The second command changes the ownership of the file's user and group, the user to jsmith and the group to admin, the owner and group being separated by a colon, :. The third and last command uses the -R switch to enable recursion. The command would change the owner of every file and directory in the /home/jsmith directory to jsmith and the group to admin.

■ **Note**   Also available is the chgrp command. It allows users to change the group of a file they own. The user can only change the group ownership to a group of which that user is a member. You use it like chgrp *groupname file*.

Size and Space

Next in our listing you see the size of the object on the disk. The size of the file is listed in bytes (a thousand and twenty four bytes is a Kibibytes, or K). We can also display sizes in a more human-readable format by adding the -h switch as follows:

```
$ ls -lh
-rw-rw-r-- 1 jsmith jsmith  51K  2016-08- 17 23:47 myfile
```

On the previous line, you can see that the myfile file is 51 kibibytes in size.

In a listing, the size next to the directory is not its total size but rather the size of the directory's metadata. To get the total size of all files in a directory, you can use the du, or disk usage, command. Specify (or change to) the directory you want to find the total size of and run the command with the -s and -h switches. The -s switch summarizes the total, and the -h switch displays the size in a human-readable form.

```
$ du -sh /usr/local/bin
4.7M    /usr/local/bin
```

The du tool has a number of additional switches and options that you can see by reviewing its man page.

In addition to the size of files and directories, you can also see the total disk space used and free on your host using another command, df. This command displays all of your disks and storage devices and the free space present on them. You can see the df command in Listing 4-13.

Listing 4-13. Displaying Disk Space

```
$ df -h
Filesystem                                    Size   Used  Avail   Use%  Mounted on
/dev/mapper/VolGroup00-LogVol01  178G    11G   159G    6%    /
/dev/sda1                                      99M    37M    58M    39%   /boot
tmpfs                                          910M     0   910M    0%    /
dev/shm
```

We've executed the command and added the -h switch, which returns human-readable sizes. It shows our current filesystems and their used and free space, as well as percentage used. There are additional options you can use with the df command, and you can review these in the command's man page. We'll revisit the df and du commands in Chapter 9.

Date and Time

The penultimate and ultimate items in our listing are the date and time the file was last modified (known as *mtime*) and the name of the file or directory. Linux also tracks the last time a file was accessed (called *atime*) and when it was created (called *ctime*). You can display the last accessed time for a file by listing it with the -u switch as follows:

```
$ ls -lu
```

You can list creation dates by using the -c switch:

```
$ ls -lc
```

■ **Note**   We will revisit atime in Chapter 17.

If you want to know the actual time and date on the current host, you can use the useful and powerful date command. Using date on the command line without any options will return the current time and date as follows:

```
$ date
Tue Aug 19 13:01:20 EST 2016
```

You can also add switches to the date command to format the output into different date or time format; for example, to display Unix epoch time (the number of seconds since January 1, 1970), you would execute the date command as follows:

```
$ date +%s
1219116319
```

Here we've used the + symbol to add a format and then specified the format, in this case %s, to display epoch time. Epoch time can be useful when calculating time differences or for adding as a suffix to a file for uniqueness. You can see additional formats in the date command's man page. You can also use the date command to set the time. Type **date** and then specify the required date and time in the format **MMDDhhmm[[CC]YY]**. You can find out more about Unix epoch time at http://en.wikipedia.org/wiki/Unix_time.

> ■ **Note** This is just one way to set the time, and we'll discuss other more effective methods such as Network Time Protocol in Chapter 10.

Working with Files

So, in the course of exploring our simple file listing, we've covered a lot of concepts, introduced you to some Linux commands, and taught you how to perform a few key administrative tasks. Leading on from these tasks, we're going to finish this chapter by covering how to view, edit, search, copy, move, and delete files. You'll need to know how to handle all these tasks in order to administer your Linux host.

Reading Files

The first thing you're going to learn is how to read files. Many files on Linux hosts, especially configuration files, are text-based and can be read using some simple command-line tools.

> ■ **Note** Always remember that in order to read a file, you must have read permissions to that file. This means you need to own it or belong to a group that has read permissions to the file, or the file has read permission set for the Other class.

The first of these tools is cat. The cat command is so named because it "concatenates and prints files." In Listing 4-14, you can see the use of the cat command on a text file.

Listing 4-14. Using the cat Command

```
$ cat /etc/hosts
# Do not remove the following line, or various programs
# that require network functionality will fail.
127.0.0.1               localhost.localdomain localhost localhost
::1             localhost6.localdomain6 localhost6
```

In Listing 4-14, we've outputted the /etc/hosts file to the screen. The /etc/hosts file contains the host entries for our Linux host (like the \WINDOWS\System32\services\etc\hosts file under Windows) that match hostnames to IP addresses. But the cat command is a pretty simple tool and just outputs the text directly. If the file is very large, the text will keep outputting and scrolling down the screen, meaning if you wanted to see something at the start of the file, you'd need to scroll back.

■ **Tip**   You can scroll a virtual console up and down via the Shift+Page Up and Shift+Page Down key combinations.

To overcome this issue, we're going to look at another command called less.

■ **Note**   You can try the cat command on the /etc/passwd and /etc/group files to see a full list of the users and groups on your host.

The less command allows you to scroll through files, both backward and forward, a screen at a time. Each time a page is displayed, you will be prompted as to how you'd like to proceed. We run less by specifying the name of the file as follows:

```
$ less /etc/services
```

From inside the less interface, you can scroll through the file. To go to the next page, you use the spacebar, and to advance one line at a time, you use the Enter key. To scroll backward, you can use the B key. You can also scroll using the arrow keys, and to quit the less command, you use the Q key.

■ **Note**   There are additional ways to navigate files using less that you can see by reviewing the command's man page.

In addition to navigating through files, it is also possible to search a file or files for specific information. To do this, we can make use of the very powerful grep command. The grep command allows you to search through a file or files for a string or pattern (using regular expressions) and return the results of that search.

■ **Note**   The word "grep" has become a commonly used term in IT for searching, much like the term "google" has for using an online search engine. In 2003, the *Oxford English Dictionary* added the word "grep" as both a noun and a verb (e.g., "John grep'ed his mailbox to find the e-mail").

In Listing 4-15, you can see a very simple grep search for the string localhost in the file /etc/hosts.

Listing 4-15. Introducing grep

```
$ grep localhost /etc/hosts
127.0.0.1       localhost.localdomain localhost localhost
::1             localhost6.localdomain6 localhost6
```

To use grep, you specify the string you're searching for, in this case localhost (grep is case sensitive, so it will only find this lowercase string), and then the name of the file you're searching in.

■ **Note**   You can make grep case insensitive by adding the -i switch to the command.

By default, grep returns those lines in the file that contain the string we're searching for. You can also search for more than one file by using the asterisk symbol, as we have demonstrated for other commands earlier in this chapter, for example:

```
$ grep localhost /etc/host*
$ grep localhost /etc/*
```

The first command would search all files starting with host* in the /etc/ directory, and the second would search all files in the /etc/ directory. Both searches are for the string localhost.

You can also recursively search down into lower directories by adding the -r switch as follows:

```
$ grep -r localhost /etc
```

■ **Tip**   On Ubuntu and Debian hosts, the rgrep command automatically recurses into directories.

You can also specify more complicated search terms, for example, multiple words, as follows:

```
$ grep "local host" /etc/hosts
```

You can see we've specified the words "local" and "host" with a space between them. In order to tell grep these words are grouped together and have them parsed correctly, we need to enclose them in quotation marks. The quotation marks are used often on the command for a number of commands to protect input from being inappropriately parsed. In this case, we're searching for the exact string "local host", and grep has returned no results because the string is not present in the /etc/hosts file.

The grep command is capable of much more than these simple examples. You can use grep to do complex regular expression searches in files, for example:

```
$ grep 'J[oO][bB]' *
```

This would find the strings JOB, Job, JOb, or JoB in all files in the current directory (remember, grep is case sensitive by default, so our regular expression has explicitly specified upper- and lowercase variations). Regular expressions allow you to do some very powerful searching across your host.

Let's look at some other useful regular expression searches using grep.

```
$ grep 'job$' *
```

In the previous line, we've searched all files in the current directory for strings ending in job. The $ symbol tells grep to search for the text at the end of strings.

You can use the ^ symbol to in turn search for strings starting with a particular string like so:

```
$ grep '^job' *
```

This would return any string starting with job. There are myriad other regular expressions that you'll find useful for employing frequently.

REGULAR EXPRESSIONS

Regular expressions, or regexes, are a formal language used to identify strings of text; for example, a regular expression might identify all the references to the string job in a file. A variety of very similar regular expression languages are used by tools like grep and by programming languages, for example, Perl. The syntax of most regular expression languages is very similar, but occasionally they have subtle differences. You can read about regular expressions further at http://en.wikipedia.org/wiki/ Regular_expression.

There are three regular expression versions you can use, BRE (basic regular expressions), ERE (extended regular expressions), and PCRE (Perl regular expressions). Depending on your version of grep, there is no difference between BRE and ERE. To make use of PCRE, you will need the following packages in Perl: libpcre3-dev (Ubuntu) or pcre-devel (CentOS).

To test your regular expressions, you can use either of the following two regular expression editors:

- http://rubular.com/

- http://pythex.org/

There are a few common patterns that are useful to know:

```
grep -o -E "([0-9]{1,3}[\.]){3}[0-9]{1,3}" /var/log/auth.log
```

The above will match all IP addresses in the /var/log/auth.log (Ubuntu log file). The -o says to only print the results of the match, otherwise you will see the whole line the match appears on. The -E says to use the ERE version (though we have said the ERE and BRE are the same here). Taking a look at the expression itself, first we look for one to three occurrences {1,3} of numbers between 0 and 9 [0-9] followed by a dot.

```
[0-9]{1,3}\.
```

This will match 0. up to 999. We expect to see exactly (...){3} of these:

```
([0-9]{1,3}[\.]){3}
```

We then expect to see one more set of octets not followed by a dot.

```
([0-9]{1,3}[\.]){3}[0-9]{1,3}
```

Putting this all together will in fact match any *IP address* from *000.000.000.000* to *999.999.999.999* which we know is technically wrong but chosen because it is clearer to explain as to match only on numbers between 0 and 255 is a more complex and long regular expression (but widely documented on the Internet).

Another useful grep regular expression is searching for e-mail addresses in the mail log.

```
egrep -o "[A-Za-z0-9._-]+@example.com" /var/log/mail.log
```

Here you can see that we are using the `egrep` command, which just executes `grep` with the `-E` flag. In this example we are searching for e-mail addresses that match `<username>@example.com`. We start by looking for any letters (Latin only), capitalized or not, `[A-Za-z...]`, or numbers, `[...0-9]`, or a dot, `[.]` or dash, `[...-]`.

`[A-Za-z0-9._-]`

These can appear one or more times `[...]+`.

`[A-Za-z0-9._-]+`

That is followed by the domain we are interested in:

`[A-Za-z0-9._-]+@example.com`

To improve our matching, let's consider the following example text file:

```
email: root@example.com
email: jsmith@example.com
iam a sentence with somewordroot@example.comsomeotherword
email: bjuice@example.com
```

With the "`[A-Za-z0-9._-]+@example.com`" regular expression we would get a match on '`somewordroot@example.com`', which is not what we want. We can use a word boundary anchor '\b', which will only capture '`root@example.com`'. That would make the regular expression look as follows:

`"\b[A-Za-z0-9._-]+@example.com\b"`

And now if we run the `grep` over our text file example we only match on the e-mail addresses we are after:

```
$ egrep -o "\b[A-Za-z0-9._%+-]+@example.com\b" file.txt
root@example.com
jsmith@example.com
bjuice@example.com
```

The `grep` command with regular expressions can be very powerful and you can do some very complex expressions, but remember the old joke:

"I solved my problem with a regular expression . . . now I have two problems," meaning that complex regular expressions can be tricky to maintain.

For further reading, we recommend picking up a book such as *Mastering Regular Expressions* by Jeffrey Friedl (O'Reilly, 2006) to help you learn about regular expressions.

Searching for Files

We've shown you how you can read a file, but what if you need to find the location of a file? A number of commands and tools on a Linux host allow you to find files in much the same way as the Windows Search function works. In Figure 4-10, you can see the Gnome search function.

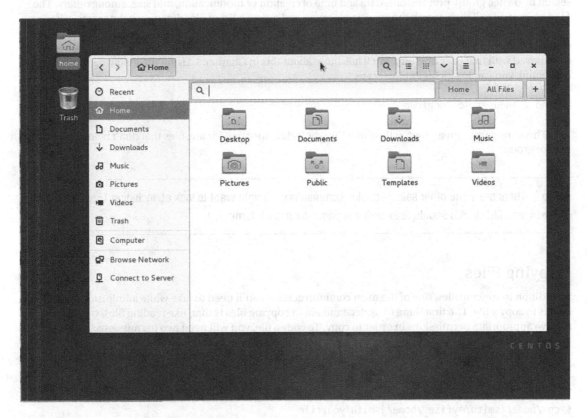

Figure 4-10. Gnome search function

On the command line, you can also search for files using the find command. Let's use the find command to search for a file called myfile in the /home directory:

```
$ find /home/ -type f -iname myfile*
```

The find command is very simple to use. First you specify where you are searching, in this case in the /home/ directory. You can also specify / for the root (and thus search the whole directory tree), or any other location that you can access.

■ **Note** If you don't have permission to search a particular directory, you'll get an error message indicating that your search has been denied.

Next, we've specified two options, -type and -iname. The first option, -type, specifies the type of file we are searching for; in this case, a normal file is represented by f. You can also specify d for directories or s for sockets (special files for interprocess communications), for example (see the man page for all the possible types you can search for). The -iname option searches for a case-insensitive pattern, in this case, all files starting with myfile. These options are just a very small selection of the possible search options; you can also search by owner, group, permissions, date and time of creation or modification, and size, among others. The find command will then search the specified location and return a list of files that match the search criteria.

You could also use the find command to locate files and directories that aren't owned by any user or group. These often exist if a user or group has been deleted and the associated files not reassigned or removed with that user or group. We'll talk more about this in Chapter 6. Using the following find command, you can list all files in this state:

```
# find / -nouser -o -nogroup
```

This command, run as root, will search the whole directory tree for any files that don't belong to a valid user or group.

■ **Tip** There are some other search-related commands you might want to look at, including locate, whereis, and which. You should read their man pages for more information.

Copying Files

In addition to viewing files, one of the most common actions you'll need to take while administering your host is to copy a file. The first thing to understand about copying files is that, like reading files, you need to have appropriate permissions in order to copy. To copy a file, you will need two permissions: read permissions on the file you are copying and write permissions in the destination you are copying to.

To copy a file, use the cp command (short for copy). In Listing 4-16, you can see a simple cp command.

Listing 4-16. Copying Files

```
$ cp /home/jsmith/myfile /home/jsmith/yourfile
```

In Listing 4-16, we've copied the file /home/jsmith/myfile to /home/jsmith/yourfile. You need to be a little bit careful with the cp command. By default, the cp command will copy over existing files without prompting you. This can be bad if you already have a file with the same name as the one you are copying to. You can change this behavior by adding the -i switch. The -i switch enables interactive mode, where you are prompted with a yes or no question if the file you are copying to already exists. You answer y to overwrite or n to abort the copy.

■ **Note** On some older Red Hat, Fedora, and CentOS distributions, the -i switch for the cp, mv, and rm commands is automatically set on by aliasing each command; for example, cp -i is aliased to cp. You can do this on other distributions using the alias command; see www.ss64.com/bash/alias.html for more details.

If we didn't have permission to read the file, we'd get an error like the following:

```
cp: cannot open `/home/jsmith/myfile' for reading: Permission denied
```

We'd get a similar error if we could not write to the target destination.

```
cp: cannot stat `/home/jsmith/yourfile': Permission denied
```

You can also do a few more things with cp. You can copy multiple files, using the asterisk symbol as follows:

```
$ cp /home/jsmith/* /home/jsmith/backup/
```

The target on the previous line, /home/jsmith/backup/, has to be a directory, and we're copying all files in the /home/jsmith directory to this directory.

You can also select a subset of files.

```
$ cp -i /home/jsmith/*.c ./
```

On the previous line, we've copied all the files with a suffix of .c to the current directory (using the ./ shortcut). We've also added the -i switch to make sure we're prompted if a file already exists.

You can also copy directories and their contents using cp by adding the –r switch.

```
$ cp -r /home/jsmith /backup
```

The previous line copies the /home/jsmith directory and all files and directories beneath it to the /backup directory.

■ **Caution** When using the -r switch, be careful to not use the *.* wildcard like you might on Windows. When used on Linux, the .. directory will also be copied recursively, which probably is not your intent!

Finally, when copying files using the cp command, some items about the file, such as dates, times, and permissions, can be changed or updated. If you want to preserve the original values on the copy, you can use the -p switch.

```
$ cp -p /home/jsmith/myfile /home/jsmith/yourfile
```

WORKING WITH DIRECTORIES

In addition to files, you can also manipulate directories. To create a directory, use the mkdir command. You must have write permissions to the location you're creating the directory in. If you want to copy directories and recursively copy their contents, you can do this with the cp command by adding the -r switch.

You can also move directories using the mv command in the same way as you can with files.

Finally, if you want to delete a directory, use the rmdir command. The rmdir command will only remove empty directories (i.e., directories with no files in them).

The `cat` command we examined earlier can also be used to copy files using a command-line function called *redirection*.

```
$ cat /home/jsmith/myfile > /home/jsmith/yourfile
```

The use of the > symbol sends the output from one command to the command or action on the other side of the > symbol. In this case, the output of the `cat` command is redirected into a file called `yourfile`. If this file doesn't exist, it will be created. If it does exist, its content will be overwritten.

■ **Caution**   Be careful when using redirection, as your target file will be overwritten without warning.

You can also append to files using the same mechanism.

```
$ cat /home/jsmith/myfile >> /home/jsmith/yourfile
```

Using the >> syntax will append the output from the `cat` of `myfile` to the end of `yourfile`. If `yourfile` does not exist, it will be created.

■ **Tip**   Redirection can be used by many other commands as well to direct output from one command to another. It is also closely linked to another Bash capability called *piping* (see the sidebar "Piping and Other Bash Tips").

PIPING AND OTHER BASH TIPS

You've had a quick look at the Bash command line and some of the things you can do with it. This includes using redirection with the > or >> symbols to redirect output from one command to another. This concept can be extended using the |, or pipe, symbol. Piping passes the output of a command to another command, for example

```
$ cat /etc/passwd | grep ataylor
```

In the previous line we've outputted the contents of the /etc/passwd file and then piped the result to the `grep` command to search for the term `ataylor`. This would output any line or lines containing the term `ataylor`. You can pretty much do this with any command that accepts input on the command line. Some useful commands that could be used with piping are `sort` (sorts input in a variety of ways), `uniq` (generates a unique list), and `wc` (counts lines, words, etc.). You can read about these commands in their `man` pages.

You can also take redirection a step further and redirect multiple times or use piping and redirection together. Let's look at an example.

```
$ cat *.txt | sort | uniq > text
```

In this example we've asked the host to output all files with a suffix of .txt, sort them alphabetically, delete duplicate lines (using the uniq command), and then output the result to a file called text (which would be created if not present and overwritten if present).

You can also redirect input as well as output.

```
$ grep accounts < /etc/group > matched_accounts
```

In the previous example, we've directed the file /etc/group into the grep command using the < symbol. We've then told grep to search for the term accounts and used the > symbol to direct the output of this command into a file called matched_accounts.

Another useful trick is the ability to run multiple commands on a single command line by separating each with a semicolon.

```
$ ./configure; make; make test
```

This command line would run the configure script in the current directory and then the make and the make test commands. The commands would run in sequence, one after the other.

These are just some very simple examples of the power of the Bash command line and redirection and piping. A lot more Bash capabilities are revealed by reviewing Bash's man page, man bash, or having a look at one of the many Bash tutorials online such as www.hypexr.org/bash_tutorial.php and http://tldp.org/LDP/Bash-Beginners-Guide/html/, or checking out the Bash reference manual at www.gnu.org/software/bash/manual/bashref.html.

Moving and Renaming Files

Moving files around in Linux is pretty straightforward. Using the mv command, you can move a file or directory from one location to another. In order to move a file, you must have write permissions to the file and write permissions to the location you want to move it to.

Listing 4-17 demonstrates how to move a file.

Listing 4-17. Moving Files

```
$ mv -i ~/myfile /home/bjones/yourfile
```

The command in Listing 4-17 moves a file called myfile from the home directory to /home/bjones and renames it to yourfile. The -i option again ensures we get prompted if the target file already exists. You can also rename files in place with the mv command.

```
$ mv -i ~/myfile ~/mynewfile
```

You can do the same for directories.

Deleting Files

Use the rm (remove) command to delete files. As with any host, deleting files should be done carefully and with thought. On Linux, however, unlike Windows, there isn't a quick and easy way to undelete files, so you need to be careful and take some precautions before you delete files. The first precaution is the use of the -i switch with the rm command. The -i switch enables interactive mode, which prompts you each time a file is deleted. You have to respond with a y or Y to delete the file or anything else to abort, as you can see in Listing 4-18.

Listing 4-18. The rm -i Switch

```
$ rm -i /home/jsmith/myfile
rm: remove regular file `/home/jsmith/myfile'? n
```

■ **Tip**   Many distributions used to alias the rm command to rm -i to force deletion checking. You can enter the command alias to see a list of all the current aliases on your host. You can create your own aliases too. For instructions, check the alias command's man page.

You can also delete directories and their contents recursively with the -r switch as follows:

```
$ rm -r /home/jsmith/backup
```

This would delete the /home/jsmith/backup directory and all its contents.
You can also override the -i switch using the -f, or force, switch like so:

```
$ rm -fr /home/jsmith/backup
```

This will also delete the backup directory and all its contents, but you will not be prompted to confirm the deletions. Be careful of using this switch and always be cognizant of where you are in the directory tree when you execute the command—the results of an inappropriate use of this command could be devastating!

■ **Caution**   Unlike Windows with its Recycle Bin, deleting files on Linux tends to be fairly permanent unless you have backups. Some methods are available to recover files, like the following: http://unix. stackexchange.com/questions/80270/unix-linux-undelete-recover-deleted-files. Your success with these methods will vary greatly. You should always delete files with extreme care, and you should make sure you have an appropriate backup. This is particularly important when editing configuration files. Always back up files before you edit, move, or delete them. Sometimes it is better to move the file or directory, wait for a period, then delete when you are sure you don't need it.

Linking Files

On Linux hosts, you can also create links to files. Links can be used like Windows shortcuts but come in two forms—hard links and soft, or symbolic, links. Hard links are not like Windows shortcuts. They are actual references to the physical file. If you delete all hard links to a file, the file they reference is also deleted.

■ **Note**   Hard links can hence only be created on the physical partition or hard drive; you can't link to a file located on another drive or partition.

Soft, or symbolic, links are more like Windows shortcuts: if they are deleted, the original file remains and only the link is removed.

You create links with the ln command. Hard links are created by default, and soft links are created by adding the -s switch. There are a few ways the ln command can be used, but the simplest is to create a link to a target file as follows:

```
$ ln -s /home/jsmith/myfile
```

The previous line would create a symbolic link called myfile to the /home/jsmith/myfile file. You can see other options you can use with the ln command by reviewing its man page.

Editing Files

Linux provides a wide variety of editing tools for files, including both GUI and command-line tools. In the GUI, you can find editors like kate or the simpler gedit. These are straightforward editors, but they are not word processors—much like Windows Notepad. Also, there are tools that allow you to edit files from the command line, like the popular vim, nano, joe, or bizarrely popular emacs.

We're going to start by taking a quick look at vim, which is a text editor that is an enhancement of an older Unix editor called vi. To edit a file, you run the vim command and specify the name of the file to edit.

```
$ vim ~/newfile
```

■ **Tip**   Some distributions also alias the vim command to vi to make it easier for people who are used to the older name.

This opens a file called newfile in your home directory. To insert some text into the file, type **i**, which is short for insert. You will see the word -- INSERT -- appear at the bottom of the screen. This means you're in insert mode, which allows you to add to the file. You can now type in the file. Let's type in **hello jsmith**. You can also use the arrow keys to move around on the line and through the file. The Enter key can be used to add lines to the file.

■ **Tip**   You can use the touch command to create empty files. Simply enter touch and the file name you want to create to create an empty file, for example, touch /home/jsmith/newfile.

When you've done that, press the Esc key. The Esc key takes you out of insert mode (you will see the text -- INSERT -- disappear from the bottom of the screen). You can now save what you've added to the file by entering the colon character (:) and the letters wq for a combination of :wq. This means write and quit. You could also just specify w, which would write but not quit. If you quit back to the command line, you can now view your file and see your typed text:

```
$ cat newfile
hello jsmith
```

■ **Tip**   You can find an introduction to vim at www.openvim.com/, or you might be able to run vimtutor on the command line to start a vim tutorial (depending on whether you have installed the vim-enhanced package).

A variety of GUI editors are also available. Some are simple in a similar style to the Microsoft Window's Notepad or WordPad applications, and others are fully fledged word processors and text editors.

An example of these is the Gnome default text editor, gedit. You can launch gedit in Gnome by clicking the Applications menu, opening the Accessories tab, and selecting the Text Editor application. This will launch the gedit editor, as you can see in Figure 4-11.

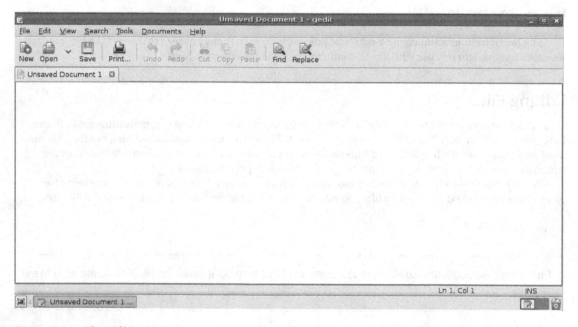

Figure 4-11. *The* gedit *editor*

Another example of these editors is kate (http://kate editor.org/), which comes with the KDE GUI. In Figure 4-12, you can see a KDE desktop with kate open.

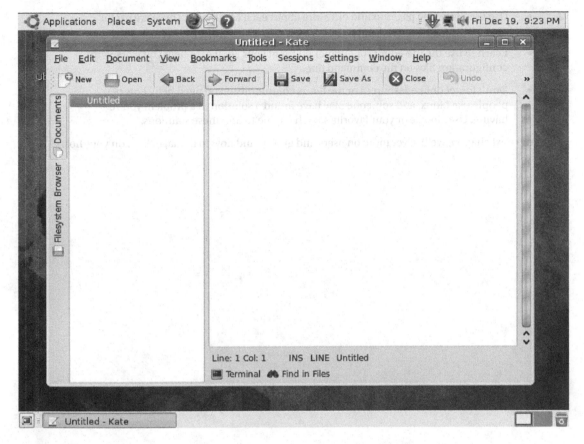

Figure 4-12. *The kate editor*

Summary

Well, what have you learned? First of all, Linux isn't that hard to understand and the command line is a very powerful tool. Compared to Window or Macs it encompasses a lot of similar concepts and principles, and this will help you get started with Linux. Some of the key things you should take away from this chapter are the following:

- You can test out lots of things using LiveCDs without any risk to your existing hosts and data, or use a virtual machine.

- Learn to use the command line—it's useful and powerful (and sometimes you won't have a choice!). The Bash shell is especially powerful, and you'll find yourself wondering how you ever got by without a command shell.

- Learn a bit more about globbing and regular expressions—you'll find both useful and powerful tools in your arsenal when administering your hosts.

- Don't use the root user to administer your host. Instead, make use of the sudo command. More on the sudo command in the next chapter.

- Use the Linux man pages to find out more about each command. These are useful resources packed with information.

- Learn to use the vim editor (or another editor of your choice) to help you work with configuration files on the command line.

- Don't forget online resources or the Linux community if you need help. Lots of people use Linux, and someone may have found a solution to a problem you're having. Use Google or your favorite search engine to find these solutions.

In the next chapter, we'll cover more on users and groups and how to manage them on your hosts.

CHAPTER 5

■ ■ ■

Users and Groups

By James Turnbull and Dennis Matotek

Chapter 4 introduced Linux basics and the concepts of users and collections of users called groups. We explained how users and groups own files and objects. We also demonstrated how that ownership, in combination with permissions, controls access to those files and objects. Users and groups are also used to initiate and run processes.

In this chapter, we'll go into detail about how users and groups work, starting with what happens when you log in, and how to control some of that process. We'll demonstrate how to create users and groups, give you some more information about passwords, and explain the process by which Linux controls access to your host.

Among the topics we're going to talk about are the su and sudo commands. These commands let you run commands as other users, specifically the root user. Thus, these commands allow you to avoid logging in as the root user to perform administrative tasks. The su and sudo commands are critical to securely administering your hosts.

What Happens When You Log In?

In Chapter 4, we talked about logging a user into a Linux host, and you saw some sample screens showing how you might enter your username and password. In this chapter, we're going to explain a bit more about what happens when you log in, and we'll begin to explore some of the options and security controls that you can manage as part of this process.

So what actually happens after you enter your username and password and before you are delivered to your command-line prompt or graphical user interface (GUI) screen? Well, this process varies slightly from distribution to distribution, but generally an application called login is executed and performs the following actions:

- Checks that the user and group exist and the user is allowed to log in

- Checks that the user is allowed to log in from a particular location (e.g., only some users can log in to the console, or the screen attached to a Linux host)

- Checks that the password is correct, and, if the password is incorrect, allows a specified number (usually three) of retries

- Checks that the password is valid and prompts the user for a new password if it has expired

- Sets environment variables like the user's home directory and path

- Starts the shell process

- Presents the user with a command-line prompt or GUI screen

© Dennis Matotek, James Turnbull and Peter Lieverdink 2017
D. Matotek et al., *Pro Linux System Administration*, DOI 10.1007/978-1-4842-2008-5_5

In the sections that follow, we'll take you through these processes and explain how you can configure and change some of these steps to suit your environment. You'll start by learning how to create, delete, and manage users and groups.

■ **Note** In this chapter, we demonstrate command-line user administration, but most things we show you is also available from a GUI tool if you prefer to administer your users and groups that way. In the application search bar, type in "users" and you'll find the Users application (CentOS) or User Accounts (Ubuntu)—or open the Settings or System Settings menu and you'll find them there.

Working with Users and Groups

At the heart of managing access to your Linux hosts is the concept of users and groups. We introduced users and the collections of users called groups in Chapter 4, and you discovered they are much like the users and groups that exist on the Microsoft Windows platform.

You can organize users and groups on your host in two ways. One way is to add users and groups to each host in your domain; the other is to centralize your user administration on one or two authentication servers. In this chapter, we will explain the former, and in Chapter 16 we will explain the latter.

As on Microsoft Windows hosts, everyone who needs to log in to your host will need a user created. Many applications, such as web and mail servers, will also require a user to be created. When they are started, these applications will then make use of that user's rights and privileges to access system resources like files, your network, or other aspects of your host.

Every user on your Linux host also needs to belong to at least one group but can belong to any number of additional groups as well. Groups are collections of users, gathered together because they are alike or require access to a particular resource. For example, all the users in your organization's sales department may belong to a group called sales. You might configure your host to ensure that only the users in the sales group have access to the sales department's applications and files.

■ **Note** When applications are installed, they often install additional users and groups required to run those applications.

Users and groups are easy to create using two commands: useradd (to create users) and groupadd (to create groups). Additionally, two commands we can use to modify existing users and groups are usermod and groupmod. Finally, to complete the life cycle, users and groups can be deleted with the userdel and groupdel commands.

■ **Tip** Working with users and groups on CentOS and Ubuntu is a very similar process that uses many of the same commands and options. We'll tell you about any minor variations between distributions.

Introducing sudo

Before we jump into explaining how to create users and groups, we want to discuss the sudo command, which we talked about a little in Chapter 4. The sudo command allows a user to run commands as if that person were signed in as the root user, Linux's equivalent of the Windows Administrator account. This ability is useful for three reasons:

- It increases security.

- It allows greater control of privileged commands.

- It provides you with a better audit trail to understand who did what on your host.

■ **Note**   Another good reason to use sudo rather than the root user on Ubuntu is that Ubuntu doesn't enable the root user by default. You cannot sign on as the root user at all.

We're going to need sudo in this chapter because almost all of the commands used to manage users and groups require the privileges of the root user to run. For example, only the root user can create another user.

When you run the sudo command, it will prompt you to enter your password (to confirm you are actually who you say you are), and then you are allowed to make use of the sudo command for a period of 5 minutes on CentOS and 15 minutes on Ubuntu. When this period expires, you will be prompted to enter your password again.

■ **Tip**   The first time you run the sudo command, it may also show you a warning to be careful with the power of the sudo command.

On Ubuntu, the sudo command is available and configured for the user you created when you installed Ubuntu. If you're logged in as that user, you can use the sudo command already. You can also enable sudo access for other users by adding them to the admin group. You can use the usermod command (which you'll see more of later in this chapter) to add a user to the group.

```
$ sudo usermod -G admin ataylor
```

Here we've used sudo and the usermod command to modify a user called ataylor. We've added the user to the admin group by specifying the -G option and the name of the group to add the user to. (Note that we've used the sudo command to do the user modification. The only user allowed to do this is the user you created when you installed the host; hence you must be logged in as that user to make this change.)

On CentOS, if you did not create the user (jsmith) as an administrator, the sudo command is not enabled by default, and you'll need to enable it. To do this, you need to use a command called visudo to edit the sudo command's configuration file, /etc/sudoers. To do this, you need to log on as the root user and run the visudo command.

```
# visudo
```

As you can see from the # command prompt, you're logging in as the root user and you're executing the visudo command. This opens an editing application that looks much like the vi or vim editor. Inside this file is the following line:

```
# %wheel ALL=(ALL) ALL
```

Shown above, in this line the # indicates the line you are working on is a comment. You need to uncomment the line. To do this put your cursor near on the # and press the x key twice. That will delete the hash (or pound sign, #) and one space character in the line. Once done, write and quit the file using the same commands you would with vim by typing the colon character, :, and w and q followed by Enter, or :wq. This enables any member of a group called wheel to use the sudo command. You can then add a user to the wheel group, as follows:

```
# usermod -a wheel ataylor
```

Again, you specify the group, wheel, with the -a option and the name of the user you want to add to the group last. Now the ataylor user can make use of the sudo command. You can also set the groups for a user using -G <group1>,<group2> and this will replace any existing groups assigned to the user.

Creating Users

Now that you know how to enable and use the sudo command, we can start looking at users and groups. Let's begin by creating a new user using the useradd command, as shown in Listing 5-1.

Listing 5-1. Creating a New User

```
$ sudo useradd -m -c 'John Smith' jsmith
```

■ **Note** In Listing 5-1, you can see we've prefixed the useradd command with the sudo command to avoid having to log on as the root user.

The useradd command has a number of options, and we're using just a couple in Listing 5-1. The first argument, -m, tells the host to create a home directory for the user. The format of the name and location of the home directory would usually resemble /home/*username*.

■ **Tip** You can prepopulate the new home directory with, for example, generic configuration files. To do this, add files to the /etc/skel (short for skeleton) directory. When a new home directory is created (using the -m option), then all the files contained in this directory are copied to the user's new home directory.

The -c option adds a description of our new user. This description is stored in the /etc/passwd file. All users have an entry in this file, and we'll examine this file and the /etc/group file that is used to store group data later in this chapter. Finally, we've specified the name of our new user, jsmith.

By default, the new user will be created disabled and with no password set. You will need to change the user's password using the passwd command (which we'll cover in more detail later in this chapter).

Table 5-1 lists some other useful useradd command-line options.

Table 5-1. *Some useradd Command-Line Options*

Option	Description
-c	Add a description of the user
-d homedir	The user's home directory
-m	Create the user's home directory
-M	Do not create the user's home directory (CentOS only)
-s shell	Specify the shell the user will use

The -d option allows you to specify the user's home directory. A home directory is the directory a user is placed in after they login. This is a private directory owned by the user for the user's files, this applies to a system user (like a user that runs a database) or a regular human user. The -M option tells Red Hat–derived distributions not to create a home directory. This option highlights the major difference between creating users on CentOS and Ubuntu distributions. On Red Hat–derived distributions, home directories are created automatically.

Ubuntu requires that the useradd command is executed with the -m option; otherwise no home directory is created.

■ **Note**   See the sidebar "Adduser: An Alternative on Ubuntu" for an alternative method to create users on Ubuntu.

Finally, the -s option allows you to specify a different shell from the default for the user.

■ **Tip**   We recommend you read the useradd command's man page for more detailed information on this command.

User Default Settings

Your new user will also be created with a variety of defaults (e.g., the setting for the user's shell). So where does the useradd command get these defaults from? On both CentOS and Ubuntu distributions, the defaults are contained in the /etc/default/useradd file, and you can display the current defaults using the following command:

```
$ sudo /usr/sbin/useradd -D
```

Listing 5-2 shows a sample of this file.

Listing 5-2. The /etc/default/useradd File

```
$ sudo cat /etc/default/useradd
# useradd defaults file
GROUP=100
HOME=/home
INACTIVE=-1
EXPIRE=
SHELL=/bin/bash
SKEL=/etc/skel
```

This file is usually populated by default when your host is installed, but you can modify it to suit your environment.

■ **Note** There are system-wide defaults that are set for the system when a user logs in. Those are found in the /etc/login.defs file. It contains things like the uid and gid ranges to use when creating users.

Table 5-2 shows the possible options you can include in the useradd file.

Table 5-2. *The /etc/default/useradd File*

Option	Description
SHELL	The path to the default shell
HOME	The path to the user's home directory
SKEL	The directory to use to provide the default contents of a user's new home directory
GROUP	The default group ID
INACTIVE	The maximum number of days after password expiration that a password can be changed
EXPIRE	The default expiration date of user accounts

Each option in the file controls a specify default; for example, the SHELL option specifies the default shell for the user. The HOME option specifies the directory in which all new home directories should be created. The SKEL option specifies which directory to use to populate the user's home directory, and as we discussed earlier, this defaults to /etc/skel. The GROUP option specifies the default group ID (GID) to use. It is set to group 100, or the "users" group, and you generally won't ever need to change this. We'll talk a bit more about groups, membership, and GIDs in the sections that follow.

Finally, two other options, INACTIVE and EXPIRE, control two different types of user account expiration. The INACTIVE value controls how long in days after a user's password expires that the user can reset his password. This allows you to specify that if a user's password expires, the user has a finite time to reset that password before he is marked inactive. The user would then require some interaction to re-enable it for access. A setting of -1 disables this setting, and a setting of 0 disables the account as soon as the password expires.

■ **Note** We'll talk more about password expiration later in this chapter.

The EXPIRE option is useful for creating temporary accounts, as it specifies a date in the format YYYY-MM-DD on which the account will be expired and disabled. The EXPIRE default allows you to specify such a date for all accounts. You can also create an individual account on the command line using the following command:

```
$ sudo useradd -e 2016-09-15 temp_account
```

This command creates an account called temp_account that would be disabled on 09-15-2016.

You can change many of the default settings in this file by executing the useradd command with the -D option. Listing 5-3 shows you how to change the default shell for your new users, and Table 5-3 shows the additional options available for use with the -D option.

Listing 5-3. Changing useradd Defaults with the -D Option

```
$ sudo useradd -D -s /bin/bash
```

■ **Tip**   You can also change your default shell with the chsh command. Use chsh -1 on CentOS to see a list of all the available shells. On Ubuntu, you can see the list in the /etc/shells file.

Table 5-3. The useradd -D Defaults

Option	Description
-b path/to/default/home	Specifies the path prefix of a new user's home directory
-e date	Specifies the default expiration date
-f days	Specifies the number of days after a password has expired before the account will be disabled
-g group	Specifies the default group
-s shell	Specifies the default shell

Creating Groups

We mentioned earlier that every user must belong to at least one group. By default on most Linux distributions, including CentOS and Ubuntu, when you create a new user, a new group with the same name as the user is also created. The new user is always the only member of this group.

But earlier we said that the default group for useradd was 100? Why isn't that used? If you use the –N (no-user-group) option to useradd or if the setting USERGROUPS_ENAB in the login.defs file is 'no' then the default group of 100 (users) will be assigned. By default the useradd command will create a group with the same name as the user.

■ **Note**   The creation of a unique group for each user is called a *user private group* (UPG) scheme. It is a flexible model for managing group permissions. You can read some details of UPG at https://wiki.debian. org/UserPrivateGroups

---

In our case, our first user, jsmith, would automatically belong to a group called jsmith. This group is called the *primary* group. Our user can also belong to other groups, and these additional groups are called *supplementary* groups.

So how do we tell what groups our new user belongs to? To check the details of a particular user, we can use the id command as shown in Listing 5-4.

Listing 5-4. The id Command

```
$ id jsmith
uid=1001(jsmith) gid=1001(jsmith) groups=1001(jsmith)
```

In Listing 5-4, we query our new user, jsmith, using the id command. But the command has returned some fairly cryptic information about uid and gid, the name of our user, and some numbers. So what exactly are these?

Each user and group is assigned a unique user ID (UID) and a GID when created. UIDs range from 0 to 65535, with the root user always having a UID of 0. GIDs also range from 0 to 65535, with the root user also always having a GID of 0.

If you run the id command for the root user, you can see the results on the following line:

```
$ id root
uid=0(root) gid=0(root) groups=0(root)
```

This shows the root user having a UID of 0 and a GID of 0.

■ **Note**   Each user and group on a host must have a unique UID and GID. A user or group cannot be created on your host with the same UID or GID as an existing user or group. Your operating system will automatically assign the numbers and prevent any conflicts.

Most distributions reserve ranges of numbers for particular types of users and groups. There are really two kinds of users on your system. One kind is a system user such as users and groups that run services—for example, a user running a database or web server. So system users like "apache" and "www-data" have set and known UID. The other kinds of users are "people," (e.g., you and I) who need to log into the system.

A CentOS distribution reserves the UID and GID ranges of 1 to 200 for assigned system UIDs (like apache). They do this by specifying the UID when the user is created. UIDs from 201 to 999 are for dynamically assigned system UIDs—these are daemons that have not defined UID and will pick a UID at installation. This is done by specifying the --system option when creating the user. Normal users are created with UIDs of 1000 and above.

Ubuntu reserves the UID and GID ranges of 1 to 99 for assigned system users. 100 to 999 for dynamically assigned system users (again by passing the --system option). On Ubuntu, the first new user would have a UID and GID of 1000 as well.

■ **Tip**   You can control the range of the UIDs and GIDs that are provided to users in the /etc/login.defs file. Edit the UID_MIN and UID_MAX range for UIDs and the GID_MIN and GID_MAX range for GIDs. It's unlikely you'll ever want to do this, but the option is there. You can also set the SYS_UID_MIN and SYS_UID_MAX as well as the group there too.

So in Listing 5-4 we've executed the id command for the jsmith user and displayed the user's UID of 1001 and GID of 1001 (with the name of the user and group in brackets after the UID and GID). The last field, groups, is where the primary and any supplementary groups are displayed.

You have two methods for adding your user to a group or groups. First, you can add the user to a group or groups upon creation with the useradd command. Second, you can modify an existing user and add groups using the usermod command.

On the following line, we're going to create a second user called ataylor and add her to some groups when we create her.

```
$ sudo useradd -m -c 'Anne Taylor' -G printing,finance ataylor
```

We have specified the –G option, which allows us to provide a comma-separated list of groups that we'd like our new user ataylor to join. The -G option allows our user to join additional groups other than her primary group, which is a unique group created when the user is created and shares her username. Here the user ataylor is a member of a unique UPG scheme primary group called ataylor, and we're trying to add her to the additional supplemental groups printing and finance.

If we execute that command now, however, it will fail because each of these groups needs to exist *before* we can add a user to them, otherwise we'll get an error message and the user will fail to be created. This is the error message that would be generated in such a scenario on Ubuntu:

```
useradd: unknown group printing
useradd: unknown group finance
```

So in this case, we need to create our groups first, and we can do that with the groupadd command, as you can see in Listing 5-5.

Listing 5-5. Creating New Groups

```
$ sudo groupadd printing
$ sudo groupadd finance
```

Table 5-4 shows some command-line options available with the groupadd command.

Table 5-4. *The groupadd Command-Line Options*

Option	Description
-g GID	Sets the GID for the group. This must be a unique number.
-r	Creates a system group (with a GID inside the system GID range).

Use the -g option if you wish to override the autogenerated GID with a specific number. Available only on CentOS, the –r option lets you create a system group and will ensure the group is assigned a GID within the range for system groups.

When we try to create the ataylor user, we succeed because the prerequisite groups now exist.

```
$ sudo useradd -m -c 'Anne Taylor' -G printing,finance ataylor
```

We can also add existing users to groups using the usermod command.

```
$ sudo usermod -a -G accounts ataylor
```

The usermod command is used to modify existing users. By specifying the –a (for append) option, the -G option, and the name of the new group to join (the group must already exist), we add the ataylor user to the accounts group.

■ **Tip** You can change many of the aspects of a user with the usermod command, and we recommend reading its man page for further information. Changes won't take effect until the user logs out and back in again if the user is currently logged in.

Also available to manage groups is the gpasswd command, which allows you to delegate responsibility for managing groups and their memberships. You can assign a particular user rights to add or remove users to a particular group. For example, you could have someone on the sales team manage the membership of the sales group. You can read about gpasswd in more detail on its man page.

Deleting Users and Groups

In addition to creating and modifying users and groups, you will also want to be able to delete them. You can use the following two commands to do this: userdel and groupdel. The userdel command deletes users, and the groupdel command removes groups. Let's now delete the ataylor user we created earlier using the userdel command, as shown in Listing 5-6.

Listing 5-6. Deleting a User

```
$ sudo userdel ataylor
```

The userdel command deletes the user, but by default it doesn't delete the user's home directory. You can force Linux to delete the user's home directory using the -r option of the userdel command. This will delete the /home/*username* directory and all files in it, but it won't delete any files outside this directory that might also belong to the user. The userdel command will also not delete a user who is currently logged in to the host.

Removing a user who owns files can be problematic. If you delete a user, then all the user's objects will no longer be owned by the user. You can identify these objects because the username will be replaced in the file listing with the former UID (the same applies for any deleted groups). As a result, if you create another user that uses the same UID or GID, that user will now own the deleted user's files. It's a very good idea to confirm the files and directories a user owns and work out what you are going to do with them prior to deleting the user. We'll show you how to assign ownership of files and directories later in this chapter. In light of this issue, it is sometimes better to disable a user rather than delete the user. But if you do decide to delete a user, you can run the command find / -user UID -o -group GID to find all the files associated with the user you have just deleted.

To delete a group, use the groupdel command and specify the name of the group to be deleted.

```
$ sudo groupdel finance
```

This command will remove the group from the host. It is important to note that the groupdel command won't delete the primary group of any user—for example, you couldn't delete the ataylor group before you deleted the ataylor user. If you want to delete a user's primary group, you must delete the user first. Like with users, deleting groups can leave files owned by those groups orphaned.

ADDUSER: AN ALTERNATIVE ON UBUNTU

Ubuntu ships with two additional user management utilities, adduser and addgroup. These provide easy-to-use and convenient alternatives to the useradd and groupadd commands. The normal way to run adduser is with the username of the new user you'd like to create. The utility will then ask you to provide additional information. For example, let's add an account for user Anne Taylor.

```
$ sudo adduser ataylor
Adding user `ataylor' ...
Adding new group `ataylor' (1001) ...
Adding new user `ataylor' (1001) with group `ataylor' ... Creating home directory `/
home/ataylor' ...
Copying files from `/etc/skel' ... Enter new UNIX password:
Retype new UNIX password:
passwd: password updated successfully
Changing the user information for ataylor
Enter the new value, or press ENTER for the default
    Full Name []: Anne Taylor
    Room Number []:
    Work Phone []:
    Home Phone []:
    Other []:
Is the information correct? [Y/n] y
```

The adduser command asks for all the variables it needs, and it then calls the useradd command with the correct parameters in order to create the account. This means that even when you use the adduser command, the default useradd options you configure in /etc/default/useradd are still honored.

You can also use the adduser script to quickly add a user to a group, by running this:

```
$ sudo adduser username groupname
```

Both the user and group need to already exist on the host.

The adduser and addgroup scripts themselves can also be configured via the /etc/adduser.conf file. By default, they will create users of the specified name, put them in a group of the same name, create the home directory, and assign the lowest available user and group IDs.

Managing Users and Groups via the GUI

Both CentOS and Ubuntu have GUIs for managing users. On CentOS and Ubuntu, the GUI tool to manage user accounts is accessed in the Settings panel launched by selecting Applications ➤ System Tools ➤ Settings (see Figure 5-1).

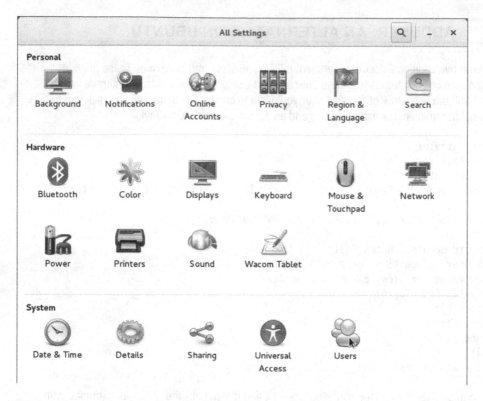

Figure 5-1. *Accessing users from the system settings*

You can change users in using this settings panel. But first you need to gain root privileges (or also referred to as administrator privileges in the GUI) to be able to change settings here. Figure 5-2 shows you that you need to click the unlock button and will then be prompted to enter your password.

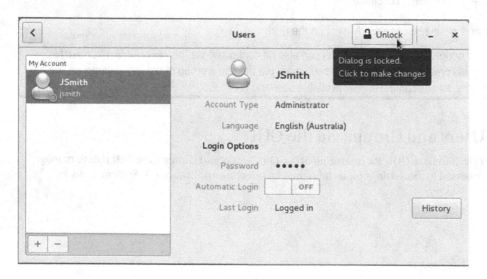

Figure 5-2. *Unlocking the Users settings interface*

In Figure 5-2 the list of the current users is in the left panel. To add a user click the + button at the bottom of that list. You can delete users by clicking the – button. In Figure 5-3 we add a new user called `ataylor`.

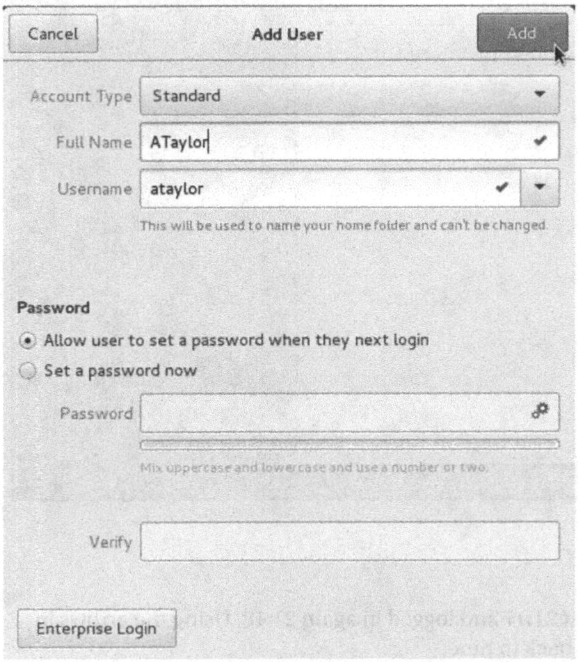

Figure 5-3. Adding user ATaylor

In Figure 5-3 we are adding the user ataylor. By selecting Allow user to set a password when they next login, ATaylor will be allowed to create their own password when they next log in. There are two types of users we can add, a Standard user or an Administrator. You can also choose to add an Enterprise Login to your users to an Active Directory domain or an IPA (Identity Policy Audit) domain. In Chapter 16 we will go further into this. By clicking the Add button we will add the user ataylor after we authenticate again with the system.

■ **Caution**   Allowing users to create their own passwords when they next log in does expose a security risk. Anybody signing in as `ataylor` will be prompted to set a new password and, by doing so, will have access to all that `ataylor` does. In this situation it is a good idea to make sure that you get `ataylor` to log in as soon as is immediately possible and confirm access.

Finally, in Figure 5-4 we show how you can view the login history of the user JSmith.

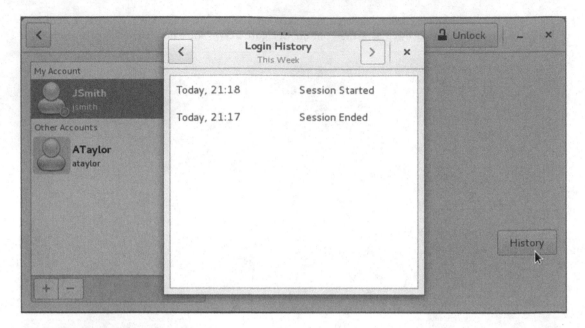

Figure 5-4. *Login history for JSmith*

In Figure 5-4 we can see that JSmith logged out at 21:17 and logged in again 21:18. Using the arrows in the title bar scroll through the history to view further back in time.

While you can add and delete users through this application you cannot administer group settings. To do this you must use the command line.

■ **Note** Remember, the Ubuntu Server version does not come with a GUI by default, and you should make use of the command-line tools provided. The Ubuntu Desktop release does come with the appropriate GUI tools, as it installs a GUI by default.

Passwords

When you create accounts via the command line, no password is set for the account. You may now want to set or at some time change the user's password. To do this, you use the `passwd` command. The `passwd` command works one of two ways depending on who runs the command. If a normal user, like `ataylor`, has a password already set and runs the command, then she will be prompted to change her own password. You can see the `passwd` command in action in Listing 5-7.

Listing 5-7. Changing Your Password

```
$ passwd
Changing password for ataylor.
(current) UNIX password:
Enter new UNIX password:
Retype new UNIX password:
```

You type in your current password and then your new password. You'll be prompted to type the new password in twice to ensure it's correct. You'll also have to provide a suitable password. By default on most distributions, some basic password checking is performed to try to prevent you from providing a weak or easy-to-guess password. On most distributions these checks are generally as follows:

- Minimum password length of four characters

- Not a palindrome (i.e., the reverse of the last password)

- Not the same as the previous password with a case change (i.e., password to PASSWORD)

- Some basic similarity checking

- Some simplicity tests based on the length of the password and the combination of characters (all alpha, all numeric, etc.)

- Simple rotation checks (i.e., rotating letters in a password, such as ginger being changed to ingerg)

If you provide a password that isn't sufficiently complex, you'll be given an error message indicating what is wrong with your password. You will then be prompted to provide a more acceptable password.

Alternatively, if you are running the passwd command as the root user, you can change the passwords of other users as you can see in Listing 5-8.

Listing 5-8. Changing Someone Else's Password

```
$ sudo passwd jsmith
```

In Listing 5-8, the passwd command prompts you to provide a new password for the user jsmith.

■ **Tip** It is important to note that as the root user you can override any warnings about bad passwords and change the user's password to a weak or easily guessable password.

Password Aging

Password aging allows you to specify a time period during which a password is valid. After the time period has expired, the user will be forced to choose a new password. This has the benefit of ensuring passwords are changed regularly and that a password that is stolen, cracked, or known by a former employee will have a time-limited value. Unfortunately for many users, the need to regularly change their passwords increases their desire to write down the passwords. We recommend you use a password age between 30 and 60 days for most passwords, depending on the nature of the host and encouraging password managers. More important, hosts should have shorter password expiration periods (e.g., 30 days), while less critical hosts could have longer periods. Some organizations choose a single expiration period so the period is consistent for all users on all hosts.

Two ways exist to handle password aging. The first uses the command-line tool called chage to set or change the password expiration of a user account individually. Listing 5-9 shows this command.

Listing 5-9. The chage Command

```
$ sudo chage -M 30 ataylor
```

Listing 5-9 uses the -M option to set the password expiration period for the user ataylor to 30 days. After 30 days the user's password will be expired and the user will be prompted to enter a new password. Table 5-5 shows several of the other variables you can set.

Table 5-5. *The chage Command Flags*

Option	Description
-m days	Sets the minimum number of days between password changes. Zero allows the user to change the password at any time.
-M days	Sets the maximum number of days for which a password stays valid.
-E date	Sets a date on which the user account will expire and automatically be deactivated.
-W days	Sets the number of days before the password expires that the user will be warned to change it.
-d days	Sets the number of days since January 1, 1970, that the password was last changed.
-I days	Sets the number of days after password expiration that the account is locked.

■ **Tip** You'll come across the date January 1, 1970, quite a few times in the Unix/Linux world. This date is also known as *Unix epoch* or *Unix time*. It is used to describe points in time and is measured in seconds since January 1, 1970 (e.g., 1229519557). You can find the Unix time on your host by using the command date +%s.

The first option, -m, allows you to specify the minimum amount of time between password changes. A setting of 0 allows the user to change the password at any time. The option -W specifies the number of days before a user's password expires that he will get a warning that the password is about to expire. The -d option is principally useful to immediately expire a password. By setting the -d option to 0, the user's last password change date becomes January 1, 1970, and if the –M option is greater than 0, then the user must change his password at the next login. The last option, -I, provides a time frame in days after which user accounts with expired and unchanged passwords are locked and thus unable to be used to log in.

If you run chage without any options and specify only the user, it will launch an interactive series of prompts to set the required values, as shown in Listing 5-10. The values between the brackets[ ] indicate the current values to which this user's password aging is set.

Listing 5-10. Running chage Without Options

```
$ sudo chage ataylor
Changing the aging information for ataylor
Enter the new value, or press return for the default
Minimum Password Age [0]:
Maximum Password Age [30]:
Last Password Change (YYYY-MM-DD) [2016-06-27]:
Password Expiration Warning [7]:
Password Inactive [-1]:
Account Expiration Date (YYYY-MM-DD) [2016-07-28]:
```

Users can also utilize the chage command with the -l option to show when a password is due to expire.

```
$ chage -l ataylor
```

The other method to handle password aging is to set defaults for all users in the /etc/login.defs file. Listing 5-11 shows the controls available for password aging in /etc/login.defs.

Listing 5-11. The login.defs Password-Aging Controls

```
PASS_MAX_DAYS    60
PASS_MIN_DAYS    0
PASS_WARN_AGE    7
```

In Listing 5-11, we have set the maximum password age to 60 days using the PASS_MAX_DAYS option, allowing users to change their passwords at any time by setting the PASS_MIN_DAYS option to 0 and providing a warning to users that their passwords will expire seven days before the password expiration date using the PASS_WARN_AGE option.

Disabling Users

As the root user, you can also use the passwd command to disable and enable user accounts using the -l, or lock, option. For example, consider the following:

```
$ sudo passwd -l ataylor
```

The previous command would lock the ataylor user and prevent ataylor from logging into the host using her password. You can then unlock the user using the -u, or unlock, option.

```
$ sudo passwd -u ataylor
```

However, this command doesn't fully disable access to the host. Users could access the host through other authentication mechanisms such as public keys for remote access using SSH (Secure Shell).

There is another way to totally disable access to the user that uses the usermod command with the --expiredate option:

```
$ sudo usermod --expiredate 1 ataylor
```

This sets the account expiration date to January 1, 1970, and disables the account immediately. The user can now do nothing on the host.

Finally, you can set the login shell to /bin/false or /usr/sbin/nologin. This doesn't lock a user out but disables the user's getting shell access.

```
$ sudo usermod -s /bin/false ataylor
```

■ **Note**   You can also set the user's shell to a command. For example, you could set the user's shell to the /bin/mail command, which is a small command-line mail reader. When the user then logs on, she can access only that command.

Storing User Data

First, your host checks that your user exists and is allowed to log in. Linux distributions store details of users, groups, and other information in three files on your host: /etc/passwd, /etc/shadow, and /etc/group. You generally won't ever need to edit these files, as there are commands and tools that allow you to add, remove, and manage users and groups. It is useful, however, to know what information they contain.

■ **Tip** If you use other forms of authentication such as NIS (Network Information Service), LDAP (Lightweight Directory Access Protocol), or Active Directory, which we'll look at in Chapter 16, then your host will usually query one of these authentication stores to confirm your user exists and is allowed to log in.

The first file, /etc/passwd, contains a list of all users and their details. Listing 5-12 shows examples of some passwd entries.

Listing 5-12. /etc/passwd Entries

```
root:x:0:0:root:/root:/bin/bash
daemon:x:2:2:daemon:/sbin:/sbin/nologin
```

Each entry can be broken into its component pieces, separated by a colon.

```
username:password:UID:GID:GECOS:Home Directory:Shell
```

The username can be up to 32 characters and is case sensitive (though it's usually all in lowercase). The x in the next field is a marker for the password. The actual password is stored in the /etc/shadow file, which we will discuss in the sidebar "Shadow Passwords."

Next is the UID and GID. As noted earlier, on a Linux host, each user account and group is assigned a numeric ID; users are assigned a UID and groups are assigned a GID. Depending on the distribution, lower-numbered UIDs and GIDs indicate system accounts and groups such as root or daemon. On CentOS and Ubuntu you will usually see system account UIDs and GIDs lower than 1000.

■ **Note** As mentioned earlier, the root user has a UID and GID of 0. This should be the only user on the host with a UID and GID of 0.

The next item is the GECOS or comment field. This field usually contains data such as the name of the user, office locations, and phone numbers. If you have more than one item of data in the GECOS field, then a comma separates each data item.

The user's home directory comes next. As we described in Chapter 4, this is usually located in the /home directory (e.g., /home/jsmith).

The last item is the user's default shell. The shell, as we discussed in Chapter 4, is a command-line environment through which the user interacts with the host. Each shell is initiated by running a binary. For example, to start the Bash shell, the /bin/bash binary would be executed. This binary is specified in the /etc/passwd file. If the default shell points to a nonexistent file, then the user will be unable to log in.

The second line in Listing 5-12 uses the shell /sbin/nologin, which is a dummy shell that not only stops the user from logging it, but also logs the login attempt to the syslog daemon.

■ **Note** The `syslog` daemon is the Linux logging server. It receives log entries from the operating system and applications and writes them to files, generally in the `/var/log` directory. We'll talk more about logging in Chapter 18.

Unless the user is set to not log in, most users will have a shell entry that references the binary that launches their shell, for example, `/bin/bash`.

SHADOW PASSWORDS

You may have noted that no password appears in `/etc/passwd` but rather the letter x. This is because modern distributions use *shadow passwords* to handle password management.

Previously, passwords were stored as one-way hashes in `/etc/passwd`, which provided limited security and exposed usernames and passwords to brute-force cracking methods. *Brute-force cracking* is a method of attacking passwords where thousands or millions of different passwords are tried until a matching password is found. The `/etc/passwd` file was especially susceptible to this attack because its use by applications requires it to be readable by all users, or world readable. This was especially dangerous when a copy of a passwd file could be stolen from a host and brute-force-cracked offline. Given the weak security of this type of password when stored in the passwd file, a modern computer can crack simple passwords in a matter of minutes or harder passwords in just days.

Shadow passwords help reduce this risk by separating the users and passwords and storing the passwords as a hash in the `/etc/shadow` file. By default, SHA512 hashes are used. These SHA512 hashes are harder to break, and to further protect the passwords, the `/etc/shadow` file is owned by the `root` user, and `root` is the only user with access to the file. The next line shows a typical line from the shadow file:

```
root:$6$RwETwzjv$ifht......7L/HiLCPR8Zc935fd0:13675:0:99999:7:::
```

You can also break down the shadow file into components, and like the `passwd` file, colons separate each component. The components of the shadow file are as follows:

- Username

- Password

- Date password last changed

- Minimum days between password changes

- Password expiration time in days

- Password expiration warning period in days

- Number of days after password expiration that account is disabled

- Date since account has been disabled

The username matches the username in the passwd file. The password itself is encrypted, and two types of special characters can tell you about the status of the user account with which the password field can be prefixed. If the password field is prefixed with ! or *, then the account is locked and the user will not be allowed to log in. If the password field is prefixed with !!, then a password has never been set and the user cannot log in to the host. The remaining entries refer to password aging, and we cover those in the section "Password Aging."

Storing Group Data

On Linux hosts, information about groups is stored in the /etc/groups file. Listing 5-13 shows a sample from this file.

Listing 5-13. Sample of the /etc/groups File

```
root:x:0:root
ataylor:x:501:finance,printing
```

The /etc/group file is structured much like the /etc/passwd file, with the data separated by a colon. The file is broken into a group name, a password, the GID, and a comma-separated list of the members of that group.

```
groupname:password:GID:member,member
```

The password in the group file allows a user to log in to that group using the newgrp command. If shadow passwords are enabled, then like the passwd file, the passwords in the group file are replaced with an x and the real passwords are stored in the /etc/gshadow file.

LOGIN MESSAGES

Your login screen is the first thing users see. It's a good idea to put some important warnings and information in that login screen. To do this, you need to edit the contents of the /etc/issue and /etc/issue.net files. The issue file is displayed when you log in via the command line on the host's console, and the issue.net file is displayed when you log in to the command line via an SSH session. Most distributions use these files for this purpose, including both CentOS and Ubuntu. These files can contain a combination of plain text and special escape characters that allow you to output colors, line feeds, and returns, for example.

You should also include a warning message stating that unauthorized access to the host is prohibited and will be prosecuted. You can use one of a series of escape characters in the files to populate the login screen with data from your host. We recommend you use a login message like the following:

```
^[c
\d at \t
Access to this host is for authorized persons only.
Unauthorized use or access is regarded as a criminal act
and is subject to civil and criminal prosecution. User
activities on this host may be monitored without prior notice.
```

The ^[c escape characters clear the screen, and the \d and \t escape characters display the current date and time on the host, respectively. Other escape characters are available to you if you check the issue, issue.net, and getty man pages.

In addition to the `/etc/issue` and `/etc/issue.net` files, the `/etc/motd` file's contents display directly after a command-line login, and you may want to adjust them to include an Acceptable Use Policy or similar information.

If you are using a GUI you can set a message on the login screen. You can do this by following these instructions for CentOS:`https://access.redhat.com/documentation/en-US/Red_Hat_Enterprise_Linux/7/html/Desktop_Migration_and_Administration_Guide/customizing-login-screen.html`

For Ubuntu you will need to see the following: `http://askubuntu.com/questions/193357/how-do-i-create-a-popup-banner-before-login-with-lightdm.`

Configuring Your Shell and Environment

After users have been authenticated and authorized, their shell is started. Most shells are highly customizable, and many users eventually tweak every aspect of their shell environment to help them work faster and more efficiently.

The Bash shell reads its initial configuration from the `/etc/profile` file. This file usually contains references to other global configuration files and is used to configure Bash for all users on the host except the root user. Finally, any configuration files in the user's home directory are processed. The `.bash_profile` and `.profile` files are most commonly used, and each user will have these in his or her home directory.

■ **Note** You can check the INVOCATION section of bash man page for a full listing of other configuration files.

Environment Variables

One of the main reasons for customizing your shell is to set environment variables. These variables act as default options that are used by many applications. They can define characteristics like your preferred text editor, your preferred language, and the colors used when listing files and directories with `ls`. You can also define your own variables for use with your own scripts.

To get a full listing of all environment variables, use the `env` command. Table 5-6 lists the most commonly customized variables.

Table 5-6. Environment Variables

Name	Used For
HOME	The user's home directory
LANG	Defines which language files applications should use
LS_COLORS	Defines colors used by the `ls` command
MAIL	The location of the user's mailbox
PATH	A colon-separated list of directories where shells look for executable files
PS1	Defines the normal prompt
SHELL	The current shell
_	Contains the last command executed in this session

You can display the contents of an environment variable via the echo command. Prefix the name of the variable you want to display with $.

```
$ echo $PS1
\u@\h:\w\$
```

The preceding is a string of special escape codes that display the username \u, hostname \h , current working directory \w, and the final character \$ in the prompt. \$ displays a pound (#) symbol if the prompt is displayed as the root user and a dollar sign ($) otherwise. For a full listing of available escape codes, see the PROMPTING section of the bash man page.

You can change environment variables either by defining them in any of the Bash configuration files or by setting them from the command line. If we wanted to change our prompt to include a timestamp and have it break to give us more space to type commands, we could add the \T and \n codes:

```
$ PS1="[\T] \u@\h:\w\n\$ "
[12:50:59] jsmith@au-mel-ubuntu-1:~
$
```

■ **Tip**   You may have noticed that we sometimes use $ and sometimes not. The simple rule here is that if we are referring to the variable and prefixing it with $, then we're interested in the value of the variable (i.e., the contents of the variable). Without $, we're talking about the variable itself.

Another useful example is adding directories to your path. You can quickly prefix or suffix directories to your path. You can add a single directory to the start of the path as follows:

```
$ PATH=/home/ataylor/scripts:$PATH
```

Here we've added the directory /home/ataylor/scripts to the front of the path and then included the existing path by separating it with a colon and specifying the $PATH value. This allows you to put binaries, scripts, or other applications in the path, which is searched every time you run a command or an application. In this case, when executing commands, Linux will look for the command first in the /home/ataylor/scripts directory before anywhere else on the host.

You can add a directory to the end of the path using the same basic construct:

```
$ PATH=$PATH:/home/ataylor/scripts
```

Then when you run a command, Linux will search all the directories in your path, and if a matching command or application isn't found, it will search your suffixed directory.

Any string of the type KEY=value is assumed to be an environment variable assignment by Bash. Making the variables uppercase is a matter of convention.

Of course, setting environment variables on the command line changes them only for the duration of your session. If you log off, they will revert back to the previous configuration. To make changes like this permanent, place them in the .bash_profile file located in your home directory, for example,

```
PATH=$PATH:/home/ataylor/scripts
export PATH
```

Here we've specified our new path and then used a special command, export, to propagate the change. Normally, changes to environment variables change only the current session or script in which they are being made. In order to use them in other sessions or scripts, you need to export them. To make a path or other environmental change for all users, add the changes to the /etc/profile file or generally you would add those to a file in the /etc/profile.d/ directory. This file is used by all users (except the root user; use the .bash_profile file in the /root directory to modify the root user's variables) to set values.

■ **Tip** You can find more information on configuring your Bash prompt at http://tldp.org/HOWTO/Bash-Prompt-HOWTO/.

Command Aliases

The second reason for configuring your shell is to create command aliases. Aliases allow you to create shortcuts or set default options for often-used commands. A prime example is an alias for the ls command we looked at in Chapter 4.

When listing files with ls, we saw in Chapter 4 that we get a simple listing of our files in a directory. By using an alias, you can have the shell execute ls -lah each time you type ll, so that you always have a full long human reading listing of your directory. You create an alias via the alias command.

```
$ alias ll='ls -lah'
$ ll
total 40K
drwx------. 4 vagrant vagrant 4.0K Mar  9 06:07 .
drwxr-xr-x. 4 root    root    4.0K Mar  3 05:37 ..
-rw-------. 1 vagrant vagrant 2.2K Mar  9 06:08 .bash_history
-rw-r--r--. 1 vagrant vagrant   18 Nov 20 00:02 .bash_logout
-rw-r--r--. 1 vagrant vagrant  225 Mar  9 06:04 .bash_profile
```

You can make an alias permanent by adding it to the .bash_profile configuration file in your home directory.

To get a listing of all aliases defined in your shell, run the alias command without any parameters.

```
$ alias
alias egrep='egrep --color=auto'
alias fgrep='fgrep --color=auto'
alias grep='grep --color=auto'
alias l.='ls -d .* --color=auto'
alias ll='ls -lah'
alias ls='ls --color=auto'
```

Here you can see our defined listing alias, other listing aliases, and several aliases that we have available to us from the /etc/profile.d/colorgrep.csh file.

You should not define an alias with the same name as an existing command, unless you're setting default options. You will still be able to run the original command by specifying the full path to the executable, but it might create nasty surprises when you don't expect them (e.g., in automated scripts).

To delete an alias, use the unalias command. To remove our interactive delete we would use this:

```
$ unalias ll
```

To read more about aliases, see the ALIASES section of the bash man page.

The Bash shell is extremely powerful and flexible, and it can make everyday administration tasks very easy. If you want to know more about Bash and what you can use it for, see www.tldp.org/LDP/Bash-Beginners-Guide/html/ and http://tldp.org/HOWTO/Bash-Prog-Intro-HOWTO.html.

Controlling Access to Your Host

You can control quite a lot of user characteristics, including when and how users can log in, what their passwords look like, and how often they have to change and reset their passwords. These controls are all checked when users log in to the host and are generally managed by a series of modules. These modules are collectively known as Pluggable Authentication Modules (PAM). Almost all Linux distributions, including CentOS and Ubuntu, rely on PAM to control how and when users can interact with hosts.

In this section, we'll introduce you to PAM and how it works. You won't generally have to change much PAM configuration, but it is important to understand how it works.

■ **Note**   We'll talk a bit more about how PAM is used with other authentication mechanisms (e.g., integration with Active Directory and LDAP) in Chapter 16.

PAM was originally designed by Sun Microsystems to provide a plug-in authentication framework. It has been heavily used and developed in the Linux world, and a large number of PAM modules exist to perform a variety of functions ranging from checking passwords to creating home directories. PAM modules were originally used to provide authentication and other services to applications that lacked authentication or a particular authentication capability. Later, as more sophisticated types of authentication became available, such as smart cards and one-time passwords (or tokens), PAM became a way to integrate and extend authentication mechanisms. Rather than having to rewrite each application for new authentication methods, all that is required is to add PAM support. PAM then takes care of the hard work of authenticating through a standard API.

Configuring PAM

Essentially PAM is a hierarchy of authentication and authorization checks that are performed when an application wants to perform some action. These checks are stacked together; for example, when logging in we check the user exists, then check that the user's password is valid, and then that the password hasn't expired. This stack is usually made up of multiple PAM modules, each of which performs some check function. Additionally, some checks must pass (e.g., your user must exist), and other checks may be optional. The best way to understand PAM is to examine some PAM configuration files.

On most Linux distributions, you have two possible locations to look for PAM configuration information. The legacy file /etc/pam.conf is used to hold PAM configuration information on Linux distributions, but now it is generally deprecated and has been replaced by the /etc/pam.d directory. Most modern versions of CentOS and Ubuntu use this directory to hold a collection of configuration files for PAM-aware services. The service shares the same name as the application it is designed to authenticate; for example, the PAM configuration for the passwd command is contained in a file called /etc/pam.d/passwd. These files are called *service configuration files*.

There are a variety of service configuration files—for example, when users log in to a host, we use an application called, appropriately, login. The login application is triggered when a user logs in, and inside the pam.d directory you'll find a file named login that contains the authentication configuration for the application. Similarly, you'll find a file called sshd that performs similar work for users who log in via an SSH connection.

Other common services that come with default PAM configurations and that you'll find in the /etc/pam.d directory are the passwd command and the cron scheduling daemon. Inside each of these files, you'll find the authentication configuration that these applications use.

■ **Note**   We'll discuss crontab and how to schedule jobs and actions in Chapter 6.

We're not going to look at each specific file, though, because most of these services rely on some common configuration for authentication. CentOS and Ubuntu both have separate files that define the common authentication configuration. Many of the service files reference and include this common configuration. On CentOS, this file is /etc/pam.d/system-auth, which is automatically generated when you install your host and is updated with a special command called authconfig. On Ubuntu, the same role is performed by four separate files: common-auth, common-password, common-session, and common-account. Let's look at the contents of the CentOS system-auth file in Listing 5-14.

Listing 5-14. The login PAM File

```
#%PAM-1.0
# This file is auto-generated.
# User changes will be destroyed the next time authconfig is run.
auth        required      pam_env.so
auth        sufficient    pam_unix.so nullok try_first_pass
auth        requisite     pam_succeed_if.so uid >= 1000 quiet_success
auth        required      pam_deny.so

account     required      pam_unix.so
account     sufficient    pam_localuser.so
account     sufficient    pam_succeed_if.so uid < 1000 quiet
account     required      pam_permit.so

password    requisite     pam_pwquality.so try_first_pass ↵
local_users_only retry=3 authtok_type=
password    sufficient    pam_unix.so md5 shadow nullok ↵
try_first_pass use_authtok
password    required      pam_deny.so

session     optional      pam_keyinit.so revoke
session     required      pam_limits.so
-session    optional       pam_systemd.so
session     [success=1 default=ignore] pam_succeed_if.so service ↵
in crond quiet use_uid
session     required      pam_unix.so
```

The system-auth and the other service configuration files have four possible directives. Let's use a single line from Listing 5-14 to examine them in more detail.

```
auth           sufficient     pam_unix.so nullok try_first_pass
```

The first directive in our line is auth, which is the management group we're configuring. Four major management groups are available in PAM, and they represent the different portions of the authentication and authorization process that can be configured:

- auth: These modules perform user authentication, for example, checking a password.

- account: This management group handles account verification tasks, for example, confirming that the user account is unlocked or if only the root user can perform an action.

- password: These modules set passwords, for example, checking to ensure your password is sufficiently strong.

- session: These modules check, manage, and configure user sessions.

■ **Note** Remember we talked about setting strong complex passwords; the password management group is one of the places you can set password rules on complexity.

Usually one or more modules are assigned to each management group, and these modules are usually checked in the order they are specified, and each module will return either a success or failure result. A particular module might also be specified more than once in a PAM configuration. For example, in Listing 5-14 you can see that all four management groups specify the pam_unix.so module.

```
auth        sufficient      pam_unix.so nullok try_first_pass
account     required        pam_unix.so
password    sufficient      pam_unix.so m5 shadow nullok try_first_pass use_authtok
session     required        pam_unix.so
```

This indicates that the pam_unix.so module, which is the module that takes care of most standard Unix authentication functions such as entering a traditional password, can perform checks and functions for each management group. For example, it can confirm that the user's password is correct in the auth group and also confirm the user exists for the account group.

The next directive, sufficient, is called a *control flag*, and it tells PAM how to treat the result of the module. As mentioned earlier, some checks are more important than others. Control flags tell PAM what to do with the success or failure result and how that result impacts the overall authentication process. Table 5-7 lists the four PAM control flags.

Table 5-7. *PAM Control Flags*

Flag	Description
required	A required module must succeed for authentication to succeed.
requisite	If a requisite module fails, then authentication will immediately fail.
sufficient	Authentication immediately succeeds if the module is successful.
optional	The success or failure of the module doesn't impact authentication.

The required flag means the module result must be a success in order for the authentication process to succeed. If the result of this module is a failure, then the overall authentication is also a failure. If more than one module is stacked together, the other modules in the stack will also be processed, but the overall authentication will still fail.

The requisite flag also indicates that the module result must be successful for authentication to be successful. Additionally, unlike the required flag, the success or failure of this module will be immediately notified to the service requesting authentication, and the authentication process will complete. This means that if any modules are stacked together and a module with a requisite control flag fails, then the modules remaining to be processed will not be executed. In comparison, with the required control flag, the remaining modules in the stack continue to be processed.

The next control flag is sufficient. The sufficient flag means that the success of this module is sufficient for the authentication process to be successful or, if modules are stacked, for the stack to succeed. This is dependent on no other required modules processed prior to this module failing. If a sufficient module fails, however, then the overall stack does not fail.

The last control flag is optional. An optional module is not critical to the overall success or failure of the authentication process or the module stack. Its success or failure will not determine the success or failure of the overall authentication process.

The next directive, pam_unix.so, indicates what PAM module will be used and its location. If you specify a PAM module without a path, then the module is assumed to be located in the /lib/security directory. You can also specify a module from another location here by providing the path to it, as you can see in the following line:

```
auth required /usr/local/pamlib/pam_local.so id=-1 root=1
```

The last directives are arguments to be passed to the PAM module—in this case, we are passing the arguments try_first_pass and nullok to the pam_unix.so module. The try_first_pass argument tells the module to see if a password has already been received by the module, and if so, to use that password to authenticate. The nullok argument tells the module that it is OK to have a blank password. Most modules will ignore invalid or incorrect arguments passed to them, and the module will continue to be processed, though some modules do generate an error message or fail.

■ **Tip** You can find man pages for most PAM modules (e.g., man pam_unix will return the pam_unix man page). You can also find documentation at www.linux-pam.org/Linux-PAM-html/Linux-PAM_SAG.html/.

There is a last PAM function we need to mention: include. The include function allows you to include one PAM file in another. This is how our common configuration is included in specific service configuration files. To see this function, let's look at a snippet from the Ubuntu login PAM service configuration file in Listing 5-15.

Listing 5-15. The Ubuntu login PAM Service Configuration File

```
@include common-auth
@include common-account
@include common-session
@include common-password
```

There is a lot more configuration in that file, but we can see that using the format @include, you can include other files in a PAM service configuration file. So @include common-account will include the content of the file common-account in the login file. Each module specified in that file will now be processed when the login file is used. The file is pulled in and parsed at the point at which it is included, and any modules in that included file are executed in order.

You can also use the `include` option as a control flag as follows:

```
auth    include system-auth
```

This will include all `auth` type lines from the file `system-auth`.

More about sudo

As discussed earlier in this chapter, the `sudo` command allows you to run some commands yourself with the privilege of another user, in most cases the `root` user. The command works much like the `RunAs` command in Microsoft Windows that allows a user to run a command as another user.

■ **Note**   Another command called `su`, also known as *substitute user* or *switch user*, allows you to open a subshell as a specific user. It is commonly used to change to the `root` user to perform some action. You can read about it through its `man` page. Note that `su` will not work if the `root` account is locked, as it is on Ubuntu. You can unlock the account by setting a password for the `root` user, but usually you will just use `sudo su` to temporarily open the root subshell. With `sudo su <user>` you don't need to know the password of the user you are trying to access as you are using privileges via `sudo`.

To use this command, you type `sudo` and then the command you want to execute. If you're allowed to run `sudo` on that command, you'll be prompted to input a password, usually your own user password. Then the specified command will be executed as the `root` user, unless you specify a different user with the `-u <username>` option to sudo.. This allows you to perform the actions the `root` user can, like creating users, without actually having to sign in as the `root` user. You can see `sudo` at work in Listing 5-16.

Listing 5-16. Using sudo

```
$ sudo userdel ataylor
We trust you have received the usual lecture from the local System Administrator.
It usually boils down to these three things:
    #1) Respect the privacy of others.
    #2) Think before you type.
    #3) With great power comes great responsibility.
Password:
```

This rather intimidating message generally appears the first time you use the `sudo` command; afterward, you'll get the password prompt only.

Once you have entered the password correctly, the `sudo` command does not prompt you for a password each time it is used. After you enter your password, the `sudo` command gives you a grace period during which you are not prompted for your password. This period is 5 minutes on CentOS and 15 minutes on Ubuntu. After this period, you will again be prompted for your password when you next run the `sudo` command.

On Ubuntu and CentOS, the `sudo` command is installed by default. Ubuntu, in fact, doesn't even set a password for the `root` user; rather, you are encouraged to always use `sudo` to run privileged commands. Any member of the admin group on Ubuntu has access to run the `sudo` command. On CentOS, we earlier configured it so that if you are a member of the `wheel` group and then you can run commands using the `sudo` command.

The sudo command is also highly configurable. You can specify exactly what commands, including grouping commands together as categories of commands, can be executed using the sudo command. You can configure the sudo command to allow users to execute all commands, some commands, or even to execute commands without prompting for their password (though this isn't recommended).

■ **Tip**   As you learned at the start of the chapter, you configure exactly what sudo can do by editing a file called /etc/sudoers using a special command called visudo. We strongly recommend that you only use visudo to edit this file, as bad configuration will make all sudo commands fail. We'll talk more about this in the section "Configuring sudo."

So, what happens if you're not allowed to execute the sudo command? In Listing 5-17 we try to use the sudo command as the user ataylor, who doesn't have the correct authority to use the sudo command.

Listing 5-17. Unauthorized sudo

```
$ sudo useradd -m -c 'Illegal User' iuser
ataylor is not in the sudoers file. This incident will be reported.
```

A failed attempt to use the sudo command will be logged by your host's syslog (or system logger) service, and then the message is sent to a file in the /var/log/ directory. On CentOS, you can see sudo command failures in the /var/log/secure file, and on Ubuntu they appear in the /var/log/auth.log file. A log message like this will be generated showing the date, time, user who tried to execute the sudo command, and unauthorized command the user tried to execute.

```
Sep 1 20:27:43 au-mel-centos-1 sudo:         ataylor : user NOT in sudoers ; TTY=pts/1 ;
PWD=/home ; USER=root ; COMMAND=/usr/sbin/useradd -m -c 'Illegal User' iuser
```

These messages allow you to monitor for people attempting to perform inappropriate actions on your hosts, and they can be used to detect attempted security breaches.

■ **Note**   In Chapter 18, we'll talk more about logging and how you can monitor for messages like the ones detailed in this section and send alerts or take some kind of action.

Configuring sudo

The sudo command checks the /etc/sudoers file for authorization to run commands. Using visudo, you can configure the sudoers file to restrict access to particular users, to certain commands, and on particular hosts.

Let's look at the /etc/sudoers file. First, you will need to use the command visudo to edit the /etc/sudoers file. The visudo command is a special editor designed to be used with the sudo command, and it is the safest way to edit the sudoers file. The command locks the file against multiple simultaneous edits, provides basic sanity checks, and checks for any parse errors. If the /etc/sudoers file is currently being edited, you will receive a message to try again later.

We'll start by looking at how we might allow our user ataylor to run the userdel command. We have added the content of Listing 5-18 to the sudoers file.

Listing 5-18. Sample sudoers

```
ataylor ALL=/bin/userdel
```

We can break down this line into its component parts.

```
username host = command
```

Listing 5-18 shows the user `ataylor` is allowed, on all hosts (using the variable ALL), to use the command /bin/userdel as if she were the root user. Any command you specify in the command option must be defined with its full path. You can also specify more than one command, each separated by commas, to be authorized for use, as you can see on the following line:

```
ataylor ALL=/bin/userdel,/bin/useradd
```

In the previous line, `ataylor` is now authorized to use the `userdel` and `useradd` commands as if she were the `root` user. All configuration lines in the `sudoers` file must be on one line only, and you can use \ to indicate the configuration continues on the next line.

A single `sudoers` file is designed to configure multiple hosts. Thus, it allows host-specific access controls. You would maintain your `sudoers` file on a central host and distribute the updated file to all your hosts.

■ **Note**   In Chapter 19 we talk about configuration management and how you could distribute this file to multiple hosts.

With host access controls, you can define different authorizations for different hosts, as shown in Listing 5-19.

Listing 5-19. Using sudo Authorization on Multiple Hosts

```
ataylor au-mel-centos-1=/bin/userdel,/bin/useradd
ataylor au-syd-ubuntu-1=ALL
```

In Listing 5-19, the user `ataylor` is allowed to use only the `userdel` and `useradd` commands on the host au-mel-centos-1, but on the host au-syd-ubuntu-1, she is allowed to use all commands as represented by the ALL option.

■ **Caution**   You should be careful when using the ALL variable to define access to all commands on a host. The ALL variable allows no granularity of authorization configuration.

You can be somewhat more selective with your authorization by granting access to the commands in a particular directory:

```
ataylor au-mel-centos-1=/bin/*
```

This applies only to the directory defined and not to any of its subdirectories. For example, if you authorize access to the /bin/* directory, then you will not be able to run any commands in the /bin/extra/ directory unless you explicitly define access to that directory, like the configuration on the next line:

```
ataylor au-mel-centos-1=/bin/*,/bin/extra/*
```

Sometimes you want to grant access to a particular command to a user, but you want that command to be run as another user. For example, say you need to start and stop some daemons as specific users, such as the MySQL or named daemon. You can specify the user you want the command to be started as by placing the username in parentheses in front of the command, as follows:

```
ataylor au-mel-centos-1=(mysql) /usr/bin/mysqld,(named) /usr/sbin/named
```

As you can imagine, lists of authorized commands, users, and hosts can become quite long. The sudo command also comes with the option of defining aliases. Aliases are collections of like users, commands, and hosts. Generally you define aliases at the start of the sudoers file. Let's look at some aliases. The first type of alias is User_Alias, which groups like users.

```
User_Alias ADMIN = ataylor,jsmith
```

You start an alias with the name of the alias type you are using, in this case User_Alias, followed by the name of the particular alias you are defining, here ADMIN. Next you specify a list of the users who belong to this alias. You can then refer to this alias in a configuration line.

```
ADMIN=/bin/userdel,/bin/useradd, \
(named) /usr/sbin/named
```

In the previous line we have specified that the users in the alias ADMIN are able to use the commands userdel, useradd, and named.

The next type of alias you can define is a command alias, Cmnd_Alias, which groups collections of commands.

```
Cmnd_Alias USER_COMMANDS = /bin/userdel,/bin/useradd
```

You can use this alias in conjunction with the user alias just created.

```
ADMIN ALL=/bin/groupadd,USER_COMMANDS
```

Now all users defined in the alias ADMIN can use the command /bin/groupadd and all those commands defined in the command alias USER_COMMANDS on ALL hosts.

You can also specify an alias that groups a collection of hosts. The Host_Alias alias can specify lists of hostnames, IP addresses, and networks.

```
Host_Alias SERVERS = au-mel-centos-1, au-mel-centos-2, au-syd-centos-1
```

You can combine this alias with the preceding ones you defined.

```
ADMIN SERVERS=USER_COMMANDS
```

Now all users specified in the ADMIN alias can run the commands specified in USER_COMMANDS on the hosts defined in the SERVERS alias group.

177

You can also negate aliases by placing an exclamation point (!) in front of them. Let's look at an example of this. First, you define a command alias with some commands you do not want users to use, and then you can use that alias in conjunction with a sudo configuration line.

```
Cmnd_Alias DENIED_COMMANDS = /bin/su,/bin/mount,/bin/umount
ataylor au-mel-centos-1=/bin/*,!DENIED_COMMANDS
```

Here the user ataylor can use all the commands in the /bin directory on the au-mel-centos-1 host except those defined in the DENIED_COMMANDS command alias.

Let's look at one of the other ways you can authorize users to use sudo. Inside the sudoers file, you can define another type of alias based on the group information in your host by prefixing the group name with %.

```
%groupname ALL=(ALL) ALL
```

You would then replace groupname with the name of a group defined on your host. This means all members of the defined group are able to execute whatever commands you authorize for them, in this case ALL commands on ALL hosts.

On CentOS hosts, a group called wheel already exists for this purpose, and if you uncomment the following line in the /etc/sudoers file on your CentOS host, then any users added to the wheel group will be able to use the sudo command to gain root privileges on your host. On Ubuntu this group is called admin rather than wheel.

```
%wheel ALL=(ALL) ALL
```

Additionally, the sudoers file itself has a number of options and defaults you can define to change the behavior of the sudo command. For example, you can configure sudo to send e-mail when the sudo command is used. To define who to send that e-mail to, you can use the option on the following line:

```
mailto "admin@au-mel-centos-1.yourdomain.com"
```

You can then modify when sudo sends that e-mail using further options.

```
mail_always on
```

To give you an idea of the sorts of defaults and options available to you, Table 5-8 defines a list of the e-mail–related options.

Table 5-8. *Sending E-mail When* sudo *Runs*

Option	Description
mail_always	Sends e-mail every time a user runs sudo. This flag is set to off by default.
mail_badpass	Sends e-mail if the user running sudo does not enter the correct password. This flag is set to off by default.
mail_no_user	Sends e-mail if the user running sudo does not exist in the sudoers file. This flag is set to on by default.
mail_no_host	Sends e-mail if the user running sudo exists in the sudoers file but is not authorized to run commands on this host. This flag is set to off by default.
mail_no_perms	Sends e-mail if the user running sudo exists in the sudoers file but does not have authority to the command he tried to run. This flag is set to off by default.

The sudoers man page details a number of other options and defaults.

The sudo command itself also has some command-line options you can issue with it. Table 5-9 shows some of the most useful options.

Table 5-9. sudo *Command-Line Options*

Option	Description
-l	Prints a list of the allowed (and forbidden) commands for the current user on the current host
-L	Lists any default options set in the sudoers file
-b	Runs the given command in the background
-u user	Runs the specified command as a user other than root

The -l option is particularly useful to allow you to determine what commands the current user on the current host is authorized and forbidden to run.

```
$ sudo -l
Password:
User ataylor may run the following commands on this host:
    (root) ALL
```

For readability, it is also a good idea to break up your rules into logically grouped files and place them in the /etc/sudoers.d directory. You would issue the following:

```
$ sudo visudo -f /etc/sudoers.d/01_operators
```

In the above file we would place things that are particular to the operators group. Sudo will look through the /etc/sudoers.d/ directory and load any files it finds, in order, if present, as above.

The sudo command is complicated and, if improperly implemented, can open your host to security breaches. We recommend you carefully test any sudo configuration before you implement it and thoroughly explore the contents of the sudo and sudoers man pages.

AUDITING USER ACCESS

Keeping track of what your users are doing is an important part of user management. In Chapter 18 we will talk about logging, and indeed one of the first resources you will use to keep track of the actions of your users is the content of your log files. But other commands and sources are also useful for keeping track of users and their activities.

The who command displays all users logged on to the host currently, together with the terminal they are logged on to. If users have connected remotely, the command shows the IP address or hostname from which they have connected.

```
$ sudo who
root       tty1        Jul  3 12:32
ataylor    pts/0        Jul  8 11:39 (host002.yourdomain.com)
```

You can modify the output of the who command, and you can see a full list of the options in the who man page. Probably the most useful command-line option is –a, which combines a variety of the command-line options to provide a detailed overview of who is logged in to your host, the login processes, and the host reboot and run-level details.

Also useful are the last and lastb commands, which display a record of when users last logged in to the host and a record of bad user logins, respectively. If you execute the last command without any options, it will print a report of the last logins to the host.

```
$ sudo last
root        tty1                             Sat  Jul  3 12:32    still logged in
ataylor     pts/0        192.168.0.23        Sat  Jul  3 14:25 - 14:26  (00:01)
reboot      system boot  2.4.20-28.8         Sat  Jul  3 12:31         (4+05:40)
```

As you can see, the last command tells you that root is logged on and is still logged in. The list also shows the user ataylor, who logged in from the IP address 192.168.0.23 and stayed logged on for one second. The last entry shows a reboot entry. Every time the host is rebooted, an entry is logged that gives the time of the reboot and the version of the kernel into which the host was booted.

The lastb command produces the same style of report but lists only those logins that were "bad." In other words, it lists those logins in which an incorrect password was entered, or some other error resulted in a failure to log in.

Related to the last and lastb commands is the lastlog command. The lastlog command displays a report that shows the login status of all users on your host, including those users who have never logged in. The command displays a list of all users and their last login date and time, or it displays a message indicating **Never Logged In** if that user has never logged in. Using command-line options, you can search records for specific users. Read the lastlog command's man page for further details.

Summary

In this chapter, you learned how to create users and groups from the command line or via the GUI interface. You also learned what happens when you sign on to your host, as well as about PAM and how to control access to your host.

This chapter also detailed the sudo command and how to use it to avoid the use of the root user to administrate your host. Additionally, we examined how to configure sudo to control who can access particular commands and how to report on sudo use. Finally, we covered a bit about how to monitor your users' logins.

In the next chapter, we'll look at what happens when your host boots up and how to start, stop, and manage services.

CHAPTER 6

Startup and Services

By Dennis Matotek

In the last few chapters, you've learned how to install a Linux host, explored some basic Linux concepts, and been introduced to the concept of users and groups. This chapter is going to delve deeper into the workings of your Linux host and examine the way it operates "under the hood."

In this chapter, we'll look at what happens when your host starts up, or *boots*. We'll step through the process and show you how to start your host in a variety of modes and how to configure and modify the startup process. To demonstrate all of this, we'll take you through the process of how your host boots from when you power it on to the login prompt.

We'll also take you beyond the boot process and look at how your host starts and stops applications, system services, and other processes. Each distribution, CentOS and Ubuntu, manages the addition, removal, starting, and stopping of these services slightly differently. We'll show you how to manage these services on each of these distributions and the nuances involved. You'll learn what services are, how to start and stop services, and how to see their status. Finally, we'll talk about how to make services start and stop automatically when your host boots or shuts down.

What Happens When Your Host Starts?

The boot process (*boot* is short for *bootstrap*) usually involves three separate but connected processes: the BIOS (Basic Input/Output System) or UEFI Unified Extensible Firmware Interface), the boot loader, and the loading of the operating system.

1. The BIOS or UEFI initiates and checks your hardware.

2. The boot loader lets you select an operating system to load.

3. Finally, your operating system is loaded and initiated.

These steps are not specific to Linux; you'll find most operating systems perform a similar set of functions and steps.

You will find modern hardware will support UEFI. It is a replacement for BIOS and older systems will use BIOS. They both perform a similar task and we will explain each of them to you, starting with BIOS.

Powering On

Let's look in a bit more detail at what happens when you boot your host. You may have noticed that when you turn on your host, it is common to hear a few beeps and whirrs and see some blinking lights on your front panel and keyboard. This is the first step of your host starting up, and this process, on a host running BIOS, is controlled by a small chip on the motherboard called the BIOS.

The BIOS

The BIOS performs rudimentary system checks or power-on self-test (POST) operations on the availability of different bits of hardware attached to your system, like the memory, hard drives, keyboard, and video card. Depending on your BIOS, you can change different settings, but we will leave that to you to investigate at your leisure.

The BIOS will also poll other hardware such as hard drive controllers and initiate their onboard chips. Depending on your hardware, you may see the BIOS screen followed by information about devices the controller has found. You may be given an option to configure controllers or other hardware by pressing a certain key sequence (usually displayed on the screen when the hardware is initiated). This menu gives you the ability to manipulate the configuration of your host; for example, it allows you to set up RAID (Redundant Array of Inexpensive Disks) on a hard disk controller or troubleshoot problems with existing hardware configuration.

■ **Caution** Changing some configurations can be dangerous; for example, incorrectly changing a RAID configuration could destroy your data, so use these menus with caution.

The BIOS also allows you to change the boot source for your host. The boot source is the media (e.g., a hard drive) where your host looks for your operating system. The boot sequence setting allows you to boot from one of a number of sources: hard drives, CD/DVDs, or even USB keys. By default, your host will usually try to boot from an attached hard drive and, if configured, look for alternatives such as a CD/DVD drive or a USB key.

Every motherboard manufacturer has a different way of getting to the boot source menu, for example, by pressing Esc, Del, or a function key such as F1, F2, or F10. Usually a message appears on your screen indicating the appropriate key to press. From here a menu is usually displayed, and you can select the boot sequence you would like.

The Unified Extensible Firmware Interface

More recent motherboards will support UEFI. When you boot your host with UEFI you will notice very little difference compared to BIOS; the lights will flash and things will whirr. It is expected to be a little faster than BIOS. However, behind the scenes things are quite different.

UEFI was created to overcome some of the very real limitations of BIOS. BIOS runs on a 16-bit processor; UEFI can run on modern processors. BIOS was limited in RAM; UEFI can run in as much RAM as required. BIOS reads from a small section of a hard drive (the master boot record, or MBR) to load the operating system. UEFI instead reads from a special FAT32 partition created at installation time and is not limited to 512 bytes. Also UEFI requires that the partition table on the disk is GPT (GUID Partition Table), and this means that we can boot off disks over 2TiB in size. It is said that UEFI is more like a modern operating system than the old BIOS; it can even run nicer graphical interfaces with mouse and keyboard support.

One of the ways that malware can be loaded on a system is via the boot loader. UEFI offers "secure boot" that is designed to protect against this by verifying signed boot loaders and hardware via public/private keys before loading them. Most modern 64-bit distros should support secure boot, but this is still relatively new and you may have problems with some hardware under secure boot. In this case you can file a bug report with the distribution and disable secure boot via the UEFI configuration screen.

Finally, it is currently not mandatory that you use UEFI. BIOS is still available in most motherboards as "legacy" and has been widely tested and supported. It is, however, mandatory under the following circumstances; you are running dual boot with a system already running UEFI and you want to access disks larger than 2TiB. The purpose of both BIOS and UEFI is to get your hardware ready and find the boot loader to load your operating system.

MORE ON DISKS

In previous chapters we have talked about partitioning disks and said that a disk is like a cake, in that you can carve up slices, but how does that work? When you slice up your disk you create table on the disk called the partition table. The partition table is normally found at the beginning of the disk and tells the computer how the disk has been laid out. That is, how much of the disk has been allocated to the '/boot' partition, how much is expected to be logical volume management (LVM), and so on.

Above we have talked about MBR and GPT and these are two types of partition tables. A partition table holds information about the block addresses (in chunks of 512 bytes or 4KB of disk). The MBR can only hold 2TiBs worth of addresses while GPT can hold 8-9ZiB.

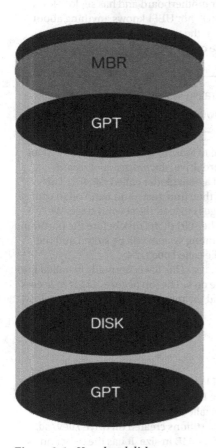

Figure 6-1. *Your hard disk*

A disk will either have a MBR at the start (in the first 512 bytes) or GPT. If it has a MBR the partition table is written after the first 446 bytes of the disk. The size of the partition table is 64 bytes and is followed by the MBR boot signature (2bytes). The remaining space up until the first partition is often called the MBR gap and varies in size as most partitioners align the start of partitions to the first 1MB.

GPT on the other hand has an address space of 16,384 bytes and can hold up to 128 partitions. GPT makes a copy of itself at the end of the disk for recovery in case of corruption. The remaining disk, excluding the partition tables, can be divided as you see fit. See the following for more detail:

- https://en.wikipedia.org/wiki/Master_boot_record

- https://en.wikipedia.org/wiki/GUID_Partition_Table

Boot Loaders

The Boot Loader with BIOS

Once your host has loaded all the checked everything attached to your motherboard and has set low-level system settings it is ready to boot up your operating system. Neither BIOS nor UEFI knows anything about the operating system you are trying to boot, but it does know how to run the code supplied by your distro. This code is called the Boot Loader and it needs to be in the right place on the disk you are booting from.

■ **Note**   It is not strictly true that UEFI "knows nothing about your operating system." It actually does know a fair bit, but the main point is that it is not your operating system but a lower-level interface with the hardware.

A host running BIOS uses the boot source setting to specify where to look for the next stage of the boot process: the boot loader. The BIOS uses the special section on your hard drive, the *master boot record*.

When we installed our operating system our installation installed a boot loader called GRUB2. This stands for GRand Unified Bootloader (2) and its job is to launch itself, then find, load, and hand off to your operating system. It does this in two *stages,* the purpose of the first stage is to load the second stage. We talked previously about the MBR and said that there was 446 bytes at the start of the disk before the partition table. This is where the first stage of the boot loader code for your operating system will be stored and the BIOS will attempt to execute the code it finds there. For Linux, this a file called boot.img.

When BIOS executes boot.img it finds and runs a file called core.img. This file is normally installed into the *MBR gap*, the space between the MBR and the first partition on the disk. The job of core.img is to access /boot/grub and load the modules it finds there. The core.img will load the menu and has the ability to load the target operating system.

The Boot Loader with UEFI

If you use an UEFI system the boot process is a little different. The UEFI can read the GPT partition table and can find and execute the boot loader code in the /EFI/ directory in the EFI system partition. Unlike BIOS, UEFI has its own partition that the boot loader and modules can be installed into.

In Figure 6-2 we can see that after our installation we have three partitions created on drive /dev/sda. The first one is our EFI System Partition and it is a FAT32 file system of 537MB in size. It has the boot and esp flags (both meaning it is a boot partition). The other thing to note is that the partition table is GPT.

```
(parted) print
Model: ATA VBOX HARDDISK (scsi)
Disk /dev/sda: 8590MB
Sector size (logical/physical): 512B/512B
Partition Table: gpt
Disk Flags:

Number  Start    End      Size     File system  Name                    Flags
 1      1049kB   538MB    537MB    fat32        EFI System Partition    boot, esp
 2      538MB    1050MB   512MB    ext2
 3      1050MB   8589MB   7539MB

(parted)
```

Figure 6-2. EFI partition on Ubuntu

So when UEFI is ready to run the boot loader it reads this partition looking for a boot loader. In this case on our Ubuntu host will find /EFI/ubuntu/grubx64.efi. This initial part of the boot loader will find the '/boot' partition that contains the GRUB2 software and load core.efi from and bring up the GRUB2 menu.

For more information on UEFI and the UEFI Shell (an interactive shell that you can use to manage your UEFI) see the following:

- https://help.ubuntu.com/community/UEFI

- https://fedoraproject.org/wiki/Unified_Extensible_Firmware_Interface

- https://www.happyassassin.net/2014/01/25/uefi-boot-how-does-that-actually-work-then/

- https://software.intel.com/en-us/articles/uefi-shell

Without any intervention GRUB2 will boot the default kernel after a brief countdown. Pressing any key will stop the countdown, show you a more detailed menu of available options, and give you the opportunity to edit your boot configuration. Later in the section "Using the GRUB2 Menu," we will explain these choices and how to manipulate them.

After picking the kernel you wish to boot into (or waiting until the default is loaded after the timeout), GRUB2 will now find the kernel binary (vmlinuz-<release-number>) and then load a special file called initrd.img into memory. This file contains the drivers your kernel needs to load to make use of the hardware of your host.

Starting the Operating System

After loading initrd.img, GRUB2 completes and hands over control to the kernel, which continues the boot process by initiating your hardware, including your hard disks. Your operating system is started, and a special program called systemd, upstart or init is called that starts your services and brings your host to life. We'll take a look at all three of these system initializers and how to manage services later in this chapter, but first, more on the boot loader.

Understanding the GRUB2 Boot Loader

So let's now delve into what the boot loader is and what it does. We'll also look a bit at how you can configure it. We're not going to cover every detail of the boot loader, because you'll rarely need to change it, and most changes to it occur automatically, for example, when you install a new kernel package. But you should understand what it does and where it fits into your host's boot process.

Some history; in the Linux world, there were two main boot loaders that existed: LILO and GRUB. The GRUB boot loader became the default for Red Hat and Ubuntu several years ago. We will be concentrating on the latest version of GRUB, GRUB2, here. GRUB2 is a powerful multiboot loader. A *multiboot loader* can enable your host to boot into many different operating systems. Unlike Microsoft Windows or Mac OS X (and their boot loader tools—NTLDR and Boot Camp, respectively), GRUB2 allows you to boot multiple versions of Linux, Microsoft Windows, and Mac OS X on a single piece of hardware. This does not mean you can run them all simultaneously, like you can with virtual machine technology, but you can boot into them individually by selecting them from the GRUB2 menu at startup.

■ **Note** LILO is a legacy boot loader used as the default boot loader on many older versions of Linux distributions. It is rarely seen today and development ceased on it in 2015. For information on the LILO boot loader, please see `http://tldp.org/HOWTO/LILO.html`.

So how does GRUB2 work? GRUB2 at its heart uses four items to boot your system: a kernel file, the name of the drive, the partition number where the kernel file resides, and optionally an initial RAM disk.

GRUB2 is capable of booting in two ways. One is directly by finding and loading the desired kernel, and this is the way most Linux distributions are booted. GRUB2 also supports a method of booting, called *chain loading*; with this method GRUB2 loads another boot loader, such as the loader for Microsoft Windows, which then loads the desired operating system kernel. This allows GRUB2 to boot other operating systems using their own boot loaders.

Using the GRUB2 Menu

When your host boots, it will boot into the default kernel (or operating system) or you can override it and display the GRUB2 menu. Once the menu is displayed, you will be presented with a list of boot options, and you can use the up and down arrows on your keyboard to choose the kernel you wish to boot. You can also edit the GRUB menu and change parameters, commands, and arguments before proceeding to boot into your chosen kernel.

For example, we could choose to boot into what is called *single-user mode*, or *maintenance mode*. This special mode, used when something is broken on your host, restricts access to the host to the root user: usually at the system console. This mode, which functions much like the Microsoft Windows Recovery Console, allows you to work with resources like disks and files without worrying about conflicts or other users manipulating the host. Let's look at booting into single-user mode now.

First, again, this is slightly different between CentOS and Ubuntu. Both show a similar GRUB2 boot menu that allows you to select which kernel you would like to run with your arrow keys. CentOS presents the two menu entries that we talked about earlier, one being the kernel and the other described as a rescue kernel. On Ubuntu you will see a *sub-menu entry* called *Advanced Options*. You can use your arrow keys to navigate to see the recovery mode kernel.

We are going to use the normal kernel of an Ubuntu host in this exercise. Press the e key to edit the highlighted kernel. You will see the configuration of that kernel, such as its location and parameters, displayed as in Figure 6-3.

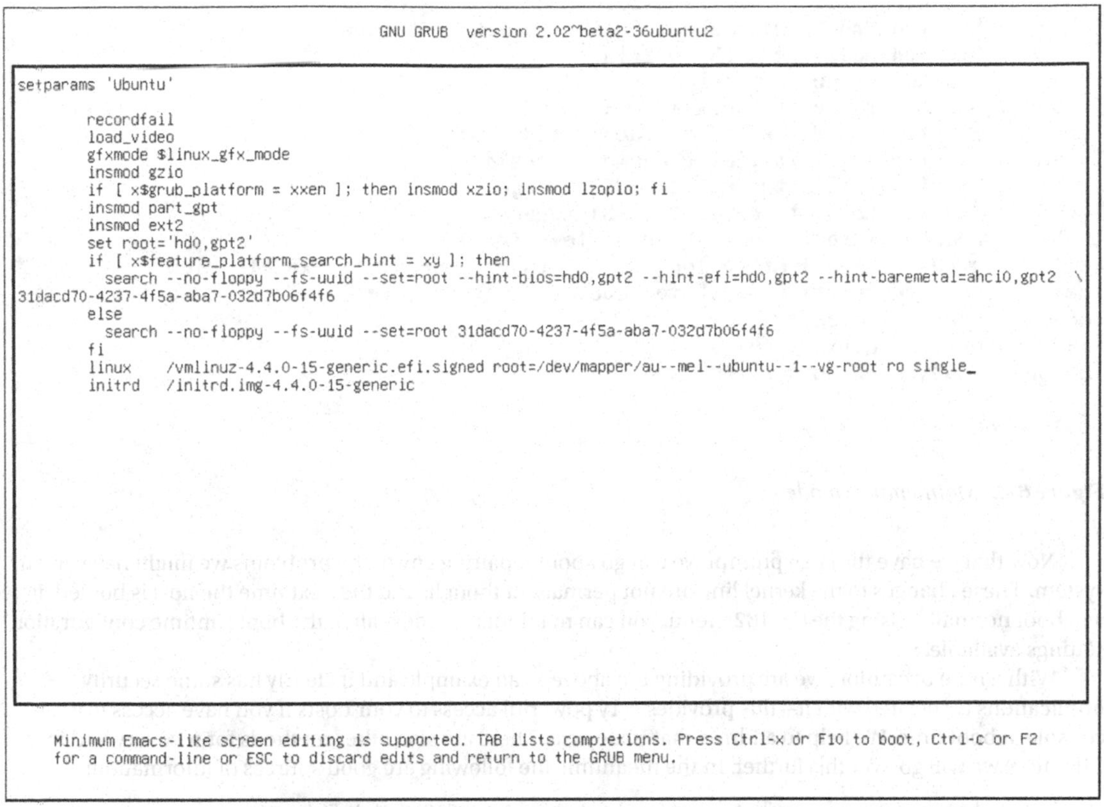

```
                          GNU GRUB   version 2.02~beta2-36ubuntu2

setparams 'Ubuntu'

        recordfail
        load_video
        gfxmode $linux_gfx_mode
        insmod gzio
        if [ x$grub_platform = xxen ]; then insmod xzio; insmod lzopio; fi
        insmod part_gpt
        insmod ext2
        set root='hd0,gpt2'
        if [ x$feature_platform_search_hint = xy ]; then
           search --no-floppy --fs-uuid --set=root --hint-bios=hd0,gpt2 --hint-efi=hd0,gpt2 --hint-baremetal=ahci0,gpt2  \
31dacd70-4237-4f5a-aba7-032d7b06f4f6
        else
           search --no-floppy --fs-uuid --set=root 31dacd70-4237-4f5a-aba7-032d7b06f4f6
        fi
        linux    /vmlinuz-4.4.0-15-generic.efi.signed root=/dev/mapper/au--mel--ubuntu--1--vg-root ro single_
        initrd   /initrd.img-4.4.0-15-generic




   Minimum Emacs-like screen editing is supported. TAB lists completions. Press Ctrl-x or F10 to boot, Ctrl-c or F2
   for a command-line or ESC to discard edits and return to the GRUB menu.
```

Figure 6-3. *Booting to single-user mode, or maintenance mode, using the GRUB2 menu*

You'll see the details here as you saw in the grub.cfg menuentry. The line we are interested in this particular example is the linux /vmlinuz-4.4.0-15-generic.efi.signed... line. Use the arrow keys to navigate to the end of that line. To boot into single-user mode, add the word 'single' (without quotes) to the end of this line. In Figure 6-3, you can see that we have already added the word single to the end of the line. At the bottom of Figure 6-3 you can see that we can now enter Ctrl-x or F10 to boot with this setting or Ctrl-c to get a command line or ESC to abandon these changes and go back to the main menu.

We can choose Ctrl-x and boot into single-user mode. We are first asked for the password to decrypt our hard drive. Then, depending on your distribution, you will either be given a maintenance password prompt that expects the root user (CentOS only) or you will be able to hit enter and be given a shell prompt (see Figure 6-4).

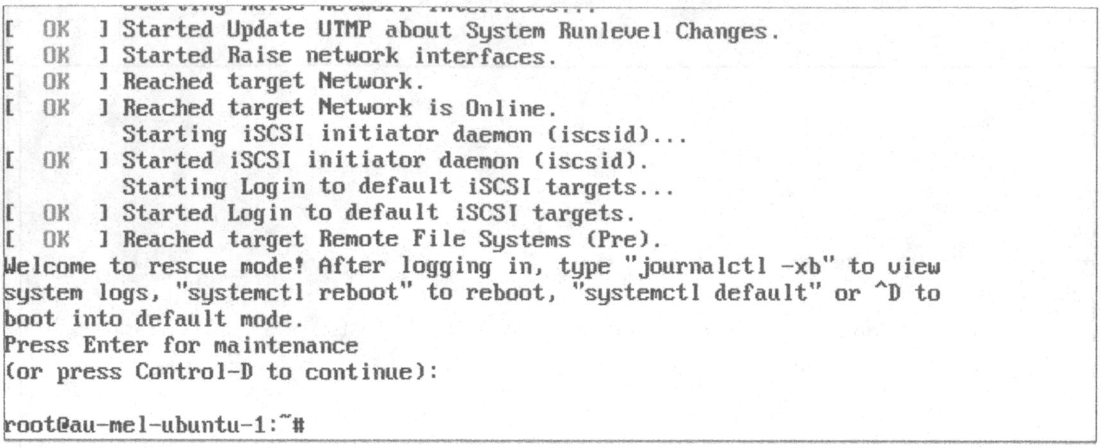

```
[  OK  ] Started Update UTMP about System Runlevel Changes.
[  OK  ] Started Raise network interfaces.
[  OK  ] Reached target Network.
[  OK  ] Reached target Network is Online.
         Starting iSCSI initiator daemon (iscsid)...
[  OK  ] Started iSCSI initiator daemon (iscsid).
         Starting Login to default iSCSI targets...
[  OK  ] Started Login to default iSCSI targets.
[  OK  ] Reached target Remote File Systems (Pre).
Welcome to rescue mode! After logging in, type "journalctl -xb" to view
system logs, "systemctl reboot" to reboot, "systemctl default" or ^D to
boot into default mode.
Press Enter for maintenance
(or press Control-D to continue):

root@au-mel-ubuntu-1:~#
```

Figure 6-4. Maintenance mode

Now that we have the shell prompt we can go about repairing any of the problems we might have on our system. These changes to the kernel line are not permanent though, and the next time the host is booted, it will boot normally. Using the GRUB2 menu, you can manipulate almost all of the boot runtime configuration settings available.

With a note of caution, we are providing the above as an example and it clearly has some security implications associated with it—this provides very powerful access to your hosts if you have access to a console at boot time. We help to address that issue next. There are also other methods for recovery and in Chapter 9 we will go over this further. In the meantime the following are good sources of information:

- https://access.redhat.com/documentation/en-US/Red_Hat_Enterprise_
  Linux/7/html/System_Administrators_Guide/sec-Terminal_Menu_Editing_
  During_Boot.html

- https://wiki.ubuntu.com/RecoveryMode

Configuring GRUB2

The GRUB2 boot loader is highly configurable, and its configuration is contained in the grub.conf configuration file. GRUB2 has made the grub.cfg more modular than its simpler predecessor. The chance that you will need to make many changes to the GRUB2 configuration is small but possible.

The GRUB2 files are located in different places on different distributions. On Red Hat-based hosts like CentOS, they can be found at /boot/grub2/grub.cfg (and the file is usually linked symbolically to /etc/grub.conf). On Ubuntu and Debian hosts, the files can be found at /boot/grub/grub.cfg.

The grub.cfg file in GRUB2 is made up of a series of configuration files. On both Ubuntu and CentOS hosts you will find the configuration files in the directory /etc/grub.d. In that directory you will see a number ordered list of files. In Listing 6-1 you can see the files found on the CentOS 7 host.

Listing 6-1. ls -la /etc/grub.d

```
total 72
-rwxr-xr-x. 1 root root  8702  Nov 25 02:49  00_header
-rwxr-xr-x. 1 root root   992  May  4 2015  00_tuned
-rwxr-xr-x. 1 root root   230  Nov 25 02:49  01_users
```

```
-rwxr-xr-x. 1 root root 10232 Nov 25 02:49  10_linux
-rwxr-xr-x. 1 root root 10275 Nov 25 02:49  20_linux_xen
-rwxr-xr-x. 1 root root  2559 Nov 25 02:49  20_ppc_terminfo
-rwxr-xr-x. 1 root root 11169 Nov 25 02:49  30_os-prober
-rwxr-xr-x. 1 root root   214  Nov 25 02:49  40_custom
-rwxr-xr-x. 1 root root   216  Nov 25 02:49  41_custom
-rw-r--r--. 1 root root   483  Nov 25 02:49  README
```

Listing 6-1 shows the files that make up a grub.cfg file. These files are read in via the grub2-mkconfig command from 00_header to 41_custom in this case. You will not need to know much about these files normally as you rarely need to touch them on a regular basis. The files you might be interested in are 01_users and 40_custom files. The 01_users file loads in the boot loader password if it set. The 40_custom file is where you may wish to add custom GRUB2 configurations.

■ **Tip**   In Linux configuration files, lines prefixed with the # symbol usually indicate comments, and these lines are skipped when processing your configuration files.

The GRUB2 configuration file is made via the grub2-mkconfig command. It takes one argument, the -o or --output option of where you would like the file to be created. You can create your own grub.cfg file now. It will probe your system and run through your configuration files and output a file that you can view. Of course, you don't have to override your current grub.cfg with this file, so we will change the output to be a file in our local directory.

Listing 6-2.   Creating a grub.cfg

```
$ sudo grub2-mkconfig --output mygrub.cfg
Generating grub configuration file ...
Found linux image: /boot/vmlinuz-3.10.0-327.el7.x86_64
Found initrd image: /boot/initramfs-3.10.0-327.el7.x86_64.img
Found linux image: /boot/vmlinuz-0-rescue-65e567f18fe84907a6f1d8519e921c97
Found initrd image: /boot/initramfs-0-rescue-65e567f18fe84907a6f1d8519e921c97.img
done
```

In Listing 6-2 you can see that we have used the sudo command to escalate our privileges to perform the grub2-mkconfig command. This command runs through the files in the /etc/grub.d directory and executes them in numbered order. The output of the command to the console shows that is has found two kernels (vmlinuz) with one being a "rescue" kernel. The grub2-mkconfig command has probed our system and found them via /etc/grub.d/30_os-prober script.

Taking a look at the mygrub.cfg file that has been produced (use $ less mygrub.cfg) you will see the output of all those files in /etc/grub.d. We are going to concentrate on the part that starts your operating system, and that starts with the following line:

```
### BEGIN /etc/grub.d/10_linux ###
```

Below that BEGIN line is the menuentry that configures our menu item.

Listing 6-3. menuentry in the grub.cfg

```
menuentry 'CentOS Linux (3.10.0-327.el7.x86_64) 7 (Core)' --class centos --class gnu-linux
--class gnu --class os --unrestricted $menuentry_id_option 'gnulinux-3.10.0-327.el7.x86_64-
advanced-f60589f6-4d39-4c5b-8ac6-b1252f28f323' {
  ....
}
```

That already seems like a lot to digest and we have reduced Listing 6-3 to just the first line. Beginning with menuentry, this tells grub that we have a new menu item for it to list. 'CentOS Linux (...) 7 (Core)' gives us the name as it will appear in the menu list. Other information is provided by the --class parameter are used to display certain themes (like splash screens and so on).

The --unrestricted option is used to allow any user to run that entry at boot time via the console menu. This can be changed with the --users option where you can list users that may be able to run that entry (note that anyone listed as a superuser will still have access). Of course, this means that any entry with --unrestricted removed will not boot automatically and will require intervention. The GRUB2 documentation says that this is not really the best form of security as it will require access to the console on reboots but might be considered in kiosk type of installations. We will talk more on this and superusers in the section "Securing Your Boot Loader."

In Listing 6-3 we have left out the code between the curly braces, {}. Let's go through that code now in Listing 6-4.

Listing 6-4. Grub Boot Menu Code

```
menuentry ... {
        load_video
        set gfxpayload=keep
        insmod gzio
        insmod part_msdos
        insmod xfs
        set root='hd0,msdos1'
        if [ x$feature_platform_search_hint = xy ]; then
          search --no-floppy --fs-uuid --set=root --hint-bios=hd0,msdos1 --hint-
          efi=hd0,msdos1 --hint-baremetal=ahci0,msdos1 --hint='hd0,msdos1'  85932bb0-c5fe-
          431f-b129-93c567e4f76f
        else
          search --no-floppy --fs-uuid --set=root 85932bb0-c5fe-431f-b129-93c567e4f76f
        fi
        linux16 /vmlinuz-3.10.0-327.el7.x86_64 root=/dev/mapper/centos-root ro
        crashkernel=auto rd.lvm.lv=centos/root rd.lvm.lv=centos/swap rhgb quiet
        initrd16 /initramfs-3.10.0-327.el7.x86_64.img
}
```

Inside the curly braces of the menuentry code the first few lines of code install various modules. For example, the first line, load_video calls a function within the grub.cfg script that inserts the various video modules for the splash screen. The modules on a CentOS 7 host can be found in /boot/grub/i386-pc/ and are loaded via the insmod command you see in the subsequent lines. The three insmod lines you see here are loading compression and file system modules.

The `set root='hd0,msdos1'` is how we set the root device for GRUB2. GRUB2 uses this setting to help find files that GRUB2 needs. What it means is the root device is on a hard drive (hd) and is the first hard drive (hd0). The `'msdos'` is the filesystem of the root device and the final '1' is the partition number on hd0. If you were booting off a USB drive you might expect it to look like `'usb0,msdos1'` instead.

■ **Note** Numbering in the Linux operating system generally starts counting from 0 and not 1. However, the first partition on a disk is partition 1, as far as GRUB2 is concerned. The first disk/device is numbered from 0.

Next in Listing 6-4 we see an *if...fi* conditional statement that has a search command inside it. The search command is different depending *if* '$feature_platform_search_hint' is set to y. What is happening here is that the search command is looking for a device by a UUID (universal unique identifier). This is used to again set the root device for GRUB2 so it can find the Linux kernel we are going to load.

In Listing 6-4 we are at last loading our Linux kernel. The first part of the line *linux16* says we are going to load the kernel using a 16-bit mode (16-bit mode is used to get around certain problems with video modes). The next part is the Linux kernel itself, `/vmlinuz-3.10.0-327.el7.x86_64`. You will find this file in the /boot directory. Next we pass in options to the kernel. We pass `root=/dev/mapper/centos-root` to provide the path to the '/' partition. Initially we load the kernel as 'ro' or read only. The `crashkernel=auto` option is a setting for kdump kernel indicating the amount of memory reserved for it. The next two options tell the kernel that there are two LVM logical volumes it needs to load: `centos/root` and `centos/swap`. Finally, we can see that we load the Red Hat Graphical Boot (rhgb), a nicer boot experience than text, and we set the `quiet` option to supress noisy output during boot time.

Finally, the last line we are concerned with in Listing 6-4 is loading the kernel initrd. The initrd is a temporary root file system that is used by the boot process to first load the needed executables and drivers and then mount the system's "true" root ('/') file system. It is only used at boot and is unmounted once the true file system has been mounted.

We have shown you only one GRUB2 menuentry and only from a CentOS host. The menuentry will be slightly different for an Ubuntu host. Normally you see at least two menu entries per kernel you have installed, with one entry being a "rescue" kernel for system recovery. It is a copy of the kernel in case one is corrupted on CentOS with no special kernel options. Ubuntu is different as it passes the `recovery` and `nomodeset` kernel options. We will talk more about these shortly.

■ **Note** You can find more information on defining kernels and kernel options to GRUB2 at `http://www.gnu.org/software/grub/manual/grub.html` and `https://wiki.archlinux.org/index.php/kernel_parameters`. You can also find information via the `info grub` command.

MANAGING YOUR KERNEL

Not all kernels need an `initrd` file. For example, kernels that you have compiled yourself with all the modules that your kernel needs for your system shouldn't require an `initrd` file.

You might, for example, wish to compile your own kernel if a later release of the kernel supported some new hardware or functionality you required. It is a great exercise to compile your own kernel just to see what the options are and how that works.

We generally recommend that you stick with the stock kernel provided by your distribution and only compile your own kernel for your own fun or if you really need to for some specific functionality. Managing "hand-rolled" kernels can be a burden to patch and update, sometimes leaving you with a system you can't update.

When you do update your kernel you will need to reboot for critical patches. In version 4 of the Linux kernel, a way of patching the kernel to no longer require a reboot, even for critical patches, has been committed since 2015. It is the result of work done by SUSE and Red Hat, inspired by original work by Oracle. It is still new at the time of writing and the supporting code still needs some work.

To get a copy of latest kernel and other information you can go here:

- www.kernel.org/

- http://kernelnewbies.org/KernelBuild

The recommended way to update your kernel is via the distribution repositories. However, this is also where having supported distributions like RHEL (Red Hat Enterprise Linux), Oracle Linux, the Canonical Enterprise Support, and others can be of enormous benefit. If you need urgent patches to the kernel, they will often update and release kernel patches for problems you have reported. Waiting for the non-commercial distributions to release patches you are interested in can be hit and miss.

Securing Your Boot Loader

Having such a versatile and configurable boot loader can have its drawbacks. One of those we have mentioned is security. An unsecured boot loader can be altered at boot time by any person with malicious intent. Many small offices will have their servers on or under a couple of desks rather than in a locked computer room, and these servers are therefore very susceptible to such attacks. We strongly suggest you consider setting a password on your boot loader and store it in a very safe place along with your other passwords.

■ **Caution**   Again, you should always put your passwords somewhere secure like a safe or other secure, locked location. Sometimes it is also good to keep this somewhere offsite (as you would with offsite backups) so that if something happens to your site, you will not only be able to restore your data, but also have the right passwords handy to access your host. You should also have a backup of all passwords and tell someone you trust in your company where to find those passwords in case of an emergency.

Luckily GRUB2 provides the ability to set a password to the boot loader so that any changes to the preconfigured boot process require the user to enter a password. CentOS hosts have tools that make this easy for us and we will explore that distribution in this exercise. First we issue the following command:

```
$ sudo grub2-setpassword
```

This will ask you for a password and confirmation and will only create a password for the root user. What this command actually does is create a file /boot/grub2/user.cfg. The contents of that file looks as follows:

```
GRUB2_PASSWORD=grub.pbkdf2.sha512.10000.00E574C[...]DDF512CC090A9B[...]CCEA3B
```

Now that is file is created, when your host is rebooted this code in the /boot/grub2/grub.cfg file will now be executed:

Listing 6-5. Adding Root User to grub.cfg

```
### BEGIN /etc/grub.d/01_users ###
if [ -f ${prefix}/user.cfg ]; then
  source ${prefix}/user.cfg
  if [ -n ${GRUB2_PASSWORD} ]; then
    set superusers="root"
    export superusers
    password_pbkdf2 root ${GRUB2_PASSWORD}
  fi
fi
### END /etc/grub.d/01_users ###
```

What that code is saying in Listing 6-5 is, if the user.cfg file exists, then we will "source" the contents. If there is a $GRUB2_PASSWORD variable declared, then we will add root to the superusers list and this locks out other users to the GRUB2 command line. Then, finally, password_pbkdf2 is a GRUB2 command that associates the user with a password. We now need to run the grub2-mkconfig -o /boot/grub2/grub.cfg to set the superuser root password.

When your host next boots, you will notice that if you interrupt the boot process at the GRUB2 stage, you will be able to select one of the kernels with the --unrestricted menuentry option. However, if you want to edit any of the GRUB2 configuration details, by pressing e, you are required to enter a password. You will then be able to edit the GRUB2 configuration as normal.

To remove the password, remove the user.cfg file. Remember the GRUB2 documentation does suggest that this is not recommended except in situations where your hosts are publicly exposed. We suggest you use your best judgment considering your circumstances.

Remember that Ubuntu doesn't provide these tools to you out of the box, but you can follow a similar process with that distribution. For an Ubuntu specific guide see https://help.ubuntu.com/community/Grub2/Passwords.

What Happens After You Boot?

So your host has found your kernel and booted it. Your operating system now starts to load, your hardware is initialized, disks are readied, IP (Internet Protocol) addresses are assigned, and a variety of other tasks are performed. To do this, Linux runs a program, which is tasked with initiating the operating system and its services. This program is the first program to be started on your system and is running until the system is shut down; unsurprisingly this process will have the process id (PID) of 1. The initialization program, or "init," will bring the system up to a known "state" by finding out what services need to started and what they're dependent on. It does this by going through a series of files on the file system and reading their instructions.

Currently Linux is in a bit of a transition. Up until recently, there were at least three different possible programs that handled the system initialization. These were the older SysV Init program, Ubuntu's Upstart program, or the much more recent Systemd.

Upstart was Ubuntu's attempt at replacing the older SysV Init initializer. Because it was compatible with SysV it was used by other distributions too as their initializer; however, not many fully implemented Upstart. It was just used as a better "init." Red Hat-based hosts have since implemented Systemd completely and Debian-based systems, such as Ubuntu, are transitioning from Upstart and SysV Init to Systemd.

```
[jsmith@au-mel-centos-1 ~]$ ps aux |head -n2
USER       PID %CPU %MEM    VSZ   RSS TTY      STAT START   TIME COMMAND
root         1  0.0  0.6  43888  6456 ?        Ss   Apr22   0:00 /usr/lib/systemd/systemd --switched-root --system --deserialize 21
```

Figure 6-5. *PID 1 on CentOS*

Systemd is a newer approach to system initialization and can be found as the default (or is said to be natively running systemd) on CentOS and you can see that systemd is PID 1 in Figure 6-5. Ubuntu on the other hand, is said to "emulate" SysV Init. It does this by using SysV initd scripts to initialize many services using compatibility scripts provided by Systemd packages.

```
jsmith@au-mel-ubuntu-1:~$ ps aux |head -n2
USER       PID %CPU %MEM    VSZ   RSS TTY      STAT START   TIME COMMAND
root         1  0.0  0.6  38160  6252 ?        Ss   08:42   0:02 /sbin/init
```

Figure 6-6. *PID 1 onUbuntu*

On Ubuntu the /sbin/init program is PID 1. That init program with PID 1 comes from the systemd-sysv package and is actually linked to the systemd binary or program. Ubuntu currently is supporting all three init types while it is transitioning to run Systemd natively.

Both distributions have the systemd-sysv package installed and that contains the compatibility utilities for running SysVInit style initd scripts. It is designed to be a drop in replacement for SysVInit but is not 100% compatible in every sense.

Let's go through how to manage Systemd native implementations. We will also briefly discuss Upstart and the older SysV init.

■ **Note** There is a long history of init programs and popular and unpopular attempts to solve the problem of how to start a system. For a good look at them please see http://blog.darknedgy.net/ technology/2015/09/05/0/.

Understanding Systemd

As we have already mentioned, Systemd is the newest system initializer that is used across many modern distributions. Systemd is the replacement for both SysV Init and Upstart. It has been criticized as being against the Unix philosophy (do one thing, do it well), but it offers many advantages over its predecessors in the following ways (to a greater or lesser degree):

- It is event driven. This means it can respond to system events (such as new hardware being plugged in, traffic starting on a network port)
- Concurrent and parallel boot processing
- It can respawn processes
- Event logging
- Tracks processes via the kernel's CGroups

For those already familiar with SysV, Systemd doesn't have runlevels like SysV but instead has "targets." Targets are used to group service dependencies together. There are some common targets in systemd like multiuser, reboot, and rescue. So much as in runlevels, we can have different targets that bring us up to certain and discrete states. For example, if we want the system to be in the state where everyone can log in and use services we would use the target multiuser. In that state, we would like sshd, logging, and networking to be available. These are considered "wants" of the multiuser target.

Remember in Figure 6-3 where we showed you how to enter "maintenance" mode from the GRUB2 menu? We typed the word "single" at the end of the line where we launched the Linux kernel. Well, with Systemd we can also do the same thing by declaring the target we wish to launch into.

Listing 6-6. Using Systemd Targets to Boot to Rescue Mode

```
linux16 /vmlinuz-3.10.0-327.el7.x86_64 root=/dev/mapper/centos-root ro crashkernel=auto
rd.lvm.lv=centos/root rd.lvm.lv=centos/swap rhgb quiet systemd.unit=rescue.target
```

From looking at Listing 6-6 you might be able to recognize that we are on a CentOS server; we can do the same on an Ubuntu server. You can see that we have issued the `systemd.unit=rescue.target` on the end of the line. We are telling the kernel that when it runs systemd we should got to the rescue target.

Systemd uses a set of "unit" files to manage the services on your system. When systemd starts it looks for the required unit files by traversing the following load path:

Table 6-1. *Systemd Load Path*

Path	Purpose
/etc/systemd/system	Localized configuration files
/run/systemd/system	Runtime unit files
/usr/lib/systemd/system	Unit files of installed packages

Because we used the `system.unit=rescue.target` parameter, when the system process starts it will look for the `rescue.target` file in these directories in order of precedence, the `/etc/systemd/system,` then the `/run/systemd/system` directories and then finally in the `/usr/lib/systemd/system` directory. The `/etc/systemd/system` and `/run/systemd/system` directories are called "drop-in" directories and systemd will search for unit and `*.conf` files there. The target file will look like the following `rescue.target.`

Listing 6-7. The rescue.target File

```
[Unit]
Description=Rescue Mode
Documentation=man:systemd.special(7)
Requires=sysinit.target rescue.service
After=sysinit.target rescue.service
AllowIsolate=yes

[Install]
Alias=kbrequest.target
```

In Listing 6-7 we have removed the comments beginning with the '#' which are ignored by the system process. The options are case sensitive. In breaking this file down you can see that it has two sections, denoted by the square brackets([...]). Systemd unit files require at least the *[Unit]* and *[Install]* sections. You have the option to include a *[Service]* section, and we will discuss that shortly.

The *[Unit]* section has a *Description* and a *Documentation* setting, and they are pretty self-explanatory. In Listing 6-7 we can see that the rescue target *Requires* the *sysinit.target* and *rescue.service*. *Requires* does not provide ordering but tells systemd that these services should be executed too. If one of the required targets or services fails, this unit will be deactivated too.

Ordering support of targets or services is provided by adding options like the *After*. The rescue.unit should now be started *after* sysinit.target and rescue.service. It is a common pattern to see the same services and targets in the *Required* option also listed in the *After* option.

The *AllowIsolate* option is a Boolean read by the systemctl isolate command. The isolate argument to the systemctl command is similar in nature to a SysV runlevel. You can use it to put your system in a particular "state," so to start your graphical environment you may choose to run systemctl isolate graphical.target. For this reason, *AllowIsolate* is set to "false/no" by default because not every target file provides a stable system state.

The *[Install]* section is used by the systemctl tool when the unit is enabled or disabled. The systemctl tool is the utility tool used to manage systemd. The Alias option here points to the kbrequest.target which is a special systemd unit that is started whenever the Alt+ArrowUp is pressed on the console. Take a look at Figure 6-7 to see how that works.

```
[jsmith@au-mel-centos-1 ~]$ sudo systemctl enable rescue.target
Created symlink from /etc/systemd/system/kbrequest.target to /usr/lib/systemd/system/rescue.target.
[jsmith@au-mel-centos-1 ~]$ ll /etc/systemd/system/kbrequest.target
lrwxrwxrwx. 1 root root 37 Apr 23 21:11 /etc/systemd/system/kbrequest.target -> /usr/lib/systemd/system/rescue.target
```

Figure 6-7. *Using systemctl to enable the Alt-ArrowUp alias*

In Figure 6-7 you can see that when we issue the $ sudo systemctl enable rescue.target, the Alias option of the Install section means that we create a symlink from kbrequest.target to the rescue.target. Now, on the console, if we hit the Alt+ArrowUp keys we get the following as shown in Figure 6-8.

```
CentOS Linux 7 (Core)
Kernel 3.10.0-327.el7.x86_64 on an x86_64

au-mel-centos-1 login: Welcome to emergency mode! After logging in, type "journa
lctl -xb" to view
system logs, "systemctl reboot" to reboot, "systemctl default" or ^D to
boot into default mode.
Give root password for maintenance
(or type Control-D to continue): _
```

Figure 6-8. *Entering rescue console from pressing the Alt+ArrowUp keys*

Let's take a quick look at a service file that configures how we manage the rsyslog daemon. Rsyslog is the logging service on Linux and we look at it in depth in Chapter 18. In Listing 6-8 we have displayed the contents of our rsyslog.service file.

Listing 6-8. The rsyslog.service systemd File

```
[Unit]
Description=System Logging Service
;Requires=syslog.socket

[Service]
Type=notify
EnvironmentFile=-/etc/sysconfig/rsyslog
ExecStart=/usr/sbin/rsyslogd -n $SYSLOGD_OPTIONS
Restart=on-failure
UMask=0066
StandardOutput=null

[Install]
WantedBy=multi-user.target
;Alias=syslog.service
```

In this file we have the *[Unit]* and *[Install]* sections as we have seen before. It is worth noting that in these sections you can see a semicolon on the Requires and Alias options. If lines start with a #or a; then they are considered comments and are ignored. In Listing 6-8 we see that there is a *[Service]* section and we use that to describe the service we are configuring to run on our system.

All *[Service]* sections require a *Type* option. It can be set to "simple," "forking," "oneshot," "dbus," "notify," or "idle." The default setting is "simple." With a type of simple you expect that the process run by the ExecStart option is to be the main process (i.e., it doesn't fork a child process). Notify is similar to simple but it will send a notification message once it has finished starting up. Systemd will then start other units once it reads this message. Since this is a logging service, it makes sense to make sure the service is up and running before starting other units dependent on recording log events.

EnvironmentFile is where we can load environmental parameters. There are many optional parameters that can be set for rsyslogd and you can add them into the /etc/sysconfig/rsyslog file. Options found in man rsyslogd can be added to the file.

Next we have the *ExecStart* option. This is the command that is executed, along with any arguments. This should be the main process of the daemon, unless you are going to fork the process (with Type=fork).

The *Restart* option controls how systemd monitors the service and reacts to any issues. The options are "no," "on-success," "on-failure," "on-abnormal," "on-watchdog," "on-abort," or "always." The rsyslog service is set to restart on failure and the default is "no" if not set. Setting on-failure means that systemd will attempt to restart the service when the process exits with a non-zero exit code, it is terminated by a signal, an operation times out, or a watch-dog timeout is triggered.

UMask sets the permissions of any files created by this process. If we remember what we learned back in Chapter 4, the umask is an octet and is used to set permissions on files and directories. When applied it means we give files created by this process permissions of 0711, or rwx-x-x. This means that the owner of the process is given read, write, and execute permission on the files, the group and everyone else will have execute only.

The last option in the *[Service]* section is StandardOutput and defines where the file descriptor 1 or standard output of the process should be connected to. The values are "inherit," "null," "tty," "journal," "syslog," "kmsg," "journal+console," "syslog+console," "kmsg+console," or "socket." The rsyslogd service has been set to null, which is to a special file on Linux called /dev/null. If you write to /dev/null you expect your data to be blackholed or lost. This means we don't care about the output of this service on standard out.

Finally, if you look at the *[Install]* section you will see a *WantedBy=multi-user.target*. This line instructs the systemctl command to create a symbolic link in the /etc/systemd/system/multi-user.target.wants directory to the /lib/systemd/system/rsyslog.service when a service is enabled, or remove the link if the service is disabled. More on this shortly.

Systemd unit files are complex and rely on many other dependency units. There are also countless options and settings available to systemd units. For further reading please see the following helpful links:

- https://access.redhat.com/videos/403833

- www.freedesktop.org/wiki/Software/systemd/

- www.freedesktop.org/software/systemd/man/systemd.html

- https://access.redhat.com/documentation/en-US/Red_Hat_Enterprise_
  Linux/7/html/System_Administrators_Guide/chap-Managing_Services_with_
  systemd.html

Once your kernel has passed off to the systemd process and it has brought up your machine to a target state you will need to know how to interact with the services running on your system. We will explore that shortly when we look at the systemctl command.

Upstart: Ubuntu's Init

The idea behind Upstart was to create a comprehensive init process that can be used to start, stop, monitor, and respond to events on behalf of services on your Linux host. It was a reworking and expansion of the SysV Init paradigm; rather than outright replacing SysV Init, the designers created Upstart to emulate SysV Init until everyone converted over.

The init process under Upstart is an event-based daemon that uses event triggers to start or stop processes. An *event* is a change of state that init can be informed of. The event can be the adding of a peripheral device, like plugging in a USB memory stick. The kernel can then inform init of this action by sending an event notice. This event in turn can trigger other jobs to be initiated or stopped depending on the job definitions under init's control.

Upstart collectively calls processes under its command jobs, and you interact with those jobs using the initctl command. Jobs can either be *services* or *tasks* or *abstract*. Services are persistent, like a mail server, and tasks perform a function and then exit to a waiting state, like a backup program. An abstract job runs forever but has no child process. The definition files (or Upstart scripts) for jobs can be found under the /etc/init directory.

Listing 6-9 illustrates what is called a *system job definition* for the rsyslogd daemon. In this case, rsyslogd is a logging daemon that needs to write to the /var/log/syslog file. As logging daemon, it is important that if this gets stopped for some reason, it is good to get it to try to restart itself. Let's run through the major points here.

Listing 6-9. /etc/init/rsyslog.conf

```
# rsyslog - system logging daemon
#
# rsyslog is an enhanced multi-threaded replacement for the traditional
# syslog daemon, logging messages from applications

Description      "system logging daemon"

start on filesystem
stop on runlevel [06]
```

```
expect fork
respawn

pre-start script
    /lib/init/apparmor-profile-load usr.sbin.rsyslogd
end script

script
    . /etc/default/rsyslog
    exec rsyslogd $RSYSLOGD_OPTIONS
end script
```

Upstart is "evented," meaning it can react to events on your system. The *start on filesystem* means that when the filesystem "event" takes place, we will automatically start rsyslog too. The *stop on* configuration option is an event definition signalling Upstart to stop rsyslogd when a runlevel 0 or 6 event is detected. As you may know, runlevels 0, 1, 6 are special runlevels that either shut down, reboot, or put your host into maintenance mode. We expect the service to fork another process and the respawn option directs Upstart to restart the job if it is stopped unexpectedly. We can write prestart scripts that run prior to executing the main script section.

While Upstart is different from SysV and has no natural concept of runlevels, it has been made backward compatible with SysV Init scripts. These help emulate the old-style SysV scripts by executing the /etc/init.d/rc script. This will in turn run through the old /etc/rcN.d directory and start and stop services for that particular runlevel.

You manage Upstart with the initclt command and that allows you to start, stop services.

```
$ sudo initctl start rsyslog
$ sudo initctl stop rsyslog
```

Upstart doesn't have a tool to enable or disable services, but you can use pre-start script section to source in a file that contains an ENABLED variable set. The Upstart Ubuntu Cookbook suggests something like this is the accepted way:

```
pre-start script

  # stop job from continuing if no config file found for daemon
  [ ! -f /etc/default/myapp ] && { stop; exit 0; }

  # source the config file
  . /etc/default/myapp

  # stop job from continuing if admin has not enabled service in
  # config file.
  [ -z "$ENABLED" ] && { stop; exit 0; }

end script
```

You can read more on Upstart at http://upstart.ubuntu.com/cookbook/.

Remembering SystemV

Let's go back in time somewhat. For a long time Linux systems were initialized by a program called SystemV Init, SysV Init, SysV, or just init. Init has since been replaced by another program called Systemd in most major distributions, including CentOS and Ubuntu. However, both of these distributions still support SysVInit startup scripts. We are going to give you a bit of a background on Init and how it works.

SysVInit has a concept of *runlevels*. Runlevels define what state a host should be in at a particular point. Each runlevel comprises a set of applications and services and an indicator of whether each should be started or stopped. For example, during the normal boot of your host, the init tool at each runlevel will initiate all the required sets of applications and services in that runlevel. Another example occurs when you shut down your host. When you tell your host to shut down, the init tool changes the runlevel to 0. At this runlevel all applications and services are stopped and the system is halted.

SysV has seven runlevels, ranging from 0 to 6, and each distribution uses different runlevels for different purposes. But some runlevels are fairly generic across all distributions. The common runlevels are 0, 1, and 6. You've already seen runlevel 0, which is used to shut down the host. Runlevel 1 is the single-user mode, or maintenance mode, that we described earlier in this chapter. Runlevel 6 is used when your host is being rebooted.

The runlevels on Ubuntu and CentOS hosts differ slightly. On Ubuntu, the runlevels 2 to 5 all run what is called multiuser mode. *Multiuser* mode is the mode where multiple users can sign in, not just a single console user. All required services are usually set to be started in this runlevel.

In comparison, CentOS generally starts in runlevel 5 if you have a GUI console installed or runlevel 3 for command line only. CentOS has the following runlevels:

- *Runlevel 0*: Shuts down the host and brings the system to a halt

- *Runlevel 1*: Runs in single-user (maintenance) mode, command console, no network

- *Runlevel 2*: Is unassigned

- *Runlevel 3*: Runs in multiuser mode, with network, and starts level 3 programs

- *Runlevel 4*: Is unassigned

- *Runlevel 5*: Runs in multiuser mode, with network, X Windows (KDE, GNOME), and starts level 5 programs.

- *Runlevel 6*: Reboots the host

Managing SysV init files

Traditionally, on most distributions the /sbin/init tool was configured using the /etc/inittab file. The inittab file specified the default runlevel the system should use. It also detailed the other runlevels and where to find the list of applications to start or stop in each runlevel. On systems running Systemd you can forget about basically ignore runlevels as they don't strictly apply in the new world and you will not find the inittab file on your system.

■ **Note** If you're looking for more detailed information than what is in the man page on the inittab, you can read information at www.cyberciti.biz/howto/question/man/inittab-man-page.php.

The traditional init program would read the inittab to determine the default runlevel and then execute a series of scripts for that runlevel (files in the /etc/rcX.d directories where X is the runlevel). Files in those directories starting with S or K' would be executed depending if the system was starting (S) or shutting down (K) (or moving between runlevels where the service is expected to be running or stopped).

With hosts with the systemd-sysv package installed, if we cannot find a systemd service file, the system will look for files in the /etc/init.d directory; for example, /etc/init.d/postfix. *This* file will be picked up and generated in to a systemd service file (more on these later).

On modern distributions running Systemd, there is no longer a need to configure SysV.

Moving Between Runlevels

On older systems you can use the telinit or init command to switch between runlevels. On today's systems you can still use these commands but the true concept of runlevels no longer applies. These now map to different systemd "targets."

However, if you happen to find yourself on the old SysV hosts you can use the telinit command as follows:

```
$ sudo telint 3
```

This would move you from your current runlevel to runlevel 3. See the man page for more information.

Understanding Initd Scripts in SysV Init

Initd scripts are scripts that stop and start processes, as well as sometimes providing the current status of the process and possibly other actions. Today's initd scripts are said to be LSB compliant in that they have a certain structure to them. Let's start by looking at an init script: take a look at the postfix script located in /etc/init.d on our Ubuntu server.

What's LSB? Short for Linux Standard Base, it is a set of standards agreed to by the various Linux distributions to make life easier for everyone using it, especially for those who develop on it. It seeks to make common standards for Linux configurations, file locations, package names, and other conventions. LSB has struggled to stay relevant in recent years and less distributions are being certified under it. You can read more about it at www.linuxfoundation.org/en/LSB.

Listing 6-10. Ubuntu Postfix Script Header

```
#!/bin/sh -e

### BEGIN INIT INFO
# Provides:          postfix mail-transport-agent
# Required-Start:    $local_fs $remote_fs $syslog $named $network $time
# Required-Stop:     $local_fs $remote_fs $syslog $named $network
# Should-Start:      postgresql mysql clamav-daemon postgrey spamassassin saslauthd dovecot
# Should-Stop:       postgresql mysql clamav-daemon postgrey spamassassin saslauthd dovecot
# Default-Start:     2 3 4 5
# Default-Stop:      0 1 6
# Short-Description: Postfix Mail Transport Agent
# Description:       postfix is a Mail Transport agent
### END INIT INFO
```

We have omitted some details here, but the important information for our discussion is between the ###BEGIN and ###END comments. LSB-compliant init scripts require a standard header. The standard says that you must have the following keywords followed by a list of arguments, some denoted by a $ prefix. These $ arguments are reserved *virtual facilities*, which are described in the LSB specification. They are designed to give more order to your init scripts. For instance, $local_fs means "all local filesystems are mounted." So when you see 'Required-Start', it means the listed services must be started before executing this script. The example in Listing 6-10 would prevent Postfix from starting unless all the filesystems are mounted, the log service is running, the named server is running, the network is up, and the time has been synchronized.

The meanings of the keywords from Listing 6-10 and listed here are:

- Provides: Gives a brief indication what this service provides. This information is used by other services.

- Required-Start: Lists services that must be available for this script to start.

- Required-Stop: Indicates this service must be stopped before the services listed here are stopped.

- Should-Start: Defines a list of what services can be started, although not mandatory, before this service starts.

- Should-Stop: Indicates this service should be stopped, although not mandatory, before the services listed here.

- Default-Start: Defines the default runlevels the service should be run in.

- Default-Stop: Defines the default runlevels this service should not run in.

- Description: Gives a description of the service.

More information about LSB init scripts can be found at

- http://refspecs.linux-foundation.org/LSB_5.0.0/LSB-Core-generic/LSB-Core-generic/iniscrptact.html

- https://wiki.debian.org/LSBInitScripts

Dissecting further the Listing 6-10 example notice the Default Start and Default Stop keywords. These map to the runlevels that we have talked about previously. In this script we are told that Postfix should start in runlevels 2 3 4 and 5. We should not be running in runlevels 0 1 and 6.

■ **Note** Older operating systems like CentOS 5 used the pre-LSB standard for writing init.d scripts. These were superseded and replaced with the LSB standard. Ubuntu has used LSB-compliant init.d scripts for many releases now.

The rest of the contents of the postfix init script (which we've omitted from Listing 6-10) are the instructions used to start, stop, and sometimes query the status of the application or service managed by the script.

HOW SYSTEMD EMULATES SYSV INIT

Systemd is has been implemented with support for backward compatibility with SysV Init (and Upstart, as it happens). It does this in the following manner:

- checking for the service unit file in the systemd directory paths

- if it can't find one, it looks in /etc/init.d/ for a service file without the .service suffix

- if it finds one it uses the systemd-sysv-generator to convert it to a systemd unit file

- it uses the LSB runlevels to decide which target it needs to be executed in.

When we have SysV Init (LSB compliant) files in /etc/init.d/ and we start the service using the systemctl command, Systemd will find those files and then run them through a generator (systemd-sysv-generator). The output of which is then converted into Systemd units.

The SysV runlevels are also mapped to Systemd targets. Systemd will map each runlevel to an appropriate target, like runlevel 3 will be linked to the multiuser.target. Here we show how Systemd maps runlevel 3 to the multiuser "target." by using symlinks.

```
$ ls -la /usr/lib/systemd/system/runlevel3.target
lrwxrwxrwx. 1 root root 17 Feb  3 22:55 /usr/lib/systemd/system/runlevel3.target ->
multi-user.target
```

So when you issue the telinit 3 command the following target is run by Systemd.

```
[Unit]
Description=Multi-User System
Documentation=man:systemd.special(7)
Requires=basic.target
Conflicts=rescue.service rescue.target
After=basic.target rescue.service rescue.target
AllowIsolate=yes
```

To the applications and packages that are not "Systemd ready," there is no difference as long as they have a LSB-compliant init.d script.

The original SysV Init actually hasn't been used on operating systems for quite some time and Upstart was swapped in to manage SysV in both Red Hat- and Debian-based systems.

Managing Services

In Chapter 4, we introduced you to the concept of processes and services. Each application and command you run creates a process. Some processes finish when the command completes, for example, listing the contents of a directory. Other processes are more long running and don't stop until you request them to do so or you reboot the host. Some of these long-running processes run applications and services like mail and web servers or print or file services. These types of long-running processes are often called daemons. *Daemons* are processes that run in the background; that is, they are not required to be attached to a console. As we explained in Chapter 4, each of these processes has a name; for example, sshd daemon or httpd, or apache for the Apache web server.

■ **Note** All processes on Linux originate from a parent process. Forking a process involves a parent process making a copy of itself, called a child process. With Systemd, the systemd process would be the parent. This means that processes can persist without requiring to be attached to a console or user session. When the parent process stops, so do all its children. For example, if you kill the `systemd` process on a host, you will stop all processes on the host. This is not a very good idea and will probably have unfortunate effects on a host. If you need to start and stop all services, you should use the commands we introduce in this chapter.

Managing Services with Systemd

As we have explained previously, in Systemd targets are used to group units so that when you boot our host to a particular target, you can expect certain services to be available and other, possibly conflicting, services to be stopped. If you change targets your services can also change from running to stopped. You can also stop and start individual services manually at any time.

Systemd has a command tool called systemctl. Systemctl is used to manage systemd resources on a local, remote, or virtual container. By issuing the `--help` argument we can see the list of arguments, unit file commands, machine commands, job commands, and more. To begin with, let's look at how we can manage an individual service and then we can look at the wider system.

■ **Note** Yes, you can use systemctl to manage remote or virtual machines. When specified with the `--host <hostname>`, systemctl uses SSH to log into the remote system and execute the systemctl command. When specified with a `--machine <machinename>` it will execute command on the specified local container.

Systemd Services—Status, Stop, and Start

So first, let's look at how to get the status of a service called postfix, which is a SMTP server for sending e-mail.

Listing 6-11. Getting the Status of the postfix Service

```
$ sudo systemctl status postfix.service
• postfix.service - Postfix Mail Transport Agent
   Loaded: loaded (/usr/lib/systemd/system/postfix.service; enabled; vendor preset:
disabled)
   Active: active (running) since Wed 2016-04-27 20:35:10 AEST; 3h 0min ago
  Process: 642 ExecStart=/usr/sbin/postfix start (code=exited, status=0/SUCCESS)
  Process: 636 ExecStartPre=/usr/libexec/postfix/chroot-update (code=exited, status=0/
SUCCESS)
  Process: 621 ExecStartPre=/usr/libexec/postfix/aliasesdb (code=exited, status=0/SUCCESS)
 Main PID: 993 (master)
   CGroup: /system.slice/postfix.service
           ├─ 993 /usr/libexec/postfix/master -w
           ├─1003 qmgr -l -t unix -u
           └─1926 pickup -l -t unix -u
```

```
Apr 27 20:35:09 au-mel-centos-1 systemd[1]: Starting Postfix Mail Transport Agent...
Apr 27 20:35:10 au-mel-centos-1 postfix/master[993]: daemon started -- version 2.10.1,
configuration /etc/postfix
Apr 27 20:35:10 au-mel-centos-1 systemd[1]: Started Postfix Mail Transport Agent.
```

We see a lot of detail here. The main things I want to draw your attention to are Loaded and Active. Loaded shows you what unit file is being used to launch this service. Active gives you the current status of the service, "active," and how long it has been running for. From this output we can also see that this service was started by running /usr/sbin/postfix start and that that process (642) ended with an exit code 0 or success. We also executed two other ExecStartPre commands which were both successful. These map nicely to the systemd postfix.service unit file on CentOS.

```
[Service]
Type=forking
PIDFile=/var/spool/postfix/pid/master.pid
EnvironmentFile=-/etc/sysconfig/network
ExecStartPre=-/usr/libexec/postfix/aliasesdb
ExecStartPre=-/usr/libexec/postfix/chroot-update
ExecStart=/usr/sbin/postfix start
```

The other thing to note in Listing 6-11 is the CGroup information. This shows that the postfix.service is under the CGroup system.slice. CGroups are implemented in the kernel and are used to group system resources for isolation and performance purposes.

The output in Listing 6-11 is very verbose and is useful for the system administrator to view the details, but if we were to do this programmatically it is a lot of data to "grok" to see the status of our service. So systemctl provides a way of condensing the same information to make it easy for a program to detect the status.

```
$ sudo systemctl is-active postfix.service ; echo $?
active
0
```

The above command provides both the state ("active," "inactive") to the standard output and an exit code (0 for active, non-zero for other state)—both of which you can test for in a script or program that might manage the service. In the line above we are making use of the special variable $? in our bash shell which holds the exit code of the last command run.

Now that we know how to see the status of our service and we can see that is it already running, let's stop the service.

```
$ sudo systemctl stop postfix.service
```

There is no noticeable output from that command so if we query the status, we can see that it is stopped.

```
● postfix.service - Postfix Mail Transport Agent
   Loaded: loaded (/usr/lib/systemd/system/postfix.service; enabled; vendor preset:
disabled)
   Active: inactive (dead) since Thu 2016-04-28 11:28:04 AEST; 1s ago
  Process: 5304 ExecStop=/usr/sbin/postfix stop (code=exited, status=0/SUCCESS)
.....
Main PID: 5267 (code=killed, signal=TERM)
```

Clearly we can see that the service is "inactive" and that the Main PID was killed with a TERM signal.

■ **Note** Processes can accept "signals" from the kill command. A TERM or SIGTERM signal tells a process to finish up what it is doing and exit. You can also send harsher signals like SIGKILL which will exit the process immediately, possibly in the middle of something important. SIGHUP can sometimes be used to reload configurations of running processes. See `http://linux.die.net/man/7/signal` for more information.

Now that the postfix service is stopped, we will start it again.

```
$ sudo systemctl start postfix.service
```

Again there is no output to the console; we run the status to confirm that it is running.

```
● postfix.service - Postfix Mail Transport Agent
   Loaded: loaded (/usr/lib/systemd/system/postfix.service; enabled; vendor preset: disabled)
   Active: active (running) since Thu 2016-04-28 11:51:45 AEST; 2s ago
```

What we have seen in this section is how to start, stop, and see the status of a service using the systemctl command. But how did those services start in the first place? How are these services enabled to be started at boot time? Let's investigate that now.

Isolated Targets

As we have said, systemd is the process that manages all the services on our host and systemctl is the command we use to manage the systemd process. We have talked about systemd targets and that they bring the system up to a certain state where the right processes are running. In SysV we called them runlevels and they were controlled by a series of files symlinked from the /etc/rcX.d directories. Well with systemd this concept of a single runlevel is not quite accurate, as many targets can be active at once. However, in systemd, some targets have a special purpose.

In systemd, targets like multiuser, if they have the Boolean *AllowIsolate=yes* set in their unit files. This means that these targets will respond to the systemctl isolate command. This command allows us to start discrete system "states" where we start one unit (and all their dependencies) and stop all others.

Let's discover our current system state. We are going to use the systemctl command again and this time we are going to list the current targets running on our system.

```
$ sudo systemctl list-units --type target
UNIT                    LOAD    ACTIVE   SUB      DESCRIPTION
basic.target            loaded  active   active   Basic System
cryptsetup.target       loaded  active   active   Encrypted Volumes
getty.target            loaded  active   active   Login Prompts
local-fs-pre.target     loaded  active   active   Local File Systems (Pre)
local-fs.target         loaded  active   active   Local File Systems
multi-user.target       loaded  active   active   Multi-User System
network.target          loaded  active   active   Network
paths.target            loaded  active   active   Paths
remote-fs.target        loaded  active   active   Remote File Systems
slices.target           loaded  active   active   Slices
```

```
sockets.target        loaded    active    active    Sockets
swap.target           loaded    active    active    Swap
sysinit.target        loaded    active    active    System Initialization
timers.target         loaded    active    active    Timers
```

Here is a list of the current targets running on our system. Some of these targets are "special" targets like swap.target which is used to manage swap partitions and swap files and slices.target, which sets up all the CGroup slice units. The multiuser target is made up of all these other targets. If you look into the unit file for multiuser.target you will see that it *Requires=basic.target*. The basic.target has *Requires=sysinit.target*. The sysinit.target has *Wants=local-fs.target swap.target*. I am leaving out some other detail here, like *Conflicts* and *After* directives, but you should be able to see that the multiuser target is made up of all these other targets and that is how systemd knows what target to pull in.

We have said that some of these targets define a "state" of a machine. These states are like rescue, multiuser, graphical, and shutdown. When your system has started you can move between these targets by issuing the following command:

```
$ sudo systemctl isolate graphical.target
```

What this command will do look at the graphical.target unit file, determine if it has *AllowIsolate=yes*, then execute the *Requires, Conflicts, After, Wants* and other directives to bring the system to that "state." You will notice when you look at the graphical.target unit file (found in /lib/systemd/system directory) that it *Requires* the multiuser target and should not start until *After* it is completed. So how does systemd know how to start our postfix service on boot?

Disabling Services

Let's explore this by looking at what happens when we disable our postfix service. If we don't want the service to start when our system reboots, we need to disable it. To disable it let's execute the following command:

```
$ sudo systemctl disable postfix.service
Removed symlink /etc/systemd/system/multi-user.target.wants/postfix.service.
```

The output of this command has told us what it is has done. It has removed a symbolic link (symlink) from the /etc/systemd/system/multi-user.target.wants directory. If we look at our postfix.service file in the /lib/systemd/system directory we will see that the *[Install]* section has the option, *WantedBy=multi-user.target*. If we remember that the *[Install]* section contains directives that tells systemctl to create the symlink or remove the symlink when we enable or disable the service, it is this option that tells systemctl to remove the symlink when we disable the service.

Enabling Services

Now that we have done that, we want to enable the service so that it starts automatically when our system boots. Let's enable the service again and see what the output is:

```
$ sudo systemctl enable postfix.service
Created symlink from /etc/systemd/system/multi-user.target.wants/postfix.service to /usr/lib/systemd/system/postfix.service.
```

The output is telling us that is has created the symlink to the postfix.service file in the /etc/systemd/system/multi-user.target.wants directory. Now when systemd initiates the multiuser.target it will look inside the multi-user.target.wants directory and start those services also.

Let's try now to get a list of all the current running services that systemd is controlling (see Listing 6-12).

Listing 6-12. Listing the Running Services

```
$ sudo systemctl --type=service --state=running
UNIT                      LOAD     ACTIVE   SUB       DESCRIPTION
atd.service               loaded   active   running   Job spooling tools
crond.service             loaded   active   running   Command Scheduler
getty@tty1.service        loaded   active   running   Getty on tty1
NetworkManager.service    loaded   active   running   Network Manager
postfix.service           loaded   active   running   Postfix Mail Transport Agent
systemd-journald.service  loaded   active   running   Journal Service
systemd-logind.service    loaded   active   running   Login Service
systemd-udevd.service     loaded   active   running   udev Kernel Device Manager
wpa_supplicant.service    loaded   active   running   WPA Supplicant daemon
```

In Listing 6-12 we can see the (trimmed) output of the systemctl command which has been run with the --*type=service* and --*state=running* options. If you run the systemctl command without any options or arguments you get a full list of every loaded unit definition (unit file) systemd has loaded. We are reducing this list by add the --type of unit we are interested in and the --state of that unit. You can see in that list that our postfix.service is loaded, active, and running. You can see all inactive units too by adding --*all* to the command.

Managing SysV style files

So far we have seen how we handle systemd unit files that control services. Remember we can also use the older SysV init.d files too. We have also said that systemd will first look in its own directory paths looking for a name.service file, or in our case postfix.service. If it cannot find one it will look in /etc/init.d/ for an executable *postfix* file (without the .service suffix). If there is one there and it is LSB compliant, it will run systemd-generate-sysv command to create a systemd wrapper file.

The Ubuntu server still uses some SysV init.d system files (whereas CentOS uses systemd natively) so we will look at how that distribution manages the postfix service. When the system starts up or after a systemctl daemon-reload is triggered, if systemd finds a postfix init.d service file it passes it to systemd-generate-sysv which will create a postfix.service and place it in /run/systemd/generator.late/postfix.service. It will also create the appropriate symlinks to multi-user.target.wants directory in the /run/systemd/generator.late directory.

The unit files generated have the same options (*[Unit]* and *[Service]*) as other unit files. The start, stop, and reload options refer to the init.d file as follows:

```
[Service]
...
ExecStart=/etc/init.d/postfix start
ExecStop=/etc/init.d/postfix stop
ExecReload=/etc/init.d/postfix reload
```

We can use the same systemctl start|stop postfix.service to manage the service. Likewise we can use the systemctl enable|disable to manage if we want it to start or not on boot.

```
$ sudo systemctl disable postfix
postfix.service is not a native service, redirecting to systemd-sysv-install
Executing /lib/systemd/systemd-sysv-install disable postfix
```

When dealing with SysV init.d scripts systemd does two things. One is to apply the same symlinks to the multi-user.target.wants directory for the postfix service (in /run/systemd/generator.late/ directory). But here you can also see that since we are not using a native systemd service we will redirect this to another compatibility script to handle the enabling and disabling in SysV land. This script executes, under the hood, the older SysV init.d manager, in this case on Ubuntu, update-rc.d. On CentOS this would be the chkconfig command.

Let's quickly go through those commands so that you are also familiar with what is happening under these circumstances.

Update-rc.d—Managing Ubuntu SysV init.d

Managing SysV init.d services onUbuntu is done via the update-rc.d command. The update-rc.d command will create symbolic links into the /etc/rc?.d directories or remove them if instructed to do so. The update-rc.d command takes the options listed in Table 6-2.

Table 6-2. update-rc.d Options

Option	Description
Start	Allows you to explicitly state the runlevels and startup sequence.
Stop	Allows you to explicitly state the sequence and runlevels you wish to stop the service.
Defaults	The update-rc.d script will create start symlinks with the default start sequence (S20) into runlevels 2, 3, 4, and 5 and stop symlinks into runlevels 0, 1, 6 with the stop sequence (K80).
Remove	Removes the symlinks from each runlevel as long as the file /etc/init.d/*script-name* has already been removed. (See -f for more information.)
-n	Gives you a dry run of what would happen without changing anything.
-f	When used with the remove option, forces the removal of the symlinks from the /etc/rcn.d directories, even if /etc/init.d/*script-name* is still present.

The update-rc.d command will simply link init.d scripts into the /etc/rcN.d directories (where N is the runlevel), usually with the defaults of runlevels 2, 3, 4, 5 and a start priority of S20, and runlevels 0, 1, 6 and a stop priority of K80.

From the command line, you can then issue update-rc.d to manipulate the services that run at particular runlevels. For example, to turn a service on with the Ubuntu defaults, you issue the following:

```
$ sudo update-rc.d postfix start defaults
```

With the defaults, as stated previously, the init.d scripts are symbolically linked to the /etc/rcN.d directories and given the standard start and stop priorities of 20 and 80.

You can specify the runlevels and priorities you wish your services to start on with the following:

```
$ sudo update-rc.d postfix start 23 40
```

Here we have set the service to start at runlevels 2 and 3 with a priority of 40.

To turn off the service in runlevel 2, issue the following:

```
$ sudo update-rc.d postfix stop 2
```

The preceding command will add a K80postfix symbolic link into the /etc/rc2.d directory.

To remove services from all runlevels, you would issue the following command:

```
$ sudo update-rc.d postfix remove
```

If the init.d script for the service you are trying to remove is still present in the /etc/init.d directory, which will be the case if you have not uninstalled Postfix, you will get an error unless you use the -f option. In this case, you issue the following:

```
$ sudo update-rc.d -f postfix remove
```

That is how you would manage Ubuntu SysV init.d. Let's look at shutting down your system next.

Shutting Down and Rebooting Your Linux Host

There are several ways to shut down and reboot a Linux host both from the GUI and the command line. From the command line, we can use the systemctl command to manage the power state of our hosts.

To shut down and power off the system we would issue the following:

```
$ sudo systemctl poweroff
```

This will power off the system immediately. You can also issue a reboot, halt, hibernate, sleep, and more. See the systemctl --help for more information.

We can still issue the older commands too to shut down the host—you can issue the appropriately named shutdown command:

```
$ sudo shutdown -h now
```

The systemctl poweroff and the shutdown command both link to the same systemd target of /lib/systemd/system/poweroff.target.

From the GUI, shutting down the host is easy. Find the power symbol, usually top right of the screen, and then select the Shutdown option.

Scheduling Services and Commands

You can schedule repeated jobs with Linux to run at specified events or at specified times or at specified intervals. There are two ways to do this. One is with systemd timers and the other is with a tool called Cron.

Systemd Timers

Systemd timers are unit files that end with *.timer suffix. They control when a service is run. It is expected that these will replace Cron for managing regularly scheduled job management.

It has advantages over Cron in that it can trigger events based on not only the wall clock (the system's time) but also things like the period after the last event was run, on boot, on startup or a combination of these sorts of things. A timer unit file can also be used to trigger another service unit that doesn't have a timer.

The configuration requires a *[Timer]* section in the unit file. Let's take this example of the daily apt schedule that manages the daily checks for the apt cache (see Listing 6-13).

Listing 6-13. Systemd timer /lib/systemd/system/apt-daily.timer

```
[Unit]
Description=Daily apt activities

[Timer]
OnCalendar=*-*-* 6,18:00
RandomizedDelaySec=12h
AccuracySec=1h
Persistent=true

[Install]
WantedBy=timers.target
```

Here you can see that we have the usual sections for *[Unit]* and *[Install]*. The OnCalendar option specifies when we should run the service, and that can be specified by the day of the week, the year, the month, the day, and then HH:MM:SS or any number of ways! There is a full list of options in man 7 systemd.timer. Asterisks (*) mean any value and this is shorthand for daily (*-*-*). It is triggered to occur at either 06:00 or 18:00Hrs, with a 12-hour random window (RandomizedDelaySec), give or take an hour (AccuracySec). The Persistence=true says to run if it missed the last start (like the system was shutdown).

Let's imagine we have a monitor.service file that makes a cURL POST request to a web site to tell us the system has booted, and checks in every 20 minutes after that.

```
[Unit]
Description=Tell the monitoring service we are up

[Timer]
OnBootSec=2min
OnUnitActiveSec=20min

[Install]
WantedBy=timers.target
```

We will put this configuration into a file called /etc/systemd/system/monitor.timer, next to our monitor.service file. Here, we can see that a unit file for a timer needs these three sections, *[Unit]*, *[Timer]*, and *[Install]*.

The *[Timer]* section is where we put our timer options. We have chosen here to trigger our cURL job 2 minutes after the boot event (OnBootSec), and then every 20 minutes after the last event (OnUnitActiveSec). The times here could be expressed as 1h (1 hour), 2w (2 weeks), or a variety of other ways. These are called *monotonic* timers as opposed to the *real-time* timer we saw in Listing 6-13.

211

The WantedBy=timers.target in the *[Install]* section creates the symlinks to the timers target which enables the timer in systemd. We can enable the timer with the following:

```
$ sudo systemctl enable monitor.timer
Created symlink from /etc/systemd/system/timers.target.wants/monitor.timer to /etc/systemd/
system/monitor.timer.
```

We can now list our timers with the following:

```
jsmith@au-mel-ubuntu-1:~$ sudo systemctl list-timers
[sudo] password for jsmith:
NEXT                        LEFT      LAST                        PASSED     UNIT                        ACTIVATES
Sun 2016-07-17 02:12:38 AEST  49s ago   Sun 2016-07-17 02:13:27 AEST  18ms ago   monitor.timer               monitor.service
Sun 2016-07-17 17:01:30 AEST  14h left  Sat 2016-07-16 22:17:17 AEST  3h 56min ago apt-daily.timer           apt-daily.service
Mon 2016-07-18 00:47:28 AEST  22h left  Sun 2016-07-17 00:47:28 AEST  1h 25min ago systemd-tmpfiles-clean.timer systemd-tmpfiles-clean.service
```

Figure 6-9. *Listing timers*

You can see our timer in Figure 6-9. You can see that it activates our monitor.service and that it was successful 18 minutes ago. You can also see the apt-daily.timer too.

One of the things it doesn't do simply is trigger an e-mail in the event of failure. Some people rely on this feature and that is why they might choose Cron instead.

For more information on timers see

- https://wiki.archlinux.org/index.php/Systemd/Timers

- www.freedesktop.org/software/systemd/man/systemd.time.html

- www.freedesktop.org/software/systemd/man/systemd.timer.html

Introducing Cron

There is a last type of service management we need to show you: scheduling. You may already be familiar with the Microsoft Task Scheduler, which you can use to schedule tasks to be run once or repeated regularly on a given minute, hour, day, week, or month. The equivalent in Linux is called *crontab* (short for chronograph table). Its purpose is to submit tasks at set times according to the host's clock. *Tasks* can be any script or application that you desire. Commonly, you will find maintenance-type tasks in the crontabs. These can be scheduled to run nightly, weekly, or monthly and perform some kind of script, like one that deletes all files in the /var/ log/httpd directory older than two months.

Cron jobs (the tasks that crontab performs) are defined in a series of scripts under the directories defined in the /etc/crontab file. These are referred to as *system cron jobs*. The lists of directories in the /etc/crontab file looks like this:

```
$ less /etc/crontab
SHELL=/bin/bash
PATH=/sbin:/bin:/usr/sbin:/usr/bin
MAILTO=root
HOME=/


# run-parts
01 *  * * *  root  run-parts  /etc/cron.hourly
02 4  * * *  root  run-parts  /etc/cron.daily
22 4  * * 0  root  run-parts  /etc/cron.weekly
42 4 1 * *  root  run-parts  /etc/cron.monthly
```

You should not edit this file because, being the system crontab file, it is likely to be replaced with a new version each time crontab is updated. This means any changes will be lost. Plus you could cause other problems if you make a mistake. It does, however, provide a good example of the syntax of a crontab file.

■ **Tip** When a single host is used to run a lot of virtualized servers, you should change the times cron jobs start on each virtual server to ensure they do not all start running at the same time. Having multiple virtual servers all start their daily cron tasks at the same time would impact system performance.

Listed at the top of the file are SHELL, PATH, MAILTO, and HOME environment variables, which we described in Chapter 4. Lines starting with # are comments and can be ignored. Further down the file, you can see five columns with either a number or *, a column with root, a column with run-parts, and finally a directory listing.

The first five columns represent minute, hour, day of the month, month, and day of the week. Let's look at the last line:

```
42 4 1 * * root run-parts /etc/cron.monthly
```

Here, 42 is the 42nd minute of the hour, the hour is 4 (with hours being based on a 24-hour clock), and 1 represents the first day of the month. So crontab will run the last line at 04:42 a.m. on the first day of every month.

■ **Note** You can also specify the standard three-letter abbreviations for the months, days in the month, and days of the week columns, for example, sun for Sunday and aug for August, respectively.

Any column with an asterisk (*) in it means all values are valid and are not restricted as to when to run. Let's take a look at our last line again:

```
42 4 1 * 3 root run-parts /etc/cron.monthly
```

Here we've changed the value in the day of the week column to 3. Our job would now run at 04:42 a.m. on the first day of the month and also every Wednesday.

■ **Note** Day of the week starts with Sunday at 0 and goes through to Saturday at 6. When specified with a value in the day of the month column, days are cumulative. So a job will execute on all the days listed in the day of the month column and on every weekday listed in the day of the week column.

You can also specify automatically reoccurring jobs as follows:

```
*/2 4 1 * 3 root run-parts /etc/cron.monthly
```

Here, instead of specifying an exact time to run, we have used the notation */2. This notation tells cron to run the job every time the number of minutes is cleanly divisible by 2. This allows you to do some powerful stuff. For example, you could use */4 in the hour column, and the job would run every other minute every fourth hour, like so:

```
*/2 */4 1 * * root run-parts /etc/cron.monthly
```

The use of the comma indicates a list of values, for example

```
2 0,1,2,3,4 1 * * root run-parts /etc/cron.monthly
```

This would run the job at 12:02 a.m., 1:00 a.m., 2:00 a.m., 3:00 a.m., and 4:00 a.m.

You can also specify ranges of numbers as follows:

```
2 0-4,12-16 1 * * root run-parts /etc/cron.monthly
```

Here the command would be run at 2 minutes past the hour between the hours of 12 a.m. and 4 a.m. and between 12 p.m. and 4 p.m.

The next column, root, represents the user that this program will run as. When you add your own cron jobs (or scripts), you can set this to be any valid user.

The run-parts option is the command that is being run. run-parts is a special command that will run any executable script within a specified directory. In this case, run-parts will change to the /etc/cron. hourly directory, /etc/cron.daily directory, and so on, and run the executable script it finds there.

Let's inspect one of the system cron directories, the /etc/cron.daily directory, for example, and examine one of the scripts already present on the Red Hat host. These are system crons that will run once every day unless otherwise defined.

■ **Note** You can edit the scripts in these crontab directories if you need to; however, any changes may be overwritten when your packages are updated. You can also add your own scripts in these directories to run them every hour, day, week, or month.

```
$ ls -l /etc/cron.daily/
-rwxr-xr-x 1 root root  379 Dec 19  2016 0anacron
-rwxr-xr-x 1 root root  118 Oct  1 00:06 cups
-rwxr-xr-x 1 root root  180 Oct 22  2017 logrotate
-rwxr-xr-x 1 root root  114 Jan 16  2018 rpm
-rwxr-xr-x 1 root root  290 Nov 26  2016 tmpwatch
```

Let's view one of these files, /etc/cron.daily/rpm, and see what is inside it.

```
$ less /etc/cron.daily/rpm
#!/bin/sh

/bin/rpm -qa --qf '%{name}-%{version}-%{release}.%{arch}.rpm\n' 2>&1 \
        | /bin/sort > /var/log/rpmpkgs
```

This daily executed script populates the /var/log/rpmpkgs file with a sorted list of all the RPM packages on your host.

■ **Note**   We'll discuss RPM packages further in Chapter 8.

Individual users can also create a crontab. You create and edit existing crontabs with the crontab -e command. If a crontab for your user does not exist already, this command creates a crontab file in /var/spool/cron/*username*.

The syntax used in a user's cron jobs is identical to that of the system crontab file you saw earlier, with one difference. You can only specify the user field in the system crontab file. Let's look at an example created by the user jsmith using the -l, or list, option for crontab.

```
$ crontab -l
*/2 * * * * [ -e /tmp/log ] && rm -f /tmp/log
```

You will see a list of all the cron jobs scheduled by this user. This is a simple series of commands that first check for the existence of a file called /tmp/log, and if it exists, remove it. It is set to run once every 2 minutes (*/2).

As a privileged user, you can view another person's cron by issuing the crontab command with the -u *username* option.

```
$ sudo crontab -u ataylor -l
1 2 * * * /usr/local/bin/changeLog.sh
```

You can also edit another person's cron by issuing the same crontab command and the -u *username* -e options.

```
$ sudo crontab -u ataylor -e
```

This allows you to edit the crontab for the user.

You can also remove your crontab or another user's crontab by issuing the crontab command with the -r option.

```
$ sudo crontab -u ataylor -r
```

This removes ataylor's crontab file: /var/spool/cron/ataylor.

Your host has a service that monitors the cron jobs and any changes to them. It also executes the individual jobs when they are scheduled. This service is called crond and can be started and stopped via the systemctl commands we talked about earlier.

```
$ sudo systemctl start|stop|reload cron(d if CentOS)
```

Summary

This chapter has explored how the host boots and the processes behind it like the `init` daemon. You have learned how to manage your services, how to start and stop them, and how to add and delete them from the different runlevels. You have also looked at the LSB project and got an overview of the new Upstart `init` daemon.

You should now be able to do the following:

- Describe the boot process for Linux.

- Use, configure, and secure GRUB2.

- Describe init scripts, including those using the LSB standard.

- Describe SysV, Upstart, and Systemd

- Start and stop services on Red Hat and Ubuntu.

- Understand targets and runlevels.

- Schedule tasks with crontab and Systemd Timers.

In the next chapter, we will show you how to configure your network, discuss firewalls, and introduce you to Linux security.

CHAPTER 7

■ ■ ■

Networking and Firewalls

By Dennis Matotek

So far we have shown you some of the basic features of Linux, but one of the most critical features is networking. It is via networking that your host talks to other hosts and your applications communicate with your users and the world. In this chapter, we will describe how to set up your host's networking and then how to protect that network from attackers using a firewall.

■ **Note** A *firewall* is a series of rules that control access to your host through the network.

We will teach you about how to configure your network cards or interfaces and how to give them IP (Internet Protocol) addresses. You will learn how to connect to other networks and how to troubleshoot your connections.

We will also be looking at a software application called Netfilter, which is a firewall common to all Linux distributions. You will learn how to manage a firewall and how to write firewall rules. To do this, we will introduce you to Netfilter's management interface, iptables. We will also show you how to use iptables tools like Firewalld and ufw. Finally, we will also show you how you can use TCP Wrappers to secure daemons running on your host and then set up a PPPOE (Point-to-Point Protocol over Ethernet) connection to an ISP (Internet Service Provider) with Linux.

Throughout this chapter, we will be using networking terminology. We don't expect you to be a networking expert, but we have assumed you do have some basic knowledge. If you don't feel that you know enough, we recommend you check out these sites and tutorials:

- www.tutorialspoint.com/ipv4/
- www.tutorialspoint.com/ipv6/
- http://ipv6.com/articles/general/ipv6-the-next-generation-internet.htm
- http://en.wikipedia.org/wiki/TCP/IP

■ **Note** iptables is used to protect your network services. You will learn more about how to run network services like DNS (Domain Name System) and DHCP (Dynamic Host Configuration Protocol) on your host in Chapter 9.

© Dennis Matotek, James Turnbull and Peter Lieverdink 2017
D. Matotek et al., *Pro Linux System Administration*, DOI 10.1007/978-1-4842-2008-5_7

Introduction to Networks and Networking

Networks are made of both hardware and software. They vary in complexity depending on their size and the level of interconnectedness they require. In a small business you will probably have a simple network. You may have a web server and mail server, and you will probably have a file/print server (sometimes all these servers are actually one host). Undoubtedly, you will have a connection to the Internet, and you will probably want to share that connection with others in your organization.

The nature of your business and the work you do will heavily dictate how you choose to set up your network. Many businesses these days make good use of SaaS (Software as a Service) providers to give them certain business functions such as e-mail, file storage, and access. These businesses can have simple network requirements. Alternatively a business that is starting out often has only one main server that pretty much does all the functions the business requires. It could be a DHCP, DNS, file, mail, and web server all rolled into one. Those familiar with Microsoft products would regard this as similar to a product like Windows Small Business Server. But as that business grows, it will probably begin to move some of these combined functions to its own hosts. Very few larger businesses would trust their entire company IT (information technology) infrastructure to an individual host that has so many roles. This single point of failure should to be avoided where possible, but a small business rarely has the luxury of having a host for each service it wishes to provide.

■ **Caution**   If your business does have single points of failure, like many services on one host, backup and recovery become critical. Losing your data could be a disaster for your business, so you should always have backups and the ability to recover your hosts and data. See Chapter 13 for details of how to implement a backup and recovery strategy for your organization.

Then there are the interconnecting pieces of hardware you may require. If you are connecting users in your office to a single network, you will need cables, patch panels switches, and most likely a wireless access point that can create a wireless network.

■ **Caution**   Wireless networks are a useful and cheap way to spread your network. They don't require expensive cabling and switches, and your staff can be a bit more mobile in the office. They present some challenges, however. It should be very common knowledge that wireless networks can allow attackers to connect and sniff your network if inappropriately secured, and they don't perform as well as wired networks (those with physical cables). For example, it is still much faster to transfer large amounts of data over wired connections rather than over wireless connections. If you're considering a wireless network for your business, we recommend you read the information at `http://en.wikipedia.org/wiki/Wireless_security`, `https://www.fcc.gov/consumers/guides/protecting-your-wireless-network`, and `https://www.communications.gov.au/what-we-do/internet/stay-smart-online/computers/secure-your-internet-connection`.

We're going to start by explaining how to configure networking on a single host and introduce you to the tools and commands you will need to configure a broader network.

In order to show you how to configure a network, we're going to use an example network that we have created. You can see this example network in Figure 7-1.

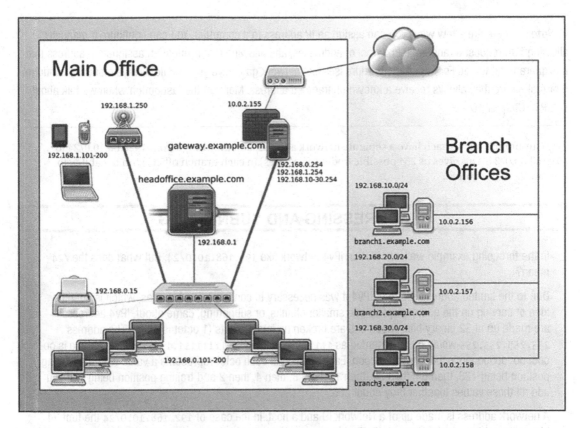

Figure 7-1. *Our example network*

Here is our complete network diagram. By the end of this chapter, this diagram will not be as daunting as it may appear now. We are going to take you through what the components of this are and how they are configured. We will also explain what all those IP addresses are for and how we can block and move from one network to another.

In this chapter, we will show you how to configure elements of our example network. We will configure a firewall/router host we're going to call gateway.example.com. It has multiple IP addresses, one for every network it acts as a router for: 192.168.0.254 on our internal network, 192.168.1.254 on our wireless network, and an external IP address of 10.0.2.155.

We will also configure a main server that we're going to call headoffice.example.com. It will have the IP address of 192.168.0.1 on our internal network. It will route to other networks, like our wireless network, branches, and the Internet via the gateway.example.com host.

As you can see, we have divided the network into separate segments, and we have chosen different network addresses to show this. As we mentioned, our wireless network has the network address of 192.168.1.0/24 and is facilitated by a wireless access point with the IP address of 192.168.1.250.

■ **Note** There are a few ways you can assign an IP address to a computer. You can configure it manually, allowing it to request a random IP in a pool of addresses, and allowing it to request an assigned IP address that it is guaranteed to get. For important IP addresses like network gateways you should always manually configure it or make sure they always receive a known guaranteed address. More on the last option when we talk about DHCP in Chapter 10.

Our branch offices each have a separate network address, and they range from 192.168.10.0/24 to 192.168.30.0/24. This gives us 254 possible nodes (or devices) in each branch office, with the ability to expand them if required.

IP ADDRESSING AND SUBNETTING

In the foregoing example we looked at an IPv4 network like 192.168.10.0/24. But what does the /24 mean?

Due to the limited address space of IPv4 it was necessary to conserve IP addresses, which is how the idea of carving up the address space into smaller chunks, or subnetting, came about. IPv4 addresses are made up of 32 binary bits. These bits are broken up into 4 octets (1 octet is 8bits). The address 255.255.255.255 would be represented as 11111111.11111111.11111111.11111111 – 0.0.0.0 is 00 000000.00000000.00000000.00000000. Each position in each octet represents a value with the leading position being 128, then 64, then 32, then 16, then 8, then 4, then 2 and trailing position being 1. If you add all those values together they equal 255.

A network address is made up of a Network ID and a host. In the case of 192.168.10.0/24 the first 24 bits of the address is the Network ID. That is represented in binary format as follows:

```
11000000.10101000.00001010
128+64.128+32+8.8+2
```

That leaves then a possible 254 possible addresses to be made out of the last octet (0 and 255 cannot be used, one being the all-zero address (or base network address) and the other being the all-ones address (or broadcast address)–these have special meaning and are reserved).

So an IPv4 address of 192.168.10.129/24 would be represented as follows:

```
11000000.10101000.00001010.10000001
128+64.128+32+8.8+2.128+1
```

With IPv6 things are slightly different, but the underlying principle is the same. Each address character you see is actually 4 bits. Meaning that the first character(f) in this local link address fe80::a00:27ff:fea4:da6b/64 is actually 1111 in binary. Each set of four characters represents 16 bits (4x4 bits) which is in total 80 bits. The full IPv6 address is 128 bits. An ISP will usually hand out a /48 address space depending on your requirements. This leaves you with 128 bits–48 bits for your available address space, or 80 bits. Considering that the whole IPv4 address space is 32 bits it is a considerable amount to work with.

It is also important to remember here that each IPv6 is intended to be world routable, unlike the private address space we are using in our IPv4 example where we have to use Source Network Address Translation (SNAT) to route our connections originating from our private address space into the world routable public address space. In the IPv6 world, your full IPv6 address is made up of your local link address and your network address and will always be unique.

As a network administrator working in IPv6, you will use the same binary calculations to determine your IPv6 subnetting, but your possible address space is now enormous!

We also have a local wired network, and this has the network address of 192.168.0.0/24. The main server, headoffice.example.com with IP address 192.168.0.1, will be able to communicate to the branch offices via the VPN networks we will establish from that host to those remote branches (we will explain VPNs in Chapter 15).

The desktops in our local wired network have been given a pool of addresses to use in a range of 192.168.0.101–192.168.0.200. This allows for 100 nodes and can be expanded upon if need be.

In reality, for a network of this size, we would probably have many more servers, and they would possibly be decentralized by placing servers in the branch offices. However, for the purpose of this chapter, we are going to concentrate on the scenario presented in Figure 7-2, in which you can see we have broken down our network into a smaller module.

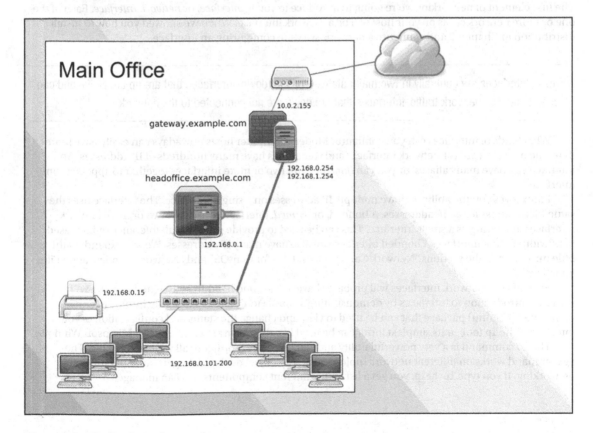

Figure 7-2. *The local wired network*

Here we can concentrate on building the principal servers for our office, gateway.example.com and headoffice.example.com.

We will show you how to set up a PPPoE connection on the gateway.example.com host to act as a firewall/router host to our ISP and the Internet.

■ **Note** PPPoE is a method used for connecting from ADSL modems to the Internet.

Our main host, headoffice.example.com, will serve mail, web, and DNS services to the public (as we will show you in Chapters 10, 11, and 12).

We will use our gateway.example.com firewall host to accept and route traffic from the Internet through our internal network to our main host. The head-office host will also provide DNS, DHCP, NTP (Network Time Protocol), SMTP (Simple Mail Transfer Protocol), IMAP (Internet Message Access Protocol), HTTP (Hypertext Transfer Protocol), and HTTPS (Hypertext Transfer Protocol Secure) services to our local network. We will also show you how to route traffic from one host to another host in our network. Let's get started by looking at setting up our interfaces.

Getting Started with Interfaces

The first element of networking we're going to introduce to you is *interface*, or *network interface*. Each of the one or more network cards on your host will be a network interface. When we showed you how to install a distribution in Chapter 2 and configure a network, we were configuring an interface.

■ **Tip** Interfaces are generally in two major states—up and down. Interfaces that are up are active and can be used to receive network traffic. Interfaces that are down are not connected to the network.

What kinds of interfaces can you configure? Modern computer hosts nowadays can easily have more than one network card (or network interface) and sometimes have many hundreds of IP addresses. An interface can have many aliases, or you can *bond* or *team* two or more interfaces together to appear as one interface.

Linux gives you the ability to have multiple IP addresses on a single interface. The interface uses the same Mac address for all IP addresses. A bonded, or *teamed*, interface consists of two or more network interfaces appearing as a single interface. This can be used to provide greater fault tolerance or increased bandwidth for the interface. A bonded interface can also have many IP addresses. We will expand on this a little further on in the sections "Network Configuration Files for CentOS" and "Network Configuration Files for Ubuntu."

Each of your network interfaces will probably have at least one IP address assigned to it. We will start this introduction to interfaces by demonstrating a simple tool called ip from the iproute (CentOS) or iproute2 (Ubuntu) package that can be used to view and change the status and configuration of your interfaces. The ip tool, in its simplest form, can be used like the ipconfig command on Microsoft Windows.

The ip command is a very powerful utility and can be used to configure all your networking. The ip command works on different network "objects." Each ip object deals with a particular part of your networking. If you type ip help, you get a list of the different components you can manage.

In Figure 7-3 we can see the output of the ip help command and you can see that we can use it to configure many parts of our networking stack. The ip command has the following basic syntax:

```
ip [ OPTIONS ] OBJECT { COMMAND | help }
```

```
jsmith@au-mel-ubuntu-1:~$ ip help
Usage: ip [ OPTIONS ] OBJECT { COMMAND | help }
       ip [ -force ] -batch filename
where  OBJECT := { link | address | addrlabel | route | rule | neighbor | ntable |
                   tunnel | tuntap | maddress | mroute | mrule | monitor | xfrm |
                   netns | l2tp | fou | tcp_metrics | token | netconf }
       OPTIONS := { -V[ersion] | -s[tatistics] | -d[etails] | -r[esolve] |
                    -h[uman-readable] | -iec |
                    -f[amily] { inet | inet6 | ipx | dnet | mpls | bridge | link } |
                    -4 | -6 | -I | -D | -B | -0 |
                    -l[oops] { maximum-addr-flush-attempts } | -br[ief] |
                    -o[neline] | -t[imestamp] | -ts[hort] | -b[atch] [filename] |
                    -rc[vbuf] [size] | -n[etns] name | -a[ll] | -c[olor]}
```

Figure 7-3. *ip help command*

The most common object you will work on are link, address, and route. Table 7-1 describes these and the rest of the objects for this command.

Table 7-1. *Describing the Full List of Objects in the ip Command*

Object	Description
link	The network device
address	The address of the interface (IPv4 or IPv6)
addrlabel	Allows you to apply labels to addresses
l2tp	Tunneling Ethernet over IP
maddress	Multicast address
monitor	Netlink message monitoring
mroute	Multicast routing cache entry
mrule	Managing rules in multicast routing policy
neighbor	ARP or NDISC cache entry
netns	Manage network namespaces
ntable	Manage the neighbor cache's operation
route	Routing table entry
rule	Rule in the routing policy database
tcp_metrics	Manage tcp metrics
tunnel	Tunnel over IP
tuntap	Manage TUN/TAP devices
xfrm	Manage IPSec policies

There are man pages for each of these objects that go further to describe their uses. For example, more information about the ip address command can be found by entering $ man ip-address. You can see all the appropriate man pages by looking at the *SEE ALSO* section of the $ man ip page.

We are now going to show you how to use the ip command to discover more about your network interfaces. To display the IP address information of all the interfaces on a host, we use this command:

```
$ ip address show
```

Running the ip command with the address show option displays all interfaces on your host and their current status and configuration. We could also use the shortened alias ip addr show.

The foregoing will list all the host interfaces and their addresses. To make it easier to explore the configuration of a particular interface, you can also display a single interface, as follows:

Listing 7-1. Status Output of ip addr show on an Active Interface

```
$ ip addr show enp0s3
2: enp0s3: <BROADCAST,MULTICAST,UP,LOWER_UP> mtu 1500 qdisc pfifo_fast state UP group
default qlen 1000
    link/ether 08:00:27:a4:da:6b brd ff:ff:ff:ff:ff:ff
    inet 192.168.0.1/24 brd 192.168.0.255 scope global enp0s3
       valid_lft forever preferred_lft forever
    inet6 fe80::a00:27ff:fea4:da6b/64 scope link
       valid_lft forever preferred_lft forever
```

The first line shows the status of the interface. The 2: is just an ordering number. The enp0s3 is the device name of the interface. In between the <> are the interface flags. BROADCAST means we can send traffic to all other hosts on the link, MULTICAST means we can send and receive multicast packets, UP means the device is functioning. LOWER_UP indicates that the cable or the underlying link is up.

In the same line we have some other information. The *state* of the interface is currently UP. This means that the interface is active and can potentially receive traffic if it is properly configured. The MTU, or maximum transmission unit, is the maximum size in bytes of packets on your network; 1,500 is the common default. The *qdisc pfifo_fast* is the queuing discipline, which is how the data is sent out to the network; this is first in, first out and the default. You can also group interfaces together and perform actions on them; this shows that ours is in the default group. Finally *qlen* is the Ethernet buffer transmit queue length and it can be referred as the speed of your network card, 1,000 mbits in this case.

The output also shows three important pieces of information, the ipv4 address, the ipv6, address and the MAC (Media Access Control) address of this host. It has an IP address assigned to it, inet 192.168.0.1, and we explain that shortly. The next line is an IPv6 address, here inet6 fe80::a00:27ff:fea4:da6b/64, that is a *link-local* IPv6 address derived from the MAC address. Every Ethernet network card has a unique hardware identifier that is used to identify it and communicate with other Ethernet devices. This *MAC address* can be seen in first line of output (link/ether 08:00:27:a4:da:6b in this example).

■ **Note**   See https://wiki.ubuntu.com/IPv6 or www.internetsociety.org/deploy360/ipv6/basics/ for more information on IPv6.

The IPv6 address can be used to communicate with other hosts using *stateless address autoconfiguration (SLAAC)*. SLAAC is used quite often by devices like PDAs and mobile phones and requires a less complicated infrastructure to communicate with other devices on the local network. This is because each SLAAC IPv6 address is intended to be world routable and is combined with the network address to make a universally unique address.

■ **Note**   See http://www.ipv6.com/articles/general/Stateless-Auto-Configuration.htm for more information on stateless autoconfiguration and IPv6.

In the next example we are going to look at a network device we have just attached to our host. This does not currently have an IP address associated with it:

```
$ ip addr show
3: enp0s8: <BROADCAST,MULTICAST> mtu 1500 qdisc noop state DOWN group default qlen 1000
    link/ether 08:00:27:13:3c:00 brd ff:ff:ff:ff:ff:ff
```

Comparing it to our previous output you can immediately notice that the *state* is DOWN and that we can only see a *MAC* address that has been assigned to the network device enp0s8. Let's now see what happens when we bring up the device or *link*. We do that by using the following ip link subcommand and then ip addr show enp0s8:

```
$ sudo ip link set dev enp0s8 up
...
3: enp0s8: <BROADCAST,MULTICAST,UP,LOWER_UP> mtu 1500 qdisc pfifo_fast state UP group
default qlen 1000
    link/ether 08:00:27:13:3c:00 brd ff:ff:ff:ff:ff:ff
    inet6 fe80::a00:27ff:fe13:3c00/64 scope link
      valid_lft forever preferred_lft forever
```

Device enp0s8 now is UP and has been assigned a qdisc (pfifo_fast). Interestingly we also have an IPv6-generated IP address, which is based on the MAC address that is assigned.

To bring down the interface, you would use the following:

```
$ sudo ip link set dev enp0s8 down
```

You can validate what you have down by issuing the following command which provides just the link status:

```
$ sudo ip link show enp0s8
3: enp0s8: <BROADCAST,MULTICAST> mtu 1500 qdisc pfifo_fast state DOWN mode DEFAULT group
default qlen 1000
    link/ether 08:00:27:13:3c:00 brd ff:ff:ff:ff:ff:ff
```

Let's now add an IPv4 address to our network device. We have checked on our network and IP address 192.168.10.1 is available. Let's add that to device enp0s8.

```
$ sudo ip addr add 192.168.10.1/24 dev enp0s8
```

Looking at the result of $ sudo ip addr show enp0s8 we see that we have the following line added to our output:

```
    inet 192.168.10.1/24 scope global enp0s8
```

This what we expect, but the status is still down, so we would now issue the following command:

```
$ sudo ip link set dev enp0s8 up
```

And on viewing the output of `ip addr show enp0s8` again, it will now be in the UP state and ready to send and receive traffic on the at interface. It should now look similar to Listing 7-1.

We can also remove an interface. When we "down" a link, we don't remove the IP address. To do that we would issue the following:

```
$ sudo ip addr del 192.168.10.1/24 dev enp0s8
```

The link is still up and the IPv4 address has gone if you now show the interface. You should notice that the IPv6 address will be available as long as the link is UP. To disable the IPv6 interface you will need to down the link.

■ **Note**   Changes to your interfaces using the ip command are not persistent across reboots; when you reboot, you will lose any changes. We will explain shortly how to permanently apply your changes to your host.

Managing Interfaces

As we have said, using the `ip` command is good for adding and managing interfaces on the fly, but we need to also be able to permanently configure interfaces too. There are several ways to do that on Linux. You can choose to either use the graphical user interfaces (GUIs) or run directly from the command line. You can also write directly to network files if you wish.

CentOS and Ubuntu can manage networking differently. CentOS now uses NetworkManager to manage its networks. Ubuntu can use NetworkManager but it is not installed by default. NetworkManager is a daemon process that manages the network connections and services. It is installed on Ubuntu as part of the Unity desktop or you can install it on its own. NetworkManager will integrate with the older style (LSB) files for managing network interfaces too via a LSB network service.

NetworkManager integrates and configures Domain Name System (DNS) resolution via the Dnsmasq program (a local DNS server) and handles configuring and setting up VPN and wireless connections.

We talked about systemd and about about the multi-user.target in Chapter 6 and this is what brings up the NetworkManager. NetworkManager has plug-ins that give it the ability to manage your network configuration files. These are `ifcfg-rh` and `ifupdown` which handle Red Hat-style and Debian-style scripts, respectively. You can disable the management of your interfaces via NetworkManager in Red Hat-style hosts by setting the `NM_CONTROLLED='no'` in the network connection profile file (explained shortly). In Debian-style hosts NetworkManager is disabled for managing interfaces listed in `/etc/network/interfaces` unless you specifically change the following in the `/etc/NetworkManager/NetworkManager.conf` to:

```
[ifupdown]
managed=true
```

Some people choose not to run NetworkManager because they find it too intrusive and they prefer to manage their networks themselves. NetworkManager was conceived to make networking "just work" and your mileage may vary, but a lot of work has gone into it since its inception and it is definitely much better than it was when it started out.

NetworkManager also provides some CLI (command-line interface) programs to help manage your configuration.

- nmcli–controls and reports status of NetworkManager
- nmtui–text-based user interface for managing NetworkManager

We are going to show you more on nmcli and nmtui later in this Chapter. For more information on NetworkManager, you can see the following:

- https://help.ubuntu.com/community/NetworkManager
- https://access.redhat.com/documentation/en-US/Red_Hat_Enterprise_
  Linux/7/html/Networking_Guide/sec-Introduction_to_NetworkManager.html

Managing Networks via a GUI

If you are using a desktop to manage your server you can use a GUI to manage your network configuration. With CentOS we access the networking settings via the *Applications* ➤ *System Tools* ➤ *Settings*.

In Figure 7-4 we can see the configured networks on our system. In the left-hand panel you can select the devices that attached to the system, here our network interface is called "Wired." The gear cog in the bottom right allows you to access the configuration. You can turn on or off the interface with the on-off toggle button. If you wish to add another type of interface, like teamed or bonded or VPN interface, you should select the + at the bottom of the left panel.

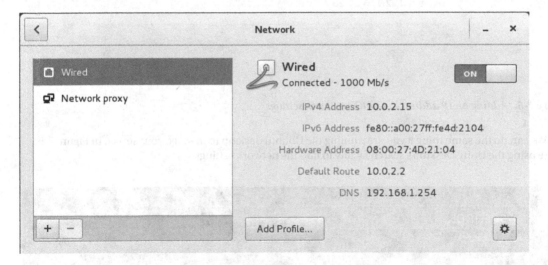

Figure 7-4. CentOS network settings

If we were to add a new interface and come there to configure it, we will see the interfaces listed in the left panel by their device names, like enp0s8. If you choose to configure one of the interfaces you can see that the options are similar to what we saw when we were installing our server.

We have seen this before; in Figure 7-5 we are adding the 192.168.10.1 address. Again we can choose to manually configure the interface, or allow it to be configured via DHCP with the drop-down option.

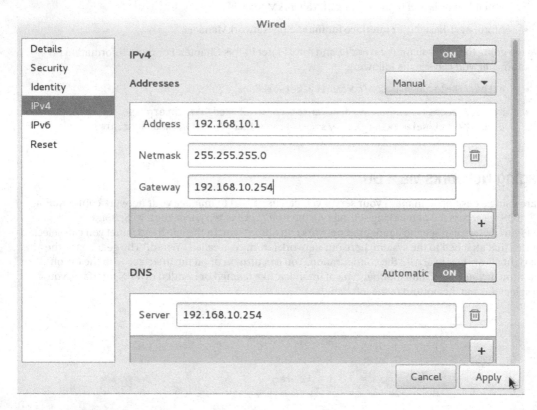

Figure 7-5. *Adding an IP address in CentOS network settings*

We can do the same thing if you are running the Ubuntu desktop to manage your server. In Figure 7-6 we are using the Unity Desktop's search facility to find the network settings.

Figure 7-6. *Network settings in Ubuntu*

On selecting Network in Figure 7-6 we get a similar user interface to configure our networks as we did with CentOS. In Figure 7-7 we can see that you plug in the same information in to this interface as we did in Figure 7-5.

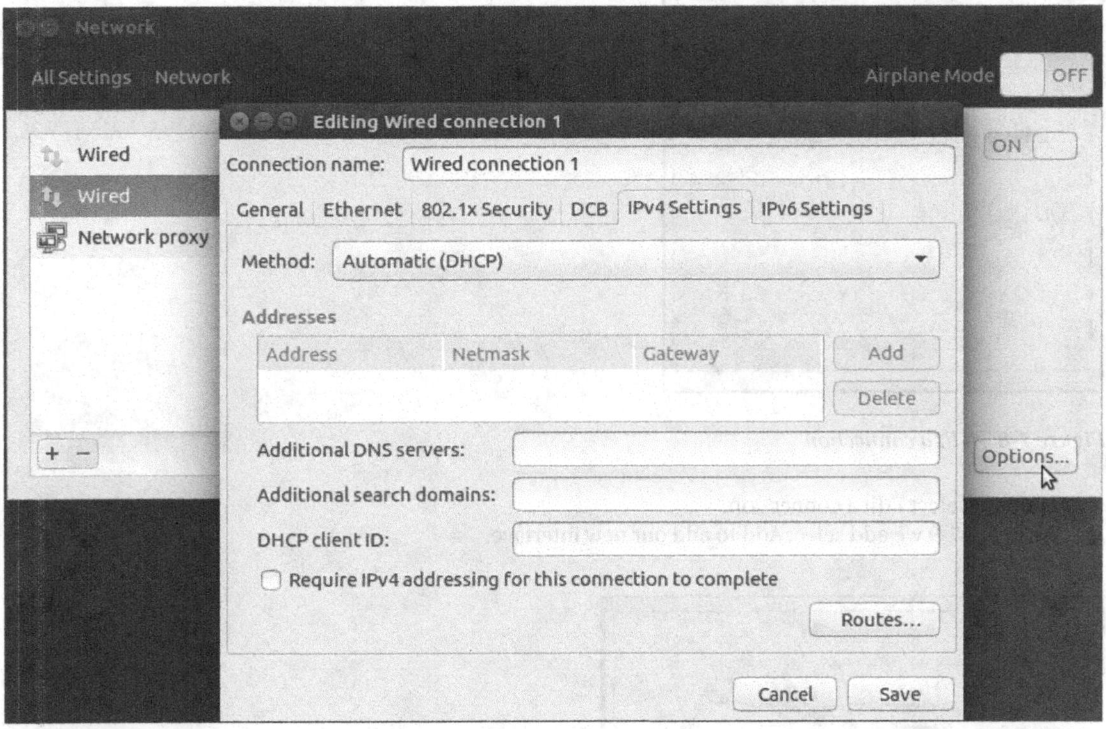

Figure 7-7. *Configuring a network interface in Ubuntu*

In Figure 7-7 we again can choose to use DHCP or manually configure the interface. Using the user interface to configure your network interfaces persist across reboots.

Let's now view the other way to persist the network configuration with network configuration files and scripts.

Configure Interfaces with nmtui

The curses-based configuration tool that comes with NetworkManager is designed to work on any type of terminal. You can create and manage interfaces as well as set the hostname via this terminal user interface (tui).

In this exercise we are going to run through the nmtui program to configure our newly attached enp0s8 Ethernet device. We can find the device name for our new interface with the use of dmesg.

```
$ sudo dmesg |grep enp
[    6.903532] IPv6: ADDRCONF(NETDEV_UP): enp0s8: link is not ready
```

We will use this information shortly. To start it you issue $ sudo nmtui.

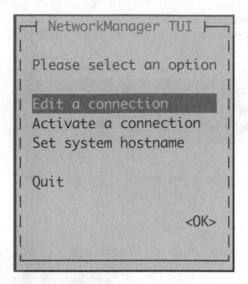

Figure 7-8. *Edit a connection*

Here we select Edit a connection.

In Figure 7-9 we add select Add to add our new interface.

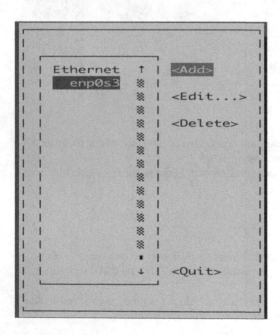

Figure 7-9. *Add a connection*

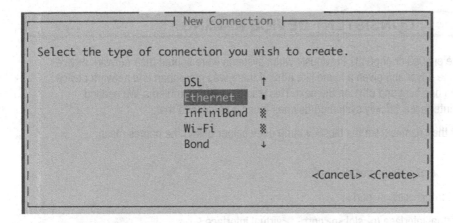

Figure 7-10. *Type of interface, Ethernet*

Here we select the type of interface we wish to add. There are several options to choose, including DSL for connecting to your ISP, Wi-Fi, and others like VLAN and team interfaces. We are going to select Ethernet.

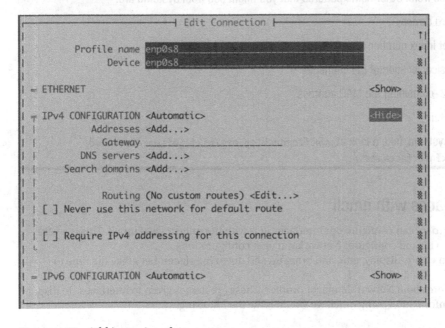

Figure 7-11. *Add in our interface*

We have provided a profile name; this name can be anything you wish, but it can often be helpful to name it something meaningful as you can use this profile name when working with the sister command, nmcli. In our case we have just named it the same as the device name which we have added to the Device section.

We can set an IP address or we can allow our interface to receive one from a DHCP server, which is what we decided to do. However, adding the IP address is simply like we have done previously. We can arrow down to <OK> and exit.

CONSISTENT DEVICE NAMING

What's with the name enpOs3 or enpOs8? Previously when systems were booted their network devices would be probed by the driver and given a name like ethO. If there was more than one network device ethO might be ethO on one boot and eth1 on the next. This lead to obvious problems. We needed predictable network interfaces. Luckily systemd/udev has found a solution to that.

Devices can now get their names from the biosdevname udev helper utility. The names mean something.

- em[1,2,3...] – embedded network interface

- p1p1 – PCI card (p<slot>p<port>)

- p2p1_1 – Virtual interface (p<slot>p<port>_<virtual interface>

Different hardware vendors have this enabled by default and some don't. You can set it to enabled on the boot command line with biosdevname=0 (or 1 to disable).

Systemd provides a fallback from this if the biosdevname is not available. This is where our device name of enpOs8 comes from. Other name patterns that you might see from systemd are:

- eno1–onboard devices

- ens1–PCI slot index number

- enpOs8–physical location of the connector

- enx7f291992–combining the MAC address

- ethO–the classic

For a closer read on systemd, take a look at `www.freedesktop.org/wiki/Software/systemd/ PredictableNetworkInterfaceNames/`.

Configuring Interfaces with nmcli

There is yet another way to we can configure our interfaces. It is with the utility called nmcli. This is a very powerful tool that works with and configures NetworkManager configurations.

With this tool we can create, display, edit, and bring up and down interfaces. Let's take the time to explore this utility first.

We have spoken before about NetworkManager profiles. These are names given to interfaces. To display the current connection information using nmcli we would issue the following:

```
$ sudo nmcli connection show
NAME        UUID                                      TYPE            DEVICE
enpOs3      da717740-45eb-4c45-b324-7d78006bb657      802-3-ethernet  enpOs3
```

There are several shortcuts for nmcli, like "c" for connection and "d" for device. To manage the actual device (connect, disconnect, delete) you use the device subcommands.

```
$ sudo nmcli d status
DEVICE  TYPE      STATE        CONNECTION
enp0s3  ethernet  connected    enp0s3
lo      loopback  unmanaged    --
```

The nmcli command takes the following format:

```
$ nmcli <OPTIONS> <OBJECT> <COMMAND|HELP>
```

So if you need help to remember how to use the add command on the connection object you can type

```
$ nmcli connection add help
Usage: nmcli connection add { ARGUMENTS | help }
....
```

What we are going to do next is add a team interface to our CentOS host. A team interface is an aggregated interface made up of two or more links. It can provide greater throughput or link redundancy than a single interface. It can support active/passive, LACP (Link Aggregation Control Protocol), and VLANs (Virtual Local Area Networks) and other protocols.

A teaming has two main parts, a teamd daemon and runners. The teamd daemon manages the API (application programming interface) between the network interfaces and the kernel. The runners are another word for modules that provide the code that implements the particular features, like active/passive and VLANs.

We are going add two devices to create a team interface with an active/passive runner. These will be enp0s8 and enp0s9.

```
$ sudo nmcli device status
DEVICE  TYPE      STATE         CONNECTION
enp0s8  ethernet  disconnected  --
enp0s9  ethernet  disconnected  --
```

To begin we add the team interface (team0) with the command in Listing 7-2.

Listing 7-2. Adding team0 Interface

```
$ sudo nmcli c add type team con-name team0 ifname team0 config ↵
 '{"device": "team0", "runner": {"name":"activebackup"}}' ip4 192.168.10.10 gw4
192.168.10.254
```

In Listing 7-2 we have used the nmcli command to add a team interface and assigned it the IP address 192.168.10.10 and the gateway address of 192.168.10.254. We did this by adding (add) a connection (c) type of team. We have given this interface the name of team0 (ifname) and a profile name of team0 (con-name) also.

With a teamed interface we need to provide a JSON configuration to describe the runner we wish to use. This can either be in a JSON file or on the command line as we have above. There are further examples of the settings that you can use in man 5 teamd.conf. In Listing 7-2 we have provided the minimum required and that is the device and the runner.

What this creates is a file called /etc/sysconfig/network-scripts/ifcfg-team0 and we can see that that has the following details:

```
DEVICE=team0
TEAM_CONFIG="{\"device\": \"team0\", \"runner\": {\"name\":\"activebackup\"}}"
DEVICETYPE=Team
BOOTPROTO=none
IPADDR=192.168.10.10
PREFIX=32
GATEWAY=192.168.10.254
DEFROUTE=yes
IPV4_FAILURE_FATAL=no
IPV6INIT=yes
IPV6_AUTOCONF=yes
IPV6_DEFROUTE=yes
IPV6_PEERDNS=yes
IPV6_PEERROUTES=yes
IPV6_FAILURE_FATAL=no
NAME=team0
UUID=2cef1621-4e56-4cb8-84f7-2d613fbc168f
ONBOOT=yes
```

We will explain these configuration files shortly, you can see our setting for the team configuration and IP address. We have created the "master" interface and we now have to add "slaves" to it.

We do this with the following commands:

```
$ sudo nmcli c add type team-slave con-name team0-port1 ifname enp0s8 master team0
Connection 'team0-port1' (4e2f4307-e026-4b1a-b19e-da8f1ad64d7a) successfully added.
$ sudo nmcli c add type team-slave con-name team0-port2 ifname enp0s9 master team0
Connection 'team0-port2' (ca1206ce-c0d3-45a5-b793-f10b8c680414) successfully added.
```

Again we have added a type of team-slave with a connection name of team-port{1,2} and attached these to interface enp0s{8,9} to master team0. Let's take a look at one of the files that this creates.

```
/etc/sysconfig/network-scripts/ifcfg-team0-port1
NAME=team0-port1
UUID=4e2f4307-e026-4b1a-b19e-da8f1ad64d7a
DEVICE=enp0s8
ONBOOT=yes
TEAM_MASTER=team0
DEVICETYPE=TeamPort
```

And now let's see if they show up in our connection list.

```
$ sudo nmcli c show
NAME          UUID                                   TYPE            DEVICE
team0-port1   4e2f4307-e026-4b1a-b19e-da8f1ad64d7a   802-3-ethernet  enp0s8
team0         2cef1621-4e56-4cb8-84f7-2d613fbc168f   team            team0
team0-port2   ca1206ce-c0d3-45a5-b793-f10b8c680414   802-3-ethernet  enp0s9
```

And the device list now looks as follows:

```
$ sudo nmcli d status
[sudo] password for jsmith:
DEVICE  TYPE      STATE      CONNECTION
enpOs8  ethernet  connected  teamO-port1
enpOs9  ethernet  connected  teamO-port2
teamO   team      connected  teamO
lo      loopback  unmanaged  --
```

We will quickly see if we can get a ping response from the interface.

```
$ ping 192.168.10.10
PING 192.168.10.10 (192.168.10.10) 56(84) bytes of data.
64 bytes from 192.168.10.10: icmp_seq=1 ttl=64 time=0.047 ms
```

So now we have a team interface. You can also manage team interfaces with team tools like teamctl and teamnl. Let's go on to see more on the configuration files.

Configuring Networks with Network Scripts

Both CentOS and Ubuntu have their network configuration files stored in the /etc directory. CentOS stores its files in a collection of network-related directories under /etc/sysconfig/network-scripts, and Ubuntu stores its files under the /etc/networks directory.

Network Configuration Files for CentOS

As we have said previously, CentOS uses NetworkManager to manage network interfaces as they are plugged in or connect. The CentOS files relating to networking can be found under the /etc/sysconfig directory. The main places to find this information are

- The /etc/sysconfig/network file
- The /etc/sysconfig/network-scripts directory

The /etc/sysconfig/network file contains global settings and can contain things like HOSTNAME and default GATEWAY. The /etc/sysconfig/network-scripts directory contains all the start-up and shutdown scripts for network interfaces. These files are general copies of files in the /etc/sysconfig/ network-script directory and are created for you by the system-config-network tool.

Taking a look at the contents of the /etc/sysconfig/network-scripts directory, you will see the files shown in Listing 7-3.

Listing 7-3. Files Found in /etc/sysconfig/network-scripts

```
$ sudo ls /etc/sysconfig/network-scripts/
ifcfg-enpOs3 ifdown-ipv6  ifdown-ppp ifdown-tunnel
ifup-ipv6 ifup-routes  ifup-wireless network-functions-ipv6
ifcfg-lo ifdown-eth ifdown-routes ifup ifup-eth ifup-post
init.ipv6-global ifdown ifdown-post ifup-aliases
ifup-ppp ifup-tunnel  network-functions
```

In Listing 7-3, you can see a reduced list of the scripts that are used to configure your interfaces and bring them up or down. A variety of files are present.

The files like `ifcfg-enpOs3` are configuration files, or connection profiles, for the Ethernet interfaces. The files with the naming convention of `if<action>-device`, for example, `ifdown-ppp`, are scripts that are used to control the state (i.e., bring the interface up or down).

We talked about NetworkManager previously. NetworkManager, if it is configured to do so, will read and write to these files. The configuration profile files, like `ifcfg-enpOs3`, are read in by NetworkManager and will pass off the device name to the `ifup` script. If the device is already connected and managed by NetworkManager, `ifup` will use the `nmcli` to manage the interface. If we have `NM_CONTROLLED="no"`, then `ifup` will use the `ip` command to manage the interface. Before doing so, it checks to see if this device is already managed by the NetworkManager and if so, it does not attempt to manage the device. To bring up the enpOs3 device you issue the following:

```
$ ifup enpOs3
```

Files like `network-functions` are scripts can that contain functions and variables. Other scripts can source (or include) the functions and variables from `network-functions` and use them in their scripts.

Let's take a look at the configuration file for enpOs3, which is called `ifcfg-enpOs3`. You can see the contents of this file in Listing 7-4.

Listing 7-4. The `ifcfg-enpOs3` File

```
$ sudo less /etc/sysconfig/network-scripts/ifcfg-enpOs3
TYPE="Ethernet"
DEVICE="enpOs3"
NAME="enpOs3"
UUID="fa56e72e-ea22-43ca-9a90-e19d64c0c431"
ONBOOT="yes"
BOOTPROTO="dhcp"
DEFROUTE="yes"
PEERDNS="yes"
PEERROUTES="yes"
IPV4_FAILURE_FATAL="no"
IPV6INIT="yes"
IPV6_AUTOCONF="yes"
IPV6_DEFROUTE="yes"
IPV6_PEERDNS="yes"
IPV6_PEERROUTES="yes"
IPV6_FAILURE_FATAL="no"
```

In Listing 7-4, you can see a number of configuration options in the form of *option=argument*. To configure a CentOS interface we set options like the name of device we are managing: DEVICE="enpOs3". We use the same value for the name.

The boot protocol, BOOTPROTO="dhcp", is set to get its address from DHCP. The UUID (universal unique identifier) of the device is "fa56e72e-ea22-43ca-9a90-e19d64c0c431", and this is a unique identifier assigned to this device and is used by the NetworkManager to map the device. You can declare whether the interface will initialize at boot up by specifying ONBOOT="yes". The type of interface is declared by TYPE="Ethernet". If you don't want to initialize our interface with an IPv6 address you can set *IPV6INIT* to "no"; here it is the default IPV6INIT="yes". When PEERDNS="yes" is declared, it means that /etc/resolv.conf file with name servers provided by the DHCP server. If we set it to no, /etc/resolv.conf will remain unmodified when this interface is brought to an up state. We will explain more about how this works in Chapter 10.

Table 7-2 lists the options you can use in your CentOS interface files.

Table 7-2. *Some of the Common Network Configuration File Options, CentOS*

Option	Description
DEVICE	The name of the device you are creating. This will appear in the interface listings.
BOOTPROTO	The protocol to use when the device starts up. The choices here are static, dhcp, and none.
ONBOOT	Whether the device is started when the host boots up.
NETWORK	The network address for this device.
NETMASK	The netmask for this device.
IPADDR	The IP address for this device.
IPV4_FAILURE_FATAL	If set to yes, if we don't get an IP address from DHCP the ifup-eth script will end immediately
MASTER	The device to which this device is the SLAVE.
SLAVE	Whether the device is controlled by the master specified in the MASTER directive.
NM_CONTROLLED	If set tono, Network manager ignores the device. The default is yes on CentOS.
DNS{1,2}	DNS host's IP address (multiple addresses are comma separated). This will be added to /etc/resolv.conf if PEERDNS is set to yes.
PEERDNS	Setting that determines whether DNS hosts specified in DNS are added to /etc/resolv.conf. If set to yes, they are added. If no, they are not added.
VLAN	Set this device as a VLAN interface ('yes', 'no')
IPV6INIT	Enable or disable the IPv6 configuration for this device.

The options in Table 7-2 are just some of what can be set in your network connection profile; for a full list of the options you can read the /usr/share/doc/initscripts-<version>/sysconfig.txt, where <version> is the version number of the initscripts package.

Creating Bonded Interfaces

We are now going to take you through how to manually configure a bonded Ethernet device by setting some options in the connection profile file. A bonded Ethernet device can also be referred to as a *trunk* device. Bonding allows you to use two or more Ethernet ports to act as one interface, giving you expanded bandwidth and some redundancy. In this way you can turn a 1 GiB link into a 2 GiB link for the one virtual interface.

So how would we do this feat? We have two devices attached to our host, enp0s8 and enp0s9. We are going to bond these two devices together so that they appear as one interface, bond0. First we have to configure each device as a SLAVE, and in Listing 7-5 you can see how we have configured enp0s8. The enp0s9 device will be a mirror of this device.

Listing 7-5. The enp0s8 Slave Device Configuration

```
$ less  /etc/sysconfig/network-scripts/ifcfg-enp0s8
DEVICE="enp0s8"
NAME="bond0-slave"
TYPE="Ethernet"
ONBOOT="yes"
BOOTPROTO="none"
SLAVE="yes"
MASTER="bond0"
```

This is a very simple configuration. We have specified the device we wish to control, enp0s8, and whether we would like it to initialize when we boot up our host by specifying ONBOOT="yes". The IP address for this bonded device will attach itself to the bond0 device, not to enp0s8 or enp0s9; therefore, we do not specify a boot protocol here and use the option BOOTPROTO="none", instead. The NAME="bond0-slave" will become clear when we bring up our bonded interface, but it provides an easy-to-read name that NetworkManager will display (remembering that unless we explicitly have NM_CONTROLLED="no", NetworkManager will manage our connection).

Next are the two options that add this device to a bonded configuration. The first, SLAVE="yes", declares that this device is to be a slave. Next, we declare to which master it belongs by specifying MASTER="bond0". The bond0 we are referring to is a device of the same name that we are about to create.

Interface enp0s9 (which is configured in the /etc/sysconfig/network-scripts/ifcfg-enp0s9 file), as we said, will mirror the copy and paste the details from enp0s8. Then we need to change the DEVICE=enp0s8 to DEVICE=enp0s9. The rest can stay the same.

Next we will create our bond0 device file. On CentOS, the configuration details will be kept in a file called /etc/sysconfig/network-scripts/ifcfg-bond0. In Listing 7-6, you see what we need to create a bonded interface.

Listing 7-6. Configuration for a Bonded Interface

```
[jsmith@au-mel-centos-1~]$ vi /etc/sysconfig/network-scripts/ifcfg-bond0
DEVICE="bond0"
NAME="bond0"
TYPE="bond"
BONDING_MASTER="yes"
BONDING_OPTS="mode=1 delayup=0 delaydown=0 miimon=100"
BOOTPROTO="none"
ONBOOT="yes"
NETWORK="192.168.0.0"
NETMASK="255.255.255.0"
IPADDR="192.168.0.1"
```

As you can see, it is very similar to a standard Ethernet device file. You need to specify the device name, bond0 in our example, and give it the appropriate network information like its IP address, network, and netmask information. Again, we want this device to be initialized at boot-up.

There are some bonding-specific options listed in Listing 7-6, like BONDING_MASTER and BONDING_OPTS. BONDING_MASTER is fairly straightforward and just means that this is a bonding master interface. BONDING_OPTS allow you to set per interface bonding options to your interface. Let's look at what we have set in the above.

Mode 1 sets the interface bonding type to active backup, and you can use "mode=active-backup" instead of "mode=1" if you prefer. With active backup, when the active interface fails, the other takes over. This primarily for network card redundancy and not throughput. The miimon is how often (in milliseconds) the interfaces are checked for being active. In high-availability configurations, when miimon notices that one interface is down, it will activate the remaining interface(s). The delayup and delaydown are settings giving the time period in milliseconds where we should wait to act on changes in the slave state. We have set these to zero and over time we would adjust these as was deemed necessary.

Depending on your network and what kind of bonding you can implement given your network equipment, you can add other options here to give fault tolerance, redundancy, and round-robin features to your bonded device. For more information, you can look at the documentation provided by the iputils package that manages bonding on CentOS hosts, specifically the /usr/share/doc/iputils-<version>/ README.bonding.

What happens when you interface comes up is that your scripts (NetworkManager or ifup-eth scripts) will insert the bonding module into the kernel. The bonding module allows the kernel to know how to handle bonded interfaces and it can be also be referred to as a driver for the kernel. The low-level tools that manage bonding interfaces, like ifenslave from the iputils package, require the bonding module to be loaded prior to bonding your interface. If you want to check to see if your bonding module is already loaded in the kernel you can issue the following, and if it is, you will see something like this:

```
$ lsmod |grep bonding
bonding     136705   0
```

If it is not, don't worry. We will check again after we bring up our interfaces. You can use the modprobe command to insert the bonding module if you wish.

```
sudo /usr/sbin/modprobe bonding
```

■ **Tip** The modprobe command is the smarter way to insert modules (instead of the insmod command) into the kernel as it handles dependencies.

We are now going to bring up the bond0 device or master interface. It is important to follow the starting order of your interfaces; for instance, when you start the master interface first, your slave interfaces *are not* automatically started, but when you start your slave interface, your master *is* automatically started. We are setting a static IP address, and our master will start IP connections and respond to "ping" even though the slave interfaces are not up. In DHCP, the master will not get an IP until the slaves are up. Also, remember that NetworkManager is going to manage these interfaces so we will begin using some of the nmcli commands to show our connections but you can also use the ip command we saw earlier.

When we make changes to our interface scripts, like ifcfg-enp0s8, we need to tell NetworkManager to reread it. We can be specific about the interface file to reread but in this case we are going to get it reread all of them by issuing

```
$ sudo nmcli connection reload
```

■ **Tip** This can be shortened to nmcli c r as many of the commands can just take the first letter of the subcommand.

Let's now check the current state of our interfaces. With nmcli we issue the following:

```
$ sudo nmcli device status
DEVICE  TYPE      STATE         CONNECTION
enp0s8  ethernet  disconnected  --
enp0s9  ethernet  disconnected  --
```

This shows our devices are currently in the disconnected state. We are now going to bring up our master (bond0) interface by starting our slave interfaces. We can do this via the nmcli command too as follows:

```
$ sudo nmcli device connect enp0s8
Device 'enp0s8' successfully activated with '00cb8299-feb9-55b6-a378-3fdc720e0bc6'.

$ sudo nmcli device status
DEVICE  TYPE      STATE         CONNECTION
bond0   bond      connected     bond0
enp0s3  ethernet  connected     enp0s3
enp0s8  ethernet  connected     bond0-slave
enp0s9  ethernet  disconnected  --
lo      loopback  unmanaged     --

$ sudo nmcli device connect enp0s9

$ sudo nmcli device status
DEVICE  TYPE      STATE         CONNECTION
bond0   bond      connected     bond0
enp0s3  ethernet  connected     enp0s3
enp0s8  ethernet  connected     bond0-slave
enp0s9  ethernet  connected     bond0-slave
lo      loopback  unmanaged     --
```

Our first command was issued to connect our enp0s8 device. When that connection can up so did our bond0 device but our enp0s9 device was still disconnected. We then brought up our enp0s9 device.

And just quickly, we can validate that our bonding driver has been loaded into the kernel by issuing the following again:

```
$ lsmod |grep bonding
bonding    136705  0
```

If we wanted to bring down the bond interface we could issue the following:

```
$ sudo nmcli connection down  bond0
Connection 'bond0' successfully deactivated (D-Bus active path: /org/freedesktop/
NetworkManager/ActiveConnection/6)

$ sudo nmcli device status
DEVICE  TYPE      STATE         CONNECTION
enp0s3  ethernet  connected     enp0s3
enp0s8  ethernet  disconnected  --
enp0s9  ethernet  disconnected  --
```

You can see here that bringing down the bond0 interface has disconnected the two slaves as well.

We can also view your new bonded device by issuing the /sbin/ip addr show command, which will produce the following output:

```
3: enp0s8: <BROADCAST,MULTICAST,SLAVE,UP,LOWER_UP> ←
mtu 1500 qdisc pfifo_fast master bond0 state UP qlen 1000
    link/ether 08:00:27:71:c3:d8 brd ff:ff:ff:ff:ff:ff
4: enp0s9: <BROADCAST,MULTICAST,SLAVE,UP,LOWER_UP> ←
mtu 1500 qdisc pfifo_fast master bond0 state UP qlen 1000
    link/ether 08:00:27:71:c3:d8 brd ff:ff:ff:ff:ff:ff
8: bond0: <BROADCAST,MULTICAST,MASTER,UP,LOWER_UP> ←
mtu 1500 qdisc noqueue state UP
    link/ether 08:00:27:71:c3:d8 brd ff:ff:ff:ff:ff:ff
    inet 192.168.0.1/24 brd 192.168.0.255 scope global bond0
       valid_lft forever preferred_lft forever
    inet6 fe80::a00:27ff:fe71:c3d8/64 scope link
       valid_lft forever preferred_lft forever
```

If you look at the interface description of enp0s8 and enp0s9, you can see that they are both set to SLAVE, and you can see that bond0 is set to MASTER. Neither slave has an IP address associated with it. It is the bond0 interface that has the IP address associated with it.

Adding Multiple IP Addresses to Interfaces

We can add multiple addresses to an interface. They do not have to be in the same network and can be used to route traffic from different networks across your host. To do this we can edit our network profile. Let's again look at our CentOS host and its enp0s3 profile.

We can use the nmcli command to do this. To do that we have to modify an existing interface. First we see the available interfaces with the following:

```
$ sudo nmcli c s
enp0s3      da717740-45eb-4c45-b324-7d78006bb657  802-3-ethernet  enp0s3
```

Take note of the device uuid (da717740-45eb-4c45-b324-7d78006bb657), we can use that to refer to our interface. We are going to use the connection object to modify our interface and add multiple IP addresses as follows:

```
sudo nmcli con mod da717740-45eb-4c45-b324-7d78006bb657 ipv4.addresses '192.168.14.10/24,
172.10.2.1/16, 10.2.2.2/8'
```

If we now look inside the /etc/sysconfig/network-script/ifcfg-enp0s3 file we can see we have our IP addresses added.

```
TYPE=Ethernet
BOOTPROTO=dhcp
DEFROUTE=yes
<snip>
NAME=enp0s3
UUID=da717740-45eb-4c45-b324-7d78006bb657
DEVICE=enp0s3
ONBOOT=yes
```

```
<snip>
IPV6_PEERROUTES=yes
IPADDR=192.168.14.10
PREFIX=24
IPADDR1=172.10.2.1
PREFIX1=16
IPADDR2=10.2.2.2
PREFIX2=8
```

Here you can see we have added two IPv4 addresses, IPADDR, IPADDR1 and IPADDR2. We can use the PREFIX, PREFIX1, and PREFIX2 to provide the network mask.

To refresh the interface to bring it up with the new addresses. We do that with nmcli too.

```
$ sudo nmcli con up enp0s3
Connection successfully activated (D-Bus active path: /org/freedesktop/NetworkManager/
ActiveConnection/2685)
```

We can now see the new addresses as follows:

```
$ ip addr show enp0s3 |grep inet
    inet 10.0.2.15/24 brd 10.0.2.255 scope global dynamic enp0s3
    inet 192.168.14.10/24 brd 192.168.14.255 scope global enp0s3
    inet 172.10.2.1/16 brd 172.10.255.255 scope global enp0s3
    inet 10.2.2.2/8 brd 10.255.255.255 scope global enp0s3
    inet6 fe80::a00:27ff:feb2:9245/64 scope link
```

The other way to add an alias is to use a script to assign IP addresses when your host boots up. We can add something like this into our rc.local file:

```
/etc/rc.d/rc.local
/sbin/ip addr add 192.168.0.24/24 brd 192.168.0.255 dev enp0s3
/sbin/ip addr add 192.168.0.25/24 brd 192.168.0.255 dev enp0s3
/sbin/ip addr add 192.168.0.26/24 brd 192.168.0.255 dev enp0s3
```

In the foregoing we are adding the IPv4 addresses 192.168.0.24-26 to our enp0s3 address when our host is rebooted. The /etc/rc.d/rc.local file needs to have the execute bit set (chmod +x rc.local) and because we are running systemd and not SysVInit we need to make sure that systemd will execute it when we restart our system. If you remember from Chapter 6 we do that by executing the following:

```
$ sudo systemctl enable rc-local.service
```

That is how we can manage different types of interfaces under CentOS. Now let's look how we do this under Ubuntu.

Network Configuration Files for Ubuntu

Ubuntu has a similar directory for its network files in /etc/network. It contains the network files and scripts that are used by Ubuntu to set up your networking. As we described earlier, Ubuntu stores interface information in the file /etc/network/interfaces. It contains all the interface information for any configured interface.

An interface that uses DHCP can be as simple as the following:

```
# The primary network interface
auto enp0s3
iface enp0s3 inet dhcp
```

First we declare that enp0s3 is automatically started with `auto enp0s3`. Next, we declare the interface enp0s3 will use an IPv4 address, which it will get from a DHCP server, `iface enp0s3 inet dhcp`. If you were to configure other Ethernet cards, enp0s8 or enp0s9, you would also use the /etc/network/interfaces file. You can put configuration file in the /etc/network/interfaces.d directory and then "source" it from the /etc/network/interface file with the following:

```
source-directory interfaces.d
```

This will automatically bring in any configuration files in the interfaces.d directory. The other parameters you can use in your interface file can be seen in Table 7-3.

Table 7-3. *Ubuntu Parameters in* /etc/network/interfaces

Parameter	Description
auto	Brings up the interface at boot time
inet	Specifies IPv4 addressing
inet6	Specifies IPv6 addressing
ppp	Specifies the device is a PPP connection
address	Specifies the IP address
netmask	Specifies the netmask
gateway	Specifies the default gateway for that interface
dns-nameserver	Specifies the name server for that interface
post-up	Specifies action to run after interface comes up
pre-down	Specifies action to run before the interface comes down
source-directory	Includes the files from the specified directory

In Table 7-3 you see most of the parameters available to you when setting up a network interface on Ubuntu. We will use some of these to set up a static network interface for enp0s3 in the /etc/network/interfaces file as follows:

```
auto enp0s3
iface enp0s3 inet static
address 192.168.0.10
netmask 255.255.255.0
gateway 192.168.0.254
dns-nameservers 192.168.0.1
```

Here we have set up our enp0s3 interface. We have set it to come up automatically when our host boots, `auto enp0s3`, and told our operating system it will have a static IP address assigned to it, `iface enp0s3 inet static`. We have given the enp0s3 interface the address 192.168.0.10 and a default gateway (default route) of 192.168.0.254. We have also specified the DNS server as 192.168.0.1, which is our internal network's primary name server.

We will now show you how they can be used in the following example. Using the interface file, we are going to create a bonded Ethernet device on our Ubuntu host.

The first thing we need to do is install an extra package if it is not installed already.

```
sudo aptitude install ifenslave
```

In this scenario we are going to enable mode "1" bonding, which as we already know can also be called active-backup. This enables some simple round-robin load balancing across your slave interfaces and enables the attaching and detaching of the slave devices.

In Ubuntu, as in CentOS, the scripts that handle the interfaces, also found in the /etc/network directories, like if-up.d, handle the inserting of the bonding module into the kernel. If you are using an older Ubuntu you can add "bonding" to the /etc/modules file which will load the modules listed there on boot.

We have added two new network cards to our Ubuntu host and they appear as devices enp0s3 and enp0s8. We need to configure these devices for bonding. To do this, we edit the Ubuntu /etc/network/interfaces file, and add the configuration for slave interfaces as well as the master, bond0. Let's begin with showing the configuration for one of the slaves.

```
# slave interface
auto enp0s8
iface enp0s8 inet manual
bond-master bond0
```

Here we have set up our first slave interface to be enp0s8. The `iface enp0s8 inet manual` means that we don't want to assign this interface an IP address. Obviously we set bond-master to the name of the master interface, bond0. The enp0s9 interface again mirrors the enp0s8 configuration.

Moving on to the bond device, we can set that like the following:

```
# The primary network interface
auto bond0
iface bond0 inet static
address 192.168.0.10
netmask 255.255.255.0
bond-mode active-backup
bond-miimon 100
bond_downdelay 25
bond_updelay 25
bond-primary enp0s8
bond-slaves enp0s8 enp0s9
```

In the first line, auto bond0, we have declared here that the bond0 device should be loaded automatically at boot time. Next, in `iface bond0 inet static`, we have declared that the inter face bond0 is an IPv4 statically assigned interface, meaning we are not going to use DHCP or another protocol to assign it an address. We then assign the IP address, netmask, gateway, and DNS servers using the key words `address`, `netmask`, `gateway`, and `dns nameservers`, respectively. We then set our bond-mode to `active-backup` (mode 1), bond-miimon to 100 and specify the slaves for this interface. We have also configured a 25 millisecond period to wait before acting on the state of our slaves coming up or down. These all have the same meanings as they do in CentOS bonding.

Now to start the interface you can choose two methods. First is using the `systemctl` command to restart the networking.service as follows:

```
$ sudo systemctl restart networking.service
```

The other is using the `ifup` command. This should be done in a particular order though. The slave interfaces will bring up the master automatically, but the master will not bring up the slaves.

```
$ sudo ifup enp0s8 && sudo ifup enp0s9
```

Here we are saying bring up the enp0s8 interface and, if the exit code is 0 ('&&'), then bring up the enp0s9 interface. We could have also rebooted our host. We can now validate that our bonded interface is working correctly by looking at the special /proc/net/bonding/bond0 file.

```
$ sudo cat /proc/net/bonding/bond0

Bonding Mode: fault-tolerance (active-backup)
Primary Slave: None
Currently Active Slave: enp0s8
MII Status: up
MII Polling Interval (ms): 100
```

That is part of the output from the cat command against that file. We can see the bonding mode is set to "fault-tolerance (active-backup)," the active slave is enp0s8 and the MII Status is "up"; that tells us the bond is working correctly. In the full output you can see the slaves listed as well.

You can also check via the `ip` command as follows:

```
$ sudo ip link show enp0s8
3: enp0s8: <BROADCAST,MULTICAST,SLAVE,UP,LOWER_UP> ←
mtu 1500 qdisc pfifo_fast master bond0 state UP mode DEFAULT group default qlen 1000
    link/ether 08:00:27:5c:94:ef brd ff:ff:ff:ff:ff:ff

$ sudo ip addr show bond0
9: bond0: <BROADCAST,MULTICAST,MASTER,UP,LOWER_UP> ←
mtu 1500 qdisc noqueue state UP mode DEFAULT group default qlen 1000
    link/ether 08:00:27:5c:94:ef brd ff:ff:ff:ff:ff:ff
    inet 192.168.0.10/24 brd 192.168.0.255 scope global bond0
        valid_lft forever preferred_lft forever
```

You can now see that the IP address 192.168.0.10 is attached to bond0, and both enp0s8 and enp0s9 are slaves to bond0: <BROADCAST,MULTICAST,SLAVE,UP,LOWER_UP> mtu 1500 qdisc pfifo_fast master bond0. You will also notice that all three devices have the same MAC address, 08:00:27:5c:94:ef, which means they can all respond to Address Resolution Protocol (ARP) requests for that MAC address. We explain ARP a little further on in the section "TCP/IP 101."

ETHTOOL

The `ethtool` command is used to further investigate and manipulate your interfaces. For example, depending on your drivers, you can change the link speed of your interface or your duplex settings.

You can see the settings your device is using by issuing the following command:

```
$ sudo ethtool enp0s8
Settings for enp0s8:
        Supported ports: [ TP ]
        Supported link modes:   10baseT/Half 10baseT/Full
                                100baseT/Half 100baseT/Full
                                1000baseT/Full
        Supported pause frame use: No
        Supports auto-negotiation: Yes
        Advertised link modes:  10baseT/Half 10baseT/Full
                                100baseT/Half 100baseT/Full
                                1000baseT/Full
        Advertised pause frame use: No
        Advertised auto-negotiation: Yes
        Speed: 1000Mb/s
        Duplex: Full
        Port: Twisted Pair
        PHYAD: 0
        Transceiver: internal
        Auto-negotiation: on
        MDI-X: off (auto)
Cannot get wake-on-lan settings: Operation not permitted
        Current message level: 0x00000007 (7)
                               drv probe link
        Link detected: yes
```

This shows the current settings of your enp0s8 device. If you want to change the duplex mode and speed, you would issue a command like the following:

```
$ sudo ethtool -s enp0s8 speed 1000 duplex half
```

Here we have changed the speed of the Ethernet card to 1000Mb/s and the duplex setting to half duplex. You can use other settings as well. For a greater understanding of the available settings, please read the man page for ethtool.

TCP/IP 101

It's time to delve a little further into TCP/IP (Transmission Control Protocol/Internet Protocol). You may be familiar with an IP address, but how does that fit in with the rest of TCP/IP? An IP address is used to find other hosts on the network and for other hosts to find you. But how does it do that?

Let's look at this simplified example when you look up a page with your Internet browser. You enter and address in the address bar and hit enter. The browser application takes this data and determines it needs to send a request for a page from a web server by opening up a session. To do this it breaks the information it needs to send into discrete packets. It then attaches the web server's address to the packet and begins trying to figure out where to send the packet. When it has this information it will initiate a connection to the webserver and then transmit the data in the packet on the physical wire and that information will find its way to web server.

You will be interested to know that when you initiate a TCP/IP connection (also known as a *socket*), a three-stage process gets that connection into an "established" state, meaning both hosts are aware of their socket to each other, agree how they are going to send data, and are ready to send that data. The first stage is the host initiating the socket by sending a packet, called a SYN packet, to the host it wants to start communications with. That host responds with another packet, known as a SYN, ACK packet, indicating that it is ready to begin communications. The initiating host then sends a packet, another SYN, ACK packet, acknowledging that packet and telling the remote host it is going to begin sending data. When they have finished communicating, the connection is closed with a FIN packet. This is a basic overview of the process of TCP/IP communications.

■ **Note** For a deeper look at how the actual packets look, read the discussion on TCP segments at `http://www.tcpipguide.com/free/t_TCPMessageSegmentFormat-3.htm`. You can also go to the following for a handy pocket guide: `http://www.sans.org/resources/tcpip.pdf?ref=3871`, and of course: `https://en.wikipedia.org/wiki/Transmission_Control_Protocol`.

The TCP/IP protocol can described under what is called the OSI model, even though it was originally conceived under a different model, called the DoD model (Department of Defense). The OSI model is made up of seven layers. Each of those layers has a special responsibility in the process of communicating data between hosts over the wire. In diagnosing your network, you will normally be interested in the layers 1, 2, and 3. You can see a description of these layers in Figure 7-12.

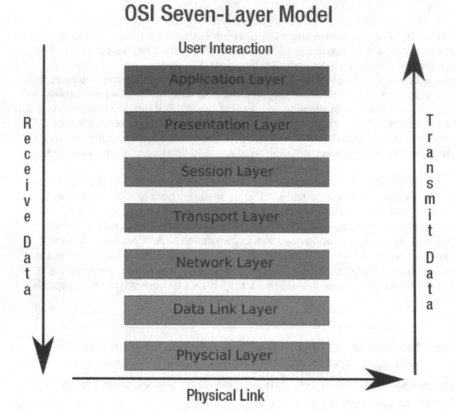

OSI Seven-Layer Model

Figure 7-12. *The OSI layer model*

■ **Note** We are going to describe the first three layers; for further information on the OSI model and layers, please see: http://www.webopedia.com/quick_ref/OSI_Layers.asp.

Layer 1 is concerned with how data is transmitted over the physical wire, and this is represented by the physical layer appearing at the bottom of Figure 7-12. When diagnosing network problems, it never hurts to jiggle the cables connecting your computer and the rest of the network. Also, when all else fails, you can try replacing cables. If cables are faulty, you will probably not see any lights on the switch/hub your host is connected to and the network card. Without these lights, your host will not be able to communicate to other hosts, so first try to replace the cable, and then the port it is connected to on the switch, and finally the network card.

Layer 2, the data link layer, provides the actual communication protocols across the wire. Problems encountered on this layer are rare. It is here that IP addresses get matched to MAC addresses by the use of ARP (Address Resolution Protocol). When two hosts on the network have the same IP address and a different MAC address, your host might start trying to send data to the wrong host. In this case, the ARP table may need to be flushed, and the host with the incorrect IP address will need to be taken offline.

Layer 3 is the network layer. It is able to discover the routes to your destination and send your data, checking for errors as it does so. This is the IP layer, so it can also be responsible for IPsec tunnelling. It is also this layer that is responsible for responding to your pings and other routing requests.

Layers 4 to 7 are described as the host layers. TCP operates in layers 4-5, the network and the session layers. The network layer is concerned with addressing and link reliability, things like error control and flow control. The session layer controls the establishing and closing out connections between computers. Layers 6 to 7 are responsible for connecting the user and this is where the HTTP and browser connects you to the web server.

General Network Troubleshooting

Things can go wrong on your network. Sometimes you aren't able to connect to services, or some part of your network is incorrectly configured. To identify and resolve these problems, you will need a set of tools. We will examine a variety of tools:

- ping: A command that sends packets between hosts to confirm connectivity
- tcpdump: A command that displays and captures network traffic
- mtr: A network diagnostic tool
- nc: The netcat, another network diagnostic and testing tool

Ping!

Probably the most common tool that people use for checking their network is a command called ping. You can ping a host or an interface to see if it responds. In the output response from issuing the ping command, you are shown the time it has taken for that response to come back. You can ping the other side of the world and receive a response in milliseconds. That is good. If you get response times in the order of whole seconds or a "host unreachable" message, that is bad. Of course, if the host you're pinging is on another continent or connected via a satellite link, ping times will be higher than if the host is sitting under your desk.

We just used the ping command to test our routes as follows:

```
$ ping 192.168.0.50
PING 192.168.0.50 (192.168.0.50) 56(84) bytes of data.
64 bytes from 192.168.0.50: icmp_seq=1 ttl=64 time=1.24 ms
```

The ping command can take the following arguments. For other arguments, refer to the man page.

```
ping -c <count> -i <interval> -I <interface address> -s <packet size> destination
```

The ping command will send pings to a host indefinitely unless you either stop it, using Ctrl+C usually, or give it the number of pings to attempt using the -c number option.

You can also express the interval between pings as -i number (in seconds) and choose the interface you wish to use as the source address, specified by -I IP address or the interface name like: -I enp0s8. This is very handy if you have multiple interfaces and wish to test one of those. If you don't define an address, it will normally ping using the primary interface on the host, usually eth0. You can also specify the packet size, using -s number of bytes, which is useful for testing bandwidth problems or problems with MTU settings.

■ **Note** As mentioned earlier in the chapter, MTU is the maximum transmission unit. It is used to limit the size of the packets to what the network devices on that network can handle. Normally it is set to 1,500 bytes, but with jumbo frames it can be up to 9,000 bytes. Having larger-sized packets should mean that you can send more data more efficiently due to less packets traveling over the wire.

One of the first things you can do to test your network is to use ping to ping the interfaces you have configured. If they respond to pings from your own host, they are up and your interface is responding to TCP traffic. You can do this as follows:

```
$ ping 192.168.0.253
PING 192.168.0.253 (192.168.0.253) 56(84) bytes of data.
64 bytes from 192.168.0.253: icmp_seq=2 ttl=128 time=1.68 ms
```

Here we have sent a ping to the local IP address of our host, and we can see a series of responses indicating that a connection has been made and the time it took. If we had received no responses, we would know something is wrong with our interface or network.

The next step is to ping another host on your network, like your default gateway or your DNS server (these two hosts are critical for your Internet communications).

```
$ ping 192.168.0.1
PING 192.168.0.1 (192.168.0.1) 56(84) bytes of data.
64 bytes from 192.168.0.1: icmp_seq=1 ttl=128 time=2.97 ms
```

If you can get there, you know that your host can reach other hosts. You would then ping a host outside your network, say www.ibm.com or www.google.com, and test its response:

```
$ ping www.google.com
PING www.l.google.com (150.101.98.222) 56(84) bytes of data.
64 bytes from g222.internode.on.net (150.101.98.222): icmp_seq=1 ttl=59 time=20.0 ms
```

When you experience problems connecting to hosts on the Internet, it can be for many reasons. There are instances in which part of the Internet will go down because a core router is broken. In this situation, all your private network pings will return, but some pings to hosts on the Internet may not. If you don't get a response from one host on the Internet, try another to see if the issue is local or somewhere else down the line. Some remote networks will actively block ICMP (Internet Control Message Protocol) traffic. These hosts will not respond to pings, and so you should check the response of other hosts before you panic. It is also handy in these situations to combine your investigations with other tools, one of which is mtr.

MTR

If you can ping hosts inside your network but can't ping hosts outside your network, you can use a tool like traceroute or mtr for troubleshooting. Both provide a similar service: they trace the route they use to get to the destination host. Both also use "TTL expired in transit" messages to record those hosts along the way. What do these messages mean? Well, as we have already explained, TTL is used to kill TCP/IP packets so they don't keep zinging around the Internet forever like some lost particle in the Large Hadron Collider. These commands take advantage of polite routers that send back "TTL expired in transit" messages when they kill your packet.

Let's take a look at an example. If we do a ping to www.ibm.com and set the TTL to 1, it gets to the first router along the path to whatever www.ibm.com resolves to. That first router looks at the TTL and sees that it is 1. It now drops the packet and sends the expired-in-transit message.

```
$ ping -t 1 -c 1 www.ibm.com
PING www.ibm.com.cs186.net (129.42.60.216) 56(84) bytes of data.
From 192.168.0.254 (192.168.0.254) icmp_seq=1 Time to live exceeded
```

```
--- www.ibm.com.cs186.net ping statistics ---
1 packets transmitted, 0 received, +1 errors, 100% packet loss, time 0ms
```

The mtr and traceroute applications use the packet sent back to discover the IP address of the router (as the TCP/IP packet containing the reply will hold this information). It then displays that information and sends the next ping, this time with the TTL set to 2. Once the ping reaches our destination, we should receive the standard echo response. Some routers are configured not to send these ICMP messages and appear as blanks in the trace output.

Have a look at the output from mtr. Here we have used mtr to trace the route between the host au-mel-centos-1 and www.ibm.com using the following command:

```
$ sudo /usr/sbin/mtr www.ibm.com --report
Start: Tue May 17 18:04:01 2016
HOST: au-mel-centos-1           Loss%  Snt   Last   Avg  Best  Wrst StDev
  1.|-- 192.168.0.254            0.0%   10    2.7   2.4   1.8   3.2   0.0
  2.|-- lnx20.mel4.something.net 0.0%   10  444.7 339.7 231.5 514.1 101.8
  3.|-- xe-0-3-2.cr1.mel4.z.net  0.0%   10  456.4 332.2 211.5 475.6 103.0
  4.|-- ae0.cr1.mel8.boo.net     0.0%   10  463.3 338.3 240.2 463.3  91.1
  5.|-- ???                      100%   10    0.0   0.0   0.0   0.0   0.0
  6.|-- a104-97-227-232.deploy.st 0.0%  10  476.3 341.9 229.3 476.3  97.0
```

Because we have used the --report switch the output isn't shown until at least ten packets are sent. What the output from this command shows is that our first hop (each host/router we pass through is called a hop) is our firewall router. Next is the default gateway of our Internet connection at our ISP. As we pass through each hop along the way, we record information about our route. At the penultimate hop, we reach the IBM gateway. If you see a ???, it will mean that the router has be set to deny returning ICMP packets, and mtr has printed ??? because it has not received the "TTL expired in transit" message. Some network administrators do this because they believe ICMP to be a security vulnerability.

For more information on some security vulnerabilities of ICMP, please read: http://resources.infosecinstitute.com/icmp-attacks/.

The tcpdump Command

You can't easily view communications at layer 1, but you can view them at layer 2 and layer 3 by using *packet-sniffing* software. One such application to view this detail is the tcpdump command-line tool. The tcpdump command, and those like it, can view traffic at the packet level on the wire. You can see the packets coming in and out of your host. The tcpdump command, when run without any expressions, will print every packet crossing the interface. You can use expressions to narrow the array of packets types it will show. See the man tcpdump page for more information.

■ **Note** Another program you can try is called Wireshark. It has a very good GUI that allows you to easily filter traffic. It also has a command-line utility called tshark, which operates in similar fashion to tcpdump. One of the good things about WireShark is that you can capture output from tcpdump (by specifying the –w option) and read it in WireShark, which does make viewing the information much easier. You can see more about Wireshark here: http://www.wireshark.org/.

To show you how a network connection is established, we are going to make a connection from our firewall to our mail server. To illustrate what happens we are going to use the tcpdump command, the output appears as follows:

```
$ sudo /usr/sbin/tcpdump -i enp0s3
tcpdump: verbose output suppressed, use -v or -vv for full protocol decode
listening on enp0s3, link-type EN10MB (Ethernet), capture size 96 bytes
19:26:35.250934 ARP, Request who-has 192.168.0.1 tell 192.168.0.254, length 46

19:26:35.475678 ARP, Reply 192.168.0.1 is-at 00:50:56:a9:54:44 (oui Unknown), length 28

19:31:17.336554 IP 192.168.0.254.33348 > 192.168.0.1.smtp: Flags [S], ↵
seq 3194824921, win 29200, options [mss 1460,sackOK,TS val 47080429 ↵
ecr 0,nop,wscale 7], length 0

19:31:17.619210 IP 192.168.0.1.smtp > 192.168.0.254.33348: Flags [S.], ↵
seq 2011016705, ack 3194824922, win 65535, options [mss 1460], length 0

19:31:17.619249 IP 192.168.0.254.33348 > 192.168.0.1.smtp: Flags [.], ↵
ack 1, win 29200, length 0

19:31:17.900048 IP 192.168.0.1.smtp > 192.168.0.254.33348: Flags [P.], ↵
seq 1:42, ack 1, win 65535, length 41

19:31:17.900081 IP 192.168.0.254.33348 > 192.168.0.1.smtp: Flags [.], ↵
ack 42, win 29200, length 0
```

We have issued the command and told it to dump all the traffic that crosses the enp0s3 interface. We use the -i option to specify which interface to examine. In the output, we can break down the lines as follows:

timestamp source.port > destination.port : flags

In the preceding output, the first two lines contain information telling you what the command is doing, in this case, listening on enp0s3. The rest are actual packets crossing the wire. The first numbers of each line, for example, 19:26:35.250934, are timestamps.

```
ARP, Request who-has 192.168.0.1 tell 192.168.0.254
```

The first field (taking away the timestamp) is the protocol in the TCP/IP model. This is an ARP request, and ARP operates at the layer 2 (or data link layer) of the TCP/IP protocol stack. ARP is used to match up MAC addresses to IP addresses. You can see that 192.168.0.254 wants to know who has 192.168.0.1. There is an ARP reply that says that 192.168.0.1 is at MAC address 00:50:56:a9:54:44.

```
ARP, Reply 192.168.0.1 is-at 00:50:56:a9:54:44
```

Now that 192.168.0.254 knows where to send its packet, it tries to establish a socket by sending a SYN packet, Flags [S]. The SYN packet carries the SYN bit set and has an initial sequence number of seq 3194824921.

```
IP 192.168.0.254.33348 > 192.168.0.1.smtp: Flags [S], seq 3194824921, ↵
win 29200, options [mss 1460,sackOK,TS val 47080429 ecr 0,nop, ↵
wscale 7], length 0
```

252

The source and destination are described by 192.168.0.254 > 192.168.0.1.smtp, where .smtp is the port we are connecting to. That port maps to port 25. This is a connection being established to an SMTP mail server.

Let's look at the next part: Flags [S]. The [S] after the source and the destination indicates that this is a SYN request and we are establishing a connection. Next is the initial sequence number of the packets, 3194824921. The sequence numbers are randomly generated and are used to order and match packets. This packet has a length of 0, that means that it is a zero-byte packet (i.e., it contains no payload).

The other flags, win 29200, options [mss 1460,sackOK,TS val 47080429 ecr 0,nop,wscale 7], provide other information in the communication like sliding window size, maximum segment size, and so on.

■ **Note**   For more information, see http://www.tcpipguide.com/free/t_
TCPMaximumSegmentSizeMSSandRelationshiptoIPDatagra.htm.

The next packet is the reply from 192.168.0.1.

```
IP 192.168.0.1.smtp > 192.168.0.254.33348: Flags [S.], seq 2011016705, ↵
ack 3194824922, win 65535, options [mss 1460], length 0
```

This packet has the Flag [S.]set and a sequence number, 2011016705. The [S.] is an SYN ACK (or no flag to be precise)—this is a response to a SYN packet. The sequence number is another randomly generated number, and the data payload is again zero, (length 0). Attached to this sequence is an ACK response, ack 3194824922. This is the original initial sequence number incremented by 1, indicating that it is acknowledging our first sequence.

The next packet is another acknowledgment packet sent by the originating host:

```
IP 192.168.0.254.33348 > 192.168.0.1.smtp: Flags [.], ↵
ack 1, win 29200, length 0
```

In this output, the dot (.) means that no flags were set. The ack 1 indicates that this is an acknowledgment packet and that from now on, tcpdump will show the difference between the current sequence and initial sequence. This is the last communication needed to establish a connection between two hosts and is called the three-way handshake.

The last two packets are the exchange of data.

```
IP 192.168.0.1.smtp > 192.168.0.254.33348: Flags [P.], ↵
seq 1:42, ack 1, win 65535, length 41
```

The mail server is sending a message to the client on 192.168.0.254, as indicated by [P.] seq 1:42, ack 1. This is pushing, [P.], 41 bytes of data in the payload and is acknowledging the previous communication (ack 1).

```
IP 192.168.0.254.33348 > 192.168.0.1.smtp: Flags [.], ↵
ack 42, win 29200, length 0
```

The last communication is 192.168.0.254 acknowledging that packet, ack 42.

So now that you know how to see the communications between two hosts at the most basic level using packet-sniffing programs such as tcpdump, let's take a look at another useful tool, netcat.

■ **Note**   If you are interested in a deeper discussion of `tcpdump` and connection establishment, try the following article: `http://www.linuxjournal.com/article/6447`.

The Netcat Tool

The other very useful tool you can use to diagnose network problems is the `nc`, or `ncat`, command. You can use this tool to test your ability to reach not only other hosts but also the ports on which they could be listening.

This tool is especially handy when you want to test a connection to a port through a firewall. Let's test whether our firewall is allowing us to connect to port 80 on host 192.168.0.1 from host 192.168.0.254.

First, on host 192.168.0.1, we will make sure we have stopped our web server. For example, we issue the following command:

```
$ sudo systemctl stop httpd
```

We will then start the `nc` command using the `-l`, or listen, option on the host with the IP address of 192.168.0.1.

```
$ sudo nc -l 80
```

This binds our `nc` command to all interfaces on the port. We can test that by running another command called netstat:

```
$ sudo netstat -lpt
tcp    0    0 *:http    *:*    LISTEN   18618/nc    .
```

We launched the `netstat` command with three options. The `-l` option tells the `netstat` command to list listening sockets. The `-p` option tells `netstat` to display what applications are using each connection, and the last option, `-t`, tells `netstat` to look for TCP connections only.

The `netstat` command displays the programs listening on certain ports on your host. We can see in the preceding output that the program `nc`, PID of 18618, is listening for TCP connections on port 80. The `*:http` indicates that it is listening on all available addresses (network interface IP addresses) on port 80 (the `:http` port maps to port 80). OK, so we know our `nc` command is listening and waiting for connections. Next, we test our ability to connect from the host with the IP address of 192.168.0.254.

We will use the `nc` command to make a connection to port 80 on host 192.168.0.1 as in the following example:

```
$ nc 192.168.0.1 80
hello host
```

The `nc` program allows us to test the connection between two hosts and send text to the remote host. When we type text and press Enter in our connection window, we will see what we have typed being echoed on the `au-mel-centos-1` host.

```
$ sudo nc -l 80
hello host
```

We now know our host can connect to the `au-mel-centos-1` host on port 80, confirming that our firewall rules are working (or too liberal as the case may be if we were trying to block port 80).

You Dig It?

dig is another handy tool for resolving DNS issues. If you use this tool in combination with others like ping and nc, you will be able to solve many problems. The dig command, short for domain information groper, is used to query DNS servers. Employed simply, the command will resolve a fully qualified domain name by querying the nameserver it finds in the /etc/resolv.conf file.

The /etc/resolv.conf file is used to store the nameserver information so your host knows which DNS server to query for domain name resolution. A /etc/resolv.conf file looks as follows:

```
$ sudo cat /etc/resolv.conf
; generated by /sbin/dhclient-script
search example.com
nameserver 192.168.0.1
nameserver  192.168.0.254
```

First you can see that the resolv.conf file was generated by the DHCP client. In general, this file should not need to be edited; often it will be overwritten by the NetworkManager. The default search domain is example.com, and any hostname searches will have that domain appended to the end of the query. Next, we have the nameserver(s) we wish to query for our domain name resolution. These should be in IP address format. If the first nameserver is unavailable, the second will be used.

The dig command will query these nameservers unless otherwise instructed. Let's look at this query.

```
$ dig www.google.com

; <<>> DiG 9.10.3-P4-Ubuntu <<>> www.google.com
;; global options: +cmd
;; Got answer:
;; ->>HEADER<<- opcode: QUERY, status: NOERROR, id: 16714
;; flags: qr rd ra; QUERY: 1, ANSWER: 12, AUTHORITY: 4, ADDITIONAL: 5

;; OPT PSEUDOSECTION:
; EDNS: version: 0, flags:; udp: 4096
;; QUESTION SECTION:
;www.google.com.                IN      A

;; ANSWER SECTION:
www.google.com.         233     IN      A       150.101.161.181
www.google.com.         233     IN      A       150.101.161.187
www.google.com.         233     IN      A       150.101.161.146
www.google.com.         233     IN      A       150.101.161.152
www.google.com.         233     IN      A       150.101.161.153
www.google.com.         233     IN      A       150.101.161.159
www.google.com.         233     IN      A       150.101.161.160
www.google.com.         233     IN      A       150.101.161.166
www.google.com.         233     IN      A       150.101.161.167
www.google.com.         233     IN      A       150.101.161.173
www.google.com.         233     IN      A       150.101.161.174
www.google.com.         233     IN      A       150.101.161.180
```

```
;; AUTHORITY SECTION:
google.com.              10960    IN      NS      ns4.google.com.
google.com.              10960    IN      NS      ns2.google.com.
google.com.              10960    IN      NS      ns1.google.com.
google.com.              10960    IN      NS      ns3.google.com.

;; ADDITIONAL SECTION:
ns1.google.com.          9192     IN      A       216.239.32.10
ns2.google.com.          13861    IN      A       216.239.34.10
ns3.google.com.          9192     IN      A       216.239.36.10
ns4.google.com.          2915     IN      A       216.239.38.10

;; Query time: 28 msec
;; SERVER: 192.168.0.254#53(192.168.0.254)
;; WHEN: Sun Jul 17 15:43:41 AEST 2016
;; MSG SIZE  rcvd: 371
```

In the ANSWER SECTION, you can see the www.google.com hostname will resolve to twelve possible IP addresses. The AUTHORITY SECTION tells us which nameservers are responsible for providing the DNS information for www.google.com. The ADDITIONAL SECTION tells us what IP addresses the nameservers in the AUTHORITY SECTION will resolve to.

IN A indicates an Internet address (or relative record). IN NS indicates a nameserver record. Numbers such as 233, 10960, and 9192, shown in the three sections in the preceding code, indicate how long in seconds the record is cached for. When they reach zero, the nameserver will query the authoritative DNS server to see whether it has changed.

At the bottom of the dig output, you can see the SERVER that provided the response, 192.168.0.254, and how long the query took, 28 msec.

You can use dig to query a particular nameserver by using the @ sign, here we are using one of the Google public DNS servers. You can also query certain record types by using the -t *type* option. For example, if we wanted to test our DNS server was working properly, we could use dig to find the IP address of Google's mail server.

```
$ dig @8.8.8.8 -t MX google.com

<snip>
;; QUESTION SECTION:
;google.com.                     IN      MX

;; ANSWER SECTION:
google.com.              392      IN      MX      20 alt1.aspmx.l.google.com.
<snip>
google.com.              392      IN      MX      10 aspmx.l.google.com.

;; AUTHORITY SECTION:
google.com.              10736    IN      NS      ns4.google.com.
google.com.              10736    IN      NS      ns3.google.com.
google.com.              10736    IN      NS      ns1.google.com.
google.com.              10736    IN      NS      ns2.google.com.
```

```
;; ADDITIONAL SECTION:
aspmx.l.google.com.      55      IN    A       64.233.189.27
aspmx.l.google.com.      112     IN    AAAA    2404:6800:4008:c03::1b
<snip>
ns3.google.com.          8968    IN    A       216.239.36.10
ns4.google.com.          2691    IN    A       216.239.38.10
<snip>
```

We could use this information and compare the response from other nameservers. If our nameserver has provided the same information, our DNS server is working correctly. If there is a difference or we return no results, we would have to investigate our DNS settings further. In Chapter 9, we discuss DNS and the dig command in more detail.

Other Troubleshooting Tools

The programs we have just discussed cover basic network troubleshooting. Many other networking tools are available to further help diagnose problems. We briefly touched on the netstat command, but there are a multitude of others. Table 7-4 lists some of the most common troubleshooting commands and their descriptions.

The list of useful tools in Table 7-4 is by no means exhaustive. However, armed with only a few of these tools, you can diagnose many common problems.

Table 7-4. *Other Handy Network Diagnostic Tools*

Tool	Description
netstat	This tool gives the status of what is listening on your host plus much more, including routes and statistics.
host	Another tool to diagnose DNS servers. We will show you how to use host in Chapter 9.
openssl s_client	This is useful to test SSL connections as it can try to establish an SSL connection to a port on a remote host.
arp	This program queries and manages the ARP cache table, and allows you to delete ARP entries.

Adding Routes and Forwarding Packets

The other common thing you will do with the ip command is add routes to your host. Routes are the pathways your host should follow to access other networks or other hosts.

IP FORWARDING

Linux hosts generally have IP forwarding turned off by default. IP forwarding allows your host to act as a router, directing packets sent to it by hosts on your network to the destination host. If your host has IP forwarding turned on, your host will be able to forward packets from one interface to another or one network to another. This is a kernel-level function that can be turned on or off by editing the /etc/sysctl.conf file. This file allows you to configure kernel parameters at runtime. You can set many other parameters in the sysctl.conf file, including memory, swap, and other network-related kernel parameters that can be tweaked during runtime.

The kernel stores this kind of information in the /proc directory. For example, the IP forwarding setting is located in the /proc/sys/net/ipv4/ip_forward file. This file system is created by the kernel at boot up, and changes made directly to it are not persistent across reboots. If this is set to o, IP forwarding is disabled, and your host will not pass on any packets not destined for it. If it is set to 1, IP forwarding will redirect those packets not destined for it to their destination host.

To make the setting persistent across reboots, you need to uncomment the following line in /etc/sysctl.conf, save the file, and then issue the sysctl -p command to load the changes into the kernel:

```
# Uncomment the next line to enable packet forwarding for IPv4
net.ipv4.ip_forward=1
```

You can also immediately turn on packet forwarding by echoing the number 1 into the file /proc/sys/net/ipv4/ip_forward like this:

```
echo 1 > /proc/sys/net/ipv4/ip_forward
```

This change is not persistent across reboots, but editing /etc/sysctl will make it permanent.

You can also configure IP forwarding for IPv6 interfaces as well. Similarly, we need to add net.ipv6.conf.all.forwarding=1to the sysctl.conf file or again echo 1 to /proc/sys/net/ipv6/conf/all/forwarding.

For more information on sysctl.conf and the use of sysctl, please read the man pages.

We want to show you an example of how to add a route using the ip command. First, we will explain what we want to achieve. We are going to route traffic from one network to another via our firewall. We are on our main server host, which has the IP address 192.168.0.1—Host A in Figure 7-13. We have our firewall/router sitting on our network with the IP address 192.168.0.254 on interface enp0s8—Host B. We have configured interface enp0s9 on our firewall host with the address 192.168.1.254/24. The network 192.168.1.0/24 is going to be our wireless network, which we will separate into its own subnet. There is a host with which we wish to communicate on that network with the IP address 192.168.1.220—Host C. Figure 7-13 provides a diagram of our network.

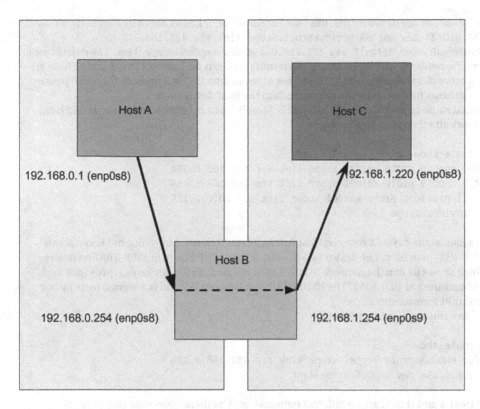

Figure 7-13. Adding a route

Host A and Host C are properly configured to route between the networks. In their routing tables, they send all requests destined for other networks via their default gateway. In this case their default gateway is the firewall/router, and the address of their default gateway is 192.168.0.254 and 192.168.1.254, respectively. Host A does not know that Host B has the 192.168.1.0/24 network attached to its enp0s9 interface, nor does Host C know that Host B has the 192.168.0.0/24 network attached to its enp0s8 interface.

■ **Note** We are going to use the ip command to explore our route tables. But first you need to know that there are different route tables. By default there is a main, local and default. You can also add your own. You can view the different tables by issuing `ip route show table local|main|default|number`. When we issue the `ip route show` command we are seeing the main table, the equivalent to `ip route show table main`.

Let's view the route table for Host A. By issuing the following command, we can list the route table of Host A:

```
$ sudo /sbin/ip route show
192.168.0.0/24 dev enp0s8 proto kernel scope link src 192.168.0.1
default via 192.168.0.254 dev enp0s8 scope link
```

The route table shows us the networks that this host knows about. It knows about its own network, as shown with `192.168.0.0/24 dev enp0s8 proto kernel scope link src 192.168.0.1`.

You can see the default route, `default via 192.168.0.254 dev enp0s8 scope link`. The default route points to the host on the network, which can handle the routing requests for hosts on its network. These are devices with usually more than one interface or IP address network attached to it and can therefore pass on the routing requests to hosts further along the routing path to the final destination.

Let's compare that route table with the one for Host B. Host B is our network router, so it should have more than one network attached to its interfaces.

```
$ sudo /sbin/ip route show
192.168.0.0/24 dev enp0s8 proto kernel scope link src 192.168.0.254
192.168.1.0/24 dev enp0s9 proto kernel scope link src 192.168.1.254
10.204.2.10 dev dsl-provider proto kernel scope link src 10.0.2.155
default dev dsl-provider scope link
```

First let's take a look at the `default` route on Host B. It indicates that anything it doesn't know about it will send out of `dev dsl-provider`. The device `dsl-provider` is our PPP link to our ISP. The first line is related to that route. It shows us that the network 10.204.2.10 is reached via the device `dsl-provider` and through the `link src` address of 10.0.2.155. The 10.204.2.10 host is in our ISP and is assigned to us by our ISP when we make our PPP connection.

On Host C we have this route configuration:

```
$ sudo /sbin/ip route show
192.168.1.0/24 dev enp0s8 proto kernel scope link src 192.168.0.220
default via 192.168.1.254 dev enp0s8 scope link
```

We know that Host A and Host C are on different networks, and by themselves they cannot reach each other. For us to make a simple connection, like a `ping` connection, from Host A to Host C, the TCP/IP packets have to go through Host B. The `ping` command sends an ICMP echo request to the host specified on the command line. The echo request is a defined protocol that says to the requesting host what would in computer speak be "I'm here."

■ **Note** Internet Control Message Protocol (ICMP) is a TCP/IP protocol that is used to send messages between hosts, normally error messages; but in the case of `ping`, it can also send an informational echo reply.

So let's see if we can reach Host C from Host A by issuing the `ping` command on Host A.

```
$ ping -c 4 192.168.1.220
PING 192.168.1.220 (192.168.1.220) 56(84) bytes of data.
64 bytes from 192.168.1.220: icmp_seq=1 ttl=64 time=1.79 ms
```

We have used the `ping` command, a way of sending network echoes, with the `-c 4` option to limit the number of echo replies to 4. This is enough to confirm that we can reach our Host C from our Host A. That was relatively easy. Let's look at a slightly different scenario in which we have to add our own route. You can see a diagram of it in Figure 7-14.

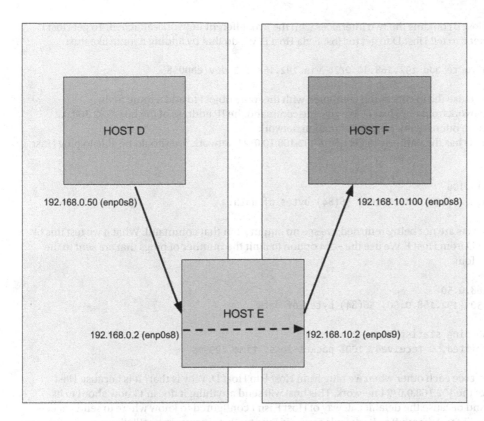

Figure 7-14. Adding another route

In this scenario, we will say that Host D is trying to reach Host F by passing through Host E. Host E has two Ethernet devices, enp0s8 and enp0s9. The device enp0s8 is attached to the 192.168.0.0/24 network with IP address 192.168.0.2, and enp0s9 is attached to the 192.168.10.0/24 network with IP address 192.168.10.2. Host D is on the 192.168.0.0/24 network with IP address 192.168.0.50. Host D has a default route of 192.168.0.254. Host F is on the 192.168.10.0/24 network with IP address 192.168.10.100. Host F has the default route 192.168.10.254.

Let's look at their route tables:

```
Host D
192.168.0.0/24 dev enp0s8 proto kernel scope link src 192.168.0.50
default via 192.168.0.254 dev enp0s8 scope link

Host E
192.168.0.0/24 dev enp0s8 proto kernel scope link src 192.168.0.2
192.168.10.0/24 dev enp0s9 proto kernel scope link src 192.168.10.2
default via 192.168.0.254 dev enp0s8 scope link

Host F
192.168.10.0/24 dev enp0s8 proto kernel scope link src 192.168.10.100
default via 192.168.10.254 dev enp0s8 scope link
```

You can see that Host E contains the two interfaces with the two different networks attached. To get Host D to see Host F, we need to tell Host D to get to Host F via Host E. We do that by adding a route like this:

```
$ sudo /sbin/ip route add 192.168.10.0/24 via 192.168.0.2 dev enp0s8
```

Here we have to use the ip command combined with the route object to add a route to the 192.168.10.0/24 network from our Host D. We give the command the IP address of the host, 192.168.0.2, which is the router on our network for the destination network.

Now that Host D has the pathway to get to the 192.168.10.0/24 network, we should be able to ping Host F, right?

```
$ ping 192.168.10.100
PING 192.168.10.100 (192.168.10.100) 56(84) bytes of data.
```

It appears packets are not being returned, we see no output from that command. What if we test this by trying to ping Host D from Host F. We use the -c 4 option to limit the number of pings that are sent to the destination host to four.

```
ping -c 4 192.168.0.50
PING 192.168.0.50 (192.168.0.50) 56(84) bytes of data.

--- 192.168.0.50 ping statistics ---
4 packets transmitted, 0 received, 100% packet loss, time 2999ms
```

Our hosts can't see each other when we ping from Host F to Host D. Why is that? It is because Host F knows nothing of the 192.168.0.0/24 network. This host will send anything it doesn't know about to its default gateway. And because the default gateway of Host F isn't configured to know where to send packets to 192.168.0.50, it will send them off to its default gateway. Eventually these packets will die.

■ **Note**   Part of the TCP/IP protocol is a TTL—*time to live*—where after a period of time the packets are ignored and dropped by upstream routers. TTL is indicated by a number, usually 64 these days, but can be 32 or 128. As packets pass through each router (or *hop*), they decrease the TTL value by 1. If the TTL is 1 when it reaches a router and that router is not the final destination, the router will drop the packet and send a "TTL expired in transit" message using the ICMP protocol. You will see how useful this is shortly in the "MTR" section.

So how do we fix this? Well, we add a route to Host F telling it how to send packets to Host D via Host E.

```
$ sudo /sbin/ip route add 192.168.0.0/24 via 192.168.10.2 dev enp0s8
```

Now when Host F tries to ping Host D, we get the following result:

```
$ ping 192.168.0.50
PING 192.168.0.50 (192.168.0.50) 56(84) bytes of data.
64 bytes from 192.168.0.50: icmp_seq=1 ttl=64 time=1.24 ms
```

After adding the route to Host F, we can now reach Host D. Combining all this information, we can use these commands in a script to bring up an interface, add an IP address, and add a route.

```
#!/bin/bash

# bring up the interface
ip link set enp0s8 up

# add an address
ip addr add 192.168.10.1/24 dev enp0s8

# add a route
ip route add 192.168.100.1 via 192.168.10.254 dev enp0s8

# ping the host
ping 192.168.100.1 -c 4

# bring down the route, remove the address and bring down the interface.
ip route del 192.168.100.1 via 192.168.10.254 dev enp0s8
ip addr del 192.168.10.1/24 dev enp0s8
ip link set enp0s8 down

exit 0
```

We have used the same command to control our interface, bringing it up, adding an address, and then adding a route. We then brought it down again with the same command. This sort of script can be used to copy files from one host to another host or make any sort of connection.

Let's now move on to further explore how you can test your connections and troubleshoot your network using a few simple utilities.

Netfilter and iptables

Many people now understand what a firewall is, as they have started to become mandatory on even the simplest of hosts. You may already be familiar with a firewall running on your desktop. These simple firewalls can be used to block unwanted traffic in and out of a single host, but that is all they can do.

Netfilter is a complex firewall application that can sit on the perimeter of a network or on a single host. Not only can it block unwanted traffic and route packets around the network, but it can also shape traffic. "Shape traffic?" you may be wondering, "What's that?"

Packet shaping is the ability to alter packets passing in and out of your network. You can use it to increase or decrease bandwidth for certain connections, optimize the sending of other packets, or guarantee performance of specific types of packets. This can be beneficial to companies that want to ensure VoIP calls are not interrupted by someone downloading GoT.

How Netfilter/iptables Work

The `iptables` command is the user-space management tool for Netfilter. Netfilter was pioneered by Paul "Rusty" Russell and has been in the Linux kernel since version 2.4. It allows the operating system to perform packet filtering and shaping at a kernel level, and this allows it to be under fewer restrictions than user-space programs. This is especially useful for dedicated firewall and router hosts as it increases performance significantly.

■ **Note** The term *user-space program* refers to a tool used by end users to configure some portion of the operating system. In this case the internal operating system component is called Netfilter, and the user-space component, the command you use to configure Netfilter, is called `iptables`.

Packet filtering and shaping is the ability to change or discard packets as they enter or leave a host according to set of criteria, or rules. Netfilter does this by rewriting the packet headers as they enter, pass through, and/or leave the host.

Netfilter is a stateful packet-filtering firewall. Two types of packet-filtering firewalls exist: stateful and stateless. A *stateless* packet-filtering firewall examines only the header of a packet for filtering information. It sees each packet in isolation and thus has no way to determine whether a packet is part of an existing connection or an isolated malicious packet. A *stateful* firewall maintains information about the status of the connections passing through it. This allows the firewall to filter packets based on the state of the connection, which offers considerably finer-grained control over your traffic.

Netfilter is part of the Linux kernel and can be controlled and configured in the user space by the `iptables` command.. In this chapter, we will frequently use `iptables` to refer to the firewall technology in general. Most Linux-based distributions will have an `iptables` package, but they may also have their own tool for configuring the rules Firewall-cmd and ufw.

Netfilter works by referring to a set of tables. These tables contain chains, which in turn contain individual rules. Chains hold groups of ordered and alike rules; for example, a group of rules governing incoming traffic could be held in a chain. Rules are the basic Netfilter configuration items that contain criteria to match particular traffic and perform an action on the matched traffic.

Traffic that is currently being processed by the host is compared against these rules, and if the current packet being processed satisfies the selection criteria of a rule, the action, known as a *target*, specified by that rule is carried out. These actions, among others, can be to ignore the packet, accept the packet, reject the packet, or pass the packet on to other rules for more refined processing. Let's look at an example; say the Ethernet interface on your web server has just received a packet from the Internet. This packet is checked against your rules and compared to their selection criteria. The selection criteria could include such items as the destination IP address and the destination port. In this example, say you want incoming web traffic on your network interface to be allowed access to the HTTP port 80 of your listening web service. If the incoming traffic *matches* these criteria, you specify an *action* to let it through.

Each `iptables` rule relies on specifying a set of network parameters as selection criteria to select the packets and traffic for each rule. You can use a number of network parameters to build each `iptables` rule. For example, a network connection between two hosts is referred to as a *socket*. This is the combination of a source IP address, source port, destination IP address, and destination port. All four of these parameters must exist for the connection to be established, and `iptables` can use these values to filter traffic coming in and out of hosts. Additionally, if you look at how communication is performed on a TCP/IP-based network, you will see that three protocols are used most frequently: Internet Control Message Protocol (ICMP), Transmission Control Protocol (TCP), and User Datagram Protocol (UDP). The `iptables` firewall can easily distinguish between these different types of protocols and others.

With just these five parameters (the source and destination IP addresses, the source and destination ports, and the protocol type), you can now start building some useful filtering rules. But before you start building these rules, you need to understand how `iptables` rules are structured and interact. And to gain this understanding, you need to understand further some of the initial `iptables` concepts such as tables, chains, and policies, which we will discuss next, along with touching a little on network address translation (NAT).

Tables

We talked about Netfilter having tables of rules that traffic can be compared against, possibly resulting in some action taken. Netfilter has four built-in tables that can hold rules for processing traffic. The first is the filter table, which is the default table used for all rules related to the filtering of your traffic. The second is nat, which handles NAT rules. Next is the mangle table, which covers a variety of packet alteration functions. There is the raw table, which is used to exempt packets from connection tracking and is called before any other Netfilter table. And lastly there is the security table which are used for Mandatory Access Control (MAC) network rules and is processed after the filter table. This is used by modules like SELinux.

Chains

Each of the Netfilter tables, filter, nat, mangle, raw and security, contain sets of predefined hooks that Netfilter will process in order. These hooks contain sequenced groupings of rules called *chains*. Each table contains default chains that are built into the table. The built-in chains are described in Table 7-5.

Table 7-5. *Built-in Chains*

Chain	Description
INPUT	Used to sequence rules for packets coming to the host interface(s). Found in the filter, mangle and security tables only.
FORWARD	Used to sequence rules for packets destined for another host. Found in the filter, mangle and security table only.
OUTPUT	Used to sequence rules for outgoing packets originating from the host interface(s). Found in the filter, nat, mangle, raw and security tables.
PREROUTING	Used to alter packets before they are routed to the other chains. Found in the nat, mangle, and raw tables.
POSTROUTING	Used to alter packets after they have left the other chains and are about to go out of the interface(s). Found in the nat and mangle tables only.

Each chain correlates to the basic paths that packets can take through a host. When the Netfilter logic encounters a packet, the first evaluation it makes is to which chain the packet is destined. Not all tables contain all the built-in chains listed in Table 7-5.

Let's look at the filter table for example. It contains only the INPUT, OUTPUT, and FORWARD chains and it is the one you configure most often. If a packet is coming into the host through a network interface, it needs to be evaluated by the rules in the INPUT chain. If the packet is generated by this host and going out onto the network via a network interface, it needs to be evaluated by the rules in the OUTPUT chain. The FORWARD chain is used for packets that have reached the local network interface but are destined for some other host (for example, on hosts that act as routers). You are able to create chains of your own in each table to hold additional rules. You can also direct the flow of packets from a built-in chain to a chain you have created, but this is only possible within the same tablespace.

Let us now explore the life of a packet as it comes into your system. We will be concerning ourselves with the filter table solely, as this is the table you will deal with most often. Remember that the table filter contains the three built-in chains: INPUT, FORWARD, and OUTPUT. These all have the default policy of ACCEPT (we talk about policies shortly). Looking at Figure 7-15, which shows how a normal network packet would flow through the filter table.

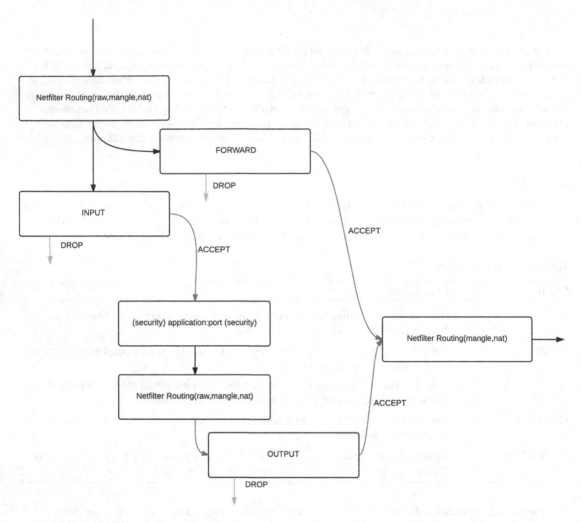

Figure 7-15. *Traffic flow through the* filter *table*

In Figure 7-15, you can see the way that packets will flow through the filter table. The Netfilter firewall program will route incoming IP packets to either the INPUT or the FORWARD chain depending on their destination address. It makes this decision in the Netfilter routing block and packets are inspected by raw, mange and nat tables before reaching filter.

If the incoming packets are destined for another host, and IP forwarding has been enabled on the firewall host, they are delivered to the FORWARD chain. Once dealt with by any rule set in that chain, the packets will leave the host if they are allowed or be dropped (DROP) if they are not. Like in the OUTPUT chain, these packets are routed by the Netfilter program and passed on to other tables (mangle, nat) before they leave on the wire.

If the packets are destined for the firewall host itself, they will be passed to the INPUT chain and if they are accepted by any rule sets in that chain will be passed to the application (via the security table). The application may then wish to send a response back. If so it, this traffic is managed by the OUTPUT chain.

The OUPUT chain is for packets originating on the actual firewall host destined for another host elsewhere. These can be new connections being initiated from the firewall to remote sockets or it can be part of an established packet flow.

■ **Tip** Think of the hooks in the preceding explanation as a set of fishing hooks with different types of bait to catch different types of fish. When a specific type of fish is swimming by it is attracted to a certain bait. Once it is hooked we determine its fate by what is at the end of the line. iptables is just like fishing for network packets!

Policies

Each built-in chain defined in the filter table can also have a policy. A *policy* is the default action a chain takes on a packet to determine whether a packet makes it all the way through the rules in a chain without matching any of them. The policies you can use for packets are DROP, REJECT, and ACCEPT. By default both Ubuntu and CentOS have ACCEPT as the default policy for all chains in all tables.

The DROP policy discards a packet without notifying the sender, often described as 'dropping to the floor.' The REJECT policy also discards the packet, but it sends an ICMP packet to the sender to tell it the rejection has occurred. The REJECT policy means that a device will know that its packets are not getting to their destination and will report the error quickly instead of waiting to be timed out, as is the case with the DROP policy. The DROP policy is contrary to TCP RFCs (Requests for Comment) and can be a little harsh on network devices; specifically, they can sit waiting for a response from their dropped packet(s) for a long time. But for security purposes, it is generally considered better to use the DROP policy rather than the REJECT policy, as it provides less information about your network to the outside world.

The ACCEPT policy accepts the traffic and allows it to pass through the firewall if it is not caught by a rule in the chain. Naturally, from a security perspective, this renders your firewall ineffective if it is used as the default policy. As we have said, by default, iptables configures all chains with a policy of ACCEPT, and it is best practice to set this to a policy of DROP for all chains is recommended – but only after careful consideration as this can stop *all* network traffic if done incorrectly.

■ **Caution** On remote hosts it is very easy to isolate the host from the network you are using to configure it. Make sure you have configured ACCEPT rules that allow you to connect before changing the policy to DROP.

The default policy of DROP falls in line with the basic doctrine of a 'default stance of denial' for the firewall. You should deny all traffic by default and open the host only to the traffic to which you have explicitly granted access. This denial can be problematic, because setting a default policy of DROP for the INPUT and OUTPUT chains means incoming and outgoing traffic are not allowed unless you explicitly add rules to allow traffic to come into and out of the firewalled host. Again some care and consideration is required when doing this as it will cause all services and tools that connect from your host or from your internal network via this firewall to fail if they are not explicitly allowed to enter or leave.

Network Address Translation

Network address translation allows your private network IP address space to appear to originate from a single public IP address. It does this with the help of IP masquerade, which rewrites IP packet headers. NAT holds information about connections traversing the firewall/router in translation tables. Generally speaking, an entry is written into the translation table when a packet traverses the firewall/router from the private to the public address space. When the matching packet returns, the router uses the translation table to match the returning packet to the originating source IP.

Many years ago, each host on the Internet was given a public IP address to become part of the Internet and talk to other hosts. It was soon realized that the available addresses would run out if every host that wanted to be on the Internet was given its own public IP address. NAT was invented to be able to have a private address space appear to come from a single IP address.

THE END OF NAT

IPv6 has of course saved us from the IPcalypse and there is no *real* need to NAT network addresses anymore. However, while NAT is a routing servicing (as opposed to a firewall service) it does provide some security for the address space it hides. NATs ability to hide our 'private' network address space means that many hosts and devices don't have to worry about network attacks (well, they should, but they don't).

When we consider that every IPv6 device is reachable from the internet and we consider the default rules for the firewall chains we have just shown, our systems could be in for a wild time without the security fig leaf of NAT'ing. We will still have the ability to perform firewall and routing operations in IPv6 to keep our devices safe but we will not be able to just 'hide' our networks.

So NAT is dead. But you will still see it around – a lot - until IPv6 is more widespread.

Using the Firewall-cmd Command

With CentOS, as we have mentioned, Firewalld is installed by default. Firewalld comes with two configuration tools, one is the GUI firewall-config and the other is the firewall-cmd command line tool. We are going to show you how to use this command to manage your host.

Firstly some background onFirewalld. Firewalld has the familiar concept of zones. Zones are names given to various levels of trust in your network. Starting with the low trust drop zone and progressing to higher levels of trust with public, external, dmz, work, home, internal and trusted zones. The idea is that you add your interfaces to one of these zones depending on your security needs. By default interfaces are added to the public zone.

It also has the ability to define a service. A service can be defined in an xml formatted file with a simple syntax. Take the `https.xml` zone file in the `/usr/lib/firewalld/services` directory:

```
<?xml version="1.0" encoding="utf-8"?>
<service>
 <short>Secure WWW (HTTPS)</short>
 <description>HTTPS is a modified ..<snip>.. be useful.</description>
 <port protocol="tcp" port="443"/>
</service>
```

You can create your own service files in the `/etc/firewalld/services` directory. These allow you reference them as service objects in your firewall configurations.

The configuration options for firewalld can be found in the `/etc/firewalld/firewalld.conf` and `/etc/sysconfig/firewalld`. In the `/etc/firewalld/firewalld.conf` you can set the default zone and other options. In the `/etc/sysconfig/firewalld` you can add any arguments to the the firewalld daemon.

By default the firewalld is not running on your system. You will need to enable it to make use of it. You can run stop|start|disable|enable|status on the firewalld service with the following commands:

```
$ sudo systemctl stop|start|disable|enable|status firewalld
```

You can check it's running state with:

```
$ sudo firewall-cmd –state
not running
```

To start firewalld, and make sure it starts again when you reboot the host, you need use systemctl to enable and then start the firewalld service. Once it is started we can view which zones we have active:

```
$ sudo firewall-cmd --get-active-zones
public
 interfaces: enp0s8 enp0s9
```

To get information about a zone, you can execute the following:

```
$ sudo firewall-cmd --zone=public --list-all
public (default, active)
 interfaces: enp0s8 enp0s9
 sources:
 services: dhcpv6-client ssh
 ports:
 masquerade: no
 forward-ports:
 icmp-blocks:
 rich rules:
```

Here we can see that the public zone is the default and that it is active. We can also see the interfaces that have been attached to it. The services describe what services are allowed access, the DHCP client and SSH. DHCP allows us to get an IP address automatically for our interface. These are defined in the services xml files and we can also use ports if you need to.

If you want to permanently change the zone for an interface you can modify the network interface with nmcli:

```
$ sudo nmcli c modify enp0s9 connection.zone dmz
```

This will add the 'ZONE=dmz' to the interface profile file /etc/sysconfig/network-scripts/ifcfg-enp0s9. This will not take any effect until we bring that interface up again.

We can add a http service to the zone labelled dmz. We do that with the following:

```
$ sudo firewall-cmd --zone=dmz --add-service=https --permanent
```

If we are going to make a change permanent we need to remember to add the --permanent option. You can reload the configuration without losing state information (does not interrupt connections) and you can reload that does lose state (people lose connections) with the complete reload:

```
$ sudo firewall-cmd reload
$ sudo firewall-cmd --complete-reload
```

Here you can see that our dmz now has the https and ssh services attached to it:

```
$ sudo firewall-cmd --zone=dmz --list-all
dmz
 interfaces:
 sources:
 services: https ssh
 ports:
 masquerade: no
 forward-ports:
 icmp-blocks:
 rich rules:
```

But you can see that it has no interfaces. We are going to add enp0s9 to this interface and like we said, the interface needs to 'upped' again.

```
$ sudo nmcli c up enp0s9
```

You should now be able to reach the HTTPS web service running on the enp0s9 interface.

Using the ufw Command

Ubuntu also has a tool for manipulating firewall rules from the command line. It is called ufw and is available from the ufw package.

■ **Tip**   We will talk more about installing packages in Chapter 8.

---

ufw is completely different to Firewalld. Under the covers it uses straight iptables directives to create firewall rules. If we look at the rule files in the /etc/ufw/ directory we can see the instructions that ufw uses to create the Netfilter rulesets.

Let's now show some of the basic commands.

You enable or disable ufw like so:

```
$ sudo ufw enable|disable
```

To get an output of current firewall status:

```
$ sudo ufw status numbered
Status: active

    To              Action      From
    --              ------      ----
[ 1] 22/tcp          ALLOW IN  Anywhere
[ 2] 22/tcp (v6)      ALLOW IN  Anywhere (v6)
```

This is saying we are going to allow traffic coming in (ALLOW IN), that originates from any network (Anywhere), and, that is destined for port TCP 22 (on both IPv4 and IPv6 interfaces).

You can add another rule like the following to allow http traffic to any local interface:

```
$ sudo ufw allow 80/tcp
Rule added
Rule added (v6)
$ sudo ufw status numbered
...
[ 3] 80                 ALLOW IN  Anywhere
[ 4] 80 (v6)            ALLOW IN  Anywhere (v6)
...
```

In the above you can see that we have added access to port 80 from anywhere on all IPv4 and IPv6 interfaces. That can be expressed like this too for common services (that is, services listed in the /etc/services file).

```
$ sudo ufw allow http
```

To remove a rule you can use the delete command:

```
$ sudo ufw delete 3
Deleting:
 allow 80
Proceed with operation (y|n)? y
Rule deleted
```

We need to answer either a y or n at the prompt to confirm if we wish to delete the rule. You can also specify the rule you wish to delete this:

```
$ sudo ufw delete allow http
```

You can also use a simplified syntax to describe rules you might need for applications. You can see the way ufw allows TCP port 22 access to the system (remembering that TCP port 22 is used for OpenSSH). The file /etc/ufw/applications.d/openssh-server is used to configure port 22 access by default.

```
[OpenSSH]
title=Secure shell server, an rshd replacement
description=OpenSSH is a free implementation of the Secure Shell protocol.
ports=22/tcp
```

Here we have the namespace [OpenSSH], followed by the title and description. The ports we need are then described, with multiple ports and protocols being separated by a '|'. For example, let's say we have a web application that requires the following TCP ports open, 80, 443 and 8080. We can create a ufw application by adding the file /etc/ufw/applications.d/web-server with the following:

```
[WebServer]
title=Application Web Server
description=Application X web services
ports=80/tcp|443/tcp|8080/tcp
```

To view our new configuration we can use the following command:

```
$ sudo ufw app info WebServer
sudo: unable to resolve host ubuntu-xenial
Profile: WebServer
Title: Application Web Server
Description: Application X web services

Ports:
 80/tcp
 443/tcp
8080/tcp
```

After creating an application configuration we need issue the update subcommand like this:

```
$ sudo ufw app update WebServer
```

Then to apply the new ruleset you can issue something like this to allow only hosts in the 192.168.0.0/24 address range.

```
$ sudo ufw allow from 192.168.0.0/24 to any app WebServer
Rule added
```

Let's break this down a little. We are saying that we want to allow any connection originating from the 192.168.0.0/24 network to any address on our localhost to any port that is listed in the app WebServer. To now list what we have done we will see the following:

```
$ sudo ufw allow from 192.168.0.0/24 to any app WebServer
$ sudo ufw status numbered
Status: active

     To          Action   From
     --          ------   ----
[ 1] WebServer   ALLOW IN 192.168.0.0/24
```

Traffic traversing this host needs to be routed with the ufw route command. For example, we have SSH traffic coming in on enp0s8 and leaving on enp0s9, we would write the ufw routing rule like this:

```
$ sudo ufw route allow in on enp0s8 out on enp0s9 to any port 22 proto tcp
```

Here we are saying allow SSH traffic (22) coming in on enp0s8 and out on enp0s9 to any destination IP address. This creates a rule in iptables that, when viewed with the iptables -L command looks like this:

```
Chain ufw-user-forward (1 references)
num target   prot opt  source        destination
1  ACCEPT    tcp  --   0.0.0.0/0     0.0.0.0/0     tcp dpt:22
```

Let's move on to explore more about iptables and what this means.

Using the iptables Command

Previously we have described the concepts of packet flows in Netfilter and we have introduced the two main commands that we can use to manage them, firewall-cmd and ufw. It is important that we now understand how they work and what they do. We will now show you how to use the `iptables` command to manage Netfilter. The `iptables` command allows you to do the following:

- List the contents of the packet filter rule set.

- Add/remove/modify rules in the packet filter rule set.

- List/zero per-rule counters of the packet filter rule set.

For IPv6 you use the ip6tables command, but syntactically it is the same command, but instructs Netfilter how to operate on IPv6 packets. In this section we are going to talk mostly about the IPv4 command but there is no difference in the commands usage for IPv6. To effectively use the `iptables` command, you must have root privileges. The basic `iptables` command structure and arguments are as follows:

```
iptables -t table-name command chain rulenumber paramaters -j target
```

Table 7-6 gives a rundown on the commands, shown in the preceding syntax *command*, we will be demonstrating and their description.

Table 7-6. *Command Options Available to the* `iptables` *Command*

Option	Description
-L	Lists the current rules of `iptables` you have in memory.
-D	Deletes a rule in a chain. The rule to delete can be expressed as a rule number or as a pattern to match.
-I	Inserts a rule into a chain. This will insert the rule at the top of the chain unless a rule number is specified.
-F	Flushes a chain. This will remove all the rules from a chain or all the rules in all the chains in a table if no chain is specified.
-A	Appends a rule to a chain. Same as -I except the rule is appended to the bottom of the chain by default.
-X	Deletes a chain. The chain must be empty and not referenced by any other chain at the time you wish to delete it.
-N	Creates a new chain. There can be no target already existing with the same name.
-R	Replace an existing rule
-C	Check if the rules exists in a chain and returns an exit code.
-S	Prints the rules (similar to –L) in the specified chain. These can be used to restore IPtables later on.
-P	Sets a default policy for a chain. Each built-in chain (INPUT, OUTPUT, FORWARD, POSTROUTING, etc.) has a default policy of either ACCEPT, REJECT, or DROP.

■ **Caution**   It is always a good idea when you are working with firewall rules to have access to a system console in the event that you make a mistake and block all your network traffic. Changing your firewall rules over the network, especially on remotely housed systems, can leave you in an *awkward* position if you make a mistake (and everyone makes at least one mistake).

```
iptables -t table-name command chain rulenumber paramaters -j target
```

A large number of parameters, shown in the iptables command syntax as *parameters* above, can be used to manipulate packets as they pass through your firewall. When we explained chains, we said they were like hooks. The parameters are the different types of bait that sit on the hook. Each parameter will attract packets depending on the information in the packet. It can be the source and destination addresses of the packet or the protocol. The packet can furthermore be matched to source or destination ports or the state the packet is in. The parameters can also be used to match packets, capture them, tag them, and release them.

```
iptables -t table-name command chain rulenumber paramaters -j target
```

The target argument, depicted by -j *target* in the iptables command syntax, is the action to be performed on the packet if it has been hooked. Common targets are ACCEPT, DROP, LOG, MASQUERADE, and CONNMARK. The target can also be another user-defined chain.

We want to now show you how to use the iptables command by running you through some examples.

The iptables command is common to both Ubuntu and CentOS and operates in the same way. Let's look at listing the contents of the iptables rule sets we currently have running. We do that by issuing the following command:

```
$ sudo /sbin/iptables -t filter -L --line-numbers
```

Here we are viewing the filter table. The -L option lists all the chains and their associated rules with line numbering, specified by --line-numbers, for each. The line numbering is important because, as has been mentioned, iptables runs through each rule sequentially starting from the first to the last. When you want to add a new rule or delete an old rule, you can use these numbers to pinpoint which rule you want to target. Here is the listed output of that command in Listing 7-7.

Listing 7-7. iptables filter table

```
sudo /sbin/iptables -t filter -L --line-numbers
Chain INPUT (policy ACCEPT)
num target   prot opt source        destination

Chain FORWARD (policy ACCEPT)
num target   prot opt source        destination

Chain OUTPUT (policy ACCEPT)
num target   prot opt source        destination
```

That is a little anti-climactic. We, by default, have no rules in any of our chains in the filter table. This of course means that any service that is started on our host can immediately begin communicating on our network. We should fix that.

It is up to you to set the minimal rule requirements and we will give help with these rules as we go along. We have the option here to create our own chain so that we can group our firewall rules. You don't have to create a new chain, but you might if you want to keep all your rules separate from the default chains, our have them relate to logical business groups. We could also define the chain by the logical network group, we are going to keep it simple and call it IPV4-INCOMING.

```
$ sudo /sbin/iptables -t filter -N IPV4-INCOMING
```

This command creates a new chain using -N IPV4-INCOMING in the filter table as denoted by -t filter. It does not have any rules associated with it yet, but by the end of this section you will be able to add and remove rules.

■ **Note**   You don't have to use the preceding naming standard for naming your chains. However, you will benefit from using something that makes sense to your configuration. Otherwise, the output of your iptables rules could look very messy and hard to diagnose for faults. You also don't need to create your own user-defined chains if you don't want to, but it will make reading your rules simpler if you do.

By listing our iptables you will now see the new chain we have created:

```
Chain IPV4-INCOMING (0 references)
num target    prot opt source          destination
```

It has no rules in it yet so we are going to create some. Let's start with a simple rule..

```
sudo iptables -t filter -A IPV4-INCOMING -d 0.0.0.0/0 -s 0.0.0.0/0 -j ACCEPT
Chain IPV4-INCOMING (0 references)
num target    prot opt source   destination
1  ACCEPT    all -- anywhere anywhere
```

This rule allows all connections from anywhere on any port and is the equivalent of the ACCEPT policy. Be we are just going to concentrate on explaining the command we have issued rather than its merits. Breaking it down we are again working on the filter table. Next we are adding (-A) a rule to the IPV4-INCOMING chain. We are using the shortened syntax for --destination (-d) and using the anywhere IP notation of 0.0.0.0/0 to show that this rule should match all IPv4 addresses on our local host. Likewise for --source (-s) we accept all source addresses for this rule (0.0.0.0/0). Lastly we provide the target for this rule (-j) which is to jump to the ACCEPT target. The ACCEPT target allows the socket to make the connection.

Okay, that was a mistake, let's remove that rule. From our iptables listing above we can see that the rule we want to remove is in position 1. We will use that when we delete that rule.

```
$ sudo /sbin/iptables -t filter -D IPV4-INCOMING 1
```

If you list the tables again we see that there are no rules associated again. We can now delete that chain because it is empty. To do that we issue the following command:

```
$ sudo /sbin/iptables -t filter -X IPV4-INCOMING
```

The whole chain has been removed. You cannot remove the default INPUT, OUTPUT FORWARD chains.

We are going re-create the chain and add a few more rules so that we show the next section. Here is our list.

```
1  ACCEPT   all -- anywhere  anywhere  ctstate INVALID
2  ACCEPT   all -- anywhere  anywhere  ctstate RELATED,ESTABLISHED
3  DROP     all -- anywhere  anywhere
4  ACCEPT   tcp -- anywhere  anywhere  tcp  dpt:ssh
```

This ruleset, if it was in the INPUT chain would be causing problems. Let's use our iptables commands to fix it. First we need to move rule 4 to above rule 1. To do that we issue the following:

```
iptables -t filter -I IPV4-INCOMING 1 -p tcp --dport 22 -j ACCEPT
```

When you look at the third line now in the IPV4-INCOMING chain, you can see that our rule has been inserted and has the target of ACCEPT.

```
num target    prot opt source    destination
1  ACCEPT   tcp -- anywhere  anywhere   tcp  dpt:ssh
2  ACCEPT   all -- anywhere  anywhere   ctstate INVALID
3  ACCEPT   all -- anywhere  anywhere   ctstate RELATED,ESTABLISHED
4  DROP     all -- anywhere  anywhere
5  ACCEPT   tcp -- anywhere  anywhere   tcp dpt:ssh
```

We will remove rule number 5 like we removed our previous rule with the -D IPV4-INCOMING 5 switch. But our rules still don't look right. Rule number 2 should not be accepting connections but dropping them. Let's replace that rule with the correct one (don't worry, we are going to explain what the conntrack does shortly).

```
sudo iptables -R IPV4-INCOMING 2 -m conntrack --ctstate INVALID -j DROP
1  ACCEPT   tcp -- anywhere  anywhere  tcp  dpt:ssh
2  DROP     all -- anywhere  anywhere  ctstate INVALID
3  ACCEPT   all -- anywhere  anywhere  ctstate RELATED,ESTABLISHED
4  DROP     all -- anywhere  anywhere
```

That looks better. So reading the rules from top to bottom like the Netfilter firewall does, we are allowing SSH traffic, dropping invalid traffic, allowing any current and established traffic, then dropping everything else.

You can also flush your chains, which means removing all the rules from all the chains or all the rules from a specified chain. This can be used to clear any existing rules before you add a fresh set.

■ **Note**   We are going to show you how to save your iptables shortly, and that is something you might want to do before this next step if you don't want to lose your current set. (Tip: `iptables-save > iptables.backup`)

You achieve this by issuing a command similar to the following:

```
$ sudo /sbin/iptables -t filter -F IPV4-INCOMING
```

Here we have flushed, as denoted by -F, all the rules from the IPV4-INCOMING chain in the filter table. If you now view the INPUT chain in the filter table, you will see there are no longer any rules associated with it.

```
$ sudo /sbin/iptables -L IPV4-INCOMING --line-numbers
Chain IPV4-INCOMING (policy ACCEPT)
num target    prot opt source        destination
```

In this case, since we have a default policy of ACCEPT, clearing this chain does not affect the way our host operates. If we changed the policy to DROP and flushed the chain, all inbound connections will be cut, making our host unusable for network-related tasks and services. This is because the policy determines what happens to packets that are not matched by any rule. If there are no rules in your chain, then iptables will use the default policy to handle packets accordingly.

Currently we have been able to make changes at will to our chain because Netfilter wasn't configured to use it. For the rules in our IPV4-INCOMING chain to be parsed, we need to add a rule in the INPUT chain that directs all the incoming packets to our host to the IPV4-INCOMING chain.

```
$ sudo /sbin/iptables -t filter -A INPUT -j IPV4-INCOMING
num target     prot opt source        destination
1 IPV4-INCOMING all -- anywhere      anywhere
```

We have included the output of the list (-L) command above. Here we have issued the command to append the rule to our INPUT chain. It is the first chain to receive packets inbound to our firewall with our host as the final destination. Like with our other rules we append it with -t filter -A INPUT. Any packets with any protocol will now be sent to chain IPV4-INCOMING, as denoted by -j IPV4-INCOMING, for further processing.

We may not want all our packets to go to our IPV4-INCOMING chain. Maybe we only want tcp packets to go to that chain and we will handle udp packets in a different chain. You can refine what you want to catch in your rules by adding other parameters. In the following incidence, we could match only on TCP traffic and send that to some target by replacing (-R) our first INPUT rule.

```
$ sudo /sbin/iptables -t filter -R INPUT 1 -p tcp -j IPV4-INCOMING
```

We can further refine our "bait" to attract different types of fish . . . er . . . packets. Maybe we only want tcp packets with a destination address in our 192.168.10.0/24 network? That would look like this:

```
$ sudo /sbin/iptables -t filter -R INPUT 1 -s 0.0.0.0/0 -d 192.168.10.0/24 -p tcp -j IPV4-
INCOMING
num target     prot opt source    destination
1 IPV4-INCOMING tcp -- anywhere  192.168.10.0/24
```

We have now replaced a rule, by specifying -R, to the INPUT chain that directs only packets with the tcp protocol and only if their destination address in the 192.168.10.0/24 network. Packet like that are directed to the IPV4-INCOMING chain.

Lastly, we will now set a default policy on our INPUT chain. We will set this to DROP so that anything not matched by our rule set will be automatically "dropped to the floor." We achieve this by specifying the table name, specified by -t filter, the chain, denoted by INPUT, and the target, DROP.

■ **Caution**   This is one of those potentially dangerous commands that can drop all your network connections. Before you run this command, make sure you have access to a physical console just in case.

```
$ sudo /sbin/iptables -t filter -P INPUT DROP
```

When we now list the INPUT chain in the filter table, the default policy is shown to be DROP.

```
$ sudo iptables -L INPUT
sudo /sbin/iptables -t filter -L --line-numbers
Chain INPUT (policy DROP)
num target      prot opt source    destination
1  IPV4-INCOMING all --  anywhere   anywhere
```

It is good practice and a good habit to remember to apply the policy of DROP to all your chains. For firewalls to be most secure, a default policy of denial should be mandatory in all your chains.

Armed with these basic commands, you will be able to perform most functions on your chains and rule sets. There are many more features that you can add to your rules to make your firewall perform very complex and interesting routing. Please refer to the iptables man page for a complete list of tasks you can do.

You can save and restore your iptables configurations fairly simply. Both Ubuntu and CentOS have the same command to do this. First, let's save our iptables rules:

```
$ sudo iptables-save > /path/to/your/iptables.bak
```

Here we have issued the iptables command and directed that output (>) to a file on our file system. If you don't redirect the output to a file it will print to screen. Restoring these files is simple also. First we can run a test on syntax of the file with the following:

```
$ sudo iptables-restore -t -v < /path/to/your/iptables.bak
Flushing chain `INPUT'
Flushing chain `FORWARD'
Flushing chain `OUTPUT'
# Completed on Fri May 20 21:49:49 2016
```

This show a verbose output (-v) of the command and will give an error if there is something wrong in your config file (like iptables-restore: line 4 failed). To restore the iptables file you remove the test switch (-t).

Starting and stopping iptables is different on both Ubuntu and CentOS. On Ubuntu you can do the following to add and remove your firewall rules. You would make any changes and additions to your rules. Then you could use the following in your /etc/network/interfaces file to activate your rules and save them again.

```
auto enp0s3
iface enp0s3 inet dhcp
  pre-up iptables-restore < /etc/network/firewall
  post-down iptables-save -c > /etc/network/firewall
```

Here we have a standard interface configuration for enp0s3. We use the pre-up command to activate the firewall rules before we bring up our interface. We then use the post-down command to save our rules once our interface has come down.

If you are using ufw on your Ubuntu host, you can use the systemctl command to stop and start ufw:

```
$ sudo systemctl start|stop|restart ufw
```

Here the `systemctl` is used to manage the `ufw` service.

On CentOS machines, since it follows closely with Red Hat, the usual tools to manage the iptables needs to be installed (if you don't already have them installed). You will need to download and install the iptables-services package (`yum install -y iptables-services`) to get access to the following commands.

To start and stop `iptables` you can use the `systemctl` command:

```
$ sudo systemctl start|stop|restart iptables
```

These actions should be self-explanatory by now. You can also use `status` to the current status as you would expect. When you execute a `stop`, your current firewall rules are saved.

Further reading

Netfilter and `iptables` are complex topics, and we recommend you read up further on them. For additional information about Netfilter and the `iptables` command, read its `man` page. Also available are some online tutorials:

- `https://help.ubuntu.com/community/IptablesHowTo`

- `http://www.linuxtopia.org/Linux_Firewall_iptables/index.html`

Ubuntu also installs some iptables documentation on the local hard disk:

- `/usr/share/doc/iptables/html/packet-filtering-HOWTO.html`

- `/usr/share/doc/iptables/html/NAT-HOWTO.html`

And for more advanced topics, these may be of interest:

- Designing and Implementing Linux Firewalls with QoS using netfilter, iproute2, NAT and L7-filter by Lucian Gheorghe (PACKT Publishing, 2006)

- Linux Firewalls: Attack Detection and Response with iptables, psad, and fwsnort by Michael Rash (No Starch Press, 2007)

- Linux Firewalls: Enhancing Security with nftables and Beyond (4th Edition) by Steve Suehring (Pearson Education 2015)

Explaining Firewall Rules

Now is a good time to explore the firewall rules you may see on your hosts more closely. Depending on your installation method, both CentOS and Ubuntu can come with a firewall configuration already installed. Tools like `ufw` and `firewalld` are both user tools to manage firewalls and they attempt to do this in a logical and sane way and hide the complexity of the rules for you.

A default rule set for just the filter table for firewalld or ufw can be over 100 lines long, Listing 7-8 shows the output (`iptables-save`) of just the INPUT chain of the filter table on a CentOS host that has firewalld installed. In Listing 7-8, we have cut down the output and added line numbers to help clarify our explanation of the output.

Listing 7-8. Firewalld INPUT chain

```
1. *filter
2. :INPUT ACCEPT [0:0]
3. :INPUT_ZONES - [0:0]
4. :INPUT_ZONES_SOURCE - [0:0]
5. :INPUT_direct - [0:0]
6. -A INPUT -i virbr0 -p udp -m udp --dport 53 -j ACCEPT
7. -A INPUT -i virbr0 -p tcp -m tcp --dport 53 -j ACCEPT
8. -A INPUT -i virbr0 -p udp -m udp --dport 67 -j ACCEPT
9. -A INPUT -i virbr0 -p tcp -m tcp --dport 67 -j ACCEPT
10. -A INPUT -m conntrack --ctstate RELATED,ESTABLISHED -j ACCEPT
11. -A INPUT -i lo -j ACCEPT
12. -A INPUT -j INPUT_direct
13. -A INPUT -j INPUT_ZONES_SOURCE
14. -A INPUT -j INPUT_ZONES
15. -A INPUT -p icmp -j ACCEPT
16. -A INPUT -j REJECT --reject-with icmp-host-prohibited
```

The Netfilter likes the configuration of iptables rules in the following format:

```
* <table name>
<CHAIN> <POLICY> [<byte:counter>]
-A <CHAIN> <rule set>
COMMIT
```

The * filter is the start of the filter table stanza each line will be read in until the COMMIT statement. Chains are then listed along with their default policies if they have one set. The byte and counter marks[0:0], can be used to see how much traffic in volume has passed through that chain as well as how many packets have passed through it (you can use iptables -Z *chain* to reset these counters to zero if you wish). We then list all our rules for that particular chain. Lastly we require the COMMIT to tell Netfilter to add the table stanza.

Lines 2-5 in Listing 7-8 are the definitions of our chains in the filter table. We have only shown the chains relating to INPUT but there are also FORWARD, OUTPUT and other user defined chains not seen here. INPUT ACCEPT on line 2 is the default INPUT chain and the default policy for that chain is ACCEPT. Lines 3-5 are the chains that Firewalld uses to group rules into more logical units. They have no policy attached (-).

In Listing 7-8, lines 6-9 do a similar thing. First thing to notice is that packets matching these rules will jump to the ACCEPT target. Lines 6-7 allow DNS queries on both udp and tcp protocols from any source to any destination on the virbr0 interface. The virbr0 interface is used for virtual interfaces to shared physical devices. Lines 8-9 are similar and provide access the bootps (DHCP) service. These rules allow virtual hosts that maybe started up (KVM or Xen virtual hosts, for example) to access these services to get DNS and DHCP services. We talk more about KVM and Xen in Chapter 20.

To understand line 10 we need to remember our talk about tcpdump and the 3 way handshake that the IP protocol uses to establish a connection (socket) with another host. In line 10 we want to accept all connections with a connection state of RELATED,ESTABLISHED. This means that any connection that has completed the handshake and has become 'established' or any connections 'relating' to an existing connection are allowed. Netfilter uses the conntrack module to track connections and know their state and it is this that makes Netfilter a stateful firewall.

NEW, ESTABLISHED, RELATED, AND INVALID STATES

The NEW connection state indicates a freshly initiated connection through which data has not passed back and forth. You must allow the NEW connection state, either incoming or outgoing, if you want to allow new connections to a service. For example, if you do not specify that the NEW connection state is accepted for incoming SMTP traffic on a mail server, remote clients will not be able to use the mail server to send e-mail.

An ESTABLISHED connection state indicates an existing connection that is in the process of transferring data. You need to allow ESTABLISHED connections if you want a service to be able to maintain a connection with a remote client or server. For example, if you want to allow SSH connections to your host, you must allow NEW and ESTABLISHED incoming traffic and ESTABLISHED outgoing traffic to ensure the connection is possible.

The RELATED state refers to a connection that is used to facilitate another connection. A common example is an FTP session where control data is passed to one connection, and actual file data flows through another one.

The INVALID state is branded on a connection that has been seen to have problems in processing packets: they may have exceeded the processing ability of the firewall or be packets that are irrelevant to any current connection.

In Listing 7-8, the rule on line 11 is set to accept all connections on the loopback device, also referred to as lo or 127.0.0.1. This is important for inter-process communications as many processes often use the loopback to send messages to each other. It is important that this is allowed to accept packets as many things stop working otherwise.

Lines 12-14 in Listing 7-8 are used to direct all our packets coming in the local interface to the Firewalld chains. They have the format:

```
-A <CHAIN> -j <CHAIN TO JUMP TO>.
```

So line 12 says to send all packets to the INPUT_direct chain managed by Firewalld. If you looked in the full output of the iptables-save command you may not see any rules associated with this chain. If we can't find any rules we move to the next rules in our INPUT chain. Line 13 also may not have any rules associated with that chain. If we follow what happens to the rule on line 14 (-A INPUT -j INPUT_ZONES) we jump to the INPUT_ZONES chain. That chain looks like this:

Listing 7-9. Iptables Jump and Goto

```
-A INPUT_ZONES -g IN_public
-A IN_public -j IN_public_log
-A IN_public -j IN_public_deny
-A IN_public -j IN_public_allow
-A IN_public_allow -p tcp -m tcp --dport 22 -m conntrack --ctstate NEW -j ACCEPT
```

Here in Listing 7-9 we have INPUT_ZONES chain with a goto (-g) switch to the IN_public chain. The -g says go to the user chain IN_public and continue processing there instead of returning to INPUT_ZONES.

A packet will land into IN_public, then jump to IN_public_log, return to IN_public, jump to IN_public_deny, return to IN_public and then jump to IN_public_allow. In IN_public_allow we have rule that allows our ssh connections.

```
-A IN_public_allow -p tcp -m tcp --dport 22 -m conntrack --ctstate NEW -j ACCEPT
```

To explain this line, let's suppose we are going to initiate an incoming connection to our local SSH service on our host. The initial incoming packet will contain the the SYN flag to try to initiate a socket. The above line tells us we match on first tcp (-m tcp) packets with a destination port of 22 (--dport 22). If we have not seen the connection before, it is not related to any packets, it also is a SYN packet so we are not yet established. The --ctstate NEW allows us to initiate the socket from the remote host. Once the connection is in the ESTABLISHED state, our firewall allows the ongoing communication. ESTABLISHED and RELATED connections are then handled by line 10 in Listing 7-8.

THE DIFFERENT PROTOCOLS

Netfilter or iptables filters traffic based on different protocols in the TCP/IP protocol stack. You can filter on protocols like TCP, UDP, AH, IPsec, PPPoE, STP, and many others.

You can get a good list of all the possible protocols in /etc/protocols along with their protocol numbers. In iptables, you can specify the protocol name, like udp, or a protocol number, like 17 (for UDP), when declaring a rule. In the following, we are filtering on UDP packets:

```
iptables -A INPUT -p 17 -m conntrack --ctstate NEW --dport 53 -j ACCEPT
```

If you do not specify a protocol, the default is to match all. You can also use ! to exclude a protocol by specifying your rule like this:

```
iptables -A INPUT -p ! udp -m conntrack --ctstate NEW -j ACCEPT
```

This rule accepts packets of all protocols except those using the UDP protocol in a NEW state. The following is a good reference on network protocols: http://www.iana.org/assignments/protocol-numbers/protocol-numbers.xhtml.

Logging and Rate Limiting and Securing Netfilter

Part of securing and managing your firewall is monitoring logging, dropping unwanted traffic and rate limiting possible vectors of attack. With Netfilter we can record in our logs connection attempts as they come into our firewall, then either accept or reject those connections. This in itself can be an attack vector as an attacker can fill your firewall logs with connection attempts and either use that to mask another attack or make the constant logging of bad connection swamp your firewall resources. Therefore it is a good idea to rate limit any firewall logging or rate limit the connection attempts themselves.

As the packet comes into the firewall we can match on the protocol, port, source address, destination address and more. Take the SSH example, we can match on protocol TCP and destination port 22. When you stand up a server that has the SSH port open to the world you will see many attempts by bots to access this port with brute force username/password combinations. Typically we would set up our Netfilter (with either iptables, firewall-cmd or ufw) like this:

```
-A INPUT_ZONES -g IN_public
-A IN_public -j IN_public_log
-A IN_public -j IN_public_deny
-A IN_public -j IN_public_allow
-A IN_public_allow -p tcp -m tcp --dport 22 -m conntrack --ctstate NEW -j ACCEPT
```

In the IN_public_log chain we could add a rule like this:

```
-A IN_public_log ! --source 10.0.0.1/32 \ ↵
 -p tcp -m tcp --dport 22 \ ↵
 -m conntrack --ctstate NEW \ ↵
 -m limit --limit 2/m --limit-burst 5 \ ↵
 -j LOG --log-prefix "IN_LOG_SSH:"
```

Here we have added a rule that says:

- If our source address is not from our trusted IP address

- And it is a TCP request on port 22

- And it has the NEW connection state

- Apply limit of 2 connections per minute after the first 5 matching packets

- LOG those connection attempts and add a prefix to the log of "IN_LOG_SSH".

This will log SSH connection attempts addresses we don't normally expect connections from (! --source 10.0.0.1/32 – the exclamation, !, says 'not from'). We can also protect our SSH service further by writing the rule in the IN_public_allow chain like this:

```
-A IN_public_allow -p tcp --dport ssh -m conntrack --ctstate NEW -m recent --set --name drop_ssh
-A IN_public_allow -p tcp --dport ssh -m conntrack --ctstate NEW \ ↵
 -m recent --name drop_ssh --update --seconds 60 --hitcount 5 -j DROP
```

Here we are using the Netfilter recent module. The recent module allows us to create a dynamic list of IP addresses that we can then apply actions on for a future match. The above creates a list of IPs that match on new TCP SSH connections that have matched destination TCP port 22 and NEW connection state. That list is given the name drop_ssh. The next line says we update the last seen timestamp each we see the connection of this type. If we see 5 hits for the that rule in the 60 second time period then DROP those connections.

You can also use the firewall-cmd to enable logging and rate limiting. If we wanted to apply the recent module with our firewall-cmd issue something similar to this from your command line:

```
$ sudo firewall-cmd --permanent --direct --add-rule ipv4 filter IN_public_allow 0 -p tcp
--dport 22 \
 -m state --state NEW -m recent --set –name ssh_drop
$ sudo firewall-cmd --permanent --direct --add-rule ipv4 filter IN_public_allow 1 -p tcp
--dport 22 \
 -m state --state NEW -m recent –name ssh_drop --update --seconds 60 --hitcount 5 -j DROP
```

This uses the firewall-cmd and the --direct configuration option to add our rule using the recent module. The direct argument is expressed like this:

```
--permanent --direct --add-rule { ipv4 | ipv6 | eb } <table> <chain> <priority> <args>
```

So in the first command, the table is filter, the chain is IN_public_allow and the priority is 0 followed by the arguments. You can read more about the --direct argument here:

- https://access.redhat.com/documentation/en-US/Red_Hat_Enterprise_Linux/7/html/Security_Guide/sec-Using_Firewalls.html#sec-Introduction_to_firewalld

In that link you will also find how to apply limit and logging with firewall-cmd as well using the Rich Language commands.

Also remember to issue the following each time you want to change your firewall rules with firewall-cmd:

```
$ sudo firewall-cmd --reload
```

■ **Caution**   These rules can sometimes be problematic if people spoof your legitimate IP address in order to trigger the DROP rule, effectively denying you access to your system.

Further to this, we can use tools like Fail2ban or Sec to parse our SSH logs and then 'jail' or 'drop' connections that match a set of unsuccessful connection attempt criteria. You can read more information about Fail2ban here:

- http://www.fail2ban.org/wiki/index.php/Main_Page
- https://www.digitalocean.com/community/tutorials/how-to-protect-ssh-with-fail2ban-on-centos-7

Now take a look at these to rules in the IN_public_allow and IN_public_deny chains respectively:

```
-A IN_public_allow -p icmp -m icmp --icmp-type echo-request –m limit --limit 1/s -j ACCEPT
-A IN_public_deny -p icmp -m icmp --icmp-type any -j DROP
```

In the IN_public_allow chain we have specified that for ICMP packet of the type echo-request we will accept 1 packets per second. ICMP packets can be a route of attack and some administrators will often block all external (and sometimes internal) ICMP packets by default because of this. Here we have made the decision to allow echo-requests, or ping, and of other ICMP types will be dropped.

DIFFERENT TYPES OF ATTACKS

There are different types of attacks that people can use to bring down your network. Some target the perimeter of your network, tying it up with bogus connections until it breaks and stops responding; these are known as Denial of Service attacks (DoS), for example, SYN flood attacks. Others will use the services you are running (like a mail or a web server) to bypass your perimeter security and launch an attack from within your network (e.g., virus attacks, Trojan attacks, script injection attacks).

Distributed Denial of Service attacks (DDoS) are also increasingly common and very hard to mitigate against. This is where the attackers use botnets (a collection of 'owned' internet computers that can be used to target a network by sending millions of bogus requests) to overwhelm network firewalls with large floods of traffic specially crafted packets. Even large companies with very expensive equipment can be subject to these attacks.

While keeping your network secure is a constant process, you can do a few things to minimize your risks:

- Track security alert mailing lists for your hosts.

- Keep your hosts up to date with the latest security patches.

- Close off unwanted ports and services.

- Get to know your logs and learn to detect anything that looks odd.

- Review your security every six months at minimum to make sure it is still working properly.

- Use an upstream DDoS mitigation service to help protect your network.

Nothing connected to the Internet is 100% secure, but you can take measures that ensure your network isn't one of those with a well-known vulnerability. It doesn't take long for the script kiddies to find your host and try for common and preventable exploits.

There are some other rules that can help prevent different network attacks. A common attack is called the SYN flood where the attacker send bogus SYN packets to the victim. A SYN flood uses the TCP three-way handshake to starve resources on your firewalls.

A fairly recent addition to the Linux kernel (v3.12) enables the use of a module called SYNPROXY. This Netfilter module is designed to mitigate SYN floods. You can read more about SYN floods, DDoS mitigation and SYNPROXY here:

- http://rhelblog.redhat.com/2014/04/11/mitigate-tcp-syn-flood-attacks-with-red-hat-enterprise-linux-7-beta/

- https://javapipe.com/iptables-ddos-protection

With ufw, we can only apply simple filtering and logging. If we wanted to limit our SSH connections we would issue the following:

```
$ sudo ufw limit ssh/tcp
```

Currently only ipv4 is supported with this and will deny the connection if there are more than 5 attempts in the last 30 seconds. If we wanted to log our SSH connections we would issue the following:

```
$ sudo ufw allow log 22/tcp
```

This will log connections for SSH. For further information on these options see the ufw man page.

Further Exploring firewall-cmd

As we have said, we can also use firewall-cmd on our CentOS hosts to manage our iptables. On a CentOS host we can perform the same iptables instructions via firewall-cmd. In this example we are going to add enpOs8 to the external zone, then configure IP masquerading on that interface. Then we are going to 'port forward' port 80 to our internal host on 192.168.0.1:80.

First we need to set our enpOs8 interface to be in the external zone. There are two ways of doing this, one is by the use of the firewall-cmd cli and the other is directly editing the network profile in /etc/sysconfig/network-scripts/ifcfg-enpOs8. If the interface is managed by NetworkManager then directly editing and adding the following to the bottom of the file:

```
ZONE=external
```

If the device is not managed by NetworkManager then you can issue the following:

```
$ sudo firewall-cmd --zone=external --add-interface=enpOs8
```

Next step is to add masquerading to the external zone. First we can check to see if it already has it and then add it like so:

```
$ sudo firewall-cmd --zone=external --query-masquerade
no
$ sudo firewall-cmd --zone=external --add-masquerade --permanent
```

We add --permanent to make the changes persistent. Now to add our port forwarding, or what we called DNATs before, we are going to issue the following:

```
$ sudo firewall-cmd --zone=external --add-forward-port=port=80:proto=tcp:toport=80:toad
dr=192.168.0.1 --permanent
```

Our zone should now look like this:

```
$ sudo firewall-cmd --zone=external --list-all
external (active)
 interfaces: enpOs8
 sources:
 services: ssh
 ports:
 masquerade: yes
 forward-ports: port=80:proto=tcp:toport=80:toaddr=192.168.0.1
 icmp-blocks:
 rich rules:
```

We are now going to setup a DMZ zone for our services that live inside our network but that are accessed by external clients, such as public websites hosted on internal servers. To do that we add our enp0s9 interface to the zone=dmz as we did for enp0s8.

Once we have that our dmz zone should look like this:

```
$msudo firewall-cmd --zone=dmz --list-all
dmz (active)
  interfaces: enp0s9
  sources:
  services: ssh
  ports:
  masquerade: no
  forward-ports:
  icmp-blocks:
  rich rules:
```

Now when we try to access our site from the public internet, with something like curl:

```
$ curl -I http://website.example.com
HTTP/1.1 200 OK
Date: Mon, 23 May 2016 12:40:16 GMT
Server: Apache/2.4.18 (Ubuntu)
Last-Modified: Tue, 10 May 2016 11:54:38 GMT
```

Definitive guide for Firewalld can be found at the Red Hat documentation site:

- https://access.redhat.com/documentation/en-US/Red_Hat_Enterprise_Linux/7/html/Security_Guide/sec-Using_Firewalls.html#sec-Introduction_to_firewalld

Here are also a few distributions that are specialised and dedicated to be firewalls. A listing can be found here, some have commercial offerings and others are community supported.

- https://en.wikipedia.org/wiki/List_of_router_and_firewall_distributions

- http://www.techradar.com/au/news/software/applications/7-of-the-best-linux-firewalls-697177

There are other non-Linux operating systems that can be quite good for firewalls such as NetBSD https://www.netbsd.org/. Linux and Unix style operating systems can also be found in commercial appliances.

TCP Wrappers

Lastly, one of the other ways of securing your host is to use TCP Wrappers. If your network service is compiled with support for TCP Wrappers, you can use TCP Wrappers to further secure the services of your hosts. TCP Wrappers control access to the daemons running on your host, not to the ports, through a series of definitions in the /etc/hosts.allow and /etc/hosts.deny files.

The rules in hosts.allow take precedence over the rules in hosts.deny. If you are going to use TCP Wrappers, it is a good idea to set the following in hosts.deny:

```
ALL: ALL
```

This will set the default action of denial to all services unless specified in the `/etc/hosts.allow` file. The rules are read in order from top to bottom.

You would then add network services. For example, for our example network, we will allow network services by setting the following:

```
ALL: localhost ACCEPT
sshd: .example.com EXCEPT .baddomain.com
```

These settings will first allow any localhost connections to be accepted. Many services require connections to services running on the loopback (localhost) interface, and these need to be accepted. Next, we are allowing the hosts on the `example.com` network to connect to our SSH daemon. Here also we are explicitly denying `baddomain.com`. For more information on configuring TCP Wrappers, please see the man page for `hosts_options` or `hosts.allow` and `hosts.deny`.

Setting Up a ppp Connection

On our gateway.example.com *bastion*, or *gateway*, host, which is another name for the router/ firewall on the perimeter of a network, we will need to set up a PPP service. The PPP service makes a connection to your ISP, provides some authentication details, and receives the IP address provided to you by the ISP. This IP address can be either a static address, meaning it doesn't't change, or a dynamic address, which means it is provided from a pool of addresses and will regularly change every few days. We are going to set up a PPP xDSL connection, which is a common way to connect to an ISP.

The most common way to set up an xDSL connection on Linux without the NetworkManager is to use the Roaring Penguin PPPoE client. To do so, first you will need to check that you have this client installed. On CentOS, again we will use nmcli to create our connection. On Ubuntu, you have to install pppoeconf.

Let's take a brief look at how you go about setting up your PPP ADSL connections using CentOS and Ubuntu.

With Ubuntu, you can use the `pppoeconf` command or create a PPP connection in your `/etc/network/interfaces` file.

ADSL Setup Using nmcli

We will look at how we can use the nmcli command for your PPPOE connection. This is relatively easy as you can see. First you will need to discover what interface your Linux server is connecting to your modem on. For this exercise we will use enp0s8 as our interface.

```
$ sudo nmcli c add type adsl ifname enp0s8 protocol pppoa username ourname password psswd ↵
encapsulation llc
Connection 'adsl-enp0s8' (ae7bc50a-c4d5-448a-8331-4a6f41c156c5) successfully added.
```

Depending on your ISP connection these may differ for you. Your ISP will provide information on your encapsulation protocol, in our case it is llc (logical link control). The nmcli command has now created a file called /etc/NetworkManager/system-connections/adsl-enp0s8. NetworkManager now controls this connection. Our `adsl-enp0s8` file looks like Listing 7-10.

Listing 7-10. adsl-enp0s3 File on CentOS

```
$ sudo cat /etc/NetworkManager/system-connections/adsl-enp0s8
[connection]
id=adsl-enp0s8
uuid=ae7bc50a-c4d5-448a-8331-4a6f41c156c5
type=adsl
interface-name=enp0s8
permissions=
secondaries=

[adsl]
encapsulation=llc
password=psswd
protocol=pppoa
username=ourname

[ipv4]
dns-search=
method=auto

[ipv6]
dns-search=
method=auto
```

This file is broken down into sections, [connection], [adsl], [ipv4] and [ipv6]. The connection section describes the interface and type. The adsl section contains the necessary configuration details for our connection. The ipv4 and ipv6 are connection information. If your ISP is providing a dedicated IP address you can modify our nmcli command to suit.

On Ubuntu you need run the pppoeconf command.

```
$ pppoeconf enp0s8
```

The first thing we do is search for a signal on the device like in 7-16. Next we are asked if we wish to modify the configuration files that pppoeconf changes.

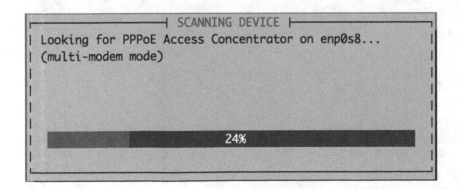

Figure 7-16. *Checking for modem/concentrators*

Select yes like in Figure 7-17.

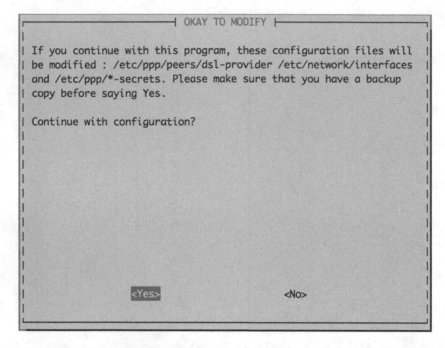

Figure 7-17. *Okay to Modify?*

Take the defaults in Figure 7-18.

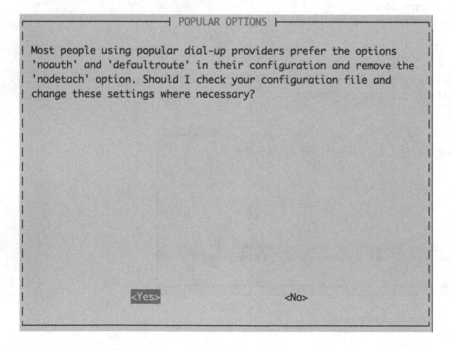

Figure 7-18. *Popular options*

Enter the ISP username you use to connect to the ISP.

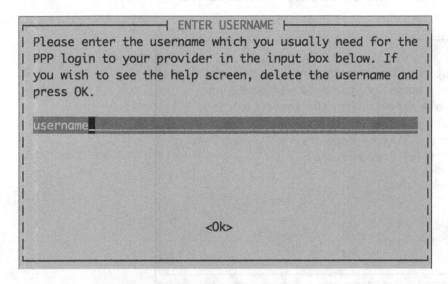

Figure 7-19. *ISP username*

Enter your ISP password.

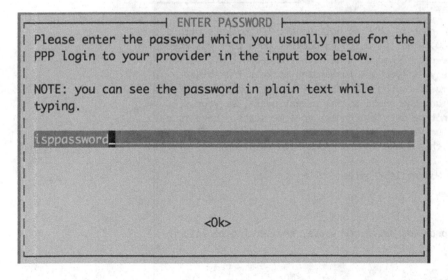

Figure 7-20. *ISP password*

We are going to say 'no', like we did with the CentOS configuration, for the DNS settings as we will manage them shortly. For the next screens we are going to select the defaults.

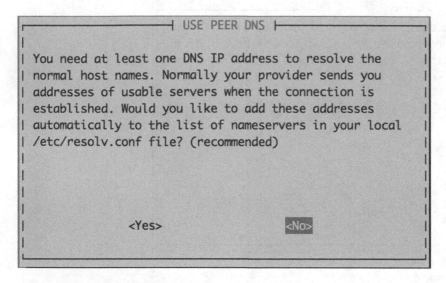

Figure 7-21. Say No ot USER PEER DNS

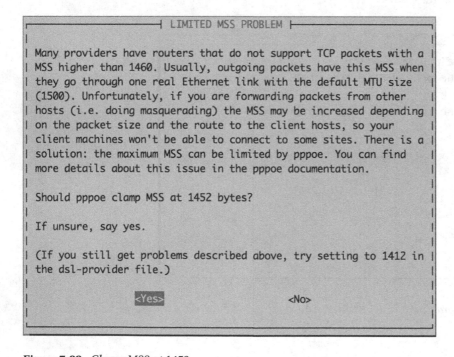

Figure 7-22. Clamp MSS at 1452.

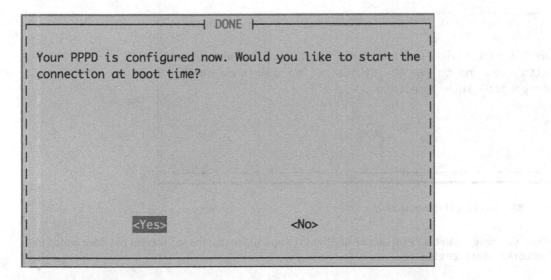

Figure 7-23. *Start the PPPOE connection at boot.*

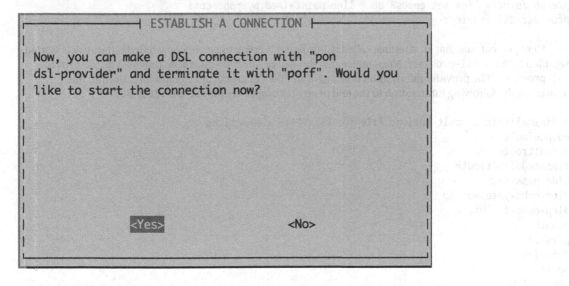

Figure 7-24. *Start the DSL connections now?*

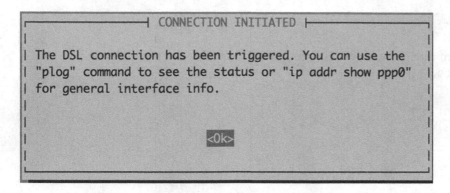

Figure 7-25. *Checking DSL connection*

Once you have created a PPPoE device on Ubuntu, you will see that the ppp section has been added to /etc/network/interfaces file:

```
auto dsl-provider
iface dsl-provider inet ppp
pre-up /bin/ip link set enp0s8 up # line maintained by pppoeconf
provider dsl-provider
```

Here you can see that an interface called dsl-provider is going to be created when the network is started, signified by auto dsl-provider. Next, notice that the device information will be provided by the provider dsl-provider. The provider information is found under the /etc/ppp/peers directory. Ubuntu has appended the following information to the end of our /etc/ppp/peers/dsl-provider file:

```
# Minimalistic default options file for DSL/PPPoE connections
noipdefault
defaultroute
replacedefaultroute
hide-password
#lcp-echo-interval 30
#lcp-echo-failure 4
noauth
persist
#mtu 1492
#persist
#maxfail 0
#holdoff 20
plugin rp-pppoe.so
nic-enp0s8
user "username"
```

The password information is stored here, in the /etc/ppp/chap-secrets file, and the contents are much like Listing 7-10.

If you are are not successful you can view connection logs via the plog command on Ubuntu or /var/log/messages on CentOS.

You should also check to make sure that your default route is set to the ISP's first hop and that it is going out the right interface.

```
$ ip route show
default via 10.1.1.1 dev adsl-enp0s8
```

In the above example, `10.1.1.1` would be your ISPs first hop and traffic will go out the adsl-enp0s8 interface if it is destined to leave your network.

For more information on setting up a connection on Ubuntu, please see:

- `https://help.ubuntu.com/community/ADSLPPPoE`

Summary

In this chapter we have taken you through networking and the Linux Netfilter firewall. We talked about basic networking, how to manage Linux network interfaces and how to trouble shoot network issues. In this chapter covered how to do the following:

- Configure interfaces on our host.

- Netfilter basics

- Firewalld and the firewall-cmd

- The ufw tool for managing Ubuntu firewalls

- The iptables tool for managing Linux firewalls

- Logging, limiting and securing your connections

- Use TCP Wrappers to secure your daemons.

- Configure a PPP connection

In the next chapter, we will look at how to manage packages on a host. In that chapter, you will learn how to install, remove, and update software on your hosts.

CHAPTER 8

■ ■ ■

Package Management

By James Turnbull, Peter Lieverdink, and Dennis Matotek

In Chapter 2 you installed your first Linux host. As you learned in that chapter, a host can be installed with a variety of different applications, ranging from a bare-bones installation to one with every application and tool installed. But this isn't the end of the line for installing and managing applications. Once you've installed your host, you'll often need to add applications, upgrade and patch them, and sometimes remove them. This chapter explains how to do these tasks on both CentOS and Ubuntu.

On Linux distributions, this sort of application management is called *package management*. This is because most applications available on Linux hosts have been made available as *packages*. Packages make it very easy to add and remove applications to and from your host. A package usually contains all the binaries, configuration files, and other supporting material required to install an application. The package also knows where these files need to be installed and usually if other packages also need to be installed to meet any prerequisites of an application. To make a comparison, a Linux package is much like a Windows installation msi or setup executable.

Packages are generally installed by an application control center called a *package manager*. Most Linux distributions come with a package manager, which usually has a set of command-line and graphical tools for managing packages, and a small database that records what has been installed.

By the end of this chapter, you'll have a good understanding of what packages are, how to install and remove them, how to find the right package for your needs, and how to install software from source code. We'll demonstrate all of these tasks using command-line tools as well as the available graphical user interfaces (GUIs) for the CentOS and Ubuntu distributions.

■ **Note** After the section "Introduction to Package Management," this chapter is divided into sections covering installation on CentOS, on Ubuntu, and from source code. You need to read only the section that relates to your chosen distribution. We also recommend that you read about how to install software from source code. You won't often need to do this (and we recommend that you stick to using packages to manage applications), but it's a useful thing to know.

Introduction to Package Management

Different distributions have different ways of packaging their software. For instance, Fedora, Red Hat Linux, and CentOS use the RPM (Red Hat Package Management) package format, while Ubuntu uses the deb (short for Debian, the distribution Ubuntu was originally based on) format. Just as the package formats differ, so do the tools that you can use to manage them.

© Dennis Matotek, James Turnbull and Peter Lieverdink 2017
D. Matotek et al., *Pro Linux System Administration*, DOI 10.1007/978-1-4842-2008-5_8

Each of these package types uses different tools to install and manage packages. On systems that use RPM packages, the basic package manager is called rpm, while on systems that use deb packages, it is called dpkg. Both are extremely powerful applications that allow you to manipulate software packages on your system. In addition to these basic package managers, there are applications that provide extra functionality such as network-based upgrading, package searching, and GUIs.

■ **Note**   Having different package formats and managers might seem strange—these are all Linux distributions, after all—but the reasons are mainly historical. When these distributions were originally created, the developers did not agree on how the package systems should work, so they created their own. Over the years, development on them has continued, and nowadays we have multiple different mature package systems and formats. Of course, if you use only one distribution, then you need to learn about just one type of package management.

Although all Linux distributions can contain thousands or tens of thousands of packages, broadly speaking these packages fall into three main categories.

- Application packages
- Library packages
- Development packages

Most *application packages* contain, as the name suggests, applications. These applications could range from a simple command-line editor to the whole LibreOffice productivity suite.

■ **Note**   LibreOffice is the open source equivalent of Microsoft Office. It contains a word processor, spreadsheet program, and presentation software, among other tools. It allows you to edit Microsoft Office documents and provides similar functionality to Microsoft Office.

Library packages contain files that are used by applications and the operating system to provide additional functionality. For instance, cryptography support is provided by the libssl package. Much like your community book library, Linux libraries are where applications can go to find the stuff they need without having to own it themselves. Because such libraries are often used by multiple applications, it makes sense to distribute them in a package of their own, rather than include a copy of each library with every application. If a library package is updated, all applications that make use of the library will now automatically use the updated version. The names of these packages often start with lib.

Development packages contain source code and header files that are required to compile software from source. These packages usually have names that end in -dev on Ubuntu or -devel on Red Hat. Most library packages have an accompanying development package, to allow for software development using these libraries. Generally, unless you are developing applications, you won't need to install these packages. But some applications do use them, and if you choose to compile applications from source and install them that way, you'll often require development packages to do this.

Because the package management tools used by CentOS and Ubuntu are completely different, we cover each in its own section. We'll first cover package management on CentOS and then on Ubuntu.

```
╔══════════════════════════════════════════════════════════════════╗
║                        WHAT'S A PACKAGE?                           ║
╚══════════════════════════════════════════════════════════════════╝
```

WHAT'S A PACKAGE?

Packages are designed to make managing applications easier. They are generally constructed from the source code of an application and have logic that tells your distribution where to put the application's binaries, files, and configuration. We're going to use two types of packages, RPMs and deb files. Both package types are archives that contain other files. So what's inside these packages? Packages contain data, metadata, and sometimes control files. The data is the files that will be installed. Control files contain descriptive information about the package, scripts for user interaction, and scripts that manage automated pre- or postinstallation tasks.

Package Management on CentOS

At the most basic level, the way applications are managed on Red Hat–based systems is via the Red Hat Package Management tool, or rpm. It is used on distributions like Red Hat Enterprise Linux, CentOS, Mandriva, and the Fedora Project. The rpm tool itself is designed for installing, manipulating, querying, and deleting packages on the local system.

■ **Tip** You can identify RPM packages by their suffix of .rpm. Each RPM package is built using information contained in a spec file. The spec file contains metadata about what is in each package and describes the way the package should be installed on your system. We will talk a little bit about spec files and how to build your own packages later in this chapter.

The rpm tool provides the basic package management tasks like installing and removing packages, but it doesn't handle a variety of other tasks, such as retrieving dependency packages (i.e., packages you need to install alongside, or prior to, a particular package installation) from online repositories or the regular automation of package updates.

■ **Note** Having worked with Linux for a long time, we can attest that managing a Linux system is now much easier thanks to smart package management. In the old days, installing a package or updating an application could involve hours of hunting for *dependencies*, packages that should be on your system before you install and use another package. Before these managers arrived, you had to build all your applications from source code and deal with all the conflicts that arose. Nowadays it is much simpler. But, of course, if you really want to do so, you can always build from source—Linux is so powerful, it gives you that choice. We'll talk about building from source in the last section of this chapter.

To provide some of the functionality that rpm lacks, most Red Hat–derived distributions have some additional tools. Most of these tools assist by retrieving packages from repositories (where the packages are stored; most distributions have a number of repositories available online) and presenting them to be installed. These sorts of tools include Red Hat's Red Hat Network (RHN, which is Red Hat's commercial update service), Duke University's Yellowdog Updater Modified or yum, Mandriva's urpmi, and the new package manager in Fedora called dnf. In this section, we're going to focus on the tools provided as part of CentOS, but the information contained within will also help with other Red Hat–based distributions like Red Hat Enterprise Linux (RHEL), Fedora, and Mandriva.

In the sections that follow, we'll take you through package installation via the GUI interface and the command line, and how to use the rpm tool itself to manage individual packages.

Getting Started

On Red Hat–based hosts like CentOS, Scientific Linux, and Fedora, managing your packages via the desktop is simple and does not require a subscription.

However, for RHEL hosts, you will need to have a subscription to get access to software updates and Red Hat's services. The subscription service for RHEL 7 is called Red Hat Subscription Management. You can find the details on how to join at

- https://access.redhat.com/documentation/en-US/Red_Hat_Subscription_Management/1/html-single/RHSM/index.html

- https://access.redhat.com/articles/11258

After logging in to your desktop you will see the usual Gnome desktop for CentOS. We are going to show you how to use the tool called Application Installer. You use the Application Installer to list, search, install, and remove your packages.

You can find both package management tools by selecting Applications ➤ System Utilities ➤ Application Installer. Or, you can search for applications by bringing up the search window by moving the mouse to the top left of the screen. This is how we did it in Figure 8-1.

Figure 8-1. Finding Application Installer on CentOS

This tool is very easy to use, as we demonstrate in the next sections.

The Application Installer

The Application Installer has a simple interface and may be similar to many other app installer interfaces you might have seen. In Figure 8-2 you can see along the top we have have the following views, "All," "Installed," and "Updates."

Figure 8-2. *Installation application*

You then have the Firefox browser and Editor's picks for common popular packages. The next section is the Categories. In Categories you can find the groups of like applications you might like. We are going to install the "Virtual Machine Manager" software that provides a management interface for KVM, Xen, or LXC.

In Figure 8-3 we select the System category. In there we will find Virtual Machine Manager as a featured application. If it is no longer featured you can find it under the Other category in the System page.

Categories			
Add-ons	Audio	Development Tools	Education
Games	Graphics	Internet	Office
Science	System	Utilities	Video

Figure 8-3. *Select System*

One of the things you will notice in Figure 8-4 is the Boxes application. You will notice that is "Installed" already on our system. We are going to select Virtual Machine Manager for installation.

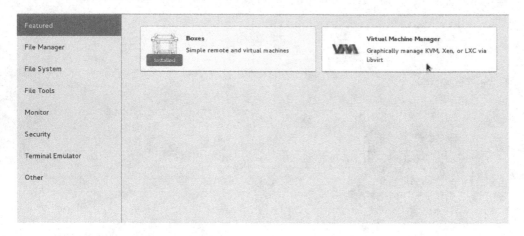

Figure 8-4. *Selecting Virtual Machine Manager*

Once selected we are presented with the information screen about the package. There is a link to the web sites, some screenshots, and even a rating of the program.

As in Figure 8-5 all we have to do is click the Install button to install. If there is a problem with the package or your system the installer will sit at Pending as in Figure 8-6.

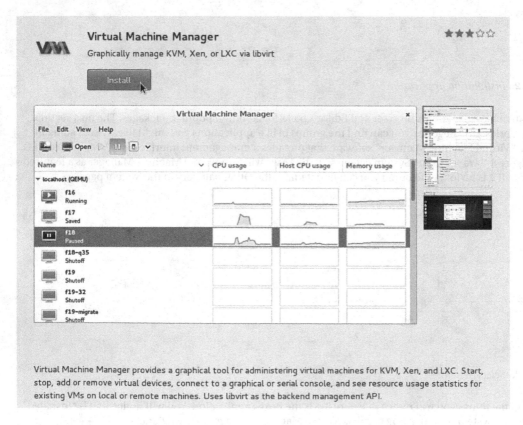

Figure 8-5. *Virtual Machine Manager information screen*

Figure 8-6. *Pending installation*

Some of the reasons your installation might be stuck at pending are the following:

- Your computer might have problems connecting to the Internet. One of the clues that this might be case is that the information screen is not showing screenshots. You should now be able to check your interface to make it work properly; if not, go back to Chapter 7 and look that the ip command again.

- There is a problem with the package and it cannot be installed. CentOS forums can usually help confirm this.

- There is a problem with the repository the package is installed from. We will talk more about repositories shortly.

Ideally, you will see the following screen instead.

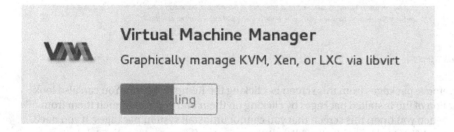

Figure 8-7. *Installing*

When the installation is complete you will now see the screen in Figure 8-8.

Figure 8-8. *Installation complete, Remove?*

If you wish to remove the application you simply hit the Remove button as in Figure 8-8. You will be asked for your password.

That is all you need to do to install and remove packages. To see all the installed packages we go back to the initial screen and select the Installed button at the top (see Figure 8-9).

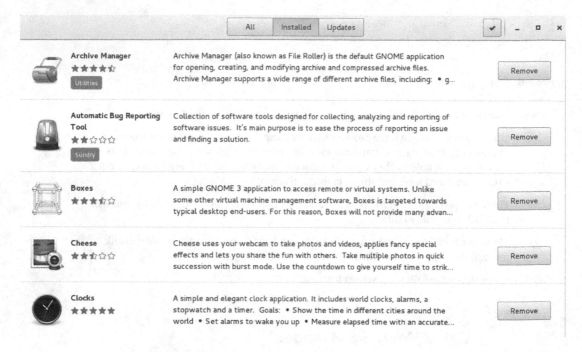

Figure 8-9. *Installed packages*

Obviously you can remove packages from this screen by clicking the Remove button. You can also look at more detailed information of the installed packages by clicking on them and you can launch them from there too. You will notice when you open this screen that you cannot uninstall system packages. If you need to remove any of these you will have to do so via the YUM package manager (more on that shortly).

You can see any updates that your system currently needs by going to the Updates tab. And in Figure 8-10 we can see that we have three updates waiting for us. We can check that this is the most recent list by clicking the refresh button in the top left.

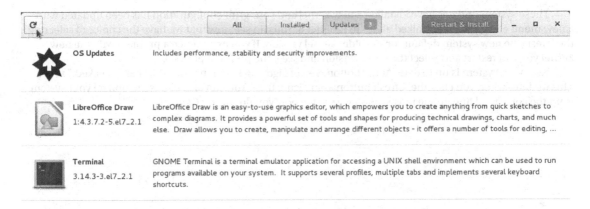

Figure 8-10. *Refresh Updates*

Because we have an OS Update we are asked to Restart & Install; normally we can just install updates without a restart.

Figure 8-11. *Restart & Install Updates message*

After clicking the Restart & Install button we are given the option to Cancel or proceed within 30 seconds before the restart and install. After the host has installed the updates we will notice that we have a new kernel installed as in Figure 8-12.

```
CentOS Linux (3.10.0-327.18.2.el7.x86_64) 7 (Core)
CentOS Linux (3.10.0-327.el7.x86_64) 7 (Core)
CentOS Linux (0-rescue-2ebc67576ed24ba08e5bbb9ab9492f47) 7 (Core)
```

Figure 8-12. *New kernel has been installed*

These system updates have installed a new kernel and your grub configuration has been updated with a new menu entry, which we talked about in Chapter 6. You can see now that we have the choice of selecting the latest (the new system default) or the older kernel version. If you experience a problem with the new kernel you can restart and select the older version and see if the problem persists.

Now your system is up to date. At the bottom you of Figure 8-13 you will see the "Last Checked:" time. This updates when you click the refresh button as in Figure 8-10. You can also choose to update your system from the command line. In the next section we see the how you do this on CentOS.

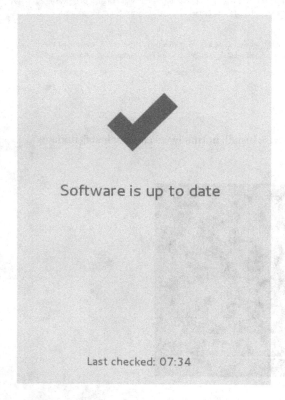

Figure 8-13. System up to date

Yellowdog Updater Modified

For Red Hat–based distributions, one of the most common tools used to install, upgrade, or update a system is a command-line-based tool called Yellowdog Updater Modified (YUM). YUM provides the ability to search and find software available to your system on remote repositories. Repositories, as explained earlier, are collections of packages made available for your distribution by the distribution's vendor, and "mirrored" by interest groups, universities, and ISPs (Internet service providers).

■ **Note**   YUM is available on Red Hat Enterprise Linux and CentOS, as well as other Red Hat–derived distributions. It is generally the default method for updating and maintaining the packages on those distributions via the command line.

YUM also has the ability to solve dependency issues by fetching the packages required to install any individual package. It uses a database to query what packages are installed on your host and then compares that to package lists provided by the repository. If you need an additional package or packages to meet any dependencies, then these are also downloaded and installed.

YUM is simple to use. On the command line, you simply type yum and one of a number of potential actions, such as **install**, **remove**, or **list**, and then potentially the name of the package or packages on which you wish to take action, for example:

```
$ sudo yum install nmap
```

■ **Note**   You need root privileges to run the yum command, either by being signed in as the root user or making use of the sudo command. We recommend using the sudo command, as we demonstrated in Chapter 5.

Table 8-1 lists the main options provided with YUM.

Table 8-1. *Options Available with YUM*

Option	Description
search	Allows you to search for packages available for download.
list	Lists all the packages available for download.
install	Installs a package or packages.
check-update	Lists packages available for update.
update	Updates the package specified or downloads and installs any available updates.
remove	Removes a package or packages from your host.
info	Provides package information about a package.
provides	Tells you what package a particular file or feature belongs to.
list updates	Lists all the packages with updates available only.
list available	Lists all the available packages only.
deplist	Lists package dependencies.
clean all	Cleans up downloaded package files that are no longer needed.
history	Shows the history of the YUM commands that have been executed on this system.
fssnapshot	This and associated subcommands can manage the creation and deletion on LVM snapshots prior to issuing YUM updates or installs.
repolist	Views the YUM repositories that are configured on your system. You can also pass -v or use the repoinfo command for more information.

Next, we'll look at each action and how we might use it.

Installing a Package with YUM

Let's get started with YUM by trying to install a package. In a normal situation, we would first search for the package to make sure it's available. We've chosen to install the nmap package (which, as mentioned previously, is a useful network-mapping and scanning tool). We will use the search option to see if the package is available, as you can see in Listing 8-1.

Listing 8-1. Searching with YUM

```
$ sudo yum search nmap
```

In Listing 8-1, we've issued the yum command with the search option and then specified the name of the package we wish to search for. This produces a list of available packages that have nmap in their name. The yum command is not smart enough to know exactly what you're looking for, so it provides you with anything with nmap in the name or description.

You can also search for parts of the package name if you are unsure of the complete name. So, for example, you could type yum **search map** and get a list of all the packages with the pattern map in their description or name.

■ **Tip** You can refine the list of packages by using the grep command we showed you in Chapter 4. For example, you could type yum search python | grep boto, and this will refine the list of the packages that are related to python by searching for the term "boto" and then displaying the resulting list of packages.

You can also use yum list see all the packages available from your repository, and you might also find yum groups list useful to see the groupings of packages (yum help groups will list the other possible subcommands for managing groups). Groups are a collection of individual packages that provide a certain application for convenience. So, for example, installing the KDE Plasma Workspaces group will provide everything for running your KDE desktop, and installing the Basic Web Server group will provide provide the Apache web server and associated packages.

With that information, to install the nmap package we run the command in Listing 8-2.

Listing 8-2. Installing the nmap Package

```
$ sudo yum install nmap
```

The will download and install a package called nmap. There is a bit of information that gets displayed in the output here from the yum install command.

```
Loaded plugins: fastestmirror, langpacks
Loading mirror speeds from cached hostfile
 * base: centos.mirror.crucial.com.au
 * extras: centos.mirror.crucial.com.au
 * updates: centos.mirror.crucial.com.au
Resolving Dependencies
--> Running transaction check
---> Package nmap.x86_64 2:6.40-7.el7 will be installed
--> Finished Dependency Resolution
```

```
Dependencies Resolved

================================================================
 Package       Arch        Version        Repository     Size
================================================================
Installing:
 nmap          x86_64      2:6.40-7.el7    base          4.0 M

Transaction Summary
================================================================
Install  1 Package

Total download size: 4.0 M
Installed size: 16 M
Is this ok [y/d/N]:
```

The first line shows any plug-ins that have been loaded with yum to provide extra features or capabilities. Then we can see the repositories we are using for this install command * base:, * extra:, and * updates:. Next we see the dependency and transaction checks and then the list of packages we are going to install, in this case one package. We have more detail about the packages we are installing, including the names of all the packages being installed, the architecture (x86_64), the Version(2:6.40-7.el7), the yum repository we are downloading this package from (base), and the size the package download (4.0M). Then the transaction summary is displayed and we are given the chance to continue with the install (y), download the packages only (d), or not install the packages (N). If you want to install the package and the dependencies without being prompted for confirmation you can issue

```
$ sudo yum install -y nmap
```

This will answer "yes" (-y) to any installation questions and is useful when you are installing packages via scripts.

You can also use the groups install command as follows:

```
$ sudo yum groups install 'Basic Web Server'
```

This will install all the packages in the group Basic Web Server. If any dependencies are required, they will also be downloaded, and you will be queried if you want to install them, too (unless you specify groups install -y). If you don't install all the required dependencies, then you will not be able to install the package you require.

Updating Your Repositories

There are several files that make up a YUM repository cache. These are small db files that contain things like file lists and package lists. Over time, your YUM repository cache data will become out of date as new packages are added to and updated in the repository.

To rebuild or refresh the cache without checking for any updated packages available for your host, you can issue the following:

```
$ sudo yum makecache
```

This will pull down from the repository the cache files. To check if there are any updates for your host you can issue the command in Listing 8-3.

309

Listing 8-3. Checking for Updated Packages

```
$ sudo yum check-update
```

The check-update subcommand will download the latest YUM repository cache data (if it is outdated) and then use that to find out what packages on your system have updates available. This will display a list of packages that have updates available for them. To install those updates you can issue

```
$ sudo yum update
```

You can also update one or more individual packages, as shown in Listing 8-4.

Listing 8-4. Updating Packages with YUM

```
$ sudo yum update nmap
$ sudo yum update nmap mutt
```

■ **Note** You should not use yum to upgrade between major versions of the operating system (e.g., from 6.5 to 7.1). Technically there is nothing stopping you from pointing your YUM repositories to the latest release and running yum update, but this will have very unpredictable results and will most likely result in system loss. You can use yum to upgrade between minor versions though (i.e., from 7.1 to 7.2).

Removing Packages with YUM

You can also remove packages with YUM, as shown in Listing 8-5.

Listing 8-5. Removing Packages with YUM

```
$ sudo yum remove nmap
```

The remove option used in Listing 8-5 will remove all the files relating to that package from your system. You can use the alias to this command, erase, and it will do the same thing. Any configuration files that have been changed from the original package versions will be saved and with a <filename>.conf.**rpmsave** extension.

Performing Additional YUM Tasks

You can do many other things with the yum command. Let's go through some other commands briefly.
The following command provides information about the package you're querying, such as its size, version, and installation status; a description of the package; and other useful information.

```
$ sudo yum info kernel
```

If you want to find what package provides a particular file, you could use the following.

```
$ sudo yum provides /bin/bash
bash-4.2.46-19.el7.x86_64 : The GNU Bourne Again shell
Repo       : base
Matched from:
Filename   : /bin/bash
```

The preceding command tells you that the /bin/bash binary is provided by the bash package and describes the version and details about the package.

To list packages provided by file paths you can also use the following:

```
$ sudo yum provides */sftp
```

This will list all packages that provide the sftp file. This will list openssh-client packages as well as others.

Another way to see the list of updates available for your host, is to issue the following command:

```
$ sudo yum list updates
```

If your host is up to date, this command should produce no results.

Next, you can list all the packages that are available to be installed on your host by issuing the following command:

```
$ sudo yum list available
```

The preceding command lists all the available packages that are not already installed for your host from your repositories.

To get a list of just security updates for your host, use the following command:

```
$ sudo yum --security check-update
```

This will provide a list of the current security packages that are waiting to be installed on your host. To install, just those security patches.

```
$ sudo yum --security update
```

You can also just install packages from a particular YUM repository with

```
$ sudo yum install --enablerepo=myrepo my-package
```

In the preceding command we told YUM to install our my-package from our myrepo YUM repository. If the repository is disabled, meaning we don't normally fetch packages from this repository, we can enable the repository while we execute this command. Subsequent yum commands will not fetch from this repository unless specified. More on YUM repositories shortly.

Finally, you can clean your cache directory (where YUM temporarily stores the packages you have downloaded). You would clear the cache if you needed to reclaim some disk space temporary disk space.

```
$ sudo yum clean all
```

The preceding command removes cached packages and headers contained in the /var/cache/yum cache directories.

Configuring YUM

The YUM application can be configured in a variety of ways. YUM has its configuration files stored under /etc/yum.conf and /etc/yum.repos.d/, and it stores state files in the directories /var/lib/yum and /var/cache/yum.

■ **Note** State files tell YUM what is already installed on your host and also hold cached versions of downloaded packages. Be careful not to delete these directories, as you can easily corrupt your package database.

You will not normally need to make changes to the default /etc/yum.conf. An example of when you might want to change configuration is to add a proxy server that YUM should use when downloading packages. The defaults will generally suit most environments. A full list of the available configuration settings for YUM is available through the yum.conf man page.

```
$ man yum.conf
```

Though you will rarely change how YUM is configured, you may wish to add additional repositories to YUM from which you can download additional packages. The files defining what repositories are available to YUM are contained in the /etc/yum.repo.d directory. Let's look at a generic repository file:

```
$ cat /etc/yum.repo.d/myrepo.repo
[myrepo]
name=myrepo
baseurl=http://myrepo.mydomain.com/pub/linux/releases/$releasever/$basearch/os/enabled=1
gpgcheck=1
gpgkey=http://myrepo.mydomain.com/linux/RPM-GPG-KEY-linux
```

Each of these options is explained in Table 8-2.

Table 8-2. *Basic Options for Adding a* yum *Repository*

Option	Description
[repo-id]	The repo_id is the unique name for the repository.
name	The name is a description of the repository.
baseurl	The baseurl is the URL to the repository. This is generally an HTTP URL, much like you would use in a web browser. It can also be a ftp:// or file:/// resource.
enabled	You can enable or disable the package by specifying 0 for disabled and 1 for enabled.
gpgcheck	This option tells yum to check the GPG keys used to "sign" packages so that you can be sure the package hasn't been tampered with. Specifying 0 turns off checking and 1 indicates checking is on.
gpgkey	This is the URL where yum should find the repository's GPG key. It can a be http://, ftp://, or file:/// resource.

In Listing 8-6, we have defined a new repository for a CentOS distribution to download source rpm files. The source rpm files are used if we wish to rebuild our own rpm packages. These source files are the ones that the CentOS maintainers used to generate the normal binary rpms we use in our packages.

Listing 8-6. Adding a CentOS Repository in a YUM Repo File

```
[source]
name=CentOS-releasever - Sources
baseurl=http://vault.centos.org/centos/$releasever/os/Source/
gpgcheck=1
enabled=1
gpgkey=file:///etc/pki/rpm-gpg/RPM-GPG-KEY-CentOS-7
```

You can see that in the baseurl option we've specified a variable called $releasever. On Red Hat and CentOS, this variable defaults to the version of the redhat-release package.

```
$ cat /etc/redhat-release
CentOS Linux release 7.2.1511 (Core)
```

In this case, $releasever will equal 7.2.1511. That release file is placed on the system by the centos-release-7-2.1511.el7.centos.2.10.x86_64 package.

You will also see that the baseurl we are using for the sources is pointing to the vault.centos.org host. This is where you can find older historical releases of CentOS and the source files for building your own RPMs. You can have more than one baseurl listed in the baseurl option.

```
baseurl=http://myrepo1.org/centos/...
        http://myrepo2.org/centos/...
```

The list of URLs can also be retrieved from a web server via the mirrorlist= option instead of baseurl=. The mirrorlist.txt file would simply contain the following:

```
mirrorlist=http://myrepo.org/mirrorlist.txt
http://myrepo1.org/centos/...
http://myrepo2.org/centos/...
```

With the fastestmirror plugin for YUM loaded, yum will find the fastest responding mirror from that list and use that when it runs.

There are other variables that can exist in your YUM repository configurations:

- $arch–the architecture of your system (as detected by yum)

- $basearch–the base architecture of your system (e.g., i686 becomes i386)

- $uuid–a unique identifier that is generated for your system and stored in /var/lib/yum/uuid

- $infra–currently unused, but you may see it in your mirrorlist URL (&repo=os&infra=$infra).

When the variables are used as follows:

```
http://myrepo.org/centos/$releasever/$arch/myapp
```

That would be extrapolated to

```
http://myrepo.org/centos/7-2.1511/x64_86/myapp
```

For a full list of configuration options to use with YUM please see man `yum.conf`. When you create a new Yum repository, you can use the `makecache` command to refresh your repository cache and add the new repository to it.

```
$ sudo yum makecache
```

On modern Fedora distributions (since release 22) and upcoming Red Hat and CentOS distributions you will newer package manager to handle rpms called DNF. Let's look at that now.

DNF –or Dandified YUM

DNF was originally a fork of the YUM package manager, and it is a replacement of YUM rather than just a new release. It is designed to maintain (roughly) CLI (command-line interface) compatibility with the current version of YUM. Therefore, you will already be familiar with the main commands of the DNF package manager.

While the end user is not supposed to notice much difference between YUM and DNF, under the hood there are a lot of differences. The differences are mainly in how the code has been rewritten to make it easier for developers to maintain and extend with a predictable and documented API (application programming interface). It is also Python3 compatible where YUM is not. Also the package dependency algorithm has been entirely rewritten. DNF will be a welcome, speedier, if mostly unnoticed, improvement.

Commands like the following perform a similar function to the equivalent YUM commands.

```
$ dnf search nmap
$ dnf info nmap
$ dnf install  nmap
$ dnf remove nmap
```

Those commands all have similar if not the same syntax as YUM. For a full list of the commands available, please see the DNF documentation at

- `http://dnf.readthedocs.io/en/latest/command_ref.html`

The repository files for DNF will also be similar to the current YUM repository files and are sourced from the same location, /etc/yum.repos.d/*.repo.

```
[fedora]
name=Fedora $releasever - $basearch
failovermethod=priority
#baseurl=http://download.fedoraproject.org/pub/fedora/linux/releases/$releasever/
Everything/$basearch/os/
metalink=https://mirrors.fedoraproject.org/metalink?repo=fedora-$releasever&arch=$basearch
enabled=1
metadata_expire=28d
gpgcheck=1
gpgkey=file:///etc/pki/rpm-gpg/RPM-GPG-KEY-fedora-$releasever-$basearch
skip_if_unavailable=False
```

As you can see, there is no real difference here in how we describe a repository to use with DNF. For a complete list of the configuration options used with DNF see man `dnf.conf`.

Red Hat Package Management

We've just looked at the yum and dnf commands and how to use them to manage packages. The sole purpose of YUM or DNF is to manage the actual Red Hat Package Management (RPM) packages on your system. Each RPM package can also be inspected, installed and removed by the rpm command. The rpm command is the basic tool for manipulating the RPM files that contain your packages. While you may not often need to use the rpm command directly, it is important that you understand how it works.

There are many options that you can pass to the rpm command. To get a complete list of these commands, we recommend that you read its man page.

```
$ man rpm
```

On the rpm man page, you can see that the rpm tool can perform three basic functions.

1. Query packages

2. Install, upgrade, and remove packages

3. Miscellaneous functions

Let's look at some of these options in more detail. Table 8-3 shows the major options you can pass to rpm and what they do. Each option has a number of flags that you add.

Table 8-3. *The Major rpm Options and Flags*

Options and Flags	Description
-q	--query	Allows you to query the RPM database and find information about installed packages on your host
-i	--install	Installs a local package on your host
-e	--erase	Removes a package from your host
-U	--upgrade	Upgrades an existing package or installs a package on your host if it is not already installed
-F	--freshen	Upgrades a package only if an earlier version is installed
-V	--verify	Verifies an installed package

Querying Packages

To begin, we'll look at querying the packages that are installed on your host, using the -q or --query option. To find out what is installed on your host, the rpm tool queries data stored in a database. This database is updated when packages are installed and removed.

■ **Note** The RPM database knows only your host's current state; it doesn't know what was removed yesterday or what the previous version of a package was. This information recorded when you use yum or dnf, but not when you use rpm.

Let's now use rpm to examine the heart of the Linux operating system, the kernel. Supposed you are asked, "What kernels do we have installed?" To find the answer, you can use the rpm command, as shown in Listing 8-7.

■ **Note**   You can also find the kernel you are currently using by issuing the uname -r command.

Listing 8-7. Querying the Installed Kernel Version

```
# rpm --query kernel
kernel-3.10.0-327.el7.x86_64
kernel-3.10.0-327.18.2.el7.x86_64
```

Here we've run the rpm command with the --query flag and specified the name of the package we want to query, in our case kernel. You can see that this has produced a list of the kernels installed.

■ **Note**   You see more than one kernel in Listing 8-7 because you can have more than one kernel installed. This does not mean you have multiple kernels running at the same time; rather, you have multiple potential kernels you *could* run.

Those numbers at the end of each kernel installed are different versions. One is 3.10.0-327.el7.x86_64 and the other is 3.10.0-327.18.2.el7.x86_64. Both are compatible with the the Red Hat Enterprise Linux 7 system (.el7).

■ **Tip**   We discuss in Chapter 6 how you can select the kernel you want to boot.

What if you don't know the name of package you are looking for? Or what if you want to see all the packages installed? In those cases, you can use the command in Listing 8-8.

Listing 8-8. Querying All Packages

```
# rpm --query --all
```

This command, which uses the --query flag together with the --all flag, indicating that you are querying all packages, lists all the packages installed.

As you will see, this list can be quite long. Suppose instead you want to find only any package whose name contains vim. You could then pipe that output through the grep tool, which searches the output for the string vim, as you can see in Listing 8-9.

Listing 8-9. Querying All Using Piping and grep

```
# rpm --query --all | grep vim
vim-minimal-7.4.160-1.el7.x86_64
vim-filesystem-7.4.160-1.el7.x86_64
vim-enhanced-7.4.160-1.el7.x86_64
vim-common-7.4.160-1.el7.x86_64
```

■ **Note** We cover the grep command and piping in Chapter 4.

Listing 8-9 shows that piping the output of the query to the grep command has reduced the list from thousands of packages to four packages with the string vim in their name (an empty list would indicate there is no package installed with that string in its name).

Let's find out a bit more information about our kernel package. In Listing 8-10, we use the query option combined with the --info option to find out more information about one of our installed kernels.

Listing 8-10. Getting Information About Packages

```
# sudo rpm --query --info kernel-3.10.0-327.18.2.el7.x86_64
Name        : kernel
Version     : 3.10.0
Release     : 327.18.2.el7
Architecture: x86_64
Install Date: Thu 26 May 2016 17:43:40 EDT
Group       : System Environment/Kernel
Size        : 142681799
License     : GPLv2
Signature   : RSA/SHA256, Thu 12 May 2016 19:41:18 EDT, Key ID 24c6a8a7f4a80eb5
Source RPM  : kernel-3.10.0-327.18.2.el7.src.rpm
Build Date  : Thu 12 May 2016 07:51:03 EDT
Build Host  : kbuilder.dev.centos.org
Relocations : (not relocatable)
URL         : http://www.kernel.org/
Summary     : The Linux kernel
Description :
The kernel package contains the Linux kernel (vmlinuz), the core of any
Linux operating system.  The kernel handles the basic functions
of the operating system: memory allocation, process allocation, device
input and output, etc.
```

Listing 8-10 has produced a lot of information. Some of it may not mean very much to you initially, but let's look at some of the data. You can see the version and release number, and the dates when it was built and installed. You can also see what group the package is in, as each package on your host belongs to a group of like packages. You saw this when you installed your host in Chapter 2 and selected the packages you wanted as part of that process.

In addition, you can see the license the package is released under (in this case, the GPLv2 license), the size of the package and, most important, a description and summary of the package and some links to more information about the package.

Sometimes you will want to know what package installed a particular file or command. You can also use the rpm tool to query this information. For example, we have the /bin/bash command installed on our host, and we can find out what installed this command by using rpm as shown in Listing 8-11.

Listing 8-11. Using query and whatprovides

```
# rpm  --query  --whatprovides /bin/bash
bash-4.2.46-19.el7.x86_64
```

Listing 8-11 tells us that the package bash is responsible for the file /bin/bash, and it also informs us of the version number of the installed bash package (you can also use the shorter format of $ rpm -qf /bin/bash).

So now we know that bash provided that file, but what other files on our system belong to the bash package? Armed with the information from --whatprovides, we can see what other files belong to the bash package by using the --query --list options as shown in Listing 8-12.

Listing 8-12. Using query and list

```
# rpm --query --list bash
/etc/skel/.bash_logout
/etc/skel/.bash_profile
/etc/skel/.bashrc
/usr/bin/alias
<snip> ...
```

Listing 8-12 displays a truncated list of all the files present in the bash package. We can also list other useful information about packages. For example, the rpm -qc <package> command will show you the configuration files associated with the package, the rpm -qd will list the documentation files.

Often packages will run pre- and post-install and uninstall scripts before or after they have been installed or uninstalled. These may create users, configure and start services, or clean up after themselves. You can view such scripts with the following:

```
# rpm -q --scripts bash
postinstall scriptlet (using <lua>):
nl      = '\n'
sh      = '/bin/sh'..nl
bash    = '/bin/bash'..nl
f = io.open('/etc/shells', 'a+')
if f then
  local shells = nl..f:read('*all')..nl
  if not shells:find(nl..sh) then f:write(sh) end
  if not shells:find(nl..bash) then f:write(bash) end
  f:close()
end
```

In the above Lua script (Lua is a programming language) we can see the script that gets executed after we install the bash program. The script performs the required additions to the /etc/shells file after installing the bash package.

As you can probably now see we can do similar tasks as these with yum or dnf. Let's move on to installing packages with rpm.

Installing Packages and Removing Packages with RPM

The rpm tool can also be used to install or upgrade packages; however, it is not recommended. It conflicts with the way that YUM works. It is also usually annoying to install via RPM. To install packages, you need to download the required RPM file, and any dependencies, and then use the rpm tool to install it on your host.

Removing packages presents the same problems and should also be avoided.

Building an RPM Package from Source

Why would you need to build a package from source? Well, sometimes you'll require a patch to the source, or perhaps you would like to build a more recent version of the package. If this is the case, you can take a couple of approaches.

Many packages have what are called *upstream* RPMs. Upstream RPMs are packages that contain a newer version of the application than the one shipped with your distribution. Frequently they are built by the developer of an application or another member of the application's development community. They will have newer patches of code or newer features that you may require, but they will be more edgy and could contain bugs and problems. These upstream RPMs will often be available on an application's web site.

■ **Caution** Upstream RPMs files can be built by anyone. They may not be stable, secure, or regularly maintained. You should exercise caution in using them.

The second approach is to download the source for the application you need to update and build your own RPMs. There are some excellent references are available online that can help you create your own RPM files:

- *Maximum* RPM: www.rpm.org/max-rpm-snapshot/

- *How to create a RPM:* https://fedoraproject.org/wiki/How_to_create_an_RPM_package

- *Packaging Software with* RPM, *Part 1:* www.ibm.com/developerworks/library/l-rpm1/

- *Creating* RPMs: http://pmc.ucsc.edu/~dmk/notes/RPMs/Creating_RPMs.html

We are going to quickly demonstrate the process of building a RPM package. This package will simply place a script on our system. To do that we need to install the rpm-build and rpmdevtools packages. If you intend to compile a program you will need the appropriate development packages as well.

```
$ sudo yum install rpm-build rpmdevtools
```

Next we need to create some basic directories required by the rpm build command. To do that we use a command from the rpmdevtools package.

```
$ rpmdev-setuptree
$ ls -l rpmbuild/
total 20
drwxrwxr-x. 2 vagrant vagrant 4096 Jul 24 09:46 BUILD
drwxrwxr-x. 2 vagrant vagrant 4096 Jul 24 09:46 RPMS
drwxrwxr-x. 2 vagrant vagrant 4096 Jul 24 09:46 SOURCES
drwxrwxr-x. 2 vagrant vagrant 4096 Jul 24 09:46 SPECS
drwxrwxr-x. 2 vagrant vagrant 4096 Jul 24 09:46 SRPMS
```

When building a RPM package we require at least the SPECS and SOURCES in the directories above. BUILD is where we build our packages. RPMS is where our packages will be placed after the build. SOURCES is where we place the source files for building. SPECS is where our spec file will be placed. SRPMS is where our RPM source files will be. We will change into our rpmbuild directory.

We have placed a compressed tarball (a compressed archive file) inside the SOURCES directory called `simple_echo.tar.gz`. It contains one file called `simple_echo.sh` and we intend to install that into the `/usr/local/bin` directory.

Before we go any further we need to create our `simple_echo.spec` file and put it in the SPECS directory. From our rpmdevtools package we use the `rpmdev-newspec` command as follows:

```
$ rpmdev-newspec simple_echo && mv simple_echo.spec SPECS/
simple_echo.spec created; type minimal, rpm version >= 4.11.
```

This has created our spec file and moved it into our SPECS directory. We can now use our vi editor to edit the file. The spec file contains the details about our package—the version number, license, and so on. It also has several macros that rpmbuild used to help create the packages. They begin with %<macro>.

Our spec file will look like this:

```
Name:           simple_echo
Version:        1.0
Release:        1%{?dist}
Summary:        Echoes your input
License:        GPLv3+
URL:            http://www.example.com/simple_echo
Source0:        %{name}-%{version}.tar.gz

BuildRequires:  bash
Requires:       bash

%description
This program echoes the first parameter entered.

%prep
%setup -q

%install
rm -rf $RPM_BUILD_ROOT
mkdir -p $RPM_BUILD_ROOT/usr/local/bin
install simple_echo.sh -m0755 $RPM_BUILD_ROOT/usr/local/bin/simple_echo.sh

%files
%doc
%attr(0755,root,root)/usr/local/bin/simple_echo.sh

%changelog
* Sun Jul 24 2016 JSmith <jsmith@example.com>
- First simple_echo package
```

In our spec file we have given the package name and version. In the Release you can see the first of the macros, %{?dist}. This adds the distribution details to the package. The Summary, License, Source, and URL are required information. You can have more than one source file if required and we have used macros again to describe it—it can be a URL or must exist in the SOURCES directory.

BuildRequires and Requires are for handling package dependencies. The required packages must be installed prior to building or installing if specified. We have chosen bash as our required package.

■ **Tip** You can create your own macros for RPM build too. For more information on macros see
www.rpm.org/wiki/PackagerDocs/Macros.

We have removed some of the standard macros that are used to compile software as we are not
compiling anything here. The prep and setup macros prepare the build space by cleaning up old files and
untarring the source file into the BUILD directory. Next we have the %install section and here we remove any
older build data and create the BUILDROOT directory structure. We then use the install command (which
copies the file to the desired location and gives them the desired mode).

The next section deals with listing the files we are installing. They can be doc files, conf files, and
directories. In this case we are listing one file with the mode 0755 and owner and group root.

Finally we have a changelog section. This should be defined in that specific date format (DayofWeek
Month Day Year name <email>). This needs to be followed by a changelog message starting with a '-'.

Once this is file is saved we can now run the build. There are primary ways to build the RPM. First is to
build the binary only. The second is to build the source and and binary. There are other options too, and you
can find these by using the man rpmbuild command.

```
$ rpmbuild –bb SPEC/simple_echo.spec
Executing(%prep): /bin/sh -e /var/tmp/rpm-tmp.7kXFJS
+ umask 022
+ cd /home/vagrant/rpmbuild/BUILD
+ cd /home/vagrant/rpmbuild/BUILD
+ rm -rf simple_echo-1.0
+ /usr/bin/gzip -dc /home/vagrant/rpmbuild/SOURCES/simple_echo-1.0.tar.gz
+ /usr/bin/tar -xf -
+ STATUS=0
+ '[' 0 -ne 0 ']'
+ cd simple_echo-1.0
+ /usr/bin/chmod -Rf a+rX,u+w,g-w,o-w .
+ exit 0
Executing(%install): /bin/sh -e /var/tmp/rpm-tmp.EJ4LAv
+ umask 022
+ cd /home/vagrant/rpmbuild/BUILD
+ '[' /home/vagrant/rpmbuild/BUILDROOT/simple_echo-1.0-1.el7.centos.x86_64 '!=' / ']'
+ rm -rf /home/vagrant/rpmbuild/BUILDROOT/simple_echo-1.0-1.el7.centos.x86_64
++ dirname /home/vagrant/rpmbuild/BUILDROOT/simple_echo-1.0-1.el7.centos.x86_64
+ mkdir -p /home/vagrant/rpmbuild/BUILDROOT
+ mkdir /home/vagrant/rpmbuild/BUILDROOT/simple_echo-1.0-1.el7.centos.x86_64
+ cd simple_echo-1.0
+ rm -rf /home/vagrant/rpmbuild/BUILDROOT/simple_echo-1.0-1.el7.centos.x86_64
+ mkdir -p /home/vagrant/rpmbuild/BUILDROOT/simple_echo-1.0-1.el7.centos.x86_64/usr/local/
bin
+ install simple_echo.sh -m0755 /home/vagrant/rpmbuild/BUILDROOT/simple_echo-1.0-1.el7.
centos.x86_64/usr/local/bin/simple_echo.sh
+ '[' '%{buildarch}' = noarch ']'
+ QA_CHECK_RPATHS=1
+ case "${QA_CHECK_RPATHS:-}" in
...
<snip>
...
```

```
Processing files: simple_echo-1.0-1.el7.centos.x86_64
Provides: simple_echo = 1.0-1.el7.centos simple_echo(x86-64) = 1.0-1.el7.centos
Requires(rpmlib): rpmlib(CompressedFileNames) <= 3.0.4-1 rpmlib(FileDigests) <= 4.6.0-1
rpmlib(PayloadFilesHavePrefix) <= 4.0-1
Requires: /bin/bash
Checking for unpackaged file(s): /usr/lib/rpm/check-files /home/vagrant/rpmbuild/BUILDROOT/
simple_echo-1.0-1.el7.centos.x86_64
Wrote: /home/vagrant/rpmbuild/RPMS/x86_64/simple_echo-1.0-1.el7.centos.x86_64.rpm
Executing(%clean): /bin/sh -e /var/tmp/rpm-tmp.LPOTLL
+ umask 022
+ cd /home/vagrant/rpmbuild/BUILD
+ cd simple_echo-1.0
+ /usr/bin/rm -rf /home/vagrant/rpmbuild/BUILDROOT/simple_echo-1.0-1.el7.centos.x86_64
+ exit 0
```

We have the output of our build process. You can see that we have the line Wrote ... simple_echo-1.0-1.el7.centos.x86_64.rpm. We are going to install that rpm now using rpm –ivh.

```
$ sudo rpm -i RPMS/x86_64/simple_echo-1.0-1.el7.centos.x86_64.rpm
```

Now we can test that the script is installed and working correctly:

```
$ simple_echo.sh hello
hello
```

It should be pointed out that creating your own packages from source can take some time depending on the complexity of the package you are trying to build and the number of dependencies it has. You also have to support it, which can sometime be more burdensome than you think. Because you may choose uncommon options, you may find yourself alone with production problems that no one else has experienced.

Before you build your own, you can also check out the EPEL packages which are upstream packages based on Fedora but rebuilt for RHEL, CentOS, and Scientific Linux. These maybe a better bet than managing your own set of RPMs but still carry the same caveats.

- https://fedoraproject.org/wiki/EPEL

That is not said to stop you from trying but more to warn you about the sometimes long and treacherous road building your own packages can become. We will show you how to compile your own packages from source in the section "Compiling from Source", and provide you a way to make both RPMs and deb packages.

Package Management on Ubuntu

Managing packages on Ubuntu servers is usually done using command-line tools, because the Ubuntu Server Edition does not install a GUI by default. In this section, we will first cover the command-line tools to manage packages. After that, we will look at the graphical package manager available from the Unity desktop.

The most common way to add software on Ubuntu hosts is to install packages from online software repositories via command-line tools. The distribution offers online software repositories containing over 22,000 ready-to-install packages. Over the years, several tools have been created to help you add applications to your Ubuntu hosts from remote repositories. These tools provide the Ubuntu equivalent of rpm and yum for Red Hat–based distributions. We're going to look at two command-line tools:

- aptitude
- dpkg

These tools are both installed by default on Ubuntu hosts. The `aptitude` tool allows you to install, remove, update, and search packages from online repositories. It is the preferred way to manage packages, so we'll cover this tool in the most detail. Another popular tool that has a similar purpose is Apt (`https://wiki.debian.org/Apt`).

The `dpkg` tool is the base command-line tool used to install and remove packages. Aptitude uses `dpkg` internally to manage packages. We'll take only a brief look at `dpkg` because you won't have much need to use it often.

Aptitude

You can work with the `aptitude` tool in two ways: interactively via menus and dialog boxes or by passing it instructions via the command line. For beginning users, the easiest way is to use `aptitude`'s menu-based user interface. Let's start it up and have a look.

```
$ aptitude
```

After processing the package lists, `aptitude` presents its main window, as shown in Figure 8-14.

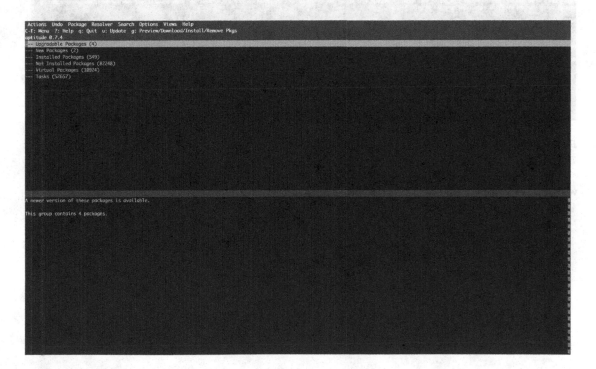

Figure 8-14. The main aptitude screen

The main screen consists of a menu bar, a command list, a window list, status information, the package list window, and an information window. Your cursor will first appear in the package list window. You can move up and down the lists using the arrow keys and expand a highlighted item by pressing Enter.

Press Enter to expand the *Installed Packages* list and then expand the *main* list. You will see an alphabetical listing of the currently installed packages in the main section. As you highlight a package, the package description is displayed in the information window. Switch to this window by pressing the Tab key,

323

and then scroll up and down the information using the arrow keys. Press Tab again to switch back to the list window. In Figure 8-15, you can see we have highlighted the adduser package.

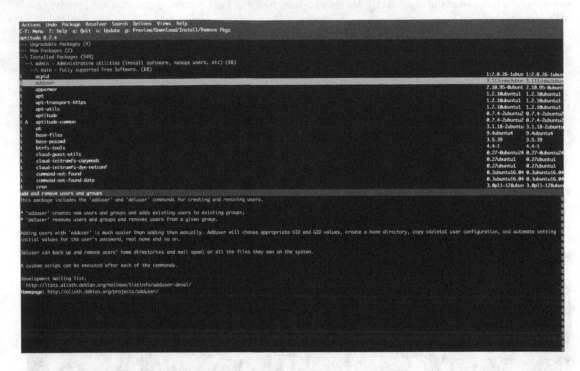

Figure 8-15. *Displaying the package description*

To display more detailed package information, scroll to highlight the package name and press Enter, as we have in Figure 8-16. You can now see information such as the dependencies, maintainer, and so on.

Since scrolling through this listing is not fast, being able to search it is useful.

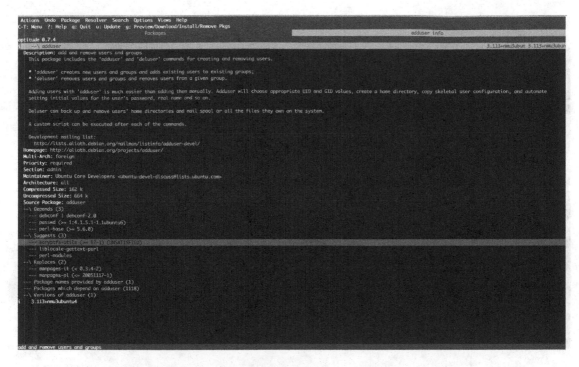

Figure 8-16. *Displaying detailed package information*

Press q to close the information window and return to the package listing.

Since scrolling through this listing is not fast, being able to search it is useful. Bring up the search dialog by pressing the forward slash (/) and entering the required search term. Let's look for the Ubuntu kernel package, called linux-image. As you type, aptitude will jump down the list to display the first matching package. You can see an example of this in Figure 8-17.

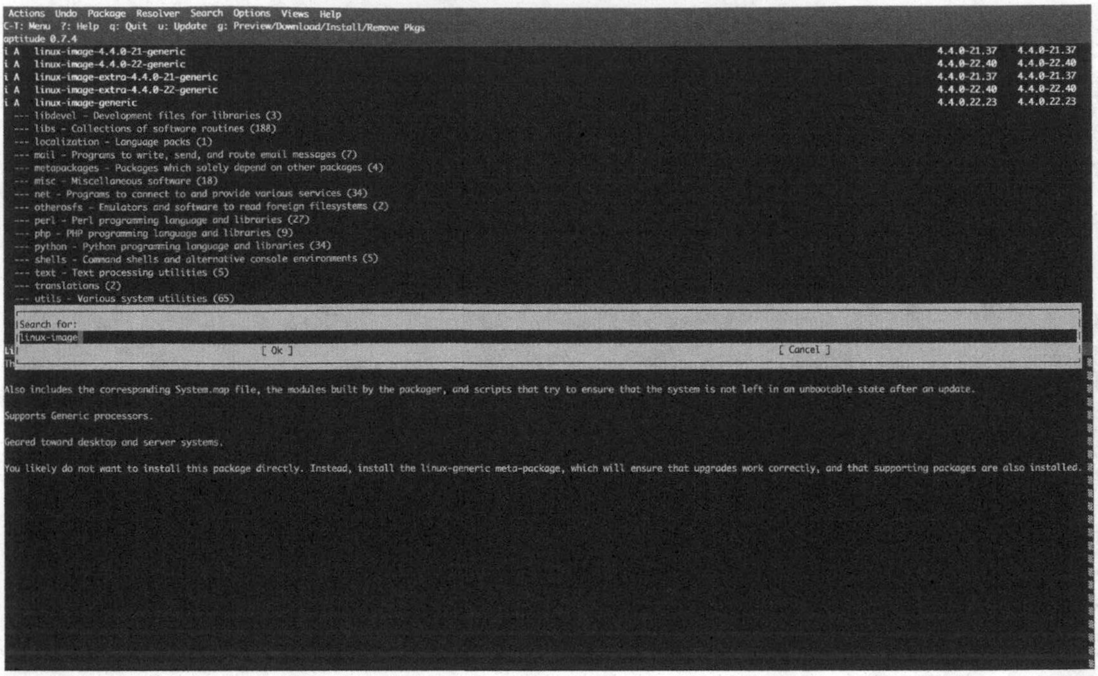

Figure 8-17. *Searching packages by name*

Press Enter to close the search dialog. To jump to the next matched package name, press n. If you keep pressing n, you will eventually find yourself in the listing of *Not Installed Packages*, which contains more kernels still. To display more package names on screen, you can toggle the information window by pressing D.

Let's now install a package. A small but helpful network utility is nmap, so we'll pick that. Use the find command to find this package in the listing, and then highlight it. To mark this package for installation, press the plus sign (+). You will see a warning dialog telling you that aptitude cannot install packages until you become the root user, as shown in Figure 8-18.

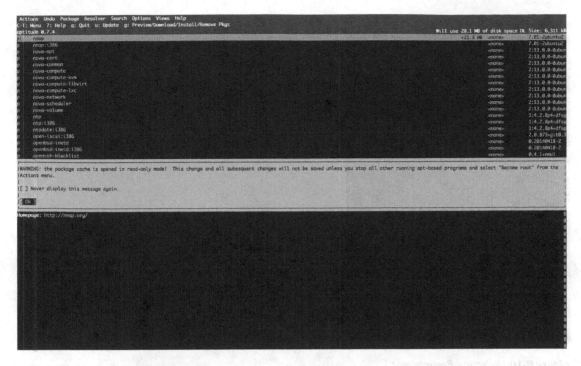

Figure 8-18. root user warning dialog

You can disable this warning from appearing in the future. You will notice there is a "Never display this message again" check box. First press Tab to jump to the check box, press the spacebar to check it, and then press Tab again to select the OK button and Enter to accept. To acknowledge this warning, press Enter.

■ **Tip** If we had started `aptitude` via `sudo`, the warning dialog would not have appeared. However, making selections as a `non-root` user adds a layer of protection from mistakes. Since it is impossible to accidentally remove packages without being the root user, running `aptitude` as a `non-root` user and becoming root only to apply pending changes is a good idea.

Rather than installing the package immediately, you'll see that the package status has changed from *p* to *pi*. It is now marked for installation. This allows you to select any number of packages for installation—or removal—before applying the changes to your system.

You are going to install just the `nmap` application for now, but first you have to become the root user. To do this, press Ctrl+T to activate the Actions menu (see Figure 8-19).

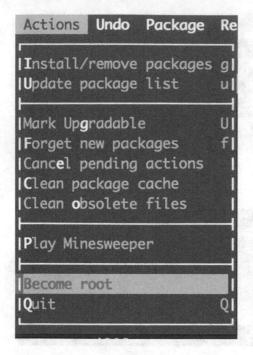

Figure 8-19. *Selecting Become root*

Use the arrow keys to select *Become root* (avoid the temptation to play minesweeper), press Enter, and aptitude will now run sudo for you. After you enter your password, it will restart itself with root user privileges. Although the package lists return to their initial collapsed state, the command to install your package was added to the internal to-do list.

To process your pending installation, press g. aptitude has found that the nmap package requires the several other package to be present on the system, and thus it is automatically selected for installation (it is flagged with *piA*), as you can see in Figure 8-20.

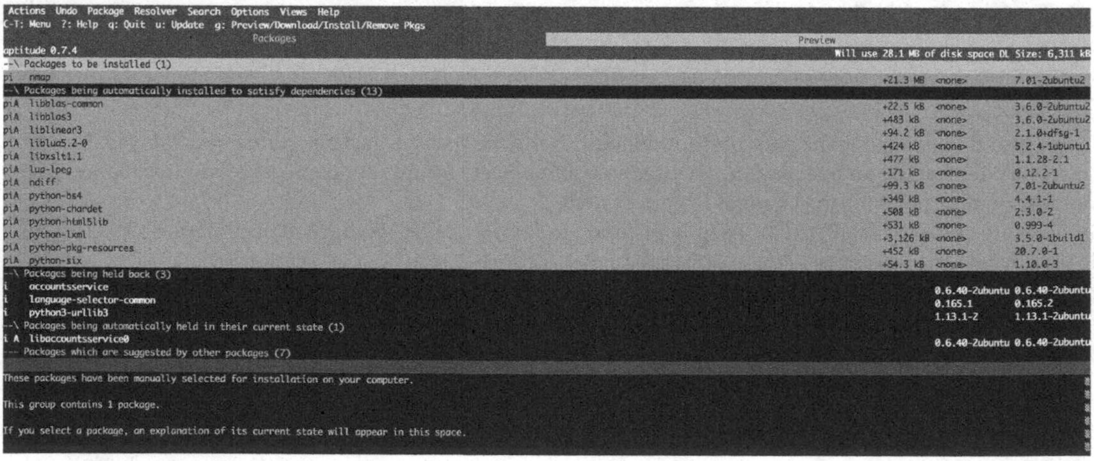

Figure 8-20. *Added package dependencies*

Confirm that you want this dependency to be installed by pressing g again, and aptitude will now download the required package files and install them. During this process, you'll be kept informed of what is happening (see Figure 8-21).

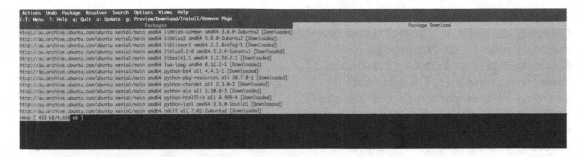

Figure 8-21. *Processing installation tasks*

After installation finishes, press Enter and you are back at the Aptitude menu. You will now learn how to remove packages by removing the nmap package you just installed (see Figure 8-22). Search for it using the / key again. You will see that it has an (i) beside it for installed. Press the hyphen (-) key to mark the package for removal. You'll see the desired package status character change from i to id. If you had customized configuration files and wanted to ensure these were removed as well at this stage, you could press the underscore (_) key to mark the package for purge; if you do so, you'll see the desired status change to p. In Figure 8-22, you can see that nmap is now set to id, as it is marked for deletion. To apply your queued changes, press g.

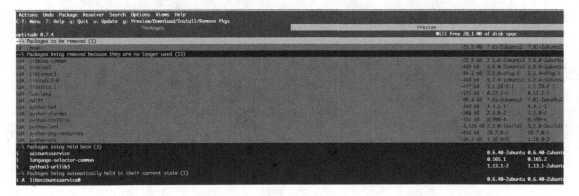

Figure 8-22. *Package removal via aptitude*

The packages that were added as dependencies when we install nmap, since they are not being used by any other package, are set to also be removed. Press g again to confirm and process the changes (see Figure 8-23).

```
Performing actions...
(Reading database ... 100407 files and directories currently installed.)
Removing nmap (7.01-2ubuntu2) ...
Removing liblinear3:amd64 (2.1.0+dfsg-1) ...
Removing libblas3 (3.6.0-2ubuntu2) ...
Removing libblas-common (3.6.0-2ubuntu2) ...
Removing liblua5.2-0:amd64 (5.2.4-1ubuntu1) ...
Removing ndiff (7.01-2ubuntu2) ...
Removing python-lxml (3.5.0-1build1) ...
Removing libxslt1.1:amd64 (1.1.28-2.1) ...
Removing lua-lpeg:amd64 (0.12.2-1) ...
Removing python-bs4 (4.4.1-1) ...
Removing python-chardet (2.3.0-2) ...
Removing python-html5lib (0.999-4) ...
Removing python-pkg-resources (20.7.0-1) ...
Removing python-six (1.10.0-3) ...
Processing triggers for man-db (2.7.5-1) ...
Processing triggers for libc-bin (2.23-0ubuntu3) ...
Press Return to continue.
■
```

Figure 8-23. *Process pending removals*

For more information on the commands available in Aptitude, press the question mark (?) key. Figure 8-24 shows a listing of the available commands.

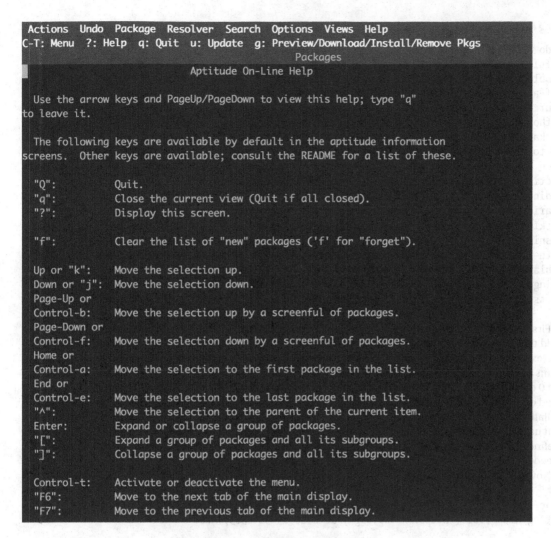

Actions Undo Package Resolver Search Options Views Help
C-T: Menu   ?: Help   q: Quit   u: Update   g: Preview/Download/Install/Remove Pkgs
                                    Packages
                        Aptitude On-Line Help

  Use the arrow keys and PageUp/PageDown to view this help; type "q"
to leave it.

  The following keys are available by default in the aptitude information
screens. Other keys are available; consult the README for a list of these.

  "Q":   Quit.
  "q":   Close the current view (Quit if all closed).
  "?":   Display this screen.

  "f":   Clear the list of "new" packages ('f' for "forget").

  Up or "k":   Move the selection up.
  Down or "j": Move the selection down.
  Page-Up or
  Control-b: Move the selection up by a screenful of packages.
  Page-Down or
  Control-f: Move the selection down by a screenful of packages.
  Home or
  Control-a: Move the selection to the first package in the list.
  End or
  Control-e: Move the selection to the last package in the list.
  "^":   Move the selection to the parent of the current item.
  Enter: Expand or collapse a group of packages.
  "[":   Expand a group of packages and all its subgroups.
  "]":   Collapse a group of packages and all its subgroups.

  Control-t: Activate or deactivate the menu.
  "F6":   Move to the next tab of the main display.
  "F7":   Move to the previous tab of the main display.

***Figure 8-24.** The aptitude command list*

You can exit the help listing by pressing q. You can then exit aptitude by pressing q again.

Noninteractive Mode

All this navigating and window switching might be user-friendly, but it's hardly quick. To this end, aptitude also has a command-line mode that does not use interactive menus but instead takes action commands and package names as parameters. To demonstrate that using aptitude this way is just as handy as using the GUI, we will install the nmap package again. When using aptitude noninteractively, you need to run it as root for install and uninstall tasks. Take a look at how to install nmap again in Listing 8-13.

Listing 8-13. Installing nmap with aptitude in Noninteractive Mode

```
$ sudo aptitude install nmap
The following NEW packages will be installed:
  libblas-common{a} libblas3{a} liblinear3{a} liblua5.2-0{a} libxslt1.1{a} lua-lpeg{a}
ndiff{a} nmap python-bs4{a} python-chardet{a} python-html5lib{a} python-lxml{a} python-pkg-
resources{a}
  python-six{a}
0 packages upgraded, 14 newly installed, 0 to remove and 4 not to upgrade.
Need to get 0 B/6,311 kB of archives. After unpacking 28.1 MB will be used.
Do you want to continue? [Y/n/?] y
Selecting previously unselected package libblas-common.
(Reading database ... 99366 files and directories currently installed.)
Preparing to unpack .../libblas-common_3.6.0-2ubuntu2_amd64.deb ...
Unpacking libblas-common (3.6.0-2ubuntu2) ...
...<snip>...
update-alternatives: using /usr/lib/libblas/libblas.so.3 to provide /usr/lib/libblas.so.3
(libblas.so.3) in auto mode
Setting up nmap (7.01-2ubuntu2) ...
Processing triggers for libc-bin (2.23-0ubuntu3) ...
```

First, aptitude checks the package database to ensure the system is able to have packages installed; should there be packages that are partially configured or pending, it will tell you and abort this installation.

Next, aptitude notifies us that nmap has a several dependencies that will be installed as well and informs us of how much disk space will be used by these packages (28.1 MB). Note that it tells us it needs to get 0 of 6,311KB of archives. Because we had previously installed nmap, the original package files are still cached on the machine, otherwise you will see aptitude download the packages once you enter y to start the installation.

It uses the dpkg command internally to handle this part. When done, it processes triggers that may be defined by the packages just added and rechecks the package status database to make sure everything succeeded.

Now we can check to see that nmap is installed by executing the following from the command line.

```
$ nmap -v
Starting Nmap 7.01 ( https://nmap.org ) at 2016-05-31 23:37 AEST
```

THE APT CACHE

When you install packages from the Internet, they are first downloaded to your computer and stored in a cache located at /var/cache/apt/archives. If you remove a package and then re-add it, it doesn't need to be downloaded all over again. Utilities are available that let you share such a cache across multiple computers, which is useful if you have a slow or expensive Internet connection. Examples of such utilities are apt-cacher, apt-cacher-ng, and apt-proxy, both of which are available as packages.

Removing Packages Using Aptitude

Listing 8-14 shows how to remove a package using aptitude. Again, like with dpkg, you can remove or purge a package. Removing, of course, removes everything but the configuration files from the host, while purging removes the package in its entirety including any configuration files.

Listing 8-14. Removing Packages with aptitude

```
$ sudo aptitude remove nmap
The following packages will be REMOVED:
  libblas-common{u} libblas3{u} liblinear3{u} liblua5.2-0{u} libxslt1.1{u} lua-lpeg{u}
ndiff{u} nmap python-bs4{u} python-chardet{u} python-html5lib{u} python-lxml{u} python-pkg-
resources{u}
  python-six{u}
0 packages upgraded, 0 newly installed, 14 to remove and 4 not to upgrade.
Need to get 0 B of archives. After unpacking 28.1 MB will be freed.
Do you want to continue? [Y/n/?] y
(Reading database ... 100407 files and directories currently installed.)
Removing nmap (7.01-2ubuntu2) ...
Removing libblas3 (3.6.0-2ubuntu2) ...
...<snip>...
Processing triggers for man-db (2.7.5-1) ...
Processing triggers for libc-bin (2.23-0ubuntu3) ...
```

If you want to also remove any configuration files, you can pass the purge option to aptitude.

```
$ sudo aptitude purge nmap
```

REPOSITORIES

Both Advanced Packaging Tool (APT) and Aptitude source packages from the online repositories. Repositories, as explained previously, are collections of packages maintained by the package maintainers for your particular distribution. Both of the tools we're going to look at use special configuration files called APT source files to define where they will go to find these repositories and what types of packages they want to have available.

APT and Aptitude use these source files to find information about tens of thousands of packages. The configuration information for your default repositories is usually stored in the /etc/apt/sources.list file, which is created during the installation of your host. Further repositories may also be defined in the /etc/apt/sources.list.d/ directory.

Generally, separate repositories exist for different distributions, and within these distributions different repositories exist for each version of a distribution. A further set of repositories exists for different types of software. Sounds complicated? Well, it isn't when you break it down. Let's look at the Ubuntu 16.04 release (codenamed Xenial Xerus). If you have this release installed, you should see a line like the following in the /etc/apt/sources.list file:

```
deb http://archive.ubuntu.com/ubuntu/ xenial main restricted
```

The repository definition starts with the repository type and a URL. The URL may be localized to your closest repository, like 'http://au.archive.ubuntu.com'. The type indicates whether the repository contains binary packages or source code. A repository type of deb contains binary packages, and a type of deb-src contains packages containing the source code for applications. You generally won't need to ever use deb-src repositories unless you are creating backports (see the sidebar "Ubuntu Backports"). The URL points at the server that hosts the repository. The next field is the release, which for Ubuntu 16.04 is "xenial" You can find other releases of Ubuntu at https://en.wikipedia.org/wiki/List_of_ Ubuntu_releases. Finally, we have a list of one or more sections that define which sets of packages you want to be available.

The packages are divided into these sections by license type and support level. Ubuntu has four sections. First is "main," which contains all free software that is supported by Ubuntu's developer, Canonical. The "restricted" packages are supported by Canonical but not completely free license, packages like Nvidia drivers. There are other types too. The "universe" packages are not supported by Canonical directly but are supported by the wider Linux community. Finally, software that may be encumbered with patents or legal issues—like MP3 players or DVD player software—are available from "multiverse." You can read more about them at https://help.ubuntu.com/community/ Repositories/Ubuntu.

By not specifying one or more of these sections, you can restrict what types of packages to install on your host. For example, you may want to install only supported and free packages from Canonical, in which case your sources line might look as follows:

deb http://archive.ubuntu.com/ubuntu xenial main

As an exercise, why not point your web browser to http://archive.ubuntu.com/ubuntu and see how a repository is laid out?

You can find out more about repositories and sections and how to set them up at https://help. ubuntu.com/community/Repositories/Ubuntu.

Updating Packages Using Aptitude

The other standard task of upgrading is accomplished by first updating the list of available packages (checking that you have the most current record of updated packages available from the repository) and performing the upgrade of packages that require upgrading on your host.

Listing 8-15 shows how to perform an update of the list of available packages. What happens here is that the aptitude program uses the list of repositories found in the /etc/apt/sources.list file (and any additional repositories contained in /etc/apt/sources.list.d/) and compiles a list of available packages for your host.

Listing 8-15. aptitude Update

```
$ sudo aptitude update
```

Now when you upgrade you have two choices: safe-upgrade and full-upgrade. The safe-upgrade will not remove installed packages to upgrade the package being upgraded, which is sometimes required. Sometimes you may have to remove a third-party package in order to upgrade a second. With safe-upgrade, this package will not be upgraded to the newer version. In that instance, you must use `full-upgrade`, which will upgrade all installed packages by removing and installing any packages it needs to get the job done.

Listing 8-16 shows the syntax of each of these commands.

Listing 8-16. Automatically Install Pending Package Upgrades

```
$ sudo aptitude safe-upgrade
$ sudo aptitude full-upgrade
```

ADVANCED PACKAGING TOOL

Before `aptitude`, the APT suite of utilities provided most of the online package management functionality on deb-based distributions. These tools are still present, but some of the functionality they provide is not present in `aptitude` or is not easily accessible, so it pays to become familiar with them. The commands that make up APT include `apt-get`, `apt-cache`, and `apt-file`. The `apt-get` command downloads, installs, and removes packages and source files. The `apt-cache` command searches package lists and displays package information. The `apt-file` command searches file content lists for which package provides a file.

The `aptitude` tool was written as a drop-in replacement for `apt-get`, so in all cases where you run `aptitude` noninteractively, you can replace it with `apt-get`. However, `aptitude` has more advanced algorithms for resolving package dependencies and conflicts, so we suggest you use `aptitude` whenever possible. For example, if you want to install the `nmap` package with `apt-get`, you use the following:

```
$ sudo apt-get install nmap
```

To find out information about a particular package using the `apt-cache` command, you use it as follows:

```
$ sudo apt-cache showpkg nmap
```

To use the `apt-file` command to find out which package provides a specific file that is not yet installed on the system, you can use `apt-file` to search the package contents files provided by the repositories:

```
$ apt-file search /usr/sbin/foo
```

This requires an up-to-date contents listing on your system. If you think these contents may be out of date, you can update to the latest versions via the following:

```
$ sudo apt-file update
```

As an alternative, you can search the package lists online at `http://packages.ubuntu.com`.

Package Management with Ubuntu Software App

If you've installed the Unity desktop on Ubuntu, you have another way of managing software installation. In Unity desktop there is an application store, Ubuntu Software, and it is very similar to the one we saw in our CentOS desktop.

You can skip this section if you don't have the Unity desktop installed on your server. Most servers sit in a rack without a screen or keyboard attached, so installing a large and complex desktop environment makes no sense. If you do want to add a full GUI, you should be able to install the unity8-desktop-session-mir package.

When installation is complete, start the display manager via sudo service lightdm start and log in with your username and password.

It is very easy to access the Ubuntu Software store, you access it from the icon shown in Figure 8-25.

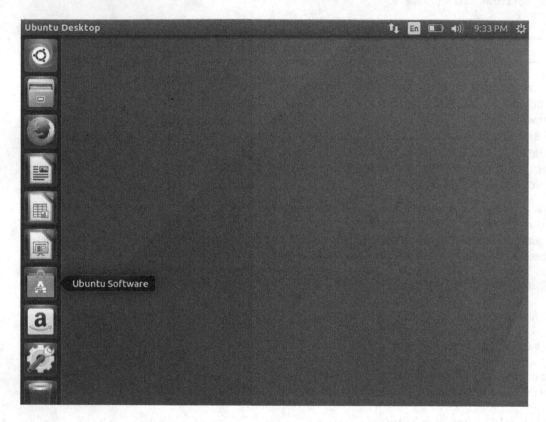

Figure 8-25. *Starting the Ubuntu Software app store*

Opening it up and it looks as shown in Figure 8-26.

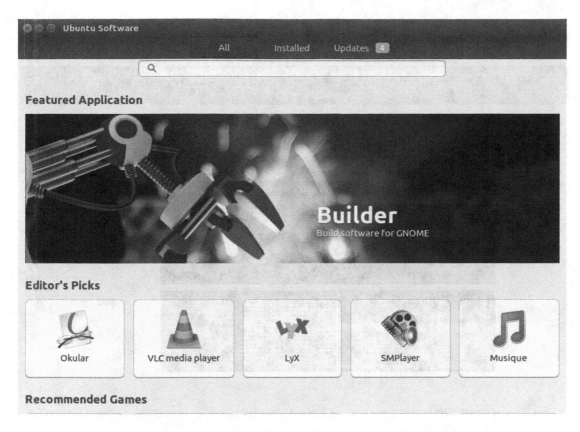

Figure 8-26. The Ubuntu Software app store

This interface is very easy to navigate around. Along the top we have the same views we saw with CentOS, All, Installed, and Updates. We see already that there are four updates waiting to be installed. Below that we have the search bar and then along the bottom we have quick links to popular and recommended applications.

Let's search for a program called "terminator," which is a great little advanced terminal. Typing that into the search bar comes back with a list of possible matches. Since this is the only "terminator," we have one package returned (see Figure 8-27).

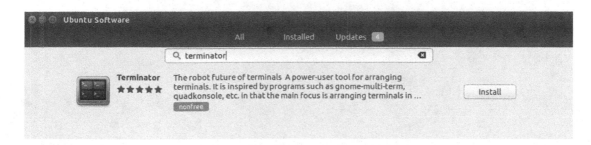

Figure 8-27. Finding the terminal package

We can click either the install button to start installing or anywhere on the listing to get more information (see Figure 8-28).

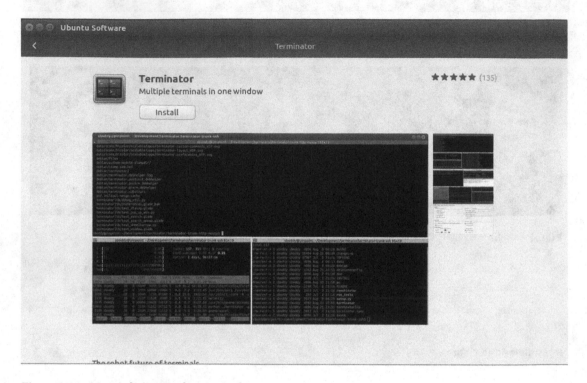

Figure 8-28. *More information for terminal*

Now we are going to install this package (see Figure 8-29).

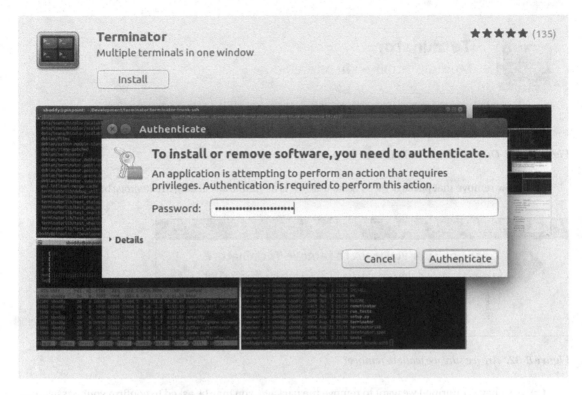

Figure 8-29. *Entering our password to get root privileges to install packages*

We are asked to enter our password before we can install software.

Once installed (see Figure 8-30), we can launch the application from here or we can remove it (see Figure 8-31).

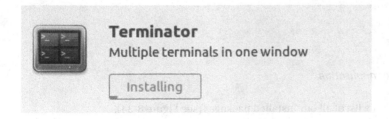

Figure 8-30. *Installing the package*

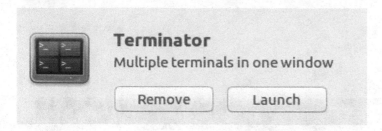

Figure 8-31. *Our installation is finished*

Let's now remove that package (see Figure 8-32). It is as simple as clicking the *Remove* button.

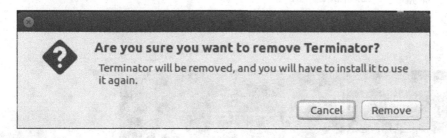

Figure 8-32. *Are we sure we want to remove?*

Once we have confirmed we want to remove the package, you may be asked to confirm your password again and then we begin removing the application (see Figure 8-33).

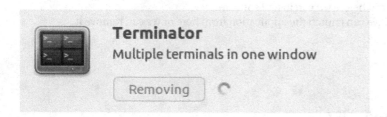

Figure 8-33. *Removing the terminator application*

If we click the Installed view we get a list of all our installed packages (see Figure 8-34).

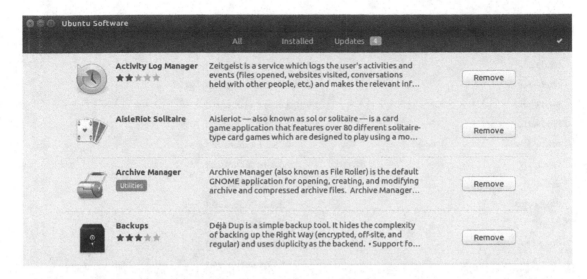

Figure 8-34. *Listing our installed packages*

From the Installed page we can click any package listed there and get more information about it or a package can be removed if that is your wish.

Moving on to the Updates page we see the following (see Figure 8-35):

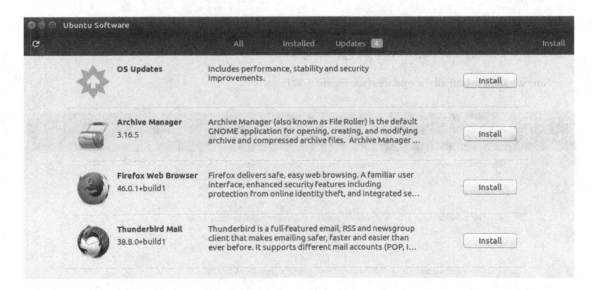

Figure 8-35. *Updates view*

Again we see that we can refresh the listing, making sure we have the most recent list, by clicking the reload icon in the top left. We can install individual updates by clicking the Install buttons or we can install all the updates with the Install button in the top right.

If we wish to see what will be installed we can click the updates.

In Figure 8-36 we see the list of packages that will be installed with the OS Updates update.

OS Updates	
accountsservice	0.6.40-2ubuntu11
bind9	1:9.10.3.dfsg.P4-8ubuntu1
bind9-doc	1:9.10.3.dfsg.P4-8ubuntu1
bind9-host	1:9.10.3.dfsg.P4-8ubuntu1
bind9utils	1:9.10.3.dfsg.P4-8ubuntu1
brltty	5.3.1-2ubuntu2.1
cpp-5	5.3.1-14ubuntu2.1
dnsutils	1:9.10.3.dfsg.P4-8ubuntu1
dosfstools	3.0.28-2ubuntu0.1
dpkg	1.18.4ubuntu1.1
dpkg-dev	1.18.4ubuntu1.1
fwupd	0.7.0-0ubuntu4.1
g++-5	5.3.1-14ubuntu2.1
gcc-5	5.3.1-14ubuntu2.1
libapache2-mod-php7.0	7.0.4-7ubuntu2.1
libdfu1	0.7.0-0ubuntu4.1
libdpkg-perl	1.18.4ubuntu1.1
libfwupd1	0.7.0-0ubuntu4.1

Figure 8-36. *Listing the packages in the OS Updates update*

Now we shall install all the updates (see Figure 8-37).

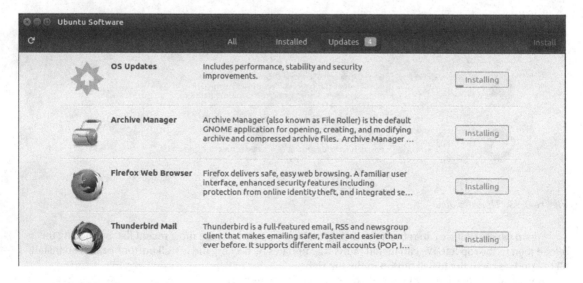

Figure 8-37. *Installing updates*

Finally, when all your updates have been installed you should see the following screen (Figure 8-38):

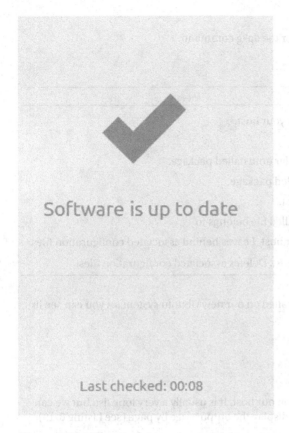

Software is up to date

Last checked: 00:08

Figure 8-38. *All up to date*

That's all for using the desktop app installer, let's now move on the most basic package tool on Ubuntu.

Using dpkg

The most basic package management tool on Ubuntu is dpkg (pronounced "dee-package"). The apt and aptitude tools are both wrappers around dpkg, much like yum is a wrapper around the rpm command.

■ **Tip** We recommend you use aptitude to manage your packages rather than dpkg. The command aptitude takes care of dependencies and manages relationships between packages; the dpkg command does not.

The dpkg command allows you to list which packages are installed, install package files you had previously downloaded, and find out to which packages files on the system belong. You can find all of the options (and there are many) that are available for dpkg by issuing the man dpkg command, as shown in Listing 8-17.

Listing 8-17. The dpkg man page

```
$ man dpkg
```

Table 8-4 lists some of the main options and flags for the dpkg command.

Table 8-4. *Options and Flags for dpkg*

Options and Flags	Description
-l	--list	Lists all installed packages on your host.
-p	--print-avail	Prints package information.
-c	--contents	Lists the contents of a particular uninstalled package.
-L	--listfiles	Lists the contents of an installed package.
-i	--install	Installs a package on your host.
-S	--search	Finds which package an installed file belongs to.
-r	--remove	Removes a package from your host. Leaves behind associated configuration files.
-P	--purge	Purges a package from your host. Deletes associated configuration files.

First, we'll get a list of packages that are already installed on our new Ubuntu system, as you can see in Listing 8-18.

Listing 8-18. Listing Installed Packages

```
$ dpkg -l
```

This produces the complete list of all the packages on our host. It is usually a very long list, but we can pipe the output from dpkg into the more command and display the output page by page (see Listing 8-19). We can then scroll through it at our leisure.

Listing 8-19. Piping the dpkg -l Output to More

```
$ dpkg -l | more
```

Notice in Figure 8-39 that dpkg lists output in four columns: status, name, version, and description. We pipe this output through the head command, which just gives us the first ten lines of output by default.

```
jsmith@au-mel-ubuntu-1:~$ dpkg -l |head
Desired=Unknown/Install/Remove/Purge/Hold
| Status=Not/Inst/Conf-files/Unpacked/halF-conf/Half-inst/trig-aWait/Trig-pend
|/ Err?=(none)/Reinst-required (Status,Err: uppercase=bad)
||/ Name                    Version              Architecture Description
+++-=====================-====================-============-=================================================
ii  accountsservice          0.6.40-2ubuntu11     amd64        query and manipulate user account information
ii  acl                      2.2.52-3             amd64        Access control list utilities
ii  acpid                    1:2.0.26-1ubuntu2    amd64        Advanced Configuration and Power Interface event daemon
ii  adduser                  3.113+nmu3ubuntu4    all          add and remove users and groups
ii  apache2                  2.4.18-2ubuntu3      amd64        Apache HTTP Server
```

Figure 8-39. *Viewing results of dpkg -l*

■ **Note**   Although is it not automatically clear from the output in Listing 8-20, the first three lines are in fact the status column.

Let's look at each of these columns for a moment. The status column actually consists of three states a package can be in.

- Desired status

- Current status

- Error

Usually, the status will be ii, which means the package is currently installed and will be upgraded if a newer version is available. Table 8-5 lists the most common status codes and their meanings.

Table 8-5. *The dpkg Status Codes*

Code	Meaning
ii	Package is installed and will install updates when available.
hi	Package is on hold and installed but will not install updates.
un	Package is not installed.
rc	Package is not installed, but there are residual configuration files (usually means the package was removed).

The other columns speak for themselves. They contain the package name, the version (if the package is currently installed), and a short description.

You would usually not want a listing of everything, so let's limit the output to packages that provide the Linux kernel by passing a string for dpkg to match. The Linux kernel in Ubuntu goes by the name linux-image, which is different from RHEL, where it is just called kernel. l lists all the linux-images installed on our host by using a glob string (meaning we catch all results with the string linux-image in them) by using the * symbol before and after the string we are targeting.

■ **Tip**   Glob strings are very useful methods for working with strings, especially strings like file names. You can read about using glob strings, known as *globbing*, at www.faqs.org/docs/abs/HTML/globbingref.html.

In this case, we are using *linux-image* (you should read a little about globbing and test the results returned when you use linux-image* and linux-image as your search string).

In Figure 8-40 you can see there are several linux-image packages, all with names based on the kernel versions they contain. This is so different kernel packages don't have the same name, thus allowing you to have multiple kernels installed. In addition, you'll find the linux-image package, which is a so-called virtual package. This package doesn't actually contain any files, but it does contain a link to the newest available kernel, so a normal upgrade always includes any available new Linux kernel package.

```
                       :~$ dpkg -l *linux-image*
Desired=Unknown/Install/Remove/Purge/Hold
| Status=Not/Inst/Conf-files/Unpacked/halF-conf/Half-inst/trig-aWait/Trig-pend
|/ Err?=(none)/Reinst-required (Status,Err: uppercase=bad)
||/ Name                            Version         Architecture    Description
+++-==============================-===============-===============-============================================================
un  linux-image                    <none>          <none>          (no description available)
ii  linux-image-4.4.0-21-generic   4.4.0-21.37     amd64           Linux kernel image for version 4.4.0 on 64 bit x86 SMP
ii  linux-image-4.4.0-22-generic   4.4.0-22.40     amd64           Linux kernel image for version 4.4.0 on 64 bit x86 SMP
ii  linux-image-extra-4.4.0-21-generic  4.4.0-21.37  amd64         Linux kernel extra modules for version 4.4.0 on 64 bit x86 SMP
ii  linux-image-extra-4.4.0-22-generic  4.4.0-22.40  amd64         Linux kernel extra modules for version 4.4.0 on 64 bit x86 SMP
ii  linux-image-generic            4.4.0.22.23     amd64           Generic Linux kernel image
```

Figure 8-40. *Listing the Linux Kernel*

■ **Tip**   Because the default Linux terminal is only 80 characters wide and dpkg wants to display information for each package on a single line only, it is unable to display the full package name if this is longer than 14 characters. For many packages, this is not a problem, but the kernel packages have long names and so don't display completely. To work around this, you can override the terminal size for dpkg, so it will display more information, using an environment variable. To do this, prefix the command like so: $ COLUMNS=200 dpkg -l '*linux-image*'. This tells your host that your screen is 200 characters wide, so it displays more of all columns.

Examining Package Details

Let's have a look at some information about a common package on Ubuntu, adduser, using dpkg. Listing 8-20 shows the output of the dpkg -p command querying for information about one of our adduser packages.

Listing 8-20. Output of the dpkg -p Command

```
$ dpkg -p adduser
Package: adduser
Priority: required
Section: admin
Installed-Size: 648
Origin: Ubuntu
Maintainer: Ubuntu Core Developers <ubuntu-devel-discuss@lists.ubuntu.com>
Bugs: https://bugs.launchpad.net/ubuntu/+filebug
Architecture: all
Multi-Arch: foreign
Version: adduser-3.113+nmu3ubuntu4
Replaces: manpages-it (<< 0.3.4-2), manpages-pl (<= 20051117-1)
Depends: perl-base (>= 5.6.0), passwd (>= 1:4.1.5.1-1.1ubuntu6), debconf | debconf-2.0
Suggests: liblocale-gettext-perl, perl-modules, ecryptfs-utils (>= 67-1)
Filename: pool/main/a/adduser/adduser_3.113+nmu3ubuntu4_all.deb
Size: 161698
MD5sum: 36f79d952ced9bde3359b63cf9cf44fb
Description: add and remove users and groups
Original-Maintainer: Debian Adduser Developers <adduser-devel@lists.alioth.debian.org>
SHA1: 6a5b8f58e33d5c9a25f79c6da80a64bf104e6268
SHA256: ca6c86cb229082cc22874ed320eac8d128cc91f086fe5687946e7d05758516a3
```

```
Homepage: http://alioth.debian.org/projects/adduser/
Description-md5: 7965b5cd83972a254552a570bcd32c93
Supported: 5y
Task: minimal
```

The adduser package contains commands for user management on your system. You can see in Listing 8-20, in addition to a description and version, each package also contains a contact e-mail for support and information about the disk space it uses when installed. The Depends section also details the packages it needs to be installed prior to the package itself being installed, which are called dependencies.

Examining Package Contents

In addition to description information about packages, you can also query what files it installed and which directories it installed them to. You can find out the package contents using the dpkg -L command as follows:

```
$ dpkg -L adduser
```

This returns a full list of the files installed by the adduser package.

■ **Tip**   An easy way to find out which commands are provided by a package is to list the files it installs to directories that hold executable applications. Make dpkg list the package contents and pipe the output to grep to limit the output to files and directories that contain the string bin, for example: dpkg -L <package name> | grep bin.

Performing a File Search

For files that are already present on the host, you can determine the package they belong to by using dpkg:

```
$ dpkg -S /usr/sbin/userdel
```

This command tells you what package provides the userdel command.

Installing Packages

All Ubuntu package files are made up of three parts: the package name, the package version, and the target architecture. For instance, version 2.17 of the foobar package for 32-bit Intel machines would be "foobar-2.17_i386.deb". If you can install the package on any architecture it will be "foobar-2.17_all.deb."

■ **Note**   The *target architecture* is the processor technology of your host (e.g., i386 or x64).

After you obtain a package file for your Ubuntu version and architecture, you can install it using dpkg. Because packages contain files that need to be installed to privileged system locations (like /bin, /usr/ sbin, etc.), the installation needs to be performed as the root user. On Ubuntu, you can use the sudo command discussed in Chapter 5 to perform the installation command as the root user:

```
$ sudo dpkg -i wget_1.17.1-1ubuntu1_amd64.deb
```

The dpkg command will keep you informed of progress during installation. Depending on the package, it may also ask you some questions about how you would like to configure the package. Don't worry, you can change the answers to these questions later.

Be careful when installing packages you manually download. If the package was not created for your Ubuntu version, other packages that it depends on may not be available in the correct version. Installing anyway might lead to an "unresolvable dependency" that can put your package system into an inconsistent state, where a package is partially installed and prevents further package management until the problem is solved. dpkg will warn you and not let you do this without forcing it to. A best practice is to always check if a package is available in the distribution itself before you download it from a third-party source.

Removing a Package

You have two different ways of removing an Ubuntu package: one is to remove the package, and the other is to purge the package from the system altogether. When you use the --remove option, you are removing everything except modified configuration files for that package from the host. When you use the --purge option, you are telling dpkg to remove everything installed by that package onto your host, including configuration files you modified yourself.

Why have the two methods? Because there are times when you want to completely remove everything and times when you want to remove something with the view of installing it again at some later stage.

Listing 8-21 shows both methods of deleting packages from a host with the dpkg command.

Listing 8-21. Package Removal

```
$ sudo dpkg --remove wget
```

or

```
$ sudo dpkg --purge wget
```

Compiling from Source

Although the list of packaged software is extensive, not everything is available as a convenient deb or RPM package. If a piece of software is not available in a packaged format, not even in a source package for backporting (see the sidebar "Ubuntu Backports"), you might need to build it from source.

UBUNTU BACKPORTS

Sometimes if a specific package version you need is not available, you may be told to create a backport. This might be the case if you are using an older version of a distribution or if a newer version of an application has not yet been packaged for your release. Creating a backport involves getting the source package from a newer (or older) release of Ubuntu and compiling it on your own machine. Backports are beyond the scope of this book, but some excellent references are available online from which you can learn how to use and create them. A good place to start is https://help.ubuntu.com/community/UbuntuBackports.

In this section we'll show you how to compile software from source and also give you some tips on how to keep such source installations manageable.

Building applications from source generally has three phases:

1. Configure the application.

2. Compile or make the application.

3. Install the application.

We'll take you through these three phases and use the nginx web server as our example. This time, rather than installing our application from a package, we'll build the latest source at the time of this writing (version 1.10.1). First, let's grab the tarball from http://nginx.org/ using the wget utility.

```
$ wget -c http://nginx.org/download/nginx-1.10.1.tar.gz
```

■ **Note** A *tarball* is a file (usually compressed) that contains a set of files and/or directories. The application used to create these tarballs is called tar (Tape ARchive), thusly named because it was initially used to write archives to magnetic tape. Tarballs have file extensions that normally indicate how the archive was compressed. Examples include tar.gz or .tgz for gzip and tar.bz2 or .tbz for bzip2 compression. You can see more information about tar on its man page.

The -c flag tells wget to resume a partial download. This means it won't restart the download from scratch if it was interrupted for some reason. With the -c option, if the download fails, you can then just rerun the command and the download will resume from the point at which it stopped.

The wget command downloads files to the current directory, so we now have a tarball we can unpack. The extension tells us it was compressed using gzip, so we need the -z flag to make tar use gzip decompression. We pass the –x to tell tar to extract the archive. The –f is used to provide the file to work on.

```
$ tar -xvzf nginx-1.10.1.tar.gz
```

■ **Tip** If you don't know what compression a tarball uses, you can find out by using the file command. Run file <tarball> and file will check the tarball for magic bytes, which indicate the file type. This list of magic bytes for thousands of file types is stored in /usr/share/file/magic. Once you know how the tarball was compressed, you can unpack it.

The -v parameter tells tar to be verbose and print the path of each file it extracts from the archive. If you know which files are contained within the archive, you might want to drop this parameter, so your terminal doesn't scroll with redundant information. As an added bonus, not printing file names means the extract operation completes a bit faster as well.

The tarball is now extracted, so we should change into the source directory and have a look around, to see which files are there.

```
$ cd  nginx-1.10.1
~/ nginx-1.10.1$ ls
```

In many cases the instructions for compiling and installing the application will be contained in a file called README or INSTALL. For nginx, there doesn't appear to be an INSTALL file, but there is an README file. By reading this file, we should be able to find the instructions for installing the application.

```
$ less README
```

We learn from this particular file that the installation documentation is online and not included in the tarball. We can refer to the nginx-specific online documentation at http://nginx.org/ for detailed information. We'll use these instructions here (http://nginx.org/en/docs/configure.html) to compile and install the application.

But before we can compile our application, we need to install a compiler and its associated libraries and utilities. These are usually packaged, so we'll simply install them via the package system. Table 8-6 shows the required packages for Red Hat and Ubuntu.

Table 8-6. *Installing a Compiler and Essential Build Tools*

Distribution	Command
CentOS	yum install gcc make
Ubuntu	aptitude install build-essential

Configure

With the compiler installed, we can now configure the sources for building. Most software is highly configurable, not just in terms of available features but also in terms of installation location. To configure an application prior to building it, we use the configure command. In Listing 8-22, we run the configure command with the --help option to display all the options available to configure our application.

Listing 8-22. Shortened List of Configuration Help

```
~/nginx-1.10.1$ ./configure --help

  --help                               print this message

  --prefix=PATH                    set installation prefix
  --sbin-path=PATH                set nginx binary pathname
  --modules-path=PATH          set modules path
  --conf-path=PATH                set nginx.conf pathname
  --error-log-path=PATH          set error log pathname
  --pid-path=PATH                  set nginx.pid pathname
  --lock-path=PATH                set nginx.lock pathname

  --user=USER                      set non-privileged user for
                                                   worker processes
  --group=GROUP                  set non-privileged group for
                                                   worker processes
```

■ **Note** Note that in Listing 7-28 we've specified ./ in front of the configure command. This tells Linux to run the configure script it finds in the current directory.

The output goes on, but we'll stop here at the most important option, --prefix. This option determines where the software will be installed, and it's important that this is a location that is not used by packaged software. Otherwise, you might end up in a situation where a file installed from source overwrites a packaged file. This would confuse the package system, and when you removed the package in question, your compiled file would be deleted.

Generally when you install applications from source, they are deployed in the /usr/local directory structure. This is usually the default option for --prefix. We are going to install nginx in another common directory for installing your own packages, /opt.

The other options to keep an eye out for are those that determine available features in the software. They determine whether third-party libraries should be checked for during configuration and used if present. These options are usually prefixed by --with- and --without-. We are going to compile the most basic default nginx server. For more on the options available refer to the document links above.

Armed with this new knowledge, we can now configure our nginx sources with default options, as you can see in Listing 8-23.

Listing 8-23. Configuring Our Source Tree

```
~/nginx-1.10.1$ ./configure --prefix=/opt/nginx
checking for OS
 + Linux 4.4.0-22-generic x86_64
checking for C compiler ... found
 + using GNU C compiler
 + gcc version: 5.3.1 20160413 (Ubuntu 5.3.1-14ubuntu2.1)
checking for gcc -pipe switch ... found
checking for -Wl,-E switch ... found
checking for gcc builtin atomic operations ... found
checking for C99 variadic macros ... found
checking for gcc variadic macros ... found
...<snip>...
checking for sha1 in system md library ... not found
checking for sha1 in system OpenSSL crypto library ... not found
checking for zlib library ... not found

./configure: error: the HTTP gzip module requires the zlib library.
You can either disable the module by using --without-http_gzip_module
option, or install the zlib library into the system, or build the zlib library
statically from the source with nginx by using --with-zlib=<path> option.
```

The configure script checks our system for the presence of a compiler, required header files, and definitions of functions and data structures in these header files. We talked about header files and libraries at the start of this chapter and mentioned that you generally only need them when compiling software from source. In Listing 7-29, note that the script was unable to find the zlib headers. We are given the option to give the path where the zlib files are installed (--with-zlib=<path>), to compile without zlib (--without-http_gzip_module). For our Ubuntu host, we are going to install the zlib1g-dev and the libpcre3-dev, which provide necessary compression and perl header files. There may be other packages you require depending on the options you include at build time.

```
$ sudo aptitude install -y zlib1g-dev libpcre3-dev
```

If you specify --without-<option>, that option will be disabled. We now run the compile command again.

```
~/nginx-1.10.1$ ./configure --prefix=/opt/nginx
checking for OS
 + Linux 4.4.0-22-generic x86_64
checking for C compiler ... found
 + using GNU C compiler
 + gcc version: 5.3.1 20160413 (Ubuntu 5.3.1-14ubuntu2.1)
checking for gcc -pipe switch ... found
checking for -Wl,-E switch ... found
checking for gcc builtin atomic operations ... found
checking for C99 variadic macros ... found
checking for gcc variadic macros ... found
...<snip>...
creating objs/Makefile

Configuration summary
 + using system PCRE library
 + OpenSSL library is not used
 + using builtin md5 code
 + sha1 library is not found
 + using system zlib library

 nginx path prefix: "/opt/nginx"
 nginx binary file: "/opt/nginx/sbin/nginx"
 nginx modules path: "/opt/nginx/modules"
 ...<snip>...
 nginx http proxy temporary files: "proxy_temp"
 nginx http fastcgi temporary files: "fastcgi_temp"
 nginx http uwsgi temporary files: "uwsgi_temp"
 nginx http scgi temporary files: "scgi_temp
```

The output shows the successful configuration of nginx and provides a summary.

Compile and Make

When complete, the configure command writes a configuration header file and a special file called Makefile. The former contains code that instructs the compiler about available functions and libraries, and the latter contains the commands needed to build the software by the make command. The make command reads the Makefile and executes the commands and the ordered steps contained in there (see http://www.tutorialspoint.com/makefile/why_makefile.htm for more information on make). We issue the make command to start building nginx in Listing 8-24.

Listing 8-24. Compiling nginx

```
~/nginx-1.10.1$ make
make -f objs/Makefile
make[1]: Entering directory '/home/jsmith/nginx-1.10.1'
cc -c -pipe  -O -W -Wall -Wpointer-arith -Wno-unused-parameter -Werror -g  -I src/core -I
src/event \
            -I src/event/modules -I src/os/unix -I objs \
        -o objs/src/core/nginx.o \
        src/core/nginx.c
cc -c -pipe  -O -W -Wall -Wpointer-arith -Wno-unused-parameter -Werror -g  -I src/core -I
src/event \
            -I src/event/modules -I src/os/unix -I objs \
        -o objs/src/core/ngx_log.o \
        src/core/ngx_log.c
sed -e "s|%%PREFIX%%|/opt/nginx|" \
        -e "s|%%PID_PATH%%|/opt/nginx/logs/nginx.pid|" \
        -e "s|%%CONF_PATH%%|/opt/nginx/conf/nginx.conf|" \
        -e "s|%%ERROR_LOG_PATH%%|/opt/nginx/logs/error.log|" \
            < man/nginx.8 > objs/nginx.8
make[1]: Leaving directory '/home/jsmith/nginx-1.10.1'
```

If the make process completes successfully, the application is now built. If it fails, you'll generally receive an error message indicating why and, it is hoped, some direction about how to fix it. There are a lot of reasons why building an application may fail—too many to detail here—but generally you'll probably have encountered a problem someone has found before. The issue you are experiencing may be detailed on the application's web site—for example, in the installation documentation or in an FAQ section. Searching for the particular error message via Google may also point to possible solutions. Also, contact the support lists and generally there are people more than willing to help.

Install

Now that our nginx application has been compiled, we need to make it available to all users on the system, by installing it to the prefix location we chose earlier when configuring. The Makefile contains commands for this as well, and you can see the installation process in Listing 8-25.

Listing 8-25. Installing nginx

```
~/nginx-1.10.1$ sudo make install
[sudo] password for jsmith:
make -f objs/Makefile install
make[1]: Entering directory '/home/jsmith/nginx-1.10.1'
test -d '/opt/nginx' || mkdir -p '/opt/nginx'
test -d '/opt/nginx/sbin' \
        || mkdir -p '/opt/nginx/sbin'
test ! -f '/opt/nginx/sbin/nginx' \
        || mv '/opt/nginx/sbin/nginx' \
                '/opt/nginx/sbin/nginx.old'
<snip>
test -d '/opt/nginx/logs' \
        || mkdir -p '/opt/nginx/logs'
make[1]: Leaving directory '/home/jsmith/nginx-1.10.1'
```

We need to use sudo, because as a normal user we're not allowed to create new files under /opt/nginx. Again, make processes rules in the Makefile and executes the commands to install nginx and its associated files on the system. We can now run our newly installed application to make sure it all went OK, as shown in Listing 8-26.

Listing 8-26. Running nginx

```
~/nginx-1.10.1$ sudo /opt/nginx/sbin/nginx -v
nginx version: nginx/1.10.1
```

Uninstall

The tricky part of managing source installations comes when you want to remove them from the system. Some, but not all, contain uninstall rules. For nginx, there is not one, but we would invoke the following:

```
~/<some-package-source>$ sudo make uninstall
```

That means we need to keep the configured sources lying about on our systems. This is less than ideal, as we need to track not only which software we installed from source but also where we keep these sources. This is one of the reasons we recommend you avoid installing applications from source but rather rely on packages to provide applications. Because we installed our application in /opt/nginx, it means we can effectively "uninstall" by issuing rm -rf /opt/nginx, which will remove the whole nginx directory.

Creating Packages with FPM

FPM is an application that builds either deb or RPM packages (among other package types) from a variety of different source types, including deb source packages and rpm source packages. We are going to build a nginx installation package as a deb, but the process works the same for a RPM package.

Starting with installing FPM, it comes as a Ruby Gem, a Gem being another way of packaging and distributing software, specifically for Ruby applications.

First, on Ubuntu, we will issue the following:

```
$ sudo aptitude install -y install ruby ruby-dev
```

If you are running CentOS:

```
$ sudo yum install -y ruby ruby-devel
```

The following steps are the same for CentOS as they are for Ubuntu. We will be building and executing this on our Ubuntu host (but you can build both RPMs and debs on either distribution if you have the required packages installed). Then FPM via the gem command:

```
$ sudo gem install fpm
```

We now create a temporary installation directory to hold our nginx installation.

```
$ sudo mkdir /tmp/installdir
```

Then we go to our nginx source directory where we compiled our nginx source, in Listing 8-25, and now issue the following command to install nginx into our temporary install directory.

```
$ sudo make install DESTDIR=/tmp/installdir
```

If you view the /tmp/installdir directory you will see we have now installed our nginx in that directory. We now instruct FPM to go into that directory and create a deb package for us. We let FPM do its magic by issuing the following:

```
$ sudo fpm -s dir -t deb -n nginx -v 1-10.1 -C /tmp/installdir/
```

Here we have specified –s for the source type of dir, which means directory. The target (-t) is a debian package. This would be -t rpm if we were building a RPM package. We name it (-n) nginx and give the version (-v) or 1-10.1. And finally we tell FPM to change to the (-C /tmp/installdir) and package up whatever is in that directory.

This creates a nginx_1-10.1_amd64.deb package in the local directory. You can now install that with the dpkg command.

```
$ sudo dpkg -i nginx_1-10.1_amd64.deb
Selecting previously unselected package nginx.
(Reading database ... 213564 files and directories currently installed.)
Preparing to unpack nginx_1-10.1_amd64.deb ...
Unpacking nginx (1-10.1) ...
Setting up nginx (1-10.1) ...
```

We can test that it work by issuing the following:

```
$ /opt/nginx/sbin/nginx -v
nginx version: nginx/1.10.1
```

And there we are, a debian package made from our compiled source. You can see more about FPM here:

- https://github.com/jordansissel/fpm

- www.digitalocean.com/community/tutorials/how-to-use-fpm-to-easily-create-packages-in-multiple-formats

Summary

In this chapter, we have seen a lot. Now you should be able to install, remove, update, and maintain the packages on your Linux server. We have shown the following:

- CentOS Application Installer

- YUM package management and DNF

- RPM package management

- Ubuntu Software App

- Aptitude package management
- Dpkg package management
- Compile from source
- Create a debian or RPM package

In the next chapter, we will look at setting up your storage for maximum reliability, and you will learn how to avoid and recover from hard disk problems.

Storage Management and Disaster Recovery

By Peter Lieverdink and Dennis Matotek

When you installed your first Linux host, you accepted all defaults when it came to setting up disks and partitions. Now that you have some basic systems administration knowledge, let's revisit the storage configuration and see how to change it to suit your needs. We'll look at various types of storage hardware and the ways in which you can use storage management software to your advantage. A critical part of any business is its data, so you need to make sure it is both safe and accessible and stays that way.

In this chapter, we will explain how to create and manage disk partitions and RAID, how to make your storage accessible to applications, and how to recover from a crash.

■ **Note** In Chapter 14, we'll cover how to back up and restore your data.

Storage Basics

We're going to start by looking at how Linux handles storage. We'll do this by adding a variety of new disks, partitioning these disks, and then formatting and managing this storage.

Drives under Windows show up as a drive letter once you format them, but Linux works differently. It has no concept of drive letters, and formatting also doesn't work quite in the same way. Instead, drives and storage appear as devices, which can be partitioned. These partitions can, in turn, be formatted or gathered into logical volumes and then formatted.

Let's start by looking at devices, which are the basic building blocks of Linux storage. We'll then move on to cover partitions and filesystems.

Devices

We briefly touched on device files in Chapter 4. These files are the way Linux makes hardware devices, such as hard disk drives, USBs, and DVD drives, accessible from within the operating system. Most, but not all, of the devices in a host are represented by files in the /dev directory.

The /dev directory is a special directory that's populated by a service called udev. When the host boots and the kernel detects a device, it tells udev, which then creates a representation of that device in the /dev directory. These device files are the way the kernel provides access to devices for applications and services.

There are several kinds of device files, but in this chapter we'll cover only the ones dealing with storage, which all fall into the category of *block devices*. This category covers hard disks, USB drives, tape drives, and CD and DVD drives. All types of hard disks—for example, ATA, Serial ATA, SCSI, SAS, and SSD—are represented by device files whose names start with sd, which stands for SCSI disk, as all these different types of drives are accessed as if they were SCSI drives.

■ **Note**   SCSI is an acronym that stands for Small Computer System Interface, a specification for how storage devices should be connected to and accessed by computers. You can read more about this specification at http://en.wikipedia.org/wiki/SCSI.

You can see which disk devices are available on your host by listing them using the ls command, as in Listing 9-1.

Listing 9-1. Listing Device Nodes

```
$ $ ll /dev/sda*
brw-rw---- 1 root disk 8, 0 Jun  7 22:45 /dev/sda
brw-rw---- 1 root disk 8, 1 Jun  7 22:45 /dev/sda1
brw-rw---- 1 root disk 8, 2 Jun  7 22:45 /dev/sda2
brw-rw---- 1 root disk 8, 5 Jun  7 22:45 /dev/sda5
```

Listing 9-1 shows four block devices, or device nodes. They are readable and writable by the root user and the disk group. Next, where normally the file size would be displayed, are two numbers separated by a comma. These are the device major number and minor number. The *major number* tells the kernel which device driver to use to access the device, and the *minor number* gives the kernel specific information about the device, in this case the partition number. Finally, the date and time the device file was last modified are shown.

The actual device file name consists of the prefix sd and a letter indicating which disk it belongs to. The first detected disk is sda, the second is sdb, the third is sdc, and so on. Finally, each partition on the disk gets its own device node as well, and the partition number is the final part of the name. This means that sda1 is the first partition on disk sda, sdb2 is the second partition on disk sdb, and so on. We'll discuss partitions shortly.

Other devices you may see are:

Device Name	Where you would find it
/dev/xvda	Xen virtual machines
/dev/vda	KVM virtual machines
/dev/hda	KVM virtual machines, older ATA hosts
/dev/md	Linux software raid
/dev/sda	Physical servers with devices like SAS, SSD.

■ **Note** Older systems could not support many drives because device minor numbers ranged from 1 to 255, and each disk could only have 16 numbers, so Linux could accommodate 16 hard disks with 16 partitions each, `/dev/sda1` through `/dev/sdp16`, before it ran out of device nodes. Now your system can theoretically support 10,000 drives (`https://access.redhat.com/articles/rhel-limits`). This is the definitive document on block and character devices in the Linux Kernel: `www.kernel.org/doc/Documentation/devices.txt`.

If you have a hardware RAID controller, it may name your array and any partitions differently. The RAID controller combines multiple disks into a Redundant Array of Inexpensive Disks (RAID). We'll talk more about RAID later on in this chapter. To find out what the device nodes for the RAID array are, you can list all block devices in the `/dev/` directory with the following command:

```
$ ls -l /dev | grep ^b
```

This command will list only lines starting with b. It would, however, be more accurate to check the contents of the kernel internal log buffer. Whenever a kernel event occurs, it is added to the kernel internal log buffer. This buffer is then written to a log file by a logging daemon, and you can query it directly using the dmesg command.

```
$ dmesg |less
```

Most RAID controllers also use at least part of the kernel SCSI subsystem, and you can search for detected SCSI devices via the built-in search function in `less`. Enter `/scsi` inside the `less` window and press Enter to search for any lines containing the string `scsi`. You can press n to jump to the next match.

Partitions

After you add a disk to your host, you need to perform a few steps to make it usable. First, you can create one or more partitions on that disk. If you create a partition, the system needs to be able to find the information about the partition geometry. It stores this information at the start of the disk (and sometimes has a copy stored elsewhere on the disk - more on this shortly).

We have previously described partitioning as slicing up a cake into smaller pieces and that is what we can do with the physical disk. We carve up the disk into smaller pieces. This way you can, for example, keep log and user data separate from the operating system, so logs or users cannot fill up your system disk and cause problems.

In Chapter 6 we introduced you to two different partition managers, the Master Boot Record (MBR) and GPT (GUID Partition Table). You might remember that the MBR, stored in the first 446 bytes of the disk, describes the partition information, which is stored in the 64 bytes directly after the boot record. You can't store a lot of data in 64 bytes, so the number of partitions a disk could hold was originally rather limited. GPT on the other hand, can hold up to 128 partitions.

DISKS AND PARTITIONS

We have previously explained the differences between MBR and GPT partitions. If you remember that MBR is held in the first 512 bytes of the disk and can only hold enough information for disk sizes less than 2 Tb. GPT does not have that restriction and can be used on any size disk. This leads to differences in the way you can carve up your disks.

With MBR, partitions come in three flavors: physical, extended, and logical. This is because only a limited amount of partition information can be stored in the 64 bytes that are available for such data. A partition needs 16 bytes of data to be described, so with information on four partitions, it's full!

As a workaround, the concept of an extended partition was invented. One of the four available physical partitions is marked as an extended partition, which then functions as a container for an unlimited number of logical partitions.

The 16 bytes describes every partition, include information about the partition type, where on the disk it can be found, and whether it is bootable, though Linux doesn't care about the latter.

You would use the fdisk utitility to manage MBR disks.

With GPT we have previously said that we can partition disks up to 2ZiB. There is a default limit of 128 partitions with GPT. GPT uses 64-bit logical block addresses. It has increased reliability with checksums. Partitions are given UUIDs and names to avoid collisions.

You can use parted or gdisk tools to manage GPT.

You can find more detailed information about these partition managers at https://wiki.manjaro.org/index.php?title=Some_basics_of_MBR_v/s_GPT_and_BIOS_v/s_UEFI.

You can create and delete partitions using the fdisk utility, or if you are using GPT, the gdisk or parted utility. Let's start by having a look at what partitions are already there by listing the partitions on the first disk on our Ubuntu host (see Listing 9-2). Because only the root user is allowed to read from and write to the raw disk device, you need to use sudo.

Listing 9-2. Listing Partitions with fdisk

```
$ sudo fdisk -l /dev/sda
Disk /dev/sda: 8 GiB, 8589934592 bytes, 16777216 sectors
Units: sectors of 1 * 512 = 512 bytes
Sector size (logical/physical): 512 bytes / 512 bytes
I/O size (minimum/optimal): 512 bytes / 512 bytes
Disklabel type: dos
Disk identifier: 0x105922fd


Device     Boot    Start       End  Sectors  Size Id Type
/dev/sda1  *        2048    999423   997376  487M 83 Linux
/dev/sda2        1001470 16775167 15773698  7.5G  5 Extended
/dev/sda5        1001472 16775167 15773696  7.5G 83 Linux
```

As you can see in the output of Listing 9-2), the installer created three partitions:

- A physical partition for the boot partition

- An extended partition to house other partitions

- A logical partition for use with LVM

You don't want to modify your system disk, but let's say you bought a new hard disk and need to partition it, so you can start using it to store data. First, you need to check that the disk was detected by the operating system and what its device name is. The kernel prints information on all devices it detects when it boots up, and you can access that information via the dmesg command once you log in.

```
$ dmesg | grep sd
[    1.838874] sd 2:0:0:0: [sda] 16777216 512-byte logical blocks: (8.59 GB/8.00 GiB)
[    1.839510] sd 2:0:0:0: [sda] Write Protect is off
[    1.839824] sd 2:0:0:0: [sda] Mode Sense: 00 3a 00 00
[    1.839834] sd 2:0:0:0: Attached scsi generic sg1 type 0
[    1.840183] sd 2:0:0:0: [sda] Write cache: enabled, read cache: enabled, doesn't support
DPO or FUA
[    1.842304]  sda: sda1 sda2 < sda5 >
[    1.842784] sd 2:0:0:0: [sda] Attached SCSI disk
[    2.178862] sd 3:0:0:0: [sdb] 16777216 512-byte logical blocks: (8.59 GB/8.00 GiB)
[    2.179508] sd 3:0:0:0: [sdb] Write Protect is off
[    2.179863] sd 3:0:0:0: [sdb] Mode Sense: 00 3a 00 00
[    2.179874] sd 3:0:0:0: Attached scsi generic sg2 type 0
[    2.180268] sd 3:0:0:0: [sdb] Write cache: enabled, read cache: enabled, doesn't support
DPO or FUA
[    2.181498] sd 3:0:0:0: [sdb] Attached SCSI disk
[   25.702112] EXT4-fs (sda1): mounting ext2 filesystem using the ext4 subsystem
[   25.711836] EXT4-fs (sda1): mounted filesystem without journal. Opts: (null)
```

By using grep to display only lines containing sd, you can limit the output to information about the SCSI disk subsystem.

DMESG AND THE KERNEL RING BUFFER

The kernel writes messages about what it is doing to a kernel ring buffer. This buffer holds a certain amount of messages and when it is full, new messages come in and old messages drop out. The kernel doesn't assume that there will be a logging daemon to write these message to a file, like during system boot-up for example. Therefore, the kernel writes all its messages to the ring buffer and you can access the messages via dmesg.

The ring buffer of the kernel contains things like how kernel was called, the hardware the kernel found, and what it did once it found it. You can find your network devices and how your disks are configured with dmesg. It can also show you times when there was a critical failure or a problem the kernel had with a component.

Some useful options for dmesg are:

- -C Clears the kernel ring buffer
- -H Human readable
- -T Human readable timestamp
- -w Follow, or wait for new messages
- -l <level> Only show messages of a certain level, like info, crit, err, emerg

In the output of dmesg we can see that the system has detected two disks, sda and sdb. When it detected sda, it also found the partitions sda1, sda2, and sda5. The angle brackets around partition sda5 (<sda5>) indicate this is a logical partition. The other disk is new and has no partition table (sdb), so let's create one using the gdisk command.

```
$ sudo gdisk /dev/sdb
sudo gdisk /dev/sdb
GPT fdisk (gdisk) version 1.0.1

Partition table scan:
  MBR: not present
  BSD: not present
  APM: not present
  GPT: not present

Creating new GPT entries.

Command (? for help): ?
B       back up GPT data to a file
c       change a partition's name
d       delete a partition
i       show detailed information on a partition
l       list known partition types
n       add a new partition
o       create a new empty GUID partition table (GPT)
p       print the partition table
q       quit without saving changes
r       recovery and transformation options (experts only)
s       sort partitions
t       change a partition's type code
v       verify disk
w       write table to disk and exit
x       extra functionality (experts only)
?       print this menu
```

The gdisk utility mirrors many of the options that you can use in fdisk, if you are going to use a MBR partition table instead. If we us the ? option from the gdisk utility, we get the help output. Let's quickly run through some of these options.

You can list the partitions on a device with the l option. The d option allows you to delete one (be careful, deleting partitions is dangerous). To erase the current partition map and create a new empty one, use the o option, which is more dangerous but sometimes necessary to delete partition map. This option will ruin *any* partitions you have on your disk.

To create a partition, use the n option, which will start a wizard to guide you through the creation process, as you'll see in a moment.

To list the current partition table, press p. This lists the partition table as it exists in memory, not as it is on the disk.

If you made changes that you do not want to save, press q. This will quit gdisk without writing the modified partition table to the disk.

Partitions also hold information about the type of filesystem they contain. The hexadecimal identifiers we got from the l option can be set using the t option.

When you're happy with a new partition map, you can press w to save it to the disk. Finally, x allows you to access advanced gdisk options, such as recovery and transformation options, changing GUID, changing the disk geometry and moving the data contained within a partition. We don't cover the use of any of these rarely used expert options.

Now press p to print the listing of partitions on the current disk. You'll see that it's empty. Normally, we recommend creating only a single partition on a data storage disk, but let's have some fun with this disk and create a few. We will create one 4 GiB partition and two 2 GiB.

Start by creating a partition, 2 GiB in size, by pressing n.

```
Command (? for help): n
Partition number (1-128, default 1):
First sector (34-16777182, default = 2048) or {+-}size{KMGTP}:
Last sector (2048-16777182, default = 16777182) or {+-}size{KMGTP}: 2G
Current type is 'Linux filesystem'
Hex code or GUID (L to show codes, Enter = 8300):
Changed type of partition to 'Linux filesystem'
```

First you are asked for the partition number, a number between 1 and 128. We will take the default, 1. We are asked next to select disk sectors, each sector being 512 bytes. Modern systems align on sector boundaries and here we choose to start at sector 2048, or at 1024 kibibyte. Next, enter 2G to indicate you want to create a partition that is 2 GiB in size. Finally, we select a partition ID, represented by a hex code, the default is 8300, or Linux filesystem.

Repeat the process to create another partititon.

```
Partition number (2-128, default 2):
First sector (34-16777182, default = 4196352) or {+-}size{KMGTP}:
Last sector (4196352-16777182, default = 16777182) or {+-}size{KMGTP}: +2G
```

For partition 2 again we took the defaults for partition number and first sector. For the last sector we have to add a +2G so that the utility will add an additional 2 GiB.

To create the last 4 GiB partition we again select the defaults for partition number, first sector, and last sector.

```
Partition number (3-128, default 3):
First sector (34-16777182, default = 8390656) or {+-}size{KMGTP}:
Last sector (8390656-16777182, default = 16777182) or {+-}size{KMGTP}:
```

This create a partition will all the remaining disk space. Now we can print what we have been doing by selecting the p option.

```
Command (? for help): p
Disk /dev/sdb: 16777216 sectors, 8.0 GiB
Logical sector size: 512 bytes
Disk identifier (GUID): 1C42CAB1-754B-4B21-A7A9-D7CE87C8965B
Partition table holds up to 128 entries
First usable sector is 34, last usable sector is 16777182
Partitions will be aligned on 2048-sector boundaries
Total free space is 4061 sectors (2.0 MiB)

Number   Start (sector)    End (sector)    Size    Code    Name
   1               2048         4194304    2.0 GiB  8300    Linux filesystem
   2            4196352         8390655    2.0 GiB  8300    Linux filesystem
   3            8390656        16777182    4.0 GiB  8300    Linux filesystem
```

We haven't written this partition table to the actual disk yet; if this doesn't look right we can exit without a worry with the q option. If we are happy we select the w option to write our GPT table.

```
Command (? for help): w

Final checks complete. About to write GPT data. THIS WILL OVERWRITE EXISTING
PARTITIONS!!

Do you want to proceed? (Y/N): y
OK; writing new GUID partition table (GPT) to /dev/sdb.
The operation has completed successfully.
```

Earlier we mentioned partition types and IDs. Linux itself doesn't generally care what the partition type is, but to make management easier, we recommend you change the type to match the intended use. As we have said, the partition id is a hex code. You get a listing of all the possible choices by issuing a l. In Table 9-1 we are giving you a listing of just those relating to Linux.

Table 9-1. *Linux Partition IDs and Types*

Hex Code/Partition id	Partition type
8200	Linux swap
8300	Linux filesystem
8301	Linux reserved
8302	Linux /home
8303	Linux x86 root (/)
8304	Linux x86-64 root (/)
8305	Linux ARM64 root (/)
8306	Linux /srv
8307	Linux ARM32 root (/)
8e00	Linux LVM

If you wanted to change your partition type you could do so by issuing the following commands. We will take a look at gdisk again on the /dev/sdb drive we have just partitioned. Here we are going to change the first 2 GiB partition from a Linux filesystem type to a Linux swap.

```
$ sudo gdisk /dev/sdb
Command (? for help): t
Partition number (1-3): 1
Current type is 'Linux filesystem'
Hex code or GUID (L to show codes, Enter = 8300): 8200
Changed type of partition to 'Linux swap'
```

Here we have used gdisk to manage our partition table and have issued the t option to change the partition's type code. We select partition 1 and it displays our current type, 'Linux filesystem'. Next we have entered the code 8200 and it has now changed the type to Linux swap. When we print that result we see the following:

```
Command (? for help): p
Disk /dev/sdb: 16777216 sectors, 8.0 GiB
Logical sector size: 512 bytes
Disk identifier (GUID): 1C42CAB1-754B-4B21-A7A9-D7CE87C8965B
Partition table holds up to 128 entries
First usable sector is 34, last usable sector is 16777182
Partitions will be aligned on 2048-sector boundaries
Total free space is 4061 sectors (2.0 MiB)

Number  Start (sector)  End (sector)  Size      Code  Name
   1     2048            4194304       2.0 GiB   8200  Linux swap
   2     4196352         8390655       2.0 GiB   8300  Linux filesystem
   3     8390656         16777182      4.0 GiB   8300  Linux filesystem
```

We have to select w to write this change to the table and q to quit. The kernel now reloads the partition map and creates new device nodes for your partitions. You'll see in the output from dmesg that the disk detection routine has run and found your new partitions. You can also check that their device nodes now exist on disk.

```
$ ls -l /dev/sdb*
brw-rw---- 1 root disk 8, 16 Jun 16 23:56 /dev/sdb
brw-rw---- 1 root disk 8, 17 Jun 16 23:56 /dev/sdb1
brw-rw---- 1 root disk 8, 18 Jun 16 23:56 /dev/sdb2
brw-rw---- 1 root disk 8, 19 Jun 16 23:56 /dev/sdb3
```

Sometimes the kernel is not able to reread the partition table, which means you can't get access to the new partition device files until you have rebooted the host. This can happen if one of the partitions on the disk you were editing was still mounted. To avoid having to reboot, make sure no partitions on the disk you're partitioning are mounted. We'll cover mounting a bit later in this chapter.

■ **Note** You can also make the kernel redetect partitions—without rebooting—by running the partprobe command.

Another utility to create and delete partitions is parted. Unlike gdisk and fdisk, this utility allows you to edit the size and ordering of partitions. We recommend you don't go down the road of resizing partitions with parted as these can be disastrous operations, but rather use LVM. We will cover LVM in detail later in this chapter. For more information about parted, visit www.gnu.org/software/parted/index.shtml.

■ **Caution**   Resizing partitions can cause unrecoverable data loss. Always back up your data first!

GIBIBYTES VS. GIGABYTES

When a hard-disk manufacturer advertises its product, it wants the available storage space to seem as large as possible, so it calculates each gigabyte as 1,000 megabytes, which in turn is 1,000,000 kilobytes, which is 1,000,000,000 bytes.

However, because all calculations on computers are done via binary arithmetic, the actual multiplication value is 1,024 (*gibi* means 2^{30}). But if a storage manufacturer used that factor, its device would seem smaller when compared to the competition, so it doesn't.

To stop confusion between these ways of calculating sizes, new terms were coined for values using the 1,024 factor: kibibyte, mebibyte, gibibyte, and so on. They are indicated with KiB, MiB, GiB, and so forth. The Linux filesystem tools use the 1,024 factor, so if you purchase a 500 GB disk, its size will always be less than 500 GiB when viewed via Linux.

For more information, see http://en.wikipedia.org/wiki/Gigabyte.

Filesystems

You've now created partitions, but you have not yet prepared them for use. The next thing you need to do is create a filesystem. You may know this as formatting.

A filesystem is a bit like a library. It stores large amounts of data and has a catalog to ensure you can find what you're looking for. The layout of the aisles and shelves and the design of the catalog determine how long it takes to find and retrieve any particular piece of information. Creating a filesystem is like initializing the catalog and moving the shelves into an otherwise empty library.

Just as there is no optimal aisle and shelf layout for all libraries, there is no "best" filesystem for all uses. We won't go into a lot of detail, but let's look at some of the most commonly used Linux filesystems. They are listed in Table 9-2 with their main features.

Table 9-2. *Linux Filesystems and Their Main Features*

Filesystem	Features
Ext2	Stable, general use, can be shrunk or expanded
Ext3	Stable, general use, quick recovery, can be shrunk or expanded
Ext4	Stable, general use, quick recovery, improves on ext3
XFS	Stable, general use, quick recovery, can be expanded online
Btrfs	Unstable, fault-tolerant, copy on write (COW), pooling, and multi-device spanning

The ext2 and ext3 filesystems are older filesystems. The general use of these filesystems was for storing many small files on them. They were a good choice of filesystem for an e-mail store, web site store, or office file store, as these usually consist of many files that are up to several hundreds of kilobytes in size. You don't see ext3 much on newer systems, but you do see ext2 as the filesystem for the /boot partition on Ubuntu 16.04 by default.

One of the major differences between ext2 and ext3 was journaling support. With ext2, if there was a crash, you can expect very long fsck waits before you could mount the disk again. To combat this issue, the journaled filesystem was created. Ext3, ext4, and XFS are such journaled filesystems, and thus don't have the long recovery wait time that ext2 does. See the sidebar "Journaled Filesystems" for more information.

With lessons learned from ext3, a further advancement, ext4, was developed. It offers some features not available in ext3, such as online defragmentation, better journal reliability, and faster filesystem checks. Ext4 is intended as an all-round filesystem with excellent performance. It can support volumes up to 1 exbibyte and a max file size of 16 tebibtyes. It is the default choice for the Ubuntu 16.04 distribution.

Another option available to you for storing video, large images, or database files is the XFS filesystem. It offers some of the same advantages as ext4; however, you cannot shrink a XFS partition (online). It is as performant as ext4. It can support up to 8 exbibytes and file sizes of 8 exibytes. It is the default choice for the CentOS 7.

Finally, Btrfs is a more recent filesystem with different features to both XFS and ext4. First, it can support ridiculously large volumes (16 exbibytes) and a max file of the same (16 exbibytes). At such a large scale, the journaling on ext4 and XFS becomes enormously slow and impossible. It aims to naturally support operations and organization like snapshotting and pooling. It also has features like automatic defragmenting and scrubbing, where it uses checksums to automatically detect and correct errors. Depending on the workload, Btrfs maybe a good choice, and at a certain scale it is the only choice. We have listed it as *Unstable* in Table 9-2 due to some recent write hole problems in Raid5/6 configurations. Check this page for the most up to date status of the filesystem: https://btrfs.wiki.kernel.org/index.php/Status.

■ **Note**   Btrfs is not the only large-scale filesystem, but it is the one that is available in the default install of Linux. Others like ZFS are also popular and performant, but ZFS cannot be redistributed due to its license (it cannot be part of a Linux distribution). You can still use it on Linux though; however, you need to download and install it yourself: http://zfsonlinux.org/.

You can find an exhaustive list of filesystems and comparisons of their features at http://en.wikipedia.org/wiki/List_of_file_systems and http://en.wikipedia.org/wiki/Comparison_of_file_systems.

JOURNALED FILESYSTEMS

Imagine a library where a returned book causes the librarian to walk off to find an empty space on a shelf somewhere to put the book and then update the catalog, before returning to the front desk in order to process the next returned book - all the while, it's not possible for anyone to borrow a book. A customer returning a book might also think, just because they are standing in the library, the library catalog knows they have returned the book. This is not an efficient system and customers can be lining up waiting to return their books, or worse, leave them on the floor and walk out.

With a book return chute, this problem can be solved. Once the book is in the return chute, the customer can go back to their business, knowing that the book has been safely accepted by the library. The librarian can process returned books when the library isn't busy with people checking out new books. And even if the books in the chute aren't processed before the library closes, they won't get lost. They will still be in the chute the next day.

A journaled filesystem makes use of circular buffer which works kind of like a library with a book chute. This is an area, or log, on the filesystem that holds changes not yet committed to the main part of the filesystem storage. Any information that needs to be written to disk is put in the journal and then put in its final place on disk later, when the operating system has a spare moment. Similarly, if the machine crashes, data in the journal is not lost. If a system crashes, the journal can be re-applied when the disk has been remounted. This helps prevent partial changes being applied and avoids corruption in the event of a system failure.

Our metaphor breaks down here, though. In our filesystem library, people are allowed to borrow books from the return chute as well, and the librarian is allowed to ignore people who want borrow a book if the chute becomes too full.

Most modern filesystems use journals, though some use the journal only for file metadata. A filesystem like Btrfs can handle metadata in different ways. You can choose to lay out your metadata differently to your file data (e.g., your metadata as raid1 and your data as raid10). And for frequently updating file data, Btrfs uses a *log tree*, which is a per sub volume journal that records changes to help maintain consistency in the event of crashes or reboots.

Creating Swap Filesystem

We are going to use the first partition you created earlier, /dev/sdb1, as a swap partition. The choice of filesystem for this one is easy, as there is only one swap filesystem format. Let's set it up first using the mkswap command, as shown in Listing 9-3.

Listing 9-3. Setting Up Swap Space

```
$ sudo mkswap /dev/sdb1
Setting up swapspace version 1, size = 2 GiB (2146430976 bytes)
no label, UUID=6d0ce2f6-f9f6-4ac2-91f6-3099a40d5624
```

You're using the mkswap utility to mark /dev/sdb1 as swap space. You can use the generated UUID to add an entry in the /etc/fstab file, which lists all filesystems to be used on the host (see the sidebar "UUID" to find out what a UUID is). We'll come back to the /etc/fstab file later in this chapter. Technically speaking, you're not formatting the partition; rather, you're writing a small amount of information to indicate to the kernel that it can be used as swap space.

You can immediately activate the new swap partition via the swapon command. This command tells the kernel it can use the specified partition as swap space.

```
$ sudo swapon /dev/sdb1
```

This command will complete without printing anything, but you can check dmesg for information on what happened. Pipe the output into tail, to limit the number of lines displayed to the specified number.

```
$ sudo dmesg | tail -n 1
[13066.031700] Adding 2096124k swap on /dev/sdb1.  Priority:-2 extents:1 across:2096124k FS
```

Another way of checking swap is seeing if the free command reports swap space. Specify the -h option to display sizes in human readable form.

```
$ sudo free -h
              total        used        free      shared  buff/cache   available
Mem:          992M        520M         62M         12M        409M        321M
Swap:         3.0G          0B        3.0G
```

Alternatively, you can use the swapon command:

```
$ swapon -s
Filename        Type            Size            Used        Priority
/dev/dm-1       partition       3145728000       0              -1
```

The command reports a total of 3.0 G of swap space, which is the original 1 G we already had plus the 2 G we just added. We'll come back to the free command in Chapter 17, when we look at performance management.

UUID

You may have seen long, random-looking strings of hexadecimal characters like "6d0ce2f6-f9f6-4ac2-91f6-3099a40d5624" while installing software or in the URIs of some web sites. These strings are universally unique identifiers (UUIDs).

UUIDs provide a convenient and computationally cheap way of identifying information without the need to check if a generated ID is already in use. Because UUIDs are generated randomly or semi-randomly, they are hard to guess and so can provide a little bit of security as well.

UUIDs are increasingly used on Linux as a way to distinguish components of RAID, logical volumes, and filesystems. It enables us to manage devices and make them persistent across reboots. While labeling devices can also serve this purpose, UUIDs are less likely to have naming collisions.

You can read more about them at http://en.wikipedia.org/wiki/Universally_Unique_Identifier .

Creating an Ext4 Partition

For your data partitions, start with the other new 2 GiB /dev/sdb2 partition. You will format this as ext4 using the mkfs.ext4 utility, as shown in Listing 9-4. If you wanted to create an ext2 filesystem, sometimes used for creating a boot partition, just run mkfs.ext2 instead.

Listing 9-4. Creating an Ext4 Filesystem

```
$ sudo mkfs.ext4 -L mail /dev/sdb2
mke2fs 1.42.9 (28-Dec-2013)
Filesystem label=mail
OS type: Linux
Block size=4096 (log=2)
Fragment size=4096 (log=2)
Stride=0 blocks, Stripe width=0 blocks
131072 inodes, 524288 blocks
26214 blocks (5.00%) reserved for the super user
First data block=0
Maximum filesystem blocks=536870912
16 block groups
32768 blocks per group, 32768 fragments per group
8192 inodes per group
Superblock backups stored on blocks:
        32768, 98304, 163840, 229376, 294912

Allocating group tables: done
Writing inode tables: done
Creating journal (16384 blocks): done
Writing superblocks and filesystem accounting information: done
```

In Listing 9-4 we have created an ext4 filesystem and specified a label using the -L parameter. This label would then allow you to refer to the partition by the label name, as opposed to the device name or UUID. On systems without many formatted partitions (and the less chance of naming collisions), using labels can help readability. In this instance, we chose a label for what will be used for.

With Ext filesystems, you then see a series of statistics about the filesystem size and how storage space was allocated. In the output you can see the settings for "Block size," "Maximum filesystem blocks," and "Inodes," which describe how your filesystem has been set up. Take a look at the sidebar "Blocks and Inodes" for a short explanation of these. Of Note are the blocks reserved for the superuser and the superblock backups.

```
26214 blocks (5.00%) reserved for the super user
...<snip>...
Superblock backups stored on blocks:
        32768, 98304, 163840, 229376, 294912
```

The superblock is part of the filesystem metadata. It contains information about the filesystem such as its size, the amount of free space in the filesystem, and where on the filesystem the data can be found. If a crash occurred and this superblock were damaged, you'd have no way of determining which parts of the filesystem contained your data. To help you in the event of such a problem, several backup copies of the superblock are maintained at well-known block numbers. We'll revisit recovery later in this chapter.

The reserved blocks for the superuser percentage exist so that a normal user cannot fill a filesystem to such an extent that the superuser (root) could no longer log in, or services running as the root user would be unable to write data to disk.

The 5% limit is historical and suitable, for instance, for the root filesystem '/', which is not normally larger than a few gibibytes. However, when you're using a 1 TiB filesystem, this limit would equate to 50 GiB of space that you could not use for storage of user data, so changing or removing it makes sense on data storage volumes.

You could have specified the -m 0 option for mkfs.ext4 to set this percentage of reserved blocks to 0 when creating the filesystem, or you can change this value later (more on this shortly).

BLOCKS AND INODES

When you create a filesystem, the available disk space is divided into units of a specific size. These units are called *blocks* and by default they are 4 KB in size.

A block can only hold one file or part of one file, so a 1 KB file still uses up a whole block—and thus 4 KB of disk space, wasting 3 KB of storage space. Larger files are spread out over multiple blocks. If you are mainly storing files smaller than 4 KB in size, you might opt to use a different, smaller, block size for your filesystem. Likewise, if your files are expected to be much larger than 4 KB you might choose a larger block size.

It is important to trial and test the performance of different block sizes when you are setting up servers for specific tasks. Database, shared filesystems, and mail systems will all have different block-size sweet spots for best performance. If you can simulate your expected workload, you should have a better idea on the best tunings for your filesystem.

Inodes are where posix-compliant filesystems store metadata such as creation and modification dates and permissions and ownership about a file or directory, as well as pointers to which blocks contain the actual file data. This means a filesystem can contain only as many files and directories as it has inodes. So, in the case with Ext filesystems, with a tiny block size and lots of files, you can run out of inodes before you run out of disk space. To read more about inodes, see http://en.wikipedia.org/wiki/Inode.

Tweaking ext2, ext3, and ext4 Filesystem Options

To change ext2, ext3, and ext4 filesystem parameters after creation, you use the tune2fs utility. To get an overview of available options, first run the utility without any parameters. You can also pull up the entire manual via man tune2fs.

```
$ tune2fs
tune2fs 1.42.13 (17-May-2015)
Usage: tune2fs [-c max_mounts_count] [-e errors_behavior] [-g group]
       [-i interval[d|m|w]] [-j] [-J journal_options] [-l]
       [-m reserved_blocks_percent] [-o [^]mount_options[,...]] [-p mmp_update_interval]
       [-r reserved_blocks_count] [-u user] [-C mount_count] [-L volume_label]
       [-M last_mounted_dir] [-O [^]feature[,...]]
       [-Q quota_options]
       [-E extended-option[,...]] [-T last_check_time] [-U UUID]
       [ -I new_inode_size ] device
```

Though it doesn't explicitly say so, the -l parameter lists current filesystem options. Let's run it on your new ext4 partition (see Listing 9-5).

Listing 9-5. Displaying Ext2, Ext3, or Ext4 Filesystem Options

```
$ sudo tune2fs -l /dev/sdb2
tune2fs 1.42.13 (17-May-2015)
Filesystem volume name:   mail
Last mounted on:          <not available>
Filesystem UUID:          71bd5774-33cb-491b-8ffe-49cb33935001
...<snip>...
Filesystem features:      has_journal ext_attr resize_inode dir_index filetype extent flex_
bg sparse_super large_file huge_file uninit_bg dir_nlink extra_isize
Filesystem flags:         signed_directory_hash
Default mount options:    user_xattr acl
Filesystem state:         clean
Errors behavior:          Continue
Filesystem OS type:       Linux
Inode count:              131072
Block count:              524288
Reserved block count:     26214
Free blocks:              498900
Free inodes:              131061
First block:              0
Block size:               4096
Fragment size:            4096
...<snip>...
Last mount time:          n/a
Last write time:          Sun Jun 19 10:42:04 2016
Mount count:              0
Maximum mount count:      -1
Last checked:             Sun Jun 19 10:42:04 2016
Check interval:           0 (<none>)
...<snip>...
Journal backup:           inode blocks
```

A lot of information is displayed, but of most interest to us are the filesystem UUID and state which tell us how to refer to the filesystem and its health. The "Errors behaviour" indicates what will happen if there are filesystem errors. In this case, we "continue" if we detect errors, but the other options are "remount-ro" (remount the filesystem as read-only), or "panic," which causes a kernel panic which halts the system. Other information that can be useful diagnosing capacity problems are "Free inodes" and "Free blocks." "Last write time," "Last mount time," and "Last mounted on" can also be useful.

■ **Note**   We'll take a closer look at some of the filesystem features in Chapter 17 when we cover capacity planning and performance.

We are now going to use tune2fs to set the reserved blocks percentage to 0, as we don't need reserved space on this partition.

```
$ sudo tune2fs -m 0 /dev/sdb2
tune2fs 1.42.9 (28-Dec-2013)
Setting reserved blocks percentage to 0% (0 blocks)
```

Table 9-3 lists the options for tune2fs that you're most likely to use.

Table 9-3. *Commonly Used* tune2fs *Options*

Option	Function
-c N	Sets the number of mounts before a filesystem check is forced to N
-l	Lists the current filesystem options
-m N	Sets the reserved blocks percentage to N% of all blocks
-r N	Sets the number of reserved blocks to N
-j	Creates a journal on this filesystem (converts ext2 to ext3)
-L label	Assigns the label "label" to the filesystem
-O feat	Toggles the filesystem feature "feat" on or off

■ **Note** We'll come back to the -O option and advanced filesystem features in Chapter 17 when we discuss performance and capacity planning.

The XFS Filesystem

The XFS filesystem was originally proprietary and closed source. XFS was developed by Silicon Graphics, Inc., for its IRIX operating system.

The filesystem driver of XFS was open sourced some years ago and IRIX helped working on integrating it into the Linux kernel, as Linux lacked a journaling filesystem at the time. The community enthusiastically embraced these newly open source filesystems, as both offered new features and excellent performance. Now they are well accepted and supported on the Linux platform including being the default on CentOS 7.

XFS

You already created an ext4 partition to store some small files on. Let's format the other partition using the XFS filesystem. To this end, we will use the mkfs.xfs tool. Depending on the distribution, you may not have the necessary utilities to manage XFS filesystems. These utilities are provided by the xfsprogs package, before you begin you should have this installed. On Ubuntu you install them as follows:

```
$ sudo aptitude install xfsprogs
```

and on CentOS, you use the command (though it is installed as the default filesystem)

```
$ sudo yum install xfsprogs
```

After installing the package, you can create your filesystem using the default options, as shown in Listing 9-6.

Listing 9-6. Creating an XFS Filesystem

```
$ sudo mkfs.xfs /dev/sdb3
meta-data=/dev/sdb3 isize=512     agcount=4,      agsize=262079 blks
                  = ectsz=512     attr=2,         projid32bit=1
                  = crc=1         finobt=1,       sparse=0
             data = bsize=4096    locks=1048315,  imaxpct=25
                  = sunit=0       swidth=0        blks
           naming = version 2     bsize=4096      ascii-ci=0 ftype=1
              log = internal log  bsize=4096      blocks=2560, version=2
                  = sectsz=512    sunit=0 blks,   lazy-count=1
         realtime = none          extsz=4096      blocks=0, rtextents=0
```

As the filesystem is created, some information about its configuration is displayed. We'll make use of this information further in Chapter 17 when we look at performance and capacity planning.

All these options, which, for instance, control block size and journal size, can be set when the filesystem is created, but the mkfs.xfs tool will choose sensible defaults based on the size of the partition it needs to format.

■ **Note**   XFS does not reserve 5% of its available space for the root user and also does not automatically force a filesystem check after a specific amount of time has passed.

The XFS filesystem can be managed via several commands. The commands begin with xfs_ and you can see the options available by typing xfs_ and hitting the tab key twice. Table 9-4 shows the main ones you will be interested.

Table 9-4. Common xfs_ Commands

Command	Purpose
xfs_repair	Helps repair damaged or corrupt filesystems
xfs_growfs	Expands an XFS filesystem.
xfs_freeze	Useful when creating snapshots.

The Btrfs Filesystem

We have already explained many of the benefits of the Btrfs filesystem and now we shall show you how to create and manage one. If you do not have the utility programs already installed, you can do so by installing the btrfs-progs package, similarly to the way we installed the XFS packages.

We have said that Btrfs uses COW (or copy on write). But what is that? When data is modified, rather than writing the modified data over the previously data location, the data is copied, modified, and then written to a new free location. The metadata, the location of the file, is then updated in the same way to reflect the new location of the data.

We will quickly demonstrate how create a Btrfs partition and mount it. We have a new disk that has been attached to our host. We have discovered via dmesg that this new disk has been given the device /dev/sdc. We are going to use the entire disk for this partition. To create the Btrfs

```
$ sudo mkfs.btrfs /dev/sdc
btrfs-progs v4.4
See http://btrfs.wiki.kernel.org for more information.

Label:                (null)
UUID:                 e1c6cbb0-4fbf-4a61-a912-0a9cda611128
Node size:            16384
Sector size:          4096
Filesystem size:      8.00GiB
Block group profiles:
  Data:               single             8.00MiB
  Metadata:           DUP              417.56MiB
  System:             DUP               12.00MiB
SSD detected:         no
Incompat features:    extref, skinny-metadata
Number of devices:    1
Devices:
   ID      SIZE     PATH
    1    8.00GiB    /dev/sdc
```

We can now simply mount that partition. We have created a directory called /data1 and we will mount it there.

```
$ mount /dev/sdc /data1
```

We can see that the filesystem is mounted.

```
$ df -h /data1
Filesystem      Size  Used  Avail  Use%  Mounted on
/dev/sdc        8.0G   60M   7.2G    1%    /data1
```

Btrfs comes with a utility to manage Btrfs filesystems. We will show you a few of the features of the utility: the first is how to resize the filesystem. We are going to decrease our filesystem by 2 GiB and then add it back again.

```
$ sudo btrfs filesystem resize -2G /data1
Resize '/data1' of '-2G'
```

One of the subcommands of the Btrfs utility is filesystem. Here we have passed the options resize -2G /data1 which tell the utility to decrease the filesystem by 2 GiB. Using the filesystem show subcommand, we can see the result.

```
$ sudo btrfs filesystem show /data1
Label: none  uuid: e1c6cbb0-4fbf-4a61-a912-0a9cda611128
        Total devices 1 FS bytes used 42.03MiB
        devid    1 size 6.00GiB used 1.64GiB path /dev/sdc
```

We are now going to add the 2 GiB back. So we simply use the following:

```
$ sudo btrfs filesystem resize +2G /data1
Resize '/data1' of '+2G'
```

In this next example we have four spare disks attached to our host. We are going to use these disks as one combined disk. The output of dmesg shows they have been assigned to the following devices:

```
[   47.815498] sdb: unknown partition table
[   47.833520] sdc: unknown partition table
[   47.848420] sdd: unknown partition table
[   47.868448] sde: unknown partition table
```

With Btrfs we can group our devices with RAID. It uses Multidevice filesystems to do this, which we talk more about later in the section "RAID." One of the possible RAID types we can use is RAID 10. This RAID type gives us mirroring and striping, meaning devices are pair mirrored and then striped. This will give us redundancy and speed.

To create the Btrfs RAID partition we issue the following:

```
$ sudo mkfs.btrfs -d raid10 -m raid10  /dev/sdb  /dev/sdc /dev/sdd /dev/sde
btrfs-progs v3.19.1
See http://btrfs.wiki.kernel.org for more information.

Turning ON incompat feature 'extref': increased hardlink limit per file to 65536
Turning ON incompat feature 'skinny-metadata': reduced-size metadata extent refs
adding device /dev/sdc id 2
adding device /dev/sdd id 3
adding device /dev/sde id 4
fs created label (null) on /dev/sdb
        nodesize 16384 leafsize 16384 sectorsize 4096 size 32.00GiB
```

Here we have issued the `mkfs.btrfs` command. We have specified the –d option which sets the profile for the data block groups. The –m option sets the profile for the metadata block group. Then we have specified the four disks we are using.

At the end it says we have created an fs label on /dev/sdb. Let's get the UUID of that device so we can put it in our fstab.

```
$ sudo blkid /dev/sdb
[sudo] password for jsmith:
/dev/sdb: UUID="0cd0e135-feb8-4f99-a973-5751549d2e4f" UUID_SUB="4d327afb-1330-43e5-b392-0e676ebab1b5" TYPE="btrfs"
```

We add our line to our fstab as follows:

```
UUID=0cd0e135-feb8-4f99-a973-5751549d2e4f  /data btrfs defaults 0 0
```

Let's know mount our disk using the mount command:

```
$ sudo mount /data2
```

Finally let's take a look at how much space we have on the /data2 partition with the df -h command:

```
$ df -h /data2
Filesystem                  Size    Used    Avail  Use%  Mounted on
/dev/sdb                    16G     18M     14G     1%    /data2
```

We have four 8 GiB disks combining for a 14 GiB usable partition. We are now going to show you briefly the ability to create a subvolume and to create a snapshot.

A subvolume is a "POSIX namespace" or a container. It is not a block device, like /dev/sda or an LVM (logical volume management) logical volume. That is, you can't mount it on its own or create a different filesystem on it, but you can mount it as a subvolume and the Linux kernel can read and write to it.

You use subvolumes as you would a normal directory. They have the following benefits:

- you can rename and remove subvolumes

- you can easily and quickly snapshot subvolumes

- you can mount snapshots

- you can nest subvolumes

- you can apply quotas to subvolumes

We are going to create a subvolume called mail and we will mount that.

```
$ sudo btrfs subvolume create /data2/mail
Create subvolume '/data2/mail'
```

We have now created a directory called /srv/mail and we are going to mount our mail subvolume there:

```
$ sudo mount -t btrfs -o subvol=mail /dev/sdc /srv/mail
```

We can now see that that filesystem is mounted.

```
$ df -h /srv/mail
Filesystem      Size   Used   Avail  Use%  Mounted on
/dev/sdb        16G    18M    14G    1%    /srv/mail
```

The great feature of BtrFS subvolumes is the speed of snapshotting. There are two types of snapshots we can create: a read-only subvolume snapshot or a writeable subvolume snapshot. Since this is a CoW filesystem, we don't change disk space until we write a change to the data. Now, let's create a snapshot of the subvolume and we can mount it elsewhere, in /mnt/snap_mail, for example.

```
$ sudo btrfs subvolume snapshot /data/mail /data2/snap_mail
```

Now to mount that on /mnt/snap_mail.

```
$ sudo mount -t btrfs -o subvol=snap_mail /dev/sdc /mnt/snap_mail
$ df -h /mnt/snap_mail
Filesystem      Size   Used  Avail  Use%  Mounted on
/dev/sdb        16G    18M   14G    1%   /mnt/snap_mail
```

A snapshot is a point-in-time copy of the subvolume. You can use it to copy off data on a busy filesystem or to take a point-in-time backup of the subvolume. To make a read-only snapshot you would issue the btrfs subvolume snapshot -r (vol_target) (vol_dest).

Filesystems for Data Sharing

So far, we've covered filesystems that are accessible only by Linux. If you need to transfer data between different operating systems—for instance, when you don't have a network between your laptop and a client's machine—you are likely to want to use a filesystem that can be accessed by Windows and Mac OS X as well as Linux.

The de facto standard for this purpose is the FAT filesystem, which was developed for MS-DOS by Microsoft. FAT comes in a few flavors. The latest version is FAT32, which supports disk sizes over 32 GiB and file sizes of up to 4 GiB.

To create a FAT32 filesystem, you use the mkfs.vfat utility. This utility is provided on both Ubuntu and CentOS by the dosfstools package, so you need to ensure that dosfstools is installed.

After plugging in the USB drive you wish to format, check its device node name via the kernel log, as shown in Listing 9-7.

Listing 9-7. Determining the Device Node for a USB Key

```
$ dmesg
[   52.464662] usb 1-1: new high speed USB device using ehci_hcd and address 2
[   52.887506] usb 1-1: configuration #1 chosen from 1 choice
[   52.967324] usbcore: registered new interface driver libusual
[   52.981452] Initializing USB Mass Storage driver...
[   52.986046] scsi3 : SCSI emulation for USB Mass Storage devices
[   52.987804] usbcore: registered new interface driver usb-storage
[   52.987831] USB Mass Storage support registered.
[   52.988661] usb-storage: device found at 2
[   52.988687] usb-storage: waiting for device to settle before scanning
[   58.982976] usb-storage: device scan complete
[   59.350262] usb 1-1: reset high speed USB device using ehci_hcd and address 2
[   59.772402] scsi 3:0:0:0: Direct-Access     SanDisk  Cruzer
8.01 PQ: 0 ANSI: 0 CCS
[   59.789834] sd 3:0:0:0: [sdg] 15682559 512-byte hardware sectors (8029 MB)
[   59.792747] sd 3:0:0:0: [sdg] Write Protect is off
[   59.792754] sd 3:0:0:0: [sdg] Mode Sense: 45 00 00 08
[   59.792766] sd 3:0:0:0: [sdg] Assuming drive cache: write through
[   59.805772] sd 3:0:0:0: [sdg] 15682559 512-byte hardware sectors (8029 MB)
[   59.815884] sd 3:0:0:0: [sdg] Write Protect is off
[   59.815891] sd 3:0:0:0: [sdg] Mode Sense: 45 00 00 08
[   59.815894] sd 3:0:0:0: [sdg] Assuming drive cache: write through
[   59.816480]  sdg: sdg1
[   59.831448] sd 3:0:0:0: [sdg] Attached SCSI removable disk
[   59.831942] sd 3:0:0:0: Attached scsi generic sg7 type 0
```

In Listing 9-7, the SanDisk Cruzer USB drive was detected as /dev/sdg. Once you know which device node the USB drive is, you can create a primary partition of type c - W95 FAT32 (LBA), and you can then format this partition using mkfs.vfat. Use the -n option to label the partition and specify that you want a FAT32 filesystem via the -F 32 option.

```
$ sudo mkfs.vfat -n "USB Key" -F 32 /dev/sdg1
mkfs.vfat 2.11 (12 Mar 2005)
```

Other Filesystems

A plethora of different filesystems are available for Linux, so you might ask why we covered only three of them. Though many other filesystems exist, we feel that most of them are not suitable or ready for use in a production environment. The foremost feature a filesystem needs to have is stability, and the filesystems we covered offer this, as well as excellent performance. If you choose ext4, XFS, or Btrfs based on the type of data you are storing, you should see excellent reliability and speed. Choosing a faster but less stable filesystem for your server is not going to be of help if as a result you need to spend time restoring your data from backups once a month.

For a brief overview of other filesystems supported by the Linux kernel, you can read the filesystems manual page.

■ **Note**   Linux can create NTFS filesystems via the mkntfs tool in the ntfsprogs package. However, we recommend you don't use NTFS filesystems to store data under Linux.

Using Your Filesystem

You've now created partitions on your new disk, /dev/sdb, and you've formatted these partitions with the filesystem of your choice. However, before you can use the filesystem to store data, you need to mount it.

As we briefly explained in Chapter 4 and at the start of this chapter, filesystems on Linux do not get assigned a drive letter. Instead, they are mounted as a directory, somewhere under the root filesystem or a subdirectory. In Chapter 4, we mentioned that the /mnt directory is commonly used as a place to temporarily mount filesystems. Next, you'll create a directory called /mnt/data, and you'll use that for your new ext4 partition.

```
$ sudo mkdir /mnt/data
```

Mounting a partition is done via the mount command. You specify the filesystem type using the -t option, then the device file, and then the directory on which you want the filesystem to become available.

```
$ sudo mount -t ext4 /dev/sdb2 /mnt/data/
```

If all goes well, the mount command will not print any information, but simply exit. To verify that the partition is now mounted, use the df command.

```
$ df -h
Filesystem                          Size   Used   Avail   Use%   Mounted on
udev                                478M      0    478M     0%   /dev
tmpfs                               100M   3.3M     96M     4%   /run
/dev/mapper/au--mel--ubuntu--1--vg-root   6.3G   2.6G    3.4G    44%   /
tmpfs                               497M      0    497M     0%   /dev/shm
```

```
tmpfs                                        5.0M     0    5.0M    0%   /run/lock
tmpfs                                        497M     0    497M    0%   /sys/fs/cgroup
/dev/sda1                                    472M   147M   301M   33%   /boot
tmpfs                                        100M     0    100M    0%   /run/user/1000
/dev/sdb2                                     2.0G   3.0M   1.8G    1%   /mnt/data
```

Our partition is listed at the bottom of the output, so the mount command has succeeded. We'll revisit df later in this chapter and explain in more detail what this output means.

You can also check for some more detailed information by examining the kernel log via the dmesg command.

```
$ dmesg
[37881.206060] EXT4-fs (sdb2): mounted filesystem with ordered data mode. Opts: (null)
```

The kernel detected an ext4 filesystem and mounted it with the default option of "ordered data mode" (which means we first write data to the main filesystem and then commit the metadata to the journal). It also started a kernel thread to flush data from the journal to the filesystem every five seconds—our librarian emptying the book chute.

Taking a look inside the newly mounted partition, we can use ls to see if it contains anything:

```
$ cd /mnt/data && ls -l
total 16
drwx------ 2 root root 16384 Jun 19 10:42 lost+found
```

Your brand-new filesystem contains a single directory called lost+found, which you didn't create! This is a special directory that exists on all ext2, ext3 and ext4 filesystems. This directory is used by Linux's filesystem repair tools, which we'll look at later in the section "Recovering from Failure."

When you no longer need the filesystem, you can unmount it from your host using the umount command.

```
$ sudo umount /mnt/data
umount: /mnt/data: target is busy
        (In some cases useful info about processes that
         use the device is found by lsof(8) or fuser(1).)
$ pwd
/mnt/data
```

What is happening here? The command umount is refusing to unmount the directory because it contains files or directories that are in use. In this case, it's because our current working directory is /mnt/data and our host can't unmount the device while we're in the directory—that is, we are sitting in the directory we are trying to unmount! A device could be busy for many reasons, and it's not always clear which user or application has opened which files or directories. To help you find out, the lsof command lists open files and directories:

```
$ sudo lsof /mnt/data
COMMAND    PID    USER     FD    TYPE    DEVICE  SIZE/OFF  NODE   NAME
bash       2750   jsmith   cwd   DIR     8,18    4096      2      /mnt/data
sudo       3999   root     cwd   DIR     8,18    4096      2      /mnt/data
lsof       4000   root     cwd   DIR     8,18    4096      2      /mnt/data
lsof       4001   root     cwd   DIR     8,18    4096      2      /mnt/data
```

Apart from lsof itself, there is a bash process owned by the user jsmith. You can make this process stop using the directory by going back to your home directory. Type **cd** and the ~ shortcut for your home directory, and then check /mnt/data again using lsof.

```
$ cd ~
$ lsof /mnt/data
```

This time the lsof command has returned no open files and directories, and as the directory is no longer listed as in use, you can now safely unmount it:

```
$ sudo umount /mnt/data
```

■ **Note** Unmounting a filesystem properly will set the Filesystem state flag you saw in the tune2fs output to clean, because it will ask the kernel to process the entire journal file and make sure all data is written to the disk. This prevents an automated filesystem check the next time your host boots.

When you run lsof as a non-root user, it will only list processes owned by that user. Someone else might still be using a file or directory on the filesystem you're trying to unmount. It is always a good idea to run lsof using sudo to check.

■ **Note** If a mounted filesystem is being used by a system service, you will have to stop the service before you can unmount the filesystem.

Automating Mounts

You've probably noticed that your other partitions don't need to be manually mounted. When you started your host they were already mounted. This was done as part of the startup process. Each partition you want to mount automatically at startup needs to be listed in the /etc/fstab file. Listing 9-8 shows the one from our Ubuntu host.

Listing 9-8. An fstab File

```
# /etc/fstab: static file system information.
#
# Use 'blkid' to print the universally unique identifier for a
# device; this may be used with UUID= as a more robust way to name devices
# that works even if disks are added and removed. See fstab(5).
#
# <file system>                    <mount point>  <type>  <options>         <dump>  <pass>
/dev/mapper/au--mel--ubuntu--1--vg-root    /      ext4    errors=remount-ro 0       1
# /boot was on /dev/sda1 during installation
UUID=d036bc4a-6f9b-4989-a377-7778a29bf16c  /boot  ext2    defaults          0       2
/dev/mapper/au--mel--ubuntu--1--vg-swap_1  none   swap    sw                0       0
```

Each line in the file consists of six fields, separated by spaces or tabs. These fields specify how and where each filesystem is mounted, and what to do if a check is to be performed. All lines starting with a hash mark (#) are comments.

The filesystem field contains the device node name of the filesystem you want to be mounted. You can also substitute a filesystem label by specifying LABEL=label or the filesystem UUID, as in the example. We'll use UUID references, as they don't change even when disks are detected in a different order and thus might be named differently. Ubuntu places the original device node name in a comment on the line directly above. Next is the mount point, which is simply a directory anywhere on the filesystem. The mount point can be on a partition that was also mounted separately.

■ **Tip** Keep in mind that entries in the /etc/fstab file are processed in order from top to bottom.

The filesystem type tells the system which type to expect. If this does not match, the mount will fail. You can specify a comma-separated list of types to try, as is the case with the DVD-ROM drive, /dev/scd0. This tries the udf DVD filesystem first and then iso9660, which is used by CD-ROMs.

Mount options are passed as a comma-delimited list as well. In our example fstab, you can see two different options being used for the ext4 filesystems. The option, errors=remount-ro, controls what happens if a filesystem error occurs. In this case, the filesystem will be immediately mounted in read-only mode. This prevents additional data corruption while keeping files readable to services and users.

The other two possible values for error behavior are continue, which would cause the system to write a log entry but otherwise ignore the problem, and panic, which would cause the system to crash ungracefully. The default error behavior can also be specified in the filesystem itself via the tune2fs -e command. In Listing 9-5 we showed you how to use tune2fs to list the options, and doing that of the root mount '/' shows that the following default mount options are used:

```
Default mount options:   user_xattr acl
```

The user_xattr is to allow support for 'user.' extended attributes (which can be used for greater filesystem security, see the man attr for more details). The acl option allows for posix acl's to be used, which again can be used for fine-grained directory access (see man acl for details).

There are many more mount options that define things like access to files and directories on filesystems, that might tweak performance, and options for filesystems that don't support Unix-style file permissions, like FAT32 and NTFS. Options for each supported filesystem can be found in the mount manual page.

The dump field contains a digit (0 or 1), which tells the system whether or not to dump some filesystem meta-information when a filesystem check is to be performed. This dump information can be used by the filesystem repair tools. A 0 means that the filesystem does not need to be dumped. We'll cover this in a bit more detail later on in the section "Recovering from Failure."

Finally, the pass field is used to determine the order in which filesystems should be checked. In our fstab file, the root filesystem is listed as 1, so it is checked first. After that the /boot filesystem would be checked. Filesystems with a 0 in this column are checked last. You can find longer descriptions of these fields on the fstab manual page.

Adding a Partition to /etc/fstab

To add your new partition to our /etc/fstab, we will map our device id, which is device path, label, or UUID, to our mount point. We are going to use the UUID and so we will need to know its UUID.

You can find this in the tune2fs -l listing with Ext filesystems, xfs_admin -u for XFS filesystems, or btrfs filesystem show for BtrFS, or you can use the blkid utility. If you run the latter without any parameters, it prints the UUID for all detected block devices, as shown in Listing 9-9.

Listing 9-9. Displaying All UUIDs

```
$ sudo blkid
/dev/mapper/sda5_crypt: UUID="MdUlYF-y6Ol-XcB5-mS9L-mxPN-jNLF-ATAImA" TYPE="LVM2_member"
/dev/mapper/au--mel--ubuntu--1--vg-root: UUID="0b9eec02-06a4-46e4-b9ac-1e1ea871ff89"
TYPE="ext4"
/dev/sda1: UUID="d036bc4a-6f9b-4989-a377-7778a29bf16c" TYPE="ext2" PARTUUID="105922fd-01"
/dev/sda5: UUID="33dcd288-27f0-4f09-ab74-617db851a552" TYPE="crypto_LUKS"
PARTUUID="105922fd-05"
/dev/mapper/au--mel--ubuntu--1--vg-swap_1: UUID="e45b953f-284f-45f5-b16d-8f5be5d5a970"
TYPE="swap"
/dev/sdb2: LABEL="mail" UUID="71bd5774-33cb-491b-8ffe-49cb33935001" TYPE="ext4"
PARTLABEL="Linux filesystem" PARTUUID="b704ec19-833d-4727-a572-189f214f2ecf"
/dev/sdb1: UUID="6d0ce2f6-f9f6-4ac2-91f6-3099a40d5624" TYPE="swap" PARTLABEL="Linux swap"
PARTUUID="db962e77-53f3-4cfe-847c-f53133f063f7"
/dev/sdb3: UUID="ccd60fc3-bbaf-40e5-a93e-43743f9176d9" TYPE="xfs" PARTLABEL="Linux
filesystem" PARTUUID="f9d90e5f-0186-4cd5-a2be-9b89e7286abb"
```

To have it print the UUID for only a single device, pass the device node name as a parameter, like

```
$ sudo blkid /dev/sdb2
```

To mount your ext4 partition (the uuid command will print the filesystem type too) with the default mount options, add the following line to the /etc/fstab file:

```
UUID="71bd5774-33cb-491b-8ffe-49cb33935001"   /mnt/
data        ext4 defaults         0            0
```

The options "defaults" provide us with the following mount options when mounting an ext4 filesystem. They are rw, which is read/write, relatime which means that the system updates inode access time relative to modify or change times (a performance improvement), and data=ordered means that the system will first write data to the main filesystem and then commit the metadata to the journal.

If you want to use the device node instead, you can do the following. However we prefer you use either a label or the UUID as device paths can change.

```
/dev/sdb2        /mnt/data      ext4      defaults         0         0
```

Now you can test this entry without the need to reboot. If you use the mount command and only pass the mount point as a parameter, it will check the /etc/fstab file for a matching entry and mount that, with the options specified in the file.

```
$ sudo mount /mnt/data
```

If the mount command exited without printing any errors, the fstab entry is correct and your filesystem will be automatically mounted each time you boot your host. If you pass the filesystem type, like with a mount -t ext4, it will mount all the ext4 filesystems. You can mount all the mount points in the fstab file with a mount -a. You can double-check that the filesystem is mounted by running the mount as in Listing 9-10.

Listing 9-10. All Mounted Filesystems

```
$ sudo mount -t ext4
/dev/mapper/au--mel--ubuntu--1--vg-root on / type ext4 (rw,relatime,errors=remount-
ro,data=ordered)
/dev/sdb2 on /mnt/data type ext4 (rw,relatime,data=ordered)
```

We have used the parameter –t ext4 to only specify ext4 fs-types in our output and you can see our /dev/sdb2 is mount on /mnt/data. Alternatively, to add a XFS partition, create the mount point directory and add the correct UUID or device node name and filesystem type to /etc/fstab:

```
UUID="ccd60fc3-bbaf-40e5-a93e-43743f9176d9" /mnt/data2 xfs defaults  0  0
```

■ **Caution**   A mistake in the fstab file might result in a system that cannot boot. If so, you may need to follow some of the steps discussed in the section "Recovering from Failure" or use single-user mode as described in Chapter 6 to boot and fix the error.

It's possible for the kernel not to have registered that the UUID on a filesystem has changed. If this happens, attempting to mount the filesystem by using the UUID reference would result in an error like the following:

```
$ sudo mount /mnt/datax
mount: special device /dev/disk/by-uuid/ccd60fc3-bbaf-40e5-a93e-43743f9176d9
    does not exist
```

You can cause the UUID to be redetected and the correct symbolic link in /dev/disk/by-uuid to be created by reloading the udev service. We can do that with the following:

```
$ sudo udevadm control --reload
```

Checking Filesystem Usage

When you start using a filesystem for data storage, you'll want to be able to keep an eye on the amount of available space. When a filesystem fills up, services that use it may refuse to start, stop working, or crash.

You can list space usage for an entire filesystem via the df command, which is usually used with the -h option. This option produces human-readable output with numbers in KiB, MiB, GiB, or TiB instead of blocks, as shown in Listing 9-11.

Listing 9-11. Filesystem Usage

```
$ df -h
Filesystem                          Size   Used   Avail   Use%   Mounted on
udev                                478M      0   478M     0%   /dev
tmpfs                               100M   4.6M    95M     5%   /run
/dev/mapper/au--mel--ubuntu--1--vg-root  6.3G   2.6G   3.4G    44%   /
tmpfs                               497M      0   497M     0%   /dev/shm
tmpfs                               5.0M      0   5.0M     0%   /run/lock
tmpfs                               497M      0   497M     0%   /sys/fs/cgroup
/dev/sda1                           472M   147M   301M    33%   /boot
tmpfs                               100M      0   100M     0%   /run/user/1000
/dev/sdb2                           2.0G   3.0M   1.8G     1%   /mnt/data
/dev/sdb3                           4.0G    33M   4.0G     1%   /mnt/data2
```

The output shows you the total size, the amounts of space used and still available, and the percentage this equates to for each mounted filesystem. This command is quick, as it simply queries the filesystem metadata. As you have seen you can also pass the mount path to only return the information for that mount.

```
$ df -h /data
Filesystem     Size  Used   Avail  Use%   Mounted on
/dev/sdb       16G   22M    14G    1%     /data
```

■ **Note**   To check the number of inodes, use the df -i command. Use this command when applications report that the disk is full, even if there is apparently a lot of free space left.

You can check the cumulative size of a directory and all the files it contains with the du command. This command needs to recursively scan files under the directory you're running it on, so it may take a long time to complete. We'll use the -h option again to give us human-readable output. By default, it will print the size for each subdirectory as well. To avoid this, we pass the -s option, so it shows us only the final total.

```
$ du -sh *
2.5M    Documents
44G     src
```

Here we are listing and calculating the files and directories in our home directory. We have two directories, Documents and src and we can see the total size of each of the files in those directories. What happens when we try one of the system directories like the /etc directory?

```
$ du -sh /etc
du: cannot read directory '/etc/ssl/private': Permission denied
du: cannot read directory '/etc/lvm/archive': Permission denied
du: cannot read directory '/etc/lvm/backup': Permission denied
du: cannot read directory '/etc/polkit-1/localauthority': Permission denied
7.0M    /etc
```

Because it scans the subdirectories in /etc, this command may encounter directories that you don't have permission to access. It cannot calculate the size of these directories, so the total that it reports is not correct in this case. To always get the correct total, you can run du as the root user:

```
$ sudo du -sh /etc
7.0M    /etc
```

And while we have the same amount shown in our result (7.0 M) this is due to rounding. If we used a –k (for KiB) instead of –h, we see values of 7,084 and 7,116 respectively. This can be helpful when determining which directories to move to a partition of their own if a filesystem becomes full. An alternative solution would be to resize the filesystem, and we'll get to that shortly.

■ **Tip**   In Chapters 17 and 18, when we look at monitoring and logging, we'll cover how to automate filesystem monitoring.

RAID

Storing data on a hard disk is great to keep it accessible on your server, but when the disk fails, you lose your data. There are several ways to combat this. One is to use LVM which can group multiple disks and present them as one device, or you can use BtrFS which can do a similar thing. In this section we are going to show you another alternative, RAID.

RAID allows you to use multiple disks as if they were a single larger disk, with optional built-in redundancy. The three broad types of RAID implementations are as follows:

- Hardware RAID

- Fake RAID

- Software RAID

Hardware RAID uses specialized hardware controllers, often called *RAID controllers*, that manage RAID transparently from the operating system. Enterprise-level servers often come with these specialized hardware controllers. On such systems, you would usually configure RAID via the BIOS (Basic Input/Output System) or UEFI (Unified Extensible Firmware Interface) (which we discussed briefly in Chapter 6). Linux will then see a single RAID array, which you would use like a normal hard disk.

Fake RAID is a lesser form of hardware RAID used on smaller systems or desktop machines. Here the manufacturer may have added RAID functionality to the mainboard via a chip. We recommend you don't use fake RAID, as any RAID array created with this implementation would work only on a host sharing an identical controller. Its performance also depends on proprietary code provided by the manufacturer. These controllers can usually be configured to run as simple Serial ATA controllers, instead of RAID. A short listing of the most common fake RAID controllers is available at `https://raid.wiki.kernel.org/index.php/DDF_Fake_RAID`.

▪ **Note** If you have fake RAID set up with Windows and want to dual boot, you can still use most fake RAID arrays under Linux via the dmraid system. Disabling fake RAID would cause Windows to stop working, and you might lose your data.

The third RAID implementation type is via software contained in the Linux kernel. This system is called md or multiple disk. The md system usually performs much better than fake RAID, and md RAID arrays are transferable between hosts. In this section, we'll focus on using md RAID.

Types of RAID

There are several types—or levels—of RAID. The level you use depends on what is most important to you. The different levels offer a trade-off between available disk space, reliability, and speed. Table 9-5 lists the most commonly used RAID levels.

Table 9-5. *Commonly Used RAID Levels*

Raid Level	Functionality	Storage capacity
RAID 0	Speed	N * size
RAID 1	Redundancy	N * size / 2
RAID 5	Redundancy, speed	N - 1 * size
RAID 6	Redundancy, reliability, speed	N - 1 * size
RAID 10	Redundancy, reliability, speed	N / 2 * size
RAID 50	Redundancy, speed	N – 1 * size

Storage capacity is calculated by the N (total number of disks) in the raid array (minus any parity disks) then multiplied by the size of the disk. You can find an exhaustive list and descriptions of RAID levels at http://en.wikipedia.org/wiki/Redundant_array_of_independent_disks.

It's common to use one hard disk as a spare as well. Should a disk in an array fail, its place can be immediately taken over by the spare disk.

■ **Note**   It's possible to run RAID without any spare devices, but you will then need to replace a failed device immediately, to avoid data loss.

Striping and Mirroring

The most basic way to use RAID is with two disks, which gives you the option to use either RAID level 0 or RAID level 1.

RAID 0, which is also known as *striping*, causes Linux to see the two disks as a combined disk of twice the size. When writing data to such a RAID array, parts of the data will end up on each of the disks. Since this is an operation Linux can execute simultaneously on both disks, writing to RAID 0 is faster than writing to a single disk. However, the drawback is that when one of the disks fails, arbitrary parts of files that were spread over both disks disappear. So you lose all your data.

■ **Caution**   Avoid using RAID 0 on a server or on any machine that holds persistent data.

RAID 1, also known as *mirroring*, allows you to store only as much data on the array as a single disk holds. It stores identical copies of all files on both disks, so if one disk fails, you can still retrieve your data from the other. Since all data needs to be written to each disk, RAID 1 does not offer any improved write performance.

Figure 9-1 shows how files are stored on disk when using RAID 0 or RAID 1. On RAID 1, each disk contains a full copy of each file. On RAID 0, each disk contains only a partial copy of each file.

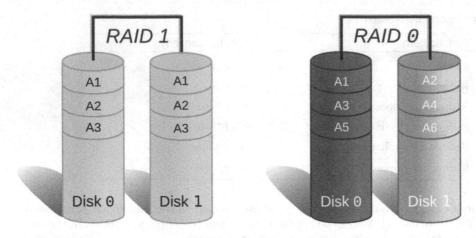

Figure 9-1. *RAID 0 and RAID 1 file storage*

When you have more disks to play with, you get more options to pick a RAID level that can give you improved performance as well as redundancy. The simplest extension is RAID 1+0 (RAID 10), which uses multiple RAID 1 mirrors as elements of a RAID 0 stripe. This way, all striped data is saved to at least two disks, which gives you the advantages of RAID 0 speed and RAID 1 redundancy. However, you can only store as much data as half the combined disk size. When disks are both large and cheap, and you have enough slots in your server to hold at least four disks, this might be a good option.

Processor to the Rescue

In order to get the best of all worlds—redundancy, storage size, and speed—you can call in the help of some processing power. RAID level 5 uses a minimum of three disks and gives you more efficient use of the available storage space and increased read and write speed. It accomplishes this by striping the data across multiple disks and also writing a checksum of each stripe to a different disk (also known as block parity - for details on how this is calcuated see `http://searchstorage.techtarget.com/definition/parity`). Should a disk fail, the checksum can be used to reconstruct the data in the missing stripes.

The trade-off is that this approach uses processing power to calculate the checksums. When data is written to the array, a checksum needs to be calculated and stored on one of the disks. If a disk fails, the checksum can then be used in combination with the data on the remaining disks to recalculate the missing parts of the data. The faster your CPU, the faster this process is.

Figure 9-2 shows a simple diagram illustrating how data and checksum are split between disks. B1, B2, and B3 are parts of file B. Bp is a checksum, or parity. If disk 1 fails, B2 can be computed from B1, B3, and Bp, so when a replacement disk is added, its contents can be restored.

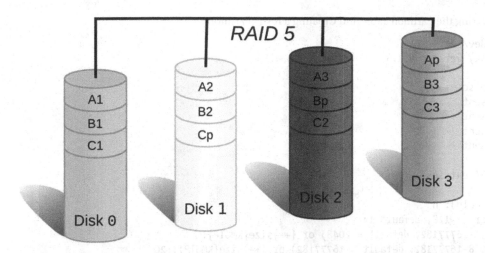

Figure 9-2. RAID 5 stripe layout across multiple disks

It's important to keep in mind that using RAID is *not* a substitute for creating regular backups. It will protect you from hardware failure but not from intentional deletion. If you accidentally delete a file from the RAID array, it will be removed from all devices in the array. We'll cover data backup and recovery in Chapter 14.

Creating an Array

You want to protect the data on your host from disk failure, so you will want to use RAID on it. To give a good overview of common RAID levels we will show you RAID 1 and RAID 5. The one you use depends on the number of hard disks you have available. First, you need to make sure you have at least three disks and create identically sized partitions on all of them.

■ **Note** If you do not have enough disks to use RAID, you can create multiple identically sized partitions on a single disk and use them as components in your RAID array. This will allow you to test RAID installation and management. Note that performance in this configuration will be quite slow, as data will need to be written to different parts of the same disk multiple times. It also doesn't provide much additional resilience against disk failures. If the single disk fails, then your RAID array will also fail.

On our example host we will again use three new disks, sdc, sdd, and sde, all of identical size. The disks need to be of identical size for RAID to work, if they are not the same size you need to create partitions on the disks of the same size. Here we create a 2 G partition and set the partition type to fd00 – Linux RAID, as shown in Listing 9-12.

Listing 9-12. Clearing the Partition Table and Creating a RAID Partition

```
$ sudo gdisk /dev/sdc
GPT fdisk (gdisk) version 0.8.6

Partition table scan:
  MBR: not present
  BSD: not present
  APM: not present
  GPT: not present

Creating new GPT entries.

Command (? for help): n
Partition number (1-128, default 1):
First sector (34-16777182, default = 2048) or {+-}size{KMGTP}:
Last sector (2048-16777182, default = 16777182) or {+-}size{KMGTP}: 2G
Current type is 'Linux filesystem'
Hex code or GUID (L to show codes, Enter = 8300): fd00
Changed type of partition to 'Linux RAID'

Command (? for help): w

Final checks complete. About to write GPT data. THIS WILL OVERWRITE EXISTING
PARTITIONS!!

Do you want to proceed? (Y/N): y
OK; writing new GUID partition table (GPT) to /dev/sdc.
The operation has completed successfully.
```

You would need to repeat this process for /dev/sdd and /dev/sde. However, if your disks are all of the same size (it is best to have the same drives from the same manufacturer for this reason) you do not need to partition the drives at all. Since our drives are the same size, we will will not partition them first.

Now that you have prepared your three disks, you can create the RAID array. For this you will need the RAID management utilities, which are provided by the mdadm package.

The command that manages all aspects of the RAID configuration is also called mdadm, and you can specify what it should do with your array via the mode option. To create an array, you need to specify create mode, which RAID level you want to use, and which partitions need to become part of the array. Listing 9-13 shows how to create a RAID 1 array.

Listing 9-13. Creating a RAID 1 Array with a Hot Spare

```
$ sudo mdadm --create /dev/md0 --level=raid1 --raid-devices=2 /dev/sdc /dev/sdd  ↵
    --spare-devices=1 /dev/sde
mdadm: Note: this array has metadata at the start and
    may not be suitable as a boot device.  If you plan to
    store '/boot' on this device please ensure that
    your boot-loader understands md/v1.x metadata, or use
    --metadata=0.90
Continue creating array? y
mdadm: Defaulting to version 1.2 metadata
mdadm: array /dev/md0 started.
```

Here we have created a device that we can mount called /dev/md0 and that is a RAID 1 device made up of two partitions /dev/sdc and /dev/sdd, with /dev/sde as a hot spare. If we were going to boot off this device (i.e., maybe create a MBR partition and install grub on it) we would need to change the metadata format we wish to use. We can do by specifying --metadata=0.90 (which is the original superblock format-see the man mdadm page for more details).

Creating or starting a RAID array will cause the md kernel modules to be loaded and display some status information. You can check the kernel log via dmesg, as shown in Listing 9-14.

Listing 9-14. Kernel RAID Information

```
$ sudo dmesg
[ 9508.794689] md: bind<sdc>
[ 9508.795609] md: bind<sdd>
[ 9508.795996] md: bind<sde>
[ 9508.806492] md: raid1 personality registered for level 1
[ 9508.807304] md/raid1:md0: not clean -- starting background reconstruction
[ 9508.807306] md/raid1:md0: active with 2 out of 2 mirrors
[ 9508.807318] md0: detected capacity change from 0 to 8584626176
[ 9508.809302] RAID1 conf printout:
[ 9508.809305]  --- wd:2 rd:2
[ 9508.809306]  disk 0, wo:0, o:1, dev:sdc
[ 9508.809307]  disk 1, wo:0, o:1, dev:sdd
[ 9508.812318] md: resync of RAID array md0
[ 9508.812320] md: minimum _guaranteed_ speed: 1000 KB/sec/disk.
[ 9508.812321] md: using maximum available idle IO bandwidth (but not more than 200000 KB/sec)
               for resync.
[ 9508.812323] md: using 128k window, over a total of 8383424k.
[ 9508.821845]  md0: unknown partition table
[ 9550.509411] md: md0: resync done.
[ 9550.516479] RAID1 conf printout:
[ 9550.516481]  --- wd:2 rd:2
[ 9550.516483]  disk 0, wo:0, o:1, dev:sdc
[ 9550.516484]  disk 1, wo:0, o:1, dev:sdd
[ 9550.517712] RAID1 conf printout:
[ 9550.517715]  --- wd:2 rd:2
[ 9550.517716]  disk 0, wo:0, o:1, dev:sdc
[ 9550.517717]  disk 1, wo:0, o:1, dev:sdd
```

Because your new array was never synchronized, the kernel will start by ensuring the data on both disks is identical. It informs you it will perform the synchronization as fast as it can, but never slower than 1,000 KB per second per disk and never faster than 200,000 KB per second in total.

■ **Tip** We'll show you how to change the synchronization speed in Chapter 17.

To check on the status of our RAID device, you can use the mdadm utility in query mode with the --detail option. This displays a wealth of information about the specified RAID device, as shown in Listing 9-15.

Listing 9-15. Querying RAID Device Status

```
$ $ sudo mdadm --query --detail /dev/md0
/dev/md0:
        Version : 1.2
  Creation Time : Mon Jun 20 09:41:18 2016
     Raid Level : raid1
     Array Size : 8383424 (8.00 GiB 8.58 GB)
  Used Dev Size : 8383424 (8.00 GiB 8.58 GB)
   Raid Devices : 2
  Total Devices : 3
    Persistence : Superblock is persistent
    Update Time : Mon Jun 20 09:42:00 2016
          State : clean
 Active Devices : 2
Working Devices : 3
 Failed Devices : 0
  Spare Devices : 1

           Name : au-mel-centos-1.example.com:0  (local to host gateway.example.com)
           UUID : ca66c4e2:49e8c87e:94d311de:01ca4f55
         Events : 17

    Number   Major   Minor   RaidDevice      State
       0       8       33          0        active sync   /dev/sdc
       1       8       49          1        active sync   /dev/sdd
       2       8       65          -        spare         /dev/sde
```

Listing 9-15 displays the metainformation about the array, as well as a detailed status for each component. In the case of our RAID 1 array, you can see that /dev/sdc and /dev/sdd are both active and in sync. This means any data written to the RAID device is immediately written to both /dev/sdc and /dev/sdd. If either of these devices should fail, our spare (/dev/sde) will be automatically activated and synchronized.

You can also quickly see your RAID device by querying the /proc filesystem:

```
$ cat /proc/mdstat
Personalities : [raid1]
md0 : active raid1 sde[2](S) sdd[1] sdc[0]
      8383424 blocks super 1.2 [2/2] [UU]

unused devices: <none>
```

We can see the [UU] and that tells us both devices [2/2] are Up. If one were degraded or down it might appear like this [U_]. The (S) after the device indicates it is being used as a spare.

At boot time, your Linux host will invoke the mdadm utility. Depending on its configuration, the utility will scan either all partitions or defined disks for RAID superblocks. If it finds any, it will analyze them and try to assemble and start all RAID arrays. You can also explicitly define your RAID arrays in the mdadm configuration file, to ensure their device node names do not change. The configuration file to define your arrays in is /etc/mdadm.conf on CentOS and /etc/mdadm/madadm.conf on Ubuntu. We've included a default mdadm.conf file from Ubuntu in Listing 9-16.

Listing 9-16. Default `mdadm.conf`

```
# mdadm.conf
#
# Please refer to mdadm.conf(5) for information about this file.
#

# by default (built-in), scan all partitions (/proc/partitions) and all
# containers for MD superblocks. alternatively, specify devices to scan, using
# wildcards if desired.
#DEVICE partitions containers

# auto-create devices with Debian standard permissions
CREATE owner=root group=disk mode=0660 auto=yes

# automatically tag new arrays as belonging to the local system
HOMEHOST <system>

# instruct the monitoring daemon where to send mail alerts
MAILADDR root

# definitions of existing MD arrays

# This file was auto-generated on Tue, 10 May 2016 21:55:12 +1000
# by mkconf $Id$
```

This configuration file will cause the host to scan for arrays at boot time and create device nodes owned by the root user and disk groups, just like regular hard drives. It specifies that when mdadm is run in monitor mode, any e-mails about device failures are sent to the root user.

■ **Note** We'll show you how to redirect all e-mail for the root user to a different address in Chapter 12.

Finally, there is a space to add the configurations for your RAID arrays. You'll add a definition for your RAID 1 array here. According to the mdadm.conf manual page, you need the following:

```
ARRAY /dev/md0 level=raid1 num-devices=2 spares=1 ↵
    UUID=ca66c4e2:49e8c87e:94d311de:01ca4f55 devices=/dev/sdc,/dev/sdd,/dev/sde
```

Note that adding this array definition is not strictly necessary. mdadm will automatically detect and assemble the array even if you leave this array definition out of the configuration file.

We already mentioned that mdadm will send an e-mail to the root user if an event occurs. We'll show you an example later on, when we start failing devices in our array.

```
┌──────────────────────────────────────────────────────────────────────────┐
│                        THE /PROC FILESYSTEM                                │
└──────────────────────────────────────────────────────────────────────────┘
```

You have likely noticed references to a directory called /proc in this chapter. This is a special directory that contains virtual, or pseudo, in memory filesystem that provides a way of interacting with the kernel. For instance, you can get information about the host processor via cat /proc/cpuinfo or you can change the kernel network stack to forward IPv4 packet by issuing echo 1 > /proc/sys/net/ipv4/ ip_forward.

Internal kernel variables are accessible via files under the /proc/sys directory. We'll come back to these in Chapter 17.

The /proc filesystem does not physically exist on disk, so it does not use any space, even though it appears to contain some very large files.

You can read more about the /proc filesystem at http://en.wikipedia.org/wiki/Procfs.

If you have minimum of four hard disks, you can create a RAID 5 array instead. Doing so allows you to use the available storage space more efficiently and, in some cases, improve performance as well. To create a new RAID 5 array, you need to disassemble the RAID 1 array first. By stopping it, you release all devices it uses:

```
$ sudo mdadm --manage /dev/md0 --stop
mdadm: stopped /dev/md0
```

You can now use these devices for the new RAID 5 array. Take care to remove the entry added to the mdadm.conf file as well. You'll add a disk, /dev/sdf, and create a single primary partition of type "Linux RAID" on it.

When that's done, you can create a RAID 5 array with three active devices and one spare, as shown in Listing 9-17.

Listing 9-17. Creating a RAID 5 Array

```
$ sudo mdadm --create /dev/md0 --level=raid5 --raid-devices=3 --spare-devices=1 /dev/sdc /
dev/sdd /dev/sde /dev/sdf
mdadm: /dev/sdc appears to be part of a raid array:
      level=raid1 devices=2 ctime=Mon Jun 20 09:41:18 2016
mdadm: /dev/sdd appears to be part of a raid array:
      level=raid1 devices=2 ctime=Mon Jun 20 09:41:18 2016
mdadm: /dev/sde appears to be part of a raid array:
      level=raid1 devices=2 ctime=Mon Jun 20 09:41:18 2016
Continue creating array? y
mdadm: Defaulting to version 1.2 metadata
mdadm: array /dev/md0 started.
```

Some of these devices were part of the previous RAID 1 array, and they still contain the old RAID superblock with array information. You want to create a new array, overwriting the old data, so answer Y. Because the old RAID 1 array was synchronized, all devices also contain a filesystem now, even though you had initially created only one on /dev/sdc. You can check the array status again via /proc/mdstat.

```
$ cat /proc/mdstat
Personalities : [raid1] [raid6] [raid5] [raid4]
md0 : active raid5 sde[4] sdf[3](S) sdd[1] sdc[0]
      16765952 blocks super 1.2 level 5, 512k chunk, algorithm 2 [3/2] [UU_]
      [===>.................]  recovery = 15.2% (1280840/8382976) finish=0.7min
      speed=160105K/sec
```

Here you can see that we have [3/2][UU_] which means two of the drives are functioning normally and the other is degraded but recovering, meaning it is getting a copy of the data it needs to bring it into the RAID array. It does not take long on this system until the array is up.

```
$ cat /proc/mdstat
Personalities : [raid1] [raid6] [raid5] [raid4]
md0 : active raid5 sde[4] sdf[3](S) sdd[1] sdc[0]
      16765952 blocks super 1.2 level 5, 512k chunk, algorithm 2 [3/3] [UUU]
```

You now have a RAID 5 array with three active devices and one spare. Provided you have enough hard disks, you can grow the size of a RAID 5 array as well. This causes data to be shifted and checksums to be recalculated, so it will take some time to complete. You'll add a sixth disk, /dev/sdg, to your host, so you can grow the array and still have a spare device available. Then you can add the new device to your array and grow the array using mdadm in manage mode via the --add option, as shown in Listing 9-18.

Listing 9-18. Expanding a RAID 5 Array

```
$ sudo mdadm --manage /dev/md0 --add /dev/sdg
mdadm: added /dev/sdf
```

To add multiple devices in a single command, just list them all after the --add option. A quick check of /proc/mdstat now shows that both sde1 and sdf1 are listed as spares.

```
$ cat /proc/mdstat
Personalities : [raid1] [raid6] [raid5] [raid4]
md0 : active raid5 sdg[5](S) sde[4] sdf[3](S) sdd[1] sdc[0]
      16765952 blocks super 1.2 level 5, 512k chunk, algorithm 2 [3/3] [UUU]

unused devices: <none>
```

And now you can expand the array from three to four active disks with mdadm in grow mode. One of the spares will automatically be used for this. Part of this process is destructive, so if a power failure occurs while you're expanding the array, you might lose data. To prevent this, specify the --backup-file option. Be sure not to store this backup file in the /tmp directory, which is emptied on boot!

```
$ sudo mdadm --grow /dev/md0 --raid-disks=4 --backup-file=/root/raid-backup-file
mdadm: Need to backup 384K of critical section..
mdadm: ... critical section passed.
```

You can keep an eye on the progress via the /proc/mdstat file again.

```
$ cat /proc/mdstat
Personalities : [linear] [multipath] [raid0] [raid1] [raid6] [raid5] [raid4]
    [raid10]
```

```
md0 : active raid5 sdg1[5](S) sde1[4] sdf1[3] sdd1[1] sdc1[0]
      16771584 blocks super 0.91 level 5, 64k chunk, algorithm 2 [4/4] [UUUU]
      [=======>.............] reshape = 35.8% (3008512/8385792) finish=22.2min
   speed=4022K/sec

unused devices: <none>
```

You now have four active devices and a single spare. The full new size of the array will not be accessible until the reshape has finished. As you can see, the reshape runs at a far slower rate than the RAID 1 re-sync.

■ **Tip** Instead of rerunning the `cat /proc/mdstat` command manually, you can automatically run it at a specified interval via the `watch` command. Log in to a second console and run `watch -n 5 cat /proc/mdstat` to automatically run the command every five seconds. Exit `watch` by pressing Ctrl+C.

We'll revisit RAID and show you how to deal with disk failures in the section "Recovering from Failure." For more information about md RAID on Linux, you can visit `http://linux-raid.osdl.org/index.php/Linux_Raid`.

Next we'll show you how to make use of these RAID devices without the need to partition them.

Logical Volume Management

We have seen how we can partition a disk and create different filesystems on them. The problem is, once you partition a disk, it's hard to resize the partitions or to add an additional one. Even if you do add disks and partitions, your data can become spread over a variety of locations and directories. This makes it harder to consolidate, back up, and manage your data, and it potentially makes it harder for your users to find their data. To overcome this issue, logical volume management (LVM) was created.

Rather than splitting a disk into a fixed number of partitions that are stored on a fixed area of the disk, LVM amalgamates one or more partitions or devices into a single logical volume group. You can then dynamically create, resize, and delete volumes in a volume group, removing the need to unmount volumes or reboot the system to update the partition map.

The LVM system has three layers. The bottom layer consists of physical volumes: disks, partitions, or RAID arrays. Physical volumes are used to create volume groups. A volume group can consist of one or more physical volumes. Finally, a volume group can contain any number of logical volumes, which are the LVM equivalent of partitions.

Both Ubuntu and CentOS have a graphical user interface (GUI) that you can use to manage disks, but they do not support LVM (there is an application called "Disks"). So what we'll do is take you through administering via the command line, starting with LVM volumes and groups.

Creating Groups and Volumes

If you want to use a partition with LVM, you need to set its type to `8e00 - Linux LVM` using gdisk. You can also use an entire disk or RAID array as storage for LVM. This is convenient, as you would not normally create partitions on a software RAID array.

For our examples, we'll be setting up LVM on the RAID 5 array created earlier. The steps are identical when setting up LVM on RAID 1, individual partitions, or whole disks.

Each of these storage devices used by LVM is called a physical volume (PV). You can mark a device as such via the pvcreate command.

```
$ sudo pvcreate /dev/md0
  Physical volume "/dev/md0" successfully created
```

This command writes a small watermark to the start of the device, identifying it for use with LVM. You can list all such devices on the system via the pvs command.

```
$ sudo pvs
PV              VG      Fmt     Attr    PSize       PFree
/dev/md0                lvm2    ---     15.99g      15.99g
/dev/sda2       centos  lvm2    a--     7.51g       40.00m
```

■ **Note** You will get more detailed information about physical volumes if you use the pvdisplay command.

Recall that we chose to use LVM when we first installed our CentOS system. You can see now that it used the /dev/sda2 partition as a physical volume. The second column, labeled VG, refers to the volume group, which is the next layer in the LVM system.

You can list all volume groups on the system via the vgs command.

```
$ sudo vgs
VG      #PV     #LV     #SN     Attr    VSize       VFree
centos  1       2       0       wz--n-  7.51g       40.00m
```

■ **Note** You will get more detailed information about volume groups if you use the vgdisplay command.

There is one volume group, called centos, which was created by the installer. It spans one physical volume and contains two logical volumes. You can list these via the lvs command. There are currently two volumes, root and swap_1.

```
$ sudo lvs
    LV      VG      Attr        LSize   Pool  Origin  Data%  Meta%  Move  Log  Cpy%Sync  Convert
    root    centos  -wi-ao---   6.67g
    swap    centos  -wi-ao---   820.00m
```

■ **Note** You will get more detailed information about logical volumes if you use the lvdisplay command.

You can now add your physical volume to an existing group via the vgextend command:

```
$ sudo vgextend centos /dev/md0
  Volume group "centos" successfully extended
```

And to check, you can display the physical volumes using pvs and vgs.

```
$ sudo pvs
  PV          VG        Fmt     Attr    PSize     PFree
  /dev/md0    centos    lvm2    a--     15.99g    15.99g
  /dev/sda2   centos    lvm2    a--      7.51g    40.00m

$ sudo vgs
  VG        #PV    #LV    #SN    Attr       VSize     VFree
  centos     2      2      0     wz--n-     23.50g    16.03g
```

The new physical volume is now part of the centos volume group. Adding the new physical volume to the group means it now has 23.50 GiB of unallocated space.

The alternative would have been to create a new volume group and use your physical volume with that. You can still do so by removing /dev/md0 from the centos group via the vgreduce command:

```
$ sudo vgreduce centos /dev/md0
Removed "/dev/md0" from volume group "centos"
```

It is now available to be used for a different volume group, which you create using the vgcreate command. You will assign the /dev/md0 device to the new raid-volume volume group. When this is complete, you can check that the new volume group exists using the vgs command.

```
$ sudo vgcreate raid-volume /dev/md0
  Volume group "raid-volume" successfully created

$ sudo vgs
  VG             #PV    #LV    #SN    Attr       VSize     VFree
  centos          1      2      0     wz--n-      7.51g    40.00m
  raid-volume     1      0      0     wz--n-     15.99g    15.99g
```

You now have a new volume group that you can use to create logical volumes. In preparation for later chapters, why don't we create a storage area for web sites? With LVM, we can easily give each of these functions its own dedicated area on disk.

First, you need to create a logical volume, which you do via the lvcreate command. You need to specify a name, a size, and the volume group to create the volume in. You can then list it via lvs.

```
$ sudo lvcreate --name www --size 2G raid-volume
  Logical volume "www" created
$ sudo lvs
  LV     VG            Attr         LSize    Pool Origin Data%  Meta%  Move Log Cpy%Sync Convert
  root   centos        -wi-ao----   6.67g
  swap   centos        -wi-ao----  820.00m
  www    raid-volume   -wi-a-----   2.00g
```

All that's left to do now is create a filesystem on the logical volume and mount it somewhere. To do so, you need the device node name for the logical volume. This is managed by a driver called device-mapper, which creates a device node entry for any volume you create.

A logical volume is accessible via /dev/mapper/<vgname>-<lvname>, which is symlinked from /dev/<vgname>/<lvname>. So for the new "www" LV, you can use /dev/raid-volume/www. We shall create a XFS filesystem for this logical volume using the following:

```
$ sudo mkfs.xfs /dev/raid-volume/www
```

You can use the volume as if it were an ordinary partition and add it to the /etc/fstab file, so it is automatically mounted on /var/www when your host boots. For this, you can use either the device node name or the UUID of the filesystem just created. blkid will provide you with both. The /etc/fstab entry looks like this:

```
# /dev/mapper/raid--volume-www
UUID=0814d564-b61c-407a-8483-9b176c684816  /var/www xfs   defaults 0  0
```

After you create the /var/www directory you can mount it using the following:

```
$ sudo mount /var/www
```

Expanding a Logical Volume

Thus far, using LVM has seemed just a more convoluted way of using your disks, but what if your web site grew beyond 2 GiB? Without LVM, you would need to create a partition on an unused disk, and then copy all data across and make sure /etc/fstab was updated. However, with LVM you can simply expand the logical volume and then resize the filesystem on it. If there was no space left in the volume group, you could add a physical volume to the group first.

You need to complete two steps to safely resize the filesystem contained in your logical volume. First, you need to resize the logical volume itself, and second, you need to resize the filesystem. LVM can do these for you and we will show you how shortly.

The volume can be expanded using the lvextend command. You need to specify either the new total size or the size increase you want, and the name of the volume. By prefixing the size parameter with +, you indicate you want the specified size added to the existing size.

```
$ sudo lvextend --size +2G --resizefs /dev/raid-volume/www
  Size of logical volume raid-volume/wwwl changed from 2.00 GiB (512 extents) to 4.00 GiB
  (1024 extents).
  Logical volume spool successfully resized.
meta-data=/dev/mapper/raid--volume-www isize = 256 agcount=4, agsize=131072 blks
                                  = ectsz=512       attr=2, projid32bit=1
                                  = crc=0           finobt=0
                           data   = bsize=4096      blocks=524288, imaxpct=25
                                  = sunit=0         swidth=0 blks
                         naming   = version 2       bsize=4096 ascii-ci=0 ftype=0
                            log   = internal        bsize=4096 blocks=2560, version=2
                                  = sectsz=512      sunit=0 blks, lazy-count=1
                       realtime   = none            extsz=4096 blocks=0, rtextents=0
data blocks changed from 524288 to 1048576
```

As you can see we have specified that we want to add 2 G (+2G) to the /dev/raid-volume/www logical volume. We also want it to be resized (--resizefs) for us. This tells LVM to simply execute xfs_growfs after the resizing the logical volume.

■ **Note**   With resizing your filesystem you are limited by the capabilities of the filesystem – lvextend and
lvreduce use the underlying filesystem tools to resize the filesystem and add nothing special. So you will be
able to extend and reduce Ext family of filesystems using LVM but only extend XFS as you cannot reduce a XFS
filesystem.

To specify the new total size, rather than adding 2G to the volume, you could also use the following:

```
$ sudo lvextend -s 4G  /dev/raid-volume/www
  Size of logical volume raid-volume/www changed from 2.00 GiB (512 extents) to 4.00 GiB
  (1024 extents).
  Logical volume www successfully resized.
```

In this case, both approaches produce the same result: a logical volume 4 GiB. However in this case
we have not told lvmextend to resize the filesystem so the filesystem size remains at 2 GiB. While we could
have got lvextend to resize the filesystem using the -r (or --resize) option, we are going to do it ourselves
manually.

We are now going to tell the filesystem about the new size of the device it is contained on, for which you
use the xfs_growfs utility. If we had an Ext4 filesystem we would use the resize2fs utility instead. You'll
start with a 2 GiB filesystem, as you can see in Listing 9-19.

Listing 9-19.   Resizing an Ext3 Filesystem

```
$ df -h /var/www
Filesystem Size Used Avail Use% Mounted on
/dev/mapper/raid--volume-www 2.0G 135M 1.9G 7% /var/www

$ sudo xfs_growfs /dev/raid-volume/www
meta-data=/dev/mapper/raid--volume-www isize=256 agcount=8, agsize=65408 blks
                                = sectsz=512   attr=2, projid32bit=1
                                = crc=0        finobt=0
                        data    = bsize=4096   blocks=523264, imaxpct=25
                                = sunit=128    swidth=256 blks
                     naming =version 2         bsize=4096 ascii-ci=0 ftype=0
                        log =internal bsize=4096 blocks=2560, version=2
                                = sectsz=512 sunit=8 blks, lazy-count=1
                   realtime =none extsz=4096 blocks=0, rtextents=0
data blocks changed from 523264 to 1048576

$ df -h /var/www
Filesystem                     Size    Used    Avail   Use%    Mounted on
/dev/mapper/raid--volume-www   4.0G    136M    4.0G    3%      /var/www
```

And you now have a 4 GiB filesystem.

Shrinking a Logical Volume

In addition to expanding a filesystem, there are some filesystems you can also shrink. To shrink a filesystem
and a logical volume, you follow the previous steps in reverse and use the lvreduce command. Just make
certain you do not shrink the logical volume to be smaller than the filesystem it contains.

We have created a new LVM group and LVM volume of 4 G. We have formatted it as an Ext4 filesystem and we are going to resize it to 2 G. Unlike growing the filesystem, if the volume you are reducing is mounted, the following command will umount and remount it.

```
$ sudo lvreduce --size -2G -r /dev/vg-mail/spool
Do you want to unmount "/tmp/block"? [Y|n] y
fsck from util-linux 2.23.2
/dev/mapper/vg--mail-spool: 11/262144 files (0.0% non-contiguous), 53326/1048576 blocks
resize2fs 1.42.9 (28-Dec-2013)
Resizing the filesystem on /dev/mapper/vg--mail-spool to 524288 (4k) blocks.
The filesystem on /dev/mapper/vg--mail-spool is now 524288 blocks long.

  Size of logical volume vg-mail/spool changed from 4.00 GiB (1024 extents) to 2.00 GiB
  (512 extents).
  Logical volume spool successfully resized.
```

And now our filesystem has been reduced.

```
$ df -h /tmp/block
Filesystem                 Size  Used Avail Use% Mounted on
/dev/mapper/vg--mail-spool 1.9G   12M  1.8G   1% /var/spool
```

LVM Commands

Although it's a little bit more work to set up than simple partitions, LVM allows you to use your storage space in a far more flexible manner. Table 9-6 lists the LVM commands you'll most often use.

Table 9-6. Basic LVM Commands

Command	Used For
pvcreate	Labeling devices for use with LVM
pvremove	Removing the LVM label from a physical volume
pvdisplay / pvs	Displaying information on the specified device or all physical volumes on the system
vgcreate	Creating a new volume group
vgremove	Removing (deleting) a volume group
vgextend	Adding physical volumes to a volume group
vgreduce	Removing physical volumes from a volume group
vgdisplay / vgs	Displaying information about the specified group or all volume groups on the system
lvcreate	Creating a new logical volume
lvremove	Removing (deleting) a logical volume
lvextend	Increasing the size of a logical volume
lvreduce	Decreasing the size of a logical volume
lvdisplay / lvs	Displaying all logical volumes on the system or in a specified volume group

Recovering from Failure

If your host suffers a crash that leaves a filesystem in an inconsistent state, the system will automatically try to repair the problem at boot time. Figure 9-3 shows how the root filesystem on our host was automatically checked and the journal on /dev/mapper/au--mel--ubuntu--1--vg--root was replayed after a crash.

```
Begin: Will now check root file system ... fsck from util-linux 2.27.1
[/sbin/fsck.ext4 (1) -- /dev/mapper/au--mel--ubuntu--1--vg-root] fsck.ext4 -f -a
 -C0 /dev/mapper/au--mel--ubuntu--1--vg-root
/dev/mapper/au--mel--ubuntu--1--vg-root: recovering journal
/dev/mapper/au--mel--ubuntu--1--vg-root: Clearing orphaned inode 20049 (uid=0, g
id=0, mode=0100666, size=0)
/dev/mapper/au--mel--ubuntu--1--vg-root: Clearing orphaned inode 20048 (uid=107,
 gid=111, mode=0100600, size=0)
/dev/mapper/au--mel--ubuntu--1--vg-root: Clearing orphaned inode 20047 (uid=107,
 gid=111, mode=0100600, size=0)
/dev/mapper/au--mel--ubuntu--1--vg-root: Clearing orphaned inode 5052 (uid=107,
gid=111, mode=0100600, size=0)
/dev/mapper/au--mel--ubuntu--1--vg-root: Clearing orphaned inode 5051 (uid=107,
gid=111, mode=0100600, size=0)
/dev/mapper/au--mel--ubuntu--1--vg-root: Clearing orphaned inode 2239 (uid=107,
gid=111, mode=0100600, size=0)
/dev/mapper/au--mel--ubuntu--1--vg-root: |=                            /   5.3%
```

Figure 9-3. *Automatic filesystem recovery*

While we don't recommend it, you can force your system to run a fsck on boot by adding fsck. mode=force to the kernel at boot, either permanently by editing grub or once off by interrupting the boot and adding it via the grub console. The fsck can take a substantial amount of time, depending on the size of your filesystem—up to hours! These automated recoveries will generally work, but on occasion the repair tools will find a problem they cannot fix automatically.

If this happens for the root filesystem, on which the repair utilities are stored, you can try to use the systemd emergency target (systemctl emergency) or you will need to boot from your installation DVD or USB. You may remember from Chapter 2, booting from the DVD or USB includes an option to boot in rescue or recovery mode. This mode boots to a minimal system running from the installation disk and drops you into a root shell. From this shell, you can then perform any steps needed to recover the filesystems. We explain boot to rescue mode in greater detail shortly.

The simplest step is to run the appropriate filesystem checker. Table 9-7 details the system check and repair tools for the filesystems you are most likely to use.

Table 9-7. *Filesystem Check and Repair Tools*

Filesystem(s)	repair tool
Ext2, ext3 and ext4	e2fsck or its aliases fsck.ext2, fsck.ext3 or fsck.ext4
XFS	xfs_repair
Btrfs	btrfs check --repair <device>

To run these repair tools, you will need to make sure the filesystem you're checking is not mounted for writing. Repairing a filesystem that is mounted in read/write mode is guaranteed to destroy data, as the filesystem will be modified directly by the repair tool without the kernel knowing about it.

To check the filesystem, you pass the appropriate device node name as a parameter to the repair tool.

■ **Note**   When repairing the root filesystem by running a tool from the root filesystem itself, make sure to mount the filesystem read-only first.

Let's take you through a problem with one of our disks. If there is a problem on a filesystem the system will inform you that the filesystem could not be mounted and drop into a maintenance mode, as shown in Figure 9-4.

```
         Activating swap /dev/mapper/au--mel--ubuntu--1--vg-swap_1...
         Starting Network Time Synchronization...
         Starting Update UTMP about System Boot/Shutdown...
[  OK  ] Activated swap /dev/mapper/au--mel--ubuntu--1--vg-swap_1.
[  OK  ] Started Network Time Synchronization.
[  OK  ] Reached target System Time Synchronized.
[  OK  ] Reached target Swap.
[  OK  ] Started Update UTMP about System Boot/Shutdown.
         Starting Update UTMP about System Runlevel Changes...
[  OK  ] Started Update UTMP about System Runlevel Changes.
[  OK  ] Found device /dev/mapper/sda5_crypt.
[  OK  ] Found device /dev/md127.
         Starting File System Check on /dev/md127...
[  OK  ] Started File System Check on /dev/md127.
         Mounting /mnt...
[  OK  ] Mounted /mnt.
[  OK  ] Started LSB: AppArmor initialization.
[  OK  ] Started ifup for enp0s9.
[  OK  ] Started ifup for enp0s8.
         Starting Raise network interfaces...
[  OK  ] Started ifup for enp0s3.
[FAILED] Failed to start Raise network interfaces.
See 'systemctl status networking.service' for details.
[  OK  ] Reached target Network.
[  OK  ] Reached target Network is Online.
         Starting iSCSI initiator daemon (iscsid)...
[  OK  ] Started iSCSI initiator daemon (iscsid).
         Starting Login to default iSCSI targets...
[  OK  ] Started Login to default iSCSI targets.
[  OK  ] Reached target Remote File Systems (Pre).
[  OK  ] Reached target Remote File Systems.
Welcome to emergency mode! After logging in, type "journalctl -xb" to view
system logs, "systemctl reboot" to reboot, "systemctl default" or ^D to
try again to boot into default mode.
Press Enter for maintenance
(or press Control-D to continue):
root@au-mel-ubuntu-1:~# journalctl -xb_
```

Figure 9-4. *A filesystem problem prevents an automatic mount*

You can press enter to access the maintenance mode and on that we are going to look at the journal log (journalctl which is the systemd logging utility). By typing journalctl -xb we access we add more detail to messages (-x) and specify this boot (-b). In Figure 9-5 we see the reason we have stopped our system.

```
Jun 22 22:19:22 au-mel-ubuntu-1 systemd[1]: Mounting /data...
-- Subject: Unit data.mount has begun start-up
-- Defined-By: systemd
-- Support: http://lists.freedesktop.org/mailman/listinfo/systemd-devel
--
-- Unit data.mount has begun starting up.
Jun 22 22:19:22 au-mel-ubuntu-1 kernel: EXT4-fs (sdg1): VFS: Can't find ext4 filesystem
Jun 22 22:19:22 au-mel-ubuntu-1 mount[924]: mount: wrong fs type, bad option, bad superblock on /dev
Jun 22 22:19:22 au-mel-ubuntu-1 mount[924]:        missing codepage or helper program, or other erro
Jun 22 22:19:22 au-mel-ubuntu-1 mount[924]:        In some cases useful info is found in syslog - tr
Jun 22 22:19:22 au-mel-ubuntu-1 mount[924]:        dmesg | tail or so.
Jun 22 22:19:22 au-mel-ubuntu-1 systemd[1]: data.mount: Mount process exited, code=exited status=32
Jun 22 22:19:22 au-mel-ubuntu-1 systemd[1]: Failed to mount /data.
-- Subject: Unit data.mount has failed
-- Defined-By: systemd
-- Support: http://lists.freedesktop.org/mailman/listinfo/systemd-devel
--
-- Unit data.mount has failed.
--
-- The result is failed.
```

Figure 9-5. *Error message on disk mount*

We can see that we have failed to mount /dev/sdg1 on the /data directory. It is saying that it can't find the filesystem. We will exit the journal and we will run the fsck check manually (see Figure 9-6).

```
root@au-mel-ubuntu-1:~# fsck.ext4 -y  /dev/sdg1
e2fsck 1.42.13 (17-May-2015)
ext2fs_open2: Bad magic number in super-block
fsck.ext4: Superblock invalid, trying backup blocks...
/dev/sdg1 was not cleanly unmounted, check forced.
Pass 1: Checking inodes, blocks, and sizes
Pass 2: Checking directory structure
Pass 3: Checking directory connectivity
Pass 4: Checking reference counts
Pass 5: Checking group summary information
Block bitmap differences:  +(32768--33280) +(98304--98816) +(163840--164352) +(229376--229888) +(294
912--295424) +(819200--819712) +(884736--885248) +(1605632--1606144)
Fix? yes


/dev/sdg1: ***** FILE SYSTEM WAS MODIFIED *****
/dev/sdg1: 11/524288 files (0.0% non-contiguous), 70287/2096891 blocks
root@au-mel-ubuntu-1:~#
```

Figure 9-6. *Manually running fsck*

Here the fsck has called e2fsck and attempted to repair the filesystem. We have told it to "assume yes" (-y) to all questions and so it will automatically try to repair your filesystem. We can now reboot our system or continue booting with ctrl-d.

On occasion there is a problem with the superblock for an ext2, ext3, or ext4 filesystem, which means the filesystem-checking tools cannot locate the filesystem metadata they need in order to repair the filesystem. For this reason, these filesystems keep backup superblocks as well. You can use the dumpe2fs tool to display their location on the disk and then specify this location for e2fsck using the -b option (use an alternative superblock), as shown in Listing 9-20.

Listing 9-20. Finding Backup Superblocks

```
$ sudo dumpe2fs /dev/sdg1 | grep Backup
dumpe2fs 1.42.13 (17-May-2015)
Journal backup:              inode blocks
  Backup superblock at 32768, Group descriptors at 32769-32769
  Backup superblock at 98304, Group descriptors at 98305-98305
  Backup superblock at 163840, Group descriptors at 163841-163841
  Backup superblock at 229376, Group descriptors at 229377-229377
  Backup superblock at 294912, Group descriptors at 294913-294913
  Backup superblock at 819200, Group descriptors at 819201-819201
  Backup superblock at 884736, Group descriptors at 884737-884737
  Backup superblock at 1605632, Group descriptors at 1605633-1605633
```

Once you know the location of a backup superblock, you can try running e2fsck and specifying the location of a backup superblock using the -b option.

```
$ sudo e2fsck -b 98304 -y /dev/sdg1
e2fsck 1.42.13 (17-May-2015)
/dev/sdg1 was not cleanly unmounted, check forced.
Pass 1: Checking inodes, blocks, and sizes
Pass 2: Checking directory structure
Pass 3: Checking directory connectivity
Pass 4: Checking reference counts
Pass 5: Checking group summary information

/dev/sdg1: ***** FILE SYSTEM WAS MODIFIED *****
/dev/sdg1: 11/524288 files (0.0% non-contiguous), 70287/2096891 blocks
```

The e2fsck command can now run and repair the filesystem.

If there are problems and file data is found in inodes that e2fsck cannot place, this data will be stored in files in the lost+found directory on the filesystem you're checking. The file name is the inode number that the data is associated with. Although this doesn't tell you which files are no longer where they should be, you can inspect these numbered files manually and get some sense of which data might be missing. If a lot of corruption occurred and there are many hundreds of files in the lost+found directory, it is probably better to restore your data from a backup.

Boot Loader Problems

If a problem occurs with a hard disk, the system may fail to boot altogether because the boot sector was corrupted. In this case, the boot loader cannot be started, and you'll see strange errors on the screen, as we showed you in Chapter 6.

Repairing the boot loader is fairly simple with the Rescue mode on the installation media. If you need to re-install your boot loader because of some issue you can use your installation media (DVD, USB) and enter the rescue section (see Figure 9-7).

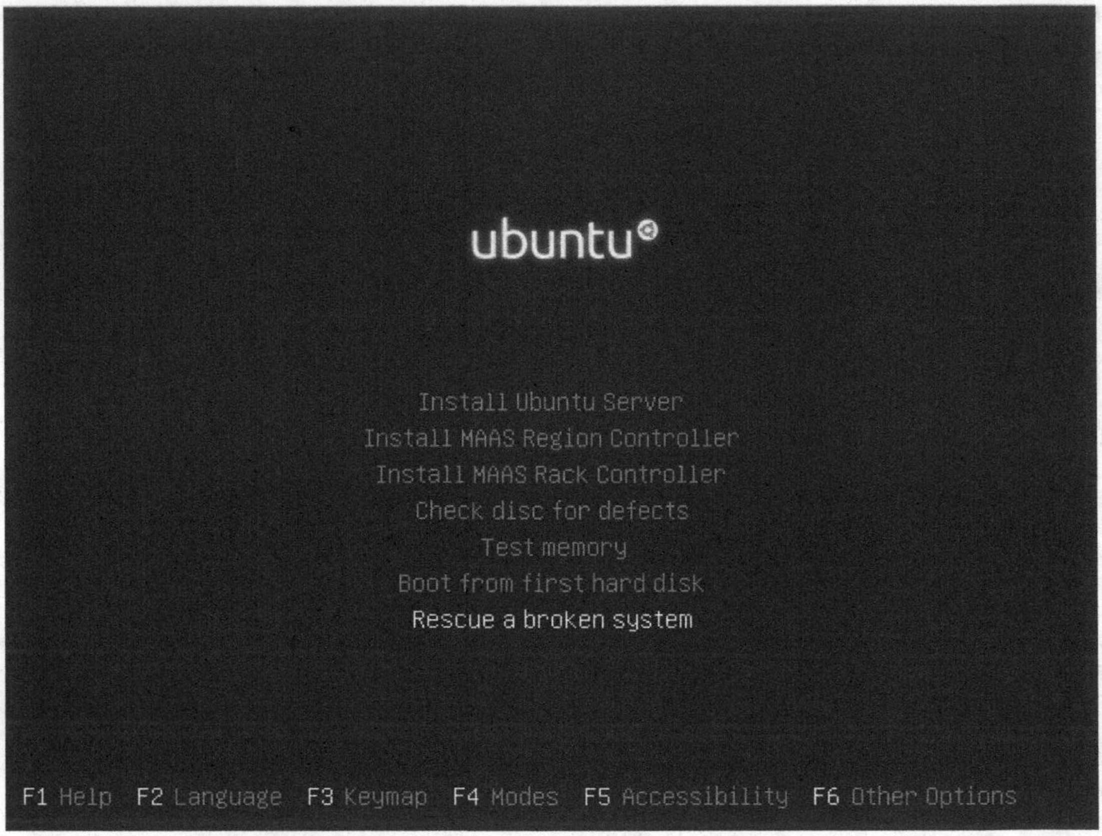

Figure 9-7. *Enter Rescue Mode*

From there we are taken through a similar installation process like the one we executed when we first installed out system, and note, this is an Ubuntu system. The CentOS procedure for entering the Rescue mode is fairly similar in concept.

The rescue process will eventually do a scan of your disks and present you with a list of possible root partitions you can choose to mount. On this Ubuntu system our root partition is similar to the one shown in Figure 9-8:

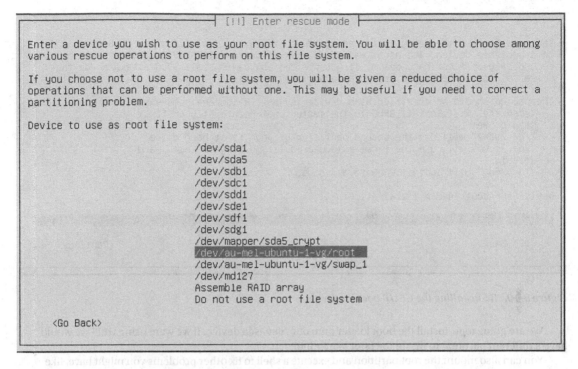

Figure 9-8. *Selecting the root partition to mount*

Our root partition is the LVM volume *au-mel-ubuntu-1-vg/root*. We select that and then we are taken to the rescue menu as in Figure 9-9.

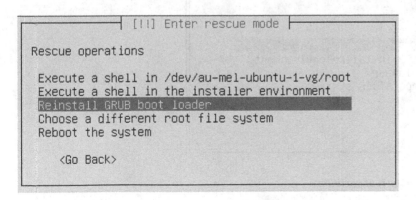

Figure 9-9. *The rescue menu*

We have selected the *Reinstall GRUB boot loader* and on entering that we are presented with the next screen to select the disk we wish to install GRUB on (see Figure 9-10).

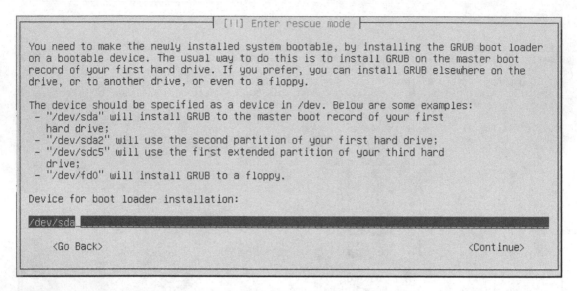

```
┤ [!!] Enter rescue mode ├

You need to make the newly installed system bootable, by installing the GRUB boot loader
on a bootable device. The usual way to do this is to install GRUB on the master boot
record of your first hard drive. If you prefer, you can install GRUB elsewhere on the
drive, or to another drive, or even to a floppy.

The device should be specified as a device in /dev. Below are some examples:
 - "/dev/sda" will install GRUB to the master boot record of your first
   hard drive;
 - "/dev/sda2" will use the second partition of your first hard drive;
 - "/dev/sdc5" will use the first extended partition of your third hard
   drive;
 - "/dev/fd0" will install GRUB to a floppy.

Device for boot loader installation:

/dev/sda

    <Go Back>                                                        <Continue>
```

Figure 9-10. *Re-installing the GRUB boot loader*

We are going to re-install the boot loader onto our /dev/sda device. If we were using UEFI we would have a different partition to install the boot loader into.

You can also mount the root partition and execute a shell to fix other problems you might have, like execute other types of disk repair and maintenance.

You do that by choosing the following from the Rescue menu shown in Figure 9-11:

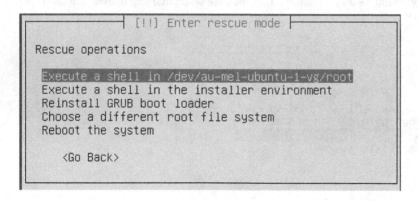

```
┤ [!!] Enter rescue mode ├

Rescue operations

 Execute a shell in /dev/au-mel-ubuntu-1-vg/root
 Execute a shell in the installer environment
 Reinstall GRUB boot loader
 Choose a different root file system
 Reboot the system

    <Go Back>
```

Figure 9-11. *Opening a shell on the root partition*

This asks us a few questions and tells us what it is doing (see Figure 9-12).

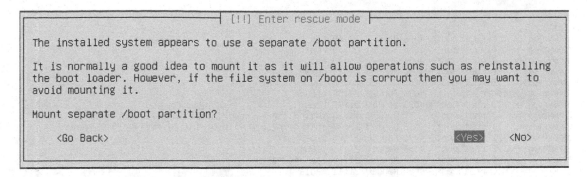

Figure 9-12. Mount /boot?

Like it says, your separate boot partition may be corrupt and you may not want to mount it at this time. Instead you may want to leave unmounted and then run e2fsck against it to do any repairs. In this case we will mount our /boot partition though.

Figure 9-13 is informational and says that there may be other partitions that you need to mount, if you have partitions mounted into other areas of your filesystem. You can continue on here and take whatever action is necessary to mount any partitions.

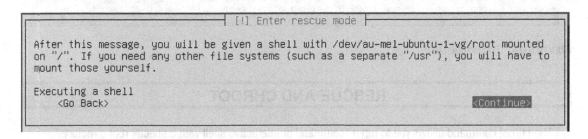

Figure 9-13. Information about other mounts

Now we have the rescue shell (see Figure 9-14). It is your system that been specially mounted via chroot. A chroot is a special mount we explain shortly.

```
# ls -l
total 93
drwxr-xr-x    2 root root   4096 May 15 22:59 bin
drwxr-xr-x    4 root root   1024 Jun 21 00:00 boot
drwxr-xr-x    2 root root   4096 Jun 22 21:43 data
drwxr-xr-x    2 root root   4096 Jun 20 21:17 data2
drwxr-xr-x   15 root root   4360 Jun 23 00:06 dev
drwxr-xr-x  100 root root   4096 Jun 22 22:55 etc
drwxr-xr-x    3 root root   4096 May 10 21:56 home
lrwxrwxrwx    1 root root     32 Jun 13 11:20 initrd.img -> boot/initrd.img-4.4.0-24-generic
lrwxrwxrwx    1 root root     32 May 10 22:07 initrd.img.old -> boot/initrd.img-4.4.0-22-generic
drwxr-xr-x   22 root root   4096 May 16 21:58 lib
drwxr-xr-x    2 root root   4096 May 10 21:11 lib64
drwx------    2 root root  16384 May 10 21:11 lost+found
drwxr-xr-x    3 root root   4096 May 10 21:11 media
drwxr-xr-x    4 root root   4096 Jun 19 19:03 mnt
drwxr-xr-x    2 root root   4096 Apr 21 08:08 opt
dr-xr-xr-x  158 root root      0 Jun 23 2016 proc
drwx------    3 root root   4096 Jun 22 23:21 root
drwxr-xr-x    8 root root    160 Jun 23 00:08 run
drwxr-xr-x    2 root root  12288 Jun 21 00:00 sbin
drwxr-xr-x    2 root root   4096 Apr 20 00:31 snap
drwxr-xr-x    3 root root   4096 Jun 20 22:11 srv
dr-xr-xr-x   13 root root      0 Jun 23 00:03 sys
drwxrwxrwt    8 root root   4096 Jun 23 00:10 tmp
drwxr-xr-x   10 root root   4096 May 10 21:11 usr
drwxr-xr-x   14 root root   4096 May 10 21:54 var
lrwxrwxrwx    1 root root     29 Jun 13 11:20 vmlinuz -> boot/vmlinuz-4.4.0-24-generic
lrwxrwxrwx    1 root root     29 May 10 22:07 vmlinuz.old -> boot/vmlinuz-4.4.0-22-generic
#
```

Figure 9-14. *The rescue shell*

RESCUE AND CHROOT

The chroot command allows you to run a "command or interactive shell with a special root directory." When we run in rescue mode we are first mounting our disks and then using chroot to change into the root directory on our mounted devices. This allows us access to all the data and commands on our system as if we had booted into it.

When using the rescue mode, you can enter the "installer environment" instead and set up the chroot environment yourself. Before we run chroot, we need to make sure we can access the device files and kernel interfaces via the dynamic /dev and /proc filesystems. We can mount the existing ones on the root filesystem on which we will run chroot via a bind mount. A *bind mount* is a way of making a directory available in multiple locations on the system, without needing to use symbolic links. In this case, we can't use symbolic links, as they would point to a target outside the chroot, which is not accessible from inside the chroot itself.

```
# mount -o bind /dev /mnt/dev
# mount -o bind /proc /mnt/proc
```

When the bind mounts are done, we can `chroot` to the mounted root filesystem and run a Bash shell there. The prompt will look somewhat odd, as the Bash startup scripts will not be run.

```
# chroot /mnt && /bin/bash
bash-2 #
```

Now that we have a shell, we can run the command to reinstall the boot loader on the first disk.

```
bash-2 # /usr/bin/grub-install /dev/sda
```

When that is done, we log out from the `chroot` and unmount the filesystems in reverse order. If we don't unmount these, our fixed root filesystem cannot be unmounted, and a check will be forced again when we next boot up.

```
bash-2 # exit
# umount /mnt/proc
# umount /mnt/dev
# umount /mnt
```

We can now reboot the host using Ctrl+Alt+Delete, the `reboot` command, or the `shutdown -r now` command. Remove the installation media, so the host boots from hard disk.

For more on chroot, see `www.cyberciti.biz/faq/unix-linux-chroot-command-examples-usage-syntax/`.

Disk Failure

Sooner or later one of your hard disks will fail. When you're using RAID, this is no longer a problem, but you will need to take action to ensure the array is fully working again before the next disk fails. As you've seen earlier in this chapter, you can keep a disk marked as a spare, and that automates part of this process.

To simulate a disk failure, we'll use `mdadm` to tell the kernel that `/dev/sdb1` has failed, as shown in Listing 9-21.

Listing 9-21. Testing Our RAID Array

```
$ sudo mdadm --manage /dev/md127 --fail /dev/sdd1
mdadm: set /dev/sdd1 faulty in /dev/md127
```

The RAID subsystem now knows the device has failed. This is identical to what happens when the RAID drivers detect that an error has occurred on one of the devices in the array. Let's have another look at the `/proc/mdstat` file.

```
$ cat /proc/mdstat
Personalities : [raid6] [raid5] [raid4] [linear] [multipath] [raid0] [raid1] [raid10]
md127 : active raid5 sdc1[1] sde1[3] sdb1[0] sdf1[5] sdd1[4](F)
      25148928 blocks super 1.2 level 5, 512k chunk, algorithm 2 [4/3] [UU_U]
      [======>..............]  recovery = 34.0% (2852268/8382976) finish=2.3min
speed=39764K/sec

unused devices: <none>
```

The sdd1 disk is now marked as failed with (F), and sdf1, which was our spare disk, is being brought up to date. We can check the system log to make sure the RAID monitor has picked up on these changes and acted appropriately. We can use the journalctl -xb command to see any messages.

```
Jun 23 01:06:01 au-mel-ubuntu-1 kernel: md/raid:md127: Disk failure on sdd1, disabling
device.
                                        md/raid:md127: Operation continuing on 3 devices.
Jun 23 01:06:01 au-mel-ubuntu-1 kernel: RAID conf printout:
Jun 23 01:06:01 au-mel-ubuntu-1 kernel:  --- level:5 rd:4 wd:3
Jun 23 01:06:01 au-mel-ubuntu-1 kernel:  disk 0, o:1, dev:sdb1
Jun 23 01:06:01 au-mel-ubuntu-1 kernel:  disk 1, o:1, dev:sdc1
Jun 23 01:06:01 au-mel-ubuntu-1 kernel:  disk 2, o:0, dev:sdd1
Jun 23 01:06:01 au-mel-ubuntu-1 kernel:  disk 3, o:1, dev:sdf1
Jun 23 01:06:01 au-mel-ubuntu-1 kernel: RAID conf printout:
Jun 23 01:06:01 au-mel-ubuntu-1 kernel:  --- level:5 rd:4 wd:3
Jun 23 01:06:01 au-mel-ubuntu-1 kernel:  disk 0, o:1, dev:sdb1
Jun 23 01:06:01 au-mel-ubuntu-1 kernel:  disk 1, o:1, dev:sdc1
Jun 23 01:06:01 au-mel-ubuntu-1 kernel:  disk 3, o:1, dev:sdf1
Jun 23 01:06:01 au-mel-ubuntu-1 kernel: RAID conf printout:
Jun 23 01:06:01 au-mel-ubuntu-1 kernel:  --- level:5 rd:4 wd:3
Jun 23 01:06:01 au-mel-ubuntu-1 kernel:  disk 0, o:1, dev:sdb1
Jun 23 01:06:01 au-mel-ubuntu-1 kernel:  disk 1, o:1, dev:sdc1
Jun 23 01:06:01 au-mel-ubuntu-1 kernel:  disk 2, o:1, dev:sde1
Jun 23 01:06:01 au-mel-ubuntu-1 kernel:  disk 3, o:1, dev:sdf1
Jun 23 01:06:01 au-mel-ubuntu-1 kernel: md: recovery of RAID array md127
Jun 23 01:06:01 au-mel-ubuntu-1 kernel: md: minimum _guaranteed_  speed: 1000 KB/sec/disk.
Jun 23 01:06:01 au-mel-ubuntu-1 kernel: md: using maximum available idle IO bandwidth (but
not more than 200000 KB/sec) for recovery.
Jun 23 01:06:01 au-mel-ubuntu-1 kernel: md: using 128k window, over a total of 8382976k.
```

After the rebuild has complete we should see something similar to this:

```
Jun 23 01:09:21 au-mel-ubuntu-1 kernel: md: md127: recovery done.
Jun 23 01:09:21 au-mel-ubuntu-1 kernel: RAID conf printout:
Jun 23 01:09:21 au-mel-ubuntu-1 kernel:  --- level:5 rd:4 wd:4
Jun 23 01:09:21 au-mel-ubuntu-1 kernel:  disk 0, o:1, dev:sdb1
Jun 23 01:09:21 au-mel-ubuntu-1 kernel:  disk 1, o:1, dev:sdc1
Jun 23 01:09:21 au-mel-ubuntu-1 kernel:  disk 2, o:1, dev:sde1
Jun 23 01:09:21 au-mel-ubuntu-1 kernel:  disk 3, o:1, dev:sdf1
Jun 23 01:09:21 au-mel-ubuntu-1 mdadm[1341]: RebuildFinished event detected on md device
/dev/md127
Jun 23 01:09:21 au-mel-ubuntu-1 mdadm[1341]: SpareActive event detected on md device
/dev/md127, component device /dev/sde1
```

Great! The monitor has picked up on the failure, activated the spare, started the rebuild, and completed rebuilding the array. The RAID system has acted to preserve our data and the array is still intact. All that's left for us to do is remove the failed disk from the array and then replace it.

First, we'll invoke mdadm to remove the failed disk from the RAID array.

```
$ sudo mdadm --manage /dev/md127 --remove /dev/sdd1
mdadm: hot removed /dev/sdd1
```

The next step depends on your hard disk controller. If it supports hot-swapping of drives, you could unplug the broken disk and replace it with a new one. If not, you will have to shut down the host to physically replace the drive.

When you've installed the new drive and started the host, you will need to partition the new disk as you have the other disks in the array. The new disk will likely have the same device node name as the disk it replaces. When partitioning is done, you can add the new partition to the array via mdadm, as shown in Listing 9-22.

Listing 9-22. Adding a New Device to a RAID Array

```
$ sudo mdadm --manage /dev/md127 --add /dev/sdd1
mdadm: added /dev/sdd1
$ cat /proc/mdstat
Personalities : [raid6] [raid5] [raid4] [linear] [multipath] [raid0] [raid1] [raid10]
md127 : active raid5 sdd1[4](S) sde1[6] sdc1[1] sdb1[0] sdf1[5]
      25148928 blocks super 1.2 level 5, 512k chunk, algorithm 2 [4/4] [UUUU]

unused devices: <none>
```

The new disk was added as the spare, ready to take over if another disk fails.

It's possible that a problem might prevent a RAID array from automatically starting. If you are booting in rescue mode from DVD or USB, the array will likely not be detected and started either. If this happens, you can manually assemble the array. To re-create a RAID array from existing components, use mdadm in assemble mode. This will try to assemble the array from the components you specify. Check the mdadm manual page for more information.

Summary

In this chapter, you learned how to manage storage on Linux and how you can most securely and flexibly store your data by making use of RAID and LVM.

- We explored the different filesystems that come with Ubuntu and CentOS

- We looked at ext4, XFS

- We saw how to create Btrfs RAID volumes and subvolumes

- We looked at mounting and auto mounting partitions

- We learned how to set up software RAID

- We looked at LVM, and resized volumes and filesystems.

- In case of disk failure, you now know how to remove components from and add components to a RAID array

- Now you can repair basic filesystem errors.

In Chapter 10, we will show you how set up infrastructure services such as an SSH server, discuss how to manage the time on your hosts using NTP (Network Time Protocol), and introduce DNS (Domain Name System) and DHCP (Dynamic Host Configuration Protocol).

PART II

■ ■ ■

Making Linux Work for You

CHAPTER 10

■ ■ ■

Infrastructure Services: NTP, DNS, DHCP, and SSH

By Peter Lieverdink and Dennis Matotek

In the previous chapters, you installed your host and got to know your way around it. You then learned how to add and configure storage hardware. Now it's time to look at how to make the software work for you. In this chapter, we will cover the infrastructure services that help you manage the basics of your network.

We'll first describe how to keep the time on your systems synchronized, which is important because a lot of applications rely on your host having the correct time. In the process, we'll introduce you to the Network Time Protocol (NTP).

We'll also cover the Domain Name System (DNS), which is the glue that allows networks like the Internet to function by allowing hosts to find one another. We'll detail the components of DNS and how to set up and manage a DNS server.

We'll then discuss the Dynamic Host Configuration Protocol (DHCP), which is used to assign addresses and network configuration to your hosts. Using DHCP means you don't have to configure individual network settings for clients in your network; rather, this can be automatically provided. You'll learn about how to use DHCP and how to set up address allocation and pass network configuration information to your hosts.

■ **Note**   We'll look at other ways to automatically configure hosts in Chapter 19.

Finally, we'll expand on the Secure Shell (SSH) service and show you how to easily access hosts and how to transfer files between hosts using SSH.

Keeping Time

Of course, having systems keep time is very important. Imagine having your Linux host powering your solid rocket boosters were out of sync with your main thrusters? When you timed both to burn you could be seconds to minutes out of sync. In the more mundane world imagine the horror of database transactions having incorrect timestamps! I don't even want to think about it.

Let's look at keeping time, or at least our server with the same relative time. The general-purpose tool for keeping time is NTP which you will find on many systems. On Red Hat-derived systems you find Chrony.

© Dennis Matotek, James Turnbull and Peter Lieverdink 2017
D. Matotek et al., *Pro Linux System Administration*, DOI 10.1007/978-1-4842-2008-5_10

Time with timedatectl

We would like to show you how to manage time on your Linux server with the `timedatactl` command. This comes as part of the systemd system. With it we can do the following:

- Set the current time

- Set the date

- Set the time zone

First let's look at the current status:

```
$ sudo timedatectl status
      Local time: Fri 2016-09-30 21:22:26 EDT
  Universal time: Sat 2016-10-01 01:22:26 UTC
        RTC time: Fri 2016-09-30 18:06:27
       Time zone: America/New_York (EDT, -0400)
     NTP enabled: yes
NTP synchronized: yes
 RTC in local TZ: no
      DST active: yes
 Last DST change: DST began at
                  Sun 2016-03-13 01:59:59 EST
                  Sun 2016-03-13 03:00:00 EDT
 Next DST change: DST ends (the clock jumps one hour backwards) at
                  Sun 2016-11-06 01:59:59 EDT
                  Sun 2016-11-06 01:00:00 EST
```

There we have our current time and date status. You can see the local time, UTC (Coordinated Universal Time), time zone, and daylight saving information.

You can see from that information that our time zone is set to New York. Let's demonstrate how to change that to our local time zone.

First we are going to list the time zones, but because the result is a very long list we are going to use grep to return only the result for Melbourne.

```
$ timedatectl list-timezones |grep Melb
Australia/Melbourne
```

Now to set the time zone we issue the following:

```
$ sudo timedatectl set-timezone Australia/Melbourne
```

Now when we check our status we have the correct time zone set.

```
$ timedatectl status
      Local time: Sat 2016-10-01 11:29:01 AEST
  Universal time: Sat 2016-10-01 01:29:01 UTC
        RTC time: Fri 2016-09-30 18:13:03
       Time zone: Australia/Melbourne (AEST, +1000)
     NTP enabled: yes
```

You can use the timedatectl --help option to list more options. For example, to set the system time you would issue timedatectl set-time. Managing your time with `timedatectl` is very easy. Let's move on to how we manage keeping your hosts time in sync with world clocks automatically.

Network Time Protocol

We'll start by showing you how to keep all system clocks on your hosts synchronized. Though this might seem a trivial issue, having system clocks match means your log entries will all carry consistent timestamps. This in turn means you can easily correlate log entries from different hosts, should the need arise. Synchronized system clocks are also a prerequisite for the functionality we'll be enabling later. You can't simply rely on your host's motherboard's onboard clocks, as their quality varies a lot and some can run out of sync by as much as several minutes each day.

We have explained a little about NTP already in Chapter 2. Time services are provided by a service called the Network Time Protocol. NTP servers provide synchronization services to a client that connects to them, and they also synchronize themselves with upstream time servers. The layers in this model are called *strata*, with the highest level, stratum 0, consisting of dedicated time hardware such as atomic clocks or satellite receivers. Servers connected to these stratum 0 time sources are called stratum 1 servers. Servers that synchronize off stratum 1 servers are stratum 2 servers, and so on.

■ **Note**   You can read more about NTP strata at http://www.akadia.com/services/ntp_synchronize.html.

You can make use of NTP servers in two ways. One is by running a client utility called ntpdate that synchronizes the system clock each time you run it. The other is to run an NTP service that automatically synchronizes whenever the system clock runs too far out of sync with the actual time. A lot of systems actually use both methods. If the system clock and atomic time differ too much, it can take a while for a system to synchronize with an upstream time server. To overcome this, the ntpdate utility is invoked and the clock is synchronized before the NTP service is started.

Let's have a look at the ntpdate utility first. On both CentOS and Ubuntu it is provided by the ntpdate package. To update the system time, run the utility with the upstream server address as the only command-line parameter. It needs to be run as root, in order to be able to update the system clock.

```
$ sudo ntpdate pool.ntp.org
24 Jun 21:25:35 ntpdate[1565]: step time server 220.233.156.30 offset 1.810551 sec
```

■ **Note**   If you already have an ntpd daemon running, the ntpdate command will fail with a message similar to this: "24 Jun 23:53:05 ntpdate[22609]: the NTP socket is in use, exiting." You can use systemctl ntpd stop and try again.

The ntpdate utility connected to one of the pool.ntp.org servers and adjusted our system time by 1.810551 seconds. There are two effect ways to make sure the system clock remains synchronized, you can add an entry in /etc/crontab that runs ntpdate once, say, every two hours. Or you can use the more effective and accurate ntp daemon.

If you are going to use the cron method, you should redirect standard input and standard output to /dev/null, so you don't receive twice-hourly e-mails.

```
0 */2 * * *    root    /usr/sbin/ntpdate pool.ntp.org > /dev/null 2>&1
```

However, you'd need to install and maintain such a crontab entry on each of your hosts, and even then, depending on the quality of the hardware, the system clock can skew quite a lot over the course of two hours. You can ensure that the system clock is adjusted whenever it attempts to run out of sync by installing and running an NTP daemon on your host. This will keep your host synchronized and also allow you to use it to synchronize other hosts on your network.

The NTP daemon and some associated utilities are provided by the ntp package. You need to install it via yum install ntp on CentOS or sudo aptitude install ntp on Ubuntu. However each distribution has a slightly different ntp.conf file and we will show you the Ubuntu version. When it starts, the ntpd service will read its options from the /etc/ntp.conf file and listen on UDP port 123. When you look at this configuration file, you can see it consists of two main sections: first is the actual time source configuration and second is the authorization configuration. We'll start with the reporting and time source configuration as shown in Listing 10-1.

Listing 10-1. ntp.conf

```
# /etc/ntp.conf, configuration for ntpd; see ntp.conf(5) for help

driftfile /var/lib/ntp/ntp.drift

# Enable this if you want statistics to be logged.
#statsdir /var/log/ntpstats/

statistics loopstats peerstats clockstats
filegen loopstats file loopstats type day enable
filegen peerstats file peerstats type day enable
filegen clockstats file clockstats type day enable

# Specify one or more NTP servers.

# Use servers from the NTP Pool Project. Approved by Ubuntu Technical Board
# on 2011-02-08 (LP: #104525). See http://www.pool.ntp.org/join.html for
# more information.
pool 0.ubuntu.pool.ntp.org iburst
pool 1.ubuntu.pool.ntp.org iburst
pool 2.ubuntu.pool.ntp.org iburst
pool 3.ubuntu.pool.ntp.org iburst

# Use Ubuntu's ntp server as a fallback.
pool ntp.ubuntu.com
```

The driftfile directive gives the server a place to store information about the idiosyncrasies of your local system clock. It stores the clock frequency offset every hour, depending on the tolerance of drift, and uses this information when the daemon is started. If the file is not there it sets the frequency offset to zero. Over time, it will use this information to report the time more precisely between synchronization attempts, as the daemon knows how the local clock behaves.

Statistics reporting is not enabled by default, as the statsdir option is not enabled. However, if you were to uncomment that line, the next directive, statistics, would enable loopstats, peerstats, and clockstats reporting to files in /var/log/ntpstats.

loopstats collects information on the updates made to the local clock by the ntpd server. peerstats logs information about all peers—upstream servers as well as clients that use your server to synchronize. Finally, clockstats writes statistical information about the local clock to the log file.

The filegen directive tells the daemon which file you want this statistical information written to and how often the file needs to be changed. In our example, a new version of each of these files is created each day due to the type day directive.

Finally, the `pool` option tells `ntpd` which upstream servers to use for synchronization. To make sure your host stays in sync, it is generally a good idea to add multiple server directives with multiple different servers. You can specify individual time servers with the `server` option or a `pool` of servers as we have done here. The `iburst` option tells ntp to send an extra eight packets if it doesn't get an initial response, originally for devices like modems and ISDN that can be slow in establishing connections. We'll explain more about the pool.ntp.org servers in a moment.

First let's quickly look at the next section in the `/etc/ntp.conf` file, which defines which hosts may access your NTP server. On CentOS, this section is listed at the top of the file, as you can see in Listing 10-2.

Listing 10-2. Access Control in `ntp.conf`

```
# By default, exchange time with everybody, but don't allow configuration.
restrict -4 default kod notrap nomodify nopeer noquery limited
restrict -6 default kod notrap nomodify nopeer noquery limited

# Local users may interrogate the ntp server more closely.
restrict 127.0.0.1
restrict ::1

# Needed for adding pool entries
restrict source notrap nomodify noquery
```

The `restrict` keyword is used to define access classes. The same access levels are defined for IPv4 and IPv6 clients here, by using the -4 and -6 parameters.

`default` is a wildcard keyword that matches all possible addresses. Kod, "kiss-of-death" is used to slow down clients that exceed a defined rate limit, by sending a special response packet. These limits are defined with the `discard` option, and since we haven't defined such limits, it's not used here. `notrap` rejects any control packets that get sent, while `nomodify` disallows attempts to modify the time on the server. `nopeer` ensures your server doesn't start using a connecting client as an upstream NTP server. The `noquery` prevents your server from being queried for peer and other statistics. Finally, `limited` is used to deny the time service if packets violate the limit set in the `discard` option.

The second set of `restrict` directives ensures that connections from the local machine, 127.0.0.1 (IPv4) and ::1(IPv6), can interrogate and reconfigure the NTP server. None of these prevent a client from synchronizing with your NTP server, though.

The last set of restrict directives allow for the pool server to become peers, meaning we can query them for time information.

```
restrict source notrap nomodify noquery
```

Here the `source` refers to the the pool servers and you will notice that `nopeer` is not set but the other restricts are still in place.

You can further restrict your ntp servers by using cryptographic keys to ensure that only servers that can participate in exchanging public key encrypted packets can use your ntp services. It is uncommon in most scenarios and impossible when using the pool.ntp.org servers. If you would like more information, please see `www.ntp.org/ntpfaq/NTP-s-algo-crypt.htm`.

■ **Note** You can find more information on NTP configuration and access control here: `http://doc.ntp.org/ 4.1.1/confopt.htm`.

The Global NTP Server Pool

Many organizations run their own time servers and make them accessible to third parties. Microsoft and Apple run time servers that are used by default by their respective operating systems, and many Linux vendors do the same.

However, when you want to add extra servers (using the server configuration) to your own ntp.conf file, you will need to know their addresses. Luckily, there is an open source project that aims to provide a pool of local NTP servers for all continents. This project is called pool.ntp.org, and the participants are individual users and organizations that allow third parties to use their servers for synchronization.

The project provides DNS-based groups for various server strata and geographical locations—for instance, 1.pool.ntp.org is provided by stratum 1 servers, au.pool.ntp.org contains only servers located in Australia, and us.pool.ntp.org is provided by servers located in the United States. By adding a selection of pool.ntp.org servers, you are assured of always having up-to-date and nearby servers available for synchronization.

■ **Note** You can read more about the project and join the pool at www.pool.ntp.org/.

Using the host command, we are going to see what 0.ubuntu.pool.ntp.org will return as shown in Listing 10-3. Listing 10-3 showspossible servers our ntpd daemon will try to synchronize against.

Listing 10-3. Ubuntu ntp Pool Servers

```
$ host 0.ubuntu.pool.ntp.org
0.ubuntu.pool.ntp.org has address 129.250.35.250
0.ubuntu.pool.ntp.org has address 129.250.35.251
0.ubuntu.pool.ntp.org has address 27.124.125.252
0.ubuntu.pool.ntp.org has address 121.0.0.41
```

Compare that with what is returned from CentOS's 0.centos.pool.ntp.org.

```
$ host 0.centos.pool.ntp.org
0.centos.pool.ntp.org has address 27.124.125.252
0.centos.pool.ntp.org has address 121.0.0.41
0.centos.pool.ntp.org has address 129.250.35.250
0.centos.pool.ntp.org has address 129.250.35.251
```

Hey look, they contain the same servers. And what if we looked at 0.au.pool.ntp.org

```
$ host 0.au.pool.ntp.org
0.au.pool.ntp.org has address 129.250.35.251
0.au.pool.ntp.org has address 27.124.125.252
0.au.pool.ntp.org has address 121.0.0.41
0.au.pool.ntp.org has address 129.250.35.250
```

Well isn't that interesting. You should test the results from 0.us.pool.ntp.org and see what you get. It is a common practice to set your local network hosts to two or three local ntp servers, which then synchronize with servers from the ntp pool.

If you choose to change these settings, your ntp.conf can restart the NTP server with sudo service ntp restart on Ubuntu or sudo systemctl restart ntpd on CentOS. The server writes any status updates to the system logger; you can find them in /var/log/syslog on Ubuntu or in /var/log/messages on CentOS. Listing 10-4 shows you the output of a server that is started and then synchronizes with upstream servers.

Listing 10-4. ntpd Status in the Ubuntu System Log

```
Jun 25 09:07:00 ubuntu ntp[13644]:  * Starting NTP server ntpd
Jun 25 09:07:00 ubuntu ntpd[13653]: ntpd 4.2.8p4@1.3265-o Fri Apr  8 20:58:07 UTC 2016 (1):
Starting
Jun 25 09:07:00 ubuntu ntpd[13653]: Command line: /usr/sbin/ntpd -p /var/run/ntpd.pid -g -u
112:116
Jun 25 09:07:00 ubuntu ntp[13644]:    ...done.
Jun 25 09:07:00 ubuntu systemd[1]: Started LSB: Start NTP daemon.
Jun 25 09:07:00 ubuntu ntpd[13655]: proto: precision = 0.059 usec (-24)
Jun 25 09:07:00 ubuntu ntpd[13655]: Listen and drop on 0 v6wildcard [::]:123
Jun 25 09:07:00 ubuntu ntpd[13655]: Listen and drop on 1 v4wildcard 0.0.0.0:123
Jun 25 09:07:00 ubuntu ntpd[13655]: Listen normally on 2 lo 127.0.0.1:123
Jun 25 09:07:00 ubuntu ntpd[13655]: Listen normally on 3 enp0s3 10.0.2.15:123
Jun 25 09:07:00 ubuntu ntpd[13655]: Listen normally on 4 lo [::1]:123
Jun 25 09:07:00 ubuntu ntpd[13655]: Listen normally on 5 enp0s3 [fe80::ff:86ff:fe2d:
ca23%2]:123
Jun 25 09:07:00 ubuntu ntpd[13655]: Listening on routing socket on fd #22 for interface
updates
Jun 25 09:07:01 ubuntu ntpd[13655]: Soliciting pool server 203.122.222.45
Jun 25 09:07:02 ubuntu ntpd[13655]: Soliciting pool server 27.124.125.251
Jun 25 09:07:02 ubuntu ntpd[13655]: Soliciting pool server 103.51.68.133
Jun 25 09:07:03 ubuntu ntpd[13655]: Soliciting pool server 130.102.128.23
Jun 25 09:07:03 ubuntu ntpd[13655]: Soliciting pool server 150.101.217.196
Jun 25 09:07:03 ubuntu ntpd[13655]: Soliciting pool server 121.0.0.41
Jun 25 09:07:04 ubuntu ntpd[13655]: Soliciting pool server 121.0.0.42
Jun 25 09:07:04 ubuntu ntpd[13655]: Soliciting pool server 202.127.210.36
Jun 25 09:07:04 ubuntu ntpd[13655]: Soliciting pool server 202.127.210.37
Jun 25 09:07:04 ubuntu ntpd[13655]: Soliciting pool server 200.160.7.186
```

We can also verify that our host is synchronized by querying the NTP server from the local host via the ntpq command, as shown in Listing 10-4. We use the -p option to list any peers we are connected to and the -4 option to resolve the hostname to an IPv4 address.

In Figure 10-1 you can see the output of our peer listing. The remote host starting with a '*' is the current time source and those with a '+' are hosts that have been selected to be used in the final set for the weighted average computation (do you remember that from Chapter 2?); those with a '-' have been discarded. The st column is the server stratum and we are peered to both stratum 1 and 2 servers via the Ubuntu stratum 16 servers (you shouldn't need to peer to any peer 1 stratum servers directly). You can also see other details about the delay, offset, and jitter.

```
ubuntu@au-mel-ubuntu-1:~$ sudo ntpq -p localhost -4
     remote         refid        st t when poll reach   delay   offset  jitter
==============================================================================
 0.ubuntu.pool.n .POOL.         16 p    -   64    0    0.000    0.000   0.000
 1.ubuntu.pool.n .POOL.         16 p    -   64    0    0.000    0.000   0.000
 2.ubuntu.pool.n .POOL.         16 p    -   64    0    0.000    0.000   0.000
 3.ubuntu.pool.n .POOL.         16 p    -   64    0    0.000    0.000   0.000
 ntp.ubuntu.com  .POOL.         16 p    -   64    0    0.000    0.000   0.000
+mail1.selcomm.c .PPS.           1 u    -   64    1   20.423   -0.822   3.033
 103.38.120.36 ( 223.252.32.9    2 u    -   64    1   24.698   -2.779   3.156
-ntp2.syrahost.c 130.217.226.49  2 u    -   64    1   45.663    0.899   1.596
-saul.foodworks. 130.194.1.96    2 u    1   64    1   21.112    6.213   1.943
*103.38.121.36 ( 203.35.83.242   2 u    1   64    1   22.940   -1.349   1.165
 xx0.nerdboy.net 202.6.131.118   2 u    2   64    1    8.280   -2.211   1.371
+203.122.222.45  17.46.99.204    2 u    -   64    1   16.685   -0.521   1.016
 b.pool.ntp.uq.e 132.163.4.101   2 u    1   64    1   32.970    1.146   1.137
-y.ns.gin.ntt.ne 249.224.99.213  2 u    2   64    1  203.101  -37.461   2.179
-ns2.unico.com.a 59.167.170.228  3 u    1   64    1   20.001   -6.653   1.056
 cachens2.onqnet 44.41.194.74    3 u    -   64    1   30.216   -7.591   0.243
 bisesa.kakaopor 198.60.73.8     2 u    1   64    1  175.623   -0.211   0.458
-golem.canonical 193.79.237.14   2 u   12   64    1  314.144   -0.675   0.000
```

Figure 10-1. *Listing connected peers*

You can now configure the hosts on your network to use the bastion host as their upstream NTP server and you can verify that they work via the ntpq command.

Chrony

Chrony is an alternative to the NTP service daemon that keeps hosts in sync with world clocks. There are several differences between Chrony and NTP in their implementation but both use the same upstream time sources. The main differences between the two implementations are the following:

- Chrony does not support multicast and manycast.
- Chrony is useful in situations where networks are intermittent.
- Chrony works better in congested networks and virtual hosts.

Install and Configure Chrony

Chrony is quick and easy to install and is available on both CentOS and Ubuntu. Let's quickly show how to install and set it up.

Installation is simple via package management on both distributions.

```
$ sudo yum install -y chrony
$ sudo aptitude install -y chrony
```

There is a configuration file placed in /etc/chrony.conf on CentOS and /etc/chrony/chrony.conf on Ubuntu. In that file you will find the public time servers and other settings.

Listing 10-5. /etc/chrony.conf from CentOS

```
# Use public servers from the pool.ntp.org project.
# Please consider joining the pool (http://www.pool.ntp.org/join.html).
server 0.centos.pool.ntp.org iburst
server 1.centos.pool.ntp.org iburst
server 2.centos.pool.ntp.org iburst
server 3.centos.pool.ntp.org iburst

# Ignore stratum in source selection.
stratumweight 0

# Record the rate at which the system clock gains/losses time.
driftfile /var/lib/chrony/drift

# Enable kernel RTC synchronization.
rtcsync

# In first three updates step the system clock instead of slew
# if the adjustment is larger than 10 seconds.
makestep 10 3

# Allow NTP client access from local network.
#allow 192.168/16

# Listen for commands only on localhost.
bindcmdaddress 127.0.0.1
bindcmdaddress ::1

# Serve time even if not synchronized to any NTP server.
#local stratum 10

keyfile /etc/chrony.keys

# Specify the key used as password for chronyc.
commandkey 1

# Generate command key if missing.
generatecommandkey

# Disable logging of client accesses.
noclientlog

# Send a message to syslog if a clock adjustment is larger than 0.5 seconds.
logchange 0.5

logdir /var/log/chrony
#log measurements statistics tracking
```

The settings listed in Listing 10-5 are similar to the ntp.conf file we have shown earlier. By default on both Ubuntu and CentOS we don't allow clients to synchronize from this time service. To do that we need to set the allow setting as follows:

```
allow 192.168/16
```

You would only set this if you were going to use these hosts in your networks as local network time clocks. Otherwise you can leave it commented out.

You may also need to add the cmdallow setting on CentOS to enable the chronyc command to access the service. We will look at chronyc shortly.

Now we use the systemctl command to enable and start our service. Replace chronyd for chrony on Ubuntu.

```
$ sudo systemctl enable chronyd && sudo systemctl start chronyd
```

Then check the service is running with

```
$ sudo systemctl status chronyd
```

Managing Chrony with Chronyc

Chrony provides a command-line interface tool to query and manage Chrony called chronyc. Again it is similar to how you can use the ntp tool.

You can enter the command-line interface by just typing chronyc or you can access the subcommands from the Linux command shell directly. You can get help with the following:

```
$ chronyc help
```

Chrony provides tracking information, different metrics about the time service, from the command line:

```
$ chronyc tracking
Reference ID    : 192.189.54.33 (warrane.connect.com.au)
Stratum         : 3
Ref time (UTC)  : Sat Oct  1 00:51:03 2016
System time     : 0.000043108 seconds slow of NTP time
Last offset     : -0.000094345 seconds
RMS offset      : 0.027604111 seconds
Frequency       : 459.036 ppm slow
Residual freq   : -0.012 ppm
Skew            : 0.430 ppm
Root delay      : 0.075154 seconds
Root dispersion : 0.012796 seconds
Update interval : 260.5 seconds
Leap status     : Normal
```

We can see from the the foregoing that we have various metrics describing our system time and our clock accuracy. We can see the stratum we are syncing against, the system time, and the offset.

Next we can view the clock sources using the following:

```
$ chronyc sources
210 Number of sources = 4
MS Name/IP address         Stratum  Poll  Reach  LastRx  Last sample
===============================================================================
^+ 0.time.itoc.com.au          2     9     377    446   +798us[ +798us] +/-  73ms
^+ dns02.ntl01.nsw.privatecl   2     9     377    249  +1507us[+1507us] +/-  52ms
^* warrane.connect.com.au      2     9     377    504  -1782us[-1876us] +/-  50ms
^+ 203.122.222.45              2     9     377    183   -200us[ -200us] +/-  85ms
```

You can use the chronyc command to add and deny access to chrony and to add and remove peers also. For more information, see the following:

- https://chrony.tuxfamily.org/faq.html

- https://chrony.tuxfamily.org/comparison.html

Domain Name System

In Chapter 2 we suggested using descriptive names for hosts. We also provided an IP (Internet Protocol) address for the host. We can, of course, use the IP address to access our host; however, humans tend to like to use names more than than "strange" numbers. But how do we map the hostname to the IP address? We can use local host's files to do address-to-name mappings, as we showed you in Chapter 4. But once your network grows beyond more than a handful of hosts, making sure that all copies of this file remain synchronized becomes an effort.

So a way of translating these names to the IP addresses of the hosts was devised. This is called Domain Name System or DNS. A DNS server maintains lists of address-to-hostname (and vice versa) mappings and can be queried by other hosts, or by users directly, using various utilities. DNS can be used to find the IP addresses of hosts on your local network or hosts on networks anywhere in the world. Let's see how it does this, starting with the root servers.

■ **Note** Before DNS existed, a single hosts.txt file was used. This file was maintained by the Network Information Center (NIC) and distributed to all ARPANET-connected machines via FTP (File Transfer Protocol).

Root Servers

Somehow, a DNS server needs to know which host or hosts to query for the correct address. An apple.com DNS server has no idea about a google.com host, so how does our own DNS server know where to look?

The entire DNS structure is like a large upside-down tree. Each period in a domain name is like a branch in this tree. As you read a domain name from left to right, each period indicates a split to a lower level in the tree, which is closer to the root. These levels are called *zones*, and for each zone a domain is a part of, a query is done to find out what the name servers are for that zone. One of these servers is then queried in turn to obtain a DNS server for the next zone. The lowest-level zone—the one that all other zones are members of—is called the *root zone*. We indicate this zone with a single period. The next level consists of top-level domains (TLDs), including generic domains such as net, com, org, and edu, as well as country codes such as au, nz, uk, and us. Figure 10-2 shows a small part of this tree structure.

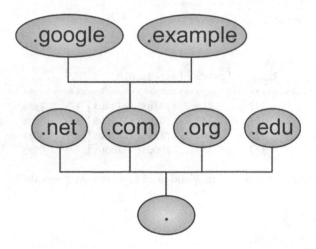

Figure 10-2. *DNS tree structure*

When writing a hostname or domain name, you usually leave off the trailing period for the root zone, but when you're dealing with DNS servers you should explicitly include it, as leaving it off may lead to unexpected results. The DNS information for these TLDs is stored in so-called root servers.

There are presently 13 globally distributed root name servers in the world that return the list of authoritive name servers for the TLDs. There are not actually just 13 servers chugging away at this but a highly distributed cluster of dedicated servers in multiple datacenters. We shall see the role these servers play in the delegation path in the upcoming "dig" section.

■ **Note**   Since the root servers are an absolute critical core of the Internet, they have been the target for network attacks. Following is summary list: `https://en.wikipedia.org/wiki/Distributed_denial-of-service_attacks_on_root_nameservers`.

WHOIS

When an organization or person buys a domain, the root DNS servers need to know which DNS servers further down the tree have been delegated to respond to queries for that domain. The organization in charge of the .com domain is the Internet Corporation for Assigned Names and Numbers (ICANN), and it manages the registrars.

When you buy a domain from a registrar, you can specify the name servers the domain is delegated to. The registrar then ensures that your DNS servers are added in the correct TLD zone, so third parties can use your DNS servers to look up hostnames on your domain. This is called the delegation path.

You can obtain a listing of DNS servers for a given domain by querying the registrar's database directly. The tool used for this, `whois`, is handy for making sure DNS delegations are correct. On CentOS and Ubuntu it's provided by the `whois` package. After installing the package, we can look at the delegation's detail for the google.com domain, as shown in Listing 10-6.

Listing 10-6. Using whois to Check Delegation Details

```
$ whois 'domain google.com'
Whois Server Version 2.0

Domain names in the .com and .net domains can now be registered
with many different competing registrars. Go to http://www.internic.net
for detailed information.

    Domain Name: GOOGLE.COM
    Registrar: MARKMONITOR INC.
    Sponsoring Registrar IANA ID: 292
    Whois Server: whois.markmonitor.com
    Referral URL: http://www.markmonitor.com
    Name Server: NS1.GOOGLE.COM
    Name Server: NS2.GOOGLE.COM
    Name Server: NS3.GOOGLE.COM
    Name Server: NS4.GOOGLE.COM
    Status: clientDeleteProhibited https://icann.org/epp#clientDeleteProhibited
    Status: clientTransferProhibited https://icann.org/epp#clientTransferProhibited
    Status: clientUpdateProhibited https://icann.org/epp#clientUpdateProhibited
    Status: serverDeleteProhibited https://icann.org/epp#serverDeleteProhibited
    Status: serverTransferProhibited https://icann.org/epp#serverTransferProhibited
    Status: serverUpdateProhibited https://icann.org/epp#serverUpdateProhibited
    Updated Date: 20-jul-2011
    Creation Date: 15-sep-1997
    Expiration Date: 14-sep-2020

>>> Last update of whois database: Sat, 25 Jun 2016 12:34:50 GMT <<<
```

We issue the whois command and we specify that we are looking only for the domain google.com. If we search without specifying the domain we are after, every domain that contains google.com in the domain name will be returned. You can see we have retrieved some information about Google's domain, including the name of the registrar; the name servers it is delegated to; and creation, modification, and expiration dates.

Some registrars also provide contact details for the domain owner via whois. This is something to keep in mind when choosing a registrar to buy your domain from, as it's a relatively convenient way for spammers to collect e-mail addresses.

___

■ **Note**   Most registrars allow only a limited number of lookups per day from a specific address against their database, to discourage address harvesting.

___

Querying Name Servers

You will already be using the DNS server or servers run by your Internet service provider to look up addresses for hosts on the Internet. Typing www.google.com is a lot more convenient than having to remember 74.125.19.147 whenever you want to do a web search. The addresses for these DNS servers are stored in the /etc/resolv.conf file. We've included ours in Listing 10-7; yours will, of course, be different.

Listing 10-7. `/etc/resolv.conf`

```
$ cat /etc/resolv.conf
search example.com
nameserver 192.168.1.1
nameserver 192.168.1.254
```

When you visit a web site or connect to a host via SSH, the application in question performs a host lookup using these DNS servers. These applications use a system library, which first checks your `/etc/hosts` file and then queries a name server only if needed.

In the following Figure 10-3 we can see a how a browser will request an IP address from their local dns, it will then query a list of root servers to find the name servers it needs to ask for the `google.com` domain.

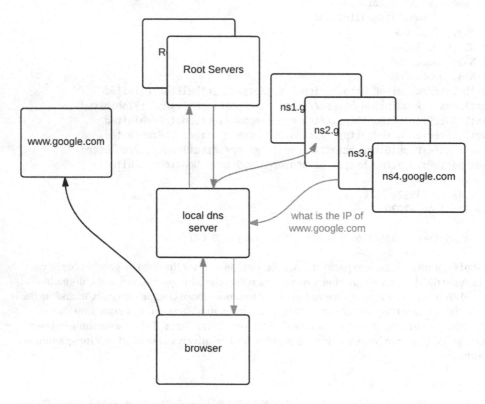

Figure 10-3. *Simple recursive DNS query*

The local dns server will first need to ask the '.' root servers for a server that can answer for the '.com.' zone. The local dns server will then ask one of the '.com.' servers which server can answer queries for ".google.com.". We then query one of the nsX.google.com. servers for the 'www' record. The browser now knows which IP address to use when looking for `www.google.com`.

The host Command

You can also query DNS servers manually. The DNS-related tools are provided by the `bind-utils` package on CentOS and the `dnsutils` package on Ubuntu, so install them. Direct host or address lookups can be done via the `host` utility.

■ **Note** You may be used to using the deprecated `nslookup` utility. The `host` command is its replacement.

You pass the hostname or address you want to look up and optionally the DNS server you want to query, as shown in Listing 10-8. If you leave off the DNS server, the utility will use one defined in `/etc/resolv.conf`.

Listing 10-8. Querying a DNS Server with host

```
$ host www.google.com 192.168.1.1
Using domain server:
Name: 192.168.1.1
Address: 192.168.1.1#53
Aliases:

www.google.com has address 150.101.161.167
www.google.com has address 150.101.161.173
www.google.com has address 150.101.161.174
www.google.com has address 150.101.161.180
www.google.com has address 150.101.161.181
www.google.com has address 150.101.161.187
www.google.com has address 150.101.161.146
www.google.com has address 150.101.161.152
www.google.com has address 150.101.161.153
www.google.com has address 150.101.161.159
www.google.com has address 150.101.161.160
www.google.com has address 150.101.161.166
www.google.com has IPv6 address 2404:6800:4006:800::2004
```

In Listing 10-8, we've asked the DNS server running on 192.168.1.1 to look up an address for www.google.com it returns several different IP addresses, including an IPv6 address. The Google web site will respond on any of these addresses and is used in a round robin, where the order of the returned list will change every so often (like we saw with the ntp pool servers earlier).

Conversely, we can do a dns lookup of a hostname for an IP addresses as well.

```
$ host 205.251.193.236
236.193.251.205.in-addr.arpa domain name pointer ns-492.awsdns-61.com.
```

What that has done is query the DNS server asking if it knows about any records for the address 205.251.193.236 and what host that refers to. It's called a reverse name lookup and may not always return any results as you don't have to record that information in your DNS records, it is just sometimes nice to have.

The dig Command

Though host is useful, it does not generally provide enough information to help resolve any DNS problem you might have, especially when you run your own DNS servers. A more flexible utility is dig, which is also provided by the bind-utils or dnsutils package.

At its most basic level, dig also does name- or address-based lookups, but it provides additional information with each lookup. Let's do the same lookup we did in Listing 10-8, but use dig instead (see Listing 10-9).

Listing 10-9. Querying a DNS Server with dig

```
$ dig www.google.com

; <<>> DiG 9.10.3-P4-Ubuntu <<>> www.google.com
;; global options: +cmd
;; Got answer:
;; ->>HEADER<<- opcode: QUERY, status: NOERROR, id: 33352
;; flags: qr rd ra; QUERY: 1, ANSWER: 12, AUTHORITY: 4, ADDITIONAL: 5

;; OPT PSEUDOSECTION:
; EDNS: version: 0, flags:; udp: 4096
;; QUESTION SECTION:
;www.google.com.                    IN      A

;; ANSWER SECTION:
www.google.com.         41      IN      A       150.101.161.153
www.google.com.         41      IN      A       150.101.161.159
www.google.com.         41      IN      A       150.101.161.160
www.google.com.         41      IN      A       150.101.161.166
www.google.com.         41      IN      A       150.101.161.167
www.google.com.         41      IN      A       150.101.161.173
www.google.com.         41      IN      A       150.101.161.174
www.google.com.         41      IN      A       150.101.161.180
www.google.com.         41      IN      A       150.101.161.181
www.google.com.         41      IN      A       150.101.161.187
www.google.com.         41      IN      A       150.101.161.146
www.google.com.         41      IN      A       150.101.161.152

;; AUTHORITY SECTION:
google.com.             2071    IN      NS      ns4.google.com.
google.com.             2071    IN      NS      ns1.google.com.
google.com.             2071    IN      NS      ns3.google.com.
google.com.             2071    IN      NS      ns2.google.com.

;; ADDITIONAL SECTION:
ns1.google.com.         179     IN      A       216.239.32.10
ns2.google.com.         4851    IN      A       216.239.34.10
ns3.google.com.         186     IN      A       216.239.36.10
ns4.google.com.         8300    IN      A       216.239.38.10
```

```
;; Query time: 11 msec
;; SERVER: 192.168.1.1#53(192.168.1.1)
;; WHEN: Sun Jun 26 00:11:48 UTC 2016
;; MSG SIZE rcvd: 371
```

In Listing 10-9 you can see that dig outputs the query results in distinct sections. First comes some information about the command you're running, including whether or not the query succeeded (opcode: QUERY, status: NOERROR, id: 33352). Next is the query section, which shows you what you actually sent to the DNS server. In this case, we are looking for an A record for the host www.google.com.

```
;; QUESTION SECTION:
;www.google.com.                    IN      A
```

An A record is one that maps names to addresses. We'll cover record types in more detail shortly.

■ **Note**   If a record doesn't exist you will get a status response of "NXDOMAIN." For a list of all the possible responses see www.iana.org/assignments/dns-parameters/dns-parameters.xhtml#dns-parameters-6.

The answer section holds the response to your query. In this case, it says that www.google.com has multiple A records assigned to it.

```
;; ANSWER SECTION:
www.google.com.         41      IN      A       150.101.161.153
www.google.com.         41      IN      A       150.101.161.159
...
```

In the authority section, dig lists the authoritative name servers for this query. Here you can see that authoritative responses for the google.com. zone can be obtained from four DNS servers.

```
;; AUTHORITY SECTION:
google.com.             2071    IN      NS      ns4.google.com.
google.com.             2071    IN      NS      ns1.google.com.
google.com.             2071    IN      NS      ns3.google.com.
google.com.             2071    IN      NS      ns2.google.com.
```

dig provides us with the IP addresses of these four servers in the additional section.

```
;; ADDITIONAL SECTION:
ns1.google.com.         179     IN      A       216.239.32.10
...
```

Finally, dig tells us how long the query took, which server was queried, when the query was run, and how much data it received.

```
;; Query time: 11 msec
;; SERVER: 192.168.1.1#53(192.168.1.1)
;; WHEN: Sun Jun 26 00:11:48 UTC 2016
;; MSG SIZE rcvd: 371
```

433

The actual response data is displayed in five columns. This format is identical to the way Berkeley Internet Name Domain (BIND) defines domains internally, where records are defined using five fields and semicolons are used for comments. These five fields are the record name, the time until the data expires (better known as *time to live* or TTL), the record class (which is virtually always IN for Internet), the record type, and finally the data for this record.

```
<record name>        <ttl>        <class>      <type>        <data>
www.google.com.        41           IN           A          150.101.161.153
```

You can use dig to query any DNS server for specific record types as well. Table 10-1 lists the most commonly used record types. We'll set up some of these later as well.

Table 10-1. *DNS Record Types*

Type	Used For
SOA	Defines a serial number and expiration information for the domain
A	IPv4 hostname to address maps
AAAA	IPv6 hostname to address maps
CNAME	Adds an alias for an existing A or AAAA record
MX	Specifies mail servers for the domain
TXT	Text records, often used with SPF or DKIM (MX record validation) and other machine-readable data
SRV	Specifies service records associated with services
NS	Specifies DNS servers for the domain
PTR	Maps an address to a hostname
DS	Delegation Signer—used in DNSSEC
DNSKEY	DNSKEY record used in DNSSEC
RRSIG	Resource record signature used in DNSSEC

Armed with this knowledge, you can now make use of the more advanced features of dig. We previously invoked it with just a hostname as parameter, but a full command usually looks like dig @server name type. In the case of our first example, the full explicit command would have been dig @192.168.1.1 www.google.com A.

■ **Note** To use the host utility for the same kind of lookup, enter host -v -t <type> <name> <server>.

We found out the main DNS servers for the google.com domain via whois earlier. To check that these DNS servers are configured properly, we can query them for all records of the NS type in the google.com domain, as shown in Listing 10-10.

Listing 10-10. Querying a DNS Server for a Specific Record Type

```
$ dig @ns1.google.com google.com NS

; <<>> DiG 9.10.3-P4-Ubuntu <<>> google.com NS
;; global options: +cmd
;; Got answer:
;; ->>HEADER<<- opcode: QUERY, status: NOERROR, id: 44887
;; flags: qr rd ra; QUERY: 1, ANSWER: 4, AUTHORITY: 0, ADDITIONAL: 5

;; OPT PSEUDOSECTION:
; EDNS: version: 0, flags:; udp: 4096
;; QUESTION SECTION:
;google.com.                    IN      NS

;; ANSWER SECTION:
google.com.             10158   IN      NS      ns2.google.com.
google.com.             10158   IN      NS      ns3.google.com.
google.com.             10158   IN      NS      ns1.google.com.
google.com.             10158   IN      NS      ns4.google.com.

;; ADDITIONAL SECTION:
ns1.google.com.         8267    IN      A       216.239.32.10
ns2.google.com.         12939   IN      A       216.239.34.10
ns3.google.com.         8274    IN      A       216.239.36.10
ns4.google.com.         1987    IN      A       216.239.38.10

;; Query time: 9 msec
;; SERVER: 10.0.2.3#53(10.0.2.3)
;; WHEN: Sun Jun 26 01:57:01 UTC 2016
;; MSG SIZE  rcvd: 175
```

Listing 10-10 shows us that the ns1.google.com DNS server does indeed have information about four name servers for the google.com domain, so it appears to be configured correctly.

Sometimes you need to know the delegation path (Listing 10-11) to your name servers. To find out that information we can use dig with the +trace option.

Listing 10-11. Seeing the Delegation Path

```
$ dig +trace www.google.com

; <<>> DiG 9.10.3-P4-Ubuntu <<>> +trace www.google.com
;; global options: +cmd
.                       9903    IN      NS      a.root-servers.net.
.                       9903    IN      NS      d.root-servers.net.
.                       9903    IN      NS      j.root-servers.net.
.                       9903    IN      NS      e.root-servers.net.
.                       9903    IN      NS      k.root-servers.net.
...<snip>...
.                       9903    IN      NS      h.root-servers.net.
...<snip>...
```

```
;; Received 913 bytes from 10.0.2.3#53(10.0.2.3) in 12 ms

com.                172800  IN    NS     a.gtld-servers.net.
com.                172800  IN    NS     b.gtld-servers.net.
com.                172800  IN    NS     c.gtld-servers.net.
com.                172800  IN    NS     d.gtld-servers.net.
com.                172800  IN    NS     e.gtld-servers.net.
...<snip>...
com.                172800  IN    NS     m.gtld-servers.net.
...<snip>...
;; Received 738 bytes from 192.58.128.30#53(j.root-servers.net) in 25 ms

google.com.         172800  IN    NS     ns2.google.com.
google.com.         172800  IN    NS     ns1.google.com.
google.com.         172800  IN    NS     ns3.google.com.
google.com.         172800  IN    NS     ns4.google.com.
...<snip>...
;; Received 664 bytes from 192.52.178.30#53(k.gtld-servers.net) in 176 ms

www.google.com.     300     IN    A      150.101.213.166
www.google.com.     300     IN    A      150.101.213.159
...<snip>...
www.google.com.     300     IN    A      150.101.213.174
;; Received 224 bytes from 216.239.34.10#53(ns2.google.com) in 177 ms
```

We have removed some of the authentication records listed in the output to make it clearer. With the +trace option we can see that the '.' root zone delegates to the servers in the 'com.' zone which then delegate to the name servers at 'google.com.'. If you are setting up a DNS server as the authority for your domain, you can validate that your delegation path is correct with the +trace option.

■ **Tip** There is often a "propagation delay" as the world of DNS reorganizes itself with updates. This delay is dependent on record TTLs and how often name servers update their records. Using dig is useful in displaying the world of DNS.

Zone Metadata

We mentioned earlier that one of the columns listed in dig results is TTL. This field defines how long DNS records are valid for, which allows your local applications to cache the results of a DNS lookup for a certain time. This way, there is no need to perform several DNS lookups for each connection you make (remember, one or more lookups are performed to find an authoritative DNS server first), which speeds up the process of establishing network connections considerably.

The other important type is called SOA, for Start of Authority. This record contains meta-information about the zone. For instance, it includes a serial number so servers can check if the zone was changed, and it defines a contact e-mail for the server administrator as well.

Let's ask one of the Google servers for the SOA record of the google.com domain (Listing 10-12). We've left the authoritative and extra sections off the output.

Listing 10-12. Querying a DNS Server for an SOA Record

```
$ dig google.com @ns1.google.com SOA
; <<>> DiG 9.10.3-P4-Ubuntu <<>> google.com @ns1.google.com SOA
;; global options: +cmd
;; Got answer:
;; ->>HEADER<<- opcode: QUERY, status: NOERROR, id: 43145
;; flags: qr aa rd; QUERY: 1, ANSWER: 1, AUTHORITY: 4, ADDITIONAL: 4
;; WARNING: recursion requested but not available

;; QUESTION SECTION:
;google.com.           IN    SOA

;; ANSWER SECTION:
google.com.    60   IN    SOA    ns2.google.com. dns-admin.google.com. 125880391 900 900
1800 60
```

Listing 10-12 shows that the SOA record consists of seven fields, which define how other DNS servers interact with this zone. After the DNS type (SOA) you will see seven fields.

```
<name server>     <admin email address>    serial #   refresh  retry expiry  nx ttl
ns2.google.com.   dns-admin.google.com.    125880391     900    900   1800       60
```

We will look at them in greater detail shortly but we would like to mention the last item in the list, which is the *negative cache* TTL, or nx ttl. This tells other the dns servers to cache negative results ("NXDOMAIN") to prevent authoritive name servers from continuously performing a lookup for a host that does not exist. In this case, a remote server should keep responding with "No such host" for 60 seconds after the initial query before it queries the authoritative name servers again. This period can be longer than 60 seconds and some might be as long as a week.

Running Caching DNS

Not all ISPs' name servers are equally reliable, and some can be slow, so why don't we run our own? A few DNS server software packages are available, but the most commonly used and well-known is Berkeley Internet Name Domain (BIND).

■ **Note** BIND is named after the place where it was developed, the University of California at Berkeley.

The software is provided by the bind package on CentOS. You install these via yum install bind. On Ubuntu, these are provided by the bind9 package, which you add via sudo aptitude install bind9. The DNS server binary itself is called named—because it is name(server) daemon.

The main configuration file shipped on Ubuntu is /etc/bind/named.conf, while on CentOS the /etc/named.conf file is used. Listing 10-13 shows you the basic file that ships with Ubuntu.

Listing 10-13. The Top of /etc/bind/named.conf in Ubuntu

```
// This is the primary configuration file for the BIND DNS server named.
//
// Please read /usr/share/doc/bind9/README.Debian.gz for information on the
```

```
// structure of BIND configuration files in Debian, *BEFORE* you customize
// this configuration file.
//
// If you are just adding zones, please do that in /etc/bind/named.conf.local

include "/etc/bind/named.conf.options";
include "/etc/bind/named.conf.local";
include "/etc/bind/named.conf.default-zones";
```

This file contains references to other files, which contain the actual configuration settings and (optionally) information about domains that are hosted locally. Comments in these configuration files are prefixed with a double slash (//) and all directives and blocks are terminated with a semicolon (;).

The include directive tells named to read the specified file and process any directives it contains, including nested include commands. In this case, the named.conf.options file contains the options section, which affects the way named operates. This is the file you would edit to make changes to your configuration on Ubuntu (see Listing 10-14).

Listing 10-14. Default named Options in Ubuntu

```
options {
        directory "/var/cache/bind";

        // If there is a firewall between you and nameservers you want
        // to talk to, you may need to fix the firewall to allow multiple
        // ports to talk.  See http://www.kb.cert.org/vuls/id/800113

        // If your ISP provided one or more IP addresses for stable
        // nameservers, you probably want to use them as forwarders.
        // Uncomment the following block, and insert the addresses replacing
        // the all-0's placeholder.

        // forwarders {
        //      0.0.0.0;
        // };

        //========================================================================
        // If BIND logs error messages about the root key being expired,
        // you will need to update your keys.  See https://www.isc.org/bind-keys
        //========================================================================
        dnssec-validation auto;

        auth-nxdomain no;    # conform to RFC1035
        listen-on-v6 { any; };
};
```

The directory directive determines that the location named will be used to look for files and also to write any files, if it's configured to do so. You can override this for individual files by specifying a full system path starting with /.

Forwarders are what named calls upstream DNS servers. If you want your caching name server to use only your ISP's name server or a set of other name servers, you can list their IP addresses in the forwarders block, each on a line by itself and terminated by a semicolon.

The next option, `dnssec-validation`, defaults to auto. This means it will try to validate the replies from dns servers with DNSSEC enabled if it receives a delegated signer record. DNSSEC is designed to prevent response tampering or dns cache poisoning, where a malicious actor can inject fake records into dns cache servers and route Internet traffic to hosts of their choosing.

In Figure 10-4 we use the dig tool to find out more information about the `google.com` dnssec records.

```
:~$ dig google.com ds +dnssec

; <<>> DiG 9.10.3-P4-Ubuntu <<>> google.com ds +dnssec
;; global options: +cmd
;; Got answer:
;; ->>HEADER<<- opcode: QUERY, status: NOERROR, id: 41375
;; flags: qr rd ra; QUERY: 1, ANSWER: 0, AUTHORITY: 6, ADDITIONAL: 1

;; OPT PSEUDOSECTION:
; EDNS: version: 0, flags: do; udp: 4096
;; QUESTION SECTION:
;google.com.                    IN      DS

;; AUTHORITY SECTION:
com.                    803     IN      SOA     a.gtld-servers.net. nstld.verisign-grs.com. 1466934134 1800 900 604800 86400
com.                    803     IN      RRSIG   SOA 8 1 900 20160703094214 20160626083214 34745 com. UjzEt9ovrWM6Bg7Cyee+Y0upNd0tvNRcHHlpqAMuinGfciMnKGfxeF4R eGuy7YbcseAtfr6qNf0Y+tFSFKTaev5lXmEvQFFOMmAPvX
0COTCgxK8N Sq9scEu7Ro/WFpogvCzlcXB0BPoegwBkCmMi3t2TdO0zI0lvg9q381J5 7AQ=
CK0POJMG874LJREF7EFN8430QVIT8BSM.com. 803 IN RRSIG NSEC3 8 2 86400 20160701045710 20160624034710 34745 com. GTFcU7b1zO3s5noMbYAvQDEMdTgLdX8Q4Uvz4Ls/BRT8wev9l31cMeoK B6VJMyMAzZT0bjlRScj/irzeyKTY3tKIUiyrCUf
j/ES56+DBxLAsZbGy FFnvEybb7RtDgXU4QrT7cOk4GFoH+7i29EF5PphPnDBAJ+8jIIeCjswF 9T0=
CK0POJMG874LJREF7EFN8430QVIT8BSM.com. 803 IN NSEC3 1 1 0 - CK0Q1GIN43N1ARRC9OSM6QPQR81H5M9A NS SOA RRSIG DNSKEY NSEC3PARAM
S84AE3BIT99DKIHQH27TRC0584HV5KOH.com. 803 IN RRSIG NSEC3 8 2 86400 20160703051044 20160626040044 34745 com. F74BIppi+vhmFXoXuds6w/bo6qrzPFQjqY2FUWRNru0489bUqQRmJFgv Y2H7ZjnJNIz/OyUNlzrIFHZDs6w6XdbdeO8QLST
Nn/i3NgC67i9bCvMf +n/Yv1D2yFkPgEXpGN4RBunWOQI7AIAH9vBXtPIztjDL2JUtetpMXXrw jfQ=
S84AE3BIT99DKIHQH27TRC0584HV5KOH.com. 803 IN NSEC3 1 1 0 - S84HQQBBMVORSCH4GNB3G868OHH33GUR NS DS RRSIG

;; Query time: 267 msec
;; SERVER: 10.0.2.3#53(10.0.2.3)
;; WHEN: Sun Jun 26 09:44:08 UTC 2016
;; MSG SIZE  rcvd: 760
```

Figure 10-4. *Google's DNSSEC records*

We apologize if you have to squint, but we used the `dig google.com ds +dnssec` command to query for the delegated signing records for dnssec. Take a look at the following sidebar for more information about what they mean.

DNSSEC

DNSSEC uses a process of exchanging cryptographic signatures and works on a "Chain of Trust" model. That means that you can validate the authenticity of the records based on the key that signed them and that they are in turn validated by someone you trust.

As we know, the top to the DNS tree is called the root '.' zone. Below them are the TLDs (like '.com.', '.org.', '.net.', '.io.', etc). Below them are the many various different domains. DNSSEC provides a way that they root zone validates records from the TLDs that can then validate the records other domains under them.

It does this by signing resource record sets, RRsets (a RRset for example, is all the MX resource records in a zone file, or all the NS resource records, or all the AAAA resource records). These RRsets are signed by a zone signing private key. These are stored in the name server as RRSIG records.

The public key of the zone signing key pair is called the DNSKEY and it is published as a record on the name server too. The DNSKEY is used to validate the RRSIG signature to verify the authenticity of the RRset.

However, we now need to validate the DNSKEY; how do we know it is the real one? For that we have a key signing key pair. That is a public key signing key (also a DNSKEY) and a private key signing key. We create a RRset of the DNSKEYs and use the private key signing key to sign them. This produces another RRSIG. In this way the public key signing key can be used to validate the public zone signing key.

At this stage we can validate the RRset and or public DNSKEYS. But do we still trust the server that gave them to us? No, we don't. This is where the TLD comes in. We give our TLD a copy of our public key signing key and they use that to create a delegated singer record (DS). This record is a hash of the key signing key DNSKEY. So every time a resolver is referred to a "child" of the TLD, this DS record is included.

This DS record is used by the resolver to validate the authenticity of the public key signing key. It does this by performing a hash on the public key signing key and comparing that to the DS record. If they match, then we can trust the rest of the keys.

ICANN, the guardian of the DNS infrastructure, controls the root and creates the RRSIG and DNSKEYs records for the whole of the Internet that we use in DNSSEC. It then provides DS records for all the TLDs. They in turn can provide DS records for anything that is under them, those can create DS records for anything under them, and so on.

In the following figure you will see that when we make a request for `www.google.com`, the root servers will send us a RRSIG and a DS for the '.com.' TLD. We will use the publicly available public key signing DNSKEY and the RRSIG to validate the RRset–at this point we have no parent or DS record to validate the DNSKEY with, so we "trust" the top-level domain.

We then use that RRset to find the address to query the '.com.' name servers. Here we make a hash of the RRSIG and the DNSKEY and compare that to the hash we received in the DS record from the root domain. If they match, they are valid and we will then use those RRsets to find the name servers for `google.com`. At the `google.com` name servers we receive the RRSIG. We hash the DNSKEY and RRSIG and compare that to what the .com DS record has; if they match, then we can trust the keys from the google name servers.

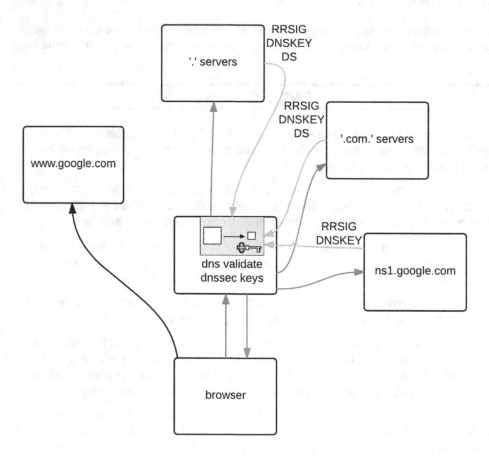

Having an explicit trust for the root domain has an interesting human side effect. For an interesting look at the root key signing ceremony, please read the following: www.cloudflare.com/dnssec/root-signing-ceremony/

For a more detailed explanation of DNSSEC please see the following:

- www.cloudflare.com/dnssec/how-dnssec-works/

- https://en.wikipedia.org/wiki/Domain_Name_System_Security_Extensions

- www.youtube.com/watch?v=yUPnI6JFTYI

The next option, auth-nxdomain, is set to no. This controls how the name server responds to lookups for domains that it thinks do not exist, which means that your local DNS server will not claim to be authoritative if it cannot find information about a domain. This in turn means that a client can continue querying other DNS servers, if this one cannot find information about a domain.

Finally, the listen-on-v6 option tells BIND that it should listen for queries on all available IPv6 addresses on all network interfaces.

To avoid the chicken-and-egg problem, a caching DNS server ships with a built-in listing of root servers. You can find them in /var/named/named.ca on CentOS and /etc/bind/db.root on Ubuntu. You can also use dig to obtain a current list of root servers, by querying a root server for all records of type NS in the "." zone.

```
$ dig @a.root-servers.net . NS > db.root.
```

Let's now take a look at the /etc/named.conf file (see Listing 10-15) that is installed when we install the BIND package on CentOS.

Listing 10-15. CentOS /etc/named.conf

```
//
// named.conf
//
// Provided by Red Hat bind package to configure the ISC BIND named(8) DNS
// server as a caching only nameserver (as a localhost DNS resolver only).
//
// See /usr/share/doc/bind*/sample/ for example named configuration files.
//

options {
        listen-on port 53 { 127.0.0.1; };
        listen-on-v6 port 53 { ::1; };
        directory       "/var/named";
        dump-file       "/var/named/data/cache_dump.db";
        statistics-file "/var/named/data/named_stats.txt";
        memstatistics-file "/var/named/data/named_mem_stats.txt";
        allow-query     { localhost; };

        /*
        - If you are building an AUTHORITATIVE DNS server, do NOT enable recursion.
        - If you are building a RECURSIVE (caching) DNS server, you need to enable
          recursion.
```

```
        - If your recursive DNS server has a public IP address, you MUST enable access
          control to limit queries to your legitimate users. Failing to do so will
          cause your server to become part of large scale DNS amplification
          attacks. Implementing BCP38 within your network would greatly
          reduce such attack surface
        */
        recursion yes;

        dnssec-enable yes;
        dnssec-validation yes;

        /* Path to ISC DLV key */
        bindkeys-file "/etc/named.iscdlv.key";

        managed-keys-directory "/var/named/dynamic";

        pid-file "/run/named/named.pid";
        session-keyfile "/run/named/session.key";
};

logging {
        channel default_debug {
                file "data/named.run";
                severity dynamic;
        };
};

zone "." IN {
        type hint;
        file "named.ca";
};

include "/etc/named.rfc1912.zones";
include "/etc/named.root.key";
```

The major difference between the CentOS and Ubuntu files is the location you use to store data for named. The dump-file directive allows named to write transient data to a file when it exits. It can then reread this data when it is started again. The statistics-file defines where named writes statistical information about the types and number of queries it receives.

This bind server is set to listen on localhost for IPv4 and IPv6. With this configuration, other hosts on the network will not be able to use this service. We will need to change the listen-on(-v6) to listen on a reachable IP address.

```
listen-on port 53 { 127.0.0.1; 192.168.1.1; };
listen-on-v6 port 53 { ::1; };
```

The next settings in Listing 10-5 are recursion (should be 'yes') as we are not using this dns server as an authoritative name server (meaning it won't be queried for any zones itself, but rather ask other dns servers). We enable dnssec and dnssec-validation by setting both to 'yes'. The bindkeys-file points to the iscdlv.key path. This key is used in dnssec validation when there is no DS record (this is less common now that DNSSEC is rolled out nearly everywhere).

We then have logging options. You can view the logs in /var/named/data/named.run on CentOS and you can dynamically adjust the severity levels.

The root zone file is next. That is output you received from dig @a.root-servers.net . NS and you would place it in the file named /var/named/named.ca. Bind uses this to find the root servers for recursive lookups.

Finally, like we saw in the Ubuntu named.conf file, we can include other configuration files with the include directive.

We can now start the name server via the sudo systemctl start named command. On Ubuntu, the name server is started automatically when it is installed, but if it were not running we could start it via sudo service bind9 start.

So that our new DNS server can be queried, we need to ensure the firewall is not blocking traffic. DNS defaults to using the UDP protocol on port number 53, but it will switch to the TCP if responses contain a large amount of data. Add the appropriate rules to the correct Netfilter chain for your network layout.

```
$ sudo /sbin/iptables -t filter -A INPUT -p udp --dport 53 -j ACCEPT
$ sudo /sbin/iptables -t filter -A INPUT -p tcp --dport 53 -j ACCEPT
```

■ **Note**   Make sure to configure the firewall on the DNS host to permit outgoing DNS responses, too. We covered firewalls and iptables in Chapter 7.

We now have our own caching DNS server, which we can use to do lookups. We call it a *caching* DNS server because it keeps the answers to any queries we do, so the next time we perform the same query, it can respond immediately with the cached information.

To make sure it works, we will query it directly, as shown in Listing 10-16.

Listing 10-16. Querying Our Local Caching DNS Server

```
$ host www.google.com localhost
Using domain server:
Name: localhost
Address: 127.0.0.1#53
Aliases:

www.google.com has address 216.58.220.132
www.google.com has IPv6 address 2404:6800:4006:806::2004
```

We asked the DNS server running on localhost to look up the address for www.google.com and it responded, so it works!

With a working caching DNS, we can replace the nameserver entries in our /etc/resolv.conf file with nameserver 192.168.0.1 to use our own server. We can also add this DNS server to the resolv.conf files on any other hosts we have in our local network.

Authoritative DNS

If you need to map hostnames to IP addresses for hosts in your own network, then a DNS caching server will not do. You will need to have an *authoritative* DNS server. An authoritive DNS server is an authoritative source of information for a zone. An authoritive DNS will provide DNS resolution for our local network, which will house our example.com domain. We do this by defining two zones: one to provide mappings from name to address and one to provide reverse mappings, from address to name.

Rezoning

Domains are described as zones. Zones are defined in zone files, much like the root zone file we mentioned earlier. Zone files always contain a header, also known as the SOA record. This header is optionally followed by DNS records that define services and hosts. We've included a sample zone file header in Listing 10-17.

Listing 10-17. Zone File Header for the example.com Domain

```
$ORIGIN example.com.
$TTL 86400
@   IN   SOA    example.com.    root.example.com. (
        2016070100  ; Serial
        604800          ; Refresh
        86400            ; Retry
        2419200        ; Expire
        3600 )             ; Negative Cache TTL
```

This header defines some meta-information about our zone that is used by caching DNS servers and also by any slave servers we may have defined. *Slave servers* are authoritative DNS servers that automatically retrieve their zone information from a master DNS server. You would use them to provide redundant DNS services, like your ISP does.

■ **Note** DNS is a read heavy database, few writes, so it can easily scale to many slaves.

We've listed the fields from our zone header and their use in Table 10-2. In our example we've listed all times in seconds, but you can also use 1d instead of 86400 to indicate one day, or 4w instead of 2419200 to indicate four weeks.

Table 10-2. *Zone Header Fields*

Field	Use
$ORIGIN	Defines the start of the zone
$TTL	Time to live, which is the default expiration for records in this zone that do not have their own expiration time set
SOA	Start of Authority, which contains seven records of zone metadata
Master	Primary authoritative DNS server for this domain
Contact	E-mail address of the contact for this domain, with the at sign (@) replaced by a period
Serial	Defines the version of this zone file, used by slave name servers
Refresh	Defines how often slave servers should update their copy of this zone
Retry	Defines the interval between attempts to refresh a slave server
Expire	Defines how long a slave server is allowed to use any version of this zone file
Negative Cache TTL	Defines how long a failed lookup result may be cached

It's also worth noting that we're using a serial number based on the current date. You can use the YYYYMMDD for the current year, month, and day, followed by a two-digit number. This allows people to easily see when the zone was last changed, while still allowing for 99 changes each day. You can also choose to use a date based on unix epoch time (number of seconds since 01/01/1970) for the zone. The format is a ten-digit string and it can be generated with the following command: $ `date +%s`. For another alternative, you can use a simple incrementing number as the serial number. The at symbol (@) in front of the SOA evaluates to the name of the current zone. We could have also typed **example.com.** in its place.

The TTL for the zone can vary greatly. Smaller values mean that records will be cached by other DNS servers for a shorter period of time. That means your DNS servers will be queried more often, whereas longer TTLs means less queries to your DNS servers. If your host IPs are changing regularly you will want to have this value small. If they are not, then longer times are suitable.

Forward Lookup Zones

It is easy to create zones files via a text editor and add their definitions to the `/etc/named.conf.local` file. We're going to store our forward lookup zone in a file called `example.com.db`.

Before we go on there are are few differences between CentOS and Ubuntu to be aware of. Zone files are stored in `/var/named/` and Ubuntu in `/var/cache/bind`. The daemon that runs the DNS service on CentOS is called named and is run by the named user. Ubuntu, on the other hand, runs the bind daemon with the bind user. In the following example we will be using an Ubuntu server. Because only the root user may write to the zone file directory, we start our editor using sudo.

```
$ sudo vim /var/cache/bind/master/example.com.db
```

We place these authoritive zone files in the master directory. We will be showing you how the slaves operate shortly. You will need to make sure that the directory `/var/cache/bind/master` or `/var/named/master` exists, depending on your distribution. Now, we simply copy and paste the zone header from Listing 10-18 into this file and save it. With the header done, we can start to add actual host and service records into this file.

You need two basic service record types to be present in your zone. One is the NS record, which defines which hosts act as DNS server for this domain, and the other is the MX record, which defines mail servers for this domain. Both records start with a blank field, as they do not define hostnames.

Listing 10-18. Our Service Records

```
IN     NS          ns.example.com.
IN     MX      10  mail.example.com.
```

The data for the MX record consists of a priority number and then the hostname that remote servers should try to deliver mail to. A properly configured remote mail server will work through a list of MX records, starting with the lowest priority number, and try to deliver e-mail. Note that we've specified a fully qualified domain name (FQDN; which is the hostname plus the full domain name) with a trailing period for these entries. If we'd left off the trailing period, the DNS server would assume we had defined hostnames only and would automatically append the $ORIGIN to the end of these records.

We've used the ns and mail hostnames in these definitions, but we've not yet defined these hosts in the zone file, so let's do that next (see Listing 10-19). Host-to-address records are called A records and remember that AAAA records are for IPv6. We'll also add an A record for our current hostname.

Listing 10-19. Creating A Records for Our Domain

```
@                IN    A    192.168.0.1
ns               IN    A    192.168.0.254
mail             IN    A    192.168.0.1
au-mel-ubuntu-1  IN    A    192.168.0.1
```

We did not specify an FQDN in the host column for these records, so the DNS server will treat them as if they have $ORIGIN (example.com.) appended to them, which is exactly what we want. The @ symbol is replaced with the origin, too, so users will be able to access a host by going to just the domain as well.

You'll note that both these names will now resolve to the same address. An IP address can have as many A records associated with it as you like. The other type ofd record in a forward zone is called a CNAME, also known as an alias.

You use a CNAME when you want to associate a number of aliased names with a single host and still be able to change the address for that host without needing to then change a long list of A records. For instance, our host au-mel-ubuntu-1 needs to provide web and SQL services, and the mail server will also provide POP and IMAP access. We can create some CNAME entries to provide aliases that all point to the mail A entry (see Listing 10-20). In the future if we migrate mail services to a different host, we only need to change the A record and all CNAME entries will automatically point at the new address as well.

Listing 10-20. Adding Some CNAME Entries

```
gateway       IN    CNAME    ns.example.com.
headoffice    IN    CNAME    au-mel-ubuntu-1.example.com.
smtp          IN    CNAME    mail.example.com.
pop           IN    CNAME    mail.example.com.
imap          IN    CNAME    mail.example.com.
www           IN    CNAME    au-mel-ubuntu-1.example.com.
sql           IN    CNAME    au-mel-ubuntu-1.example.com.
```

We've also created CNAMEs called gateway and headoffice, which we will use when we set up a Virtual Private Network in Chapter 15. That's all we need for now. We'll save the file and create an accompanying reverse zone file, which will provide an address-to-name mapping.

Reverse Lookup Zones

In order to set up a reverse zone, you need to first find out what it is called. Unlike a forward zone, it has no domain name, but it does have a unique address range. To provide lookups for addresses, a special domain named in-addr.arpa. is used. This is essentially the root zone for reverse mappings.

Just like forward zones, you prepend the parts of your network address to this zone, with the most significant parts to the right. For our network of 192.168.0.x, this results in a 0.168.192.in-addr.arpa. reverse zone name.

■ **Note**   In-addr.arpa. zones are always prefixed with up to three-quarters of a dotted quad. There is no standard way of having reverse zones for a subnet with fewer than 255 addresses.

We once again fire up our editor (as the root user) to create a new zone file.

```
$ sudo vim /var/cache/bind/192.168.0.db
```

The header in this file needs to be a bit different from our forward zone, as the zone name is different. Add in the contents of Listing 10-21.

Listing 10-21. The Reverse Zone Header

```
$ORIGIN 0.168.192.in-addr.arpa.
$TTL  86400
@  IN  SOA    ns.example.com.    root.example.com. (
          2016070100 ; Serial
          604800     ; Refresh
          86400      ; Retry
          2419200    ; Expire
          3600 )     ; Negative Cache TTL
```

With the header created, we can now start adding PTR records, which map addresses to names. Let's add one for our bastion host and one for our host on 192.168.0.254 and the mail A records, as shown in Listing 10-22.

Listing 10-22. Adding PTR Records for Our Hosts

```
IN      NS     ns.example.com.
1       PTR    mail.example.com
1       PTR    au-mel-ubuntu-1.example.com.
254     PTR    ns.example.com.
```

We save the reverse zone file and exit the editor. All that's left to do now is add the zone definitions for these two zones to /etc/bind/named.conf.local. We open this file and add in the definitions, as shown in Listing 10-23. Each zone directive block contains a reference to the file that defines the zone. By default, the server expects these in the directory specified in the main configuration file. Since we're the authoritative DNS server providing these zones, we need to set the zone type to master.

Listing 10-23. Adding Zone Definitions

```
zone "example.com" {
    type master;
    file "master/example.com.db";
};

zone "0.168.192.in-addr.arpa" {
    type master;
    file "master/192.168.0.db";
};
```

Then we save the file and quit the editor. We need to tell the server to reload its configuration, either by restarting the server via systemctl reload or service, or using the rndc utility. The latter is much faster and does not interrupt services, so let's do that.

```
$ sudo rndc reload
server reload successful
```

The rndc utility is used to control the named (bind) server. Not only can it reload the named configuration (after you have edited files), it can reload particular zones, change logging levels, and flush caches. We will show you more uses for rndc throughout the chapter.

The name server should know about our new zones, and we can query it to check this. Let's start by looking up the address for ns.example.com, as shown in Listing 10-24.

Listing 10-24. Testing Forward Name Resolution

```
$ host ns.example.com localhost
Using domain server:
Name: localhost
Address: 127.0.0.1#53
Aliases:

ns.example.com has address 192.168.0.254
```

That works fine. Let's also check that the reverse zone works by looking up the name associated with the 192.168.0.1 address, as shown in Listing 10-25.

Listing 10-25. Testing Reverse Name Resolution

```
$ host 192.168.0.1 localhost
Using domain server:
Name: localhost
Address: 127.0.0.1#53
Aliases:

1.0.168.192.in-addr.arpa domain name pointer au-mel-ubuntu-1.example.com.
1.0.168.192.in-addr.arpa domain name pointer mail.example.com.0.168.192.in-addr.arpa.
```

That isn't quite right! The name server has appended the reverse zone name to the mail.example.com host. We know what usually causes this, though, so if we go and check the reverse zone file, we can see that we did indeed forget the trailing period at the end of the entry for mail.example.com.

But let's take the time to investigate how we can see the query logs on our bind server. Using the rndc utility again we can issue the following command:

```
$ sudo rndc querylog on
```

If we tail the /var/log/syslog (on Ubuntu) we will see the following:

```
Jun 28 12:23:26 localhost named[2548]: received control channel command 'querylog on'
Jun 28 12:23:26 localhost named[2548]: query logging is now on
```

We will now be able to see the DNS queries in the system log as follows:

```
Jun 28 12:25:31 localhost named[2548]: client 127.0.0.1#47616 (1.0.168.192.in-addr.arpa):
query: 1.0.168.192.in-addr.arpa IN PTR + (127.0.0.1)
```

To turn off the query logging we simply issue the following:

```
$ sudo rndc querylog off
```

We'll add the period now and increment the zone serial number and the records should now look as follows:

```
$ORIGIN 0.168.192.in-addr.arpa.
$TTL  86400
@  IN  SOA    ns.example.com.    root.example.com. (
       2016070100  ; Serial
       604800          ; Refresh
       86400           ; Retry
       2419200         ; Expire
       3600 )          ; Negative Cache TTL

       IN  NS     ns.example.com.


1       PTR    mail.example.com.
1       PTR    au-mel-ubuntu-1.example.com.
254     PTR    ns.example.com.
```

When we finish, we issue the sudo rndc reload command again. If we test the reverse resolution again, we can see the problem has been fixed.

```
$ host 192.168.0.1 localhost
Using domain server:
Name: localhost
Address: 127.0.0.1#53
Aliases:

1.0.168.192.in-addr.arpa domain name pointer au-mel-ubuntu-1.example.com.
1.0.168.192.in-addr.arpa domain name pointer mail.example.com.
```

Security Considerations

We're now running the DNS server on the bastion host as both an authoritative and caching DNS server. Though the software can handle this fine, there are some security considerations. The main one of these is due to an attack known as *DNS cache poisoning*, which allows an attacker to make your caching DNS server hand out incorrect addresses. This can cause a user to click a malicious web link or open an e-mail with an embedded link.

■ **Note**   You can read more about DNS cache poisoning at http://en.wikipedia.org/wiki/ DNS_cache_poisoning.

Luckily BIND provides a way for us to mitigate this problem with DNSSEC, the security extension of the DNS protocol. With recent versions of bind (bind v9.7 and above), we can use auto key signing which will automatically sign and resign zones at the defined intervals. From version 9.9 onward we can use a feature called "inline" key signing.

There are two kinds of records we can create, NSEC and NSEC3. Depending on your requirements you can implement whichever is appropriate. They both provide "authenticated denial of existence," meaning that if a record is not available then you can trust the response from the server. The main difference between

449

the two records is that NSEC3 prevents zone walking, where you can build a map of the domain by what records are not there. You can read more about the differences at www.internetsociety.org/deploy360/resources/dnssec-nsec-vs-nsec3/.

■ **Tip** The next couple of steps will require a good amount of system entropy to create good-quality encryption keys. You should install haveged which is a daemon that will provide an additional source of entropy. See details at www.issihosts.com/haveged/.

We are going to create and store our keys in the /etc/bind/keys directory. We will need create that directory and then change our bind configuration file for the local zones to be like the following:

```
zone "example.com" {
    type master;
    file "master/example.com.db";
    key-directory "/etc/bind/keys";
    auto-dnssec maintain;
    inline-signing yes;
};

zone "0.168.192.in-addr.arpa" {
    type master;
    file "master/192.168.0.db";
    key-directory "/etc/bind/keys";
    auto-dnssec maintain;
    inline-signing yes;
};
```

We use the key-directory directive to tell bind where to find the keys we are going to creating. We will create those keys now. To do that we need the dnssec-keygen command to create a zone signing key (ZSK) and a key signing key (KSK). Change to the /etc/bind/keys directory and we will create our ZSK.

```
$ sudo dnssec-keygen -a RSASHA256 -b 2048 -3 example.com
Generating key pair..................................................+++ ...............+++
Kexample.net.+008+50331
```

Now we need a KSK to verify our zone key.

```
$ sudo dnssec-keygen -a RSASHA256 -b 2048 -f KSK -3 example.com
Generating key pair..................................................................+
++ .........................+++
Kexample.net.+008+62695
```

Looking inside the directory we see that there are four keys produced. Two private keys, ending with .private, and two public keys, ending in .key.

```
-rw-r--r-- 1 root bind  606 Jul  3 02:41  Kexample.net.+008+50331.key
-rw------- 1 root bind 1776 Jul  3 02:41  Kexample.net.+008+50331.private
-rw-r--r-- 1 root bind  605 Jul  3 02:44  Kexample.net.+008+62695.key
-rw------- 1 root bind 1776 Jul  3 02:44  Kexample.net.+008+62695.private
```

A copy of the private keys should be stored somewhere safe like we do with all highly sensitive information. You will notice that the keys are owned by the root user. We will need to change the owner of the files to bind (Ubuntu). With the keys in place we will start up our bind server using the $ sudo systemctl start bind9 command or if your bind server is already running we can run $ sudo rndc reconfig. We can view the logs using the $ sudo journalctl -x -u bind9 command in another terminal window or shell.

We will issue the following commands to make sure our zones are signed.

```
$ sudo rndc sign example.com
$ sudo rndc signing -list example.com
Done signing with key 814/RSASHA256
Done signing with key 62760/RSASHA256
```

In Listing 10-26 we can see the logs from the journalctl command.

Listing 10-26. bind journalctl Log

```
Jul 06 13:01:59 ubuntu-xenial named[12461]: received control channel command 'sign example.com'
Jul 06 13:01:59 ubuntu-xenial named[12461]: zone example.com/IN (signed): reconfiguring zone keys
Jul 06 13:01:59 ubuntu-xenial named[12461]: zone example.com/IN (signed): next key event: 06-Jul-2016 14:01:59.665
Jul 06 13:02:09 ubuntu-xenial named[12461]: received control channel command 'signing -list example.com'
Jul 06 13:04:40 ubuntu-xenial named[12461]: received control channel command 'sign 0.168.192.in-addr.arpa'
Jul 06 13:04:40 ubuntu-xenial named[12461]: zone 0.168.192.in-addr.arpa/IN (signed): reconfiguring zone keys
Jul 06 13:04:40 ubuntu-xenial named[12461]: zone 0.168.192.in-addr.arpa/IN (signed): next key event: 06-Jul-2016 14:04:40.598
```

You can see that the bind server has automatically signed our zones (zone example.com/IN (signed): loaded serial 2016070100). You can also see that we have a "next key event," which is when the keys will be regenerated. Now take a look at our zone file directory.

```
$ ll /var/cache/bind/master/
total 48
drwxr-xr-x 2 bind bind  4096 Jul  3 12:46 ./
drwxrwxr-x 3 root bind  4096 Jul  3 12:47 ../
-rw-r--r-- 1 bind bind   346 Jul  3 12:35 192.168.0.db
-rw-r--r-- 1 bind bind   512 Jul  3 12:35 192.168.0.db.jbk
-rw-r--r-- 1 bind bind   349 Jul  3 12:35 192.168.0.db.signed
-rw-r--r-- 1 bind bind   899 Jul  3 12:25 example.com.db
-rw-r--r-- 1 bind bind   512 Jul  3 12:35 example.com.db.jbk
-rw-r--r-- 1 bind bind   839 Jul  3 12:35 example.com.db.signed
-rw-r--r-- 1 bind bind 13384 Jul  3 12:46 example.com.db.signed.jnl
```

We now have zone files that have been signed (example.com.db.signed). We can now validate that our keys are signed as we expect.

```
$ dig +dnssec +multiline @127.0.0.1 mail.example.com
mail.example.com.       86400 IN A 192.168.0.1
mail.example.com.       86400 IN RRSIG A 8 3 86400 (
                        20160802120825 20160703120630 6513 example.com.
                        <snip>
                        TorDjrwEutOJnt1HLxoJ/+EVJ6K9l+sZfrfG4ZM4lB5i
                        eVxmZe3quQ3M+HHDHPVwZu1XwJkNz97Kuw== )
mail.example.com. 86400 IN RRSIG A 8 3 86400 (
                        20160802124245 20160703120630 65028 example.com.
                        <snip>
                        qGxaP6lJ+WKbIhw3NoqSd++E6bVUU5L46qaxczIhact3
                        xZEOwrAnAQ2MSq9Qx1b41ghbwfVBUOMQZQ== )
```

Adding a Slave Server

In order to provide reliable DNS services, virtually all domain registrars require you to enter a minimum of two DNS servers for any domain. It is, of course, possible to maintain multiple copies of all your zone files, but you can make use of the master/slave functionality in BIND to automate this process.

In this section we are going to add a DNS slave using our CentOS server. First we will show you how to configure the master.

■ **Note** We do note that some people object to using the "master/slave" terminology when describing leader/ follower relationships. BIND still uses this terminology and we have chosen to use the same in order not to confuse readers, rather than out of indifference to the subject.

Ubuntu

If you want to set up the master to allow transfers from slave hosts on Ubuntu, you need to change the zone definitions in /etc/bind/named.conf.local. You need to ensure that the master server contacts the slaves when a zone is updated, and you do this by adding the notify yes directive. This means you don't need to wait until the slave reaches the zone expiration time, as any zone changes on the master server will be replicated to the slave immediately.

Next, you add an allow-transfer directive, which should contain the IP address of the slave server. We've included the new definition for the example.com zone in Listing 10-27.

Listing 10-27. Adding Zone Definitions

```
acl "transfer-hosts" {
        192.168.0.254 ;
        127.0.0.1 ;
};
zone "example.com" {
    type master;
    file "master/example.com.db";
    notify yes;
```

```
allow-transfer {
  transfer-hosts ;
};
key-directory "/etc/bind/keys";
auto-dnssec maintain;
inline-signing yes;
};
```

What we have done in Figure 10-26 is use a variable called "transfer-hosts," which we created with the acl option in our bind zone configuration file. We have then used that in the allow-transfer section to allow the IP addresses we have defined in transfer-hosts. Creating acl variables is good practice as you can quickly update your configuration in one place. It makes reading and validation of your configuration easier. If we add more slaves, we can add them to the transfer-hosts acl.

When you've added the addresses for all slaves, save the file and then tell BIND to reload its configuration via sudo rndc reload.

■ **Tip** To test the master configuration, you can use dig on the slave to simulate a zone transfer. Use the AXFR query type: dig example.com @127.0.0.1 AXFR.

By default, the bind server listens on the localhost address (127.0.0.1). You will need to set the listen-on named.conf option to get the bind server to listen on the local network interface. For the master you will need to add the following to the /etc/bind/named.conf.options file.

```
listen-on port 53 { 127.0.0.1; 192.168.0.1; };
```

On the slave you will need to add the following to the /etc/named.conf file:

```
listen-on port 53 { 127.0.0.1; 192.168.0.254; };
...
allow-query     { localhost; 192.168.0.0/24; };
```

The next step is to tell the slave server where to find the master. Open the /etc/named/named.conf. local file on the slave server and add a zone definition for the example.com domain. Set the zone type to slave. To make sure that the server can retrieve the zone data, you need to specify the address for the master server in the masters configuration block. We've included the configuration for our network in Listing 10-28.

Listing 10-28. Slave Server Zone Configuration

```
zone "example.com" {
    type slave;
    masters {
        192.168.0.1;
    };
    file "slaves/example.com.db";
};
```

When you've finished, save the configuration file and tell the slave server to reload it via sudo rndc reload. You can check the /var/log/syslog file to verify that the zone is being transferred, or you can query the slave server using host or dig to ensure the zone data is present.

While watching the bind log (sudo journalctl -xf -u bind9) you and send a $ sudo rndc notify example.com command to tell the slaves to check in and transfer the zones. On the slave log (sudo journalctl -xf -u named) after triggering the notify you will see something similar to the following:

```
Jul 05 09:35:47 au-mel-centos-1 named[4266]: client 192.168.0.1#47692: received notify for
zone 'example.com'
Jul 05 09:35:47 au-mel-centos-1 named[4266]: master 192.168.0.1#53 (source 0.0.0.0#0)
deleted from unreachable cache
Jul 05 09:35:47 au-mel-centos-1 named[4266]: zone example.com/IN: Transfer started.
Jul 05 09:35:47 au-mel-centos-1 named[4266]: transfer of 'example.com/IN' from
192.168.0.1#53: connected using 192.168.0.254#34645
Jul 05 09:35:47 au-mel-centos-1 named[4266]: zone example.com/IN: transferred serial
2016070107
Jul 05 09:35:47 au-mel-centos-1 named[4266]: transfer of 'example.com/IN' from
192.168.0.1#53: Transfer completed: 1 messages, 82 records, 17410 bytes, 0.001 secs
(17410000 bytes/sec)
```

The last line shows us that we have transferred 82 records. This shows that the master will transfer zone files to the slave. You should now be able to dig the slave and resolve the following:

```
$ dig @192.168.0.254 mail.example.com
...
;; ANSWER SECTION:
mail.example.com.        86400    IN    A      192.168.0.1
...
;; SERVER: 192.168.0.254#53(192.168.0.254)
...
```

Dynamic DNS

If your ISP is assigning your host a new random address each time you connect to the Internet, running your own authoritative DNS doesn't make a lot of sense. Your server's address will keep changing, and you will need to keep changing the delegation information in the WHOIS database.

An alternative solution is dynamic DNS, which is available from various providers on the Internet. With this solution, the dynamic DNS provider hosts DNS servers. A small client application runs on one of your systems and remotely updates host records on the DNS servers whenever your IP address changes. The TTL on these dynamic DNS services is low enough not to interrupt services like mail delivery. Of course, you can also use such a service even if your external IP address never changes.

There are various dynamic DNS providers, a non-exhaustive list of which is available at www.dmoz. org/Computers/Internet/Protocols/DNS/DNS_Providers/Dynamic_DNS. If you choose to outsource DNS hosting this way, the dynamic DNS provider you choose will provide you with DNS server details to enter in your registrar's registration form.

If you require dynamic updates, you should choose a provider that offers a client utility that works under Linux. A few of these utilities are available as packages in Ubuntu, such as ddclient:

- https://help.ubuntu.com/community/DynamicDNS

- *ddclient*: http://sourceforge.net/projects/ddclient/ and http://dag.wieers. com/rpm/packages/ddclient/

- *noip (source)*: www.noip.com/download?page=linux

For CentOS, you will need to download the tarball for one of these tools and install it by hand, or find an RPM package created by a third party. The instructions here for Ubuntu should work the same for CentOS: www.noip.com/support/knowledgebase/installing-the-linux-dynamic-update-client-on-ubuntu/.

Of course, many home/business firewall routers also support dynamic dns updating and may be a better choice if you have one.

Dynamic DNS is not to be confused with local dynamic dns updates, which is in principle similar but different. We are going to go through dynamic dns updates shortly.

Dynamic Host Configuration Protocol

Now that we have naming of hosts sorted, it might be nice to have network addresses assigned automatically to some hosts, like workstations or laptops. The service used for this is Dynamic Host Configuration Protocol. It consists of a server, which defines which addresses can be assigned to which clients, and a client, which requests addresses from the server and uses the response to configure the local network interface.

This is great for random machines that you may want to add to your network, where you don't really care what address is assigned to them. However, for servers, if you use DHCP on them, you'll usually want static allocation. If a server's address changes unpredictably, you may not be able to use the services it provides.

Luckily, the DHCP server allows you to split your range of available network addresses into pools. Each of these pools can then be configured to be assigned to known hosts, or to unknown hosts. This way, it's possible to have visiting laptops assigned a random free address in a specific range from a specific pool.

Installing and Configuring

The DHCP server is provided by the `isc-dhcp-server` package on Ubuntu and the `dhcp` package on CentOS. On Ubuntu and CentOS, a sample configuration file is installed as `/etc/dhcp/dhcpd.conf`. On CentOS this file doesn't have any configuration. It does have instructions on where to find an example file, which you can see by issuing:

```
$ cat /usr/share/doc/dhcp*/dhcpd.conf.example
```

The configuration file consists of a set of global directives followed by one or more subnet definitions. Comments are prefixed with hash marks (#). We've included the global directives from the Ubuntu file in Listing 10-29 (removing the comments).

Listing 10-29. dhcpd.conf Global Settings

```
ddns-update-style none;
option domain-name "example.org";
option domain-name-servers ns1.example.org, ns2.example.org;
default-lease-time 600;
max-lease-time 7200;
log-facility local7;
```

The first directive specifies that our DHCP server will not do DNS updates for addresses that it hands out. You'll see a bit later how to change this. The `default-lease-time` directive specifies how long a DHCP lease will be active if a connecting client does not specify a time. If it does specify a time, this time cannot be longer than `max-lease-time`. Both settings specify a time in seconds. Finally, the `log-facility` specifies how the system logger should handle log entries generated by the DHCP server. We'll show you how to configure the syslog side of things in Chapter 18. The options are passed to the dhcp-client and used to update the `resolv.conf` file. These current options are examples and not something we have set.

Let's change this configuration somewhat to suit our own needs. As we don't expect to have many machines turn on and off every minute, we can increase the lease times as well. Let's set the default to six hours and the maximum to 24 hours.

```
default-lease-time 21600;
max-lease-time 86400;
```

With that done, we can add a subnet on which our DHCP server should hand out leases.

```
subnet 192.168.0.0 netmask 255.255.255.0 {
}
```

The DHCP server will check the network addresses assigned to the local network interfaces when it starts and automatically assign each subnet declaration to the correct network interface.

We can now add subnet-specific options within this configuration block. We'll start with options that define which address to use as the default route on our network and which host to use as the name server.

```
subnet 192.168.0.0 netmask 255.255.255.0 {
    option routers 192.168.0.254;
    option domain-name "example.com";
    option domain-name-servers 192.168.0.1;
    option broadcast-address 192.168.0.255;
}
```

Here we have defined which network settings should be sent to a client when it requests a lease. The router option specifies the default gateway to be used by the client. The domain-name option speaks for itself. In the domain-name-servers option, we can add one or more DNS server addresses, separated by spaces. The broadcast address is a special address on the network that is used to send requests to all hosts on the same network range, and we specify it via the broadcast-address option.

However, we have not yet specified any addresses that the DHCP server is allowed to hand out. We do this via the range directive.

```
subnet 192.168.0.0 netmask 255.255.255.0 {
    option routers 192.168.0.254;
    option domain-name "example.com";
    option domain-name-servers 192.168.0.1;
    option broadcast-address 192.168.0.255;
    option subnet-mask 255.255.255.0;
    range 192.168.0.101 192.168.0.200;
}
```

This tells the server that if a client requests a lease, it may assign any address from 192.168.0.101 through 192.168.0.200. We don't specify the full network range here, so that we have some addresses left to assign manually to servers or other hosts.

All that is left for us to do now is tell the DHCP server which network interfaces it should listen on. If we don't do this, it won't start. On Ubuntu, we can specify this by editing the /etc/default/isc-dhcp-server file and adding each interface on which we want the server to listen to the INTERFACES variable.

```
INTERFACES="enp0s3"
```

On CentOS, we do not need to set an interface on which to listen on. When dhcpd starts it will listen on any interface it can associate with a subnet declaration. So if interface enp0s100 has an ip address of 192.168.100.1/24, and we have a subnet declared in dhcpd.conf of 192.168.100.0/24 – the enp0s100 interface will automatically be used for that subnet.

We save the file and then start the server using `sudo system start isc-dhcp-server` on Ubuntu or `sudo systemclt start dhcpd` on CentOS.

When the server assigns a lease to a specific client, it records the client MAC (Media Access Control) address and the assigned lease to a file. Generally, it tries to reassign the same address to a client when it reconnects, even if more time than `max-lease-time` has passed. Of course, if the address isn't available because it has been assigned to a different client, the server will need to issue a different one.

Static Lease Assignments

Sometimes you want to be able to assign the same IP address to a host or device-for instance, a networked printer or a workstation that hosts a development web site. You can manually edit the configuration on the client, but that means you need to log in to a client to make changes to the network configuration. You might also end up with IP address clashes if DHCP assigns the same address to a new host that someone has assigned to another.

DHCP allows you to assign the same IP address to a host by matching it with the host's MAC address. If you make use of this, you can change address assignments to any host by simply editing `dhcpd.conf`, restarting the DHCP service, and waiting for a host to renew its lease.

Recall that you can obtain the MAC address for a host by running the `ip link show` command. You can also run the `arp` command to list IP addresses and associated MAC addresses on the local network, but that might be hard to match the address to the right machine.

These configuration directives all go within the subnet block in the `dhcpd.conf` file. You start by defining a group, which you can give any name you like; here we've chosen "static."

```
subnet ... {
    group "static" {
    }
}
```

Next, you add a host definition. Each host is defined in a block of its own, within your group definition. The `hardware ethernet` option specifies the MAC address that will have the address specified with the `fixed-address` option assigned to it.

■ **Note**   You can find out the MAC address for a network interface via the `ip link show` command.

This option can contain either an IP address or a resolvable FQDN. We'll use the FQDN, as DNS is working fine for us. It also means that if we want to change the IP address that is assigned to the host, but don't want to change its hostname, we only need to update the DNS zone file and not the DHCP server as well.

```
subnet ... {
    group "static" {
        host au-mel-ubuntu-2 {
            hardware ethernet 00:16:3E:15:3C:C2;
            fixed-address au-mel-ubuntu-2.example.com;
        }
    }
}
```

We set the use-host-decl-names flag to on. This ensures that the name we set on the host block—au-mel-ubuntu-2 in our case—will be sent to the DHCP client as the hostname it should use. If we did not set this, we would have to add a specific hostname option to each static host we define this way. Because we define it within the group, it does not apply to any configurations that fall outside this group.

```
subnet ... {
    group "static" {
        use-host-decl-names on;
        host au-mel-ubuntu-2 {
            hardware ethernet 00:16:3E:15:3C:C2;
            fixed-address au-mel-ubuntu-2.example.com;
        }
    }
}
```

Finally, we will want to make sure that the addresses we use for static DHCP leases never get assigned to clients the DHCP server doesn't know about. We can reserve some of our 100 addresses for this purpose by defining address pools. We'll first define a pool for hosts the DHCP server knows about. Again, these pool definitions go within the subnet block.

```
subnet ... {
    ...
    pool {
        range 192.168.0.101 192.168.0.150;
        deny unknown clients
    }
}
```

This reserves 50 addresses for use with hosts that need a static assignment. Next we'll define a pool for all other clients. On this pool we will also override the lease times, as visiting machines generally won't need an address all day long.

```
subnet ... {
    ...
    pool {
        range 192.168.0.101 192.168.0.150;
        deny unknown clients
    }
    pool {
        range 192.168.0.151 192.168.0.200;
        allow unknown clients;
        default-lease-time 7200;
        max-lease-time 21600;
    }
}
```

We have split our original range of IP addresses into two. To make sure the server doesn't think it's allowed to assign the same range twice, we comment out the original statement near the top of the file.

```
subnet ... {
    ...
    // range 192.168.0.101 192.168.0.200;
...
```

We can now restart the DHCP server. All that is left to do is make sure DHCP requests reach our server through the firewall. A DHCP client by definition does not have an IP address assigned yet, so it cannot send a packet to a specific network address.

What it does instead is broadcast a UDP packet to port 67 at the address 255.255.255.255, which is the broadcast address for the 0.0.0.0 network. The DHCP server knows to listen for these packets and will respond if it receives one. We thus need to configure the firewall on the DHCP server host to accept packets to port 67 at any address.

```
$ sudo /sbin/iptables -t filter -A INPUT -p udp --dport 67 -j ACCEPT
```

We now have a DHCP server configuration that assigns specific reserved IP addresses to defined hosts and uses a different address range for other hosts. By having these hosts use a predetermined set of IP addresses, we can also regulate their access by setting firewall rules and changing server configurations to either grant or deny access based on the address a host is connecting with.

Dynamic DNS Updates

You might also want to assign fixed DNS names to specific hosts, regardless of which IP address they were assigned by the DHCP server. This allows you to refer to machines by name, even if their address changes. This is accomplished by setting up a cryptographic key that is shared by both the DNS and DHCP servers. The DHCP server will then contact the DNS server when it issues a new lease and update the associated A and PTR entries, if required.

Configuring DNS

On Ubuntu, we start by generating the key, and for this we will use the ddns-confgen tool. We will specify the hmac-sha512 algorithm with the -a option, give the key a name with -k option and declare the zone with -z option.

```
# ddns-confgen -a hmac-sha512 -k dynamic-update-key -z example.com
# To activate this key, place the following in named.conf, and
# in a separate keyfile on the system or systems from which nsupdate
# will be run:
key "dynamic-update-key" {
        algorithm hmac-sha512;
        secret "kHATLZ8hl4RbSoe7W71pqaGZ3oCIP3WIgZZI/UcXYzbOooCOTS3cN7lFdQ/+97VYVfFYEGmzRCq
RKyj4AcLfdg==";
};

# Then, in the "zone" definition statement for "example.com",
# place an "update-policy" statement like this one, adjusted as
# needed for your preferred permissions:
update-policy {
        grant dynamic-update-key zonesub ANY;
};
```

```
# After the keyfile has been placed, the following command will
# execute nsupdate using this key:
nsupdate -k <keyfile>
```

We are shown a helpful output of what we need to do next. If you don't want to see this output, you can use the -q option.

We are going to add key "dynamic-update-key" to our /etc/bind/named.conf.options file.

```
key "dynamic-update-key" {
      algorithm hmac-sha512;
      secret "kHATLZ8hl4RbSoe7W71pqaGZ3oCIP3WIgZZI/UcXYzbOooCOTS3cN7lFdQ/+97VYVfFYEGmzRCqRKy
j4AcLfdg==";
};
```

Next we need to add the update-policy to the zone definition for the example.com zone file.

```
zone "example.com" {
    type master;
    file "master/example.com.db";
    notify yes;
    allow-transfer {
      transfer-hosts ;
    };
    update-policy {
      grant dynamic-update-key zonesub ANY;
    };
    key-directory "/etc/bind/keys";
    auto-dnssec maintain;
    inline-signing yes;
};
```

We then reload the name server configuration via sudo rndc reload.

■ **Tip** You can also use key-based authentication between master and slave DNS servers.

Configuring DHCP

The next step is to tell the DHCP server about this key as well, and to configure it so it sends DNS update requests to named when it hands out a new lease. We start by changing the ddns-update-style variable from none to interim. We also want a fairly low TTL on these dynamic DNS entries, so they don't remain active after a host disappears off the network. We'll specify an hour.

```
ddns-update-style interim;
ddns-ttl 3600;
```

Under that, still in the global configuration section, we add the key definition. It is important to use exactly the same key name used on the name server, or the updates will not work.

```
key "dynamic-update-key" {
  algorithm hmac-sha512;
  secret "kHATLZ8hl4RbSoe7W71pqaGZ3oCIP3WIgZZI/UcXYzbOooCOTS3cN7lFdQ/+97VYVfFYEGmzRCqRKyj4A
cLfdg==";
}
```

You will notice that we have removed the ';' from the {}. And finally we need to tell the DHCP server that we want to perform dynamic updates on the forward and reverse zones. We need to add a zone definition for each zone in the global section of the configuration file. We also need to specify which key should be used for updates and which DNS server the updates need to be sent to, as shown in Listing 10-30.

Listing 10-30. Adding Zone Update Definitions in dhcpd.conf

```
zone 0.168.192.in-addr.arpa. {
    key dynamic-update-key;
    primary 192.168.0.1;
}
zone example.com. {
    key dynamic-update-key;
    primary 192.168.0.1;
}
```

We restart the DHCP server as well, and when that is done, the server-side configuration is complete. All that remains to do now is tell the DHCP clients to send a hostname string to the server when they ask for a lease. This hostname string will then be used to create the FQDN for the DNS entries.

To set it, we edit the file /etc/dhclient.conf on the client and add the send host-name option. On a host that we'd like to be named au-mel-centos-2.example.com, we add the following:

```
send host-name "au-mel-centos-2";
```

■ **Note** The configuration in /etc/dhclient.conf is applied to all network interfaces. You can use the /etc/dhclient-enp0s3.conf file instead to apply it to the first interface only.

We can then run the dhclient utility to renew our address lease, as shown in Listing 10-31. This would also run automatically at boot time if we'd configured the host to use DHCP. If that is the case, and you want to manually renew a lease, you should first kill the running dhclient process.

Listing 10-31. Obtaining a Lease with dhclient

```
$ sudo dhclient enp0s3
Internet Systems Consortium DHCP Client V3.0.5-RedHat
Copyright 2004-2006 Internet Systems Consortium. All rights reserved.
For info, please visit http://www.isc.org/sw/dhcp/

Listening on       LPF/eth1/00:0c:29:7b:b1:77
Sending on         LPF/eth1/00:0c:29:7b:b1:77
Sending on         Socket/fallback
DHCPREQUEST on enp0s3 to 255.255.255.255 port 67
DHCPACK from 192.168.0.1
bound to 192.168.0.200 -- renewal in 7181 seconds.
```

We can check the system log on the server to see what happened. We've included a snippet in Listing 10-32. On CentOS this log file would be /var/log/messages, and on Ubuntu it would be /var/log/syslog. We'll show you how you can redirect specific log messages to different files in Chapter 18.

Listing 10-32. The DHCP Server Log

```
Jun 11 11:23:15 au-mel-ubuntu-1 dhcpd: DHCPDISCOVER from 00:0c:29:7b:b1:77 via enp0s3
Jun 11 11:23:16 au-mel-ubuntu-1 dhcpd: DHCPOFFER on 192.168.0.200 to
    00:0c:29:7b:b1:77 (au-mel-centos-2) via enp0s3
Jun 11 11:23:16 au-mel-ubuntu-1 named[5187]: client 192.168.0.1#46749: updating
    zone 'example.com/IN': adding an RR at 'au-mel-centos-2.example.com' A
Jun 11 11:23:16 au-mel-ubuntu-1 named[5187]: client 192.168.0.1#46749: updating
    zone 'example.com/IN': adding an RR at 'au-mel-centos-2.example.com' TXT
Jun 11 11:23:16 au-mel-ubuntu-1 named[5187]: journal file example.com.db.jnl does
    not exist, creating it
Jun 11 11:23:16 au-mel-ubuntu-1 dhcpd: Added new forward map from
    au-mel-centos-2.example.com to 192.168.0.200
Jun 11 11:23:16 au-mel-ubuntu-1 named[5187]: zone example.com/IN:sending
    notifies (serial 2009020102)
Jun 11 11:23:16 au-mel-ubuntu-1 named[5187]: client 192.168.0.1#58073: updating zone
    '0.168.192.in-addr.arpa/IN': deleting rrset at '200.0.168.192.in-addr.arpa' PTR
Jun 11 11:23:16 au-mel-ubuntu-1 named[5187]: client 192.168.0.1#58073: updating zone
    '0.168.192.in-addr.arpa/IN': adding an RR at '200.0.168.192.in-addr.arpa' PTR
Jun 11 11:23:16 au-mel-ubuntu-1 named[5187]: journal file 192.168.0.db.jnl does
    not exist, creating it
Jun 11 11:23:16 au-mel-ubuntu-1 dhcpd: added reverse map from
    200.0.168.192.in-addr.arpa. to au-mel-centos-2.example.com
Jun 11 11:23:16 au-mel-ubuntu-1 dhcpd: DHCPREQUEST for 192.168.0.200 (192.168.0.1)
    from 00:0c:29:7b:b1:77 (au-mel-centos-2) via enp0s3
Jun 11 11:23:16 au-mel-ubuntu-1 dhcpd: DHCPACK on 192.168.0.200 to
    00:0c:29:7b:b1:77 (au-mel-centos-2) via enp0s3
```

You can see the server received a DHCP request from a host with MAC address 00:0c:29:7b:b1:77. It then offered this host the address 192.168.0.200 and was told the host's name is au-mel-centos-2. Next, you can see the name server adding an A and a TXT record for the au-mel-centos-2.example.com FQDN. The TXT entry contains a checksum that is used to track whether a DNS entry was created by the DHCP server. If it is not present, the server will not change or remove the associated A entry.

The changes to the zone are then written to a journal file that is associated with the zone file created earlier. The actual zone file itself is not modified. After the forward zone is updated, it sends a notification to any slave servers that are configured for this zone. If we had any, this would trigger the slaves to transfer the updates zone file from the master.

Next, the same process is repeated for the reverse zone. When that is also done, the DHCP server allows the client to obtain the lease it offered and updates its internal leases file. We can quickly double-check that these new DNS entries work by performing a lookup via the host command.

```
$ host 192.168.0.200
200.0.168.192.in-addr.arpa domain name pointer au-mel-centos-2.example.com.
$ host au-mel-centos-2.example.com.
au-mel-centos-2.example.com has address 192.168.0.200
```

Both lookups work, so we can now configure any other hosts on the network that we also want to have dynamically updated in the DNS server.

Manually Changing DNS Entries

Because these dynamic updates use a journal file, you need to perform an extra step if you want to manually change any DNS entries. If you simply change the zone file, these changes will be ignored because the data in the journal file will supersede it.

You can tell the DNS server you want to lock the zone journal files and reject any dynamic changes while you're editing a zone by issuing the sudo rndc freeze command before you start editing. When you're done editing the zone file, you can permit dynamic updates again by unlocking the zone via sudo rndc unfreeze.

THE INTERNET SUPERSERVER

Not all network services need to run all the time. For some of them, it would be handy to have a way of listening for traffic on a specific port number and start the service only when it is needed. Once a client disconnects, the service can be shut down again. Not all services support this, but if they do, it is a nice way to conserve system resources.

This "supervisor" functionality is provided by the Internet superserver. The latest and most feature-rich version of this software is provided by the xinetd package.

Each service that is managed by xinetd has its own configuration file snippet in the /etc/xinetd.d directory, and by default it will install configuration files for some very basic services, such as echo, which simply repeats any character you send to it. These services are not enabled until you edit their configuration files, though.

We'll show you how to add a service to xinetd in Chapter 19.

Secure Shell

Thus far, you've really only used SSH to connect from a workstation to a server, in order to make configuration changes or add new software. We'll now show you how you can get the most out of SSH. We'll set up key-based authentication, use ssh to copy files between hosts, and make use of tunnels to access remote services through a firewall.

When you connect to a host via SSH, you are asked to enter your password. This is fine if you need to type it once a day, but if you connect to remote hosts often, it can become time-consuming, especially if you have a secure, long password.

SSH allows you to use key-based authentication instead. To make use of this, you create public and private keys and then copy the public key to the remote servers you want to connect to. When you connect, the remote host will verify that you have the private key that belongs to the public key component on that host. If you do, you are authenticated.

■ **Note** The public and private keys are used to authenticate you. The connection encryption is provided by the SSH host keys, which are generated when the service is installed.

Creating and Distributing Keys

We'll start by creating a public/private key pair using the ssh-keygen utility. We can define the key type (two encryption algorithms are supported) and key size in bits, as well as the output file names to use. For the latter we'll use the defaults, and for the former we'll specify the RSA algorithm with the -t option and a 4096-bit key using the -b option, as shown in Listing 10-33.

Listing 10-33. Generating a New SSH Key Pair

```
$ ssh-keygen -t rsa -b 4096
Generating public/private rsa key pair.
Enter file in which to save the key (/home/jsmith/.ssh/id_rsa):
Enter passphrase (empty for no passphrase):
Enter same passphrase again:
Your identification has been saved in /home/jsmith/.ssh/id_rsa.
Your public key has been saved in /home/jsmith/.ssh/id_rsa.pub.
The key fingerprint is:
c9:62:dd:da:cd:71:33:78:3d:08:93:3e:8c:25:b0:f3 jsmith@au-ubuntu-1.example.com
```

It is important to add a passphrase to your private key, as without one anyone who gets hold of your private key can use it to log in (without the need for a password) to any host that contains your public key.

Now that we have a key pair, we can copy the public part to a remote host. We need to store the public key in a file called authorized_keys in the .ssh directory in our home directory in order to be able to use it to log in. We can either add the key to that file by hand or use the ssh-copy-id utility to do this for us, as in Listing 10-34.

Listing 10-34. Copying a Public SSH Key to a Remote Host

```
$ ssh-copy-id au-mel-centos-1.example.com
The authenticity of host 'au-mel-centos-1.example.com (192.168.0.1)' can't be
    established.
RSA key fingerprint is 67:e3:50:bf:8c:2c:a0:d5:0c:e9:fc:26:3f:9f:ea:0e. Are you sure you
want to continue connecting (yes/no)? yes
Warning: Permanently added 'au-mel-centos-1.example.com,192.168.0.1' (RSA) to the
    list of known hosts.
jsmith@au-mel-centos-1.example.com's password:
```

Now we'll try logging in to the machine with the following:

```
$ ssh au-mel-centos-1.example.com
```

Since we had not yet connected to au-mel-centos-1 from the host we're logged in to, we're prompted to accept the remote SSH host key. The fingerprint that uniquely identifies this key is printed, so you can visually verify whether it matches with the key on the remote host.

■ **Note** To obtain a host key fingerprint, you can use the ssh-keygen tool. In this case, use ssh-keygen -l -f /etc/ssh/ssh_host_rsa_key.pub to obtain the fingerprint for the host RSA key.

You'll note that SSH assumes our username on the remote host is the same as the user we're logged in as locally. If this is not the case, we can copy the key to username@remotehost instead.

Next, we're prompted for the login password, since our key is not yet listed in the correct file on the remote host. Once we're authenticated, ssh-copy-id appends the public key to the correct file and asks us to test it. We do this by logging in to the remote host, as shown in Listing 10-35.

Listing 10-35. Logging In Using an SSH Key

```
$ ssh au-mel-centos-1.example.com
Enter passphrase for key '/home/jsmith/.ssh/id_rsa':
Last login: Tue Feb 10 15:14:42 2009 from au-mel-ubuntu-1.example.com
[jsmith@au-mel-centos-1 ~]$
```

This time, we were not asked for our login password on au-mel-centos-1, which is exactly what we wanted. We can now check the .ssh/authorized_keys file on au-mel-centos-1 to make sure we haven't added extra, unexpected keys.

Of course public keys can also be installed into user's home directories at the time we provision our servers. They can also be provisioned by configuration management services like Puppet, Ansible, Chef, or SaltStack. We will look at configuration management service later in Chapter 19.

Using SSH Agent

However, we did still have to enter the password we set on the private SSH key. If you have to do this each time you want to connect to a remote host, it defeats the purpose of setting up key-based authentication. Enter the SSH agent, a small daemon that keeps unlocked private SSH keys in memory. Once we start it, we can unlock one or more private keys and add them to the agent. SSH can then use the agent to provide a private key and authenticate us to a remote host.

The way to tell SSH about the agent is by setting two environment variables, SSH_AUTH_SOCK and SSH_AGENT_PID. If these are set, ssh can communicate with the agent. The agent outputs shell code to set these variables when it starts, as you can see in Listing 10-36.

Listing 10-36. Starting ssh-agent

```
$ ssh-agent
SSH_AUTH_SOCK=/tmp/ssh-SZGGF11534/agent.11534; export SSH_AUTH_SOCK; SSH_AGENT_PID=11535;
export SSH_AGENT_PID;
echo Agent pid 11535;
```

If we then paste these lines into the shell, the variables will be set.

```
$ SSH_AUTH_SOCK=/tmp/ssh-SZGGF11534/agent.11534; export SSH_AUTH_SOCK;
$ SSH_AGENT_PID=11535; export SSH_AGENT_PID;
$ echo Agent pid 11535;
Agent pid 11535
```

Having to copy and paste these lines is a bit cumbersome, so instead we can use the eval shell function to make life a bit easier. This function executes any parameters passed to it as if they were commands. First, we'll stop the agent via ssh-agent -k, and then we'll restart it and set the environment variables in one fell swoop. The backquotes around the parameter cause it to be executed as a command by the shell. The output this command generates is then interpreted by eval.

```
$ ssh-agent -k
unset SSH_AUTH_SOCK;
unset SSH_AGENT_PID;
echo Agent pid 11535 killed;
$ eval `ssh-agent`
Agent pid 11541
```

All we need to do now is unlock the private key and add it to the agent.

```
$ ssh-add
Enter passphrase for /home/jsmith/.ssh/id_rsa:
Identity added: /home/jsmith/.ssh/id_rsa (/home/jsmith/.ssh/id_rsa)
```

We are able to connect to any host that contains the matching public key, without any further need to enter a password.

```
$ ssh jsmith@au-mel-centos-1
Last login: Tue Feb 10 15:17:19 2009 from au-mel-ubuntu-1.example.com
[jsmith@au-mel-centos-1 ~]$
```

■ **Tip**   You can tell multiple shells on the same host that you are using the agent by simply setting the SSH_ AUTH_SOCK and SSH_AGENT_PID variables to the correct values in the shell.

Tweaking SSH Configuration

When all your SSH servers listen on the same port and you use a single key pair for all hosts, the default server configuration will suit you fine. If not (e.g., port 22 traffic might be firewalled or the remote username is different for each host), you might want to tweak the configuration for your server or client somewhat.

Basic Server Configuration

The server side of SSH reads its configuration from the /etc/ssh/sshd_config file. By default, it listens on port 22 on all available network interfaces. You can change this by changing the Port and ListenAddress options in the configuration file.

The Port option takes a single parameter, which is the port number you want the server to listen on. To have the server listen on multiple ports, you can add extra Port directives, one for each port number.

This also applies to the ListenAddress directive. As long as no such directive is present, the server will listen on all interfaces. When you add one, it will start listening on all defined ports on only the address specified. You can have it listen on multiple addresses by adding additional ListenAddress directives.

For instance, to make the SSH server on our bastion host listen on ports 22 and 2022 only on the internal network interfaces, we can add these directives to the configuration file:

```
Port 22
Port 2022
ListenAddress 192.168.0.1
ListenAddress 19.168.1.1
```

We can now tell the server to reload its configuration file via sudo systemctl reload sshd on CentOS or sudo systemctl reload ssh on Ubuntu. This will not affect current connections, so you can run this command remotely.

■ **Caution** Make sure you do not reconfigure the SSH server to the point where you can no longer access it! If you're worried, do not log out after a configuration change. Try creating a new connection first, to ensure it still works.

The other basic server option we'll cover is designed to make your life easier when working with GUI applications on remote hosts. When the X11Forwarding option is set to on and you pass the -X parameter to the SSH client when you connect to such a host, you can run any graphical applications and their windows will be displayed on your local desktop. This feature takes advantage of the client/server modes of the X Window System by forwarding any connection attempts to an X server on the remote host through your SSH connection to the X server on your local host.

To force all users to use key-based authentication, you can add PasswordAuthentication no in the server configuration file. This will prevent everyone from being able to log in with a password. Note that if you lose your private key, you will no longer be able to log in to hosts with this option set.

You can find a full listing of all available server configuration options on the man sshd_config manual page.

Client Configuration

The SSH client can be configured globally for all users on a host and locally as well, specifically for each user. The global configuration file is /etc/ssh/ssh_config and the per-user file is .ssh/config in the user's home directory.

The most basic client configuration directives allow you to define which username and port number to use when you connect to a given host or all hosts. Each of these configuration blocks starts with a Host directive, which is followed by a hostname or a shortened alias if the section should apply to a single host only, or an asterisk if it should apply to all hosts.

For instance, we can easily customize our connection options for the bastion host by adding the following snippet to our .ssh/config file.

```
Host gateway
    Hostname au-mel-centos-1
    Port 2022
    User ataylor
```

This configuration is used each time we use the ssh gateway command. It tells the client to connect to the au-mel-centos-1 host on port number 2022 and log in as user ataylor. By adding these options in the client configuration file, we don't need to keep specifying the port number and login name on the command line.

Similarly, we can tell the client to use a different private key file when connecting to a remote host, by adding it using the `IdentityFile` directive. We'll generate a key pair to use for `ataylor` on the gateway host via `ssh-keygen -t rsa -s 2048 -f .ssh/gateway-ataylor`. Once done, we can tell the client to use this key for connections to the bastion host.

```
Host gateway
     Hostname au-mel-centos-1
     Port 2022
     User ataylor
     IdentityFile ~/.ssh/gateway-ataylor
```

The final options we'll cover are designed to make your life easier when working on remote hosts. First, the `ForwardAgent yes` option allows you to tell a server that it should use the SSH agent on the originating host for authentication. This allows you to hop from host to host via SSH, without needing to enter passwords to start an SSH agent on each of these hosts.

So you don't have to keep adding the -X parameter to ssh in order to enable X forwarding, you can enable it on a per-host basis in the configuration file as well. For each host on which you want to remotely run GUI applications, add a `ForwardX11 yes` directive to automatically enable this option.

Finally, you may have a jump host, or bastion host, that you have to first ssh to before getting access to a network beyond it. From a security point of view, it is easier to manage one jump host that proxies SSH connections into a private network, than to have every host in that private network exposed. We can use the PoxyCommand in the SSH config to configure a jump host.

```
Host jumphost
   Hostname jumphost.foo.com

Host private.foo.com
   Hostname 10.0.1.1
   ForwardAgent yes
   ProxyCommand ssh -qxT jumphost nc %h %p
```

To make a connection to `private.foo.com`, we first set up a proxying connection to jumphost. It works by setting up a netcat connection (nc) to the hostname 10.0.1.1(%h) with %p (22 is the default). We use the -q to not display annoying connection information, -x disables X11 forwarding, and –T disables the pseudo terminal on the jumphost (we don't require one for proxying).

In newer versions of OpenSSH (7.3 and above) you will use the ProxyJump configuration option which will handle this for you. It is also quite common for people to use the ProxyCommand ssh -W %h:%p jumphost instead of the nc command.

With this we can now issue a `ssh private.foo.com` command and ssh will connect to the jumphost and then establish a connection to `private.foo.com` directly.

Tunnelng

You can also use SSH to access protected services on remote hosts and networks without first setting up a VPN (Virtual Private Network). If two sites share the same private network ranges, a VPN would not work, as the address ranges on both sides of the VPN would be identical. In this case, you can use SSH to forward connections from a local host to a remote address or vice versa. Such forwards act as a single-port tunnel.

You can do this each via command-line parameters, or you can define forwards for each host in your .ssh/config file. For instance, you could create an SSH tunnel that forwards connections to port 8080 on your local host to port 80 on a machine on the remote network. This way, you are able to access a remote web site by browsing an address on your local network. You create a local forward by passing the -L option to the SSH client and specifying an optional local address followed by a mandatory local port as the start for the tunnel, and then a remote host and a remote port as the end for the tunnel, all separated by colons.

```
$ ssh -L 8080:192.168.1.12:80 ataylor@192.168.1.1
```

This command connects us to the host 192.168.1.1 as the user ataylor and sets up a tunnel that allows us to browse the web site on the host 192.168.1.12 by visiting http://localhost:8080 in our web browser. The connection will be forwarded over our SSH connection, and the web server on host 192.168.1.12 will see an incoming connection from the address 192.168.1.1.

■ **Note** Accessing them via a tunnel may not work for all web sites due to the way they are hosted. We will cover such name-based virtual hosting in Chapter 12.

Conversely, you can provide users on a remote host access to a service on your local network by creating a remote forward using the -R option. This option takes the same parameters as the -L option, but instead specifies an optional remote address and mandatory port number to listen on the remote host, followed by a local address and port number for the tunnel end point.

To allow a remote user to connect to a normally inaccessible SSH server on our local network, we can create a remote tunnel on port 2022 that forwards connections to port 22 on a host on our local network.

```
$ ssh -R 192.168.1.1:2022:192.168.0.15:22 ataylor@192.168.1.1
```

After we're logged on to the host 192.168.1.1 as user ataylor, we can SSH to port 2022 on the local host, which will then log us in to SSH on the host at 192.168.0.15.

For security reasons, the start of the tunnel will only ever bind to the loopback network interface, so users on different hosts on the network are not able to use the tunnel. We can change this behavior by adding the GatewayPorts directive to the SSH server configuration file. This option applies only to the starting point of the forward, so for local tunnels we add it on the local host, and for remote forwards we add it on the remote host.

To allow us to specify whether users on other hosts should be able to use a forward, we set the GatewayPorts option to clientspecified. If we do not specify an IP address for the forward starting point, it will be accessible only to local users, while it will be available to any users on the same network as the tunnel starting point if we specify an accessible address.

Since this requires quite a lot of typing, it's easier to define commonly used tunnels in the SSH client configuration file. We do this via the LocalForward and RemoteForward directives. Each of these takes two parameters, the forward starting address and port, separated by a colon, and the end point address and port, again separated by a colon.

We can add the forwards we used previously to our client configuration file:

```
Host gateway
    Hostname 192.168.1.1
    Port 22
    User ataylor
    IdentityFile ~/.ssh/gateway-ataylor
    LocalForward 8080 192.168.1.12:80
    RemoteForward 192.168.1.1:2022 192.168.0.15:22
```

Finally, the ForwardAgent yes option makes SSH configure the remote shell to use the SSH agent on your local host for any authentication. Provided your public key is available on all remote hosts, this allows you to hop from host to host without needing to re-enter your password or starting a new ssh-agent instance on each intermediate host. This is an extremely useful option, so you may as well enable it for all users by adding it to the global section of the /etc/ssh/ssh_config file.

Performing Quick and Secure File Transfers

The SSH protocol allows for more than just remote logins. You can also use it to securely transfer files between hosts. One way is to use the scp command, which works just like cp, except the source or target files can be prefixed by a remote username and hostname, as shown in Listing 10-37.

Listing 10-37. Using scp to Transfer a File to a Remote Host

```
$ scp data.txt jsmith@au-mel-centos-1:/tmp
data.txt                                    100% 3072KB    3.0MB/s    00:00
```

Because we had sent our public SSH key to au-mel-centos-1 previously, scp was able to use the SSH agent to authenticate and we weren't asked for a password. We can log in to the au-mel-centos-1 host and see the file data.txt is now in the /tmp directory.

We can also copy from a remote host back to a local host, by specifying a remote file path as the first parameter and a local file or directory second.

```
$ scp jsmith@au-mel-centos-1:/tmp/data.txt /tmp
data.txt                                    100% 3072KB    3.0MB/s    00:00
```

We can even copy files or directories from one remote host to another remote host without logging in to either of them. For instance, on au-mel-ubuntu-1 we could run the following:

```
$ scp jsmith@au-mel-centos-1:/tmp/data.txt ataylor@au-mel-centos-2:/tmp
data.txt                                    100% 3072KB    3.0MB/s    00:01
```

SSH also provides a replacement for the FTP. If you want to be able to interactively move files or directories, you can use the sftp command, as shown in Listing 10-38. Again, this command will use the SSH agent if present.

Listing 10-38. Using sftp

```
$ sftp jsmith@au-mel-centos-1
Connecting to au-mel-centos-1...
jsmith@au-mel-centos-1's password:
sftp> cd /tmp
sftp> ls
data.txt        ssh-IWYooo5675 sftp>
get data.txt
Fetching /tmp/data.txt to data.txt
/tmp/data.txt                               100% 3072KB    3.0MB/s    00:00
sftp> quit
```

▓ **Tip**   In combination with SSH port forwards, you can also easily copy files to hosts that aren't directly accessible. Note that `scp` uses the `-P` option to specify a port number, whereas `ssh` uses `-p`.

Summary

In this chapter, you learned about basic infrastructure services like NTP, DNS, and DHCP. We've also shown you how to connect to remote hosts, to make system administration and maintenance easier. You should now be able to do the following:

- Set and keep the correct time on all your hosts.

- Create forward and reverse DNS records for all your hosts and have these records replicate to multiple DNS servers.

- Set up DHCP to automate address assignment and link it to DNS to automatically update relevant DNS records.

- Use ssh, scp, and sftp to easily and securely work on remote hosts and transfer files.

In the next chapter, we'll introduce you to mail services and teach you how to run your own mail server.

CHAPTER 11

■ ■ ■

Web and SQL Services

By Peter Lieverdink and Dennis Matotek

One of the more common things you will do is set up web services. Most likely the web services will have a requirement for a Structured English Query Language (SEQUEL) database. In this chapter we are going to explore the major components of a secure web service.

In this chapter, you will learn how to securely set up the Apache web server and MariaDB database server. To secure communications with our new web server, we will use Let's Encrypt to create Secure Sockets Layer (SSL) /Transport Layer Security (TLS) certificates. This will provide us with certificates for securing other services too. Then we will show how to install a content management system and a webmail application. Finally, we will show you how to make web browsing a faster and safer experience for your staff by protecting them via a web proxy.

Apache Web Server

Apache is one of the most widely used pieces of open source software today. While its popularity has declined over the last few years, it is still used to host more than 30 percent of all web sites in existence[1] and is usually chosen for its maturity, stability, and the nature of the application. It is designed to be modular, so extra functionality can be added or removed by enabling or disabling modules. Packages are available for virtually all Linux distributions, so you can install it on your hosts via the package management system.

The Apache server can run as a single web server for a single site or, more commonly, can serve hundreds of sites as *virtual hosts*. That is, many web sites share the underlying resources, such as central processing unit (CPU), disk resources, and Internet Protocol (IP) addresses, of a single web server.

Apache currently has three multiprocessing modules (MPMs) that you can choose to use. They are prefork, worker, and event.

- The prefork module is where connections are handled by a separate process. It is suitable for nonthreadsafe web applications. In the prefork module, a control process creates a child process that listens for connections.

- The worker module is a mixture of process-based and thread-based processing. It is suitable for threadsafe applications. In the worker model, the parent process creates a child process that launches several threads; one thread is assigned to each incoming connection. One listens for incoming connections and passes them off to waiting server threads.

---

[1]See http://news.netcraft.com/archives/web_server_survey.html.

© Dennis Matotek, James Turnbull and Peter Lieverdink 2017
D. Matotek et al., *Pro Linux System Administration*, DOI 10.1007/978-1-4842-2008-5_11

- The event module is newer and based on the worker module. Its threading model is similar to worker but is optimized for handling keepalive connections. It dedicates several threads to handle keepalives, which hand active connections to waiting threads.

The other popular alternative to Apache web servers is Nginx. Nginx is a fast and modular web server that is often used in conjunction with the Apache server as a caching server or on its own as a web server. We will show how to install an Nginx server as part of the discussion on Ansible in Chapter 19.

Installation and Configuration

Both CentOS and Ubuntu install Apache version 2.4, but the packages are named differently. On CentOS, you run sudo yum install httpd, while on Ubuntu you run sudo aptitude install apache2. Adding these packages will cause some additional libraries to be installed.

Also, both CentOS and Ubuntu allow you to choose the MPM via loading the specific module you want to use. We will show how to do that shortly. Along with loading a specific MPM, you can load modules to load the necessary software to run different web server applications, such as PHP or Django. We are going to show you this shortly too.

■ **Note** If you run a high-volume, high-traffic web site, you might consider changing to a different Apache engine or different web server altogether, such as Nginx. Nginx differs from Apache as it is truly a nonblocking, event-driven, large-scale web server. For a good write-up on the differences and capabilities of these web servers, see https://www.digitalocean.com/community/tutorials/apache-vs-nginx-practical-considerations.

You can also find a list of web servers at http://en.wikipedia.org/wiki/Comparison_of_web_servers.

We'll start by showing how to do a basic configuration for Apache. Later, we'll show how to add some modules to extend functionality.

CentOS

In this section we are going to show how to configure our Apache web server. The Apache web server stores its configuration files in /etc/httpd, with the main configuration file being /etc/httpd/conf/httpd.conf. We are going to first edit the /etc/httpd/conf/httpd.conf file and then create a virtual host file.

The default MPM module for CentOS is prefork. You can change the module by editing /etc/httpd/conf.modules.d/00-mpm.conf and comment and uncomment the appropriate module. We are going to use the worker module as it provides a better performance profile over the prefork module.

```
#LoadModule mpm_prefork_module modules/mod_mpm_prefork.so
LoadModule mpm_worker_module modules/mod_mpm_worker.so
```

The main `httpd.conf` file is more than 350 lines long, so we will not be showing every option. As with many other Linux configuration files, # signifies comments, and options are in the form of <name> <directive>. Let's start with the basics: the server name (ServerName) and the webmaster e-mail address (ServerAdmin).

```
ServerName au-mel-centos-1.example.com
ServerAdmin webmaster@example.com
```

The server name and webmaster e-mail address are used by Apache when it displays default error pages. We have entered the values for our own host, au-mel-centos-1.example.com and webmaster@ example.com. By default, Apache will listen and serve requests on all available network addresses. If you want to select a specific address, you can use the `Listen` directive to change that. You can also configure the port you want to listen on. To change the default, you can specify something like this:

```
Listen 192.168.0.1:8080
```

The previous line specifies to listen only to a specific IPv4 address and on the port 8080. Be careful, because multiple `Listen` directives with the same IP and port will give an error ((98)Address already in use) when Apache tries to start. In our example, we will set `Listen` to listen on all addresses on port 80.

```
Listen 80
```

It is possible to change which user and group the web server runs as by setting the `User` and `Group` fields.

```
User apache
Group apache
```

If you change the `User` and `Group` fields, it is important that you do not change them to a user and group used elsewhere on the system, like a database user, for instance. The Apache service is started by the root user, so it can bind to port 80 (a *privileged* port) and launch child processes as the user defined here. This user should have as few privileges as possible and should be able to read the content it is serving.

Lastly, we will highlight these configuration items:

```
Include conf.modules.d/*.conf
IncludeOptional conf.d/*.conf
```

The first loads the modules, such as the MPMs described earlier. Modules provide different software capabilities; there are authorization modules, web language modules like PHP, and other kinds of features. The `IncludeOptional` directive can be used to store configuration files such as virtual hosts or other configuration files, such as `php.conf`. If these files are numbered, like `00-php.conf`, then they will be loaded in numeric order.

Creating a Virtual Host

We are ready now to create our first virtual host. A single Linux host running Apache can serve hundreds or thousands of web sites, all with their own hostnames. We call this *virtual hosting* because each of these sites is running on a single web server. There are two kinds of virtual hosting: IP based and name based. Apache can provide both.

IP-based virtual hosting causes Apache to serve a web page from a specific directory, based on the IP address the request was received on. For each IP-based virtual host, the Linux host needs to have an IP address assigned to a network interface. This is done by adding additional addresses to an interface, as we discussed in Chapter 7. This should be less common now that Server Name Indication (SNI; www.ietf.org/rfc/rfc4366.txt) is available, which is a way to provide the server name to the web server when using SSL/TLS certificates. Because some older browsers can't support SNI, you can still see IP-based virtual hosting where it makes sense to do so.

Name-based virtual hosting causes Apache to serve a web page for a specific directory based on the name of the site a remote user connected to. Any number of name-based virtual hosts can share a single IP address. The name of the site is determined by a special header that is sent in the request to the web server.

We are going to create a named virtual host. To do this, we need to create a configuration file for our site. We create this file in the Apache `conf.d` directory `/etc/httpd/conf.d/www.example.com.conf`. Let's start with how we describe the virtual host.

```
<VirtualHost *:80>
...
</VirtualHost>
```

Apache has a special syntax for describing virtual hosts. All configuration for each virtual host needs to be enclosed in the `<VirtualHost *:80>` ... `</VirtualHost>` directives. The opening directive declares the start of the virtual host and, in this case, specifies that you should listen on all network interfaces on port 80 for this host (`*:80`). We then close the virtual host configuration with the closing directive `</VirutalHost>`.

For a basic virtual host, we can use the following configuration:

```
<VirtualHost *:80>

  ServerName www.example.com
  ServerAdmin webmaster@example.com
  DocumentRoot  /var/www/html/www.example.com

</VirtualHost>
```

`ServerName` tells the Apache server that it should direct requests for the `www.example.com` web site to this virtual host. The `DocumentRoot` directory setting is where Apache serves the files for the web site from. You are able to override the webmaster e-mail address for this virtual host.

We can create an `index.html` file in our document root directory and start the Apache server.

```
$ sudo mkdir -p /var/www/html/www.example.com
$ sudo bash -c "echo www.example.com > /var/www/html/www.example.com/index.html"
```

Now we simply need to restart our Apache server. Prior to this, though, we should validate our Apache configuration. We do this with the following:

```
$ sudo apachectl configtest
Syntax OK
```

Here we are using the `apachectl` command to manage our Apache service. The `apachectl` program can be used to start, stop, restart, gracefully restart, and check the configuration, as we have done here. See the man `apachectl` page for more information. To start the Apache service, you can also use the `systemctl` command on CentOS. Let's go ahead and do that.

```
$ systemctl start httpd.service
```

You will see logs for the Apache service in the /var/log/httpd directory. You can follow the logs with following command:

```
$ sudo tail -f /var/log/httpd/access_log /var/log/httpd/error_log
```

Now we can check to see whether our host is responding as we expect. To do this, we will use the curl command. The curl command will allow us to make a request to the web server from within our shell.

```
$ curl -H 'Host: www.example.com' http://localhost
www.example.com
```

This shows that our server has responded correctly with our virtual host. With the curl command we made a request to the web server listening on the localhost. We also sent a Host header (-H 'Host:') with the name of the web server we wanted to send our request to. Apache will read this header and pass this request to the corresponding virtual host. If it cannot find a virtual host with the same ServerName field, it will route the request to the "base" virtual host or, in other words, the first it loaded. For this reason, it is a good idea to add a number as a suffix to the configuration file like 00-www.example.com.conf, which will determine the order the virtual hosts are loaded.

Before we open this up to the wide world, we should ensure that our firewall allows Hypertext Transfer Protocol (HTTP) traffic to our host. First, let's see the current list of services allowed by the firewall.

```
$ sudo firewall-cmd --list-services
dhcpv6-client ssh
```

We need to add the http service. We do that with firewall-cmd again.

```
$ sudo firewall-cmd --add-service http --permanent
$ sudo firewall-cmd --reload
```

This will add the service to the public zone by default. Now we should be able to access our site from remote clients.

On Ubuntu, the basic configuration has been divided among multiple files. The main file loaded by Apache on Ubuntu is /etc/apache2/apache2.conf. We've included the basic configuration directives from this file in Listing 11-1. While this file contains common Apache directives, it references additional files to configure virtual hosts, modules, ports, and IP addresses via include statements like we saw in the CentOS httpd.conf file.

Listing 11-1. Defaults in Ubuntu's apache2.conf File

```
ServerRoot "/etc/apache2"
Mutex file:${APACHE_LOCK_DIR} default
PidFile ${APACHE_PID_FILE}

Timeout 300

KeepAlive On
MaxKeepAliveRequests 100
KeepAliveTimeout 5

User ${APACHE_RUN_USER}
Group ${APACHE_RUN_GROUP}
```

477

```
AccessFileName .htaccess
<FilesMatch "^\.ht">
        Require all denied
</FilesMatch>

HostnameLookups Off
ErrorLog ${APACHE_LOG_DIR}/error.log
LogLevel warn
LogFormat "%v:%p %h %l %u %t \"%r\" %>s %O \"%{Referer}i\" \"%{User-Agent}i\"" vhost_
combined
LogFormat "%h %l %u %t \"%r\" %>s %O \"%{Referer}i\" \"%{User-Agent}i\"" combined
LogFormat "%h %l %u %t \"%r\" %>s %O" common
LogFormat "%{Referer}i -> %U" referer
LogFormat "%{User-agent}i" agent

IncludeOptional mods-enabled/*.load
IncludeOptional mods-enabled/*.conf
Include ports.conf

# Include generic snippets of statements
IncludeOptional conf-enabled/*.conf

# Include the virtual host configurations:
IncludeOptional sites-enabled/*.conf
```

The default configuration on Ubuntu is mostly the same as on CentOS. However, Ubuntu and Debian differ in how they manage their virtual hosts, or site configurations. Most obviously you see that there are several environment variables declared in the configuration. The values that these resolve to can be found in the /etc/apache2/envvars file.

Also of note is the AccessFileName directive. It specifies the name of a file that may contain server configuration directives. This file is named .htaccess, and any web directory may contain such a file. The server will check whether the file exists and process any directives it contains before attempting to serve files to a connecting client.

Because the .htaccess file can contain sensitive information, we should restrict access to this file. The following directive does this:

```
<FilesMatch "^\.ht">
        Require all denied
</FilesMatch>
```

This is an example of a match directive, where we can match any file starting with .ht (<FilesMatch "^\.ht">) and deny all requests to access these files (Require all denied).

■ **Note**   .htaccess files are not really recommended as using them incurs a negative performance impact.

The logging directives describe how we will be logging our Apache information. You can decide what is recorded in your Apache logs by using the LogFormat directive.

```
LogFormat "%v:%p %h %l %u %t \"%r\" %>s %O \"%{Referer}i\" \"%{User-Agent}i\""
vhost_combined
```

Apache interprets each %<value> in the string and allows you to format your logging output in a way that is useful to you. In this LogFormat directive we are getting Apache to include the virtual host (%v) and port (%p) of the virtual host accepting the request. Next we have the remote hostname (%h) and remote username (%l), the authenticated user (%u). The request is recorded (%r) along with the final status (%>s) and byte size (%O). Lastly, we log the referrer (%{Referer}i) and user agent (%{User-Agent}i), which makes use of Apache *VARNAME*s - variable names available to the logging format. These are derived from the headers sent by the browser. We then give this log format the name vhost_combined. We can now use this format in our configuration by declaring the CustomLog like this:

```
<VirtualHost *:80>
...
  CustomLog ${APACHE_LOG_DIR}/access.log vhost_combined
...
</VirtualHost>
```

You can find more information on the LogFormat options at https://httpd.apache.org/docs/2.4/mod/mod_log_config.html#formats. You can see the variables you can use in *VARNAME*s at http://httpd.apache.org/docs/current/expr.html.

In the CentOS httpd.conf file we had the Listen directive; on Ubuntu, Apache loads information about which IP addresses and ports it should listen on from the ports.conf file; the default of that file is as follows:

```
Listen 80

<IfModule ssl_module>
    Listen 443
</IfModule>

<IfModule mod_gnutls.c>
    Listen 443
</IfModule>
```

In this file you will see how to defensively add directives for modules. The Hypertext Markup Language (HTML)–like syntax <IfModule ssl_module>…</IfModule> denotes that the Listen 443 directive should be loaded only if the ssl_module is loaded. This can prevent Apache from erroring when modules have not been enabled yet.

Ubuntu also differs from CentOS in the way that you include modules and configuration files, like virtual hosts. You will see that there are directives such as IncludeOptional <resource>-enabled/*.conf. Ubuntu (and Debian, of course) makes use of symlinks to *enable* a module or configuration option.

Managing Modules

Let's take a look at the /etc/apache2/mod-available directory. We have changed into the /etc/apache2 directory and will execute a listing of the mod-available directory. In that directory you will find modules that are currently *available* to be loaded when Apache starts. In fact, this is how we choose the MPM we want to load for Ubuntu.

```
$ ll mods-available/mpm*
-rw-r--r-- 1 root root 668 Mar 19 09:48 mods-available/mpm_event.conf
-rw-r--r-- 1 root root 106 Mar 19 09:48 mods-available/mpm_event.load
-rw-r--r-- 1 root root 571 Mar 19 09:48 mods-available/mpm_prefork.conf
-rw-r--r-- 1 root root 108 Mar 19 09:48 mods-available/mpm_prefork.load
-rw-r--r-- 1 root root 836 Mar 19 09:48 mods-available/mpm_worker.conf
-rw-r--r-- 1 root root 107 Mar 19 09:48 mods-available/mpm_worker.load
```

In the previous listing, you can see the three different Apache MPM engines we have talked about. If we now look inside the /etc/apache2/mod-enabled directory, we can see which of these modules is loaded when Apache is started.

```
$ ls -l mods-enabled/mpm*
lrwxrwxrwx 1 root root 32 Aug  5 12:18 mods-enabled/mpm_event.conf -> ../mods-available/
mpm_event.conf
lrwxrwxrwx 1 root root 32 Aug  5 12:18 mods-enabled/mpm_event.load -> ../mods-available/
mpm_event.load
```

Now you can see that by default Ubuntu will run the event MPM. There is a .conf file and a load file, with one file for configuration directives and the other for actually loading the module. While you could add symlinks yourself to enable modules, the preferred method is to use the commands provided by Ubuntu for this. These commands are a2enmod for enabling modules (creating the symlinks) and a2dismod for disabling modules (removing the symlinks).

To show how to use these commands, we will enable and disable the status module, a module that allows us to see the current status of the web server. First, to enable it, we will issue the following:

```
$ sudo a2enmod status
Enabling module status.
To activate the new configuration, you need to run:
  service apache2 restart
```

This can be executed from any directory and will require a restart of the apache2 service like it says. The command has created the following symlinks:

```
$ ls -l mods-enabled/status*
lrwxrwxrwx 1 root root 29 Aug  6 05:08 mods-enabled/status.conf -> ../mods-available/status.conf
lrwxrwxrwx 1 root root 29 Aug  6 05:08 mods-enabled/status.load -> ../mods-available/status.load
```

Now let's disable that module with the following:

```
$ sudo a2dismod status
Module status disabled.
To activate the new configuration, you need to run:
  service apache2 restart
```

Rather than checking for symlinks in directories, Ubuntu provides another command to check the current Apache settings. The a2query command can be used to find the state of a module like this:

```
$ a2query -m status
No module matches status (disabled by site administrator)
```

Because we have just disabled the module, the status module is listed as disabled. If the module does not exist, you will just see "No module matches fakemodule" only. The a2query is also useful for querying other configuration options, as described in Table 11-1.

Table 11-1. *a2query Options*

-q	Quiet output, for scripting
-m <module>	Lists enabled modules or all if no module specified
-M	Lists current MPM
-s <site>	Checks whether the site is enabled or all if no site specified
-c <conf>	Lists enabled configuration files or all if no configuration specified
-d	Returns the Apache2 module directory

Managing Sites on Ubuntu

We are going to add a virtual host to the Ubuntu web server, much like we did with the CentOS host. Traditionally, Debian (and Ubuntu) system administrators tend to put service-related files in the /srv directory. In this example we are not going to follow that idiom, but there is no reason why you cannot place web server files in the /srv/www or /var/local directory or any other place on the filesystem that makes sense. To define the virtual host, we'll add the directives from Listing 11-2 in /etc/apache2/sites-available/www.example.com.

Listing 11-2. Our New Virtual Host Definition

```
<VirtualHost *>
    ServerName www.example.com
    ServerAlias example.com
    ServerAdmin webmaster@localhost
    DocumentRoot /var/www/html/www.example.com
    <Directory /var/www/html/www.example.com>
        Options Indexes FollowSymLinks Includes IncludesNOEXEC SymLinksIfOwnerMatch
        AllowOverride None
    </Directory>
</VirtualHost>
```

This is similar to our CentOS virtual host declaration. In this one we have added some extra directives. We start by opening the VirtualHost tag and specifying that the definition will apply to all addresses. Next, we specify the names we want this virtual host to reply to. Only a single ServerName can apply to any given virtual host, but others can be added via ServerAlias. You can add extra aliases by using more ServerAlias directives or by adding extra hostnames to a single ServerAlias separated by spaces.

As we have said, the DocumentRoot directive specifies the directory from which this virtual host will serve files. Once this is defined, you can use the Directory directive to specify options for this directory and all files and directories it contains. You specify the same list as on the CentOS machine. The Options directive lists what features are enabled in any particular directory. In Table 11-2 we provide an explanation of what has been included here. By setting AllowOverride to None, you deny the server to modify these options with settings from an .htaccess file. You could allow this by setting AllowOverride to All or be more descriptive about what is allowed by using something like Options=Indexes,MultiViews. Finally, you close the Directory and VirtualHost directives and save the file.

Table 11-2. *Options*

Option	Function
All	All options except MultiViews.
ExecCGI	Scripts are executed as applications, and their output is sent to the browser.
FollowSymLinks	The server may follow a symbolic link and serve the file or directory it points to.
Includes	The server will process server-side include directives that can be embedded in pages.
IncludesNOEXEC	Server-side include directives may not execute scripts on the server.
Indexes	If no index page exists in a directory, display the directly contents in a listing.
SymLinksIfOwnerMatch	The server may follow a symbolic link only if the owner of the link is the same as the owner of the link target.
MultiViews	With the mod_negotiation module, you can specify how content is selected, based on the client's capabilities.

We can enable the virtual host by using the utility a2ensite. This, like a2enmod, will create the symlinks from /etc/apache2/sites-available to /etc/apache2/sites-enabled.

```
$ sudo a2ensite www.example.com
Enabling site www.example.com.
To activate the new configuration, you need to run:
  service apache2 reload
```

You can now do as the script suggests or use sudo apache2ctl graceful to manually reload the server configuration. You can also use a2query to check that the site is enabled like this:

```
$ sudo a2query -s www.example.com
www.example.com (enabled by site administrator)
```

We can also make sure that our firewalls allow HTTP traffic through to our host by issuing the following:

```
$ sudo ufw allow http
```

This allows web traffic through to our web service.

httpd Performance

There are several nobs and dials that can be tweaked for Apache performance. An Apache web server, without any changes to the default settings, can handle many hundred concurrent users. We will go over just some of these here. Performance is a relative topic, and you should be using your metrics collected from your web service and hosts to guide you through this. Chapter 17 will deal with metrics collection.

Most documentation will tell you that random access memory (RAM) is the first concern. You will need enough for your web application and for system processes. Write-heavy applications will need appropriately fast disks. For this, data collected from system metrics will be your guide.

The following settings determine how Apache manages connection timeouts and keepalives:

```
Timeout 300

KeepAlive On
MaxKeepAliveRequests 100
KeepAliveTimeout 5
```

Timeout is the connection timeout setting, measured in seconds. This can be lengthened or shortened depending on your requirements. The KeepAlive settings determine how Apache deals with longer-running sessions. Instead of creating new TCP connections for sessions, you can specify that the Apache server should use the same TCP connection. You can fine-tune these settings with MaxKeepAliveRequests and KeepAliveTimeout.

The different MPMs also have ways to tune their performance. We will look here at the worker and event MPMs.

For both worker and event performance, there are two primary performance options that can be adjusted. The first is ThreadsPerChild, and the second is MaxRequestWorkers. ThreadsPerChild describes how many server threads are created from each child process. MaxRequestWorkers determines the maximum threads launched in total. Many web browsers make multiple connections to a web server, so they can download style sheets and images simultaneously. Therefore, a single web connection from a user can launch more than one thread. This means each user connection increases the amount of system resources, such as RAM and CPU time. These settings should be adjusted, monitored, and refined if you are experiencing poor performance.

The Apache httpd documentation provides some guidance as to some sensible performance settings. But, the following are the default settings for the worker MPM:

```
ServerLimit          16
StartServers          3
MaxRequestWorkers   400
MinSpareThreads      75
MaxSpareThreads     250
ThreadsPerChild      25
```

As for the settings, ServerLimit defines a hard limit on the number of active threads. MaxRequestWorkers is set to 400, which is the total threads. This value comes from the ServerLimit value multiplied by the ThreadsPerChild value, which is set to 25. StartServers is the initial number of threads launched. MinSpareThreads and MaxSpareThreads define the minimum and maximum spare idle threads. Apache will reduce or increase the idle threads available depending on these settings.

With the event MPM, there is also one other performance consideration that you can use along with the tunings for the worker MPM, AsyncRequestWorkerFactor. With the event MPM, situations can lead to thread starvation as there are no threads to handle new requests. AsyncRequestFactor can provide a fine-tuning of idle threads by limiting the number of concurrent connections.

It is recommended that you use the mod_status module in conjunction with any metrics collection tools available to you when measuring and tuning your Apache server.

Access Restriction

In the configuration section we talked about the use of the Require directive to limit access to a directory. In this section we will show you more on that directive and how to secure your site with a basic username and password.

The Require directive can be used to limit access to directory (and location) paths. You have seen it already being used to protect the access to .htacess files.

```
<FilesMatch "^\.ht">
        Require all denied
</FilesMatch>
```

Here we have denied access to any file beginning with .ht. This directive comes from the mod_authz_core module. There are others that extend this module, like mod_authz_host, which allows us to authorize access based on IP.

In an example, let's say we had a directory called /var/www/html/www.example.com/uploads. We can restrict access to this from only internal IP addresses.

```
<Directory /var/www/html/www.example.com/uploads>
    Options -Indexes -FollowSymLinks
    AllowOverride None
    Require ip 192.168.0
</Directory>
```

The module mod_authz_host provides us with the facility to restrict access to parts of the site based on IP address. In the previous lines, only hosts that have a remote IP address in the 192.168.0.0/24 subnet will be allowed to access this directory. In Table 11-3, you can see the other options available to the Require directive.

Table 11-3. *Require Options*

Require all granted	Allow access unconditionally.
Require all denied	Deny access unconditionally.
Require env <envvar>	Access is granted if an environment variable is set.
Require method <method>	Access is granted to certain HTTP methods.
Require expr <expression>	Access is granted if the expression is true.
Require user <userid>	Access is granted only to these users (mod_authz_user).
Require group <group-name>	Access is granted to users in specified groups (mod_authz_groupfile).
Require valid-user	Access is granted to an authorized user.
Require ip <IPaddress>	Access is granted to clients within the IP address range.

The other way to restrict access to resources is by requiring users to enter a username and password. Many web applications manage this internally, but you can also have Apache manage a list of usernames and passwords, allowing you to protect specific directories without needing additional software. The authentication sources can be a file, a database, or Lightweight Directory Access Protocol (LDAP). We will show you how to perform authentication backed by a file.

First, we need to create a file that contains the usernames and passwords we want to use via the htpasswd utility. We do not want to place this file in the directories that our Apache server serves, so we create a directory called /opt/apache/www.example.com and place our password files there. Normally, we pass the file name to use and the user to create as parameters, but if the file does not yet exist, we also need to pass the -c option.

```
$ sudo htpasswd -c /opt/apache/www.example.com/passwords jsmith
New password:
Re-type new password:
Adding password for user jsmith
```

We can now add additional users without needing the -c option. If we don't want to be asked for a password to use, we can set that on the command line as well, via the -b option.

```
$ sudo htpasswd -b /opt/apache/www.example.com/passwords ataylor s3kr@t
Adding password for user ataylor
```

Next, we need to tell Apache to ask for authentication. If you choose to do this in a .htaccess file inside the /var/www/www.example.com directory, you will need to add the ability to override the AuthConfig option. We would need to set AllowOverride AuthConfig for this to work fine. We are not going add the .htaccess directive; we are going to add our authentication at the directory level in the virtual host config.

```
<Directory /var/www/html/www.example.com/uploads>
    Options -Indexes -FollowSymLinks
    AllowOverride None
    AuthType Basic
    AuthName "Restricted Uploads"
    AuthBasicProvider file
    AuthUserFile "/opt/apache/www.example.com/passwords"
    Require valid-user
</Directory>
```

First, we specify the authentication type we want to use via the AuthType directive, which in our case is basic. We then need to tell Apache which module will provide the basic authentication using AuthBasicProvider, which is file. Next, we need to tell Apache which file holds our authentication information via the AuthUserFile directive.

To help users determine what they're trying to access, we can specify a name for the protected resource via the AuthName directive. This name will be displayed to users when they are asked for credentials, as shown in Figure 11-1, so it helps to make this name fairly descriptive.

Finally, Apache needs to be told that access must be granted only if a user successfully authenticates. We do this by specifying Require valid-user.

If we now browse to www.example.com/uploads, our browser will ask us for a username and password, as shown in Figure 11-1.

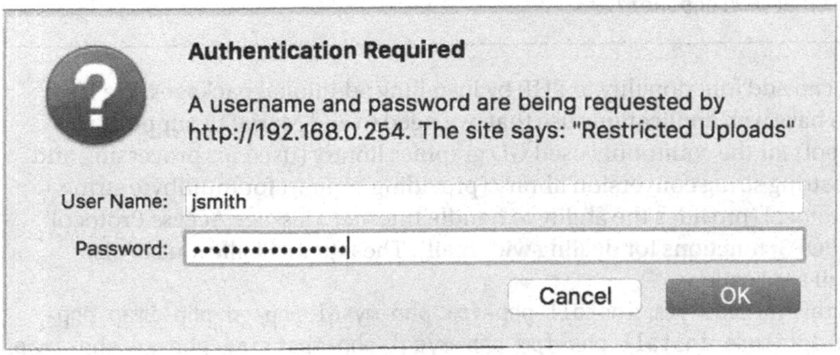

Figure 11-1. *Apache authentication*

We won't be granted access if we don't provide a valid username and password, but if we enter valid credentials, Apache will let us view the site. It should be noted that we are passing credentials over an unencrypted HTTP session, which is a dangerous practice. We will show you how to set up an HTTP Secure (HTTPS) server shortly.

You can read more about host-and user-based access control on the Apache documentation site.

- `https://httpd.apache.org/docs/2.4/howto/auth.html`

- `https://httpd.apache.org/docs/2.4/howto/access.html`

Modules

We have talked about modules and how they provide extra functionality to Apache and are enabled using the `LoadModule` directive. This directive specifies the path to the module file that should be loaded.

On CentOS, extra modules are usually enabled by a configuration snippet in `/etc/httpd/conf.modules.d` that is installed by the module package. When the server is restarted, it picks up these new files and processes their directives. You can order how these modules are loaded by prefixing a number to the file name, and this is the default on CentOS. To prevent such a snippet from being included, thus disabling the module, you can rename it so its file name no longer ends in `.conf` or move or remove the file from the directory. You can also comment (#) any of the directives in the file.

On Ubuntu, module packages add these snippets in the `/etc/apache2/mods-available` directory and then create links to them in the `/etc/apache2/modules-enabled` directory. These links can also be managed manually using the `a2enmod` and `a2dismod` commands, similar to `a2ensite` and `a2dissite`.

Information on all included Apache modules and the functionality they provide is available at `http://httpd.apache.org/docs/2.4/mod/`.

Installing PHP Support

Many web applications are written in PHP, a scripting language developed by Rasmus Lerdorf that powers many web sites around the world including the popular WordPress content management system (CMS). As your web browser requests a page from such an application, the web server processes the code in the page and displays the output to your browser. To be able to host these web applications, the web server needs to be able to understand and execute PHP code.

Executing PHP can be done two ways. You can add PHP support to Apache by installing a module and using the prefork Apache MPM. We, however, are going to be using the worker MPM, and since PHP is not threadsafe, we will use a FastGGI process manager to link Apache to PHP.

■ **Note** You can read all about PHP at `www.php.net/`.

PHP itself is modular, so you can add functionality to PHP by installing additional packages. We'll set up a MariaDB server shortly, so to have web applications use that, we need to add MariaDB support in PHP. In addition, we'll install support for the commonly used GD graphics library (used for processing and manipulating image files), the mbstring string conversion library (providing support for multibyte string encodings), and the IMAP mail protocol (provides the ability to handle Internet Message Access Protocol [IMAP] and Post Office Protocol [POP3] functions for dealing with mail). The latter will allow us to also install and use PHP-based webmail applications.

On CentOS, we can install all this via `sudo yum install php-fpm php-mysql php-gd php-imap php-mbstring` and on Ubuntu via `sudo aptitude install php-fpm php-mysql php-mbstring php-gd php-imap`.

We are going to set up a web site that uses PHP later in this chapter. But here we are going to show you how to use PHP-FPM in our virtual host on our CentOS host.

First we need to make sure that we have the following modules loaded. As you know, modules are loaded in via the /etc/httpd/conf.modules.d/ directory. We are searching for two proxy files to be present.

```
$ grep -E '(proxy.so|fcgi)' /etc/httpd/conf.modules.d/00-proxy.conf
LoadModule proxy_module modules/mod_proxy.so
LoadModule proxy_fcgi_module modules/mod_proxy_fcgi.so
```

These modules are provided by the httpd package and apache2 package for CentOS and Ubuntu, respectively.

Next we are going to move off our /etc/httpd/conf.d/php.conf file, as this is the configuration file for the php module.

```
$ sudo mv /etc/httpd/conf.d/php.conf /etc/httpd/conf.d/php.conf_bak
```

PHP-FPM is a daemon that will translate requests from the HTTP server and respond with an appropriate response from the PHP code. The php-fpm.conf file configures this daemon. PHP-FPM can separate applications into pools. You create pools in the /etc/php-fpm.d directory. We now have to edit the /etc/php-fpm.d/www.conf file and add the following line:

```
; Start a new pool named 'www'.
[www]

; The address on which to accept FastCGI requests.
; Valid syntaxes are:
;   'ip.add.re.ss:port'   - to listen on a TCP socket to a specific address on
;                           a specific port;
;   'port'                - to listen on a TCP socket to all addresses on a
;                           specific port;
;   '/path/to/unix/socket' - to listen on a unix socket.
; Note: This value is mandatory.
listen = 127.0.0.1:9000
listen = /run/php-fcgi.sock
```

You will need to restart php-fpm after you have edited this file. You can do this on CentOS with $ sudo systemctl restart php-fpm. You should now notice a socket file has been created in the /run directory (which is a special in-memory directory).

```
$ ll /run/php-fcgi.sock
srw-rw-rw-. 1 root root 0 Aug 16 09:49 /run/php-fcgi.sock
```

Once that is done, we are ready to run PHP web sites. All that is left to do is to add a ProxyPassMatch directive to our HTTP config to match on *any* .php files and pass those to the PHP-FPM daemon.

```
<VirtualHost *:80>

  ServerName www.example.com
  ServerAdmin webmaster@example.com
  DocumentRoot /var/www/html/www.example.com
  DirectoryIndex index.php
  ProxyPassMatch ^/(.*\.php(/.*)?)$ unix:/run/php-fcgi.sock|fcgi://127.0.0.1:9000/var/www/
html/www.example.com/
```

```
<Directory /var/www/html/www.example.com>
    Require all granted
</Directory>
</VirtualHost>
```

The virtual host is now ready to handle our PHP applications, which we will install later in this chapter. ProxyPassMatch allows us to use a regular expression to match on the uniform resource locator (URL) and pass that request to the proxy back end. We provide where the proxy is listening and give it the location of the directory where we will install our PHP code.

You can read more on the directives available for mod_proxy, including the ProxyPassMatch directive, here:

- https://httpd.apache.org/docs/current/mod/mod_proxy.html

File and Directory Permissions

When you're working with web sites, you need write access to the document root directories where sites are installed. At the same time, the Apache user needs to not be able to write to the same directories, as that could allow anonymous web users to write files to your system, if they find a vulnerability in a web site.

If multiple users will be managing sites, it's a good idea to create a group for this purpose. As long as the group in question has write permissions to the document root, any users you add to this group will be able to write to files and create directories. Many times, a web application is deployed automatically by a deploy user.

■ **Tip** Using a specific system group to manage web sites also means you can allow members of this group to use the apachectl or apache2ctl command via sudo without giving them full root access.

To ensure that files created by one user can be modified by another user in the same group, you need to set the umask option so that any new files and directories created are writable by the group. You also need to set the setgid bit so that new files and directories will inherit ownership from the group that owns the parent directory, not the primary group of the user who happened to create the file or directory in question. We'll show you an example of this a bit later, when we install some web applications.

■ **Tip** You can find more information and the Apache documentation at http://httpd.apache.org/.

SQL Database

Because many web-based applications use a SQL server to store data, we'll also show you how to install a SQL server. We are going to show you how to install a fork of the MySQL database server called MariaDB. The database server provides data storage and retrieval, while the client can be any application that uses the database server — that can be a command-line utility, LibreOffice, or a library that is used by a web site.

Because MariaDB is a fork of MySQL, it is a drop-in replacement for the MySQL database. Many of the commands for MySQL are the same in MariaDB, and the configuration and environment variables are the same, making it easy to swap these databases in and out. The reason that MariaDB came into being is that the former developers of MySQL wanted to keep it free under the GNU General Public License (GNU GPL) license after MySQL was bought by Oracle Corporation.

MariaDB still merges code, or ports code, from MySQL into its code base, and while they are not the same, the releases of MariaDB can map to releases of MySQL. Up until version 5.5 of MariaDB, MariaDB kept the same release number as MySQL. But recently it has changed its release number to be 10.*x*, which can make things more confusing. The following Table 11-4 illustrates the versions.

Table 11-4. *MariaDB to MySQL Versions*

MariaDB 5.5	MariaDB 5.3 and MySQL 5.5
MariaDB 10.0	MariaDB 5.5 and backported MySQL 5.6
MariaDB 10.1	Contains ports of MySQL 5.6 and 5.7
MariaDB 10.2	Alpha release

■ **Note**   For an explanation of the reasoning behind these version number changes, see `https://mariadb.org/explanation-on-mariadb-10-0/`.

Installation

On both CentOS and Ubuntu you can install MariaDB easily using the package managers. On CentOS, MariaDB is installed via the `mariadb-server` package.

```
$ sudo yum install mariadb-server
```

On Ubuntu, the server component is provided by the `mariadb-server-core-10.0` package (at the time of writing). You can install it via the virtual package.

```
$ sudo aptitude install mariadb-server.
```

Initial Configuration

You'll need to make a few basic configuration changes. By default on CentOS, the MariaDB server listens for connections on all configured network interfaces and addresses. Since we are going to have the web server and the database on the same host, we are going to limit the database to listen only on the loopback address. This is more secure, but in an ideal world we would have the database server and the web server on separate hosts. For Ubuntu, if you examine the `/etc/mysql/mariadb.conf.d/50-server.cnf` configuration file, you will see that the following bind-address directive is already there.

On CentOS, we open `/etc/my.cnf` in a text editor and add the following line under the `[mysqld]` section:

```
bind-address = 127.0.0.1
```

Here we are instructing the database server to listen only on the loopback address, which prevents other hosts from accessing our database. When and if we want other hosts to access our database, we will need to change this to listen on an appropriate interface. Our new configuration file will look like Listing 11-3.

Listing 11-3. Our /etc/my.conf on CentOS

```
[mysqld]
bind-address = 127.0.0.1

datadir=/var/lib/mysql
socket=/var/lib/mysql/mysql.sock
# Disabling symbolic-links is recommended to prevent assorted security risks
symbolic-links=0

[mysqld_safe]
log-error=/var/log/mariadb/mariadb.log
pid-file=/var/run/mariadb/mariadb.pid

!includedir /etc/my.cnf.d
```

There are many different settings that can be configured for the MariaDB server. You can find some useful documentation here:

- https://mariadb.com/kb/en/mariadb/configuring-mariadb-with-mycnf/
- https://mariadb.com/kb/en/mariadb/server-system-variables/

We can now start the MariaDB server via the systemctl command, as shown in Listing 11-4.

Listing 11-4. MariaDB First Run on CentOS

```
$ sudo systemctl start mariadb
```

The server is now running, so we can set a root password and clean up the default tables. We can do this on both CentOS and Ubuntu. There is a utility called mysql_secure_installation that will do this for us.

```
$ sudo mysql_secure_installation

NOTE: RUNNING ALL PARTS OF THIS SCRIPT IS RECOMMENDED FOR ALL MariaDB
      SERVERS IN PRODUCTION USE!  PLEASE READ EACH STEP CAREFULLY!

In order to log into MariaDB to secure it, we'll need the current
password for the root user.  If you've just installed MariaDB, and
you haven't set the root password yet, the password will be blank,
so you should just press enter here.

Enter current password for root (enter for none):
OK, successfully used password, moving on...

Setting the root password ensures that nobody can log into the MariaDB
root user without the proper authorisation.

Set root password? [Y/n] y
New password:
Re-enter new password:
Password updated successfully!
Reloading privilege tables..
 ... Success!
```

By default, a MariaDB installation has an anonymous user, allowing anyone
to log into MariaDB without having to have a user account created for
them. This is intended only for testing, and to make the installation
go a bit smoother. You should remove them before moving into a
production environment.

Remove anonymous users? [Y/n] y
... Success!

Normally, root should only be allowed to connect from 'localhost'. This
ensures that someone cannot guess at the root password from the network.

Disallow root login remotely? [Y/n] y
... Success!

By default, MariaDB comes with a database named 'test' that anyone can
access. This is also intended only for testing, and should be removed
before moving into a production environment.

Remove test database and access to it? [Y/n] y
 - Dropping test database...
 ... Success!
 - Removing privileges on test database...
 ... Success!

Reloading the privilege tables will ensure that all changes made so far
will take effect immediately.

Reload privilege tables now? [Y/n] y
... Success!

Cleaning up...

All done! If you've completed all of the above steps, your MariaDB
installation should now be secure.

Thanks for using MariaDB!

Our server is now secured. It will not accept connections from remote hosts, and it will not allow
users without MariaDB accounts to connect. To ensure that it is started on boot, we will use the `systemctl`
command to enable `mariadb` on boot.

```
$ sudo systemctl enable mariadb
```

Let's now test our server to make sure we can connect to it.

Testing the Server

To check that the MariaDB server is running, we can connect to it via the command-line client. We need
to specify the -u option to specify a user to connect as (Figure 11-2). The -p option will prompt us for the
associated password.

```
[vagrant@au-mel-centos-1 ~]$ mysql -h localhost -p -u root
Enter password:
Welcome to the MariaDB monitor.  Commands end with ; or \g.
Your MariaDB connection id is 3
Server version: 5.5.47-MariaDB-log MariaDB Server

Copyright (c) 2000, 2015, Oracle, MariaDB Corporation Ab and others.

Type 'help;' or '\h' for help. Type '\c' to clear the current input statement.

MariaDB [(none)]> SELECT VERSION();
+--------------------+
| VERSION()          |
+--------------------+
| 5.5.47-MariaDB-log |
+--------------------+
1 row in set (0.00 sec)

MariaDB [(none)]> ▮
```

Figure 11-2. *Signing in to MariaDB*

We are able to connect and run a query; the MariaDB server is working fine. Note that the version string that is returned on your host may differ, depending on which MariaDB server version is installed. On Ubuntu you can access the mysql command line via the sudo command.

```
$ sudo mysql
```

MariaDB Storage Engines

MariaDB has several different storage engines designed to perform better with different data set requirements. The default engine is called XtraDB and is a database compliant with the atomicity, consistency, isolated, durability (ACID) attributes and multiversion concurrency control (MVCC); it is generally a good pick for most application types.

There are several others available too. The main ones that might be of interest to you are listed in Table 11-5.

Table 11-5. *MariaDB Storage Engines*

Archive	Data archiving
Aria	An enhanced MyISAM database
Cassandra	NoSQL storage engine to access data in a Cassandra cluster
Connect	Allows access to text files as if they were database tables
ScaleDB	Commercial large-scale high availability (HA)/durable database storage engine
Spider	Allows access distributed databases via sharded share-nothing architecture
TokuDB	High-performance write-heavy database
XtraDB	A fork and drop-in replacement of MySQL InnoDB

You can see the list of engines you have installed by issuing the command in Figure 11-3.

```
MariaDB [(none)]> show engines;
+--------------------+----------+----------------------------------------------------------------+--------------+------+------------+
| Engine             | Support  | Comment                                                        | Transactions | XA   | Savepoints |
+--------------------+----------+----------------------------------------------------------------+--------------+------+------------+
| InnoDB             | DEFAULT  | Percona-XtraDB, Supports transactions, row-level locking, and foreign keys | YES | YES | YES |
| CSV                | YES      | CSV storage engine                                            | NO           | NO   | NO         |
| MRG_MYISAM         | YES      | Collection of identical MyISAM tables                         | NO           | NO   | NO         |
| BLACKHOLE          | YES      | /dev/null storage engine (anything you write to it disappears) | NO          | NO   | NO         |
| MEMORY             | YES      | Hash based, stored in memory, useful for temporary tables     | NO           | NO   | NO         |
| PERFORMANCE_SCHEMA | YES      | Performance Schema                                            | NO           | NO   | NO         |
| ARCHIVE            | YES      | Archive storage engine                                        | NO           | NO   | NO         |
| MyISAM             | YES      | MyISAM storage engine                                        | NO           | NO   | NO         |
| FEDERATED          | YES      | FederatedX pluggable storage engine                          | YES          | NO   | YES        |
| Aria               | YES      | Crash-safe tables with MyISAM heritage                       | NO           | NO   | NO         |
+--------------------+----------+----------------------------------------------------------------+--------------+------+------------+
10 rows in set (0.00 sec)
```

Figure 11-3. *Showing database engines*

In Figure 11-3 you can see the database engines that have been installed by default. You can see that XtraDB is still called the InnoDB engine, and you can see what each supports.

Basic Tuning for XtraDB

All performance tunings usually concern these three areas: hardware, operating system, and database configuration. Hardware is pretty easy; with databases, the general rule is a faster disk, a faster CPU, and more and faster memory are better. The operating system has many performance tweaks available to it, including disk mount options, sysctl settings, kernel schedulers, and many more. With database tuning we have many configuration options as well as database optimization strategies. We are going to concentrate on basic tunings for the XtraDB engine in MariaDB.

To show the current settings of the MariaDB, you can issue the following command from the command line:

```
MariaDB [(none)]> show variables;
```

This command produces a long list of all the variables currently stored in MariaDB. To see individual settings, we can use the SQL shown in Figure 11-4.

```
MariaDB [(none)]> show variables like '%innodb_fast_shutdown';
+-----------------------+-------+
| Variable_name         | Value |
+-----------------------+-------+
| innodb_fast_shutdown  | 1     |
+-----------------------+-------+
1 row in set (0.00 sec)
```

Figure 11-4. *Listing environment variables*

In Figure 11-4 we have used the SQL like clause to search the show variables listing for the innodb_fast_shutdown variable and to show its setting.

| HOW INNODB STORES DATA |

InnoDB, and therefore XtraDB, has a two-tiered data storage design. The data stored on disk lives in the /var/lib/mysql directory. Inside this directory are the ibdata1, ib_logfile0, and ib_logfile1 files. The ibdata1 file contains system and user data, and the ib_logfile0 and ib_logfile1 files are redo, or transaction, logs. Databases are created in directories inside the /var/lib/mysql/<databasename> directory. Tables in those databases are stored in /var/lib/mysql/<databasename>/<tablename.frm>.

When data in a table changes in memory (e.g., because you insert a record), InnoDB stores it in its redo logs. When these transaction logs fill up, the MariaDB server flushes these changed data records to the table files.

One of the reasons for this is performance, just like with a journaling filesystem. By performing all these operations at once, disk writes are more efficient. Another reason is for durability, as these logs can be used to replay transactions when the system comes back up from an unexpected crash.

When the MariaDB server shuts down, it does not process these transaction logs, so they usually contain live data. This means they cannot be simply deleted and re-created in order to increase or decrease their size.

One simple performance tuning we can do is to change the default size of the redo logs. If the file is too small, it fills up quickly, and this means the SQL server is continuously emptying this file, which degrades performance. If the file is too large, then the recovery time can be lengthened.

In Figure 11-5, we can see the log file size of MariaDB 5.5, which has the default of 5MB. Versions of MariaDB 10.0 and above have a default of 48MB. For older MariaDB 5.5 versions, before we change the InnoDB transaction log file size, we need to ensure the transaction log files no longer contain any live data.

```
MariaDB [(none)]> show variables like 'innodb_log_file_size';
+----------------------+---------+
| Variable_name        | Value   |
+----------------------+---------+
| innodb_log_file_size | 5242880 |
+----------------------+---------+
1 row in set (0.00 sec)
```

Figure 11-5. Redo log file size

We can do this by forcing the server to process all entries in the transaction log and write them to the table files when we shut the server down. This behavior is controlled by the variable innodb_fast_shutdown, which we can change on a running server by connecting to it as the root user and then running the query SET GLOBAL innodb_fast_shutdown=1, as shown in Listing 11-5.

Listing 11-5. Forcing an InnoDB Transaction Log Flush at Shutdown

```
MariaDB [(none)]> SET GLOBAL innodb_fast_shutdown = 1;
Query OK, 0 rows affected (0.00 sec)
```

We can now shut down the MariaDB server, and it will flush all pending changes from the transaction logs to the table files. That means we can safely move the existing files out of the way and change the transaction log file size. On CentOS, we do this via `sudo systemtctl stop mariadb`.

The log files are called `ib_logfile0` and `ib_logfile1`, and they can be found in the `/var/ lib/mysql` directory. We'll move both of these files out of the way so the MariaDB server can create new ones when we next start it.

```
$ cd /var/lib/mysql
/var/lib/mysql$ sudo mv ib_logfile* /root
```

■ **Caution** Do not delete these log files until you've verified that the MariaDB server works with its new configuration.

We can now edit the configuration file. On CentOS, that file is `/etc/my.cnf.d/server.cnf`. The file is relatively empty on CentOS, so you can simply add in the configuration directives we'll give you shortly.

On Ubuntu, MariaDB 10.0.25 is installed. This has the 48MB log file size by default, so it normally does not need to be changed. However, if you do need to change it, you just need to edit the file `/etc/mysql/mysql.conf.d/mysqld.cnf` and add, or make a change to, `innodb_log_file_size`. Then, on Ubuntu, you need to restart the `mysql` service (yes, Ubuntu currently runs MariaDB with the `mysql` service).

All changes we're making here go under the `[mysqld-5.5]` section (CentOS) or the `[mysqld]` section (Ubuntu).

```
innodb_log_file_size = 48M
innodb_log_buffer_size = 16M
innodb_log_files_in_group = 2
innodb_buffer_pool_size = 128M
innodb_flush_method = O_DIRECT
```

We set the InnoDB transaction log file size to 48Mb and the in-memory log buffer to 16Mb. These values mean the server will use a bit more RAM, but it will need to access the disk less often, resulting in better performance. We tell the server it has two transaction log files via `innodb_log_files_in_group`, which is the default.

Next, we need to assign some RAM for the server to use to keep table data and perform queries. This amount is controlled by the `innodb_buffer_pool_size` variable, and we've set it to 128Mb. This should be a reasonable amount on a modern server that runs MariaDB as well as other services. On a dedicated server it can be set to up to 80 percent of the available memory.

We can tell the server not to cache any data in the operating system disk cache by setting `innodb_flush_method`. After all, the data is stored in the memory we've reserved for the InnoDB buffer pool. By specifying `O_DIRECT`, we prevent the system from keeping two copies of the data in RAM by flushing data to disk regularly. It is unset by default, and there are several options available to choose. Depending on your situation and version, you might choose `ALL_O_DIRECT` (for large InnoDB database files).

When data is not in RAM and needs to be written from disk, MariaDB defaults to read data one tiny 128KB chunk at a time. This saves on memory use but is very slow when many megabytes of data need to be read. We'll increase this chunk size via the `read_buffer_size` and `read_rnd_buffer_size` variables.

```
read_buffer_size = 1M
read_rnd_buffer_size = 1M
```

We'll also allow the server to perform very large queries, so larger amounts of data can be stored. The default is 1Mb (on older releases); we'll change this to 16Mb.

```
max_allowed_packet = 16M
```

Finally, we'll enable the binary log by setting the `log_bin` variable. This will help us recover in case of a crash.

```
log_bin  = /var/log/mariadb/mariadb-bin.log
expire_logs_days = 14
max_binlog_size = 128M
```

The bin logs, or binary logs, are used to replication transactions on the database. Inserts, updates, and deletes are recorded in them, and they can be replayed on a secondary server to keep them in sync. They can also be used by administrators to restore backups of databases. In the previous code, we tell the server to automatically purge binary logs after 14 days. This means we should do a backup of the MariaDB data at *least* every two weeks. (We'll cover how you can automate the backup process in Chapter 14.) Finally, we tell the server to start a new binary log file once the current one reaches a size of 128Mb. This makes the bin logs more manageable and quicker to transport to any secondary or tertiary databases. We have also created them in a separate location to the primary database files, ideally on their own disk or partition.

We've now completed our basic MariaDB server tweaks, so we can turn it back on via `sudo systemctl start mariadb` on CentOS or `sudo systemctl start mysql` on Ubuntu. To verify that the MariaDB server is happy and has created the new InnoDB transaction log files, you can check the logs. On CentOS, `mariadb` writes to the `/var/log/mariadb/mariadb.log` file; on Ubuntu, it uses the `/var/log/syslog` file.

Note that we have not tuned the MariaDB server for high-end performance; we've just modified the basic configuration to give us better data integrity and to perform a bit better than it would normally. If you need extremely high performance or advanced features such as data replication across multiple servers, we suggest you read *High Performance MySQL, Third Edition* by Baron Schwartz et al. (O'Reilly Media, Inc., 2012).

Basic MariaDB Administration

As you've seen already, MariaDB has an internal list of users and passwords. This means you need to know how to manage MariaDB users, as you do not want all applications to connect to the MariaDB server as `root`. We'll demonstrate how to create and remove databases and users via the command-line `mysql` client.

Databases

Creating databases in MariaDB is easy. You connect to the server via the command-line utility and issue the `CREATE DATABASE` statement, giving it the database name as a parameter, as shown in Figure 11-6. (Note that we've used uppercase in the SQL statements for clarity only; if you use lowercase, they'll still work fine.)

```
MariaDB [(none)]> CREATE DATABASE `mydb`;
Query OK, 1 row affected (0.00 sec)

MariaDB [(none)]> USE mydb;
Database changed
MariaDB [mydb]> SHOW TABLES;
Empty set (0.01 sec)
```

Figure 11-6. *Creating a new database in MariaDB*

In Figure 11-6 you can see that we created a database called mydb, and then we switched to that database and checked whether it contained any tables. You will notice that when we switched to the mydb database our prompt also changed from [(none)] to [mydb] indicating the current database we are working on. Note that we used backquotes, or backticks, to quote the database name. There is no explicit need to do so in this case, but database, table, and column names can sometimes contain a reserved character such as a hyphen. For instance, if you want to create a database called my-db, you need to use backquotes; otherwise, MariaDB would interpret my-db as subtracting the value in the db column from the value in the my column. Since neither of these columns exists, an error would be generated, as shown in Figure 11-7.

```
MariaDB [mydb]> CREATE DATABASE my-db;
ERROR 1064 (42000): You have an error in your SQL syntax; check the manual that correspo
nds to your MariaDB server version for the right syntax to use near '-db' at line 1
MariaDB [mydb]> CREATE DATABASE `my-db`;
Query OK, 1 row affected (0.00 sec)
```

Figure 11-7. *The importance of proper quoting*

With quotes, the database is created with the specified name.

■ **Tip**   When naming databases and tables, it's generally best to use only alphanumeric characters and the underscore character. Even then, proper quoting is a good habit.

We don't need this database, though, so we'll delete it again. We do this via the DROP DATABASE statement.

```
MariaDB [mydb]> DROP DATABASE `my-db`;
Query OK, 0 rows affected (0.00 sec)
```

■ **Caution**   You cannot undo a DROP DATABASE command, not even if you run it within a transaction and then roll back. Consider carefully before you do so and make sure you create a backup before dropping data.

Users and Privileges

Privileges are managed via the GRANT statement. This statement takes a set of parameters that defines a set of operations a user on a given host is allowed to perform on a specific object.

In practice, you usually just create a user who is allowed to perform all operations on a single database.

This means that each application that uses its own database gets its own MariaDB login. If an application turns out to contain a bug that allows access to the database server, only the data used by that application is at risk.

We connect to the MariaDB server as root and then create a user called jsmith, just like our host account, who can access all databases and tables and create new users. This way we do not need to keep using the MariaDB root account.

The code in Figure 11-8 creates a user called jsmith who can connect from localhost only with the password "secret." The ALL keyword specifies the user has all privileges. We use the shorthand *.* to indicate all tables in all databases.

```
MariaDB [(none)]> GRANT ALL PRIVILEGES ON *.* TO `jsmith`@`localhost` IDENTIFIED BY 'secret' WITH GRANT OPTION;
Query OK, 0 rows affected (0.00 sec)

MariaDB [(none)]> \q
Bye
```

Figure 11-8. *Creating a GRANT for users*

We could limit access to tables in a single database called mydb by using mydb.* instead. Finally, we specify GRANT OPTION, which gives this user permission to use the GRANT statement. Table 11-6 shows the possible privileges.

Table 11-6. *GRANT Privileges*

SELECT	Gives the ability to perform SELECT statements
INSERT	Gives the ability to perform INSERT statements
UPDATE	Gives the ability to perform UPDATE statements
DELETE	Gives the ability to perform DELETE statements
INDEX	Gives the ability to create indexes on tables
CREATE	Gives the ability to create databases tables
ALTER	Gives the ability to alter database tables
DROP	Gives the ability to drop database tables
GRANT OPTION	Gives the ability to grant the same privileges to other users
ALL	Gives all privileges except GRANT OPTION

Let's log in as the user we just created and create a user with access only to the mydb database. We don't need to specify a MariaDB user to connect as now, as we just created a MariaDB user with the same name as our host account.

To do that, like we have in Figure 11-9, pass the following arguments to the mysql client. We use -h to connect to the localhost, -u to indicate the user we want to connect as, and -p to signify we will provide a password.

```
[vagrant@au-mel-centos-1 ~]$ mysql -h localhost -u jsmith -p
Enter password:
Welcome to the MariaDB monitor.  Commands end with ; or \g.
Your MariaDB connection id is 5
Server version: 5.5.47-MariaDB-log MariaDB Server

Copyright (c) 2000, 2015, Oracle, MariaDB Corporation Ab and others.

Type 'help;' or '\h' for help. Type '\c' to clear the current input statement.

MariaDB [(none)]> GRANT ALL PRIVILEGES ON `mydb`.* to `mydb`@`localhost` identified by 'passwd';
Query OK, 0 rows affected (0.00 sec)

MariaDB [(none)]> FLUSH PRIVILEGES;
Query OK, 0 rows affected (0.00 sec)
```

Figure 11-9. *Creating user accounts*

We now have a user called mydb who can access tables only in the mydb database. Since we have no need for this user at the moment, we'll show you how to delete the user by removing mydb from the system.

```
MariaDB [(none)]> DROP USER `mydb`@`localhost`;
Query OK, 0 rows affected (0.00 sec)
```

And since we also have no need for the mydb database, we'll remove that, too.

```
MariaDB [(none)]> DROP DATABASE `mydb`;
Query OK, 0 rows affected (0.00 sec)
```

Teaching SQL and MariaDB administration skills is beyond the scope of this book, but these basic skills will allow you to set up most MariaDB-based web applications by following their installation instructions. Many web sites are dedicated to teaching MySQL and therefore MariaDB skills, and the following resources are also excellent sources of information:

- https://mariadb.com/kb/en/mariadb/getting-started/
- www.techonthenet.com/mariadb/index.php
- http://dev.mysql.com/doc/
- *Learning MySQL and MariaDB* by Russell JT Dyer (O'Reilly Media, 2015)

Managing Web Site Contents

With a working web and SQL server, you can now install some web applications to enhance your online presence. In this section, we will show you how to install a few web applications on their own virtual hosts. We will not show you how to use these web applications, as most come with excellent documentation and a support community.

We'll start by creating a group called www to which we will add any users who need to be able to modify the web site installations, and we'll add ourselves to that group. We can override the default umask for this group via the -K parameter.

```
$ sudo groupadd -K UMASK=0002 www
$ sudo usermod -G www jsmith
```

Once we log out and log back in, the group membership change will be active.

Next, we'll change the ownership and permissions of the /var/www/html/www.example.com directory and any directories it contains so the www group has full access to it.

```
$ sudo chgrp -R www /var/www/html/www.example.com
$ sudo chmod u+rwx,g+srwx,o+rx /var/www/html/www.example.com
```

Instead of the full permission string, we could have also specified octal mode 2775. On CentOS, the web server runs as the apache user, and on Ubuntu it runs as www-data, you will need to chown the file and directory as required.

```
$ sudo chown www-data -R /var/www/html/www.example.com
```

Web Presence

Of course, you will want your business to have a web presence, and of course this has never been easier to achieve. To this end, we will install a CMS to use as our web site.

A CMS allows us to focus our energy on creating content and making it look good, while providing us with a framework that can save multiple revisions of pages, separates the web content from the graphic design, and manages access permissions for users and staff.

One of the most popular web site frameworks around the world is PHP, and one of the most popular tools used to develop web sites is called WordPress. We will install WordPress on the www.example.com virtual host. There are of course many CMSs; we have chosen WordPress because out of the other PHP-based CMSs, it is the simplest and most widespread. There are other options for you; you might consider one of the following:

- Joomla! (http://joomla.org), PHP based

- Drupal (www.drupal.org), PHP based

- Jekyll (https://jekyllrb.com/), Ruby based

- Django (https://www.django-cms.org), Python based

The software is available as a tarball from https://wordpress.org/download/. The latest version at the time of this writing is WordPress 4.5.3. We'll download it to our home directory using the curl command.

```
$ curl https://wordpress.org/latest.tar.gz -o wordpress.tar.gz
```

Next, we unpack the tarball. We can unpack it here and then move the required files and directories to the web root, or we can unpack it directly to the web root. We'll do the latter by telling tar to strip the first directory component from the archive and specifying a target directory using the -C option.

```
$ sudo tar -xz --strip-components=1 -C /var/www/html/www.example.com/ -f wordpress.tar.gz
```

■ **Tip** To find out which directories a tar archive contains, use the -t and -v options to display a list of files without extracting them (e.g., `tar -tvzf wordpress.tar.gz`).

We need to now create a new database and create a new database user. We do that like we have previously shown you.

```
MariaDB [(none)]> CREATE DATABASE example;
MariaDB [(none)]> GRANT CREATE, SELECT,  INSERT,  UPDATE,  DELETE  ON example.* ↪
  TO `wpexample`@`localhost` IDENTIFIED BY 'secret';
```

What have we done there? We have granted only the necessary privileges to the database that WordPress should normally need. This is following the access of least privilege principle where we provide only the rights a user needs and no more. We have also used a poor example of a good password for that user.

A WordPress site has a configuration file that requires editing and describes the database details and some secret keys. We can make a copy of this file and rename it to the required name. We will change into the www.example.com directory to edit these files.

```
$ sudo cp wp-config-sample.php wp-config.php
```

Before we edit the `wp-config.php` file, go to this site, which creates the randomized keys required in the configuration file: `https://api.wordpress.org/secret-key/1.1/salt/`. These keys are used to sign session cookies, and you can change them at any time (and any signed-in user would have to sign in again). We just take a copy of these keys.

```
define('AUTH_KEY',         'yr-[fb[mc=Oef:L9 Px|6~alOPwR<KrxOy!|%g??@hD&hPh(=1J-DWO9pSWGiuic');
define('SECURE_AUTH_KEY',  '24|Nn+<)pFE@6Ity9LwMrDT!|JYe*JQFQm+qb(#[2-J?|c!U|$5/$rr;_wln~p-a');
define('LOGGED_IN_KEY',    'D_OYeZJLx~,/bB^]l1-?dDIni1StB(z-/-2FQSd^:}2.1|]uJXlMW%,<h6Q!k9x^');
define('NONCE_KEY',        ' 7=5Z7c4%tO!b@HAD= [nOby2Unrp^Et@.h-&3S2SrxdLL6gKV>3<o+dVj;,BI^h');
define('AUTH_SALT',        'ZYV|3qST=QVlH^MsccnF;k,-yKa=oq&x8iA|ohNN,6j.Y:o_,9zp$XBPzO3UcI^i');
define('SECURE_AUTH_SALT', 'vvC.{}1RjuE2I!yRs?]D/iHmZ3rbf->bHzpAlz?tR]$Nt..#=5{WC52#ty#C93+]');
define('LOGGED_IN_SALT',   'JZ>-u/:oUbhdK4qgJ.n_ReUi%Lj~J(t8{MI?kme#.U[qF:aZw*zpwIoc^:#4/[$O');
define('NONCE_SALT',       'T%|]FT^^!.:[sL}S4-DXz{o)R*TasHB.eh}<hknQjuK|R&yW^5ff9M-f{KlC-I@4');
```

Now when you edit the `wp-config.php` file, you can paste your keys in the "Authentication Unique Keys and Salts" section after deleting those lines with the put your unique phrase here string. Next you should also add the database details that we created in the previous section.

With the site content in the correct location, we can now point our web browser at www.example. com/wp-admin/install.php. This will allow us to start the web-based installation process, as shown in Figure 11-10.

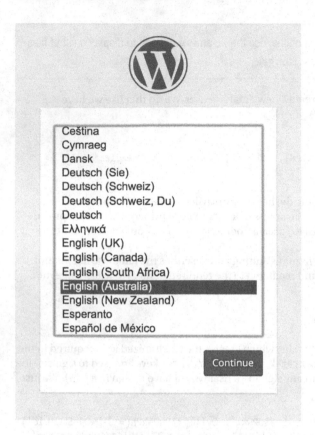

Figure 11-10. *WordPress installation*

To proceed, we click Continue to install WordPress in our local language. The next page, shown in Figure 11-11, gives us the opportunity to name our web site and provide the administration details.

Figure 11-11. Entering the web site details and admin credentials

Remember to record your password somewhere safe; you will need it shortly. Once that is done, we are shown the success page and offered a login button (Figure 11-12).

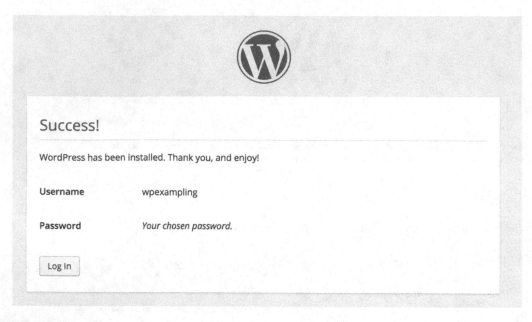

Figure 11-12. *Successfully installed WordPress*

Let's quickly show you the login process. First we gain access via our username and password we just created (Figure 11-13).

Figure 11-13. *Logging in*

On signing in, we are given access to the WordPress administration console (Figure 11-14).

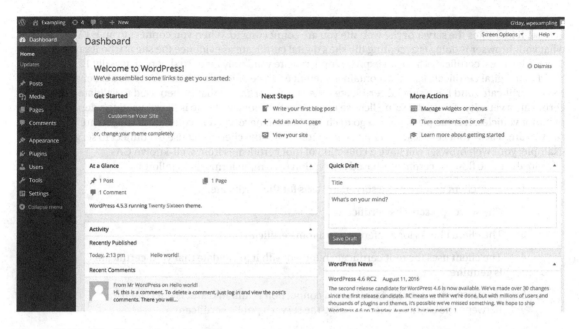

Figure 11-14. *WordPress admin console*

Securing Your Web Services with SSL/TLS Certificates

It is almost considered mandatory to have secured web services. There are many reasons to secure your web services and few to keep them unsecured. Not only do properly secured web server communications prevent any eavesdropping on your communications for things such as usernames and passwords or credit card information, they also stop spying on cookies or session information and help to prevent cross-site scripting and malicious code injection. Google now uses HTTPS as a ranking signal, meaning that if your site is fully encrypted, then your rank will be higher than an unencrypted site of the same content.

We are going to talk about TLS and then show you how to create your own certificate authority (CA), and finally we will install a certificate provided by Let's Encrypt.

TLS and Certificates

TLS works using digital certificates and a type of cryptography called *public key encryption*. Public key encryption works with two keys: the public key is available publicly, and the private key is stored on the server and kept secret. Anything that is encrypted using the public key can be decrypted only with the corresponding private key; this is the same concept described in the "DNSSEC" sidebar section in Chapter 10.

■ **Note**   Digital certificates and public key cryptography are complicated topics. This is really only an introduction to give you the basics for using TLS. If you're really interested in the math behind this, we recommend this excellent book: *Applied Cryptography: Protocols, Algorithms, and Source Code in C, 20th Anniversary Edition* by Bruce Schneier (John Wiley & Sons, 2015).

When using TLS, the digital certificate is the server's public key and acts like an electronic driver's license. It identifies the server or the web site you are connecting to. When you connect to an HTTPS web site, what your browser is doing is accepting the site's digital certificate as evidence the site is who it says it is. Like driver's licenses, certificates have an expiry period and are valid only for a fixed period, usually 12 months.

Each digital certificate can also contain a reference to a certificate authority. A CA is a mechanism that issues certificates and has a special certificate called a *root certificate* that is then used to validate the server certificate's veracity. To use the same license metaphor, the root certificate is like your state's department of motor vehicles. It is the place people go to check that you have a valid license and that you are who you say you are. These root certificates are usually bundled with the clients you use to connect to servers; for example, your web browser will have a collection of root certificates from well-known CAs.

So, the basic flow for certificate-based encryption (in simple terms) is as follows:

1. Your client connects to a server and asks for the certificate.

2. The server presents its certificate.

3. The client checks for a reference to a root certificate.

4. The client uses the root certificate bundled with it to validate that your certificate is genuine.

5. If your client trusts the certificate, a connection is initiated and is encrypted between the client and server using the server's public certificate.

■ **Tip** In some cases your client will tell you it isn't sure whether to trust the certificate and will prompt you to make a decision about whether you trust the server.

There are four types of certificates that you need to know about, and there are pros and cons with using each type.

- Certificates issued by a commercial CA

- Certificates issued by a noncommercial CA

- Certificates issued by a self-managed CA

- Self-signed certificates

Certificates from Commercial Certificate Authorities

Certificates from commercial CAs are issued by popular providers such as VeriSign, Thawte, or Comodo. These certificates generally require regular payment, for example, yearly or biannually. The prices vary depending on the type and number of certificates. The root certificates of most commercial CAs are bundled with clients such as browsers, mail clients, and other tools that use SSL/TLS connections. Commercial CAs are usually regularly audited for security, and a certificate issued by them is generally assumed to be secure.

Certificates from Non-commercial Certificate Authorities

In addition to the commercial certificate providers are a small number of noncommercial providers. These providers don't charge for their certificates, but correspondingly their root certificates are sometimes not bundled with many browsers. This means if you use these certificates for a web site or to secure a service like Simple Mail Transfer Protocol (SMTP), your client will most likely warn you that the validity and security certificates can't be determined.

If the CA's root is not installed in the browser, the only way to overcome this is to manually add a noncommercial CA's root certificate to the browser. If you have a lot of client browsers, this can add a lot of overhead and maintenance to your environment. In many cases, such as a web site, you don't have access to the clients, and these errors may result in someone getting the message that the client cannot validate the certificate and hence not trust your web site. For example, this makes using noncommercial certificates for an e-commerce site problematic.

However, things have changed more recently. There has been a big push to encrypt the Internet in an effort to make the Internet more secure. One of the reasons for not using HTTPS on sites is that certificates are too expensive and noncommercial certificates are not widely supported, as we have mentioned. The Internet Security Research Group (ISRG) decided to create Let's Encrypt to solve this problem.

Let's Encrypt is a nonprofit organization dedicated to helping encrypt the Internet by providing a simple and automated mechanism for getting and installing TLS certificates. The Let's Encrypt root CA is also bundled in a lot of modern browsers, which solves many of the issues faced by noncommercial CAs. You can find more information about Let's Encrypt at `https://letsencrypt.org/`.

An alternative way of getting noncommercial certificates is using CAcert. It provides free temporary certificates (like Let's Encrypt) but also allows you to have longer certificates if you pass a "key of trust" that validates domain owners. For more information, see the CAcert web site and wiki: `www.cacert.org/` and `http://wiki.cacert.org/wiki/`.

Certificates from Self-Managed Certificate Authorities

You can also create and manage your own certificates. These certificates are issued by a certificate authority that you create and manage yourself. As a result, the certificates don't cost any money, but they do have other issues. First, as it is your own CA, you can't expect others to trust your certificates. This leads us to the second issue: usability. The root certificate of your CA is not bundled with clients and will never be. So if you want to install our root certificate, you will need to do so via software management (like Ansible or Puppet, discussed in Chapter 19).

■ **Note**   In the case of noncommercial CAs, there are at least a small number of clients with their root certificate bundled. In the case of your own self-managed CA, the clients with your root certificates are ones you install it on yourself.

Hence, when your web client attempts to validate certificates provided by your CA, for example, an error message is generated indicating that the client does not trust the CA. Other services may just refuse to connect altogether with a valid certificate. To overcome this error, you need to install your CA's root certificate on the client. This is something you can do for clients you manage, for example, your internal desktops, but for others this isn't feasible.

■ **Tip**   In this model, you have to secure and manage your own CA. This isn't overly complicated for a small number of certificates, but it does pose some issues and risks that we will discuss.

Self-Signed Certificates

Self-signed certificates don't use a CA. They are signed by you and hence don't cost any money either. Like certificates generated by a self-managed CA, they are not trusted and will generate a similar error message on your clients. Unlike those generated by a self-managed CA, you can't remove this error by adding a root certificate because you have no root certificate to add to the client. Self-signed certificates are generally used only for testing and are rarely used in production environments.

Choosing a Certificate Type

If you want to buy a certificate for a long period of time, the best certificates to use are those issued by commercial CAs. The key issue here is cost. A certificate from a commercial CA can cost hundreds of dollars a year. This is a considerable expense just to secure your e-mail or your business marketing site. As a result, if you don't want the expense of buying certificates, we recommend a Let's Encrypt certificate.

If we choose a commercial certificate, we will need to create the private key and a certificate signing request (CSR). We show that next.

Creating Certificates for TLS

As you've discovered, for TLS to work we need two certificates: a server certificate and the root certificate from a CA (either a commercial CA, a noncommercial CA, or your own CA). Let's start by generating our first server certificate. This first step is generating a server key and a CSR. We would take these steps whether we were generating a certificate from a commercial or a self-managed CA.

The process creates our private key and a CSR. This CSR is then submitted to a CA, in our case our own CA, but also to a commercial CA. It is this signing process that allows a client to confirm the identity of a server certificate.

In Listing 11-6, we generate a key and the request using the `openssl` command that is part of the OpenSSL application. The OpenSSL application is an open source SSL implementation that allows Linux and other operating systems to encrypt and secure applications using SSL.

Listing 11-6. Generating a Server Key and Request

```
$ openssl genpkey -algorithm RSA -out www.example.com.key -pkeyopt rsa_keygen_bits:2048
..............................................................+++
.................+++
```

In Listing 11-6 we've used the `openssl` command to generate a private key using the RSA cipher. The key is 2,048 bits long, which is the current standard for the Internet but can be higher if you want. The issue is that some CAs will not support larger key lengths.

■ **Note**   Higher key lengths increase the security of your encryption, but there is a (slight) processing penalty, and doubling the key does not result in double the encryption security. As a result, most keys used for web sites are 2,048 bits long and are expected to remain secure until around 2030. You can increase the key length to 4,096 if you want.

We pass the `-algorithm` option to tell the `openssl` command to use the RSA cipher, and the `-out` option tells the `openssl` command where to write the key, here to the `www.example.com.key` file. We pass the bit size to `openssl` via `-pkeyopt rsa_keygen_bits:2048`.

■ **Tip**   You can see more details about the `openssl genpkey` options by entering `man genpkey`.

Next we want to generate a CSR. It is this that we would give to the CA for signing. This is generated from our private key we just generated. This way we do not have to give *anyone* our private key in order to get our certificate. While the private key is precious and needs to be secured, the CSR is public and doesn't need such restrictions. We create a CSR as shown in Listing 11-7.

Listing 11-7. Generating the CSR

```
$ openssl req -new -sha256 -key www.example.com.key -out www.example.com.csr
You are about to be asked to enter information that will be incorporated
into your certificate request.
What you are about to enter is what is called a Distinguished Name or a DN.
There are quite a few fields but you can leave some blank
For some fields there will be a default value,
If you enter '.', the field will be left blank.
-----
Country Name (2 letter code) [XX]:AU
State or Province Name (full name) []:Victoria
Locality Name (eg, city) [Default City]:Melbourne
Organization Name (eg, company) [Default Company Ltd]:Example Inc
Organizational Unit Name (eg, section) []:IT
Common Name (eg, your name or your server's hostname) []:www.example.com
Email Address []:admin@example.com

Please enter the following 'extra' attributes
to be sent with your certificate request
A challenge password []:
An optional company name []:
```

During the request creation process, you will be prompted for some information about your new certificate. If you don't want to answer a specific query, you can type **Enter** to skip the field. You will be prompted for the two-letter country code, for example, US for the United States, GB for Great Britain, and AU for Australia.

■ **Note** You can find a full list of country codes at www.nationsonline.org/oneworld/country_code_list.htm.

You will also be prompted for the state, municipality, and name of your organization and optionally an organizational unit in your organization. This data will be displayed in your certificate when a client or user queries it. It's a good idea to be specific and accurate here—especially if you are submitting your CSR to be signed by a commercial CA.

Next, and most important, we need to specify the common name of the certificate. This must be the exact hostname of the server that is going to use the certificate. If you specify an incorrect hostname, you will get an error about a mismatch between the server and certificate name. In this case, we specify mail.example.com, which is the fully qualified hostname of the e-mail server.

Then specify the e-mail address of the contact for the certificate, in this case admin@example.com.

Last, you are prompted for some extra attributes for the certificate. You don't need to worry about these, and you can type **Enter** to skip the fields.

This process will leave you with two files: www.example.com.key and www.example.com.csr. We will keep these two files, as we'll need them later in this process.

The next step in the process is signing the CSR with a CA. If you're going to create your own CA, see the next section, "Creating Your Own Certificate Authority."

Otherwise, you need to provide the contents of the www.example.com.csr file that you would provide to your commercial CA, and it will then deliver a certificate to you. Your commercial CA will provide instructions as to how to provide your CSR file. Usually, you would cut and paste the contents of the CSR into a web page and submit it. The CA would then sign it and notify you when a signed certificate was available to download.

In the next chapter we are going to show you how you can create another certificate and use it in your Postfix installation.

Creating Your Own Certificate Authority

Creating your own CA is an easy task. First, you create a directory to hold your CA and some subdirectories inside that directory. CentOS stores all OpenSSL files in the /etc/pki directory. Ubuntu uses /etc/ssl. In this example, we're going to put our CA in the /etc/pki directory on our CentOS host. The following directories should already exist:

```
$ sudo mkdir /etc/pki/CA
$ sudo mkdir /etc/pki/CA/{private,newcerts,crl,certs}
$ sudo chown -R root:root /etc/pki/CA
$ sudo chmod 0700 /etc/pki/CA/private
```

The private directory will hold the CA's private key, and the newcerts directory will contain a copy of each certificate the CA will sign. We also ensure the root user owns all the directories, and we secure the private directory so that only the root user can access it.

Next, you need to create a database to hold details of your signed certificates.

```
$ echo '01' | sudo tee /etc/pki/CA/serial
$ sudo touch /etc/pki/CA/index.txt
```

■ **Note** In the first line, we've echoed the number 01 to the /etc/pki/CA/serial file. To do this, we've used a command called tee, which can read from standard output and then write to standard output and files. You can find more information in the tee command's man page.

The serial file tracks the last serial number of certificates issued through this CA, starting with the number 01. Each certificate issued by the CA has a unique serial number.

The index.txt file will contain a list of the certificates currently being managed by this CA. Next to each certificate will be a letter indicating the status of that certificate.

- R: Revoked

- E: Expired

- V: Valid

OpenSSL has a configuration file that controls defaults and CA settings. There is a template file available on most distributions. This file, called openssl.cnf, is located in the /etc/pki/tls/ directory on CentOS distributions and in the /etc/ssl/ directory on Ubuntu.

If you are using a nonstandard directory for your CA or have some other settings, you can make a copy of this file and edit it in your CA directory. To do this, find the section in the configuration file that starts with the following:

```
[ CA_default ]
```

In the following example, we change the configuration option called dir. If we wanted to change the openssl command to read CA information from the current directory, we would do the following:

```
dir = .
```

This tells OpenSSL to look in the current directory for directories and files needed to configure and sign certificates. For CentOS, this is already set to /etc/pki/CA. Ubuntu has this set to ./demoCA. This means when you sign a certificate, you must change your working directory to the CA directory, in our case, /etc/pki/CA.

■ **Tip** Have a look at the default settings in the openssl.cnf file for your CA. It should show the default directories and files you've created for your CA; in our case, these are the private directory and the serial file.

Now you need to create a self-signed certificate and a private key for your CA.

```
$ cd /etc/pki/CA
$ sudo openssl req -new -x509 -newkey rsa:4096 -keyout private/cakey.pem \ ↩
    -out certs/cacert.pem -days 3650 \ ↩
    -subj '/C=AU/ST=Victoria/L=Melbourne/O=Example Inc/OU=IT/CN=ca.example.com/
emailAddress=admin@example.com/'
Generating a 4096 bit RSA private key
...............................++
.....................................................................................................
..................................................++
writing new private key to 'private/cakey.pem'
Enter PEM pass phrase:
Verifying - Enter PEM pass phrase:
-----
```

First, as we mentioned, we change our working directory to /etc/pki/CA. Next, we're creating a key, this one also RSA and 4,096 bits long. We store that key in the /etc/pki/CA/private/cakey.pem file. We're also creating the certificate as self-signed because we don't have another CA to sign it. We specify the age of the certificate as 3,650 days (or 10 years). We have specified some other options: -x509, which indicates the certificate is self-signed, and -extensions v3_ca, which specifies that we're creating a CA certificate. The last option, -subj, allows us to answer the attributes we add to the certificate subject.

■ **Tip** It's worth reading through the openssl.cnf configuration file to understand what other options are available to you.

You'll be prompted for a passphrase or password for your CA private key. Choose a good password and remember it. You'll need this password every time you create a new certificate.

As you can see, the CA is made up of a private key and a public certificate. You now have your own CA and can use it to sign certificates.

```
                    SECURING YOUR CERTIFICATE AUTHORITY
```

If you are using your CA to secure production or any sensitive data transmissions, you will want to keep your CA (private keys, CRLs, and so on) very secure. If you are just using it for fun and experimenting, you can be less strict with how you secure it.

In this example we have created a CA on the same host we are using for a web server. This is not really ideal in the real world, and having a dedicated host for this activity is preferable. Ideally this host should be restricted or disconnected from the network when it is now being used, and having this on a web server is dangerous. Having a dedicated host is our strong recommendation.

One good way of securing your CA is to have a dedicated virtual image that resides on a password-protected encrypted disk. When you want to sign a certificate, you can mount the encrypted disk, spin up the virtual image, sign the certificates, power down the virtual host, and unmount the disk.

We can create a private key for www.example.com on any host we like. You don't need to be on a host with the same hostname to create a private key. You would then have to copy the private key to the www.example.com host for it to use it. It is recommended that you do not leave private keys lying around on hosts that are not using them. They should be securely deleted (like using the shred program) if they are not needed.

If your CA is compromised, depending who is using it, you *can* re-create it and re-sign all your certificates. If other organizations are using your CA or the numbers of certificates issued is large, then the effort to re-create CAs can be annoying and disruptive.

Of course, the passwords associated with the CA would be stored securely in a password manager, and a copy of the CA's private key could be stored on an encrypted thumb drive and stored in a secure vault.

Signing Your Certificate with Your Certificate Authority

Now that you've created your CA, you can use it to sign your certificate request. In our case, the CA is on the same host that we have created our CSR requests. You would normally need to copy the CSR file to the CA host. This takes your CSR and signs it with your CA and outputs a signed certificate. In Listing 11-8, we've signed our CSR.

Listing 11-8. Signing Our Certificate Request

```
$ cd /etc/pki/CA
$ sudo openssl ca -out /root/www.example.com.cert -infiles /root/www.example.com.csr
Using configuration from /etc/pki/tls/openssl.cnf
Enter pass phrase for /etc/pki/CA/private/cakey.pem:
Check that the request matches the signature
Signature ok
Certificate Details:
        Serial Number: 1 (0x1)
        Validity
            Not Before: Aug 21 02:05:11 2016 GMT
            Not After : Aug 21 02:05:11 2017 GMT
```

```
Subject:
    countryName              = AU
    stateOrProvinceName      = Victoria
    organizationName         = Example Inc
    organizationalUnitName   = IT
    commonName               = www.example.com
    emailAddress             = admin@example.com
X509v3 extensions:
    X509v3 Basic Constraints:
        CA:FALSE
    Netscape Comment:
        OpenSSL Generated Certificate
    X509v3 Subject Key Identifier:
        3E:37:13:CB:D3:84:58:9D:47:73:89:A6:80:12:DD:90:FE:C7:06:4B
    X509v3 Authority Key Identifier:
        keyid:54:57:27:C4:82:CA:C2:97:CE:5E:C7:64:A8:99:D3:A8:D1:1E:EC:77

Certificate is to be certified until Aug 21 02:05:11 2017 GMT (365 days)
Sign the certificate? [y/n]:y

1 out of 1 certificate requests certified, commit? [y/n]y
Write out database with 1 new entries
Data Base Updated
```

In Listing 11-8, we've used the ca option to sign our request. The -out option specifies the signed certificate we're going to output, and the -infiles option specifies the CSR we want to sign (we've assumed our CSR file is in the /root directory).

■ **Tip**   You can see the other options available with the openssl ca command by entering man ca.

You will be prompted for the passphrase you created for the CA's private key, then the details of your certificate will be displayed, and finally you will be prompted to sign the certificate and write its details to the CA's database. Answer y for yes to both questions.

At the end of the process, you will have a signed certificate, a private key, and a certificate request all located in the /root directory. Your certificate is valid for one year (you can override this period using the -days option to specify a different validity period).

You can examine the details of your certificate using the openssl command.

```
$ openssl x509 -in /root/www.example.com.cert -noout -text -purpose | more
```

■ **Tip**   You can keep a hold of your CSR. When you want to renew your certificate, after a year in our case, you can just re-sign this request using the command in Listing 11-8. This means you don't need to keep re-creating your CSR.

Remember, to avoid your clients indicating that your certificates are not trusted, you must install your root certificate in the relevant client, for example, the user's browser! The CAcert site has instructions for installing its root certificate into a variety of clients at http://wiki.cacert.org/FAQ/BrowserClients. To install your certificate, replace its certificate with yours in the instructions.

Creating HTTPS Certificates with Let's Encrypt

Let's Encrypt (`https://letsencrypt.org`) has a mission to encrypt the Internet! It is a free, automated, and open certificate authority from the nonprofit Internet Security Research Group (ISRG). Let's Encrypt is a free CA that will automatically create, request, and sign certificates, primarily for web servers. We are going to be using Let's Encrypt for many of our services as it is a secure and convenient way to encrypt all your traffic.

How does it work? Well, like we said, the heart of it is just like a normal CA. Let's Encrypt provides an agent that uses the Automated Certificate Management Environment (ACME) protocol to first validate the web server domain and second create the private keys and CSR requests to create valid certificates. Renewals and revocations are also done by Let's Encrypt. For a greater explanation, please refer to the documentation here: `https://letsencrypt.org/how-it-works/`.

We are going to use the Certbot agent provided by Let's Encrypt to manage our certificates. For this to work, your web server will need a valid Domain Name System (DNS) public record and be able to accept HTTP and HTTPS connections from the Internet. We are also going to use the Let's Encrypt staging environment so that our testing will not impact their services.

To install Certbot, we can see the instructions here: `https://certbot.eff.org`. We selected the instructions for Apache and CentOS 7. We need to issue the following:

```
$ sudo yum install epel-release
```

Then we need to install the `python-certbot-apache` package.

```
$ sudo yum install python-certbot-apache
```

For Apache HTTPS on CentOS, we require that the `mod_ssl` package be installed. On Ubuntu the SSL module is part of the core Apache packages. For CentOS the module is loaded via `/etc/httpd/conf.modules.d/00-ssl.conf` and should be present after installing the package.

What we are going to do now is use the `certbot` command to create and install our certificates. Certbot will handle the certificate creation and installation, and it will make a copy of our virtual host and redirect `http://` traffic to `https://`. Because we are using the Let's Encrypt staging server, we will be making useless certificates, but we will not be restricted to the access limits while testing that the production Let's Encrypt systems have.

■ **Note**   We cannot use the `example.com` domain to create Let's Encrypt certificates as we obviously don't own that domain. Instead, we are using another domain in these examples.

The `certbot` command has several options available to it. You can see them by typing `certbot --help`, or for *all* available options, you can issue `certbot --help all`. Let's use `certbot` to create our certificates for `www.example.com`.

```
$ sudo certbot --test-cert -d www.example.com
```

Here we have issued `certbot` with the `--test-cert` argument, which will mean we will use the staging application programming interface (API) instead of the real endpoint for Let's Encrypt. This staging API will do everything we need except create a valid certificate (certificates are issued by Fake LE). We also passed the `-d` option to Certbot to provide the hostname we want to certify. We can provide multiple hostnames by adding additional `-d <hostname>` arguments as long as you have virtual hosts for them.

When we first run `certbot`, we provide an e-mail address for correspondence about our certificates (Figure 11-15).

Figure 11-15. *Adding e-mail address to Certbot*

This process creates a series of files in the `/etc/letsencrypt/accounts` directory for the staging API. When we first run `certbot`, we provide an e-mail address for correspondence about our certificates (Figure 11-16).

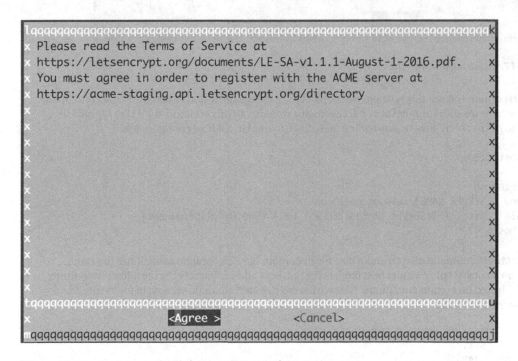

Figure 11-16. *Agreeing to the Let's Encrypt terms of service*

In Figure 11-17 we are presented with two options.

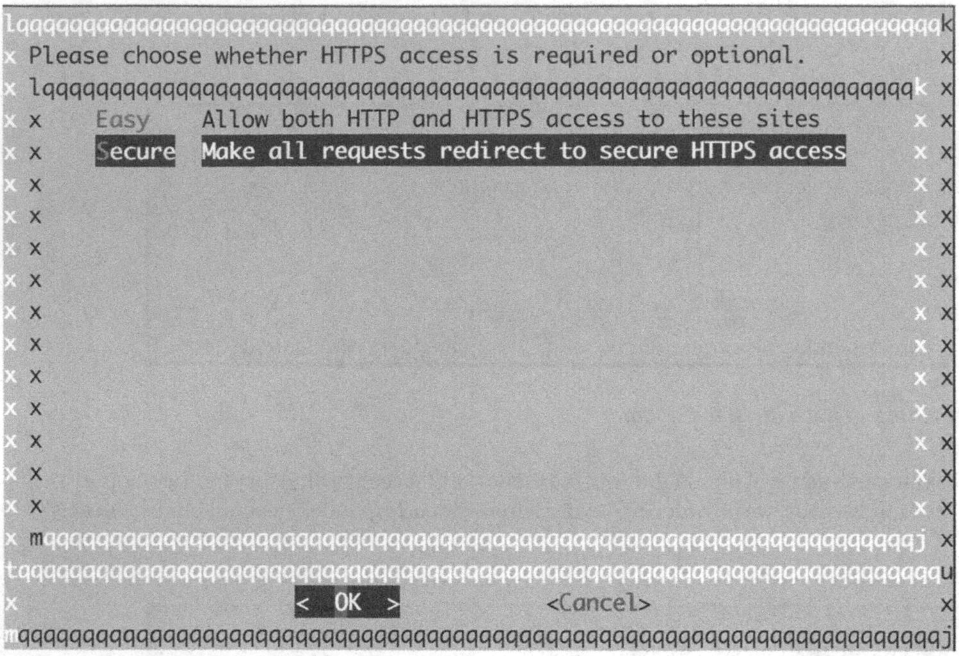

```
Lqqqqqqqqqqqqqqqqqqqqqqqqqqqqqqqqqqqqqqqqqqqqqqqqqqqqqqqqqqqqqqqqqqqqqqqk
x Please choose whether HTTPS access is required or optional.        x
x lqqqqqqqqqqqqqqqqqqqqqqqqqqqqqqqqqqqqqqqqqqqqqqqqqqqqqqqqqqqqqqqqqqk x
x x    Easy    Allow both HTTP and HTTPS access to these sites     x x
x x    Secure  Make all requests redirect to secure HTTPS access   x x
x x                                                                 x x
x x                                                                 x x
x x                                                                 x x
x x                                                                 x x
x x                                                                 x x
x x                                                                 x x
x x                                                                 x x
x x                                                                 x x
x x                                                                 x x
x x                                                                 x x
x x                                                                 x x
x x                                                                 x x
x mqqqqqqqqqqqqqqqqqqqqqqqqqqqqqqqqqqqqqqqqqqqqqqqqqqqqqqqqqqqqqqqqqqj x
tqqqqqqqqqqqqqqqqqqqqqqqqqqqqqqqqqqqqqqqqqqqqqqqqqqqqqqqqqqqqqqqqqqqqqqqu
x               <  OK  >              <Cancel>                      x
mqqqqqqqqqqqqqqqqqqqqqqqqqqqqqqqqqqqqqqqqqqqqqqqqqqqqqqqqqqqqqqqqqqqqqqqj
```

Figure 11-17. *Securing our web site*

The first option is Easy; this is where we keep `http://` alongside `https://` access. The second option (Secure) is where we allow only `https://` access to our web site. In this scenario, the `http://` traffic is redirected to `https://`. It does this by adding these lines to our virtual host configuration:

```
<VirtualHost *:80>
...
RewriteEngine on
RewriteCond %{SERVER_NAME} =www.example.com
RewriteRule ^ https://%{SERVER_NAME}%{REQUEST_URI} [END,QSA,R=permanent]
</VirtualHost>
```

The `certbot` command also creates a new file to contain our SSL configuration. It has the same configuration as our `http://` virtual host but has the SSL keys added. `RewriteEngine` allows us to route HTTP traffic based on certain conditions. Here we have redirected all traffic coming in for `http://` to the `https://` version of the site.

```
/etc/httpd/conf.d/www.example.com-le-ssl.conf
<IfModule mod_ssl.c>
<VirtualHost *:443>

  ServerName www.example.com

  ServerAdmin webmaster@example.com
  DocumentRoot  /var/www/html/www.example.com
  DirectoryIndex index.php
  ProxyPassMatch ^/(.*\.php(/.*)?)$ unix:/run/php-fcgi.sock|fcgi://127.0.0.1:9000/var/www/
  html/www.example.com/
```

```
<Directory /var/www/html/www.example.com>
   Require all granted
</Directory>

SSLCertificateFile /etc/letsencrypt/live/www.example.com/cert.pem
SSLCertificateKeyFile /etc/letsencrypt/live/www.example.com/privkey.pem
Include /etc/letsencrypt/options-ssl-apache.conf
SSLCertificateChainFile /etc/letsencrypt/live/www.example.com/chain.pem
</VirtualHost>

</IfModule>
```

Here we have a copy of the virtual host we created earlier, but Let's Encrypt has added the SSL certificate details it has just created. In doing so, it will restart the Apache server, and we can access the `https://` version (Figure 11-18).

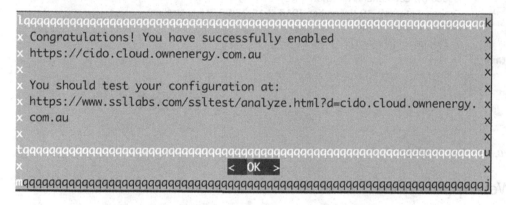

Figure 11-18. *We have our certificates.*

As we said earlier, we can't test with `www.example.com` for real, so you can see the pretend URL (Figure 11-19).

Figure 11-19. *Our fake certificate*

The staging API will give us certificates that we can use but that will not be trusted by anyone. To make it a true trusted certificate, we just remove -test-cert from our certbot command and add our e-mail address again, and we will have a working certificate (Figure 11-20).

```
$ sudo certbot -d cido.cloud.ownenergy.com.au
```

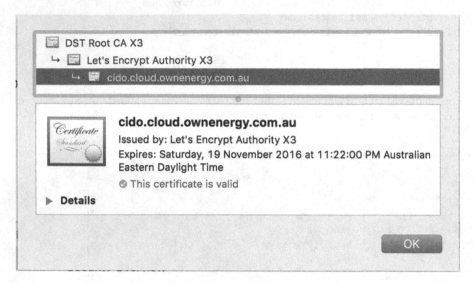

Figure 11-20. *Our true certificate*

Other Web Applications

We've shown you how to install two web applications in a virtual host of their own, which should provide you with a basic understanding of the process. We can't include installation guidance for all web applications here, but we can suggest some that you might find useful.

MediaWiki is a collaboration tool that runs Wikipedia (among other sites). You can download it from www.mediawiki.org/.

Moodle is a course or learning management system. It is used by many schools to provide web-based learning to their students. You can download it from www.moodle.org/.

SugarCRM is customer relationship management (CRM) software that can help you and your organization's salespeople manage clients and client relationships. You can download it from www.sugarcrm.com/.

Web Caching

Web caching is use to speed up the delivery of web pages by returning cached responses to multiple clients. This can be internal users or external public clients and can save your web servers from handling every request that comes into your site, freeing them to better handle dynamic content generation.

There are different types of caching software and services. There are content delivery networks (CDNs) services such as Akamai, Cloudflare, CloudFront, and Fastly as well as software such as Varnish, Nginx, Apache, and Squid-Cache.

Web caching works by using HTTP headers. The Cache-Control and ETag headers are used by the browser to determine when the resource it is requesting has changed and should be fetched again. For files such as images, JavaScript, and CSS, you can set a Cache-Control header like max-age=120, which means the browser will store a resource object in its cache for 120 seconds before it considers it stale. After this time, it will fetch the resource again.

However, if the resource hasn't changed at all in that time, it would be a waste of resources to download it again. It is better to renew the cached version. The browser can determine if the resource has changed by using the ETag value. The browser asks the web server if the resource with this particular ETag has changed by setting a header in the request, IF-NONE-MATCH, with the ETag value it has. If it has changed, then the resource is downloaded again; if not, then the web server sends back a 304 Not Modified response, and the object in the cache is renewed for another 120 seconds.

Some organizations will use a web caching server in front of their main web servers. For instance, you may use a Varnish or Nginx server in front of your Apache server, or you may want your global users to be able to benefit from a CDN that provides a web presence closer to your clients. It depends on your infrastructure and the nature of how your web site will be used. If you are getting only several thousands of users a month, there may be little benefit. If you are distributing content to tens of thousands of people around the world, you will definitely want to look at a CDN.

In our example, we are going to install a web caching server to help reduce our local bandwidth and speed up our browsing.

Squid-Cache

When multiple users in your office start browsing the Web simultaneously, they can end up using quite a lot of bandwidth. To help minimize the impact of web browsing on other network users, you can install a cache or proxy server.

One of the commonly used web cache servers on Linux is Squid-Cache. When your browser is configured to use the cache, Squid keeps a local cached copy of any files you retrieve from a web site, so the next time the same file is accessed, it can be served from the local Squid cache instead.

The other mode of operation for Squid is as a *reverse proxy*, which sits in front of one or more web servers on the web server side of the connection. A reverse proxy is used when sites serve large amounts of content that doesn't change very often. By allowing the data that does not change to be cached by the reverse proxy, the load on the underlying web servers can be reduced. This kind of proxy is also known as a *web accelerator*.

Configuration

Squid is provided by the squid package. Install it via sudo yum install squid on CentOS or sudo aptitude install squid on Ubuntu. Both distributions use the same configuration file for Squid, which is /etc/squid/squid.conf. Because this file can contain sensitive information (e.g., passwords), you cannot even view it without using sudo.

The default configuration file on Ubuntu is well commented, so we won't go into great detail about most options. The squid.conf file on CentOS has been striped to the recommended minimum settings. We will show you how to configure which address and port Squid should listen on and how to configure it so your users are actually permitted to access the Web via the cache.

Squid listens on port 3128 on all network interfaces by default, though port 8080 is used commonly as well. The directive to modify the port in the configuration file is http_port. This directive allows you to specify a port number or an address and port number combination.

If you want Squid to listen on multiple addresses and ports, you can add more http_port directives.

Because we're setting up Squid on the gateway host, we don't want it to listen for connections on all interfaces; users not on our local networks should not be able to access it. We thus need to add two http_port lines: one for the wireless network address range and one for the wired range.

```
http_port 192.168.0.254:3128
http_port 192.168.1.254:3128
```

Next, we need to tell Squid which ranges of IP addresses are allowed to connect to it and access web sites. Squid uses access control lists (ACLs) for this. For each network range you want to control, you need to define an ACL. You then create rules that control access for each ACL. The configuration file contains a few basic ACLs, which we've included in Listing 11-9.

Listing 11-9. ACL Definitions

```
acl all src 0.0.0.0/0.0.0.0
acl localhost src 127.0.0.1/255.255.255.255
acl to_localhost dst 127.0.0.0/8
```

The `acl` directive tells Squid the rest of the line is an ACL definition. Next, we give the ACL a label so we can refer to it later. Then we specify the ACL type we're creating. Squid supports many types, but we'll be using only `src`, `dst`, and `port`, which control whether we're dealing with source addresses, destination addresses, or port numbers. Finally, we define the source, destination, or port using a string. To get a full list of ACL types, you can read through the ACL section on the Squid web site at `www.squid-cache.org/Versions/v2/2.6/cfgman/acl.html`.

In our case, we've defined an ACL called `all` that encompasses all Internet addresses. The next ACL allows us to refer to all traffic originating on the local network interface as localhost. The third does the same but for traffic *to* the local network interface.

Let's add in some ACLs for our network addresses. We can add these directly under the line that defines `to_localhost`.

```
acl wired src 192.168.0.0/255.255.255.0
acl wireless src 192.168.1.0/255.255.255.0
```

We've defined two new ACLs, one for the wired network range and one for the wireless range. We could have combined them by simply specifying the same label for both ACLs. However, giving them different names means we can give them different levels of access to the Web, should we want to.

Another configuration option that might be useful is to set the time you want to allow access from any particular network or zone.

```
acl wireless_hours time M T W T F 8:30-17:30
```

Squid contains an ACL called `Safe_ports` that contains commonly used ports for web and FTP traffic. This way, you can control which ports on remote servers you want local users to be able to connect to. If a site you need to access runs on a nonstandard port, you can add the port number to the `Safe_ports` ACL and so permit browsers to connect to it.

```
acl Safe_ports port 80  # http
acl Safe_ports port 21     # ftp
acl Safe_ports port 443 # https
```

Now that we have defined all the ACLs we need, we can complete our configuration by defining access rules for these ACLs. Squid uses the `http_access` directive to determine whether a given ACL is allowed to use the cache. This directive has two parameters, an action and an ACL. These directives are processed in order, and processing stops when a rule matches.

The first rule prevents browsers from connecting to ports we haven't explicitly listed in the `Safe_ports` ACL.

```
http_access deny !Safe_ports
```

Next, localhost is permitted to connect, and all other connections are rejected.

```
http_access allow localhost
http_access deny all
```

If no http_access rule matches, the opposite of the last seen action is applied. This is why it's important to always leave http_access deny all in place as the final rule; it means Squid will deny access unless it encounters a rule to allow access.

We should insert our new rules in between, as shown in Listing 11-10.

Listing 11-10. Granting Access for Our Networks

```
http_access allow localhost
http_access allow wired
http_access allow wireless wireless_hours
http_access deny all
```

We are going to add some logging to help track down any issues with our configuration. To do this, we add the access_log directive. Logs will be written to /var/log/squid.

```
access_log daemon:/var/log/squid/access.log squid
```

This is will give us some logging details for our access logs like this example:

```
1471953526.429    934 192.168.0.1 TCP_MISS/200 10265 GET http://blahblah.com/ - HIER_
DIRECT/64.207.180.61 text/html
1471953526.961    493 192.168.0.1 TCP_MISS/200 19834 GET http://blahblah.com/blah.jpg -
HIER_DIRECT/64.207.180.61 image/jpeg
...
1471953633.942    389 192.168.0.1 TCP_REFRESH_UNMODIFIED/304 305 GET http://blahblah.com/ -
HIER_DIRECT/64.207.180.61 -
```

In this example of our access log, you can see that we first get the resource we are after, and then we can see a subsequent request returns a 304 unmodified status.

Finally, we can change the directory on the disk that Squid uses to store its cached objects using the cache_dir directive. This is commented out, which means it will use the built-in default, as follows:

```
# cache_dir ufs /var/spool/squid 100 16 256
```

The preceding line tells Squid to store cache objects under the /var/spool/squid directory in ufs format. It will store a maximum of 100Mb of objects; after that, older objects will be expired from the cache and replaced by newer ones. The final two numbers control how many subdirectories Squid will create in the main cache directory. In this case, it will create 16 main subdirectories, each containing another 256 subdirectories.

This subdirectory schema came about because most filesystems are quite slow at accessing directories containing a large number of files. For example, if each of the Squid subdirectories contained about 100 cached files, the total number of files in the cache would exceed 400,000. If they were all stored in a single directory, each time one of these files was requested by a browser, the host would need to search through up to 400,000 entries in the directory inode to find out where the data it needs is stored. By subdividing the cache, the number of inodes that need to be searched for any given file is much smaller, resulting in less performance degradation as the cache grows.

Since disk space is generally cheaper than bandwidth, we'll allow our cache to grow bigger.

```
cache_dir ufs /var/spool/squid 2000 16 256
```

We save the configuration file and start Squid. On CentOS, we should create the startup links via `systemctl` first.

```
$ sudo systemctl enable squid
```

We can now start Squid via `sudo systemctl start squid` on CentOS or restart it on Ubuntu via `sudo service squid restart`. On CentOS, the cache directory we specified will be created when Squid first starts. This already happened on Ubuntu, when we installed the package.

Client Configuration

All that is left for us to do is configure the web browser to use the proxy. In Chrome, we choose Settings ➤ Network ➤ Change proxy settings. On this Apple Mac host, we can configure the proxy service as shown in Figure 11-21 for `http://`-only traffic.

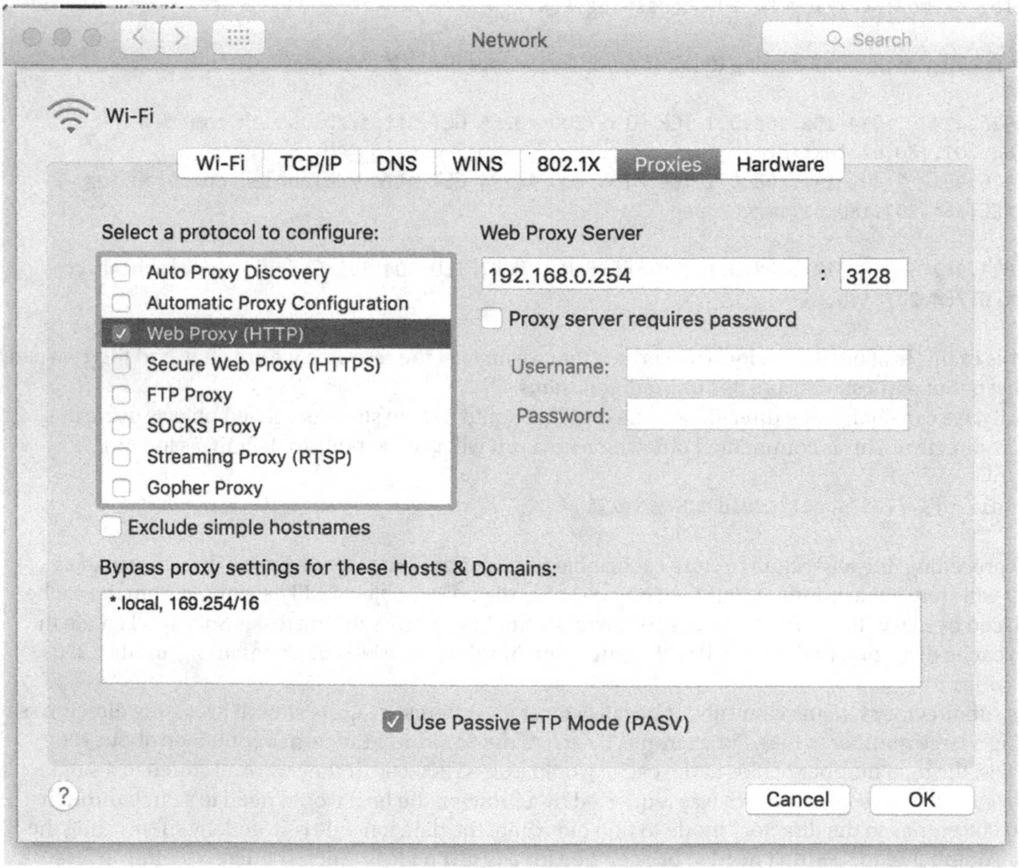

Figure 11-21. *Setting a proxy server in Chrome*

We could configure the traffic for `https://` also if we so choose to. We then close the network and Chrome settings and visit our favorite web site. We can verify that the proxy is being used by looking at the Squid access logs.

Transparency

If you don't want to make your users change their proxy settings in order to use the Squid cache, you can run Squid as a transparent proxy instead. A *transparent proxy* is one that has all outbound web traffic redirected to it via firewalling rules. Browsers accessing the Web don't know they're using a cache, and you don't need to explicitly configure any web browsers to use it.

■ **Note** If you want to use authentication with your proxy services, you will not be able to use transparent proxying. The client thinks it is talking directly to the origin servers.

To turn our current configuration into a transparent proxy, we have to make two small changes to the configuration file. For each `http_port` directive, we need to add the option `transparent`.

```
http_port 192.168.0.254:3128 transparent
http_port 192.168.1.254:3128 transparent
```

After restarting Squid, we add firewall rules on the gateway host. These rules should intercept all connections to remote web sites and redirect them to our proxy instead. We want to change the destination address and port number on packets before the gateway sends them out to the Internet. This is a form of network address translation (NAT), and it is done by Netfilter in the NAT table. The command `firewall-cmd` can be used for this again.

■ **Note** We cover firewalls in Chapter 7.

To change the destination address of a packet, we need to create a DNAT target and mangle the HTTP traffic outbound. First make sure that we masquerade our connection. Then we forward traffic coming in to the firewall on port 80 to be redirected to port 3128 where Squid will be waiting.

```
$ sudo firewall-cmd --permanent --zone=public --add-masquerade
$ sudo firewall-cmd --permanent --zone=public --add-forward-port=port=80:proto=tcp:toport=31
28:to_addr=192.168.0.254
$ sudo firewall-cmd --reload
```

We then reload the firewall to make the changes permanent.

■ **Caution** If your transparent proxy host is not the gateway host, you should make sure it can access remote web sites directly, without being redirected to itself.

Summary

In this chapter, we showed you how to use your Linux host as a flexible web server with SQL support and how to make use of this by installing web services. You should now be able to do the following:

- Create and manage virtual web sites

- Add functionality to Apache via modules

- Control access to sites based on hostname or username and password

- Create and manage MariaDB databases and users

- Install and configure third-party web applications

- Configure a web proxy to save on bandwidth costs and increase speed

In the next chapter, we will look at setting up our mail server.

CHAPTER 12

■ ■ ■

Mail Services

By James Turnbull and Dennis Matotek

One of the most common reasons to deploy a Linux host is to provide mail services including receiving and sending e-mail and retrieving e-mail via mechanisms such as Internet Message Access Protocol (IMAP) and Post Office Protocol (POP3). In this chapter, we'll briefly explain how e-mail works, and we'll introduce you to the component parts of an e-mail solution, including

- *Mail transfer agents (MTAs)*: The servers that send and receive e-mail

- *Mail user agents (MUAs)*: Clients through which your users send and receive e-mail

- *Mail delivery agents (MDAs)*: Tools that help you deliver e-mail to mailboxes

We'll also introduce you to these applications to perform these functions:

- *Postfix*: A Simple Mail Transfer Protocol (SMTP) e-mail server

- *Dovecot*: An IMAP and a POP3 server

The Postfix e-mail server will allow your users to send and receive e-mail both from internal users and externally, such as from the Internet. The Dovecot server provides IMAP and POP3 daemons. IMAP and POP3 are two different ways for your users to retrieve their e-mail from a mailbox located on your e-mail server (we'll explain those differences and why you might use one over the other).

We'll also show you how to protect your users from unsolicited e-mail or spam and from viruses.

In this chapter we'll explain basic mail services—sending, receiving, and managing e-mail. Many users expect much more from e-mail servers now, such as calendaring, messaging, and even document management. They expect these features to work seamlessly on different devices. These collaboration services are available under Linux with varying degrees of polish. Some are proprietary licensed, and some are GPL or variations. Some will provide a basic service, some will be free for a small per-user amount, and some will be free except for certain proprietary modules. We will cover some of these at the end of this chapter.

How Does E-mail Work?

E-mail is still ubiquitous for personal and business communications. While social media is also now used for communications, e-mail is still core to most companies. Most people don't need to worry beyond composing e-mails and clicking the Send button. To run your own mail server, however, you need to understand a bit more about the inner workings of e-mail. In Figure 12-1, you can see the typical e-mail life cycle.

© Dennis Matotek, James Turnbull and Peter Lieverdink 2017
D. Matotek et al., *Pro Linux System Administration*, DOI 10.1007/978-1-4842-2008-5_12

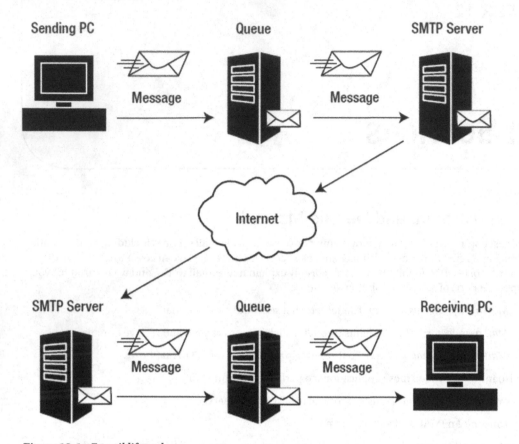

Figure 12-1. *E-mail life cycle*

What Happens When You Send an E-mail?

E-mail is based around a protocol called SMTP (defined in RFC 5321; www.ietf.org/rfc/rfc5321.txt). Each e-mail has a series of headers that tell your mail server what to do with it and where to send it. So when users create a new e-mail, they address that e-mail. They add a recipient (or To field) and perhaps "cc" or "bcc" the e-mail to others. They then send the e-mail.

The user's e-mail client is configured with a server, and your client now contacts this server (on TCP port 25) and says "Hello! I have mail from this person to these people—please send it to them!" Actually, our client doesn't precisely say "hello," it says something pretty close—a command called EHLO (or more rarely HELO).

■ **Note** There are a lot of names for e-mail servers. They can be called SMTP servers or SMTP daemons, but their proper name is *mail transfer agents*. The client that sends e-mail is known in this nomenclature as a *mail user agent*. We'll also look at another component called the *mail delivery agent* that can be used to deliver e-mail to a user's mailbox later in this chapter.

EHLO is an SMTP command that is part of SMTP's "language." Commands are how SMTP clients and servers (or MUAs and MTAs) communicate with one another. Originally, SMTP had only about ten words, or commands, in its language. In more recent times, an enhanced version of SMTP called Extended SMTP (ESMTP) has been created that adds many more useful commands to the language to provide features such as authentication and encryption.

We are going to make a connection to a mail server now using the netcat (nc) command. We are going to use nc to show you the actual commands that mail servers send to each other when sending e-mail. For that, we will issue $ nc mail.example.com 25. In this case, the client is telling the server who it is, and in Listing 12-1, you can see a simple conversation in SMTP's "language."

Listing 12-1. A Simple SMTP Conversation

```
220 mail.example.com ESMTP Server
EHLO client.example.com
250-mail.example.com
250-PIPELINING
250-SIZE 10240000
250-VRFY
250-ETRN
250-ENHANCEDSTATUSCODES
250-8BITMIME
250 DSN
```

When you initiate a connection to a mail server, it should respond with status code 220 and its name and capabilities. The first line in Listing 12-1 is the server telling the client who it is, mail.example.com, and that it is an SMTP server that supports ESMTP.

On the next line, we have entered the command EHLO client.example.com. When a client says hello and tells the server who it is, it should provide a fully qualified domain name like client.example.com. There is no validation whether this is a legitimate hostname at all, so it can be anything (and unfortunately this is how a lot of spam can be delivered—more on that shortly). Lastly, the server responds, acknowledges the connection (status code 250), and returns a list of capabilities.

Next we are going to send an e-mail to a user in the example.com domain via this server. This starts with sending the sender and recipient details, what is commonly called the *envelope*.

```
MAIL FROM: <ataylor@example.com>
250 2.1.0 Ok
```

Here the sender, ataylor@example.com, has used the MAIL FROM command. The server checks, returns the 250 response code, and indicates that this sender is allowed to submit e-mail. This acceptance can be based on a number of criteria, including a properly constructed e-mail address, and we'll talk about mechanisms like authentication later in this chapter, but again there is little validation that this sending address is legitimate.

Next, the server expects the RCPT TO command, or whom the e-mail is being sent to.

```
RCPT TO: <jsmith@example.com>
250 2.1.5 Ok
```

Here the acceptance of the address is dependent on criteria such as having a properly formed e-mail address and that this server is configured to accept mail on behalf of the example.com domain. If this mail server is poorly configured and accepts mail for domains not under its control, it is called an *open relay*.

Next, in our simple example, we need the content of the actual e-mail. The client sends a command called DATA to the server.

```
DATA
354 End data with <CR><LF>.<CR><LF>
Message-ID:
Date: Mon, 17 Aug 2016 12:29:26 +1100
From: Anne Taylor ataylor@example.com
To: John Smith jsmith@example.com
Subject: Email is cool
This is an email message.
.
250 2.0.0 Ok: queued as DF44644A9
```

The server responds with a request for the content of the e-mail and then a marker of a single period or full stop on a line by itself that indicates the end of the e-mail.

You can see we've passed some fairly default headers like the date, the To and From headers, the subject, and the content of the e-mail. We've specified the . marker, and the server has responded by saying that it has accepted the e-mail. Each e-mail is then submitted to a mail queue, processed, and sent on by your server.

You can now continue to send e-mails by repeating the MAIL FROM command, or you can disconnect from the server using the QUIT command.

```
QUIT
221 2.0.0 Bye
```

This is a simple scenario for sending e-mail. It's the most basic exchange of commands possible. Most of your normal e-mail sending will be a little more complicated when you factor in elements such as encryption and authentication.

E-MAIL ADDRESSES

So what is acceptable as an e-mail address? What is a properly formed e-mail address? An e-mail address in its most basic form is a username and a hostname, domain name, or fully qualified domain name, separated by an @ symbol, for example, jsmith@example.com. The rules around what characters are allowed and the appropriate structure of e-mail addresses are often confusing. E-mail addresses can take many forms, and different e-mail servers or MTAs accept varying formats as valid. The MTA we're going to show you, Postfix, accepts e-mail addresses in a variety of formats. Postfix's e-mail address rewriting guide demonstrates some of the many e-mail address formats accepted: www.postfix.org/ADDRESS_REWRITING_README.html.

What Happens After You Send an E-Mail?

After the server (or MTA) has received the e-mail from your client and places it in a mail queue, a whole new set of commands and steps gets executed. First, the server needs to find out where to send the e-mail. To do this, the server takes the portion of the e-mail address to the right of the @ symbol. This is usually the fully qualified domain name, for example, example.com. The e-mail server then uses a Doman Name System (DNS) query to contact the remote domain and ask it where to send the e-mail.

■ **Note** We discussed DNS in Chapter 10.

The e-mail server does this by querying a special kind of DNS record called an MX record. Querying the MX record returns one or more entries that tell your e-mail server where to send the e-mail, usually a specific host or IP address. If there is more than one e-mail server returned, a priority is also returned that tells your e-mail server which entry to use first, and then second, and so on. Later in the chapter we will show how to configure our DNS MX record.

■ **Note** If the DNS query indicates that there isn't an MX record, your e-mail server will be unable to deliver the e-mail and will send you a message indicating this. This can often occur if your user has mistyped or specified an incorrect e-mail address.

The e-mail server then submits your outgoing e-mail to another queue, and from there it is sent on to the destination e-mail server. To do this, your e-mail server tries to connect, via TCP port 25 or a secured transport port of TCP 465, to each e-mail server returned by the MX query in the priority sequence the record specifies. The e-mail server then follows a submission sequence to see whether it can deliver your e-mail.

1. If an e-mail server responds, it will try to submit the e-mail.

2. If an e-mail server does not respond, your e-mail server will try the next server returned from the MX record in sequence.

3. If no e-mail servers respond, your e-mail server will usually queue your e-mail to try again later.

4. If, after continued failures, the e-mail still can't be delivered, the e-mail server will report failure to the user via an e-mail.

The destination server your e-mail server tries to send to could be the final destination of your e-mail, or it could merely be a gateway that your e-mail passes through onto one or more further e-mail servers until it finally reaches its destination. This depends on how the destination has configured its e-mail environment. Many environments have an Internet-facing e-mail gateway that receives mail and then internal e-mail servers that process internal mail. This configuration allows features such as spam and virus filtering on your e-mail gateway that are different from what you may have on your internal servers. However, as we have said, a properly configured e-mail server should be set to accept mail only for the domain under its control.

■ **Note** It's important to note that e-mail is classified as "best effort" and is not guaranteed. Meaning, a mail server will try to send mail for normally 4 hours before it gives up. While usually mail is delivered anywhere around the world in less than a minute, it is not something that is guaranteed.

Configuring E-mail

We're going to show you how to create a basic e-mail server configuration that allows you to send and receive e-mail and helps protect your users from spam, viruses, and malware. We'll also make use of Transport Layer Security (TLS), a form of encryption that can be used to encrypt your e-mail, and talk about SMTP AUTH, which is a way to authenticate your users when they send e-mail.

We're going to use the headoffice.example.com host as our e-mail server, and our gateway.example.com will pass e-mail traffic through to that host, as we described in our example network configuration in Chapter 7.

Our mail server will be called mail.example.com (which is a DNS CNAME we created in Chapter 10) and have an internal IP address of 192.168.0.1. You can see our example network in Figure 12-2.

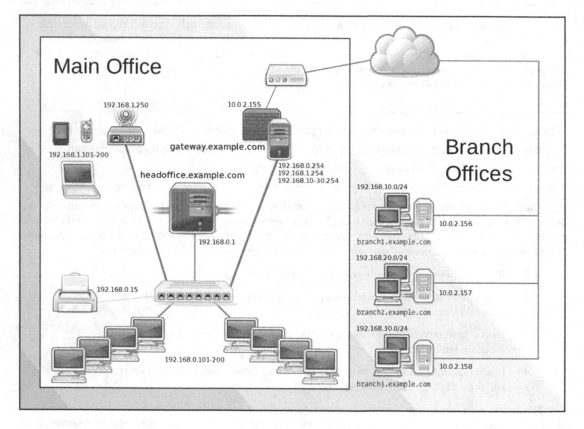

Figure 12-2. *Example network*

Installation

We're going to start by installing the packages we're going to need—the Postfix and Dovecot applications.

CentOS Installation

On later versions of CentOS, the default MTA is Postfix and is installed as part of a minimal install. The other common MTA is called Sendmail. We're going to use the Postfix MTA, which is much easier to understand, configure, and troubleshoot.

■ **Note**   There is always a lot of argument over which MTA is best, and many are available including Sendmail, Postfix, Exim, and others. Our recommendation is to start with Postfix and see how it goes. We think you'll find Postfix powerful and easy to use and that it meets all your needs.

First, let's see whether Postfix and Dovecot are already installed.

```
$ sudo rpm -q postfix dovecot
postfix-2.10.1-6.el7.x86_64
package dovecot is not installed
```

If one or more packages are not installed, we need to install them. We've done it here using the yum command:

```
$ sudo yum install -y postfix dovecot
```

■ **Note**   Some additional prerequisite packages can also be installed by either of these commands. We'll also install some additional packages later in the chapter to provide support for other functions.

Ubuntu Installation

The Postfix MTA is also the default MTA on Ubuntu distributions, so it is usually already installed. Indeed, you saw in Chapter 2 that our Ubuntu installation prompted us to perform some basic MTA configuration. We'll revisit that configuration dialog shortly (see the "Editing Postfix Configuration" sidebar).

If the Postfix MTA is not installed, we want to install the Postfix and Dovecot packages. Let's first check to see whether they are installed.

```
$ sudo aptitude show postfix
Package: postfix
State: installed
...
$ sudo aptitude show dovecot-core
Package: dovecot-core
State: installed
...
```

Here we have checked whether the postfix package and the dovecot-core packages are installed. If both are installed, you already have what's needed.

If they are not installed, you can use the aptitude command to install them.

```
$ sudo aptitude install postfix dovecot-core dovecot-imapd dovecot-pop3d
```

Starting Postfix

After installation, it is easy to start Postfix using the service management tools we introduced to you in Chapter 6. For CentOS and Ubuntu, you start Postfix using the systemctl command.

```
$ sudo systemctl start postfix.service
```

531

■ Tip It is also important to reload or restart Postfix after making configuration changes, and you'll see we mention that throughout the chapter. If you can't work out why something isn't working, a restart is often a good start to your troubleshooting.

You can confirm Postfix is started by checking its log files. Postfix logs its output to the system logger, or *syslog*, which in turn logs to files located on your host. You can find its log files in the /var/log directory. On CentOS, we need to look in the /var/log/maillog file. On Ubuntu, Postfix sends all log messages to /var/log/mail.log. On Ubuntu, error and warning messages are also logged to the /var/log/mail.err and /var/log/mail.warn files, respectively. It's a good idea to monitor these files for error messages. A good way to do this is with the tail command using the -f option, which monitors files in real time and scrolls down your screen as new log messages are added to the file.

```
$ sudo tail -f /var/log/maillog
```

When Postfix is started successfully, you should see the following log messages:

```
Jul 10 03:21:34 au-mel-centos-1 postfix/postfix-script[4500]: starting the Postfix mail
system
Jul 10 03:21:34 au-mel-centos-1 postfix/master[4502]: daemon started -- version 2.10.1,
configuration /etc/postfix
```

Understanding Postfix Configuration

The majority of Postfix configuration is handled by two files, located in the /etc/postfix directory. These files are called main.cf and master.cf. The main.cf file contains a subset of the major configuration options you can use to customize Postfix. You can add any additional options you need to configure Postfix to this file. The master.cf file controls how clients connect to your server and how the services that make up the server are configured. Most of the time you won't change much in the master.cf file.

Let's start by taking a quick look at how each file is structured.

■ Note Most distributions install preconfigured main.cf and master.cf files. These usually include extensive inline documentation describing each option.

Inside main.cf each option is structured as follows:

option = value

Options do not have to be placed in any order, and empty lines are ignored.

■ Note The Postfix configuration files are in what's called the INI format, with option = value. Like most Linux configuration files, any lines starting with # are comments.

In Listing 12-2, you can see a sample of a typical main.cf file.

Listing 12-2. The main.cf File

```
...
# LOCAL PATHNAME INFORMATION
#
# The queue_directory specifies the location of the Postfix queue.
# This is also the root directory of Postfix daemons that run chrooted.
# See the files in examples/chroot-setup for setting up Postfix chroot
# environments on different UNIX systems.
#
queue_directory = /var/spool/postfix
...
```

We'll talk about some of the configuration options in the main.cf file during this chapter; you can see a full list with $ man 5 postconf or at www.postfix.org/postconf.5.html.

In the master.cf file, you can see a structured list of the daemons, services, and processes you can enable and configure in Postfix. In Listing 12-3, you can see some sample lines from this file.

Listing 12-3. The master.cf File

```
...
# ==========================================================================
# service      type       private     unpriv        chroot       wakeup
maxproc      command + args
#                         (yes)       (yes)         (yes)        (never)      (100)
# ==========================================================================
smtp         inet                     n                          n
-            -                        smtpd
...
submission   inet                     n             -            n
-            -                        smtpd
  -o syslog_name=postfix/submission
  -o smtpd_tls_security_level=encrypt
  -o smtpd_sasl_auth_enable=yes
  -o smtpd_reject_unlisted_recipient=n
...
```

Here two services are defined, smtp and submission. Each service is generally a daemon process that runs in the background and performs a specific function.

■ **Note**   Unlike many other services, Postfix isn't a single monolithic daemon but rather a collection of small processes that perform individual functions and communicate with each other. As such, when you start Postfix, you may see a number of processes start rather than a single process.

In this case, the smtp service is the basic SMTP service that receives mail for your host on TCP port 25, and the submission service is an alternative service that listens on TCP port 567 and is sometimes used to receive e-mail from internal mail clients (MUAs).

Next on the line, we define the type of service; here `inet` defines these as network-based services (i.e., services that run on your network interface). Other types of services also available include local Unix sockets and named pipes. Unix domain sockets and named pipes are used to send messages between services; see http://en.wikipedia.org/wiki/Unix_domain_socket and http://en.wikipedia.org/wiki/Named_pipe.

Next, we have a series of settings for each service. Each setting is specified on the line in sequence and separated with spaces. You won't need to worry about these settings for your basic configuration, but you can find more details of them at $ `man 4 master` or www.postfix.org/master.5.html.

Last, each service needs to have the command that starts the service specified together with any arguments to be passed to that command. In Listing 12-3, both services are started with the command `smtpd`, but the `submission` service has several options passed to the command. These are the same options available in the `main.cf` configuration file, which allows us to configure a particular service in a way that varies from our main configuration. We'll look at how to pass these options to an individual service in the section "Combating Viruses and Spam" later in the chapter.

EDITING POSTFIX CONFIGURATION

There are three ways to edit your Postfix configuration files, most particularly the `main.cf` file.

- You can use the `postconf` command.

- On Ubuntu, the `dpkg-reconfigure` command can perform basic Postfix configuration.

- You can employ a text editor such as `vim` or `gedit`.

We generally recommend the last option, using a text editor to edit your configuration files, but first let's quickly look at the other two options. The file can be long, and you can mistakenly have the same option with two values. In this case, the last value will win, and you may spend hours scratching your head wondering why it is not working like you expect.

The `postconf` command is a special command that allows you to manipulate the `main.cf` file and display your existing configuration. The command also has some useful command-line options for debugging and displaying your configuration. For example, to display any configuration options that have been changed from the default (i.e., modified for your host), you can use the –n configuration flag.

```
$ sudo postconf -n
```

If you are looking for troubleshooting, you will be usually asked to provide the output of the `postconf -n` command. You can also display every configuration option and its default setting using the –d flag. Lastly, you can use the command to actually edit your configuration files via the -e option like so:

```
$ sudo postconf -e 'inet_interfaces = all'
```

Here the `inet_interfaces` option (which controls which network interfaces Postfix binds itself to) has been set to a value of `all`.

On Ubuntu, you can use the `dpkg-reconfigure` command to configure the basic state of Postfix.

```
$ sudo dpkg-reconfigure postfix
```

This command offers you a selection of basic configuration models, for example, a basic Internet host that sends and receives e-mail. Another model uses a smarthost; in this case, e-mail is sent to an intermediate relay server. This model is often used in Internet service provider (ISP) environments where you are sometimes restricted from sending and receiving e-mail directly to port 25. This is designed to reduce spam volumes by preventing the sending and relaying of e-mail from compromised desktop hosts in xDSL or cable networks. We'll discuss smarthosts in the "Smarthosting" sidebar later in this chapter.

A number of other configuration options are also set by the same utility. We don't recommend you use the utility, though; instead, you should manually edit your configuration files using a text editor so you become more familiar with all the options.

Always remember that after any Postfix configuration changes, you must reload or restart the `postfix` service.

Initial Configuration

Despite all the rather complicated-looking configuration processes and options, Postfix is actually easy to configure. A simple e-mail server, designed to send and receive e-mail for a domain, can be set up in minutes.

The first step is telling Postfix what domains it should be handling mail for. To do this, we update the `mydestination` configuration option in the `main.cf` configuration file by adding our domain to it, in this case `example.com`. We could make this change by editing the `main.cf` file directly and changing the option as shown here:

```
mydestination = mail.example.com, localhost.localdomain, localhost, example.com
```

We could also change it using the `postconf` command.

```
$ sudo postconf -e "mydestination = mail.example.com, localhost.localdomain, ↵
localhost, example.com"
```

On the previous line, we've added two items: our mail server and our local domain. Postfix now knows that if it receives mail destined to either of these, for example, ataylor@mail.example.com or ataylor@example.com, it should accept and process this e-mail.

■ **Note** Postfix will receive mail only for users it knows about. Generally, this will be a user created on the host, but we'll briefly look at "virtual" users in the "Virtual Domains and Users" section later in this chapter. In some cases, Postfix knows about users on other e-mail servers and can be configured to forward mail to another host. But generally, if Postfix can't find a recipient for the e-mail (e.g., if an e-mail is sent to bjones@example.com and Postfix doesn't know about this user), the e-mail will be rejected.

When we want Postfix to receive e-mail for other domains (for example, we want to receive e-mail from the example.net domain also), we'd add that domain to the `mydestination` option.

```
mydestination = mail.example.com, localhost.localdomain, localhost,↵
example.com, example.net
```

The other entries, which will generally already be present, include localhost, which tells Postfix to process e-mail that is local to the host, for example, e-mail sent by a local process. It is also this setting that stops your mail becoming an *open relay* like we talked about earlier. The mail server will only accept mail that is configured for the domains listed here. If you're domain is not listed here in mydestination, you will receive something like this when you send mail to a user:

```
RCPT TO: <bobby@unlisted.org>
554 5.7.1 <bobby@unlisted.org>: Relay access denied
```

Next, we need to add our local networks to the mynetworks configuration option. This tells Postfix what trusted IP address ranges SMTP clients will have to process e-mail. Trusted SMTP clients are allowed to relay (send e-mail to other e-mail servers) through our e-mail server. In our case, we only care about the 192.168.0.0/24 and 192.168.1.0/24 ranges, which are our local wired and wireless network ranges. The 127.0.0.1, or localhost, address should already be present in the option.

```
mynetworks = 127.0.0.0/8, 192.168.0.0/24, 192.168.1.0/24
```

If we had external users that required access to our e-mail server from other networks, they need to authenticate before being allowed to relay. We can again use the postconf command to edit the option.

```
$ sudo postconf -e "mynetworks = 127.0.0.0/8, 192.168.0.0/24, 192.168.1.0/24"
```

Now we need to bind Postfix to the network interfaces we want it to listen on. In this case, we're going to bind to all network interfaces, which is the default.

```
inet_interfaces = all
```

Or we could use the postconf command.

```
$ sudo postconf -e "inet_interfaces = all"
```

You can be more selective, though, and if you wanted to bind Postfix to listen only on a single interface, you could do so as follows:

```
inet_interfaces = enp0s3
```

■ **Tip** There is a setting called inet_protocols that controls which IP version Postfix will attempt to use when making or accepting connections. By default, it is set to all, but you can specify ipv6 or ipv4 depending on your needs. On CentOS, setting all to inet_protocol will also make the default interface we listen on IPv6, which will mean our e-mail server will need to be IPv6 capable to avoid errors.

Finally, after making all the relevant changes, we need to restart Postfix. We can issue the following:

```
$ sudo systemctl reload postfix.service
```

■ **Note** Every time you change a Postfix configuration option, you should reload or restart Postfix.

536

In addition to restarting Postfix, you'll need to ensure TCP port 25 is open on your host to allow incoming connections. If you have the iptables firewall running, you'll need to create appropriate rules to allow access. Here's an example:

```
$ sudo iptables -A INPUT -p tcp -m conntrack --ctstate NEW -m tcp --dport 25 -j ACCEPT
```

■ **Tip**   We talked about the iptables firewall, writing rules, and opening ports in Chapter 7.

We should now configure our MX record in our DNS server that we set up in Chapter 10. Remember that the MX record is short for mail exchange, and your MTA server will look for this record when it sends mail to another domain.

First we need to freeze any nsupdate (name server updates) to our example.com zone from services like DHCP on our master DNS server.

```
$ sudo rndc freeze example.com
```

Now open the zone file and increment the serial number to the appropriate date. To add an MX record, we will add one after the NS record in our example.com.db file, like the following:

```
        IN      NS              ns.example.com.
        IN      MX  10  mail.example.com.
```

We have the name of the record, the Internet type (IN), the record type (MX), the mail server priority (10), and the host it maps to (mail.example.com). Save the zone file and exit.

Next we need to thaw the zone again.

```
$ sudo rndc thaw example.com
```

And lastly let's validate that the change has worked with the dig command.

```
$ dig -t MX example.com @192.168.0.1
;; ANSWER SECTION:
example.com. 86400 IN MX 10 mail.example.com.
```

That looks like we expect it to. We are ready to begin testing.

Testing Postfix

We can now test to see whether Postfix is working by sending ourselves an e-mail. Like we did at the start of this chapter, we are going to do this through the useful tool called netcat (nc). As we have seen, the nc command is the Swiss Army knife of network tools and can be used to create and manipulate Transmission Control Protocol (TCP) and User Datagram Protocol (UDP) connections.

■ **Note**   There are others ways of sending a test e-mail (e.g., using the mail command from the command line), but the nc command allows you to view the SMTP commands and displays any error messages on the command line where you can see them.

Let's use the nc command to script a session with our Postfix e-mail server again, as you can see in Listing 12-4.

Listing 12-4. A Scripted E-mail Session with nc

```
$ nc mail.example.com 25
220 mail.example.org ESMTP Postfix
ehlo example.com
250-mail.example.com
250-PIPELINING
250-SIZE 10240000
250-VRFY
250-ETRN
250-ENHANCEDSTATUSCODES
250-8BITMIME
250 DSN
mail from: jsmith@example.com
250 2.1.0 Ok
rcpt to: ataylor@example.com
250 2.1.5 Ok
data
354 End data with <CR><LF>.<CR><LF>
Subject: My first mail for my domain
This is a test.
Thanks
Mr Testing
.
250 2.0.0 Ok: queued as 61A703FA5E
quit
221 2.0.0 Bye
```

In Listing 12-4, we've started by specifying the nc command, the e-mail server we want to connect to, and the port, 25, that we want to connect to. Next, we've stepped through the SMTP commands (lowercase this time; the commands are case insensitive) needed to send an e-mail. In Listing 12-4, all the text in bold represents commands we've entered, and you will need to enter these to send your e-mail. Adjust the text to suit your environment, for example, replacing example.com with the name of your domain. The nonbolded text is the expected response from our e-mail server.

■ **Note**   You can see that each line is prefixed with the SMTP response code, for example, 250. You can see a full list of these codes at https://www.iana.org/assignments/smtp-enhanced-status-codes/smtp-enhanced-status-codes.xml#smtp-enhanced-status-codes-3.

We tell the server who we are with the EHLO command, and it responds with its own identity and a list of its available features. We then indicate to whom we want to send an e-mail and whom it is from. In our case, we're sending an e-mail to ataylor@example.com and from jsmith@example.com.

■ **Note**   We created these users in Chapter 5. If you are following along, you should substitute the names of users on your local host or create some new users to test your e-mail with.

We then tell our server we're sending the e-mail with the DATA command. We input our e-mail, marking its end with a period (.) and quitting.

■ **Tip** As mentioned earlier, another way to send local e-mail from the command line is to use the mail command, available from the mailutils package (Ubuntu) or the mailx package (CentOS). This doesn't give us a diagnostic view of our server, but it is easier to use to send mail. To start the command, type **mail** on the command line together with the e-mail address you'd like to send e-mail to, for example, **mail root@example. com**. Entering the mail command on its own will open a simple command-line mail client.

We can now check that our e-mail has arrived. In our case, we want to check whether the e-mail has been received by the user ataylor. By default, both CentOS and Ubuntu use a mailbox format called *mbox* to store received e-mail. The mbox format has all of your e-mail held in a single file. Both Ubuntu and CentOS store these files in different locations, but both use symlinks to make sure the files appear in similar locations.

■ **Note** See http://en.wikipedia.org/wiki/Mbox for more details of the mbox format.

On Ubuntu, a mailbox file named for the user is created in the /var/mail directory, for example, /var/mail/ataylor. But there is a symlink to the /var/mail directory for the /var/spool/mail directory.

On CentOS, each user has an mbox-format mailbox file contained in the /var/spool/mail directory. The file is named after the user, for example, /var/spool/mail/ataylor. Again, there is a symlink to the /var/spool/mail directory for the /var/mail directory.

Let's look inside one of these mbox files in Listing 12-5.

Listing 12-5. An mbox File

```
$ more /var/mail/ataylor
From jsmith@example.com  Sun Jul 10 12:12:46 2016
Return-Path: <jsmith@example.com>
X-Original-To: ataylor@example.com
Delivered-To: ataylor@example.com
Received: from example.com (ns.example.com [192.168.0.254])
    by mail.example.com (Postfix) with ESMTP id 2625C3FA5A
    for <ataylor@example.com>; Sun, 10 Jul 2016 12:12:18 +0000 (UTC)
Subject: My first mail for my domain

This is a test.
Thanks
Mr Testing
```

In Listing 12-5, you can see the mbox file contains our e-mail, including all the headers and the content of the e-mail. Additional e-mails would be appended to this file. As a result, if you have a large volume of e-mail, these files can become unwieldy to manage, search, and back up.

ALIASES

When e-mail reaches your host, Postfix looks at the recipient to determine who to deliver it to. Some applications use recipients such as the postmaster address (for example, errors from MTAs are usually sent to the user postmaster at your domain) and the `root` user. Since people do not generally log in as either of these users, this e-mail might never get seen. Postfix uses a function called *aliases* to allow you to redirect mail sent to these recipients to other users. Postfix uses a configuration option called `alias_maps` in the `main.cf` configuration file to specify a file that matches recipients to the user who will actually receive the e-mail. The default aliases file is usually `/etc/aliases`. Inside this file you'll find a list of users like so:

```
user1:user2
```

Here all mail for `user1` will be redirected to `user2`, with each username separated by a colon. You should check this file and ensure that both the postmaster and the `root` user's e-mail direct to an appropriate user. You can also send e-mail to a user at another host by specifying an external e-mail address, like `username@example.com`. A common pattern is to direct all e-mail for system users to the `root` user and then redirect the `root` user to someone who needs to see this e-mail, for example:

```
postmaster: root
operator: root
lp: root
root: ataylor
```

Here the `postmaster`, `operator`, and `lp` users' e-mail all redirect to the `root` user, whose mail in turn is redirected to the user `ataylor`.

You can direct mail for one user to more than one subsequent user as well. If we wanted to redirect the mail for the root user to both `ataylor` and `jsmith`, we would do the following:

```
root: ataylor,jsmith
```

Now when root receives an e-mail, both `ataylor` and `jsmith` receive the same e-mail.

After making any change to the `/etc/aliases` file, you need to run a command called `newaliases` to update Postfix with the changes.

```
$ sudo newaliases
```

We are going to look deeper into how this works in the "Postfix Lookup Tables and Virtual Domains" section coming up.

Choosing a Mailbox Format

In addition to the potential to become a large and difficult-to-handle file, the default mbox format has another issue: the potential for file corruption. For example, if your MTA is delivering a message to your mbox file at the same time your MUA or mail client is deleting a message, there is the potential that your mbox file could become corrupted or return unpredictable results.

An alternative to mbox is the Maildir mailbox format. Rather than a single file, Maildir stores your e-mails in separate files under a directory. This allows multiple processes to interact with your mailbox without risking any conflicts or corruption. It's also easier to back up and restore.

The Maildir format is a directory, appropriately called `Maildir`, containing three subdirectories: `cur`, `new`, and `tmp`. You can see the listing of the Maildir-format directory here:

```
$ ls -l Maildir
total 168
drwxr-xr-x 2 ataylor ataylor 28672 2009-01-01 13:53 cur
drwxr-xr-x 2 ataylor ataylor  4096 2009-01-01 13:53 new
drwxr-xr-x 2 ataylor ataylor  4096 2009-01-01 13:53 tmp
```

E-mail messages are first delivered into the `tmp` directory and given a unique name (usually constructed from the current time, the hostname, and other pseudorandom characteristics). The e-mail is then moved into the `new` directory where they sit in a sort of "unread" status. When your MUA or mail client connects to the mailbox, it detects the e-mail in the `new` directory and then moves them to the `cur` directory.

■ **Note**   This sounds a little complicated, but it ensures that e-mail isn't corrupted or misplaced when e-mail is being delivered, read, sent, and deleted from your mailbox.

To use Maildir instead of mbox, we need to tell Postfix that we're using a different mailbox format. We're also going to change our default mailbox location from its existing location, either /var/mail or /var/spool/mail, to the user's home directory. To do both of these things, we're going to update a Postfix option called home_mailbox like so:

```
home_mailbox = Maildir/
```

or using the `postconf` command, like so:

```
$ sudo postconf -e "home_mailbox = Maildir/"
```

The home_mailbox option tells Postfix the location of the user's mailbox, relative to the user's home directory, so that `Maildir/` translates to `/home/ataylor/Maildir`.

■ **Note**   The trailing / is important. It needs to be there, and it tells Postfix that the directory is a `Maildir` directory.

We also need to confirm that another option, `mailbox_command`, is blank. The `mailbox_command` option can specify an external command, for example, the mail processing tools like `procmail` or `maildrop`. These tools, called MDAs or mail filters, can perform actions on incoming mail as it is delivered to your mailbox. We'll talk a bit more about these applications in the "Mail Delivery Agents and Mail Filtering" sidebar later in this chapter. So we now set this option to a blank value.

```
mailbox_command =
```

or again using the postconf command.

```
$ sudo postconf -e "mailbox_command = "
```

Finally, we need to reload Postfix for all this to take effect, for example:

```
$ sudo systemctl reload postfix
```

Now, if you send another e-mail, you'll find a new directory created in the home directory of the recipient called Maildir. Inside this directory will be the tmp, new, and cur subdirectories, and inside the new directory will be your e-mail in a single file. You can use the less command to display the contents of this file, for example:

```
$ less /home/jsmith/Maildir/new/1468154018.V801I3fa69M48418.mail.example.com
Return-Path: <ataylor@au-mel-centos-1.example.com>
X-Original-To: jsmith@example.com
Delivered-To: jsmith@example.com
Received: from au-mel-centos-1.example.com (ns.example.com [192.168.0.254])
        by mail.example.com (Postfix) with ESMTP id 09F9E3FA66
        for <jsmith@example.com>; Sun, 10 Jul 2016 12:33:38 +0000 (UTC)
Received: by au-mel-centos-1.example.com (Postfix, from userid 1000)
        id 1F5EF61A55; Sun, 10 Jul 2016 08:33:38 -0400 (EDT)
Date: Sun, 10 Jul 2016 08:33:38 -0400
To: jsmith@example.com
Subject: My first email to my new Maildir mailbox
User-Agent: Heirloom mailx 12.5 7/5/10
MIME-Version: 1.0
Content-Type: text/plain; charset=us-ascii
Content-Transfer-Encoding: 7bit
Message-Id: <20160710123338.1F5EF61A55@au-mel-centos-1.example.com>
From: ataylor@au-mel-centos-1.example.com (ataylor)

This is also a test.
Thanks
Mr Testing
```

Here you can see that the individual Maildir file will contain an individual e-mail with all its headers.

■ **Note**   Each Maildir must be owned by the user it belongs to. For example, the Maildir directory belonging to the user ataylor must be owned and writable (with permissions of 0700) only by that user. If needed, you can use the chown and chmod commands to change the ownership and permissions, respectively.

Although in this case Postfix automatically created the Maildir directory, it is usually a good idea to prepopulate your user's home directories with an empty Maildir directory. You can do this by adding an empty Maildir directory to the /etc/skel directory. You saw the /etc/skel directory in Chapter 5 and discovered that its contents are copied to the home directory of any newly created user.

To create a new `Maildir` directory on Ubuntu, there is a useful command called `maildirmake.dovecot` that can automatically create the `Maildir` structure.

```
$ sudo maildirmake.dovecot /etc/skel/Maildir
```

The command will also create the `tmp`, `new`, and `cur` subdirectories.

■ **Tip** You can also create folders, for example, a `Sent` folder, in your `Maildir` structure. Folders can be used to sort and store e-mail so that it is easier to find e-mails. Folders are subdirectories prefixed with a period (.); a `Sent` folder would have the structure `/home/ataylor/Maildir/.Sent` created by using the command `maildirmake.dovecot /etc/skel/Maildir/.Sent`. Be careful to avoid folder names containing spaces, like "My Personal Mail," as sometimes your mail client can get confused. You should use an underscore or dash to link the words together like so: "My-Personal_Mail."

On Ubuntu, there is another, potentially easier, way to create your `Maildir` directories and folders. To do this, you can install a package called `maildrop`, which contains the `maildirmake` command, a more sophisticated version of the `maildirmake.dovecot` command.

You can then use the `maildirmake` command to create the skeleton directory and any required folders.

```
$ sudo maildirmake /etc/skel/Maildir
$ sudo maildirmake -f Sent /etc/skel/Maildir
$ sudo maildirmake -f Trash /etc/skel/Maildir
$ sudo maildirmake -f Drafts /etc/skel/Maildir
$ sudo maildirmake -f Spam /etc/skel/Maildir
```

Here we've used the `-f` option of the `malldirmake` command to create folders. We specify the name of the folder we want created and the `Maildir` to create it in.

If you don't want to install the `maildrop` package, you can create the directories using the `mkdir` command, as shown in Listing 12-6.

Listing 12-6. Manually Creating Maildir

```
$ sudo mkdir -p /etc/skel/Maildir/{cur,new,tmp}; chmod -R 0700 /etc/skel/Maildir
```

■ **Note** In Listing 12-6 we've used a clever Bash shortcut and listed all three directories enclosed in brackets ({ }) and separated by commas. This technique, *brace expansion*, tells `mkdir` to create all three subdirectories. You can use this with a variety of other commands without needing to type the command three times. The –p option creates all the parent directories as well as the target directories.

Listing 12-6 creates the `Maildir` and the required subdirectories and changes the permissions on the resulting directories to 0700, hence allowing only the user who owns `Maildir` to access it.

MAIL DELIVERY AGENTS AND MAIL FILTERING

Earlier in this chapter, we talked about MDAs. These tools sit between your MTA and the user's mailbox, and you can tell Postfix what MDA, if any, to use with the `mailbox_command` configuration option you saw earlier. When an MDA is specified in this option, Postfix will deliver e-mail to this MDA, and the MDA will deliver the e-mail to the user's mailbox.

During the delivery process, the MDA can perform a variety of actions; for example, it can look for a characteristic of an e-mail, like whom it is from, and redirect it to a specific mailbox folder. Many people use MDAs to sort e-mails from mailing lists into separate folders. MDAs are also used to sort e-mail based on headers added by other applications; for example, many spam filters add headers indicating whether an e-mail is spam. MDAs can read these headers and place e-mails into an appropriate folder—for example, into a spam folder. You can also use MDAs to generate out-of-office notices, forward particular e-mails to others, and perform a variety of other tasks.

You can also call other applications from some MDAs. For example, some people don't run spam filters in their MTA, instead running a spam filter with their MDA.

In this chapter we are going to be using Dovecot to deliver mail from the MTA to the user's mailboxes. Using Dovecot LDA (local delivery agent - MDA and LDA are synonyms) we can use the Sieve plugin to do mail filtering, forwarding and auto e-mail replies.

Extending Postfix Configuration

So far we've just touched on the basics of Postfix configuration that allow our local users to send and receive e-mail. However, Postfix has a lot of other facets to make your environment more secure and your user's experience better, including the following:

- *Encryption*: To secure the transmission of both e-mail and the user credentials

- *Authentication*: To ensure only appropriate and authenticated users can send e-mail

Using Encryption

The Postfix MTA is able to encrypt e-mail transmission via an encryption protocol called TLS. TLS is a successor protocol to Secure Sockets Layer (SSL) and is commonly used for encrypting Transmission Control Protocol/Internet Protocol (TCP/IP) traffic. TLS for mail traffic is the same as when connecting to a web site using the Hypertext Transfer Protocol Secure (HTTPS) protocol, for example, `https://www.gmail.com`.

TLS provides two key features for our e-mail communication.

- Prevents eavesdropping on our e-mail contents

- Encrypts communication between the client and server and hence protects authentication

Unfortunately, you should be aware that TLS in e-mail transportation is not really as secure as everyone would like. Mail servers can be configured to encrypt the sending and receiving of e-mail via STARTTLS. Because mail servers are not required to use STARTTLS, many will downgrade to clear text, or they can be vulnerable to malicious downgrade attacks. So while we recommend using a secure transport like TLS, it is not a guaranteed protection against eavesdropping. E-mail clients are different, and you can ensure that clients use a secure transport only with the right configuration.

Creating SSL Certificates for Postfix

We are going to use Let's Encrypt to get our SSL certificates. We do that with the certbot command we saw in the previous chapter. The Certbot process requires a web server to manage the validation process to get your certificate. The good news is that the certbot command has the option to run a stand-alone web server while we run the process to get the certificates.

The certbot stand-alone web service will need port 80 (HTTP) or port 443 (HTTPS) access to your host. We can do this with the ufw or firewall-cmd command. For Ubuntu, we would issue the following:

```
$ for h in http https ;do sudo ufw allow $h ;done
```

Or on CentOS we would issue the following:

```
$ for h in http https; do sudo firewall-cmd --zone public --add-service=$h ;done
```

Once this is done, we can use Certbot to create our certificates for our mail host. Again, if we are testing the creation of our certificates, we should use the --test-cert option to use the staging API at Let's Encrypt.

```
$ sudo certbot certonly --test-cert --standalone --uir --hsts --agree-tos -n -m admin@
example.com -d mail.example.com
IMPORTANT NOTES:
- Congratulations! Your certificate and chain have been saved at
  /etc/letsencrypt/live/mail.example.com/fullchain.pem.
  Your cert will expire on 2016-11-22. To obtain a new or tweaked
  version of this certificate in the future, simply run certbot
  again. To non-interactively renew *all* of your certificates, run
  "certbot renew"
```

When we are happy that we are ready to generate our certificate for real, we would remove --test-cert. The other options that we have used are certonly, which says we just want the certificate and not to install that into our web configuration. The --standalone option tells certbot to start its own web service to generate the certificates. The next two options, --uir and --hsts, are to make sure that every communication to the Certbot API is under https://. With the --agree-tos option, we agree to the terms of service. The -n option is for noninteractive, which is good for scripting. We then provide the registration contact (-m) and the hostname we want to register (-d). The certificate is then stored in the /etc/letsencrypt/live/mail.example.com/ directory.

Configuring Postfix for TLS

Now, you have a certificate and a key from Let's Encrypt, or you could have gotten either a commercial certificate or one signed by your self-managed certificate authority (CA). You will also need the root certificate from either your commercial CA or your self-managed CA. If you've gone with a commercial certificate, your CA will generally provide a link to a downloadable root certificate, or if you are using your own CA, the certificate will be in /etc/pki/CA/cacert.pem.

Now that you have your certificates and key, you need to configure Postfix's main.cf configuration file. In Listing 12-7, you can see the options you need to add to your main.cf configuration file, and we'll walk you through each of these settings.

Listing 12-7. Postfix TLS Configuration

```
smtp_tls_security_level = may
smtp_tls_CAfile = /etc/letsencrypt/live/mail.example.com/chain.pem
smtp_tls_cert_file = /etc/letsencrypt/live/mail.example.com/cert.pem
smtp_tls_key_file = /etc/letsencrypt/live/mail.example.com/privkey.pem

smtpd_tls_security_level = may
smtpd_tls_CAfile = /etc/letsencrypt/live/mail.example.com/chain.pem
smtpd_tls_cert_file = /etc/letsencrypt/live/mail.example.com/cert.pem
smtpd_tls_key_file = /etc/letsencrypt/live/mail.example.com/privkey.pem
smtpd_tls_loglevel = 1
smtpd_tls_mandatory_exclude_ciphers = aNULL, MD5
smtpd_tls_mandatory_protocols = TLSv1
```

If you look at the options in Listing 12-7, you can see they look similar except for a difference in the initial prefix. One starts with `smtp`, and the other starts with `smtpd`. Configuration options starting with `smtp` are used when Postfix is sending e-mail to another e-mail server. Options starting with `smtpd` are used when Postfix receives e-mail, for example, from a client. By specifying both `smtp_tls_security_level` and `smtpd_tls_security_level`, we are telling Postfix we want to potentially encrypt both incoming and outgoing connections.

The may value for both options enables a mode called *opportunistic TLS*. This basically means that if TLS is supported by the remote client or server, it should be used. Otherwise, plain-text connections are acceptable. Unfortunately, not all e-mail servers will support TLS. So, currently may is a sensible choice given that not all clients and servers support TLS, and restricting the server to encrypted connections would mean some e-mail servers could not send you e-mail.

The next three options, `smtpd_tls_key_file`, `smtpd_tls_cert_file`, and `smtpd_tls_CAfile`, specify the locations of our certificate, key file, and CA certificate.

The next option, `smtpd_tls_loglevel`, controls how much logging of TLS connections Postfix will generate. Specifying 0 here disables logging, specifying 1 provides basic logging, and specifying 3 and 4 produce the highest level of logging (and are not recommended unless you are troubleshooting). We recommend leaving it at 1 for day-to-day operations, and this will produce some brief information about the connection and any certificates used.

We also set some options that determine what ciphers we will accept and what protocol we want to use. The `smtpd_tls_mandatory_exclude_ciphers` option determines which ciphers we will not accept; since aNULL and MD5 are weak ciphers, we will not them in our TLS transmissions. With `smtpd_tls_mandatory_protocols`, we are declaring that we will only support TLSv1 and above as, again, anything lower is considered vulnerable.

After making the changes, you will need to restart the Postfix service.

```
$ sudo service postfix restart
```

Once the Postfix service has restarted, you can test to see whether TLS is enabled using the same nc command we introduced earlier, as you can see in Listing 12-8.

Listing 12-8. Testing Postfix with TLS

```
$ $ openssl s_client -connect localhost:25 -starttls smtp
CONNECTED(00000003)
depth=1 CN = Fake LE Intermediate X1
verify error:num=20:unable to get local issuer certificate
```

```
verify return:0
---
Certificate chain
 0 s:/CN=mail.example.com
   i:/CN=Fake LE Intermediate X1
 1 s:/CN=Fake LE Intermediate X1
   i:/CN=Fake LE Root X1
---
Server certificate
-----BEGIN CERTIFICATE-----
MIIE+zCCA+OgAwIBAgITAPpVz+iRXsKC43OYQrhOPwEhdjANBgkqhkiG9wOBAQsF
ADAiMSAwHgYDVQQDDBdGYWtlIExFIEludGVybWVkaWF0ZSBYMTAeFwOxNjA4MjQx
...<snip>...
iIVJyRvMWqW2x9iOo/t9bheRaoSX/Vt7X4ZF8vClEQQOiSNTC956WxAiyFOXLU7A
86RIlXw3ZmO1CtiP4rHi2ZzoIChvcSBfdNG5kOCy5w==
-----END CERTIFICATE-----
subject=/CN=mail.example.com
issuer=/CN=Fake LE Intermediate X1
---
Acceptable client certificate CA names
/CN=Fake LE Intermediate X1
Server Temp Key: ECDH, prime256v1, 256 bits
---
SSL handshake has read 3421 bytes and written 428 bytes
---
New, TLSv1/SSLv3, Cipher is ECDHE-RSA-AES256-SHA
Server public key is 2048 bit
Secure Renegotiation IS supported
Compression: NONE
Expansion: NONE
SSL-Session:
    Protocol  : TLSv1
    Cipher    : ECDHE-RSA-AES256-SHA
    Session-ID: 419EB576C7D51B5818CD1F64564275F8104AEB4ABAE8FAA0C9EA300A0F44B8F3
    Session-ID-ctx:
    Master-Key: 6FD71DE08D3888747E57D506FCDB710BCCEBE7557810DC92F1E4FBCC77CCAD0CCA2DE0616E882
    E0B9BC1775E8054298D
    Key-Arg   : None
    Krb5 Principal: None
    PSK identity: None
    PSK identity hint: None
    TLS session ticket lifetime hint: 3600 (seconds)
    TLS session ticket:
    0000 - 5d e2 39 53 22 6b 33 9e-d9 4e 14 de 63 6d de 73   ].9S"k3..N..cm.s
    0010 - d0 1c e9 55 7a 1e 70 32-b3 02 30 93 e5 f5 d3 d4   ...Uz.p2..0.....
    0020 - 8e a6 e5 bf c8 d5 20 a2-88 0e 20 88 15 29 4c f4   ...... .. ..)L.
    0030 - f1 88 eb b8 a1 47 1a 2c-3e 74 2e f0 b5 c1 f5 d2   .....G.,>t......
    0040 - 97 ec 26 a9 65 c8 e9 b6-92 3a 07 a0 30 56 5f e5   ..&.e....:..0V_.
    0050 - ad 73 a7 46 42 47 7f a2-82 b8 ed 08 6a da 25 6b   .s.FBG......j.%k
    0060 - ae 44 a6 c7 b3 b8 e4 f9-8f 73 64 b6 47 01 79 36   .D.......sd.G.y6
    0070 - 7d 91 3a 26 e7 03 74 5d-4f db 1a d4 28 65 e1 f7   }.:&..t]O...(e..
```

```
0080 - b8 d0 a5 91 81 96 0a 3a-cd fa a1 f0 97 c7 b5 37    ......:.......7
0090 - 0e bd 29 7b 1d 56 ad 91-81 a9 50 6e c4 ee 0f 94    ..){.V....Pn....

Start Time: 1472046666
Timeout   : 300 (sec)
Verify return code: 20 (unable to get local issuer certificate)
---
250 DSN
EHLO o.yeah.com
250-mail.example.com
250-PIPELINING
250-SIZE 10240000
250-VRFY
250-ETRN
250-ENHANCEDSTATUSCODES
250-8BITMIME
250 DSN
```

In Listing 12-8, we have connected to our e-mail server and issued the EHLO command. We used the openssl s_client command to connect to our e-mail server and pass the STARTTLS command. You can see that the e-mail server responded and that we set up an encrypted session. After we issued the EHLO command, the e-mail server responded with the supported commands available.

If you connect with just netcat, you'll see a new command listed here, STARTTLS. This tells us that Postfix is now offering TLS to clients and other servers.

```
$ nc localhost 25
220 mail.example.com ESMTP Postfix
EHLO ah.ah.com
250-mail.example.com
250-PIPELINING
250-SIZE 10240000
250-VRFY
250-ETRN
250-STARTTLS
250-ENHANCEDSTATUSCODES
250-8BITMIME
250 DSN
STARTTLS
220 2.0.0 Ready to start TLS
```

We've then entered the STARTTLS command to tell Postfix we'd like to initiate an encrypted connection. Postfix responds to say it's ready to start an encrypted connection. This indicates that TLS is successfully set up and awaiting connections.

Another way to test if your server is set up correctly to send secure e-mail is to check it against something like www.checktls.com/testreceiver.html. This will try to make connections to your e-mail server and give you a report on whether it can do so securely.

If you have issues with configuring Postfix TLS/SSL encryption, see the pointers and links in the upcoming "Getting Help for Postfix" section.

■ **Caution** It is important to note a few issues about using Postfix TLS encryption to ensure the confidentiality of the content of your e-mails. Postfix sends e-mail to other servers but encrypts it only when the other server supports TLS. As not all servers support encryption, some e-mail may not be encrypted. The only way to ensure all your e-mail is encrypted is to make use of content-based encryption solutions like S/MIME (http://en.wikipedia.org/wiki/S/MIME), PGP (www.pgp.com/), and GnuPG (http://www.gnupg.org/).

Authentication

So now that we have TLS configured, we can encrypt sessions between our clients and the server as well as between our servers and other servers that support TLS. This leads us to the next stage of our Postfix configuration: authentication.

In its default configuration, your Postfix server will accept e-mail only from clients in its trusted networks as defined in the mynetworks configuration option, in our case, the 192.168.0.0/24 and 192.168.1.0/24 networks. This prevents inappropriate users from using our e-mail server. E-mail servers without these restrictions are called *open relays*. An open relay allows anyone to send it e-mail, and the server will send it on. Spammers make extensive use of open relays to pollute the Internet with unwanted e-mail.

■ **Caution** Open relays are highly problematic, and incorrect configuration that results in your server becoming an open relay can be greatly troublesome for your organization. Open relays generally get blacklisted when they are detected. This blacklist process means the open relay's IP address is added to a list of servers from which e-mail will not be accepted. If your server is an open relay, even after closing the relay and fixing your server, it can be quite hard to remove yourself from these blacklists and allow your users to send e-mail. You should regularly test that your server isn't behaving like an open relay using a service like www.mailradar. com/openrelay/.

Postfix's configuration prevents your server from behaving like an open relay by default. But, although this configuration stops open relaying, it leaves a security hole and creates a functionality gap.

Regarding the hole, anyone who can get an IP address on your network can send e-mail to your e-mail server. If an attacker compromises your wireless network, for example, she could make use of your e-mail server to send spam.

This configuration also leaves a functionality gap for mobile users. You almost certainly have users who travel, work from home, or have mobile devices such as cell phones or tablets. These users cannot make use of your e-mail server, because being mobile, they don't have an IP address on your network. These users must rely on a service provider's e-mail server that allows relaying, an open relay, or a virtual private network (VPN) into your organization. Often this isn't an ideal situation.

With authentication, your users can send e-mail from anywhere as long as they are authenticated. It also means internal users on your trusted network need to provide authentication credentials before they will be allowed to send e-mail. This reduces the risk that someone can just jump onto your network and use your e-mail server.

Your authentication is in turn protected by the TLS encryption you've just configured, allowing your users to authenticate without the potential for their credentials to be exposed across the network.

■ **Note**   This is a good thing because people commonly "sniff" networks using tools like `tcpdump` or Wireshark (both mentioned in Chapter 7). These people are "sniffing" for things such as encrypted or exposed passwords to steal. With wireless networks, this is particularly easy, as an attacker doesn't even need to physically plug into your network.

SMTP AUTH and SASL

Authentication for e-mail servers is provided by a mechanism called SMTP AUTH. This is another SMTP command that prompts a user for a username and password before allowing him to send e-mail. That username and password can be provided via a variety of mechanisms including in plain text and in encrypted forms. Also available are mechanisms that support *one-time passwords* such as smart cards or tokens. What mechanisms are used very much depends on what mechanisms are supported by your client. The Microsoft Outlook client, for example, supports only a small number of mechanisms, while the Mozilla Thunderbird supports a wider variety.

■ **Note**   You can learn about one-time passwords at `http://en.wikipedia.org/wiki/One-time_password`.

To confirm the user's credentials are valid, the AUTH command makes use of an authentication framework called Simple Authentication and Security Layer (SASL). SASL is much like Pluggable Authentication Modules (PAM), which we looked at in Chapter 5, and it abstracts authentication. It allows multiple types of authentication to be hidden behind the Simple Authentication and Security Layer (SASL) protocol. This means your e-mail server can check a variety of back-end services to validate that the user is allowed to send e-mail without needing to understand how to authenticate to those services.

These back-end services can include PAM (which can be used to allow users to authenticate with their Linux login and password), databases of users and passwords, and even user repositories like LDAP or Active Directory. Postfix doesn't have SASL built in. It relies on integration with other applications to provide SASL capabilities. We're going to use the Dovecot server to provide these SASL capabilities to Postfix.

If you've been following along with the example so far, you should have already installed Dovecot when we showed you how to install Postfix earlier in this chapter. If not, install it now using those instructions if you want to work through the upcoming instructions. Then you need to ensure Postfix supports SASL authentication with Dovecot. This can be done with the `postconf` command using the `-a` option.

```
$ sudo postconf -a
cyrus
dovecot
```

Here the `postconf` command has returned all the SASL authentication plug-ins supported by Postfix. We're looking for the `dovecot` entry. This support should be available on all recent versions of CentOS and Ubuntu.

Configuring Dovecot for SASL

Now, we need to configure Dovecot's SASL support and start the Dovecot daemon. The Dovecot configuration files are located at `/etc/dovecot/dovecot.conf` and at `/etc/dovecot/conf.d`. The files in the `conf.d` directory are for configuring different services and mechanisms for Dovecot.

We're going to edit /etc/dovecot/dovecot.conf and set up Dovecot's SASL authentication service. We open the configuration file and look for the first option we want to edit: protocols. We first want to turn off all the services other than authentication. We do this by setting it to none.

```
protocols = none
```

■ **Note**   We'll come back to this option when we look at IMAP and POP3 and how to enable them in the "Configuring IMAP and POP3" section later in this chapter.

Next, we need to configure the authentication, or auth, service. To do this, we will edit /etc/dovecot/conf.d/10-master.conf, finding the service auth configuration option. You can see the service auth configuration options we're going to set in Listing 12-9.

Listing 12-9. Configuring Dovecot auth

```
service auth {
...
  # Postfix smtp-auth
  unix_listener /var/spool/postfix/private/auth {
    mode = 0660
    user  = postfix
    group = postfix
  }
....
}
```

service auth consists of a series of directives enclosed in brackets ({ }). The service may be already partially configured in your existing 10-master.conf configuration file. You will need to ensure the configuration present in your existing configuration file matches that of Listing 12-9.

The unix_listener directive in Listing 12-9 is the socket that provides the connection between Postfix and Dovecot. The socket listens for authentication requests from Postfix and then returns the results. It does this by using a special type of file called a *socket*, which we briefly discussed in Chapter 4, that allows interaction between applications. This socket is located in a Postfix directory that stores files and sockets used by the daemon, /var/spool/postfix/private/, and has a file name of auth. The mode, user, and group options control the permissions and ownership of the socket that we restrict to just the postfix user.

When the Dovecot daemon is running, you can see this file in the directory.

```
$ sudo ls -l /var/spool/postfix/private/auth
srw-rw----. 1 postfix postfix 0 Aug 25 09:33 /var/spool/postfix/private/auth
```

Next we have to change a setting in /etc/dovecot/conf.d/10-auth.conf. This file controls the mechanisms for authenticating. The directive in this file we want to change is mechanisms, which specifies which authentication mechanisms this Dovecot instance supports. By default, the PLAIN mechanism that accepts users and passwords in plain text is usually always enabled.

■ **Caution**   You should use the PLAIN mechanism only if you have TLS enabled; otherwise, an attacker could steal your user's credentials from the network.

You can see the other types available to Dovecot in Table 12-1.

Table 12-1. *Dovecot Authentication Mechanisms*

Mechanism	Description
PLAIN	Plain-text authentication.
LOGIN	A Microsoft authentication mechanism used in the Microsoft Outlook client.
CRAM-MD5	Encrypted password mechanisms. This has some support in mail clients.
DIGEST-MD5	Like CRAM-MD5 but with stronger ciphers. This has limited support in clients.
NTLM	Microsoft Windows–based authentication, generally supported only in Microsoft clients.
GSSAPI	Kerberos v5 support. This has limited support in clients.
ANONYMOUS	Supports anonymous logins. This is not recommended and not secure.
OTP	One-time password mechanism.
SKEY	One-time password mechanism.

■ **Note** You can't specify an authentication mechanism that Dovecot is not configured to support. For example, without the correct supporting configuration, you can't specify the NTLM mechanism.

In Listing 12-9, we've also enabled the LOGIN authentication mechanism in case any of our users have a Microsoft client, but we're not going to enable any other types. The vast majority of clients will support PLAIN, and many others will also support the LOGIN authentication type. You can find a full list of mail clients and the authentication mechanisms they support at http://en.wikipedia.org/wiki/Comparison_of_e-mail_clients#Authentication_support.

Also in the 10-auth.conf file we determine which authentication service we will use. At the bottom of the file you will see that we include !include auth-system.conf.ext. The !include statement says we want to include the configuration settings from this file. That file is located here: /etc/dovecot/conf.d/auth-system.conf.ext.

If we look in that file, we need to make sure it matches Listing 12-10.

Listing 12-10. Specifying the Authentication Service

```
passdb {
  driver = pam
  # [session=yes] [setcred=yes] [failure_show_msg=yes] [max_requests=<n>]
  # [cache_key=<key>] [<service name>]
  #args = dovecot
}
userdb {
  # <doc/wiki/AuthDatabase.Passwd.txt>
  driver = passwd
  # [blocking=no]
  #args =

  # Override fields from passwd
  #override_fields = home=/home/virtual/%u
}
```

The directives in Listing 12-10 control the authentication store that Dovecot checks to perform authentication. The default driver for the authentication store is pam. The pam store is a password database that makes use of the PAM application to authenticate users against the local host's users. So for a user to authenticate to the host to send e-mail, he would need to have a user with a valid password created on the host.

When authenticating users, Dovecot then looks for a PAM service definition called dovecot in the /etc/pam.d directory. This file is installed when you install the Dovecot packages on your distribution. In Listing 12-11, we've shown the /etc/pam.d/dovecot file for Ubuntu.

Listing 12-11. Dovecot PAM Service

```
#%PAM-1.0
auth       required      pam_nologin.so
auth       include       password-auth
account    include       password-auth
session    include       password-auth
```

You can see in Listing 12-11 that an authentication query to Dovecot uses the same PAM authentication check that a user logging on to the host would experience (as you saw in Chapter 5).

■ **Note** You can find more information on password databases for Dovecot at http://wiki.dovecot.org/PasswordDatabase and on PAM authentication for Dovecot at http://wiki.dovecot.org/PasswordDatabase/PAM.

The other directive in Listing 12-10, userdb, is set to driver = passwd. This performs a user lookup to return some information about the user. It returns the user's UID, GID, and home directory among other information, and it retrieves this information from the /etc/passwd file. As you can see, you can choose to override values that you might have in the passwd file, like the home directory of the user to put their mail in a different directory to their normal home directory.

■ **Note** You can read more about the user database lookups at http://wiki.dovecot.org/UserDatabase.

After you have configured Dovecot, you'll need to start (or restart) it. We start Dovecot using the systemctl command.

```
$ sudo systemctl start dovecot
```

Or, you can check that the Dovecot process is running like so:

```
$ systemctl status dovecot
● dovecot.service - Dovecot IMAP/POP3 email server
   Loaded: loaded (/usr/lib/systemd/system/dovecot.service; disabled; vendor preset: disabled)
   Active: active (running) since Thu 2016-08-25 09:33:09 EDT; 37min ago
  Process: 7172 ExecStartPre=/usr/libexec/dovecot/prestartscript (code=exited, status=0/
  SUCCESS)
 Main PID: 7177 (dovecot)
```

```
CGroup: /system.slice/dovecot.service
        ├─7177 /usr/sbin/dovecot -F
        ├─7180 dovecot/anvil
        ├─7181 dovecot/log
        ├─7183 dovecot/config
```

```
Aug 25 09:33:09 ip-10-0-10-154.ap-southeast-2.compute.internal systemd[1]: Starting Dovecot
IMAP/POP3 email server...
Aug 25 09:33:09 ip-10-0-10-154.ap-southeast-2.compute.internal systemd[1]: Started Dovecot
IMAP/POP3 email server.
Aug 25 09:33:09 ip-10-0-10-154.ap-southeast-2.compute.internal dovecot[7177]: master:
Dovecot v2.2.10 starting up without any protocols (core dumps disabled)
```

Here you can see the dovecot and dovecot-auth processes running, indicating that Dovecot has started successfully.

On CentOS, Dovecot logs to the /var/log/maillog file and on Ubuntu to the /var/log/mail.log file, and you can confirm it is running if you see a log entry like the following:

```
Jan  7 18:37:03 au-mel-rhel-1  dovecot: Dovecot v1.0.7 starting up
```

Configuring Postfix for SASL

Next, we need to configure Postfix to use the Dovecot SASL service we've just configured. Add the entries in Listing 12-12 to the main.cf configuration file.

Listing 12-12. Configuring Postfix for Dovecot SASL

```
smtpd_sasl_type = dovecot
smtpd_sasl_path = private/auth
smtpd_recipient_restrictions = permit_sasl_authenticated,permit_mynetworks,reject_unauth_
destination
smtpd_sasl_auth_enable = yes
smtpd_tls_auth_only = yes
```

In Listing 12-12, we've used the smtpd_sasl_type option to specify that we're using Dovecot to perform our SASL authentication. The smtpd_sasl_path option specifies the location of the authentication socket relative to Postfix's spool directory, usually the /var/spool/postfix directory. This matches the Dovecot client socket we defined earlier in Listing 12-9. The smtpd_sasl_auth_enable option tells Postfix to enable SASL authentication.

The next option, smtpd_tls_auth_only, tells Postfix to announce and use authentication only if TLS is enabled and running. This means the STARTTLS command needs to have been issued with an encrypted connection created between the client and server.

The last option, smtpd_recipient_restrictions, is one of Postfix's restriction lists. It tells Postfix what to allow or deny when the RCPT TO command is issued, for example, when an e-mail is received from a client. By default, as we mentioned earlier, Postfix will accept e-mail

- From clients whose IP addresses match the values in the mynetworks option

- To remote destinations that match the value of the relay_domains option, which defaults to the value of the mydestination option

- To and from the local host

We're going to adjust this default behavior by telling Postfix to also accept e-mails from users authenticated by SASL.

So first, we have the `permit_mynetworks` option, which maintains access for the networks in the `mynetworks` options. We then add the `permit_sasl_authenticated` option that tells Postfix to accept mail from SASL-authenticated users. Lastly, for Postfix to receive e-mail and have a valid configuration, we must finish with a reject restriction, in this case the `reject_unauth_destination` option. This option rejects any e-mail not in accordance with the last two criteria we just established: to the specified remote destinations or to and from the local host.

■ **Note**   You can see a bit more about recipient restrictions at `www.postfix.org/postconf.5.html#smtpd_recipient_restrictions`.

Testing Postfix Authentication

Now, once we've restarted Postfix, our SASL configuration should be active, and we can test this. There are a number of ways we can test this now. The first is to configure a client to send authenticated e-mail to our server. But since we haven't enabled a way for a client to browse a mailbox yet, such as the IMAP or POP3 protocols, this isn't overly useful. We can employ the `openssl s_client` command again to test.

To test the connection, we need to create a base64-encoded username and password. To do this, we are going to use Python.

```
$ python  -c 'import base64; print base64.b64encode("jsmith")'
anNtaXRo
$ python  -c 'import base64; print base64.b64encode("secret")'
c2VjcmV0
```

In the previous snippet, we have used the `python` command to execute (`-c`) the code that will create a base64 encoding of the username and password we need. We are now going to use these values to test whether we can authenticate against our SMTP server and send an e-mail.

In Listing 12-13, you can see a `openssl s_client` session that tests SASL authentication.

Listing 12-13. Using swaks to Test SASL

```
$ openssl s_client -connect mail.example.com:25 -starttls smtp
CONNECTED(00000003)
depth=2 O = Digital Signature Trust Co., CN = DST Root CA X3
verify return:1
depth=1 C = US, O = Let's Encrypt, CN = Let's Encrypt Authority X3
verify return:1
depth=0 CN = mail.example.com
verify return:1
---
Certificate chain
 0 s:/CN=mail.example.com
   i:/C=US/O=Let's Encrypt/CN=Let's Encrypt Authority X3
 1 s:/C=US/O=Let's Encrypt/CN=Let's Encrypt Authority X3
   i:/O=Digital Signature Trust Co./CN=DST Root CA X3
---
```

```
Server certificate
-----BEGIN CERTIFICATE-----
MIIFGjCCBAKgAwIBAgISAofRIzPUESQUdGrLEPG8niSXMAOGCSqGSIb3DQEBCwUA
...
<snip>
...
PLCtj2aR+DrP2jz7IKO3CmzrvSbPxs+wtmIpgmV96HLE6zc94xAV6bQEoZWvav5F
I2Ra8G/fFEYE1/nNvinV1ikOQa68vHqYhLOhemU/2Z8/pBCFWg1txqfSSUq4G4mH
NsOPhphTx/QyYjeU7KO=
-----END CERTIFICATE-----
subject=/CN=mail.example.com
issuer=/C=US/O=Let's Encrypt/CN=Let's Encrypt Authority X3
...
< snip>
...
Verify return code: 0 (ok)
---
250 DSN
ehlo me.com
250-mail.example.com
250-PIPELINING
250-SIZE 10240000
250-VRFY
250-ETRN
250-AUTH PLAIN LOGIN
250-ENHANCEDSTATUSCODES
250-8BITMIME
250 DSN
AUTH LOGIN
334 VXNlcm5hbWU6
anNtaXRo
334 UGFzc3dvcmQ6
c2VjcmVO
235 2.7.0 Authentication successful
MAIL FROM: me@here.com
250 2.1.0 Ok
rcpt to: jsmith@example.com
250 2.1.5 Ok
DATA
354 End data with <CR><LF>.<CR><LF>
Subject: hello you
You're ace
.
250 2.0.0 Ok: queued as 5F2051866087
DONE
```

In Listing 12-13, we've initiated the openssl s_client command with the –starttls smtp option, which tells openssl to pass the STARTTLS command when making a connection to our e-mail server. We have specified the –connect option and passed the host and port we are going to connect to.

When the command is executed, you can see a connection is initiated, the STARTTLS command is initiated, and the server's public key details are displayed. We get the return code 250 DSN (for "delivery status notification"). We then issue the ehlo me.com command, and the SMTP server responds with its server name and the list capabilities it has, one of them being AUTH PLAIN LOGIN showing the two available authentication mechanisms being offered: PLAIN and LOGIN.

We then issue the AUTH LOGIN command, and we are presented with 334 VXNlcm5hbWU6, which is the base64-encoded word *Username*. We submit the username, and then we are asked for the password (334 UGFzc3dvcmQ6). We submit the password, all in base64 encoding. The authentication succeeded, and the test e-mail was submitted. If the authentication mechanism had failed, Postfix would have kept trying authentication mechanisms, in our case LOGIN and then PLAIN, until one mechanism succeeds or all have failed. If all have failed, the client will receive an error message.

■ **Note** We used the lowercase RCPT TO: (rcpt to: jsmith@example.com) in the previous example. This is because openssl will *renegotiate* the TLS session if a line starts with a capital *R* and you will not be able to sign in.

You can also confirm that the session has succeeded by checking the syslog log files for Postfix.

```
$ sudo less /var/log/maillog
Aug 26 20:38:31 ip-10-0-10-154 postfix/smtpd[10683]: initializing the server-side TLS engine
Aug 26 20:38:31 ip-10-0-10-154 postfix/smtpd[10683]: connect from ↵
  ppp12-29-41-55.bras1.mel11.internode.on.net[12.29.41.15]
Aug 26 20:38:31 ip-10-0-10-154 postfix/smtpd[10683]: setting up TLS connection from ↵
  ppp12-29-41-55.bras1.mel11.internode.on.net[12.29.41.15]
Aug 26 20:38:31 ip-10-0-10-154 postfix/smtpd[10683]: ppp12-29-41-15.bras1.mel11.internode.
on.net[12.29.41.15]: ↵
  TLS cipher list "aNULL:-aNULL:ALL:!EXPORT:!LOW:!MEDIUM:+RC4:@STRENGTH:!aNULL:!MD5"

Aug 26 07:52:14 mail postfix/smtpd[9215]: 5F2051866087: ↵
  client=ppp12-29-41-55.bras1.mel11.internode.on.net[12.29.41.15], sasl_method=LOGIN,
sasl_username=jsmith
Aug 26 07:52:29 mail postfix/anvil[9162]: statistics: max connection rate 1/60s for
(smtp: 12.29.41.15) at Aug 26 07:42:29
Aug 26 07:52:29 mail postfix/anvil[9162]: statistics: max connection count 1 for
(smtp: 12.29.41.15) at Aug 26 07:42:29
Aug 26 07:52:29 mail postfix/anvil[9162]: statistics: max cache size 1 at Aug 26 07:42:29

Aug 26 07:52:37 mail postfix/cleanup[9227]: 5F2051866087: message-id=<>
Aug 26 07:52:37 mail postfix/qmgr[1186]: 5F2051866087: from=<me@here.com>, size=270,
nrcpt=1 (queue active)
Aug 26 07:52:37 mail postfix/local[9228]: 5F2051866087: to=<jsmith@example.com>,
relay=local, delay=235, delays=235/0.01/0/0, dsn=2.0.0, status=sent (delivered to mailbox)
Aug 26 07:52:37 mail postfix/qmgr[1186]: 5F2051866087: removed

Aug 26 07:52:44 mail postfix/smtpd[9215]: disconnect from ppp12-29-41-15.bras1.mel11.
internode.on.net[12.29.41.15]
```

Notice the TLS connection is established in the first section, then authentication is initiated, the e-mail is sent, and, lastly, the disconnection takes place.

If your authentication has succeeded, you've now got Postfix authentication running, your server can now be used by remote users, and your internal users can securely submit e-mail.

If you have issues with configuring Postfix authentication, see the pointers and links in the upcoming "Getting Help for Postfix" section.

SMARTHOSTING

As we mentioned earlier in the chapter, some ISPs block outgoing SMTP traffic. This is designed to help reduce spam. In addition, some SMTP servers are configured not to receive e-mail from certain types of networks, such as ADSL and those using dynamic IP addresses. If you cannot send outbound e-mail or some servers refuse connections from your server, this may be the issue. An easy way to check this is to see whether you can connect to an external MTA using a tool like swaks or if you can contact your ISP to find out if it restricts outgoing SMTP traffic.

If you are being blocked, you can overcome this with smarthosting. A smarthost is a relay server that receives and forwards your e-mail. Many ISPs offer smarthosts to their users.

There are two types of smarthost—unauthenticated and authenticated. Both types are specified with the relayhost configuration option in the main.cf configuration file (see www.postfix.org/postconf.5.html#relayhost) like so, where mail.isp.net is the hostname of your smarthost:

```
relayhost = mail.isp.net
```

This will tell your Postfix e-mail server to send all outgoing e-mail to mail.isp.net. This assumes that the smarthost will accept e-mail from you; for example, some ISP smarthosts are happy to accept e-mail from any IP address that the ISP manages.

Sometimes, however, your smarthost won't accept e-mail from you without SASL authentication. If so, you need to configure smarthost authentication. To do this, you need to configure SASL authentication where Postfix is a client rather than the server. Remember, when you configured it as a server, all the configuration options started with smtpd_, indicating it was for connections incoming to the server. Now you need to configure Postfix to be a client, and you use configuration options starting with smtp. To do so, set the following options in the main.cf file:

```
smtp_sasl_password_maps = hash:/etc/postfix/smtp_sasl_passwd
smtp_sasl_auth_enable = yes
smtp_sasl_mechanism_filter = plain, login
smtp_sasl_security_options = noanonymous
```

This configures SASL authentication for your server when it is a client. The smtp_sasl_password_maps option (see www.postfix.org/postconf.5.html#smtp_sasl_password_maps) specifies a database file containing a list of smarthosts and their required credentials. This is created by editing a file and using the postmap command to create a database from that file. The /etc/postfix/smtp_sasl_passwd file needs to contain the name of the smarthost and the username and password (separated by a colon) required to authenticate like so:

```
mail.isp.net          username:password
```

You need to make sure these files are readable only by the root user and have appropriate permissions to stop anyone viewing your passwords.

```
$ sudo chown root:root /etc/postfix/smtp_sasl_passwd
$ sudo chmod 0600 /etc/postfix/smtp_sasl_passwd
```

We then use the postmap command to create a database.

```
$ sudo postmap hash:/etc/postfix/smtp_sasl_passwd
```

A file called smtp_sasl_passwd.db is then created.

The remaining options are pretty simple. The smtp_sasl_auth_enable option turns on SASL authentication for Postfix as a client. The smtp_sasl_mechanism_filter option specifies what types of authentication mechanisms are supported by the smarthost, and the smtp_sasl_security_options option disables anonymous mechanisms.

After your configuration is updated, you will need to reload or restart Postfix, and you can then test to see whether your server can send SASL-authenticated e-mail to the smarthost. You can also specify more granular smarthosting with the transport option (see www.postfix.org/transport.5.html).

Postfix Lookup Tables and Virtual Domains

We have talked throughout this chapter about lookups and maps, either for aliases or for things like passwords. These are generally known as *lookup tables*. Postfix lookup tables are used to store information concerning access, routing, rewriting, and filtering content. Lookup tables can be text file–based databases, LDAP databases, or SEQUEL databases. We are going to look at two examples of lookup tables: aliases and virtual alias domains.

Earlier we talked about the newaliases command. This command uses the postalias command to take the names and aliases listed in the /etc/aliases file and makes an index file used by the local delivery daemon. We can use the postalias command to create and manage the index directory; however, the newaliases command manages this for us as we also need to reload the configuration into the daemon after every change and so is easier to use (and is compatible with the Sendmail program too).

We can use the postalias command to query the alias hash.

```
$ sudo postalias -c /etc/postfix/ -q root hash:/etc/aliases
ataylor
```

We tell Postfix which table to use via the alias_database configuration in the main.cf file. We can view that easily with the following:

```
$ postconf -n |grep alias_database
alias_database = hash:/etc/aliases
```

We can move on to more complex uses. Our host can be the final destination for mail bound for the example.com domain. But it can also be used to "host" other domains. In this scenario, our server can be the final destination for example.com, example.net, example.id, or any other kind of registered domain name with an MX record pointing at our mail server.

We can do this via the `mydestination` setting in the `main.cf` file.

```
mydestination = mail.example.com example.net example.id example.com
```

This means that mail for ataylor@example.com will need a local ataylor Linux user account, and that address will be delivered to the same mailbox for ataylor@example.com, ataylor@example.net, and ataylor@example.id. You might want admin@example.com to go to ataylor but admin@example.net to go to bsingh. You may not want this to happen at all, and you may not want to have to give every mail user a Linux user account on your mail servers. If you are hosting for multiple different domains, this also becomes unwieldly.

Postfix can solve this problem in two different ways.

- Virtual alias domains
- Virtual mailbox domains

The first step you can take is to create virtual domains. This allows you to map virtual domains to user accounts for each domain. So, in the previous example, admin@example.com can go to a different user than admin@example.net. To do that, we use a lookup table in Postfix that will manage users for each domain.

We need to set the following in our `main.cf` file.

```
virtual_alias_domains = example.net example.id example.com
virtual_alias_maps = hash:/etc/postfix/virtual
```

We have told Postfix that if it gets mail for example.com or .net or .id, to use the indexed file alias_map /etc/postfix/virtual, which will be a file containing our listings.

```
/etc/postfix/virtual
admin@example.com ataylor
sales@example.com  jsmith
....
admin@example.net bsingh
sales@example.net jsmith ataylor@example.com
```

Here we have two domains, example.com and example.net. The admin@example.com address is aliased to ataylor, and admin@example.net will be sent to bsingh. The address can be local Linux addresses or remote addresses, like you can see in the sales@example.net address. After we have created this file and after each time we change it, we need to use the postmap command to re-create the indexes and restart Postfix to pick up the changes.

```
$ sudo postmap /etc/postfix/virtual
$ sudo systemctl reload postfix
```

Say we don't want to create Linux user accounts on our mail servers. We can still deliver mail for our mail users with virtual mailboxes. We cannot have virtual alias domains and virtual mailbox domains for the same domains, so it is either one or the other.

To set up virtual mailbox domains, we will need to set the following:

```
/etc/postfix/main.cf:
mydestination = localhost
virtual_mailbox_domains = hash:/etc/postfix/virt_domains
virtual_mailbox_maps = hash:/etc/postfix/virt_mailbox
virtual_alias_maps = hash:/etc/postfix/virtual
virtual_transport = lmtp:unix:private/dovecot-lmtp
```

In the previous example, we have reset the `mydestination` option to `localhost`, and we get our list of destinations from the `virtual_mailbox_domains` setting. The `virtual_mailbox_maps` setting will list the mail addresses we accept. The `virtual_alias_maps` setting will contain the aliases for our mail users, like the aliases file would.

Here are the virtual domains we accept mail for. They are in the format `<domain> <action>`.

```
/etc/postfix/virt_domain
example.com        OK
example.net        OK
example.id         OK
```

Here we are setting the `OK` action to all our domains. Other actions that could be set include `DISCARD`, `FILTER`, `REJECT`, and more. The `virtual_mailbox` file has a similar syntax.

```
/etc/postfix/virt_mailbox:
ataylor@example.com      OK
ataylor@example.net      OK
bsingh@example.com       OK
jsmith@example.net       OK
```

Here we are listing the e-mail addresses we accept. Again, we could set other actions instead of `OK` such as `REJECT` or `FILTER` or `BCC`.

Finally, we can also use virtual aliases like we did with the `/etc/aliases` file. Here we list the e-mail address we accept on the left side and the destination on the right:

```
/etc/postfix/virtual:
admin@example.com  ataylor@example.com
```

Once we have configured or changed these, we need to run the `postmap` command again.

```
$ sudo postmap /etc/postfix/virt_domains
$ sudo postmap /etc/postfix/virt_mailbox
$ sudo postmap /etc/postfix/virtual
$ sudo systemct reload postfix
```

Now that we have this working for our domains, we could change the lookup tables to be SQL or LDAP backed. There are many other options for lookup tables too; for a full list, you can visit the following:

- www.postfix.org/DATABASE_README.html

Getting Help for Postfix

Postfix is not only one of the easiest applications to configure, with a simple configuration model and lots of documentation, but also one of the friendliest to troubleshoot, with most error messages being descriptive and helpful.

■ **Note**   Not all MTAs are as easy to configure, and others have complex syntax and bewildering error messages. You'll find Postfix easy to configure, but others like Exim and Qmail are also easy.

You can find useful documentation at the Postfix home page (`www.postfix.org/`). This includes documentation (`www.postfix.org/documentation.html`) and how-tos and FAQs (`www.postfix.org/docs.html`).

There are some useful resources for specifically configuring and troubleshooting for SSL/TLS encryption and SASL. For encryption, you can find resources at `www.postfix.org/TLS_README.html`. For SASL, you can find a useful how-to at `www.postfix.org/SASL_README.html`, another for Ubuntu at `http://adomas.org/2006/08/postfix-dovecot/`, and a more advanced version at `www.lxtreme.nl/index.pl/docs/linux/dovecot_postfix_pam`.

The following documentation can also be helpful: `www.postfix.org/DEBUG_README.html`. It shows how to debug Postfix problems from increasing verbosity of logs to stracing Postfix processes. One of the most useful debugging tools is the `debug_peer_list` option.

By setting `debug_peer_list`, you can increase the information in the mail logs about a peer. You can set it like this:

```
debug_peer_list = troubled.domain.com
```

On the next connection from `troubled.domain.com`, you will see an increase in logging, which you will find immensely useful.

You can also find some tips on running Postfix in a small office/home office environment at `www.postfix.org/SOHO_README.html`, and you might want to consider joining the Postfix mailing list at `www.postfix.org/lists.html`.

Remember that if you submit a question or a bug, you should include the following information:

- Your Postfix configuration (run `postconf -n`)

- Your platform (run `uname -a`)

- Any log messages generated (either in the `/var/log/mail.log` file on Ubuntu or in the `/var/log/maillog` file on CentOS)

Also available is an IRC channel called `#postfix` on the Freenode IRC server (`http://freenode.net/`) where you can seek assistance.

Combating Viruses and Spam

Now that you have Postfix running with encryption and authentication, we're going to show you how you can defend your users and your organization from spam and viruses. We're going to look at two tools.

- *SpamAssassin*: An open source antispam tool

- *ClamAV*: An open source antivirus scanner and engine

We're going to integrate both these tools with Postfix and teach you how to use them.

Fighting Spam

Spam is unsolicited e-mail ranging from requests to help with myriad illegal financial transactions to offers for medicine that will enlarge portions of human anatomy. Spam is one of the biggest threats to the happiness of your users. Nothing is more irritating than coming to work to find a huge collection of spam e-mail and your actual e-mail buried. It is also a threat to your organization and users, as spam often hides phishing attacks (`http://en.wikipedia.org/wiki/Phishing`), virus distributions, and other types of malware attacks.

We're going to configure our Postfix server to reject some spam on its own and then introduce you to a popular antispam tool called SpamAssassin. SpamAssassin is a Bayesian spam filter (http://en.wikipedia.org/wiki/Bayesian_spam_filtering). *Bayesian spam filtering* in the simplest terms is a method that predicts the likelihood that the presence of a word, phrase, or other characteristic in an e-mail means that e-mail is spam.

Each e-mail is marked spam or not according to a numeric score calculated through a series of customizable tests or rules; by default, a score higher than 5.0 is marked as spam. Each rule either adds or subtracts from this score depending on the weighting of the rule. For example, a rule might check a particular characteristic of the e-mail, and if it matches, SpamAssassin might add 0.5 to the score assigned to that e-mail.

Bayesian spam filters also learn patterns from your users' incoming mail and can be trained by telling them which mail is spam and which is not, called *ham* by SpamAssassin (http://en.wikipedia.org/wiki/Spam_(food)). The data from its learning is added to a database and used to make future analysis of incoming e-mail more accurate.

SpamAssassin runs as a daemon on your host, and e-mail is submitted to the daemon, analyzed, and then returned marked, via the addition of a new header, as either spam or not.

Configuring Postfix for Antispam

Before we configure SpamAssassin, we're going to tighten our Postfix configuration. To do this, we add some configuration options to our main.cf configuration file. Most of these options reject e-mail that isn't compliant to the SMTP RFC, for example, by rejecting e-mail whose source address isn't a valid e-mail.

We're principally going to update the restriction lists we introduced when we were looking at Postfix authentication. Table 12-2 presents these restriction lists.

Table 12-2. Postfix Restriction Lists

Restriction List	Description
smtpd_client_restrictions	Restrictions when the clients connect
smtpd_helo_restrictions	Restrictions when the HELO/EHLO command is issued
smtpd_sender_restrictions	Restrictions when the MAIL FROM command is issued
smtpd_relay_restrictions	Restrictions applied to RCPT TO prior to the smtpd_recipient_restrictions
smtpd_recipient_restrictions	Restrictions when the RCPT TO command is issued for spam blocking
smtpd_data_restrictions	Restrictions when the DATA command is issued

Restriction lists are triggered when particular events occur; for example, the smtpd_client_restrictions are checked when the client connects, and the smtpd_helo_restrictions are checked when the EHLO command is issued by the client. If the client does not send the EHLO command, these restrictions are ineffective. With the postconf command, we can add directives to the main.cf file with postconf -e. We will add the following:

```
$ sudo postconf -e 'smtpd_helo_restrictions = reject_unknown_helo_hostname'
$ sudo postconf -e 'smtpd_helo_required = yes'
```

With the first option, `smtpd_helo_restrictions`, we reject the connecting e-mail server if it doesn't have an A or MX record in DNS. For this to work, `smtpd_helo_required` tells Postfix to deny connections from clients that don't send a proper EHLO and announce their name. The `smtpd_helo_required` makes the connecting MTAs send the EHLO command.

In this case, we're going to add some options to the sender, recipient, and data restriction lists. First, add the `smtpd_sender_restrictions` options to `main.cf` like so:

```
$ sudo postconf -e 'smtpd_sender_restrictions = reject_non_fqdn_sender, reject_unknown_
sender_domain'
```

The `reject_non_fqdn_sender` option rejects e-mails where the sender mailing address is not in the proper format. This means the value passed by the MAIL FROM command must be in the form of a valid e-mail address, for example, ataylor@example.com. An address such as Anne Taylor or ataylor or Anne or anything else that you will not be able to respond to will not be accepted, and the e-mail is thereby rejected.

The `reject_unknown_sender_domain` option rejects e-mail where the domain of the sender has no DNS A or MX record. This is usually when the e-mail has been sent from a bogus domain, as is often the case with spam e-mail.

We can protect our e-mail server from becoming a relay server by adding the following:

```
$ sudo postconf -e 'smtpd_relay_restrictions = permit_mynetworks, permit_sasl_authenticated, ↵
reject_unauth_destination'
```

Here we are saying that we will permit any specified networks (`permit_mynetworks`) to send mail to other destination mail servers. Next we will permit any authenticated (via SASL) clients (`permit_sasl_authenticated`) to send e-mail to other destination servers. Finally, we will reject any mail to unauthorized destinations (`reject_unauth_destination`).

Next, we want to add another rejection criterion to our `smtpd_recipient_restrictions` option.

```
$ sudo postconf -e 'smtpd_recipient_restrictions = reject_rbl_client zen.spamhaus.org, ↵
   reject_rhsbl_reverse_client dbl.spamhaus.org, ↵
   reject_rhsbl_helo dbl.spamhaus.org, reject_rhsbl_sender dbl.spamhaus.org, reject_unauth_
   pipelining '
```

In this section we are attempting to reduce the amount of spam by rejecting known blacklisted servers and domains. The Spamhaus Project is a not-for-profit organization that tracks spam and other cyber threats. It provides a service that you can query to help reduce the amount of spam you receive. These real-time blackhole lists (RBLs) will allow you to query their databases of known open relays and bad to and from addresses.

The `reject_rbl_client` queries the DNS block list (DNSBL) at zen.spamhaus.org and rejects any positive entries there. The `reject_rhsbl_reverse_client` queries dbl.spamhaus.org based on the client, which is a domain block list (DBLs). It can help reject spam based on several elements (HELO, IP/DNS, to and from, and so on). The other two DBLs work on the HELO (`reject_rhsbl_helo`) and sender (`reject_rhsbl_sender`), respectively.

We have included the `reject_unauth_pipelining` restriction that rejects e-mails submitted using a special technique called *pipelining* without checking to see whether pipelining is supported. This is a common technique used by spam mailers to submit e-mail.

We're also going to add this same option to the `smtpd_data_restrictions` to catch spammers who use the same technique when the DATA command is issued.

```
smtpd_data_restrictions = reject_unauth_pipelining
```

Lastly, we're going to configure an option not related to restriction lists that foils some spam.

```
$ sudo postconf -e 'disable_vrfy_command = yes'
```

The `disable_vrfy_command` option disables the SMTP VRFY command. The VRFY command allows a sender to query the Postfix server and verify that an address exists. This is used by spammers to validate addresses and occasionally by hackers to harvest the names of users on your host prior to attacks.

■ **Note**   There are other restrictions you can enable, but these are the simplest, easiest, and least likely to restrict legitimate e-mail to your Postfix server. See `www.postfix.org/uce.html` for more details.

After making the changes, restart the Postfix daemon.

■ **Note**   It's a good idea to confirm that you can still send and receive e-mail after making your changes.

Installing and Configuring SpamAssassin

To supplement our Postfix changes, we're going to install and configure SpamAssassin. We'll start by installing the required packages. On CentOS, we need to install the `spamassassin` package and tell it to start the SpamAssassin daemon automatically.

```
$ sudo yum install spamassassin
```

On Ubuntu, we need to install the `spamassassin` and `spamc` packages.

```
$ sudo aptitude install spamassassin
```

When SpamAssassin opens, it launches a daemon called `spamd`. We are going to create a system user that will run this daemon called `spamd`.

```
$ sudo useradd -r -m -s /sbin/nologin spamd
```

-r indicates we want a system user (a UID below 1000), -m indicates that we want the home directory created, and -s is the shell. The previous is for CentOS; for Ubuntu you would change the shell to `/usr/sbin/nologin`.

Then we enable the SpamAssassin daemon by issuing the following on both distributions:

```
$ sudo systemctl enable spamassassin
```

■ **Note**   The SpamAssassin packages have some additional prerequisite packages that will also be installed on both CentOS and Ubuntu when you install them.

For SpamAssassin you can make changes to the configuration by editing the files found in /etc/mail/ spamassassin on both distributions. You might like to edit the local.cf file that has the threshold at which mail is classified spam (required_score).

The other file we need to change is /etc/sysconfig/spamassassin on CentOS or /etc/default/ spamassassin on Ubuntu. This file controls the options (SPAMDOPTION on CentOS, OPTION on Ubuntu) we provide to spamd. We are going to add the user and group that will run the spamd daemon.

```
SPAMDOPTIONS="-d -c -m5 -H -u spamd -g spamd"
```

Here we are adding the –u and –g options to the default settings. These defaults are –d for daemonize, -c for create user preference files, -m is the number of child processes, and -H is to specify a different help directory (for third-party services).

We then need to start the SpamAssassin spamd daemon. We use the systemctl command.

```
$ sudo systemctl start spamassassin
```

■ **Tip** Like Postfix, it is a good idea to restart SpamAssassin after you make configuration changes.

Configuring Postfix for SpamAssassin

There are a number of different ways to integrate spam filters like SpamAssassin into your e-mail environment. One is to scan your user's incoming e-mail using an MDA before delivering them to the user. The spam filter then usually adds a header to the e-mail, which your MDA detects, and directs spam e-mail to a particular folder.

Another method is to analyze the e-mail while it is still inside the MTA. This allows us to pass the e-mail from Postfix's mail queue to SpamAssassin. The e-mail is then scanned and sent back to Postfix for delivery. A client or MDA can then make use of the results of that scanning, again a header added to the e-mail, to determine what to do with the e-mail. In Figure 12-3 you can see the proposed flow of e-mail through Postfix.

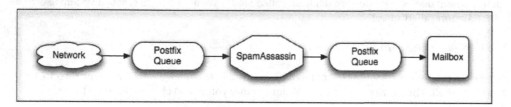

Figure 12-3. *SpamAssassin and Postfix filtering*

We're going to choose this latter method because it's a lot more efficient and scalable for most environments.

First, we update the master.cf file to send e-mail to SpamAssassin. To do this, we adjust the smtp service in the master.cf file like so:

```
smtp    inet    n    -    n    -    -    smtpd
    -o content_filter=spamassassin
```

This adds the line -o content_filter=spamassassin (the -o should be indented with spaces to show it is a follow-on from the previous line). The content_filter option tells Postfix that we want all e-mail delivered to the smtp service to be sent to a filter called spamassassin.

We now need to define this filter. To do this, we add the filter to the bottom of the master.cf file. Define the filter like so:

```
spamassassin   unix   -   n   n   -   -   pipe ↩
  user=spamd argv=/usr/bin/spamc -e /usr/sbin/sendmail -oi -f ${sender} ${recipient}
```

This creates a new service in the master.cf file, of the type unix, which is a Unix socket, and it calls another Postfix daemon called pipe, which delivers e-mail to an external command. In the next lines (again indented), we specify that external command.

We specify the external command will run, the user to run it as, and then the command and arguments we're going to pass to that command. We're calling the spamc command, a binary that connects to the spamassassin daemon, submits our e-mail, and then receives the scanned results.

To the spamc command, we're passing the -e argument. This argument (which must be specified last on the command line) tells the spamc command what to do with the e-mail after it's been scanned. In this case, we're submitting it to the /usr/sbin/sendmail command, which is the Postfix command that delivers our e-mail back to Postfix to be delivered to the user (the sendmail program here is a symlink to /usr/sbin/sendmail.postfix).

We've also specified some options for the sendmail command. The –oi option tells the sendmail command not to stop processing e-mail when it finds a line with a single period (.) on it (remember our test e-mails earlier ended when a line with a period on it was sent). This is because the e-mail might have a line with a period on it that might not indicate the end of the e-mail. The -f ${sender} option makes sure the sender of the e-mail is sent on to Postfix. Lastly, the ${recipient} option contains the recipient of the e-mail so Postfix knows to whom to send the e-mail.

Testing SpamAssassin

To test SpamAssassin, let's send an e-mail using the swaks tool, an e-mail testing tool that can be installed via the package manager, and examine the results.

```
$ swaks -tls -a -au ataylor -ap password -t jsmith@example.com -f ↩
ataylor@example.com --body /usr/share/doc/spamassassin-3.4.0/sample-spam.txt
```

This command connects to your mail server and sends an e-mail to the user jsmith@example.com from the SASL-authenticated user ataylor. We've also added the --body option to specify the contents of our e-mail. In this case, we're using a sample spam e-mail provided with the SpamAssassin package. The e-mail is located in the /usr/share/doc/spamassassin-<version>/ directory (substitute your SpamAssassin version for version, for example, 3.4.0). This sample spam is guaranteed to trigger SpamAssassin's spam filters and hence test our spam detection.

If we check in our Postfix logs, we can see this e-mail get received and processed, as shown in Listing 12-14.

Listing 12-14. Postfix Logs with SpamAssassin

```
$ sudo less /var/log/mail.log
Aug 27 08:11:35 ip-10-0-10-154 postfix/qmgr[12743]: 564B21866089: from=<ataylor@example.
com>, size=1316, ↩
  nrcpt=1 (queue active)
```

```
Aug 27 08:11:35 ip-10-0-10-154 spamd[12345]: spamd: connection from localhost [::1]:46002 to
port 783, fd 6
Aug 27 08:11:35 ip-10-0-10-154 spamd[12345]: spamd: setuid to mail succeeded
Aug 27 08:11:35 ip-10-0-10-154 spamd[12345]: spamd: creating default_prefs: /home/spamd/.
spamassassin/user_prefs
Aug 27 08:11:35 ip-10-0-10-154 spamd[12345]: spamd: failed to create readable default_prefs: ↵
  /var/spool/mail/.spamassassin/user_prefs
Aug 27 08:11:35 ip-10-0-10-154 spamd[12345]: spamd: processing message (unknown) for mail:8
Aug 27 08:11:36 ip-10-0-10-154 spamd[12345]: spamd: identified spam (999.1/5.0) for mail:8
in 0.3 seconds, 1280 bytes.
Aug 27 08:11:36 ip-10-0-10-154 spamd[12345]: spamd: result: Y 999 - ALL_TRUSTED,GTUBE,
MISSING_MID ↵
  scantime=0.3,size=1280,user=mail,uid=8,required_score=5.0,rhost=localhost,raddr=::1,rpo
rt=46002, ↵
  mid=(unknown),autolearn=no autolearn_force=no
Aug 27 08:11:36 ip-10-0-10-154 spamd[12344]: prefork: child states: II
Aug 27 08:11:36 ip-10-0-10-154 postfix/pipe[12758]: 564B21866089: to=<jsmith@example.com>,
relay=spamassassin, ↵
  delay=0.89, delays=0.57/0.01/0/0.3, dsn=2.0.0, status=sent (delivered via spamassassin
service)
Aug 27 08:11:36 ip-10-0-10-154 postfix/qmgr[12743]: 564B21866089: removed
Aug 27 08:11:36 ip-10-0-10-154 postfix/pickup[12742]: 0AF49181186C: uid=8 from=<ataylor@
example.com>
Aug 27 08:11:36 ip-10-0-10-154 postfix/cleanup[12757]: 0AF49181186C: message ↵
  id=<20160827121136.0AF49181186C@mail.example.com>
Aug 27 08:11:36 ip-10-0-10-154 postfix/qmgr[12743]: 0AF49181186C: from=<ataylor@example.
com>, size=2091, ↵
  nrcpt=1 (queue active)
Aug 27 08:11:36 ip-10-0-10-154 postfix/local[12762]: 0AF49181186C: to=<jsmith@example.com>,
relay=local, ↵
  delay=0.04, delays=0.03/0.01/0/0, dsn=2.0.0, status=sent (delivered to mailbox)
Aug 27 08:11:36 ip-10-0-10-154 postfix/qmgr[12743]: 0AF49181186C: removed
```

In Listing 12-14, we've connected to our Postfix server, been authenticated, and submitted our e-mail. During the transaction the e-mail is submitted to SpamAssassin (see the lines with spamd, which is the SpamAssassin daemon).

```
Aug 27 08:11:35 ip-10-0-10-154 spamd[12345]: spamd: connection from localhost [::1]:46002 to
port 783, fd 6
Aug 27 08:11:35 ip-10-0-10-154 spamd[12345]: spamd: setuid to mail succeeded
Aug 27 08:11:35 ip-10-0-10-154 spamd[12345]: spamd: creating default_prefs: /home/spamd/.
spamassassin/user_prefs
Aug 27 08:11:35 ip-10-0-10-154 spamd[12345]: spamd: processing message (unknown) for mail:8
Aug 27 08:11:36 ip-10-0-10-154 spamd[12345]: spamd: identified spam (999.1/5.0) for mail:8
in 0.3 seconds, 1280 bytes.
Aug 27 08:11:36 ip-10-0-10-154 spamd[12345]: spamd: result: Y 999 - ALL_
TRUSTED,GTUBE,MISSING_MID ↵
  scantime=0.3,size=1280,user=mail,uid=8,required_score=5.0,rhost=localhost,raddr=::1,rpo
rt=46002, ↵
  mid=(unknown),autolearn=no autolearn_force=no
```

We can see our SpamAssassin daemon gets a connection from the server, changes our user to the `mail` user, and processes our e-mail message. It has returned a line indicating that the message is a spam e-mail, with a score of `999.1/5.0` (significantly larger than 5.0 and hence spam).

SpamAsssassin works by doing several checks against known spam patterns.

- Header tests
- Body phrases
- Bayesian filters
- Whitelist/blacklist
- Reputational checks
- Collaborative checks
- RBLs and DNSRBLs

Each one of those adds to the overall score, and if they are over 5, it is considered spam. The list of checks that were triggered on the previous test spam message were `ALL_TRUSTED`,`GTUBE`,`MISSING_MID`. You will see others triggered when you see spam like `ADVANCE_FEE_5_NEW_FRM_MNY`, `FILL_THIS_FORM`,`FILL_THIS_FORM_LOAN`.

You can also train your Bayesian filters to better detect spam from ham. If you have a mailbox that is known to be full of spam, you can train your filters by issuing the following:

```
$ sudo sa-learn --showdots --mbox --spam file-of-spam
```

You should also teach your filter about ham, and to do that, you would issue the following:

```
$ sudo sa-learn --showdots --mbox --ham file-of-ham
```

We can also look at our actual e-mail and see the details of the headers SpamAssassin has added.

```
$ sudo cat /home/jsmith/Maildir/new/1472350940.Vca02I203b0aaM132480.mail.example.com
Return-Path: <ataylor@example.com>
X-Original-To: jsmith@example.com
Delivered-To: jsmith@example.com
Received: by mail.example.com (Postfix, from userid 993)
id 1F0C4181186F; Sat, 27 Aug 2016 22:22:20 -0400 (EDT)
X-Spam-Checker-Version: SpamAssassin 3.4.0 (2014-02-07) on
mail.example.com
X-Spam-Flag: YES
X-Spam-Level: **********************************************
X-Spam-Status: Yes, score=999.1 required=5.0 tests=ALL_TRUSTED,GTUBE,
MISSING_MID autolearn=no autolearn_force=no version=3.4.0
X-Spam-Report:
* -1.0 ALL_TRUSTED Passed through trusted hosts only via SMTP
* 1000 GTUBE BODY: Generic Test for Unsolicited Bulk Email
*  0.1 MISSING_MID Missing Message-Id: header
Received: from me.here (me.here [63.38.238.98])
by mail.example.com (Postfix) with ESMTPSA id 901A2181186E
for <jsmith@example.com>; Sat, 27 Aug 2016 22:22:19 -0400 (EDT)
Date: Sat, 27 Aug 2016 22:22:17 -0400
To: jsmith@example.com
```

```
From: ataylor@example.com
Subject: [SPAM] test Sat, 27 Aug 2016 22:22:17 -0400
X-Mailer: swaks v20130209.0 jetmore.org/john/code/swaks/
X-Spam-Prev-Subject: test Sat, 27 Aug 2016 22:22:17 -0400
Message-Id: <20160828022220.1F0C4181186F@mail.example.com>

Subject: Test spam mail (GTUBE)
Message-ID: <GTUBE1.1010101@example.net>
Date: Wed, 23 Jul 2003 23:30:00 +0200
From: Sender <sender@example.net>
To: Recipient <recipient@example.net>
Precedence: junk
MIME-Version: 1.0
Content-Type: text/plain; charset=us-ascii
Content-Transfer-Encoding: 7bit
```

We can see that SpamAssassin has added six headers.

- `X-Spam-Checker-Version`: The SpamAssassin version

- `X-Spam-Level`: The total score in asterisks

- `X-Spam-Flag`: Present only if e-mail is identified as spam

- `X-Spam-Status`: The spam status (No or Yes), the total the e-mail scored, and a list of the spam tests checked

- `X-Spam-Report`: The breakdown of how the spam score was derived

- `X-Spam-Prev-Subject`: The previous spam subject heading

The first three in the list are added to all e-mail; the last three are added only if the e-mail is considered spam.

Getting Help with SpamAssassin

Like with Postfix, getting help with SpamAssassin is easy. Abundant documentation as well as a helpful and extensive community are available online. The best place to start when seeking help is the SpamAssassin home page at `http://spamassassin.apache.org/`. The page includes a wiki, FAQ, and documentation. You can also join the active mailing list at `http://wiki.apache.org/spamassassin/MailingLists`, and you can submit bugs at `https://issues.apache.org/SpamAssassin/index.cgi`.

You can increase the debug level of `spamd` by adding a `-D` to the `spamd` daemon options we described earlier. This will increase your logging levels and give you great insight into what `spamd` is doing.

Remember that if you submit a question or a bug, you should include the following information:

- Your SpamAssassin and Perl version (run the `spamassassin` command with the `--version` option)

- Your platform (run `uname -a`)

- Any log messages generated (either in the `/var/log/mail.log` file on Ubuntu or in the `/var/log/maillog` file on CentOS)

Also available is an IRC channel called #spamassassin on the Freenode IRC server (http://freenode. net/) where you can seek assistance.

What to Do with the Spam?

If we have e-mail identified as spam by SpamAssassin, we alter the Subject line by adding "[SPAM]" to it, but that is all. It is still delivered into the user's inbox as a new message. In most cases, people put their spam e-mail into a separate folder to review and usually delete. Some people reject or delete any e-mail marked as spam, leading to loss of possibly important e-mail. Spam detection tools, including SpamAssassin, are not infallible, and false positives are sometimes generated. This means a legitimate e-mail can be marked as spam. If you delete your spam, you've lost this e-mail. Storing it in a folder for a period of time allows you to potentially find and retrieve these false positives.

We're going to use the first method and move our spam e-mail into a special folder in our Maildir directory for later review. To do this, we can use two main methods to leverage our newly acquired headers to move the e-mail to where we want it to go. These methods are

- Use a Local Mail Transfer Protocol (LTMP) agent like Dovecot
- Use MDAs like procmail or maildrop
- Use Mail client rules or filtering

Using Dovecot

We have seen Dovecot before for configuring our SMTP authentication. We are now going to configure it to transport our mail from the MTA and into the users' home directories. Dovecot allows us to use Sieve (http://sieve.info/) to filter what e-mail gets delivered to where for our users.

To use Dovecot, we are going to set an LMTP (Local Mail Transfer Protocol), which is a long-running process started by the Dovecot master process. This describes the difference between this Dovecot solution and the procmail and maildrop solutions, which are binaries fired with each mail that is delivered. Also, the LMTP can be running on a separate server as it can read from TCP and unix sockets.

The first step is to download the Dovecot Sieve support packages. For CentOS we will install this:

```
$ sudo yum install dovecot-pigeonhole
```

For Ubuntu we will install the following:

```
$ sudo aptitude install dovecot-sieve dovecot-lmtp
```

We configure Dovecot to start accepting connections with LMTP. We do that by adding the following to /etc/dovecot/dovecot.conf.

```
protocols = lmtp
```

Now we need to configure the following file, /etc/dovecot/conf.d/20-lmtp.conf:

```
protocol lmtp {
  postmaster_address = postmaster@example.com
  mail_plugins = quota sieve
}
```

We need to add the LMTP process, or Unix socket, to the Dovecot master process so Postfix can pass messages through it. We edit the `/etc/dovecot/conf.d/10-master.conf` file like so:

```
service lmtp {
 unix_listener /var/spool/postfix/private/dovecot-lmtp {
   group = postfix
   mode = 0600
   user = postfix
   }
}
```

Lastly, we need to tell Dovecot to strip the domain away from the username when delivering the mail. The LMTP process gets the username from `RCPT TO:`, and we need to strip the domain off. Otherwise, it will try to deliver the mail to `jsmith@example.com` instead of just `jsmith` (which will error with `550 5.1.1 User doesn't exist`). We do this in the `/etc/dovecot/conf.d/10-auth.conf` file.

```
auth_username_format = %Ln
```

Now we need to edit the Postfix configuration to tell it to use the LMTP socket. We do this via the following:

```
$ postconf -e 'mailbox_transport = lmtp:unix:private/dovecot-lmtp'
```

We need to restart Postfix and Dovecot now to push the changes through the following:

```
$ sudo systemctl restart dovecot
$ sudo systemctl restart postfix
```

Filtering with Sieve

The syntax for filtering your mail with Sieve is fairly simple. You can set global filters or individual filters in the users' home directories. In this example, we are going to show you how mail that has been marked as spam can be moved to your spam folder for later inspection.

Sieve has several easy-to-understand commands and conditionals. You require those you need at the top of your Sieve file, which you usually find in `~/.dovecot.sieve`. Here is an example:

```
require ["fileinto" ];
```

There are many other commands to use, and you can find the list available to you by running the following command:

```
$ doveconf -n managesieve_sieve_capability
fileinto reject envelope encoded-character vacation subaddress comparator-i;ascii-numeric
relational regex imap4flags copy include variables body enotify environment mailbox date
ihave
```

We are going to use a conditional `if` statement to store our spam into our spam folder. We are going to test against the headers that SpamAssassin makes available to us.

```
require ["fileinto"];
if header :contains "X-Spam-Flag" "YES" {
        fileinto "Spam";
}
```

This says if the header X-Spam-Flag contains the word YES, file the mail into the Spam folder. You can see how simple it is.

Before we test this, we need to make sure that the Spam folder exists. We can this by using the doveadm command. First we list to see whether the folder exists.

```
$ doveadm mailbox list -u jsmith
INBOX
```

In this case it doesn't, so we are going to create it.

```
$ doveadm mailbox create -u jsmith Spam
$ doveadm mailbox list -u jsmith
Spam
INBOX
```

Next, when we send our test spam e-mail like we did previously, we will now see the following:

```
Aug 28 05:17:10 ip-10-0-10-154 dovecot: lmtp(18407): Connect from local
Aug 28 05:17:10 ip-10-0-10-154 dovecot: lmtp(18407, jsmith): Kl1sKRaswlfnRwAArNTl4g: sieve:
msgid=<20160828091710.A40A21811885@mail.example.com>: stored mail into mailbox 'Spam'
Aug 28 05:17:10 ip-10-0-10-154 dovecot: lmtp(18407): Disconnect from local: Successful quit
```

Excellent. We have mail being delivered into our mailboxes, and we have it filtering out the spam.

Antivirus

We all should know that viruses are malicious code designed to attack your hosts, steal your data, or compromise other aspects of your organization. While extremely rare on Linux distributions, some viruses have targeted Linux distributions. But we're not particularly worried about viruses attacking our Linux hosts via e-mail; instead, we're concerned with viruses that might spread via e-mail onto other, more susceptible hosts such as Microsoft Windows desktops or be spread from your organization to other organizations.

We're going to introduce an application called ClamAV and show you how to integrate it with Postfix as a *milter*, or a *mail filter*. ClamAV is an open source antivirus engine much like similar tools from companies such as Symantec and McAfee. Unlike these commercial products, the ClamAV software and its update signatures are free.

■ **Note**   ClamAV uses special rules called *signatures* to scan your incoming e-mail for data that looks like a virus. Each signature contains information about a particular virus, for example, a string of data the virus file contains that, when found, tells ClamAV a virus has been detected.

We're going to show you how to integrate ClamAV into Postfix as a milter. Postfix allows for mail to be sent to a filter and then re-queued. There are two types of Postfix milters, smtpd only and non-smtpd only. We are going to show you how to set up the smtpd filter.

```
network -> smtpd -> filter -> smtpd -> delivery
```

The previous is the simplified version of the process that we will show you.

Installing ClamAV

First, you need to install and configure the ClamAV scanner and its daemon, called clamd. You also need to install an update tool called FreshClam that automatically downloads and updates the virus signatures that ClamAV uses to detect viruses.

On CentOS, the process of installing ClamAV is via these packages:

```
$ sudo yum install -y clamav-scanner clamav-update clamav-server-systemd clamav-milter-
systemd sendmail-milter
```

On Ubuntu, you install the clamav and clamav-daemon packages. Some additional packages may also be installed as prerequisites of these packages.

```
$ sudo aptitude install clamav clamav-daemon clamav-milter
```

Once again, the distributions put the configuration files into different locations. For CentOS we find clamav-milter in /etc/mail/clamav-milter.conf, and for the clamav daemon we find them in /etc/clam.d/scan.conf. For Ubuntu you find the files in /etc/clamav.

For CentOS we want to remove the word *Example* from /etc/mail/clamav-milter.conf and set the following:

```
MilterSocket /var/run/clamav-milter/clamav-milter.socket
MilterSocketGroup mail
MilterSocketMode 660
AllowSupplementaryGroups yes
ClamdSocket unix:/var/run/clamd.scan/clamd.sock
OnInfected Accept
AddHeader Add
ReportHostname mail.example.com
```

In the previous lines, we have set some configuration options like socket files for clamav-milter and the socket we talk to the scanner (clamd) on. Of note is OnInfected Accept. Normally we would have this set to Quarantine, but for the coming example we want our infected mail delivered so we can see the headers that we have added.

For the scanner on CentOS we have to edit /etc/clamd.d/scan.conf and make sure the following is set as well as Example if removed:

```
LocalSocket /var/run/clamd.scan/clamd.sock
```

Ubuntu doesn't need much configuration. The file /etc/clamav/clamav-milter.conf needs the following:

```
MilterSocket inet:7357@localhost
OnInfected Accept
AddHeader Add
```

Again, for testing we are accepting infected files and adding the header. Also, for Ubuntu, we are going to set up the milter to listen on the loopback address instead of using a named socket like we did in the CentOS setup. Both distributions can use this method. We don't need to change /etc/clamav/clamd.conf although this file contains different scanning settings that you might like to look at (as does the /etc/clamd/scan.conf in CentOS).

Now, we need to add the postfix and clamilt users to the mail group on CentOS.

```
$ sudo usermod –aG mail postfix && sudo usermod –aG mail clamilt
```

And for Ubuntu, unless we are using the named socket, we don't need to make any changes. But we will need to make some changes to the Postfix main.cf file to reflect our smtpd_milter. We do that by adding the following to our CentOS host:

```
milter_default_action = accept
smtpd_milters = unix:/var/run/clamav-milter/clamav-milter.socket
```

Because with Ubuntu we are talking to the milter over the loopback address, we will need to have the following:

```
milter_default_action = accept
smtpd_milters = inet:7357
```

Lastly, on CentOS, we need to make some adjustments to our SELinux policies. The following requires that the policycoreutils-python package be installed. Normally you can start your service, wait for it to fail, check /var/log/audit/audit.log, and run the audit2allow command to remedy any SELinux permission issues. In this example, we are going to use the target entry file to generate our policy package file and then load that into SELinux (see the upcoming "SELinux and Apparmor" sidebar for more information on SELinux). The contents of our clamav-write.te target entry file look like this:

```
module clam-write 1.0;

require {
        type unconfined_t;
        type var_run_t;
        type postfix_smtpd_t;
        type init_t;
        class sock_file write;
        class unix_stream_socket connectto;
}

#============= postfix_smtpd_t ==============
allow postfix_smtpd_t init_t:unix_stream_socket connectto;
allow postfix_smtpd_t unconfined_t:unix_stream_socket connectto;
allow postfix_smtpd_t var_run_t:sock_file write;
```

The first line consists of the module name and the version. The require section contains the different types and classes we will require. Lastly, we have the lines that allow the smtpd daemon to connect and write to the Unix sockets like /run/clamav-milter/clamav-milter.socket. We now have to compile the policy package, which we load into the SELinux policy configuration. We do that by first compiling a policy module file with the following commands:

```
$ sudo checkmodule -M -m -o clamav-write.mod clamav-write.te
```

The checkmodule command takes the following arguments, -M to enable LSM support, -m to generate the module binary, and –o, which is the output file name. Now we create the policy package with the following command:

```
semodule_package –o clamav-write.pp -m clamav-write.mod
```

We have created the policy package by passing the module (-m) file to the semodule_package command and have written it (-o) to the clamav-write.pp file. Now we are ready to load this policy package into SELinux. This is done by simply issuing the following:

```
$ sudo semodule –i clamav-write.pp
```

We have told semodule to install (-i) the clamav-write.pp policy into SELinux. We are now ready to start the ClamAV services.

Once all the relevant packages have been installed, you need to ensure the ClamAV daemon has been enabled and started. Let's start the clamd service.

```
$ sudo systemctl enable clamd@scan && sudo systemctl start clamd@scan (CentOS)
$ sudo systemctl enable clamav-daemon && sudo systemctl start clamav-daemon (Ubuntu)
```

Next we will start the clamav-milter service and freshclamd service, which polls for the latest virus signature updates.

```
$ sudo systemctl enable clamav-milter && sudo systemctl start clamav-milter (Both)
$ sudo systemctl enable clamav-freshclam && sudo systemctl start clamav-freshclam (Ubuntu)
```

We should now be able to look a bit more at the configuration of ClamAV.

SELINUX AND APPARMOR

There are different types of access controls available in Linux provided via the Linux Security Module (LSM), which is part of the Linux kernel. One of these is called Mandatory Access Control (MAC), which is provided by SELinux on RHEL-based and Debian distributions and by Apparmor on Ubuntu and Debian. Each provides the ability to allow or restrict access to files, processes, and network resources, and, of course, each does it differently.

MAC is different from Discretionary Access Control (DAC), which is the core of the Linux operating system and the one we are more familiar with. DAC allows the owner of a resource, for example, a file, to set the permissions for that file. MAC, on the other hand, mandates the permissions for resources in the kernel, and the permissions can be changed only by loading access policies into the kernel from user space.

SELinux was developed by the US National Security Agency (NSA) and works by tagging each object on the system and then using the SELinux security module to validate access to the resources. It will log access violations to the audit log, usually /var/log/audit/audit.log. From there you can use the audit2allow command to create new target entry files and policy packages. The target entry files (usually ending in .te) explain the policy in plain text. From that we can create the policy package (ending in .pp) that we can load into the kernel.

```
type=AVC msg=audit(1472477657.569:13159): avc:  denied  { write } for  pid=24859
comm="smtpd" name="clamav-milter.socket" dev="tmpfs" ino=281983 scontext=system_u:sys
tem_r:postfix_smtpd_t:s0 tcontext=unconfined_u:object_r:var_run_t:s0 tclass=sock_file
```

Here we can see the log SELinux output in the `audit.log`. We can break it down into three parts, the access required, the source context, and the target context.

`type=AVC` is the access vector cache, and then there is an audit time stamp. Then the `avc` action that was denied, write (`denied { write }`), by the command `smtpd` trying to write to `clamav-milter.socket`. The source context (`scontext`) is `system_u:system_r:postfix_smtpd_t:s0`, and the target context (`tcontext`) is `tcontext=unconfined_u:object_r:var_run_t:s0`. This means that the process with the `postfix_smtpd_t` type tried to access the socket file with the `var_run_t` type and couldn't. The solution is to allow the *write* on the socket file by the Postfix `smtpd` process. If we collect these messages and pass them to the `audit2allow` program, we will be able to create the policy package we need to allow the correct access.

```
sudo grep "denied" /var/log/audit/audit.log |grep clamav | audit2allow -M clamav-
write
```

This command will create `clamav-write.te` and `clamav-write.pp`, which you can then load in via the following:

```
sudo semodule -i clamav-write.pp
```

For Apparmor it is a different concept. Whereas SELinux uses tags on objects, Apparmor applies a security policy to path names. You create profiles for applications by defining what permissions an application will need, and you can manage this fairly easily with the tools that Apparmor comes with.

To view the status of Apparmor, you can issue the following:

```
$ sudo apparmor_status
apparmor module is loaded.
15 profiles are loaded.
15 profiles are in enforce mode.
   /sbin/dhclient
   /usr/bin/freshclam
   /usr/bin/lxc-start
...
4 processes have profiles defined.
4 processes are in enforce mode.
   /usr/bin/freshclam (2153)
   /usr/sbin/clamd (11998)
   /usr/sbin/mysqld (2997)
0 processes are in complain mode.
0 processes are unconfined but have a profile defined.
```

You can see that there is already a policy for the `clamd` service. These profiles are installed with their relevant package, the `clamd` profile supplied with the `clamav-daemon` package.

To create your own profile, you need to create a test plan, which is a plan that runs and executes the process you are profiling. You then run the program with the `aa-genprof` command. The profile is built after answering questions about the application access. The resultant profile can then be copied into the `/etc/apparmor.d/` directory and enabled by issuing the following:

```
$ sudo aa-enforce /etc/apparmor.d/<your profile>
```

Apparmor is distributed on Ubuntu and OpenSUSE but can be installed on Debian and CentOS.

We have only touched on these subjects. It would be good for you to read the following documents:

- https://www.linux.com/learn/overview-linux-kernel-security-features
- https://access.redhat.com/documentation/en-US/Red_Hat_Enterprise_Linux/7/html/SELinux_Users_and_Administrators_Guide/index.html
- https://wiki.centos.org/HowTos/SELinux
- https://wiki.ubuntu.com/AppArmor
- https://help.ubuntu.com/lts/serverguide/apparmor.html

It is a sensible idea to use either one of the two with any Internet-facing system.

Configuring ClamAV

You generally won't need to change any of ClamAV's configuration options, but you should know a bit about how it is configured. On CentOS, the ClamAV daemon is configured via the `/etc/clamd.d/scan.conf` file. The `scan.conf` file configures the ClamAV daemon. The package installation process also creates a cron entry (in the `/etc/cron.daily` directory) for the FreshClam update tool that updates ClamAV's signatures once a day.

On Ubuntu, the ClamAV daemon is configured via the `/etc/clamav/clamd.conf` configuration file and the `freshclam` update daemon via the `/etc/clamav/freshclam.conf` configuration file. Rather than a cron job on Ubuntu, the FreshClam service is run as a daemon and will try to download any available signatures several times per day.

On both CentOS and Ubuntu, running the ClamAV daemon will create a Unix socket file. This special type of file is used by the ClamAV milter to communicate with the antivirus scanner. E-mail is submitted to the socket, scanned, and then returned to the ClamAV milter with an assessment of whether it is a virus. This assessment is then added in the form of the `X-Spam-Virus` header to the scanned e-mail.

On CentOS, this socket is located by default in `/var/run/clamd.scan/clamd.sock`, and you can see a listing of it here:

```
$ sudo ls -l /var/run/clamd.scan/clamd.sock
srw-rw-rw-. 1 clamscan clamscan 0 Sep  3 04:07 /var/run/clamd.scan/clamd.sock
```

On Ubuntu, the socket is located in the `/var/run/clamav` directory and is called `clamd.ctl`.

```
$ sudo ls -lart /var/run/clamav/clamd.ctl
srw-rw-rw- 1 clamav clamav 0 Sep  3 11:20 /var/run/clamav/clamd.ctl
```

Testing Postfix with ClamAV

Now that you have the ClamAV milter enabled, you need to test to see whether your incoming e-mail is being scanned for viruses. To do this, use the swaks command and a special file that contains a test virus signature called eicar.txt, as we demonstrate here:

```
$ swaks -tls -a -au ataylor -ap password -t jsmith@example.com -f ataylor@example.com --body
eicar.txt
```

We've again used the swaks command to send an e-mail to jsmith@example.com. The file eicar.txt contains this string, which will trigger the virus scanner.

```
X5O!P%@AP[4\PZX54(P^)7CC)7}$EICAR-STANDARD-ANTIVIRUS-TEST-FILE!$H+H*
```

■ **Note** You would substitute the appropriate values for a user in your environment to test this.

This e-mail will be received and processed by your MTA and then passed to the ClamAV milter that will talk to the ClamAV scanner and, then based on your configuration, passed to SpamAssassin for analysis. The e-mail will be submitted to the user jsmith's mailbox, and you can then examine the contents of the e-mail's headers. In Listing 12-15, you can see the headers of the e-mail we've just sent.

Listing 12-15. E-mail Headers After SpamAssassin with ClamAV Scan

```
X-Spam-Checker-Version: SpamAssassin 3.4.0 (2014-02-07) on
X-Spam-Level: *
X-Spam-Status: No, score=-0.9 required=5.0 tests=ALL_TRUSTED,MISSING_MID
X-Mailer: swaks v20130209.0 jetmore.org/john/code/swaks/
X-Virus-Scanned: clamav-milter 0.99.2 at mail.example.com
X-Virus-Status: Infected (Eicar-Test-Signature)
```

In Listing 12-15, you can see that a header called X-Spam-Virus has been added to the e-mail. The header in Listing 12-15 has a value of Infected and the signature it matched. If a virus had been detected, the header would be marked Clean.

What to Do with an Infected E-mail?

Like with the X-Spam-Status header, you can use this header to process e-mail identified as containing a virus differently, for example, if you wanted to move all such e-mail to a separate folder called Viruses. You can do this using the Sieve configurations you previously used to sort spam e-mail into a separate folder. To do this using Sieve, you add a recipe like the following to your user's ~/.dovecot.sieve file:

```
require ["fileinto"];
if header :contains "X-Virus-Status" "" {
        fileinto "Spam";
}
if not header :contains "X-Virus-Status" "Clean" {
        fileinto "Virus";
}
```

However, it may be better to not pass on infected files to your users at all. You can quarantine your infected files on the mail server by setting the `OnInfected Quarantine` value in the `clamav-milter.conf` file. We set it earlier to accept so that we could see the mail arrive in our inbox. However, it would be prudent now to stop that mail from getting through and being mistakenly opened by someone.

Getting Help with ClamAV

You can find a variety of resources for troubleshooting ClamAV. You should start with the ClamAV home page (`www.clamav.net/`). On the same site, you'll find a variety of support resources available (`www.clamav.net/support/`), and you can join the ClamAV mailing list (`www.clamav.net/support/ml/`). You can find a list of current bugs at `www.clamav.net/bugs/`.

Remember, if you submit a question or a bug, you should include the following information:

- Your ClamAV version (run the `clamscan` command with the `--version` option)

- Your platform (run `uname -a`)

- Any log messages generated (either in `/var/log/clamav/clamav.log` or in the `/var/log/clamav/freshclam.log` file on Ubuntu, or the `/var/log/clamav/clamd.log` or `/var/log/clamav/freshclam.log` file on CentOS)

Also available is an IRC channel called #clamav on the Freenode IRC server (`http://freenode.net/`) where you can seek assistance.

SPF and DKIM, Controlling Your E-mail

There are further actions that we can take to help defeat spam. Neither of these methods by themselves will stop spam, but each is a part of tools that help make it harder for spam to get through. They do help stop spammers from forging your domain name when they send their mail.

The Sender Policy Framework (SPF) is used to identify an e-mail server that can send e-mail on behalf of your domain. Domain Keys Identified Mail (DKIM) is a way that mail coming from your servers can be identified by validating a header against your publicly available key.

SPF

SPF uses text records added to your DNS for your domain. Your SPF record tells the e-mail servers receiving your e-mail if they should accept or reject it based on the server sending it. Let's take an example where you send the company's marketing newsletter to your clients via MailChimp or Sendgrid or one of the many alternative bulk e-mail services. When the e-mail comes into your client's e-mail server, it will come from the one of the bulk e-mail provider's e-mail servers. How can the client's e-mail server be sure it really came from your marketing team?

With SPF we can tell our client's e-mail server that it should accept e-mail from this bulk e-mail service on our behalf. In this way, we can say that e-mail server `1.bulk.mailer.net` can send mail for the `example.com` domain.

Let's take a look at an example DNS record for our `example.com` domain. We are going to add a TXT record for the `example.com` domain.

```
example.com.    IN  TXT "v=spf1 mx -all"
```

Here we are editing the zone file for `example.com` and adding the TXT record. You may also commonly see this as an SPF record that has been depreciated. The TXT record itself contains the version of SPF (`spf1`), what e-mail servers can send for our domain (all listed MX servers), and if we should accept or reject e-mail from servers not in that list (`-all`).

In this example, we say that any server listed as an MX record is able to send mail on our behalf. So how would we allow 1.bulk.mailer.net to be able to send e-mail on our behalf? Instead of specifying mx, we can specify hostnames, IPv4 or IPv6, CIDRs, and combinations of these. The bulk e-mail service will generally have an address range of IP addresses it uses to send mail. You would add those to your SPF records. This RFC has more details on what is accepted: https://tools.ietf.org/html/rfc7208#section-3.

The –all option indicates that we want the receiving e-mail server to reject any e-mail not from one of our determined e-mail servers. You can set this to ~all, which tells the receiving e-mail server to not reject it but to flag it as forged. If you are in full control of the e-mail for your domain, you should be able to set it to –all.

For help in creating your SPF record, you can go to the following site. It will generate the SPF record based on the information you enter: http://spfwizard.com/.

Once this is done for our e-mail services, we need to set it up so that our e-mail server receiving e-mail also uses SPF to validate e-mail being sent to it. To do that, we need to add another package that will handle this validation.

For Ubuntu, we have to add the following package:

```
$ sudo aptitdue install -y postfix-policyd-spf-python
```

For CentOS, we will add this package:

```
$ sudo yum install -y pypolicyd-spf.noarch
```

Then the configuration for Postfix simply consists of adding the following to /etc/postfix/main.cf:

```
smtpd_recipient_restrictions =
....
    reject_unauth_destination
    check_policy_service unix:private/policyd-spf
    reject_rbl_client zen.spamhaus.org
...
policyd-spf_time_limit = 3600
```

Then to /etc/postfix/master.cf, we need the following:

```
policyd-spf  unix -     n      n      -      0      spawn
 user=nobody argv=/usr/libexec/postfix/policyd-spf
```

We can change the configuration for our Postfix SPF by editing either /etc/postfix-policyd-spf-python/policyd-spf.conf (Ubuntu) or /etc/python-policyd-spf/policyd-spf.conf (CentOS). The man page for policyd-spf.conf describes the configuration options. The defaults should be fine, but you might want to adjust skip_addresses and set the debug_level (1 to 5 with 5 being most verbose).

Now when you send a test e-mail, you will see the following header being added to the e-mail (which SpamAssasin will use in the calculation of spam scores):

```
X-Spam-Checker-Version: SpamAssassin 3.4.0 (2014-02-07) on
        ip-10-0-10-154.ap-southeast-2.compute.internal
X-Spam-Level: *
X-Spam-Status: No, score=1.8 required=5.0 tests=MISSING_SUBJECT autolearn=no
        autolearn_force=no version=3.4.0
Received-SPF: Pass (sender SPF authorized)  identity=mailfrom; client-ip=31.28.208.98;
helo=mail.example.net; envelope-from=ataylor@example.net; receiver=jsmith@example.com
X-Virus-Scanned: clamav-milter 0.99.2 at mail.example.com
X-Virus-Status: Clean
```

You can see now we have `Received-SPF: Pass (sender SPF authorized)`, which means that we have looked up the TXT record for `example.net` and found that `mail.example.net` was able to send mail for the `example.net` domain.

Let's now look at setting up Domain Key Identified Mail.

DKIM

Domain Key Identified Mail is where we will add a signature header to the mail we send so that other mail servers can verify it came from us via our published public key. You have seen the public key infrastructure (PKI) being used to validate web servers and domain records. Now we can use the framework to validate e-mail we are sending.

We are going to publish our public key again via DNS so that other mail servers can validate our signature. Also, we will need the OpenDKIM package to manage our DKIM service.

```
$ sudo yum install -y opendkim (CentOS)
$ sudo aptitude install -y opendkim (Ubuntu)
```

This will install the OpenDKIM packages as well as create the `opendkim` user. On both Ubuntu and CentOS you can configure OpenDKIM via the configuration file `/etc/opendkim.conf` file, and we will make the following configuration settings:

```
Mode                sv
SubDomains          no
SignHeaders         From,Subject,Date
OversignHeaders     From,Subject,Date
Syslog              yes
UMask               002
UserID              opendkim
KeyTable            /etc/opendkim/KeyTable
SigningTable        refile:/etc/opendkim/SigningTable
ExternalIgnoreList  /etc/opendkim/TrustedHosts
InternalHosts       /etc/opendkim/TrustedHosts

Canonicalization    relaxed
AutoRestart         yes
AutoRestartRate     10/1M
Background          yes
DNSTimeout          5
SignatureAlgorithm  rsa-sha256
Socket              /var/spool/opendkim/opendkim.socket
```

We will not go through each line, but we will draw you to the first two lines that declare `Mode` and `SubDomains`. `Mode` can be `s` or `v` or `sv`. The `s` means signing, the `v` means verifying, and `sv` means both. `SubDomains` `no` means that we will not sign the subdomains of the domains we have listed in our table files. We have also set a socket file, which we will connect to Postfix later.

Last, we will talk about `SignHeaders` and `OversignHeaders` `From`. We include headers in our signatures, and we tell OpenDKIM to include the `From,Subject,Date` headers. You can include others if you want, but the From header must be signed. `OverSignHeaders` tells OpenDKIM to include these headers, even if they are absent, and record them as null, which prevents them from being added at a later date.

On Ubuntu we will create the required OpenDKIM directories with the following:

```
$ sudo mkdir -p /etc/opendkim/keys && sudo touch /etc/opendkim/{KeyTable,SigningTable,Trust
edHosts}
$ sudo mkdir -p /var/spool/opendkim
$ sudo chown opendkim:opendkim -R /etc/opendkim/* /var/spool/opendkim && sudo chmod 0640 /
etc/opendkim/*
$ sudo chmod 0750 /etc/opendkim/keys
```

Next we are going to address the cryptographic configuration now. We need to add our domain to the table files. First we will edit /etc/opendkim/SigningTable. We will add the following:

```
*@example.com    example
```

This tells OpenDKIM to sign all addresses in the example.com domain (*@example.com), and it has the shortened name of example. Next we edit the /etc/opendkim/KeyTable file with the following:

```
example    example.com:201609:/etc/opendkim/keys/example.com.private
```

Here we are using the shortened name to like in the KeyTable to the match like the one in the SigningTable. Then we see the domain and the selector, which is a unique and arbitrary value (used during the DNS lookup and is in YYYYMM format), followed by the private key we will use for the signing.

We are now going to edit the TrustedHosts file to add our trusted hosts we will be mailing from.

```
127.0.0.1
::1
localhost
mail
mail.example.com
example.com
```

This covers the different names our hosts can be referred to. We are now going generate our keys. We do that with the following commands:

```
$ opendkim-genkey -D /etc/opendkim/keys -a -d example.com -b 2048 -r -s 201609
$ sudo ls -l /etc/opendkim/keys
total 8
-rw-------. 1 root root 1679 Sep  5 09:21 201609.private
-rw-------. 1 root root  504 Sep  5 09:21 201609.txt
```

Here we have created a 2,048-bit private key (-b 2048) and a public key in the /etc/opendkim/keys directory (-D). We append the domain (-a), which appends our domain to the zone file stub. The -d says we are generating the keys for a particular domain. You can remove this if you want to use the same key for multiple domains. We have also restricted this key (-r) to e-mail only. The -s is the selector, which, as we have said, is used in the DNS name lookup.

We are going to move these two generated file to the names we specified in our KeyTable file.

```
$ sudo mv /etc/opendkim/keys/201609.private /etc/opendkim/keys/example.com.private
$ sudo mv /etc/opendkim/keys/201609.txt /etc/opendkim/keys/example.com.txt
$ sudo chown opendkim /etc/opendkim/keys/ownenergy.com.au.private
```

We now need to update our DNS again with the text in the example.com.txt file. If we look inside that, we will see the following:

```
201609._domainkey.example.com. IN TXT ( "v=DKIM1; k=rsa; s=email; "
"p=MIIBIjANBgkqhkiG9w0BAQEFAAOCAQ8AMIIBCgKCAQEAz5DbbqRCsZ564tDCDeonTkr4ggYrVr5H19qBCYPwnks
FyqzmQtpntQq78hpt7lcYghwmhDT9V3o72lUKYn151p6e3rsvtSXmNHuhgxHRwozDf7NdQeDEzpEa7+/
UdWvDDtmg9Bbsx6kLhOfTZU8TvnOW3UCJPFkzKNhCg5rrZGLXUqsoS762T4gLDJYCrgkIxUW1KEazkRn1mr" "XvcvE+
wt6QL4GPcz6ddPYw4DS9sdZ17DZMa7ngv2COEjrQwfTcIfoTkfc2G6GgjayVM+RgAs234Eo6+7tX+W7ZmXpzgk2YtHah
1cNjHV2dAgGRo/B6H2WoKK89LkZsfTzMYjasfQIDAQAB" )  ; ----- DKIM key 201609 for example.com
```

DNS TXT records cannot have strings longer than 255 characters; we will need to break this up into multiple lines. We need to copy the data between the (). For our Bind DNS, we can add this as a multiline DNS record:

```
201609._domainkey IN TXT ("v=DKIM1 ; k=rsa, s=email; "
    "p= MIIBIjANBgkqhkiG ... "
    "XvcvE+wt6Q ... jasfQIDAQAB")
```

If you are using an external DNS provider, you may need to use multiline too (AWS Route53, for example). It is best to consult any of the documentation on DKIM. We can now validate our DNS record using the following command:

```
opendkim-testkey -d example.com -s 201609
```

No output means we are successful. We are now going to enable and start opendkim.

```
$ sudo systemctl enable opendkim
$ sudo systemctl start opendkim
```

To configure Postfix, we need to add another milter. We do that by editing the main.cf file again.

```
smtpd_milters = unix:/var/run/clamav-milter/clamav-milter.socket unix:/var/spool/opendkim/
opendkim.socket
```

We will add the opendkim group to the postfix user.

```
$ sudo usermod -aG opendkim postfix
```

We then will need to fix our SELinux policy.
We can restart Postfix now too.

```
$ sudo systemctl restart postfix
```

We can now send ourselves an e-mail to one of our external addresses. We chose a Gmail address, and if we view the headers of that e-mail, we see this:

```
Authentication-Results: mx.google.com;
      dkim=pass header.i=@example.com;
      spf=pass (google.com: domain of jsmith@example.com designates 52.82.67.42 as
      permitted sender) smtp.mailfrom=jsmith@example.com
Received: by mail.example.com (Postfix, from userid 1000)
```

```
id 99CFA187135A; Tue,  6 Sep 2016 07:59:43 -0400 (EDT)
DKIM-Signature: v=1; a=rsa-sha256; c=relaxed/simple;
d=example.com; s=201609; t=1473163183;
bh=ShAzA6t1zCobzHEAhrmK5udJcy/7FvQ3DqD9cIsQ/Lk=;
h=Date:Subject:From:From:Subject:Date;
b=ecfUXsieztVsVnngyFtsY1RrAeApoCCt+MoAclGdrS4XmSEOQIMrq3olstlsLm8WO
 /qmV5MSxvFzpQoEXZ5RnRMyoOVPAgaHx4gSP5mjEpWozawD4KYC6WAO9jxVNSX8fzU
 McOJn7wQdDIWAjXjvOubEkFFn9AyLs77aUhwRjOT2CwpJhSzzPYvWOR+LZrO6PymTf
 FQ6C9t4jMSRfGDHnWMTp/QkleeSjCzLlebaQFaDgo38phdNYx2LOKLxdyqzJq/nkeK
 2XXM7rGRM9fllTMy4OHDiabvjSg2GfubOMkwKiJaEv7SOFc5MrW6nGFR+3s5u4jdq8
 kKDmm2pyeR+oQ==
```

The `Authentication-Results` header is now added to the e-mail we have sent, and you can see that our public key has been added too. You can also use an external validator service like this:

```
echo 'hello' | mail check-auth@verifier.port25.com
```

This sends an e-mail to `check-auth@verfier.port25.com`, which will run a report on your DKIM and SPF settings and e-mail a detailed report to you.

Configuring IMAP and POP3

Unlike what you've seen in most of the earlier sections of this chapter, your users aren't going to be directly accessing their e-mail via the command line. They will want to access it from an e-mail client on their local desktop. This is where an IMAP or POP3 server comes into its own. These protocols represent two different methods of accessing mailboxes from a mail client or MUA. We're going to examine both methods, explain the pros and cons of each, and demonstrate how to configure and implement them in your environment.

IMAP

IMAP is used for accessing e-mail mailboxes from a remote client, like a desktop or laptop. Your client connects to the IMAP server, and you can read, manage, and delete any e-mail in your mailbox. You can also search messages, create and delete folders, and perform a variety of other management tasks.

POP3

POP3 is also used for accessing e-mail mailboxes from a remote client. E-mail is received and held in the users' mailboxes until they check their e-mail. When a user's e-mail client connects, all waiting e-mail is downloaded to the client and removed from the server.

What's the Difference?

The IMAP protocol acts much like a file server. Your e-mail stays on the server and can be read, deleted, and manipulated. POP3 is a store-and-forward mechanism. Each of the basic protocols offers advantages and disadvantages.

Advantages of IMAP:

- Allows users to access e-mail from multiple locations, not just their client

- Allows webmail access

- Protects your messages from accidental deletion

- Centralizes e-mail, making backup and recovery easier

Advantages of POP3:

- You don't need to be connected to the server (or indeed the network) to have access to your e-mail.

- It doesn't use any storage on your server—all mail is stored on your clients after retrieval.

Disadvantages of IMAP:

- You need to be able to connect to the server (and hence the network and/or Internet) to access your e-mail.

- It requires sufficient storage on your server.

Disadvantages of POP3:

- Mail is present only on the client and can't be accessed from elsewhere.

- Users can lose e-mail if they lose, damage, or rebuild their client desktop, laptop, and so on, without sufficient backups.

- If users require e-mail to be backed up, a per-client backup and recovery strategy can be complex and difficult to implement.

Choosing Between IMAP and POP3

For the vast majority of circumstances, we recommend you use IMAP. The reasons for this are simplicity and ease of use. IMAP allows your users to roam with or without their client; for example, an IMAP server allows a user to have access to her e-mail via her laptop and a smart phone or other mobile device.

Your user's e-mail is also in a central location, which makes it easy for you to back it up (and recover it when one of your users inevitably deletes a vital e-mail). Additionally, with the cheap cost of storage, it is no longer an issue in most organizations to store e-mail centrally on a server or disk array.

The major caveat is that if your users cannot connect to the IMAP server, they will not be able to retrieve their e-mail. We consider the benefit of IMAP's other advantages outweigh the risk in this case.

In this section, we'll demonstrate how to configure IMAP in our examples. If you are interested in configuring POP3 instead, you can see some instructions, tips, and caveats at `http://wiki.dovecot.org/POP3Server` and `http://wiki.dovecot.org/QuickConfiguration`.

Introducing Dovecot IMAP

You've already been introduced to the Dovecot server because we're using it in our example as an authentication service for Postfix. There is some good news as a result. If you've been following along up to this point, you've already installed, started, and partially configured Dovecot. This means you have a limited number of steps you need to take to get it working now.

In this section, we're going to show you how to turn on IMAP, specifically the secure version of the IMAP protocol called IMAPS (with the *S* meaning *Secure*). This uses SSL encryption to protect both user authentication and the content of users' e-mail as it flows between the client and the server. The other main difference between IMAP and IMAPS is the TCP port they run on. The IMAP protocol runs on port 143, while the IMAPS protocol runs on port 993. You will need to specify this port number (and potentially tell your client to use SSL) in your mail client.

■ **Tip**   The POP3 protocol runs on TCP port 110, and its secure counterpart, SSL-POP3, runs on TCP port 995.

We're also going to configure Dovecot to find our local Maildir mailboxes. We don't need to configure authentication because we've already done it. The same authentication mechanism we enabled for Postfix, using the PAM authentication to check the local user's username and password, will work fine for IMAP connections.

Configuring Dovecot

The Dovecot server is configured using the `dovecot.conf` configuration file, as you discovered earlier in this chapter. On both distributions this file is located at `/etc/dovecot/dovecot.conf`. Let's start our configuration process by enabling the IMAPS protocol and specifying the location of the SSL certificates we're going to use. To make this easy, we're going to reuse the same certificates we created for our Postfix encryption.

First, we enable IMAP by editing the `protocols` configuration option and changing it from `lmtp` to `lmtp imap` like so:

```
protocols = lmtp imap
```

We specify how IMAP listens in the `/etc/dovecot/conf.d/10-master.conf` file. We need to change the `service imap-login` to the following:

```
service imap-login {
  inet_listener imap {
    port = 0
  }
  inet_listener imaps {
    port = 993
    ssl = yes
  }
}
```

This turns off the non-SSL plain-text port and listens only on the SSL port 993.

Next, we specify our SSL certificate and key files. To do this, we need to uncomment and update the `ssl_cert_file` and `ssl_key_file` options and add the location of our certificate and key. The file is located at `/etc/dovecot/conf.d/10-ssl.conf`.

```
ssl = required

ssl_cert = </etc/letsencrypt/live/mail.exmaple.com/cert.pem
ssl_key = </etc/letsencrypt/live/mail.example.com/privkey.pem
ssl_ca = </etc/letsencrypt/live/mail.example.com/chain.pem
# SSL protocols to use
```

```
ssl_protocols = !SSLv2 !SSLv3
ssl_cipher_list = ALL:!LOW:!SSLv2:!SSLv3:!EXP:!aNULL
# Prefer the server's order of ciphers over client's.
ssl_prefer_server_ciphers = yes
```

The certificate and key files we're going to use are the same ones we used to provide Postfix's encryption. You could follow the same steps we followed in that section to create Dovecot-specific certificates, or you could even buy additional certificates specifically for Dovecot if you want, but we don't feel this is necessary.

■ **Note** Remember, your certificate is tied to a hostname, in our case `mail.example.com`. If you are running your Dovecot server on another host, you should create a new key and certificate with the hostname of the server running Dovecot. Additionally, as the certificate is tied to the hostname, you must specify this hostname (`mail.example.com` for this example) in your mail client rather than any other DNS name the host may be known as.

Next, we uncomment and change the `disable_plaintext_auth` option to yes in the `/etc/dovecot/conf.d/10-auth.conf` file.

```
disable_plaintext_auth = yes
```

This option disables any plain-text authentication unless SSL is enabled and an encrypted connection is running. This protects our user's authentication credentials from attacks that might sniff or grab them off the network or Internet.

Finally, make sure we have the right location of our mailboxes using the `mail_location` option (which we set up previously). You will need to edit `/etc/dovecot/conf.d/10-mail.conf`.

```
mail_location = maildir:~/Maildir
```

This tells Dovecot we're using `Maildirs` located in the user's home directory, or ~, and in the directory `Maildir`.

Now we need to restart the Dovecot server, and then we can test to see whether we can make a connection and retrieve our e-mail on our server, for example:

```
$ sudo systemctl restart dovecot
```

Testing Dovecot

Now that we've configured Dovecot, we can enable a client and test its access. We're going to configure a Mozilla Thunderbird client to test Dovecot; of course, you can use any IMAP client.

■ **Note** Mozilla Thunderbird is a popular open source mail client released by the Mozilla Foundation, which also developed the Firefox browser.

To configure the client, we first need to install it. On both CentOS and Ubuntu, the required package is called `thunderbird`, and you should use your Application Installer tool (or package manager) to install it.

Now, let's review what we need to know in order to configure our client:

- The name of our server

- Our username and password

We're going to launch the Mozilla Thunderbird mail client by selecting the menu options Applications ➤ Internet ➤ Thunderbird, as shown in Figure 12-4.

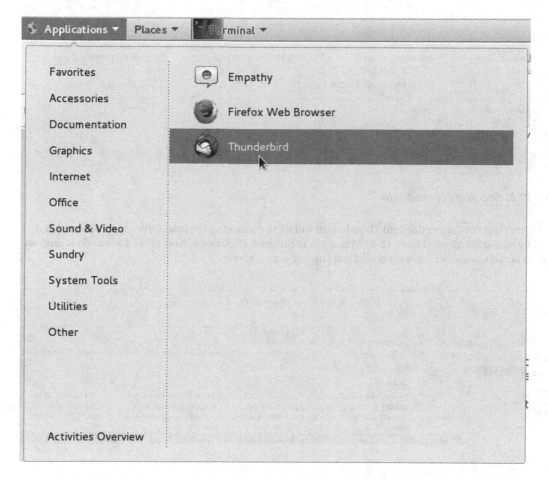

Figure 12-4. *Launching Mozilla Thunderbird*

If this is the first time you've launched Thunderbird, the Account Wizard will start. This wizard allows you to create an account with a service provider. You can create a new account by selecting Preferences ➤ Account Settings and clicking Add Account.

By now most people will be familiar with setting up an e-mail client. You will need details similar to Figure 12-5.

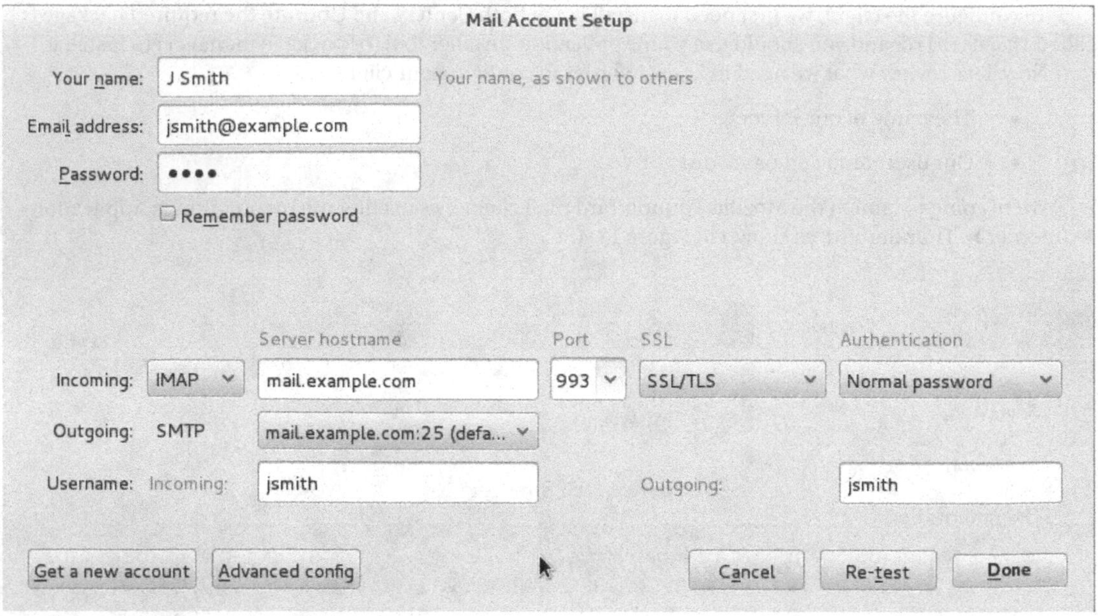

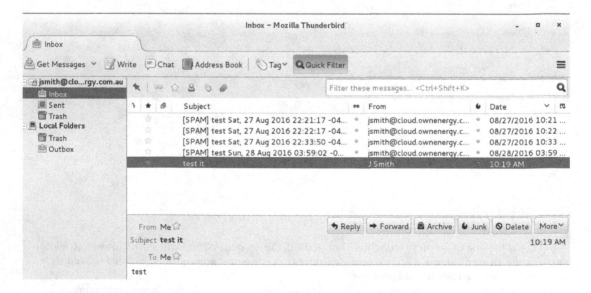

Figure 12-5. *Specifying server details*

You can test the connection and Thunderbird will try to connect to the mail server and validate that it is actually an e-mail server (Figure 12-6). When you're finished, click Done. Now all we have to do is send an e-mail to ourselves and we have successfully set up our e-mail server.

Figure 12-6. *Testing our ability to send and receive e-mail*

You should also be able to see a record of your connection and authentication in the appropriate log file for your distribution: /var/log/maillog on CentOS and /var/log/mail.log on Ubuntu, as you can see in Listing 12-16.

Listing 12-16. Dovecot Authentication Log Entries

```
Sep  6 10:19:49 ip-10-0-10-154 dovecot: imap-login: Login: user=<jsmith>, method=PLAIN,
rip=203.217.94.151, lip=10.0.10.154, mpid=2762, TLS, session=<aqdGfdc72ADL2V6X>
Sep  6 10:25:18 ip-10-0-10-154 dovecot: imap(jsmith): Disconnected: Disconnected in IDLE
in=1186 out=120979
```

Troubleshooting Dovecot

If something doesn't work or you can't connect to your Dovecot server, then we recommend the first place you look is in the log files. You can make this process easier as Dovecot has some useful debugging settings you can enable to get more verbose output if you are having an issue. Table 12-3 provides a list of these options.

Table 12-3. *Dovecot Debugging Options*

Option	Description
mail_debug	When set to yes, it shows more information about the mail process.
auth_verbose	When set to yes, it shows more information about the authentication process.
auth_debug	When set to yes, it shows debugging information about the authentication process.
auth_debug_ password	If both auth_debug and this option are set to yes, the authentication mechanisms and password are displayed.

Turn on one or more of these options to see verbose debugging information. This information is sent to the syslog daemon and hence onto either your /var/log/maillog or /var/log/mail.log log files. The additional information should make it much easier to determine whether anything is wrong with your Dovecot installation.

■ **Note**   You must restart the Dovecot server after changing any of these options, and we recommend setting the options back to no after you've fixed any issues. Leaving debugging on can impact the performance of your Dovecot server.

Getting Help with Dovecot

A considerable amount of useful information is available to help you resolve any potential issues with Dovecot. The best place to start when trying to get help is the Dovecot home page at www.dovecot.org/. The site includes a comprehensive wiki (http://wiki.dovecot.org/) including a number of how-tos and examples for configuring Dovecot in variety of implementations. Also available are the Dovecot mailing lists (www.dovecot.org/mailinglists.html) and bug submission instructions (www.dovecot.org/bugreport.html).

Remember that if you submit a question or a bug, you should include the following information:

- Your Dovecot version (run the dovecot command with the --version option)

- Include your configuration, which you can get with doveconf -n

- Your platform (run uname -a)

- Any log messages generated (either in the /var/log/mail.log file on Ubuntu or in the /var/log/maillog file on CentOS)

Also available is an IRC channel called #dovecot on the Freenode IRC server (http://freenode.net/) where you can seek assistance.

Virtual Domains and Users

We've introduced the basics of providing e-mail to your users in this chapter. Here we'll discuss the ways you can extend the mail services we've introduced in this chapter.

The primary way you can extend Postfix and Dovecot is into virtual domains and virtual users. Up until now, we've assumed that the domain we're delivering mail for and the users who receive that mail are all physical instantiations. The domain we're accepting e-mail for is the domain the mail server belongs to, and our users actually exist on our mail server. With virtual domains and users, you can configure destinations and recipients for e-mail that aren't physical. We're not going to demonstrate these concepts, but we'll explain them and refer you to documentation that will allow you to extend what we've built in this chapter to do all of this.

Hosting virtual domains allows you to receive e-mail for additional domains. For example, say you currently receive mail for the domain example.com. Your company might also have the domains product. com and anotherproduct.com. You can configure Postfix to receive e-mail for these additional domains.

Virtual users are a similar concept. Thus far, all our users have existed as actual Linux users, jsmith and ataylor, for example. Their mailboxes have been stored in the /home directory tree. With virtual users, your mail users don't need to be created as operating system users. Each e-mail address is mapped to a virtual user or a user contained in a database such as MySQL or LDAP. This reduces the need to create and manage large numbers of operating system users.

You can find a complete how-to on configuring virtual domains and users with Postfix at www.postfix. org/VIRTUAL_README.html. You can find a more Ubuntu-specific guide at https://help.ubuntu.com/ community/PostfixCompleteVirtualMailSystemHowto. You can also find instructions for extending Dovecot in a similar way at http://wiki.dovecot.org/VirtualUsers and on the Dovecot how-to page at http://wiki.dovecot.org/HowTo.

Alternative Mail Servers for Linux

There are several free and commercial e-mail solutions that provide more features than those described in this chapter. Many people expect things such as calendaring, enterprise authentication, file sharing, and collaborative features to be part of their daily work experience and requirements.

Table 12-4 lists some of the solutions that have been around for many years. They offer their software under different licenses, but each has an open source edition. Many offer additional features at commercial rates and support agreements.

Table 12-4. *List of Alternative E-mail Solutions*

Kolab Community	Free Software (`https://www.gnu.org/philosophy/free-sw.en.html`).
Open-Xchange	Free for noncommercial use. Payment for commercial license (`https://www.open-xchange.com/terms-and-conditions`).
Zimbra	Open source edition free. Commercial licenses available to get certain features (`https://www.zimbra.com/legal/licensing/`).
iRedMail	Open source with commercial add-ons (`https://creativecommons.org/licenses/by-nd/3.0/us/`).

Summary

In this chapter, we introduced you to mail services on a Linux host that allow your users to send and receive e-mail from your organization. We discussed IMAP and POP3, protocols that allow your users to connect to your host and retrieve and manage their e-mail in mailboxes.

In the process, we covered some important concepts:

- Protecting your users' e-mail and their authentication credentials via encryption

- Enabling SASL authentication to allow your users to safely and securely authenticate to your mail server to send and receive e-mail

- Making use of SpamAssassin to filter your e-mail and stop spam from reaching your users

- Using the open source ClamAV antivirus engine to check your user's e-mail for viruses and malware

- Using LMTPs such as Dovecot and Sieve to filter your e-mail

- Further protecting your server and its reputation by using SPF and DKIM

- Implementing the Dovecot server to allow users to connect to their mailboxes and retrieve e-mail

In the next chapter, we'll introduce you to file and print services and teach you how to run your own NFS server and look at clustered network file systems.

CHAPTER 13

■ ■ ■

File Sharing and Printing

By Dennis Matotek

One of the most common office functions is sharing/printing documents and files. In this chapter, we will show you how this can be done using Linux. Linux provides many ways to share information. It can share information with Microsoft Windows clients or macOS using an integration tool called Samba. It can also share documents between Linux (and other Unix) hosts using a tool called Network File System (NFS).

In heterogeneous environments, it has become increasingly common to move document management and storage into cloud-based providers. These services are widespread and have several key advantages over traditional file sharing such as version control, multiple device support, collaboration features, and some support workflows. Businesses now expect this ease of access to documents, and neither Samba nor NFS is particularly suited for this work.

To go beyond basic file sharing, though, we are going to introduce you to different platforms that can be cheap and effective for document management. We will give a list of possible alternatives for this.

Lastly, we'll show you how to configure printing and print services on your Linux host. We'll demonstrate both how to print from your host and how to make your host act as a print server. Printing on Linux is easy to implement, and both CentOS and Ubuntu share a common toolset that makes it easy to implement and manage.

File Sharing with Samba and NFS

File sharing is the ability to share documents between your users. Rather than everyone keeping company documents on their individual desktop computers and passing them via means such as e-mail, we centralize the documents in one place and allow our staff to access them in a controlled and secure way. The benefits of this are enormous, as it cuts down on the proliferation of multiple copies of one document on everyone's desktops and makes restricting access and backing up documents much easier. Certain applications require a file share before they can be accessed by desktop clients, and file sharing can be used for this.

On your desktops, you can mount a network drive. A file share can be assigned when you log in to your host either via a domain controller that runs login scripts or manually when you require one. You can also mount file shares on your Linux desktop. Linux desktops can easily mount a Samba or NFS share; however, they can't run Windows executable files without some modification.

■ **Note**   You may get some success running some Windows applications using software developed by Wine (www.winehq.org). This open source community works on integrating a selected group of Windows applications to run on Linux operating systems (or macOS). There is also a supported version offered by sister organization CodeWeavers (www.codeweavers.com).

© Dennis Matotek, James Turnbull and Peter Lieverdink 2017
D. Matotek et al., *Pro Linux System Administration*, DOI 10.1007/978-1-4842-2008-5_13

File sharing can be achieved in many ways using Linux, depending on your needs for access, security, and the clients you have to support. Linux can provide a good platform for traditional file sharing, as it gives you the ability to mount a network drive on your client host. This allows for access to common data shared by a centralized file server host. The two main tools for achieving this are Samba for Microsoft Windows desktops and NFS for Linux or Unix hosts (macOS can use either).

Samba can provide user authentication for file shares and printer services. NFS on its own does not provide any user authentication, but it can be integrated into a Kerberos domain for authentication. This is complicated to set up, and we will not attempt to cover it in this book.

Next, we give you an up-close look at Samba.

Samba

Samba is a file-sharing and printing service for Linux. It operates in the standard client-server model with a daemon accepting requests from network clients. It is based on the Common Internet Filesystem (CIFS) and Server Message Block (SMB) protocols, the protocols that handle interhost communications of the filesystem on Microsoft products, making Samba compatible with Microsoft Windows desktop clients and Microsoft Windows domain services.

There are currently two supported versions of Samba, version 3.*x* and version 4.*x*. What you are trying to achieve will form your view as to which is best for you. Version 4.*x* is emulating Active Directory (AD), while version 3.*x* is more like NT 4. Version 3.*x* supports Lightweight Directory Access Protocol (LDAP) integration, while LDAP integration in version 4.*x* is still experimental. Also, Samba 4 currently supports up to Windows Server 2012 R2, but 2012 servers will require a Windows 2008 server to join the Samba AD first. Windows Server 2012 or 2012 R2 directory schemas are currently experimental. Please see `https://wiki.samba.org/index.php/Joining_a_Windows_Client_or_Server_to_a_Domain` to find out what clients are supported and how to join a domain for Windows clients and servers (2008 and 2012).

In this example, we are going to show you how to implement version 4.*x* of Samba and mount a drive on our macOS host. We show you how to set up a simple file using Samba that will allow you to share documents with your co-workers. You will also learn how to set up a Samba AD domain server so your users can authenticate, as well as how to set up a departmental share that you can also mount to your desktop.

Also, in this example, it is important to note that we are going to create a `samba.example.com` Domain Name System (DNS) subdomain. This is because Samba is going to manage this subdomain, which would conflict with our `example.com` domain. We are also setting up only one domain controller and having that act as our file server. The Samba documentation recommends that this setup is not suitable for production use, but instead we should have one or two Samba AD and a couple of file servers that hang off the ADs. Having more than one AD allows for ease of maintenance (you can perform maintenance on one while still serving with the other), reliability, and availability.

First you need to install the software. Both CentOS and Ubuntu require the same packages to get Samba up and running.

On CentOS, you issue the following:

```
$ sudo yum install samba-client samba-common samba winbind
```

However, CentOS 7 does not provide the samba-tool binary that we require to configure Samba AD. You can configure Samba as a classic NT4 server or you can buy a Samba software subscription from `https://www.sernet.de/en/samba/samba/` for CentOS. We suggest that you just use Samba with Ubuntu instead.

On Ubuntu, you issue the following:

```
$ sudo aptitude install samba-client samba-common samba winbind
```

Configuring Samba AD

We are going to install Samba on our Ubuntu server. To do that, we need to do several things.

- Set the hostname
- Update Apparmor
- Update DNS

Once these tasks are done, we can configure Samba.

First we need to make sure that our hostname is set correctly. We are going to use the hostname `dc1.samba.example.com`, which is unique in our domain. For a complete understanding of Samba naming recommendations, please read `https://wiki.samba.org/index.php/Active_Directory_Naming_FAQ`. Our host needs to match the following configuration:

```
$ hostname -s
dc1
$ hostname -d
samba.example.com
```

It is a good idea to add `dc1.samba.example.com` to your `/etc/hosts` file too.

```
127.0.0.1    localhost dc1 dc1.samba.example.com
```

Also, because we are going to let Samba manage its own DNS subdomain, we need to allow it access to bind configuration. The `bind9` server must be on the same server as the Samba AD server as it requires access to certain directories. Because we are using an Ubuntu server, we need to make some changes to Apparmor that will allow the `bind9` service to access Samba directories. Remember, we spoke about Apparmor in Chapter 12; it is a security module that describes security access for system resources (such as ports and files).

We will add the following to our `/etc/apparmor.d/local/usr.sbin.named` file, remembering that we add localhost changes into the `/etc/apparmor.d/local` directory:

```
# Samba4 DLZ and Active Directory Zones
/var/lib/samba/lib/** rm,
/var/lib/samba/private/dns.keytab r,
/var/lib/samba/private/named.conf r,
/var/lib/samba/private/dns/** rwk,
```

After saving this file, we then need to load this into Apparmor with the following:

```
$ sudo apparmor_parser -r /etc/apparmor.d/usr.sbin.named
```

To configure our `bind9` service in preparation for our Samba configuration, we are going to add the following to the bottom of our `/etc/bind/named.conf.options` file:

```
include "/var/lib/samba/private/named.conf";
```

We will need to reload our `bind9` configuration with the following:

```
$ sudo rndc reload
```

Now it's time to configure Samba. Samba provides a tool, called `samba-tool`, to help configure the Samba server. You may need to remove or copy off any existing `/etc/samba/smb.conf` file that is present on your system as the following command will create a new file for you.

In Listing 13-1, we have used `samba-tool` in interactive mode (`--interactive`). For a full list of options that you can provide on the command line, see `samba-tool provision --help`. We have provided the `--use-rfc2307` option, which tells Samba to store user and group information in the internal LDAP directory. This is useful for maintaining consistent user IDs/group IDs (UIDs/GIDs) across domain members and has some associated benefits; see `https://wiki.samba.org/index.php/Setting_up_RFC2307_in_AD`. We have also provided our preferred hostname (`--host-name`), dc1.

Listing 13-1. Configuring Samba with samba-tool

```
$ sudo samba-tool domain provision --use-rfc2307 --host-name=dc1 --interactive
Realm [SAMBA.EXAMPLE.COM]:
 Domain [SAMBA]:
 Server Role (dc, member, standalone) [dc]:
 DNS backend (SAMBA_INTERNAL, BIND9_FLATFILE, BIND9_DLZ, NONE) [SAMBA_INTERNAL]: BIND9_DLZ
Administrator password:
Retype password:
Looking up IPv4 addresses
More than one IPv4 address found. Using 192.168.0.10
Looking up IPv6 addresses
No IPv6 address will be assigned
Setting up secrets.ldb
Setting up the registry
Setting up the privileges database
Setting up idmap db
Setting up SAM db
Setting up sam.ldb partitions and settings
Setting up sam.ldb rootDSE
Pre-loading the Samba 4 and AD schema
Adding DomainDN: DC=samba,DC=example,DC=com
Adding configuration container
Setting up sam.ldb schema
Setting up sam.ldb configuration data
Setting up display specifiers
Modifying display specifiers
Adding users container
Modifying users container
Adding computers container
Modifying computers container
Setting up sam.ldb data
Setting up well known security principals
Setting up sam.ldb users and groups
Setting up self join
Adding DNS accounts
Creating CN=MicrosoftDNS,CN=System,DC=samba,DC=example,DC=com
Creating DomainDnsZones and ForestDnsZones partitions
Populating DomainDnsZones and ForestDnsZones partitions
See /var/lib/samba/private/named.conf for an example configuration include file for BIND
and /var/lib/samba/private/named.txt for further documentation required for secure DNS updates
Setting up sam.ldb rootDSE marking as synchronized
Fixing provision GUIDs
A Kerberos configuration suitable for Samba 4 has been generated at /var/lib/samba/private/
krb5.conf
```

```
Setting up fake yp server settings
Once the above files are installed, your Samba4 server will be ready to use
Server Role:           active directory domain controller
Hostname:              dc1
NetBIOS Domain:        SAMBA
DNS Domain:            samba.example.com
DOMAIN SID:            S-1-5-21-295742502-4045385941-247307200
```

In interactive mode we are given the defaults in the [ ] brackets, and we have chosen the defaults for Realm, Domain, and Server Role. The Server Role setting is dc, which stands for domain controller, meaning we are the authority for the Samba Windows domain, SAMBA.

For DNS, we have the options SAMBA_INTERNAL, BIND9_FLATFILE, BIND9_DLZ, and NONE. We have chosen BIND9_DLZ, which will tells Samba to manage our DNS subdomain dynamically through the special Samba module we included in our named.conf.options file previously. Samba will create all the necessary DNS records required during the setup process. SAMBA_INTERNAL is also suitable if you want to let Samba own and manage your DNS setup. BIND9_FLATFILE is not a recommended option, and you should choose NONE if you want to completely manage your own DNS.

You will be asked to provide the administrator password. The password needs to be eight or more characters and complex, requiring symbols, letters, and numbers. Once that has been entered, the setup of Samba completes quickly. Once it is complete, we can start our service.

```
$ sudo systemctl start samba-ad-dc
```

This starts the Samba service, and you can use the systemctl status samba-ad-dc command to check it has started alright. Also, remember to enable it on boot with systemctl enable samba-ad-dc.

Testing Samba

Now we can test that we can authenticate against the service. To do that, we use the smbclient command, which is the tool used to interact with the Samba service.

```
$ smbclient -L dc1 -U Administrator
Enter Administrator's password:
Domain=[EXAMPLE] OS=[Windows 6.1] Server=[Samba 4.3.9-Ubuntu]

	Sharename       Type        Comment
	---------       ----        -------
	netlogon        Disk
	sysvol          Disk
	IPC$            IPC         IPC Service (Samba 4.3.9-Ubuntu)
Domain=[EXAMPLE] OS=[Windows 6.1] Server=[Samba 4.3.9-Ubuntu]

	Server          Comment
	---------       -------

	Workgroup       Master
	---------       -------
	WORKGROUP       DC1
```

Here we have gotten a listing (-L) from our dc1 Samba service using the Administrator user (-U) to authenticate. If you get errors here, then you have made an error in your setup. There is a troubleshooting page that might help you here: https://wiki.samba.org/index.php/Samba_AD_DC_Troubleshooting.

You can see from the test that we have two disk shares (netlogon and sysvol) and one IPC$ (interprocess connection for communicating with Samba). We can run the ls command (-c) to get a listing of the netlogon share, again testing that we can list the netlogon share.

```
$ smbclient //localhost/netlogon -UAdministrator -c 'ls'
Enter Administrator's password:
Domain=[EXAMPLE] OS=[Windows 6.1] Server=[Samba 4.3.9-Ubuntu]
  .                                   D        0  Sat Sep 24 14:02:06 2016
  ..                                  D        0  Sat Sep 24 14:02:15 2016

        10098468 blocks of size 1024. 7667640 blocks available
```

Testing DNS

We can test our DNS responses now too. For Samba to act as a domain controller, it must respond to the following text record requests:

```
$ host -t SRV _ldap._tcp.samba.example.com.
_ldap._tcp.samba.example.com has SRV record 0 100 389 dc1.samba.example.com.
$ host -t SRV _kerberos._udp.samba.example.com.
_kerberos._udp.samba.example.com has SRV record 0 100 88 dc1.samba.example.com.
$ host -t A dc1.samba.example.com.
dc1.samba.example.com has address 192.168.0.10
```

Here we have tested that we can resolve the LDAP service record, the Kerberos service record, and the A record for dc1.samba.example.com. If this resolves correctly, then Samba can use our bind9 DNS service correctly.

If this does not work, check the bind service for any errors, starting with /var/log/syslog.

Testing Kerberos

Kerberos is a network authentication protocol that can be used to join Active Directory services together and authenticate users and machines. Kerberos is installed as part of the automatic installation of Samba. Since we have only one Samba server, it is not really required unless we are joining another Active Directory domain controller or we want to authenticate our Linux user accounts via the Samba service as a single sign-on authority.

Before we can test our Kerberos configuration, we first need to create a symlink. The output in Listing 13-1 tells us that the Kerberos configuration file has been generated and placed in /var/lib/samba/private/krb5.conf. We are going to symlink that to /etc/krb5.conf.

```
$ sudo ln -sf /var/lib/samba/private/krb5.conf /etc/krb5.conf
```

Taking a look at that file, we can see that it looks like this:

```
[libdefaults]
    default_realm = SAMBA.EXAMPLE.COM
    dns_lookup_realm = false
    dns_lookup_kdc = true
```

The dns_lookup_ option determines whether we use DNS lookups for SRV records. We have already tested the SRV record (host -t SRV _kerberos._udp.samba.example.com.) in our DNS tests previously and have confirmed that it is working for our KDC (Kerberos Domain Controller).

Let's now test the implementation to make sure it is working correctly. We are going to obtain a Kerberos ticket and then verify it.

```
$ kinit administrator@SAMBA.EXAMPLE.COM
Password for administrator@SAMBA.EXAMPLE.COM:
Warning: Your password will expire in 41 days on Mon 07 Nov 2016 11:04:17 PM UTC
```

You do need to specify capital letters for the domain. Now let's look at our ticket:

```
$ klist
Ticket cache: FILE:/tmp/krb5cc_1000
Default principal: administrator@SAMBA.EXAMPLE.COM

Valid starting        Expires            Service principal
09/26/2016 23:34:37   09/27/2016 09:34:37   krbtgt/SAMBA.EXAMPLE.COM@SAMBA.EXAMPLE.COM
    renew until 09/27/2016 23:34:30
```

That proves Kerberos is working correctly. We are all set to create a share now.

■ **Note**   Kerberos can be a pretty complex and daunting topic. You may like to read the following for a gentle introduction: www.roguelynn.com/words/explain-like-im-5-kerberos/.

Configuring Samba Shares

To access Samba shares, there will be several things we will need to do:

- Add the share to smb.conf
- Create the directory and add permissions
- Create any system users that are necessary
- Add Samba users to Samba

Let's start by looking at the Samba configuration file we are going to use. This is what is created by the provision process.

The configuration file can be broken up into two sections, the [global] configuration options and then the specific configuration options, such as [netlogon], [sysvol], and so forth (see Listing 13-2). The [global] section, as the name implies, defines the configuration options that affect the whole server, and the specific configurations in [netlogon] and [sysvol] affect only those services they are trying to define.

Listing 13-2. Samba /etc/samba/smb.conf File

```
# Global parameters
[global]
    workgroup = SAMBA
    realm = SAMBA.EXAMPLE.COM
    netbios name = DC1
    server role = active directory domain controller
    server services = s3fs, rpc, nbt, wrepl, ldap, cldap, kdc, drepl, winbindd, ntp_signd, kcc, dnsupdate
    idmap_ldb:use rfc2307 = yes
```

```
[netlogon]
    path = /var/lib/samba/sysvol/samba.example.com/scripts
    read only = No

[sysvol]
    path = /var/lib/samba/sysvol
    read only = No
```

Let's go through the [Global] section. First you see the option workgroup. This option should be familiar to you if you are a Windows user. It is the workgroup name that will appear in your network neighborhood. A *workgroup* is a collection of computers sharing information. Usually, in a workgroup, the computers do not have central authentication, and each host in the workgroup takes care of its own authentication. In other words, you maintain a list of users with access *to each* host *on each* host.

Central authentication is achieved when one of the hosts in the workgroup becomes a primary domain controller (PDC). Hosts join the domain and then use the PDC to authenticate user access to their resources. If the host is not part of a domain, it can still share resources, but it will have to maintain its own authentication and access lists.

Setting the workgroup here does not make our host a PDC, just part of a workgroup. We have set this to our domain name, EXAMPLE.

```
workgroup = SAMBA
```

Next you need to configure NetBIOS. NetBIOS is a local broadcast protocol that is used to handle connection information between hosts. NetBIOS information is used to match names to Internet Protocol (IP) addresses in WINS servers, kind of like DNS. The NetBIOS protocol itself is used for a name service, session service, and datagram server. As you can see in Listing 13-2, we are setting the netbios name option to dc1, and we will be able to use this NetBIOS name to refer to our host.

■ **Note**   If you are interested in a further explanation of NetBIOS, please read http://en.wikipedia.org/wiki/NetBIOS.

The server role directive is set to active directory domain controller. This obviously means that we are operating an AD DC. If you were to use the *classic* domain controller, you would set it here (NT4). The server services directive defines the services that this server supports. You can add or remove services here with a + or -, like -kdc.

You can further control access to your Samba service by specifying what hosts can access your service by using the hosts allow option. In our configuration, we specify the loopback network and the 192.168.0. network. The notations 127. and 192.168.0. are equivalent to specifying the network masks 127.0.0.0/8 and 192.168.0.0/24, respectively. Here you can also specify individual hosts by using their full IP address and exclude certain hosts by using the EXCEPT clause. For example, if we want to allow access to all hosts on our 192.168.0. network except a naughty host with the address 192.168.0.15, we would use the following in hosts allow:

```
hosts allow = 127. 192.168.0. EXCEPT 192.168.0.15
```

You can also use fully qualified domain names (FQDNs) like headoffice.example.com or gateway.example.com to specify individual hosts. We don't show it here, but hosts deny allows you to list the hosts and networks you do not want to access this service.

We are going to have the networks 192.168.0.0 to 192.168.30.0 access this Samba service, so we will specify the following, which will allow any address in the 192.168.0.0/16 range to connect:

```
hosts allow = 127. 192.168.
```

Samba considers some of the services, demarcated in sections beginning with the [ ] brackets, to be "special." Specifically, [global], [printers], and [homes] describe special services. Samba treats these services differently from, say, a [sales] or [tmp] share.

For example, as you would expect, when Samba receives a file via the [printer] service, it deals with it differently from a file received via a user-defined [tmp] service. Samba has functions that are associated with definitions only in these "special" services. In this example, a path definition in [printer] defines a spooling directory. When your printer spools your printout to this path via the [printer] service, Samba automatically passes it on to CUPS for printing. Setting the value for path in another service will not trigger this behavior. This special behavior also applies to [homes], where Samba will create home directories dynamically if required. You can read more under the "Special Sections" section in the smb.conf man page.

When you define your own services, you use a set of directives that are common to special services and user-defined services. In Table 13-1, we have listed the directives that we will use in our example. You would use these directives to alter or create your own services.

Table 13-1. *Samba Service Directives*

Directive	Description
path	Defines the path of the share you are describing (e.g., /tmp).
browseable	Describes whether the share is visible in the browser list of shares.
comment	Gives a description of the share.
writable	Indicates the share can be written to, as opposed to being read-only.
readonly	Signifies the share is read-only.
printable	Allows spool files to be created and submitted to the share. Applies to printing only.
guest ok	Indicates no password is required for the share. Default is no. Also called public.
valid users	Specifies a list of users allowed to use this service.
write list	Specifies a list of users/groups that can read/write to a share regardless of the readonly setting.
force user	Assigns a default user to all connections to this share.
force group	Assigns a default group to all connections to this host.
force create mode	Forces Unix permissions on files that are created.
force directory mode	Forces Unix permissions on directories that are created.
create mask	Sets Unix permissions on files that are created.
directory mask	Sets Unix permissions on directories that are created.

You can use these service directives to define the path and access rights to your shares. There are many more directives available, and you can find a comprehensive explanation of them in the man smb.conf page.

The [netlogon] share is not classified as a special service in Samba, but it is a standard service in many default smb.conf files and is included by default in the Ubuntu and CentOS Samba packages. That and [sysvol] have been created as part of the default configuration process. The [netlogon] service is used to authenticate Windows clients and can contain things such as login scripts and other information. The [sysvol] service is required by each domain controller and is a folder that is replicated on other domain controllers.

We are going to add the following to the section at the end of the file to set up a sales share that members of the sales group can share:

```
[sales]
        comment = shared sales directory
        path = /data/staff/sales
        readonly = yes
        public = no
        browseable = yes
        valid users = +SAMBA\sales
        write list = jsmith, bsingh
        force create mode = 0770
        force directory mode = 2770
        create mask = 0770
        directory mask = 2770
        force group = sales
        force user = exbackup
```

We have added a share called [sales]. This share is to be made available to our sales staff only. We have decided to put our staff-shared documents into the /data/staff directory, and the sales directory will be under that. We have specified that it should be read-only by default (readonly = yes). This stops unintended users from writing to this directory. We have also denied public or guest users (public = no). It is browsable (browserable = yes), so it will appear in share browser lists for this Samba server. We have also specified here a valid users list, which is set to the sales group (valid users = +SAMBA\sales). The + indicates to Samba to look through the local Unix user/group lists. The people in the sales group will have read-only access to the [sales] share. We then specify exactly who we want to have read/write access, jsmith and bsingh. We could use group lists here as well. If we had a group called sales_admins, we could add write list = @sales_admins.

The last section ensures that files and directories are created with the correct ownership, group, and permissions. We don't want users owning their own documents throughout the directory tree and then having to get someone to change the permissions or ownership for them later when they want to share those documents with others. We want the owner to always be exbackup so that we will always be able to access the shares with our backup scripts, and we want the shares to have group ownership according to their departmental group. We want files to be readable and writable, and for directories we should give full access to the specified users and groups but no access for the general public.

```
force create mode = 0770
force directory mode = 2770
create mask = 0770
directory mask = 2770
force group = sales
force user = exbackup
```

As you saw in Chapter 4, the permissions here are read, write, and execute/access on all files and directories. This might be too liberal for your requirements, but it gives you an idea how to use the permissions. You might want to create files with only 0660 permissions, which is entirely reasonable but might entail some administration overhead.

Samba should automatically load your new configuration without a need to restart the service; however, if you do not see your configuration, you can restart the service with the following:

```
$ sudo systemctl restart samba-ad-dc
```

SAMBA VARIABLE SUBSTITUTIONS

Samba has some standard variable substitutions we will take a look at here. The following list is a subsection of the available variables listed on the man page:

- %U: Session username (the username that the client wanted, not necessarily the same as the one it got).

- %G: Primary group name of %U.

- %S: Name of the current service, if any.

- %L: NetBIOS name of the server. This allows you to change your config based on what the client calls you. Your server can have a dual personality.

- %M: Internet name of the client machine.

- %D: Name of the domain or workgroup of the current user.

- %H: Home directory of the user given by %u.

We have not shown all the variables here; for the complete list of variables, please see the man smb.conf page.

Adding Users to Samba

We now have a basic Samba configuration. You can add your own shares to this configuration as you see fit. There are several things we need to do now to the host to get it ready for users. We are shortly going to create our Samba users and groups via the samba-tool command, and once that is done, we will create our directories and assign permissions.

We have set up Samba in such a way that requires user accounts to be administered on the Samba host. Samba provides a subcommand to samba-tool to administer user accounts on your Samba host. The tool samba-tool uses the following syntax:

```
$ sudo samba-tool user --help
Usage: samba-tool user <subcommand>

User management.

Options:
  -h, --help  show this help message and exit

Available subcommands:
  add        - Create a new user.
  create     - Create a new user.
  delete     - Delete a user.
```

```
disable     - Disable an user.
enable      - Enable an user.
list        - List all users.
password    - Change password for a user account (the one provided in authentication).
setexpiry   - Set the expiration of a user account.
setpassword - Set or reset the password of a user account.
For more help on a specific subcommand, please type: samba-tool user <subcommand> (-h|--help)
```

Let's list the current users we have.

```
$ sudo samba-tool user list
Administrator
dns-dc1
krbtgt
Guest
```

You can see that we have four current users that have been created by the Samba provisioning. We are going to add two more users, jsmith and bsingh, who are part of the sales team.

```
$ sudo samba-tool user create jsmith
New Password:
Retype Password:
User 'jsmith' created successfully
```

We have added a new user called jsmith. We will do the same for bsingh. The password should be at least 8 characters and complex.

Unfortunately, tbear has just left the firm, and his Samba account needs to be disabled. To do that, we disable tbear's details like so:

```
$ sudo samba-tool user disable tbear
Disabled user tbear
```

If we wanted to remove him completely, we would use samba-tool user delete.

Next we are going to create our sales group, and then we will add jsmith and bsingh to it. We use samba-tool again via the group subcommand. Issuing help shows our options.

```
$ sudo samba-tool group
Usage: samba-tool group <subcommand>

Group management.

Options:
  -h, --help  show this help message and exit

Available subcommands:
    add            - Creates a new AD group.
    addmembers     - Add members to an AD group.
    delete         - Deletes an AD group.
    list           - List all groups.
    listmembers    - List all members of an AD group.
    removemembers  - Remove members from an AD group.
For more help on a specific subcommand, please type: samba-tool group <subcommand> (-h|--help)
```

As you can see, it is similar to the user subcommand. First let's add the sales group.

```
$ sudo samba-tool group add sales
Added group sales
```

That is simple, and you should add the group staff too. We can now add our users to the sales group.

```
$ sudo samba-tool group addmembers sales jsmith,bsingh
Added members to group sales
```

We can list the members of the sales group now.

```
$ sudo samba-tool group listmembers sales
jsmith
bsingh
```

We can delete groups and remove members of groups with the following:

```
$ sudo samba-tool group removemembers sales tbear
Removed members from group sales
```

We have removed the user tbear from the sales group; we can also delete the fails group with the following:

```
$ sudo samba-tool group delete fails
Deleted group fails
```

Samba will authenticate our users and provide them with access to any shares they have access to. Samba will use Winbind to authenticate and map users and groups for us. We still need to create one Linux system user, though. This user will own the files and therefore needs to exist on each Samba server. This user will be our backup user. We will show you more on how we will use this user in our backup strategies in Chapter 14.

```
$ sudo useradd -u 903 exbackup
```

Next, we need to create the directory /data/staff/sales. We will make exbackup the owner of the files and directories in /data/staff. We need to make sure that the appropriate groups can access the shares we have defined, and we will do that shortly.

```
$ sudo mkdir -p /data/staff/sales
$ sudo chown exbackup -R /data/staff
```

■ **Note** Any of these user and group IDs are arbitrary, and they may already be used on your host. You may want to choose a different range for your network. Remember, ID values less than 1000 are reserved for system accounts.

We have set up the `sales` group in Samba. We need to query Winbind now to get the GID that has been assigned to the `sales` group, and then we will change the group ownership on our directories. These users and group don't exist in the normal Linux /etc/passwd or /etc/group file, so we need to use the GID that Samba will use when accessing files and directories.

```
$ wbinfo --group-info sales
SAMBA\sales:x:3000010:
```

We can see that `wbinfo` has queried the group information for the sales group and the GID 3000010 has been assigned to it. We will use this GID to change the group ownership.

```
$ sudo chgrp 3000010 /data/staff/sales
```

We also found that the staff GID was 3000012, and we will use that here:

```
$ sudo chgrp 3000012 /data/staff
```

Now we have set permissions on those directories. We want to prevent general access to the directories and allow only defined users and groups.

```
$ sudo chmod 0750 /data && sudo chmod 2750 /data/staff ↵
&& sudo chmod 2770 -R /data/staff/sales
```

We are now ready to use our Samba service.

Required iptables Rules for Samba

Samba 4 requires the following ports to be open in your firewall:

- UDP protocol on ports 137 and 138 for NetBIOS name services
- TCP protocol on port 139 for NetBIOS sessions
- The Microsoft-dn TCP port 445 for the Samba server

For Ubuntu we just need to add the following commands:

```
$ sudo ufw allow samba
$ sudo ufw allow bind9
```

There are many ports that are listening with Samba. It is a good idea to change your ufw default policy to deny to deny access to ports unless explicitly allowed.

```
$ sudo ufw default deny
```

This should be done with some caution as it can block other legitimate processes listening on the host.

■ **Note** We discussed `iptables` in Chapter 7.

Mounting Samba Shares on Linux

Linux hosts can also mount Windows shares using the mount command and the cifs type. You will need to install the cifs-utils package. However, some Linux distributions do not include the ability to read and write to NTFS shares, as Microsoft considers it a breach of its patent to do so. Both distributions allow the ability to mount NTFS and FAT filesystems, and you can find it in the cifs-utils package.

You will need to create the /data/sales directory. To mount the Samba share on a Linux host, you would do something similar to the following:

```
$ sudo mount -t cifs //dc1.samba.example.com/sales /data/sales -o username=jsmith
Password for jsmith@\dc1.samba.example.com\sales:  *****************
```

This will mount the remote Samba share /data/staff/sales under the /data/sales directory. You pass the remote host and your username. You will be asked to provide a password, and then the share should be mounted under the /data directory. For more information on mounting Samba shares, read the man mount.cifs page.

We can see the mounted share with our mount command.

```
$ sudo mount
\\dc1.samba.example.com\sales on /data/sales type cifs (rw,relatime,vers=1.0,cache=strict,us
ername=jsmith,domain=SAMBA,uid=0,noforceuid,gid=0,noforcegid,addr=192.168.0.1,unix,posixpath
s,serverino,acl,rsize=61440,wsize=65536,actimeo=1)
```

The default options for cifs mount can be found in the previous example, the full details of which can be found in the man mount.cifs page. You can see the username we attach as; the domain is SAMBA. You can see rsize and wsize, which are the maximum byte size of data that can be sent between the host and the Samba server, and this is configurable if need be. cache=strict sets the caching strategy to support and follows the CIF/SMB2 protocol; other options are none and loosely.

If we want to automount this via fstab, we will need to provide credentials at boot time. These credentials need to be provided in plain text in a file on the filesystem, preferably the user's home directory. This, of course, is a security concern as storing plain-text credentials on filesystems can be snooped on compromised systems and be used to gain access to other systems. However, if you choose this path, you might like to have separate credentials for Samba from other systems (which adds to the administration burden).

So, you will first need to create the .smb_credentials file in the home directory. It should contain the following:

```
username=bsingh
password=COmpl#xp$sSw0rd
```

You should secure it with the following:

```
$ chmod 0600 .smb_credentials
```

You will need to edit your /etc/fstab file and add the following for automounting:

```
//dc1.samba.example.com/sales /data/sales cifs _netdev,credentials=/home/bsingh/.smb_
credentials
```

This is useful for single desktop access but becomes more complicated if you have people sharing development servers.

Where you have many people sharing one server, you can share access to shared directories using the multiuser mount option. The users gain access to these shares via a local user and a shared mount connection. For example, users jsmith and bsingh can share one common mount, via a common local user.

In this example, the group sales does not need to exist on the local Linux server we are mounting the share on, but the user exbackup also needs to exist. There are local user accounts on the Linux server for jsmith and bsingh too.

On the Samba server, we will create a user that we will use as a set of shared credentials for mounting. Remember to give this user a unique complex password.

```
$ sudo samba-tool user add sharedcreds
```

We will add them to sales group.

```
$ sudo samba-tool group addmembers sales sharedcreds
```

When we normally mount the share, we provide a username and password, and we use that to manage our mount. This allows for only one mount of /data/sales and only one set of user credentials being able to access it. In the shared multiuser environment, we can mount the share with one common user. From our user session on the local Linux server, we can then provide our credentials to the kernel, and it will allow us to access the share with those credentials.

On the local Linux server we are going to mount /data/sales as the sharedcreds user (a user that does not exist on the local Linux server). We do this via the cifscreds command like so:

```
$ sudo cifscreds add -u sharedcreds dc1.samba.example.com
```

We can use any user that has sudo access to do this. We provide the add argument, the user, and the hosts that we want to provide access to. To remove these credentials, we can issue the following:

```
$ sudo cifscreds clear –u sharedcreds
```

Take a look at the man page for cifscreds for other options. We can now mount the share on the local server with the following command:

```
$ sudo mount -tcifs //dc1.samba.example.com/sales /data/sales/ -o
multiuser,username=sharedcreds, \
uid=exbackup,gid=3000017
```

This mounts the /data/sales share using the sharedcreds user. But because there is no local sharedcreds user, we don't have access to write into /data/sales. If we see the perspective from jsmith, we can see that it too does not have access.

```
[jsmith@backup]
$ cp text.file /data/sales/
cp: cannot create regular file '/data/sales/text.file': Permission denied
[jsmith@backup ~]$ ll /data/
ls: cannot access /data/sales: Permission denied
total 20
d?????????? ? ?        ?          ?       ? sales
```

The user jsmith cannot even see the permissions on the /data/sales directory, which is the reason for ????. We need to provide our credentials to the kernel for jsmith too so that it can manage our session to that mount.

```
$ sudo cifscreds add -u jsmith  dc1.samba.example.com
```

The jsmith user will need sudo access to cifscreds; otherwise, it will not be able to execute that command. Now that we have added our credentials to the kernel, we can list the sales directory and read and write from and to it using the exbackup and sales group permissions.

```
[jsmith@backup ~]$ ll /data/sales/
total 1405408
-rwxrwx---+ 1 exbackup 3000017       66376 Nov 26 17:14 logo.png
-rwxrwx---+ 1 exbackup 3000017 479678976 Nov 27 13:21 forecast-2016.xls
-rwxrwx---+ 1 exbackup 3000017 479678976 Nov 27 14:04 media.docx
```

Now, bsingh also needs to access to the sales directory. We need to add the user to the Samba sales group and then set their Samba credential in their user session on the local Linux server. So, on the Samba server, we issue the following:

```
$ sudo samba-tools group addmembers sales bsingh
```

Now in bsingh's local Linux server sign-in, we issue the following:

```
$ sudo cifscreds add -u bsingh dc1.samba.example.com
```

Now bsingh too can access the Samba share mounted on /data/sales.

Mounting Shares on macOS

We are going to show you how to mount your Linux Samba shares on macOS using the graphical interface. This is an easy procedure on macOS or Windows desktops and follows the same pattern.

We will need to be able to resolve the hostname of the Samba server. If you can't resolve the dc1.samba.exmaple.com hostname, check your /etc/resolv.conf or, if you are using Windows, your network settings.

First we use Finder to mount our Samba share. Once the application is started, select Go ➤ Connect to Server, or you can press ⌘ K and get to the same screen.

In Figure 13-1 we just add our server address and click Connect.

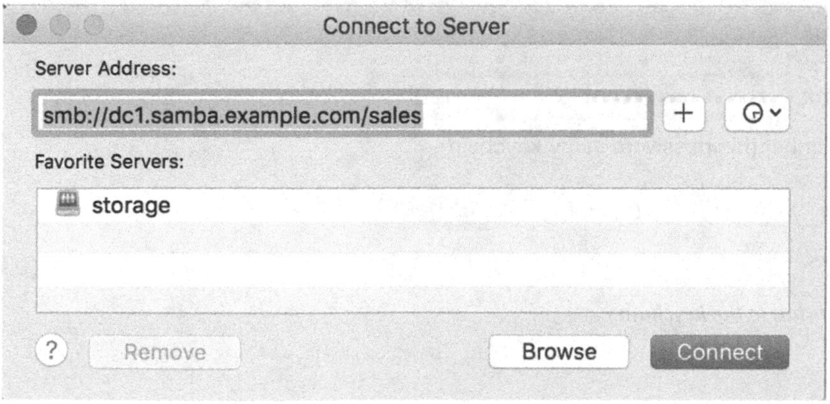

Figure 13-1. *Adding server address*

The next step is to add credentials, as shown in Figure 13-2.

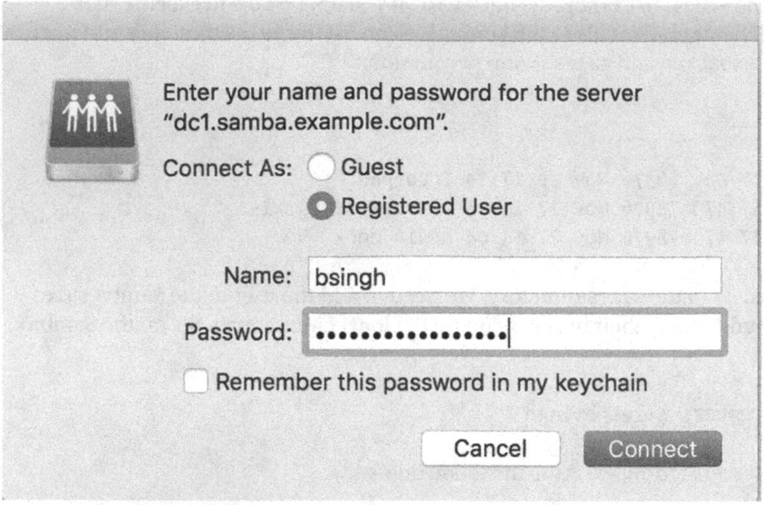

Figure 13-2. *Adding Samba credentials*

If we want to keep these credentials securely, we can add them to our keychain, which is an encrypted safe for credentials (Figure 13-3).

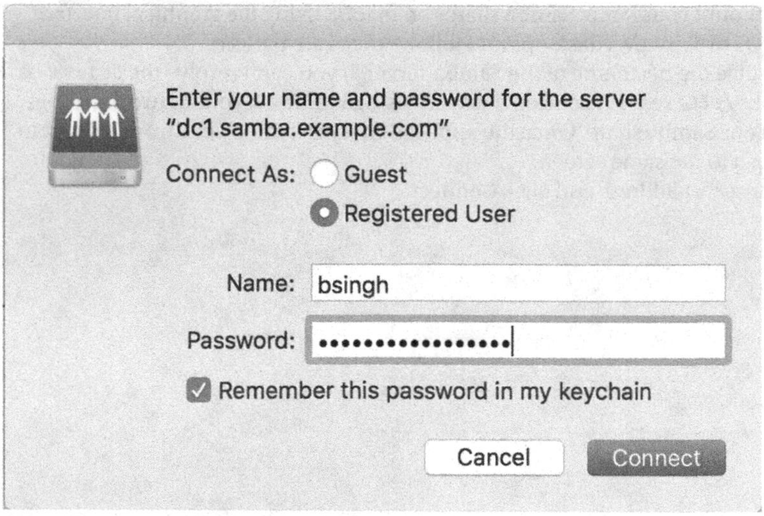

Figure 13-3. *Adding credentials to the keychain*

Now all we need to do is click Connect (Figure 13-4).

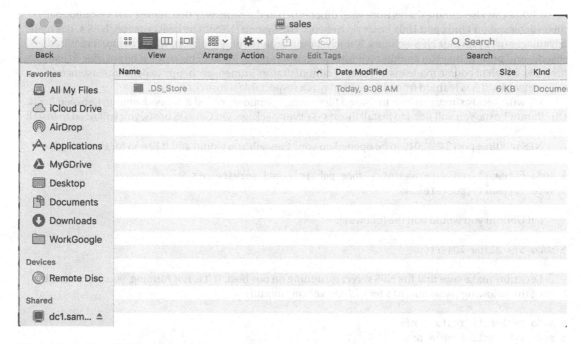

Figure 13-4. *Successfully mounted*

As shown in Figure 13-4 we have a successfully mounted sales directory. There are plenty of instructional pages on the Internet that can help you with your particular version of software or help you with different errors that may pop for both Windows and macOS.

There are already several resources about mounting drives for Windows hosts available online, like this one: www.laptopmag.com/articles/map-network-drive-windows-10. We will leave that as an exercise for you. The process is similar to how we mounted the drive for our Mac and is similar to mounting other Windows network drives.

Resources

For more information on setting up Samba, please see the following resources:

- https://wiki.samba.org/index.php/Main_Page

- https://www.samba.org/samba/docs/

- www.samba.org/samba/docs/man/Samba-HOWTO-Collection/-v3.5

NFS Shares: Linux to Linux

Linux hosts can also mount shares from each other much in the same way that Samba does. Traditionally, this is achieved on Linux and Unix hosts via Network File System (NFS). The latest version, NFS 4, has many advantages over previous NFS versions. Namely, now it requires only one port, where before it required several, and prior to that you couldn't tell what ports it was going to use! This made it impossible to use firewalls, which of course made many security administrators immensely happy to deny its existence on their networks. It has learned from this and today is a respectable network citizen.

We will quickly show you how to share a filesystem, commonly called a *network mount*, between hosts. On Ubuntu hosts, you will need to install the nfs-server package. On CentOS hosts, you will need to install nfs-utils.

NFS requires port TCP 2049 to be opened on your firewall. You would add it like so for CentOS:

```
$ sudo firewall-cmd --permanent --zone public --add-service nfs
$ sudo firewall-cmd --reload
```

On Ubuntu you would add the following:

```
$ sudo ufw allow 2049/tcp
```

Let's now make sure that the NFS server is running on our host. If it is not running, you can start it by issuing the following (swapping nfs for nfs-server on Ubuntu):

```
$ sudo systemctl restart nfs
$ sudo systemctl enable nfs
```

Once done, you need to edit the /etc/exports file.

NFS reads its share instruction from the /etc/exports file. Here you add the directories you want to share along with some options as to how you want them shared. You need to use the following syntax:

```
directory network(nfs_options),network(nfs_options)
```

You select the directory you want to share, the network to which you want it shared, and then several NFS options. Take a look at the one we are going to use:

```
/data/staff 192.168.0.2/255.255.255.255(rw,root_squash,fsid=0)
```

Here we are going to share the /data/staff directory to the host at 192.168.0.2/32. This IP address can also be an FQDN, like fileserver2.example.com, or a whole domain, like *.example.com, like this:

```
/data/staff 192.168.0(rw,root_squash,fsid=0) *.example.com(rw,root_squash,fsid=0)
```

Next, we set the following options: rw,root_squash,fsid=0. The first option (rw) allows the share to be readable and writable. The option root_squash means that the root user on the remote host has the UID/GID set to the anonymous UID/GID—which means this user's root powers are valid on this share. This is to protect the network mount from being compromised by the remote root user.

The fsid option identifies the filesystem that NFS is exporting. This (fsid=0) is telling NFS that /data/staff is the root of all the exported filesystems and not /data. This means that when we issue the following mount command:

```
$ sudo mount nfs1:/ /path/to/mountpoint
```

only /data/staff, and everything under it, will be mountable from nfs1:/. This also means that you don't have to specify nfs1:/data/staff with your mount command. You will also not be able to see any other directory in the /data directory when you mount nfs1:/.

There are many other options that can be specified, and we suggest you read the man page for exports to get further details. To make these settings active, you need to run the following command:

```
$ sudo exportfs -a
```

The previous command will export or unexport all listed directories in /etc/exports. You can also use exportfs -rv, which will also update exported directories and remove unexported directories. These options synchronize the exports with /var/lib/nfs/etab and the Linux kernel.

Now that the new network mounts have been defined, we will try to mount our share on our remote host. Let's see whether our NFS mount is being served. You can use the showmount command to check your NFS shares by issuing the following:

```
$ sudo showmount -e localhost
Export list for localhost:
/data/staff 192.168.0
```

You can see that the output shows our NFS mount and the host IP address that can connect to it.

On the remote host, 192.168.0.2, we need to issue the following command to mount the share /data/staff to /data/remote (/data/remote needs to exist prior to running this command):

```
$ sudo mount -t nfs4 -o rw,intr,hard 192.168.0.1:/data/staff /data/remote
```

This will mount the /data/staff directory to the /data/remote directory on the remote host. You will notice that we have specified the share name, /data/staff, followed by the host to mount from, as indicated by the setting 192.168.0.1:/data/staff. This is because we are specifically requesting the directory that we have access to on that remote host; however, we could specify / if we wanted, and we would mount all shares that we have access to.

We use the mount command to mount a filesystem of type nfs4. We have set the following options on that mount: read/write, interruptible (as specified by intr), and hard. The first is self-explanatory; the last two are not. NFS traditionally had the quirk that if the host sharing the filesystem had a hiccup, it would cause all hosts joined to it to be severely affected until that service was restored or the hosts rebooted. The intr, or interrupt, allows for NFS 4 operations to be interrupted while waiting for a response from the server. The hard option means that the filesystem will be treated like a local mounted filesystem. If it is set to soft, the alternative to hard, the filesystem would automatically be unmounted if it is idle for a period of time. For more information on mount options, please see the man page for mount.

To set this to automatically mount when our host is rebooted, we would add this to the /etc/fstab file:

```
192.168.0.1:/ /data/remote nfs4 rw,hard,intr,_netdev 0 0
```

Here we are accessing the NFS filesystem from host 192.168.0.1 and mounting the remote shares under the /data/remote directory. We are specifying the same options we did previously and adding one more. The _netdev option tells our host not to try to mount our filesystem until after our network devices are up. If this is not set, the host will fail to mount the filesystem and wait for ages until it fails and the attempt times out.

Troubleshooting NFS

NFS is notoriously hard to troubleshoot as it provides limited logging and obscure error messaging. It is getting better, and you can try some basic troubleshooting by adding –v to the mount command, which should give you more information.

```
$ sudo mount -v -tnfs4 192.168.0.30:/data/cows /data/remotes/cows -oro
mount.nfs4: timeout set for Fri Sep 30 03:29:32 2016
mount.nfs4: trying text-based options 'addr=192.168.0.30,clientaddr=192.168.0.1'
mount.nfs4: mount(2): No such file or directory
mount.nfs4: mounting 192.168.0.30:/data/cows failed, reason given by server: No such file or
directory
```

There is a "user space" or FUSE-based alternative to the kernel NFS server that is part of the mainline Linux operating system. It is called NFS-Ganesha and can be found here:

- https://github.com/nfs-ganesha/nfs-ganesha/wiki

FUSE is short for Filesystem in UserSpacE, which means that the NFS server doesn't execute in the kernel but uses kernel modules to access necessary resources and executes in user space (see https://en.wikipedia.org/wiki/Filesystem_in_Userspace).

NFS servers are not designed to be highly available without substantial modification. There is no native concept of clustering, and they need block-level device replication or clustered filesystems, floating IP addressing, and more to make them scale. It's time now for us to show you an alternative: distributed network filesystems.

Resources

You can find more information about NFS here:

- http://nfs.sourceforge.net/nfs-howto/
- https://help.ubuntu.com/community/NFSv4Howto

Distributed Network Filesystems

A distributed network filesystem (DNFS) is a large, distributed and scalable filesystem using commodity hardware. Distributed network filesystems are useful for handling disk image files, media files, and scalable data for analysis processing. The benefits of DNFS over the simple NFS are several:

- Distributed (the loss of one server does not affect the service)
- Scalable up to several petabytes
- Geodistributed, with ability to be available across data centers

There are several different solutions to choose from. We are going to show you how to set up GlusterFS, but you could also choose from several alternatives depending on your workload or preference.

- *CephFS*: http://ceph.com/
- *BeeGFS (formerly FhGFS)*: www.beegfs.com/content/
- *Hadoop (HDFS)*: http://hadoop.apache.org/

For a straight filesystem to share files across many servers, you probably wouldn't want Hadoop HDFS as it is more suited to the Hadoop `map-reduce` workloads and requires you to use the Hadoop API for filesystem access. The others all provide POSIX-compliant filesystems that you can mount and access the files and directories natively on your servers.

CephFS and GlusterFS are most similar in architecture in that they both don't require a metadata server, where the architecture of BeeGFS and HDFS are similar in that they do. Ceph itself is object block storage and a reliable autonomous distributed object store (RADOS) that can support huge amounts of data. All can be supported by commercial support licenses or the relevant communities that create them.

GlusterFS

GlusterFS is a network filesystem, and the company that initiated its development (Gluster Inc.) was acquired by Red Hat. Red Hat offers a support model of the software, and if you have complex requirements, then you should consider purchasing that. You can run the open source version that can be found at the web site (`https://www.gluster.org/`).

Since we are installing a distributed service, we will require at least three hosts. As with all distributed services, having an odd number of hosts is usually preferred as it helps to avoid "split brain." There are other things you can think about too when designing your cluster, such as housing the physical servers in different racks or different data centers to help with your data resiliency.

■ **Note**   Split brain is where at least two servers serving the same application in a cluster can no longer see each other and yet they still respond to clients. In this situation, data integrity and consistency start to drift apart as both servers continue to serve and store data but can no longer sync any data between each other.

GlusterFS Key Concepts

There are several key concepts when thinking of GlusterFS.

- The GlusterFS network filesystem is a "no metadata" distributed filesystem, which means that it does not have a dedicated metadata server that is used to handle file location data. Instead, it uses a deterministic hashing technique to discover the file location (see DHT; `http://gluster.readthedocs.io/en/latest/Quick-Start-Guide/Architecture/`).

- GlusterFS exports a fully POSIX-compliant filesystem, which basically means you can mount, read, and write to GlusterFS from Unix and Unix-like operating systems (such as Linux).

- GlusterFS is a user space filesystem, meaning it doesn't run in the Linux kernel but makes use of the FUSE module.

- A *trusted pool* is a network of servers operating in the GlusterFS cluster. Each server is called a *peer*.

- A *brick* is a basic unit of storage for the GlusterFS. It is exported a server in the trusted pool.

- A *volume* is a logical collection of bricks.

There are several ways that data can be stored inside GlusterFS. These concepts are similar to those found in RAID. Files can be stored in Gluster volumes either with or without levels of redundancy depending on your configuration options.

- *Distributed volume*: By default, if no distribution type is specified, GlusterFS creates a distributed volume. In this setup, a file can be stored on any brick in the volume with no redundancy.

- *Replicated volume*: In a replicated volume setup, your files are replicated across all bricks in the volume. This requires a minimum of two bricks and provides a level of redundancy.

- *Distributed replicated volume*: Files in this configuration are stored across replicated sets of bricks. Here the number of bricks must be a multiple of the replica count. This is a configuration for highly available file storage.

- *Striped volume*: For large files frequently accessed by many clients, this configuration will store the large file in chunks (the same number of chunks as there are bricks). This configuration provides zero redundancy.

- *Distributed striped volume*: Here we stripe (chunk) the data across a number of bricks. The number of bricks must be a multiple of the number of stripes. This can provide greater speed but still doesn't provide redundancy.

Installing GlusterFS

Luckily GlusterFS is easy to install. Both Ubuntu and CentOS have native packages available to them. But to install the latest GlusterFS on CentOS, we are going to install packages provided by the CentOS Special Interest Group (SIG; see https://wiki.centos.org/SpecialInterestGroup). To do that, we are going install its YUM repository for GlusterFS version 3.7.*x* like so:

```
$ sudo yum install centos-release-gluster37
$ sudo yum install -y glusterfs-server
```

For Ubuntu, we are going to add the Gluster team PPA (this PPA, or Personal Package Archive, is not directly associated with Gluster but a group of Ubuntu maintainers). This will provide us with the latest 3.7.*x* version of Gluster too.

```
$ sudo add-apt-repository ppa:gluster/glusterfs-3.7 && sudo aptitude update
$ sudo aptitude install -y glusterfs-server
```

Now for both Ubuntu and CentOS let's make sure that the service starts on boot. Do this on Ubuntu:

```
$ sudo systemctl enable glusterfs-server
```

Do this for CentOS:

```
$ sudo systemctl enable glusterd glusterfsd
```

Now that they are installed, we can configure GlusterFS.

Configuring GlusterFS

Let's look at how we are setting up our servers. We have three servers each with a 50GB drive attached for data. We will have one Ubuntu and two CentOS servers. The Ubuntu server has attached the 50GB disk to /dev/sdc, and on CentOS it's attached to /dev/sdb.

We are going to format those drives with the XFS filesystem as it is the recommended filesystem. With that in mind, you could format with ext4, if you wanted. We do that with the following:

```
$ sudo mkfs.xfs -L brick1_r1 /dev/sdb
$ sudo mkdir -p /data/brick1_r1 && sudo bash -c 'echo LABEL=brick1_r1  /data/brick1_
r1 xfs  defaults  1  2 >> /etc/fstab'
$ sudo mount -a
```

We have chosen to create our device labels and bricks with the brickN_rN suffix, with brickN being an incrementing number and _rN being the replication set they belong to. This allows us to add and replace bricks into replication sets. Naming things is hard, and there is no reason to follow this if you have a better naming scheme. Let's start Gluster on our Ubuntu server; to do that, we execute the following:

```
$ sudo systemctl start glusterfs-server
```

If we had chosen our CentOS server, we would issue the following:

```
$ sudo systemctl start glusterd && sudo systemctl start glusterfsd
```

Of course, we can check that the services started properly by issuing sudo systemctl status <service.name>, but we are going to run one of the gluster commands. If everything is right, we should not receive an error.

```
$ sudo gluster peer status
Number of Peers: 0
```

This is great. We have used the gluster command to query the Gluster cluster and check the status of our peers. We have not added any peers, so we expect this to be 0 at this stage.

You access and configure the GlusterFS service via the gluster command utility. The syntax looks like this:

```
$ sudo gluster <subcommand> <options> <args...>
```

The gluster help option is useful in describing the subcommands, options, and arguments to each instruction. Table 13-2 lists some of the common subcommands you will use.

Table 13-2. *Gluster CLI Commands*

volume info	Shows information on any volumes configured
volume list	Lists the current volumes
volume create	Creates volumes
volume delete	Deletes volumes
volume start/stop	Starts or stops volumes
volume add-brick	Adds a brick to a volume
volume replace-brick	Replaces bricks
volume top	Gives Gluster volume metrics
volume set	Turns on or sets options on volume <key> <value>
peer status	Gives status of the peers in the cluster
peer probe	Probes and adds other peers
pool list	Lists all nodes in the trusted storage pool

GlusterFS: Adding Peers and Creating Volumes

Let's select one host (it doesn't matter which one); we are going to start our cluster. We are going to choose our Ubuntu server, but any would do. We are going to do the following from this one server:

- Add peers to our cluster
- Create a volume directory on our brick
- Create a volume

We have named our hosts au-mel-dfs-1 to au-mel-dfs-3 and have added them to our DNS zone. The Ubuntu host has been assigned au-mel-dfs-3. To add our peers to the cluster, we issue the following:

```
$ sudo gluster peer probe au-mel-dfs-1
peer probe: success.
```

We do the same for au-mel-dfs-2. Now we can show the status of our peers again.

```
$ sudo gluster peer status
Number of Peers: 2

Hostname: au-mel-dfs-1
Uuid: a605a82d-fa77-48dd-8183-95a960547b1f
State: Peer in Cluster (Connected)

Hostname: au-mel-dfs-2
Uuid: 5ceee284-616b-4c2d-87d7-1c44f4cbdca0
State: Peer in Cluster (Connected)
```

We can now see these hosts in the gluster trusted storage pool too.

```
sudo gluster pool list
UUID                                    Hostname        State
a605a82d-fa77-48dd-8183-95a960547b1f    au-mel-dfs-1    Connected
5ceee284-616b-4c2d-87d7-1c44f4cbdca0    au-mel-dfs-2    Connected
30cf104f-00b2-4371-8935-d91719a2e17b    localhost       Connected
```

Each peer has been given a UUID, and you can see the hostname and current state. Only peers in this list can probe new peers. Now we will create our volume directory on all our peers. This can be any name, but we are calling ours vol1.

```
$ sudo mkdir /data/brick1_r1/vol1
```

We shall now create our Gluster volume. We do that with the following command:

```
$ sudo gluster volume create vol1 replica 3 \
        au-mel-dfs-1:/data/brick1_r1/vol1 \
        au-mel-dfs-2:/data/brick1_r1/vol1 \
        au-mel-dfs-3:/data/brick1_r1/vol1
volume create: vol1: success: please start the volume to access data
```

We have created a new Gluster volume called vol1. It is going to replicate each file over the three bricks. Those bricks we are adding are on our three peers, and we have listed the peers previously.

■ **Note**   It is worth noting here that having three replicas of each file increases your storage requirements by at least three.

We can see the information associated with this volume now; let's run the following command:

```
$ sudo gluster volume info
Volume Name: vol1
Type: Replicate
Volume ID: e9964568-feef-4f2f-a61d-14ba643b76e5
Status: Created
Number of Bricks: 1 x 3 = 3
Transport-type: tcp
Bricks:
Brick1: au-mel-dfs-1:/data/brick1_r1/vol1
Brick2: au-mel-dfs-2:/data/brick1_r1/vol1
Brick3: au-mel-dfs-3:/data/brick1_r1/vol1
Options Reconfigured:
performance.readdir-ahead: on
```

Our Gluster volume has been created, and we can see the details in the previous lines. We can see the type (Replicate) and the number of bricks (1 × 3 = 3). This tells us that each file is going to be stored on each brick, and we have one set of three bricks for a total of three bricks.

We can check the status of our volume. We can do that with the following:

```
$ sudo gluster volume status
Volume vol1 is not started
```

So, like the message from when we created our volume, it is not started, and we will have to start it. Let's do that now with the following command:

```
$ sudo gluster volume start vol1
volume start: vol1: success
```

With that we have created and started our Gluster volume, and we are now ready to test that we can mount and write to it.

Testing GlusterFS

In this testing scenario, we are going to mount our Gluster volume onto another server. We are going to perform some write tests. Then we are going perform those same write tests and shut down the server we mounted Gluster from.

The first thing we will do is install the Gluster client. Now, you don't have to do this if you intend to use Gluster with NFS or SMB (Samba). The Gluster client does provide one great feature that we will demonstrate.

You need to install the glusterfs-fuse package for CentOS or glusterfs-client for Ubuntu.
Now we will mount our Gluster volume. To do that, we issue the following:

```
$ mount -t glusterfs au-mel-dfs-1:/vol1 /mnt
```

We have mounted our GlusterFS volume to our /mnt directory. Taking a look at df shows the following:

```
$ df -h /mnt
Filesystem          Size  Used  Avail  Use%    Mounted on
au-mel-dfs-1:/vol1  50G   33M   50G    1%      /mnt
```

As shown, we have our 50GB volume mounted successfully. We can do a write test to see whether we can write data to it. For this we are going to use a for loop bash one-liner. It is going to write zeros in 100 files in the mount directory of incrementing sizes.

```
$ for a in {1..100} ; do sudo dd if=/dev/zero of=/mnt/datafile${a} bs=4096 count=$a ;done
....
100+0 records in
100+0 records out
409600 bytes (410 kB, 400 KiB) copied, 0.0287382 s, 14.3 MB/s
```

We can see that the test data files have been created, and when take a look at df, we will see that all hosts are reporting the same disk usage for their bricks.

```
$ df -h /data/brick1_r1/
Filesystem      Size  Used Avail Use% Mounted on
/dev/sdc        50G   62M  50G   1%   /data/brick1_r1
```

Let's do another exercise. When you mount your GlusterFS volume, the Gluster FUSE client will receive a volfile from one of the peers. It will then mount the volume from any one of the peers listed, not necessarily the one we first contacted. This time we are going to drop the host we had in our mount command, au-mel-dfs-1, and we will see what happens when we are in the middle of copying a file.

```
$ while true ; do sudo cp /var/log/syslog /mnt/ ; date ; done
....
Sat Sep 17 15:09:05 UTC 2016
Sat Sep 17 15:09:05 UTC 2016
Sat Sep 17 15:09:05 UTC 2016
....
```

The previous command says, let's copy the syslog file to /mnt indefinitely and, in between copies, print the current date. You will see the date firing rapidly on your screen after each copy. While it is doing that, on au-mel-dfs-1 enter the reboot command.

```
$ sudo reboot
```

The host will immediately reboot. While this is happening, two things can happen.

If our host had mounted the volume from au-mel-dfs-1, you would see a pause in the copying. You can tell that we are paused because the date output will stop incrementing. We need to wait for the Gluster network ping to time out or the host to be restarted and the service to come back up. If the host does not come up and the network ping times out, the Gluster client will request access to one of the other peers in the volfile and try to require the resources it needs (file locks and so on; this can take up to a minute). The network timeout is configurable, and we will show you how to change that shortly. Once it does, we will resume the copy.

If our host mounted the volume from one of the other peers, nothing exciting will happen, and the copy will continue. If this is the case, reboot one of the other peers when `au-mel-dfs-1` comes up and see what happens.

Managing GlusterFS

In this section, we are going to show you how to manage your GlusterFS server. We would like to show you the following:

- Set a volume option

- Expand our storage

- Replace a brick

Setting Configuration Options

We can change the option settings per volume. Starting with changing the cluster volume configuration for vol1, we are going to set our network ping timeout from the default 42 seconds to 15 seconds. This setting tells the GlusterFS client that it should wait 15 seconds before giving up and reacquiring all the resources from another Gluster peer. This an expensive operation, and really we should delay this action for as long as possible. Here, as a demonstration only, we are going to show you how to change it.

We use the `gluster volume` subcommand to change options on the volume. The syntax is the following:

```
$ sudo gluster volume set <volume name> <option> <value>
```

So in our case, we would issue the following to change the `network.ping-timeout` setting:

```
$ sudo gluster volume set vol1 network.ping-timeout 15
```

If we look at the volume information, we will now see our change in the `Options Reconfigured` section.

```
$ sudo gluster volume info
Volume Name: vol1
Type: Replicate
Volume ID: e9964568-feef-4f2f-a61d-14ba643b76e5
Status: Started
Number of Bricks: 1 x 3 = 3
Transport-type: tcp
Bricks:
Brick1: au-mel-dfs-1:/data/brick1_r1/vol1
Brick2: au-mel-dfs-2:/data/brick1_r1/vol1
Brick3: au-mel-dfs-3:/data/brick1_r1/vol1
Options Reconfigured:
network.ping-timeout: 15
performance.readdir-ahead: on
```

There are a large number of configuration options that can be changed using the volume set subcommand; you can see them here:

- http://gluster.readthedocs.io/en/latest/Administrator%20Guide/ Managing%20Volumes/#tuning-options

Expanding GlusterFS Volume Storage

Of course, there will be time you need to expand the size of your storage, and that is where Gluster is a great performer, compared to alternatives like plain old NFS. The options to expand come down to adding new bricks to existing peers or adding new peers and bricks into the volume. We have added a new 50GB hard drive to our existing peers, and we are going to add them to the vol1 volume.

We are going to create another three 50GB drives and add them into the volume as another set. This will give us a total of 100GB of usable storage with a redundancy factor of 3. We are going to follow the same instructions for our first brick.

```
$ sudo mkfs.xfs -L brick1_r2 /dev/sdc && sudo mkdir -p /data/brick1_r2 && \
        sudo bash -c 'echo LABEL=brick1_r2 /data/brick1_r2 xfs defaults 1 2 >> /etc/
        fstab' && sudo mount -a
$ sudo mkdir /data/brick1_r2/vol1
```

Here we have created and mounted our new device (/dev/sdc on our CentOS hosts) and created a vol1 directory on the new device. This is just like we did earlier, but we've condensed our commands into two lines. Now we create our new replica set and add it to the vol1 volume.

```
$ sudo gluster volume add-brick vol1 replica 3  \
        au-mel-dfs-1:/data/brick1_r2/vol1  \
        au-mel-dfs-2:/data/brick1_r2/vol1  \
        au-mel-dfs-3:/data/brick1_r2/vol1
volume add-brick: success
```

We have now added these new bricks to the vol1 volume. If we run the volume info subcommand, we will see we have a new replica set.

```
$ sudo gluster volume info
Volume Name: vol1
Type: Distributed-Replicate
Volume ID: e9964568-feef-4f2f-a61d-14ba643b76e5
Status: Started
Number of Bricks: 2 x 3 = 6
Transport-type: tcp
Bricks:
Brick1: au-mel-dfs-1:/data/brick1_r1/vol1
Brick2: au-mel-dfs-2:/data/brick1_r1/vol1
Brick3: au-mel-dfs-3:/data/brick1_r1/vol1
Brick4: au-mel-dfs-1:/data/brick1_r2/vol1
Brick5: au-mel-dfs-2:/data/brick1_r2/vol1
Brick6: au-mel-dfs-3:/data/brick1_r2/vol1
Options Reconfigured:
network.ping-timeout: 15
performance.readdir-ahead: on
```

As you can see, we have added three new bricks to our volume, bricks 4–6. You can also see that we now have two sets of three disks for a total of 6 (2 × 3 = 6). Looking at our mounted volume on our test server, we can see that the volume has increased to 100GB.

```
$ df -h /mnt
Filesystem              Size    Used    Avail   Use%    Mounted on
au-mel-dfs-1:/vol1      100G    85M     100G    1%      /mnt
```

Replacing a Brick

We are stupid. We have just wiped out the /data/brick1_r2/vol1 directory on au-mel-dfs-1. This now puts that brick into a failed state. We can view that from our system log and from the volume status subcommand.

```
$ sudo gluster volume status
Status of volume: vol1
Gluster process                             TCP Port    RDMA Port   Online   Pid
-------------------------------------------------------------------------------
Brick au-mel-dfs-1:/data/brick1_r1/vol1     49152       0           Y        1292
Brick au-mel-dfs-2:/data/brick1_r1/vol1     49152       0           Y        3198
Brick au-mel-dfs-3:/data/brick1_r1/vol1     49152       0           Y        1978
Brick au-mel-dfs-1:/data/brick1_r2/vol1     N/A         N/A         N        N/A
Brick au-mel-dfs-2:/data/brick1_r2/vol1     49153       0           Y        11652
Brick au-mel-dfs-3:/data/brick1_r2/vol1     49153       0           Y        2133
```

As you can see, the current status shows that service for au-mel-dfs-1:/data/brick1_r2/vol1 is not listening on a port and does not have a PID. We are going to replace it. We have added another device to our peer of 50GB and have formatted and mounted it similarly as we did when we expanded the volume.

```
$ sudo mkfs.xfs  -L brick2_r2 /dev/sdd && sudo mkdir -p /data/brick2_r2 && \
        sudo bash -c 'echo LABEL=brick2_r2 /data/brick2_r2 xfs defaults 1 2 >> /etc/fstab' && \
        sudo mount -a
$ sudo mkdir /data/brick2_r2/vol1
```

Now to replace the damaged brick, we use the following command:

```
$ sudo gluster volume replace-brick vol1 au-mel-dfs-1:/data/brick1_r2/vol1 au-mel-dfs-1:/
data/brick2_r2/vol1 commit force
volume replace-brick: success: replace-brick commit force operation successful
```

Now we can see the health with the volume status.

```
$ sudo gluster volume status
Status of volume: vol1
```

```
Gluster process                          TCP Port  RDMA Port  Online    Pid
------------------------------------------------------------------------------
Brick au-mel-dfs-1:/data/brick1_r1/vol1    49152       0         Y      12252
...
Brick au-mel-dfs-3:/data/brick2_r2/vol1    49154       0         Y       2280
```

The brick has been replaced, and we can see from the df command that data has been synced to it.

```
$ df -h /data/brick2_r2
Filesystem      Size  Used  Avail Use% Mounted on
/dev/sde        50G   42M   50G   1%  /data/brick2_r2
```

Managing Documents

File sharing is an important part of distributing documents in your company. However, it does have certain limitations when it comes to tracking and versioning documents. Without excessive overhead in writing and checking permissions, you can't get great fine-grained control of who is accessing your documents. Also, you can't lock the file being edited, so two people can access the same file, make separate changes, and, when one user saves it back to the file share, destroy the other's work. There is still clearly a need for file sharing, but a better way to manage the documents in your business exists.

A good document management system (DMS) will ideally achieve these five things for you:

- Securely share your documents with other staff members

- Provide version control for documents so that previous edits are not lost

- Require documents to be checked out so that two people can't edit the same document at the same time

- Style the DMS to match your company's workflow for creating, reviewing, and publishing documents

- Have a single entry point for all your document sharing without having to manage several file servers and their file shares

With a good document management system, you typically have a web portal that becomes the central point for all access to your documents. This can be part of a secured intranet with remote offices accessing it via your virtual private network (VPN) links into your main office.

Using Document Management Systems

Your company doesn't need to be a large firm to have a good document management system. A little thought put into designing a DMS early on in your business will save you a lot of problems later as your business grows and your need to control documents becomes more evident. A good DMS helps not only with workflow but also with securing your documents. Add to this version control of your documents, and you have greater security of the data you are sharing with your colleagues.

Of course, we have online document management like Google Docs, Quip, and Microsoft360, and these may be just fine for your needs. In many cases, using these solutions are great for small businesses that don't have the infrastructure and are relatively low cost. Of course, documents are online (or partly online) and so can be subject to network problems, but in general they are very secure, highly available, and low cost.

There are several open source, or partly open source alternatives, that you might like to try.

- *Alfresco*: Community edition LGPLv3 license, limited features compared to commercial editions

- *LogicalDoc*: Community edition LGPLv2 license, limited features compared to commercial editions

- *OpenKM*: Community edition GPLv2, limited features compared to commercial editions

Each of these solutions has online documentation and the ability for you to purchase support if needed. We provide this because it is most likely a better choice for document management compared to either Samba or NFS.

Print Servers

Setting up printer servers on CentOS and Ubuntu is easy. Both distributions use the same print server software to manage print services. We will show you how to set up the CUPS printer server, which is the standard for Linux distributions and which also has a consistent web interface available across both CentOS and Ubuntu.

In many circumstances, setting up CUPS servers for printing has become redundant as many modern printers now have their own print servers and are available on the network, Wi-Fi, or even Bluetooth. Also, we really hope fewer people require printing as there are many alternative ways to transport and read documents in this day and age.

If you still need to set up a printer on your network (for example, you have a USB printer and you want to share that among the hosts on your network), you can attach it to a Linux server or even attach it to a small Raspberry Pi and use the CUPS print server.

■ **Note** There are many uses for a Raspberry Pi; one of them is being a print server. A Raspberry Pi is a microcomputer that can be attached to a printer via USB and can act as a print server. It normally comes with the Raspberian operating system, which is a Debian-based distribution of Linux. A Raspberry Pi is even better used for learning! See https://www.raspberrypi.org/.

CUPS

We will begin by showing you how to configure a new printer that is attached via USB to your host. You can then share that with other hosts in your network. To demonstrate this, we will then attach our printer to a client.

Installing and Configuring CUPS

You can configure your printers from the command line and by hand-editing your CUPS configuration files (though it's not recommended). CUPS also comes with a web UI that we will use to add and share our printer.

When you plug in your printer, the kernel will send an event notice to both Udev and the Hardware Abstraction Level (HAL) manager. Udev is a user-space device management application, and HAL provides a consistent interface for the desktop programs. This means that applications such as word processors can consistently know how to use a printer device, and a calendar can talk to a smart device using a consistent and defined set of rules.

Let's look at what happens when we plug in an Epson USB printer on our Ubuntu host. To make sure everything is working properly, first we issue the `tail` command on the log to make sure our device has been picked up by the kernel.

```
$ sudo dmesg
[13433828.652994] usb 2-1: new high-speed USB device number 4 using ehci-pci
[13433828.786834] usb 2-1: New USB device found, idVendor=04b8, idProduct=0811
[13433828.786847] usb 2-1: New USB device strings: Mfr=1, Product=2, SerialNumber=3
[13433828.786855] usb 2-1: Product: USB2.0 MFP(Hi-Speed)
[13433828.786860] usb 2-1: Manufacturer: EPSON
[13433828.786865] usb 2-1: SerialNumber: L76010502151505100
[13433828.789721] usblp 2-1:1.1: usblp0: USB Bidirectional printer dev 4 if 1 alt 0 proto 2
vid 0x04B8 pid 0x0811
[13433828.790798] usb-storage 2-1:1.2: USB Mass Storage device detected
[13433828.791051] scsi9 : usb-storage 2-1:1.2
[13433829.790811] scsi 9:0:0:0: Direct-Access     EPSON    Stylus Storage   1.00 PQ: 0 ANSI: 2
[13433829.791627] sd 9:0:0:0: Attached scsi generic sg5 type 0
[13433829.795826] sd 9:0:0:0: [sdf] Attached SCSI removable disk
```

Here you can see that our host has recognized that we have attached a USB printer and has registered the device as usblp. We can check that the device exists by issuing `ls /dev/usblp`. Now we can be content that our device has been recognized and is ready to be added under the control of the CUPS printing service.

We first need to set up some things on our print server. We will need to add an administration user to administer the setup of our print devices. This can be any user, and we will make bsingh our printer administrator by adding them to the lpadmin group.

```
$ usermod -aG lpadmin bsingh
```

Next, unless this CUPS server is running locally, we are going to allow it to be administratively accessible remotely.

```
$ sudo cupsctl --remote-admin
```

Now we are going make sure it can reached by our print server hostname. We will edit the /etc/cups/cupsd.conf file and add the following:

```
LogLevel warn
PageLogFormat
MaxLogSize 0
Port 631
Listen print-srv.example.com
ServerAlias *
```

Here we have added the Listen directive to allow it to listen on our printer server interface and have added a ServerAlias * so that we can use the print-srv.example.com hostname to connect to the administration web page.

We should also add the hostname `print-srv.example.com` and map that to 192.168.0.1 in our DNS server.

```
$ sudo nsupdate -k /etc/bind/dynamic-update-key
> server ns1.example.com
> update add print-srv.example.com 86400 A 192.168.0.1
> send
<ctrl d>
```

Here we have used the `nsupdate` command to add our `print-srv.example.com` record. We should now restart our `cups` service and make sure it is available on boot.

```
$ sudo systemctl enable cups
$ sudo systemctl start cups
```

Now we can go to the web administration page and add our printer. Open a web page and go to the URL `https://print-srv.example.com:631`. Since we don't have a valid Secure Sockets Layer (SSL) certificate installed, we will get a warning that this site is untrusted. We will accept that risk, which brings us to the following page, as shown in Figure 13-5.

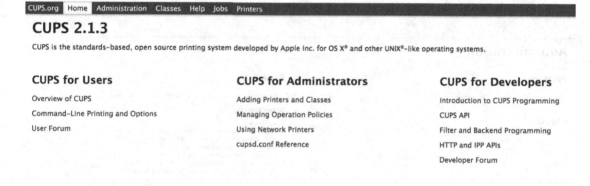

Figure 13-5. *The CUPS home page*

From this page we are going to click Adding Printers and Classes under the CUPS for the Administrators column. We will be prompted for a username and password; we will use `bsingh`'s credentials (Figure 13-6).

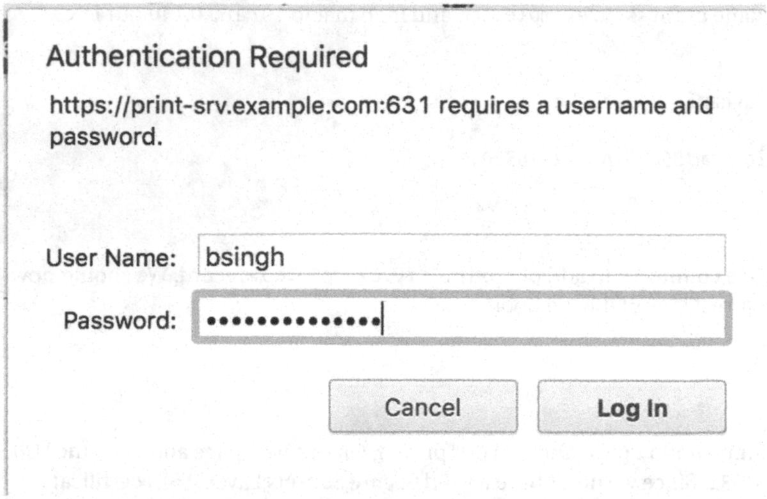

Authentication Required

https://print-srv.example.com:631 requires a username and password.

User Name: bsingh

Password: ●●●●●●●●●●●●●●

Cancel   Log In

Figure 13-6. Using the administrator's credentials

From here we will add a printer using the Add Printer button (Figure 13-7).

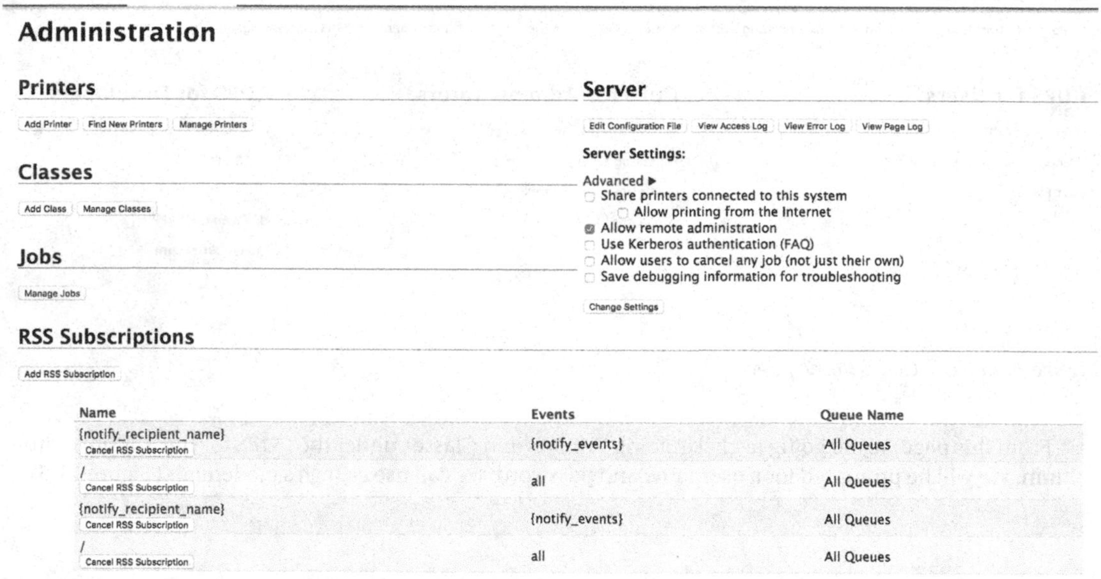

Administration

Printers

Add Printer Find New Printers Manage Printers

Classes

Add Class Manage Classes

Jobs

Manage Jobs

RSS Subscriptions

Add RSS Subscription

Server

Edit Configuration File View Access Log View Error Log View Page Log

Server Settings:
Advanced ►
☐ Share printers connected to this system
  ☐ Allow printing from the Internet
☑ Allow remote administration
☐ Use Kerberos authentication (FAQ)
☐ Allow users to cancel any job (not just their own)
☐ Save debugging information for troubleshooting

Change Settings

Name	Events	Queue Name
{notify_recipient_name} Cancel RSS Subscription	{notify_events}	All Queues
/ Cancel RSS Subscription	all	All Queues
{notify_recipient_name} Cancel RSS Subscription	{notify_events}	All Queues
/ Cancel RSS Subscription	all	All Queues

Figure 13-7. Administration page for CUPS

Clicking the Add Printer button brings up the first of our printer dialogs. We have a local Epson Stylus printer attached to our host via USB, as shown in Figure 13-8.

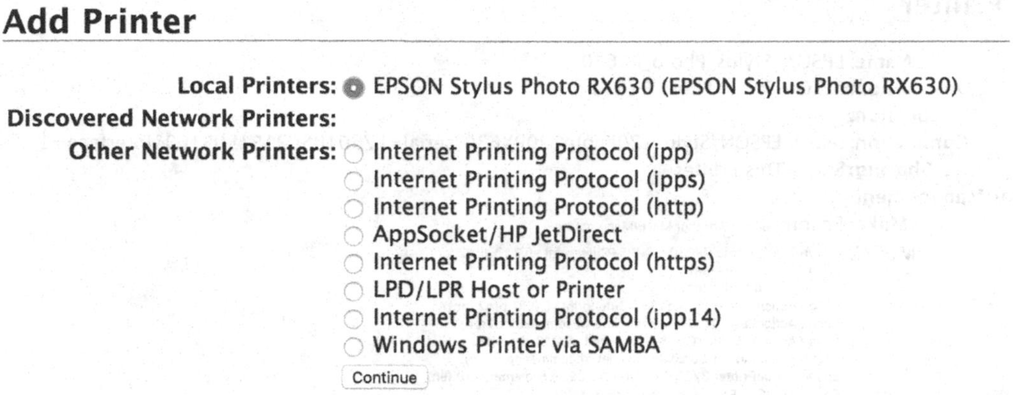

Add Printer

Local Printers: ⦿ EPSON Stylus Photo RX630 (EPSON Stylus Photo RX630)
Discovered Network Printers:
Other Network Printers: ○ Internet Printing Protocol (ipp)
○ Internet Printing Protocol (ipps)
○ Internet Printing Protocol (http)
○ AppSocket/HP JetDirect
○ Internet Printing Protocol (https)
○ LPD/LPR Host or Printer
○ Internet Printing Protocol (ipp14)
○ Windows Printer via SAMBA

Continue

Figure 13-8. *Selecting the USB printer*

You will also notice that we can add other types of network printers, including printing via our Samba server. You can see how to set up Samba printer shares here:

- `https://wiki.samba.org/index.php/Setup_a_Samba_print_server`

We are now asked a series of questions about the printer. We are asked to give the printer a name, description, and location. These can be whatever makes sense to you. We are going to enable sharing of this printer and allow color management, as shown in Figure 13-9.

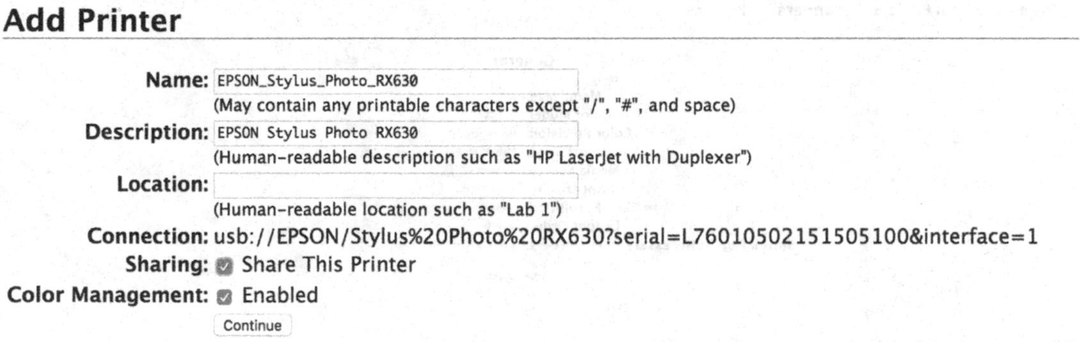

Add Printer

Name: EPSON_Stylus_Photo_RX630
(May contain any printable characters except "/", "#", and space)
Description: EPSON Stylus Photo RX630
(Human-readable description such as "HP LaserJet with Duplexer")
Location:
(Human-readable location such as "Lab 1")
Connection: usb://EPSON/Stylus%20Photo%20RX630?serial=L76010502151505100&interface=1
Sharing: ☑ Share This Printer
Color Management: ☑ Enabled

Continue

Figure 13-9. *Printer information*

We are then asked more information, this time about the model of the printer. We will choose from the drop-down list (Figure 13-10).

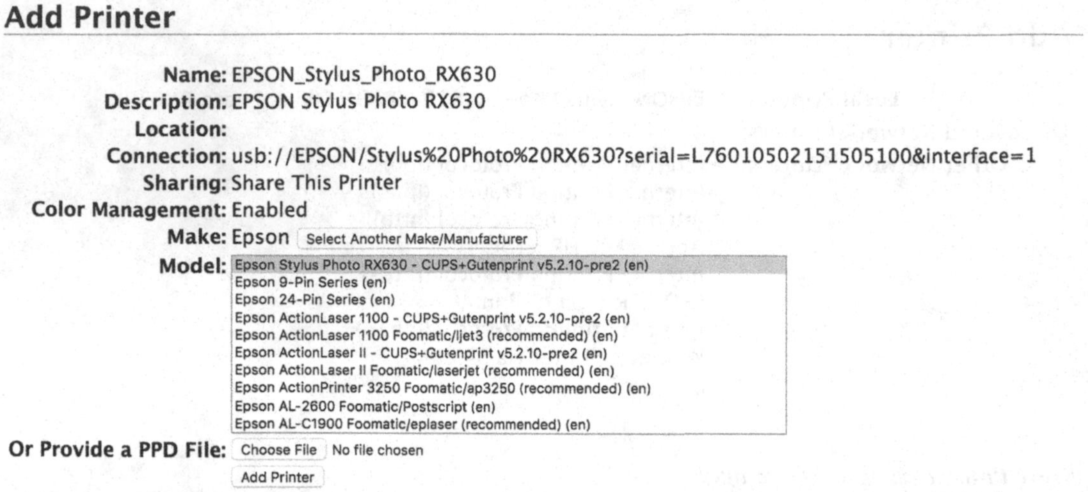

Add Printer

Name: EPSON_Stylus_Photo_RX630
Description: EPSON Stylus Photo RX630
Location:
Connection: usb://EPSON/Stylus%20Photo%20RX630?serial=L76010502151505100&interface=1
Sharing: Share This Printer
Color Management: Enabled
Make: Epson `Select Another Make/Manufacturer`
Model:

```
Epson Stylus Photo RX630 - CUPS+Gutenprint v5.2.10-pre2 (en)
Epson 9-Pin Series (en)
Epson 24-Pin Series (en)
Epson ActionLaser 1100 - CUPS+Gutenprint v5.2.10-pre2 (en)
Epson ActionLaser 1100 Foomatic/ljet3 (recommended) (en)
Epson ActionLaser II - CUPS+Gutenprint v5.2.10-pre2 (en)
Epson ActionLaser II Foomatic/laserjet (recommended) (en)
Epson ActionPrinter 3250 Foomatic/ap3250 (recommended) (en)
Epson AL-2600 Foomatic/Postscript (en)
Epson AL-C1900 Foomatic/eplaser (recommended) (en)
```

Or Provide a PPD File: `Choose File` No file chosen
`Add Printer`

Figure 13-10. *Selecting the printer model*

If we don't find the printer model, we can add a PPD file. Next comes the printer defaults (Figure 13-11).

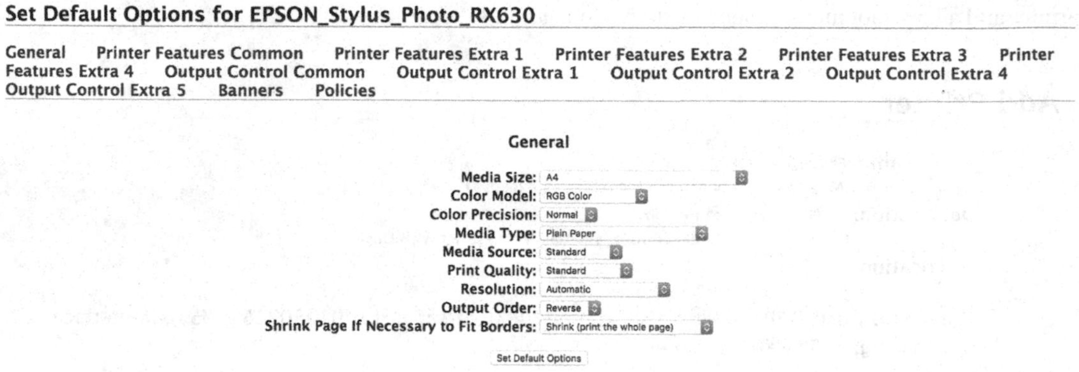

Set Default Options for EPSON_Stylus_Photo_RX630

General   Printer Features Common   Printer Features Extra 1   Printer Features Extra 2   Printer Features Extra 3   Printer Features Extra 4   Output Control Common   Output Control Extra 1   Output Control Extra 2   Output Control Extra 4   Output Control Extra 5   Banners   Policies

General

Media Size: A4
Color Model: RGB Color
Color Precision: Normal
Media Type: Plain Paper
Media Source: Standard
Print Quality: Standard
Resolution: Automatic
Output Order: Reverse
Shrink Page If Necessary to Fit Borders: Shrink (print the whole page)

`Set Default Options`

Figure 13-11. *Editing or selecting defaults*

You can edit or select defaults for your printer. We will just keep the defaults (Figure 13-12).

EPSON_Stylus_Photo_RX630 (Idle, Accepting Jobs, Shared, Color-Managed)

Maintenance ◇   Administration ◇

Description: EPSON Stylus Photo RX630
   Location:
      Driver: Epson Stylus Photo RX630 – CUPS+Gutenprint v5.2.10-pre2 (color, 2-sided printing)
Connection: usb://EPSON/Stylus%20Photo%20RX630?serial=L76010502151505100&interface=1
   Defaults: job-sheets=none, none media=iso_a4_210x297mm sides=one-sided

Jobs

Search in EPSON_Stylus_Photo_RX630: [   ] Search Clear

Show Completed Jobs   Show All Jobs

No jobs.

Figure 13-12. *Ready and waiting for jobs*

Our printer is now ready for jobs. We will now attach that to a client. On our macOS client we can again select our printer and add it (Figures 13-13 and 13-14).

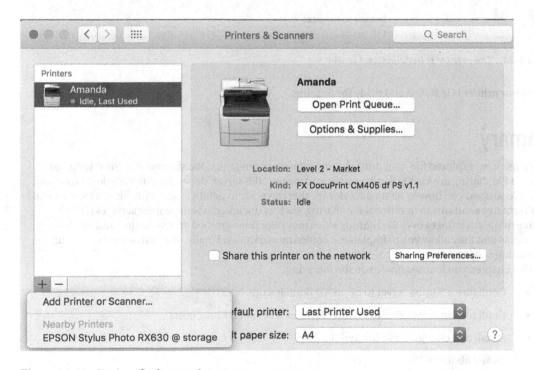

Figure 13-13. *Bonjour finds our print server*

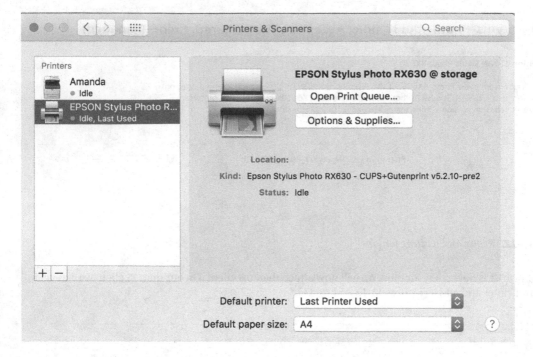

Figure 13-14. *The printer is installed and ready*

Now our printer is installed and ready for printing.

Summary

In this chapter, we explored file- and print-sharing offerings from Linux. We showed that the traditional methods of file sharing are via the Samba server and via the NFS server, depending on the clients you want to serve. We showed you how to set up data storage that can scale to petabyte size with GlusterFS. We talked about alternative solutions to traditional file sharing, such as document management services (DMS). They have many advantages over file sharing, since they offer finer-grained access control and versioning of documents and they allow you to implement company workflows. Finally, you learned how to set up the CUPS printing service.

In this chapter, you learned how to do the following:

- Configure a Samba server to be an AD domain controller

- Configure an NFS server to mount filesystems between Linux hosts

- Install and configure the GlusterFS

- Talked about DMSs

- Configure CUPS printer servers and attach them to a host

In the next chapter, we will look at backup and recovery for your office.

CHAPTER 14

■ ■ ■

Backup and Recovery

By Dennis Matotek

The ability to back up and restore data is critical in any organization. You need high-quality backups not only to restore deleted or overwritten data but also in many cases for legal requirements you might have in your country (e.g., related to keeping tax or customer records).

We will begin this chapter by discussing disaster recovery planning (DRP) and business continuity management (BCM), giving you a grounding in these concepts. We will show you how to securely copy data from a remote host, whether it is on your network or on the other side of the world. We will then introduce you to the backup server Bareos and show you how to use it to save and restore your files. Also using Bareos, we will demonstrate how to back up and restore a database. Finally, we will discuss the Web-UI console, which is a web-based UI for Bareos.

By the end of this chapter, you should be able to do the following:

- Be aware of the requirements needed for DRP and BCM

- Use the `rsync` command to securely copy data from one host to another and use a script to automate that process

- Install and configure Duply to back up to Amazon S3

- Install and configure a backup server called Bareos

- Manage your backups and create jobs within Bareos

- Restore files to your host using Bareos

- Install and configure the Web-UI management console

We'll start off with a general discussion on DRP.

Disaster Recover Planning

Of course, we all hope that nothing disastrous happens to our business, but it's important to prepare for any number of scenarios, just in case. There are two main categories of disaster: man-made disasters and natural disasters. An e-mail server going down for a day, causing vital, time-sensitive business matters to be missed, is a man-made disaster related to human error or mechanical malfunction that can have a process of recovery associated with it. On the other hand, an earthquake that destroys your office is a natural disaster that would require a completely different recovery response. Both scenarios can be planned for, depending on the likelihood of them occurring.

© Dennis Matotek, James Turnbull and Peter Lieverdink 2017
D. Matotek et al., *Pro Linux System Administration*, DOI 10.1007/978-1-4842-2008-5_14

Disaster recovery planning is all about recognizing, managing, and mitigating risk. It is part of an overarching process called *business continuity management,* or making sure a business can continue in the face of unknown adversity to at least a predetermined minimum level. BCM covers various aspects of your organization and should detail timelines that your business agrees upon for the restoration of particular services.

The following are questions to consider when formulating your organization's BCM and DRP strategy:

- Can we predict the most likely disruptions our business could face? What are the steps required to recover from them? What are timelines for expected recovery?

- What are the costs associated with mitigating the risks for and recovering from each potential event?

- Do we need a co-location where we can move our business?

- Do we need to rent extra equipment, such as power generators, in any potential crisis scenario?

- Who are the people and organizations that need to reached/communicated with in the event of disruption to the business? How should the disruption be communicated to the public?

- In the case of a large-scale catastrophic event, what are the points that determine whether continuation of the business can be achieved? Losses can quickly accumulate if key infrastructure or business assets are disrupted.

Developing BCM and DRP plans can be a complex process. Within your organization, you should have a BCM plan that contains the findings of risk analysis, business impact analysis, and crisis management investigations that can be signed off on by the major business units. Even small businesses can benefit from a semiformal arrangement, though the resources to develop a full BCM may not be required. For further information on BCM and DRP, we recommend the following resources:

- *Ready Business (U.S. Homeland Security)*: www.ready.gov/business/index.html

- *Australian National Security, Business Continuity Planning*: www.ag.gov.au/agd/www/nationalsecurity.nsf/Page/Information_For_BusinessBusiness_Continuity

- *Wikipedia, Business Continuity Planning*: http://en.wikipedia.org/wiki/Business_continuity_planning

- *Wikipedia, Disaster Recovery*: http://en.wikipedia.org/wiki/Disaster_recovery

- *Business Continuity and Disaster Recovery Checklist for Small Business Owners*: http://www.continuitycentral.com/feature0501.htm

- *Disaster Recovery Using Bareos*: https://www.bareos.org/en/HOWTO/articles/relax-and-recover-with-bareos.html

In this chapter, we're going to focus on the process of backing up and restoring your data, which should be part of your organization's BCM and DRP plans. The next section covers backup strategies.

Backup Process

You have many different questions to think about when choosing a backup regimen. Answering these questions will give your company its backup strategy.

- What is it we are trying to back up?

- How often do we need to back up the data?

- How long do we want to keep the data backed up?

- Where should we store our backups and on what media?

The important thing here is to know your data. You need to know how often it changes and in what volume. You also need to know your storage media and how much data it can store, and for how long. Data volumes can be tricky things—without planning, you could have too much data to back up or not enough time to back up your data. In these situations, you may find yourself backing up data you don't need, or you may need to get different storage appliances for faster performance or larger backup volumes.

Data retention periods, called the *data life cycle*, are also important to consider. You may need to keep your data for legal or tax purposes for specific periods of time, usually a few years. You may want to keep client data for several years, and you may want to keep other types of data for shorter periods of time. Depending on what you are backing up, there may be absolutely no point in keeping data on media with the aim to restore data that is months old; in such cases, you could look at shortening your backup cycles to free up that media.

Another thing to think about is scheduling. What time window do you have available to schedule backups in? You may be running 24/7 shops that leave little time for offline backup regimens. You may have to perform *hot backups* (i.e., backups of live hosts at a moment in time), and you may not have much time to do this in. For scheduling, you may need to think in terms of daily, weekly, or monthly backup regimens.

Finally, you'll need to determine the type of backup you'll perform. In most backup regimens, you can break backups into three types: full, incremental, and differential. *Full* backups are definitive backups of data, and they will be the largest and longest backups performed. *Incremental* backups are backups of files and directories that have changed since the last backup (be it full, differential, or incremental). Incremental backups are smaller than full and differential backups, and they are normally much quicker to perform. *Differential* backups are backups of all changed files since the last full backup. These can be larger than incremental backups but are useful when doing restores, as you need only the full backup and the latest differential (if you are not running incremental backups at all). In scheduled backups, you may take one full backup every week with nightly incremental or differential backups.

With full, incremental, and differential backups, your restore operations are done in the following order: the last full backup is restored first, followed by the most recent differential backup, and then any subsequent incremental backups. If you are not using differential backups, then it is the last full backup followed by each subsequent incremental, from the oldest to the most recent.

■ **Caution**   In backup operations, you may restore unwanted, deleted files and directories along with good data. You should take care to examine what has been restored before proceeding.

Your network will have its own special backup requirements, and a plethora of hardware appliances and even online storage options are available for you to choose from. Hardware appliances can come bundled with different vendor software, or you can buy your hardware and run open source software to run your backups. The following are some hardware storage options:

- *Magnetic tapes*: Different types depending on the volume of your backups

- *Hard disks*: Different speed and volume options

- *Optical*: DVD/CD-ROM low-volume data backups

Online storage options can also be used for large volumes of data, as long as you have a fast, reliable Internet connection and low data-charge rates. Storing data in AWS S3 (life-cycling your data through S3 storage classes and then moving off to Glacier storage after a period) can be economical for large data sets. Google Cloud Storage also has competitive data storage services but without the super-cheap long-term storage of Glacier.

Here are some AWS storage offerings:

- *S3 Standard*: Fastest object store

- *S3 Standard-IA*: Intermediate, infrequent access

- *Glacier*: Long-term, infrequent access

Here are some Google storage offerings:

- *Standard*: Fastest object store

- *DRA*: Intermediate, infrequent access

- *Nearline*: Long-term, infrequent access

Both AWS, with an option, and Google, by default, provide Server Side Encryption (SSE) of your data at rest, but you can also use your own encryption key to secure your data. Both comply with PCI DSS (3.*x*) and the various ISO standards on securing hardware and servers, storing data, and securing data centers. Combining this security with running highly reliable and durable services makes AWS or Google a good choice for intermediate and long-term storage.

AWS also offers an AWS Storage Gateway, which is a virtual appliance (a virtual machine) that you install inside your data center and use as a gateway to S3 and Glacier. It also has the capability to act as a virtual tape library (VTL), which software like Bareos can use to back up to. The AWS Storage Gateway will then sync the data to AWS storage while maintaining a local cache. It has a significant price associated with it, but that could be offset by the costs of tape drives and storage tapes.

Things to Think About

We have talked about disaster recovery and business continuity and the importance of securing your data, but there is one other thing we want to talk about. What we really need to think about is how quickly we can recover from a data loss or hardware failure. You have hosts, and you have data. In the event of hardware loss, can you recover your hosts and data quickly?

If you have a database, your database will probably be the single most important data and server you will have. A database server is usually built lovingly, with disk arrays created and the operating system installed and tuned. In this scenario, provided you have recent data, rebuilding this host can take a long time.

Of course, there are a couple of ways around this time recovery time.

- The best is having primary/secondary databases. Your secondary database can be promoted to primary, providing time for you to rebuild your host.

- You can make use of virtualization technology. Your host can be rebuilt quickly from a template or image, or it can be moved off failing hardware without interruption. Combined with configuration management, like Puppet or Ansible, you will be able to recover your systems quickly.

- If you have bare-metal hosts, then you need to back up the disk architecture as well as the operating system and the data. Something like Relax-and-Recover might be a good idea, or something like Mass or Cobbler would help rebuild your servers quickly from a known build.

The worst situation we can have is relying on a running list of how we might have built the host 6 months ago while never having tried to build a host like it since. Actually, there probably is one worse situation: not having the running list.

For other types of hosts, like web servers, you might not need to back them up. You should take careful consideration of things like logs, but if you can rebuild your hosts quicker than restoring them, that would be your best option. If the rebuilding process is automated via configuration management, then you are in a great position as an administrator. This is the notion of treating servers as cattle and not pets and leaves your backup regimes much simpler.

Network Backups

Our network is simple: we have one main host, headoffice.example.com, and hosts in remote branch offices that may have data we need to back up.

Figure 14-1 shows our network. (This is a variation on the diagram from Chapter 7.)

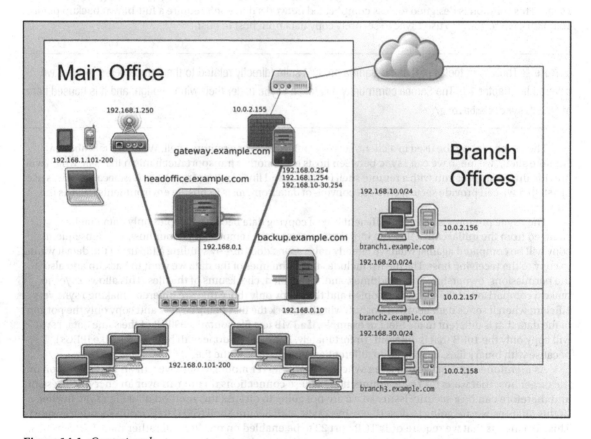

Figure 14-1. *Our network*

We are going to show you two methods of how we can back up our network. We will copy the data from the remote hosts to the headoffice.example.com central server. After copying these remote files, we can then back them up using a full-featured backup application that will reside on backup.example.com.

We have chosen to use a separate host to house our backup server. Ideally, you do not want your main server to also be your backup host because if you lose your main server, you also lose the ability to restore your backups. However, if you can't afford to buy an extra host, any backups are better than no backups, and you should then back up to external media such as DVDs or data tapes.

■ **Note**   Traditionally, Linux backups have been a combination of `tar`, `gzip`, `rsync`, `dd`, `cpio`, `dump`, `restore`, and `mt` commands in hand-rolled scripts. This approach *may be* worthwhile for one or two hosts, but it can become unwieldy with a few cross-platform hosts.

Using rsync

We'll begin by showing you how to copy data from remote hosts securely and efficiently using a tool called `rsync`. This solution is designed for less complicated networks that don't require a full-blown backup plan. To do this, we're going to use `rsync` to securely copy data from host to host.

■ **Note**   The `rsync` tool is part of the Samba product suite (directly related to the Samba server project we covered in Chapter 13). The Samba community has taken `rsync` under their wing, though, and it is housed here: `http://rsync.samba.org/`.

The `rsync` tool can be used in a client/server configuration or a remote shell. When we talk about a "remote shell," we mean we can `rsync` between hosts over another transport mechanism like `ssh`, which will provide the `rsync` program with a remote shell (or command line) on the target host. It is because of this use of `ssh` that we can provide secure, efficient copying of data from hosts in hostile environments such as the Internet.

The `rsync` program is a fast and efficient way of copying data because it copies only data that has changed from the initial copy. After the initial `rsync` copy of the remote data to our host, any subsequent copy will be compared against what we already have. `rsync` does this by sending a file list of the data it wants to copy to the receiving host. The file list includes the pathnames of the data we want to back up and also the permissions, ownership, size, modtimes, and, if specified, checksums of the files. This allows `rsync` to make a comparison of the files being copied and then copy only those that are different, making `rsync` very efficient when it sends data between hosts. It will also check the files being copied and copy only the portion of the data that is different in the file. For example, if a 1MB text file contains 990KB of the same data, `rsync` will copy only the 10KB that is different. Unfortunately, this can't be done with binary files (like JPEGs), because with binary files, it is harder to differentiate any changes to the file.

As mentioned earlier, we can use `rsync` in a client/server model, where we run an `rsync` daemon on the target host that waits for `rsync` connections. These connections do not run over an encrypted session and therefore can be a security issue, so we are not going to discuss this method of using `rsync` further. In this chapter, we are going to describe using `rsync` with Secure Shell (SSH) to provide secure transport. This also means that we require only TCP port 22 to be enabled on our firewall rather than TCP port 873, which is required by the `rsync` daemon. You can read more about setting up the `rsync` daemon in the following tutorials:

- `https://www.digitalocean.com/community/tutorials/how-to-use-rsync-to-sync-local-and-remote-directories-on-a-vps`

- `http://everythinglinux.org/rsync/`

Using rsync over SSH

It is not uncommon to have a requirement to back up remote hosts outside your immediate network, across hostile environments like the Internet. In these situations, you can use rsync to remotely access those hosts via SSH and pull data off them or make a backup. With the implementation of a simple Bash script, you can automate your backups by connecting to the remote host and copying the files back to your backup host.

In this section, we are going to do the following:

- Create a user to manage our backups

- Create our passphrase-less SSH keys

- Copy our keys to our remote hosts

- Create a script that allows only certain commands via SSH

- Create a script that uses rsync to sync files from remote hosts

- Add that script to cron

We introduced you to SSH communications in Chapters 4 and 10. Normally, you would create your SSH keys with a suitable passphrase, which you would use to authenticate your session when you signed on to a remote host. The reason we need an SSH key without a passphrase to make our connection is that we are going to run this script via crontab, which we introduced in Chapter 6, so we can regularly do the backup of our remote host without any user interaction. Not having a passphrase on our keys is a security concern, so we will take steps to mitigate any chance of them being abused a little later.

First, we are going to create a new user, exbackup, to control these backups, if you haven't created them already. Then we will generate our SSH keys.

```
$ sudo /usr/sbin/useradd -m -d /data/backups -u 903 -g adm exbackup
```

Here we have created a user called exbackup with a UID of 903 and default group of adm. We have chosen a UID for this user that is lower than 1000, as we are creating a service user (any user UID less than 1000 is fine) and we prefer to have service users between 900 and 999. We have added this user to the adm, or administrator, group because this group traditionally has access to read log files. The exbackup home directory is /data/backups, and that is where we will store all our backups. Next, we will sudo into the user's account and create our SSH keys.

```
$ sudo su - exbackup
$ mkdir .ssh && chmod 0700 -R .ssh && cd .ssh
$ ssh-keygen -b 4096 -t rsa -f exbackup
Generating public/private rsa key pair.
Enter passphrase (empty for no passphrase):
Enter same passphrase again:
Your identification has been saved in exbackup.
Your public key has been saved in exbackup.pub.
The key fingerprint is:
c1:0c:1f:a5:e4:cf:b9:a5:30:c3:4b:45:23:4f:c9:96 exbackup@backup
$ ls -l total 16
-rw-------. 1 exbackup adm 3243 Oct 12 23:10 exbackup
-rw-r--r--. 1 exbackup adm  741 Oct 12 23:10 exbackup.pub
```

First, we issue sudo su - exbackup to change to the shell of exbackup. Then we create the .ssh directory to store our keys in, and if that was successful (as signified by &&), we change the permissions on the directory and change into that directory. We then use the ssh-keygen command to create our keys. We chose to make the key length 4,096 bytes, -b 4096, and of type rsa, and we called the key exbackup so that we recognize it easier. As the key was being generated, we were asked for the passphrase, and we just pressed Enter twice. You can see that we have listed the contents of our .ssh directory, and we have the two keys, one private and one public, as indicated by the .pub suffix. We keep the private one (exbackup) secured on this host, and we copy the contents of the public key (exbackup.pub) to the authorized_keys file for the user on our remote host.

We need to now talk a little about security. Having passphrase-less keys whizzing across the Internet to your remote hosts is a potential security risk. The data will be encrypted to prevent casual snooping, but a committed attacker could potentially use the keys as an access point to attack your hosts. We could also create a security mechanism called a *chroot jail* on our remote hosts, but this will limit our ability to access the rest of the host's file systems.

■ **Tip**   For information on how to set up chroot jails, visit https://www.debian.org/doc/manuals/ securing-debian-howto/ap-chroot-ssh-env.en.html.

We could use passphrases with our keys and use a tool called key-chain to cache our passphrase for our connection, but we would have to enter the passphrase each time we rebooted the host, which is not ideal. What we will do to make it slightly harder for an attacker is limit the commands our SSH keys can be used for. On our remote hosts, we will create an executable file called ssh_limiter.sh. When we log on to our remote host with our SSH key, this script will be called, which allows only one command to be executed by anyone with this key.

You can limit what SSH can do by adding some options to the authorized_keys file. authorized_keys is a file in the .ssh directory of the user on the remote host that holds copies of the public keys authorized to make connections to our host. We create them in the home directory of our user on our remote host. We can use these options to limit what our keys can do, as shown in Table 14-1.

Table 14-1. *authorized_keys Options*

Option	Description
From="hostname.example.com"	Limits where connections can come from. Takes domain, FQDN, and IP addresses.
Command="/command/to/execute"	Specifies the command to be executed whenever this key is used for authentication.
Environment	Sets user environment if it is allowed by sshd.
no-agent-forwarding	Prevents SSH authentication agent forwarding, meaning we cannot use these keys to make connections to other hosts using the ssh agent.
no-port-forwarding	Prevents SSH port forwarding, meaning we cannot use ssh port forwarding to open connections to other hosts.
no-X11-forwarding	Prevents X11 forwarding. This means we cannot use the X protocol; therefore, we cannot open new X windows or terminals.
no-pty	Prevents interactive shell. This means the user with this key can only run commands and not have an interactive shell.

Table 14-1 is a subset of the complete options available. For more information, read the man page for sshd.

Let's use this information to create an authorized_keys file that we will send to our remote host. First, we'll copy the existing exbackup.pub key to a file called remote_authorized_keys. This creates a file containing the public key for the exbackup user. We are shortly going to edit this file copy, add some restrictions to it, and send it to the authorized_keys file on remote hosts.

```
$ cp exbackup.pub remote_authorized_keys
```

If we want to simply copy our public keys to any remote host, we can use ssh-copy-id, which will create the authorized_keys file on the remote server for the user, like so:

```
$ ssh-copy-id -i .ssh/exbackup jsmith@headoffice.example.com
/usr/bin/ssh-copy-id: INFO: Source of key(s) to be installed: ".ssh/exbackup.pub"
/usr/bin/ssh-copy-id: INFO: attempting to log in with the new key(s), to filter out any that
are already installed
/usr/bin/ssh-copy-id: INFO: 1 key(s) remain to be installed -- if you are prompted now it is
to install the new keys
jsmith@headoffice.example.com's password:

Number of key(s) added: 1

Now try logging into the machine, with:   "ssh 'jsmith@headoffice.example.com'"
and check to make sure that only the key(s) you wanted were added.
```

But we are going to do a few more tasks than simply copying the authorized_keys file. In fact, we are going to do these extra things:

- Create a wrapper script to deny unauthorized commands

- On the remote host, create a user and home directory containing .ssh and bin directories

- Move the SSH wrapper script with authorized commands to the bin directory

- Move the authorized_keys to the .ssh directory

- Make sure the permissions are correct for each file and directory

Creating the Wrapper Script

First up, we are going to create a file called ssh_limiter.sh, and that will be the script we'll force our connection to run when we connect with the exbackup SSH key. This script will live on our remote hosts. This provides some security to the range of commands anybody with this SSH key can execute.

When we make an SSH connection to a host, the variable $SSH_ORIGINAL_COMMAND holds the command we want to execute on our remote host. So if we make the following SSH connection:

```
$ ssh somehost@example.com ls -l /tmp
```

the variable $SSH_ORIGINAL_COMMAND will hold the value ls -l /tmp. When presented with an SSH key, we can now test that variable and decide whether it's the kind of command we will accept this key to use. When we perform an rsync on our remote host, the variable will contain rsync --server <some other arguments for rsync>. We want to allow this and exclude anything else.

We do this with a wrapper script, as shown in Listing 14-1.

Listing 14-1. Limiting the Commands ssh Can Do Using Keys

```
$ vi ssh_limiter.sh
#!/bin/bash
# Command to be used by exbackup at example.com to limit what exbackup can
# do on a remote host.
# SSH2 stores the original command sent by the remote host in a variable
# $SSH_ORIGINAL_COMMAND. We will use case to test and limit the commands
# we are running.

case "$SSH_ORIGINAL_COMMAND" in
  *\&*)
  echo "UNAUTHORIZED COMMAND"
  ;;
  *\;*)
  echo "UNAUTHORIZED COMMAND"
  ;;
  *\|*)
  echo "UNAUTHORIZED COMMAND"
  ;;
  rsync\ --server*)
  $SSH_ORIGINAL_COMMAND
  ;;
  *)
  echo "UNAUTHORIZED COMMAND"
  ;;
esac
```

In Listing 14-1, we are using the Bash scripting language to test the commands that are being presented by the ssh user.

The case statement tests the variable $SSH_ORIGINAL_COMMAND to make sure it contains only the command rsync --server. First, we deny control commands &, ;, and |, which can be used to add other commands to the end of our intended command. If the command starts with rsync --server, then we accept it (\ --server is making sure Bash escapes the <space>--). Anything else that may be passed as a command is denied by *.. The case statement is ended by the esac statement.

We now need to edit our remote_authorized_keys file to add options for our key.

```
$ vi remote_authorized_keys
command="~/bin/ssh_limiter.sh",from="*.example.com", no-port-forwarding,no-X11-↵
forwarding,no-agent-forwarding,no-pty ssh-rsa↵
AAAAB3NzaC1yc2EAAAABIwAAAgEAp7jGL2il3QKREVTpNWkdPqiEbG4rKdCLt/nx57PHkZvz↵
SGI64GlscloIz92PBN/ZjNb4Z1ZaOGS7UYQOg4SHKXsw5/VHchIN1k3p9Vwm9rZUiDg3azKr9J+R↵
+r9TDhwReyYtOQhR/j1aZf1gYS3+xRLs+bQb6UXVRrccygCFtxvrA2B5Kkgw2QJhctSlNRyi8XobUK↵
7kOs2Bw4zIY8hEZMRBFEibqi/diXPngWsMeo2UQQGICo6yXmgUKqiuQq1azdDuTbEstLS97/LdT↵
qWd9MNAsYk= exbackup@backup.example.com
```

Here we added the options to the remote_authorized_key file that will eventually be on our remote host. We specified the command to be run when we use the key and the hosts that can connect with it, and we limited the functions normally allowed with general users. Anyone connecting with this key will now be able to run only the ssh_limiter.sh script, which allows only the rsync command to be executed and only connections originating from the *.example.com domain. We could be stricter in the from= option if we wanted and put in the IP address of the host originating the connection.

We also specify that we cannot port forward to other hosts (no-port-forwarding), x11 terminals, or X Windows (no-X11-forwarding); we can't use the ssh agent to forward our keys to other hosts (no-agent-forwarding); and we will also fail to get an interactive shell (no-pty).

Deploying to the Remote Host

We are going to set up our remote host with the username and directory, mirroring what we previously did for exbackup. We need to make sure that the exbackup home directory on the remote host has an .ssh directory and that it has the permissions of 0700 set on it. We will now copy the remote_authorized_keys file to our remote server using a normal user. First, we'll copy the remote_authorized_keys file somewhere we can access by the user jsmith; /tmp should be OK. We'll copy the ssh_limiter.sh file to /tmp, too.

Using jsmith, who has an account on the remote hosts with administrative sudo access, we do the following:

```
$ scp /tmp/remote_authorized_keys /tmp/ssh_limiter.sh ↵
 jsmith@branch1.example.com:~/
```

This securely copies the remote_authorized_keys file to the home directory of jsmith on the remote host. Now we issue the following series of ssh commands:

```
$ ssh jsmith@branch1.example.com 'sudo useradd -u 903 -g adm -m ↵
-d /data/backups exbackup && sudo -u exbackup mkdir -p /data/backups/.ssh && ↵
sudo chmod 0700 /data/backups/.ssh'
```

This sets up our exbackup user on our remote host. It also creates a directory called .ssh in the home directory and sets the permission of 0700 on it, which is a requirement of SSH security. We would like to point out that we used sudo -u exbackup to make the directory so it has the correct ownership permissions. The double ampersand (&&) indicates that we want to execute the next set of commands if the first set was successful.

■ **Caution** Adding any user to the adm group can give them elevated sudo privileges.

We have the wrapper script (ssh_limiter.sh) and the remote_authorized_keys file in the home directory of jsmith, and we have created the exbackup user. Next, we will copy the remote_authorized_keys file to its proper location on the remote host, renaming it on the way and setting the required permissions. We will also create the /data/backups/bin directory and move ssh_limiter.sh there.

```
$ ssh jsmith@branch1.example.com ↵
'sudo mv remote_authorized_keys /data/backups/.ssh/authorized_keys \ ↵
&& sudo chown exbackup:adm /data/backups/.ssh/authorized_keys \ ↵
&& sudo chmod 0600 /data/backups/.ssh/authorized_keys \ ↵
&& sudo -u exbackup mkdir /data/backups/bin \ ↵
&& sudo mv ssh_limiter.sh /data/backups/bin \ ↵
&& sudo chown exbackup:adm /data/backups/bin/ssh_limiter.sh \ ↵
&& sudo chmod 0750 /data/backups/bin/ssh_limiter.sh'
```

In the preceding code, we used the backslash (\) to break up the lines; the backslash tells Bash that our command continues on the next line rather than to execute the line of code when we press the Enter key. As far as Bash is concerned, it could be all one line, but this makes this somewhat easier to see what is happening.

The sudo command, unless used in conjunction with the -u <username> option, will create all the new files and directories with root being the owner. Therefore, we need to change the permissions and ownership of the directories and files we are creating. We also created a bin directory in the /data/backups directory, which is the home directory of exbackup. In the authorized_key file, we specified command=~/bin/ssh_limiter.sh, so our ssh_limiter.sh script needs to be copied to the bin directory with the appropriate permissions as well.

■ Tip   This rather convoluted setup process can be made infinitely easier with configuration management tools, like those explained in Chapter 19.

Testing rsync

We are going to create a file on our remote host to test the rsync script we are about to show you. On our remote host, we will create a text file in the /tmp directory called /tmp/test_sync.txt and fill it with garbage text.

```
$ vi /tmp/test_sync.txt
fldjfsl
lfdsjfsla
fsdjfsl
fjsdl
fsjfs
fsl
fsa
23433
```

Here we created a file on remotehost.example.com and added random text to a file called /tmp/test_sync.txt. If you use the cat command on the file (cat /tmp/test_sync.txt), you will see that it contains all that random text.

We are now going to test our backup of this file on the remote host using rsync and our SSH keys.

```
$ sudo su - exbackup
[sudo] password for jsmith:
$ rsync -av -e 'ssh -i .ssh/exbackup' remotehost.example.com:/tmp/test_sync.txt /tmp
receiving file list ... done
test_sync.txt
sent 42 bytes received 194 bytes 472.00 bytes/sec
total size is 58 speedup is 0.25
$ cat /tmp/test_sync.txt
fldjfsl
lfdsjfsla
fsdjfsl
fjsdl
fsjfs
fsl
fsa
23433
LDJAS
```

We used the `rsync` command to perform a simple copy of the file `test_sync.txt` to our local `/tmp` directory. You can see that the file has been copied by using `cat` to display its contents. We will explain the details of the `rsync` command a little later.

Next, let's add some more lines to the file and sync it again.

```
$ vi /tmp/test_sync.txt
fldjfsl
...
<snip>
...
fsa
23433
ldjas
dfald
asd
12344556
```

We'll then save the file and do the `rsync` again.

```
$ rsync -av -e 'ssh -i .ssh/exbackup' branch1.example.com:/tmp/test_sync.txt /tmp
receiving file list ... done
test_sync.txt

sent 48 bytes received 213 bytes 174.00 bytes/sec
total size is 77 speedup is 0.30
```

When we use the `cat` command on the `/tmp/test_sync.txt` file, on our localhost you will notice that it contains the new changes to the file.

```
$ cat /tmp/test_sync.txt
fldjfsl
...
<snip>
...
fsa
23433
ldjas
dfald
asd
12344556
```

So, we can securely sync a file from a remote host without needing to use a password. Let's quickly test our `ssh_limiter.sh` script to check that it works as expected. Here we will test to see whether we can use our key to `ssh` across to the remote host and run the `top` command.

```
$ ssh -i .ssh/exbackup remotehost.example.com top
UNAUTHORIZED COMMAND
```

Perfect—sending prohibited or unexpected commands elicits the `UNAUTHORIZED COMMAND` response.

Setting a rsync Script in crontab

Now we can set up `crontab` scripts to regularly sync our remote host files down to our backup directory.
Table 14-2 lists some of the options that can be used with `rsync`.

Table 14-2. rsync Options

Option	Description
-a	Archive, general-purpose option that copies recursively with these options: -rlptgoD.
-r	Recursively copy directories.
-l	Copy symlinks as symlinks.
-p	Copy permissions.
-t	Copy timestamps.
-g	Copy group permissions.
-o	Copy ownership permissions.
-D	Preserve device (character and block devices) and special files (fifo and named sockets).
--exclude	Exclude directories or file; can be patterns. An example is .svn/ to exclude .svn directories.
--include	Include directories or files; fine-tune the files you want to copy. Same syntax as --exclude.
-n, --dry-run	Dry run. Show what would happen but do not actually perform sync.

In general, you will primarily use the `rsync` command with the archive options set, which is –a. This is
a bundled option that represents the following options: -rlptgoD. These options are –r, recursive; -l, copy
symlinks as symlinks; -p, copy permissions; -t, copy file and directory modified times; -g, preserve groups; -o,
preserve ownership; and -D, preserve devices and special files. These options are usually sufficient to archive
your systems, but if you need to, you can add more options, which are explained in the `rsync` man page.

You will probably make use of the `--exclude` and `--include` options, which allow you to fine-tune the
file or directory you want to sync. You can also use `--exclude-from=<file>` and `--include-from=<file>` to
list multiple selections of files or directories you want to target.

The rsync Backup Script

Let's take a look at a typical script we can use to sync our remote hosts to our local host. On our remote hosts,
we will have a directory called /data/staff/sales that we want to sync down to our local host, and then we
will back that up with our backup application. We will have two remote hosts, branch1.example.com and
branch2.example.com, and we will use `rsync` to sync the contents of their /data/staff/sales directory,
except the /data/staff/sales/temp directory, which we want to exclude. We also want this script to be run
by the exbackup user using the passphrase-less key we have created.

First, let's set up the .ssh/config file that will handle all the SSH configuration we need. In that file, we
will add the hostname, the IP address or FQDN name, and the user to connect with. We will also define the
SSH key we will use in our connection.

```
$ cat .ssh/config
Host *.example.com
  User exbackup
  Identityfile ~/.ssh/exbackup
```

The preceding code adds the username exbackup with the identity file in ~/.ssh/exbackup to every ssh connection made to a host in the example.com domain space. It is the equivalent of specifying $ ssh -I ~/.ssh/exbackup exbackup@somehost.example.com.

The script that we will use to run rsync between our hosts looks like Listing 14-2.

Listing 14-2. The nightly_remote_sync.sh Script

```
1. #!/usr/bin/env bash
2.
3. # This uses rsync to sync down remote files to the /data/backups/<hostname>
4. # directories.
5. # The rsync command we will use.
6. RSYNC='which rsync'
7. RSYNC_OPTS="-av "
8.
9. # Host list - Bash array
10. HOSTLIST='
11. branch1.example.com
12. branch2.example.com
13. '
14. # Back up directory on local host and source directory on remote host
15. BACKUP_DIR='/data/backups/'
16. SALES_DIR='/data/staff/sales'
17.
18. # excluded directory
19. EXCLUDED="temp/"
20.
21. # error function
22. error_check() {
23.     if [ $1 -eq 0 ] ; then
24.         echo "backup successful"
25.     else
26.         echo "backup failed: see error number: $1"
27.     fi
28. }
29.
30. # The rsync functions
31. get_sales() {
32.   ${RSYNC} ${RSYNC_OPTS} --exclude $EXCLUDED $HOST:$SALES_DIR $BACKUP_DIR/$HOST ↵
      2>&1 > /dev/null
33. }
34.
35. # Bash for loop to go through each host and rsync the data.
36. for HOST in $HOSTLIST ; do
37.   get_sales
38.   error_check $?
39. done
40.
41. exit 0
```

The purpose of the script in Listing 14-2 is to sync files from one or more remote hosts to the /data/ backups directory of the host the script is running on. This can be the local network's backup host, backup. example.com, where we will have installed proper backup software. This is just one approach among many to achieve this outcome.

Line 1 contains the call to set the environment as a Bash script. We could also use the traditional shebang (#!/bin/bash) to let Linux know we are running a Bash script.

Lines 2–5 are comments describing our script. Lines 6–7 set RSYNC variables, and lines 10–13 declare the list of hosts we want to sync from. Lines 15–19 are more variables. The backup directory we will be directing our backups to is BACKUP_DIR='/data/backups'. The sales directory, SALES_DIR='/data/staff/sales', is the target directory we are backing up. The temp/ directory is the one we want to exclude.

■ **Note** The user exbackup must have read permissions on all the files and directories you want to back up and write permissions on the directories you are backing up to. You can look at using groups to achieve this.

Lines 22–28 are a Bash function that handles our error checking. If the script ends in anything other than a zero, then it fails; if it ends in zero, the script is successful. The error_check() subroutine or function takes the $? argument, the exit code from another function call, and tests it for a zero. We know that if everything goes well, rsync will exit with a zero; otherwise, it exits with another error code. We can use this error-check function to test for the success or failure of any other function that exits with a zero on success.

The get_sales function declared in lines 31–33 describes the rsync function that calls the rsync command and syncs the /data/staff/sales directory to the /data/backups/<hostname> directory. In line 32, 2>&1 >/dev/null directs the stdout and stderr (or standard out and standard error) to /dev/null. Note that /dev/null is a Linux black hole; if you send things to it, like stdout or stderr, they disappear into nothingness.

■ **Note** When you run a program on Linux/Unix hosts, three standard special file descriptors are used: stdin (standard input), stdout (standard output), and stderr (standard error). When your program receives input, it can receive that input by attaching to the stdin file descriptor. Likewise, when it produces its output, it can write that to stdout. If there is an error in the program, it can write that to stderr. For more information on handling and redirecting stdin, stdout, and stderr, please visit www.tldp.org/LDP/abs/html/io-redirection.html.

Finally, lines 36–39 loop through each host in the host list with the for loop function and perform rsync on each host. Then the script checks the error code of each to see whether it is zero, and if so, it prints the success message.

■ **Note** A good resource for learning more about Bash programming is located at www.tldp.org/LDP/abs/html/index.html. Another reference is the book *Beginning the Linux Command Line* by Sander Van Vugt (Apress, 2015).

When we run the script from the command line, we get the following result:

```
exbackup@au-mel-ubuntu-1:~$ ./bin/nightly_remote_rsync.sh
backup successful
backup successful
```

■ **Note**   When you first run this script, you will be presented with SSH asking you to confirm the new key signature of the remote hosts. Type **yes** to confirm the signature and the script should proceed as normal from then on.

We will now put this script into a crontab file so we can run it on a regular basis. Recall that we discussed crontab files in Chapter 5. Let's create the file /etc/cron.d/example_nightly_sync and add the following:

```
# run the nightly rsync script at 5 minutes past 12 every morning.
MAILTO=jsmith@example.com
5       0       *       *       *       exbackup ↵
  /data/backups/bin/nightly_remote_rsync.sh
```

Here we are setting the script to run every night at five minutes past midnight as the user exbackup. If there is an error, an e-mail will be sent to jsmith@example.com. This is a great way to sync up files from one host to another, but it is not really a great backup strategy. For instance, every night we sync over all the changed files, including mistakes. If they are not noticed early enough, then the mistakes are propagated to our backup host and we lose our good copy of data. When we use a proper backup strategy, the potential for losing our ability to restore good data is minimized.

■ **Tip**   When running commands from crontab, it is a really good idea to consider using flock. This uses file locking to prevent scheduled commands being executed while existing commands are already running. See man flock for more details.

A few backup tools have been developed around rsync.

- *BackupPC*: http://backuppc.sourceforge.net/
- *RSnapshot*: http://rsnapshot.org/
- *Duplicity*: http://duplicity.nongnu.org/

Next, we'll take a look at an open source backup server application called Bareos, which can back up Linux, Microsoft Windows, and macOS hosts.

Backing Up with Duply

Duply is a backup program that makes using the Duplicity program dead simple. Duplicity is a program that uses rsync, and rsync can sync large amounts of data. Around the world rsync has been used by many companies as their remote backup strategy successfully. rsync by itself is great at syncing, but it does not easily manage discrete backups. Duplicity manages discrete backups effectively, but it can have many options to choose from. Duply provides a simple way to configure Duplicity backups.

Duplicity can back up to various cloud storage providers. We are going to use AWS in this example, but you could just as easily use Dropbox, RackSpace Cloudfiles, Google Cloud Storage, or more, as listed in the Duplicity man page.

In this exercise, we are going to do the following things:

- Create an S3 bucket with a retention policy
- Create a policy that allows access to our bucket
- Configure Duply
- Test our backup
- Set up a cron job to trigger the backup nightly

We will assume that you already have an AWS account and that you have created a user to access it. You will need the credentials, SECRET_ACCESS_KEY_ID and SECRET_ACCESS_KEY, for this user handy as we are going to need to add them to our configuration. If you need help creating an AWS user, you should start with this documentation:

- *To set up an account*: https://aws.amazon.com/
- *To create users*: https://aws.amazon.com/iam/getting-started/

Setting Up S3 Buckets

To back up our data, we are going to use Amazon's S3 object store. For this we need to create an S3 *bucket*. An S3 bucket is used to store S3 objects. S3 objects are made up of a unique key, data, and metadata and are stored in a flat structure. While the keys can have prefixes (such as nightly/backupfile.zip, where nightly is the prefix and nightly/backupfile.zip is the key), they are not nested hierarchically but instead all live in the one bucket.

- We are going to set up an S3 bucket.
- We are to create a life-cycle version policy.
- Set the access policy to allow our backup user to put files in S3, list them, and get them.

When you have logged into the AWS web console for your account, you will need to make your way to the S3 service tab like in Figure 14-2.

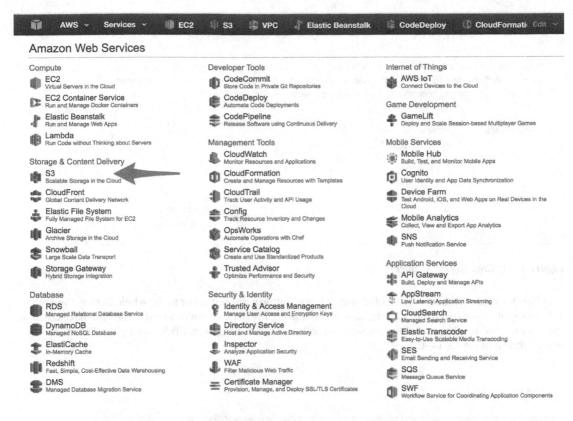

Figure 14-2. *Going to S3*

From there we are going to create a bucket called our-backups. You are free to choose an appropriate name. Click the Create Bucket button to proceed.

As shown in Figure 14-3, we have created an S3 bucket called our-backups. We are next going to make sure that we have a life-cycle versioning policy on this bucket so that we don't have to pay too much for any old data. What this policy will do is to move to lower-cost storage after 35 days and delete any objects just older than one year. The reason is that if we haven't used the data after a month, the likelihood we will need it beyond that is small and so we will move it to a lower-cost tier of storage. We allow 5 days (30+5) after the month for a little buffer like we do at the expiration of 1 year. This does mean that retrieval will be slower, but the chance of us actually needing it is much lower after only a few weeks. There may be times when this is not the case, and we should revise as we went along.

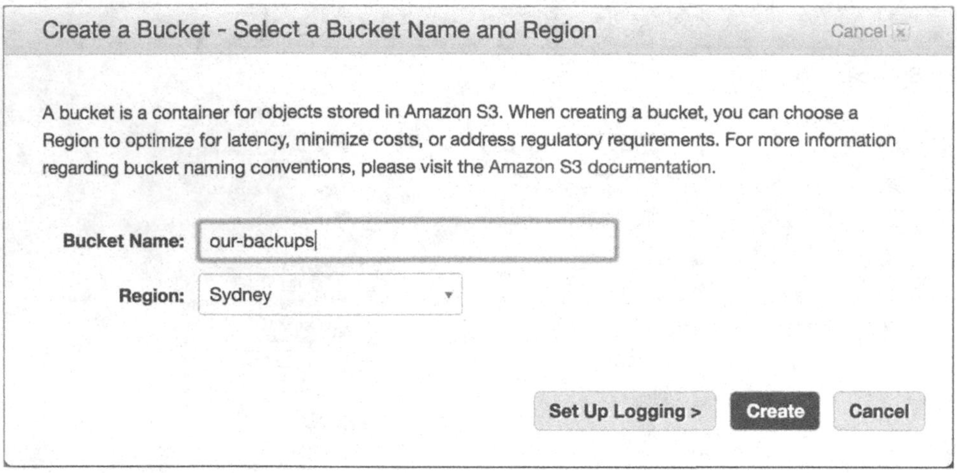

Create a Bucket - Select a Bucket Name and Region   Cancel x

A bucket is a container for objects stored in Amazon S3. When creating a bucket, you can choose a
Region to optimize for latency, minimize costs, or address regulatory requirements. For more information
regarding bucket naming conventions, please visit the Amazon S3 documentation.

Bucket Name: our-backups

Region: Sydney   ▼

                    Set Up Logging >   Create   Cancel

Figure 14-3. *Creating an S3 bucket*

We can apply these life-cycle policies to different paths in our bucket or to the whole bucket. We are
going to apply these to a prefix nightly, as these are the nightly backups for our hosts. After you have created
the bucket, on the right pane of the console you will see a Lifecycle option. Click it and you will see the
screen shown in Figure 14-4.

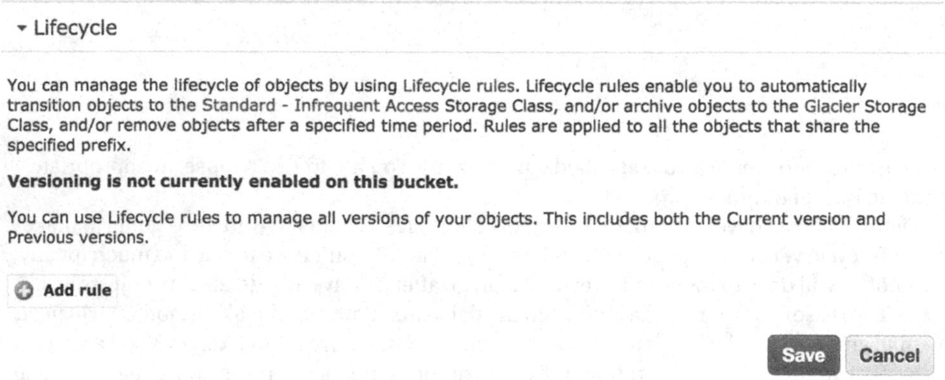

▾ Lifecycle

You can manage the lifecycle of objects by using Lifecycle rules. Lifecycle rules enable you to automatically
transition objects to the Standard - Infrequent Access Storage Class, and/or archive objects to the Glacier Storage
Class, and/or remove objects after a specified time period. Rules are applied to all the objects that share the
specified prefix.

Versioning is not currently enabled on this bucket.

You can use Lifecycle rules to manage all versions of your objects. This includes both the Current version and
Previous versions.

⊕ **Add rule**

                                                        Save   Cancel

Figure 14-4. *Adding a life-cycle rule*

Click "Add rule" to start adding our rule.

In Figure 14-5 we are creating a life-cycle policy that is concerned only with objects that have the
"nightly" prefix in their keys. Now we click Configure Rule.

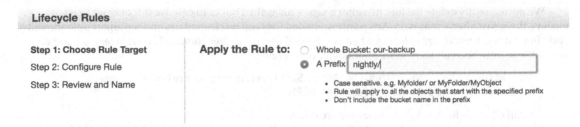

Figure 14-5. Setting life-cycle policy target

In Figure 14-6 you can see there are three nobs we can tweak. Remember we talked about the S3 tiers earlier? We back up originally to the Standard tier. The next below that is Standard Infrequently Accessed (Standard-IA) and then below that is the Glacier storage. The Standard tier costs the most, so we want to transition off that as soon as possible, and we have chosen 35 days. This gives us the standard month plus a couple of days for holidays or people being off work as a buffer. We will not bother moving to Glacier storage because if we need it, we will need it relatively quicker than Glacier will take retrieve. Standard-IA also has a minimum object size of 128Kb, which means objects smaller than that will not be transitioned and will be deleted after the year is up. Also, once we have transitioned the files into Standard-IA, they need to remain there for 30 days before we can transition them to another tier like Glacier.

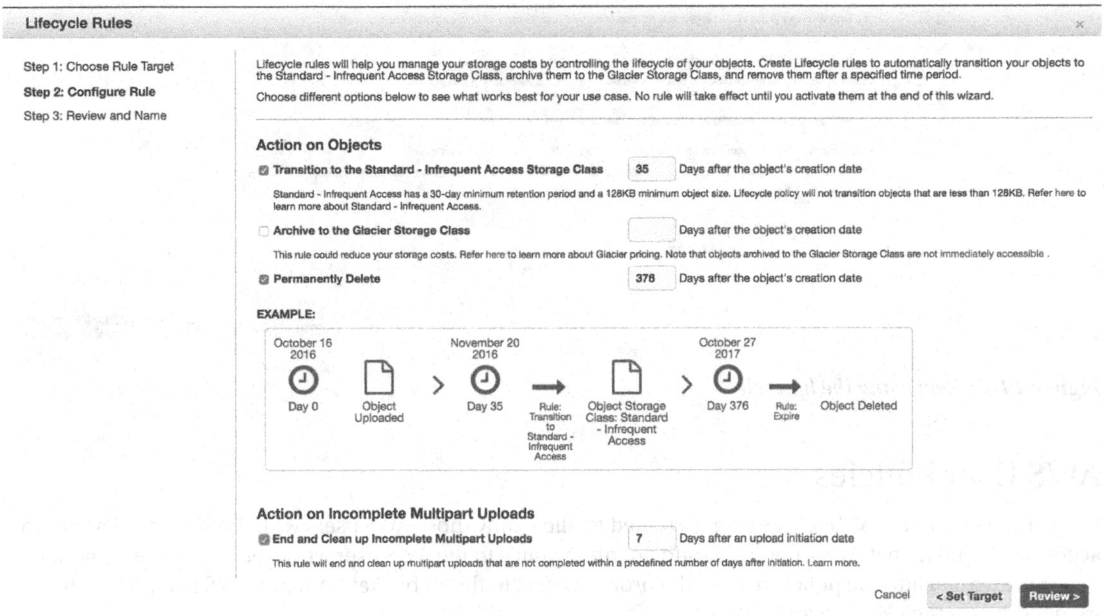

Lifecycle Rules

Step 1: Choose Rule Target
Step 2: Configure Rule
Step 3: Review and Name

Lifecycle rules will help you manage your storage costs by controlling the lifecycle of your objects. Create Lifecycle rules to automatically transition your objects to the Standard - Infrequent Access Storage Class, archive them to the Glacier Storage Class, and remove them after a specified time period.

Choose different options below to see what works best for your use case. No rule will take effect until you activate them at the end of this wizard.

Action on Objects

☑ **Transition to the Standard - Infrequent Access Storage Class**   `35`   Days after the object's creation date

Standard - Infrequent Access has a 30-day minimum retention period and a 128KB minimum object size. Lifecycle policy will not transition objects that are less than 128KB. Refer here to learn more about Standard - Infrequent Access.

☐ **Archive to the Glacier Storage Class**   Days after the object's creation date

This rule could reduce your storage costs. Refer here to learn more about Glacier pricing. Note that objects archived to the Glacier Storage Class are not immediately accessible .

☑ **Permanently Delete**   `376`   Days after the object's creation date

EXAMPLE:

October 16 2016 — Day 0 — Object Uploaded > November 20 2016 — Day 35 — Rule: Transition to Standard - Infrequent Access → Object Storage Class: Standard - Infrequent Access > October 27 2017 — Day 376 — Rule: Expire → Object Deleted

Action on Incomplete Multipart Uploads

☑ **End and Clean up Incomplete Multipart Uploads**   `7`   Days after an upload initiation date

This rule will end and clean up multipart uploads that are not completed within a predefined number of days after initiation. Learn more.

Cancel   < Set Target   Review >

Figure 14-6. Configuring life-cycle rules

We permanently delete the files just after a year with again a buffer in case we discover we need to retrieve them just after a year is up. Any partly uploaded files will be cleaned up, and multipart uploads will end after 7 days. A *multipart upload* is when you upload files in smaller chunks. This will clean up and end any of those jobs. You can learn more about that process here:

- https://docs.aws.amazon.com/AmazonS3/latest/dev/mpuoverview.html#mpu-abort-incomplete-mpu-lifecycle-config

We can click the Review button when we are done.

We have the opportunity in Figure 14-7 to give our policy a name, and we have called it `nightly-lifecycle`. You can have more than one policy on a bucket. You use this page to review the settings; we are just going to click the Create and Activate Rule button.

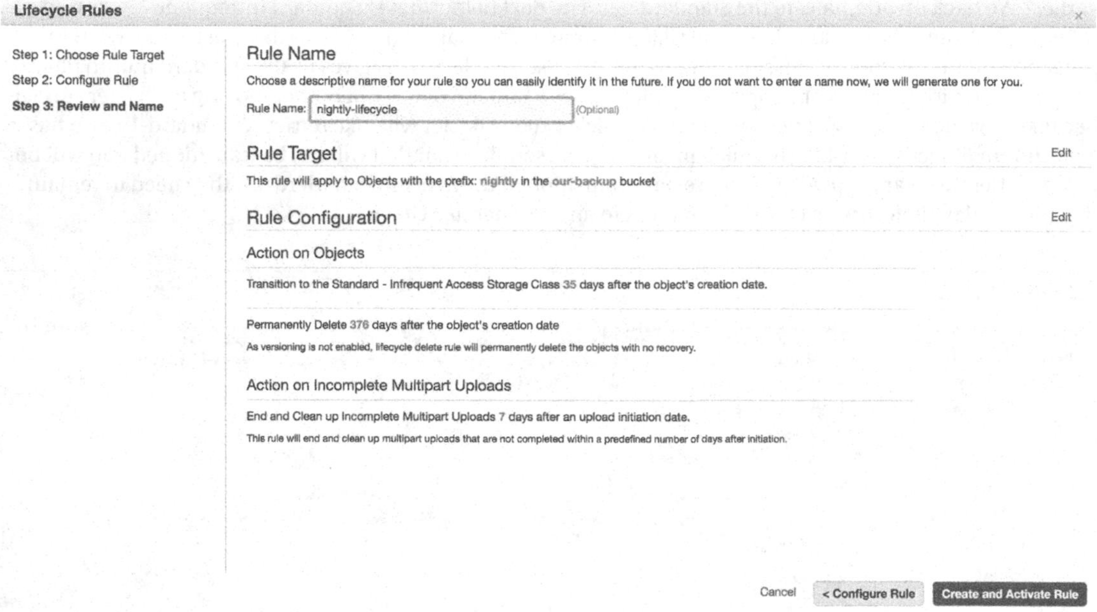

Figure 14-7. *Reviewing the life cycle*

AWS User Policies

We want to secure the S3 bucket we have created to allow only those AWS users with the right credentials to access and upload to it. We are going to add an inline policy to the AWS user we asked you to create earlier.

Now we can add the policy to allow the proper access to the S3 bucket from our AWS user. To do that, we need to use the IAM service in AWS.

■ **Tip**   In general, the preferred way to attach a policy to a user is to not use an *inline policy* like we will do here but to make a *managed policy* and attach that to the user or even a role. That way you can centralize your policies and share them more easily.

In Figure 14-8 we can see the policy we are going to attach to our AWS backup user. Lines 3–11 allow us to list all our S3 buckets. It is made up of three parts: the effect, the action, and resource. The effect can be Allow or Deny. The action is the API action being performed (in this case ListAllMyBuckets). The resource is the AWS resource (the Amazon resource name) you are applying this to; arn:aws:s3:::* is our S3.

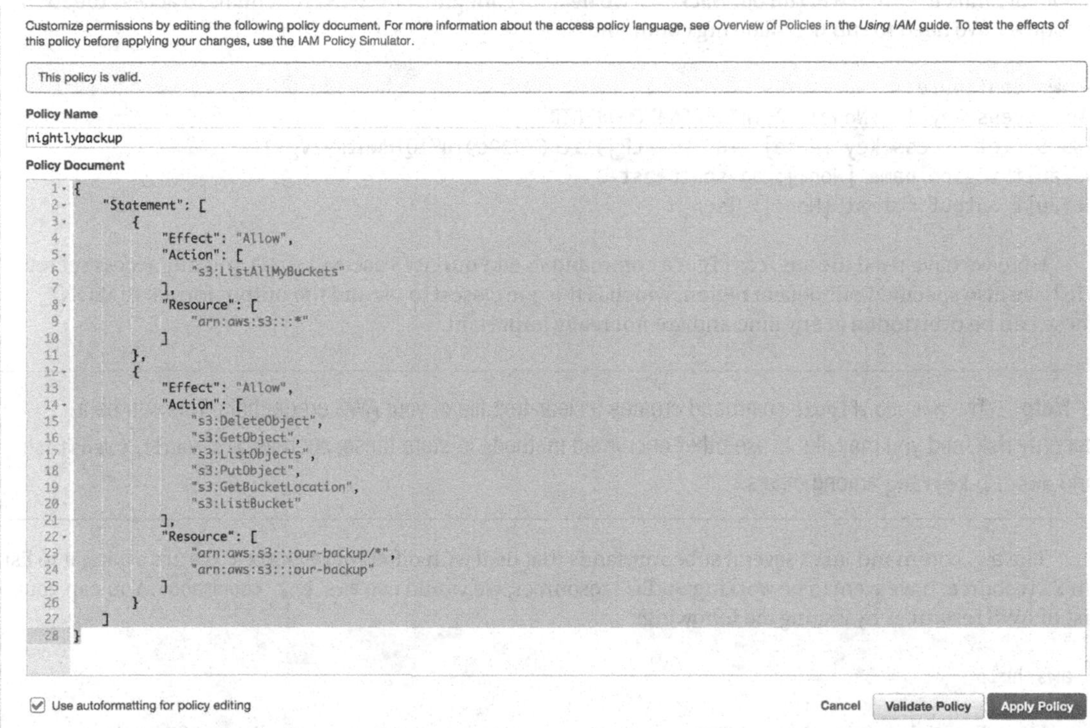

Customize permissions by editing the following policy document. For more information about the access policy language, see Overview of Policies in the *Using IAM* guide. To test the effects of this policy before applying your changes, use the IAM Policy Simulator.

This policy is valid.

Policy Name

nightlybackup

Policy Document

```
 1   {
 2       "Statement": [
 3           {
 4               "Effect": "Allow",
 5               "Action": [
 6                   "s3:ListAllMyBuckets"
 7               ],
 8               "Resource": [
 9                   "arn:aws:s3:::*"
10               ]
11           },
12           {
13               "Effect": "Allow",
14               "Action": [
15                   "s3:DeleteObject",
16                   "s3:GetObject",
17                   "s3:ListObjects",
18                   "s3:PutObject",
19                   "s3:GetBucketLocation",
20                   "s3:ListBucket"
21               ],
22               "Resource": [
23                   "arn:aws:s3:::our-backup/*",
24                   "arn:aws:s3:::our-backup"
25               ]
26           }
27       ]
28   }
```

☑ Use autoformatting for policy editing   Cancel   **Validate Policy**   **Apply Policy**

Figure 14-8. *Attaching an inline policy to our user*

The second part of the policy statement shows the other API actions we allow. They manage our objects and allow us to put (PutObject), get (GetObject), and list (ListObject). In lines 22–25 we see that we are limiting these actions to the backup bucket ARN, arn:aws:s3:::our-backup, only.

For further information on this, please read the following:

- http://docs.aws.amazon.com/AmazonS3/latest/dev/using-iam-policies.html

Testing S3 Bucket Access

We are going to test our access to our backup S3 bucket. To do that, we are going to download and configure the awscli program that allows us to interact with AWS resources from our command line.

The first thing we will do is download the awscli package. This can be done using your native package manager or by downloading via PIP, the Python package manager.

```
$ sudo aptitude install -y awscli
```

If you use PIP, try this:

```
$ sudo pip install awscli
```

Once that has been installed, we can begin to use the aws command to interact with AWS resources. As the local Linux user that will run our backups, we need to configure our AWS credentials to access the AWS resources. We need to run the following command:

```
$ aws configure
AWS Access Key ID [None]: ALIAIJBASN4NOMJ4FLTR
AWS Secret Access Key [None]: +GDHpm+FLPj311tu6YJ29c9luMlQTHwntgy7vgs2
Default region name [None]: ap-southeast-2
Default output format [None]: json
```

Here we have used the aws configure command to add our AWS access key ID and our access secret. We have also specified our default region, which is the one closest to us, and the output format of JSON; these can be overridden at any time and are not really important.

■ **Note**　The aws configure command creates a clear-text file of your AWS credentials. This can be a security risk, and you may like to use other encrypted methods to store these, such as aws-vault, credstash, and awscli-keyring among others.

The aws command takes several subcommands that deal with different resources. We are asking it to list an S3 resource. If we were to be working on EC2 resources, we would use aws ec2 <command>. You can get a list of AWS resources by issuing the following:

```
$ aws help
```

Now that we have our AWS credentials set up, we are going to test that we can list our S3 bucket.

```
$ aws s3 ls our-backup/
```

If there are no errors, that shows we can list our S3 bucket. We can try to copy, or put, a local file up into our S3 bucket. To do that, we issue the following:

```
$ aws s3 cp afile s3://our-backup/
upload: ./afile to s3://our-backup/afile
$ aws s3 ls our-backup/
2016-10-16 05:02:47        32768 afile
```

There you can see we have uploaded a small file to our S3 bucket. Let's now see if we can copy the file back down to our host and then delete that file from S3.

```
$ aws s3 cp s3://our-backup/afile afile2
download: s3://our-backup/afile to ./afile2
$ aws s3 rm s3://our-backup/afile
delete: s3://our-backup/afile
```

These are all the actions that our backup program will perform, and we can see that our credentials allow us to perform these actions. Let's now move on to creating our nightly backup with Duply.

Installing and Configuring Duply

Duply, as we have said, is the convenient way to manage our Duplicity backups. Duplicity can run multiple methods to securely back up files to remote systems. With AWS, it is going to copy our backup in file chunks of about 25Mb. It does this because it is easier to manage several small files than one rather large file.

There are two ways you can secure your data with Duplicity, one with GPG symmetric keys and the other using GPG asymmetric keys. We are going to use symmetric keys, but if you have GPG asymmetric keys available, please use those. We also store our data encrypted at rest with S3, and we could further encrypt our files using server-side encryption.

Installing Duply will install Duplicity as a requirement. It may not, however, install python-boto, and you may have to install this also. However, by installing awscli previously, we should have already installed python-boto.

```
$ sudo aptitude install -y duply
```

For CentOS, you will need to use YUM, of course.

Now that Duply is installed, we can investigate how to use the command. Table 14-3 shows the command usage to get help information (--help or help do not work).

Table 14-3. *$ duply usage*

create	Creates a configuration profile.
backup	Creates a backup (full if it doesn't exist and incremental if it does) and executes pre- and post-scripts.
pre/post	Executes '<profile>/pre', '<profile>/post' scripts.
bkp	Backs up without executing pre- and post-scripts.
full	Forces a full backup.
incr	Forces an incremental backup.
list [<age>]	Lists all files in the backup (as it was at <age>). The default is now.
status	Prints backup sets and chains currently in repository.
verify [<age>] [--compare-data]	Lists files changed since <age>, if given.
verifyPath <rel_path_in_bkp> <local_path> [<age>] [--compare-data]	Lists changes of a file or folder path in backup compared to a local path since <age>, if given.
restore <target_path> [<age>]	Restores the complete backup to <target_path> (as it was at <age>).
fetch <src_path> <target_path> [<age>]	Fetches single file/folder from backup (as it was at <age>).
purge [<max_age>] [--force]	Lists outdated backup files (older than $MAX_AGE). Use --force to actually delete these files.
purgeFull [<max_full_backups>] [--force]	Lists number of full backups and associated incrementals to keep, counting in reverse chronological order. Use --force to actually delete these files.

(continued)

659

Table 14-3. (*continued*)

purgeIncr [<max_fulls_with_incrs>] [--force]	Lists outdated incremental backups ($MAX_FULLS_WITH_INCRS being the number of full backups that associated incrementals will be kept, counting in reverse chronological order). Use --force to actually delete these files.
cleanup [--force]	Lists broken backup chain files archives (e.g., after unfinished run). Use --force to actually delete these files.
version	Shows version information of Duply and needed programs.

When we interact with our backups, we will need to use the duply command like so:

```
$ duply <profile> command
```

To configure Duplicity via Duply, we need to create a backup profile. This is going to store our configuration details for Duplicity to use.

```
$ duply nightly create

# although called exclude, this file is actually a globbing file list

Congratulations. You just created the profile 'nightly'.
The initial config file has been created as
'/home/exbackup/.duply/nightly/conf'.
You should now adjust this config file to your needs.

IMPORTANT:
  Copy the _whole_ profile folder after the first backup to a safe place.
  It contains everything needed to restore your backups. You will need
  it if you have to restore the backup from another system (e.g. after a
  system crash). Keep access to these files restricted as they contain
  _all_ informations (gpg data, ftp data) to access and modify your backups.

  Repeat this step after _all_ configuration changes. Some configuration
  options are crucial for restoration.
```

This command creates a directory (~/.duply) in the home directory of the user issuing the command. In that directory, a profile (~/.duply/nightly) directory is created, and in that directory, a ~/.duply/nightly/conf file is created. Created is an excludes file (~/.duply/nightly/exclude) that can contain the directories we want to include or exclude from our backup profile.

In this nightly profile directory we can also include pre- and post-scripts that can be run before or after our backups. These should be included in .duply/nightly/pre or .duply/nightly/post files.

Also, the output in the end of the create command tells us to make a safe copy of the whole profile directory after the first backup as we may need it when we restore our systems.

Configuring Duply Backups

As we said previously, the create command will create a conf file in the profile directory. We are going to edit that to manage our backups now.

■ **Note**   If you want to configure Duply for the root user, you can configure Duply in the /etc/duply directory.

There are many options available to us in the configuration file, but we need to set only a couple to create our backups. We will need to set the following:

```
GPG_PW='mygeniusbigbikeisnice'
```

First we have provided the GPG_PW value. This is the password we will use to encrypt and decrypt our backups. You can use a more random password than this simple example. You should copy it to your password safe or manager for future reference. Alternatively, you can also use asymmetric encryption where we use private and public GPG keys to encrypt our data.

Next we can set our target and target credentials. The target can be any of the accepted Duplicity back-end types; see the man duplicity page for the list. In general, the type should conform to the following:

```
<scheme://><uid>:<password>@<other.host>/<some_dir>
```

We are going to use the S3 scheme that does not require user and password information in the URL.

```
TARGET='s3://s3-ap-southeast-2.amazonaws.com/our-backup/nightly'
```

This is similar to the URL we used to copy our test file via the aws cli command. Next we need to set our AWS access credentials.

```
TARGET_USER='ALIAIJBASN4NOMJ4FLTR'
TARGET_PASS='+GDHpm+FLPj311tu6YJ29c9luMlQTHwntgy7vgs2'
```

We have set the AWS credentials here, but we may not like to do this as it means we are scattering our AWS credentials over many files in our home directory. Alternatively, we could do something like the following:

```
TARGET_USER=`awk '/aws_access_key_id/ {print $3}' ~.aws/credentials`
TARGET_PASS=`awk '/aws_secret_access_key/ {print $3}' ~.aws/credentials`
```

Here we use the awk command to search the ~/.aws/credentials file for the access and secret AWS keys, printing the third (print $3) column. Another alternative is to have something like this where we use environment variables that are populated from a secured keychain:

```
TARGET_USER=`echo $AWS_ACCESS_KEY_ID`
TARGET_PASS=`echo $AWS_SECRET_ACCESS_KEY`
```

A list of alternatives to storing your secrets for AWS would look like this:

- https://github.com/fugue/credstash
- https://github.com/99designs/aws-vault
- https://github.com/pda/aws-keychain

Next we list the base root, or source, of all our backups.

```
SOURCE='/'
```

If you are doing home directories, you might like to use your home directory as the source.

```
SOURCE='/home/jsmith'
```

Lastly, we are going to set MAX_AGE to 1 month. When we run a purge on our backup files, the actual files are not deleted until we run a --force option with our command. We can still keep our files in S3 for 12 months, but they will not be in the duply catalog. Having many months of backups can slow our duply commands down.

```
MAX_AGE=1M
```

That is all we need to configure for the conf file. Next we are going to edit the ~/.duply/nightly/ exclude file to not back up certain files. The exclude file takes the following syntax:

```
- /path/to/exclude
+ /path/dir/of/directory/to/include
+ /path/*/**.py
```

We can use various conditions to select the paths that we want to include (+) or exclude (-). The file list is included unless it is specifically excluded. Ordering is important as files included will take precedence over files excluded.

In our example, we are going to do a full system backup. The following are files we want to exclude:

```
- /data/
- /dev/
- /lost+found/
- /media/
- /mnt/
- /proc/
- /run/
- /srv/
- /sys/
- /tmp/
- /var/tmp
```

By default, all files are included under the / directory as determined by the SOURCE='/' configuration in our Duply conf file. This example shows we are going to exclude all the normal system directories, like /dev, /proc, and /sys. These are ephemeral and don't need backing up. There are others that don't need backing up, including /data, which will hold remote network filesystems, and the /run and /tmp directories, which are volatile.

You can learn more about how to include and exclude directories and files in the duplicity man page. We are ready to back up or system now.

Running a Duply Backup

Now it is time to back up our system. The first backups are always the longest, as are any full backups. However, to make sure that our exbackup user can access all the parts of the system when running duply, we must first make this change in our sudoers file.

```
$ sudo visudo
# Cmnd alias specification
Cmnd_Alias BACKUPS = /usr/bin/duply

%backup ALL=(ALL) NOPASSWD:  BACKUPS
```

We will then need to add exbackup to the backup group. On CentOS you may have to create the group prior to this step; on Ubuntu the backup group should exist already.

```
$ sudo usermod -aG backup exbackup
```

To make sure that we back up all our system files, we are going to use the sudo command to elevate our permission.

```
$ sudo duply nightly backup
Start duply v1.11, time is 2016-10-15 23:57:21.
Using profile '/home/exbackup/.duply/nightly'.
Using installed duplicity version 0.7.06, python 2.7.12, gpg: unsafe (Home: ~/.gnupg), awk
'GNU Awk 4.1.3, API: 1.1 (GNU MPFR 3.1.4, GNU MP 6.1.0)', grep 'grep (GNU grep) 2.25', bash
'4.3.46(1)-release (x86_64-pc-linux-gnu)'.
Signing disabled. Not GPG_KEY entries in config.
Checking TEMP_DIR '/tmp' is a folder and writable (OK)
Test - Encryption with passphrase (OK)
Test - Decryption with passphrase (OK)
Test - Compare (OK)
Cleanup - Delete '/tmp/duply.12989.1476575841_*'(OK)

--- Start running command PRE at 23:57:21.238 ---
Skipping n/a script '/home/exbackup/.duply/nightly/pre'.
--- Finished state OK at 23:57:21.252 - Runtime 00:00:00.013 ---


--- Start running command BKP at 23:57:21.262 ---
Reading globbing filelist /home/exbackup/.duply/nightly/exclude
Local and Remote metadata are synchronized, no sync needed.
Last full backup date: none
No signatures found, switching to full backup.
Error accessing possibly locked file /var/lib/lxcfs
--------------[ Backup Statistics ]--------------
StartTime 1476588974.26 (Sun Oct 16 03:36:14 2016)
EndTime 1476591675.63 (Sun Oct 16 04:21:15 2016)
ElapsedTime 2701.37 (45 minutes 1.37 seconds)
SourceFiles 140466
SourceFileSize 2375250457 (2.21 GB)
NewFiles 140466
NewFileSize 2375250457 (2.21 GB)
DeletedFiles 0
ChangedFiles 0
ChangedFileSize 0 (0 bytes)
ChangedDeltaSize 0 (0 bytes)
DeltaEntries 140466
RawDeltaSize 2281512996 (2.12 GB)
TotalDestinationSizeChange 198548201 (189 MB)
```

```
Errors 1
-------------------------------------------------

--- Finished state OK at 04:39:42.342 - Runtime 01:03:29.436 ---

--- Start running command POST at 04:39:42.354 ---
Skipping n/a script '/home/exbackup/.duply/nightly/post'.
--- Finished state OK at 04:39:42.375 - Runtime 00:00:00.020 ---
```

With the backup finished, we can see that we have captured 2.21GB of data in our backup. The backup started with several checks, then we read the exclude file, and then we started the backup. There was one file that was not successfully backed up (/var/lib/lxcfs, which is a docker view of the /proc filesystem cgroups and can be excluded too). Despite this, we had a successful backup. Checking in with our S3 bucket, we can see that there are now several files related to our backup.

```
$ aws s3 ls our-backup/nightly/
2016-10-16 03:35:34              0
2016-10-16 04:25:55       36877167 duplicity-full-signatures.20161015T235721Z.sigtar.gpg
2016-10-16 04:39:28         634738 duplicity-full.20161015T235721Z.manifest.gpg
2016-10-16 03:35:37       26244347 duplicity-full.20161015T235721Z.vol1.difftar.gpg
2016-10-16 03:35:37       26194091 duplicity-full.20161015T235721Z.vol10.difftar.gpg
2016-10-16 03:35:37       26196749 duplicity-full.20161015T235721Z.vol11.difftar.gpg
2016-10-16 03:35:38       26227650 duplicity-full.20161015T235721Z.vol12.difftar.gpg
...
```

In the S3 listing, we can see the files that make up our backup. The backups of the files themselves are in the *.difftar.gpg files. There are *.manifest.gpg and *.sigtar.gpg files too. The manifest file is the listing of files, and the sigtar is the signatures of the files to see if they change between backups.

We can now also run a list command to get a few of the files we have backed up.

```
$ sudo duply nightly list
Start duply v1.11, time is 2016-10-16 10:41:48.
Using profile '/home/exbackup/.duply/nightly'.
Using installed duplicity version 0.7.06, python 2.7.12, gpg: unsafe (Home: ~/.gnupg), awk
'GNU Awk 4.1.3, API: 1.1 (GNU MPFR 3.1.4, GNU MP 6.1.0)', grep 'grep (GNU grep) 2.25', bash
'4.3.46(1)-release (x86_64-pc-linux-gnu)'.
Signing disabled. Not GPG_KEY entries in config.
Checking TEMP_DIR '/tmp' is a folder and writable (OK)
Test - Encryption with passphrase (OK)
Test - Decryption with passphrase (OK)
Test - Compare (OK)
Cleanup - Delete '/tmp/duply.18655.1476614508_*'(OK)

--- Start running command LIST at 10:41:49.064 ---
Local and Remote metadata are synchronized, no sync needed.
Last full backup date: Sun Oct 16 10:01:58 2016
Thu Oct 13 07:21:56 2016 .
Thu Sep 29 23:57:15 2016 bin
Fri Jun 24 15:44:14 2016 bin/bash
Tue Jan 19 23:11:42 2016 bin/btrfs
Tue Jan 19 23:11:41 2016 bin/btrfs-calc-size
```

```
...<snip>...
Thu May 26 23:31:30 2016 sbin/wipefs
Tue Feb 16 13:19:00 2016 sbin/xfs_repair
Fri Feb 19 15:21:11 2016 sbin/xtables-multi
Thu May 26 23:31:30 2016 sbin/zramctl
Thu Sep  1 17:37:32 2016 snap
Tue Oct 11 14:07:06 2016 vmlinuz
Thu Sep 29 12:36:50 2016 vmlinuz.old
--- Finished state OK at 10:41:58.667 - Runtime 00:00:09.603 ---
```

This is a long list of all the files we have backed up. We can use a time argument to reduce the output and grep to further narrow what we are looking for (`duply nightly list 2016-10-15 | grep /usr/sbin`).

From the list we are going to now fetch one of the files (`/bin/bash`) from our backup and copy it to the local `/tmp` directory.

```
$ sudo duply nightly fetch bin/bash /tmp/restores/bash
Start duply v1.11, time is 2016-10-16 11:41:15.
Using profile '/home/exbackup/.duply/nightly'.
Using installed duplicity version 0.7.06, python 2.7.12, gpg: unsafe (Home: ~/.gnupg), awk
'GNU Awk 4.1.3, API: 1.1 (GNU MPFR 3.1.4, GNU MP 6.1.0)', grep 'grep (GNU grep) 2.25', bash
'4.3.46(1)-release (x86_64-pc-linux-gnu)'.
Signing disabled. Not GPG_KEY entries in config.
Checking TEMP_DIR '/tmp' is a folder and writable (OK)
Test - Encryption with passphrase (OK)
Test - Decryption with passphrase (OK)
Test - Compare (OK)
Cleanup - Delete '/tmp/duply.20766.1476618075_*'(OK)

--- Start running command FETCH at 11:41:15.242 ---
Synchronizing remote metadata to local cache...
Copying duplicity-full-signatures.20161015T235721Z.sigtar.gpg to local cache.
Copying duplicity-full-signatures.20161016T100158Z.sigtar.gpg to local cache.
Copying duplicity-full.20161015T235721Z.manifest.gpg to local cache.
Copying duplicity-full.20161016T100158Z.manifest.gpg to local cache.
Last full backup date: Sun Oct 16 10:01:58 2016
--- Finished state OK at 12:04:32.407 - Runtime 00:23:17.164 ---
```

The duply `fetch` process will download the signature files and manifest files locally so they can be processed. This can take some time. Once done, Duply will restore the file. Here you can see that we have restored the bin/bash file successfully. To restore the whole backup, we use the duply `restore <path_to_restore_to>` command.

Now that we have successfully backed up and restored files on our host, we will add a `cron` job to do this for us on a nightly basis. We will add this to the exbackup crontab with the following command:

```
$ crontab -e
0 2 * * * env HOME=/home/exbackup sudo duply nightly backup
```

We will run this Duply backup at 2 a.m. every morning and guarantee that the `HOME` environment variable is set correctly as many parts (gpg, duply) rely on the correct home directory.

Using Bareos

The cost of a commercial backup solution can be extremely high. Bareos provides a robust, reliable, customizable, and efficient open source backup service for Linux, Unix, and Windows desktops and servers. It works with most storage devices, DAT, LTO, and autoloaders, and it can also back up to disk, including GlusterFS. Bareos is easy to configure, secure, and upgrade, and it is a complete, free, and robust backup server.

Bareos is a fork of the popular Bacula backup server software. Bacula is still available in an open source community version, but it has dedicated development for the commercial version of its software. Bareos and Bacula have since diverged significantly in features but still remain similar in configuration and installation. In most instances, in this section you could swap *Bareos* for *Bacula* and you would be fine for configuring either.

Bareos works on the client/server model and requires a Bareos client installed on the target host to be backed up. The components of the Bareos are as follows:

- A Director daemon

- A Storage daemon

- A File daemon

- A catalog of what has been backed up to where

- A console to manage Bareos

The Bareos backup server itself requires at least these two daemons to be running: the Director daemon and the Storage daemon.

The Director daemon controls what will be backed up, when it will be backed up, and the location to which it will be backed up. It also provides similar services for any restoration jobs that might need to take place. It has a configuration file that contains the details that control the running of the Director daemon itself, as well as the Storage daemon and the File daemon that run on the target host.

The Storage daemon communicates with the Director daemon and the File daemon running on the target host and controls the access to the devices where your data will be stored, either on disk or on tape. The Storage daemon controls access to the backup media, tape drives, and autoloaders. It can be configured to even write to GlusterFS, and we will demonstrate this shortly.

The File daemon sits on the target host waiting for connections from the Bareos Director daemon. When it receives the instructions to start a backup, the target host gets a list of the files it is to back up. It then makes a direct connection to the Storage daemon and sends the backup data to the Storage daemon to be written to the backup media. The File daemon communicates what files have been backed up to the Director daemon, and that information is written to the Bareos catalog.

The catalog records the files that have been backed up, the location from which they were backed up, when they were backed up, and onto what media (or volume) they were backed up. This catalog is kept in a SQL database for future reference. Once the backup is complete, the Bareos program can verify the backup was successful by comparing what was written to the catalog and what was written to the tape.

When a restore operation is requested, Bareos will read the contents of the catalog and request that the appropriate media be loaded. It will then contact the target client and the Storage daemon, and they will begin the restoration process.

The backup and restore operations are referred to as *jobs* in Bareos. You can schedule backup and restore jobs in the Bareos Director configuration file, /etc/bareos/bareos-dir.conf. Each job is made up of a series of definitions, and these definitions can inherit a set of common definitions that can make your configurations easier to manage. Each job acts on a client that is the target host. The jobs back up on or restore from a *volume*, which refers to the storage media you are using (e.g., tape, DVD, or disk). These volumes can be grouped into *pools* and given common definitions concerning retention periods, usage, and rotation. The scheduler can, of course, manage the coordination of the jobs, clients, volumes, and pools to run a one-off operation or repeated ones.

You control Bareos operations via the bconsole, a terminal console program that you can use to run jobs and view the status of the Director, Storage, or File daemons. You can also use it to manage volumes, pools, and restore operations. It is simple to set up, and you can place it anywhere on the network.

■ **Note** We will look at setting up Bareos's console in the "Introducing the Bareos Web-UI" section.

The Bareos server requires the following TCP ports open on your server:

- The Bareos Director daemon requires port 9101 (on the Bareos server only).

- The Bareos Storage daemon requires port 9102 (on the Bareos server only).

- The Bareos File daemon requires port 9103 (on any target host or client).

You add them with the following command on the backup server:

```
$ sudo firewall-cmd --zone public --permanent --add-service bacula
$ sudo firewall-cmd --reload
```

On the clients, you only need to open TCP port 9103, and on CentOS hosts you will find that there is a bacula-client service provided in firewalld.

```
$ sudo firewall-cmd --zone public --permanent --add-service bacula-client
$ sudo firewall-cmd -reload
```

If you are running this on Ubuntu, you can use ufw to add the application file (/etc/ufw/applications.d/bareos) like so:

```
[Bareos]
title=Bareos Backup Server
description=The Bareos Backup Server.
ports=9101,9102,9103/tcp
```

And you do similar for the client by just allowing port 9103 access. We then would execute the following:

```
$ sudo ufw reload && sudo ufw allow bareos
```

Getting the Software

The Bareos download page (https://www.bareos.org/en/download.html) provides links to RPM and DEB packages of the latest releases for you to download. Distributions can be several versions behind the latest release, and only Ubuntu is currently shipping with Bareos. CentOS still has Bacula available but not Bareos. You can get the packages and tarballs here: http://download.bareos.org/bareos/.

For CentOS we will install the following YUM repo contents into the file /etc/yum.repos.d/bareos. repo, as shown here:

```
[bareos_bareos-15.2]
name=Backup Archiving Recovery Open Sourced 15.2 (CentOS_7)
type=rpm-md
baseurl=http://download.bareos.org/bareos/release/15.2/CentOS_7/
gpgcheck=1
gpgkey=http://download.bareos.org/bareos/release/15.2/CentOS_7/repodata/repomd.xml.key
enabled=1
```

We are then able to install the following packages:

```
$ sudo yum install bareos-client bareos-director bareos-storage bareos-storage-glusterfs
bareos-bconsole
```

On Ubuntu, you have to use the following:

```
$ sudo aptitude install bareos-filedaemon bareos-bconsole bareos-director bareos-storage
```

On Ubuntu, you will be asked to give a username and password for your MariaDB service via the `dbconfig-common` helper. At this stage we are not ready to provide that information, so we are going to choose <No>. If you have your details or are setting this up on your localhost, you can select yes and go through the steps for setting up the database. We are going to go through the database configuration shortly.

The installation process installs all the required packages and any dependencies and creates the default configuration files in the configuration directory /etc/bareos. The bareos user is also created at this point. To get Bareos up and running, you will have to edit the following files in the configuration directory to access the Bareos management console: `/etc/bareos/bareos-dir.conf`, `/etc/bareos/bareos-sd.conf`, `/etc/bareos/bareos-fd.conf`, and `/etc/bareos/bconsole.conf`.

Configuring the Database

We talked about MariaDB servers in Chapter 11. We are now going to create a database on that host to house our catalog. Along the way, we'll configure the MariaDB host to be backed up. First, we need to create the correct accounts and the database on our MariaDB host.

We will assume that the `headoffice.example.com` host has the MariaDB database server installed and that we are running our backups from `backup.example.com`. We can, of course, house this database on the one host, `headoffice.example.com`, if we didn't have an extra host available to be the separate backup host. In that case, you should use localhost in the following examples where we have used `backup.example.com`. The other alternatives are to store a separate MariaDB database server (or PostgreSQL, if you want) on your backup host or to use a SQLite database on the backup host.

On the `headoffice.example.com` MariaDB host, we will create a new database for Bareos and grant access to the user bareos from our `backup.example.com` host. We will then make sure that our `backup.example.com` host can connect to port 3306 on `headoffice.example.com` by making a change to the firewall. While we do that, we will also make sure that our Bareos File daemon is installed on `headoffice.example.com` and that we have firewall access for TCP port 9103 on that host from `backup.example.com`.

We need to install the following packages on the host that will house the Bareos database; they contain the helper scripts that help manage the database:

```
$ sudo aptitude install -y bareo-database-common bareos-database-mysql
```

Of course, on CentOS, you would use the yum command.
On `headoffice.example.com` we will do the following:

```
$ sudo mysql -u root -p
Enter Password:
...
mysql> CREATE DATABASE 'bareos';
Query OK, 1 row affected (0.00 sec)
mysql> GRANT ALL PRIVILEGES ON bareos.* to bareos@backup.example.com ↵
```

```
IDENTIFIED BY 'somepassword';
Query OK, 0 rows affected (0.00 sec)
mysql> FLUSH PRIVILEGES;
Query OK, 0 rows affected (0.00 sec)
mysql> \q;
Bye
```

In the previous code, we have created a database called bareos. On that database, we have given the user bareos signing in from backup.example.com all privileges if they use the somepassword password. If you were setting this up for a localhost, you would change bareos@backup.example.com to bareos@localhost. Finally, we use FLUSH PRIVILEGES, which reloads the grants table with all the recent changes.

On CentOS and Ubuntu hosts, there are scripts to create, drop, update, and back up your Bareos databases. You will find them in /usr/lib/bareos/scripts/.

To create the database tables for the Bareos database, we will run the following on the backup.example.com host:

```
$ sudo /usr/lib/bareos/scripts/create_bareos_database
Creating mysql database
Creating of bareos database succeeded.
$ sudo /usr/lib/bareos/scripts/grant_bareos_privileges
Granting mysql tables
Privileges for user bareos granted ON database bareos.
```

Running these scripts supplied by Bareos will create the necessary tables for our catalog and appropriate grants for the Bareos user.

We confirm that the database was created by running the following command from backup.example.com:

```
$ sudo -u bareos mysql -h headoffice.example.com -u bareos -p -D bareos ↵
-e 'show tables;'
```

This command connects to the MariaDB database running on the headoffice.example.com host using the Bareos username and password. -p prompts for a password, and -psomepassword is how you would submit the password on the command line (there is no space between –p and the password). Getting the output will do two things: confirm that our username and password are working correctly and that the scripts actually did create some tables.

■ **Note**   You can find additional information on using Bareos with MySQL and MariaDB at
http://doc.bareos.org/master/html/bareos-manual-main-reference.html#x1-41100032.1.2.

Other things to be aware of are that the /data/backups/bareos/FileStorage directory must exist, and it must also be writable by the Bareos user, as should the /var/log/bareos.log file.

Configuring Bareos

We'll now examine the configuration files that need to be defined for your Bareos server. As mentioned earlier, there are three files for dealing with the Bareos server itself and one for the management console.

What we are going to do in these exercises is the following:

- In the bareos-dir.conf file:

  - Configure the director with the correct name

  - Configure the default Linux backup job definition

  - Configure a backup job for the headoffice server

  - Configure the set of files to back up

  - Configure the schedule of the backup

  - Configure the client to back up

  - Add the Storage daemon configuration for the Director

  - Configure the pools

  - Configure the console

  - Configure the messages

- In the bareos-sd.conf file:

  - Configure the storage daemon

- In the bareos-fd.conf file:

  - Configure the client daemon

Before we configure anything in Bareos, we should explain the relationship these files have with each other. For the Bareos daemons to communicate with each other, they require the exchange of a set of passwords. Each Storage daemon (you can have more than one) and each File daemon (you will generally have more than one) must contain the name of the Bareos Director and the password it uses to verify itself. The password is set in two places for each daemon that wants to communicate with the Bareos Director.

Figure 14-9 shows the relationship between the configuration files and their common definitions.

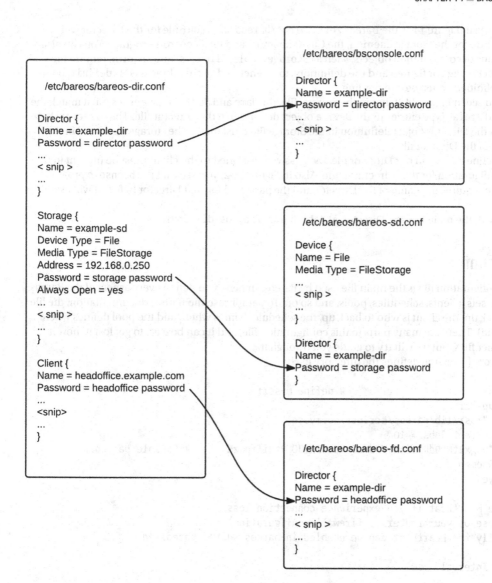

```
                                              /etc/bareos/bsconsole.conf

                                              Director {
   /etc/bareos/bareos-dir.conf                Name = example-dir
                                              Password = director password
   Director {                                 ...
   Name = example-dir                         < snip >
   Password = director password               ...
   ...                                        }
   < snip >
   ...
   }

   Storage {                                  /etc/bareos/bareos-sd.conf
   Name = example-sd
   Device Type = File                         Device {
   Media Type = FileStorage                   Name = File
   Address = 192.168.0.250                    Media Type = FileStorage
   Password = storage password                ...
   Always Open = yes                          < snip >
   ...                                        ...
   < snip >                                   }
   ...
   }                                          Director {
                                              Name = example-dir
   Client {                                   Password = storage password
   Name = headoffice.example.com              }
   Password = headoffice password
   ...
   <snip>
   ...
   }
                                              /etc/bareos/bareos-fd.conf


                                              Director {
                                              Name = example-dir
                                              Password = headoffice password
                                              ...
                                              < snip >
                                              ...
                                              }
```

Figure 14-9. *Bareos common configuration file definitions*

As you can see in Figure 14-9, the Bareos /etc/bareos/bareos-dir.conf file for the Director will contain information for the Storage daemon, the Client daemon, and the bconsole program. You can also see that definitions of configuration objects, such as Storage, Pools, FileSets, and so forth, require the name of the object being configured and the definitions to be enclosed in curly brackets: {<definition = value>}. The definitions must be one per line.

You can also see in Figure 14-9 that in the Storage file, the Name and Media Type entries must match the Device Type and Media Type entries in the Device object definition in the Director file. The Director Name and Password in the Director object definition in the Storage file must match the storage password in the Storage section of the Director file.

When we define a client in our Director file, the password assigned to the client must be present in the File daemon configuration for that Director name. Also in Figure 13-2, you see that the bconsole program configuration file requires the name of the Director and the password for that Director before it will establish a connection.

Let's start with the main file, the Director, at /etc/bareos/bareos-dir.conf.

bareos-dir.conf

The Director configuration file is the main file used by Bareos. In here, you define every aspect of the Bareos service: jobs, file sets, clients, schedules, pools, and so on. To paraphrase the Bareos documentation, the file set is what to back up, the client is who to back up, the schedule defines when, and the pool defines where (i.e., what volume). There are many parts to this configuration file, and it can be easy to get lost in how it relates to the other files, but we will try to guide you through it.

The Director {} section defines the directory itself.

```
Director {                           # define myself
  Name = backup-dir
  QueryFile = "/usr/lib/bareos/scripts/query.sql"
  Maximum Concurrent Jobs = 10
  Password = "uogx2tNL9dRUwGfNvY/b+uQrU8osZn+JOM7t8iIrpszN"      # Console password
  Messages = Daemon
  Auditing = yes

  # Enable the Heartbeat if you experience connection losses
  # (eg. because of your router or firewall configuration).
  # Additionally the Heartbeat can be enabled in bareos-sd and bareos-fd.
  #
  # Heartbeat Interval = 1m

  # remove comment in next line to load dynamic backends from specified directory
  # Backend Directory = /usr/lib64/bareos/backends

  # remove comment from "Plugin Directory" to load plugins from specified directory.
  # if "Plugin Names" is defined, only the specified plugins will be loaded,
  # otherwise all director plugins (*-dir.so) from the "Plugin Directory".
  #
  # Plugin Directory = /usr/lib64/bareos/plugins
  # Plugin Names = ""
}
```

When we install Bareos, a lot of our basic configuration is ready to go. The installation should configure the passwords automatically. Here we have changed the Name definition; the password was autogenerated. The rest of the entries are defaults and are fine. The Director port is sitting on 9101. The QueryFile directive points to /usr/lib/bareos/scripts/query.sql and is a SQL file that contains various "precanned" SQL statements that can be used to query the database from the console. You could add your own SQL queries to this script if you believe that Bareos console doesn't have the information you are looking for.

JobDefs

A JobDefs section groups similar backup job requirements together. They are then referenced in one of the Job sections. For instance, to group the requirements for our web servers that define their FileSet, Schedule, and Storage media, we can create a JobDefs section for them, and mail servers can be defined in another. All the options that you use to define a Job can be put into the JobDefs section. The following creates a generic DefaultLinux job definition:

```
JobDefs {
  Name = "DefaultLinux"
  Type = Backup
  Level = Incremental
  Client = bareos-fd
  FileSet = "Linux"
  Schedule = "WeeklyCycle"
  Storage = File
  Messages = Standard
  Pool = Incremental
  Priority = 10
  Write Bootstrap = "/var/lib/bareos/%c.bsr"
  Full Backup Pool = Full
  Incremental Backup Pool = Incremental
}
```

The preceding code is taken from the provided /etc/bareos/bareos-dir.conf. All the definitions here can also be defined in the Job resource. First, we declare the JobDefs section between the curly brackets, { }. Next, we name the JobDefs as DefaultLinux.

The Type of job can be Backup, Restore, Verify, or Admin. The Backup job type performs a backup, the Restore type performs a restore, the Verify type compares the contents of the catalog to the file system you have just backed up, and the Admin type can be used to perform catalog maintenance, if required.

The Level of backup required is not really required, but it must be specified either here in the JobDefs or in the Schedule section. Any setting within the Schedule overrides the setting here.

The value for Level can be Full, Incremental, or Differential. The full backup takes a backup of all files in the specified FileSet regardless of their backup history. The incremental backup will back up files changed since the last full, differential, or incremental backup. The differential backup will do a very similar job as the incremental, but it will back up *all* files changed since the last full save. Let's discuss that a little more.

Whenever a differential or incremental backup is performed, the Bareos File daemon clients will check the file list for modified file timestamps and changed file timestamps and compare them to the previous full backup. If the timestamps are different, then the files will be backed up by the incremental or differential backup process. However, what differentiates the differential from the incremental is that the differential backup merges all changed files into one backup since the last full backup. This means that although the backup may take up more space on your volumes (storage media), when you restore from the backups, you will need only the last full backup and the most recent differential backup. If you had been using incremental backups, you would need the last full backup plus each incremental since the last full backup. The other point we will make here is that if there is no full backup for this `FileSet` on this client for the retention time period, Bareos will upgrade your backup to a full backup automatically. We are going to leave `Level = Incremental` in this `JobDefs`.

ALWAYS INCREMENTAL

Bareos also provides another option to the more traditional full, differential, incremental backup regime called Always Incremental. This, as the name suggests, is where you only ever do incremental backups of your file data (it works only for file-based backups).

It is useful for reducing the amount of network traffic that occurs during backups and of course makes backups quicker as it does away with full backups. The incremental backups can be set to be stored depending on number of days or job numbers.

After that backup age has expired, a consolidation job merges the incremental backups into a new backup. That backup itself can be copied off to longer-term storage at particular points or via a virtual full job that can take all backups into a new long-term backup.

The backup starts with a full backup, of course, but then subsequent incremental backups are performed, possibly nightly, and then consolidation jobs are run on the backup server daily or when appropriate. This frees the clients from long-running backup jobs and transfers the bulk of the mundane full backup processing to the backup server.

The `Client` directive here is set to `bareos-fd`. This is overridden by the `Client {}` definition but is needed by the configuration file. The client `bareos-fd` resource has to exist in the configuration file; otherwise, an error will occur. We will leave this as is.

The `FileSet = "Linux"` directive defines the resource that describes the files we want to back up for our hosts. The `FileSet` will be defined later in our Director configuration file. In the `FileSet`, you can include and exclude directories and file names or types. You can also define Linux, Microsoft Windows, or Mac files to be backed up or excluded. The default `FileSet` included here refers to a typical Linux file set, which will be seen shortly.

Next is the `Schedule` resource we are assigning to the `JobDefs`, which defines when we should run this type of job. The default definition for the `WeeklyCycle` included in Bareos is a simple monthly full backup with a differential once a week. It also runs a nightly incremental backup from Monday to Saturday. We will alter this so that it runs another full backup every third week; we will cover how to do this shortly.

In the default `JobDefs`, we can also see that the `Storage` resource has been defined as `File`. This points to the name of the storage device defined by `Name = File`. We just explained that this points to our Storage configuration file, and our backups will go to a portion of hard disk we have set aside for backups, `/data/backups/FileStorage`.

`Messages = Standard` refers to the `Messages` resource. Here, you can set the way your messages are handled. They can be either written to a log or sent to an e-mail address.

The `Pool = Full` definition points the job to a particular pool of volumes where they are backed up. As mentioned earlier, volumes are groups of storage media. You might have a group for your daily backups, a group for your weekly backups, and a group for your monthly backups. In this instance, we have defined a default group, Full, for our backups. We have, however, defined `Full Backup Pool = Full` and `Incremental Backup Pool = Incremental` to make sure that the full and incremental backups go to the right media.

Lastly in our JobDefs we have `Priority` = 10. This setting helps prioritize jobs; the lower the number, the higher the priority Bareos will give to the job. Some settings in the JobDefs can be overridden by definitions in other areas, like in the Job, Schedule, and Client definitions.

Jobs

Jobs define the actual backups that can occur. The most basic job must have a name, a client, a JobDefs name, and if it is enabled. If the job is enabled, it will be listed in the schedule.

```
Job {
  Name = "BackupCatalog"
  JobDefs = "DefaultJob"
  Level = Full
  FileSet="Catalog"
  Schedule = "WeeklyCycleAfterBackup"

  # This creates an ASCII copy of the catalog
  # Arguments to make_catalog_backup.pl are:
  #  make_catalog_backup.pl <catalog-name>
  RunBeforeJob = "/usr/lib/bareos/scripts/make_catalog_backup.pl MyCatalog"

  # This deletes the copy of the catalog
  RunAfterJob  = "/usr/lib/bareos/scripts/delete_catalog_backup"

  # This sends the bootstrap via mail for disaster recovery.
  # Should be sent to another system, please change recipient accordingly
  Write Bootstrap = "|/usr/bin/bsmtp -h localhost -f \"\(Bareos\) \" -s \"Bootstrap for Job
%j\" root@localhost" # (#01)
  Priority = 11                   # run after main backup
}

Job {
  Name = "RestoreFiles"
  Type = Restore
  Client=au-mel-centos-1-fd
  FileSet = "Linux All"
  Storage = File
  Pool = Incremental
  Messages = Standard
  Where = /tmp/bareos-restores
}

Job {
  Name = headoffice.example.com
  Client = headoffice-fd
  Enabled = yes
  JobDefs = "DefaultLinux"
}
```

The first two job definitions are standard in Bareos. We need the first job, named `BackupCatalog`, to back up our MariaDB database, which holds the catalog. The second job definition is used by restore jobs. These are both defaults in the current Bareos installation.

You can also see we have now described a new job. In the `headoffice.example.com` job, we have declared the `Name` and the `Client` (which we will define shortly), `Enabled` the job, and given it a `JobDef`. We have used `JobDefs = "DefaultLinux"` to define the other options we can use in our job.

The remaining items we need to address are `FileSet`, `Pool`, and `Schedule`, and we need to set a `Client`. Let's look at the `FileSet` definition first.

FileSets

A `FileSet` describes what you want to back up on your hosts. You can declare as many as you like, and you can declare these file sets for Windows, Linux, and Mac hosts. We are going to create a new `FileSet` called `Linux`.

```
FileSet {
  Name = "Linux"
  Include {
    Options {
      Compression = GZIP
      Signature = SHA1
    }
    File = "/etc"
    File = "/var/lib" File = "/data" File = "/home"
    }
  Exclude {
    File = "/proc"
    File = "/sys"
    File = "/dev"
    File = "/run"
    File = "/tmp"
    File = "/data/backups/FileStorage"
  }
}
```

In this `FileSet` we first define the `Name`. This can be used in the `JobDefs` or `Job` resource definition. As you can see, we can divide the `FileSet` into two parts: the `Include` section and the `Exclude` section. In the `Include` section, we have specified a couple of options: `Compression` and `Signature`. These settings allow our backup data to be compressed with the gzip program and define the signature of either SHA1 or MD5. If we were using a tape drive that did hardware compression on the data as it was written to tape, we would not use the software compression here. It also supports other compression formats like LZO, LZ4, and LZ4HC. The LZ formats tend to provide greater speed in compression/decompression but a smaller compression ratio. You can also choose your GZIP compression ratio with choosing between GZIP1 to GZIP9 (with GZIP9 being the best, and slowest, compression).

With the signature, you can use either SHA1 or MD5, but MD5 will add an extra overhead to each file saved in both data size and CPU time. The signature is stored in the catalog for use with verification of the file's contents and if they have changed. SHA1 is recommended as it has less chance of collision and greater integrity than MD5.

Next we define the files we want to include in our backup. These are the /etc, /var/lib, /data, and /home directories. We chose /etc because it contains the main configuration files for our system, the /var/lib/ directory because some of our Samba and MariaDB data will be stored there, and the /data and /home directories because that is where our user data will be stored.

We are also excluding some directories (or at least making sure that they will not be backed up by mistake): /proc, /sys, /dev, and others. These directories are nonpermanent and change at every boot of the host, so there is no point in saving them. The /data/backups/FileStorage directory is being excluded because that is where we are backing up to. There is no point making backups of backups here—if we did, our backups would double in size with every backup.

It is also interesting to note that we are not backing up the whole system here; for example, we are not backing up /usr or /lib or /boot, which are important in full system restores. The reason behind this is that we are confident that we will be able to rebuild this host as fast or faster than we can restore it. This way we can reduce the size of our backups without increasing our risk of not being able to restore data if we need it. If you want to back up the whole Linux system, take a look at the Linux All file set instead.

Our file lists can also be kept in a separate file that we include into the FileSet with the @ symbol. For example, say we have a Windows list like the following that we have saved to a file called /etc/bareos/windows.list:

```
File = "C:/"
File = "D:/"
```

In our FileSet we would include that file list like so:

```
FileSet {
  Name = "Windows All Drives"
  Enable VSS = yes
  Include {
    Options {
      Signature = MD5
      Drive Type = fixed
      IgnoreCase = yes
      WildFile = "[A-Z]:/pagefile.sys"
      WildDir = "[A-Z]:/RECYCLER"
      WildDir = "[A-Z]:/$RECYCLE.BIN"
      WildDir = "[A-Z]:/System Volume Information"
      WildDir = "*/Cache/*"
      WildDir = "*/cache/*"
      Exclude = yes
    }
    @/etc/bareos/windows.list
  }
}
```

Here we have included the C: and D: drives on our Windows host via the @/etc/bareos/windows.list file. We are using the SHA1 signature for our catalog. We are also excluding some unwanted directories using the [A-Z] regular expression to handle any drive letter between A and Z. We don't want any temp or cache directories, as these tend to hold lots of data that doesn't require backing up and can be quite large.

```
FileSet {
  Name = "Catalog"
  Include {
    Options {
      signature = MD5
    }
```

```
    File = "/var/lib/bareos/bareos.sql" # database dump
    File = "/etc/bareos"                 # configuration
  }
}
```

This last FileSet has been defined in the BackupCatalog resource job.

Schedules

Next, we have the Schedule resources. A Schedule defines when a job should run. We can also describe the level of our backup (if it is declared in the schedule, it overrides the setting in the Job or JobDefs resource). For the WeeklyCycle we are using, we need to change it slightly from the default. We want to take a full backup of our data bimonthly, so we change the Schedule to look like this:

```
Schedule {
  Name = "WeeklyCycle"
  Run = Full 1st 3rd sun at 23:05
  Run = Differential 2nd 4th 5th sun at 23:05
  Run = Incremental mon-sat at 23:05
}
Schedule {
  Name = "WeeklyCycleAfterBackup"
  Run = Full sun-sat at 23:10
}
```

As described in the Schedule named WeeklyCycle, we are running a full backup on the first and third Sundays of every month. We run a differential every second, fourth, and fifth Sunday, with an incremental nightly between Monday and Saturday. These date-time specifications are made up of several well-defined keywords, and it is easy to create complex schedules if you want.

■ **Note**   You can read more about the terms you can use in the Schedule resource documentation at http://doc.bareos.org/master/html/bareos-manual-main-reference.html#x1-1300009.4.

Clients

Before we can run any backups, we need to create the Client resource. We do that by providing an Address, a Name, and a Password. The Name in the Client definition will match the Client defined in the Job resource. The Password must match the password defined in the File daemon configuration file (bareos-fd.conf) Director resource. The Address can be the fully qualified domain name or the IP address. Our Client resource will look like the following:

```
Client {
  Name = headoffice-fd
  Address = headoffice.example.com
  Password = "6rZQQqVsOJeeTPefrG2AslT5ODxtPWO1hNsd7Re1u6J/"
}
```

Storage

Let's now configure the Storage definition. Again, this will be within the Storage {} section of the bareos-dir.conf file. We will use this information in the bareos-sd.conf file soon.

```
Storage {
  Name = File
# Do not use "localhost" here
  Address = backup.example.com
  Password = "4ncvx7V+Mw4NOMDMyuYjCHsNg1nKgcdh8nlOszWpi6t4"
  Device = FileStorage
  Media Type = File
}
```

This is the default configuration for the Storage section. We have changed only the Address details, the password being created during the installation process. In Figure 14-9, you saw that the Name, Password, Device, and Media Type details should also be in the /etc/bareos/bareos-sd.conf file.

Catalog

Next, we should add these details to the Bareos Director configuration file. The configuration for the catalog will begin with the Catalog definition.

```
Catalog {
  Name = MyCatalog
  # Uncomment the following lines if you want the dbi driver
  # dbdriver = "dbi:postgresql"; dbaddress = 127.0.0.1; dbport =
  #dbdriver = "postgresql"
  dbdriver = "mysql"
  dbname = "bareos"
  dbuser = "bareos"
  dbpassword = "somepassword"
  dbaddress = headoffice.example.com
}
```

The Name can be anything, and we will stick with the default MyCatalog. By default Bareos will use the PostgreSQL driver and database. Here we are specifying the dbdriver mysql for the MariaDB database we are using. The dbname should be bareos, as should the user. The dbpassword is the password we created previously. The dbaddress should be the address of the host the Catalog is on.

Pools

Pools, as described earlier, are media volumes that are grouped together to reflect their purpose. You could have pools of media in groups like monthly, weekly, daily, or archive, or even by things like web servers, database servers, and so forth. In the Pool definition, you specify things like retention policies, labeling formatting, and so on. We are using our hard disk as our storage device, so we won't have any physically different media to load in or rotate out like you do with tape media. Our main interest here will be retention or how long we hold the data for before we wipe it.

In our Pool definition we have made the following changes to the default:

```
Pool {
  Name = Full
  Pool Type = Backup
  Recycle = yes
  Recycle Oldest Volume = Yes
  AutoPrune = yes
  Volume Retention = 365 days
  Maximum Volume Bytes = 50G
  Maximum Volumes = 100
  Label Format = "Full-${Year}-${Month:p/2/0/r}-${Day:p/2/0/r}"
}

Pool {
  Name = Differential
  Pool Type = Backup
  Recycle = yes
  Recycle Oldest Volume = Yes
  AutoPrune = yes
  Volume Retention = 90 days
  Maximum Volume Bytes = 10G
  Maximum Volumes = 100
  Label Format = "Differential-${Year}-${Month:p/2/0/r}-${Day:p/2/0/r}"
}

Pool {
  Name = Incremental
  Pool Type = Backup
  Recycle = yes
  Recycle Oldest Volume = Yes
  AutoPrune = yes
  Volume Retention = 30 days
  Maximum Volume Bytes = 1G
  Maximum Volumes = 100
  Label Format = "Incremental-${Year}-${Month:p/2/0/r}-${Day:p/2/0/r}"
}
```

The Name of the Pool will be used to reference the Pool in other resource definitions. Each has the Pool Type of Backup, which is currently the only available type, according to the Bareos documentation. We have set two different Maximum Volume Bytes, one at 50GB, 10GB, and one at 1GB. This will roll over the volume to the next available volume (or Bareos will create a new volume for us) when the volumes reach those size limits. This means that we will have small files to deal with, rather than one huge file containing all our backup data.

■ **Note**   With tape media, you probably won't set the Maximum Volume Bytes limit, as in general you will want the tape to hold as much as its capacity. If a volume is created with this limit, it will remain at that limit regardless of the setting in the Pool resource. You will have to update the volume itself to change this limit using the Bareos console.

In our `Pool` definition we have also set `AutoPrune = Yes`, which enables Bareos to delete backup details from the catalog once the `Volume Retention` period has expired. There are times when you would not want this to occur. For example, with archive backups—that is, when you want to keep your data for as long as possible—you will not want the records of those backups to be deleted from the catalog. In this case, you would set `AutoPrune` to No, just to be safe.

■ **Caution**   Even if you have set your `Pool` to `AutoPrune = No` and `Volume Retention = 10 years`, your backup data will last only as long as the data on the tape or the disks lasts. Overwriting the data or corruption of the data will make restoring the data impossible, regardless of what the Bareos catalog says.

`Volume Retention` tells Bareos how long it should consider the data on the volume as current. We have set our pools to different values: we want to keep the data in our full volumes for 12 months and 90 days for differentials and our incremental volumes for 30 days. You may want to consider longer retention periods. After this retention period has expired, Bareos considers the volume data to have expired and that data can be overwritten.

Setting `Recycle = Yes` in our `Pool` definition means that once the data on the volume is considered expired, that volume will become available again to the general pool, to be used for writing again. Setting `Recycle Oldest Volume = Yes` means the oldest volume will be used before any other volume when more than one volume is available. This has the obvious advantage of destroying any existing data on those volumes at the latest possible time, so you will still be able to restore from those volumes up until that time.

Last in our `Pool` resource is the `Label` definition. Bareos gives a name or label to volumes based on this format. Tapes from autoloaders with barcode labels are not automatically read into Bareos and need to be manually labeled when you add a new tape. In the case of tape media, a small section of data is written to the start of the tape, giving it the label name for that volume. Once a tape is labeled, Bareos will always know which tape is inserted into the tape unit. We are using `"Full-"` and `"Incremental-"` and adding the suffix `"${Year}-${Month:p/2/0/ r}-${Day:p/2/0/r}"` to produce a labeled volume like `Full-2016-01-01`. For full details on the variable expansions available with Bareos, please visit `http://doc.bareos.org/master/html/bareos-manual-main-reference.html#x1-1190008.3.3`.

■ **Note**   For a discussion on backup strategies in relation to managing your tapes and rotations using Bareos, go to `http://doc.bareos.org/master/html/bareos-manual-main-reference.html#x1-23200019`.

Console

The `Console` service gives the Director the ability to poll the File or Storage daemons and report on their status. This ability is verified by the password provided and requires the name of the Bareos service allowed to monitor it. In the Director configuration file, we have the following:

```
Console {
  Name = example-mon
  Password = "tcqT4bG9NLl11YoZ5GXFLrcb8o9mSuM2U4rxl7mgH8eD"
  CommandACL = status, .status
  JobACL = *all*
}
```

Messaging

The messaging service is defined in the Director configuration and is a way for all communications from Bareos to be sent via the Director and not from the individual clients. When an incident occurs or a job completes, the messages are sent to the standard messaging service configured in the Director. The resource named Standard is defined in the Messages section and looks like the following:

```
Messages {
  Name = Standard
  mailcommand = "/usr/bin/bsmtp -h localhost -f \"\(Bareos\) \<%r\>\" -s \"Bareos: %t
  %e of %c %l\" %r"
  operatorcommand = "/usr/bin/bsmtp -h localhost -f \"\(Bareos\) \<%r\>\" -s \"Bareos:
  Intervention needed for %j\" %r"
  mail = admin@example.com = all, !skipped, !audit # (#02)
  operator = admin@example.com = mount        # (#03)
  console = all, !skipped, !saved, !audit
  append = "/var/log/bareos/bareos.log" = all, !skipped, !audit
  catalog = all, !audit
}


#
# Message delivery for daemon messages (no job).
#
Messages {
  Name = Daemon
  mailcommand = "/usr/bin/bsmtp -h localhost -f \"\(Bareos\) \<%r\>\" -s \"Bareos daemon
  message\" %r"
  mail = admin@example.com = all, !skipped, !audit # (#02)
  console = all, !skipped, !saved, !audit
  append = "/var/log/bareos/bareos.log" = all, !skipped, !audit
  append = "/var/log/bareos/bareos-audit.log" = audit
}
```

Bareos uses the mailcommand and operatorcommand commands to send e-mail messages indicating the status of Bareos, either alerts or completion messages. It uses its own mailer binary, bsmtp, to send messages to the appropriate addresses. -f sets the From header, and -s sets the Subject header of the e-mail. You need to change the mail and operator settings to suit your environment by setting the e-mail address to the person responsible for administering the Bareos server (in our case, admin@example.com). You can set operator type messages, such as "Please mount tape," to a different e-mail address compared to success/failure messages defined in the mail definition. We have also added the -h mail.example.com setting, which points to our mail server for the mailcommand and operatorcommand commands. For more information, see the following documentation: http://doc.bareos.org/master/html/bareos-manual-main-reference.html#x1-16500012.

In the next section, we'll look at the file we are going to configure to describe our Storage daemon.

bareos-sd.conf

Bareos stores the configuration details for the Storage daemon in the /etc/bareos/bareos-sd. conf file. The Storage configuration file that is supplied by Bareos has many examples of different ways to configure your devices. You should use the file as a guide to setting up different types of storage devices. In our Storage file we have the following:

```
Storage {                               # definition of myself
  Name = example-sd
  Maximum Concurrent Jobs = 20

  # remove comment from "Plugin Directory" to load plugins from specified directory.
  # if "Plugin Names" is defined, only the specified plugins will be loaded,
  # otherwise all storage plugins (*-sd.so) from the "Plugin Directory".
  #
  # Plugin Directory = /usr/lib64/bareos/plugins
  # Plugin Names = ""
}

#
# List Directors who are permitted to contact Storage daemon
#
Director {
  Name = example-dir
  Password = "4ncvx7V+Mw4NOMDMyuYjCHsNg1nKgcdh8nlOszWpi6t4"
}
```

In the file /etc/bareos/bareos-sd.conf, we have defined the Name of our Storage daemon, example-sd. We could have other storage daemons on our network, so this name must be unique. The Director section defines the name of our Bareos Director and the storage password that was defined in /etc/bareos/bareos-dir.conf and was automatically also created here by the installation process.

```
Director {
  Name = example-mon
  Password = "/H9QQD9YJOcd9jTnX1w/aFMMghxFuHmPYuJv882Sk54F"
  Monitor = yes
}
Messages {
  Name = Standard
  director = example-dir = all
}
```

The Monitor, or Console, section in bareos-dir.conf defines the resource Director { ... Name = example-mon ... }. This is used to monitor the resource and allows the Director to get the status of the Storage daemon. It requires that the password be declared in the Director configuration as well as here. Again, that password was generated during installation.

The messages resource allows the Storage daemon to send informational messages via the Bareos Director daemon.

In the Device section, the Name matches the Device in the Storage section of the Director configuration file. Media Type = FileStorage matches in both the Director and Storage configuration files.

```
Device {
  Name = FileStorage
  Media Type = File
  Archive Device = /data/backups/FileStorage
  LabelMedia = yes;
  Random Access = Yes;
  AutomaticMount = yes;
  RemovableMedia = no;
  AlwaysOpen = no;
}
```

Here we have defined the device that our backups will be stored on. We don't have any tape drives or autoloaders, so this will be a simple disk-based storage setup. We define where on our host the backup files will be stored. In this instance, we are going to store them in the /data/backups/FileStorage directory. Most of the other options are not really relevant when talking about backing up to the filesystem, and we've left the other options at their defaults.

Also, it is worth noting that the Plugin Names = "" directive is where you can load any particular plug-in that you might like to use. There are file daemon plug-ins and storage daemon plug-ins. File daemon plug-ins concern themselves mainly with how to back up things from, and storage deals with how to back up things to.

■ **Note**   You can read more on the configuration of the Storage daemon at http://doc.bareos.org/
master/html/bareos-manual-main-reference.html#x1-15000010.

---

bareos-fd.conf

The last thing we have to do before we can take a backup is to install the bareos-fd software on our headoffice.example.com host. CentOS and Ubuntu hosts require bareos-common and bareos-client, which will download any dependencies we may also need. Once these are installed, we will edit the /etc/bareos/bareos-fd.conf file and add the following information:

```
Director {
FileDaemon {                            # definition of myself
  Name = headoffice-fd
  WorkingDirectory = /var/lib/bareos
  Maximum Concurrent Jobs = 20

  # remove comment from "Plugin Directory" to load plugins from specified directory.
  # if "Plugin Names" is defined, only the specified plugins will be loaded,
  # otherwise all storage plugins (*-fd.so) from the "Plugin Directory".
  #
  # Plugin Directory = /usr/lib64/bareos/plugins
  # Plugin Names = ""
```

```
# if compatible is set to yes, we are compatible with bacula
# if set to no, new bareos features are enabled which is the default
# compatible = yes
}


#
# List Directors who are permitted to contact this File daemon
#
Director {
  Name = example-dir
  Password = "6rZQQqVsOJeeTPefrG2AslT5ODxtPWO1hNsd7Re1u6J/"
}


#
# Restricted Director, used by tray-monitor to get the
#   status of the file daemon
#
Director {
  Name = example-mon
  Password = "WOhEm9JC+uBvpNBJta1RuA7NJSmUgQrz3QPRgPYhRzyZ"
  Monitor = yes
}


# Send all messages except skipped files back to Director
Messages {
  Name = Standard
  director = example-dir = all, !skipped, !restored
}
```

In the File daemon configuration script, we declare the Director {} stanza for connecting to the Bareos Director daemon. That requires the Name of the Director we are connecting to and the Password we have defined in the Client resource for headoffice-fd. The FileDaemon defines primarily the Name and Maximum Concurrent Jobs settings. The Name setting must match the Name in the Client resource in the bareos-dir. conf file. Maximum Concurrent Jobs defines the number of jobs that can connect to this host at any one time.

The Director and Messages sections are the same as described in the Storage file. They are used to allow the Director to get the status of the File daemon and define where to send messages if there is an error.

Testing the Syntax

We can now test the syntax of our bareos-dir.conf configuration file by issuing the following command:

```
$ sudo /usr/sbin/bareos-dir -t -c /etc/bareos/bareos-dir.conf
```

For the File and Storage daemons, we would issue this command:

```
$ sudo /usr/sbin/bareos-fd -t -c /etc/bareos/bareos-fd.conf
```

or this one:

```
$ sudo /usr/sbin/bareos-sd -t -c /etc/bareos/bareos-sd.conf
```

If neither command returns an error, then each has a syntactically correct configuration, and we can enable and start our service using systemctl. Great! They're running, aren't they? You're right—how can we tell? We can use the status argument to see whether they are running.

```
$ sudo systemctl enable bareos-dir bareos-sd bareos-fd
$ sudo systemctl start bareos-dir bareos-sd bareos-fd
$ sudo systemctl status bareos-dir bareos-sd bareos-fd
```

bconsole.conf

We now have to set up the console so we can administer and monitor the backup service. The file that holds the configuration for our bconsole is called /etc/bareos/bconsole.conf.

Several consoles are available, and depending on your own preferences, you can set up either a GUI or a screen-based console. We'll first set up the screen-based console, and then we'll set up the Web-UI console later in the chapter. In the /etc/bareos/bconsole.conf file, we define the following:

```
Director {
  Name = example-dir
  DIRport = 9101
  Address = backup.example.com
  Password = "uogx2tNL9dRUwGfNvY/b+uQrU8osZn+JOM7t8iIrpszN"
}
```

This has the same details (Name, port, Address, and Password) as the Directory resource in the bareos-dir.conf configuration file. Again, the password was created and installed during the installation process.

Managing Bareos with bconsole

After you configure Bareos, you can start the services by using the systemctl command, like we just did previously. We can now start the Bareos console program using the bconsole command like so:

```
$ sudo /usr/sbin/bconsole
```

First, we can list the current status of the Director by issuing the status all command. Issuing this command gives a detailed list of what is happening on the Bareos Director, including the attached Storage daemons and File daemons.

To find out what the Director itself is doing, we use the stat dir command. This command gives an overview of the pending jobs, the current running jobs, and the jobs that have been completed. We access the console by issuing the following command:

```
$ sudo /usr/sbin/bconsole
Connecting to Director backup.example.com:9101
1000 OK: example-dir Version: 15.2.2 (16 November 2015)
Enter a period to cancel a command.
* stat dir
example-dir Version: 15.2.2 (16 November 2015) x86_64-redhat-linux-gnu redhat CentOS Linux
release 7.0.1406 (Core)
Daemon started 10-Oct-16 00:56. Jobs: run=0, running=0 mode=0 db=mysql
 Heap: heap=274,432 smbytes=86,156 max_bytes=86,156 bufs=321 max_bufs=322
```

```
Scheduled Jobs:

Level          Type      Pri   Scheduled        Name                      Volume
=================================================================================
Incremental    Backup    10    10-Oct-16 23:05  headoffice.example.com    *unknown*
Full                     Backup    11    10-Oct-16
23:10      BackupCatalog                    *unknown*

Running Jobs:
Console connected at 10-Oct-16 00:57
No Jobs running.
====
No Terminated Jobs.
====
*
```

As you can see, we have no jobs completed and no jobs currently running. We have two jobs scheduled to run on October 11 at 23:05, one that backs up headoffice.example.com and one that backs up the catalog (BackupCatalog). Take some time to explore bconsole a little more. For example, type help and then press Enter to see a list of commands available to you on the command line. Table 14-4 lists the most useful commands.

Table 14-4. Useful Bareos bconsole Commands

Command	Description
run	Starts a job (a backup)
cancel	Cancels the current job
mess	Shows any current messages
restore	Manages restore jobs
label	Labels a tape or media volume
update volume	Allows you to update the properties of any particular volume
stat dir	Gets the current status of the Director daemon
stat client	Gets the current status of a File daemon
stat storage	Gets the current status of the Storage daemon
mount	Mounts a volume (e.g., loads a media volume into a tape drive)
unmount	Unmounts a media volume (e.g., unloads the tape from a drive)

■ **Note** Another resource for useful commands is in the Bareos documentation at http://doc.bareos.org/master/html/bareos-manual-main-reference.html#x1-18400015.

You can run a job or a backup in two ways. One is to use the run command and press Enter. You are then presented with an easy-to-understand menu-driven way to submit your backup. The other is to place the commands directly on the command line like this:

```
* run job=headoffice.example.com level=full priority=7 yes
```

When we run the * `stat dir` command, we can see that our job is running.

```
Running Jobs:

Console connected at 10-Oct-16 01:21
 JobId Level    Name                          Status
==========================================================
     1 Full     headoffice.example.com.2016-10-10_01.21.34_04 is running
====
```

From that status you can see that we have a job ID of 1 and that we are running a full backup, since we do not have a full backup yet. Bareos will automatic start a full backup if it does not exist yet. A new volume has been created, and the backup is restoring to it. If you type **mess** at the command line, you will receive any messages that are available about your job.

Now if we wanted to stop this job, we would use the `cancel` command with `JobId` 1 as an argument. You can see in the previous `Running Jobs` output the `JobId` to use.

```
*cancel jobid=1
```

The `cancel` command can be run without arguments and will automatically select the `JobId` for you (if only one job is running; otherwise, it presents a list to choose from). We have run the job again, this time without canceling it, and it has completed. When we do a `stat dir` in the `Terminated Jobs` section, we find the following:

```
Terminated Jobs:
 JobId Level    Files       Bytes  Status  Finished          Name
==================================================================
  2     Full    8,908      140.1 M  OK      10-Oct-16 01:21 headoffice.example.com
```

The preceding output shows that we have a full save of the `Linux FileSet` for the host headoffice. example.com. You can see the number of files it holds and the data volume. Let's try to restore the /etc/ hosts file using the `restore` command.

```
* restore
To select the JobIds, you have the following choices:
     1: List last 20 Jobs run
     2: List Jobs where a given File is saved
     3: Enter list of comma separated JobIds to select
```

The list of options to use here actually goes to 12, but we will use option 2 to find out the `JobId` (which we already know from the `Terminated Jobs` output to be 4).

```
Select item: (1-12): 2
Automatically selected Client: headoffice-fd
Enter Filename (no path):hosts
+--------+------------+----------------------+---------+-----------+----------+-------------+
| JobId  | Name       | StartTime            | JobType | JobStatus | JobFiles | JobBytes    |
+--------+------------+----------------------+---------+-----------+----------+-------------+
| 2      | /etc/hosts | 2016-10-10 01:21:36  | B       | T         | 8908     | 140144767   |
+--------+------------+----------------------+---------+-----------+----------+-------------+
```

Now that we know our JobId, we would then use option 3 to restore our hosts file, as follows:

```
Select item: (1-12): 3
Enter JobId(s), comma separated, to restore: 4
You have selected the following JobId: 4

Building directory tree for JobId 4 ... ++++++++++++++++++++++++++++++++++++++++
1 Job, 1,174 files inserted into the tree. cwd is: /
$ cd /etc
cwd is: /etc/
$ mark hosts
1 file marked.
$ done
Bootstrap records written to /var/lib/bareos/example-dir.restore.1.bsr

The job will require the following
   Volume(s)                 Storage(s)                SD Device(s)
===========================================================================

   Full-0001                    File                     FileStorage

Volumes marked with "*" are online.

1 file selected to be restored.

Run Restore job
JobName:         RestoreFiles
Bootstrap:       /var/lib/bareos/example-dir.restore.1.bsr
Where:           /tmp/bareos-restores
Replace:         Always
FileSet:         Linux All
Backup Client:   headoffice-fd
Restore Client:  headoffice-fd
Format:          Native
Storage:         File
When:            2016-10-10 01:32:35
Catalog:         MyCatalog
Priority:        10
Plugin Options:  *None*
OK to run? (yes/mod/no): yes
Job queued. JobId=4
```

When selecting the files you want to restore, you can use the ls and cd commands to list and change directories as you search for the files.

```
cwd is: /
$ cd /etc
cwd is: /etc/
$ mark hosts
1 file marked.
$ done
```

Here we have used the `mark` command to select the file we want to restore after using the `cd` command to navigate through the backed-up file system. To select everything recursively in a directory, you can use the `mark *` command. When you are finished selecting the files you want to restore, use the done command.

You are given a list of the media volumes required to perform this restore. You will have to load them if they are not already available to your backup host. Then you are given the rundown of the restore job you are going to run. Make a note of `Where: /tmp/bareos-restores`, as this is where your restored file will be found.

Looking at `stat dir` and the `Terminated Jobs` section, a complete restore will look like this:

```
JobId  Level   Files     Bytes    Status   Finished          Name
=========================================================================
  4      1      403        OK     10-Oct-16 01:32            RestoreFiles
```

Now we can check that the file has been restored to the `/tmp/bareos-restores` directory.

```
$ $ sudo ls -l /tmp/bareos-restores/etc/
total 4
-rw-r--r--. 1 root root 403 Oct 10 00:53 hosts
```

We could always use the `restore` command to restore to a different host and a different destination by changing the `Client` and `Where` options before we confirm that we want to run the restore job.

Using GlusterFS for Backup Storage

We are going to quickly go through how to set up your Bareos server to use the GlusterFS storage as our backup device. As you can remember, GlusterFS provides us with reliable and expandable storage options on commodity hardware and can be a great option for safely keeping backups on disk. In this section, we are going to do the following:

- Create a new backup volume in GlusterFS and update our GlusterFS configuration
- Add a new record to our DNS server
- Mount volume and setup directories
- Configure Bareos storage

Bareos can talk directly to the Gluster daemon via the `libgfapi` provided by the `bareos-storage-glusterfs` package. This means we don't FUSE mount the Gluster volume but allow Bareos direct access to the daemon.

Creating Backup Gluster Volume

Like in Chapter 13, to create a new volume on our GlusterFS cluster, we first need to add our new devices (disks) and format and mount them. Once we have done that, we then need to create the new volume with those new bricks.

We will assume that we have added our new disks to our Gluster servers. We can execute the following:

```
$ sudo mkfs.xfs -f -L brick3_r1 /dev/sdf && \
   sudo mkdir -p /data/brick3_r1 && \
   sudo bash -c 'echo LABEL=brick3_r1 /data/brick3_r1 xfs defaults 1 2 >> /etc/fstab' && \
   sudo mount -a && \
   sudo mkdir /data/brick3_r1/backups
```

We have seen this command previously, and we are formatting the disks, making the directories where we will mount the devices, adding the disks to automount in our fstab, mounting the device, and finally creating a backup directory on the mounted disk. We have done this on all our three servers, and now we are ready to create our GlusterFS volume.

```
$ sudo gluster volume create backups replica 3 \
  au-mel-dfs-1:/data/brick3_r1/backups \
  au-mel-dfs-2:/data/brick3_r1/backups \
  au-mel-dfs-3:/data/brick3_r1/backups
```

We now start the volume.

```
$ sudo gluster volume start backups
```

Our volume is now ready to be mounted, but first we need to make some changes to our Gluster configuration to allow the Bareos server to directly contact our glusterd daemons. To do that, we need to do the following.

First we need to edit the /etc/glusterfs/glusterd.vol file and add the following on each Gluster server:

```
volume management
    type mgmt/glusterd
    option working-directory /var/lib/glusterd
...<snip>...
    option rpc-auth-allow-insecure on
end-volume
```

We will need to restart the glusterd service after making this change. This change allows unprivileged connections from our backup server. We are going to also make this change to the Gluster backup volume only.

```
$ gluster volume set backups server.allow-insecure on
```

This need to be executed on only one of the Gluster peers. We are now ready to move on to the next step.

Update DNS Records

We are going to use a single hostname to contact our GlusterFS service. We are going to call this storage. example.com, and we need to create a series of A records to respond.

We need to be on our DNS server, and we are going to issue the following:

```
$ sudo nsupdate -k /etc/bind/ddns_update.key
> server localhost
> update add storage.example.com 360 A 192.168.0.240
> update add storage.example.com 360 A 192.168.0.241
> update add storage.example.com 360 A 192.168.0.242
> send
> quit
```

Using dig, we can see that our DNS returns the correct records:

```
$ dig @localhost storage.example.com
....
;; ANSWER SECTION:
storage.example.com.     360    IN    A    192.168.0.242
storage.example.com.     360    IN    A    192.168.0.240
storage.example.com.     360    IN    A    192.168.0.241
```

Now when we query storage.example.com, we will receive one of these IP addresses in a round-robin fashion.

Preparing the Bareos Server

Now it is time to prepare the Bareos server. On backup.example.com we are going to mount the Gluster volume, create the storage directory, and set the ownership of that directory.

We will need to mount the Gluster volume via the FUSE package. We are going to make sure that the package glusterfs-fuse is installed on our CentOS backup server. Once it is, we are going to mount our volume.

```
$ sudo mount -t glusterfs storage.example.com:/backups /mnt
```

Now that we have mounted our Gluster volume, we are going to create a directory and change the ownership. We first get the UID and GID of our bareos user. We can do that by issuing the following:

```
$ id bareos
uid=899(bareos) gid=986(bareos) groups=986(bareos),6(disk),30(tape)
```

Now we will create the directory and then change the ownership and mode of the directory.

```
$ sudo mkdir /mnt/FileStore && \
  sudo chown 899:986 /mnt/FileStore && \
  sudo chmod 2770 /mnt/FileStore
```

We can now unmount the directory.

```
$ sudo umount /mnt
```

Now we need to change the /etc/bareos/bareos-dir.conf and /etc/bareos/bareos-sd.d/device-gluster.conf files. Let's begin with the latter.

```
/etc/bareos/bareos-sd.d/device-gluster.conf
Device {
  Name = GlusterStorage
  Archive Device = "Gluster Device"
  Device Options = "uri=gluster://storage.example.com/backups/FileStore"
  Device Type = gfapi
  Media Type = GlusterFile
  Label Media = yes
  Random Access = yes
```

```
Automatic Mount = yes
Removable Media = no
Always Open = no
}
```

Once this is done, we can change bareos-dir.conf. Let's do that now.

```
/etc/bareos/bareos-dir.conf
Storage {
  Name = Gluster
  Address = backup.example.com              # N.B. Use a fully qualified name here
  Password = "4ncvx7V+Mw4NOMDMyuYjCHsNg1nKgcdh8nlOszWpi6t4"
  Device = GlusterStorage
  Media Type = GlusterFile
  Maximum Concurrent Jobs = 10
}
```

This maps the directory storage to the device storage file. We are now going to change the JobDefs named DefaultLinux for the Storage option.

```
JobDefs {
  Name = "DefaultLinux"
  Type = Backup
...<snip> ...
  Storage = Gluster
...<snip>...
}
```

Lastly we need to tell the Storage daemon to load in our Gluster device. We need to remove the # from the following line:

```
/etc/bareos/bareos-sd.conf
...<snip>...
@/etc/bareos/bareos-sd.d/device-gluster.conf
...<snip>...
```

We now need to reload our configuration so that the Bareos Storage daemon will add in the device-gluster.conf file. Using bconsole, we can issue the reload command, or we can restart using the normal systemctl commands. We are now ready to back up to our GlusterFS servers.

From bconsole we will issue the following command to see that we have everything ready for our backups to Gluster:

```
*status Storage=Gluster
... <snip>...
====

Device status:

Device "GlusterStorage" (Gluster Device) is not open.
==
...<snip>...
```

We are ready to do our backups now. Let's test with our database backups in the next section.

Backing Up Databases with Bareos Plug-Ins

We now want to show you a more advanced scenario. We have a MariaDB database running on our headoffice.example.com host. Currently it holds our Bareos catalog database, but it could also contain the WordPress database that we created in Chapter 11 or any other databases we use.

As we have mentioned, you can install Bareos plug-ins on your Storage and File daemons to do special tasks. We are going to install a Python plug-in on the database server so the File daemon can back up the MariaDB database for us. This plug-in will make use of the mysqldump and mysql commands to make a database backup, consisting of a file for each database found.

The plug-in we are going to use can be found here:

- https://github.com/bareos/bareos-contrib/tree/master/fd-plugins/mysql-python

We are going to install it in /usr/lib64/bareos/plugins and then make a configuration change to update our bareos-fd.conf file. To do that, we going to copy two files from the GitHub repository with the curl command.

```
# curl -s https://raw.githubusercontent.com/bareos/bareos-contrib/master/fd-plugins/mysql-
python/BareosFdMySQLclass.py \
  -o /usr/lib64/bareos/plugins/BareosFdMySQLclass.py
# curl -s https://raw.githubusercontent.com/bareos/bareos-contrib/master/fd-plugins/mysql-
python/bareos-fd-mysql.py \
  -o /usr/lib64/bareos/plugins/bareos-fd-mysql.py
```

These two files have been copied via curl into the plugins directory as the root user. Now we have to configure the /etc/bareos/bareos-fd.conf file on the headoffice.example.com server where the database lives.

```
FileDaemon {                         # definition of myself
  Name = headoffice-fd
  Maximum Concurrent Jobs = 20

  # remove comment from "Plugin Directory" to load plugins from specified directory.
  # if "Plugin Names" is defined, only the specified plugins will be loaded,
  # otherwise all storage plugins (*-fd.so) from the "Plugin Directory".
  #
  Plugin Directory = /usr/lib64/bareos/plugins
  Plugin Names = "bareos-fd-mysql.py"
...
}
```

You will need to restart the File daemon on the headoffice.example.com server. Now we are going to change the Director configuration and create a new FileSet for the database server.

```
FileSet {
  Name = "DBLinux"
  Include {
    Options {
      Compression = GZIP
```

```
   Signature = SHA1
   }
   File = "/etc"
   File = "/var/lib" File = "/data" File = "/home"
   Plugin = "python:module_path=/usr/lib64/bareos/plugins:module_name=bareos-fd-mysql"
   }
 Exclude {
   File = "/proc"
   File = "/sys"
   File = "/dev"
   File = "/run"
   File = "/tmp"
   File = "/data/backups"
 }
}
```

We are going to create a new JobDefs for headoffice.example.com also.

```
JobDefs {
  Name = "DBLinux"
  Type = Backup
  Level = Incremental
  Client = headoffice-fd
  FileSet = "DBLinux"
  Schedule = "WeeklyCycle"
  Storage = Gluster
  Messages = Standard
  Pool = Incremental
  Priority = 10
  Write Bootstrap = "/var/lib/bareos/%c.bsr"
  Full Backup Pool = Full
  Incremental Backup Pool = Incremental
}
```

We have created a new JobDefs and added the DBLinux FileSet for the database server. We can change other defaults for the job as we require, like schedules or storage. Lastly we need to change the job for the database server.

```
Job {
  Name = headoffice.example.com
  Client = headoffice-fd
  Enabled = yes
  JobDefs = "DBLinux"
}
```

We need to reload or restart the Director service before this becomes active. Let's try to run our backup for headoffice.example.com.

```
*  run job=headoffice.example.com client=headoffice-fd
Automatically selected Catalog: MyCatalog
Using Catalog "MyCatalog"
```

```
Run Backup job
JobName:  headoffice.example.com
Level:    Incremental
Client:   headoffice-fd
Format:   Native
FileSet:  DBLinux
Pool:     Incremental (From Job IncPool override)
Storage:  Gluster (From Job resource)
When:     2016-10-11 22:29:37
Priority: 10
OK to run? (yes/mod/no): yes
Job queued. JobId=15
```

Here you can see our job being scheduled and run with the DBLinux FileSet. As this job runs, we can follow it in /var/log/bareos/bareos.log, and we can see the databases being backed up here:

```
11-Oct 22:29 example-sd JobId 15: Ready to append to end of Volume "Full-0004"
size=145926917
11-Oct 22:29 headoffice-fd JobId 15:      /var/lib/nfs/rpc_pipefs is a different filesystem.
Will not descend from /var/lib into it.
11-Oct 22:29 headoffice-fd JobId 15: Starting backup of /_mysqlbackups_/test.sql
11-Oct 22:29 headoffice-fd JobId 15: Starting backup of /_mysqlbackups_/mysql.sql
11-Oct 22:29 headoffice-fd JobId 15: Starting backup of /_mysqlbackups_/bareos.sql
11-Oct 22:29 example-sd JobId 15: Elapsed time=00:00:08, Transfer rate=18.22 M Bytes/second
```

When we issue the restore command in bconsole and select the jobid for the last restore, we can see the backups of our database files.

```
cwd is: /
$ cd _mysqlbackups_/
cwd is: /_mysqlbackups_/
$ ls
bareos.sql
mysql.sql
test.sql
$ mark bareos.sql
1 file marked.
$ done
```

The contents of the bareos.sql file when restored contain the full backup of our bareos database.

■ **Caution**   Make sure you have enough space on your host to handle the size of your database dump—you could find yourself in trouble if you run out of room. It is a good idea to dump this file into a separate partition so that if you do run out of space, it does not impact other processes on your host.

Bareos also provides two instructions in the Job resource that we can take advantage of when running complex jobs: Client Run Before Job and Client Run After Job. As their names imply, these instructions can be used to run scripts on the target host. Client Run Before Job will execute the command or script on the target host and require a successful completion before it continues. If it does not succeed, the job will terminate and produce an error message. `Client Run After Job` also requires a successful completion of the script or command on the target host; otherwise, it stops further processing for that job and submits an error message. If we did not want to use the Python plug-ins, we could write our own scripts. To use these, we could change the `headoffice.example.com` Job resource we defined earlier. We would change it as follows:

```
Job {
  Name = headoffice.example.com
  Client = headoffice-fd
  Enabled = yes
  JobDefs = "DefaultLinux"
  Client Run Before Job = "/usr/local/bin/mysql_backup start"
  Client Run After Job = "/usr/local/bin/mysql_backup stop"
}
```

The script `mysql_backup` must exist on our target host in the `/usr/local/bin` directory.

You can now see how you can manage complex backups on the Bareos backup server. You can use Bareos to back up a complete file system, or you can target data directories only. If you are going to target data directories only, be sure to look at how you are going to rebuild your hosts in the event of a problem with the hosts.

Next, we're going look at using the Web-UI console to manage our Bareos configurations.

Introducing the Bareos Web-UI

Using a text-based console is a quick and easy way to set up and manage your Bareos services. Some people prefer a GUI, however, so Bareos created a nice, clean web interface called Web-UI for managing the Bareos Director.

We set up a PHP web service in Chapter 11 and now would be a good time to review that if you have forgotten. The Web-UI can be installed on any web host; it does not require a Bareos Director to be installed. You install the Web-UI via the `bareos-webui` package, which is available from the online repository. It will install the required dependencies for you.

The `bareos-webui` package will install the web files into `/usr/share/bareos-webui` and install an Apache configuration file in `/etc/httpd/conf.d/bareos-webui.conf`.

We can restart the Apache service, and then we will create a user to access the web interface. We will create a file `/etc/bareos/bareos-dir.d/admin.conf` if it is not already created by your installation process.

```
Console {
  Name = "admin"
  Password = "secret"
  Profile = "webui"
}
```

Next we will need to create the file `/etc/bareos/bareos-dir.d/webui-consoles.conf` and enter the following contents for the file:

```
Profile {
  Name = webui
  CommandACL = status, messages, show, version, run, rerun, cancel, .api, .bvfs_*, list,
  llist, use, restore, .jobs, .filesets, .clients
  Job ACL = *all*
  Schedule ACL = *all*
```

```
Catalog ACL = *all*
Pool ACL = *all*
Storage ACL = *all*
Client ACL = *all*
FileSet ACL = *all*
Where ACL = *all*
}
```

This profile relates to the commands that the admin user can access using the webui profile. If you wanted to restrict access to certain profiles, you would edit this file by listing the resources the profile has access to (see http://doc.bareos.org/master/html/bareos-manual-main-reference.html#x1-1510009.12 for more details).

We now need the Bareos Director to read these files in when it starts. To do that, we need to add the following to the bottom of our bareos-dir.conf file:

```
@/etc/bareos/bareos-dir.d/webui-consoles.conf
@/etc/bareos/bareos-dir.d/webui-profiles.conf
```

Again, we are using the @ symbol to tell the Bareos Director to read in these files. We now have to restart or reload the Director.

Once all this is done, we should be able to restart the Apache server and log in to the Bareos Web-UI. Let's log in, as shown in Figure 14-10.

Figure 14-10. *Log Web-UI page*

We use the password *secrets* and the username *admin*, which we specified in webui-consoles.conf earlier. In Figure 14-11 we see the main dashboard.

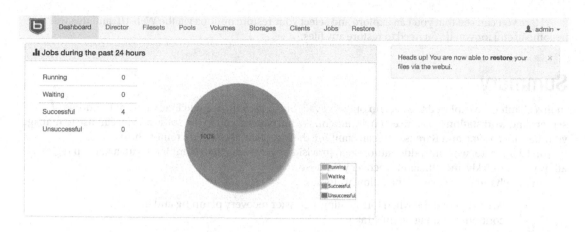

Figure 14-11. *Dashboard page of Web-UI*

We will not go through every page; as you can see, there are many parts to explore that maps to parts of the Bareos configuration. We do want to show you the Restore page, as you can use this to find and restore your backups like in Figure 14-12.

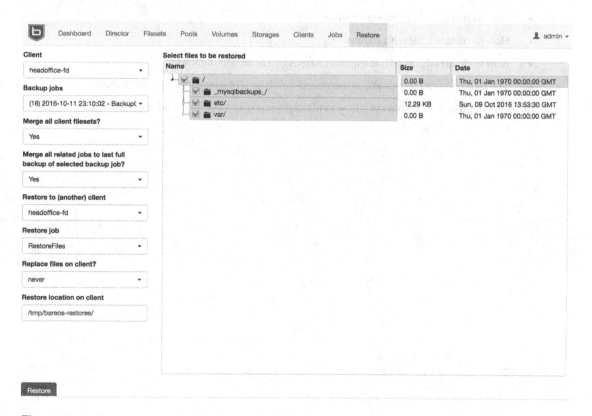

Figure 14-12. *Restore page on Web-UI*

Here you can see that you can explore and select your restore options via the Web-UI, and this will become useful for you if you need to restore any files.

Summary

In this chapter, we explored the backup options available to back up a single Linux host or hundreds of servers and workstations in a mixed environment. We introduced you to the software you can use to manage your backups, rsync and Bareos. You can combine them to securely back up remote hosts.

In Chapter 19, we'll introduce automated provisioning systems that, combined with a backup regimen, allow you to quickly and efficiently recover your hosts.

In this chapter, we covered the following topics:

- Issues to consider when formulating a disaster recovery planning and business continuity management strategy

- How to back up remote hosts to a central host using rsync and SSH

- How to write a simple Bash script that can rsync your remote hosts regularly

- How to install and configure Duply and Duplicity

- How to install and configure Bareos

- How to run a backup job with Bareos

- How to restore a file with Bareos

- How to do an advanced backup with Bareos of a MariaDB database

- The Bareos Web-UI console, an advanced web-based management GUI for Bareos

In the next chapter, we will show you how to manage your own VPN links and internetwork security.

CHAPTER 15

■ ■ ■

Networking with VPNs

By James Turnbull and Dennis Matotek

In previous chapters, we talked about a lot of the services your organization might implement (e.g., e-mail and web services). We showed you a variety of ways to deliver those services to your users and customers, including over the Internet, and to mobile users and users located at other sites. Some services, however, are simply easier and safer to deliver locally (e.g., file and print services). If your users are not located locally, then you need some way of connecting them as if they were local. Enter the *virtual private network* (VPN).

A VPN is, in essence, a private network that runs over a public, or hostile, network. VPNs are often called *tunnels*, and they are used to secure and protect traffic you'd like to keep private over an otherwise public network like the Internet. VPNs can be initiated to and from network devices or to and from hosts. They can be made between two offices, for example, or from a client such as a desktop or laptop to an office. The traffic running over a VPN is usually encrypted and authenticated via a mechanism such as an TLS/SSL certificate, a password, or a two-factor authentication mechanism such as a token or smartcard.

VPNs are commonplace and home and business-grade firewalls will usually have support for them.

In this chapter, we're going to show you how to install the required software (in our case, an open source VPN tool called OpenVPN) to create a VPN and how to configure and generate VPN tunnels.

Our Example Network

We're going to demonstrate a variety of VPN connections in this chapter, and we'll use the example network we created in Chapter 7 for our sample environment and network to configure. Figure 15-1 shows that network again.

© Dennis Matotek, James Turnbull and Peter Lieverdink 2017
D. Matotek et al., *Pro Linux System Administration*, DOI 10.1007/978-1-4842-2008-5_15

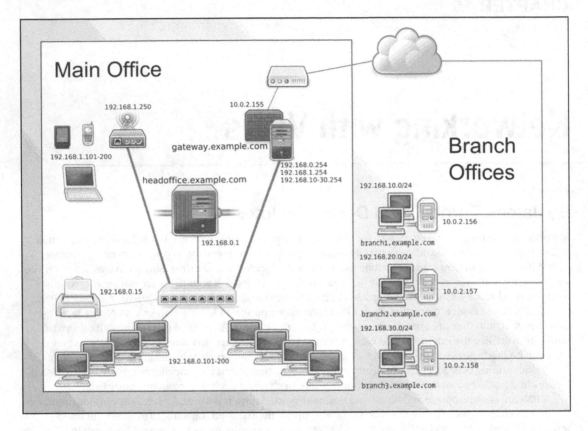

Figure 15-1. *Our example network*

Currently in our example network we have a head office with two main hosts:

- *gateway.example.com*: Our bastion host. It has an external IP address of 10.0.2.155 and an internal IP address of 192.168.0.254.

- *headoffice.example.com*: Our main head office server host. It has an internal IP address of 192.168.0.1, and external connections go out through the gateway host.

■ **Note**   We show how you can create these DNS CNAMEs (e.g., gateway and headoffice) in Chapter 10.

We also have three branch offices, each with its own internal and external IP address ranges.

- *branch1.example.com*: A branch office host with an external IP address of 10.0.2.156. The branch has an internal IP address range of 192.168.10.0/24.

- *branch2.example.com*: A branch office host with an external IP address of 10.0.2.157. The branch has an internal IP address range of 192.168.20.0/24.

- *branch3.example.com*: A branch office host with an external IP address of 10.0.2.158. The branch has an internal IP address range of 192.168.30.0/24.

Introducing OpenVPN

OpenVPN (http://openvpn.net/) is an open source SSL VPN application written by James Yonan that is available under the GNU GPLv2 license (OpenVPN v2) and AGPL (OpenVPN v3). There is also a commercial version under a separate EULA. You can also choose to use an AWS Marketplace–bundled EC2 instance that allows you to pay an hourly price and removes some of the administrative burden to set it up.

It works in a client/server model, with a server running on your host and clients connecting to the server and creating VPN tunnels.

■ **Note**   Other Linux-based VPN solutions are available, including IPsec implementations such as Openswan.

OpenVPN runs on a variety of platforms including Linux, Solaris, macOS, and Microsoft Windows. This allows you to connect a variety of clients to your Linux host; for example, you can connect a VPN tunnel from a desktop or laptop running Microsoft Windows. OpenVPN will even run on mobile devices running Android, Apple's iPhone, or Windows Mobile. You can use it to create VPN tunnels from these sorts of devices to allow you to securely access resources in your internal networks.

OpenVPN can also be configured to use several different authentication services. We will show you how to authenticate using normal Linux PAM modules but you can use PAM to authenticate against services like LDAP and RADIUS.

In the sections that follow, we will demonstrate how to install and set up OpenVPN in a variety of configurations.

Installing OpenVPN

You will need to install OpenVPN on both ends of your connection. For hosts, this means installing the OpenVPN server on both ends. If one end of your connection is a network device that supports connecting to OpenVPN, then you'll need to install the server only on the host that you will be using as the tunnel endpoint.

We're going to start by installing the server on our bastion host, gateway.example.com, which has the internal IP address of 192.168.0.254 and external IP address of 192.0.2.155, in the head office branch of our example network.

OpenVPN works on both CentOS and Ubuntu, and it can be installed via normal package management methods. On CentOS, you will get the most recent OpenVPN package from the EPEL repository. Ubuntu is currently a few minor releases behind.

To view what version is currently available on your operating system, issue either of the following:

```
$ sudo aptitdue show openvpn (Ubuntu)
$ sudo yum info openvpn (CentOS)
```

On CentOS we first issue the installation of the EPEL repository, if it is not already installed, and then install the package.

```
$ sudo yum install epel-release
$ sudo yum install openvpn
```

On Ubuntu, you install the openvpn package, and some additional prerequisites will generally also be installed.

```
$ sudo aptitude install openvpn
```

Let's look at stopping and starting the service now.

Starting and Stopping OpenVPN

OpenVPN runs as a service on your hosts. The openvpn package on both Ubuntu and CentOS will install appropriate Systemd service scripts.

However, with OpenVPN, the way we start and stop the services is slightly different. Taking a look at CentOS, for example, we need to pass the name of the OpenVPN configuration we want to start. The systemctl command can take arguments. Looking at the Systemd service file for OpenVPN, you will see the following:

```
ExecStart=/usr/sbin/openvpn --daemon --writepid /var/run/openvpn/%i.pid --cd /etc/openvpn/
--config %i.conf
```

Do you notice the %i? We need to specify the configuration file (--config %i.conf) when we start the openvpn service. We use the systemctl command with the @ symbol to do this.

```
$ sudo systemctl start service@configuration
```

The systemctl command will extrapolate %i.conf to the configuration name we passed in after the openvpn@. In the following command, we will start configuration defined in /etc/openvpn/gateway.conf:

```
$ sudo systemctl start openvpn@gateway
```

You use the Systemd enable command to ensure it starts at bootup.

```
$ sudo systemctl enable openvpn@gateway
```

On Ubuntu, we just run the following:

```
$ sudo systemctl start openvpn
```

When we start OpenVPN, these configuration service files will be automatically loaded, and the server will attempt to start the specified VPNs.

Configuring OpenVPN

As we mentioned earlier, we need to configure OpenVPN on both ends of any connection. We're going to start our configuration by setting up the OpenVPN server on our bastion host in our head office, and then we'll configure connections to our branch offices. A connection between two offices like this is called a *static* or *point-to-point* VPN. Finally, we'll show you how to configure a client, such as a laptop or desktop, for a mobile user.

Our Proposed VPN Configuration

Let's quickly look at a network diagram of our proposed VPN tunnel configuration (see Figure 15-2). We're going to create tunnels between our head office branch and each of our branch offices.

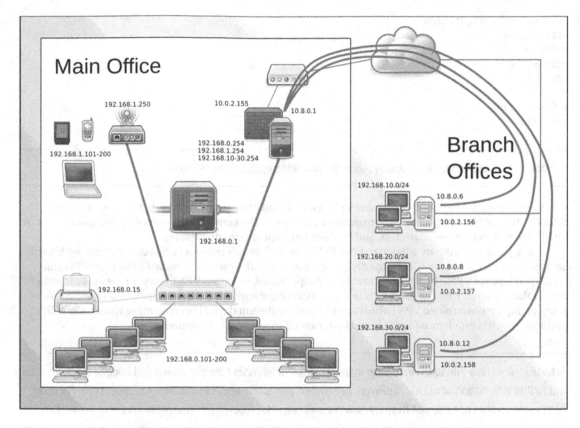

Figure 15-2. *Point-to-point VPN configuration between the head office and branches*

Configuring OpenVPN on Our Gateway Server

We've installed OpenVPN on our head office's bastion server, gateway.example.com, and now we're going to start configuring it. We start by telling OpenVPN a few basics about our configuration. We're going to create a file called gateway.conf in the /etc/openvpn directory, as shown in Listing 15-1.

Listing 15-1. The gateway.conf Configuration File

```
# Network configuration
dev tun
port 1194
proto udp
server 10.8.0.0 255.255.255.0
keepalive 10 120

# Logging configuration
log-append /var/log/openvpn.log
status /var/log/openvpn-status.log
verb 4
mute 20
```

```
# Security configuration
user nobody
group nobody
persist-key
persist-tun

# Compression
comp-lzo
```

■ **Note**   We'll expand on the `gateway.conf` file with additional options as we go along.

In Listing 15-1 we've specified a number of options. The first of these options is `dev tun`, or tunnel device. A tun device is a special software network interface in the kernel that user space programs can use. A tun device will receive raw IP packets, and its sister, tap, expects Ethernet frames.

We're going to configure a tun to run our VPN over, and we will create a virtual device, `tun0`, which will be used for the VPN connection. By specifying `dev tun`, we're also creating a routed VPN. OpenVPN can create two types of VPNs: bridged and routed. In simple terms, a *bridged* VPN joins your networks together at the Ethernet level, while a *routed* VPN relies on TCP/IP networking to join your networks together. We're going to implement a routed VPN (which is the reason for the tun device) because these types use the IP protocol, which is much more scalable and better suited to our network requirements.

■ **Note**   If you are interested in reading more about the differences between routed and bridged VPNs, you can find further information at `http://openvpn.net/index.php/documentation/howto.html#vpntype`. For more information on taps or tuns, visit `https://www.kernel.org/doc/Documentation/networking/tuntap.txt`.

Next, we've specified two options, `port 1194` and `proto udp`. These tell OpenVPN to listen for UDP traffic on port 1194 when making VPN connections. The firewall needs to be configured to allow traffic on this port to accept incoming connections.

■ **Tip**   If required, you can change the port and use TCP instead by changing these options to the required port and protocol.

Using the Netfilter firewall and the `iptables` command, you can ensure traffic passes through the appropriate port on your host, as you can see in Listing 15-2.

Listing 15-2. OpenVPN Firewall Rules CentOS

```
$ sudo firewall-cmd --zone public --permanent --add-port=1194/udp && sudo firewall-cmd
--reload
```

Here we've added a rule allowing incoming UDP traffic to the `tun0` interface on port 1194.
Or, if you are using TCP instead, you use a rule like the following:

```
$ sudo firewall-cmd --zone public --permanent --add-port=1194/tcp && sudo firewall-cmd -
reload
```

And of course for Ubuntu that would be as follows:

```
$ sudo ufw allow 1194/udp
```

■ **Tip**   The most common reason for a failed VPN configuration is a firewall issue. You should always check that your firewall rules allow access to this port by using the `tcpdump` or `nmap` command. We discuss firewall setup, rules, and troubleshooting in Chapter 7.

Next in Listing 15-1, the server option tells OpenVPN the IP address of the server and the pool of IP addresses available to our VPN clients. We've specified the default network, 10.8.0.0/24. By default, our OpenVPN server will take the address 10.8.0.1 and assign the remaining addresses to incoming VPN connections.

We've specified an option called `keepalive` that is used to keep our connection open. We specify the `keepalive` option and two values, 10 and 120. The value 10 indicates that OpenVPN will ping the connection every 10 seconds to check it is active. The value 120 indicates the time in seconds that OpenVPN will wait for a response. If no response is received within 120 seconds, then OpenVPN will assume the connection is down and notify us.

Then we've added some logging functions. The first is `log-append`, which tells OpenVPN to log to the `/var/log/openvpn.log` file. The second option, `status`, outputs a status file that shows current connections to a log file, in our case `/var/log/openvpn-status.log`. The third option, verb, tells OpenVPN how much logging to do. It ranges from 0 to 15, where 0 is no logging and 15 is maximum logging. A value of 4 generates sufficient logging to suit most purposes. Finally, `mute` reduces consecutive messages from the same category.

The next block of configuration options provides some additional security for our OpenVPN server. The first two options, `user` and `group`, allow us to specify a user and group for OpenVPN to run as. This drops any privileges (e.g., from the `root` user) the process has and ensures that if someone were to compromise the process, he would have limited privileges to exploit that compromise on your host. On CentOS, you use the nobody user and the nobody group. On Ubuntu, we recommend you use the user nobody and the group nogroup.

```
user nobody
group nogroup
```

The next two options, `persist-tun` and `persist-key`, are related to this dropping of privileges. They allow OpenVPN to retain sufficient privileges to work with network interfaces and SSL certificates.

The last option in the file, `comp-lzo`, tells OpenVPN to use compression for VPN tunnels. This improves performance across the tunnel.

So, we've configured the basics of our VPN, but is it now ready? Not quite yet—we have one more step: authentication.

Configuring OpenVPN Authentication

Authentication ensures that only authorized hosts can initiate VPNs and connect. OpenVPN allows a wide variety of authentication mechanisms including preshared keys, two-factor authentication such as tokens, and TLS/SSL certificates.

The most basic authentication is *preshared keys*, which are static keys generated on your host and then distributed to the host you want to connect to. You can generate a static key with the --genkey option of the openvpn command like so:

```
$ sudo openvpn --genkey --secret /etc/openvpn/secret.key
```

This will create a file containing a key in a file called secret.key in the directory /etc/openvpn, the file name and directory being specified with the --secret option. You specify the location of this file in your OpenVPN configuration using the secret option.

```
secret /etc/openvpn/secret.key
```

You would then copy this file, preferably in a secure way such as via scp or GPG-encrypted file sharing (like that offered by https://keybase.io) or by encrypting and using a configuration management system and applying it to the other host's OpenVPN configuration.

We're not going to use preshared keys, though, because they have some limitations. Their biggest limitation is that you can have only one server and client connection (i.e., you can connect only one host to each VPN tunnel). This isn't an ideal model if you have more than one host or office you want to connect. For example, it won't be effective to allow multiple mobile users to connect to your head office.

Instead, we're going to use certificates to secure the VPNs between our head office and branch offices. To use certificates, we need to create and sign them with a certificate authority (CA). The alternative to this is to use Let's Encrypt or commercial certificates. Commercial certificates can get expensive, and Let's Encrypt certificates require frequent renewing. We will use our own CA because it will be cheaper and we can manage the renewal cycle.

■ **Note** We discuss the CA process extensively in Chapter 11 (refer there now if you like).

We're going to show you how to create and sign your own using the CA we created in Chapter 11.

We first need to create a server certificate for the VPN server. You will remember the first step in the process of creating a new certificate is to create a certificate signing request (CSR) and a secret key. Let's do that now by first changing into the /etc/pki/tls directory and executing the following:

```
$ openssl req -new -newkey rsa:4096 -nodes -keyout private/gateway.example.com.key ↵
-out gateway.example.com.req
```

We've generated a 4,096-bit RSA key in the /etc/pki/tls/private directory and created a CSR. You will be prompted to populate the required fields (State, City, etc.). You need to use the same values as your certificate authority. For the Common Name field, you should specify the fully qualified domain name of your server, in our case gateway.example.com.

We need to sign on to our host that manages our CA to sign our CSR request and generate our public certificate. We need to copy the CSR to the CA host and then run the command shown in Listing 15-3.

Listing 15-3. Signing Our Server Certificate

```
$ cd /etc/pki/CA
$ sudo openssl ca -out gateway.example.com.cert -cert certs/cacert.pem -infiles gateway.
example.com.req
Using configuration from /etc/pki/tls/openssl.cnf
Enter pass phrase for /etc/pki/CA/private/cakey.pem:
Check that the request matches the signature
```

```
Signature ok
Certificate Details:
        Serial Number: 1 (0x1)
        Validity
                Not Before: Oct 22 11:47:26 2016 GMT
                Not After : Oct 22 11:47:26 2017 GMT
        Subject:
                countryName              = AU
                stateOrProvinceName      = Victoria
                organizationName         = Example Inc
                organizationalUnitName   = IT
                commonName               = gateway.example.com
                emailAddress             = admin@example.com
        X509v3 extensions:
                X509v3 Basic Constraints:
                    CA:FALSE
                Netscape Comment:
                    OpenSSL Generated Certificate
                X509v3 Subject Key Identifier:
                    A6:A4:16:17:32:D2:7B:03:D2:5C:5A:DE:85:29:51:BE:E4:73:EA:20
                X509v3 Authority Key Identifier:
                    keyid:98:3E:03:EB:FF:8A:FF:E8:1A:BC:56:04:CA:BE:BC:DB:D2:FA:68:12

Certificate is to be certified until Oct 22 11:47:26 2017 GMT (365 days)
Sign the certificate? [y/n]:y

1 out of 1 certificate requests certified, commit? [y/n]y
Write out database with 1 new entries
Data Base Updated
```

First, on our CentOS CA server, we change into our /etc/pki/CA directory and then run the openssl ca command to sign our CSR. This outputs a certificate signed by our CA. We now have our public certificate file, gateway.example.com.cert. We need to copy this file to the /etc/pki/tls/certs directory on our gateway host. We will also need to copy the CA root certificate.

To do this, we have an OpenSSH shell open on both the CA server and the gateway server. Then we use the cat program to print the public and cacert certificates to the screen. For each file we copy and paste them into the gateway.example.com.cert and cacert.pem files to the following directories:

```
[ca.example.come] $ sudo cat gateway.example.com.cert
[gateway.example.com] $ sudo vi /etc/pki/tls/certs/gateway.example.com.cert
[ca.example.come] $ sudo cat certs/cacert.pem
[gateway.example.com] $ vi /etc/pki/tls/certs/cacerts.pem
```

Then on the gateway host we make sure we move the private key to the proper directory.

```
[gateway.example.com] $ sudo mv gateway.example.com.key /etc/pki/tls/private/gateway.
example.com.key
```

In the previous lines, we have copied our TLS certificates to their proper locations on our gateway host, including the CA's root certificate, cacert.pem. In addition, the gateway.example.com.key should be on our gateway.example.com host and moved into the proper location.

■ **Note** In addition to the private key and certificate files, you have a CSR request file. It's worth hanging on to this for when your certificate expires. You can use this request again to create a new certificate, as we mentioned in Chapter 11.

We want to protect our certificate and key with the right ownership and some restricted permissions for our key.

```
$ sudo chown root:root /etc/pki/tls/{private,certs}/gateway.example.com.*
$ sudo chmod 0400 /etc//pki/tls/private/gateway.example.com.key
```

We also need to create some *Diffie-Hellman parameters*, cryptographic parameters that enhance the security of our VPN session. This is on the server only. This key is used to generate a public key that communicating parties use to generate a shared secret that both parties will use to communicate. (You can read about Diffie-Hellman in more detail at https://wiki.openssl.org/index.php/Diffie_Hellman). We can use the openssl command to create these.

```
$ sudo openssl dhparam -out /etc/openvpn/dh2048.pem 2048
Generating DH parameters, 2048 bit long safe prime, generator 2
This is going to take a long time
.............................................+..............................................
```

Here we've created a file called dh2048.pem in the /etc/openvpn directory. It's a 2,048-bit DH parameter file, and we've specified the size using the 2048 option. This will be a sufficiently safe key size for several years, but you can increase this to 4,096 if you want longer protection from future cracking.

One more thing we will quickly do is create a tls-auth key. This is also used to provide greater security to the TLS channel by using a pre-shared key. This PSK should be deployed to all servers and clients.

```
openvpn --genkey --secret /etc/openvpn/ta.key
```

Now we tell OpenVPN about our new certificates and the location of our CA certificate and our DH parameter file (see Listing 15-4).

Listing 15-4. The gateway.conf Configuration File

```
# Network configuration
dev tun
port 1194
proto udp
server 10.8.0.0 255.255.255.0
keepalive 10 120

# Certificate configuration
ca /etc/pki/tls/certs/cacert.pem
dh /etc/openvpn/dh2048.pem
cert /etc/pki/tls/certs/gateway.example.com.cert
key /etc/pki/tls/private/gateway.example.com.key
tls-auth ta.key 0
```

```
# Logging configuration
log-append /var/log/openvpn.log
status /var/log/openvpn-status.log
verb 4
mute 20

# Security configuration
user nobody
group nobody
persist-key
persist-tun

# Compression
comp-lzo
```

You can see we've added four options. The first is the ca option to specify the location of the CA certificate, in our case /etc/pki/tls/certs/cacert.pem. The next, dh, specifies the location of the Diffie-Hellman parameter file we created, in our case /etc/openvpn/dh2048.pem. Lastly, we've used the cert and key options to specify the location of our certificate and key files, respectively, in our case /etc/pki/tls/certs/gateway.example.com.cert and /etc/pki/tls/private/gateway.example.com.key.

The tls-auth key needs to be specified as tls-auth <key> 0 on the server and tls-auth <key> 1 on the clients. We will need to copy the tls-auth key to all the clients.

We can start our OpenVPN server as follows:

```
$ sudo systemctl start openvpn@gateway
$ sudo systemctl status openvpn@gateway.service
● openvpn@gateway.service - OpenVPN Robust And Highly Flexible Tunneling Application On
gateway
   Loaded: loaded (/usr/lib/systemd/system/openvpn@.service; enabled; vendor preset:
disabled)
   Active: active (running) since Sat 2016-10-22 22:37:09 UTC; 1h 39min ago
  Process: 7779 ExecStart=/usr/sbin/openvpn --daemon --writepid /var/run/openvpn/%i.pid --cd
/etc/openvpn/ --config %i.conf (code=exited, status=0/SUCCESS)
 Main PID: 7780 (openvpn)
...
```

You can see that we've started the OpenVPN server, and you can see when it started the VPN called gateway.service. The VPN is named for the gateway.conf configuration file.

We are also able to see some log entries in the /var/log/openvpn.log file, as shown in Listing 15-5.

Listing 15-5. The /var/log/openvpn.log Log File

```
Sat Oct 22 22:37:09 2016 us=712503 OpenVPN 2.3.12 x86_64-redhat-linux-gnu [SSL (OpenSSL)]
[LZO] [EPOLL] [PKCS11] [MH] [IPv6] built on Aug 23 2016
Sat Oct 22 22:37:09 2016 us=712511 library versions: OpenSSL 1.0.1e-fips 11 Feb 2013, LZO 2.06
Sat Oct 22 22:37:09 2016 us=724495 Diffie-Hellman initialized with 2048 bit key
Sat Oct 22 22:37:09 2016 us=724919 TLS-Auth MTU parms [ L:1542 D:1212 EF:38 EB:0 ET:0 EL:3 ]
Sat Oct 22 22:37:09 2016 us=724982 Socket Buffers: R=[212992->212992] S=[212992->212992]
Sat Oct 22 22:37:09 2016 us=725172 ROUTE_GATEWAY 10.0.2.2/255.255.255.0 IFACE=eth0
HWADDR=52:54:00:c5:83:ad
Sat Oct 22 22:37:09 2016 us=733863 TUN/TAP device tun0 opened
Sat Oct 22 22:37:09 2016 us=733929 TUN/TAP TX queue length set to 100
```

```
Sat Oct 22 22:37:09 2016 us=733946 do_ifconfig, tt->ipv6=0, tt->did_ifconfig_ipv6_setup=0
Sat Oct 22 22:37:09 2016 us=733963 /usr/sbin/ip link set dev tun0 up mtu 1500
Sat Oct 22 22:37:09 2016 us=740224 /usr/sbin/ip addr add dev tun0 local 10.8.0.1 peer
10.8.0.2
Sat Oct 22 22:37:09 2016 us=745857 /usr/sbin/ip route add 10.8.0.0/24 via 10.8.0.2
Sat Oct 22 22:37:09 2016 us=755742 Data Channel MTU parms [ L:1542 D:1450 EF:42 EB:143 ET:0
EL:3 AF:3/1 ]
Sat Oct 22 22:37:09 2016 us=756240 GID set to nobody
Sat Oct 22 22:37:09 2016 us=756256 UID set to nobody
Sat Oct 22 22:37:09 2016 us=756265 UDPv4 link local (bound): [undef]
Sat Oct 22 22:37:09 2016 us=756270 UDPv4 link remote: [undef]
Sat Oct 22 22:37:09 2016 us=756279 MULTI: multi_init called, r=256 v=256
Sat Oct 22 22:37:09 2016 us=756297 IFCONFIG POOL: base=10.8.0.4 size=62, ipv6=0
Sat Oct 22 22:37:09 2016 us=756313 Initialization Sequence Completed
```

Listing 15-5 shows that the OpenVPN server has started, our interface tun0 was created, and our IP address of 10.8.0.1 was added and bound to the UDP port of 1194.

■ **Note**   Ensure you have the right firewall rules in place to allow VPN connections to your host—in this case, incoming connections on UDP port 1194 need to be accepted.

Our server is running, but we're still not quite done. We need to configure our clients, install the OpenVPN software, and create certificates for our clients to use to connect.

■ **Note**   Going forward in this chapter, we'll refer to two hosts. When a command needs to be run on a particular host, we're going to prefix it with the same of that host: [ca]$, [gateway]$, or [branch1]$.

Configuring OpenVPN on Our Branch Office Servers

First, we need to install the OpenVPN packages on our branch server, branch1.example.com. Follow the appropriate instructions for your distribution and set OpenVPN to start when your host boots, for example:

```
[branch1]$ sudo systemctl enable openvpn@branch1
```

■ **Note**   You can tell we're running the preceding command on the branch1.example.com host by the command prefix, [branch1]$.

The next step is to create a certificate and key for each of our branch offices. We're going to create our certificate and key on the ca.example.com host and sign it using the CA on that host. We'll start with one branch office, branch1.example.com.

```
[ca]$ openssl req -new -newkey rsa:4096 -nodes -keyout branch1.example.com.key ↵
-out branch1.example.com.req
```

We've generated a 4,096-bit RSA key and created a CSR. You will be prompted to populate the required fields: State, City, and so forth. You need to use the same values as your certificate authority. For the Common Name field, you should specify the fully qualified domain name of your server, in our case branch1.example.com.

Then we use our CA to sign our certificate as we did earlier.

```
[ca]$ cd /etc/pki/CA
[ca]$ sudo openssl ca -out branch1.example.com.cert -cert certs/cacert.pem ↵
-infiles branch1.example.com.req
```

Now we need to send our certificate and key as well as the CA certificate to the branch server. There are a number of ways you can do this, but you must do it securely—don't e-mail them, for example, as they can be readily intercepted. Take them on a USB key, add them to your configuration management system (encrypted), and install them locally on the target server/client. Or if you are able to directly connect to the host, use the scp (secure copy) or sftp (secure FTP) command to send the files. These commands use an SSH connection to securely connect to another host and transfer files.

In this example, we're going to use the sftp command to connect to our branch office server and transfer the required files.

```
[ca]$ sftp jsmith@branch1.example.com
Connecting to branch1.example.com...
jsmith@branch1.example.com's password:
sftp> put branch1.example.com.cert
Uploading /home/jsmith/branch1.example.com.cert to ↵
/home/jsmith/branch1.example.com.cert
/home/jsmith/branch1.example.com.cert 100%   5881    12.0KB/s    00:03
```

We have connected to the branch1.example.com host and, using the put command, transferred the branch1.example.com.cert certificate file from its location, here the /home/jsmith directory, to the equivalent directory /home/jsmith on the branch1 host. You can use the cd command to change to an appropriate directory on the remote host where you want to write your files.

```
sftp> cd /tmp
```

You'll need permission to write to that location. You can use the cd command to change the directory on the local gateway.example.com host if your files are located elsewhere.

We use the put command to also put the branch1.example.com.key and the cacert.pem CA certificate file onto the branch1 host. Since this is an Ubuntu server, we're now going to move our files to the /etc/ssl directory and secure their ownership and permissions. On CentOS we would be using the /etc/pki/tls directory again.

```
[branch1]$ sudo mv branch1.example.com.cert /etc/ssl/certs/
[branch1]$ sudo mv branch1.example.com.key /etc/ssl/private/
[branch1]$ sudo mv cacert.pem /etc/ssl/certs/
```

We want to protect our certificate and key with the right ownership and some restricted permissions for our key.

```
branch1$ sudo chown root:root /etc/ssl{certs,private}/branch1.example.com.*
branch1$ sudo chown root:root /etc/ssl/certs/cacert.pem
branch1$ sudo chmod 0400 /etc/ssl/private/gateway.example.com.key
```

Next, we need to create a configuration file for our client. We're going to create a file called branch1.conf in our /etc/openvpn directory, as you can see in Listing 15-6.

Listing 15-6. The branch1.conf Configuration File

```
# Network configuration
dev tun
client
remote gateway.example.com 1194
keepalive 10 120

# Certificate configuration
ca /etc/ssl/certs/cacert.pem
cert /etc/ssl/certs/branch1.example.com.cert
key /etc/ssl/private/branch1.example.com.key
tls-auth ta.key 1

# Logging configuration
log-append /var/log/openvpn.log
status /var/log/openvpn-status.log
verb 4
mute 20

# Security configuration
user nobody
group nogroup
persist-key
persist-tun

# Compression
comp-lzo
```

■ **Note** If you're using CentOS, your group setting should be set to nobody rather than nogroup.

The file in Listing 15-6 is similar to the gateway.conf configuration file, but we've specified some different options because of the host's role as a client. Again, we've specified dev tun for a routed VPN. We've also specified the client option, which indicates that this is a client, and the remote option, which tells OpenVPN where to connect our VPN tunnel. We've specified gateway.example.com and port 1194.

■ **Note** OpenVPN must be able to resolve this host (i.e., it must be able to find an IP address for this host). If you don't have a DNS (you should), then you can specify an IP address directly in this option.

We've also specified the location of our CA certificate with the ca option and the location of our client's certificate and key using the cert and key options, respectively.

Starting OpenVPN on Our Branch Office Server

With the VPN configured on our server, we can now start OpenVPN on our client. For example, we use the following command on CentOS:

```
[branch1]$ sudo systemctl start openvpn@branch1
```

Testing Our OpenVPN Tunnel

You can determine whether your connection has worked in a number of ways, and we'll take you through them all. First, you should see some entries in the /var/log/openvpn.log file on the branch1 host. You should see similar entries to those in Listing 15-5, but you'll also see the negotiation process as our client connects to the server.

```
Sun Oct 23 06:24:58 2016 us=729639 [gateway.example.com] Peer Connection Initiated ↵
  with [AF_INET]10.0.2.155:1194
```

■ **Note**   You will see factious public IPv4 addresses here (10.0.2.155 and 10.0.2.156) in these examples that match the diagram in Figure 15-2.

You should also see some entries on the gateway host in the /var/log/openvpn.log file showing the connection.

```
gateway$ less /var/log/openvpn.log
Sun Oct 23 06:25:06 2016 us=416152 branch1.example.com/10.0.2.156:1194 SENT CONTROL
[branch1.example.com]: 'PUSH_REPLY,route 10.8.0.1,topology net30,ping 10,ping-restart
120,ifconfig 10.8.0.6 10.8.0.5' (status=1)
```

In addition, you can see a new interface created on both the gateway and branch1 hosts, starting with tun. On the gateway host you can see a new interface called tun0 with an IP address of 10.8.0.1 (as mentioned earlier).

```
[gateway]$ ip addr show tun0
5: tun0: <POINTOPOINT,MULTICAST,NOARP,UP,LOWER_UP> mtu 1500 qdisc pfifo_fast state UNKNOWN
qlen 100
    link/none
    inet 10.8.0.1 peer 10.8.0.2/32 scope global tun0
       valid_lft forever preferred_lft forever
```

On the branch1 host an interface, also called tun0, has been created with an IP address of 10.8.0.6 from the pool of addresses our server is offering.

```
[branch1]$ ip addr show tun0
5: tun0: <POINTOPOINT,MULTICAST,NOARP,UP,LOWER_UP> mtu 1500 qdisc pfifo_fast state UNKNOWN
group default qlen 100
    link/none
    inet 10.8.0.6 peer 10.8.0.5/32 scope global tun0
       valid_lft forever preferred_lft forever
```

You can also see the route table on the branch1 host (using the ip command introduced in Chapter 7) has a route for our 10.8.0.0/24 network.

```
branch1$ ip route show
sudo ip route show
default via 10.0.2.2 dev enp0s3
10.0.2.0/24 dev enp0s3  proto kernel  scope link  src 10.0.2.15
10.8.0.1 via 10.8.0.5 dev tun0
10.8.0.5 dev tun0  proto kernel  scope link  src 10.8.0.6
192.168.0.0/24 dev enp0s8  proto kernel  scope link  src 10.0.2.156
```

There is a route to the 10.8.0.1 host via the tun0 interface.

You'll notice that on both hosts a file called /var/log/openvpn-status.log has been created. This file contains a list of the current connections and is refreshed every 60 seconds. Let's look at this file on the gateway host.

```
gateway$ less /var/log/openvpn-status.log
OpenVPN CLIENT LIST
Updated,Sun Oct 23 06:44:43 2016
Common Name,Real Address,Bytes Received,Bytes Sent,Connected Since
branch1.example.com,10.0.2.156:1194,16384,16774,Sun Oct 23 06:24:30 2016
ROUTING TABLE
Virtual Address,Common Name,Real Address,Last Ref
10.8.0.6,branch1.example.com,10.0.2.156:1194,Sun Oct 23 06:33:01 2016
GLOBAL STATS
Max bcast/mcast queue length,0
END
```

You can see a connection listed from the branch1 host with an IP address of 10.0.2.156.

Lastly, you can use network tools to test your actual connection. Let's start by using the ping command on our gateway host to ping our branch1 host. We're going to ping the address used as the end of our VPN tunnel on the branch1 host, which we discovered earlier is 10.8.0.6.

```
[gateway]$ ping 10.8.0.6 -c 3
PING 10.8.0.6 (10.8.0.6) 56(84) bytes of data.
64 bytes from 10.8.0.6: icmp_seq=1 ttl=64 time=0.593 ms
64 bytes from 10.8.0.6: icmp_seq=2 ttl=64 time=0.588 ms
64 bytes from 10.8.0.6: icmp_seq=3 ttl=64 time=0.807 ms
```

The preceding code shows us that the gateway host can see the branch1 host using ICMP and the 10.8.0.6 IP address on that branch1 host responds to ICMP traffic.

We can do the same thing from the branch1 host by trying to ping IP address 10.8.0.1 on the gateway host end.

```
branch1$
ping 10.8.0.1 -c 3
PING 10.8.0.1 (10.8.0.1) 56(84) bytes of data.
64 bytes from 10.8.0.1: icmp_seq=1 ttl=64 time=0.682 ms
64 bytes from 10.8.0.1: icmp_seq=2 ttl=64 time=0.672 ms
64 bytes from 10.8.0.1: icmp_seq=3 ttl=64 time=0.751 ms
```

If both ends respond, then your VPN is up, and you can use it to route traffic to and from your branch office to your head office.

If you now want, you can repeat this configuration for any additional branch offices. For example, in our case we could add tunnels from the `branch2.example.com` and `branch3.example.com` offices.

Exposing Head Office Resources with OpenVPN

With our configuration so far, we can route traffic between our branch offices and our head office over our VPN tunnel. Let's take a look at how our head office and our branch offices now interact.

Take another look at Figure 15-2. Currently, we have two paths from our branch offices to our head office. The first is across the 10.0.2.0/24 network you saw in Chapter 7. This is our DSL or ASDL (or similar type) Internet connection between our offices and the Internet. Each individual office will generally have an individual Internet connection. We've used the 10.0.2.0/24 network as their IP address, but it's more likely that each office has an individual address acquired from the ISP.

This network is not secure, as it runs over the Internet. Unless we secure a particular application or protocol (e.g., in the way we used SSL/TLS in Chapter 12 to protect our SMTP and IMAP services), then an attacker could read our data from that network. Because of this potential security issue, across this connection we've instantiated our second path between these hosts, the 10.8.0.0/24 network that we are using for our VPN tunnels. Our head office is the OpenVPN server with an IP address of 10.8.0.1. Each branch office has an IP address from that range—for example, you've seen the 10.8.0.6 IP address assigned to the `branch1.example.com` office.

Currently through our VPN tunnel, however, we can reach only the IP address 10.8.0.1. This isn't much use to us because we can't access any of the resources available on the internal network (e.g., a file share on the `headoffice.example.com` host). We can test this from our branch office host by trying to ping the `headoffice` host:

```
branch1$ ping 192.168.0.1
```

We'll get no reply from these pings because there is no route to this network. To access these resources, we need to ensure two elements are in order: routing and firewall rules. We'll discuss these in the sections that follow.

Routing

We first need to configure our branch offices to route to the internal network of our head office. To do this, we tell our branch office that when it wants to route to the 192.168.0.0/24 network, it needs to go through the VPN tunnel to the gateway host. We do this as shown in Listing 15-7 by adding a line to the `gateway.conf` configuration file on the gateway host to push a route to our branch hosts.

Listing 15-7. Push Route Added to gateway.conf

```
push "route 192.168.0.0 255.255.255.0"
```

This line adds a route to all clients that connect to the OpenVPN server. For the new route to be pushed, we need to restart the openvpn service on both the gateway host and the branch office hosts.

If we look at the route table on our branch1 host, we can see a new route to the 192.168.0.0/24 network in our routes (in bold).

```
[branch1]$ ip route
default via 10.0.2.2 dev eth0  proto static  metric 100
10.0.2.0/24 dev eth0  proto kernel  scope link  src 10.0.2.15   metric 100
10.8.0.1 via 10.8.0.5 dev tun0
10.8.0.5 dev tun0  proto kernel  scope link  src 10.8.0.6
169.254.0.0/16 dev eth1  scope link  metric 1003
10.0.2.0/24 dev eth1  proto kernel  scope link  src 10.0.2.156
192.168.0.0/24 via 10.8.0.5 dev tun0
192.168.10.0/24 dev eth1  proto kernel  scope link  src 192.168.10.254
```

We can now ping this network from the branch1 host.

```
branch1$ ping 192.168.0.1
PING 192.168.0.1 (192.168.0.1) 56(84) bytes of data.
64 bytes from 192.168.0.1: icmp_seq=1 ttl=64 time=1.18 ms
64 bytes from 192.168.0.1: icmp_seq=2 ttl=64 time=1.31 ms
64 bytes from 192.168.0.1: icmp_seq=3 ttl=64 time=2.33 ms
64 bytes from 192.168.0.1: icmp_seq=4 ttl=64 time=1.25 ms
64 bytes from 192.168.0.1: icmp_seq=5 ttl=64 time=0.923 ms
```

You can see we're getting a response from the host 192.168.0.1 on our branch1 host. We are able to access anything that the firewall on the gateway host allows us to on the 192.168.0.0/24 network.

If the branch1 host is the default route for 192.168.10.0/24 (the local network at the branch1 site), then all our users in the 192.162.10.0/24 network will be able to access resources in the 192.168.0.0/24 network at our head office.

■ **Note**   We're not going to tell our head office how to route to the internal networks of our branch offices, but this is also possible.

Firewall

We also need to ensure the firewall rules on our gateway and branch hosts allow traffic to and from the relevant networks. On our gateway host, this involves forwarding IP traffic from our gateway host into the internal network and back, much like the configuration we created in Chapter 7 for forwarding our services from our bastion host, gateway.example.com.

First, we direct traffic that we want to forward through our gateway host from the VPN tunnel interface tun0 using the public zone. We will add the tun0 interface to the public zone.

```
[gateway]$ sudo firewall-cmd --zone public --permanent --add-interface tun0
```

We then need to create a rule set for this zone to allow our gateway host to forward particular traffic through the host, as shown in Listing 15-8.

Listing 15-8. Some Sample firewalld Rules for OpenVPN Routing

```
[gateway]$ sudo firewall-cmd --zone public --permanent --add-service=http
success
[gateway]$ sudo firewall-cmd --zone public --permanent --add-service=https
success
[gateway]$ sudo firewall-cmd --zone public --permanent --add-service=smtp
success
[gateway]$ sudo firewall-cmd --zone public --permanent --add-service=dns
success
[gateway]$ sudo firewall-cmd --zone public --permanent --add-service=ntp
success
[gateway]$ sudo firewall-cmd --zone public --permanent --add-service=imaps
success
```

Now we have to reload the firewall configuration.

```
[gateway]$ sudo firewall-cmd --reload
```

We've created a variety of simple rules to allow traffic through the VPN tunnel and forward it into our internal network. We've forwarded SMTP, HTTP/HTTPS, and IMAP, among other protocols.

■ **Note** You can use the instructions provided in Chapter 7 to add these rules to your gateway host.

VPN Connections for Mobile Users

OpenVPN is capable of more than just allowing point-to-point connections from your branch offices to your head office. You can also use it to allow mobile users to connect to your head office and access resources such as file shares, printers, and applications. To do this, we need to set up another VPN tunnel on our gateway host and install OpenVPN on our clients. As we mentioned earlier in this chapter, OpenVPN can run on platforms including Linux, Microsoft Windows, macOS, and others.

We're going to do a few things differently with our mobile users. We're not going to use certificates (although we could use them) to authenticate our client because the overhead of potentially generating a lot of certificates can be quite high.

■ **Note** A tool that makes certificate management easier with OpenVPN is easy-rsa. The documentation is available here: https://openvpn.net/index.php/open-source/documentation/miscellaneous/77-rsa-key-management.html.

Instead, we're going to show you how to use PAM (which we introduced you to in Chapter 5) to authenticate your users. As a result of PAM's ability to plug in a variety of authentication mechanisms, we can use it to include authentication mechanisms such as the following:

- Local Linux users
- Two-factor authentication such as RSA tokens or smartcards

- Kerberos

- RADIUS

- IMAP (against an IMAP server)

- LDAP

We're going to show you how to configure basic local-user authentication—that is, your users will have a Linux user on the gateway host, and they will be authenticated as if they were logging on to that host using the console or via SSH. Using PAM, you can easily extend this to other forms of authentication.

Configuring Our Mobile VPN

To start our configuration, we need a new `.conf` file. We're going to create one called `mobile.conf` in `/etc/openvpn`, as you can see in Listing 15-9.

Listing 15-9. Mobile User's mobile.conf Configuration File

```
# Network configuration
dev tun
port 1195
proto udp
server 10.9.0.0 255.255.255.0
keepalive 10 120

# Certificate configuration
dh /etc/openvpn/dh2048.pem
ca /etc/pki/tls/certs/cacert.pem
cert /etc/pki/tls/certs/gateway.example.com.cert
key /etc/pki/tls/private/gateway.example.com.key
tls-auth ta.key 0

plugin /usr/lib64/openvpn/plugins/openvpn-plugin-auth-pam.so login

# Logging configuration
log-append /var/log/openvpn-mobile.log
status /var/log/openvpn-status-mobile.log
verb 4
mute 20

# Security configuration
user nobody
group nobody
persist-key
persist-tun

# Compression
comp-lzo
```

■ **Note** We'll expand on this configuration later in this section when we look at configuring routing and related functionality on our client.

You can see that our `mobile.conf` configuration is similar to our `gateway.conf` VPN tunnel. We are separating the two so that machines use the server on 1194 and roaming users use 1195, which will be further secured by their username and password.

Let's focus on the differences. We've changed some networking configuration: we've used a different port, 1195, because our other VPN tunnel is bound to the 1194 port. It can be common for administrators to use the TCP protocol and port 443 for mobile users; this is because ports like 1195 or 1194 can be blocked at places like airports. We've also specified an additional IP subnet for our mobile users, 10.9.0.0/24.

We need to ensure we have suitable firewall rules in place for this subnet. First, we open the 1195 port for our tunnel on the `tun1` interface (the interface number has incremented for our new tunnel).

```
[gateway]$ sudo firewall-cmd --zone public --permanent --add-port=1195/udp
```

■ **Note** Our new interface will be `tun1` because we already have a `tun0` interface. If you don't have another VPN tunnel, then your interface may be `tun0`.

We've specified the same certificate, key, `tls-auth`, and DH parameters, but we've added a new option called `plugin`. The `plugin` configuration option allows us to specify external plug-ins, in our case a PAM plug-in called `openvpn-pluging-auth-pam.so` that ships with the OpenVPN package.

On Ubuntu, the plug-in is located at `/usr/lib/openvpn/openvpn-plugin-auth-pam.so`.

We also need to specify the name of a PAM authentication file that OpenVPN will use to authenticate the VPN tunnel. On Ubuntu, we've specified the standard shadow password PAM authentication file, `passwd`, as the authentication mechanism to use. On CentOS, we could specify the `system-auth` default PAM authentication file.

For other forms of authentication, you specify here an appropriate PAM authentication file for that mechanism. For example, to enable two-factor authentication, you might specify a file that uses the Google Authenticator PAM module, `pam_google_authenticator.so` (see `https://www.linux.com/learn/how-set-2-factor-authentication-login-and-sudo` for an example of how to implement it). This module allows you to integrate your Google Authenticator with PAM to allow you to provide a token to authenticate users.

We've updated the logging files to create new files for our mobile connection. We've also specified the `user` and `group` options (in this case, we've used the `nobody` group on CentOS).

Next, we need to restart our OpenVPN service to start our mobile VPN tunnel.

Configuring Mobile VPN Clients

You need to configure your clients to connect to the gateway, which you can do in a variety of ways depending on the client. A number of clients are available, ranging from the normal OpenVPN binary right through to sophisticated GUI clients. We'll provide a list of some of the available clients in this section, and we'll show you how to connect via OpenVPN.

The simplest client is the OpenVPN binary. We will create and sign a key and certificate for `mobile1.example.com` like we have for our other TLS certificates. We will put them in similar place as before, either in the `/etc/pki/tls` directories or in the `/etc/ssl` directories depending on our host.

If you're using the OpenVPN binary, you're also going to need to create a client configuration file. We'll call ours `mobileclient.conf` and store it in the `/etc/openvpn` directory on our client, as shown in Listing 15-10.

Listing 15-10. The mobileclient.conf Configuration File

```
# Network configuration
dev tun
client
remote gateway.example.com 1195
keepalive 10 120

# Certificate configuration
ca /etc/ssl/certs/cacert.pem
cert /etc/ssl/certs/mobile1.example.com.cert
key /etc/ssl/private/mobile1.example.com.key
tls-auth ta.key 1

auth-user-pass

# Logging configuration
log-append /var/log/openvpn.log
status /var/log/openvpn-status.log
verb 4
mute 20

# Security configuration
user nobody
group nobody

persist-key
persist-tun

# Compression
comp-lzo
```

You can see the options we've used previously with one addition and some minor changes. We've changed the remote port we're connecting on to 1195. We've also added the `auth-user-pass` option, which tells the client that we're going to use usernames and passwords rather than just certificate authentication.

Now, if we start OpenVPN on our client, it will connect to the gateway, prompting the user to enter appropriate credentials.

```
$ sudo /etc/init.d/openvpn restart
Shutting down openvpn                                    [ OK ]
Starting openvpn:
Enter Auth Username:jsmith
Enter Auth Password:********
```

Notice the auth username and password prompts. We've entered the username of a user on the gateway host, `jsmith`, and his password.

The client will then connect, and you should be able to see a new interface (tun1, in our case).

```
$ ip addr show tun0
10: tun0: <POINTOPOINT,MULTICAST,NOARP,UP,LOWER_UP> mtu 1500 qdisc pfifo_fast state UNKNOWN
qlen 100
    link/none
    inet 10.8.0.6 peer 10.8.0.5/32 scope global tun0
       valid_lft forever preferred_lft forever
```

The interface has the IP address of 10.9.0.6 issued by the gateway host (remember, we set our mobile client VPN network as 10.9.0.0/24). You can then ping this IP address of the gateway host (in our case, 10.9.0.1) and vice versa back to 10.9.0.6.

```
$ ping 10.9.0.1
PING 10.9.0.1 (10.9.0.1) 56(84) bytes of data.
64 bytes from 10.9.0.1: icmp_seq=1 ttl=64 time=10.3 ms
64 bytes from 10.9.0.1: icmp_seq=2 ttl=64 time=10.64 ms
64 bytes from 10.9.0.1: icmp_seq=3 ttl=64 time=10.59 ms
64 bytes from 10.9.0.1: icmp_seq=4 ttl=64 time=10.73 ms
64 bytes from 10.9.0.1: icmp_seq=5 ttl=64 time=10.59 ms
```

OpenVPN Client Profile

The other way we can distribute the OpenVPN client configuration is to create an OpenVPN profile file. These can be distributed via the OpenVPN Access Server or by other means. In this example, we will create an .ovpn profile file for our mobile client, upload that to our OpenVPN app in iTunes, and connect to our OpenVPN server.

A profile is basically the same as a normal OpenVPN configuration file. The difference is we include the TLS certificates, including the private key. The following is the mobile1.ovpn file we have created for our profile:

```
client
proto udp
remote gateway.example.com
port 1195
dev tun
nobind
auth-user-pass
key-direction 1

<ca>
-----BEGIN CERTIFICATE-----
# TLS root ca
-----END CERTIFICATE-----
</ca>

<cert>
-----BEGIN CERTIFICATE-----
# TLS public certificate
-----END CERTIFICATE-----
</cert>
```

723

```
<key>
-----BEGIN PRIVATE KEY-----
# TLS private key
-----END PRIVATE KEY-----
</key>

<tls-auth>
-----BEGIN OpenVPN Static key V1-----
# tls-auth key
-----END OpenVPN Static key V1-----
</tls-auth>
```

Now we need to install the app from the App Store on the iPhone (Figure 15-3).

Figure 15-3. *Installing the app*

Now we need to add the `mobile1.ovpn` file to the app via iTunes (Figure 15-4).

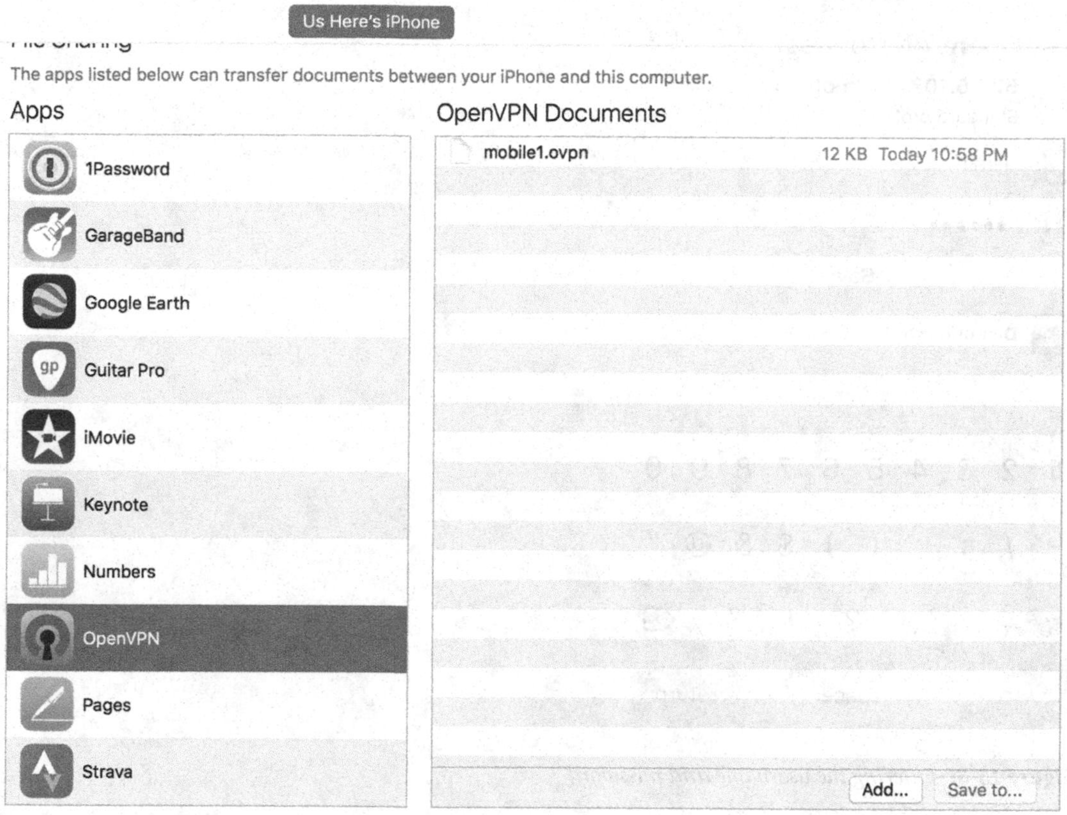

Figure 15-4. Adding mobile1.ovpn to the OpenVPN client

Once this is done, we are ready to make our connection to the OpenVPN server. From the app we add the profile using the green plus button. Then we are ready sign in. In Figure 15-5 we enter the username and password for `jsmith` and then toggle the connection button.

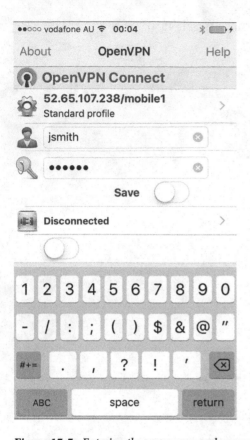

Figure 15-5. *Entering the username and password*

Figure 15-6 shows we are connected via the iPhone app.

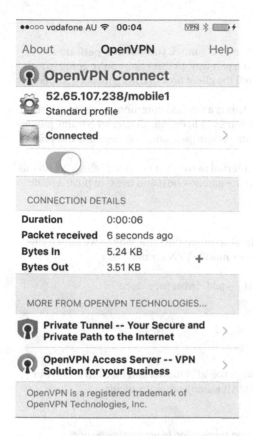

Figure 15-6. Connected via the iPhone app

We can confirm this in our server logs on the gateway machine.

```
AUTH-PAM: BACKGROUND: received command code: 0
AUTH-PAM: BACKGROUND: USER: jsmith
AUTH-PAM: BACKGROUND: my_conv[0] query='Password: ' style=1
Mon Oct 24 09:50:48 2016 us=779104 118.209.127.108:55174 PLUGIN_CALL: POST /usr/lib64/
openvpn/plugins/openvpn-plugin-auth-pam.so/PLUGIN_AUTH_USER_PASS_VERIFY status=0
Mon Oct 24 09:50:48 2016 us=779146 118.209.127.108:55174 TLS: Username/Password
authentication succeeded for username 'jsmith' [CN SET]
...
<snip>
...
Mon Oct 24 09:50:48 2016 us=801096 118.209.127.108:55174 [jsmith] Peer Connection Initiated
with [AF_INET]118.209.127.108:55174
```

We have completed the authentication, and now our iPhone is connected via our OpenVPN server to the local network.

There are a variety of other clients for various platforms available as many networking tools will support OpenVPN. You can also download the client for most systems here:

- https://openvpn.net/index.php/open-source/downloads.html

Mobile VPN Routing

Just as you can create a point-to-point head office to branch office VPN tunnel, you can also perform a variety of routing configurations between your client host and the gateway. In this case, you're going to not just help the client see hosts behind the gateway host but also tell the client how to configure itself, especially its DHCP settings.

You'll also see how to force all traffic up through the VPN. This is a method commonly used to ensure a user's traffic goes only to your organization. For example, it is often used to ensure all user web traffic passes through your organization's proxy, thus ensuring it complies with your organization's acceptable use policy or similar standards.

First, let's allow our mobile user to see the 192.168.0.0/24 internal network at our head office. We do this by adding the push option to our mobile.conf configuration on the gateway host and use it to push a route.

```
push "route 192.168.0.0 255.255.255.0"
```

We also need to update the firewall rules on our gateway host, in much the same way as we added rules for the branch to head office tunnel. We add another chain for our mobile VPN tunnel.

```
[gateway]$ sudo firewall-cmd --zone public --permanent --add-interface tun1
```

Now we have reload the firewall configuration.

```
[gateway]$ sudo firewall-cmd --reload
```

We've created a variety of simple rules to allow traffic through the VPN tunnel and forward it into our internal network. We've forwarded SMTP, HTTP/HTTPS, and IMAP, among other protocols.

■ **Note**   You can use the instructions provided in Chapter 7 to add these rules to your gateway host.

We can also pass a variety of options to our client, for example, to help set DHCP options like DNS and WINS servers.

■ **Note**   We set up DHCP in Chapter 10.

Different types of clients (e.g., Linux and Microsoft Windows clients) require different methods to push down the required options. When passing options to a Microsoft Windows client, we can simply pass the required options along using the push option. For example, to push a DNS server IP address to the client, we do the following:

```
push "dhcp-option DNS 10.0.2.155"
```

Here we're telling OpenVPN to tell a Microsoft Windows client to push the DNS server 10.0.2.155 to its DHCP option.

In a Microsoft Windows environment, we can also push down a variety of other options, as shown in Table 15-1.

Table 15-1. DHCP Options

Option	Description
DOMAIN *name*	Sets the client's DNS suffix.
DNS *address*	Sets the DNS server address. Repeat to set secondary DNS servers.
WINS *address*	Sets the WINS server address. Repeat to set secondary WINS servers.
NBDD *address*	Sets the NBDD server address. Repeat to set secondary NBDD servers.
NTP *address*	Sets the NTP server address. Repeat to set secondary NTP servers.
DISABLE-NBT	Disables NetBIOS over TCP/IP.

On Linux and other hosts, you can't directly set these sorts of options using the push option. Instead, you need to tell OpenVPN to run scripts when the tunnel goes up and down. To do this, you use the appropriately named up and down options. We can add the following options to the mobileclient.conf on our VPN client:

```
up /etc/openvpn/tunnelup.sh
down /etc/openvpn/tunneldown.sh
```

Each option specifies scripts or commands that will be run when the VPN tunnel goes up and down. If we wanted to set the DNS configuration of our client, we might use an up script, tunnelup.sh, like this:

```
#!/bin/sh
mv /etc/resolv.conf /etc/resolv.conf.bak
echo "search example.org" > /etc/resolv.conf
echo "nameserver 10.0.2.155" >> /etc/resolv.conf exit 0
```

We could then use a down script, tunneldown.sh, to revert our configuration options, like so:

```
#!/bin/sh
mv /etc/resolv.conf.bak /etc/resolv.conf
```

■ **Note**   You need to transfer these scripts to the client yourself or use a configuration management tool, as we'll show you in Chapter 19.

Lastly, we can force all traffic from the client to the VPN. This is often used to force users to comply with some policy or standard or to ensure all traffic is scanned for viruses and malware through a proxy or virus scanner.

There are some issues with pushing all traffic through your tunnel, though. Most notably, performance can be impacted by pushing traffic through the tunnel to your office and then onto the Internet. You will also need a proxy or NAT redirection for all the traffic generated by the client, as every protocol—not just web traffic—will need a means to connect.

To force all traffic up the VPN tunnel from the client, we add the following directive to the `mobile.conf` configuration file on our gateway host:

```
push "redirect-gateway def1"
```

If your VPN setup is over a wireless network and all clients and the server are on the same wireless network, you need to add to this directive.

```
push "redirect-gateway local def1"
```

You can see we've added the `local` option to the directive.

Troubleshooting OpenVPN

Troubleshooting OpenVPN requires you to take into consideration all elements of a connection: networks, firewalls, and OpenVPN itself. OpenVPN's extensive logging (you saw the `log-append`, `status`, and `verb` options earlier in the chapter) allows you to quickly see errors. Additionally, OpenVPN's error messages usually provide a clear and accurate indication of the actual problem.

But you also need to ensure you check that you have network connectivity and appropriate firewall rules, both `iptables` rules on your host(s) and potentially rules on any intervening network devices, to allow connections. You need to check that the connection is up, that firewall rules allow the VPN tunnel to connect, and finally that rules and routing exist that allow your traffic to flow across the VPN and to the intended destination.

■ **Tip**   Chapter 6 covers network and firewall troubleshooting.

The best place to start to look for troubleshooting help is the OpenVPN web site (`http://openvpn.net/`). There you can find documentation, including a comprehensive HOWTO page:

```
http://openvpn.net/index.php/documentation/howto.html
```

and a FAQ page:

```
http://openvpn.net/index.php/documentation/faq.html
```

You can find OpenVPN's man page here:

```
https://openvpn.net/index.php/open-source/documentation/manuals.html
```

Also available is a mailing list you can join here:

```
http://openvpn.net/index.php/documentation/miscellaneous/mailing-lists.html.
```

For more complex implementations, the OpenVPN developers provide commercial support, or you can turn to the book *OpenVPN: Building and Integrating Virtual Private Networks* by Markus Feilner (Packt Publishing, 2006) for help.

Summary

In this chapter, we took you through the process of configuring and managing VPN tunnels. We introduced point-to-point tunnels, such as between a head office and remote branches. We also explained how you can use VPN tunnels to allow your mobile users to securely and safely connect to resources at your head office or other locations. You've learned how to do the following:

- Configure VPN tunnels

- Create and configure certificates for authentication

- Make use of PAM to allow alternative forms of authentication

- Configure your `iptables` firewall to allow VPN tunnels

- Configure your networks and routing to allow users to traverse VPN tunnels and access resources

- Configure networking options on your clients using OpenVPN

In the next chapter, we'll discuss LDAP services.

CHAPTER 16

■ ■ ■

Directory Services

By Dennis Matotek

Directory services are widespread throughout major computer networks. A Lightweight Directory Access Protocol (LDAP) directory is an example of this type of service. LDAP directories are special databases that usually contain usernames, passwords, common names, e-mail addresses, business addresses, and other attributes. Organizations first used directory services to facilitate the distribution of address books and user information. Since that time, directory services have grown to take on roles as the central repositories for all user information and authentication services. Applications are developed with the ability to authenticate against directory services, further enhancing their importance within an organization.

In this chapter, we are going to show you how to install and configure an OpenLDAP server. We are also going to talk about extending your OpenLDAP directory server by adding your own schema. We will show you how to design the access control lists to secure your installation, as well as how to manage your LDAP server via command-line tools and a web-based GUI. Finally, you'll see how to integrate your LDAP server with your existing network and applications, including the ability to implement single sign-on services and Apache web authentication.

Directory services implementations can be complicated. While installation is simple, they are often intricate to configure securely. OpenLDAP does not have a commercially supported version, but even the simplest question to the OpenLDAP mailing list is regularly answered by senior engineers and designers of the project (which is an enormous help and absolute credit to their dedication). That said, you would be well served by purchasing a book dedicated to the subject before you begin your installation to further your understanding of this software. We would like to recommend to you the following:

- Checking the technical support page if you require expert support: `www.openldap.org/support/`

- *Deploying OpenLDAP* by Tom Jackiewicz (Apress, 2004)

- *Mastering OpenLDAP: Configuring, Securing, and Integrating Directory Services* by Matt Butcher (Packt Publishing, 2007)

■ **Tip**   The OpenLDAP web site also contains a good administration guide and FAQ at `www.openldap.org`.

© Dennis Matotek, James Turnbull and Peter Lieverdink 2017
D. Matotek et al., *Pro Linux System Administration*, DOI 10.1007/978-1-4842-2008-5_16

Overview

In this chapter we will be exploring OpenLDAP and using it as an authentication service. We can use it as a single sign-on service for any authentication mechanisms that support LDAP. It can be used to centrally hold identity information for all our users, including usernames, passwords, e-mail addresses, and other user and group information. In this chapter we are going to take you through the following:

- Installing and setting up the OpenLDAP service
- Explaining schemas and creating an attribute that we can use as a filter to check for active and inactive users
- Adding users to our LDAP service
- Securing the service to protect sensitive data with access control lists
- Using the LDAP tools such as `ldapmodify`, `ldapadd`, and `ldapsearch`
- Setting up a web GUI to manage LDAP
- Performing single sign-on with SSSD and LDAP
- Implementing web authentication with LDAP

You can search, add, modify, delete, and authenticate against entries in your LDAP service. These actions are restricted with access lists, and different users can have different access rights. There is an authentication process that happens in this initial phase that determines access level, and this is called *binding*. This can be done by a user on behalf of another user or anonymously depending on how you configure your access lists. Once this is done, we can get access to the entries in the service.

Read on and we will explain what LDAP is and give you an understanding of the components that make up the LDAP service.

What Is LDAP?

Lightweight Directory Access Protocol is used to access X.500-based directory services derived from the Directory Access Protocol (DAP). X.500 is a set of protocols that outline how user information should be stored and how that information should be accessed. LDAP resulted from the Directory Access Protocol not having TCP/IP capabilities.

■ **Note** For more information on the X.500 OSI protocol, please see `http://en.wikipedia.org/wiki/X.500`.

Several common types of directory services exist, and they are all derived from the X.500 DAP OSI model. Examples of some common ones are these: Microsoft's Active Directory, Red Hat's Directory Services, and Oracle Directory Server Enterprise Edition.

In this chapter, we will be concentrating on the commonly used and robust OpenLDAP server. OpenLDAP was forked from the original project originally designed by the University of Michigan and now continues through the work of a community of engineers and developers from the OpenLDAP project (`www.openldap.org/project/`).

■ **Note**   An alternative recommendation, though not explored in this book, is the FreeIPA project. It allows you to manage identities (user accounts and the like), perform policy authorization such as Kerberos policies for DNS and `sudo`, and create mutual trusts between other identity services (such as Microsoft AD). You can view more information about it at `https://www.freeipa.org/page/Main_Page`. There is also a good write-up on migrating from OpenLDAP to FreeIPA at `https://www.dragonsreach.it/2014/10/12/the-gnome-infrastructures-freeipa-move-behind-the-scenes/`.

The X.500 DAP OSI model describes some fundamental concepts to which LDAP complies. First, you need to have a single directory information tree (DIT). This is a hierarchical organization of entries. Each of these entries requires a distinguished name (DN). The DN of an entry consists of the relative distinguished name (RDN) and the ancestor entries that it belongs to. Figure 16-1 shows the basic relationships between DIT, DN, and RDN.

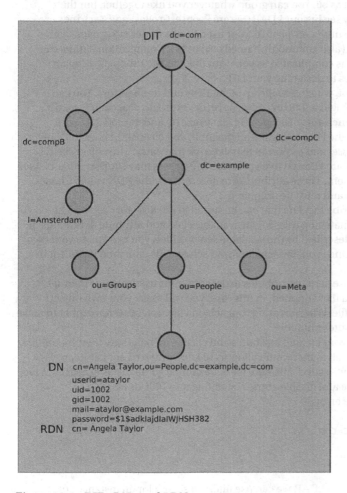

Figure 16-1. DITs, DNs, and RDNs

The DIT is the directory tree, and in this case it has the root DN of dc=com. There are several ways to define your root and main branches. Some people choose a layout based on their DNS domains, as we have here, and some people use geographic locations, such as o=US, o=AU, or o=DE, as their root. In our case, we choose to use the DNS naming standard as we are not overly concerned about the geographic locations of our organization. We can always introduce the LocalityName attribute further down the tree if we want, as we have with the compB branch where we specify a locality of l=Amsterdam. Some thought should be given to how you want to lay out your directory structure, but ultimately you want it to be as simple and easy to understand as possible.

■ **Tip** It is important to define a standard way of naming your branches and describing your organization now and stick to it.

The branches are used to organize your information into logical groups. These logical groups are called *organizational units* and represented as ou. You can group whatever you like together, but the main organizational units you will normally see in your LDAP tree are People, Groups, and Machines. You store everything to do with your people under ou=people, your user groups under ou=groups, and your nonhuman assets under ou=Machines (also commonly named ou=hosts). Organizational units can hold other organizational units and can be as complicated as you want them to be, although we again recommend simpler as better when it comes to designing your DIT.

The DN is a unique entry under the root, which is made up of the RDN and its ancestors. You can see in Figure 16-1 that we have a DN of cn=Angela Taylor,ou=people,dc=example,dc=com. It is made up of the RDN cn=Angela Taylor and the ancestors of ou=people, dc=example, and dc=com. Likewise, ou=people,dc=example,dc=com is a DN for the People organizational unit, and ou=people is an RDN of it.

Each DN entry is made up of *object classes* and *attributes* that describe that entry. The object classes describe what attributes must be present or are allowed to be present. The classes may support other classes in order to provide extended attributes to them. These attributes are described by the RDN value. Classes and attributes must be defined in a schema and must be unique.

A *schema* is set of definitions that describe the data that can be stored in the directory server. The schema is used to describe the syntax and matching rules for an available class and attribute definitions. If you find your organization is not properly described by the available schema files, you can create your own schema file for your company if you want. Once you have created your schema file, you then include it in your OpenLDAP configuration files.

It is common for organizations to require certain attributes to describe your users or your internal systems that are not provided in the schema files supplied. In this case, you will make your own object classes and attributes in your own schema file. When creating your schema file, you must remember to make the names for your object classes and attributes unique.

It is good practice to add a prefix to all your created attributes and classes to make sure they are unique. Suppose we wanted to add an attribute ourselves that would allow us to know when a user has been disabled. In this instance, we could define an "active" attribute for our example company as exampleActive. We could then use exampleActive to enable and disable entries by setting it to TRUE or FALSE.

Here's how this would look in an LDAP entry:

```
dn: uid=user1,ou=people,dc=example,dc=com
uid: user1
exampleActive: TRUE
```

Once this attribute is added to an entry in LDAP, we can use filters to search for all instances of exampleActive = TRUE in our LDAP directory, which would speed up the results for active users. This is just an example of how you can use your own schema definitions; there may be other ways to achieve the same outcome.

■ **Note** The *OpenLDAP Administrator's Guide* has an explanation of how to create your schema files here: www.openldap.org/doc/admin24/schema.html.

OpenLDAP can use a variety of back ends. By default, OpenLDAP uses the Memory Mapped Database (MDB), which is based on the Lightning Memory Mapped Database (LMDB). The LMDB was developed by Symas, a software organization founded by many, if not all, the core OpenLDAP development team. It is extremely fast and scalable, with databases holding millions of records. It is optimized for reading, searching, and browsing. OpenLDAP can use other databases as the back end if you desire.

■ **Note** You can read more about LMDB at https://symas.com/products/lightning-memory-mapped-database/.

General Considerations

Ubuntu and CentOS offer different releases of OpenLDAP. Both CentOS and Ubuntu offer a recent OpenLDAP 2.4 release. The following are some of the features it supports:

- MirrorMode and MultiMaster replication
- Proxy sync replication
- Expanded documentation
- LDAP version 3 extensions
  - LDAP chaining operation support
  - No use of copy control support
  - LDAP dynamic directory services (RFC 2589)
- Added overlays for greater functionality

If you were seeking support for MultiMaster replication capabilities (i.e., the ability to have more than one LDAP master directory service), MultiMaster enhances redundancy of your LDAP installation.

You can also make use of overlays. Overlays give OpenLDAP advanced functionality to alter or extend the normal LDAP behavior. Overlays such as the Password Policy (ppolicy) overlay enable password controls that are not provided in the base code of OpenLDAP. The ppolicy overlay allows you to set things such as password aging and minimum character length.

You will also need to decide what kind of authentication methods you are going to support in your organization. OpenLDAP supports two authentication methods, simple and SASL. The simple method has three modes of operation.

- *Anonymous*: No username or password is supplied.
- *Unauthenticated*: A username but no password is supplied.
- *Username/password authentication*: A valid username and password must be provided.

737

Of the SASL method, the *OpenLDAP Administrator's Guide* says you need an existing working Cyrus SASL installation to provide the SASL mechanism. This is not entirely true, depending on the mechanism of SASL you want to implement. You can set up PLAIN/LOGIN and DIGESTMD5 mechanisms pretty easily. However, you must have Cyrus SASL installed. SASL provides the following mechanisms:

- PLAIN/LOGIN
- DIGESTMD5
- GSSAPI (Kerberos v5)
- EXTERNAL (X.509 public/private key authentication)

■ **Note** SASL (PLAIN/LOGIN, DIGESTMD5) requires clear-text passwords to be used in the userPasswd attribute. Whether this is good or not for security is heavily debated. One side of the argument goes something like this: "Once I access your database, I've got access to all your passwords." The counter to this is, "If you've got access to my database, the game is over anyway. At least I'm not sending passwords over the wire where they can be intercepted."

You can read more about these different authentication methods at the following pages in the *OpenLDAP Administrator's Guide*:

- www.openldap.org/doc/admin24/security.html#Authentication%20Methods
- www.openldap.org/doc/admin24/sasl.html

Implementation

Before we show you how to install the OpenLDAP server on our example system, we need to go over a few details of the implementation.

- We will set a CNAME in our DNS that will point ldap.example.com to the headoffice.example.com record or define some other DNS A record to the host on which we are installing our LDAP server. See Chapter 10 for instructions on DNS.

- We are not using any replication of our directory service. Replication is where we can have more than one LDAP server on our network sharing all or part of our LDAP data and answering client requests. It takes additional configuration to enable this.

Let's view just one piece of our network. Suppose that we have a web server on our network and we want to make sure only people from a certain group within our organization are able to access it. Normally, we would need to add a complicated login mechanism to our web site, have some kind of user database to store the information, and so on. With our Apache web server, we can use the Apache LDAP module to get our web server to use an LDAP server to authenticate requests. Without this authentication, the web site will not be accessible. We can also have other services authenticating against our OpenLDAP directory server. In Figure 16-2, you can see how we would authenticate our web servers.

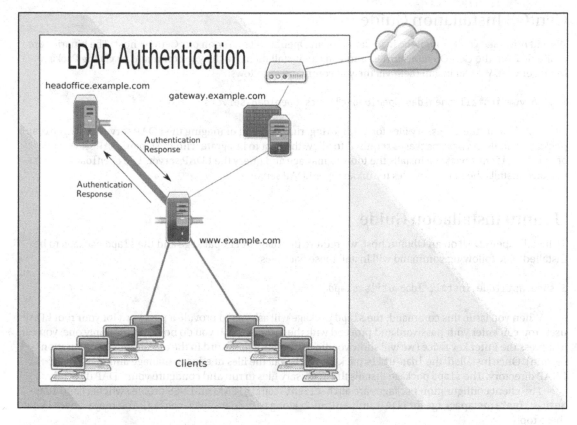

Figure 16-2. LDAP authentication of web services

Figure 16-2 presents a simple diagram showing a web server using LDAP to authenticate our desktop or Internet clients to web services (the LDAP service and the web service can be on the same host if you do not have the necessary hardware resources). When a request is received by a web site, the user making the request requires validation before access is granted. An authentication request is sent to the LDAP service on headoffice.example.com. If the user is validated, the LDAP server sends the response to the web service, and the user can access the site.

Many of the services that we have described in this book can be made to use an LDAP service. This allows you to centralize your authentication services on the one host, reducing complexity, increasing authentication security, and providing a central repository for all your staff details.

We are going to show you how to set up both your LDAP service and authentication for an Apache web service.

Installation

OpenLDAP is available on both CentOS and Ubuntu via their online repositories. Again, for OpenLDAP, subtle differences exist between the two distributions, and we'll detail them next.

CentOS Installation Guide

We will now take you through the installation of an OpenLDAP server on our CentOS host. The binaries are available from the CentOS repositories, and you can install them via the yum command or via the Package Manager GUI. We will install them via the yum command as follows:

```
$ sudo yum install openldap openldap-clients openldap-servers
```

This installs the necessary files for configuring, running, and managing the LDAP server. The openldap package installs the base packages required to allow the host to integrate with the OpenLDAP server. The openldap-clients package installs the tools to manage and query the LDAP server. The openldap-servers package installs the necessary files to run an OpenLDAP server.

Ubuntu Installation Guide

To install OpenLDAP on an Ubuntu host, we require the ldap-utils package and the slapd package to be installed. The following command will install these packages:

```
$ sudo aptitude install ldap-utils slapd
```

When you issue this command, the slapd package will ask you to provide a password for your root LDAP user. You can enter your password and proceed with the installation. If you do not want to supply one, you can just press the Enter key twice (we will show you how to create a password in the upcoming "Configuration" section). Once installed, the ldap-utils package will install the files needed to manage and search your LDAP directory. The slapd package installs the necessary files to run and configure your LDAP directory.

The client configuration packages are auth-client-config (PAM and NSS profile switcher) and ldap-auth-client (metapackage for LDAP authentication along with ldap-auth-config). You may want to install these too.

Configuration

We are going to show you how to configure an LDAP directory service. The LDAP server is called *SLAPD*. We are going to show you how to configure that service.

OpenLDAP uses a dynamic runtime configuration to manage SLAPD, meaning that it configures itself via its own DIT (directory tree). That means that SLAPD configuration changes can be done dynamically through changing records in the DIT using the standard tools used to change other LDAP records, with commands such as ldapmodify.

In our example, we'll configure our SLAPD on our Ubuntu host; some of the directory paths will be different for CentOS. For CentOS hosts, the configuration directory is called /etc/openldap instead of /etc/ldap that you will find on Ubuntu hosts. Both distributions store the databases in /var/lib/ldap.

For example, the configuration files for OpenLDAP on a CentOS host are stored in /etc/openldap/.

```
$ sudo ls -l /etc/openldap/
total 12
drwxr-xr-x. 2 root root   85 Oct 26 12:46 certs
-rw-r--r--. 1 root root  121 Mar 31  2016 check_password.conf
-rw-r--r--. 1 root root  365 Oct  3 13:47 ldap.conf
drwxr-xr-x. 2 root root 4096 Oct 26 12:46 schema
drwx------. 3 ldap ldap   43 Oct 26 12:46 slapd.d
```

Secrets are stored in the `certs` directory. The configuration file specifically for the configuration of LDAP clients is `ldap.conf`. The `schema` directory contains the schema files for our `ldap` service. In there you will find `.schema` files and `.ldif` files. The *LDIF* files are LDAP interchange format files, a special format to specify data changes in LDAP. In the `slapd.d` directory you will find the files comprising the SLAPD DIT. We will explain these as we go through the chapter.

Requirements

Prior to configuring OpenLDAP we are going to set up a few requirements. We need to create a TLS certificate and key and a DNS name entry.

The first step is to create the DNS record. Authentication systems like LDAP are not normally exposed to the public and if they are they can be subjected to external attacks. For this reason we would not normally provide a public IP address. For your external offices that need to authenticate against the service we recommend you use the private VPN for access.

This OpenLDAP service is going to be installed on our `headoffice.example.com` host. We are going to provide our DNS server with the `CNAME` record to point `ldap.example.com` to `headoffice.example.com`. We need to be on our DNS server and issue the following command:

```
$ sudo nsupdate -k /etc/bind/ddns_update.key
> server localhost
> update add ldap.example.com 8600 CNAME headoffice.example.com
> send
> quit
$ host ldap.example.com
ldap.example.com is an alias for headoffice.example.com.
headoffice.example.com has address 192.168.0.1
```

Since this points to an internal private IPv4 address, we will not be able to use Let's Encrypt to create our TLS certificate and will have to use our own private CA. Clients that connect to our LDAP server will need to have the CA root certificate installed.

First, create a new directory called `/etc/ldap/certs` and then change the permissions on it.

```
$ sudo mkdir /etc/ldap/certs
```

We will create the key and the CSR on our `ldap.example.com` host and run the following from inside the `/etc/ldap/certs` directory:

```
$ sudo openssl req -new -newkey rsa:4096 -nodes -keyout ↵
ldap.example.com.key -out ldap.example.com.req
```

Go ahead and sign the request like we did in Chapters 11 and 15 by our private CA. We then need to add the public cert that is produced to the `/etc/ssl/certs` directory along with the root CA if it is not already there, `cacert.pem`.

When the certificates are installed into the `certs` directory, we should change the ownership and permissions to the following:

```
$ sudo chown openldap:openldap -R /etc/ldap/certs
$ sudo chmod 600 /etc/ldap/certs/ldap.example.com.key
```

The user running the LDAP service on CentOS is `ldap` and would need to be used in the previous chown command.

Configuring SLAPD

With the requirements in place, we can now get on to configuring our OpenLDAP server. When we installed our slapd packages and were asked for the administrator password on Ubuntu, the basic OpenLDAP server was configured, installed, and started (on CentOS you will have to start the slapd service prior to running this command).

In Listing 16-1 we have the output of the ldapsearch command. This command is part of the suite of commands used to interact with the LDAP server (or any LDAP server). In this example, we have passed in the –Q argument to ldapsearch to enable SASL quiet mode (as we are using elevated sudo privileges). The three Ls (-LLL) all have a meaning. Having one means print in the LDIF format; the other two reduce the output. The –H argument is the URI we want to attach to, ldapi:///, which is saying, connect to local LDAP server via the Unix socket on the local host. With this we can pass the UID and GID of the user to the LDAP server for authentication. Next, -b defines the search base; we are searching in the cn=config DIT for each dn (or distinguished name) by using dn as a filter.

Listing 16-1. Viewing the Default Configuration

```
$ sudo ldapsearch -Q -LLL -Y EXTERNAL -H ldapi:/// -b cn=config dn
dn: cn=config
dn: cn=module{0},cn=config
dn: cn=schema,cn=config
dn: cn={0}core,cn=schema,cn=config
dn: cn={1}cosine,cn=schema,cn=config
dn: cn={2}nis,cn=schema,cn=config
dn: cn={3}inetorgperson,cn=schema,cn=config
dn: olcBackend={0}mdb,cn=config
dn: olcDatabase={-1}frontend,cn=config
dn: olcDatabase={0}config,cn=config
dn: olcDatabase={1}mdb,cn=config
```

In Listing 16-1 you can also see we have passed the –Y option. This specifies the SASL authentication mechanism we want to use. EXTERNAL here says use the localhost's authentication in this case. We pass the root user's UID and GID via the Unix socket to LDAP for authentication. The default installation allows local root access to the installed LDAP server.

LDIF FORMAT

The LDAP Directory Interchange Format (LDIF) is a specification of how to add and remove entries in a LDAP database. It has its own RFC (https://www.ietf.org/rfc/rfc2849.txt) and can be used by the LDAP tools to change the records in the LDAP database.

The format of a LDIF file looks like so:

```
dn: <the distinguished name you wish to change>
changetype: optional change type of either add, replace, or delete
<attribute or objectclass>: value
```

The following is an example:

```
dn: dc=example,dc=com
objectclass: dcObject
objectclass: organizationalUnit
dc: example
ou: example
```

Here we have described the top level of the DIT. The DN dc=example,dc=com will be made up of those particular object classes and attributes.

To modify an existing DN entry, we could use something like this:

```
dn: uid=ffrank,ou=people,dc=example,dc=com
changetype: replace
replace: userPassword
userPassword: <new password>
-
```

Here we have changed ffrank's userPassword using an LDIF-formatted text file. You can see the DN we want to change, the change type we want to perform (replace), and the attribute we are going to replace (userPassword); finally we assign the new value to the attribute. We can have many of these statements in the one file, and we separate each with - on a new line.

Then in Listing 16-1 we have the list of global directive DNs that are in the cn=config global configuration DIT. You can see that the global DIT is comprised of the root cn=config, and then the DNs are nested under that, like in Figure 16-3.

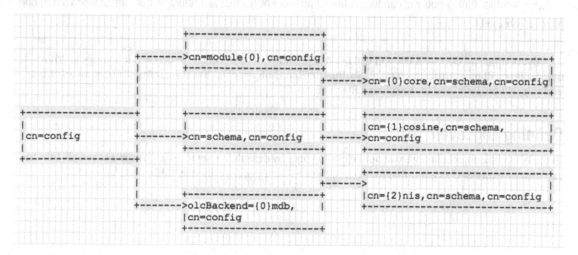

Figure 16-3. *cn=config DIT*

You can see from Listing 16-1 and Figure 16-3 that the LDAP schema, cn={1} cosine,cn=schema,cn=config, is found under the cn=schema DN, which is found under cn=config. The {1} denotes an index of the schema DN.

Also, in Listing 16-1 there are several other global directives like olcBackend and olcDatabase. These, as their names imply, describe the back-end data storage.

```
dn: olcBackend={0}mdb,cn=config
dn: olcDatabase={-1}frontend,cn=config
dn: olcDatabase={0}config,cn=config
dn: olcDatabase={1}mdb,cn=config
```

To get a full listing, or a backup, of the cn=config DIT, you can issue the following command:

```
sudo ldapsearch -Q -LLL -Y EXTERNAL -H ldapi:/// -b cn=config > slapd.ldif
```

We have used the same command as previously but have removed the dn filter from the end and directed the output to the slapd.ldif file. If you look at that file, you will see how the directives have been configured.

Looking at the first declaration, we have the DN for cn=config. It has an ObjectClass of olcGlobal, which is the object class that defines the global DIT. You can also see that we can declare the common name (cn:), an arguments file for slapd (olcArgsFile:), log level (olcLogLevel:), process ID (olcPidFile:), and threads to use (olcToolThreads:).

The olcToolThreads directive tells the slapd daemon to use only one CPU to run indexes on. If you have more than one CPU, you can set this to a higher number, but not higher than the number of CPUs you have. Other performance settings can be turned on, including olcThreads, olcTimeLimits, olcSockBuffMaxIncoming, and olcSockBuffMinIncoming.

■ **Tip** Another tuning nob you can turn is the number of entries that are returned from an ldapsearch in one hit, olcSizeLimit.

Every time you declare a DN you will need to provide the object class (or classes) it belongs to. That object class will have attributes it takes. So, the olcGlobal object class has the olcArgsFile as an attribute, and this will be described in the schema file.

Defining LogLevels

In the olcGobal object class we can define our logging. By default it is set to none. This is a keyword, but this can also be expressed as a number (or even in hexadecimal), as described in Table 16-1.

Table 16-1. *Additive Logging Levels*

Level	Keyword/Description
-1	(any) Turns on all debugging information. This is useful for finding out where your LDAP server is failing before you make your logging level more fine-grained.
0	Turns all debugging off. This is recommended for production mode.
1	(0x1 trace) Traces function calls.
2	(0x2 packets) Debugs packet handling.
4	(0x4 args) Provides heavy trace debugging (function args).
8	(0x8 conns) Provides connection management.
16	(0x10 BER) Prints out packets sent and received.
32	(0x20 filter) Provides search filter processing.
64	(0x40 config) Provides configuration file processing.
128	(0x80 ACL) Provides access control list processing.
256	(0x100 stats) Provides connections, LDAP operations, and results (recommended).
512	(0x200 stats2) Indicates stats log entries sent.
1024	(0x400 shell) Prints communication with shell back ends.
2048	(0x800 parse) Parses entries.
16384	(0x4000 sync) Provides LDAPSync replication.
32768	(0x8000 none) Logs only messages at whatever log level is set.

The log level is important to help debug your installation. To be honest, to the new user it can be very confusing as to what is being reported. However, the logging level is additive, and you can get finer-grained detail in the logs. In a production environment, we recommend setting this value to 0 and, if you want, using the audit overlay to monitor what is happening to your installation (an *overlay* being a software module that can hook into the back end to provide particular information, in this case an audit trail).

We will like to set our logging level to 480. This will show search filters, configuration file processing, access controls, and connection information in our logs. As mentioned, the Loglevel setting is additive, meaning you can enable more logging by adding the values of the things you want to log. As you may have already worked out, our Loglevel of 480 comprises the level 32 (search filter), 64 (configuration processing), 128 (access control list processing), and 256 (connections and LDAP operations results). This is a good setting while we are setting up our LDAP service, as it provides a nice level of information. If we get stuck, we can change Loglevel to -1 to turn on debugging, which turns on all logging features. Also, remember that in a production environment, you would normally want to have Loglevel set at 0. To set Loglevel, you can also list the hexadecimal numbers on one line to achieve the same result; in this case, we would set the log level to Loglevel 0x20 0x40 0x80 0x100.

Modifying the LogLevel Configuration with ldapmodify

Let's modify LogLevel to our wanted level. To do that we will use the ldapmodify command. This takes similar arguments to the ldapsearch command we used previously. We are going to provide a file called loglevel.ldif to the command, which will look like this:

```
dn: cn=config
changetype: modify
replace: olcLogLevel
olcLogLevel: 480
```

To modify an attribute, we need to provide the dn value we want to modify (dn: cn=config), the type of change (changetype: modify), the attribute we want to replace (replace: olcLogLevel), and finally the attribute we are setting (olcLogLevel: 480).

Now, let's use ldapmodify to modify the logging attribute.

```
$ sudo ldapmodify -Q -Y EXTERNAL -H ldapi:/// -f loglevel.ldif
```

To confirm that this has been set, we can issue the ldapsearch command again to verify.

```
$ sudo ldapsearch -Q -LLL -Y EXTERNAL -H ldapi:/// -b cn=config cn=config
dn: cn=config
objectClass: olcGlobal
cn: config
olcArgsFile: /var/run/slapd/slapd.args
olcPidFile: /var/run/slapd/slapd.pid
olcToolThreads: 1
olcLogLevel: 480
```

Great, there we have our requested log setting. As we have set this attribute, any other SLAPD configuration attribute can be set in a similar way.

Adding Modules

In the slapd.ldif file we have the modules section. Modules are added to the configuration to provide access to certain functionality.

```
dn: cn=module{0},cn=config
objectClass: olcModuleList
cn: module{0}
olcModulePath: /usr/lib/ldap
olcModuleLoad: {0}back_mdb
```

Here we are declaring the path in which to find our modules, olcModulePath: /usr/lib/ldap. We have one module that is loaded, back_mdb, which is the hierarchical Memory Mapped database we spoke of earlier.

We want to also enable the ppolicy overlay module. The ppolicy module allows us to have greater control of the passwords in our database via password expiry and other password control features. If we check the module path described earlier, we can verify that the required files are in there.

```
$ ll /usr/lib/ldap/pp*
-rw-r--r-- 1 root root 39328 May 11 17:11 /usr/lib/ldap/ppolicy-2.4.so.2.10.5
-rw-r--r-- 1 root root   948 May 11 17:11 /usr/lib/ldap/ppolicy.la
```

To load the policy, we are going to create a file called ppolicy_module.ldif and use ldapmodify to add it.

```
dn: cn=module{0},cn=config
changetype: modify
add: olcModuleLoad
olcModuleLoad: ppolicy.la
```

When we execute the ldapmodify command, you can see we are now asking it to add the module ppolicy.la. If we now do an ldapsearch filtering only for those DNs that contain the object class olcModuleList, we see the following:

```
$ sudo ldapsearch -H ldapi:// -Y EXTERNAL -b "cn=config" -LLL -Q ↵
"objectClass=olcModuleList"
dn: cn=module{0},cn=config
objectClass: olcModuleList
cn: module{0}
olcModulePath: /usr/lib/ldap
olcModuleLoad: {0}back_mdb
olcModuleLoad: {1}ppolicy.la
```

We will add further to the ppolicy overlay configuration when we load our LDIFs into the OpenLDAP database in the "Password Policy Overlay" section.

Setting Suffix, RootDN, and RootPW

We are now going to configure the back-end database that will hold our DIT. We can change the default database back end if we wanted, and there are several options here. Normally, you will choose the default mdb. The other types you can choose from (ldap, ldif, metadirectory, perl, etc.) are used for proxying your LDAP server.

■ **Note** For more information on the choices for back-end databases available to you, please see the online documentation: www.openldap.org/doc/admin24/backends.html.

To view the current database settings, we can issue the following ldapsearch:

```
$ sudo ldapsearch -H ldapi:/// -Y EXTERNAL -b "olcDatabase={1}mdb,cn=config" -LLL  -Q
dn: olcDatabase={1}mdb,cn=config
objectClass: olcDatabaseConfig
objectClass: olcMdbConfig
olcDatabase: {1}mdb
olcDbDirectory: /var/lib/ldap
olcAccess: {0}to attrs=userPassword by self write by anonymous auth by * none
olcAccess: {1}to attrs=shadowLastChange by self write by * read
olcAccess: {2}to * by * read
olcLastMod: TRUE
olcDbCheckpoint: 512 30
olcDbIndex: objectClass eq
olcDbIndex: cn,uid eq
olcDbIndex: uidNumber,gidNumber eq
```

```
olcDbIndex: member,memberUid eq
olcDbMaxSize: 1073741824
olcSuffix: dc=nodomain
olcRootDN: cn=admin,dc=nodomain
olcRootPW: {SSHA}EEyEuYme4zBPYbRzHc+l4rApfvrXjXnV
```

The default for our database type is defined here: olcDatabase: {1}mdb. You can declare more than one database instance. The next detail we configure is the top of the DIT, the suffix, and a user that will have full access to it, like a root user.

■ **Note** If you configured your OpenLDAP server when you installed it on your Ubuntu server, you won't need to do this step.

Here we will create a file called db.ldif that has the following contents:

```
dn: olcDatabase={1}mdb,cn=config
changetype: modify
replace: olcSuffix
olcSuffix: dc=example,dc=com
-
replace: olcRootDN
olcRootDN: cn=admin,dc=example,dc=com
-
replace: olcRootPW
olcRootPW: {SSHA}QN+NZNjLxIsG/+PGDvb/6Yg3qX2SsX95
```

The olcSuffix directs queries for dc=example,dc=com to this database instance. Because there are already values for these attributes, we are using the replace directive in our LDIF file, for example: replace: olcRootPW. You can have more than one suffix declared here. The olcRootDN is the root user, who has full access to database; the password is declared in olcRootPW. You can create a password using the slappasswd command as follows:

```
$ sudo slappasswd
```

The password that is printed can then be copied and pasted to olcRootPW like earlier. Before we apply this LDIF, we will view our indexes.

Creating Indexes

Next, we can set our indexes. Indexes are used to speed up searches on the database. You can view the current indexes on your database by running the following:

```
$ sudo ldapsearch -H ldapi:/// -Y EXTERNAL -b "olcDatabase={1}mdb,cn=config" -LLL -Q
olcDbIndex
olcDbIndex: objectClass eq
olcDbIndex: cn,uid eq
olcDbIndex: uidNumber,gidNumber eq
olcDbIndex: member,memberUid eq
```

As a rule, you should index what your clients are commonly going to search for. An e-mail client's address book may search for the common name, or `cn`, when it looks for people's names to populate its address book entries. In such a case, you would want to have an index of the cn attribute optimized for substrings, `sub`. Table 16-2 lists the common types of indexes available.

Table 16-2. *Common Index Types*

Type	Description
sub	Useful for optimizing string searches that contain wildcards like `cn=Jane*`
eq	Useful for optimizing searches for exact strings like `sn=Smith`
pres	Useful for optimizing searches for object classes or attributes, like `objectclass=person`
approx	Useful for optimizing searches for sounds-like searches, like `sn~=Smi*`

Other index types are available, and you can read about them on the `slapd.conf` man page. We want to index the `objectclass`, `cn`, and `uid`, which we know will be commonly searched when users try to authenticate. In the previous code, you can see that we are already indexing these things. We are going to add an index to an attribute we will create shortly called `exampleActive`. We will add the following to our `db.ldif`:

```
add: olcDbIndex
olcDbIndex: exampleActive pres,eq
```

Let's now go ahead and use `ldapmodify` to apply our `db.ldif` changes.

```
$ sudo ldapmodify -Q -Y EXTERNAL -H ldapi:/// -f db.ldif
```

■ **Note** You can read more about the configuration engine database here: `www.openldap.org/doc/admin24/slapdconf2.html`.

Listing, Adding, and Creating a Schema

A schema provides the structure of your object's classes and attributes to the SLAPD server. While not the same as a database schema, the LDAP schema describes the object classes and attributes your LDAP server will hold, much like a database schema would describe tables and rows. You can view the currently loaded schemata with the following `ldapsearch`:

```
$ sudo ldapsearch -Q -LLL -Y EXTERNAL -H ldapi:/// -b cn=schema,cn=config dn
dn: cn=schema,cn=config
dn: cn={0}core,cn=schema,cn=config
dn: cn={1}cosine,cn=schema,cn=config
dn: cn={2}nis,cn=schema,cn=config
dn: cn={3}inetorgperson,cn=schema,cn=config
```

The top dn is cn=schema,cn=config, and that is the parent of our schemata. We then have some default schemata that are provided by our installation. The core schema provides such object classes as the dcObject (dc) and organizationalUnit (ou). The cosine schema provides the dNSDomain object class and host attribute. The nis schema provides user account objects and attributes, such as posixAccount and shadow password settings. The inetorgperson holds other various employee-related objects and classes. You may or may not use objects and attributes that these provide.

To see all the schemata available to you, you can list the /etc/ldap/schema directory. For example, we can see that in that directory the ppolicy.schema and ppolicy.ldif files for the ppolicy schema are present.

```
$ ls /etc/ldap/schema/pp*
/etc/ldap/schema/ppolicy.ldif  /etc/ldap/schema/ppolicy.schema
```

The ppolicy.ldif file has been derived from the ppolicy.schema file for us. We are going to add our ppolicy.ldif schema to our SLAPD. We do that by using the ldapadd command. It takes similar arguments to ldapsearch and ldapmodify.

```
$ sudo ldapadd -Q -Y EXTERNAL -H ldapi:/// -f /etc/ldap/schema/ppolicy.ldif
adding new entry "cn=ppolicy,cn=schema,cn=config"
```

Let's see if that has been loaded.

```
$ sudo ldapsearch -Q -LLL -Y EXTERNAL -H ldapi:/// -b cn=schema,cn=config dn
dn: cn=schema,cn=config
dn: cn={0}core,cn=schema,cn=config
dn: cn={1}cosine,cn=schema,cn=config
dn: cn={2}nis,cn=schema,cn=config
dn: cn={3}inetorgperson,cn=schema,cn=config
dn: cn={4}ppolicy,cn=schema,cn=config
```

There you can see that our ppolicy schema has been added at index {4}. Remember that index number as we are going to need it when we add our own schema. Let's see how we create and add our own schema.

Creating Our Schema

We will create a file called /etc/ldap/schema/exampleactive.schema. In this schema file, we will include a simple class and attribute that we will use to indicate whether a user account is active or not.

To get started, let's look at how to declare an object class in the schema. The following appears in the core.schema file in the schema directory:

```
objectclass ( 1.3.6.1.4.1.1466.344 NAME 'dcObject'
       DESC 'RFC2247: domain component object'
       SUP top AUXILIARY MUST dc )
```

This is one of the main object classes that will be included in the DIT. We need to declare what type of entity we are using, and for an object class we start with objectclass (schema detail). Whitespace is important when declaring your object classes and attributes, and there must be a space inside the ( ) at each end. An object class declaration should follow this format:

```
objectclass ( <OID> NAME <name> DESC <description> SUP <parent class> <class type>
<MUST|MAY> attritubutes )
```

The number you see, `1.3.6.1.4.1.1466.344`, is the private enterprise number (PEN), or object identifier (OID), which is a unique series of numbers for identifying objects; if you are familiar with things like SNMP, you should recognize this as they use the same OID concept.

■ **Note** You can register for your own OID or PEN at the Internet Assigned Numbers Authority (IANA) web site: `http://pen.iana.org/pen/PenApplication.page`.

The object class is given a name, `dcObject`, and a description (DESC). The next line tells you that this will inherit the object class `SUP` `top`. The `SUP` stands for superior, and `top` means that this object class has no parent object class; it is the highest in the object class hierarchy. Other subsequent object classes may use this object class as their `SUP`, or inherited, object class.

The `AUXILIARY` indicates the type of object class. There are three types of object classes.

- `AUXILIARY`: Allows you to add attributes to the entry but not create an entry

- `STRUCTURAL`: Allows you create a valid entry

- `ABSTRACT`: The base object from which other object classes can be defined; `top` is an `ABSTRACT` example

The `MUST` `dc` says that if this object is declared in the directory server, the attribute `dc` must also be added. Attributes that are not mandatory but available to the object class can be declared as `MAY`.

■ **Note** The full details of declaring object classes are contained in this RFC: `www.rfc-editor.org/rfc/rfc4512.txt`. A quick explanation of extending your schemata can be found here: `www.openldap.org/doc/admin24/schema.html`.

Attributes have certain rules also. They must be declared in the schema, and the same attribute can be included in one or more object class. Also, by default, attributes are `MULTI-VALUE`, meaning we can have more than one value declared for our DN. The common example is e-mail address; a user can have more than one e-mail address. Other attributes are declare `SINGLE-VALUE` and can be declared only once, like the users' password.

Attributes can be hierarchical and can inherit the properties of its parent. They are expressed differently to object class hierarchies in these ways:

- They are not terminated with a *top*.

- The absence of the *SUP*erior definition indicates the end of the hierarchy.

The common example of attribute inheritance is the name attribute. The name attribute is the parent of *common name* (`cn`), *given name* (`gn`), and *surname* (`sn`).

Let's take a look at our own schema file that we have created, `/etc/ldap/schema/exampleactive.schema`:

```
# $Id$

attributetype ( 1.1.3.10 NAME 'exampleActive'
DESC 'Example User Active'
SINGLE-VALUE
EQUALITY booleanMatch
SYNTAX 1.3.6.1.4.1.1466.115.121.1.7)
```

```
objectclass ( 1.1.1.2 NAME 'exampleClient'
SUP top AUXILIARY
DESC 'Example.com User objectclass'
MAY ( exampleActive ))
```

In these two schema objects, we have two OIDs, which we made up. The ones in this example may conflict with other existing schema files and are for demonstration only. To avoid this, so we would normally apply for our own PEN. We'll pretend we did so and that we received an OID of 1.3.6.1.4.1.111111, where 1.3.6.1.4.1 is the IANA *arc*, or node, and 111111 is the special number that distinguishes our company from other companies. We can now use our OID in place of the ones in the preceding schema.

■ **Caution**   As we mentioned, we have made up the 1.3.6.1.4.1.111111 OID for the purpose of this demonstration. Please do not make up numbers or use this OID in your production environment. You should really get your own PEN; otherwise, you risk having conflicts and things breaking. For more information on OIDs and LDAP, please also view the following: www.zytrax.com/books/ldap/apa/oid.html.

```
attributetype ( 1.3.6.1.4.1.111111.3.1.1 NAME 'exampleActive'
DESC 'Example User Active'
SINGLE-VALUE
EQUALITY booleanMatch
SYNTAX 1.3.6.1.4.1.1466.115.121.1.7 )

objectclass ( 1.3.6.1.4.1.111111.3.2.1 NAME 'exampleClient' SUP top AUXILIARY DESC
'Example.com User objectclass'
MAY ( exampleActive ))
```

Once you have a PEN or an OID, you can divide it into useful segments (also called *nodes* or *arcs*). Generally, you can use an OID for not only LDAP schema objects but also for things like SNMP MIBs. As you can see, we have branched off 1.3.6.1.4.1.111111.**3** for our LDAP schema definitions. Under that, we will place all our object class definitions under 1.3.6.1.4.1.111111.**3.2** and our attributes under 1.3.6.1.4.1.111111.**3.1**.

■ **Note**   Assigning 1.3.6.1.4.1.111111.**3.1** and 1.3.6.1.4.1.111111.**3.2** to LDAP classes and attributes is completely arbitrary. You can choose whatever numbering scheme you desire.

Our attribute exampleActive can only ever be declared once, so we will make it a SINGLE-VALUE. If we try to declare this attribute more than once for a particular DN, we will get a violation error.

We set the exampleActive attribute to be a Boolean match, meaning it can be either true or false. Setting this attribute to TRUE will mean that our account is active. Setting it to FALSE will mean the account is inactive. We can index this attribute, which will again speed up our searches. This is why we added the following in our db.ldif earlier:

```
olcDbIndex: exampleActive pres,eq
```

The exampleClient object class defines that we may have the exampleActive attribute present (as indicated by MAY) when we include that object class in our DN entry. If we wanted to enforce its presence, we can specify MUST instead. The object class is of type AUXILARY and has the superclass defined by SUP top. The default object type is STRUCTURAL. You must have one STRUCTURAL object class in your entries, and you cannot have two STRUCTURAL object classes pointing to the same parent or superior class.

■ **Note** You can find the RFC that describes the LDAP schema files at www.rfc-editor.org/rfc/rfc4512.txt.

Adding Our Schema

To add our schema, we need to go through the following process:

- Convert our schema to LDIF via slaptest
- Edit the output in preparation for inputting the schema
- Add that into our SLAPD via ldapadd

To convert the schema file into LDIF, we use the slaptest command. The slaptest command is useful for converting the text-based schema files to LDIF format.

We will pass the /etc/ldap/schema/exampleactive.schema into slaptest, and the output file will be generated in a temporary SLAPD config directory.

First create a temporary directory to hold our converted files.

```
$ sudo mkdir /etc/ldap/ldif_converted && cd /etc/ldap
```

In this directory we will now create a file called schema_load.conf in the old slapd.conf format that will be used to direct the slaptest command to read in our schema file. It has the following contents:

```
include /etc/ldap/schema/exampleactive.schema
```

Now we can use that as the input file to our slaptest command.

```
$ sudo slaptest -f schema_load.conf -F ldif_converted
```

This creates an LDIF-formatted file.

```
/etc/ldap/ldif_converted/cn\=config/cn\=schema/cn={0}exampleactive.ldif
```

If you get the following error:

```
58180fbb schema/exampleactive.schema: line 1 attributetype: Missing closing parenthesis
before end of input
```

this indicates that there are whitespace errors in the schema file. You can put your declarations on a single line, without carriage returns, and take note of white spacing. Here's an example:

```
attributetype ( attribute detail )
```

```
objectclass ( object detail )
```

We are going to edit the LDIF file that has been outputted using our vi editor and using sudo to elevate our privileges.

```
# AUTO-GENERATED FILE - DO NOT EDIT!! Use ldapmodify.
# CRC32 39f1bf5a
dn: cn={0}exampleactive
objectClass: olcSchemaConfig
cn: {0}exampleactive
olcAttributeTypes: {0}( 1.3.6.1.4.1.111111.3.1.1 NAME 'exampleActive' DESC '
 Example User Active' EQUALITY booleanMatch SYNTAX 1.3.6.1.4.1.1466.115.121.
 1.7 SINGLE-VALUE )
olcObjectClasses: {0}( 1.3.6.1.4.1.111111.3.2.1 NAME 'exampleClient' DESC 'E
 xample.com User objectclass' SUP top AUXILIARY MAY exampleActive )
structuralObjectClass: olcSchemaConfig
entryUUID: 53a98d60-3432-1036-9ae2-35c34321a848
creatorsName: cn=config
createTimestamp: 20161101035217Z
entryCSN: 20161101035217.399551Z#000000#000#000000
modifiersName: cn=config
modifyTimestamp: 20161101035217Z
```

We need to remove the lines that are in bold, like from structuralObjectClass: olcSchemaConf to modifyTimestamp: 20161101035217Z and the top two # lines. Next, you can see the following line:

```
dn: cn={0}exampleactive
```

Remembering that the {0} refers to the index, if we try to load this DN, we will conflict with any existing schema that has cn={0}, which, going back to our ldapsearch output, is the core schema. When we add the ppolicy schema, we said to remember the index number ({4}), and now we need to add one to it to make sure our indexes don't conflict.

```
dn: cn={5}exampleactive
```

Then we will save that file to /etc/ldap/schema/exampleactive.ldif. You can now use the ldapadd command to add the created LDIF into our SLAPD server.

```
$ sudo ldapadd -Q -Y EXTERNAL -H ldapi:/// -f schema/exampleactive.ldif
adding new entry "cn={5}exampleactive,cn=schema,cn=config"
```

We will use the exampleactive.schema file when we declare our users in the "LDIFs and Adding Users" section of this chapter.

Access Control Lists

Every connection that accesses your LDAP server has to be given specific access to various parts of the tree if you want it to be secure. The default access for OpenLDAP is read, and you will want to lock this down if you store secret such as passwords. You can specify from where you accept connections, the level of security, or the encryption that connection must have to gain access, right down to the branch or attribute that you allow access to. You also have several levels of access that you can then grant to the requesting connection: manage, write, read, search, and auth.

Listing Access Controls

Access controls are attached to the database configuration. To see the current access control lists, we need to execute the following:

```
$ sudo ldapsearch -H ldapi:/// -Y EXTERNAL -b "olcDatabase={1}mdb,cn=config" -LLL  -Q
dn: olcDatabase={1}mdb,cn=config
objectClass: olcDatabaseConfig
objectClass: olcMdbConfig
olcDatabase: {1}mdb
olcDbDirectory: /var/lib/ldap
olcSuffix: dc=example,dc=com
olcAccess: {0}to attrs=userPassword by self write by anonymous auth by * none
olcAccess: {1}to attrs=shadowLastChange by self write by * read
olcAccess: {2}to * by * read
olcLastMod: TRUE
...
```

In the previous lines, you can see the access lists. They begin with olcAccess and have been assigned an index number, {0}. We can view index {0} as follows:

```
(access) to attrs=userPassword
    by self write
    by anonymous auth
    by * none
```

This allows a user to write to their own userPassword attribute, and the anonymous user can authenticate. Everything else cannot do anything (by * none).

How to Define Access Control Lists

You will see documentation for access control lists in "old slapd.conf" style and in dynamic or LDIF format. In the older format, you will have the access directive leading the access list. In the LDIF format, you will have the index number.

In its most basic form, access is given using the following syntax:

```
[access|{n}]to what [ by who [ access-level ] [ control ] ]
```

what is an entity in the LDAP database, who is the client requesting the information, and access-level is the level of access you want that client to have on it. control specifies how the list is processed after this entry and is optional.

■ **Note**   In this section, when we show the access list directive, from this point we will ignore the access directive or index number. The final access list will be in LDIF format.

In the following simple example, we give read access to everything in our DIT.

```
to *
    by * read stop
```

You can use the wildcard * to allow general unrestricted access. The access control here indicates any user has read access to anything. Next is a control statement that tells slapd to stop processing any other directives. Order is important in your access control list, with directives of a higher order being processed before those of a lower order. When you give a privilege or access level, it implies all the previous ones. For example, read access automatically grants the preceding disclose, auth, compare, and search access levels, including read access rights. Table 16-3 lists the access levels you can assign to a request for access to an entity.

Table 16-3. Access Privileges

Access	Privileges
none	Allows no access at all
disclose	Allows no access but returns an error
auth	Enables bind operations (authenticate)
compare	Allows you to compare the entity
search	Allows you to search that part of the DIT
read	Allows read access
write	Allows write access
manage	Allows all access and the ability to delete entities

When you choose none, you are denying all access to the entity without returning an error to the requestor. This helps prevent information leakage of what is and what isn't in your DIT. The disclose access, unlike none, will return an error to the requesting client.

Defining who

Looking further at requesting access to an entity, you need to know who is requesting the access. There can be more than one who declaration, each using certain keywords. These keywords can be combined with a style qualifier, which can be something like regex or exact. The regex style refers to a regular expression that can be used to match various parts of a DN. It is more costly in processing your access control list.

■ **Tip** See the *OpenLDAP Administrator's Guide* for tips on using regular expressions as well other topics we are discussing here: www.openldap.org/doc/admin24/access-control.html.

It is always less costly, in processing terms, yet more precise to describe exactly what you would like to give access to and to whom. Here's an example:

```
to dn.subtree=ou=people,dc=example,dc=com
  by dn.exact="cn=admin,ou=meta,dc=example,dc=com" read
```

Here we are again granting read access to everything under the organizational unit People. We are being specific and defining that this access be granted only to the DN cn=admin,ou=meta, dc=example,dc=com.

Defining what to grant access to can get tricky. Several standard methods are available for granting access. You can use the following:

```
dn.base
dn.one
dn.subtree
dn.children
```

To explain how these relate to the objects we are working on, we will borrow an example from the *OpenLDAP Administrator's Guide*. Imagine we have the following lists:

```
0: dc=example,dc=com
1: cn=Manager,dc=example,dc=com
2: ou=people,dc=example,dc=com
3: uid=jsmith,ou=people,dc=example,dc=com
4: cn=addresses,uid=jsmith,ou=people,dc=example,dc=com
5: uid=ataylor,ou=people,dc=example,dc=com
```

When we try to work on parts of the DIT, we can declare the scope of our pattern matches.

```
dn.base="ou=people,dc=example,dc=com" match 2;
dn.one="ou=people,dc=example,dc=com" match 3, and 5;
dn.subtree="ou=people,dc=example,dc=com" match 2, 3, 4, and 5; and
dn.children="ou=people,dc=example,dc=com" match 3, 4, and 5.
```

Declaring the right scope will capture the right part of the DIT tree. As you can see, the scope dn.base will just reference the level of the declared tree, ou=people,dc=example,dc=com. The scope of dn.one will act on the immediate part of the tree after ou=people,dc=example,dc=com.

The dn.subtree scope will act on everything under ou=people,dc=example,dc=com and itself, whereas dn.children will work on everything under ou=people,dc=example,dc=com.

Defining who by Filters

In LDAP, you can use filters, which are a means of weeding out undesirable data and leaving behind the exact results you want. In access control lists, you can use filters to be more specific about what you are granting access to. Take a look at the following line:

```
to dn.subtree="ou=people,dc=example,dc=com" attrs="userPassword"
    by dn.exact="cn=admin,ou=meta,dc=example,dc=com" write
    by * none
```

In this example, we have declared we would like this to apply to everything under and including ou=people,dc=example,dc=com and to any attribute called userPassword that might be found under there. In this case, the attribute userPassword is the filter. We are giving the admin user write access to the userPassword, and everything will be silently refused.

The man pages are excellent resources for further information on access control lists, and the *OpenLDAP Administrator's Guide* is also very good: www.openldap.org/doc/admin24/access-control.html.

Defining Our Access Control Lists

We'll now take you through the access control list we are going to use in our `example.com` LDAP DIT. This is what we want to do:

- We want users to change their own passwords and bind.

- We want to create a `meta` users group that can bind on behalf of users.

- We want an admin group to able to manage the user's entries.

We are going to give our system root user manage access to our DIT. This can be removed at a later stage, but it provides us with access in the event we get something wrong in our access lists. This is the same access as the default provided on the `cn=config` database.

```
to *
    by dn.exact=gidNumber=0+uidNumber=0,cn=peercred,cn=external,cn=auth manage
    by * break
```

This says the root user (`uid 0, gid 0`) is allowed to manage the whole DIT (to *). We then `break` processing and go to the next access list. This user, as we have spoken of before, is authenticated by an external provider (the system authentication, or PAM). When we provide `-Y EXTERNAL`, LDAP will allow access to the UID and GID 0 (or the root user) without prompting for authentication itself.

Next we are defining access to our password information. As we have previously mentioned, the access control lists are read and implemented from top to bottom. It is important to keep the sensitive access control lists at the top so that they are not overridden by a higher entry.

In this section, we have restricted access to the users' password information, stored in the attributes `userPassword`, `shadowLastChange`, `entry`, and `member` throughout the DIT. `entry` is a special pseudo-attribute that we must specify to access an entry, and `member` is to access group memberships.

We are going to allow only the administrators to have special access. The `webadmin` user will be used to bind to our LDAP server from our web server so that our web users can authenticate. We only allow access to these attributes by connections with a TLS security strength factor (`tls_ssf`) equal to or greater than 128. We will explain `ssf` further in the "Securing SLAPD with TLS" section of this chapter, but for now, the `tls_ssf` specifies the minimum TLS key size required to access these attributes, meaning we will allow access to these attributes only if they have an adequately secured transport layer.

■ **Note**   We will explain security strength factors shortly. You can use other options to restrict access to your attributes, like specifying a peer name or domain from which to accept connections. For more information on this and access control lists in general, please see `www.openldap.org/doc/admin24/access-control.html`.

We are granting anonymous `auth` access; that is, clients need not bind (or authenticate) to our LDAP server to authenticate. There are three ways to authenticate; one is to not provide a username or password (anonymous), another is to provide only a username, and the other is to provide a username and password. Anonymous is not particularly recommended without strict access conditions. Anonymous should never be used if your LDAP server is publicly available on the Internet.

■ **Note**   You can use a user and password to initially authenticate against the LDAP server to perform a bind operation (authenticate a user). We will show you how to do this when we authenticate with Apache later in this chapter.

Anonymous auth is required for how we implement single sign-on services, which we will explain later in the "Single Sign-On: Centralized Linux Authentication" section of this chapter. We have secured anonymous to auth only if it has a TLS security strength factor (tls_ssf) of 128. We also give users the ability to change their own password details by allowing self write access.

The last line in Listing 16-2 is important. It is a control statement to prevent access further down the access list.

Listing 16-2. Access List for Sensitive Attributes

```
olcAccess: {1}to attrs=userPassword,shadowLastChange,entry,member
        by dn.exact="cn=webadmin,ou=meta,dc=example,dc=com" tls_ssf=128 auth
        by anonymous tls_ssf=128 auth
        by group.exact="cn=admins,ou=groups,dc=example,dc=com" tls_ssf=128 write
        by self tls_ssf=128 write
        by * tls_ssf=128 search
        by * none stop
```

```
by * none stop
```

It says any other user (*) has no access (none) and then stop processing further.

As we have said, order is important. When an access request comes into your LDAP host, the access control list is parsed, and if a match is found, access is either granted or denied. You can speed your access requests by putting your access control list in order of most requested access to least. You want all those common requests to be toward the top of your access control list and the less common requests closer to the bottom. Assume for this example some *meta users* will have access to various parts of our directory server and that these users will have the most commonly requested access requests. That is why we have our access controls dealing with the *meta users* group toward the top of the list just below our user passwords entry.

The branch ou=meta holds the users that we use to proxy our authentication to our directory server. We don't always require a user to bind directly to our directory server, but sometimes we want them to still authenticate against it, such as when we are performing web authentication. You have already seen that we have granted auth access to the user password entries to webadmin. Now we are declaring the ability of those DNs to see their own information.

```
to dn.children="ou=meta,dc=example,dc=com"
        by dn.exact="cn=webadmin,ou=meta,dc=example,dc=com" read
        by group.exact="cn=admins,ou=groups,dc=example,dc=com" write
        by self read
```

We allow write access to this organizational unit by the cn=admins group, in which we will put our system administrator user and read access by the meta users themselves. This prevents the users defined under the ou=meta organizational unit from being able to change any of their own entries, and this gives greater security to those users.

Next, we grant access to everything under the ou=people branch, bearing in mind that we have already defined access to the user password attributes earlier in the access control list. The earlier access definition will override any access we detail here for the previously defined attributes. The administrator accounts require at least read access, and we have given the admins group write access. We will want the admins group to also change details from time to time. The webadmin user just requires read access only. We give read access to the entry itself with the self keyword.

```
to dn.children="ou=people,dc=example,dc=com"
        by dn.exact="cn=webadmin,ou=meta,dc=example,dc=com" read
        by group.exact="cn=admins,ou=groups,dc=example,dc=com" write
        by self write
        by users read
```

You may have different requirements in your network, and it is quite common to have the self access as write instead. This setting will give the users the ability to change their own attribute details that define their personal information, whereas read access does not.

In the following code, we grant access to the ou=groups branch where we will hold all our group information.

```
to dn.children="ou=groups,dc=example,dc=com"
        by dn.exact="cn=webadmin,ou=meta,dc=example,dc=com" read
        by group.exact="cn=admins,ou=groups,dc=example,dc=com" write
        by anonymous read
```

As you can see, this is similar to the ou=people branch with the same administrator accounts having the same access. However, we have allowed authenticated users the ability to read the groups by specifying users read.

Next, we have the ou=hosts organizational unit. Some people name this unit machines, but the choice is yours. It will hold all your host information, IP addresses, locations, and so forth. We have used the scope of subtree, and there is minimal write access granted to everything except the cn=admins group.

```
to dn.children="ou=hosts,dc=example.com"
        by group.exact="cn=admins,ou=groups,dc=example,dc=com" write
        by anonymous read
```

Here the cn=admins group will require write access. We give anonymous clients, which are clients that have not made a bind connection (nonauthenticated), read access. Various applications can make use of the ou=hosts organizational unit including such applications as Samba.

The final rule we will have is a blanket denial rule. This will enforce the rejection of all other access. This is basically superfluous, as anything not granted explicit access will be denied; however, it shows the end of your access control list set and prevents any access control lists that might be present below it being read in by mistake.

```
to * by * none stop
```

The wildcards here match everything, meaning that any access sort is denied, and all further processing is stopped by the stop option in the control field. Other processing controls available are break and continue.

The break control option will, on a match, stop further processing in that access control group and jump to the next. The continue option, after a match, will continue processing further down the access control group, allowing for incremental privileges to be granted. The stop option just immediately stops any further processing and is the default control. Listing 16-3 shows our complete access control list.

■ **Note** The listing of olcAccess: directives you see in Listing 16-3 are separated onto different lines only for clarity of this documentation. If you have any errors about white spacing, try putting each directive on a single line.

Listing 16-3. The Complete Access Control List

```
dn: olcDatabase={1}mdb,cn=config
changetype: modify
replace: olcAccess
olcAccess: {0}to *
        by dn.exact=gidNumber=0+uidNumber=0,cn=peercred,cn=external,cn=auth manage
        by * break
-
add: olcAccess
olcAccess: {1}to attrs=userPassword,shadowLastChange,entry,member
        by dn.exact="cn=webadmin,ou=meta,dc=example,dc=com" tls_ssf=128 auth
        by anonymous tls_ssf=128 auth
        by group.exact="cn=admins,ou=groups,dc=example,dc=com" tls_ssf=128 write
        by self tls_ssf=128 write
        by * tls_ssf=128 search
        by * none stop
-
add: olcAccess
olcAccess: {2}to dn.children="ou=meta,dc=example,dc=com"
        by dn.exact="cn=webadmin,ou=meta,dc=example,dc=com" read
        by group.exact="cn=admins,ou=groups,dc=example,dc=com" write
        by self read
-
add: olcAccess
olcAccess: {3}to dn.children="ou=people,dc=example,dc=com"
        by dn.exact="cn=webadmin,ou=meta,dc=example,dc=com" read
        by group.exact="cn=admins,ou=groups,dc=example,dc=com" write
        by self write
        by users read
-
add: olcAccess
olcAccess: {4}to dn.children="ou=groups,dc=example,dc=com"
        by dn.exact="cn=webadmin,ou=meta,dc=example,dc=com" read
        by group.exact="cn=admins,ou=groups,dc=example,
dc=com" write
        by anonymous read
-
add: olcAccess
olcAccess: {5}to dn.children="ou=hosts,dc=example.com"
        by group.exact="cn=admins,ou=groups,dc=example,dc=com" write
        by dn.exact="cn=webadmin,ou=meta,dc=example,dc=com" search
-
add: olcAccess
olcAccess: {6}to * by * none
```

There are some things to note about updating access control lists. In Listing 16-3 we see we are using the LDIF format to add these access lists. Let's take the first section and explain it.

```
dn: olcDatabase={1}mdb,cn=config
changetype: modify
replace: olcAccess
olcAccess: {0}<access list>
-
add: olcAccess
olcAccess: {1}<access list>
```

The first line is the DN, the main config database in this case, we want to work on. The second line is the change type, which is modify. For the first index element {0} we need to use the replace modify type. For the access lists after that, we need to add the lists. When working with dynamic access lists and ldapmodify, there are some rules to remember.

- If you replace an index element, you need to load in the full access list.

- You can append to the end of the access list only with an add directive.

- The access list is read from first to last.

We can now put these access list directives into a file called access.ldif and then use ldapmodify to apply them.

```
$ sudo ldapmodify -H ldapi:/// -Y EXTERNAL  -f access.ldif
```

We will explain how to search test these shortly.

Working with the slapd Daemon

You can run your slapd daemon in two ways: with the slapd.d configuration engine (dynamic configuration) or without it. As mentioned previously, the configuration engine enables the SLAPD configuration to be changed on the fly using LDIF syntax and LDAP commands.

The other way is to load in a slapd.conf file that has the older style directives. We saw an example of the slapd.conf syntax when we included our exampleactive.schema file to convert it to LDIF format.

Both ways are supported, but running with the old-style slapd.conf will be deprecated, so we don't recommend starting slapd with it. You can convert your old-style slapd.conf into the dynamic LDIF configuration engine by issuing the following command (SLAPD cannot be already running):

```
$ sudo slapd -f slapd.conf -F slapd.d -u openldap -g openldap
```

This is similar to our slaptest command we ran previously. You will notice that this is being run in the foreground, and you can see whether there are any problems when it tries to start. For CentOS hosts, you would use -u ldap -g ldap for the user that runs OpenLDAP instead of -u openldap, which is for Ubuntu hosts. Then -f slapd.conf points to the configuration file we want to read in, and -F points to the slapd.d directory, which will hold the LDIF files for your configuration engine.

When your slapd instance starts, you will see that the slapd.d directory now contains several files and directories. These files contain the LDAP settings you have specified in slapd.conf and other included files in an LDIF file format.

■ **Note** You can see more about managing the configuration of your OpenLDAP server at https://help.
ubuntu.com/lts/serverguide/openldap-server.html.

For troubleshooting, it can often be useful to run the SLAPD daemon in debug mode in the foreground
to see exactly what the service is doing. To do that, you would issue the following (on Ubuntu, use –u ldap
and –g ldap for CentOS):

```
$ sudo slapd -F /etc/ldap/slapd.d -d -1 -u openldap -g openldap -h ldapi:///
```

You can manually start or stop an SLAPD server service using the following on either CentOS or Ubuntu:

```
$ sudo systemctl start slapd
$ sudo systemctl stop slapd
```

You can then check the status of the daemon with the following:

```
$ sudo systemctl status slapd
```

You can enable at boot with the following:

```
$ sudo systemctl enable slapd
```

Once the service is started, you can tail the journal logs to see any logging information.

```
$ sudo journalctl -xfe -u slapd
```

You can use the logs to monitor and solve problems with your access requests.

Securing SLAPD with TLS

Because LDAP can often contain sensitive data, it is a good precaution to make sure that the data transferred
between your LDAP clients and your LDAP server is encrypted. LDAP can be used for things like address
books, but it can also be used to store more sensitive data such as passwords, employee details, and so on.

We can configure Transport Layer Security (TLS) to secure our transport over the wire. TLS is used for
encrypting communications between our server and its clients. We will create an LDIF file to add these records.

```
dn: cn=config
changetype: modify
add: olcTLSCACertificateFile
olcTLSCACertificateFile: /etc/ldap/certs/cacert.pem
-
add: olcTLSCertificateFile
olcTLSCertificateFile: /etc/ldap/certs/ldap.example.com.cert
-
add: olcTLSCertificateKeyFile
olcTLSCertificateKeyFile: /etc/ldap/certs/ldap.example.com.key
-
add: olcTLSVerifyClient
olcTLSVerifyClient: allow
```

Here we create a certificate file from our private key and add the details. The issuing certificate file is added to the `cacert.pem` file. We have also specified `allow` for `TLSVerifyClient`. This means that we will verify any client certificates presented to us during the TLS exchange but not fail if we can't verify the certificate. Other options are `never`, `allow`, `try`, and `demand`. `try` and `demand` will fail connections for unverified certificates.

We apply `tls.ldif` with `ldapmodify` like before.

```
$ sudo ldapmodify -Q -Y EXTERNAL -H ldapi:/// -f tls.ldif
```

We can validate that we can still use the root user to query the LDAP server and view our TLS entries.

```
$ sudo ldapsearch -H ldapi:/// -Y EXTERNAL -b "cn=config" -LLL  -Q |grep TLS
olcTLSCACertificateFile: /etc/ldap/certs/cacert.pem
olcTLSCertificateFile: /etc/ldap/certs/ldap.example.com.cert
olcTLSCertificateKeyFile: /etc/ldap/certs/ldap.example.com.key
```

We will not be able to issue `ldapsearch` requests against the `ldap:///` URI until we make some adjustments to the `/etc/ldap/ldap.conf` file. We will do that in the next section (in the earlier section we used the Unix socket `ldapi:///`).

Working with SSF

We will now talks about the security strength factor directive, or `ssf`. We can define the minimum security strength we allow for our connections and specify higher-security-strength communications for more sensitive roles.

For example, if we had a `sec.ldif` file like that shown next, it describes the factors of security we require for certain connection types:

```
dn: cn=config
changetype: modify
add: olcSecurity
olcSecurity: ssf=128 update_ssf=256 simple_bind=128 tls=256
```

The `ssf=128` setting describes the overall security strength factor we require for our service based on the encryption key size. Higher key sizes imply greater encryption strength.

If we define the `ssf` security in the global DIT, it is defined for all other DITs. We have set it to 128, which is reasonable, and we can restrict more sensitive DITs with stronger security requirements. The `update_ssf=256` setting describes the overall security strength required for directory updates, and the `simple_bind=128` setting is the required security factor for `simple_bind` operations. The `ssf` values are as follows:

- 0 (zero) implies no protection.

- 1 implies integrity protection only.

- 56 allows DES or other weak ciphers.

- 112 allows triple DES and other strong ciphers.

- 128 allows RC4, Blowfish, and other strong ciphers.

- 256 allows AES, SHA ciphers.

The default is 0. You can combine them in your access control lists to control what those connections can access, depending on the security strength of the connection.

We are not going to apply this configuration at present, but we have already secured our sensitive user data with `ssf_tls=128` in our access control list.

We now have to set up our LDAP client with our TLS certificate details if we want to make adjustments to user passwords or other sensitive data.

Setting Up Your LDAP Client

Ubuntu and CentOS both use the `ldap.conf` file to configure system-wide LDAP defaults for clients (there is also another method using the `sssd` program that we will discuss in the "Single Sign-On: Centralized Linux Authentication" section). Applications that use the OpenLDAP libraries will use these files to get the LDAP details. You will find Ubuntu's file in the directory `/etc/ldap` and CentOS's in `/etc/openldap`.

■ **Note**   It is important that you don't get this confused with the file provided by the `libnss-ldap` file, which is also called `ldap.conf` and can be found here on both distributions: `/etc/ldap.conf`. This file is for configuring user and host information for your system, while `/etc/(open)ldap/ldap.conf` is used by the OpenLDAP tools such as `ldapmodify`, `ldapadd`, etc.

You will need to edit your `ldap.conf` file by adding the following lines of text. In our case, we are going to cheat a little and not worry about setting up client SSL certificates for our LDAP clients. If this host was being used to replicate our LDAP server, we would definitely ensure that both the server and client had SSL verification enabled. Check the man page for `ldap.conf` for details.

```
URI ldap://ldap.example.com/
BASE dc=example,dc=com
TLS_CACERT /etc/ldap/certs/cacert.pem
TLS_REQCERT demand
```

The `URI` points to our LDAP server. The `BASE` is the default base DN for LDAP operations. `TLS_CACERT` points to our CA certificate file, which will contain our `example.com` CA certificate. On some clients you may have installed the CA cert into the default location of `/etc/ssl/certs`. The `demand` we specify in the `TLS_REQCERT` field means that we will try to verify the certificate, and if it cannot be verified, we cancel the connection (this is the default). Other options are `try`, which means the connection will continue if no certificate is provided, but if a bad certificate is provided, the connection is stopped immediately; `allow`, which means that if the certificate provided is bad, the session can continue anyway; and `never`, which means your host will not request or check the server certificate before establishing the connection.

If you were looking at a CentOS host, you would most likely find your SSL CA certificate in the `/etc/pki/tls/certs` directory.

LDAP Management and Tools

So how do you manage entries with LDAP? Several tools are available for just this purpose. Using the command line, you can add entries from text files, search for existing entries, and delete entries. The text files are required to be in a format called LDIF. The format of the LDIF file is as follows:

```
dn: <dn entry>
objectclass: <objectclass to be included>
attribute: <attribute value described in an objectclass>
```

It is generally a good idea to create separate LDIF files for the different sections you are dealing with. For example, everything under ou=people,dc=example,dc=com can be in people.ldif, and everything under ou=groups,dc=example,dc=com can be in groups.ldif. Alternatively, for fresh LDAP servers, you can have all your entries in the one file, but be wary that in LDAP servers with existing entries, you will get errors if you try to add an existing entry again. You can use the # symbol at the start of each line of an entry to comment out that entry in your LDIF file in such cases. LDIF files can be used by the LDAP tools by using the -f *filename* option that we will detail in the following sections.

The other way to manage entries is to use one of the many GUI tools that are available. We will show how to install and configure a web-based GUI in the "LDAP Account Manager: Web-Based GUI" section.

LDIFs and Adding Users

At the top of the DIT sits the rootDN. The DIT starts with the declaration of the dcObject class. The following is a snippet of the LDIF text file we will use to populate our LDAP server:

```
dn: dc=example,dc=com
objectclass: dcObject
objectClass: organization
dc: example
o: example
```

This declares that we are going to create the rootDN dc=example,dc=com. According to the dcObject object class in the core.schema on Ubuntu, we must include the dc attribute. Let's look at the object class declaration from the core.schema file:

```
objectclass ( 1.3.6.1.4.1.1466.344 NAME 'dcObject'
        DESC 'RFC2247: domain component object'
        SUP top AUXILIARY MUST dc )
```

You can see how we use the preceding object class in the declaration of the DN: dc=example, dc=com. We specify the dc attribute as we are directed to use, indicated by the MUST clause in the object definition. Remember, this is an AUXILLARY object class and cannot be used to create an entry. We need a STRUCTUAL object class, and organization is such a class. It requires the o attribute for organization. We will add this entry when we add our users in the next section. This should be the first entry you add to your LDAP server.

It should be noted here that depending on if you are using Ubuntu, rootDN may already exist. You can find out by running the following:

```
$ sudo ldapsearch -D "cn=admin,dc=example,dc=com" -b "dc=example,dc=com" -ZZ ↵ -H ldap://
ldap.example.com -W
# example.com
dn: dc=example,dc=com
objectClass: top
objectClass: dcObject
objectClass: organization
o: example
dc: example
```

If this is the case, do not include this in `users.ldif` or you will get an error like the following when you try to add it:

```
adding new entry "dc=example,dc=com"
ldap_add: Already exists (68)
```

Next, we want to set up the users in our organization, so we will now declare our people organizational unit. We could separate this section into a new file for just our people entries if we wanted.

```
dn: ou=people,dc=example,dc=com
objectclass: organizationalUnit
ou: people
```

You can see that the LDIF format requires the declaration of the DN, followed by the object classes we want to use and the attributes. Each declaration should be separated by a blank line. The order of declaration is also important; you can't create a user in `ou=people,dc=example,dc=com` until that organizational unit is created. The object class `organizationalUnit` requires that we declare the ou attribute as we have here, `ou: people`.

Now we are going to add a user, `jsmith`.

```
dn: uid=jsmith,ou=people,dc=example,dc=com
objectclass: top
objectclass: person
objectclass: posixAccount
objectclass: exampleClient
cn: Jane Smith
sn: Smith
uid: jsmith
uidNumber: 1000
gidNumber: 1000
exampleActive: TRUE
homeDirectory: /home/jsmith
userPassword: {SSHA}IZ6u7bmw12t345s3GajRt4D4YHkDScH8
```

So, let's look at the DN first. You can see that we declare our DN using the uid attribute. We could have used a couple variations here other than `uid=jsmith`: `cn=Jane Smith` or `uid=jane.smith@example.com`. Which of these you end up using on your system depends on what you think will be best for your server (keeping indexes in mind), and you should be aware that these must be unique (`SINGLE-VALUE`).

Next, we have to declare the object class `top` and `person`. The `top` object class, an ABSTRACT superclass, is required to provide the other object classes and is used to terminate the hierarchy.

The `person` object class provides the sn (surname) and cn (common name) attributes. Let's quickly view the schema for this object class.

```
objectclass ( 2.5.6.6 NAME 'person'
        DESC 'RFC2256: a person'
        SUP top STRUCTURAL
        MUST ( sn $ cn )
        MAY ( userPassword $ telephoneNumber $ seeAlso $ description ) )
```

The parent of the person object class is top (SUP top), and it is a STRUCTURAL object class, meaning that its attributes can form an entry in the DIT. For the person class, we MUST provide a cn and an sn entry. We MAY provide userPassword, telephone, seeAlso, and description.

It is optional to include the posixAccount and exampleClient object classes. The object class posixAccount will provide the attributes useful for Unix/Linux hosts such as userPassword, uid, uidNumber, gidNumber, and homeDirectory. The exampleClient object class that we created in the schema section provides the exampleActive attribute, which we can use to activate and deactivate our users. Please note that the attribute value for Boolean attributes such as exampleActive must be uppercase, and because it is an SINGLE-VALUE attribute, we can declare it only once.

We'll now add groups as an organizationalUnit so that we can make use of groups to manage access to our users. Again, we can create a new LDIF text file for our groups.

```
dn: ou=groups,dc=example,dc=com
objectclass: top
objectclass: organizationalUnit
ou: groups
```

You can see that creating the organizational unit for groups is similar to the way we declared the people organizational unit earlier. As required by the schema definition, we have used and declared the ou attribute to name our DN. Next, we declare the group admins that we will use to group our administrators.

```
dn: cn=admins,ou=groups,dc=example,dc=com
objectclass: top
objectclass: groupOfNames
cn: admins
member: uid=ataylor,ou=people,dc=example,dc=com
```

We declare a group list with the groupOfNames object class, which allows us to just add members. We could have also used the posixGroup object class, which would allow us to use gidNumbers as well. We can add as many members to the group as we like by adding member: DN on a separate line.

Now we can look at adding our details to the LDAP database. To do so, we will use the ldapadd tool that comes with OpenLDAP.

Adding Users from LDIF Files

The LDAP tools all share a common set of options that you can provide to connect to your LDAP server. The OpenLDAP client tools can be used to connect to other LDAP servers provided by other software manufacturers. Table 16-4 lists the common options that are available to most LDAP tools.

Table 16-4. *Common LDAP Tool Options*

Option	Description
-x	Performs a simple bind.
-v	Specifies verbose output.
-W	Prompts for a password.
-f	Points to an input file, which can be a different type under a different tool context.
-D	Specifies the DN to bind as. This DN must have proper access rights to work on the entries.
-Z	Tries using TLS to make the LDAP connection. ZZ indicates that use of TLS must be successful before continuing with the connection.
-Y	Specifies the SASL authentication mechanism to connect to your LDAP server. You must have SASL configured to use this option.
-X	Specifies the SASL authzid, or the requested authorization ID for a SASL bind.
-U	Specifies the SASL authcid, or the authentication ID for a SASL bind.
-b	Specifies the base DN. Instead of querying the whole tree, you can specify a base to start from, like ou=people,dc=example,dc=com.
-s	Indicates the scope of the search query. Can be either base, one, sub, or children.

Most commonly you will use the –D option to specify the user you are binding as to make a query or modification and will use the -xW option to perform a simple bind and be prompted for a password (as opposed to a SASL bind -Y). Some of the options we have shown in Table 16-4 will not be available to all LDAP tools. The syntax of the LDAP tool commands usually looks like this:

ldaptool <options> filter entry

Several LDAP tools are available. The main ones are ldapadd, ldapmodify, ldapsearch, and ldapdelete, and as we said, they all share some or all of the common options shown previously. For the exact options available, please refer to the man pages for those tools. We are going to give you examples of how to use these commands and options in the upcoming next sections.

Adding users to our LDAP server is easy now that we have created our LDIF file. Let's look at the complete LDIF file. As we have mentioned, we need to add the dc entry, or the top level of our DIT, at the top of this file (remember to remove it from the file if it already exists). If you are adding hundreds of users, you may want to use a script or program that handles the existing users (or LDAP errors generated from trying to re-add an existing user or DN).

```
$ sudo cat users.ldif
dn: dc=example,dc=com
objectclass: dcObject
objectclass: organizationalUnit
dc: example
ou: example

dn: ou=people,dc=example,dc=com
objectclass: organizationalUnit
ou: people
```

```
dn: uid=jsmith,ou=people,dc=example,dc=com
objectclass: top
objectclass: person
objectclass: posixAccount
objectclass: exampleClient
cn: Jane Smith
sn: Smith
uid: jsmith
uidNumber: 1000
gidNumber: 1000
exampleActive: TRUE
homeDirectory: /home/jsmith
userPassword: {SSHA}IZ6u7bmw12t345s3GajRt4D4YHkDScH8

dn: uid=ataylor,ou=people,dc=example,dc=com
objectclass: top
objectclass: person
objectclass: posixAccount
objectclass: exampleClient
cn: Angela Taylor
sn: Taylor
uid: ataylor
uidNumber: 1002
gidNumber: 1000
exampleActive: TRUE
homeDirectory: /home/ataylor
userPassword: {SSHA}PRqu69QU5WK5i8/dvqQuvFXoOxJ74OFG

dn: ou=meta,dc=example,dc=com
objectclass: organizationalUnit
objectclass: top
ou: meta

dn: cn=webadmin,ou=meta,dc=example,dc=com
objectClass: organizationalRole
objectclass: simpleSecurityObject
userPassword: {SSHA}KEOJMvJjYjQ/9lpigDCbLla5iNoBb8O8

dn: ou=groups,dc=example,dc=com
objectclass: top
objectclass: organizationalUnit
ou: groups

dn: cn=staff,ou=groups,dc=example,dc=com
objectclass: top
objectclass: posixGroup
gidNumber: 1000
cn: staff
```

```
dn: cn=admins,ou=groups,dc=example,dc=com
objectclass: top
objectclass: groupOfNames
cn: admins
member: uid=ataylor,ou=people,dc=example,dc=com

dn: ou=hosts,dc=example,dc=com
objectclass: top
objectclass: organizationalUnit
ou: hosts
```

We are now going to add our users using the file users.ldif. The ldapadd tool is versatile and takes many options. The way we will use it is as follows:

```
$ sudo ldapadd -D "cn=admin,dc=example,dc=com" -ZZ -H ldap://ldap.example.com ↵
 -xWv -f users.ldif
```

The ldapadd command can use the SASL authentication method or the simple method. As we have mentioned earlier, if you have SASL set up, you can bind without sending the password across the wire, with the simple authentication method the password is sent to be verified on the LDAP server, so it should be sent over a secure transport like TLS. The -x will make ldapadd use the simple method. -W tells ldapadd that we want to be prompted for a password. -v is to be verbose in its information. When you specify -D, you give the username you want to bind with. In this case, we are using the cn=admin,dc=example,dc=com user, and as you may remember, this is the rootDN we added to the SLAPD server earlier. The -h switch is the hostname, ldap.example.com. -Z tells the command to use STARTTLS, or make a TLS connection to the LDAP host, but if you have TLS already set in /etc/ldap/ldap.conf or /etc/openldap/ldap.conf, your command will fail. Finally, -f indicates the file we want to use to add our users, users.ldif.

The options you use here are the same for all the other LDAP tools; see the man page for more details. When you issue this command, you will get something like this:

```
jsmith@ldap:/etc/ldap$ ldapadd -xWv -D cn=admin,dc=example,dc=com ↵
-h ldap.example.com -Z -f users.ldif
ldap_initialize( ldap://ldap.example.com )
Enter LDAP Password:
add objectclass:
        top
        person
        exampleClient
        posixAccount
add cn:
        Jane Smith
add sn:
        Smith
add uid:
        jsmith
add uidNumber:
        1000
add gidNumber:
        1000
add exampleActive:
        TRUE
```

```
add homeDirectory:
        /home/jsmith
add userPassword:
        {SSHA}IZ6u7bmw12t345s3GajRt4D4YHkDScH8
adding new entry "uid=jsmith,ou=people,dc=example,dc=com"
modify complete
```

If successful, you will see a "Modify complete" message. If something goes wrong, you will receive an error on the console output, and you can use journalctl to further examine the log entries produced.

```
$ journalctl -xe -u slapd
```

Remember to adjust your LogLevel entry like described previously if you are not seeing enough detail in the logs.

Searching Your LDAP Tree

Now that we have some entries in our LDAP database, we can search it to make sure we can return useful information. Let's look at ways we can search our LDAP directory.

```
$ ldapsearch -xvW -H ldap://ldap.example.com -ZZ \
-D cn=admin,dc=example,dc=com \
-b ou=people,dc=example,dc=com -s sub \
'(&(&(objectclass=person)(uid=jsmith))(exampleActive=TRUE))' cn
```

The arguments we use for the search are similar to the ones we use for the ldapadd command. We first specify that we are performing a simple bind with verbose output, and we want to be prompted for a password, -xvW. -h declares the host we want to connect to, and -Z says try to make a connection using TLS (a -ZZ would mean to confirm that the TLS connection was successful before proceeding). Angela Taylor is a user that we have put in cn=admins,ou=groups,dc=example,dc=com; remember that we have given write access to all entries under ou=people,dc=example,dc=com through our access control list. We have just added the user Jane Smith to our LDAP directory, and we will conduct a search to look at her details.

In our ldapsearch command, you can see we include a filter to make use of indexes and to reduce our search response time. We know that all user entries have the object class person. As we explained, in our slapd.conf file all object classes are indexed, so choosing one that you know is in the entity you are looking for will speed your searches. The uid attributes are also indexed, so we also want to filter on the uid of the entry we are looking for. Our search filter looks like this:

```
(&(&(objectclass=person)(uid=jsmith))(exampleActive=TRUE)),
```

These are read inside out; let's take the first part.

```
&(objectclass=person)(uid=jsmith)
```

This means to filter on entries where the object class is person AND uid is jsmith. The second part looks like this:

```
(&(<first match>)(exampleActive=TRUE))
```

Here we match on the first match AND that the account is active, as indicated by exampleActive=TRUE. The & operator indicates that we are searching for one AND the other. We can also use the | symbol to indicate we want to search for one OR the other.

We specify the base of the DIT tree we wish to start searching from, -b ou=people, dc=example,dc=com, and the scope of our search is -s sub, or everything under it. And finally, we are searching for Jane's common name, or cn. The results of this search will look like the following:

```
ldap_initialize( ldap://ldap.example.com )
filter: (&(&(objectclass=person)(uid=jsmith))(exampleActive=TRUE))requesting: cn
# extended LDIF
#
# LDAPv3
# base <ou=people,dc=example,dc=com> with scope subtree

# filter: (&(&(objectclass=person)(uid=jsmith))(exampleActive=TRUE))
# requesting: cn
#

# jsmith, People, example.com
dn: uid=jsmith,ou=people,dc=example,dc=com
cn: Jane Smith

# search result
search: 3
result: 0 Success

# numResponses: 2
# numEntries: 1
```

Here you can see that we have returned the DN we were looking for and the common name for that entry. Next, let's look at deleting entries.

Deleting Entries from Your LDAP Directory

The other thing you are going to want to do often is delete entries in your LDAP directory. To delete entries, use the ldapdelete command. Again, this takes the same arguments as ldapadd and ldapsearch. For deleting more than one entry, you can input a text file, or you can delete entries individually. Assume we have the following entries in a new users.ldif file, and we want to delete them.

```
uid=jbob,ou=people,dc=example,dc=com uid=tbird,ou=people,dc=example,dc=com
```

We can now add these two entries to a file called deluser.ldif and then run the ldapdelete command with the -f argument as follows:

```
ldapdelete -xvW -D uid=ataylor,ou=people,dc=example,dc=com \
-h ldap.example.com -Z -f deluser.ldif
ldap_initialize( ldap://ldap.example.com )
deleting entry "uid=jbob,ou=people,dc=example,dc=com"
deleting entry "uid=tbird,ou=people,dc=example,dc=com"
```

As a result, these entries are no longer in our directory and have been deleted.

■ **Note**   OpenLDAP is case insensitive, meaning that uid=jsmith,ou=people,dc=example,dc=com is treated the same as uid=jSmith,ou=people,dc=example,dc=com. Trying to add two Jane Smiths, one with a lowercase *s* and one with an uppercase *S*, will return a duplicate error.

Password Policy Overlay

Setting the password policy overlay allows us greater control over password aging and change history. Overlays, as explained earlier, provide extra functionality for your OpenLDAP server. We want to set our password aging to 7776000 (90 days in seconds) and our password history to 3, meaning we will store the previous three passwords supplied by users so they can't keep using the same one. The password will need to have a minimum of eight characters.

Adding Our PPolicy Overlay

It is time to add our Password Policy overlay. An overlay, as previously mentioned, provides certain additional functionality not normally supplied by the OpenLDAP server. In this case, we are declaring the ppolicy overlay, which helps manage our passwords.

We are going to create a file called ppolicy.ldif with the following contents:

```
dn: ou=policies,dc=example,dc=com
objectClass: organizationalUnit
ou: policies

dn: olcOverlay={0}ppolicy,olcDatabase={1}mdb,cn=config
objectClass: olcOverlayConfig
objectClass: olcPPolicyConfig
olcOverlay: {0}ppolicy
olcPPolicyDefault: cn=default,ou=policies,dc=example,dc=com
olcPPolicyHashCleartext: FALSE
olcPPolicyUseLockout: TRUE
olcPPolicyForwardUpdates: FALSE
```

First you can see that we create an organizationalUnit, a way of collecting similar items in our DIT, called ou=policies,dc=example,dc=com. This provides the structure to place our default polices that we will define later.

The ppolicy overlay provides certain functions that allow you to better control password security on your LDAP server. OpenLDAP itself provides no password management features, such as password expiry and password history. This overlay allows you to declare a policy or associate different policies with different parts of the DIT tree. Here we declare a default policy with the DN cn=default,ou=Policies,dc =example,dc=com. We also declare that we want to use the lockout feature of the ppolicy. This allows us to send a message back to the requesting client if it is locked out. This can provide information to attackers who will then know whether a username exists or not, so you might want to turn this off. We also turn off HashCleartext and ForwardUpdate at this stage.

We now have to define the actual policy that sets the values we want to enforce on our password regime. To do that, we will need to add the following LDIF to our LDAP server:

```
dn: cn=default,ou=policies,dc=example,dc=com
objectClass: top
objectClass: device
objectClass: pwdPolicy
cn: default
pwdAttribute: userPassword
pwdMaxAge: 7776000
pwdExpireWarning: 6912000
pwdInHistory: 3
pwdCheckQuality: 1
pwdMinLength: 8
pwdMaxFailure: 4
pwdLockout: TRUE
pwdLockoutDuration: 1920
pwdGraceAuthNLimit: 0
pwdFailureCountInterval: 0
pwdMustChange: TRUE
pwdAllowUserChange: TRUE
pwdSafeModify: FALSE
```

We have now added the password policy to our LDAP server, and it has some basic settings like password age (90 days in seconds) and passwords in history (3). This overlay will now make all password accounts comply with the password policy.

We will use ldapadd to apply this ppolicy.ldif file. In this instance, since we are modifying the SLAPD database config, we will use the powers of the local root user to make this change:

```
$ sudo ldapadd -H ldapi:/// -Y EXTERNAL -f ppolicy.ldif
```

■ **Note**   See the man slapo-ppolicy page for more details on the Password Policy overlay.

Testing Your Access Control Lists

From time to time, you will run into permission issues because of incorrectly functioning access control lists. There is a tool you can use to test your ACLs called slapacl. This tool tests access to attributes and object classes by the DN you want to grant access to. For example, if we want to make sure that the DN cn=webadmin ,ou=meta,dc=example,dc=com, which is the user we use to bind our web services during authentication, has auth access to the userPassword attribute of our user Angela Taylor, we would issue the following:

```
sudo slapacl -F /etc/ldap/slapd.d \
  -b uid=ataylor,ou=people,dc=example,dc=com \
  -D cn=webadmin,ou=meta,dc=example,dc=com \
  -o tls_ssf=128 \
  -v userPassword/auth
```

The slapacl command requires sudo access. You need to specify the slapd config directory you want to test against with -F /etc/ldap/slapd.d on an Ubuntu host; on a CentOS host, you would need to use the /etc/openldap/slapd.d directory. The -b uid=ataylor,ou=people,dc=example,dc=com DN is the DN we want to test our access on. -D cn=webadmin,ou=meta,dc=example,dc=com is the DN that we want to confirm has auth access to the DN of uid=ataylor,ou=people,dc=example,dc=com. The -o allows us to provide options that are related to slapd access. In this case, since we need to mimic our TLS security strength factor, we add the tls_ssf=128. The -v is for verbose. We specify the attribute and authentication level we want to test, in this case the attribute userPassword against the access auth. As you know, we need at least auth access for the DN cn=webadmin,ou=meta,dc=example,dc=com to authenticate with userPassword. If we are successful, we will get the following result:

```
authcDN: "cn=webadmin,ou=meta,dc=example,dc=com"
auth access to userPassword: ALLOWED
```

This confirms that the line in our access control list is working like we expect.

```
olcAccess: {1}to attrs=userPassword,shadowLastChange,entry,member
        by dn.exact="cn=webadmin,ou=meta,dc=example,dc=com" tls_ssf=128 auth
```

We'll test to see whether we can get write access to the same attribute to confirm that our access control list doesn't have a security hole in it.

```
sudo slapacl -F /etc/ldap/slapd.d \
  -b uid=ataylor,ou=people,dc=example,dc=com \
  -D cn=webadmin,ou=meta,dc=example,dc=com \
  -o tls_ssf=128 \
  -v userPassword/write
 authcDN: "cn=webadmin,ou=meta,dc=example,dc=com"
write access to uid: DENIED
```

This is as we expect: we should be denied everything but auth access and below. You can also pass in other options that allow you to test access against such things as peernames and ssf.

One of the other useful ways to figure out what is going on with your access control lists, which can be hard to get right, is to have the following in your access control list while you are testing:

```
access to * by * search
```

You can combine this with modifying the logging configuration in your SLAPD, changing your log level to something like this:

```
olcLogLevel:  416
```

This will show the search filter and the access control list processing as well as connection management and configuration file processing. You can use the journalctl command to access the logs. When a request comes in, it will produce output like the following:

```
$ journalctl -xe -u slapd
slapd[1350]: conn=1011 op=2 SRCH base="ou=people,dc=example,dc=com" scope=2 deref=0
filter="(&(objectClass=person)(uid=jsmith))"
slapd[1350]: conn=1011 op=2 SRCH attr=uid
```

```
...<snip>...
slapd[1350]: => access_allowed: read access to "uid=jsmith,ou=people,dc=example,dc=com"
"uid" requested
slapd[1350]: => acl_get: [1] attr uid
slapd[1350]: => acl_mask: access to entry "uid=jsmith,ou=people,dc=example,dc=com", attr
"uid" requested
slapd[1350]: => acl_mask: to value by "uid=ataylor,ou=people,dc=example,dc=com", (=0)
slapd[1350]: <= check a_dn_pat: gidNumber=0+uidNumber=0,cn=peercred,cn=external,cn=auth
slapd[1350]: <= check a_dn_pat: *
slapd[1350]: <= acl_mask: [2] applying +0 (break)
slapd[1350]: <= acl_mask: [2] mask: =0
slapd[1350]: => dn: [3] ou=people,dc=example,dc=com
slapd[1350]: => acl_get: [3] matched
slapd[1350]: => acl_get: [3] attr uid
slapd[1350]: => acl_mask: access to entry "uid=jsmith,ou=people,dc=example,dc=com", attr
"uid" requested
slapd[1350]: => acl_mask: to value by "uid=ataylor,ou=people,dc=example,dc=com", (=0)
slapd[1350]: <= check a_dn_pat: cn=webadmin,ou=meta,dc=example,dc=com
slapd[1350]: <= check a_group_pat: cn=admins,ou=groups,dc=example,dc=com
slapd[1350]: <= acl_mask: [2] applying write(=wrscxd) (stop)
slapd[1350]: <= acl_mask: [2] mask: write(=wrscxd)
slapd[1350]: => slap_access_allowed: read access granted by write(=wrscxd)
slapd[1350]: => access_allowed: read access granted by write(=wrscxd)
```

The first line shows the search string of the request, SRCH base="ou=people,dc=example,dc=com" scope=2 deref=3 filter="(&(objectClass=*)(uid=jsmith))", and we are looking for the attribute UID.

The output also shows the user making the request, uid=ataylor,ou=people,dc=example,dc=com. You can see the process of the request for access starts with a search of ou=people,dc=example,dc=com and then the final acceptance for the search (and read), via the check a_group_pat: cn=admins,ou=groups,dc=example,dc=com, and that gives ataylor write access.

With a combination of logs, the slapacl and ldapsearch tools, and the useful OpenLDAP mailing list, you can achieve intricate access control lists. Let's look at the other tools you can use to manage your LDAP servers, including the ldapsearch tool we just mentioned.

Backing Up Your LDAP Directory

Text-based files are great for building or restoring your LDAP directory. Once your directory is implemented, we suggest that you set up a script that might regularly output your LDAP database into a text file and save it. In Chapter 14, we introduced you to the Bareos backup server and showed you how to use the Client Run Before Job and Client Run After Job options when we backed up our MySQL database. You can do a similar thing with the LDAP database, as shown in Listing 16-4.

Listing 16-4. slapcat LDIF Dump

```
#!/bin/bash

case $1 in
start)
    slapcat -b dc=example,dc=com -l /var/lib/ldap/backup.ldif
      if [ $? -eq 0 ] ; then
          echo "backup successful"
      else
          echo "backup failed"
          exit 1;
    fi
;;

stop)
  if [ -e /var/lib/ldap/backup.ldif ] ; then
      rm -f /var/lib/ldap/backup.ldif
      if [ $? -eq 0 ] ; then
          echo "removal of file successful"
      else
          echo "failed to remove file"
          exit 1;
      fi

  fi
 ;;
esac
exit 0
```

To get a perfect backup, you would want to stop the OpenLDAP directory server before you run the command in Listing 16-4; however, this is not always possible, and hot backups are preferable over no backups at all.

You use the slapcat command to dump the LDAP database to a file on disk using the Client Run Before Job script. You then get Bareos to back it up; Bareos can delete it by running the Client Run After Job script (see Listing 16-5).

Listing 16-5. The Job Definition for Bareos Backup Service

```
Job {
    Name = ldap.example.com
    Client = ldap-fd
    Enabled = yes
    JobDefs = "DefaultLinux"
    Client Run Before Job = "/usr/local/bin/ldap_backup start"
    Client Run After Job = "/usr/local/bin/ldap_backup stop"
}
```

This is based on the proviso that you have your LDAP backup script installed in /usr/local/bin on your ldap.example.com host.

Restoring your LDAP database is then simply a matter of restoring the file on your host and running the slapadd command with the following parameters (OpenLDAP should be shut down for this process):

```
$ slapadd -b dc=example,dc=com -F /etc/ldap/slapd.d -l restored.ldif.backup.file
```

Here we have restored our LDAP database to how it was when we performed the last save. Because LDAP has no write-ahead logs, you cannot replay your most recent updates to your LDAP directory server like you can in a fully featured transactional relational database, so regular backups are important. We suggest at minimum you make backups nightly.

Managing your directory server via text files can get tiresome. Luckily, we have a solution if you're one of those who prefer a web-based GUI to do all the fiddly work for you, and we'll discuss this next.

LDAP Account Manager: Web-Based GUI

Several tools are available to manage your LDAP directories. We have decided to focus on one of them in this book, LDAP Account Manager (LAM). This is a web-based GUI that can take some of the administrative pain away from updating text files. It is available in two versions: a free version and an enterprise version that requires a fee. If you discover you do not like using this tool, you might want to try some of the others that exist, such as the following:

- *Luma*: http://luma.sourceforge.net/

- *GQ*: http://sourceforge.net/projects/gqclient/

- *phpldapAdmin*: http://phpldapadmin.sourceforge.net/

- *web2ldap*: https://web2ldap.de/web2ldap.html

- *LDAPAdmin*: https://github.com/ibv/LDAP-Admin (Linux version)

Some of these are old, and some more are recent. OpenLDAP hasn't changed very much over the years, so you are free to try any you choose. We chose to show you LAM because it is designed not only to manage LDAP but also to provision user accounts. It allows you to create users based on templates that are easy to follow. It is also flexible enough to allow you to integrate your Samba user administration if you choose to do so.

Installation and Configuration

LAM is available for download with Ubuntu from its online repositories. It is a few releases old, and if you are looking for a more recent version, you can get the .deb packages from the web site's download page (https://www.ldap-account-manager.org/lamcms/releases) or from the Debian repository.

For LAM, you will need a version of PHP installed on your host higher or equal to 5.2.4.

To install it, you issue the following:

```
$ sudo aptitude install php-mcrypt php-zip ldap-account-manager apache2
```

At the time of writing, the version provided in the Ubuntu repository (5.2-1ubuntu1) does not support the default PHP (7.x) installed with Xenial. The solution is to install the .deb package first from the download page and manually install it similar to how we will do it with CentOS.

For CentOS hosts you have to download the Fedora/CentOS RPMs from the web site (https://www.ldap-account-manager.org/lamcms/releases). This will link to a SourceForge download, and you can get a copy to the direct link (removing the mirror information from the URL). Then use yum to install the package like in this example:

```
$ sudo yum install -y httpd php php-ldap php-xml
$ sudo yum install -y http://downloads.sourceforge.net/project/lam/LAM/5.5/ldap-account-
manager-5.5-0.fedora.1.noarch.rpm
```

The CentOS installation puts all the LAM files under /usr/share/ldap-account-manager. All the configuration files are installed under /var/lib/ldap-account-manager/config/.

LAM is fairly easy to configure. On Ubuntu, some configuration files are installed into /etc/ldap-account-manager. You will find an example configuration for your Apache web server and the configuration file, /etc/ldap-account-manager/config.cfg, containing the default username and password for your LAM installation.

```
$ sudo vi /etc/ldap-account-manager/config.cfg
# password to add/delete/rename configuration profiles
password: {SSHA}tj1yDeQfLJbmISXwh8JfjMb2ro3v5u44

# default profile, without ".conf"
default: lam
```

In the config.cfg file, you can see we have set our own password to {SSHA} tj1yDeQfLJbmISXwh8JfjMb2ro3v5u44 (be careful with your ownership and permissions). We also need to change the following file to add our own LDAP directory details. First, we make a copy of the file /var/lib/ldap-account-manager/config/lam.conf. We then make the changes in bold to the /var/lib/ldap-account-manager/config/lam.conf file.

```
$ sudo vi /var/lib/ldap-account-manager/config/lam.conf
# LDAP Account Manager configuration

# server address (e.g. ldap://localhost:389 or ldaps://localhost:636)
ServerURL: ldaps://ldap.example.com

# list of users who are allowed to use LDAP Account Manager
Admins: cn=admin,dc=example,dc=com

# password to change these preferences via webfrontend
Passwd: somepassword

# suffix of tree view
treesuffix: dc=example,dc=com

# maximum number of rows to show in user/group/host lists
maxlistentries: 30

# default language (a line from config/language)
defaultLanguage: en_GB.utf8:UTF-8:English (Great Britain)

# Number of minutes LAM caches LDAP searches.
cachetimeout: 5
```

```
# Module settings
modules: posixAccount_minUID: 1000
modules: posixAccount_maxUID: 30000
modules: posixAccount_minMachine: 50000
modules: posixAccount_maxMachine: 60000
modules: posixGroup_minGID: 1000
modules: posixGroup_maxGID: 20000
modules: posixGroup_pwdHash: SSHA
modules: posixAccount_pwdHash: SSHA
```

In the first section of this file, we add the details for our LDAP directory including the connection details, tree information, Posix UID, GID, and machine numbers. The UID and GIDs are used when we create new users in the LAM interface; they will be incremented in those ranges listed previously.

```
# List of active account types.
activeTypes: user,group,host

types: suffix_user: ou=people,dc=example,dc=com
types: attr_user: #uid;#givenName;#sn;#uidNumber;#gidNumber
types: modules_user: person,posixAccount,shadowAccount,exampleClient

types: suffix_group: ou=groups,dc=example,dc=com
types: attr_group: #cn;#gidNumber;#memberUID;#description
types: modules_group: posixGroup

types: suffix_host: ou=hosts,dc=example,dc=com
types: attr_host: #cn;#description;#uidNumber;#gidNumber
types: modules_host: account,posixAccount

# Access rights for home directories scriptRights: 750
```

In the last section of the file, we detail the account types we want to enable in the `activeTypes` section and the LDAP branches that house these. The LAM administration tool will use these details to create the user accounts for us in our LDAP server.

Adding the Apache Virtual Host for LAM

We are going to add an Apache virtual host to our web server to host our LAM site. In Chapter 11, we showed you how to set up an Apache virtual host. The web service can run on any host; it does not have to be on the same host as the LDAP server, but in our example, this will be the case. We have chosen to house this site on our host with the IP address 192.168.0.1 and DNS name of `ldap.example.com`, also known as `headoffice.example.com`.

■ **Note** Our `headoffice.example.com` host may now be overloaded with secure virtual hosts (https), and we may have to choose a nonstandard port, like 8443, to run our `ldap.example.com` web site. Alternatively, we could run it on a completely different host.

On our Ubuntu host, we will have the following configuration: the main sections of this virtual host have been provided by the LAM package and can be found in /etc/ldap-account-manager/apache.conf. We are going to include this file in our VirtualHost information. The VirtualHost will be placed in /etc/apache2/ sites-available and will be called ldap.example.com.conf. On CentOS, we would include the file in the / etc/httpd/conf.d/ directory.

```
$ sudo vi /etc/apache2/sites-available/ldap.example.com.conf
<VirtualHost 192.168.0.1:443>
  ServerName ldap.example.com
  SSLEngine on
  SSLCertificateFile /etc/ldap/certs/ldap.example.com.cert
  SSLCertificateKeyFile /etc/ldap/certs/ldap.example.com.key
  SSLCACertificateFile /etc/ldap/certs/cacert.pem

  LogFormat "%v %l %u %t \"%r\" %>s %b" comonvhost
  CustomLog /var/log/apache2/ldap.example.com_access.log comonvhost
  ErrorLog /var/log/apache2/ldap.example.com_error.log
  Loglevel debug

  Include /etc/ldap-account-manager/apache.conf

</VirtualHost>
```

We have created a VirtualHost enclosed between the <VirtualHost> </VirtualHost> tags. In this VirtualHost we have added our TLS/SSL keys pointing to our /etc/ldap/certs directory and have created separate log files in the /var/log/apache2 directory to aid diagnosis of any problems relating to this VirtualHost.

We have included (Include /etc/.../apache.conf) the Apache configuration file provided by the LAM package. This allows that package to be managed by the package manager and updated accordingly.

On Ubuntu we need to enable the site and make sure SSL is also enabled. We do that with the following:

```
$ sudo a2ensite ldap.example.com.conf
$ sudo a2enmod ssl
```

On CentOS hosts, there is a lam.apache.conf file placed in the /etc/httpd/conf.d/ directory. You may like add the VirtualHost directives in our Ubuntu example into a copy of this file to include the SSL and logging directives. If you don't, the LAM GUI will be available from http://ldap.example.com/lam. Refer to Chapter 11 for more information on managing CentOS virtual hosts.

Next, we start the Apache web server and point our browser at https://ldap.example.com/lam. We are now presented with the login page for the LAM configuration tool, as shown in Figure 16-4.

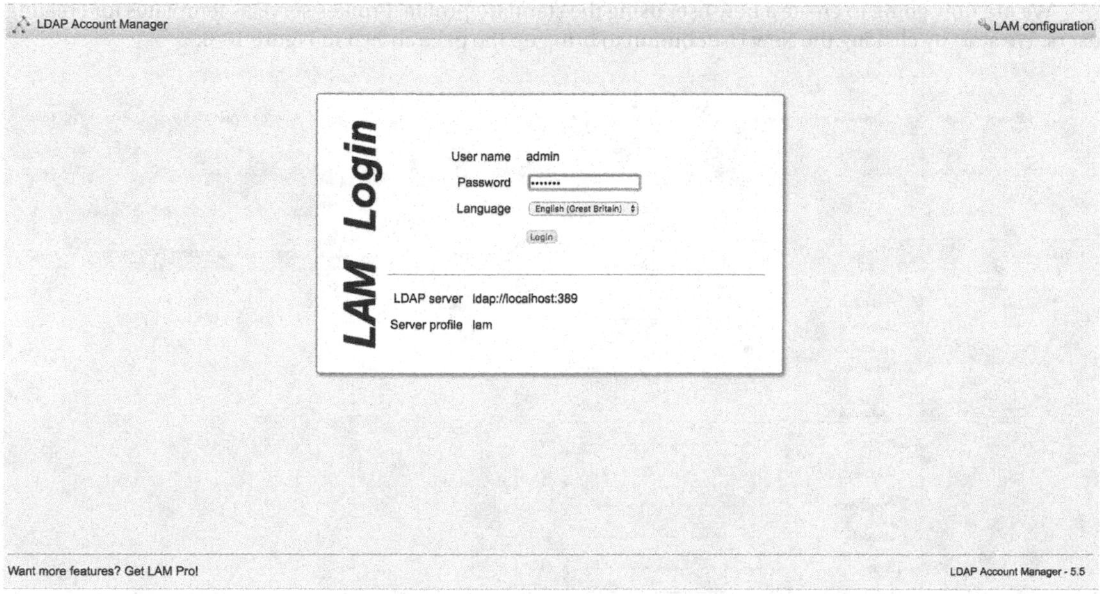

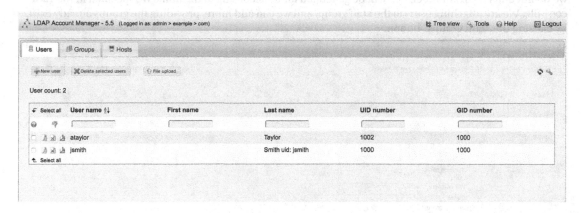

Figure 16-4. *LAM login page*

In the top right notice the LAM configuration link. This is used to perform general maintenance on the LAM configuration tool. On the login page, you will be asked for the password you have added to /var/lib/ldap-account-manager/config.cfg. Here you can change the general login settings as well as the password for your manager.

The admin user you can see in Figure 16-4 refers to the rootDN we specified in /var/lib/ldap-account-manager/config/lam.conf. When we enter the password for our rootDN, we are presented with the users we have already configured, as shown in Figure 16-5.

Figure 16-5. *Front page of the LAM web GUI*

We are now going to create a new user using the standard profile. Profiles serve as templates for creating users. We start by clicking the New User button to bring up the page shown in Figure 16-6.

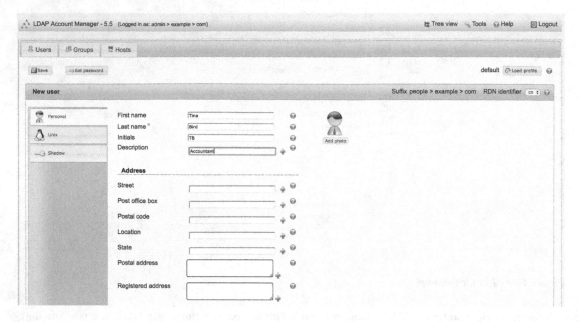

Figure 16-6. *Creating a new user*

We now need to click the Personal tab and fill out the details required there. The only details we will enter in the Personal tab are first name, last name, and description (see Figure 16-6); you can, of course, add as much detail as you want.

In the Unix tab, we fill in the details required to add a Unix/Linux account, as shown in Figure 16-7. If we do not enter a UID number, one will be generated for us according to the limits we specified in the `lam.conf` file. We are attaching users to the staff group, and we can add more, providing the groups already exist, by clicking the "Edit groups" button.

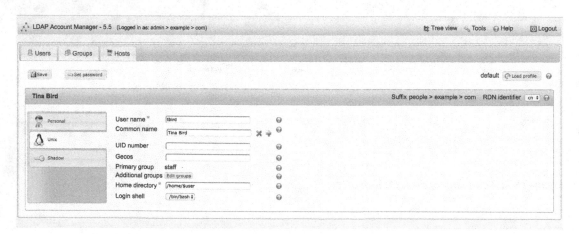

Figure 16-7. *Linux(Unix) details*

Prior to the enabling the Shadow section, we need to enable the shadow extension. Once this is done, you will see the screen in Figure 16-8.

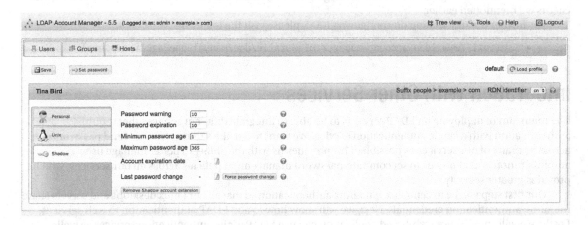

Figure 16-8. *Shadow details*

In the Shadow tab, we will leave the defaults as is. You can see these defaults in Figure 16-9.

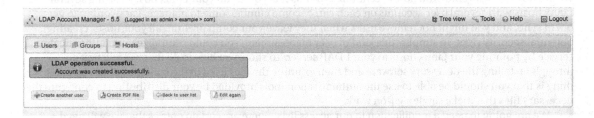

Figure 16-9. *User add complete*

To finish creating our user, we go back to the Main tab and click the Create Account button. We then see a confirmation screen like the one in Figure 16-9 indicating a successful operation.

As you can see in Figure 16-10, our new user, tbird, has been created.

LDAP Account Manager - 5.5   (Logged in as: admin > example > com)   ‡ Tree view   Tools   Help   Logout

| Users | Groups | Hosts |

New user   Delete selected users   File upload

User count: 3

Select all	User name ↑↓	First name	Last name	UID number	GID number
ataylor			Taylor	1002	1000
jsmith			Smith uid: jsmith	1000	1000
tbird		Tina	Bird	10000	1000
Select all					

Figure 16-10. *Listing the new user*

You can use LAM to add and remove group and host entries in your LDAP directory, which we will leave you to explore further on your own. Remember, LAM is not the only LDAP management tool. If you do not like this LDAP management client for managing your LDAP service, we suggest you try one of the other clients we mentioned earlier.

For further documentation on configuring LAM, please visit the following:

- `https://www.ldap-account-manager.org/static/doc/manual-onePage/index.html`

Integration with Other Services

The main aim of deploying an LDAP server is to be able to integrate different services that require authentication with a single authentication service. We want to use the same usernames and passwords across as many of our services as possible. This provides us with the ability to better manage user administration and allows us to set common password management policies across all our services, which provides greater security.

Our first step will be to centralize our Linux authentication so that all our Linux desktops and servers share the same authentication credentials. Next, we will show how to add LDAP authentication to web services. Lastly, we will show how a web-based application can use LDAP for its authentication services as well.

Single Sign-On: Centralized Linux Authentication

We are now going to show you how to centralize your user accounts on your Linux hosts. Having several Linux hosts with several user accounts on each can become cumbersome to manage. Passwords can get out of sync, and you might not remove users when they leave your company from all your hosts, creating potential security risks. To simplify this kind of user management, you could centralize your authentication service by pointing your Linux hosts to your LDAP server. To show you how to do that, we will first go through installing the necessary software and then examine the files used in the configuration. The good thing is that you should be able to use the authentication tools provided by your distribution to configure the necessary files that make single sign-on work.

We are going to need a modification to our access lists. There are certain entries that we will need anonymous access. When we authenticate against our LDAP server, we need to first access certain entries. There are two ways to do this; the first is with a bind DN and password, like a proxy, that will bind and get access to the entries, and the second is with anonymous bind, where no bind is done (remember that bind is another word for authentication). If we use a proxy bind DN, we need to set a password in clear text on every host that connects. In this exercise, we have chosen not to do that.

There are several other authentication methods you could choose to use instead of simple authentication. You can set up authentication with SASL or Kerberos if you wanted, and we talked about these authentication methods in Chapter 13.

The access control list now looks like this. You will see the changes in bold; we have given anonymous the ability to read certain attributes that are looked up during authentication and have given `auth` access to the `userPassword` attribute. We have also prevented users from changing certain attributes that they shouldn't have write access to, such as `uidNumber`, `homeDirectory`, and so on.

```
dn: olcDatabase={1}mdb,cn=config
changetype: modify
replace: olcAccess
olcAccess: {0}to *
        by dn.exact=gidNumber=0+uidNumber=0,cn=peercred,cn=external,cn=auth manage
        by * none break
-
```

```
add: olcAccess
olcAccess: {1}to attr=entry,member,objectClass,uid,uidNumber,gidNumber,homeDirectory,cn,shad
owWarning,modifyTimestamp
        by group.exact="cn=admins,ou=Groups,dc=example,dc=com" tls_ssf=128 write
        by dn.exact="cn=webadmin,ou=meta,dc=example,dc=com" tls_ssf=128 read
        by anonymous tls_ssf=128 read
        by self tls_ssf=128 read
-
add: olcAccess
olcAccess: {2}to attrs=userPassword
        by dn.exact="cn=webadmin,ou=meta,dc=example,dc=com" tls_ssf=128 auth
        by group.exact="cn=admins,ou=Groups,dc=example,dc=com" tls_ssf=128 write
        by self tls_ssf=128 write
        by anonymous tls_ssf=128 auth
        by * none stop
-
add: olcAccess
olcAccess: {3}to dn.children="ou=People,dc=example,dc=com"
        by dn.exact="cn=webadmin,ou=meta,dc=example,dc=com" read
        by group.exact="cn=admins,ou=Groups,dc=example,dc=com" write
        by self write
        by users read
-
add: olcAccess
olcAccess: {4}to dn.children="ou=Groups,dc=example,dc=com"
        by dn.exact="cn=webadmin,ou=meta,dc=example,dc=com" read
        by group.exact="cn=admins,ou=Groups,dc=example,dc=com" write
-
add: olcAccess
olcAccess: {5}to dn.children="ou=meta,dc=example,dc=com"
        by dn.exact="cn=webadmin,ou=meta,dc=example,dc=com" read
        by group.exact="cn=admins,ou=Groups,dc=example,dc=com" write
        by self read
-
add: olcAccess
olcAccess: {6}to dn.children="ou=Hosts,dc=example.com"
        by group.exact="cn=admins,ou=Groups,dc=example,dc=com" write
        by dn.exact="cn=webadmin,ou=meta,dc=example,dc=com" search
-
add: olcAccess
olcAccess: {7}to * by * none
```

Setting Up sssd

To authenticate against an LDAP server from our Linux clients, we will install a package called sssd. It is designed as a daemon that will authenticate against a wide range of authentication services, including LDAP.

On Ubuntu, you need these packages installed:

```
$ sudo aptitude install sssd
```

On CentOS, of course, you would use YUM to install the same package name. They also take the same configuration. We need to create a file called /etc/sssd/sssd.conf. This file needs to have the 0600 permission set.

This file itself will have the following contents:

```
[sssd]
config_file_version = 2
services = nss, pam
domains = LDAP

[domain/LDAP]
cache_credentials = true

id_provider = ldap
auth_provider = ldap

ldap_uri = ldap://ldap.example.com
ldap_search_base = dc=example,dc=com
ldap_id_use_start_tls = true
ldap_tls_reqcert = demand
ldap_tls_cacert = /etc/ssl/certs/cacert.pem
chpass_provider = ldap
ldap_chpass_uri = ldap://ldap.example.com
entry_cache_timeout = 6
ldap_network_timeout = 2
ldap_group_member = uniquemember
ldap_pwdlockout_dn = cn=ppolicy,ou=policies,dc=example,dc=com
ldap_access_order = lockout
```

The main directives in this file can be found in man sssd.conf and sssd-ldap. But the first section tells sssd that we are going to use nss and pam to run our LDAP domain. In the LDAP domain section we have the provider for id and auth and then the connection details including TLS settings and password policy details.

When Linux looks for a piece of information such as a host or a password, it checks a file called /etc/nsswitch.conf for where to find that information. The nsswitch.conf file will need to be updated with the following information to tell it to use sssd for passwd, group, and shadow files; this is the information required to log in.

```
passwd:     files sss
group:      files sss
shadow:     files sss
gshadow:    files

hosts:      files mdns4_minimal [NOTFOUND=return] dns
networks:   files

protocols:  db files
services:   db files sss
ethers:     db files
rpc:        db files
```

```
# pre_auth-client-config # netgroup:          nis
netgroup:   nis sss
sudoers:    files sss
```

We have the information we seek on the left, and then we have where to look for that information on the right and the order to look for it. For example, when we require information that is normally contained in the /etc/passwd file (like username), we first look in that file. If the username is not found in the file, we then query the sssd daemon (or sss). The same applies for group and shadow.

The next part we need to update is the PAM authentication modules. We need to allow us to use sss(d) for authentication via PAM. On Ubuntu we do that by changing the following (we have removed the comments from the example):

```
/etc/pam.d/common-auth
auth     [success=3 default=ignore]    pam_unix.so nullok_secure
auth     [success=2 default=ignore]    pam_sss.so use_first_pass
auth     [success=1 default=ignore]    pam_ldap.so use_first_pass
auth     requisite                     pam_deny.so
auth     required                      pam_permit.so

/etc/pam.d/common-password
password requisite                     pam_pwquality.so retry=3
password [success=3 default=ignore]    pam_unix.so obscure use_authtok try_first_pass sha512
password sufficient                    pam_sss.so use_authtok
password [success=1 user_unknown=ignore default=die]   pam_ldap.so use_authtok try_first_pass
password requisite                     pam_deny.so
password required                      pam_permit.so
password optional                      pam_gnome_keyring.so

/etc/pam.d/common-account
account  [success=2 new_authtok_reqd=done default=ignore]    pam_unix.so
account  [success=1 default=ignore]  pam_ldap.so
account  requisite                     pam_deny.so
account  required                      pam_permit.so
account  sufficient                    pam_localuser.so
account  [default=bad success=ok user_unknown=ignore]     pam_sss.so

/etc/pam.d/common-session
session  [default=1]                   pam_permit.so
session  requisite                     pam_deny.so
session  required                      pam_permit.so
session  optional                      pam_umask.so
session  required                      pam_unix.so
session  optional                      pam_sss.so
session  optional                      pam_ldap.so
session  optional                      pam_systemd.so
session  required                      pam_mkhomedir.so skel=/etc/skel umask=0022
```

These files should be updated for you when you have installed sssd on Ubuntu, and we will not need to change them. You will note that at the end of the common-session file we are allowing authenticated users to make their own home directories and populate them with the contents of /etc/skel.

On CentOS you may have to add these pam directives to /etc/pam.d/system-auth yourself. They are slightly different but basically the same for both distributions.

```
auth        required        pam_env.so
auth        sufficient      pam_fprintd.so
auth        sufficient      pam_unix.so nullok try_first_pass
auth        sufficient      pam_sss.so use_first_pass
auth        requisite       pam_succeed_if.so uid >= 1000 quiet_success
auth        required        pam_deny.so

account     required        pam_unix.so
account     sufficient      pam_localuser.so
account     sufficient      pam_succeed_if.so uid < 1000 quiet
account     [default=bad success=ok user_unknown=ignore]  pam_sss.so
account     required        pam_permit.so

password    requisite       pam_pwquality.so try_first_pass local_users_only retry=3 authtok_
type=
password    sufficient      pam_unix.so sha512 shadow nullok try_first_pass use_authtok
password    sufficient      pam_sss.so use_authtok
password    required        pam_deny.so

session     optional        pam_keyinit.so revoke
session     required        pam_limits.so
-session    optional        pam_systemd.so
session     [success=1 default=ignore] pam_succeed_if.so service in crond quiet use_uid
session     optional        pam_mkhomedir.so skel=/etc/skel umask=0022
session     required        pam_unix.so
```

We discussed configuring PAM in Chapter 5, but we are going to talk about it some more in the "How PAM Works" section coming up.

Now that we have PAM and sssd configured, we only need to make sure that we can connect to the LDAP server from the client. In our sssd.conf file, we specified the ldap_tls_cacert. We need to make sure that we have /etc/ssl/certs/cacert.pem installed in the correct location; otherwise, we will be rejected from the LDAP server.

Once we have placed cacert.pem in the correct place, we can test to see whether we can query the LDAP server for users.

```
$ grep ataylor /etc/passwd
```

On our host, this returns no result, meaning that the user ataylor has not been created, but we did create her in our LDAP configuration. We are going to use a command called getent to query the passwd file and the sssd (as directed by our configuration in nsswitch.conf; getent is a tool for querying those entries).

```
$ getent passwd ataylor
ataylor:*:1002:1000:Angela Taylor:/home/ataylor:
```

We have been returned the user details for Angela Taylor, including the UID/GID and home directory information. This means we can talk and return information from our LDAP server successfully.

The next step is to prove that we can log in as her. To do that, we are going to use the su command, or superuser command. This command allows you to sign in as the root user or into another account. When we issue this command, we will be asked to provide Angela's password.

```
jsmith@au-mel-ubuntu-2:~$ su - ataylor
Password:
ataylor@au-mel-ubuntu-2:~$
```

Here we have successfully signed into a user that exists only in LDAP. A home directory has been created as we signed in for the first time. Now any LDAP user can sign into our hosts and have their home directories created.

We can further refine our sssd.conf file to filter for certain users, like only if they have exampleActive set to TRUE.

```
ldap_access_filter = (exampleActive=TRUE)
```

If you are using the Ubuntu Unity desktop, you will need to make a change to the following file to allow other users to log in from the desktop:

```
/usr/share/lightdm/lightdm.conf.d/50-unity-greeter.conf
[Seat:*]
greeter-session=unity-greeter
greeter-show-manual-login=true
```

This will allow you to see a screen like in Figure 16-11 after a reboot of your Ubuntu desktop. After you enter your username, you'll enter your password, as shown in Figure 16-12.

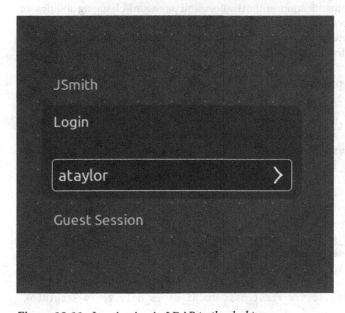

Figure 16-11. *Logging in via LDAP to the desktop*

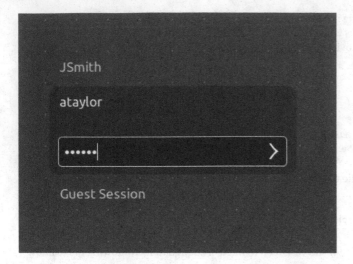

Figure 16-12. *Providing the LDAP password*

You will be able to provide an LDAP username and password with CentOS too, without having to configure anything special.

How PAM Works

As explained in Chapter 5, Linux can use Pluggable Authentication Modules (PAM) to authenticate services against your LDAP service. PAM provides authentication, authorization, and password-changing abilities for hosts against LDAP servers. PAM is configured via the files located in the /etc/pam.d directory. As described in Chapter 5, the main PAM file on your CentOS host is the /etc/pam.d/system-auth file. Listing 16-6 shows an example of the settings required to establish LDAP authentication on your host.

Listing 16-6. PAM Settings for system-auth on CentOS

```
auth        required      pam_env.so
auth        sufficient    pam_fprintd.so
auth        sufficient    pam_unix.so nullok try_first_pass
auth        sufficient    pam_sss.so use_first_pass
auth        requisite     pam_succeed_if.so uid >= 1000 quiet_success
auth        required      pam_deny.so

account     required      pam_unix.so
account     sufficient    pam_localuser.so
account     sufficient    pam_succeed_if.so uid < 1000 quiet
account     [default=bad success=ok user_unknown=ignore]  pam_sss.so
account     required      pam_permit.so

password    requisite      pam_pwquality.so try_first_pass local_users_only retry=3 authtok_
type=
password    sufficient    pam_unix.so sha512 shadow nullok try_first_pass use_authtok
password    sufficient    pam_sss.so use_authtok
password    required      pam_deny.so
```

```
session     optional     pam_keyinit.so revoke
session     required     pam_limits.so
-session    optional     pam_systemd.so
session     [success=1 default=ignore] pam_succeed_if.so service in crond quiet use_uid
session     optional     pam_mkhomedir.so skel=/etc/skel umask=0022
session     required     pam_unix.so
```

This file is generated for you, and you should not have to alter it yourself unless there is a good reason. You can see from Listing 16-6 that the file is made up of four independent management groups: auth, account, password, and session.

Take a look at the following line, which is an example of the auth management group:

```
auth        sufficient   pam_sss.so use_first_pass
```

This group authenticates the user usually by some password challenge-response mechanism. The sufficient control value says that if this module is successful, consider the user authenticated. pam_sss. so is the PAM shared object to be used, the code that determines how a user is authenticated. Lastly, use_first_pass is the optional syntax that says instead of asking for your password again, use the first one provided by one of the higher modules in the stack.

On Ubuntu hosts, the corresponding files are common-auth, common-password, common-session, and common-account in the /etc/pam.d directory.

■ **Note**   You can read more about PAM in the *System Administrator's Guide* here: www.linux-pam.org/
Linux-PAM-html/Linux-PAM_SAG.html.

The other file central to PAM authenticating against an LDAP service is /etc/nsswitch.conf. This file requires the passwd, group, and shadow keywords to have these values:

```
passwd: files ldap
group:  files ldap
shadow: files ldap
```

As we have explained, these tell PAM what authentication databases to use and the order in which to use them. So when we are looking for information we would normally find in /etc/passwd, we would first use the files on the host and then use LDAP. The same goes for group and shadow. The PAM and nsswitch.conf files should be configured for you by the authentication configuration tools provided by your distribution.

■ **Note**   When using different authentication services, you may have to map certain attributes. Mapping of attributes is done when the authentication service requires a certain attribute that is not normally provided with OpenLDAP, say, an attribute required by an AD server. You'll find the Red Hat docs for doing this at https://
access.redhat.com/documentation/en-US/Red_Hat_Enterprise_Linux/7/html/Windows_Integration_
Guide/sssd-ad-integration.html.

LDAP and Apache Authentication

Let's now look at how we get our web server to use our LDAP server to authenticate clients. When clients try to access the `https://ldap.example.com` web site, they will be required to enter their LDAP username and password before they gain access. We will do two things to our web server to achieve this: make all our communications with our web server secure by enabling SSL on our web host and add the LDAP details to the `ldap.example.com` virtual host.

■ **Note**   Chapter 11 discussed Apache virtual hosts.

We will assume this is being run from the `ldap.example.com` host and that there is no other Apache service running on it.

Next, let's examine the changes we will make to our `ldap.example.com` virtual host file.

```
$ sudo vi /etc/apache2/sites-available/ldap.example.com.conf
LDAPTrustedGlobalCert CA_BASE64 /etc/ldap/certs/cacert.pem
LDAPTrustedMode TLS

<VirtualHost 192.168.0.1:443>
  ServerName ldap.example.com
  SSLEngine on
  SSLCertificateFile /etc/ldap/certs/ldap.example.com.cert
  SSLCertificateKeyFile /etc/ldap/certs/ldap.example.com.key
  SSLCACertificateFile /etc/ldap/certs/cacert.pem

  LogFormat "%v %l %u %t \"%r\" %>s %b" comonvhost
  CustomLog /var/log/apache2/ldap.example.com_access.log comonvhost
  ErrorLog /var/log/apache2/ldap.example.com_error.log
  Loglevel debug

  <Location /lam >
     AuthType Basic
     AuthName "LDAP example.com"
     AuthBasicProvider ldap
     AuthLDAPBindAuthoritative on
     AuthLDAPURL ldap://ldap.example.com/ou=people,dc=example,dc=com?uid?sub
     AuthLDAPBindDN cn=webadmin,ou=meta,dc=example,dc=com
     AuthLDAPBindPassword <thewebadminpasswordincleartext>
     Require valid-user
     Require ldap-group cn=admins,ou=groups,dc=example,dc=com
  </Location>

  Include /etc/ldap-account-manager/apache.conf

</VirtualHost>
```

■ **Note**   On CentOS hosts, this file can be found in `/etc/httpd/conf.d/vhost.conf`, depending on how you manage your virtual hosts on CentOS.

Inside the <VirtualHost> tags, we have added a Location directive. The Location directive says that any URI matching /lam will now trigger the following configuration, prompting the user to authenticate against LDAP:

```
AuthType Basic
AuthName "LDAP example.com"
AuthBasicProvider ldap
AuthLDAPBindAuthoritative on
AuthLDAPURL ldap://ldap.example.com/ou=people,dc=example,dc=com?uid?sub
AuthLDAPBindDN cn=webadmin,ou=meta,dc=example,dc=com
AuthLDAPBindPassword Zf3If7Ay
Require valid-user
Require ldap-group cn=admins,ou=groups,dc=example,dc=com
```

We have set AuthType to Basic and AuthName to LDAP example.com. AuthType defines the method of authentication, and you have a choice between Basic and Digest. LDAP authentication requires Basic. AuthName is the name in the authentication window that pops up.

AuthBasicProvider ldap defines the server we are going to use, in this case the LDAP server, to provide our authentication mechanism. We indicate that we want the LDAP server to be the authoritative service to accept or decline access by specifying AuthzLDAPAuthoritative on. Next is the LDAP URL we are going to use for our authentication service, AuthLDAPURL ldap:// ldap.example.com/ou=people,dc=example, dc=com?uid?sub. It specifies the base of our searches, ou=people,dc=example,dc=com; the attribute we are interested in, uid; and the scope of our searches, sub. Here you can now see where we are using the cn=web admin,ou=meta,dc=example,dc=com meta account, which will bind to our LDAP server with the password also provided. You don't have to provide the password as clear text; if it makes you uncomfortable, you can try these other methods as well:

- https://httpd.apache.org/docs/2.4/mod/mod_authnz_ldap.html#authldapbind
  password

Finally, we specify that we require a valid user, and the authenticating user must also belong to the LDAP group cn=admin,ou=groups,dc=example,dc=com.

■ **Note** To find out more on LDAP and Apache authentication, read the following: https://httpd.apache. org/docs/2.4/mod/mod_authnz_ldap.html.

Before we proceed, we will need to make sure that the modules are added to our web host, and on Ubuntu we would do the following:

```
$ sudo a2enmod authnz_ldap
$ sudo a2enmod ldap
$ sudo a2enmod ssl
```

For CentOS, we need to make sure that the packages mod_ssl and mod_ldap are installed; this will create the file in the conf.modules.d directory.

```
$ cat /etc/httpd/conf.modules.d/01-ldap.conf
# This file configures the LDAP modules:
LoadModule ldap_module modules/mod_ldap.so
LoadModule authnz_ldap_module modules/mod_authnz_ldap.so
```

We need to now restart our Apache service (restart apache2 for Ubuntu).

```
$ sudo systemctl restart httpd
```

We use our web browser now to connect to the LAM web GUI at the following address: https://ldap.example.com/lam.

In Figure 16-13, you can see the authentication challenge provided by Apache. We have entered the uid of ataylor, whom we know is a member of the cn=admins,ou=groups,dc=example,dc=com group, which is required by our Apache configuration.

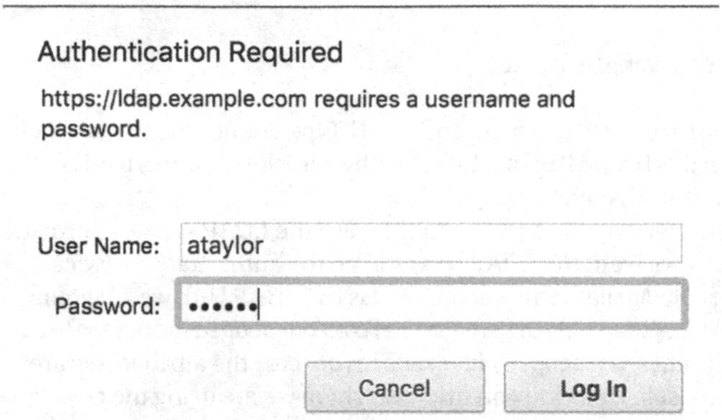

Authentication Required

https://ldap.example.com requires a username and password.

User Name: ataylor

Password: ••••••

Cancel   Log In

Figure 16-13. *The Apache request for username and password*

You should now be able to access LAM, and you should see the successful login in the Apache logs.

```
...authorization result of Require ldap-group cn=admins,ou=groups,dc=example,dc=com...
...auth_ldap authenticate: accepting ataylor....
...authorization result of Require valid-user : granted...
```

This shows that the LDAP server is authenticating our request using the username ataylor and testing that this user is a member of the cn=admin,ou=groups,dc=example,dc=com group. This level of detail is provided by the debug logging option in the virtual host LogLevel directive.

Summary

In this chapter, we discussed what a directory server is and how the entries are organized in the directory information tree. We showed you how to configure and install an OpenLDAP directory server and populate it with user accounts and management accounts. We discussed schemata, indexes, and access control lists. We showed you how to use the various client tools provided by OpenLDAP to query and manage the LDAP server. You can now set up a web GUI to manage your LDAP directory and integrate LDAP into your network and existing applications.

You should now be able to do the following:

- Install and configure OpenLDAP on Ubuntu and CentOS hosts

- Understand and configure access control lists

- Query and manage your LDAP directory

- Install and configure the LAM web GUI

- Set up single sign-on for Linux to LDAP

- Configure Apache web server to use LDAP authentication to authenticate client access

Directory services, as we have said, can play a central part in your network, and there are many things about this topic we have not even touched on in this chapter. We recommend that you purchase a book dedicated to the subject, read the online documentation at `www.openldap.org`, and use the mailing lists to help you further your knowledge in this area.

In the next chapter, you will read about performance monitoring and optimization.

CHAPTER 17

■ ■ ■

Performance Monitoring and Optimization

By Peter Lieverdink and Dennis Matotek

Now that your host is providing you services, it is important that it continue to do so. As your business grows, so will the workload on your servers. In this chapter, we will show you how to monitor resources such as disk space and processor and RAM usage. This will help you identify performance bottlenecks and make better use of the resources you have.

A small amount of tuning can alleviate the need to purchase additional hardware, so monitoring performance can help you save money as well as time.

Basic Health Checks

In this section, we look at some basic tools that help you determine the status of your hosts.

CPU Usage

When applications are running slow, the first thing you should check is whether the system is in fact busy doing anything. The quickest way to find out is via the uptime command, as shown in Listing 17-1.

Listing 17-1. The uptime Command

```
$ uptime
12:51:04 up 116 days, 7:09, 3 users, load average: 0.01, 0.07, 0.02
```

This command prints a short overview of the system status, including the current time, the amount of time the system has been on (or up), the number of logged-in users, and three numbers representing the system's workload.

In our example, the system was last booted 116 days, 7 hours, and 9 minutes ago. If you lose connectivity with a remote server, this allows you to easily determine whether the system was rebooted once you can log back in.

The number of logged-in users is the total number of current logins via the terminal console, in X, and via SSH. If you are logged in twice, you will be counted as two users. Users connected to a service like Samba or Apache are not counted here.

© Dennis Matotek, James Turnbull and Peter Lieverdink 2017
D. Matotek et al., *Pro Linux System Administration*, DOI 10.1007/978-1-4842-2008-5_17

Finally, the system load is displayed in three numbers. These numbers form an index that indicates the average ratio of work scheduled to be done by a CPU versus the work actually being done, over the past 1-minute, 5-minute, and 15-minute periods.

A load of 1.00 means the amount of work being scheduled is identical to the amount of work a CPU can handle. Confusingly, if a host contains multiple CPUs, the load for each CPU is added to create a total; on a host with four CPU cores, a load of 4.00 means the same as a load of 1.00 on a single-core system.

In our example, the average workload over the past minute was about 1 percent. Some extra tasks were running and probably completed a few minutes ago, as the average workload over the past 5 minutes was 7 percent.

Though these numbers should by no means be taken as gospel, they do provide a quick way to check whether a system is likely to be healthy. If the system load is 6.00 on a host with eight CPU cores, a lot of tasks may have just finished running. If the load is 60, a problem exists.

This problem can be that the host is running a few processes that monopolize the CPU, not allowing other processes enough cycles. We'll show you how to find these processes with the top utility a bit later. Alternatively, your host might be trying to run far more processes than it can cope with, again not leaving enough CPU cycles for any of them. This may happen if a badly written application or daemon keeps spawning copies of itself. See the "Fork Bomb" sidebar for more information. We'll show you how to prevent this using the ulimit command later.

Finally, it's possible that a process is waiting for the host to perform a task that cannot be interrupted, such as moving data to or from disk. If this task must be completed before the process can continue, the process is said to be in uninterruptible sleep. It will count toward a higher load average but won't actually be using the CPU. We'll show you how to check how much the disk is being used in the "Advanced Tools" section a bit later.

FORK BOMB

We explained in Chapter 5 that when a daemon or service runs in the background, it forks a child process and makes init the parent process, while the original process exits. It's perfectly possible for a misbehaving application to do the wrong thing and keep forking child processes, rather than exiting. This is called a *fork bomb*.

A fork bomb creates new copies of itself as fast as the host will allow. One process creates two, two create two more, four leads to eight, and so on, thus starving other processes of resources such as CPU cycles and, eventually, RAM.

Memory Usage

Another cause of reduced performance is excessive memory use. If a task starts using a lot of memory, the host will be forced to free up memory for it by putting other tasks into swap memory. Accessing swap memory, which after all is just a piece of disk that is used as if it were memory, is very slow compared to accessing RAM.

You can quickly check how much RAM and swap memory a host is using via the free command. We'll pass it the -h (human-readable) option so it displays the sizes in gigabytes (-g), megabytes (-m), or kilobytes (-k), as in Listing 17-2.

Listing 17-2. The free Command

```
$ free -h
              total      used       free      shared      buff/cache     available
Mem:          3.1G       59M        2.7G      13M         350M           2.8G
Swap:         1.5G       0B         1.5G
```

This listing gives you an instant overview of whether the system is running low on available memory. The first line tells you the status of RAM use. The total is the amount of RAM that is available to this host. This is then divided into RAM that is in use and RAM that is free. Different versions of the free program may show different memory values on the same system.

The shared refers to shared memory, mainly tmpfs. This matches the /proc/meminfo Shmem value (space used by the kernel).

The buffers column tells you the amount of memory the kernel is using to act as a disk write buffer. This buffer allows applications to write data quickly and have the kernel deal with writing it to disk in the background. Data can also be read from this buffer, providing an additional speed increase. The last column, cached, tells you how much memory the kernel is using as a cache to have access to information quickly.

Both the buffer and cache are resized as needed. If an application needs more RAM, the kernel will free up part of the cache or buffer space and reallocate the memory. If swap space is available, the kernel can move inactive memory to the swap space.

Finally, the last line tells us how much swap space the host is using. Over time, this number will rise slightly, as services that aren't being used can be parked in swap space by the kernel. Doing this allows it to reclaim the otherwise idle RAM and use it as buffer or cache.

This means that having your host use swap space is not necessarily a bad thing. However, if all memory and all swap space are in use, there is obviously a problem. In our case, we are not using any swap space and so it is showing as 0s out of a possible 1.5GB available to us.

■ **Note** On Linux, free memory means wasted memory, as it is not being utilized, not even as buffer or cache.

We'll show you how to find out how much memory individual tasks are using in the "Advanced Tools" section.

Disk Space

The other finite resources a computer system has are disk space and disk speed. Generally speaking, a system won't slow down when a disk becomes full, but services may crash and cause your users grief, so it pays to keep an eye on usage and make more storage available when needed.

We'll show you how to check for disk speed problems in the next section.

■ **Note** We covered the df and du tools for checking available and used disk space in Chapter 9.

Logs

Finally, if something untoward has occurred with an application or the kernel, you'll likely find a log entry in your system or kernel log. You will of course want to restart any service that crashed, but checking the logs for the cause of the problem will help you prevent the same thing from happening again.

If the log daemon itself has stopped, you can still check the kernel log buffer via the dmesg command.

■ **Note** We will cover logging in detail in Chapter 18.

Advanced Tools

The basic tools give you a quick overview but don't provide any information to help you determine the cause of a problem, if there is one. To this end, we'll show you some tools that can help you pinpoint bottlenecks.

CPU and Memory Use

To list details about currently running tasks, Linux provides the top utility. This is similar to the Task Manager you may be used to from Windows or Activity Monitor on macOS, but it runs in a terminal window, as shown in Figure 17-1. It provides a sortable and configurable listing of running processes and threads on the host. You access it with the following command:

```
$ top
```

```
×   vagrant@localhost:~                                                    ≡
top - 10:53:51 up 1 day,  5:40,  1 user,  load average: 0.00, 0.01, 0.05
Tasks:  90 total,   2 running,  88 sleeping,   0 stopped,   0 zombie
%Cpu(s):  0.0 us,  0.0 sy,  0.0 ni,100.0 id,  0.0 wa,  0.0 hi,  0.0 si,  0.0 st
KiB Mem :  3045392 total,  2737276 free,    95400 used,   212716 buff/cache
KiB Swap:  1572860 total,  1572860 free,        0 used.  2794264 avail Mem

  PID USER      PR  NI    VIRT    RES    SHR S %CPU %MEM     TIME+ COMMAND
    1 root      20   0   44520   7216   2620 S  0.0  0.2   0:02.11 systemd
    2 root      20   0       0      0      0 S  0.0  0.0   0:00.00 kthreadd
    3 root      20   0       0      0      0 S  0.0  0.0   0:00.03 ksoftirqd/0
    4 root      20   0       0      0      0 S  0.0  0.0   0:00.00 kworker/0:0
    6 root      20   0       0      0      0 S  0.0  0.0   0:00.00 kworker/u2:0
    7 root      rt   0       0      0      0 S  0.0  0.0   0:00.00 migration/0
    8 root      20   0       0      0      0 S  0.0  0.0   0:00.00 rcu_bh
    9 root      20   0       0      0      0 S  0.0  0.0   0:00.00 rcuob/0
   10 root      20   0       0      0      0 S  0.0  0.0   0:00.95 rcu_sched
   11 root      20   0       0      0      0 R  0.0  0.0   0:01.59 rcuos/0
   12 root      rt   0       0      0      0 S  0.0  0.0   0:00.70 watchdog/0
   13 root       0 -20       0      0      0 S  0.0  0.0   0:00.00 khelper
   14 root      20   0       0      0      0 S  0.0  0.0   0:00.00 kdevtmpfs
   15 root       0 -20       0      0      0 S  0.0  0.0   0:00.00 netns
   16 root       0 -20       0      0      0 S  0.0  0.0   0:00.00 perf
   17 root       0 -20       0      0      0 S  0.0  0.0   0:00.00 writeback
   18 root       0 -20       0      0      0 S  0.0  0.0   0:00.00 kintearitvd
```

Figure 17-1. *The top utility*

The top of the output gives you a few header lines, which includes the information from uptime, as well as some aggregated data from the free and vmstat commands, which we'll discuss in the "Swap Space Use" and "Disk Access" sections a bit later. You can toggle these headers on and off. The L key toggles the display of the load average line. You can toggle the task summary via the T key and memory information via M.

The rest of the display consists of several columns of information about running processes and threads. The columns you see here are shown by default, but you can enable or disable others as well. We've listed their headers and meaning in Table 17-1.

Table 17-1. *top Column Headers*

Header	Meaning
PID	Task's process ID. This unique identifier allows you to manipulate a task.
USER	The username of the task's owner; the account it runs as.
PR	The task priority.
NI	The task niceness; an indication of how willing this task is to yield CPU cycles to other tasks. A lower or negative niceness means a high priority.
VIRT	The total amount of memory allocated by the task, including shared and swap memory.
RES	The total amount of physical memory used by the task, excluding swap memory.
SHR	The amount of shared memory used by the task. This memory is usually allocated by libraries and also is usable by other tasks.
S	Task status. This indicates whether a task is running (R), sleeping (D or S), stopped (T), or zombie (Z).
%CPU	Percentage of CPU cycles this task has used since the last screen update.
%MEM	Percentage of available RAM used by this task.
TIME+	Total CPU time the task has used since it started.
COMMAND	The name of the task being monitored.

You can obtain full descriptions for these and all other available fields in the man top manual page.

By default, the tasks are displayed in descending order and sorted by %CPU. The process consuming the most CPU time will be at the top of the list, which is immediately useful for problem solving.

We can sort on many columns in top. To sort on CPU usage, we will need to sort the %CPU column. We can choose a column to sort by pressing the F key, which brings up a list of available columns, as shown in Figure 17-2.

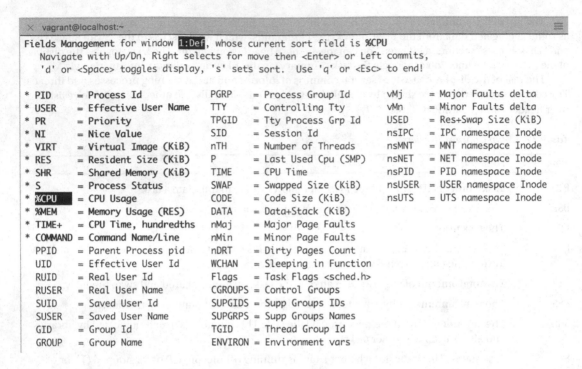

```
✕  vagrant@localhost:~                                                    ≡

Fields Management for window 1:Def, whose current sort field is %CPU
   Navigate with Up/Dn, Right selects for move then <Enter> or Left commits,
   'd' or <Space> toggles display, 's' sets sort. Use 'q' or <Esc> to end!

* PID     = Process Id          PGRP   = Process Group Id    vMj    = Major Faults delta
* USER    = Effective User Name TTY    = Controlling Tty     vMn    = Minor Faults delta
* PR      = Priority            TPGID  = Tty Process Grp Id  USED   = Res+Swap Size (KiB)
* NI      = Nice Value          SID    = Session Id          nsIPC  = IPC namespace Inode
* VIRT    = Virtual Image (KiB) nTH    = Number of Threads   nsMNT  = MNT namespace Inode
* RES     = Resident Size (KiB) P      = Last Used Cpu (SMP) nsNET  = NET namespace Inode
* SHR     = Shared Memory (KiB) TIME   = CPU Time            nsPID  = PID namespace Inode
* S       = Process Status      SWAP   = Swapped Size (KiB)  nsUSER = USER namespace Inode
* %CPU    = CPU Usage           CODE   = Code Size (KiB)     nsUTS  = UTS namespace Inode
* %MEM    = Memory Usage (RES)  DATA   = Data+Stack (KiB)
* TIME+   = CPU Time, hundredths nMaj  = Major Page Faults
* COMMAND = Command Name/Line   nMin   = Minor Page Faults
  PPID    = Parent Process pid  nDRT   = Dirty Pages Count
  UID     = Effective User Id   WCHAN  = Sleeping in Function
  RUID    = Real User Id        Flags  = Task Flags <sched.h>
  RUSER   = Real User Name      CGROUPS = Control Groups
  SUID    = Saved User Id       SUPGIDS = Supp Groups IDs
  SUSER   = Saved User Name     SUPGRPS = Supp Groups Names
  GID     = Group Id            TGID   = Thread Group Id
  GROUP   = Group Name          ENVIRON = Environment vars
```

Figure 17-2. *Choosing a sort field*

The first line tells us the current sort field, %CPU. Below that we have instructions on how to choose a different sort field. The up and down arrows navigate to the different fields. If you press s, you will see that that field is now selected. The d key and spacebar toggle whether that field will be displayed. You can use q or the Escape key to go back to the top screen with your selection. We can press s to make the %CPU column our sort field and then press q to go back to the task list. All processes are now sorted by the number of CPU cycles they use, so if a process is running amok, you'll be able to spot it easily.

■ **Note**   It is possible to select more fields than will fit onscreen. If this happens, you will need to unselect some other fields to make space.

ORPHANS AND ZOMBIES: UNDEAD TASKS

Apart from the initial process, systemd or init, every task on a Linux host is controlled by a parent process, and it reports its status to this parent when it completes execution.

Sometimes things go wrong, though, and a parent process might crash, leaving a completed child waiting to report its status to its parent. This creates an orphan process, and it is adopted by systemd (or init). When it is finished, it reports and is reaped (or cleaned up).

A zombie process is a child process that has terminated but still exists in the process table awaiting its parent to read its exit status. This is how every child process ends. A parent will send a wait system call to the child process to read its exit status. If this does not happen, the process cannot be removed from the process list and remains there. It is not necessarily a problem as it should be eventually reaped by the parent or by systemd (init). In this state, it has already deallocated its memory and is not using CPU. However, it can point to a problem with a program whose parent crashes and does not reap its children.

You can view a zombie process by grepping the process list output.

```
$ ps aux |grep Z
USER    PID    %CPU %MEM   VSZ   RSS   TTY    STAT   START   TIME   COMMAND
ubuntu  7814   0.0  0.0    0     0     pts/0  Z+     11:52   0:00   [zombie] <defunct>
```

You can read more about zombies at http://en.wikipedia.org/wiki/Zombie_process.

Many more display options are available in top, and you can find them on the help menu. Press ? to access it. When you have customized the way top displays information to your liking, you can save the configuration by pressing W. This will write the settings to a file called .toprc in your home directory.

If you find a misbehaving task, you can use top to quit it. To do this, press k and enter the PID of the task in question. You will then be asked for the signal to send to the process. The signal to make a process terminate normally is 15. If this doesn't work, you might want to try sending signal 3, which is a bit sterner, or signal 9, which is akin to axe-murdering the process.

To find out more about signals, read the "Killing Is Not Always Murder" sidebar.

■ **Note**   You need to be the process owner or root user to be allowed to send signals to a process.

KILLING IS NOT ALWAYS MURDER

Though the act of sending signals to processes is called *killing* and is usually done via the kill command, it won't necessarily quit the process. It uses a facility in the kernel to send processes a signal.

Provided services have been designed to listen for this signal; they can be made to perform an action. Most commonly used is signal 1—also known as HUP. This signal causes most services to reload their configuration files, removing the need to stop and restart them.

If you want an application or process to quit, you can ask it to do so by sending it the SIGTERM or SIGQUIT signal, which are 15 and 3, respectively. A task that is ignoring polite requests to stop may be forced to via the 9, or SIGKILL, signal.

Sending SIGKILL will immediately stop the process regardless of what it is doing. This could leave your process (and possibly data) in a messy state, so use with care. SIGTERM will allow the process to close down gracefully before exiting.

You can read more about signals and what they do in the man 7 signal manual page.

If you have a process that is using too much CPU time and interrupting more important processes, you can try making it nicer, by lowering its priority. This means it will yield more easily to other processes, allowing them to use some of the CPU cycles that were assigned to it. You can change process niceness by pressing the R key. top will ask you for the process ID and then the new niceness value.

Unless you run top as root or via sudo, you can only make processes nicer. You cannot raise their priority, only lower it.

When done, press q to quit top.

■ **Note**   You can also use the renice utility to change niceness and priority without using top. For instance, to change the niceness of process 8612, you would run renice +5 8612.

Swap Space Use

If you see a lot of swap space in use, it may indicate the system is running low on memory. Swap space and RAM make up the total allocatable memory available to your system. The kernel will swap out less used memory pages into the swap space when it requires memory for a particular process and does not have that immediately available. This isn't necessarily a bad thing, but if the system is "heavily swapping" (that is, moving memory pages in and out of swap space frequently, then because swap is much slower than RAM, it can lead to poor performance).

You can check whether this is the case via the vmstat utility. You normally want to tell this utility to print information every few seconds so you can spot any trends. Pass the -n option to prevent the headers from being reprinted and tell it to redisplay statistics every 5 seconds, as shown in Figure 17-3. Press Ctrl+C to quit vmstat.

```
jsmith@au-mel-ubuntu-2:~$ vmstat -n 5
procs -----------memory---------- ---swap-- -----io---- -system-- ------cpu-----
 r  b   swpd   free   buff  cache   si   so    bi    bo   in   cs us sy id wa st
 1  0 219864 594068   4420  82392    6   59   406   181   65  159  4  0 95  0  0
 2  1 561236  69688    464  57800 30671 100278 31640 100278 5163 38782  0 81  0 19  0
 1  1 535840  70620    144  57140 62829 61596 64317 61596 3786 55019  0 49  0 51  0
 3  3 529512  74820    140  52764 64014 65162 65675 65162 3882 55585  0 51  0 49  0
 1  1 549424  75896    140  56024 61751 60935 63279 60935 3871 55520  1 49  0 50  0
 1  1 485616  62332    136  54924 62087 58051 64278 58051 3689 53115  0 48  0 52  0
 2  2 541520  76692    136  54532 62319 64746 64188 64746 3939 52545  2 51  0 47  0
```

Figure 17-3. vmstat output on heavily swapping host

This rather impressive jumble of numbers gives us an indication of how much data is moving through the system. Each line consists of sets of numbers in six groups, which provide information on processes, memory, swap, input/output, system, and CPU.

Reduced performance due to excessive swap space usage will show up in two of these groups: swap and cpu.

The si and so columns in the swap group display the amount of swap memory that is being read from (si—swap in) and written to (so—swap out) your swap space. The wa and sy columns in the cpu group tell you the percentage of time the CPU is waiting for data to process system (or kernel) requests—and thus not processing system instructions.

If a host is spending most of its CPU cycles moving applications from and to swap space, the si and so column values will be high. The actual values will depend on the amount of swapping that is occurring and the speed of your swap device. The wa column will usually display values in the high 90s as well, indicating the CPU is waiting for an application or data to be retrieved from swap space.

You can solve this problem by using top to find out which application is using too much RAM and possibly changing its configuration to use less. Mostly you will see your main application is the one using the most memory. In that case, either allocate or install more memory to your system.

■ **Note**   top itself is fairly resource hungry, so if a system is unresponsive and under extremely heavy load, it might be easier and quicker to reboot it than to wait for top to start.

```
procs - ---------memory------------- ---swap-- ---io--- --system-- ------cpu-----
 r  b   swpd   free    buff  cache   si   so    bi   bo    in    cs    us sy id wa st
 0  0  422336 750352  8252 130736    0    0     0    0     27    56     0  0 100  0  0
 0  0  422332 750352  8252 130736    1    0     1    0     27    55     0  0 100  0  0
```

In the previous example, this is an example of a host under light load. This host has low swap space, and the CPU spends most of its time idle.

Disk Access

The vmstat utility will also give us information on how much data is being read from and written to disk. We've highlighted the bi (blocks in) and bo (blocks out) columns in the io group in Figure 17-4. By passing a second number as a parameter, we've told vmstat to quit after five intervals.

```
jsmith@au-mel-ubuntu-2:~$ vmstat 5 5
procs ----------memory---------- ---swap-- ----io---- system-- ------cpu-----
 r  b   swpd   free    buff  cache   si   so    bi   bo    in    cs us sy id wa st
 0  0 421060 150756  6308 730944    92  135   187  458    45   167  1  0 99  0  0
 0  0 421060 147920  6308 733776     1    0   570    0    45    93  0  0 99  0  0
 0  0 421060 147920  6308 733776     0    0     0    0    28    54  0  0 100  0  0
 0  0 421060 147920  6308 733776     0    0     0    0    25    58  0  0 100  0  0
 0  0 421060 147920  6308 733776     0    0     0    0    25    53  0  0 100  0  0
```

Figure 17-4. vmstat with low disk I/O

These two numbers tell you exactly how many blocks of data are being read from (bi) and written to (bo) your disks during each interval. In our case, the system is reading more data from disk than it is writing back, but both numbers are low. Because the block size on our disks is 4KB, this means they aren't very heavily loaded.

■ **Tip**   If you have forgotten the block size of your disk or partition, you can issue the following: blockdev -getbsz <partition>.

What constitutes a heavy load will depend on the block size and the speed of the disks. If a large file is being written, this number will go up for the duration of the write operation but drop down again later.

You can get an idea of what your host is capable of by checking the numbers you get when creating a large file on an otherwise idle system. Run a dd command to create a 1Gb file containing only zeroes in the background, while running vmstat simultaneously, as shown in Figure 17-5.

On the same host we will run the following command:

```
$ dd if=/dev/zero of=./largefile bs=1M count=1024
```

Then when we run the vmstat command at the same time, you will see something similar to Figure 17-5.

```
jsmith@au-mel-ubuntu-2:~$ vmstat 5 5
procs -----------memory---------- ---swap-- -----io---- -system-- ------cpu-----
 r  b   swpd   free   buff  cache   si   so    bi     bo   in   cs us sy id wa st
 2  1 420348  76168  11456 794476   93  136   188    209   44  165  1  0 99  0  0
 0  0 420348  72012  11608 799752    3    1    33   6947   58  128  0  2 98  0  0
 0  0 420456  77440  10276 796020    0   22    10 222955 1240 3704  0 66 33  0  0
 2  0 420572 379396   8928 493384    0   23    30 268810  666 1265  0 62 37  0  0
 2  0 420864  77644   7620 797580    0   58     2 295894 1214 3483  0 81 19  0  0
```

Figure 17-5. *vmstat with high disk I/O*

The bo column is low for the two runs, as the file data is still in the kernel buffer. At the next interval, however, you can see it spike to more than 222,000 blocks. Keep in mind that this is over 5 seconds, though, so we can calculate the peak write rate on this particular host to be around 45,000 blocks per second.

If you notice degraded performance and vmstat shows a bo value that is up near the maximum rate that the system could manage when you tested it for a long time, you have an application or service that is trying very hard to write a lot of data. This usually indicates a problem, so you should find out which application is the culprit and rectify the problem.

Deeper with dstat

How could you find out which application might have a problem? The vmstat command is great to see a problem, but it doesn't allow you to go deeper in your investigations. The dstat command, on the other hand, is a great tool at digging.

You can install dstat via the dstat package on both Ubuntu and CentOS using the package manager YUM or Apt. Once one is installed, you can issue the output shown in Figure 17-6.

```
jsmith@au-mel-ubuntu-2:~$ dstat
You did not select any stats, using -cdngy by default.
----total-cpu-usage---- -dsk/total- -net/total- ---paging-- ---system--
usr sys idl wai hiq siq| read  writ|  recv  send|   in   out | int   csw
  1   0  99   0   0   0|   k     k|    0     0 |    k     k|  45   164
  0   0 100   0   0   0|   0     0 |  300B 1186B|    0     0 |  36    70
  0   0 100   0   0   0|   0     0 |  120B  428B|    0     0 |  31    60
  0   0 100   0   0   0|   0     0 |  120B  428B|    0     0 |  36    68
  0   0 100   0   0   0|   0     0 |  120B  428B|    0     0 |  29    59
  0   0 100   0   0   0|   0     k|  120B  428B|    0     0 |  36    86
  1   0  99   0   0   0|   0     0 |  120B  436B|    0     0 |  32    58
```

Figure 17-6. dstat output

So far it's not that much different from vmstat, except that we have disk reads and writes calculated for us, and we also we have network send and receive information. The CPU, paging, and system are the same as vmstat.

Let's suppose that we have noticed that our application is performing poorly and we think it is due to disk performance. When we look at vmstat, we see the results in Figure 17-7.

```
jsmith@au-mel-ubuntu-2:~$ vmstat 2 2
procs -----------memory---------- ---swap-- -----io---- -system-- ------cpu-----
 r  b   swpd   free   buff  cache   si   so    bi    bo   in   cs us sy id wa st
 1  0 176072 284092   2756 284224    5  262   808 28281  135  402  1  5 93  0  0
 1  0 177600 383668   2856 187228    8  766    10 783502 1200 1122  2 98  0  0  0
```

Figure 17-7. Checking I/O with vmstat

We can see that we have a fair bit of data being written (bo), but we have no idea to what disk. With our pretend application, we have three partitions that are mounted to /app/log, /app/sys, and /app/data. The partitions are sdc1, sdb1, and sdb2 respectively. We will use this information to see what dstat says.

In Figure 17-8 we can see that we have used the –D switch to dstat to pass in the partitions we want to monitor. We have a significant amount of data being written to sdc1, which is our application logging. In our pretend world I would suspect that our application has been started with debug logging.

```
jsmith@au-mel-ubuntu-2:~$ sudo dstat -D sdb1,sdb2,sdc1
You did not select any stats, using -cdngy by default.
----total-cpu-usage---- --dsk/sdb1----dsk/sdb2----dsk/sdc1- -net/total- ---paging-- ---system--
usr sys idl wai hiq siq| read  writ: read  writ: read  writ|  recv  send|   in   out | int   csw
  1   6  88   0   0   4|6590B    k:7403B    k:6629B  66M|    0     0 |4503B    k| 192   438
  2   0   0   0   0   0|   0     0 :   0     0 :   0  640M| 360B 1628B|    k     k|1116  1070
  2   0   0   0   0   0|   0     0 :   0     0 :   0  695M| 540B 1406B|    0     k|1270  2921
  3   0   0   0   0   0|   0     0 :   0     0 :   0  703M| 540B 1398B|    0     0 |1135  1061
  1   0   0   0   0   0|   0     0 :   0     0 :   0  683M| 420B 1106B|    0     0 |1080   802
```

Figure 17-8. dstat disk access

Similarly, you can use the –N switch to supply network interfaces to dstat (-N em1,em2) to report network traffic per interface. The –C will do a similar job for CPUs. You should check the help or man page for more information.

We'll come back to how you can get notifications when system performance degrades when we cover Nagios in Chapter 18.

Continuous Performance Monitoring

Now that you have the basic tools to diagnose where a performance bottleneck is, we will show you how to automate ongoing monitoring. This will give you access to longer-term performance and resource usage data, which in turn allows you to make a better determination on whether and when to upgrade hardware or migrate services to other hosts. We are going to introduce you to the following tools:

- *Collectd*: System statistics collection daemon

- *Graphite*: A store to collect and graph metrics

- *Grafana*: A nice front-end interface for presenting graphs of metrics

Collectd

Collectd is a robust system metrics collection daemon that can collect information about your system and various applications and services. It is highly configurable and works out of the box to collect metrics for you.

We are going to use Collectd to gather metrics from our hosts and send them to Graphite, a metrics collection store. However, you can write metrics to many other back ends using the Write HTTP or Network plug-in.

You can install Collectd on both Ubuntu and CentOS via your package manager. For CentOS you will need to have the epel-release package installed as the Collectd packages aren't available in the standard repositories.

The Ubuntu version available from the standard Ubuntu repositories is slightly behind the current version, but the CentOS version is fairly recent; depending on the features you require, this may affect your install decisions.

Installation is simple. On CentOS you would issue the following to install Collectd and the mysql plug-in:

```
$ sudo yum install collectd collectd-mysql
```

There are several plug-in packages that you can install in the same way, depending on your requirements (use yum search collectd for a list). On Ubuntu it is simply as follows:

```
$ sudo aptitude install collectd
```

Collectd Configuration

The Collectd service is configured from the main collectd.conf file. Of course, there is a slight difference where these are installed. On Ubuntu it is installed into the /etc/collectd directory, and on CentOS it is installed into the /etc/ directory.

You can also drop in configuration files into the collectd.d directory. This of course is different on Ubuntu (/etc/collectd/collectd.conf.d/) compared to CentOS (/etc/collectd.d/).

There is a required format for the configuration files used with Collectd. It is as follows:

```
global options

# plugin without options
LoadPlugin plugin_name
# loading a plugin and overriding options
<LoadPlugin plugin_name>
    ...plugin options...
</LoadPlugin>
# provide an option block to plugins without a LoadPlugin stanza (requires AutoLoadPlugin
true)
<Plugin plugin_name>
    ... plugin options...
</Plugin>
```

There are two types of plug-ins: read plug-ins and write plug-ins (some can be read and write plug-ins). Read plug-ins will collect data, and write plug-ins will put collected data somewhere. Each plug-in can be placed in its own configuration file; however, if there are duplicates that LoadPlugin calls, the first that is read in will be executed, and any other configuration for that plug-in will be silently ignored. The configuration is similar to Apache web server configuration files. Configuration blocks are enclosed in <>...</>.

In this example, we will collect the basic system metrics, such as CPU, memory, and disk space, and we will measure some database stats with the mysql plug-in. Our database server happens to be CentOS, and the installation of the mysql collectd plug-in has placed a mysql.conf file in the /etc/collectd.d directory. The Collectd configuration is the same no matter which distribution you are using.

We will first look at the collectd.conf file (Listing 17-3).

Listing 17-3. collectd.conf Configuration Global Options

```
#Hostname "localhost"
FQDNLookup true
#BaseDir "/var/lib/collectd"
#PluginDir "/usr/lib/collectd"
#TypesDB "/usr/share/collectd/types.db" "/etc/collectd/my_types.db"
#AutoLoadPlugin false
#CollectInternalStats false
#Interval 10
#MaxReadInterval 86400
#Timeout         2
#ReadThreads     5
#WriteThreads    5
#WriteQueueLimitHigh 1000000
#WriteQueueLimitLow   800000
```

The Global options for Collectd apply to the Collectd service itself and define things like the base directory, plug-in directory, interval and read/write threads, and queue limits. These can mostly remain as the defaults. The FQDNLookup line means that it will look up the hostname of the computer this is running on, or you can force this via the Hostname setting.

```
LoadPlugin syslog
<Plugin syslog>
    LogLevel info
</Plugin>
```

We load our first plug-in, and it is used to direct our logs to the `syslog` service with the `LogLevel` of `info`. The debug value is available only if Collectd has been compiled with debugging support, notice, warning, and err are acceptable also.

```
LoadPlugin cpu
LoadPlugin df
LoadPlugin disk
LoadPlugin interface
LoadPlugin load
LoadPlugin memory
LoadPlugin mysql
LoadPlugin swap
LoadPlugin rrdtool
```

In this section we are loading in our plug-ins that we will use for metrics collection. We are covering the basics of `cpu`, `df`, `disk`, `interface`, `load`, `memory`, and `swap`. These should be fairly self-explanatory to you by now. The `mysql` plug-in will be used to collect some InnoDB statistics from our MariaDB database. Finally, we have the `rrdtool` plug-in that will be used to output the metrics as RRD files.

RRD stands for "round-robin database" files, which are normally used to hold time-series data. Time-series databases hold `db` record types such as counts, gauges, and histograms. They can hold these records at different granularities. You might have records that are collected every second, and they can be stored at that granularity in the RRD files. Or we might choose a granularity of 5 minutes for those metrics, and 1-second metrics are rolled up as 5-minute averages.

There are other options for storing your metrics, and we will show you how they can be configured in the next section.

```
<Plugin cpu>
    ReportByCpu true
    ReportByState true
    ValuesPercentage false
</Plugin>
```

When we declare our configuration options for our CPU, we are giving the options to report by CPU and report by state, and we are not showing values as percentages. This will give us an accurate picture of our CPU workloads.

```
<Plugin df>
    FSType rootfs
    FSType sysfs
    FSType proc
    FSType devtmpfs
    FSType devpts
    FSType tmpfs
    FSType fusectl
    FSType cgroup
    IgnoreSelected true
</Plugin>
```

The `df` plug-in shows another example of how to refine the metrics we want to select. In this example we are listing the values we do not want to collect in our metrics, and then we use `IgnoreSelected true` to exclude them from our collection. The file types listed are pseudo-filesystems that just add noise.

```
<Plugin disk>
    Disk "/^(xv)?[hs]?d[a-z]\d?$/"
    IgnoreSelected false
    UseBSDName false
    UdevNameAttr "DEVNAME"
</Plugin>
```

With the disk plug-in, we are doing the opposite of what we did with the df plug-in. Here we are selecting the devices we want to monitor and naming them via a regular expression. We may have disks that are named in the following ways:

```
/dev/sda2
/dev/hdb4
/dev/xvda3
```

We need to be able to match on any of these disk naming conventions. First, we look for the x and v together (^(xv)?) and match this pattern zero or more times at the start of string (^). Next, we may have an h or an s zero or more times ([hs]?). Then we anchor around the d, followed by any a to z disk ([a-z]). Then, we expect zero or more partition numbers (\d?). Finally, the end of the line is also matched ($).

When we match with IgnoreSelected false, we should be able to match on our disk names. UseBSDName false is used only on Macs, and UdevNameAttr "DEVNAME" means we try to use the Udev name for the disk device.

```
<Plugin interface>
    Interface "localhost"
    IgnoreSelected true
</Plugin>
```

Again, with the interface configuration, we make use of the IgnoreSelected option. We want to collect metrics for each network interface except the localhost or loopback interface.

```
<Plugin load>
    ReportRelative true
</Plugin>
```

```
<Plugin memory>
    ValuesAbsolute true
    ValuesPercentage false
</Plugin>
```

The previous are the defaults for memory and load and are similar to other system metrics we are gathering.

```
<Plugin mysql>
    <Database no_db>
        Host "localhost"
        Port "3306"
        User "monitor"
        Password "monitorpasswd"
        ConnectTimeout 10
        InnodbStats true
    </Database>
</Plugin>
```

813

The mysql plug-in will work just as good with our MariaDB server. It requires a user with USAGE privileges only and will gather internal metrics the equivalent of the mysql SHOW STATUS; command. If you are after query metrics, you can look at the dbi plug-in, which you can use to run metrics against your database.

In the mysql plug-in, you can specify the database or several databases in <Database> </Database> blocks.

```
<Plugin rrdtool>
    DataDir "/var/lib/collectd/rrd"
    CacheTimeout 120
    CacheFlush 900
    WritesPerSecond 30
    CreateFilesAsync false
    RandomTimeout 0
</Plugin>
```

The rrdtool plug-in is a write plug-in and is used to write rrd files to local disk. Once you start your Collectd service, you will see many files being created in /var/lib/collectd/rrd. While this works fine for small systems, it does not scale very well and, under heavy system usage, can task disk performance. This is why many people have moved away from this to other metric storage and collection systems, like Graphite, which will use to replace this shortly.

```
<Include "/etc/collectd/collectd.conf.d">
    Filter "*.conf"
</Include>
```

Lastly we have an include statement that says, include any files ending with the .conf suffix in the /etc/collectd/collectd.conf.d directory.

Starting and Stopping Collectd

Starting and stopping Collectd is again very straightforward. On both Ubuntu and CentOS you would issue the following commands:

```
$ sudo systemctl start collectd
$ sudo systemctl status collectd
$ sudo systemctl enable collectd
```

In the previous lines, we have started Collectd, checked the status, and enabled it on bootup. Successful status output will look like this:

```
-- Unit collectd.service has begun starting up.
Nov 15 21:55:26 backup collectd[8000]: plugin_load: plugin "syslog" successfully loaded.
Nov 15 21:55:26 backup collectd[8000]: plugin_load: plugin "cpu" successfully loaded.
Nov 15 21:55:26 backup collectd[8000]: plugin_load: plugin "interface" successfully loaded.
Nov 15 21:55:26 backup collectd[8000]: plugin_load: plugin "load" successfully loaded.
Nov 15 21:55:26 backup collectd[8000]: plugin_load: plugin "memory" successfully loaded.
Nov 15 21:55:26 backup collectd[8000]: plugin_load: plugin "mysql" successfully loaded.
Nov 15 21:55:26 backup collectd[8000]: plugin_load: plugin "rrdtool" successfully loaded.
Nov 15 21:55:26 backup collectd[8000]: Systemd detected, trying to signal readyness.
Nov 15 21:55:26 backup collectd[8000]: Initialization complete, entering read-loop.
Nov 15 21:55:26 backup systemd[1]: Started Collectd statistics daemon.
```

```
-- Subject: Unit collectd.service has finished start-up
-- Defined-By: systemd
-- Support: http://lists.freedesktop.org/mailman/listinfo/systemd-devel
--
-- Unit collectd.service has finished starting up.
--
-- The start-up result is done.
Nov 15 21:55:26 backup collectd[8000]: mysql plugin: Successfully connected to database
<none> at server Localhost via UNIX socket with cipher <none> (server version:
5.5.50-MariaDB, protocol version: 10)
```

You can see that we have successfully connected to our database. You should check the `systemctl` status or `syslog` if you have any issues.

Now that we have this successfully set up, we will look at setting up Graphite so we can collect metrics and store them centrally.

Graphite

According to the web site, Graphite does only three things: kicks arse, chews bubble gum, and makes it easy to store and graph metrics. We are unqualified to verify the first two statements, but the third statement is correct.

There are four components to Graphite.

- *Carbon*: A high-performance listener for receiving time-series data

- *Whisper*: A time-series database for metrics data

- *Graphite-web*: A web UI that renders graphs and dashboards

- *Graphite-API*: An API that fetches JSON data from the time-series Whisper database

In this exercise we are going to be installing Carbon, the time-series Whisper database and the Graphite-API. We will be using Grafana to display our metrics (in the next section) and so do not need install Graphite-web.

The Carbon components are comprised of carbon-relays and carbon-aggregators and carbon-cache. We are interested in installing the carbon-cache and a carbon-relay. All three components help to scale the Carbon service to enable the collection of thousands of metrics per second.

The carbon-cache is a required component and forms the basic collection model, carbon-cache, Whisper, and Graphite-API. It is able to listen on UDP or TCP ports (2003, 2004, 2007) and supports Python pickle and newline-delimited formats. The carbon-cache also configures how data will be stored in the Whisper databases. You can store different retention periods based on certain metric patterns. These are referred to as the storage-schema.

The carbon-relay is used to send metrics to certain back-end servers based on metric patterns. There are two ways a carbon-relay can be used, for sharding requests (using consistent hashing) to multiple backends and for replication, sending metrics to any number of different carbon-cache servers or aggregators.

Carbon-aggregators are used to buffer metrics that are destined for the carbon-cache to help reduce I/O. Averages or sums can be made of the metrics and pushed into Whisper as a single metric, reducing I/O on the carbon-cache and Whisper database.

Whisper is a time-series database for long-term storage of your metrics data. It is written in Python and allows for high-precision data resolution to degrade over time. When data degrades, the data points are "rolled up" or aggregated. You can choose to aggregate using the following functions:

- Average (default)
- Sum
- Max
- Min
- Last

You can find more information on Whisper here:

- `http://graphite.readthedocs.io/en/latest/whisper.html`

■ **Note**   There are a number of back-end time-series databases that can be used instead of Whisper. Some are listed here: `https://graphite.readthedocs.io/en/latest/tools.html#storage-backend-alternates`.

Graphite-web is one of the ways you can view your data. It is a Python app that requires the backing of a database, either SQLite (for very small deployments), MariaDB, or PostgreSQL. It also supports LDAP authentication.

If you want to present your metrics via a different graphical presentation service, you can just install Graphite-API, which will return JSON responses to metric queries. This provides a lighter, stateless interface into your metrics from any number of third-party graphical web UIs.

Graphite Installation

The Graphite components are easily installed using the common packaging tools, YUM and Apt, or via Pip (the Python packaging tool).

On CentOS you can install Graphite with the following:

```
$ sudo yum install -y python-carbon
```

This will install carbon-cache and the Whisper database (python-whisper). Graphite-API is installed via the graphite-api package.

```
$ sudo yum install -y graphite-api
```

On Ubuntu you need to install the following to install carbon-cache and Whisper:

```
$ sudo aptitude install -y graphite-carbon
```

Again, to install the Graphite-API component, you need to issue the following:

```
$ sudo aptitude install -y graphite-api
```

An alternative exists to install and experiment with Graphite. The developers of Graphite have provided a quick way to install and configure it.

- https://graphite.readthedocs.io/en/latest/install-synthesize.html

At the time of writing, this will spin up a Vagrant Ubuntu 14.04 and install version 0.9.5 of the Graphite software. You will have an environment up and running quickly to begin testing it.

Configuring Carbon-Cache

Most of the configuration for Graphite is in how we configure the carbon-cache. We use the same file for configuring the carbon-cache, aggregator, and relay. To achieve this, the file can be divided up into sections: [cache], [aggregator], and [relay]. This configuration file is well commented and is the source of truth for options available to you.

Carbon-cache and carbon-relays can be run on the same instance; aggregators should be one separate hosts. In this exercise, we are going to configure the carbon-cache and a carbon-relay.

To begin with, we will configure the carbon-cache. We can configure generic, or global, options under the [cache] section.

```
[cache]
STORAGE_DIR     = /var/lib/graphite/
LOCAL_DATA_DIR  = /var/lib/graphite/whisper/
CONF_DIR        = /etc/carbon/
LOG_DIR         = /var/log/carbon/
PID_DIR         = /var/run/
ENABLE_LOGROTATION = False
USER = _graphite
```

Here we are describing the general configuration of where we will store or retrieve data and service housekeeping. The important note here is that USER will be carbon on CentOS and _graphite on Ubuntu. These must be set for the [relay] and [aggregator] sections as well. The next section further describes the service. In Listing 17-4 are the default settings that are installed with package; these are the same for both distributions.

Listing 17-4. Default Carbon-Cache Settings

```
ENABLE_UDP_LISTENER = False
UDP_RECEIVER_INTERFACE = 0.0.0.0
MAX_CACHE_SIZE = inf
MAX_UPDATES_PER_SECOND = 500
MAX_CREATES_PER_MINUTE = 50
CACHE_WRITE_STRATEGY = sorted
WHISPER_AUTOFLUSH = False
WHISPER_FALLOCATE_CREATE = True
USE_FLOW_CONTROL = True
LOG_LISTENER_CONNECTIONS = True
LOG_UPDATES = False
LOG_CACHE_HITS = False
LOG_CACHE_QUEUE_SORTS = True
USE_INSECURE_UNPICKLER = False
```

First, the UDP listener is disabled by default, leaving the TCP listener as the default. Then we have some settings for our cache writing. MAX_CACHE_SIZE is set to inf, or infinite. You should limit this if you are seeing a lot of swapping or CPU-bound processes. As the cache size grows, the more expensive sorts and queries of the cache become. MAX_UPDATES_PER_SECOND and MAX_CREATES_PER_MINUTE are set to limit high disk I/O contention.

CACHE_WRITE_STRATEGY can have three possible settings.

- sorted (default): Data points are flushed to disk as an ordered list.

- max: Frequently updated data points are flushed to disk, and infrequent data points will be flushed at shutdown or low disk I/O periods (if there are any).

- naive : Data points are flushed in an unordered list.

There is further detail on these settings in comments of the carbon.conf file. WHISPER_AUTOFLUSH and WHISPER_FALLOCATE_CREATE are related to kernel options. WHISPER_AUTOFLUSH set to True will cause Whisper to write synchronously, handled by the carbon-cache, and WHISPER_FALLOCATE_CREATE (Linux only) can speed up file creation (and therefore allow you to increase MAX_CREATES_PER_MINUTE).

Setting USE_FLOW_CONTROL to True (default) means that if MAX_CACHE_SIZE is reached, carbon-cache will stop accepting connections until the cache is below 95 percent.

Next we have a set of logging options. Setting these to True can produce high I/O and should be turned on and off if you need to further investigate issues; we have left the default settings.

Finally, in Listing 17-4 there is an option to allow the older and less secure version of unpickler, USE_INSECURE_UNPICKLER = False. Unless you have a really strong need, leave this as it is.

In this next section we define the interfaces and ports for our carbon-cache service:

```
LINE_RECEIVER_INTERFACE = 0.0.0.0
PICKLE_RECEIVER_INTERFACE = 0.0.0.0
CACHE_QUERY_INTERFACE = 0.0.0.0
LINE_RECEIVER_PORT = 2003
PICKLE_RECEIVER_PORT = 2004
CACHE_QUERY_PORT = 7002
```

Here you can target your listeners to listen on certain IP addresses (IPv4); you should leave the ports as the defaults here. The line receiver supports the newline-delimited format (which means a newline signals the end of the metric). The pickle receiver supports the Python pickle object serialization (https://docs.python.org/3/library/pickle.html).

You can improve carbon-cache performance by having multiple cache declarations. A declaration like [cache:1] with different receiver ports specified looks like so:

```
[cache:1]
LINE_RECEIVER_PORT = 2103
PICKLE_RECEIVER_PORT = 2104
```

You can have one carbon-cache per CPU if you are running on a host with several CPUs.

The last piece of a carbon-cache is the way we store our metric data in our Whisper database. We do this by the file /etc/carbon/storage-schemas.conf. The file can look like this:

```
[carbon]
pattern = ^carbon\.
retentions = 60s:90d
```

```
[default_1min_for_1day]
pattern = .*
retentions = 60s:1d
```

Different metrics can have different retentions periods. You define them after giving them a [name]. You can see that we can match metrics that match the pattern ^carbon\. (that is, metrics starting with the word *carbon*). Metrics generated by carbon itself can look like this:

```
carbon.agents.host1.cache.queries
```

For this pattern we can see that they have a 60-second resolution and are stored at this resolution for 90 days (frequency:retention). As a default, we will record all metrics at a minute resolution for 1 day as a catchall collector.

Suppose we wanted to collect metrics from our databases. Collecting metrics from something like a database can produce a significant amount, so we can change the frequency and retention accordingly. As an example, you might choose something like this:

```
[database_metrics]
pattern = ^collectd_(db|backup)_*
retentions = 15s:7d,1m:90d,15m:180d
```

Here we are selecting metrics based on the pattern collectd_ followed by either db_ or backup_, and we will retain that for 15-second frequency for 7 days, 1 minute for 90 days, and 15 minutes for 180 days. That means, by default, our 15-second metrics will be averaged over a minute after 7 days, losing that precise resolution. That will continue until 90 days when they will again be averaged over a 15-minute period.

You may need to update your firewalls to allow access to ports 2003 and 2004. That is all you need to configure a basic carbon-cache.

Configuring Carbon-Relay

In this section we are going to configure the carbon-relay. In small networks you won't need to do this as a single Graphite carbon-cache can manage a significant number of metrics per host. In this scenario our hosts will send their metrics to our relay.example.com host on port 2013 (which is a line-delimited receiver). From there we will send the metrics on to our monitor.example.com host, which has a carbon-cache daemon listening on port 2004.

Configuring a carbon-relay requires a carbon.conf file and a file called relay-rules.conf. Taking a look at carbon.conf you will see that we have a [cache] section that is similar to our carbon-cache configuration seen previously.

```
[cache]
STORAGE_DIR    = /var/lib/graphite/
LOCAL_DATA_DIR = /var/lib/graphite/whisper/
CONF_DIR       = /etc/carbon/
LOG_DIR        = /var/log/carbon/
PID_DIR        = /var/run/
ENABLE_LOGROTATION = False
USER = carbon
LOG_LISTENER_CONNECTIONS = True
USE_INSECURE_UNPICKLER = False
USE_FLOW_CONTROL = True
CACHE_WRITE_STRATEGY = sorted
```

Next we are going create a [relay] section.

```
[relay]
LINE_RECEIVER_INTERFACE = 0.0.0.0
PICKLE_RECEIVER_INTERFACE = 0.0.0.0
LINE_RECEIVER_PORT = 2013
PICKLE_RECEIVER_PORT = 2014
DESTINATIONS = monitor.example.com:2004
LOG_LISTENER_CONNECTIONS = True
RELAY_METHOD = rules
MAX_DATAPOINTS_PER_MESSAGE = 500
MAX_QUEUE_SIZE = 10000
QUEUE_LOW_WATERMARK_PCT = 0.8
USE_FLOW_CONTROL = True
```

It has similar settings to a carbon-cache. We will listen on the ports 2013 (line-delimited metrics) and 2014 (pickle format). With a carbon-relay we need to provide a destination (or destinations) for our metrics. If using RELAY_METHOD rules, like we are, then you need to specify each carbon-cache you have listed in your relay-rules.conf file. The relay-rules.conf file is an ordered list of relay destinations based on particular matching patterns. We will discuss this shortly, but for now we will include the monitor.example.com destination, and because we are talking carbon-relay to carbon-cache, we will use the pickle port.

MAX_DATAPOINTS_PER_MESSAGE, MAX_QUEUE_SIZE, QUEUE_LOW_WATERMARK_PCT, and USE_FLOW_CONTROL are options for flow control. MAX_QUEUE and MAX_DATAPOINTS should be adjusted with caution. LOW_WATERMARK means that if the queue exceeds 80 percent, we will stop accepting metrics.

The relay-rules.conf file enables us to direct certain metrics to particular carbon-cache destinations. Each rule requires a unique name, a pattern, a destination, and whether we continue processing after this rule. In our example we have gone with a simple relay-rules.conf file like the following:

```
[default]
default = true
destinations = monitor.example.com:2004
```

There can be only one rule with default = true. By default we are sending all metrics to monitor.example.com on port 2004. Pretending that we want to send metrics from backup.example.com to a different carbon-cache, we could do the following:

```
[backup_example]
pattern = ^collectd_backup_example_com\.*
destination = 192.168.0.250:2004
continue = true
```

We would need to add 192.168.0.250 to the DESTINATIONS field in the carbon.conf file.

You can start and stop your carbon-relay service like this on CentOS:

```
$ sudo systemctl start carbon-relay
```

and like this for Ubuntu where we pass the instance name to the systemd service:

```
$ sudo systemctl start carbon-relay@default
```

Updating Collectd Configuration

Now we need to make our changes to the Collectd configuration to send metrics to our carbon-relay. There is a plug-in called `write_graphite`, which will send Collectd metrics to a Graphite carbon-cache or relay. The configuration is simple and looks like the following:

```
LoadPlugin write_graphite

<Plugin write_graphite>
  <Node "monitor">
    Host "relay.example.com"
    Port "2013"
    Protocol "tcp"
    ReconnectInterval 0
    LogSendErrors true
    Prefix "collectd_"
    StoreRates true
    AlwaysAppendDS false
    EscapeCharacter "_"
  </Node>
</Plugin>
```

This is the same plug-in format we saw earlier. In the Node block we are setting the relay host and port. We can add prefixes to our metrics and suffixes as well. Here we are adding `collectd_` as a prefix to each metric to more easily track the metric origins.

We can now restart the Collectd, service and metrics should begin to be sent via the relay to the monitor server. However, if you are running CentOS, you will not be able to send metrics to port 2013 without modifying SELinux.

You can issue the following to allow Collectd to connect to the network using `tcp`:

```
$ sudo getsebool collectd_tcp_network_connect
collectd_tcp_network_connect --> off
$ sudo setsebool collectd_tcp_network_connect on
```

You should also check /var/log/audit/audit.log for any denied messages.

Checking Logs

Once we have restarted our carbon-cache, carbon-relay, and collectd service, you should see them making connections to the services in the logs.

Collectd will log to syslog in our configuration, and Graphite will log into the /var/log/carbon directory. Taking a look at Collectd, we want to see the following in our logs:

```
Nov 22 23:19:06 backup collectd[5999]: plugin_load: plugin "write_graphite" successfully loaded.
```

On our relay host, we want to see our hosts connecting to us in the /var/log/carbon/listener.log.

```
22/11/2016 12:29:56 :: MetricLineReceiver connection with 192.168.0.30:38309 established
```

Then on our monitor host, we want to see this in the /var/log/carbon/listener.log.

```
20/11/2016 10:19:03 :: MetricPickleReceiver connection with 192.168.0.251:52146 established
```

So, we can see from our logs that our connections are being established between our Collectd service running on our backup host to our relay to our monitor. Now we will quickly check that metrics are being created for our backup host. The /var/log/carbon/creates.log file on the monitor host will show us if we are getting metrics from our backup hosts.

```
21/11/2016 11:35:48 :: new metric collectd_backup_example_com.cpu-0.cpu-user matched schema
default_1min_for_1day
```

Here you can see that we have a metric being created for our CPU. Alright, now we have metrics being generated on our backup host and being sent to our monitor via the relay. Let's now set up our Graphite-API service so that we can use Grafana to view them.

Configuring Graphite-API

As we have said, Graphite-API is the lightweight front end for Graphite. It allows applications to query metrics from our carbon-cache. To run it, we need to other components, Gunicorn and Nginx.

Gunicorn is a Python fork of the unicorn project, a web server gateway interface that powers many Ruby on Rails applications. We will use this to glue the Nginx web server requests to the Graphite-API application.

Nginx we have spoken of briefly. It is a very fast, low-resource web server that will sit in front of Gunicorn and pass web requests to it. We will use Nginx as a proxy service for our application.

Setting Up Gunicorn

We are going to set up Gunicorn to serve our Graphite-API application. To do that, we will get it to start our application listening on a loopback interface and listening on a particular port. This will allow Nginx to proxy requests to this port and serve the responses.

We can install Gunicorn via the pip command, which is the Python package manager. On Ubuntu we need to use pip3, or version 3 of pip, to install Gunicorn as Graphite-API is a Python 3 install. On CentOS the standard pip command will suffice as it is a Python 2.7 install.

```
$ sudo pip3 install gunicorn
```

Again, specifically for Ubuntu, we are going to create a symlink for /usr/local/bin/gunicorn to be /usr/bin/gunicorn. This will enable us to write one systemd service file for both Ubuntu and CentOS.

```
$ ln -s /usr/local/bin/gunicorn /usr/bin/gunicorn
```

Now we will create the systemd file to start the Gunicorn service. We will create a service file and socket file as we expect to run a socket for Nginx to connect in to. As you may recall, local systemd files live in /etc/systemd/system. We will create the file /etc/systemd/system/graphite-api.socket.

```
[Unit]
Description=graphite-api socket
```

```
[Socket]
ListenStream=/run/graphite-api.sock
ListenStream=127.0.0.1:8881

[Install]
WantedBy=sockets.target
```

Here we are saying to systemd, create a socket /run/graphite-api.sock that listens on the loopback address on port 8881. The WantedBy will mean that this will be started when the socket.target is activated.

Looking now at the service file, /etc/systemd/system/graphite-api.service, we can see the following details:

```
[Unit]
Description=Graphite-API service
Requires=graphite-api.socket

[Service]
ExecStart=/usr/bin/gunicorn -b 127.0.0.1:8881 -w2 graphite_api.app:app
Restart=on-failure
ExecReload=/bin/kill -s HUP $MAINPID
ExecStop=/bin/kill -s TERM $MAINPID
PrivateTmp=true

[Install]
WantedBy=multi-user.target
```

Here you can see that we call the gunicorn command to start graphite_api.app. We ask it to connect to 127.0.0.1 on port 8881. We also require graphite-api.socket. The –w2 says to start two worker processes to handle requests.

We can now use the systemctl command to start and stop the service and the socket.

```
$ sudo systemctl start graphite-api.service
```

You can read more about Gunicorn here:

- http://gunicorn.org/

Setting Up Nginx

While Gunicorn is a web server, it is recommended to deploy behind a proxy server. The proxy server can handle thousands of connections and acts as a buffer between the clients and the Gunicorn processes.

All that is required is for us to put the following graphite.conf file in a place where the Nginx server can find it:

```
upstream graphite {
    server 127.0.0.1:8881 fail_timeout=0;
}

server {
    server_name monitor;
    listen 80;
    root /var/www;
```

```
    location / {
        try_files $uri @graphite;
    }

    location @graphite {
        proxy_pass http://graphite;
    }
}
```

With Nginx, a proxy server is declared as an upstream server. That is declared in the upstream <name> { .. } section. In this section we tell Nginx to direct any requests for Graphite upstream servers to server 127.0.0.1:8881 where our Gunicorn server will be listening. If you have more than one back-end server listed, Nginx will round-robin between the two.

The server { ... } section is the front-end server declaration. We provide a server name, port we listen on, and root path. The root does not need to exist as all requests will be passed off to the back-end servers. We do this with the location / { ... } directive. When we make a request to any URI, we try first to return the URI, and then, if it is not found, we send the request to the @graphite location. The location @graphite { ... } then sends the request to the upstream server at http://graphite (which is the upstream server we have declared at the top of the file).

Depending on your distribution, you will do either one of the following. On Ubuntu you place graphite.conf in the /etc/nginx/sites-available/ directory. We then need to make the symlink to sites-enabled and start Nginx like so:

```
$ sudo ln -s /etc/nginx/sites-available/graphite.conf /etc/nginx/sites-enabled/graphite.conf
$ sudo systemctl start nginx
```

On CentOS we need to place graphite.conf in the following directory, /etc/nginx/conf.d/. Then we can start Nginx like normal.

```
$ sudo systemctl start nginx
```

By default both distributions will log to /var/log/nginx. We can test that our API is working correctly with the following:

```
$ curl -H 'Host: monitor' http://127.0.0.1:80/metrics/find?query=*
[{"text": "carbon", "expandable": 1, "allowChildren": 1, "id": "carbon", "leaf": 0},
{"text": "relay", "expandable": 1, "allowChildren": 1, "id": "relay", "leaf": 0}]
```

This shows that we can contact the Nginx web server, and that will make a request to the back-end Gunicorn service that will return our query request for our metrics.

Grafana

Grafana is a visualization web application for graphing time-series data. It can talk to a variety of data sources including Graphite-API. With your newly created metrics, you can now create dashboards and display those metrics.

Grafana supports LDAP authentication and can use a database to store users' dashboards. It has a stand-alone web service that you interact with. You can install it on your localhost or a central server; it does not store metric data locally but will make request to back-end storage services, in our case Graphite.

Installing Grafana

We are going to install Grafana on our Ubuntu server. We are going to follow the instructions from here: `http://docs.grafana.org/installation/debian`. You can follow the instructions here for CentOS: `http://docs.grafana.org/installation/rpm/`. You can also install Grafana on macOS or Windows.

First we will add the Grafana repository.

```
$ sudo bash -c 'echo "deb https://packagecloud.io/grafana/stable/debian/ jessie main" > /
etc/apt/sources.list.d/grafana.list'
$ curl https://packagecloud.io/gpg.key | sudo apt-key add -
$ sudo aptitude update
$ sudo aptitude install -y grafana
```

Once it is installed, we can start the Grafana service. This is the same for both Ubuntu and CentOS:

```
$ sudo systemctl start grafana-server
```

Now we can access Grafana on the following URL: `http://monitor:3000`. By default the username and password are admin (Figure 17-9).

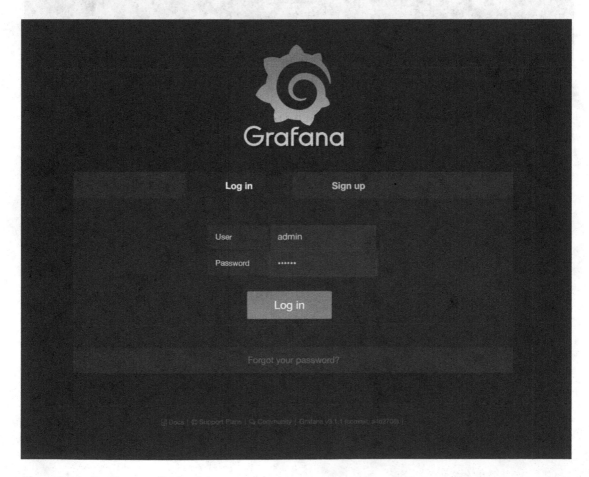

Figure 17-9. *Logging into Grafana*

Adding Storage Back End

Before we can graph any of our newly Collectd metrics, we need to add our Graphite back end. We need to add it as a data source (Figure 17-10).

Figure 17-10. *Selecting data sources*

From the Data Sources screen we click the green "Add data source" button and fill in the details (Figure 17-11).

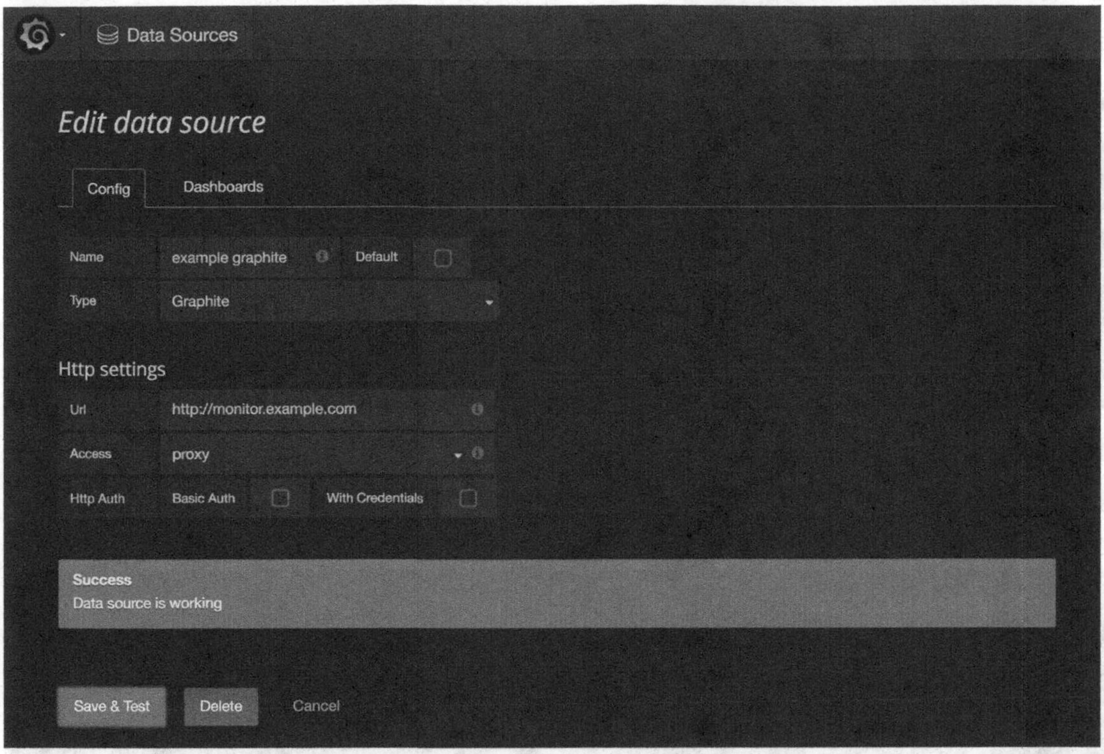

Figure 17-11. *Adding Graphite as our data source*

Clicking Save & Test will try to make a request to our Graphite host and test that it can get appropriate data back. If we click the Dashboards tab, we will import the Graphite metrics dashboard (Figure 17-12).

Figure 17-12. *Clicking Import*

After you have imported the dashboard, you can click Graphite Carbon Metrics and you will be shown Figure 17-13.

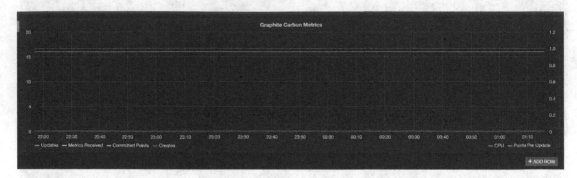

Figure 17-13. *Carbon Metrics graph*

Let's create a new dashboard by selecting Create New, as shown in Figure 17-14.

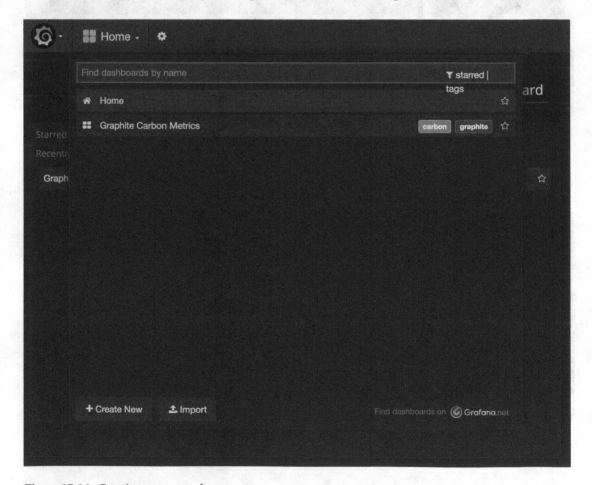

Figure 17-14. *Creating a new graph*

When you create a dashboard, a green bar will appear on the left side. Then select Add Panel and Graph, as shown in Figure 17-15.

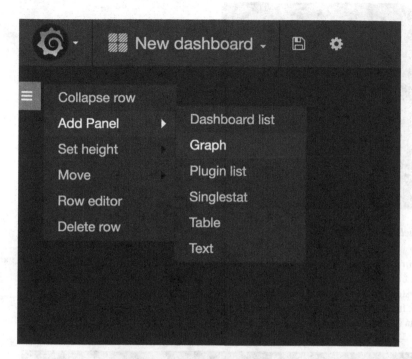

Figure 17-15. *From the left drop-down, select Graph*

When you add a panel, you get a test metric graph based on fake data (Figure 17-6).

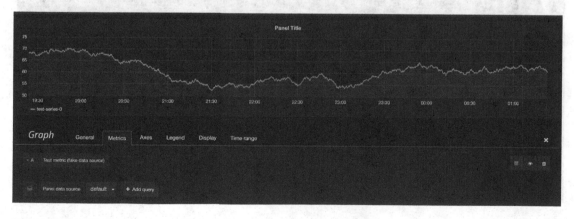

Figure 17-16. *Test metric*

To create our own graphs, we have to select the data source first. Let's do that, as in Figure 17-17.

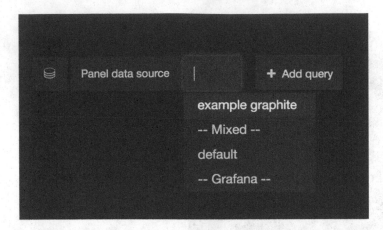

Figure 17-17. *Selecting the Panel data source*

Once we select the data source, the test data will disappear. You can click "select metric" and choose the origin of the metric you want to graph. We have selected "collectd_backup_example_com," and then we can select the metrics we interested in. We will choose "load" out of the list. We then select all the metrics available (*) and then again (*). In Figure 17-18 you can see we have tracked the host's load over 15 minutes. You can see more about Grafana in this YouTube tutorial by Grafana: `https://youtu.be/1kJyQKgk_oY`.

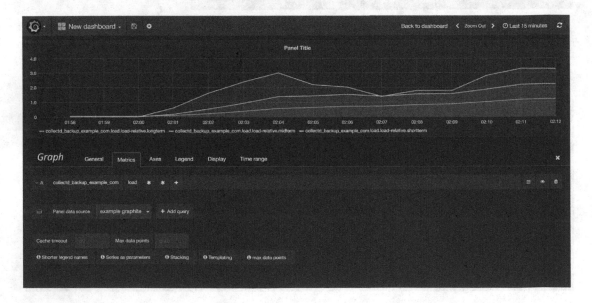

Figure 17-18. *Seeing load metrics on backup host*

Now that you have your metrics being collected and discoverable, you look at making performance tweaks and be able to measure their effect.

Performance Optimization

When your host was installed, it was set up with defaults that offer reasonable performance for most configurations. However, since each host is different, you can usually tweak settings to make the configuration more optimal for a specific workload.

In this section, we'll show you some tips and tricks that should help speed up your host for most server-related tasks.

Resource Limits

Linux allows you to enforce resource limits on users via the ulimit command. This is actually a built-in function of the Bash shell. Any limits you set via this command apply only to the current shell and the processes it starts.

To report current limits, run ulimit with the -a option, as shown in Figure 17-19.

```
ubuntu@monitor:~$ ulimit -a
core file size          (blocks, -c) 0
data seg size           (kbytes, -d) unlimited
scheduling priority             (-e) 0
file size               (blocks, -f) unlimited
pending signals                 (-i) 3909
max locked memory       (kbytes, -l) 64
max memory size         (kbytes, -m) unlimited
open files                      (-n) 1024
pipe size            (512 bytes, -p) 8
POSIX message queues     (bytes, -q) 819200
real-time priority              (-r) 0
stack size              (kbytes, -s) 8192
cpu time               (seconds, -t) unlimited
max user processes              (-u) 3909
virtual memory          (kbytes, -v) unlimited
file locks                      (-x) unlimited
```

Figure 17-19. ulimit -a

To prevent a fork bomb from being run by this shell user, you can change the maximum number of running processes, for instance, from 3909 to 1, using the -u option. If you then try to run a new process, the system will prevent you from doing so.

```
$ ulimit -u 1
$ ls
bash: fork: Resource temporarily unavailable
```

You receive an error to indicate the shell could not fork the command you tried to run. We are not suggesting that you manage users in this way but instead demonstrating the effect of this command.

■ **Caution**   If you are logged in via SSH or X, you will already have several running processes.

The other useful limits are the maximum memory size, which can be set via the -m option, and the number of open files, which you set via -n. The most common change you may make when tuning for resource limits is the number of open files a user can have.

You can obtain a full listing of options and their functions in the ulimit section of the man bash page.

Setting Limits for All Users

The ulimit command sets limits for the current shell, so you can add limits via /etc/profile or / etc/bashrc for users who log in. However, most daemons don't use shells, so adding limits to the shell configuration files won't have any effect.

You can instead use the limits module for PAM. This module is invoked when a user creates a new process, and it sets limits that you can define in /etc/security/limits.conf. This file defines both soft and hard limits for users and groups. We've included the sample limits.conf from CentOS in Figure 17-20.

```
#<domain>        <type>   <item>           <value>
#

#*               soft     core             0
#*               hard     rss              10000
#@student        hard     nproc            20
#@faculty        soft     nproc            20
#@faculty        hard     nproc            50
#ftp             hard     nproc            0
#@student        -        maxlogins        4

-
```

Figure 17-20. *Setting limits for all users*

Each line specifies a domain that the limit applies to. This domain can be a wildcard, a username, or a group name. Next comes the limit type, which can be either soft or hard. A hard limit can be set only by the root user, and when a user or process tries to break this limit, the system will prevent this. The soft limit can be adjusted by the user using the ulimit command, but it can be increased only to the value of the hard limit.

Next is the resource that is being limited. A full listing of available resources is included in the sample file, and it also available on the man limits.conf page. Last on each line is the value that the limit should be set to. Lines beginning with # are comments or examples.

In the case of the sample file, the @faculty group is allowed to run 20 concurrent processes (nproc) according to their soft limit. However, any member of this group is allowed to change that limit to any value up to 50 but no higher than that.

sysctl and the proc File System

We briefly mentioned the proc file system in Chapter 9 as a way to obtain system information directly from the kernel. It also provides a way to tweak a running kernel to improve system performance. To this end, you can change values in virtual files under the /proc/sys directory.

The virtual files are grouped in subdirectories, based on the parts of the system they affect, as listed in Table 17-2.

Table 17-2. */proc/sys Subdirectories*

Directory	Used By
abi	System emulation (e.g., running 32-bit applications on a 64-bit host).
crypto	Cryptography-related information, like ciphers, modules, and so on.
debug	This is an empty directory; it's not used.
dev	Device-specific information.
fs	File system settings and tuning.
kernel	Kernel settings and tuning.
net	Network settings and tuning.
sunrpc	Sun Remote Procedure Call (NFS) settings.
vm	Memory, buffer, and cache settings and tuning.

We won't go into detail on every single file, but we'll give you an idea of the kinds of tweaking that can be done.

Each of the virtual files contains one or more values that can be read via cat or the sysctl utility. To list all current settings, we can use the following:

```
$ sysctl -a
abi.vsyscall32 = 1
crypto.fips_enabled = 0
debug.exception-trace = 1
debug.kprobes-optimization = 1
dev.hpet.max-user-freq = 64
dev.mac_hid.mouse_button2_keycode = 97
...
vm.percpu_pagelist_fraction = 0
vm.stat_interval = 1
vm.swappiness = 30
vm.user_reserve_kbytes = 29608
vm.vfs_cache_pressure = 100
vm.zone_reclaim_mode = 0
```

To read a particular value, pass its key as a parameter to sysctl.

```
$ sudo sysctl vm.swappiness
vm.swappiness = 30
```

The key is the full path to the file, with /proc/sys/ removed and the slashes optionally replaced with full stops. For instance, to check how likely your host is to use swap memory, you can check the contents of /proc/sys/vm/swappiness.

```
$ cat /proc/sys/vm/swappiness
30
```

This particular value is an indication of how likely the kernel is to move information from RAM into swap space after it hasn't been used for a while. The higher the number, the more likely this is. The value in this case can range from 0 to 100, with 60 being the default. If you wanted to ensure your host is less likely to use swap memory, you could set the value to 20 instead via the sysctl utility and the -w option. You would need to then pass the key whose value you want to change and the new value.

```
$ sudo sysctl -w vm.swappiness=20
```

Another example is the number of files and directories that can be open at any single moment on the system. This is defined in /proc/sys/fs/file-max, and you can read the value via the command sysctl fs.file-max. To increase the maximum number of open files to half a million, run sudo sysctl -w fs.file-max=500000.

■ **Caution**   Changing kernel variables in the proc filesystem can have not only a positive impact but also a large adverse impact on system performance. We recommend you do not change anything unless you have a good reason to. A good approach for tuning is measure, change, measure. If you can't measure, be very careful.

When the system is rebooted, these variables are reset to their default values. To make them persist, you can add an appropriate entry in the /etc/sysctl.conf file. When the system boots, all settings in this file are applied to the system via the sysctl -p command.

On Ubuntu, instead of directly editing /etc/sysctl.conf, you can create a file in /etc/sysctl.d/<number>-<option-name>.conf, and they will be read in at boot.

On CentOS you will find the default system settings in /usr/lib/sysctl.d. You can override these in /etc/systctl.conf or by placing a file like on Ubuntu in /etc/sysctl.d/.

More information on sysctl settings can be found with man sysctl.d. A comprehensive list of available variables, with documentation, is available at https://www.kernel.org/doc/Documentation/sysctl/.

Storage Devices

In Chapter 9 you saw that in the event of a disk failure, the kernel needs to rebuild the RAID array once a replacement disk is added. This task generates a lot of I/O and can degrade performance of other services that the machine may be providing. Alternatively, you might want to give priority to the rebuild process, at the expense of services.

While a rebuild occurs, the kernel keeps the rebuild speed between set minimum and maximum values. We can change these numbers via the speed_min_limit and speed_max_limit entries in the /proc/sys/dev/raid directory.

A more acceptable minimum speed would be 20,000K per second per disk, and you can set it using sysctl.

```
$ sudo sysctl -w dev.raid.speed_limit_min=20000
```

Setting the minimum too high will adversely affect performance of the system, so make sure you set this number lower than the maximum throughput the system can handle, divided by the number of disks in your RAID array.

The maximum, which can be changed by setting the `dev.raid.speed_limit_max` variable, is fairly high already. If you want a RAID rebuild to have less of a performance impact, at the cost of a longer wait, you can lower this number.

To make these changes permanent, add these key-value pairs to `/etc/sysctl.conf`.

File System Tweaks

Each time a file or directory is accessed, even if it's only for reading, its last accessed time stamp (or `atime`) needs to be updated and written to the disk. Unless you need this timestamp, you can speed up disk access by telling your host to not update these.

By default, your system should mount your disks with the `relatime` option. This option means that each file access does not initiate an update to the file metadata, which increases performance by not issuing unnecessary operations. It is synonymous with `noatime`.

If it is not set, you simply add the `noatime` option to the `options` field in the `/etc/fstab` file for each filesystem on which you want to enable this option.

```
UUID=f87a71b8-a323-4e8e-acc9-efb0758a0642 / ext4 defaults, ↵
    errors=remount-ro,relatime 0 1
```

This will enable the option the next time the filesystem is mounted. To make it active immediately, you can remount the filesystem using the `mount` command.

```
$ sudo mount -o remount,relatime /
```

In addition to mount options, filesystems themselves provide some features that may improve performance; these vary depending on what a particular file system is used for. The main one of these is `dir_index`, and it applies to the ext2, ext3, and ext4 file systems. Enabling this feature causes the file system to create internal indexes that speed up access to directories containing a large number of files or subdirectories. You can use the `tune2fs` utility to check whether it's enabled.

```
$sudo tune2fs -l /dev/md0 | grep features
Filesystem features: has_journal ext_attr resize_inode dir_index filetype needs_recovery
extent 64bit flex_bg ↵
    sparse_super large_file huge_file uninit_bg dir_nlink extra_isize
```

If you need to change features, and you rarely do, you could use `tune2fs` to enable a particular feature.

```
sudo tune2fs -O dir_index /dev/md0
```

Alternatively, features can be turned off by prefixing their name with a caret.

```
sudo tune2fs -O ^dir_index /dev/md0
```

You can set which options should be enabled on the various ext file systems by changing the defaults in the `/etc/mke2fs.conf` file.

I/O Schedulers

I/O schedulers, also called I/O elevators, are algorithms that kernel will use to order I/O to disk subsystems. Schedulers can be changed to improve the efficiency of this process. Three schedulers are available to the kernel.

- *Cfq*: This is the default scheduler for SATA devices and tries to implement completely fair queues for processing I/O.

- *Deadline*: This is the default scheduler for block devices. It preferences read requests and tries to provide certainty to requests by imposing a deadline on the start time.

- *Noop*: This is a first in/first out queue, where the I/O is left to lower subsystems to order; it is suitable for virtual machines.

You can find the scheduler on your device by executing a command similar to this:

```
$ cat /sys/block/sda/queue/scheduler
noop deadline [cfq]
```

The scheduler in [ ] is the current setting. You can change it with the following command:

```
$ sudo bash -c 'echo deadline > /sys/block/sda/queue/scheduler'
$ cat /sys/block/sda/queue/scheduler
noop [deadline] cfq
```

You can set the scheduler at boot time by making an edit to GRUB. You will need to edit the following file by adding this:

```
$ vi /etc/default/grub
GRUB_CMDLINE_LINUX="console=tty0 ... rhgb quiet elevator=deadline"
```

This sets deadline as the default scheduler across the whole server. You then need to remake GRUB with the following:

```
$ sudo grub2-mkconfig -o /boot/grub2//grub.cfg
```

Now when you reboot your host, the default scheduler is deadline.

```
$ cat /sys/block/sda/queue/scheduler
noop [deadline] cfq
```

Remember that on Ubuntu grub2-mkconfig needs to be like this:

```
$ sudo grub2-mkconfig -o /boot/grub/grub2.cfg
```

Now your changes will persist across reboots.

Summary

In this chapter, we showed you simple tools that allow you to easily determine the basic health of a running host. You learned how to do the following:

- Check CPU usage

- Check memory and swap space usage

We also introduced more advanced system metric collection tools such as Collectd and Graphite, which will help you monitor resource usage and performance on an ongoing basis. You learned how to do the following:

- Install and configure Collectd

- Install and configure Graphite

- Use Grafana to monitor and visualize the health of your hosts

We also gave a little information on some common performance tunings and how to change the kernel settings using `sysctl`.

In the next chapter, you'll see how to configure some monitoring of your hosts and services. We'll also show you how to configure logging and monitor the logs for unusual or suspicious activity.

CHAPTER 18

■ ■ ■

Logging and Monitoring

By James Turnbull and Dennis Matotek

Throughout this book, we've talked about logging and monitoring and their value in troubleshooting your applications and services. In the first section of this chapter, we're going to look at how logs work on the Linux operating system and how to make use of that data. We'll look at how to store, aggregate, analyze, send alerts on, and rotate log entries and logs. We'll also look at some tools to make it easier to interact with your logs.

In the second section of this chapter, we'll show how you can use an open source tool called Nagios to monitor the applications and services we've introduced. Nagios allows you to define your hosts and the services that run on them. You can then ensure these hosts are up and that your services are functioning correctly. If they are not functioning, your monitoring system can then notify you about what has gone wrong. This process can greatly speed up the time it takes to identify and fix issues.

Logging

You've seen throughout the book that many applications and tools log data about their actions and status. You have seen that we can use the `journalctl` command to view logs and also that logs can end up in the /var/log directory in a variety of files. Logging is, usually, done by two daemons: the `journald` daemon and the `rsyslogd` daemon. We will look at each of these now.

journald

As part of `systemd`, a new logging capability was introduced. Journald creates binary structured log files and can be used instead of, or with, traditional (r)syslog logging. These are some of the features of the Journald log file:

- Log tampering can be detected and cannot easily be manually edited.

- Logs are indexes, making faster searching.

- Logs are in a structured format with well-defined fields.

- `journald` collects extra log metadata for each log message.

- Journald supports export formats (such as JSON).

The logs are by default stored in system memory or a ring buffer and are not stored permanently. Because of the extra metadata, the log events are larger in size than normal logs and take more space. You can persist them to disk, and we will show you how to do that a little later in the chapter.

© Dennis Matotek, James Turnbull and Peter Lieverdink 2017

D. Matotek et al., *Pro Linux System Administration*, DOI 10.1007/978-1-4842-2008-5_18

We access the journal files with the journalctl command that we have already used several times. If you execute the journalctl command without any arguments or filters, you will see something like Listing 18-1.

Listing 18-1. The journalctl Command

```
$ sudo journalctl
-- Logs begin at Fri 2016-11-25 22:16:00 AEDT, end at Mon 2016-11-28 21:07:54 AEDT. --
Nov 25 22:16:00 au-mel-centos-1 systemd-journal[89]: Runtime journal is using 8.0M...current
limit 92.0M).
Nov 25 22:16:00 au-mel-centos-1 systemd-journal[89]: Runtime journal is using 8.0M...current
limit 92.0M).
Nov 25 22:16:00 au-mel-centos-1 kernel: Initializing cgroup subsys cpuset
Nov 25 22:16:00 au-mel-centos-1 kernel: Initializing cgroup subsys cpu
Nov 25 22:16:00 au-mel-centos-1 kernel: Initializing cgroup subsys cpuacct
Nov 25 22:16:00 au-mel-centos-1 kernel: Linux version 3.10.0-327.4.5.el7.x86_64 ...CentOS
4.8.3-9) (GCC)...
Nov 25 22:16:00 au-mel-centos-1 kernel: Command line: BOOT_IMAGE=/vmlinuz-3.10.0-
327.4.5.el7.x86_64...
Nov 25 22:16:00 au-mel-centos-1 kernel: e820: BIOS-provided physical RAM map:
```

The output of journalctl will show our logs from when we booted our host, and we have truncated some long lines for clarity. You first see the journal starting, and then you see the initialization of cgroups, followed by the Linux kernel version and how it was built. Then we see the kernel-loading command followed by low-level memory initialization.

The first line in Listing 18-1 shows us the date of the first entry and the date of the last entry. You can see that each log here consists of four things.

- A timestamp

- The hostname

- The service emitting the log

- The log message

Looking further at the journalctl command, we will explore some of the options available with it. For instance, to view the last ten lines of the journal, we will issue the following:

```
$ sudo journalctl -n 10
-- Logs begin at Fri 2016-11-25 22:16:00 AEDT, end at Mon 2016-11-28 21:24:54 AEDT. --
Nov 28 21:01:01 backup run-parts(/etc/cron.hourly)[9627]: starting 0yum-hourly.cron
...
Nov 28 21:24:54 backup sudo[9647]:   bsingh : TTY=pts/0 ; PWD=/home/bsingh ; USER=root ;
COMMAND=/bin/journalctl -n 10
```

Here we see the last ten lines (eight lines are omitted), with the last log entry being the sudo command we just entered. What we are seeing here is the simplified view of the log made up of the four fields we just talked about. There is a lot of data about the logs we don't see. Let's take a look at the last entry more closely with the verbose output (see Listing 18-2).

Listing 18-2. Journal Metadata

```
$ sudo journalctl -n 1 -o verbose
-- Logs begin at Fri 2016-11-25 22:16:00 AEDT, end at Mon 2016-11-28 21:29:46 AEDT. --
Mon 2016-11-28 21:29:46.407435 AEDT [s=1798dd89d9ff412b8edcc9e7b5cb8484;i=1c0b;b=11ffa7916ba
a42a89cbbc756af6d26bc;m=2486cb476a;t=54259f362b5ab;x=68026ef74697a39]
    _BOOT_ID=11ffa7916baa42a89cbbc756af6d26bc
    _MACHINE_ID=e3c7fd86ed8b4ef69e569a93e30db6ab
    PRIORITY=5
    _CAP_EFFECTIVE=1ffffffff
    _HOSTNAME=backup
    _TRANSPORT=rsyslog
    SYSLOG_FACILITY=10
    _AUDIT_LOGINUID=1000
    _SYSTEMD_OWNER_UID=1000
    _SYSTEMD_SLICE=user-1000.slice
    SYSLOG_IDENTIFIER=sudo
    _COMM=sudo
    _EXE=/usr/bin/sudo
    _SELINUX_CONTEXT=unconfined_u:unconfined_r:unconfined_t:s0-s0:c0.c1023
    _AUDIT_SESSION=40
    _SYSTEMD_CGROUP=/user.slice/user-1000.slice/session-40.scope
    _SYSTEMD_SESSION=40
    _SYSTEMD_UNIT=session-40.scope
    _UID=1005
    _GID=1006
    MESSAGE=  bsingh : TTY=pts/0 ; PWD=/home/bsingh ; USER=root ; COMMAND=/bin/journalctl -n
1 -o verbose
    _PID=9653
    _CMDLINE=sudo journalctl -n 1 -o verbose
    _SOURCE_REALTIME_TIMESTAMP=1480328986407435
```

You can see that each log contains a wealth of associated metadata. The first line after the log date range information is the cursor position information, or the entry's position in the journal. The rest are key/value pairs with a wealth of filterable data. Let's now look at some common filters.

journalctl Filters

The great thing about the journal logging facility is that it is structured, meaning that we can filter information we are interested in easily. Anyone with Linux experience will tell you their favorite incantations to investigate logs. With filters we no longer need to rely on piping logs through commands such as grep and awk so much.

We will start with filtering the `journalctl` output by just kernel messages by using the –k option.

```
$ sudo journalctl -k
-- Logs begin at Fri 2016-11-25 22:16:00 AEDT, end at Mon 2016-11-28 22:06:08 AEDT. --
Nov 25 22:16:00 au-mel-centos-1 kernel: Initializing cgroup subsys cpuset
Nov 25 22:16:00 au-mel-centos-1 kernel: Initializing cgroup subsys cpu
...
Nov 28 21:01:01 backup kernel: SELinux: initialized (dev tmpfs, type tmpfs), uses transition SIDs
Nov 28 22:01:01 backup kernel: SELinux: initialized (dev tmpfs, type tmpfs), uses transition SIDs
```

Now let's reduce that long list to only those kernel log messages that are of an ERROR priority (-p).

```
$ sudo journalctl -p err -k
-- Logs begin at Fri 2016-11-25 22:16:00 AEDT, end at Mon 2016-11-28 22:10:14 AEDT. --
Nov 25 22:16:13 backup kernel: CIFS VFS: Send error in SessSetup = -127
Nov 25 22:16:13 backup kernel: CIFS VFS: cifs_mount failed w/return code = -127
Nov 25 22:17:13 backup kernel: CIFS VFS: Send error in SessSetup = -13
```

Here we have listed all the kernel logs that are in error. There are seven priorities available to use; either the word or the number will do.

- emerg(0)— emergency
- alert(1)
- crit(2)— critical
- err(3)— error
- warning(4)
- notice(5)
- info(6)—information
- debug(7)

The –k option is the same as using the dmesg command to view logs, but as you can see, journalctl is easier to read and filter.

We can combine filters. We can see messages since the last system boot with the –b option.

```
$ sudo journalctl -p info -b
```

This can often still be a lot of messages, so we can further refine this with more specific time filters.

```
$ sudo journalctl -p info --since "2016-11-28 22:44:00" --until "2016-11-28 22:54:00"
```

Here we are displaying the logs at priority info for the last ten minutes. The times are in local time. If you want to see UTC times, you can issue the following:

```
$ sudo journalctl --utc
```

In Listing 18-2 we saw the full list of fields that are included in our logs. We can use this metadata as filters too. One of the fields from Listing 18-2 is _COMM, which records the command that was used in generating the log. We can list all the different values for that field with the following:

```
$ sudo journalctl -F _COMM
unix_chkpwd
request-key
freshclam-sleep
run-parts
pickup
usermod
...
```

Let's say we want to search for any usermod changes that have happened since the last boot.

```
$ sudo journalctl _COMM=usermod -b
-- Logs begin at Fri 2016-11-25 22:16:00 AEDT, end at Mon 2016-11-28 23:09:04 AEDT. --
Nov 25 22:48:41 backup usermod[4844]: add 'jsmith' to group 'sales'
Nov 25 22:48:41 backup usermod[4844]: add 'jsmith' to shadow group 'sales'
```

We can also combine any of these fields with the --since and --until time filters to get a more narrow view. Having two fields listed (separated by a space) provides a logical AND listing (_COMM=usermod _COMM=useradd). Using a + will give you a logical OR listing (_COMM=usermod + _HOSTNAME=backup), which will provide a listing with usermod and any listing with the hostname backup.

> ■ **Tip** Typing journalctl and pressing the Tab key twice will give you a list of available fields.

We can also list logs by their systemd unit names. Here we are going to follow (like the tail command) the httpd log using the following:

```
$ sudo journalctl -f -u httpd.service
-- Logs begin at Fri 2016-11-25 22:16:00 AEDT. --
Nov 28 23:27:11 backup systemd[1]: Starting The Apache HTTP Server...
Nov 28 23:27:11 backup systemd[1]: Started The Apache HTTP Server.
```

Here you can see the output of the Apache service as it starts up.

Securing Journald with FSS

We said earlier that we can detect whether journal logs have been tampered with. This is done with a feature called Forward Secure Sealing (FSS), which signs the logs with one of a generated key pair. A *sealing key* will seal the logs at a specified interval, and the *verify key* can be used to detect tampering. The logs are singed, or sealed, at regular configurable intervals. This provides some level of security for your logs.

However, it does not stop people who attack your system from covering their tracks, and they can get around this by either deleting the logs or editing between the sealing time interval. It does not provide any extra information in the event of someone tampering with your logs but will give you a timeframe in which such an event happened. It can be seen as one small piece of your overall system security.

To use FSS, you first need to enable the persistent storage of your journal log files. This is easily done by issuing the following:

```
$ sudo mkdir /var/log/journal
$ sudo systemctl restart systemd-journald
```

Then to generate the key pair, we will issue the command in Figure 18-1.

```
[bsingh@backup ~]$ sudo journalctl --setup-keys
Generating seed...
Generating key pair...
Generating sealing key...

The new key pair has been generated. The secret sealing key has been written to
the following local file. This key file is automatically updated when the
sealing key is advanced. It should not be used on multiple hosts.

        /var/log/journal/e3c7fd86ed8b4ef69e569a93e30db6ab/fss

Please write down the following secret verification key. It should be stored
at a safe location and should not be saved locally on disk.

        4f5f8f-9eb38b-eff95a-bc0bc8/191914-35a4e900

The sealing key is automatically changed every 15min.

The keys have been generated for host backup/e3c7fd86ed8b4ef69e569a93e30db6ab.

To transfer the verification key to your phone please scan the QR code below:
```

Figure 18-1. *FSS key generation and QR code*

As the text in Figure 18-1 says, we should store the secret verification key in a safe place, and it gives us the handy ability to use the QR code to store it on our phone. The signing key has been place in the `fss` file in the /var/log/journal/ e3c7f…db6ab/ directory. That will be rotated every 15 minutes.

Let's verify the logs with our key to make sure they haven't been tampered with.

```
$ sudo journalctl --verify-key 4f5f8f-9eb38b-eff95a-bc0bc8/191914-35a4e900
PASS: /var/log/journal/e3c7fd86ed8b4ef69e569a93e30db6ab/system.journal
PASS: /var/log/journal/e3c7fd86ed8b4ef69e569a93e30db6ab/user-1005.journal
```

Journal-Remote

Another way to secure our logs from loss or tampering is to send them to a centralized logging host as quickly as we can. Systemd Journal provides a `systemd-journal-remote` service that can receive journal messages from other hosts and provide a centralized logging service. This is quite new, and it currently has a few detractors since the TLS service isn't really secure (doesn't enforce client certificate verification), but it shows great promise as it matures.

The service can act either passively (wait for journal messages) or actively (pull messages from a remote host). It can be configured to listen over HTTP or HTTPS. We are going to set up one host, `gateway.example.com`, that will upload logs to our main `backup.example.com` server.

We are going to use `https://` transport for our logs, and we will assume that we have already created the TLS keys required with our CA. We are also using two CentOS hosts in this example, but the configuration should be the same for both CentOS and Ubuntu.

First with CentOS you will need to install the `systemd-journal-gateway` package. On Ubuntu it is the `systemd-journal-remote` package. Both packages provide the `systemd-journal-gateway`, `systemd-journal-upload`, and `systemd-journal-remote` services.

The gateway service is an HTTP server that can be used to query journal logs. The remote service is used to receive logs from other servers. The upload, of course, is used to upload logs to a remote server. We are only going to show the upload and remote services here.

We will first set up the remote service that will listen for log messages. To do this, we need to edit the following:

```
$ sudo vi /etc/systemd/journal-remote.conf
[Remote]
ServerKeyFile=/etc/pki/tls/private/backup.example.com.key
ServerCertificateFile=/etc/pki/tls/certs/backup.example.com.cert
TrustedCertificateFile=/etc/pki/tls/certs/cacert.pem
```

This provides the details of the TLS keys and certs we need. The `systemd-journal-remote` user will need to be able to read the private key file. Next we need to make some additional filesystem changes.

```
$ sudo mkdir -p /var/log/journal/remote && sudo chown systemd-journal-remote /var/log/journal/remote
```

By default the remote journal service will listen on port 19532. We will need to add this to our allowed rules in our firewall.

```
$ sudo firewall-cmd --permanent --zone public --add-port=19532/tcp
$ sudo firewall-cmd --reload
```

By default the service is configured to listen with `https://`. This is configurable in the `/usr/lib/systemd/system/systemd-journal-remote.service` file. Now we can start the remote journal service with the following:

```
$ sudo systemctl enable systemd-journal-remote
$ sudo systemctl start systemd-journal-remote
$ sudo systemctl status systemd-journal-remote
```

We check the status before proceeding to make sure our service has started successfully. The next service we need to configure is on the gateway host. We need to edit the following file:

```
$ sudo vi /etc/systemd/journal-upload.conf
[Upload]
URL=https://backup.example.com:19532
ServerKeyFile=/etc/pki/tls/private/gateway.example.com.key
ServerCertificateFile=/etc/pki/tls/certs/gateway.example.com.cert
TrustedCertificateFile=/etc/pki/tls/certs/cacert.pem
```

This is similar to the remote service file with only one significant difference, as you can no doubt see. The URL option points to the backup.example.com host on port 19532. Again, the private key must be readable by the systemd-journal-upload user. We need now to make some similar filesystem changes like we did for the remote service.

First we need to give access to the state file that keeps track of what journals we have sent and give access to the journal logs that are stored in /run/log/journal.

```
$ sudo chown systemd-journal-upload /var/lib/systemd/journal-upload
$ sudo usermod –aG systemd-journal systemd-journal-upload
```

We are now ready to start our journal uploader.

```
$ sudo systemctl enable systemd-journal-upload
$ sudo systemctl start systemd-journal-upload
```

We should, very shortly, start seeing logs coming into the /var/log/journal/remote directory on the backup.example.com host.

```
[jsmith@backup ~]$ sudo ls -l /var/log/journal/remote/
total 16388
-rw-r-----. 1 systemd-journal-remote systemd-journal 8388608 Nov 29 22:58 remote- ↵
gateway@3a016bda55334bcd88d8a6fa52b1dc61-0000000000000001-0005426ea713ed3c.journal
```

Now we have our remote host sending logs to our backup server. In the next section we will further explore how to get the journal logs into rsyslog as an alternative.

rsyslogd

Applications output data to the rsyslog daemon with log entries in a special format that the daemon can parse. The daemon then takes the log entries and can perform a variety of actions with them, including writing them out to a file.

You've seen a few syslog entries earlier in this book. Let's look at a few rsyslog lines now:

```
Nov 30 00:54:25 backup systemd: Stopping System Logging Service...
Nov 30 00:54:25 backup systemd: Starting System Logging Service...
Nov 30 00:54:28 backup systemd: Started System Logging Service.
```

An rsyslog entry is constructed of a date, the name of the host that logged the entry (usually the service that emitted it), and the log data itself. Here we've shown a restart of the rsyslog service that is first stopped and started and then confirm it is started.

syslog, the predecessor to rsyslog, has been the ubiquitous Unix format for logging. It has been present on all flavors of Linux and indeed on almost all flavors of Unix. You could add it using third-party tools to Windows systems, and most network devices such as firewalls, routers, and switches are capable of generating syslog messages. This resulted in the syslog format being the closest thing to a universal logging standard that exists. rsyslog is an advancement on syslog, which provides things like TCP (SSL/TLS), extra modules, and reliable event logging protocol (RELP).

■ **Tip**   RFC 5424 documents the core rsyslog functionality, and you can read it at https://tools.ietf.org/html/rfc5424.

The syslog format is used by a variety of tools that vary in function and complexity and are generally all collectively called syslog daemons. These daemons include the basic syslog tool as well as more advanced variants such as syslog-NG (the NG means "next generation") and rsyslog. rsyslog has benefitted greatly from the work done on syslog and syslog-NG.

We will cover the basic rsyslog tool because it is the default on both CentOS and Ubuntu. It also lays down the groundwork for understanding how logging works on Linux systems.

The rsyslog utility is designed to generate, process, and store meaningful event notification messages that provide the information required for administrators to manage their systems. syslog is both a series of programs and libraries, including rsyslogd, the rsyslog daemon, and a communications protocol.

The most frequently used component of rsyslog is the rsyslogd daemon. This daemon runs on your system from startup and listens for messages from your operating system and applications. It is important to note that the rsyslogd daemon is a passive tool. It merely waits for input from devices or programs. It does not go out and actively gather messages.

The next major feature of the rsyslog tools is the RELP communications protocol. With this protocol it is possible to send your log data across a network to a remote system where another rsyslog daemon can collect and centralize your logs.

■ **Tip**   rsyslog traffic is usually transmitted via TCP on port 514.

Configuring rsyslog

The rsyslog daemon is controlled by a configuration file located in /etc called rsyslog.conf. This file contains the information about what devices and programs rsyslogd is listening for, where that information is to be stored, and what actions are to be taken when that information is received.

You can see the default rsyslog.conf configuration file from Ubuntu here:

```
#################
#### MODULES ####
#################

module(load="imuxsock") # provides support for local system logging
module(load="imklog")   # provides kernel logging support
#module(load="immark")  # provides --MARK-- message capability
```

```
# provides UDP syslog reception
#module(load="imudp")
#input(type="imudp" port="514")

# provides TCP syslog reception
#module(load="imtcp")
#input(type="imtcp" port="514")

# Enable non-kernel facility klog messages
$KLogPermitNonKernelFacility on


############################
#### GLOBAL DIRECTIVES ####
############################

#
# Use traditional timestamp format.
# To enable high precision timestamps, comment out the following line.
#
$ActionFileDefaultTemplate RSYSLOG_TraditionalFileFormat

# Filter duplicated messages
$RepeatedMsgReduction on

#
# Set the default permissions for all log files.
#
$FileOwner syslog
$FileGroup adm
$FileCreateMode 0640
$DirCreateMode 0755
$Umask 0022
$PrivDropToUser syslog
$PrivDropToGroup syslog

#
# Where to place spool and state files
#
$WorkDirectory /var/spool/rsyslog

#
# Include all config files in /etc/rsyslog.d/
#
$IncludeConfig /etc/rsyslog.d/*.conf
```

The first section, as you can see, loads the base modules. We load the imuxsock module (module(load="imuxsock")), which is needed to deliver syslog system calls to rsyslog, and the imklog (module(load="imklog")), which allows for kernel logging. There are many modules that can be loaded, and you can find a list of those that are bundled with rsyslog in the man rsyslog.conf page. You can also install other modules; those will be provided by related packages like rsyslog-mysql, which provides logging support for MySQL.

848

The Modules section is followed by the Global Directives section. This defines the user, file, and directory modes and other housekeeping. These are rarely edited. In the bottom of the file you will find the IncludeConfig statement that will tell rsyslog to load any file it finds in the rsyslog.d directory that ends with a *.conf.

In the rsyslog.d directory on Ubuntu there is a file that contains some defaults called 50-default. conf; the file contains extra directives. The CentOS rsyslog.conf file is a combination of these two files and is mostly similar.

```
#
# First some standard log files.  Log by facility.
#
auth,authpriv.*                 /var/log/auth.log
*.*;auth,authpriv.none          -/var/log/syslog
#cron.*                         /var/log/cron.log
#daemon.*                       -/var/log/daemon.log
kern.*                          -/var/log/kern.log
#lpr.*                          -/var/log/lpr.log
mail.*                          -/var/log/mail.log
#user.*                         -/var/log/user.log

#
# Logging for the mail system.  Split it up so that
# it is easy to write scripts to parse these files.
#
#mail.info                      -/var/log/mail.info
#mail.warn                      -/var/log/mail.warn
mail.err                        /var/log/mail.err

#
# Logging for INN news system.
#
news.crit                       /var/log/news/news.crit
news.err                        /var/log/news/news.err
news.notice                     -/var/log/news/news.notice

#
# Some "catch-all" log files.
#
#*.=debug;\
#       auth,authpriv.none;\
#       news.none;mail.none     -/var/log/debug
#*.=info;*.=notice;*.=warn;\
#       auth,authpriv.none;\
#       cron,daemon.none;\
#       mail,news.none          -/var/log/messages
```

```
#
# Emergencies are sent to everybody logged in.
#
*.emerg                                 :omusrmsg:*

#
# I like to have messages displayed on the console, but only on a virtual
# console I usually leave idle.
#
#daemon,mail.*;\
#       news.=crit;news.=err;news.=notice;\
#       *.=debug;*.=info;\
#       *.=notice;*.=warn       /dev/tty8

# The named pipe /dev/xconsole is for the `xconsole' utility.  To use it,
# you must invoke `xconsole' with the `-file' option:
#
#       $ xconsole -file /dev/xconsole [...]
#
# NOTE: adjust the list below, or you'll go crazy if you have a reasonably
#       busy site..
#
daemon.*;mail.*;\
        news.err;\
        *.=debug;*.=info;\
        *.=notice;*.=warn       |/dev/xconsole
```

As you've discovered, both CentOS and Ubuntu store their log files in the /var/log directory but use different file names to store different types of log entries; for example, you saw in Chapter 12 (and you can see in the preceding 50-default.conf configuration file) that Ubuntu stores mail-related rsyslog entries in the mail.log file. On CentOS, however, mail-related rsyslog entries are written to the maillog file. You can check your host's rsyslog.conf configuration file to determine where the information you want will be written.

Each line in the rsyslog.conf file is structured into two fields: a selector field and an action field. These fields are separated by spaces or a tab. You can see an example of a line in Listing 18-3.

Listing 18-3. rsyslog.conf Syntax

```
mail.*          -/var/log/mail.log
```

This example shows a selector, mail.*, together with the action /var/log/mail.log. The selector specifies a facility and a priority, separated by a period. Facilities tell you the source of log messages; for example, the mail facility is used for log messages related to mail services such as Postfix. A number of facilities are available, and we'll look at each in the next section. Each application specifies the facility it will use for its log entries.

The priority (.*) tells rsyslog the importance of the message being sent. A range of priorities are available, and we'll explain each shortly. Again, applications choose the priority of each message when they send them to rsyslog.

The action tells rsyslog what to do with the message; generally this means writing it to a file. In Listing 18-3, all messages from the mail facility with the any priority will be written to the file /var/log/mail.log.

Facilities

The facility identifies the source of the `rsyslog` message. Some operating system daemons and other common application daemons have standard facilities attached to them. The `mail` and `kern` facilities are two good examples, being mail-related event notification messages and all kernel-related messages, respectively.

Other processes and daemons that do not have a specified facility can use the `local` facilities, which range from `local0` to `local7`. Table 18-1 lists all `rsyslog` facilities.

■ **Tip** On CentOS systems, `local7` is, by default, used for boot messages, and these are directed to `/var/log/boot.log`.

Table 18-1. *syslog Facilities on Linux*

Facility	Purpose
auth	Security-related messages
auth-priv	Access control messages
cron	cron-related messages
daemon	Daemons and process messages
kern	Kernel messages
local0–local7	Reserved for locally defined messages
lpr	Spooling (printing) subsystem messages
mail	Mail-related messages
mark	Time-stamped messages generated by rsyslogd (internal use only)
news	Network news–related messages (for example, Usenet)
syslog	syslog-related messages
user	The default facility when no facility is specified
uucp	UUCP-related messages

■ **Note** The `mark` facility is a special case. It is used by the time-stamped messages that `rsyslogd` generates when you use the `-m` (minutes) flag.

There are also two special facilities: *, a wildcard that indicates all facilities, and none, which negates a facility selection.

You can see the wildcard selector in Listing 18-4.

Listing 18-4. rsyslog.conf * Wildcard Selector

```
*.emerg                          :omusrmsg:*
```

This will send all messages of the emerg priority, regardless of facility, to everyone who is logged in.

■ **Tip** The *om* in omusrmsg stands for output module. These are used for processing messages and transmitting them to different targets; you can see more of them here: `www.rsyslog.com/doc/v8-stable/configuration/modules/idx_output.html`.

You can use the none wildcard selector to not select messages from a particular facility. The example shown in Listing 18-5 will tell rsyslog to not log any kernel messages to the file /var/log/messages.

Listing 18-5. rsyslog.conf none Wildcard Selector

```
kern.none                        /var/log/messages
```

Priorities

Priorities are organized in an escalating scale of importance. They are debug, info, notice, warning, err, crit, alert, and emerg. Each priority selector applies to the priority stated and all higher priorities, so mail.err indicates all mail facility messages of err, crit, alert, and emerg priorities.

Like with facilities, you can use the wildcard selectors * and none. Additionally, you can use two other modifiers: = and !. The = modifier indicates that only one priority is selected; for example, cron.=crit indicates that only cron facility messages of crit priority are to be selected. The ! modifier has a negative effect; for example, cron.!crit selects all cron facility messages except those of crit *or higher priority*. You can also combine the two modifiers to create the opposite effect of the = modifier so that cron.!=crit selects all cron facility messages except those of critical priority. Only one priority and one priority wildcard can be listed per selector.

Actions

Actions tell rsyslogd what to do with the event notification messages it receives. Depending on the output modules loaded, rsyslog can perform several potential actions.

- Logging to a file
- Logging to a device
- Logging to a named pipe
- Logging to a specific user or the console
- Sending logs to another host
- Logging to a database table
- Executing a command
- Discarding

Listing 18-6 shows examples of the first four actions `rsyslogd` can take, including logging to a file, device file, named pipes, and the console or a user's screen.

Listing 18-6. File, Device, and Named Pipe Actions

```
cron.err        /var/log/cron
auth.!=emerg    /dev/lpr1
news.=notice    |/tmp/pipe
auth-priv       root,jsmith
```

In the first line, all `cron` messages of `err` priority and higher are logged to the file `/var/log/cron`.

■ **Note** When logging to files, `rsyslogd` allows you to add a hyphen (-) to the front of the file name like this: `-/var/log/auth`. This tells `rsyslog` to not sync the file after writing to it. This is designed to speed up the process of writing to the log. But it can also mean that if your system crashes between write attempts, you will lose data.

The second line has all `auth` messages except those of `emerg` priority being sent to a local printer `lpr1`. The third sends all `news` messages of `notice` or greater priority to a named pipe called `/tmp/pipe`.

■ **Note** Sending to a named pipe allows you to send `rsyslog` data to other applications; for example, you use named pipes to collect log messages and pass them to a log correlation engine or a database.

The fourth and last line sends all `auth-priv` messages to the users `root` and `jsmith` if they are logged in. There is one last action you can perform, sending logs to another host, as you can see in Listing 18-7.

Listing 18-7. Logging to a Remote System

```
mail    @backup.example.com
```

In this example, all `mail` messages are sent to the host `backup.example.com`.
To send all logs, we'd use this syntax:

```
*.*     @backup.example.com
```

`rsyslog` uses UDP port 514 to transmit log messages. This assumes the `rsyslog` daemon on the remote host has been configured to receive logs and that you have suitable firewall rules in place to receive the log entries. Here's an example:

```
$ sudo firewall-cmd --permanent --zone public --add-port=514/udp
```

Here we've created a firewall rule that allows the host to receive `rsyslog` data from the host 192.168.0.254 on UDP port 514. However, since this is UDP, remembering that UDP is a fire-and-forget protocol, there is no guarantee that the server at the other end will receive it.

To get around this and prevent possible message loss, we would use RELP, which is the reliable event logging protocol (see `www.rsyslog.com/doc/v8-stable/configuration/modules/omrelp.html`).

```
*.*     :omrelp:backup.example.com:2514
```

Of course, we need to load the module in the module section of our `rsyslog.conf` file, and we will show how to configure RELP shortly.

Combining Multiple Selectors

You can also combine multiple selectors in your rsyslog.conf file, allowing for more sophisticated selections and filtering. For example, you can list multiple facilities separated by commas in a selector (see Listing 18-8).

Listing 18-8. Multiple Facilities

```
auth,auth-priv.crit                 /var/log/auth
```

This sends all auth messages and all auth-priv messages with a priority of crit or higher to the file / var/log/auth.

You cannot do this with priorities, though. If you want to list multiple priorities, you need to list multiple selectors separated by semicolons, as shown in Listing 18-9.

Listing 18-9. Multiple Priorities

```
auth;auth-priv.debug;auth-priv.!=emerg       /var/log/auth
```

This example shows you how to send all auth messages and all auth-priv messages with a priority of debug or higher, excluding auth-priv messages of emerg priority to the file /var/log/auth.

■ **Tip**   Just remember with multiple selectors that filtering works from left to right; rsyslogd will process the line starting from the selectors on the left and moving to the right of each succeeding selector. With this in mind, place the broader filters at the left, and narrow the filtering criteria as you move to the right.

You can also use multiple lines to send messages to more than one location, as shown in Listing 18-10.

Listing 18-10. Logging to Multiple Places

```
auth                      /var/log/auth
auth.crit                 jsmith
auth.emerg                /dev/console
```

Here all auth messages are logged to /var/log/auth as previously, but auth messages of crit or higher priority are also sent to user jsmith, if he is logged in. Those of emerg priority are also sent to the console.

It is also common to use the omfwd output module, which allows you to send logs to a remote server via TCP or UDP. If we wanted to send log messages to a local file and to a remote server, we could use something like this:

```
mail.*    action(type="omfile" sync="no" file="/var/log/maillog")
                action(type="omfwd" Target="monitor.example.com"
                Port="10514" Protocol="tcp")
```

You can read more about this module at www.rsyslog.com/doc/v8-stable/configuration/modules/ omfwd.html.

Configuring RELP

RELP allows us to set up central logging servers that can collect and store logs from any number of client servers. RELP is more mature than the remote logging of Journald and has been battle tested by thousands of installations. It is also fairly simple to configure, and the modules can be installed with package management.

```
$ sudo yum install -y rsyslog-relp rsyslog-gnutls
$ sudo aptitude install -y rsyslog-relp rsyslog-gnutls
```

We will need to configure the client and server. RELP allows you to relay logs from clients to servers that can push logs onto other servers. We will use TLS to encrypt our log traffic and avoid rouge clients from connecting and potentially sending bogus log traffic or staging DoS attacks, which is possible with the plain UDP/TCP modules.

On Ubuntu the `syslog` user runs the `rsyslogd` service. Therefore, you will need to make sure that the `syslog` user can read the TLS private keys. You can use the `setfacl` command for this:

```
$ sudo setfacl -m u:syslog:rx /etc/ssl/private
$ sudo setfacl -m u:syslog:r /etc/ssl/private/nfs.example.com.key
```

The `root` user runs the `rsyslogd` service on CentOS and does not need changing.

Configuring RELP Client

We will start with the RELP client configuration. We will assume that the hosts already have a TLS key and public certificate that has been signed by our private CA. We will again use the gateway host, and it will connect and send its logs to the `backup.example.com` host.

```
$ sudo vi /etc/rsyslog.d/relp.conf
# make gtls driver the default
$DefaultNetstreamDriver gtls

# certificate files
$DefaultNetstreamDriverCAFile /etc/pki/tls/certs/cacert.pem
$DefaultNetstreamDriverCertFile /etc/pki/tls/certs/gateway.example.com.cert
$DefaultNetstreamDriverKeyFile /etc/pki/tls/private/gateway.example.com.key

$ActionSendStreamDriverAuthMode x509/name
$ActionSendStreamDriverPermittedPeer backup.example.com
$ActionSendStreamDriverMode 1
*.* @@backup.example.com:6514
```

We have created a file called `relp.conf` and have configured it to use an encrypted transport between the client and the `backup.example.com` host. We do this via a NetStreamDriver called `gtls`, which implements our TLS transport (GnuTLS). A NetStreamDriver can provide sequenced delivery, authentication, and secure transport.

We need to provide our TLS certificate files, and they are described as shown previously. Remember that on Ubuntu the TLS files will have a different path.

We handle authentications via our certificate names (`x509/name`). That means we verify our connection to our peer by testing their common name in their TLS certificate. If it matches the peer `backup.example. com`, then we will permit the connection; if not, we will fail it. The mode 1 signifies that we will use TLS.

The last line says that we will ship all facilities and priorities (*.*) to backup.example.com on port 6514. You will now restart the rsyslog daemon.

```
$ sudo systemctl restart rsyslog
```

Configuring RELP Server

Now we can configure our RELP server. This is going to collect our logs from our network and store them. The configuration is similar to the client, and our backup host looks like this:

```
$ sudo vi /etc/rsyslog.d/relp.conf
$ModLoad imtcp

$DefaultNetstreamDriver gtls

$DefaultNetstreamDriverCAFile /etc/pki/tls/certs/cacert.pem
$DefaultNetstreamDriverCertFile /etc/pki/tls/certs/backup.example.com.cert
$DefaultNetstreamDriverKeyFile /etc/pki/tls/private/backup.example.com.key

$InputTCPServerStreamDriverAuthMode x509/name
$InputTCPServerStreamDriverPermittedPeer *.example.com
$InputTCPServerStreamDriverMode 1
$InputTCPServerRun 6514
```

First we will need to load our imtcp module, which will provide TCP connections. Then we have the same configuration options as we had in the client for our TLS keys except we change the names. We accept all peers that are signed by our CA with example.com in their common name. The last line tells rsyslogd to run a TCP server on port 6514.

Now we will need to make sure that port 6514 is open on our backup server, which is a CentOS server, so we use the firewall-cmd command.

```
$ sudo firewall-cmd --permanent --zone public --add-port=6514/tcp
$ sudo firewall-cmd --reload
```

Then we restart the rsyslog daemon on the backup server too.

```
$ sudo systemctl restart rsyslog
```

On the backup server we can now inspect our /var/log/messages file, and we should see logs similar to these:

```
Dec  1 12:01:17 gateway chronyd[608]: Selected source 27.124.125.250
Dec  1 12:01:19 gateway chronyd[608]: Selected source 27.124.125.250
Dec  1 12:01:21 backup systemd: Starting user-0.slice.
Dec  1 12:01:01 backup systemd: Started Session 143 of user root.
Dec  1 12:05:51 gateway chronyd[608]: Selected source 202.127.210.37
Dec  1 12:08:22 dc1 systemd[1]: Started CUPS Scheduler.
```

The logs are coming in with the timestamp, hostname, service, and message being written. There we can see that the host gateway, the host dc1 and the backup server are all now logging to our backup server.

Starting and Stopping rsyslog

The rsyslogd daemon is usually started when your system boots up. You can manually start and stop the rsyslog daemon with the systemctl command.

```
$ sudo systemctl start rsyslog
$ sudo systemctl stop rsyslog
$ sudo systemctl status rsyslog
```

On both CentOS and Ubuntu, you can customize rsyslogd's options using the /etc/sysconfig/rsyslog and /etc/default/rsyslogd files, respectively.

When setting up your host, it is important to note the following. If your logs are located in the root partition, your system can potentially crash. To reduce the risk of this potential crash, we recommend you store your logs on a nonroot (non-/) partition. This means that even if all the space on your disk is consumed, the system will not crash.

Testing Logging with logger

Present on both CentOS and Ubuntu, logger is a useful command-line tool to test your logging configuration.

```
$ logger -p mail.info "This is a test message for facility mail and priority info"
```

This would write the message "This is a test message for facility mail and priority info" to your rsyslog daemon and into whatever destination you have configured for messages with a facility of mail and a priority of info.

As you can see, the -p parameter allows you to specify a facility and priority combination, and then the test message is contained in quotation marks.

We often use logger inside bash scripts to generate multiple messages for testing purposes. The script in Listing 18-11 generates an rsyslog message for every facility and priority combination.

Listing 18-11. Log Testing bash Script

```
#!/bin/bash


for f in
{auth,authpriv,cron,daemon,kern,lpr,mail,mark,news,rsyslog,user,uucp,local0,local1,
local2,local3,local4,local5,local6,local7}

    do
     for p in {debug,info,notice,warning,err,crit,alert,emerg}
    do
      logger -p $f.$p "Test rsyslog messages from facility $f with priority $p"
    done
    done
exit 0
```

You can also use logger to pipe a growing file into rsyslog.

```
$ tail -f /tmp/logfile | logger -p daemon.info
```

Here we've tailed the file /tmp/logfile into the logger command. Each line in the file would be written to the daemon facility with a priority of info.

Log Management and Rotation

An important part of managing your logging environment is controlling the volume of your log files and keeping your log files to a manageable size. To do this, you can rotate your logs.

Log rotation is the process of periodically copying the log file and usually adding a suffix like the date or an incrementing number. The rsyslog daemon then logs to a new file. You would usually keep rotated log files for a fixed period, for example, a week or a month.

Let's look at an example. We've got the /var/log/mail.log file. We could rotate this file daily and keep the rotated files for seven days. The log rotation process would kick off at a time we specified, copy the existing mail.log file to mail.log.1, for example, and then create an empty mail.log file. The log rotation process would also increment; if a mail.log.1 file existed, this file would be renamed to mail.log.2, and so on. If there were a mail.log.7 file, this file would be deleted, and the mail.log.6 file incremented to mail.log.7.

Log rotation can be quite complicated to manually manage, so we recommend you use the logrotate tool. Both CentOS and Ubuntu come with the logrotate tool, and it is usually installed and configured for you already. The default configuration handles most typical log files from applications installed on the host.

The logrotate command is simple to configure and relies on crontab to run on a scheduled basis. The base logrotate configuration is located in /etc/logrotate.conf, and you can see a typical file in Listing 18-12.

Listing 18-12. logrotate.conf

```
weekly
rotate 4
create
dateext
include /etc/logrotate.d
/var/log/wtmp {
    monthly
    create 0664 root utmp
    minsize 1M
    rotate 1
}
/var/log/btmp {
    missingok
    monthly
    create 0600 root utmp
    rotate 1
}
```

This simple file contains the global options that logrotate uses to handle log files. In this example, we have removed empty lines and comments. All logs files rotate weekly, logs are rotated four times before they are deleted, new log files are created, rotated files have a date extension added to them, and the logrotate tool checks the logrotate.d directory for any new logrotate files. You can use other options, some of which are shown in Table 18-2. You can delve into the logrotate man file for other options.

Table 18-2. logrotate.conf Options

Option	Description
daily	Logs are rotated on a daily basis.
weekly	Logs are rotated on a weekly basis.
monthly	Logs are rotated on a monthly basis.
compress	Old log files are compressed with gzip.
create mode owner group	New log files are created with a mode in octal form of 0700 and the owner and group (the opposite is nocreate).
ifempty	The log file is rotated even if it is empty.
include directory or filename	The contents of the listed file and directory to be processed by logrotate.
are included.	
mail address	When a log is rotated out of existence, it is mailed to address.
nomail	The last log is not mailed to any address.
missingok	If the log file is missing, it is skipped and logrotate moves on to the next without issuing an error message.
nomissingok	If the log file is missing, an error message is issued (the default behavior).
rotate count	The log files are rotated count times before they are removed. If count is 0, old log files are removed, not rotated.
size size[M,k]	Log files are rotated when they get bigger than the maximum size; M indicates size in megabytes, and k indicates size in kilobytes.
sharedscripts	Prescripts and postscripts can be run for each log file being rotated. If a log file definition consists of a collection of log files (for example, /var/ log/samba/*) and sharedscripts is set, then the pre-script/post-scripts are run only once. The opposite is nosharedscripts.

Listing 18-12 shows the last command, include, which principally drives logrotate. The logrotate.d directory included in Listing 18-12 holds a collection of files that tell logrotate how to handle your various log files.

You can also define additional directories and files and include them in the logrotate.conf file to suit your environment. Most distributions, however, use the logrotate.d directory and come with a number of predefined files in this directory to handle common log rotations such as mail, cron, and rsyslog messages. We recommend you add any new log rotation files here.

■ **Note** Many packages will also add log rotation files to this directory when installed.

Listing 18-13 shows you one of these files.

Listing 18-13. CentOS rsyslog logrotate File

```
/var/log/messages /var/log/secure /var/log/maillog /var/log/spooler ↵
/var/log/boot.log /var/log/cron
{
daily
rotate 7
sharedscripts
postrotate
    /bin/kill -HUP 'cat /var/run/rsyslogd.pid 2> /dev/null' 2> /dev/null || true
endscript
}
```

Inside these files you can override most of the global options in `logrotate.conf` to customize your log rotation for individual files or directories. Listing 18-13 first lists all the files to be rotated. This could also include directories using the syntax /path/to/log/files/*.

Then enclosed in { } are any options for this particular set of files. In this example, we have overridden the global logging options to rotate these files on a daily basis and keep seven rotations of the log files.

Next, we run a script. You can run scripts using the `prerotate` command, which runs the script prior to rotating any logs, or using `postrotate`, which runs the script after rotating the log file (or log files).

Listing 18-13 shows a script that restarts the `rsyslog` daemon after the log file (or log files) has been rotated. As the option `sharedscripts` is enabled, the script will be run only once no matter how many individual log files are rotated. The script statement is terminated with the `endscript` option.

So, how does `logrotate` run? By default on both CentOS and Ubuntu, `cron` runs `logrotate` at scheduled times (through a script `/etc/cron.daily`; it is executed by Anacron). You can also manually run it on the command line.

If running on the command line, `logrotate` defaults to a configuration file of `/etc/logrotate.conf`. You can override this configuration file, as you can see on the following line:

```
$ sudo logrotate /etc/logrotate2.conf
```

The `logrotate` command also has several command-line options to use, as shown in Table 18-3.

Table 18-3. *logrotate Command-Line Options*

Option	Description
-d	Debug mode in which no changes will be made to log files; it will output the results of what it may have rotated. Implies verbose mode also.
-v	Verbose mode.
-f	Forces a log rotation even if not required.

By default on most systems, `logrotate` is run on a daily basis by `cron`, and this is the model we recommend you use.

Log Analysis and Correlation

Now that you have all of these log files, what can you do with them? Well, logs are useful for two purposes.

- To identify when something has gone wrong
- To help diagnose the problem when something has gone wrong

To achieve the first objective, you need a tool that will identify particular log messages and alert you to their presence. This process is called *log analysis and correlation,* and it is often considered a black art. The good news is we're going to introduce you to a tool called Logstash.

Logstash is going to feed all our logs into a distributed search and analytics tools called Elasticsearch. From there we can view the log data we collect with an interface called Kibana. This will help make log analysis and correlation a simple part of your daily monitoring routine.

The first thing to remember is that analysis and correlation are two very different things. *Analysis* is the study of constituent parts and their interrelationships in making up a whole. As a system administer, the best analysis tool available is you. System administrators learn the patterns of their hosts' operations and can often detect a problem far sooner than automated monitoring or alerting systems have done on the same problem.

There are two problems with this model, though. The first is that you cannot be everywhere at once. The second is that the growing volume of the data collected by the systems can become overwhelming.

This is where correlation comes in. *Correlation* is best defined as the act of detecting relationships between data. You set up tools to collect your data, filter the "wheat from the chaff," and then correlate that remaining data to put the right pieces of information in front of you so you can provide an accurate analysis.

Properly set up and managed tools can sort through the constant stream of data from the daily operations of your hosts. They can detect the relationships between that data and either put those pieces together into a coherent whole or provide you with the right pieces to allow you to put that analysis together for yourself.

But you have to ensure those tools are the right tools and are configured to look for the right things so you can rely on them to tell you that something is wrong and that you need to intervene.

The first stage of building such an automated log-monitoring system is to make sure you are collecting the right things and putting them in the right place. Make lists of all your applications, devices, and hosts and where they log. The second stage is bringing together all that information and working out what you really want to know. Make lists of the critical messages that are important to you and your hosts.

Group those lists into priority listings; some messages you may want to be paged for, others can go via e-mail, and some may trigger automated processes or generate attempts at self-recovery such as restarting a process.

The third stage is implementing your log correlation and analysis, including configuring your correlation tools and designing the required responses. Make sure you carefully document each message, the response to the message, and any special information that relates to this message.

Introducing Beats and Logstash

We looked at how the system write logs and manages them; now we want to take a look at the next level of logging, namely, shipping and transforming those logs into useful information. Logstash and Beats help us move the log information off our hosts and process them ready for storage so that we can use discovery tools to see analysis of what is happening on our systems. The storage and discovery are handled by Elasticsearch and Kibana, and we will look those in the next section.

Beats are lightweight forwarders of logs, metrics, network packets data, and Windows events. Lightweight means that they do nothing other than ship data to a remote location, keeping track of what they have shipped. We will look at Filebeat, which will ship our logs to Logstash.

Logstash is a tool that can transform logs (or other data such as metrics and so on) into data that can be indexed and tagged and then stored (or shipped again) to make discovery of that data easier. Logstash can ingest a wide variety of inputs and has a wide variety of outputs, one of those being the ability to write to Elasticsearch.

Logstash has a good selection of plug-ins that can help parse, filter, and transform your data, or you can write your own. Plug-ins are written in Ruby, and you can create input, codec, filter, and output plug-ins to suit your needs if you cannot find any existing plug-ins.

Input plug-ins, as the name suggests, handles the ingestion of data into Logstash. Codec plug-ins are used to change the data representation of an event or stream filter. Filters allow for processing of events before sending to the output (dropping events on certain conditions, anonymize data, and so on). Outputs write the outputs of the Logstash processing to a stash or some kind of storage like Elasticsearch. Other outputs could be S3 or Graphite. The combination of input, codec, filter, and output creates a pipeline.

For a deeper discussion into how Logstash works, see here:

- https://www.elastic.co/guide/en/logstash/current/pipeline.html

Installing and Configuring Beats

Let's take a look now at the first step of the path of our logs. With Beats, particularly Filebeat, we are going to gather data from our host and ship it to a Logstash server. In this scenario, the Filebeat will run on our gateway host and send its data to our monitor server. The monitor server we talked about in Chapter 17 had our Graphite service set up and was used to store the metrics we collected from our hosts via Collectd.

For simplicity we are going to run the Logstash service and Elasticsearch on our monitor host. In a real-world scenario you would have at least three Elasticsearch nodes in a cluster, depending on the amount of transforming and data collection, and you may have a few tiers of Logtash services that would run on one or two other separate nodes.

On the gateway node, we will install Filebeat. We can download Filebeat from https://www.elastic.co/downloads/beats/filebeat, and we can choose the most appropriate package format (RPM, DEB, tar.gz). The gateway host happens to be a CentOS host, so we will install an RPM version.

```
$ sudo yum install -y https://artifacts.elastic.co/downloads/beats/filebeat/filebeat-
5.0.2-x86_64.rpm
```

■ **Tip** You can also set up the APT or YUM repositories on your machines too; see here for details: https://www.elastic.co/guide/en/beats/libbeat/current/setup-repositories.html.

For both Ubuntu and CentOS, the configuration file for Filebeat is stored in /etc/filebeat/filebeat.yml. We are going to send all our logs from /var/log to our Logstash server that will be on the monitor server. We do that with the configuration shown in Listing 18-14.

Listing 18-14. Filebeat.yml

```
filebeat.prospectors:
- input_type: log
  paths:
    - /var/log/messages
    - /var/log/*.log
    - /var/log/audit/audit.log
```

```
tags: ["security", "network"]
fields:
  env: production
output.logstash:
  hosts: ["monitor.example.com:5044"]
  ssl.certificate_authorities: ["/etc/pki/tls/certs/cacert.pem"]
  ssl.certificate: "/etc/pki/tls/certs/gateway.example.com.cert"
  ssl.key: "/etc/pki/tls/private/gateway.example.com.key"
```

It is common to send data to a local Logstash service instead of a remote one as we have done here. This way you can locally transform the data prior to sending across the network. You may want to do this if you require only anonymized data to traverse the network, or you may want to use the distributed processing power of your hosts rather than relying on a centralized Logstash service to transform your data.

The format of Filebeat configuration file is YAML (see the "YAML Format" sidebar for more information). In Listing 18-14 the first line declares our `filebeat.prospectors`. You can have different types of input, and the prospectors file is where you declare them. In Listing 18-14 you can see we declare an `input_type` value of `log`. The other alternative is an input type of `stdin`. We can then list the paths that we want to ingest our logs from. Of course, we would like to gather logs from /var/log/messages. You can use globs to catch all logs (/var/log/*.log), or you can target specific logs (/var/log/audit/audit.log). Here we are capturing any in the /var/log directory (excluding any .gz or -20161131 rotated logs), and we are not capturing anything in /var/log/*/*.log except for those we have specified (audit.log).

YAML FORMAT

YAML Ain't Markup Language, or just YAML, is a human-readable data serialization language. YAML is a superset of the JSON data serialization format and is used commonly for configuration files.

It is structured data that can contain strings, lists, associative arrays, and block scalars.

```
---
key: value
- lista
- listb
keya:
  - valuea
  - valueb
```

You can read more about YAML at www.yaml.org/start.html.

If we wanted a different to capture our Apache logs, we would do that separately like this:

```
- input_type: log
  paths:
    - /var/log/*.log
- input_type: log
  paths:
    - /var/log/apache/httpd-*.log
  document_type: apache
```

We don't run an Apache server on our gateway, but here you can see that we would target the Apache logs as a different input type, and we would apply a document_type of apache. This changes the event type field, one of the metadata tags we apply to our logs, to apache instead of log. This helps us with transformations further down the processing chain.

In Listing 18-14 you will also see that there are global directives we apply to all our data. We tag our data with security and network, and we give it an environment tag of production. This again adds richness to the data we can later use to extract and transform and filter our data.

Our output is going to our Logstash server on the monitor.example.com host. We are going to use TLS-encrypted transport to send our data. We are not anonymizing our logs here, so anything that is sent to the monitoring host can be read in clear text, making us vulnerable to snooping. Encrypting the data prevents this.

There are more configuration options that you can use on your Filebeat prospectors. You can include or exclude specific lines, exclude files, add specific tags, add specific fields, and add multiline pattern matching. You can read more about these here:

- https://www.elastic.co/guide/en/beats/filebeat/current/configuration-filebeat-options.html

We will not start our Filebeat service straightaway, but you can start and stop it using systemctl as you would normally.

```
$ sudo systemctl enable filebeat
$ sudo systemctl start filebeat
```

Before we start our Filebeat service, we will configure our Logstash service to accept the logs.

Installing and Configuring Logstash

Logstash is a Java process that is used to transform data prior to "stashing" the output in some kind of storage for further analysis or viewing. It is very powerful, and you can do a lot with it. This chapter will not do it justice as we are only able to show the barest essentials of its power. In this section we are going to show you how to install and then do a basic configuration so that we can output our log data to Elasticsearch.

The current version of Logstash requires Java 8. We are going to be installing this service on our Ubuntu monitoring host via the APT repository provided at https://www.elastic.co, a company that helps design and support the open source projects of Kibana, Elasticsearch, Logstash, and Beats.

Let's first add the APT repository by first adding the public GPG key, then adding the package apt-transport-https (if it is not already installed), and finally adding the actual repository to APT.

```
wget -qO - https://artifacts.elastic.co/GPG-KEY-elasticsearch | sudo apt-key add -
sudo aptitude install -y apt-transport-https
echo "deb https://artifacts.elastic.co/packages/5.x/apt stable main" | sudo tee -a /etc/apt/
sources.list.d/elastic-5.x.list
sudo aptitude update
```

Here we have used the aptitude package manager, which we have installed rather than apt-get, which you can also use. Now we can install Logstash.

```
$ sudo aptitude install -y logstash
```

For CentOS and the latest installation notes, you can see the instructions here:

- https://www.elastic.co/guide/en/logstash/current/installing-logstash.html

The configuration files for Logstash are kept in /etc/logstash. Mostly you do not need to change any configuration on how the service starts, but if you want, you can do so with the /etc/logstash/startup. options file. That file contains the user that runs the service, the JAVA_OPTS you may like to include, and so on.

We are now going to create a pipeline for processing our logs. We can do this in two ways. We can edit and add to the /etc/logstash/logstash.yml file, which is the main pipeline configuration file, or we can create a file in /etc/logstash/conf.d/, which will be read in by the Logstash service. Let's see how we can collect our log file from the gateway host and any other Beats service.

```
$ sudo vi /etc/logstash/conf.d/general.conf
input {
  beats {
    port => 5044
    ssl  => true
    ssl_certificate => "/etc/ssl/certs/monitor.example.com.cert"
    ssl_key => "/etc/ssl/private/monitor.example.com.key"
    ssl_certificate_authorities [ "/etc/ssl/certs/cacert.pem" ]
    ssl_verify_mode => force_peer
  }
}
output {
  stdout { codec => rubydebug }
}
```

Taking a look at this file, you can see that it is made of two sections: an input and an output. Typically you will see three sections including a filter section.

```
Input {
  ...
}
filter {
  ...
}
output {
  ...
}
```

Those of you familiar with Ruby will recognize this as Ruby hash syntax. JRuby, for Java Ruby, is used with Logstash, and the configuration files are in native Ruby syntax.

In our input section, we have included our beats plug-in, and the beats plug-in accepts the port and SSL configuration options like earlier. This should already be familiar to you, but the important thing to note is that here we are specifying a ssl_verify_mode value of force_peer. This means that if the client does not provide the server with a certificate, we will drop the connection immediately. This will make our system more secure and drop unauthorized connections early.

The output section describes where we will send the data after we have processed it. We can see that we will output the data to stdout, and to help us debug that output, we will use a codec called rubydebug. This is good for viewing what Logstash is doing while we begin our journey. We will also specify elasticsearch as an output, but we don't want to do so at this stage.

We are ready to start our Logstash service and start seeing how it works. We do that via the following command:

```
$ sudo -u logstash /usr/share/logstash/bin/logstash -f /etc/logstash/conf.d/general.conf
WARNING: Could not find logstash.yml which is typically located in $LS_HOME/config or /etc/
logstash. You can specify the path using --path.settings. Continuing using the defaults
Could not find log4j2 configuration at path /usr/share/logstash/config/log4j2.properties.
Using default config which logs to console
04:20:40.036 [[main]-pipeline-manager] INFO  logstash.inputs.beats - Beats inputs: Starting
input listener {:address=>"0.0.0.0:5044"}
04:20:40.072 [[main]-pipeline-manager] INFO  logstash.pipeline - Starting pipeline
{"id"=>"main", "pipeline.workers"=>2, "pipeline.batch.size"=>125, "pipeline.batch.delay"=>5,
"pipeline.max_inflight"=>250}
04:20:40.075 [[main]-pipeline-manager] INFO  logstash.pipeline - Pipeline main started
04:20:40.087 [[main]<beats] INFO  org.logstash.beats.Server - Starting server on port: 5044
04:20:40.134 [Api Webserver] INFO  logstash.agent - Successfully started Logstash API
endpoint {:port=>9600}
```

In the first section we will see the startup output giving us details on what is being started with what parameters. You will see that we are starting the Beats input on port 5044, the main pipeline, and a web API on port 9600.

Now, on the gateway host we can start our `filebeat` service. We do that with the `systemctl` command like so, and then we can tail the logs that are produced by the service.

```
$ sudo systemctl start filebeat && tail -f /var/log/filebeat/filebeat
```

Now on the `monitor` host, we can start the `logstash` service, and we should see a rapid amount of data coming in from our Filebeat on the gateway server.

In Listing 18-15 we see the one of the captured log messages from the gateway host. Each Beat is given its own timestamp, and we are given a bunch of other related metadata like `input_type`, the host it can from, tags we have associated with the Beat, and so on. Each of these Beats will have a host, a source, and a message. The message will have the `rsyslog` format we have already seen.

Listing 18-15. Beat from Gateway Server Logs

```
{
    "@timestamp" => 2016-12-04T06:33:33.868Z,
    "offset" => 11979,
    "@version" => "1",
    "input_type" => "log",
    "beat" => {
        "hostname" => "gateway.example.com",
            "name" => "gateway.example.com",
         "version" => "5.0.2"
    },
    "host" => "gateway.example.com",
    "source" => "/var/log/messages",
     "message" => "Dec  4 06:33:24 gateway jsmith: tesing this is a test",
     "fields" => {
          "env" => "production"
        },
```

```
    "type" => "log",
    "tags" => [
        [0] "security",
        [1] "network",
        [2] "beats_input_codec_plain_applied"
    ]
}
```

Let's briefly take a look at the audit log we are collecting too:

```
    "host" => "gateway.example.com",
    "source" => "/var/log/audit/audit.log",
    "message" => "type=SERVICE_STOP msg=audit(1480834167.796:997): pid=1 uid=0
auid=4294967295 ses=4294967295 subj=system_u:system_r:init_t:s0 msg='unit=NetworkManager-
dispatcher comm=\"systemd\" exe=\"/usr/lib/systemd/systemd\" hostname=? addr=? terminal=?
res=success'",
    "type" => "log",
```

Immediately you will notice that audit.log is not is the same format as your normal rsyslog. The
auditd file is a set of key/value pairs (key=value). They can appear very different from what we see here,
but basically they consist of a type and a message (which includes a timestamp and unique ID). Then,
depending on the type, they can have any number of other keys and values. In this example we have stopped
the openvpn service, and this is the resultant log notification.

This is not in the format that we would like and is not like an rsyslog message. Let's change that so that
we record this as a different type of event. To do that, we will edit the Filebeat configuration on the gateway
host and change the following:

```
filebeat.prospectors:
- input_type: log
  paths:
    - /var/log/messages
    - /var/log/*.log
- input_type: log
  paths:
    - /var/log/audit/audit.log
  document_type: auditd
```

We have moved the audit.log into its own input_type section. To that section we have added the
document_type option and set it to auditd. Now let's show you what that does; go ahead and reload the
Filebeat service.

```
    "host" => "gateway.example.com",
    "source" => "/var/log/audit/audit.log",
    "message" => "type=SERVICE_STOP msg=...terminal=? res=success'",
    "fields" => {
        "env" => "production"
    },
    "type" => "auditd",
```

Now when we get the same message from stopping the openvpn service on the gateway host, the `type` is set to `auditd`. We can now use this in our filter section to make the audit log easier to further process.

Logstash Filters

Logstash filters are a way of parsing and transforming data to make it easier to discover what's in your logs. We are going to take our `auditd` log and extract information and add it to our event data.

When we look at a raw `audit.log` file, we see information like this:

```
type=SERVICE_STOP msg=audit(1480844911.323:1080): pid=1 uid=0 auid=4294967295 ses=4294967295
subj=system_u:system_r:init_t:s0 msg='unit=openvpn@gateway comm="systemd" exe="/usr/lib/
systemd/systemd" hostname=? addr=? terminal=? res=success'
```

These are key=value logs. You can see `type=SERVICE_STOP`, `uid=0`, and `msg='...'` are all key/value pairs. Logstash can understand how to deal with key=values. We do this by telling the filter to take each key and value and assign it. You can also see that there we have an `audit(1480844911.323:1080)`, which is the timestamp (`1480844911.323`, in Unix epoch time) plus a unique ID (`1080`) that marks the event.

So, how do we tell Logstash to work on these events? In our Beat configuration we marked `audit.logs` with the document_type of `auditd`. We saw that the events coming into Logstash from the Filebeat now have the type `auditd` attached to them. We can now match this value and work on the logs that specifically have that data. We do that with a conditional `if` statement in our filter section.

```
filter {
  if [type] == "auditd" {
    # audit.log get matched and worked on here
  }
}
```

Here we are using a conditional `if { ... }` statement that matches on the tag `[type]` if it equals the string `"auditd"`. Now that we are working on the right logs coming through, we can now tell Logstash to create key/value pairs from what it sees. We do this with the following lines:

```
filter {
  if [type] =~ "auditd" {
    kv { }
  }
}
```

This simply will create more labels in our metadata on which we can further work on and use for discovery. Let's take a look at what this does to our Logstash data:

```
{
    "msg" => [
        [0] "audit(1480844911.323:1080):",
        [1] "unit=openvpn@gateway comm=\"systemd\" exe=\"/usr/lib/systemd/systemd\"
        hostname=? addr=? terminal=? res=success"
    ],
    "uid" => "0",
    "ses" => "4294967295",
    "auid" => "4294967295",
    "pid" => "1",
```

```
"source" => "/var/log/audit/audit.log",
"message" => "type=SERVICE_STOP msg=audit(1480844911.323:1080): pid=1 uid=0
auid=4294967295 ses=4294967295 subj=system_u:system_r:init_t:s0 msg='unit=openvpn@
gateway comm=\"systemd\" exe=\"/usr/lib/systemd/systemd\" hostname=? addr=?
terminal=? res=success'",
"type" => "SERVICE_STOP",
"subj" => "system_u:system_r:init_t:s0"
"tags" => [
    [0] "security",
    [1] "network",
    [2] "beats_input_codec_plain_applied"
],
"offset" => 5738705,
"input_type" => "log",
"@timestamp" => 2016-12-04T09:48:31.650Z,
"@version" => "1",
"beat" => {
    "hostname" => "gateway.example.com",
    "name" => "gateway.example.com",
    "version" => "5.0.2"
},
"host" => "gateway.example.com",
"fields" => {
    "env" => "production"
},
}
```

Now you can see that we are adding further texture to our data by labeling it with more usable data. We have ordered the output to be more human readable, but you can see that the first few lines of the output are the key/value pairs from the message contents. We can make it more readable too if we give greater detail to some of those labels. We do this with the mutate and rename functions.

```
filter {
  if [type] =~ "auditd" {
    kv { }
    mutate {
      rename => {
        "type"       => "audit_type"
        "auid"       => "audit_uid"
        "fsuid"      => "audit_fs_uid"
        "suid"       => "audit_set_uid"
        "subj"       => "audit_subject"
        "ses"        => "session_id"
        "hostname    => "audit_hostname"
      }
    }
  }
}
```

Now when we look at our Logstash data, it will look similar to this:

```
{
...
    "audit_uid"      => "4294967295",
    "audit_subject" => "system_u:system_r:init_t:s0",
    "audit_type"     => "SERVICE_STOP",
    "session_id"     => "4294967295",
...
}
```

The mutate function has changed the state of the log information. It has allowed us to take certain fields in the log message and rename them to clearer labels.

Lastly, if we look at the timestamp in the log message it, it doesn't get extracted. We are going to make sure that the data ends up as a label as well. To do that, we use a function called grok. A grok function is made up of two parts, the syntax and the semantic, and is written like this:

```
%{SYNTAX:SEMANTIC}
```

The SYNTAX is a name of a pattern that matches your text. There are quite a few that come with Logstash, and you can view them all here:

- https://github.com/logstash-plugins/logstash-patterns-core/blob/master/patterns/grok-patterns

The patterns are regular expressions that map to a name. The timestamp we are dealing with is in epoch or Unix epoch and is the number of seconds since 1970. Since it is a number, we can use the native Logstash NUMBER pattern to match it.

The SEMANTIC is just the identifier we will give it so that we add greater value to our metadata labels. We will give it audit_epoch.

As we have said, there are two parts to the timestamp audit(1480844911.323:1080): the time and the unique identifier. We will use grok to search for the string containing the epoch and the unique ID and extract them as labels for us.

```
grok {
  match => { "msg" => "audit\(%{NUMBER:audit_epoch}:%{NUMBER:audit_counter}\):" }
}
```

Here we are telling grok to match the msg key and find the audit(<somenumber>:<somenumber>): string. For the first match we will give it the name audit_epoch, and for the second we will give it audit_counter. Now when we run our Logstash service again, we will see the following appear:

```
{
...
    "offset" => 5745528,
    "audit_epoch" => "1480846476.689",
   "audit_counter" => "1106",
...
}
```

We now have our audit log being successfully transformed and adding extra labels to our Logstash data. We can now begin to add that into Elasticsearch.

Elasticsearch for Log Stashing

We have our logs being shipped from our Filebeat, we have the logs going into our Logstash service, and we are transforming some of our logs to be more discoverable after we store them. Let's now take a look at where we will store our log data, namely, Elasticsearch.

Elasticsearch is an Apache Lucene–based full-text search and analytics engine. (Lucene is a code library and API: `http://lucene.apache.org/core/`.) Elasticsearch is great at searching and making sense of text-based data. It has a RESTful API that allows you to query and store data. It is based on a distributed architecture and can store petabytes of searchable data.

Elasticsearch will store our log data from Logstash in an index. An *index* is a logical namespace for data. With Logstash, by default, we create an *index* for each day's log data. An *index* is made up of *documents*, which are the equivalent of relational database rows. Each *index* has a *mapping* that defines the *types* in the index and other index settings and describe how the *index* can be searched. A *type* is the type of document, like a *user* or a *log*, and is used by the API as a filter. The *document* is a JSON object, and each has a *type* and an *ID*. The *document* is made up of one or more *key/value pairs*.

Each document is stored in one primary shard and can have zero or more replica shards, which are for redundancy and performance. Shards are distributed among the nodes in the Elasticsearch cluster. When a node goes down, replica shards can be promoted to primary shards, and shards can be redistributed across the cluster.

We are going to install it and configure it on our monitoring host, which is a single node. Depending on how much data you intend to have, you will obviously need to make some decisions about your deployment. For distributed systems, it is always good to deploy in odd numbers, as in 1, 3, 5, 7, and so on. This helps reduce the risk of split-brain events like those we talked about with GlusterFS in Chapter 13.

Elasticsearch Installation and Configuration

Elasticsearch installations require a minimum of 4GB of RAM to run the service and will fail to start without it. The installation is simple once we have the APT repository configured provided by Elastic Co. (the one we configured in the installation of Logstash).

Not surprisingly, the installation is simply using the aptitude package manager:

```
$ sudo aptitude install -y elasticsearch
```

In our one server scenario, we do not need much extra configuration. We can start the Elasticsearch service now, and we can start storing our logs in it. However, if we want to create an Elasticsearch cluster, we will need to edit the /etc/elasticsearch/elasticsearch.yml file.

To create an Elasticsearch cluster, you need to supply the cluster name and the node name. Let's edit the file like so:

```
cluster.name: monitor
node.name: monitor-node-1
```

Also within the elasticsearch.yml file, we can set the data path where we store data, the log directory, network options, and so on.

For service discovery, or how Elasticsearch finds other nodes in the cluster, Elasticsearch has a Zen Discovery module. The Zen Discovery module is used to discover other cluster nodes, perform master elections, detect faults, and notify of cluster updates. It does this by sending either network pings to nodes or unicast packets that participating hosts can react to.

Since we are not setting up a cluster, we can just start the service now without changing the configuration.

```
$ sudo systemctl start elasticsearch
```

Of course, we can always use the status subcommand of systemctl to check the status of our Elasticsearch service, but we can also issue the following command from the command line:

```
$ curl http://localhost:9200
{
  "name" : "7mf_JBi",
  "cluster_name" : "elasticsearch",
  "cluster_uuid" : "69nMGfoYRYiwatKO6Nj1BA",
  "version" : {
    "number" : "5.0.2",
    "build_hash" : "f6b4951",
    "build_date" : "2016-11-24T10:07:18.101Z",
    "build_snapshot" : false,
    "lucene_version" : "6.2.1"
  },
  "tagline" : "You Know, for Search"
}
```

This curl command to port 9200 shows that our Elasticsearch server is responding. The response is in JSON format. We can query Elasticsearch further with something like this:

```
curl -H "Content-Type: application/json" "http://localhost:9200/logstash-*/_search" -d '{
  "query": {
    "match": {
      "event_type": "SERVICE_STOP"
    }
  },
  "sort": [ "_doc" ]
}'
```

This curl command now queries the _search URI on Elasticsearch to check whether we have any matches for audit_type "SERVICE_STOP". The -d option for curl allows us to send a data POST, which we send as a JSON-formatted query.

The result of this query can look like this:

```
{
  "took":2,
  "timed_out":false,
  "_shards": {
    "total":5,
    "successful":5,
    "failed":0
  },
  "hits": {
    "total":74,
    "max_score":null,
    "hits":[...the events...]
  }
}
```

The first section tells us how long it took to run the query and that we successfully queried five shards. In the hits section, we have a total of 74 hits for SERVICE_STOP audit_type. There will be list of events that match printed also. So, now we can see that our Logstash service is sending data in from our gateway server as we expected.

Rather than using `curl` commands to search your logs, there is another open source tool that can help visualize our logs, Kibana. We will now show you how to install and configure it.

Kibana Installation and Configuration

Kibana has been packaged by Elastic Co. as well and is available from their APT (and YUM) repository. This makes installation again easy for us. As you can guess, installation is as follows:

```
$ sudo aptitude install -y kibana
```

The configuration of Kibana will by default look at `localhost:9200` for an Elasticsearch service. The configuration file is located here: `/etc/kibana/kibana.yml`.

```
server.port: 5601
server.host: "192.168.0.250"
elasticsearch.url: "http://localhost:9200"
```

Here we are setting up our Kibana server with the following settings. We specify the port to listen on, the IP address to listen on, and where it can find the Elasticsearch service. Now we can start the Kibana service.

```
$ sudo systemctl start kibana
```

We can now open a browser to `http://192.168.0.250`, and we will be presented with the front page of Kibana.

In Figure 18-2 we are presented with the first page for Kibana. This allows us to configure our index pattern. The default, `Logstash-*`, makes sense in this instance since we are dealing with indexes with the naming format of `Logstash-<date>`. We can also set the timestamp field that tells Kibana which field represents the time, but we will leave it as the default. Click Create to continue.

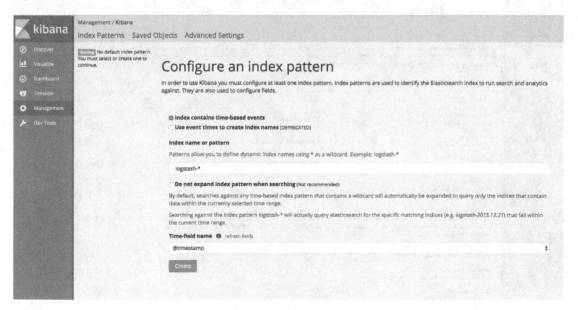

Figure 18-2. *Configuring index pattern*

Figure 18-3 shows all the fields and their associated types in the `Logstash-*` index. To change these, you need to use the mappings API. We are not going to change anything here.

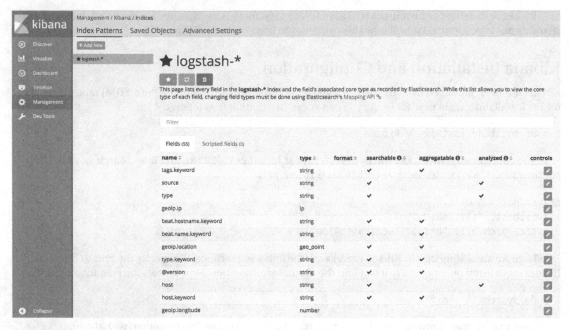

Figure 18-3. *Index patterns*

Figure 18-4 shows the Advanced Settings tab. We can change things such as the default index, date formats, and default columns. We do not need to change anything here.

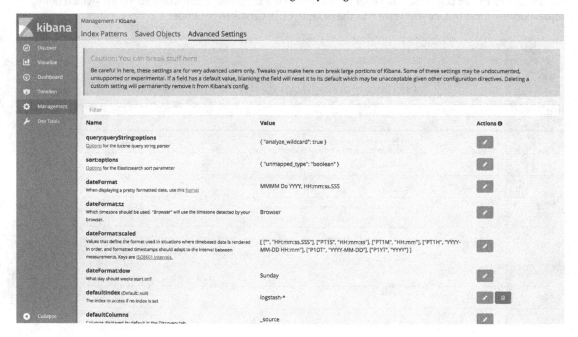

Figure 18-4. *Advanced Settings tab*

The Saved Objects tab in Figure 18-5 shows nothing at the moment. As you create dashboards and visualizations, you will be able to manage them on this tab.

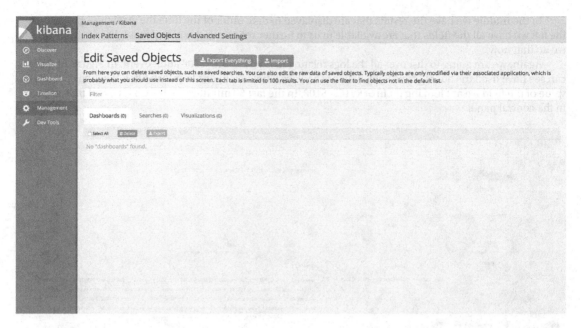

Figure 18-5. *Saved Objects tab*

Figure 18-6 shows the search interface of Kibana. The default view here is the last 15 minutes of our log events. In the top left we can see how many events we can search over (14,094 hits). Just below that is the search bar where we can enter our search queries. Currently, the * means we are searching (and displaying) all 14,094 events. There is a visual display showing how many events we have for a particular time period. We can change the time period by picking a time period from the drop-down in the top right.

Figure 18-6. *All logs for the last 15 minutes*

In the middle we have the results that are displayed in date order of the time the event was created. To the left we have all the fields that are available to us to further refine our query and result list. Let's see how we do that now.

Again, we are going to discover all the logs relating to the SERVICE_STOP audit event. In Figure 18-7 we can see have used the audit_type field, which is how we labeled it in our Logstash filter. We then specify the value of the field we are looking for in SERVICE_STOP. In the last 30 minutes, we have 3 hits, and they appear in the central panel.

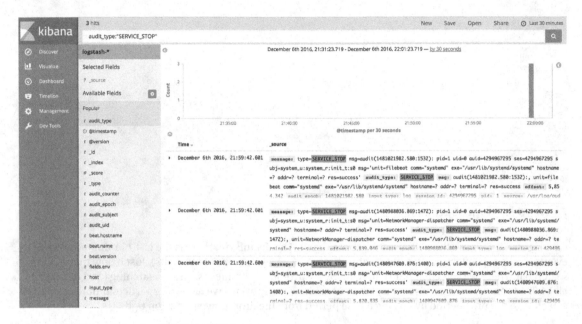

Figure 18-7. *Searching for SERVICE_STOP*

Further Information

For further information on Beats, Logstash, Elasticsearch, and Kibana, you can see the following:

- `https://logstashbook.com/`
- `https://www.elastic.co/products`

Monitoring

Once you have all your applications and services running, you need to have some mechanism available to monitor them. This ensures your host lets you know when important events occur, such as when disk space runs out on a host or when a service unexpectedly stops.

In the IT world, this monitoring mechanism is called *enterprise monitoring*. Like the other applications and tools we've introduced you to in this book, a number of open source tools are available that can perform this monitoring.

- Hyperic (www.hyperic.com/)

- M/Monit (http://mmonit.com/)

- Nagios (www.nagios.org)

- OpenNMS (www.opennms.org/)

- Zenoss (http://zenoss.com/)

- Zabbix (www.zabbix.com/)

Probably the most well-known of these is Nagios, which we'll take a closer look at next.

Introducing Nagios-Core

Nagios-Core is a popular GPL-licensed monitoring tool that allows you to monitor infrastructure, applications, and even environmental characteristics such as power and air conditioning. It comes with a simple web console that gives you a visual view of the state of your hosts and services. You can see an example console screen in Figure 18-8.

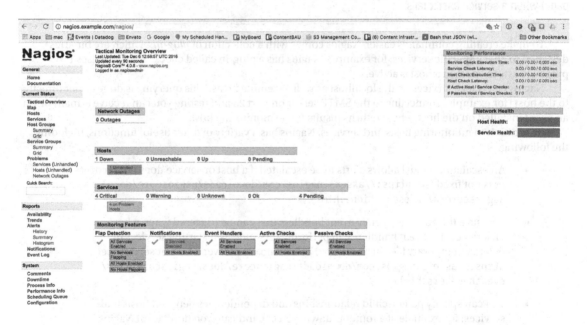

Figure 18-8. *An example console*

We're going to introduce you to Nagios-Core and how to use it to monitor your hosts and services. Nagios-Core is an open source version of Nagios that has been around for many years. There is now a commercial version of Nagios available if you require extra features or support. We're going to show you how to set up some basic monitoring for your host and for some of the services we've introduced you to earlier in the book.

For this book, we'll look at the latest version, version 4, of Nagios—it is packed full of features and functions. Nagios, however, is too complex to explain completely in this single chapter. Luckily, Nagios is very well documented, and you can find the documentation for version 4 at `https://assets.nagios.com/downloads/nagioscore/docs/nagioscore/4/en/`. CentOS has version 4 available from the EPEL repository. Ubuntu is still on version 3, but you can download the source code for version 4 from the Nagios web site and compile it.

Nagios is capable of monitoring a wide variety of hosts and services on a number of platforms including Linux, BSD, Solaris, and even Windows (see `https://assets.nagios.com/downloads/nagioscore/docs/nagioscore/4/en/monitoring-windows.html` for instructions on monitoring on Windows).

Nagios runs as a daemon and monitors the services on your hosts and their state. It can monitor to confirm both that a service is running and that it is performing appropriately. For example, if we were to monitor that a host is active using an ICMP ping (which we discussed in Chapter 7), we could configure it to alert if it can't contact the host or if responses take longer than a specified time to return.

To do this monitoring, you tell Nagios about your hosts and services by defining them as objects in the Nagios configuration. Each host is defined to Nagios, and then the services that run on that host are defined.

You also tell Nagios how you are going to monitor each host and service by defining commands. Each service uses particular commands to check its status, and each command specifies the binary or script used to check the status of a service.

■ **Note** You will also define commands to send notifications (for example, to generate an e-mail or send a page) when a service check fails.

To make creating commands easier, Nagios comes with a collection of *plug-ins*, which are binaries designed to check specific services; for example, Nagios has a plug-in called `check_icmp` that uses IMCP ping requests to confirm a host is active.

Nagios can query services on the localhost as well as remote hosts. This querying is done either directly to the host (for example, connecting to the SMTP server on port 25 and testing you can receive e-mail) or via an agent installed on the host, which returns results to the monitoring host.

In addition to monitoring hosts and services, Nagios has a variety of other useful functions, including the following:

- An escalation model allows alerts to be escalated if a host or service does not recover or is not fixed (see `https://assets.nagios.com/downloads/nagioscore/docs/nagioscore/4/en/escalations.html`).

- You have the ability to specify event handlers that can be triggered when a host or service fails. Event handlers can perform tasks such as restarting services or deleting temporary files in an effort to automatically recover a host or service (see `https://assets.nagios.com/downloads/nagioscore/docs/nagioscore/4/en/eventhandlers.html`).

- You can specify parent-child relationships and dependencies between hosts and services; for example, if a router is down, you can indicate you don't want Nagios to bother to check hosts behind that router because they won't be contactable (see `https://assets.nagios.com/downloads/nagioscore/docs/nagioscore/4/en/dependencies.html`).

- You can design a distributed monitoring environment where there are redundant monitoring servers or where checks are distributed over multiple sites or locations (see `https://assets.nagios.com/downloads/nagioscore/docs/nagioscore/4/en/distributed.html` and `https://assets.nagios.com/downloads/nagioscore/docs/nagioscore/4/en/redundancy.html`).

Installing Nagios

Nagios is easy to install, and packages are available for both CentOS and Ubuntu.

Installing Nagios on CentOS

On CentOS, we can install our Nagios package with the following:

```
$ sudo yum install nagios nagios-plugins nagios-plugins-ssh nagios-plugins-smtp
nagios-plugins-bacula ↵
nagios-plugins-disk nagios-plugins-fping nagios-plugins-http nagios-plugins-ldap
nagios-plugins-mysql
```

We have chosen a selection of plug-ins to install as well. While we won't show you how to use each plug-in, you can see that there are plug-ins available for most of the services we have shown in this book.

Installing Nagios on Ubuntu

On Ubuntu, the default version of Ubuntu is version 3. If we want to install version 4, we will have to install from source.

```
$ sudo apt-get install nagios3 nagios-plugins
```

This will install Nagios version 3 and all the required supporting packages including the Nagios plug-ins.

If you want to install from source (for either CentOS or Ubuntu, but this is for Ubuntu), you need to do the following.

First we need to create users and groups to run and manage the Nagios service.

```
$ sudo useradd nagios  && \
sudo groupadd nagcmd && \
sudo usermod -aG nagcmd www-data && \
sudo usermod -aG nagcmd nagios
```

We have added the nagcmd group to the www-data and nagios users so that the web service can read the Nagios results. Now we need to download the source, untar it, and then enter the directory.

```
$ wget https://assets.nagios.com/downloads/nagioscore/releases/nagios-4.2.3.tar.gz && \
tar zxf nagios-4.2.3.tar.gz && \
cd nagios-4.2.3/
```

If you remember when we compiled Nginx in Chapter 8, we will do something similar now to Nagios. We first have to configure any special requirements for our installation, then compile any binaries, and finally install Nagios onto our system.

```
$ ./configure --with-httpd-conf=/etc/apache2/conf-available \
   --with-nagios-user=nagios \
   --with-nagios-group=nagcmd \
   --sysconfdir=/etc/nagios
```

Here we have configured our Nagios service to place the Apache configuration into the appropriate place (you may like to choose /etc/apache2/sites-available instead here). We have declared the user and group, and we have placed our --sysconfdir (system configuration directory) in /etc/nagios, which is common in CentOS (in Ubuntu it is normally /etc/nagios<version number>, but we are not choosing that here).

Now we need to compile the source code and then install the various components.

```
$ sudo make all
$ sudo bash -c 'make install
make install-init
make install-config
make install-commandmode
make install-webconf'
```

The configuration files are installed in /etc/nagios, and the Nagios binary is installed in /usr/local/nagios/bin/nagios. If you want to install the latest plug-ins, you can do so like this:

```
$ wget https://nagios-plugins.org/download/nagios-plugins-2.1.4.tar.gz && \
tar zxf nagios-plugins-2.1.4.tar.gz && \
cd nagios-plugins-2.1.4/ && \
./configure --with-nagios-user=nagios --with-nagios-group=nagcmd && \
make && sudo make install
```

This will install the plug-ins into the /usr/local/nagios/libexec/ directory. The last thing we need to do is make sure we have a systemd service file to start the service.

```
$ sudo vi /etc/systemd/system/nagios.service
[Unit]
Documentation=man:systemd-sysv-generator(8)
SourcePath=/etc/init.d/nagios
Description=LSB: nagios host/service/network monitoring and management system
Before=multi-user.target
Before=multi-user.target
Before=multi-user.target
Before=graphical.target
Before=shutdown.target
After=local-fs.target
After=remote-fs.target
After=systemd-journald-dev-log.socket
After=nss-lookup.target
After=network-online.target
After=time-sync.target
Wants=network-online.target
Conflicts=shutdown.target
```

```
[Service]
Type=forking
Restart=no
TimeoutSec=5min
IgnoreSIGPIPE=no
KillMode=process
GuessMainPID=no
RemainAfterExit=yes
ExecStart=/etc/init.d/nagios start
ExecStop=/etc/init.d/nagios stop
ExecReload=/etc/init.d/nagios reload
```

Because there is no native systemd service file available for Ubuntu just yet, the Nagios installation will deploy the /etc/init.d/nagios file, and we just have to point this service file at it (we spoke about Ubuntu's adoption of systemd in Chapter 6 and how it still uses some LSB init files to start services).

Starting Nagios

On both CentOS and Ubuntu, we start and stop Nagios with the systemctl command.

```
$ sudo systemctl start nagios
```

The nagios daemon logs to the /var/log/nagios/nagios.log log file. You can confirm that the daemon has successfully started. If it has not, you will see errors in this file. Or course, you can also use the journalctl and systemctl status commands.

Nagios Configuration

We're going to quickly walk you through how to configure Nagios. In simple terms, the steps for configuring Nagios are as follows:

1. Create definitions for the hosts you want to monitor.

2. Create definitions for the services you want to monitor on your hosts.

3. Create commands to monitor your services.

4. Tell Nagios when you want them monitored.

5. Tell Nagios who should be told if a check fails.

6. Tell Nagios how people should be informed if a check fails—e-mail, IM, SMS, pager, chatbot, and so on.

Nagios configuration is made up of objects. You define the host you want to monitor as a host object and each service you want to monitor as a service object. A variety of other object types also exist, such as time-period objects for monitoring periods and contact objects to tell Nagios whom to notify when something occurs.

We're going to show you how to configure your hosts in Nagios and then how to configure a variety of types of services. Along the way, we'll show you a variety of the other elements in the Nagios configuration.

The Nagios configuration is stored in /etc/nagios on CentOS and, depending how you configured your Ubuntu installation, in /etc/nagios as well. Nagios configuration files are suffixed with .cfg, and the main configuration file for Nagios is called nagios.cfg.

Both CentOS and Ubuntu come with some sample configuration to help you get started with Nagios. On both distributions, the /etc/nagios/objects/localhost.cfg configuration file contains some basic configurations for your localhost and some services on it. Also, in that same directory, you will see a few other configuration examples for printers, Windows hosts, time periods, templates, and switches.

Nagios also has a mode that enables you to check your configuration for errors prior to running the daemon. This is useful to confirm you don't have any errors.

On CentOS, we would run the following:

```
$ sudo nagios -v /etc/nagios/nagios.cfg
```

On Ubuntu, depending if you chose Nagios version 3 or built version 4 like we did earlier, you will find it here:

```
$ sudo nagios3 -v /etc/nagios3/nagios.cfg
```

or here:

```
$ sudo /usr/local/nagios/bin/nagios -v /etc/nagios/nagios.cfg
```

The -v option checks that all configuration is correct and, if so, outputs a statistical report showing the number of configuration objects defined.

■ **Note** After changing Nagios configuration, you need to restart the daemon for the new configuration to be parsed.

The nagios.cfg File

The nagios.cfg configuration file contains the base configuration for your Nagios installation. Each option in this file is in the form of an option-value pair. For example, the location of the Nagios log file is specified using the log_file option; on CentOS, this would be done as follows:

```
log_file=/var/log/nagios/nagios.log
```

This is usually the first option in your nagios.cfg file followed by the cfg_file and cfg_dir options that specify the location of your object configuration files. The cfg_file option allows you to specify an individual file that contains the Nagios object configuration. Here's an example:

```
# Definitions for monitoring the local (Linux) host
cfg_file=/etc/nagios/objects/localhost.cfg
```

You can specify multiple files; indeed, many people specify each object type in a separate file to organize them.

```
cfg_file=/etc/nagios/objects/commands.cfg
cfg_file=/etc/nagios/objects/contacts.cfg
cfg_file=/etc/nagios/objects/timeperiods.cfg
cfg_file=/etc/nagios/objects/templates.cfg
...
```

■ **Note** It's a good idea to put your files into a *version control system* (VCS), like Subversion or Git. Such systems track your files and the changes to them. They are commonly used by programmers to track source code and used more and more by system administrators to track configuration files. In Chapter 3 we showed you how to install Git.

Further in the configuration file you will find the `cfg_dir` option, which specifies a directory. Nagios will load any file in this directory with a suffix of `.cfg`. Here's an example:

```
cfg_dir=/etc/nagios/conf.d
```

The `nagios.cfg` file contains a number of other useful options, some of which you can see in Table 18-4.

Table 18-4. nagios.cfg Configuration File Options

Option	Description
resource_file	A separate configuration file used to hold system variables such as paths and passwords.
nagios_user	The user to run Nagios as. This defaults to nagios.
nagios_group	The group to run Nagios as. This defaults to nagios.
log_rotation_method	When to rotate logs. Values are n for no rotation, h for hourly, d for daily, w for weekly, and m for monthly.
log_archive_path	The directory to store archived, rotated log files.
use_syslog	Whether to log Nagios output to syslog (rsyslog). This defaults to 1 for syslog logging. Set to 0 for no syslog logging.

You can also turn on and off checking of hosts and services and the sending of alerts at a global level on the `nagios.cfg` configuration file. For a full list of the available options, see https://assets.nagios.com/downloads/nagioscore/docs/nagioscore/4/en/configmain.html.

Host Configuration

Let's start examining Nagios's configuration by opening CentOS's `/etc/nagios/objects/localhost.cfg` configuration file and looking at its contents, starting with a host object definition.

■ **Note** We've included both the CentOS and Ubuntu sample configuration files with the source code for this chapter.

We're going to start with the host object definition in the file that you can see in Listing 18-16.

Listing 18-16. A Host Object

```
define host {
        use                       linux-server    ; Name of host template to use
                                                   ; This host definition will inherit
                                                   all variables that are defined
                                                   ; in (or inherited by) the linux-
                                                   server host template definition.
        host_name          localhost
        alias              localhost
        address            127.0.0.1
        }
```

You can see that an object definition starts with `define`, the type of object to define (in our case a host object), and the definition, which is enclosed in the { } curly braces. Inside the definition are the attributes of the object defined by a series of key/value statements, separated by spaces. Our host object definition has four attributes: `use`, `host_name`, `alias`, and `address`.

■ **Tip** Some attributes are mandatory for certain object definitions, meaning you must specify the attribute and a value for them. In the Nagios documentation, these values are specified in red at `https://assets.nagios.com/downloads/nagioscore/docs/nagioscore/4/en/objectdefinitions.html`.

The `use` attribute tells our host object to refer to a template. A template is a technique Nagios uses to populate an object definition with values that might be the same across many objects. For example, host objects will share many of the same attributes and characteristics. Rather than specify every single attribute in each host object definition, you can instead refer to a template. Nagios then creates the host object with all the attributes in the host definition plus those attributes in the template. We'll look at the additional attributes defined in the `linux-server` template in Listing 18-17 in a moment.

In this case, the rest of the attributes of our host object define its identity. The `host_name` attribute defines the name of the host object. This name must be unique. You can have only one host object called `localhost` or `headoffice.example.com`. Nagios also makes the `host_name` attribute available as a macro called `$HOSTNAME$`.

■ **Note** Macros allow Nagios to embed information about hosts and services in other object definitions, most specifically the commands Nagios uses to check services and send notifications. You'll see more macros later in this chapter; in the meantime, you can see a full list of these macros at `https://assets.nagios.com/downloads/nagioscore/docs/nagioscore/4/en/macros.html`.

The `alias` attribute is another name for the object; in this case, we've used an alias of `localhost`. This alias is usually used as a longer description of the host and is also available as a macro called `$HOSTALIAS$`.

The last attribute, `address`, provides the IP address of the host; in this case we're monitoring our local host, 127.0.0.1. This IP address must be contactable by Nagios to allow monitoring to take place. It is also available as the macro `$HOSTADDRESS$`.

Host Templates

Now let's see what additional attributes are provided by our linux-server template. In Listing 18-17, you can see the linux-server host object template.

Listing 18-17. A Host Object Template

```
define host {
        name                    linux-server
        use                        generic-host
        check_period        24x7
        check_interval      5
        retry_interval       1
        max_check_attempts  10
        check_command       check-host-alive
        notification_period   workhours
        notification_interval 120
        notification_options  d,u,r
        contact_groups      admins
        register               0
        }
```

You can see we've defined a lot more attributes in our template. First, we define what sort of object this is a template for, in our case a host object. Next, using the name attribute, we give our template a name that must be unique. You can't have two templates named linux-server.

The next attribute is one you've seen before, use, and it allows us to specify a template that this template in turn inherits from. Confused? Simply put, Nagios allows you to chain templates together. This enables you to build quite complex template models that minimize the amount of typing needed to define your monitoring environment. We'll also look at the generic-host template in a moment.

```
dns-servers <- critical-servers <- linux-servers <- generic-host
```

You can define the defaults you want in the generic-host template, override or add to those in linux-servers, override or add to those in critical-servers, and finally override or add to those definitions in the dns-servers template. The host definition again can override or add to those definitions defined in the templates.

The next five attributes in Listing 18-17, check_period, check_interval, retry_interval, max_check_attempts, and check_command, are all related.

Time Periods

The first attribute, check_period, tells Nagios when to check the host. In our case, we've specified a time period called 24x7. We also need to define this time period in our Nagios configuration.

```
define timeperiod{
        timeperiod_name         24x7
        alias                   24 Hours A Day, 7 Days A Week
        Sunday                  00:00-24:00
        monday                  00:00-24:00
        tuesday                 00:00-24:00
        wednesday               00:00-24:00
        Thursday                00:00-24:00
        friday                  00:00-24:00
        saturday                00:00-24:00
        }
```

This is a simple time-period definition, which has a timeperiod_name, in our case 24x7, and an alias description. We've then defined each day of the week and the times during those days that we want the time period to cover. In this time-period definition, we're defining every day of the week and 24 hours a day.

To not cover a particular day, you simply don't specify it. The times are specified in 24-hour time, and you can specify multiple ranges. Here's an example:

```
Sunday      00:00-02:00,17:00-19:00
```

Here our time period is Sunday from midnight to 2 a.m. and from 5 p.m. to 7 p.m.

Time periods are used in number of places in Nagios, but most commonly they specify when hosts and services should be checked and when notifications (messages generated when hosts and services fail or vary from their required state) should be sent.

The next attribute, max_check_attempts, specifies the number of times Nagios checks a host or service before determining that there is a problem.

The check_interval specifies how long between checks, and if there is a failure, we can use retry_interval to check more or less frequently.

Commands

The last attribute, check_command, tells Nagios what command to use to check the host's status, in this case check-host-alive.

This is one of the commands we discussed earlier. Let's look at it now.

```
define command{
        command_name    check-host-alive
        command_line    $USER1$/check_ping -H $HOSTADDRESS$ -w 3000.0,80% -c 5000.0,100% -p 1
        }
```

Commands are defined just like other objects. They are named with the command_name attribute, and the actual command to be executed is specified via the command_line attribute. In this case, we've specified the following line:

```
$USER1$/check_ping -H $HOSTADDRESS$ -w 3000.0,80% -c 5000.0,100% -p 1
```

The first part of the command, $USER1$, is another Nagios macro. The $USERx$ macros are configuration variables, usually configured in a file called resource.cfg (or another file specified in the nagios.cfg configuration file using the resource_file configuration option). In this example, the value of the $USER1$ macro is the directory that contains the Nagios plug-ins.

```
$USER1$=/usr/lib64/nagios/plugins
```

The next part of the command is the Nagios plug-in the command will employ, check_ping, which uses ICMP pings to check the status of your host.

■ **Note**   This assumes your host's firewall is configured to accept ICMP pings, as we discussed in Chapter 7.

In this command, you can see the use of one of Nagios's macros, $HOSTADDRESS$, that you learned earlier contains the IP address of the host. Whenever a host executes the check command, its address replaces the macro. This allows the same command to be used by multiple host objects. The macro is specified as the value of the -H option, which specifies the host to ping.

■ **Note**   You can get the help text from most Nagios plug-ins by running the command with the --help option. You can also run most Nagios plug-ins on the command line to see how they work, their command-line options, and what results they return.

The next two options, -w and -c, specify the thresholds for this check. If these thresholds are broken, Nagios will update the status of the host or service.

Hosts and services have different statuses. A host can be in the UP, DOWN, or UNREACHABLE state, and a service can be in the UP, WARNING, CRITICAL, or UNKNOWN state.

■ **Note**   The UNREACHABLE status is used when dependencies and parent-child relationships have been configured and a host is not available because a parent or host it depends on is not available.

The plug-ins themselves, though, return only the WARNING, CRITICAL, and UNKNOWN states (the UNKNOWN state is generally set when a plug-in fails to run or an error is returned rather than a valid status). When these plug-ins are run for a host, Nagios interprets and converts these statuses into the appropriate UP and DOWN statuses, as you can see in Table 18-5.

Table 18-5. *Nagios Plug-in Status Conversions*

Plug-in Status	Host Status	Status Description
OK	UP	The host is up.
WARNING	UP or DOWN	The host could be up or down but by default is up.
UNKNOWN	DOWN	The host is down.
CRITICAL	DOWN	The host is down.

■ **Note**   This host state is also available to Nagios as a macro called $HOSTSTATE$. Also, see further information about host checking options here: https://assets.nagios.com/downloads/nagioscore/docs/nagioscore/4/en/configmain.html.

The -w and -c options take two values: the round-trip time in milliseconds and the percentage of successful pings needed not to break the threshold. So, if the -w threshold is broken, the WARNING status is generated, and Nagios will mark the host as UP. However, if the -c threshold is broken, the CRITICAL status is generated, and Nagios will mark the host as DOWN. A notification will usually then be generated. The last option on our command line, -p, specifies the number of pings to send.

■ **Note**   In addition to the status returned by a plug-in, for example, WARNING or CRITICAL, you will also get some output describing that state, which you can use in notifications or display in the console. For example, the check_ping plug-in returns PING OK - Packet loss = 0%, RTA = 3.98 ms. This output is also available as a macro called $HOSTOUTPUT$ for hosts and $SERVICEOUTPUT$ for service checks.

Notification Period

The next attribute in Listing 18-17 is the notification_period attribute. This differs slightly from the check period. While checks occur during the check_period time, in our case the 24x7 period, notifications (the alerts that get generated when a status changes) will get sent only during the workhours time period.

```
define timeperiod{
        timeperiod_name     workhours
        alias               "Normal" Working Hours
        monday              09:00-17:00
        tuesday             09:00-17:00
        wednesday           09:00-17:00
        thursday            09:00-17:00
        Friday              09:00-17:00
        }
```

You can see that the workhours time period is 9 a.m. to 5 p.m., rather than 24 hours every day of the week as specified by our 24x7 check period.

The next attribute in Listing 18-17, notification_interval, configures how often Nagios will resend notifications if the status of the host doesn't change; here it's every 120 minutes, or 2 hours.

The notification_options attribute specifies when Nagios should send a notification. Here it is set to d, u, and r, which means Nagios will send notifications when the host is DOWN (d) or UNREACHABLE (u). The last option, r, sends a notification if the host has recovered (i.e., gone from a DOWN or UNREACHABLE state to an UP state).

Contacts and Contact Groups

The next attribute, contact_groups, tells Nagios whom to notify when a notification is generated. In our case, the value of this is admins, which refers to a contactgroup object. Contact groups are collections of contacts, which are the people you want to notify, for example, yourself or another system administrator, when a notification is generated. A contactgroup object looks like this:

```
define contactgroup{
        contactgroup_name       admins
        alias                   Nagios Administrators
        members                 nagios-admin
        }
```

A contact group has a name defined via the contactgroup_name attribute, a description provided by the alias attribute, and a list of the contacts in that group, specified using the members attribute. In this case, the only member of the contact group is nagios-admin, which you can see here:

```
define contact{
        contact_name                    nagios-admin
        alias                           Nagios Admin
        service_notification_period     24x7
        host_notification_period        24x7
        service_notification_options    w,u,c,r
        host_notification_options       d,r
        service_notification_commands   notify-by-email
        host_notification_commands      host-notify-by-email
        email                           nagios-admin@localhost
        }
```

Contacts are simple to define. Each has a name provided via the contact_name attribute and an alias.

For each contact, we specify when they should receive notifications and what notifications they should receive.

For specifying when to receive notifications, we use service_notification_period and host_ notification_period. In our case, the nagios-admin contact will receive notifications during the 24x7 time period you saw earlier, or in real terms 24 hours every day of the week, for both hosts and services.

For specifying which notifications, we use the service_notification_options and host_ notification_options attributes. For services, the nagios-admin contact will receive WARNING, UNKNOWN, or CRITICAL as indicated by the w, u, and c options, respectively; the r option means it will also receive recovery notifications. For hosts, the contact will receive only DOWN (d) and recovery (r) notifications.

The service_notification_commands and host_notification_commands attributes specify the commands Nagios uses to send the notifications. You can specify multiple commands by separating each with a comma. These commands are defined just like the commands used to check your hosts and services. Let's look at one of these commands, notify-by-email.

```
define command{
        command_name      host-notify-by-email
        command_line     /usr/bin/printf "%b" "***** Nagios *****\n\nNotification Type:
$NOTIFICATIONTYPE$\nHost: $HOSTNAME$\nState: $HOSTSTATE$\nAddress: $HOSTADDRESS$\nInfo:
$HOSTOUTPUT$\n\nDate/Time: $LONGDATETIME$\n" | /usr/bin/mail -s "** $NOTIFICATIONTYPE$ Host
Alert: $HOSTNAME$ is $HOSTSTATE$ **" $CONTACTEMAIL$
    }
```

Like the previous command you saw, a name is provided with the command_name attribute, and the actual command to be executed by the command_line attribute. In this case, we're printing some text including a number of macros to the /bin/mail binary.

This would send an e-mail to any required contacts notifying them of the change in status. For example, if Nagios was monitoring our gateway.example.com host and a check of this host failed, a notification much like this would be generated:

```
***** Nagios *****

Notification Type: PROBLEM
Host: gateway.example.com
State: DOWN

Address: 192.168.0.254
Info: PING CRITICAL - Packet loss = 100%

Date/Time: Fri Feb 13 00:30:28 EST 2009
```

■ **Tip** Nagios can issue alerts through more than just e-mail. Indeed, Nagios can issue alerts to anything you can build an alert command for, for example, via API webhooks, ChatBots (Hubot, HipChat, Slack), instant messaging like Jabber, a pager like PagerDuty, or even a ticketing system via their APIs.

Table 18-6 provides a list of the macros used in our notification command.

Table 18-6. Macros in the Notification Command

Macro	Description
$NOTIFICATIONTYPE$	The type of notification, for example, PROBLEM for an issue or RECOVERY sif the host has recovered
$HOSTNAME$	The name of the host you are being notified about
$HOSTSTATE$	The current host state, for example, UP or DOWN
$HOSTADDRESS$	The IP address of the host
$HOSTOUTPUT$	Text output from the command used to check the host's status
$LONGDATETIME$$	The date and time in long format (e.g., Fri Feb 13 00:30:28 EST 2009)
$CONTACTEMAIL$	The e-mail address of the contact to be e-mailed

■ **Note**   You can see a full list of macros and where you can use them at `https://assets.nagios.com/downloads/nagioscore/docs/nagioscore/4/en/macrolist.html`.

Let's get back to our contact definition; you can see the last attribute, `email`, which specifies an e-mail address for notifications to be sent to, which you've seen is available as the `$CONTACTEMAIL$` macro.

In our template, you can see the last attribute in our Listing 18-17 template is `register`. This attribute is what tells Nagios that this is a template rather than a real host definition; when `register` is set to 0, Nagios doesn't try to create the host object. Instead, it ignores it. The default setting for `register` is 1, which means any object definition that doesn't explicitly specify `register` 0 will be assumed to be a real host object and will be monitored by Nagios.

Now let's take a quick look at the parent template, `generic-host`, shown in Listing 18-18.

Listing 18-18. The generic-host Template

```
define host{
        name                           generic-host
        notifications_enabled          1
        event_handler_enabled          1
        flap_detection_enabled         1
        failure_prediction_enabled     1
        process_perf_data              1
        retain_status_information      1
        retain_nonstatus_information   1
        notification_period            24x7
        register                       0
        }
```

■ **Note**   We're not going to explain these options in any detail here; you can see read about them at `https://assets.nagios.com/downloads/nagioscore/docs/nagioscore/4/en/objectdefinitions.html - host`.

Defining Our Host

We are going to define our own hosts. We inherit some of our definitions from the `linux-server` template, which in turn will inherit from the `generic-host` template in the same way as we've shown here. For example, our `gateway.example.com` host would be defined like so:

```
define host{
        use              linux-server
        host_name        gateway.example.com
        alias            gateway.example.com
        address          192.168.0.254
        }
```

■ **Tip**   Don't forget you need to restart Nagios after adding any new configuration.

Here we've defined a host object for gateway.example.com and specified we're going to use the host templates we've just explored. We've specified its internal IP address, 192.168.0.254, and Nagios will use this address to try to monitor the host via ICMP. The firewall on our gateway.example.com host would have to allow ICMP packets to ensure monitoring is possible.

■ **Note** There are several other object definitions related to host monitoring that we haven't looked at that allow you to group hosts together, enable dependencies between hosts, and provide similar functionality. You can see a full list of object types and their attributes at https://assets.nagios.com/downloads/ nagioscore/docs/nagioscore/4/en/objectinheritance.htmlxodtemplate.html.

Service Configuration

Now that you know something about host objects, we're going to examine a service object. Services are defined using the service-type object and are linked to their underlying host. For example, based on our existing configuration examples, Listing 18-19 shows a service that checks the disk space of our root partition.

Listing 18-19. A Service Definition

```
define service{
        use                          local-service
        host_name                    localhost
        service_description      Root Partition
        check_command            check_local_disk!20%!10%!/
        }
```

Our service definition is simple. The use attribute specifies a template our service is going to use. The host_name attribute specifies what host the service runs on, in our case localhost. The service_ description describes the service. Lastly, the check_command attribute specifies the command that the service uses to check the status of whatever is being monitored. This check_command is slightly different; after the command we want to use, you can see a string.

```
!20%!10%!/
```

This string consists of variables we're passing to the command definition, with each variable value prefixed with an exclamation mark (!). So here we are passing the values 20%, 10%, and / to the command. This allows us to reuse a command for multiple services, as you'll see in a moment.

Let's take a quick look at the check_local_disk command:

```
define command{
          command_name     check_local_disk
          command_line         $USER1$/check_disk -w $ARG1$ -c $ARG2$ -p $ARG3$
          }
```

Like our previous command, with command_line we've specified the $USER1$ macro to give us the path to the plug-in being executed. That plug-in is check_disk, which checks the status of a local disk.

You can also see the -w and -c options—which we told you earlier set the threshold values for the WARNING and CRITICAL statuses. Lastly, we have the -p option, which specifies the disk partition we're monitoring. In this command, however, the value of each option is $ARGx$: $ARG1$, $ARG2$, and $ARG3$, respectively. Each of these arguments represents one of the arguments we passed in our check_command attribute in Listing 18-19, so our command_line command in fact looks like the following:

```
command_line    $USER1$/check_disk -w 20% -c 10% -p /
```

This results in a WARNING status being generated when only 20 percent of disk space is available and a CRITICAL status being generated when 10 percent of disk space is free, with both statuses applying to the root filesystem, or /.

To create a service that monitors disks on another partition, for example, /var, we would create a service like the following:

```
define service{
        use                     local-service
        host_name               localhost
        service_description     Var Partition
        check_command           check_local_disk!20%!10%!/var
        }
```

Before we discuss some other services, let's take a quick look at the local-service template our service is using:

```
define service{
        name                    local-service
        use                     generic-service
        max_check_attempts      4
        normal_check_interval   5
        retry_check_interval        1
        register                    0
        }
```

The service template, local-service, is similar to previous templates you've seen but with some additional attributes. The first of these new attributes, normal_check_interval, specifies how often Nagios should check that the service is OK, in this case every 5 minutes. The second new attribute, retry_check_interval, is related. If, when checking the service, Nagios discovers that the service is not OK, it retries the check the number of times specified in the max_check_attempts attribute. This is done before it marks the service as not OK. During this retry period, instead of checking once every 5 minutes as specified in normal_check_interval, the check is made every 1 minute as specified in retry_check_interval.

■ **Note** Nagios has the concepts of *soft* and *hard* states. When a check fails, we've discovered Nagios checks it the number of times specified by max_check_attempts. Until Nagios exhausts all its check attempts, the host or service is marked as a soft fail state. When the check attempts are exhausted and a notification is generated, the host or service is now in a hard fail state. This soft fail mode means that if a host or service has temporarily failed and then recovers, you don't get a notification, thereby reducing the number of potential false positive alerts from your monitoring system. You can read more about this at https://assets.nagios.com/downloads/nagioscore/docs/nagioscore/4/en/statetypes.html.

Note that this template also has a parent template, generic-service, which we're not going to discuss in detail. Suffice to say that options like notification_options, notification_period, contact_groups, and check_period are defined there and can be overridden in downstream templates. The options used in that template are explained at https://assets.nagios.com/downloads/nagioscore/docs/nagioscore/4/en/objectdefinitions.html - service.

■ **Note**   Nagios tries to be smart about monitoring and usually doesn't check hosts for their status unless a service running on that host has an issue. If a service on a host fails, Nagios usually schedules a check of the underlying host, too. You can read more about this at https://assets.nagios.com/downloads/nagioscore/docs/nagioscore/4/en/hostchecks.html.

Let's look at another service definition, this one to monitor a network-based service, in Listing 18-20.

Listing 18-20. A Network-Based Service Definition

```
define service{
        use                             local-service   ; Name of service template to use
        host_name                   gateway.example.com
        service_description     Check SMTP
        check_command           check_smtp!25
        }
```

In Listing 18-20, we have a new service, called Check SMTP, that uses our local-service template and a check_command of check_smtp!25. This passes the value 25 to a command called check_smtp. Let's look at that command now:

```
define command{
        command_name    check_smtp
        command_line     $USER1$/check_smtp -H $HOSTADDRESS$ -p $ARG1$
        }
```

Here we have a command that runs a plug-in called check_smtp. It accepts the $HOSTADDRESS$ macro, which is the IP address of the SMTP server we want to check. The -p option specifies the port (the plug-in defaults to port 25), and we pass in this value as the $ARG1$ macro.

You can see a service alert generated by this service from the nagios.log log file here:

```
[1481325559] SERVICE ALERT: gateway.example.com;Check SMTP;CRITICAL;HARD;4; ↩
CRITICAL - Socket timeout after 10 seconds
```

The nagios.log entry specifies the Unix epoch time (1481325559, or Fri Dec 9 23:19:19 UTC 2016), the type of alert, the host and service, and the nature of the alert including the output from the plug-in.

■ **Note**   You can convert epoch time from the command line: date --date='@1235270465'.

REMOTE MONITORING

So far you've seen only how to monitor services on a local host, such as our local disk, or services that are accessible via the network, such as SMTP, IMAP, or SSH. Nagios can also monitor services on remote hosts that aren't exposed to the network. Nagios comes with a variety of instructions on how to monitor a variety of such remote hosts, but two of the principal popular mechanisms are the NRPE and NSCA plug-ins. There are several others too that can be found here: `https://www.nagios.org/downloads/nagios-core-addons/`.

For operating systems that are unsuitable for installing either plug-in, you can also check via SSH with the `check_by_ssh` plug-in.

NRPE is a tool that allows you to execute the Nagios plug-ins on remote hosts and get the results back to the `nagios` daemon. The Nagios server will schedule and execute each check. In large distributed environments, this can be troublesome because latency and the number of checks really affect performance. You can find the NRPE documentation at `https://github.com/NagiosEnterprises/nrpe`.

NSCA is a service that allows for passive checking. Passive checking is where, instead of the Nagios server reaching out to the monitored client and executing a command, the NSCA service on the monitored client will run checks and then send the results to the Nagios server. This is useful in distributed environments. Details are here: `https://exchange.nagios.org/directory/Addons/Passive-Checks/NSCA--2D-Nagios-Service-Check-Acceptor/details`.

NCPA is designed to be both active and passive. It supports a wide variety of operating systems (including Macs and Windows) and includes a local monitoring interface. See it here: `https://exchange.nagios.org/directory/Addons/Monitoring-Agents/NCPA/details`.

The `check_by_ssh` plug-in allows you to log in to a remote host by SSH, execute a command, and return results. This useful when the operating system supports only SSH access.

You'll find more information on monitoring methods in the following documentation:

- *Monitoring using SNMP:* `https://assets.nagios.com/downloads/nagioscore/docs/nagioscore/4/en/monitoring-routers.htmlhtml`

- *Monitoring Linux/Unix:* `https://assets.nagios.com/downloads/nagioscore/docs/nagioscore/4/en/monitoring-linux.html`

- *Monitoring Windows:* `https://assets.nagios.com/downloads/nagioscore/docs/nagioscore/4/en/monitoring-windows.html`

Simple Remote Monitoring

You can create a variety of network-based services using Nagios plug-ins, but what if you want to monitor services that aren't network facing or on the local host? One of the methods to do this is a special plug-in called `check_by_ssh` (for others, see the "Remote Monitoring" sidebar).

The `check_by_ssh` plug-in uses SSH to connect to a remote host and execute a command. So to make use of the plug-in, you have an SSH daemon running on the remote host, and any intervening firewalls have to allow SSH access to and from the host.

You also need to use key-based authentication between the hosts because Nagios has no capability to input a password when checking the service. So we're going to start by creating a key to use between our Nagios server and the remote host.

■ **Note**   We introduced key-based SSH authentication in Chapter 10.

To create this key, we should be the user who runs Nagios, usually `nagios`. We can do this using the `sudo` command to execute the `ssh-keygen` command from the Nagios home directory of `/var/spool/nagios`.

```
# sudo -u nagios ssh-keygen -t rsa -b 4096
Generating public/private rsa key pair.
Enter file in which to save the key (/var/spool/nagios/.ssh/id_rsa):
Created directory '/var/spool/nagios/.ssh'.
Enter passphrase (empty for no passphrase):
Enter same passphrase again:
Your identification has been saved in /var/spool/nagios/.ssh/id_rsa.
Your public key has been saved in /var/spool/nagios/.ssh/id_rsa.pub.
The key fingerprint is:
df:fc:d6:d2:50:66:65:51:79:d1:f8:56:a1:78:a4:df nagios@nagios.example.com
```

We use the `-t rsa` option to create an RSA key. We are prompted to enter a location for the key, usually in the `.ssh` directory under the home directory of the nagios user—in this case, `/var/spool/nagios/.ssh`. The private key is in the `id_rsa` file, and the public key is in the `id_rsa.pub` file. Instead of entering a passphrase for the key, we press Enter to specify an empty passphrase, because we need the connection to be made without a passphrase or password prompt.

We then need to copy the public key, `id_rsa.pub`, to the remote host and store it in the `authorized_keys` file for the user we're going to connect to. If you are following along with this example, you should create a user on the remote host and specify a password for it. In our case, we do so on the remote `gateway.example.com` host as follows:

```
gateway$ sudo useradd nagios
```

We also need to create the `.ssh` directory on the remote host and protect it.

```
gateway$ sudo mkdir /home/nagios/.ssh
gateway$ sudo chmod 0700 /home/nagios/.ssh
```

We can then copy the file, assuming `jsmith` has the appropriate access to the gateway server.

```
nagios$ scp .ssh/id_rsa.pub jsmith@gateway.example.com:/tmp/authorized_keys
nagios$ ssh jsmith@gateway.example.com
gateway$ sudo mv /tmp/authorized_keys /home/nagios/.ssh/authorized_keys && \
sudo chown nagios /home/nagios/.ssh/authorized_keys && \
sudo chmod 0644 /home/nagios/.ssh/authorized_keys
```

If this succeeds, we should now be able to SSH from the Nagios server to the gateway host without requiring a password. As root, issue the following (as the Nagios user account cannot access a shell as it is set to /sbin/nologin for their account; see the /etc/passwd file):

```
nagios# sudo -u nagios -E ssh nagios@gateway
The authenticity of host 'gateway (192.168.0.254)' can't be established.
ECDSA key fingerprint is 2d:94:d5:bd:3e:40:93:fe:d4:9b:eb:6f:93:4d:f3:a1.
Are you sure you want to continue connecting (yes/no)? yes
Warning: Permanently added 'gateway,192.168.0.254' (ECDSA) to the list of known hosts.
```

Here we have used sudo to execute the ssh command as the nagios user. The –E says use the Nagios user's environment. This is important because this command will write the host key to the Nagios user's ~/.ssh/known_hosts file. We now configure Nagios to use this connection to check services. The check_by_ssh plug-in also relies on having the command to be executed installed on the remote host. This command is usually a Nagios plug-in, and hence the easiest way to do this is to install the Nagios plug-in package on the remote host. On CentOS, we issue the following:

```
gateway$ sudo yum install nagios-plugins nagios-plugins-load
```

On Ubuntu, you can install the plug-ins like we did on the Nagios server, or you should be able to install them from the APT repository.

```
gateway$ sudo apt-get install nagios-plugins
```

We can then define a command that uses the check_by_ssh plug-in to monitor a service on the remote host. For example, to monitor the load on a remote host, we could use the following command:

```
$ sudo vi /etc/nagios/objects/commands.cfg
# ssh_check_commands
define command{
        command_name       check_load_ssh
        command_line       $USER1$/check_by_ssh -H $HOSTADDRESS$ -l nagios  ↵
-C "/usr/lib64/nagios/plugins/check_load -w $ARG1$ -c $ARG2$"
        }
```

We have added the previous command definition to the /etc/nagios/objects/commands.cfg file. We call our command check_load_ssh. The command_line part specifies that we're executing the check_by_ssh plug-in and connecting to the host specified by the -H option.

The -l option specifies the name of the user we want to connect to on the remote host; here we're using the nagios user we just created.

The -C specifies the command we want to run on the remote host. In this case, we're running another, locally installed, Nagios plug-in called check_load and passing two arguments to it as the values of the -w and -c (WARNING and CRITICAL) thresholds.

■ **Tip**   The check_by_ssh command can do a whole lot more. Run it with the --help option to see all its capabilities.

We are going to create a file called `linux-servers-base.cfg` in the `/etc/nagios/objects` directory. This is going to be used to define our gateway host and define the service check we will use to check the load on the gateway server. The file will look like Listing 18-21.

Listing 18-21. linux-servers-base.cfg

```
define host{
        name            basic-ssh-checks
        use                 linux-server
        hostgroups  linux-group
        register        0
        }

define host{
        host_name       gateway
        alias                   gateway.example.com
        use                 basic-ssh-checks
        }

define service{
        use                             local-service
        hostgroup_name          linux-group
        service_description     Current Load
        check_command           check_load_ssh!5.0,4.0,3.0!10.0,6.0,4.0
        }

define hostgroup{
        hostgroup_name  linux-group
        }
```

In Listing 18-21 we have defined one host template, one host, one service, and one hostgroup. The host template is basically used to attach any hosts that use this template to the `linux-group` hostgroup. We are using the hostgroup here to link the host template and the service together. Every host that uses the template `basic-ssh-checks` will get the Current Load service because they share the same hostgroup.

Taking a look at our service definition closer, we can see that we have declared it like this:

```
define service{
        use                             local-service
        hostgroup_name          linux-group
        service_description     Current Load
        check_command           check_load_ssh!5.0,4.0,3.0!10.0,6.0,4.0
        }
```

Our service, called `Current Load`, executes the `check_load_ssh` command and passes two arguments, which specify the average load over the 1-, 5-, and 15-minute intervals required to trigger a WARNING or CRITICAL status.

■ **Note**   We discussed load in Chapter 17.

Finally in Listing 18-21 we have the host definition for the gateway server. This uses the template `basic-ssh-checks`, which calls in the Current Load service check via the hostgroup. It also will have all the notification and check period definitions provided by the `linux-server` template and the `generic-host` templates as we do not override anything here or in the templates.

This is a simple example of how to perform remote monitoring; it is not ideal (the key-based SSH connection could be a security vulnerability), but it is the simplest method. For more complicated environments, using the NRPE server and corresponding command is usually a better approach. NCAP and NRDP are also available and require a combination of different plug-ins with a mix of languages (which makes them awkward to install and configure).

■ **Note**   As with hosts, we haven't covered all the available functionality for services. You can also group services together, make them dependent on each other, and perform a variety of other useful tricks with them. We recommend you read the available Nagios documentation and many of the other useful resources for more information.

Logging and Debugging

You can view the logs for Nagios in the `/var/log/nagios/nagios.log` file. You may also have these notifications being replicated to the `syslog` (`rsyslog`) daemon.

If you do not want this functionality, you can set your `use_syslog` directive to the following:

```
use_syslog=0
```

When you need to debug Nagios, you will need to edit the `/etc/nagios/nagios.cfg` file and edit the following:

```
debug_level=0
```

Do you remember from LDAP logging when we had additive logging directives that give different log levels by adding binary numbers together? Nagios is the same. Here is the list of possible logging levels:

```
#           -1 = Everything
#           0 = Nothing
#           1 = Functions
#           2 = Configuration
#           4 = Process information
#           8 = Scheduled events
#           16 = Host/service checks
#           32 = Notifications
#           64 = Event broker
#           128 = External commands
#           256 = Commands
#           512 = Scheduled downtime
#           1024 = Comments
#           2048 = Macros
```

So if we wanted to see host and service checks in our logs and the external commands, we would change debug=0 to debug=144, which is 16 (host/service checks) + 128 (external commands).

You will need to restart Nagios for this to take effect, and the debug logs will appear in a `/var/log/nagios/debug.log` file.

Nagios Plug-ons

You can choose from a large collection of plug-ins to create services and commands to check them. You can see a partial list of the available plug-ins in Table 18-7.

Table 18-7. *Nagios Plug-Ins*

Plug-in	Description
check_ntp	Checks the status of an NTP service
check_swap	Checks your swap
check_ifstatus	Checks the status of network interfaces
check_tcp	Checks the status of a TCP-based network service
check_by_ssh	Checks the status of a service via SSH
check_imap	Checks the status of an IMAP service
check_clamd	Checks the status of a ClamAV daemon
check_udp	Checks the status of a UDP-based network service
check_dig	Checks the DNS status via dig
check_ping	Checks the status of a host via ICMP
check_simap	Checks the status of an IMAP service
check_nagios	Checks the status of the Nagios process
check_snmp	Checks via SNMP
check_http	Checks the status of a web server
check_ssh	Checks the status of an sshd service

This is a small selection of the available plug-ins, but it should give you a good basis for creating appropriate checks for your environment. Most Nagios plug-ins are simple and self-explanatory. Almost all of them provide the `--help` option to display their function and options.

Other plug-ins outside of the Nagios plug-in pack are also available. For example, you can find a huge collection of such plug-ins at `https://exchange.nagios.org/directory/Plugins`.

■ **Note**   You can also find some useful add-ons at `https://www.nagios.org/downloads/nagios-core-addons/`.

You can develop your own plug-ins, if required. Some simple guidelines and examples for such development are located at `https://assets.nagios.com/downloads/nagioscore/docs/nagioscore/4/en/pluginapi.html`.

Setting Up the Nagios Console

Now that you understand how hosts and services can be defined, you can create your own hosts and services to supplement the examples provided with both distributions. Once you have created these hosts and services, it is useful to have a console to view them in. Nagios comes with a fully functional web-based console, and we're going to show you how to set it up.

■ **Tip** Alternatives to the Nagios console are also available. You can see a good list of these at `https://exchange.nagios.org/directory/Addons/Frontends-(GUIs-and-CLIs)/Web-Interfaces`.

The Nagios console can run inside the Apache web server we demonstrated in Chapter 11. Both CentOS and Ubuntu include default installations of the web console. On CentOS, you can find the Apache configuration for Nagios at `/etc/httpd/conf.d/nagios.conf`; on Ubuntu, it's at `/etc/apache2/conf-available/nagios.conf`.

The console can be found in a web service directory of `/nagios`. If your web server is running, browsing to `http://nagios.example.com/nagios/` (replacing the hostname with the name of your Nagios host) should display your console.

■ **Note** You can use what you learned in Chapter 11 to move your Nagios console to a virtual host or other location.

Console Authentication

To protect against people making malicious use of your Nagios console, the web server has some basic authentication. Nagios uses Apache's basic HTTP authentication to protect the console. When you open the console, you will be prompted for a username and password, as you can see in Figure 18-9.

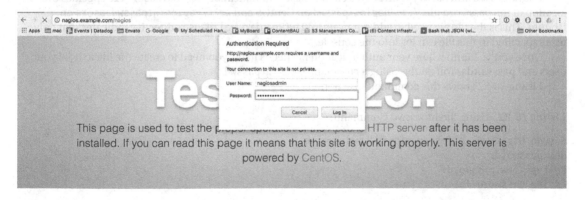

Figure 18-9. *Nagios authentication*

Apache basic authentication is configured by specifying a file holding usernames and passwords to the web server. This file is then queried by web sites that are secured by basic authentication. The default username and password are *nagiosadmin*.

■ **Caution** This is basic authentication with an emphasis on *basic*, however. Apache basic authentication uses simple encrypted passwords that are easy to intercept and decrypt. To ensure better protection of your Nagios console, you should consider enabling SSL for it.

Let's look inside our Nagios Apache configuration for the location of our password file. On CentOS, inside our /etc/httpd/conf.d/nagios.conf file, we find the following:

```
AuthName "Nagios Access"
AuthType Basic
AuthUserFile /etc/nagios/passwd
<IfModule mod_authz_core.c>
      # Apache 2.4
    <RequireAll>
        Require all granted
        Require valid-user
    </RequireAll>
</IfModule>
```

On Ubuntu, in the /etc/apache2/conf-available/nagios.conf file, we have this:

```
AuthName "Nagios Access"
AuthType Basic
AuthUserFile /etc/nagios/htpasswd.users
Require valid-user
```

The AuthName and AuthType directives enable basic authentication. The AuthUserFile specifies the location of the password file, /etc/nagios/passwd on CentOS and /etc/nagios/htpasswd.users on Ubuntu. This is the file we need to add our users to. The Require valid-user directive indicates that only users specified in this file can log into the console.

Once you've found where your authentication file needs to be, you need to create the file to hold your users and passwords. You do this using a command called htpasswd.

Listing 18-22 shows this command in action.

Listing 18-22. Using the htpasswd Command

```
$ sudo htpasswd -c /etc/nagios/passwd jsmith
New password:
Re-type new password:
Adding password for user jsmith
```

The htpasswd command has two variables: the location of the file that holds our usernames and passwords and the username of the user. We also use a command-line switch, -c. The -c switch is used when you first create a password file. After that, you can drop this switch and merely specify the file and the user to be added.

In Listing 18-22, we added a new password to the file with the -c option called /etc/nagios/passwd. We specify the user we're adding, jsmith, and are prompted for a password and then a verification of the entered password. Both passwords must match. If they do, the command will be successful, and the user will be added to the specified password file.

We can then use this username and password to sign in to the Nagios console and display the console screen, as you can see in Figure 18-10.

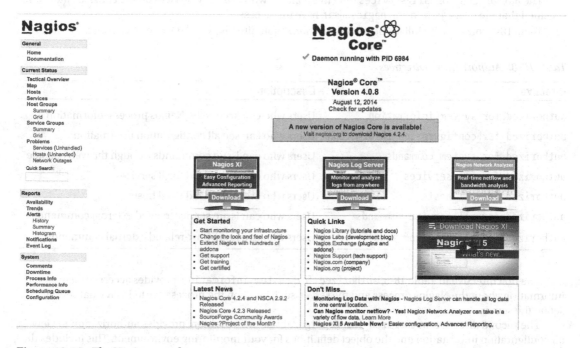

Figure 18-10. *The Nagios console*

Once we have users and passwords created, we can sign on to the console, but we also need to configure what access each user has. This is done by editing a configuration file called cgi.cfg, located in the /etc/nagios directory.

Nagios has two types of users on the console: authenticated users and authenticated contacts. Both types of users need a username and password to sign on to the console. Authenticated users have their access specified in the cgi.cfg configuration file. Authenticated contacts are authenticated users, with the username of each matching the name of a Nagios contact.

Hence, if the username jsmith, for example, matches the name of a contact, which is the value of the contact_name directive, this authenticated user becomes an authenticated contact.

So, what's the difference? Authenticated users are granted some generic rights to view the web console. Authenticated contacts are granted further rights to view and manipulate the hosts and services for which they are contacts.

Let's look at the cgi.cfg file. The first directive in the cgi.cfg file is called use_authentication. It controls whether authentication is enabled for the Nagios web console and whether Nagios will use the authentication credentials provided from the web server. The directive looks like this:

```
use_authentication=1
```

A setting of 1, which is the default, enables authentication, and a setting of 0 disables it. Authorization for particular functions on the console is provided by a series of directives in the `cgi.cfg` file that take lists of users, separated by commas, as options. Here's an example:

```
authorized_for_all_services=jsmith,nagiosadmin
```

The `authorized_for_all_services` directive controls who can view services on the console, and we've specified that the users `jsmith` and `nagiosadmin` have this access.

Table 18-8 contains the full list of possible authorization directives and describes each one.

Table 18-8. *Authorization Directives*

Directive	Description
`authorized_for_system_information`	Users who can access the Nagios process information
`authorized_for_configuration_information`	Users who can see all configuration information
`authorized_for_system_commands`	Users who can issue commands through the web console
`authorized_for_all_services`	Users who are authorized to all services
`authorized_for_all_hosts`	Users who are authorized to all hosts
`authorized_for_all_service_commands`	Users who can issue service-related external commands
`authorized_for_all_host_commands`	Users who can issue host-related external commands

The first directive in Table 18-8, `authorized_for_system_information`, provides access to view information about the Nagios process and the server, such as when the process started and what settings are set on the server.

The second directive, `authorized_for_configuration_information`, provides authorization to view all configuration information and the object definitions for your monitoring environment. This includes the configuration of your hosts, services, contacts, and commands, as well as all other object types.

The third directive, `authorized_for_system_commands`, controls who has access to start, stop, or restart the Nagios process from the web console.

The next two directives, `authorized_for_all_services` and `authorized_for_all_hosts`, control which users can view all service and host information on the web console. Remember, authenticated contacts can view the information about the hosts and services for which they are contacts.

The last two directives in Table 18-8, `authorized_for_all_service_commands` and `authorized_for_all_host_commands`, allow you to specify users who are authorized to issue external commands to services and hosts, respectively. This allows you to perform actions such as disabling active checks of the host or service or enabling or disabling notifications for the host or service.

■ **Note** By default, all the authorization directives are commented out in the `cgi.cfg` file. You will need to uncomment them and add any required users to the directives.

If you want to specify that all users have access to a particular function, use the * symbol.

```
authorized_for_all_services=*
```

This directive setting would provide all authenticated users with access to view information about all services defined on the Nagios server. The * symbol will work for all authorization directives.

As we mentioned earlier, in addition to any authorization granted to them, users who are also contacts have access to the hosts and services for which they are contacts. For services, this access includes

- Viewing of service status

- Viewing of service configuration

- Ability to view service history and notifications

- Ability to issue commands to the service (start and stop checking, for example)

For hosts, this access includes

- Viewing of host status

- Viewing of host configuration

- Ability to view host history and notifications

- Ability to issue commands to the host (start and stop checking, for example)

Authenticated contacts that have access to a particular host because they are a contact for that host also have the same access to all the services on that host just as if they were a contact for those services. For example, if you are an authenticated contact for the server1 host, you are able to view the status, configuration, service history, and notifications as well as issue commands to all the services defined on that host.

Console Functions

The Nagios console provides not only an interface through which to view your hosts and services but also the ability to control how they are monitored. We're going to walk you through a few of the screens available in the console, but we recommend you take a look at the views, graphs, lists, and controls available on the console.

For a summary of the status of your environment, the best view is the Tactical Monitoring Overview screen, which you can see in Figure 18-11.

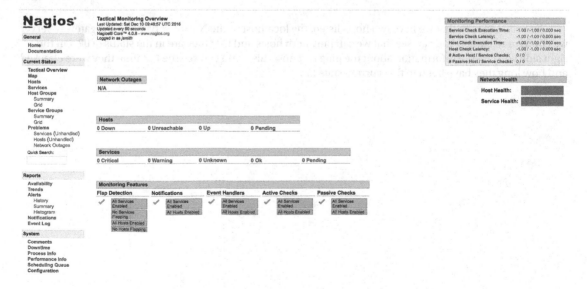

Figure 18-11. *The Tactical Monitoring Overview screen*

This screen displays the current status of the Nagios server and a summary of your host and service statuses. It is reached by clicking the Tactical Monitoring Overview link in the left menu.

To see your hosts and services in more detail, the Host Detail and Service Detail links in the left menu display a full list of the hosts and services being monitored. You can see the Service Detail screen in Figure 18-12.

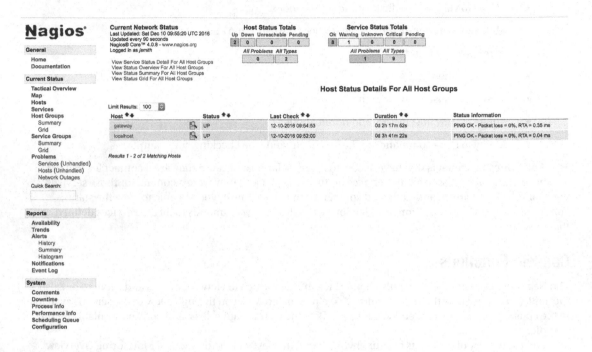

Figure 18-12. *The Hosts Detail screen*

You can see here that we have two hosts listed: the localhost or the Nagios server and the gateway server we configured earlier. You can see that we can ping both hosts and that they are in the status of UP. On the right side you can see information about the ping response; also, you can see the last time they were checked and how long they have been in that current state for.

In Figure 18-13 we show the Service Detail screen.

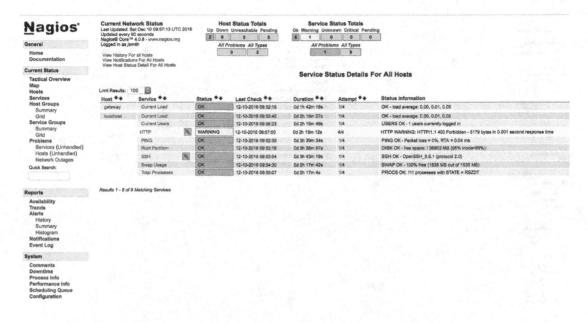

Figure 18-13. *The Service Detail screen*

Here in Figure 18-13 we can see the status of the services that we are checking on our hosts. You can see the check for Current Load is working on our gateway server. The HTTP check is in a WARNING state because the httpd service is responding but the result is not 200 OK but rather 403. We would have to change the check to handle the authentication the Nagios web service requires before we will get a 200 OK and for it to be green.

On both these screens, you can click the hosts and services to drill down into their status and configuration.

The last console screen we're going to show you in Figure 18-14 is the Process Info screen, which displays the status of the Nagios process and its configuration. You can also configure a variety of Nagios options, such as enabling and disabling checking and notifications, through this screen.

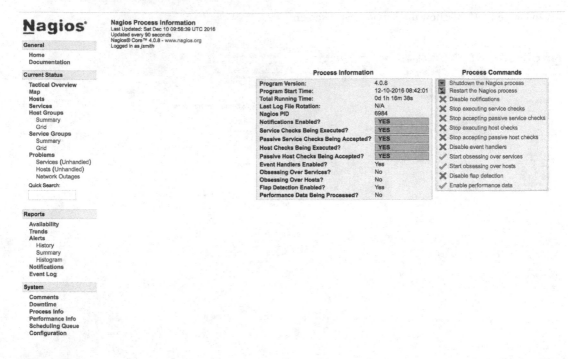

Figure 18-14. *The Nagios Process Information screen*

You can do other things through this console, such as host and service reports, check the event log, and see and schedule downtime for hosts and services.

Troubleshooting Nagios

Lots of resources are available to help you with Nagios including web sites, forums, and books, such as *Pro Nagios 2.0* by James Turnbull, one of the authors of this book (Apress, 2006). You may also find *Art of Monitoring* by the same author to be useful; see `https://www.artofmonitoring.com/`.

You can find a number of support options, including commercial support, at `https://www.nagios.org/support/`, comprehensive documentation at `https://www.nagios.org/documentation/`, and a FAQ for Nagios at `https://support.nagios.com/knowledge-base/`. You can also subscribe to the active and helpful mailing list available at `http://lists.nagios.com/mailman/listinfo` through the Nagios forum at `https://support.nagios.com/forum/index.php`, which is the preferred way of getting user help.

Summary

In this chapter, you learned about logging and monitoring and how to make them work for you. You discovered how `rsyslog` works and how to make the most out of your `rsyslog` daemon. You also learned how to search your log data using Kibana and how to get your log data into Elasticsearch via Logstash and Filebeats.

In addition, the chapter explored Nagios, an enterprise monitoring tool. You saw how to install and configure Nagios. You also discovered how to configure your hosts and services and the supporting configuration needed to monitor your environment.

In the next chapter, we'll discuss provisioning hosts and show you how to manage your configuration with automated configuration tools.

CHAPTER 19

■ ■ ■

Configuration Management

By James Turnbull and Dennis Matotek

Now that you have learned how to build the components for a few systems, we are going to show you how you can build thousands of them quickly, at the same time, and all having the right configuration for each type of system! In the last 18 chapters we wanted to show you just how each part of the Linux system was configured, what switch applied to what command, and what outcome each switch had. All this was essential to understanding what automated provisioning and configuration management are now going to do for you.

In this chapter, we're going to look at three facets of configuration management.

- Automated provisioning and installation of new hosts

- Automated management of your configuration including files, users, and packages

- How to test your configuration as code

The first process we're going to examine, automated provisioning or installation of new hosts, is sometimes called *bootstrapping*. In the CentOS world, bootstrapping is often referred to as *kickstarting* (after the Kickstart tool used to perform it). On Ubuntu and Debian, the process is called *preseeding*.

Provisioning is a way of automatically installing a distribution to a host. When we first looked at installing distributions in Chapter 2, we demonstrated how to do it manually. You inserted a DVD and followed the onscreen prompts to install your distribution. Automated provisioning is a way of installing a distribution without being prompted by the configuration questions. This makes provisioning quick and simple, and it also has the advantage of ensuring every build is identical.

■ **Tip**   You can use provisioning for both server hosts and desktop hosts. Not only is it a quick way of building (or rebuilding) server hosts, but it can also be a quick way to automatically install desktops for your users.

The second process we're going to examine is configuration management and automation. By now you've seen that you can accumulate a lot of installed packages, users, configuration files, and other settings. Your environment can quickly get complicated and difficult to manage if you don't take steps to control and automate it. Configuration management allows you to centralize your configuration, document it, and automate it. This allows you to manage and control changes to your environment and protects you against accidental or malicious configuration changes.

The third is testing your infrastructure just like you would your application code. Because configuration management is just code, this makes testing your configurations easier and helps to ensure fewer bugs creep into your production servers. This can lead to fewer administration mistakes as things can be tested and reviewed prior to being pushed into production. This can be all hooked into your normal Jenkins or other continuous integration/continuous deployment (CI/CD) infrastructure to make this a seamless operation.

© Dennis Matotek, James Turnbull and Peter Lieverdink 2017
D. Matotek et al., *Pro Linux System Administration*, DOI 10.1007/978-1-4842-2008-5_19

Provisioning, configuration management, and testing are meant to be used in a workflow. In your system provisioning process you can install the operating system with Cobbler, or different provisioning system, and then use Ansible or Puppet to apply the tested configuration as part of that process. This means that by the time you first get access to your console, it has the right disk layout, it has the right operating system, it has the right network configuration, it has the right users and packages, it has the right configuration for services, and those services have been started. Not only that, but every system you build after that is also just right, even if it consists of thousands of them. And it can be done automatically for you after you have completed your CI builds!

Provisioning

We've talked a little about what provisioning is, but how you go about it varies between distributions. We are going to explain how to automatically provision both CentOS and Ubuntu hosts.

Provisioning is usually a two-stage process.

1. Boot your host and send it the files required for installation.

2. Automate the installation steps.

The process starts with a host booting up. Remember in Chapter 5 when we told you about the boot sequence? On many hosts, you can configure that boot sequence to look in alternative places to get its boot instructions; for example, you can boot from a DVD or a USB stick. In addition to these methods, you can also get your boot instructions from a network source.

The technology behind this boot process is called Preboot Execution Environment (PXE). A network boot server is hence called a PXE boot (pronounced "pixie boot") server. The host that we intend to build uses a network query to find a PXE boot server, usually a network query to a DHCP server, that might offer it the files required to boot and then transfers those files to the host using a file transfer protocol called Trivial File Transfer Protocol (TFTP).

■ **Note**   You can read more about PXE at `http://en.wikipedia.org/wiki/Preboot_Execution_` `Environment`.

Once this initial boot takes place, your provisioning process continues by installing a prepackaged version of your distribution, usually with a series of automated scripted responses to the various configuration questions you are prompted for when installing.

■ **Note**   We're using network-based provisioning to create our hosts rather than any of the alternatives, such as CD or DVD. This is because we believe network-based provisioning is the simplest, easiest, and most efficient way to automatically build hosts.

Provisioning with CentOS Cobbler

CentOS has a variety of tools for provisioning hosts, ranging from the most basic, Kickstart, which automates installations, to full-featured GUI management tools for host configuration such as Cobbler (`http://cobbler.github.io/`) and Spacewalk (`http://spacewalk.redhat.com/`).

We're going to look at a combination of three tools:

- *Kickstart*: An installation automation tool for Red Hat–based operating systems
- *Preseed*: An installation automation tool for Debian-based operating systems
- *Cobbler*: A provisioning server that provides a PXE boot server

We'll take you through the process of creating a Cobbler server and a build to install. Later in this chapter, we'll show you how to configure Kickstart to automate your configuration and installation options.

Installing Cobbler

Let's start by installing Cobbler on your host. To run Cobbler, you need to install the EPEL repositories.

```
$ sudo yum install -y epel-release
```

Then we need to install Cobbler.

```
$ sudo yum install -y cobbler
```

This will install some additional YUM utilities and the createrepo package, which assist in repository management. We've also installed some additional packages Cobbler uses: the DHCP daemon, a TFTP server, and the Apache web server. You may already have these packages installed, in which case YUM will skip them.

■ **Note** We talk about DHCP in Chapter 10 and Apache in Chapter 11.

Once everything is installed, we need to enable cobblerd, the daemon process, at boot and start it.

```
$ sudo systemctl enable cobblerd httpd
$ sudo systemctl start cobblerd
$ sudo systemctl start httpd
```

Cobbler requires access to the Apache server to be started. Also, we need to ensure that the cobblerd service can access the httpd server port. SELinux by default will prevent this, so we need to issue the following:

```
$ sudo setsebool -P httpd_can_network_connect true
```

Cobbler has some specific SELinux settings, and you can view them with the following command:

```
$ sudo getsebool -a|grep cobbler
cobbler_anon_write --> off
cobbler_can_network_connect --> off
cobbler_use_cifs --> off
cobbler_use_nfs --> off
httpd_can_network_connect_cobbler --> off
httpd_serve_cobbler_files --> off
```

We will enable the following SELinux Booleans:

```
$ sudo setsebool -P httpd_serve_cobbler_files on
$ sudo setsebool -P httpd_can_network_connect_cobbler  on
```

Configuring Cobbler

After you've installed the required packages, you need to configure Cobbler. Cobbler comes with a handy check function that tells you what needs to be done to configure it. To see what needs to be done, run the following:

```
The following are potential configuration items that you may want to change:


1 : The 'server' field in /etc/cobbler/settings must ... by all machines that will use it.
2 : For PXE to be functional, the 'next_server' field ... the IP of the boot server on the
    PXE network.
3 : SELinux is enabled. Please review the following ... https://github.com/cobbler/cobbler/
    wiki/Selinux
4 : change 'disable' to 'no' in /etc/xinetd.d/tftp
5 : some network boot-loaders are missing from /var/lib/cobbler/loaders, ...is the easiest
    way to resolve these requirements.
6 : debmirror package is not installed, it will be required to manage debian deployments and
    repositories
7 : ksvalidator was not found, install pykickstart
8 : The default password used by the sample templates ...  'your-password-here'" to generate
    new one
9 : fencing tools were not found, and are required to use ... cman or fence-agents to use
    them

Restart cobblerd and then run 'cobbler sync' to apply changes.
```

You can see there are a few things you need to do to get Cobbler running. Let's work through each of these issues.

First, you configure the /etc/cobbler/settings file. You need to update two fields in this file: server and next_server. You need to replace the existing values (usually 127.0.0.1) with the IP address of your host so a PXE-booted host can find your Cobbler host. In our case, we specify the following:

```
server 192.168.0.1
next_server 192.168.0.1
```

To update Cobbler's configuration, you then run this:

```
$ sudo cobbler sync
```

■ **Note**   You need to run the $ sudo cobbler sync command any time you change the /etc/cobbler/settings file. Common errors include leaving trailing spaces after options in the settings file. Make sure you delete any extra spaces from the file.

You also need to configure a DHCP server (like the one we introduced in Chapter 10). You have two choices here: you can get Cobbler to manage your existing DHCP server, or you can tell your existing DHCP server to point to Cobbler.

After you have run `cobbler sync` and rerun `cobbler check`, you will notice the list of outstanding things to check has been reduced. We are going to now install the Cobbler loaders and `debmirror` binary.

```
$ sudo cobbler get-loaders
```

For `debmirror`, you need to download the file from Debian, untar it, and copy it to a common location (alternative, you could use FPM, like we showed you in Chapter 9, to create a package to do this for you in a repeatable way!).

We need at least these Perl modules installed:

```
$ sudo yum install -y perl-LockFile-Simple perl-IO-Zlib perl-Digest-MD5 perl-Net-INET6Glue
perl-LWP-Protocol-https
```

Next we will download and install the `debmirror` package, untar it, and place it in the `/usr/local/bin` directory.

```
$ curl -s http://archive.ubuntu.com/ubuntu/pool/universe/d/debmirror/debmirror_2.25ubuntu2.
tar.xz -o debmirror_2.25.tar.xz
$ tar xf debmirror_2.25.tar.xz && sudo cp debmirror-2.25ubuntu2/debmirror /usr/local/bin/
```

To test we have everything installed correctly for `debmirror`, run `debmirror --help` and make sure you don't get any Perl module errors.

Lastly, we are going to change the default root password that gets placed on the hosts. First you can create a secure SHA-512 password using `python3` with the following:

```
python3 -c 'import crypt; print(crypt.crypt("yourpasswordhere", crypt.mksalt(crypt.METHOD_
SHA512)))'
$6$KnsQG.tEetSCSmid$HpqUNyEk1UPkt9Dc9MPcwPY...guKOGdUeNXoA7.ugUBGGaDIk8RY8FRYVOwzmsM.uO1
```

Then you need to update the `default_password_crypted:` setting in the `/etc/cobbler/settings` file. Remember to run `cobbler sync` after each change.

■ **Note**   Python 3 is not installed by default on CentOS but can be available on Ubuntu. The previous script for generating the password can be run on any host that has Python 3 installed already and can be copied across.

Now when we run `$ sudo cobbler check`, the list contains only three items, which we don't need to address.

Cobbler Managing Your DHCP

If you want to enable Cobbler to manage your DHCP server, then you need to enable another option in the `/etc/cobbler/settings` file.

```
manage_dhcp: 1
```

You also need to update a template file that Cobbler will use to configure your DHCP server, /etc/cobbler/dhcp.template. Listing 19-1 shows an example of this file.

Listing 19-1. The /etc/cobbler/dhcp.template File

```
# ****************************************************************
# Cobbler managed dhcpd.conf file
#
# generated from cobbler dhcp.conf template ($date)
# Do NOT make changes to /etc/dhcpd.conf. Instead, make your changes
# in /etc/cobbler/dhcp.template, as /etc/dhcpd.conf will be
# overwritten.
#
# ****************************************************************

ddns-update-style interim;

allow booting;
allow bootp;

ignore client-updates;
set vendorclass = option vendor-class-identifier;

option pxe-system-type code 93 = unsigned integer 16;

key dynamic-update-key {
        algorithm hmac-sha256;
        secret "RZqM/JutbhgHiBR8ICGOLDyN+9c1LpNU83ycuU9LPaY=";
}

zone 0.168.192.in-addr.arpa. {
    key dynamic-update-key;
    primary 192.168.0.1;
}

zone example.com. {
    key dynamic-update-key;
   primary 192.168.0.1;
}

subnet 192.168.0.0 netmask 255.255.255.0 {
    option routers 192.168.0.254;
    option domain-name "example.com";
    option domain-name-servers 192.168.0.1;
    option broadcast-address 192.168.0.255;

    next-server $next_server;
    filename "/pxelinux.0";
    group "static" {
       use-host-decl-names on;
         host au-mel-rhel-1 {
                hardware ethernet 00:16:3E:15:3C:C2;
```

```
        fixed-address au-mel-rhel-1.example.com;
    }
  }
  pool {
      range 192.168.0.101 192.168.0.150;
      deny unknown clients;
  }
  pool {
    range 192.168.0.151 192.168.0.200;
    allow unknown clients;
   default-lease-time 7200;
    max-lease-time 21600;
  }
}
```

If you have an existing DHCP server with a configuration, you should update this template to reflect that configuration. You can see we've adjusted the template in Listing 19-1 to reflect the DHCP configuration we used in Chapter 10. We've added two settings.

```
allow booting;
allow bootp;
```

These two options tell the DHCP server to respond to queries from hosts who request network boots.

The other two important settings to note in Listing 19-1 are next-server and filename configuration options. The next-server option is set to $next_server. This value will be replaced by the IP address we just configured in the next_server option in the /etc/cobbler/settings file. This tells our DHCP server where to route hosts that request a net boot.

The filename option is set to /pxelinux.0, which is the name of the boot file that PXE-booted hosts should look for to start their boot process. We'll set up this file shortly.

Now, after changing these files, you need to run the following command:

```
$ sudo cobbler sync
```

■ **Caution**   If you have an existing DHCP server, this template will *overwrite* its configuration by overwriting the /etc/dhcpd.conf configuration file. Only do this if you are sure you know what you are doing, and make a copy of your existing /etc/dhcpd.conf file *before* running the command.

Cobbler Not Managing Your DHCP

If you don't want Cobbler to manage your DHCP, then you just need to adjust your existing DHCP configuration file, /etc/dhcpd.conf, to add the next-server and filename options. Let's update the relevant portions of the configuration we created in Chapter 9 with this option, as shown in Listing 19-2.

Listing 19-2. Existing dhcpd.conf Configuration File

```
allow booting;
allow bootp;

subnet 192.168.0.0 netmask 255.255.255.0 {
    option routers 192.168.0.254;
    option domain-name "example.com";
    option domain-name-servers 192.168.0.1;
    option broadcast-address 192.168.0.255;
    filename "/pxelinux.0";
    next-server 192.168.0.1;
    group "static" {
      use-host-decl-names on;
       host au-mel-rhel-1 {
            hardware ethernet 00:16:3E:15:3C:C2;
          fixed-address au-mel-rhel-1.example.com;
         }
     }
     pool {
       range 192.168.0.101 192.168.0.150;
       deny unknown clients;
     }
     pool {
      range 192.168.0.151 192.168.0.200;
      allow unknown clients;
      default-lease-time 7200;
      max-lease-time 21600;
     }
}
```

You can see we've added two options to the start of the DHCP section.

```
allow booting;
allow bootp;
```

These two options tell the DHCP server to respond to queries from booting clients.
We've also added the next-server option to our subnet definition.

```
next-server 192.168.0.1
```

The next-server option tells DHCP where to send hosts that request a PXE network boot. We need to specify the IP address of our Cobbler server.

Lastly, we've added the filename option, set to /pxelinux.0, which is the name of the boot file that PXE-booted hosts should look for to start their boot process. We'll set up this file shortly.

■ **Tip**   After configuring your DHCP server, you will need to restart the Cobbler server for the new configuration to be applied.

Configuring TFTP

Once the daemon is started, you need to enable your TFTP server to send your boot file to the host to be installed. To do this, you edit the /etc/xinet.d/tftp file to enable a TFTP server. Inside this file, find this line:

```
disable = yes
```

and change it to this:

```
disable = no
```

Next, you enable the TFTP server like so:

```
$ sudo systemctl enable tftp
$ sudo systemctl start tftp
```

You need to ensure your hosts can connect to the Cobbler server through your firewall by opening some required ports, 69, 80, 25150, and 25151, for example, by creating firewalld rules such as the following:

```
$ sudo firewall-cmd --zone=public --add-service=tftp --permanent
$ sudo firewall-cmd --zone=public --add-service=httpd –permanent
$ sudo firewall-cmd --zone=public --add-port=25150:25151/tcp –permanent
```

These rules allow access for any host on the 192.168.0.0/24 subnet to the boot server on the appropriate ports. You can find more information on firewall rules in Chapter 7.

Using Cobbler

Once you've configured Cobbler, you can start to make use of it. Cobbler allows you to specify a distribution you'd like to build hosts with, imports that distribution's files, and then creates a profile. You can then build hosts using this distribution and profile.

We have mounted our ISO files to /mnt/centos and /mnt/ubuntu, respectively. This is done like so:

```
$ sudo mount -o loop /path/to/downloaded.iso /path/to/mountpoint
```

Let's start by creating our first profile using the import command.

```
$ sudo cobbler import --path=/mnt/centos --name=CentOS7 --arch=x86_64
task started: 2016-12-22_055922_import
task started (id=Media import, time=Thu Dec 22 05:59:22 2016)
Found a candidate signature: breed=redhat, version=rhel6
Found a candidate signature: breed=redhat, version=rhel7
Found a matching signature: breed=redhat, version=rhel7
Adding distros from path /var/www/cobbler/ks_mirror/CentOS7-x86_64:
creating new distro: CentOS7-x86_64
trying symlink: /var/www/cobbler/ks_mirror/CentOS7-x86_64 -> /var/www/cobbler/links/
CentOS7-x86_64
creating new profile: CentOS7-x86_64
associating repos
checking for rsync repo(s)
```

```
checking for rhn repo(s)
checking for yum repo(s)
starting descent into /var/www/cobbler/ks_mirror/CentOS7-x86_64 for CentOS7-x86_64
processing repo at : /var/www/cobbler/ks_mirror/CentOS7-x86_64
need to process repo/comps: /var/www/cobbler/ks_mirror/CentOS7-x86_64
looking for /var/www/cobbler/ks_mirror/CentOS7-x86_64/repodata/*comps*.xml
Keeping repodata as-is :/var/www/cobbler/ks_mirror/CentOS7-x86_64/repodata
*** TASK COMPLETE ***
```

We will import our Ubuntu ISO also.

```
$ sudo cobbler import --path=/mnt/ubuntu --name Ubuntu-16.04 --breed=ubuntu --os-
version=xenial
```

You issue the cobbler command with the import option. The --path option specifies the source of the distribution you want to import—in our case, /mnt/ubuntu and /mnt/centos. The --name is any name you want to give the distribution, and you can add --breed and --os-version to help the import command find the right signature to match your distribution.

■ **Note**   If you get errors when doing an import, make sure you run $ sudo cobbler signature update and try again. Learn more about signatures here: http://cobbler.github.io/manuals/2.8.0/3/2/3_-_Distro_Signatures.html.

You can also sync with online repositories. Here's an example:

```
$ sudo cobbler reposync
task started: 2016-12-22_063019_reposync
task started (id=Reposync, time=Thu Dec 22 06:30:19 2016)
hello, reposync
run, reposync, run!
running: /usr/bin/debmirror --nocleanup --verbose --ignore-release-gpg --method=http
--host=archive.ubuntu.com --root=/ubuntu --dist=xenial,xenial-updates,xenial-security
--section=main,universe /var/www/cobbler/repo_mirror/Ubuntu-16.04-x86_64 --nosource -a amd64
```

This will sync with online repositories and, in this case, uses the debmirror binary we installed earlier to sync our Ubuntu Xenial release.

■ **Tip**   You will need sufficient disk space on your host to copy whatever distributions you want to keep. Hosting your own syncs of repositories will speed up your deployments greatly and reduce online network downloads.

Cobbler will run the import process and then return you to the prompt. Depending on the performance of your host (and, if you are importing over the network, the speed of your connection), this may take some time.

You can view the distributions install via this command:

```
$ sudo cobbler distro list
   CentOS7-x86_64
   Ubuntu-16.04-x86_64
```

The import will create two profiles as well; we can see them with this command:

```
$ sudo cobbler profile list
   CentOS7-x86_64
   Ubuntu-16.04-x86_64
```

After you've created your distribution and profile, you can see the full details in Cobbler using the report option, as shown in Listing 19-3.

Listing 19-3. A Cobbler Report

```
$ sudo cobbler report
distros:
==========
Name                         : CentOS7-x86_64
Architecture                 : x86_64
TFTP Boot Files              : {}
Breed                        : redhat
Comment                      :
Fetchable Files              : {}
Initrd                       : /var/www/cobbler/ks_mirror/CentOS7-x86_64/images/pxeboot/
                               initrd.img
Kernel                       : /var/www/cobbler/ks_mirror/CentOS7-x86_64/images/pxeboot/
                               vmlinuz
Kernel Options               : {}
Kernel Options (Post Install) : {}
Kickstart Metadata           : {'tree': 'http://@@http_server@@/cblr/links/
                               CentOS7-x86_64'}
Management Classes           : []
OS Version                   : rhel7
Owners                       : ['admin']
Red Hat Management Key        : <<inherit>>
Red Hat Management Server     : <<inherit>>
Template Files               : {}

Name                         : Ubuntu-16.04-x86_64
Architecture                 : x86_64
TFTP Boot Files              : {}
Breed                        : ubuntu
Comment                      :
Fetchable Files              : {}
Initrd                       : /var/www/cobbler/ks_mirror/Ubuntu-16.04/install/netboot/
                               ubuntu-installer/amd64/initrd.gz
```

```
Kernel                         : /var/www/cobbler/ks_mirror/Ubuntu-16.04/install/netboot/
                                 ubuntu-installer/amd64/linux
Kernel Options                 : {}
Kernel Options (Post Install)  : {}
Kickstart Metadata             : {'tree': 'http://@@http_server@@/cblr/links/Ubuntu-
16.04-x86_64'}
Management Classes             : []
OS Version                     : xenial
Owners                         : ['admin']
Red Hat Management Key         : <<inherit>>
Red Hat Management Server      : <<inherit>>
Template Files                 : {}
```

This option displays all the distributions, and their profiles are currently imported into Cobbler.

■ **Note**   You may see more than one distribution and profile created from importing a distribution.

Listing 19-3 shows our vanilla CentOS7-x86_64 distribution and the profile we created, CentOS7-x86_64. Most of the information in Listing 19-3 isn't overly important to us; we are going to use these profiles to create a new system shortly.

■ **Note**   You can see the other options you can edit on your profile by looking at the cobbler command's man page or visiting the documentation at http://cobbler.github.io/manuals/2.8.0/.

Building a Host with Cobbler

Now that you've added a profile and a distribution, you can boot a host and install your distribution. Choose a host (or virtual machine) you want to build and reboot it. Your host may automatically search for a boot device on your network, but more likely you will need to adjust its BIOS settings to adjust the boot order. To boot from Cobbler, you need to specify that your host boots from the network first.

We have created a VirtualBox host on the same Host-only Adapter interface as our Cobbler server. We created VirtualBox hosts in Chapter 3 and created a basic host with an 8Gb hard drive. In the System settings, we are going to select Network for the boot device.

In Figure 19-1 we are selecting the Network Boot option. We will come back to here and set it to Hard Disk when we are finished. We now start the hosts like we would normally.

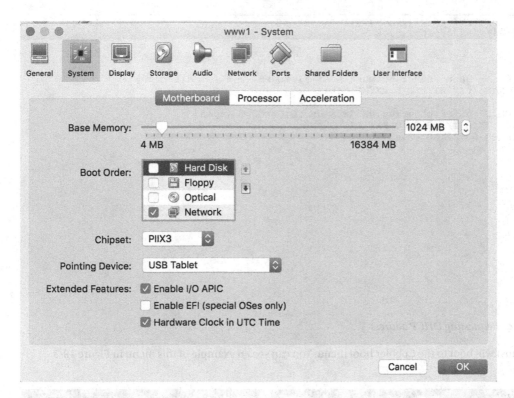

Figure 19-1. *Setting Network Boot*

When your host boots, it will request an IP address from the network and get an answer from your DHCP server, as you can see in Figure 19-2.

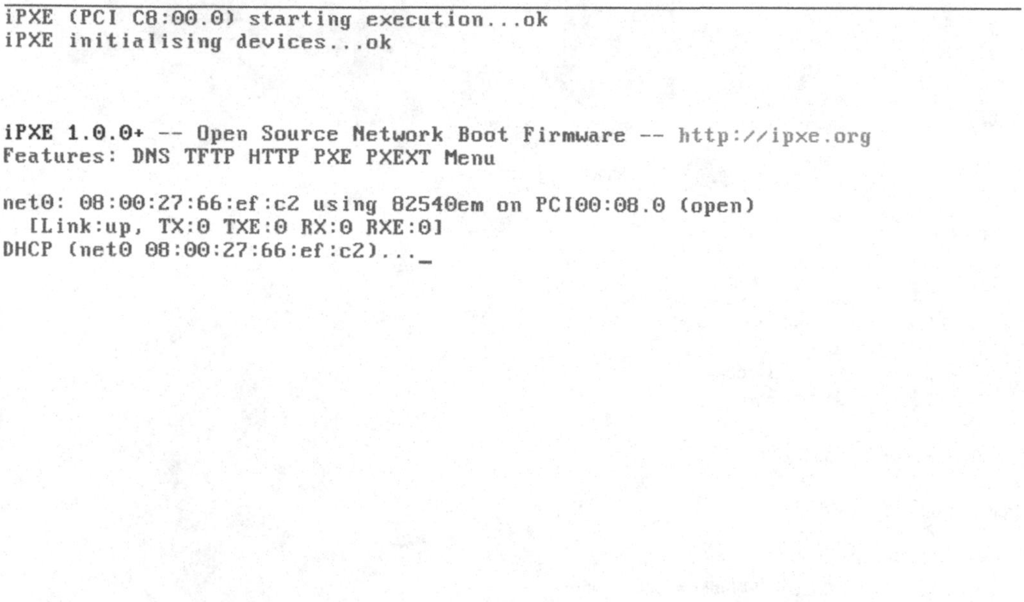

iPXE (PCI C8:00.0) starting execution...ok
iPXE initialising devices...ok
iPXE 1.0.0+ -- Open Source Network Boot Firmware -- http://ipxe.org
Features: DNS TFTP HTTP PXE PXEXT Menu
net0: 08:00:27:66:ef:c2 using 82540em on PCI00:08.0 (open)
[Link:up, TX:0 TXE:0 RX:0 RXE:0]
DHCP (net0 08:00:27:66:ef:c2)..._

Figure 19-2. *Requesting DHCP address*

Your host will boot to the Cobbler boot menu. You can see an example of this menu in Figure 19-3.

Cobbler | http://cobbler.github.io
(local)
CentOS7-x86_64
Ubuntu-16.04-x86_64
Press [Tab] to edit options

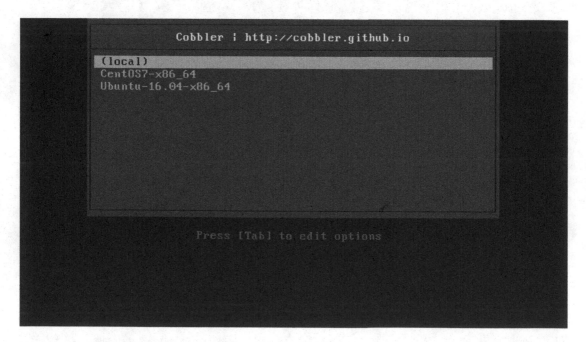

Figure 19-3. *The Cobbler menu*

From this menu, you can select the profile you'd like to install (e.g., CentOS7-x86_64). If you don't select a profile to be installed, Cobbler will automatically launch the first item on the menu (local), which continues the boot process on the localhost.

■ **Note**   If you don't have an operating system installed on this host, the local boot process will obviously fail.

We will select CentOS7-x86_64, which will automatically install CentOS onto our host. If we select Ubuntu-16.04-x86_64, we will install Ubuntu; Figures 19-4 through 19-6 tell that story.

```
Installing openssh (170/297)
Installing dhcp-libs (171/297)
Installing dhcp-common (172/297)
Installing selinux-policy (173/297)
Installing python-pycurl (174/297)
Installing python-urlgrabber (175/297)
Installing lsscsi (176/297)
Installing hardlink (177/297)
Installing pth (178/297)
Installing gnupg2 (179/297)
Installing gpgme (180/297)
Installing pygpgme (181/297)
Installing rpm-build-libs (182/297)
Installing rpm-python (183/297)
Installing yum-plugin-fastestmirror (184/297)
Installing yum (185/297)
Installing libmnl (186/297)
Installing libnetfilter_conntrack (187/297)
Installing iptables (188/297)
Installing iproute (189/297)
Installing qrencode-libs (190/297)
Installing kpartx (191/297190/297)
Installing kpartx (191/297)
Installing device-mapper (192/297)
```

Figure 19-4. *Installing CentOS*

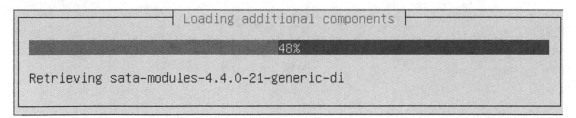

Figure 19-5. *Installing Ubuntu*

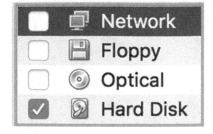

Figure 19-6. *Selecting Boot from Hard Disk*

Remember, when we have finished installing our host on VirtualBox, we need power on the host and need to change the boot device and then start the host again.

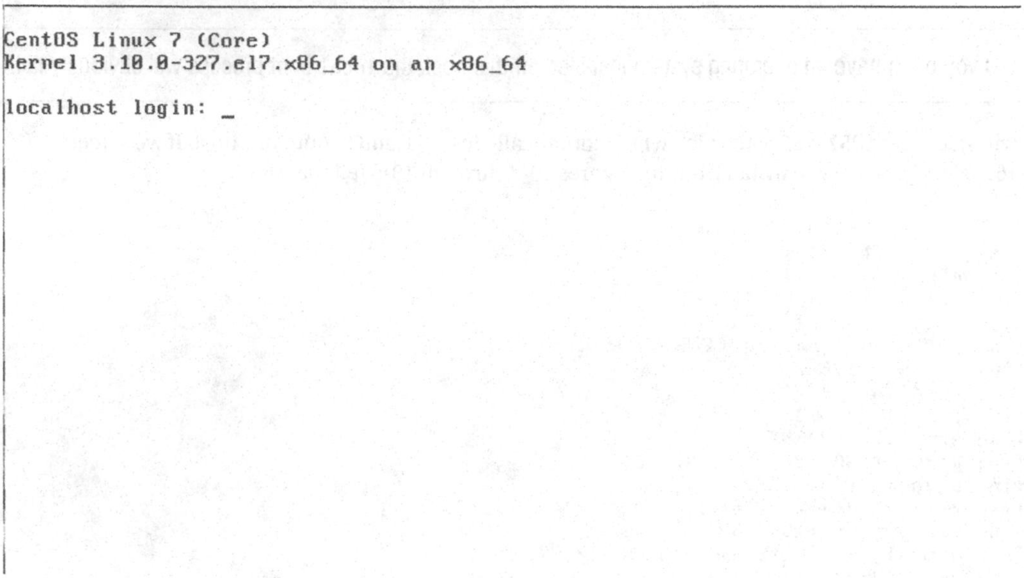

```
CentOS Linux 7 (Core)
Kernel 3.10.0-327.el7.x86_64 on an x86_64

localhost login: _
```

Figure 19-7. *CentOS installed*

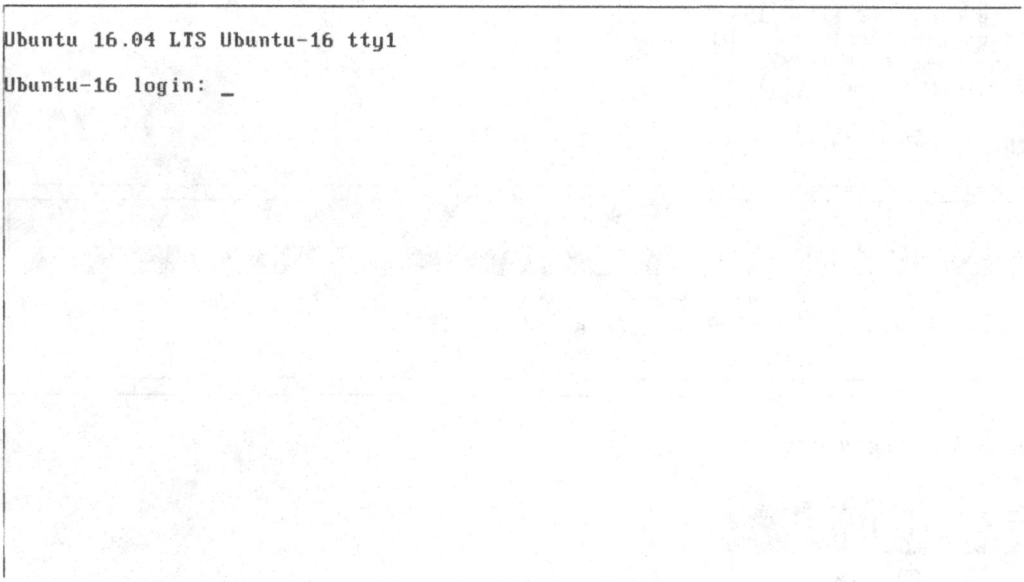

```
Ubuntu 16.04 LTS Ubuntu-16 tty1

Ubuntu-16 login: _
```

Figure 19-8. *Ubuntu installed*

We selected a profile, and then this profile started the installation process using the instructions contained in the associated Kickstart or Preseed file. If you are watching your installation process, you will see the installation screens progress—all without requiring input from you to continue or select options.

Using Cobbler, you can also specify configuration options for particular hosts. You don't need to do this, but it is useful if you have a specific role in mind for a host and want to specify a particular profile or Kickstart configuration.

To do this, you add hosts to Cobbler, identifying them via their MAC or IP addresses, using the system command.

```
$ sudo cobbler system add --name=web1.example.com --mac=08:00:27:66:EF:C2 ↵
--profile=CentOS7-x86_64 --interface eth1
```

Here we've added a system named web1.example.com with the specified MAC address.

■ **Note**   You can usually see your MAC address during the network boot process, or you can often find it printed on a label on your network card. Alternatively, you may have a way of seeing your virtual interfaces, like you can in VirtualBox.

The new host uses the CentOS7-x86_64 profile. So far it is no different from the hosts we have built previously. If a host with the appropriate MAC address connects to our Cobbler host, then Cobbler will use these configuration settings to provision the host.

If you need to change the way you build a host, you can create a new profile. Your new profiles can inherit settings from other profiles, which are regarded as their parents. We are going to create a profile called centos-base that will inherit the distro and other settings from the parent CentOS7-x86_64.

```
$ sudo cobbler profile add --name centos-base --parent CentOS7-x86_64
```

This is how we can use different common Kickstart or preseed files for different host groups. Kickstart and Preseed files may have different disk configurations or package lists that are tailored for particular profiles. To add a particular Kickstart or Preseed file, you first copy and modify any existing one to the way you like it and add it to the /var/lib/cobbler/kickstarts directory. Then you can add it to the profile with the --kickstart option.

You can list the configured hosts using the list and report options.

```
$ sudo cobbler system list
web1.example.com
```

A full listing of the gateway.example.com system definition can be seen using the report option.

```
$ sudo cobbler system report -name=web1.example.com
```

We can also delete a system using the remove command.

```
$ sudo cobbler system remove --name=web1.example.com
```

■ **Note**   You can read about additional Cobbler capabilities on the cobbler command's man page.

Cobbler Web Interface

Cobbler also has a simple web interface you can use to manage some of its options. It's pretty simple at this stage, and the command-line interface is much more fully featured, but it is available if you want to implement it. You can find instructions at `http://cobbler.github.io/manuals/2.8.0/5_-_Web_Interface.html`.

Troubleshooting Cobbler

You can troubleshoot the network boot process by monitoring elements on your host, including your log files, and by using a network monitoring tool like the `tcpdump` or `tshark` command.

You can start by monitoring the output of the DHCP process by looking at the `/var/log/messages` log files. Cobbler also logs to the `/var/log/cobbler/cobbler.log` file and the files contained in the `kicklog` and `syslog` directories also under `/var/log/cobbler`.

You can also monitor the network traffic passing between your booting host and the boot server. You can use a variety of network monitoring tools for this.

```
$ sudo tcpdump port tftp
```

Cobbler has a wiki page available that contains documentation at `http://cobbler.github.io/manuals`. The documentation includes some useful tips for troubleshooting at `http://cobbler.github.io/manuals/2.8.0/7_-_Troubleshooting.html`. The Cobbler community also has a mailing list and other support channels that you can see here: `http://cobbler.github.io/community.html`.

Kickstart

On CentOS, the language used to automatically install your host is called Kickstart. On Ubuntu, it is called Preseed. For simplicity's sake and because it's an easier language to use, we're going to show you how to use Kickstart to automate your installation for both CentOS and Ubuntu. Where something isn't supported on Ubuntu, we'll show you how to use Preseed to configure it.

A Kickstart configuration file contains the instructions required to automate the installation process. It's a simple scripted process for most installation options, but it can be extended to do some complex configuration.

You can find the latest detailed documentation for Kickstart at `http://pykickstart.readthedocs.io/en/latest/kickstart-docs.html`.

You can find documentation on Preseed and its directives at `https://wiki.debian.org/DebianInstaller/Preseed`. We'll work with a few of these directives later in this section.

You've already seen how to specify Kickstart files to your provisioning environments, using Cobbler. Let's start by looking at some of the contents of a simple Kickstart file in Listing 19-4.

Listing 19-4. A Kickstart File

```
install
# System authorization information
auth --enableshadow  --passalgo sha512
# System bootloader configuration
bootloader --location=mbr
# Partition clearing information
clearpart --all --initlabel
# Use text mode install
text
```

Listing 19-4 shows a list of configuration directives starting with the `install` option, which dictates the behavior of the installation process by performing an installation.

You can then see configuration directives with options, for example, `auth --enableshadow --passalgo sha512`, which tell Kickstart how to answer particular installation questions. The `auth` statement has the values `--enableshadow` and `--passalgo sha512` here, which enable shadow passwords and specify that passwords hashes must use the SHA512 password algorithm, respectively.

The option that follows, `bootloader` with a value of `--location=mbr`, tells Kickstart to install the boot loader into the MBR. Next is the directive `clearpart`, which clears all partitions on the host and creates default labels for them. The final option, `text`, specifies we should use text-based installation as opposed to the GUI.

■ **Tip**   You can use Kickstart to upgrade hosts as well as install them. If you have an existing host, you can network boot from a new version of your operating system and use a Kickstart file to script and upgrade.

There are too many directives to discuss them individually, so we show you in Table 19-1 the directives that must be specified and some of the other major directives that you may find useful.

Table 19-1. *Required Kickstart Directives*

Directive	Description
auth	Configures authentication.
bootloader	Configures the boot loader.
keyboard	Configures the keyboard type.
lang	Configures the language on the host.
part	Configures partitions. This is required for installation, but not if upgrading.
rootpw	Specifies the password of the root user.
timezone	Specifies the time zone the host is in.

You can also find a useful list of the available directives with explanations at `http://pykickstart.readthedocs.io/en/latest/kickstart-docs.html#chapter-2-kickstart-commands-in-fedora`.

■ **Tip**   If you are on CentOS, you can see an example Kickstart file that was created when you installed your host in the `/root/anaconda-ks.cfg` file. This will show you how your current host is built and can be used as an example to build similar hosts.

Installation Source

You've already seen the `install` and `upgrade` directives that specify the behavior of the installation. You can also specify the source of your installation files.

```
url --url http://192.168.0.1/centos/
```

For Cobbler, we define a variable to specify the location of our installation source.

```
url --url=$tree
```

The url directive can also be used to specify an FTP server.

```
url --url ftp://jsmith:passsword@192.168.0.1/centos
```

We can specify some alternative sources, including cdrom, when installing from a locally mounted CD or DVD and hard drive to install from a local partition.

```
harddrive --dir=/centos --partition=/installsource
```

Keyboard, Language, and Time Zone

The next snippet we're going to show you configures our keyboard, language, and time zone.

```
# System keyboard
keyboard us
# System language
lang en_AU
# System timezone
timezone Australia/Melbourne
```

Here we've specified us as the value for the keyboard directive to indicate a U.S. keyboard. We've specified our language as en_AU (English Australian) and our time zone as Australia/ Melbourne.

Managing Users

You can also set the root user's password with the Kickstart rootpw directive.

```
rootpw --iscrypted $6$D7CxLkSBeC9.k.k3$S8G9s3/Y5LJ4dio....S5GS78p2laxALxaJ.
lCN9tzKB1zIpYz38Fs9/
```

The rootpw directive is a required Kickstart option for all Kickstart files. It can take either a plain-text value or an encrypted value for the root user's password when the --iscrtypted option is specified. You can lock the root user account so that no one can log in with it using the --lock option too (if --lock is specified, then you don't need a password as well).

You can create a new user with Kickstart using the user directive.

```
user jsmith --password password
```

The preceding code creates a new user called jsmith, with a password of *password*. By adding the --iscrypted option, you can add a user with an encrypted password. We would create our encrypted password as we did with the rootpw directive.

Firewall and Network

On CentOS, you can configure your host's initial firewall and network configuration.

```
# Firewall configuration
firewall --enabled --http --ssh --smtp
# SELinux configuration
selinux --enabled
```

Here we enabled the firewall with the `firewall` option and allowed access via HTTP, SSH, and SMTP. (You can disable the firewall with the `--disabled` option.) We also enabled SELinux—if you *really* need to, you can disable using the `selinux --disabled` option.

You can configure your network connections with Kickstart like so:

```
# Network information
network --bootproto=static --device=eth0 --gateway=192.168.0.254 ↵
--ip=192.168.0.1 --nameserver=192.168.0.1 --netmask=255.255.255.0 --onboot=on
```

You can also specify network configuration for one or more interfaces using the `network` option. You can see we've set the various options required to configure the eth0 interface. You can also specify DHCP, for example:

```
network --bootproto=dhcp --device=eth0 --onboot=on
```

On CentOS with Cobbler, if you're working with a specific host (one created with the `cobbler system` command), you can pass specific network configuration values to the Cobbler system configuration.

```
$ sudo cobbler system edit --name=gateway.example.com --mac=00:0C:29:3B:22:46 ↵
--profile=centos-base --interface=eth0 --ip=192.168.0.1 --subnet=255.255.255.0 -- ↵
gateway=192.168.0.254 --hostname=gateway --bootproto=static
```

Here we've specified the `edit` command to change an existing Cobbler-defined system and passed network configuration values to our system. This would define a static network configuration for interface eth0. We specify that the boot protocol is static using the `--static=1` option; we would specify `--static=0` for a DHCP configuration. The interface to be configured is specified using the `--interface=eth0` option.

Then, instead of specifying a network line, in our Kickstart file we specify what Cobbler calls a *snippet*.

```
$SNIPPET('network_config')
```

When building your host, Cobbler passes the network configuration you've specified to this snippet and a template it contains. This is then converted into the appropriate network line, and your host is configured.

■ **Tip** This snippet is a simple use of Cobbler's snippet system. You can define a variety of other actions using snippets, and you can see a selection of these in the `/var/lib/cobbler/snippets` directory, including the `network_config` snippet we used in this section. You can see how to use these snippets in the `sample.ks` file, and you can find instructions on how to make use of templates and snippets at `http://cobbler.github.io/manuals/2.8.0/3_5_-_Kickstart_Templating.html` and `http://cobbler.github.io/manuals/2.8.0/3/6_-_Snippets.html`.

Disks and Partitions

You've already seen one option Kickstart uses to configure disks and partitions, `clearpart`, which clears the partitions on the host. You can then use the part option to configure partitions on the host like so:

```
# Partition clearing information
clearpart --all --initlabel
part /boot --asprimary --bytes-per-inode=4096 --fstype="ext4" --size=150
part / --asprimary --bytes-per-inode=4096 --fstype="ext4" --size=4000
part swap --bytes-per-inode=4096 --fstype="swap" --size=512
```

■ **Note**   On CentOS, you can create a similar configuration just by specifying the `autopart` option. The `autopart` option automatically creates three partitions. The first partition is a 1GB or larger root (/) partition, the second is a swap partition, and the third is an appropriate boot partition for the architecture. One or more of the default partition sizes can be redefined with the `part` directive.

You use the `part` option to create specific partitions. In the preceding code, we first created two partitions, /boot and /, both ext4. We specified a size of 150MB for the /boot partition and a size of 4000MB (or 4GB) for the / or root partition. We also created a swap partition with a size of 512MB.

Using Kickstart on CentOS, we can create software RAID configurations, for example:

```
part raid.01 --asprimary --bytes-per-inode=4096 --fstype="raid" --grow --ondisk=sda ↵
--size=1
part raid.02 --asprimary --bytes-per-inode=4096 --fstype="raid" --grow --ondisk=sdb ↵
--size=1
part raid.03 --asprimary --bytes-per-inode=4096 --fstype="raid" --grow --ondisk=sdc ↵
--size=1
part raid.04 --asprimary --bytes-per-inode=4096 --fstype="raid" --grow --ondisk=sdd ↵
--size=1
part raid.05 --asprimary --bytes-per-inode=4096 --fstype="raid" --grow --ondisk=sde ↵
--size=1
raid / --bytes-per-inode=4096 --device=md0 --fstype="ext4" --level=5 raid.01 raid.02 ↵
raid.03 raid.04 raid.05
```

We specified five RAID disks, and each disk uses its entire contents as indicated by the --grow option. The respective disk to be used is specified with the --ondisk option, here ranging from sda to sde. Lastly, we used the raid option to specify the md0 RAID disk as the / or root partition.

You can also create partitions using LVM during an automated installation. On CentOS, for example, you would create them like so:

```
part /boot --fstype ext4 --size=150
part swap --size=1024
part pv1 --size=1 --grow
volgroup vg_root pv1
logvol / --vgname=vg_root --size=81920 --name=lv_root
```

In the preceding sample, we created a 150MB boot partition, a 1GB swap partition, and a physical volume called pv1 on the remainder of the disk, using the --grow option to fill the rest of the disk. We then created an 80GB LVM logical volume called vg_root.

Package Management

Using Kickstart, you can specify the packages you want to install. On CentOS, you specify a section starting with %packages and then the list of package groups or packages you want to install.

```
%packages
@ Administration Tools
@ Server Configuration Tools
@ System Tools
@ Text-based Internet
dhcp
```

We specify an at symbol (@), a space, and then the name of the package group we want to install, for example, Administration Tools. We can also specify individual packages by listing them by name without the @ symbol and space, as we have here with the dhcp package.

Ubuntu uses a similar setup.

```
%packages
@ kubuntu-desktop
dhcp-client
```

Here we've installed the Kubuntu-Desktop package group and the dhcp-client package. For more information, see http://pykickstart.readthedocs.io/en/latest/kickstart-docs.html#chapter-7-package-selection.

■ **Note** We discuss package groups in Chapter 8.

Pre- and Post-installation

You can run scripts before and after Kickstart installs your host. The prerun scripts run after the Kickstart configuration file has been parsed, but before your host is configured. Any prerun script is specified at the end of the Kickstart file and prefixed with the line %pre.

Each %post and %pre section must have a corresponding %end.

The postrun scripts are triggered after your configuration is complete and your host is installed. They should also be specified at the end of the Kickstart file and prefixed by a %post line. This is the %post section from our sample.ks configuration file:

```
%post
$SNIPPET('post_install_kernel_options')
$SNIPPET('post_install_network_config')
%end
```

Here we've specified two postrun Cobbler snippets that configure kernel and network options.

This postrun scripting space is useful to run any required setup applications or scripts.

Preseed

Preseed is the Debian installation automation tool. It is more opaque than Kickstart, but it performs the same function of automating an installation.

To provide some context, each `d-i` line that you see is a call to the Debian installer. The format of the file is the same as instructions passed to the `debconf-set-selection` command. It takes the following form:

```
<owner> <question name> <question type> <value>
```

So something like setting the locale for your system would look something like this:

```
d-i debian-installer/locale string en
```

The owner is the `debian-installer`, the question is `debian-installer/locale`, the type is `string`, and the value is en, or English.

Installation Source

Cobbler is selected as the initial installation source via the `live-installer` question.

```
d-i live-installer/net-image string http://$http_server/cobbler/links/$distro_name/install/
filesystem.squashfs
```

During the install, you can set up your apt repositories. This points your apt sources to the Ubuntu mirrors.

```
d-i mirror/country string manual
d-i mirror/http/hostname string archive.ubuntu.com
d-i mirror/http/directory string /ubuntu
d-i mirror/http/proxy string
```

You can choose the different apt pools with these settings to get to packages available from backports and the like:

```
#d-i apt-setup/restricted boolean true
#d-i apt-setup/universe boolean true
#d-i apt-setup/backports boolean true
```

You can just uncomment what pool you would like.

Keyboard, Language, and Time Zone

Setting the keyboard and language can be a time-consuming process but not with the installer. You can select the following in Preseed:

```
d-i debian-installer/locale string en
d-i debian-installer/country string AU
d-i debian-installer/locale string en_AU.UTF-8
d-i debian-installer/language string en
d-i console-setup/ask_detect boolean false
d-i console-setup/layoutcode string us
```

```
d-i console-setup/variantcode string
d-i keyboard-configuration/layoutcode string us
d-i clock-setup/ntp boolean true
d-i clock-setup/ntp-server string ntp.ubuntu.com
d-i time/zone string UTC
d-i clock-setup/utc boolean true
```

Here we set the locale and country, and we disabled the keyboard prompt to ask for our selection and answered all the questions concerning keyboard layout. Then we enable NTP for our clocks and set their time to UTC.

Managing Users

With Cobbler and Preseed we enable the root user, which Ubuntu doesn't normally do.

```
d-i passwd/root-login boolean true
d-i passwd/root-password-crypted password $default_password_crypted
d-i passwd/make-user boolean false
```

So when you build your hosts, you will need to sign in as root. To keep your familiar setup, you could add a user ubuntu either in the Preseed or in a SNIPPET at the end of the installation.

```
#d-i passwd/user-fullname string Ubuntu User
#d-i passwd/username string ubuntu
```

Firewall and Network

You can set up the network in whichever fashion suits you with Preseed, but you cannot do any firewall configurations. You can also add firewall configurations in post-install scripts in Cobbler if that is a requirement.

```
# IPv4 example
#d-i netcfg/get_ipaddress string 192.168.1.42
#d-i netcfg/get_netmask string 255.255.255.0
#d-i netcfg/get_gateway string 192.168.1.1
#d-i netcfg/get_nameservers string 192.168.1.1
#d-i netcfg/confirm_static boolean true
```

You can set a static IP or allow for DHCP in your network settings.

Disks and Partitions

Disk partition can be fairly complex in Preseed. Here we are just creating a simple LVM partition setup:

```
d-i partman-auto/method string lvm
d-i partman-lvm/device_remove_lvm boolean true
d-i partman-lvm/confirm boolean true
d-i partman-auto/choose_recipe select atomic
d-i partman/confirm_write_new_label boolean true
d-i partman/choose_partition select finish
d-i partman/confirm boolean true
```

Package Management

Using Preseed, you can specify the packages you want to install. For group packages, you can use `tasksel` (or task select owner) to multiselect a package group—like `ubuntu-desktop`.

```
tasksel tasksel/first multiselect ubuntu-desktop
```

For individual packages, you can just use the following:

```
d-i pkgsel/include string openssh-server
```

You can have more than one package selected if you like.

```
d-i pkgsel/include string openssh-server build-essential
```

MAAS

We're going to briefly introduce you to the MAAS tool—or Metal As A Service by Ubuntu. You may remember we saw "Install MAAS rack or region servers" in the initial splash screen when we first created our Ubuntu installation. This is an Ubuntu service used for managing bare metal, or physical computers, like you manage virtual computers. This service is able to install bare-metal Ubuntu and CentOS servers—as well as RHEL and Windows.

The MAAS service strives to provide cloud functionality on your metal servers. The technology underlying this tool is not new. It uses PXE, Trivial File Transfer Protocol (TFTP), and Debian Preseed to build up nodes. It is designed to manage physical data centers and is very scalable to manage thousands of nodes.

Once MAAS spins up a host, you can provision it with Juju, an Ubuntu provision framework. This can install software, user accounts, and other resources onto your server, or you can use other provisioning services like Puppet or Ansible. You can read more about that here: `https://maas.ubuntu.com/docs/juju-quick-start.html`.

You can see how it works here: `https://maas.io/how-it-works`. There is a quick get-started tutorial here: `https://maas.io/get-started`. You can even try to run up a Vagrant test suite here: `https://github.com/battlemidget/vagrant-maas-in-a-box`.

Configuration Management

We've shown you throughout this book that configuring a Linux server includes quite a few tasks, for example, configuring hosts; creating users; and managing applications, daemons, and services. These tasks can be repeated many times in the life cycle of one host in order to add new configurations or remedy a configuration that has changed through error, entropy, or development. They can also be time-consuming and are generally not an effective use of time and effort.

The usual first response to this issue is to try to automate the tasks, which leads to the development of custom-built scripts and applications. Few scripts developed in this ad hoc manner are ever published, documented, or reused, so the same tool is developed over and over again. These scripts also tend not to scale well, and they often require frequent maintenance.

Configuration management tools can automate these tasks efficiently and allow a consistent and repeatable life cycle for your hosts. We're going to show you how to use one of these tools, Puppet, to automate your configuration.

Introducing Puppet

Puppet (https://puppet.com/, formerly Puppetlabs) is an open source configuration management tool that in most installations relies on a client/server deployment model. Puppet is as available as open source or the commercial enterprise product. The enterprise product combines the multiple Puppet open source products and provides an enterprise dashboard to coordinate and configure your resources as well as commercial support agreements. The open source version doesn't have the fancy enterprise features, is community supported, and is licensed using the Apache 2.0 license. We're going to give you an overview of Puppet and how to use it to configure your environment and your hosts.

> ■ **Note** At the time of writing, the Puppet world is changing from version 3.*x* to version 4.*x*. Version 3.*x* will be end of lifed by the end of 2016, so you should be using version 4.*x*. Version 4 is substantially different under the hood than version 3. The current version at the time of writing is v4.8.

When using Puppet, central servers, called Puppet *masters*, are installed and configured. Client software is then installed on the target hosts, called *nodes*, that you want to manage. When a node connects to the Puppet master, a configuration *manifest* for that node is *compiled* on the master, sent to the node, and then applied on the node by the Puppet agent.

> ■ **Tip** There is another way to apply the manifest to a node, and that is called *master-less puppet*, or a puppet apply. It does not rely on the Puppet master architecture and certificate signing.

To provide client/server connectivity, Puppet uses RESTful web services running over HTTPS on TCP port 8140. In version 4.*x*, the Puppet server is a JVM-based application. To provide security, the sessions are encrypted and authenticated with internally generated self-signed certificates. Each Puppet client generates a self-signed certificate that is then validated and authorized on the Puppet master.

Thereafter, each client contacts the server—by default every 30 minutes, but this interval is customizable—to confirm that its configuration is up-to-date. If a new configuration is available or the configuration has changed on the node, the configuration manifest is recompiled and then applied to the client. This way, if any existing configuration has varied on the client, it is corrected with the expected configuration from the server. The results of any activity are logged and transmitted to the master.

At the heart of how Puppet works is a language that allows you to articulate and express your configuration. This is called the Puppet Declarative Scripting Language (Puppet DSL). Your configuration components are organized into entities called *resources*, which in turn can be grouped together in *collections*. Resources consist of the following:

- Type
- Title
- Attributes

Listing 19-5 shows an example of a simple resource.

Listing 19-5. A Puppet Resource

```
file { '/etc/passwd':
     owner => 'root',
     group => 'root',
     mode => '0644',
}
```

The resource in Listing 19-5 is a `file` type resource. The `file` resource configures the attributes of files under management. In this case, it configures the `/etc/passwd` file and sets its owner and group to the root user and its permissions to 0644.

■ **Tip** There is a style guide for writing your Puppet manifests that you should become familiar with early on. You can see it here: `https://docs.puppet.com/guides/style_guide.html`.

The resource type tells Puppet what kind of resource you are managing—for example, the `user` and `file` types are used for managing user and file operations on your nodes, respectively. Puppet comes with a number of resource types by default, including types to manage files, services, packages, `cron` jobs, and repositories, among others.

■ **Tip** You can see a full list of the built-in resource types at `https://docs.puppet.com/puppet/4.8/type.html`. You can also develop your own types in the Ruby programming language.

The resource's title identifies it to Puppet. Each title is made up of the name of the resource type (e.g., `file`) and the name of the resource (e.g., `/etc/passwd`). These two values are combined to make the resource's title (e.g., `File['/etc/passwd']`).

■ **Note** In a resource title, the name of the resource type is capitalized (`File`), and the name of the resource is encapsulated in block brackets and single quotes (`['/etc/passwd']`).

Here the name, `/etc/passwd`, also tells Puppet the path of the file to be managed. Each resource managed by Puppet must be unique—for example, there can be only one resource called `File['/etc/passwd']`.

The attributes of a resource describe the configuration details being managed, such as defining a particular user and the attributes of that user (e.g., the groups the user belongs to or the location of the user's home directory). In Listing 19-5, we are managing the owner, group, and mode (or permissions) attributes of the file. Each attribute is separated from its value with the `=>` symbols and is terminated with a comma.

Puppet also uses the concept of collections, which allow you to group together many resources. For example, an application such as Apache is made up of a package, a service, and a number of configuration files. In Puppet, each of these components would be represented as a resource (or resources) and then collected and applied to a node. We'll look at some of these collection types later in this chapter.

Installing Puppet

Let's start by installing Puppet. For Puppet, the client and server installations are slightly different, and we'll show you how to install each.

The Puppet master will require at least 3Gb of memory for the JVM and operating system to have enough room. Also, TCP port 8140 needs to be open on the Puppet master.

CentOS Installation

With the latest packages from Puppet, all the required packages are installed by default when we install the server. On CentOS, on both servers and clients, you will need to add the Puppet repositories for Red Hat-based machines.

```
$ sudo yum install -y https://yum.puppetlabs.com/puppetlabs-release-pc1-el-7.noarch.rpm
```

There are several components that make up the Puppet ecosystem such as Facter, a tool for discovering system facts on nodes. System facts are things like operating system, IP addresses, and any custom facts. Another one is Hiera, a key/value lookup database for declaring Puppet configuration data. Finally, there's MCollective, an orchestration tool for managing Puppet nodes.

On the master, you install the puppetserver, and this will install facter, hiera, the agent, and other required packages from the Puppet repository.

```
$ sudo yum install puppetserver
```

On the Puppet nodes, or clients, we can install the puppet-agent package by itself, and it will contain or require all that it needs to run.

```
$ sudo yum install -y puppet-agent
```

This of course will require the installation of the YUM repository, like earlier, first.

Ubuntu Installation

On Ubuntu, we again install the apt repository and then install puppetserver on the master server, which will bring down all the necessary Puppet components, like Facter and Hiera and the agent.

On the server or master, we need to do this:

```
$ wget https://apt.puppetlabs.com/puppetlabs-release-pc1-xenial.deb -O xenial.deb && sudo
dpkg -i xenial.deb
$ sudo apt-get update
$ sudo apt-get install -y puppetserver
```

```
On the client, you need the following:
$ sudo apt-get install -y puppet-agent
```

You will now have all the necessary components installed on your systems.

Configuring Puppet

We'll start configuring Puppet by setting up our Puppet master. Our configuration for the Puppet master will be located under the /etc/puppetlabs directory.

As we have said, Puppet has several components that make up the ecosystem. Puppet's principal server configuration file is located at /etc/puppetlabs/puppetserver/conf.d/puppetserver.conf. You will rarely need to edit this file, but it has things like various path settings and TLS ciphers being used.

The other main configuration file is on both the agent and the master. It is located at /etc/puppetlabs/puppet/puppet.conf. You can define global configuration settings or service-specific settings under the [service] sections, such as [main], [master], [agent], or [user].

Configuring the Master

Typically the master's /etc/puppetlabs/puppet/puppet.conf will look something like this:

```
[main]
certname = puppetmaster.example.com
server = puppet
environment = production
runinterval = 30m
strict_variables = true

[master]
dns_alt_names = puppetmaster,puppet,puppet.example.com
```

The [main] section contains the defaults for both the master and agents. Here we determine the certname, which will be the common name specified in the TLS certificate that we will generate on startup. This is related to the dns_alt_names setting that provides alternative DNS names that agents can use to verify the Puppet master. The server = puppet is the name of the Puppet master this Puppet agent will try to connect to. You can see that this matches one of the dns_alt_names.

The Puppet agents can specify the environment that they should use to collect their catalog when they connect to the Puppet master. This is often used to test version control system (VCS) branches of your Puppet code or can be used to multihome your Puppet master for more than one organization.

Do not fall into the mistake of making environments that mirror the roles your hosts may perform. That is, don't have an environment for development, UAT, staging, and production and assign relevant hosts to those environments. It is easier to treat all your hosts as production and handle the different roles and profiles these hosts may take on in the Puppet manifest itself. It often leads to a horrible divergence of your Puppet code between systems and VCS branches. By all means create an environment to test your Puppet code, but roll that as soon as you can into the production branch. Use alternatives like Hiera and the "roles and profiles" patterns to achieve this. See https://docs.puppet.com/hiera/3.2/ and https://docs.puppet.com/pe/2016.4/r_n_p_full_example.html.

The runinterval is the time between each Puppet run, that is, when the agent will call into the Puppet master for its catalog. strict_variables means that the parse will raise an error when referencing unknown variables.

In the [master] section, we define setting for the Puppet master server. We are not going to set anything here except the dns_alt_names value. Settings that might belong in here are codedir, where Puppet will look for the Puppet code, or the manifest, which we are going to write. However, we are going to take the defaults, which means our codedir will be /etc/puppetlabs/code.

It is in here you will set reporting settings and configuration for using PuppetDB. Using PuppetDB is a great idea as it allows you to do complex catalogs as it collects data from multiple nodes but is outside the scope of this exercise. See here for more details: https://docs.puppet.com/puppetdb/.

We recommend you create a DNS CNAME for your Puppet host (e.g., puppet.example.com) or add it to your /etc/hosts file.

```
# /etc/hosts
127.0.0.1 localhost
192.168.0.1 au-mel-ubuntu-1 puppet puppetmaster puppet.example.com puppetmaster.example.com
```

■ **Note** We cover how to create CNAMEs in Chapter 10.

Writing the Manifest

We're going to store our actual configuration in a directory called manifests under the /etc/puppetlabs/ code/environments/production directory. In this directory, you will most likely see the following directories and files:

```
ll /etc/puppetlabs/code/environments/production/
-rw-r--r-- 1 root root  879 Dec  5 23:53 environment.conf
drwxr-xr-x 2 root root 4096 Dec  5 23:53 hieradata/
drwxr-xr-x 2 root root 4096 Dec  5 23:53 manifests/
drwxr-xr-x 2 root root 4096 Dec  5 23:53 modules/
```

There is an environment.conf file that the Puppet server will read to determine the specific settings this environment will need. The hieradata directory will contain the Hiera database for variable lookups. The manifest directory is where the Puppet looks for the site.pp file. This file is used to create the root of our configuration. The modules directory is where we install Puppet modules. Modules are collections of Puppet files that perform a specific set of tasks. We will explain them in greater detail shortly.

The manifests directory needs to contain a file called site.pp that is the root of our configuration. Let's create that now.

```
$ sudo touch /etc/puppetlabs/code/environments/production/manifests/site.pp
```

■ **Note** Manifest files containing configuration have a suffix of .pp.

We're also going to create three more directories at the base of our production directory, first site and in that directory profile and role.

```
$ sudo mkdir -p /etc/puppetlabs/code/environments/production/site/{profile,role}
```

The site directory is actually another module and, like role, will be used to contain specific role and profile information for this particular environment. We will need to edit our environment.conf file to get Puppet to see these. We need to add the following to the modulepath directive:

```
$ sudo vi /etc/puppetlabs/code/environments/production/environment.conf
modulepath = ./sites:./modules:$basemodulepath
```

MODULES

In Puppet you can create *.pp files that contain collections of resources, classes, and definitions, but Puppet has another, more complex type of collection called a *module*. You can combine collections of classes, definitions, templates, files, and resources into modules. Modules are portable collections of configuration; for example, a module might contain all the resources required to configure Postfix or Apache.

You can read about how to use modules here:

- https://docs.puppet.com/puppet/4.8/modules_fundamentals.html

Also, there is a huge number of user-contributed modules on the https://forge.puppet.com/ site. Someone else has almost certainly written a module to configure a service or application you may want, and in many cases you can just download and reuse these modules to save having to write ones yourself. To install these modules, you can use something like r10k (https://docs.puppet.com/pe/latest/r10k.html) to help manage the installation of your modules.

You can use the puppet module command to manage modules as well. The puppet module command will create skeleton modules for you, search for existing modules from the Puppet Forge, install modules, and manage the life cycle of modules for you. For example, you can install a module from the Forge like this:

```
$ puppet module search apache
NAME                        DESCRIPTION                AUTHOR          KEYWORDS
puppetlabs-apache           Installs, configures, ...  @puppetlabs     apache web
example42-apache            Puppet module for apache   @example42      apache
herculesteam-augeasproviders_apache  Augeas-based apache ty... @herculesteam   types apache
...
$ sudo /opt/puppetlabs/bin/puppet module install puppetlabs-apache
Notice: Preparing to install into /etc/puppetlabs/code/environments/production/sites ...
Notice: Created target directory /etc/puppetlabs/code/environments/production/sites
Notice: Downloading from https://forgeapi.puppet.com ...
Notice: Installing -- do not interrupt ...
/etc/puppetlabs/code/environments/production/sites
└─┬ puppetlabs-apache (v1.11.0)
  ├── puppetlabs-concat (v2.2.0)
  └── puppetlabs-stdlib (v4.14.0)
```

You can see that we first searched for an apache module and found more than 900 modules that have the keyword apache. We then installed the puppetlabs-apache module. You can then read the documentation for this module and create your Apache services (https://forge.puppet.com/puppetlabs/apache).

You can read more about how to create your own modules and how they are structured at https://docs.puppet.com/puppet/4.8/modules_fundamentals.html#writing-modules.

We are now going to create a node definition so that we can match each of our nodes to a *profile*. A profile can be described as the kind of host it is. A *role* in comparison is like the service that host performs. For example, we can have a *role* of web_server. We can have a *profile* of UAT web_server. That is, it is a web server that has things that the UAT people require that might make it slightly different from our *production* web servers—different database back-end configurations, different authentication requirements, or the like—but still essentially it still has a *role* of being a web server that might have our application deployed to it.

It can take a bit to get your head around, and there are no perfect answers for how you should implement this structure into your Puppet manifest. Individual companies will have different implementations based on practices that work best for their companies. For a greater discussion of the Role and Profile pattern, see https://www.youtube.com/watch?v=RYMNmfM6UHw.

We'll continue our configuration by defining our site.pp file, as shown in Listing 19-6.

Listing 19-6. The site.pp File

```
sudo vi /etc/puppetlabs/code/environments/production/manifests/site.pp
node /^web\d+\.example\.com$/ {
  include profile::web_server
}
```

The node declaration in Listing 19-6 is how the Puppet master knows what to do with nodes when they "check in." Here we have used a regular expression, but you can also use plan strings like the following:

```
node 'web1.example.com' { ... }
node 'web1.example.com', 'web2.example.com' { ... }
```

In our declaration we are saying any node that checks in with a TLS certificate name starts with web (^web) and has one or more numbers following that (^web\d+) and then the domain name (\.example\.com) and nothing more (\.com$). Then we provide this node with the profile::web_server profile.

There is a special node declaration for when there is no match, the default node definition.

```
node default { ... }
```

You can use this default node declaration to notify people that a node has no definition or to apply a set of default security restrictions. If there is no default node, and no matching definition for a node, Puppet will fail to compile a manifest for this node.

■ **Note** You can find more information on defining nodes here: https://docs.puppet.com/puppet/latest/lang_node_definitions.html.

Starting Puppet Server with the RAL

Here is a neat trick. You can use the Puppet resource command to start your Puppet master server (puppetserver). The Puppet resource command allows you to directly interact with the Puppet Resource Abstraction Layer (RAL). The RAL is how Puppet interacts and manages the system. With the Puppet resource we will start puppetserver and make it start on boot like this:

```
sudo /opt/puppetlabs/bin/puppet resource service puppetserver ensure=running enable=true
```

We have not yet described how Puppet manages resources, and you will get a deeper understanding of what this command is doing shortly, but briefly what this is doing is the following:

- Starting a service (ensure=running)

- Making the necessary changes to start a service at boot (enable=true)

- Using whatever underlying system to start the service (service puppetserver)

In our case, it will use systemctl commands (start and enable) under the hood. You can run this same command on CentOS, Ubuntu, or any other supported system, and it will start the puppetserver process. If you were on a Mac and starting an Apache service, it would use launchctl—it uses whatever is appropriate for the system it is run on.

We can see if it has started using the normal systemctl command, and we can see the logs here:

```
$ sudo journalctl -u puppetserver -f
-- Logs begin at Tue 2016-12-20 09:24:04 UTC. --
Dec 21 09:25:29 puppetmaster systemd[1]: Starting puppetserver Service...
Dec 21 09:25:29 puppetmaster puppetserver[4877]: OpenJDK 64-Bit Server VM warning: ignoring
option MaxPermSize=256m; support was removed in 8.0
Dec 21 09:26:30 puppetmaster systemd[1]: Started puppetserver Service.
```

Also, the running server logs can be found in /var/log/puppetlabs.
We can use this for keeping an eye on the tasks in the next section.

Connecting Our First Client

Once you have the Puppet master configured and started, you can configure and initiate your first client. On the client, as we mentioned earlier, you need to install the puppet-agent package using your distribution's package management system. We're going to install a client on the web.example.com host and then connect to our puppet.example.com host. This installation will also create a /etc/puppetlabs/puppet/ directory with a puppet.conf configuration file.

When connecting our client, we first want to run the Puppet client from the command line rather than as a service. This will allow us to see what is going on when we connect. The Puppet client binary is called puppet agent, and you can see a connection to the master initiated in Listing 19-7.

Listing 19-7. Puppet Client Connection to the Puppet Master

```
web$ sudo /opt/puppetlabs/bin/puppet agent --server puppet.example.com --test --waitforcert 15
Info: Creating a new SSL key for web1.example.com
Info: Caching certificate for ca
Info: csr_attributes file loading from /etc/puppetlabs/puppet/csr_attributes.yaml
Info: Creating a new SSL certificate request for web1.example.com
Info: Certificate Request fingerprint (SHA256): 3E:D9:02:08:98:79:FB:8C:40:65:75:4E:15:7C:51
:89:4C:14:25:90:16:2A:DB:29:D6:3C:F4:82:64:7E:C8:62
Info: Caching certificate for caNotice: Did not receive certificate
```

In Listing 19-7, we executed the puppet agent binary with a number of options. The first option, --server, specifies the name or address of the Puppet master to connect to. We can also specify this in the main section of the /etc/puppetlabs/puppet/puppet.conf configuration file on the client.

```
[main]
server=puppet.example.com
```

The --test option runs the Puppet client in the foreground and prevents it from running as a daemon, which is the default behavior. The --test is commonly mistaken, and people think that it only "tests" a Puppet run and isn't destructive. This sadly misnamed option is actually a meta parameter for onetime, verbose, no-daemonize, no-usecacheonfailure, detailed-exitcodes, no-splay, show_diff, and no-use_cached_catalog. If you want a nondestructive Puppet run, you need to specify --noop.

■ **Tip** The --debug option provides further output that is useful for troubleshooting.

In Listing 19-7, you can see the output from our connection. The client has created a certificate signing request and a private key to secure our connection. Puppet uses TLS certificates to authenticate connections between the master and the client. The client is now waiting for the master to sign its certificate and enable the connection. At this point, the client is still running and awaiting the signed certificate. It will continue to check for a signed certificate every 15 seconds until it receives one or is canceled (using Ctrl+C or the like).

■ **Note** You can change the time the Puppet client will wait using the --waitforcert option like we have done. You can specify a time in seconds or 0 to not wait for a certificate.

Now on the master, we need to sign the certificate. We do this using the puppet cert command.

```
puppet$ sudo /opt/puppetlabs/puppet/bin/puppet cert list
  "web1.example.com" (SHA256) 3E:D9:02:08:98:79:FB:8C:40:65:75:4E:15:7C:51:89:4C:14:25:90:16
:2A:DB:29:D6:3C:F4:82:64:7E:C8:62
```

The --list option displays all the certificates waiting to be signed. We can then sign our certificate using the sign option. You can use the certificate fingerprint to verify you are signing the correct certificate.

```
puppet$ sudo /opt/puppetlabs/puppet/bin/puppet cert sign web1.example.com
Signing Certificate Request for:
  "web1.example.com" (SHA256) 3E:D9:02:08:98:79:FB:8C:40:65:75:4E:15:7C:51:89:4C:14:25:90:16
:2A:DB:29:D6:3C:F4:82:64:7E:C8:62
Notice: Signed certificate request for web1.example.com
Notice: Removing file Puppet::SSL::CertificateRequest web1.example.com at '/etc/puppetlabs/
puppet/ssl/ca/requests/web1.example.com.pem'
```

■ **Note** You can sign all waiting certificates with the puppet cert sign --all command.

On the client, after we've signed our certificate, we should see the following entries:

```
Notice: Did not receive certificate
Info: Caching certificate for web1.example.com
Info: Caching certificate_revocation_list for ca
Info: Using configured environment 'production'
Info: Retrieving pluginfacts
Info: Retrieving plugin
Info: Loading facts
```

```
Error: Could not retrieve catalog from remote server: Error 500 on SERVER: Server
Error: Evaluation Error: Error while evaluating a Function Call, Could not find class
::profile::web_server for web1.example.com at /etc/puppetlabs/code/environments/production/
manifests/site.pp:2:3 on node web1.example.com
Warning: Not using cache on failed catalog
Error: Could not retrieve catalog; skipping run
```

The client is now authenticated with the master, but we have an error, and nothing has been applied.

```
Error: Could not retrieve catalog from remote server: Error 500 on SERVER: Server
Error: Evaluation Error: Error while evaluating a Function Call, Could not find class
::profile::web_server for web1.example.com at /etc/puppetlabs/code/environments/production/
manifests/site.pp:2:3 on node web1.example.com
Warning: Not using cache on failed catalog
Error: Could not retrieve catalog; skipping run
```

The error is fairly detailed. We expected this error, so let's see what it is telling us. It says that on line 2 in /etc/puppetlabs/code/environments/production/manifests/site.pp we could not find the class ::profile::web_server for web1.example.com. Looking on line 2 of the site.pp file we see the following:

```
include profile::web_server
```

We have told it to include a profile that we have not created yet. We have to create it. Let's do that next.

■ **Tip** In the error do you notice that ::profile is preceded by ::? That indicates that the error is in the top scope in Puppet.

Creating Our First Configuration

Now our client has connected, and we're going to add some configuration for it. On the Puppet master, we need to add our profile module and add some configuration to apply to our client.

A module should have the following structure:

```
modulename/
                |- manifests
                                        |- init.pp
                |- files
                |- templates
```

At the least, you need the manifests directory; you may see other modules with more directories, like spec and lib as well—for testing and module code, respectively.

We have created the profile module directory in /etc/puppetlabs/code/environments/production/ sites already. Let's create a manifests file inside the profile directory. In that directory we will create a file called init.pp. This file is not technically necessary and will not hold any configuration. You can see the contents of this file in Listing 19-8.

Listing 19-8. Our init.pp Configuration

```
class profile {

}
```

It is simply an empty Puppet file. This is the standard format of a Puppet file. The `class` declaration is a Puppet *type*. The `profile` is a *title*. Then the *class type* expects the Puppet code in that class to be between curly braces `{...}`. See `https://docs.puppet.com/puppet/4.8/lang_resources.html` for the basics on the Puppet language.

Now inside the profile directory, we will create our `web_server.pp` file. The Puppet master autoloader, the mechanism that looks for and loads the Puppet files, will, when it sees `include profile::web_server`, look in its module path for first the directory profile and then in the `manifests` directory in that. Then it will load all the `*.pp` files until it finds the class `profile::webserver { ... }` directive like declared here:

```
$ sudo vi /etc/puppetlabs/code/environments/production/sites/profile/manifests/web_server.pp
class profile::web_server {

}
```

In this file, between the `{...}` we are going to declare a resource. This resource is called `notify`, and a resource is declared like the following:

```
notify { "profile::webserver - loaded": }
```

The `notify` is the resource type. The `"profile::webserver - loaded":` is the title. What it does is print a message in the runtime log of the Puppet run. As with all resource types, you can add attributes, and `notify` can take a name, `message`, and `withpath` attributes. So, you could write it like this:

```
notify { "profile::webserver - loaded":
  name    => 'a name',
  message => 'this is our message'
}
```

Feel free to experiment. You will find all the resources and their attributes at the following link: `https://docs.puppet.com/puppet/latest/type.html`. Save that file, and let's run the Puppet agent on `web1.example.com` again.

```
$ sudo /opt/puppetlabs/bin/puppet agent --server puppet.example.com --test
Info: Using configured environment 'production'
Info: Retrieving pluginfacts
Info: Retrieving plugin
Info: Loading facts
Info: Caching catalog for web1.example.com
Info: Applying configuration version '1482320904'
Notice: profile::webserver - loaded
Notice: /Stage[main]/Profile::Web_server/Notify[profile::webserver - loaded]/message:
defined 'message' as 'profile::webserver - loaded'
Notice: Applied catalog in 0.01 seconds
```

There you can see the output of our `notify`. Notify can be a handy way to debug your Puppet code as you can print out variables and the like to see that your code is working as you expect.

947

We now have our profile::web_server module working. Now inside this *profile* we are going to soon include the *role* apache_web. This is maybe starting to sound a little like Russian dolls, but the idea is that you abstract designation logic from the type of server it is. For the time being, let's move on to configuring our role.

Create the following directory: /etc/puppetlabs/code/environments/production/sites/role/ manifests. In there we create the file in Listing 19-9.

Listing 19-9. The role::apache_web Class

```
$ sudo vi /etc/puppetlabs/code/environments/production/sites/role/manifests/apache_web.pp
class role::apache_web (
  String $vhost_name,
  String $vhost_doc_root,
  Numeric $vhost_port
) {
  include apache

  apache::vhost { $vhost_name:
    port    => $vhost_port,
    docroot => $vhost_doc_root,
  }
}
```

This class has a bit more meat to it. Here we declare the class role::apache_web, and we provide a list of parameters we expect this class to be provided with when it is used. Class parameters in Puppet can either be declared when we create the class or be looked up from a key/value database like Hiera at the time this class is compiled for a node. They are declared right after the class name and inside parentheses separated by a comma. Read more about class parameters here: https://docs.puppet.com/puppet/4.8/ lang_classes.html.

In Puppet you can define the data types of the variables you are passing in, and if they are not the correct types, Puppet will error. We have used String and Numeric, but the others, like Boolean, Array, and Hash are described here: https://docs.puppet.com/puppet/4.8/lang_data_type.html.

In Listing 9-11 we have included the apache module. This is a module we are now going to install using the Puppet module command like we described earlier, and it will be the puppetlab/apache module. Looking at the documentation, we can declare a virtual host by giving a name, a port, and doc_root, and we have used the parameters provided to the class.

The apache::vhost is what is called a defined resource type. Defined resource types are normal blocks of Puppet code that can be evaluated multiple times. You still cannot have multiple defined resources with the same name, so you could not have two declarations of apache::vhost {'www.example.com': } for instance, but you can declare apache::vhost {'www.example.com': } and apache::vhost {'api. example.com': } in the same manifest just fine.

Let's install the puppetlabs-apache module on the Puppet server now.

```
$ sudo /opt/puppetlabs/puppet/bin/puppet module install puppetlabs-apache
Notice: Preparing to install into /etc/puppetlabs/code/environments/production/sites ...
Notice: Created target directory /etc/puppetlabs/code/environments/production/sites
Notice: Downloading from https://forgeapi.puppet.com ...
Notice: Installing -- do not interrupt ...
/etc/puppetlabs/code/environments/production/sites
└─┬ puppetlabs-apache (v1.11.0)
  ├── puppetlabs-concat (v2.2.0)
  └── puppetlabs-stdlib (v4.14.0)
```

This has installed the puppetlabs-apache module and the required concat and stdlib modules as well and installed them into the /etc/puppetlabs/code/environments/production/sites directory. You can see the documentation for that module here: https://forge.puppet.com/puppetlabs/apache.

Now let's go to the profile::web_server class again and add in our virtual host we want to install.

```
sudo vi /etc/puppetlabs/code/environments/production/sites/profile/manifests/web_server.pp
class profile::web_server {
  class { role::apache_web:
    vhost_name       => 'www.example.com',
    vhost_doc_root => '/var/www/html',
    vhost_port       => 80
  }
}
```

We have now called in the class role::apache_web and provided the vhost_ parameters that we required in the role::apache_web class. In this profile you may also include some Puppet code that deploys the site to /var/www/html.

Applying Our First Configuration

Let's now run our Puppet agent on web1 and see what happens.

■ **Caution**   This next action is destructive and will purge any existing Apache configuration from your Puppet node.

```
$ sudo /opt/puppetlabs/bin/puppet agent --server puppet.example.com --test
Info: Using configured environment 'production'
Info: Retrieving pluginfacts
Info: Retrieving plugin
Info: Loading facts
Info: Caching catalog for web1.example.com
Info: Applying configuration version '1482323449'
Notice: profile::webserver - loaded
Notice: /Stage[main]/Apache/Package[httpd]/ensure: created
Info: /Stage[main]/Apache/Package[httpd]: Scheduling refresh of Class[Apache::Service]
Info: Computing checksum on file /etc/httpd/conf.d/README
Info: /Stage[main]/Apache/File[/etc/httpd/conf.d/README]: Filebucketed /etc/httpd/conf.d/
README to puppet with sum 20b886e8496027dcbc31ed28d404ebb1
...
Notice: /Stage[main]/Apache::Service/Service[httpd]/ensure: ensure changed 'stopped' to 'running'
Info: /Stage[main]/Apache::Service/Service[httpd]: Unscheduling refresh on Service[httpd]
Notice: Applied catalog in 20.26 seconds
```

That is a shortened output of our Puppet run. You can see that the Apache package was installed. We removed the README (and saved it to a file bucket; see https://docs.puppet.com/puppet/latest/man/filebucket.html) and started the Apache service.

We can now test that the Apache service is up and running with the following command:

```
$ curl -I http://localhost
HTTP/1.1 200 OK
Date: Wed, 21 Dec 2016 13:07:46 GMT
Server: Apache/2.4.6 (CentOS)
Connection: close
Content-Type: text/html;charset=UTF-8
```

Every subsequent run of the Puppet agent will make sure the node stays in its current configuration. If you do another Puppet run, nothing will be changed. Try it yourself now. On our web server node we are going to remove the /etc/httpd/conf.d/25-www.example.com.conf file that was created during our Puppet run. Then we will run Puppet again on that node.

```
$ sudo rm -f /etc/httpd/conf.d/25-www.example.com.conf
$ sudo /opt/puppetlabs/bin/puppet agent --server puppet.example.com --test
Info: Using configured environment 'production'
...
Notice: /Stage[main]/Role::Apache_web/Apache::Vhost[www.example.com]/Concat[25-www.example.
com.conf]/File[/etc/httpd/conf.d/25-www.example.com.conf]/ensure: defined content as '{md5}6
bee975590cb7b26b89cfd48d8d65bdf'
Info: Concat[25-www.example.com.conf]: Scheduling refresh of Class[Apache::Service]
Info: Class[Apache::Service]: Scheduling refresh of Service[httpd]
Notice: /Stage[main]/Apache::Service/Service[httpd]: Triggered 'refresh' from 1 events
Notice: Applied catalog in 1.71 seconds
```

Here you can see that the file was replaced and the Apache service was restarted.

CREATING A PUPPET CONFIGURATION

The best way to convert your existing configuration to Puppet is to start small. Choose a function or application, such as sudo or the SSH daemon, and convert its configuration management from manual to managed with Puppet. When these functions are stable, add additional components to your Puppet configuration. A good way to approach this task is to classify your hosts by their functions. For example, our www.example.com host can run a number of services such as Apache or Postfix, so a logical first step would be to configure these services and then slowly add the additional functions also supported on this host.

Specifying Configuration for Multiple Hosts

We've barely scratched the surface of Puppet's configuration capabilities, so let's look at extending our current configuration to multiple clients or nodes. We'll demonstrate how to differentiate configuration on two clients and apply a slightly different configuration to each.

To implement this differentiation, we're going to use Puppet's partner tool, Facter. Facter is a system inventory tool that returns facts about your hosts. We can run Facter from the command line using the facter binary to see what it knows about our web1.example.com client.

```
web1$ sudo /opt/puppetlabs/bin/facter -p
...
facterversion => 3.5.0
filesystems => ext2,ext3,ext4
identity => {
  gid => 0,
  group => 'root',
  privileged => true,
  uid => 0,
  user => 'root'
}
is_virtual => true
kernel => Linux
kernelmajversion => 3.10
kernelrelease => 3.10.0-327.28.3.el7.x86_64
kernelversion => 3.10.0
load_averages => {
  15m => 0.05,
  1m => 0.05,
  5m => 0.04
}
...
```

We've shown you a small selection of the facts available in Facter, but you can see that it knows a lot about our host, including its name, network information, operating system, and even the release of the operating system.

So, how is this useful to Puppet? Well, each of these facts is available to Puppet as a variable. Puppet runs Facter prior to applying any configuration, collects the client's facts, and then sends them to the Puppet master for use in configuring the client. For example, the hostname fact is available in our Puppet configuration as the variable $hostname – or as $fact['hostname']. Let's look at an example in Listing 19-10.

MORE ABOUT FACTER

Facts are provided as structured facts or as either an array or a hash. This means you can use them via the $facts variable using a structured syntax, in other words, $facts['hostname']. You can learn more them here: https://docs.puppet.com/puppet/4.8/lang_facts_and_builtin_vars.html.

Certain facts are called *trusted facts*. These are facts that cannot be self-reported by the node. They are derived from the TLS certificate. This provides some level of assurance when dealing with sensitive data. You can access them via $trusted['fact_name']. You can read more about this here: https://docs.puppet.com/puppet/latest/lang_facts_and_builtin_vars.html#trusted-facts.

For more information, you can visit https://docs.puppet.com/facter/.

Facter is also highly extensible. With a small amount of Ruby code, you can add your own facts, for example, information customized to your environment. You can read about how to add these custom facts at https://docs.puppet.com/facter/3.5/fact_overview.html.

Listing 19-10. Using Facts

```
class sudo {
    package { sudo:
        ensure => 'present',
    }

  file { '/etc/sudoers':
        source => [
          "puppet:///modules/sudo/sudo_${hostname}",
          "puppet:///modules/sudo/sudo_${os['family']}",
          'puppet:///modules/sudo/sudo_default'
        ]
        owner => 'root',
        group => 'root',
        mode => '0440',
    }
}
```

Here we are defining a class that provides sudo. You can see in this sudo class we have defined a file
resource type that specifies the basic security requirements of that file and a source file, or a file local to the
Puppet master that we will send to the node when the agent checks in.

When the agent checks in, the Puppet master will search in the sudo module for a file in the modules/
sudo/files directory called sudo_web1; if it can't find that, it will look for sudo_Redhat (for CentOS hosts,
sudo_Debian for Ubuntu), and if it cannot find a match, then it will provide the sudo_default file.

Depending on which client connected, they would get a file appropriate to them. But this isn't the only
use for facts. We can also use facts to determine how to configure a particular node, as shown in Listing 19-11.

Listing 19-11. A Fact in a case Statement

```
node default {

  case $facts['os']['name'] {
        'CentOS', 'RedHat':    { include centos } # include the centos
        /^(Ubuntu|Debian)$/:  { include ubuntu } # include the ubuntu class
        default:                    { include common } # include the common class
    }
}
```

Here we created our default node definition, which is the node configuration used for all nodes that
don't explicitly have a node defined. Inside this node definition, we used a feature of the Puppet language, a
case statement. The case statement, a concept common to many programming languages, specifies a result
based on the value of a variable—in this case we use the $facts['os']['name'] fact, which contains the
name of the operating system running on the client (e.g., CentOS or Red Hat or Debian or Ubuntu).

■ **Tip** Puppet has two other types of conditionals: selectors and if/else clauses. You can read about these
at https://docs.puppet.com/puppet/4.8/lang_conditional.html.

In Listing 19-11, if the value of the `$facts['os']['name']` is CentOS, then the centos class is included on this client. We can define more than one case, as long as they are strings separated by a comma. If the value is Ubuntu, then the ubuntu class is included; here you can see we can use a regular expression to match on Ubuntu or Debian. The last value, default, is the behavior if the value does not match either redhat or ubuntu. In this case, the common class is applied to the client.

We've used another Puppet conditional, a selector, in Listing 19-12.

Listing 19-12. A Selector

```
$ssh_service = $facts['os']['name'] ? {
    'CentOS' => 'sshd',
    'Ubuntu' => 'ssh',
    default => 'ssh',
  }

service { $ssh_service:
  ensure => 'running',
}
```

In Listing 19-12, we introduced a new type, service, that manages services on hosts. We've titled our service resource $ssh_service, and we've defined that variable just above it. We've used a Puppet language construct called a *selector*, combined with the `$fact['os']['name']` fact, to specify the name of the SSH service. This is because on each operating system we've specified, the SSH daemon is called something different. For example, on CentOS the SSH daemon is called sshd, while on Ubuntu it is called ssh.

The title attribute uses the value of the $ssh_service to specify what the daemon will be called on each distribution. Puppet, in turn, uses this to determine what service to start or stop. The default value is used when the value of `$facts['os']['name']` is neither CentOS nor Ubuntu.

Lastly, the ensure attribute has been set to running to ensure the service will be started. We could set the ensure attribute to stopped to ensure it is not started.

■ **Note**   The Puppet language has a lot of useful features and lots of different ways you can express your code. Remember to consult the style guide for Puppet at `https://docs.puppet.com/guides/style_guide.html`.

Relating Resources

Resources in Puppet also have the concept of *relationships*. For example, a service resource can be connected to the package that installs it. Using this, we could trigger a restart of the service when a new version of the package is installed. This allows us to do some useful things. Consider the simple example in Listing 19-13.

Listing 19-13. Requiring Resources

```
class ssh {
    service { 'sshdaemon':
        name => $facts['os']['name'] ? {
            'CentOS' => 'sshd',
            'Ubuntu' => 'ssh',
            default  => 'ssh',
        },
        ensure => 'running',
        require => File['/etc/ssh/sshd_config'],
    }

    file { '/etc/ssh/sshd_config':
        owner  => 'root',
        group  => 'root',
        mode   => '0644',
        source => 'puppet://modules/ssh/sshd_config',
        notify => Service['sshdaemon'],
    }
}
```

Listing 19-13 shows a new class called ssh, which contains the service resource we created in Listing 19-12. We have created a file resource to manage the /etc/ssh/sshd_config file. We've created the ssh service a little differently here; we have made a selector on the name attribute to the service type. It works exactly the same as in Listing 19-12. You've seen almost all the attributes in these resources except require in the service resource and notify in the file resource. These are not, however, normal attributes—they are called *metaparameters*. Let's look at each metaparameter and see what it does.

The require metaparameter allows you to build a relationship to one or more resources. Any resource you specify in the require metaparameter will be configured *before* this resource; hence, Puppet will process and configure the File['/etc/ssh/sshd_config'] resource before the Service['sshdaemon'] resource. This approach ensures that the appropriate configuration file is installed prior to starting the SSH daemon service. You could do a similar thing with a package resource.

```
class httpd {
    package { 'httpd':
        ensure => 'present',
    }

    service { 'httpd':
        ensure  => 'running',
        enabled => true,
        require => Package['httpd'],
    }
}
```

Here the package resource, Package['httpd'], must be installed before the Service['httpd'] service can be started.

■ **Tip** We've also added the `enabled` attribute to the `Service['http']` resource. When set to `true`, this attribute ensures our service starts when the host boots (similar to using the `systemctl enable` command).

We've also specified another metaparameter, this one called `notify`, in Listing 19-13. This metaparameter has been added to the `File['/etc/ssh/sshd_config']` resource. The `notify` metaparameter tells other resources about changes and updates to a resource. In this case, if the `File['/etc/ssh/sshd_config']` resource is changed (e.g., if the configuration file is updated), then Puppet will notify the `Service['sshdaemon']` resource, causing it to be run and thus restarting the SSH daemon service.

■ **Tip** Two other relationships you can construct are `subscribe` and `before`. You can see both of these at `https://docs.puppet.com/puppet/latest/metaparameter.html` and also read about other available metaparameters you may find useful.

Using Templates

In addition to retrieving files from the Puppet file server, you can also make use of a template function to apply specific values inside those files to configure a service or application. Puppet templates use a Ruby template language called EPP (see `https://docs.puppet.com/puppet/latest/lang_template_epp.html`). It's a function that happens during compilation on the Puppet master and is simple to use, as you can see in Listing 19-14.

Listing 19-14. Using Templates

```
file { '/etc/ssh/sshd_config':
        path       => '/etc/ssh/sshd_config',
        owner    => 'root',
        group     => 'root',
        mode      => '0644',
        content => epp('ssh/sshd_config.epp', { 'root_login' => 'no' }),
        notify    => Service['sshdaemon'],
    }
```

In Listing 19-14, we used the same `File['/etc/ssh/sshd_config']` resource we created earlier, but we exchanged the source attribute for the `content` attribute. With the `content` attribute, rather than a file being retrieved from the Puppet file server, the contents of the file are populated from this attribute. The contents of the file can be specified in a string like so:

```
content => 'this is the content of a file',
```

Or, as Listing 19-14 shows, we can use a special Puppet function called epp. To use the template function, we specify a template file, and Puppet populates any EPP code inside the template with appropriate values that have been passed in as a hash to the function. Listing 19-15 shows a simple template.

Listing 19-15. sshd_config Template

```
Port 22
Protocol 2
ListenAddress <%= $ipaddress %>

SyslogFacility AUTHPRIV
PermitRootLogin <%= $root_login %>
PasswordAuthentication no
ChallengeResponseAuthentication no
GSSAPIAuthentication yes
GSSAPICleanupCredentials yes
UsePAM yes
X11Forwarding yes
Banner /etc/motd
```

We've used only one piece of EPP in Listing 19-15, to specify the ListenAddress of our SSH daemon, <%= $ipaddress %>. The <%= $value %> syntax is how you specify variables in a template. Here we specified that Puppet should set ListenAddress to the value of the $ipaddress variable. This variable is, in turn, the value of the ipaddress fact, which contains the IP address of the eth0 interface. We also have passed in the { 'root_login' => 'no' } key/value as a hash. This is now available as a variable <%= $root_login %>.

When we now connect a client that applies the File['/etc/ssh/sshd_config'] resource, the value of the ipaddress fact on the client will be added to the template, and the root_login will be evaluated to no and then applied on the client in the /etc/ssh/sshd_config file.

You can perform a wide variety of functions in an EPP template—more than just specifying variables. You can read about how to use templates in more detail at https://docs.puppet.com/puppet/latest/lang_template_epp.html.

You can also explore the older style of Puppet templating using Ruby's ERB templating language. It is similar EPP syntactically; you can see the page for it here: https://docs.puppet.com/puppet/latest/lang_template_erb.html.

More Puppet

We've barely touched on Puppet in this chapter—there's a lot more to see. In the sections that follow, we'll describe some of the topics we haven't covered that you can explore further to make the best use of Puppet.

Functions

Puppet also has a collection of functions. *Functions* are useful commands that can be run on the Puppet master to perform actions. You've already seen two functions: template, which we used to create a template configuration file, and include, which we used to specify the classes for our nodes. There are a number of other functions, including the generate function, which calls external commands and returns the result, and the notice function, which logs messages on the master and is useful for testing a configuration.

You can see a full list of functions at https://docs.puppet.com/puppet/latest/function.html.

Reports

Puppet has the ability to report on events that have occurred on your nodes or clients. Combined with PuppetDB, you can get extensive reports about your systems; if you have the enterprise version, you will be able to see these in the Puppet dashboard. You can read more about reporting at `https://docs.puppet.com/puppet/latest/reporting_about.html`.

External Nodes

As you might imagine, when you begin to have a lot of nodes, your configuration can become quite complex. If it becomes cumbersome to define all your nodes and their configuration in manifests, then you can use a feature known as *external nodes* to better scale this. External nodes allow you to store your nodes and their configuration in an external source.

The ENC runs as a command on the Puppet master and returns a YAML document describing the manifest for any particular node. It can be from any source, such as a database.

You can read more about external nodes classifiers at `https://docs.puppet.com/guides/external_nodes.html`.

Documenting Your Configuration

A bane of many system administrators is documentation, both needing to write it and needing to keep it up-to-date. However, Puppet has some suggestions on how to write the documentation for any modules you create and want to publish to the broader community via sites like Puppet Forge. You can read about manifest documentation at `https://docs.puppet.com/puppet/latest/modules_documentation.html`.

Troubleshooting Puppet

Puppet has a big and helpful community as well as extensive documentation. Start at these Puppet sites:

- `https://puppet.com/resources`

- `https://docs.puppet.com/puppet/4.8`

- `https://puppet.com/community/get-help`

The following books are recommended:

- *Pro Puppet* by Spencer Krum, William Van Hevelingen, Ben Kero, James Turnbull, and Jeffrey McCune (Apress, 2014)

- *Extending Puppet* by Alessandro Franceschi and Jaime Soriano Pastor (Packt, 2016)

These and more can be found here: `https://puppet.com/resources/books`.

Introducing Ansible

Ansible has a different approach than Puppet. At its heart is the open source Ansible software that can orchestrate the provisioning of large-scale fleets. It was originally designed by Michael DeHaan, the same person who wrote Cobbler. The Ansible Inc., the company that was formed for the commercial support of Ansible (the Tower product), was acquired by Red Hat, which continues to support the open source community as well as provide subscription-based commercial support service.

Written in Python, it was designed to be agentless. It uses SSH as its transport mechanism, which means there is no certificate management like with Puppet; instead, you use your existing SSH key management to provide secure transport. It works by sending an Ansible payload (a *playbook*) via SSH to the target server. The payload is a set of Python scripts, executed on the target system.

■ **Note**   At the time of writing, Ansible currently support versions 2.6 and 2.7 of Python. It has preliminary support for Python version 3 as of Ansible version 2.2.

Like Puppet, Ansible can install files and manage packages and many other resources, including creating cloud resources. It does this by calling playbooks. Ansible playbooks are made up of sequential tasks. As you step through each task, you execute a module.

A module is an action that should be performed on target node. There is an extensive set of core modules. They are called to manage files, packages, and services; they can also manage cloud service infrastructure. There are many core modules shipped with Ansible, and they are documented here: `http://docs.ansible.com/ansible/modules_by_category.html`.

The target systems, or inventory, are a collection of hosts and can be grouped together into groups. These can be static or dynamically collected with helper scripts. You can assign variables to these hosts and groups that can be used in your playbooks. You can see more about hosts and groups here: `http://docs.ansible.com/ansible/intro_inventory.html`.

Any variables that are declared in hosts or groups can be used throughout your playbooks. Ansible uses the Jinja2 Python templating engine to allow for complex filtering and playbook compilation. You can also declare variables on the command line or in the playbooks themselves.

You can also find system facts, like Puppet Facts, that can also be used by the templating engine inside your playbooks. We can also perform lookups that can be read from external services or from local files. You can find more information on variables at `http://docs.ansible.com/ansible/playbooks_variables.html#variables`.

In this section we are going to build up a web server. We are then going to use ServerSpec to validate our configuration.

Ansible Installation and Configuration

Ansible is simple to install and is available from either `.deb` or `.rpm` packages, Python Pip installation or tar files, and more, depending on your system. We are going to use the Debian package as we are running this on our Xenial server.

Let's run the `aptitude` command like so:

```
$ sudo aptitude install -y ansible
```

It is also available via `yum install`. You can also install it via Python Pip, which is a Python package manager. This is available on most operating systems.

```
$ sudo pip install ansible
```

Once it's installed, you can edit the global configuration file, `ansible.cfg`, that will be in the `/etc/ansible` directory. When Ansible starts, it looks for the configuration file, first in the environment variable `ANSIBLE_CONFIG`, then in `ansible.cfg` in the local directory, then in `~/.ansible.cfg` in the home directory, or lastly the system default in `/etc/ansible/ansible.cfg`.

When you start out, you don't need to edit this file. If you have downloaded third-party Ansible modules to a particular location, you can declare that location in in the `ansible.cfg` file. Other things like SSH options that you want to use as defaults can also go in there.

```
inventory      = /etc/ansible/hosts
library        = /usr/share/my_modules/
roles_path     = /etc/ansible/roles
log_path       = /var/log/ansible.log
fact_caching   = memory
ssh_args       = -o ControlMaster=auto -o ControlPersist=60s -o
                 ProxyCommand="ssh  -W %h:%p -q jumphost"
```

Here you can see a small subset of things you may want to change or add to. The inventory is where Ansible expects to see you host list or a program that will dynamically gather your host list. The library is for your own or shared modules. The `role_path` is where you might install roles. Roles are collections of tasks, variables, templates, files, and handlers that can be used to configure a particular service, like Nginx (see https://galaxy.ansible.com/ for a whole bunch of roles that people have created and shared).

The `fact_caching` can be stored either in memory on your local host or in different shared service like Redis (Redis being an open source key/value store database). This can help to speed up fact collection for multiple users of Ansible.

For the `ssh_args` the default SSH options are `ControlMaster=auto` and `ControlPersist=60s`, which allow for the sharing of multiple sessions over the one connection (meaning we don't need to connect the target host, execute a task, disconnect, connect again, execute another task, and so on). The option we have added here is how you can run your commands via a jump host, so any target hosts will be accessed via this SSH proxy server.

There is no `ansible` service to start. However, you may want to automate the process of running playbooks on your hosts; that is where Ansible Tower (https://www.ansible.com/tower) comes in. It is a commercial automation and job scheduling tool provided by Red Hat.

You can also, of course, automate your Ansible playbooks by using other continuous delivery (CD) solutions like executing runs as part of a build step in tools like Jenkins (https://jenkins.io/).

Using the ansible Command

Ansible is great for running ad hoc command across multiple hosts. Any of the modules (documented at http://docs.ansible.com/ansible/modules_by_category.html) can be used to execute ad hoc commands via the `ansible` command. If we bundle up the ad hoc tasks into a list of tasks, that is called a *playbook*, which is invoked with the `ansible-playbook` command.

Let's look first at the `ansible` command to run a simple task. At the basic level, Ansible needs to know three things.

- How to find the host to target

- The host to target

- The module to run and any arguments for that module

While there are many more options to the ansible command, we can apply this to run our first task. We are going to use the setup module, a module that gathers the facts that we can use in our tasks or playbooks.

```
$ ansible -c local localhost -m setup
localhost | SUCCESS => {
    "ansible_facts": {
        "ansible_all_ipv4_addresses": [
            "192.168.0.61",
            "10.0.2.15"
        ],
...
        "ansible_virtualization_type": "virtualbox",
        "module_setup": true
    },
    "changed": false
}
```

There is a long list of Ansible facts returned as a JSON string; we have shown only a small portion. The ansible command is using a local connection (-c local) and operating on the target host localhost. We executed on that host the setup module (-m setup).

Let's now take it one step further; on this local host we will install the Nginx package. To do that, we use the apt or yum module, depending on which host operating system we are targeting.

```
$ ansible -c local localhost -m apt -a 'name=nginx state=latest update_cache=yes'
localhost | FAILED! => {
    "changed": false,
    "cmd": "apt-get update '&&' apt-get install python-apt -y -q --force-yes",
    "failed": true,
    "msg": "W: chmod 0700 of directory /var/lib/apt/lists/partial failed -
SetupAPTPartialDirectory (1: Operation not permitted)\nE: Could not open lock file /var/
lib/apt/lists/lock - open (13: Permission denied)\nE: Unable to lock directory /var/lib/
apt/lists/\nW: Problem unlinking the file /var/cache/apt/pkgcache.bin - RemoveCaches
(13: Permission denied)\nW: Problem unlinking the file /var/cache/apt/srcpkgcache.bin
- RemoveCaches (13: Permission denied)\nE: Could not open lock file /var/lib/dpkg/lock -
open (13: Permission denied)\nE: Unable to lock the administration directory (/var/lib/
dpkg/), are you root?",
    "rc": 100,
    "stderr": "W: chmod 0700 of directory /var/lib/apt/lists/partial failed -
SetupAPTPartialDirectory (1: Operation not permitted)\nE: Could not open lock file /var/
lib/apt/lists/lock - open (13: Permission denied)\nE: Unable to lock directory /var/lib/
apt/lists/\nW: Problem unlinking the file /var/cache/apt/pkgcache.bin - RemoveCaches
(13: Permission denied)\nW: Problem unlinking the file /var/cache/apt/srcpkgcache.bin
- RemoveCaches (13: Permission denied)\nE: Could not open lock file /var/lib/dpkg/lock -
open (13: Permission denied)\nE: Unable to lock the administration directory (/var/lib/
dpkg/), are you root?\n",
    "stdout": "",
    "stdout_lines": []
}
```

We have an error! You can see from the output that we have tried to execute the "apt-get update '&&' apt-get install python-apt -y -q --force-yes" commands and we have been denied permission. This should not be a surprise; we don't let unauthorized users install packages without appropriate sudo privileges. Let's provide Ansible with the ability to use sudo with the request.

```
$ ansible -c local localhost --become -m apt -a 'name=nginx state=latest update_cache=yes'
localhost | SUCCESS => {
    "cache_update_time": 1481951319,
    "cache_updated": true,
    "changed": true,
    "stderr": "",
    "stdout": "...."
}
```

Now we have added the --become argument to the ansible command, and now it will attempt to execute the commands via sudo. The output has again been shortened, but you can see that we have "change": true, which means that the task was executed on the system and the system was changed.

What happens if we run that ansible task again?

```
$ ansible -c local localhost --become -m apt -a 'name=nginx state=latest update_cache=yes'
localhost | SUCCESS => {
    "cache_update_time": 1481951681,
    "cache_updated": true,
    "changed": false
}
```

Again, we are successful but this time, because Nginx is already install there was nothing to change, so "changed" is false. That is installing one thing on one host, how do you do that on many hosts?

Ansible Inventory

Ansible inventory is a way of defining our list of hosts that we want to execute our commands over. This can be dynamically discovered with the help of scripts or as a plain static host list. We are going to show you how to configure the static host list. If you want, you can read about dynamic host lists here: http://docs.ansible.com/ansible/intro_dynamic_inventory.html.

The inventory file can be in the local directory or in the systemwide /etc/ansible/hosts file. In our host inventory we can define our hosts and host groups. Host groups are defined in square brackets and can have nested host groups in them.

```
$ sudo vi /etc/ansible/hosts

somehost.example.com

[all_centos]
gateway.example.com
backup.example.com

[all_ubuntu]
mail.example.com
monitor.example.com
```

```
[dbs]
db.example.com

[all_servers:children]
all_centos
all_ubuntu
dbs
```

In our host list we have defined a single host, somehost.example.com for an example. Then we have defined three host groups with the [ ] brackets. They include hosts that are of a particular operating system, either all CentOS or all Ubuntu, but the groups can be anything that makes sense to your installation. Lastly, we have a group of groups [all_servers:children] host group that contains the all_ubuntu and all_centos host groups as well as the [dbs] host.

Let's see how we now execute something across a few hosts. We will assume that the user we are running this command as has had their public SSH key deployed to all the hosts already. In some situations, like running Vagrant hosts, you will find that the username you are using is different on each host. Xenial hosts will use the ubuntu user, and CentOS will use the vagrant user as defaults. We can cater for these kinds of differences in our host file by adding the following variable declaration:

```
[all_ubuntu:vars]
ansible_user=ubuntu

[all_centos:vars]
ansible_user=vagrant
```

You will notice that hosts in the [dbs] group have not been declared as either Ubuntu or CentOS, so we can manage those hosts with this similar declaration.

```
[dbs]
db.example.com ansible_user=vagrant
```

We may also want particular hosts to be reached via a particular jumphost (sometimes called a *bastion* or *proxy*). We can declare the following:

```
[remote:vars]
ansible_ssh_common_args: '-o ProxyCommand="ssh  -W %h:%p -q jumphost"'
```

In this way, all hosts classified in the [remote] group will reached via the host jumphost.

■ **Tip**   Not sure what the ProxyCommand does? Check out this page for this and other interesting SSH tricks: https://en.wikibooks.org/wiki/OpenSSH/Cookbook/Proxies_and_Jump_Hosts.

With that host configuration now in place, we can run a test to see that we can see all our hosts with the following `ansible` command:

```
$ ansible all_servers -m ping
gateway.example.com | SUCCESS => {
    "changed": false,
    "ping": "pong"
}
...
db.example.com | SUCCESS => {
    "changed": false,
    "ping": "pong"
}
```

We have successfully connected, authenticated, and executed the module `ping` on the host. That module responds with pong if we are successful. If we are not able to get a successful connection, we will get an error similar to this:

```
mail.example.com | UNREACHABLE! => {
    "changed": false,
    "msg": "ERROR! SSH encountered an unknown error during the connection. We recommend you
re-run the command using -vvvv, which will enable SSH debugging output to help diagnose the
issue",
    "unreachable": true
}
```

Make sure you can SSH to the target host as the user executing `ansible`. You can use the –vvv option to increase the verbosity of the `ansible` command output, which should help you track down any connection issues.

Imagine we needed for some reason to restart `sshd` on all our hosts. That would be a difficult task to manage each host individually. We have only around five different hosts, but you could have thousands. With Ansible, it is the same command to do 1 as it is to do 1,000.

```
$ ansible all_servers --become -m service -a "name=sshd state=restarted"
```

Here we have provided the hosts to target (`all_servers`), we will execute our command using `sudo` on the target host (`--become`), we want to use the service module (`-m service`), and that module will take the arguments `-a "name=sshd state=restarted"`.

Each module has different arguments, and you can pass them as key/value pairs (`key=value`). They are all clearly listed in the module document link we gave earlier.

The `--become` option has further options available to it. The default `--become-method` is `sudo`, but depending on your system, you can choose `su`, `pbrun`, `pfexec`, `runas`, or `doas`. If you need to provide an authentication password with those options, you can with `--ask-become-pass`, which will prompt you for a password. If don't run operations as the root user, you can choose a different user with the `--become-user` option.

You can now issue ad hoc commands across the entire fleet of systems or target just smaller groups or individual hosts. But how do we execute several tasks? Well, that's where we use playbooks.

Ansible Playbooks

Now that we have configured Ansible and we can execute modules on our hosts, we are going to run several tasks to bring up a particular service. Ansible provides a command called `ansible-playbook`, and it is designed to connect to particular hosts and run a series of tasks. Playbooks are quite powerful, they can run in serial or parallel across your hosts, and they can delegate tasks to other hosts and wait for those to complete before moving on to the next task. In this way, you can build complex deployment playbooks.

Playbooks are YAML files. We have spoken previously about YAML files. YAML files are a markup language for data serialization that lets us describe key/values including lists and associative arrays. Playbooks can describe tasks to run on a collection of hosts or include other playbooks as well as Ansible roles. Let's take a look at one now.

```
---
- hosts: ahostgroup
  become: true
  gather_facts: true
  vars:
    - akey: avalue
  tasks:
    - name: do something
      module: module=arguments
  handlers:
  - name: a handler
    module: module=arguments
```

This is a basic playbook layout. We declare the key hosts and give it a value of the hosts we want to run this on, either a group or an individual host. We can declare other key values like `become` and `gather_facts`, which are Boolean values that can be `true` or `false`.

The `gather_facts` option will trigger an initial request to all the target hosts and gather all their available facts. If you are not using any facts in your plays, you can set this to `false`, and it will speed up your runs. If you use it, you can then use those facts in your plays as conditionals or as values in your plays.

We can list our own variables in the `vars` key as an associate array. These key/value pairs can be used by our templating engine. Tasks and handlers are similar and are essentially tasks. The handlers are used to "handle" restarts of services mainly. You can notify a handler from a task to perform a task, such as restart a service.

Let's take a look at the following playbook. In this example we are going to create a playbook that installs our backup software, Bareos. In this example, we are going to install Bareos and the MariaDB it requires on the same host. The first part of the playbook looks like this:

```
$ vi playbooks/backup.yml
- hosts: backup.example.com
  become: true
  gather_facts: true
  vars:
    url: http://download.bareos.org/bareos/release/latest/{{ ansible_distribution }}_{{
ansible_distribution_major_version }}
    bareos_db_packages: bareos-database-mysql
    sql_import: '/usr/lib/bareos/scripts/ddl/creates/mysql.sql'
```

Here we have targeted one host, `backup.example.com`. We will actions that require escalated privileges with `sudo` (so the user executing this playbook must already have `sudo` privileges on the target host). We are going to gather facts about the host and use them in our playbook.

In the vars section we have specified some variables that we will use in our playbook. These can be seen and edited easily, making ongoing management of our playbook easier. You will notice the {{ words }}. This is our templating engine syntax. It tells Ansible that the values in {{ }} are variables, either facts or like the ones we have just created.

Remembering back to when we ran the setup module with the ansible command, the output list from there contained the key values for ansible_distribution and ansible_distribution_major_version.

```
"ansible_distribution": "CentOS",
"ansible_distribution_major_version": "7",
```

On a CentOS system, when we run the play, the Jinja2 templating engines will substitute the variables like this:

```
url: http://download.bareos.org/bareos/release/latest/CentOS/7
```

VARIABLES AND CONDITIONALS

Ansible and Jinja2 can be powerful. With Jinja2 you have a great deal of power and can use Python methods on variables to add to or modify the values in your playbooks.

To show how this works, let's take this example. We have a file path like this:

```
/etc/bareos/bareos-dir.conf
```

Often you will just want to see the file name without the path. With Ansible and Jinja2, we can do this:

```
{{ /etc/bareos/bareos-dir.conf | basename }}
```

We can use Ansible to test our results. Using the ansible command with the debug module, we can print the results of our substitutions like this:

```
$ ansible -c local localhost -m debug -a "msg={{ '/etc/bareos/bareos-dir.conf'
|basename }}"
localhost | SUCCESS => {
    "msg": "bareos-dir.conf"
}
```

Here we have taken the full path, and using the pipe (|) into the Jinja2 basename filter, we can extract just the file name. Using the debug module allows you to print out the result of that substitution.

For more information on filters, see http://docs.ansible.com/ansible/playbooks_filters.html.

You can provide variables to Ansible using host group names and YAML files also. You can create a directory called group_vars in your /etc/ansible directory or local directory. In there, if you create a directory with the same name as your host group, then when you execute an Ansible command, any *.yml files will be used to look up any variables (they can also be named *.yaml or be JSON files, *.json).

See here for more information: `http://docs.ansible.com/ansible/intro_inventory.html#group-variables`.

Ansible also provides the ability to encrypt sensitive variables with the tool Ansible Vault. Ansible Vault allows for secrets, like database passwords, private SSH keys, and other sensitive data, to stored alongside the Ansible playbooks. You encrypt the secrets with a password that you can pass in on the command line when you run the `ansible` or `ansible-playbook` command.

The encrypted files are just normal YAML files and can live in your `group_vars` subdirectories. We will show more about this shortly.

See here for more details: `http://docs.ansible.com/ansible/playbooks_vault.html`.

With conditionals we can determine when to run a task based on some value. With Jinja2 you can also execute complex conditionals inside the templating engine to return a desired result or action. Ansible provides a simple `when` conditional that you will use frequently.

```
- name: install mariadb
  apt: name=mariadb-server state=latest
  when: ansible_distribution == "Ubuntu"
```

Here we are selecting to run this task when the `ansible_distribution` is equal to `Ubuntu`. When the distribution is not Ubuntu, this task will be skipped.

If we had a data structure like this:

```
our_config: {
    our_url:   'https://endpoint.example.com'

}
```

then we could use a complex conditional like this in our Jinja2 template file to make sure our URL is given the default value if it is not declared.

```
{% if our_config["our_url"] is not defined -%}
  url: {{ our_url | default('https://www.example.com') }}
{% endif %}
```

Here we are saying if the associative array `our_config` does not have the key `our_url` defined, then we should get the `default` URL of `https://www.example.com`. In this particular case, since `our_url` is defined, then the URL will be `https://endpoint.example.com`.

Defining Playbook Tasks

Let's move on to defining our playbook tasks. We have defined our hosts and our variables, and now we have to execute tasks in the order in which we want them to occur. In general, we want to make sure we have the necessary repositories installed, we download and install the right packages, and then we configure any services before finally starting them.

Let's view the tasks required to install Bareos on our backup server.

```
tasks:
- name: install epel
  yum: name=epel-release state=latest
```

In the first section we are using the yum module to install first the epel repository. We are specifying that we want the latest release. The name is optional but helps tell the story of each step. The yum and apt modules take similar arguments, but of course can be run only on systems that support either package managers. The format of a task is as follows:

```
- name: optional or description
  module_name: module_arg1=value1.... module_argx=valuex
```

We can also install repositories this way.

```
- name: add bareos
  get_url:
    url: "{{ url }}/bareos.repo"
    dest: /etc/yum.repos.d/bareos.repo
    mode: 0444
```

Of course, this can also apply to other types of files if you want. This time we are using the get_url that will make a http:// connection, download the URI, and copy the contents to the /etc/yum.repos.d/ bareos.repo file. The contents, evidently, are the Bareos repository, and we have used the url variable listed in our variable section and combined that with /bareos.repo to complete the URI. We could use the yum_repository to create the repository for us using the details of the URI (you can add Apt repositories in a similar way too).

For more on managing packages and repositories, see http://docs.ansible.com/ansible/list_of_packaging_modules.html.

```
- name: install pip
  yum: name={{ item }} state=latest update_cache=yes
  with_items:
    - python-pip
    - python-devel
- name: install mariadb
  yum: name={{ item }} state=latest
  with_items:
    - mariadb-devel
    - mariadb-server
  notify: mariadb_restarted
```

This next tasks are similar to the first but use a loop. We are saying we want to use the yum module to install some packages. To install the packages, we could write out a task for each package saying install the latest package and make sure we have an up-to-date repository cache (update_cache=yes). But since this is repetitive, we will use a loop.

We say, loop through the items listed in the with_items: list and install them. Ansible will replace {{ item }} with those packages listed for us.

You can read more on loops here: http://docs.ansible.com/ansible/playbooks_loops.html.

You will also notice that there is a notify: mariadb_restarted call to a handler. Handlers are just tasks that are run at the end of a block of playbook tasks. What this says is to tell the handler named mariadb_restarted to execute the task associated with it if these packages change. This does not immediately start the database, however, and we will do that shortly. The actual mariadb_restarted handler will be described a little later too.

```
- name: install pre-reqs
  pip: name=mysql state=latest
```

In this task we are again installing a Pip package called mysql. Pip is a package manager for Python modules and takes similar arguments to both the apt and yum modules. Next we will start the database.

```
- name: start db service
  service: name=mariadb enabled=yes state=started
```

The previous is an example of using the service module to start (started) the database. Other service states are stopped, restarted, and reloaded. The enabled here indicates that we would like this service started on boot. We require this step to run prior the create db step coming up.

Next we will continue installing the Bareos packages.

```
- name: install bareos
  yum: name={{ item }} state=installed
  with_items:
    - bareos-database-mysql
    - bareos-client
    - bareos-director
    - bareos-storage
    - bareos-storage-glusterfs
    - bareos-bconsole
    - bareos-filedaemon
```

Here we are installing the Bareos packages and again using the with_items loop to avoid repetition. The bareos-database-mysql package will create the file in our {{ sql_import }} variable that we use in the next step to create our database.

```
- name: create db
  mysql_db: login_user=root name=bareos state=import target={{ sql_import }}

- name: create db user bareos
  mysql_user: login_user=root name=bareos password={{ backup_database_password }}
encrypted=yes priv=bareos.*:ALL state=present
```

Next we will create the database for Bareos using the mysql_db module. We can import the database structure, and this is the purpose of the state=import and target={{ sql_import }}. We are using the default root user access in this instance, but we could also use a user/password combination in this module to gain access to the database. The sql_import variable is defined at the top of our playbook and is the import SQL script provided by the Bareos installation.

We go on to create the Bareos user on the MariaDB database. We provide the user, password, password type, and privileges for the user. The state is present, meaning we want to create the user; if we want to remove the user, we can choose absent.

The password variable (password={{ backup_database_password }}) we use here is interesting. This is a sensitive secret, so we need to make sure that we do not have it in plain text anywhere, but Ansible still needs access to it. With Ansible Vault we can provide that protection.

We have generated a strong password using a password generator and stored that successfully. Then, using an existing MySQL install, we created a mysql password hash.

```
SELECT PASSWORD('strongpasswordstring');
+-----------------------------------------------------------+
| password('strongpasswordstring')                          |
+-----------------------------------------------------------+
| *35D93ADBD68F80D63FF0D744BA55CF920B2A45BD |
+-----------------------------------------------------------+
```

We then created a playbooks/group_vars/dbs directory and a vars.yml file and vault.yml file. In the vars.yml file, we will add the following:

```
backup_database_password: "{{ vault_backup_database_password }}"
```

Then in the vault.yml file, we will add our hashed MySQL password like this:

```
vault_backup_database_password: '*35D93ADBD68F80D63FF0D744BA55CF920B2A45BD'
```

The reason we do this is because once we encrypt this file, we will have no way of seeing the keys that we are using. By setting the plain-text variable (backup_database_password) to look at the encrypted variable (vault_backup_database_password), we make it easier for people following us to know how these variables are stored. So to be clear, when the ansible commands look for the backup_database_password, it will then do a lookup for the vault_backup_database_password and return that value.

We will now encrypt this file with the ansible-vault command.

```
$ ansible-vault encrypt playbooks/group_vars/dbs/vault.yml
```

We are asked to create and enter a password, which we will also store securely.

Next we have the configuration files. We have created a playbooks/files directory, and in there we have added our bareos-*.conf files.

```
- name: add bareos-dir.conf
  copy: src=files/bareos-dir.conf dest=/etc/bareos/bareos-dir.conf owner=bareos
  group=bareos mode=0640

- name: add bareos-sd.conf
  copy: src=files/bareos-sd.conf dest=/etc/bareos/bareos-sd.conf owner=bareos group=bareos
  mode=0640

- name: add bareos-fd.conf
  copy: src=files/bareos-fd.conf dest=/etc/bareos/bareos-fd.conf owner=bareos group=bareos
  mode=0640

- name: add bconsole.conf
  copy: src=files/bconsole.conf dest=/etc/bareos/bconsole.conf owner=root group=bareos
  mode=0640
```

We use the copy module to copy local files to the server and place them in the appropriate destination file. The copy module supports assigning owner, group, and mode permissions to the file we create. The path of src is relative to the playbooks directory.

In this simple playbook, we are not taking advantage of the templating engine that comes with Ansible. If you remember to Chapter 14 where we set up Bareos, we needed to add clients and passwords to our Bareos configuration files. We could use templating to create these values and make the coordination of setting up these files easier.

A template is like a file, but it is parsed by the templating engine to find and replace variables. So, values like the following:

```
$ vi playbooks/files/bareos-fd.conf
Client {
  Name = bareos-fd
  Description = "Client resource of the Director itself."
  Address = localhost
  Password = "YVcb9CkOMvIXpZkZCM8wBV1qyEi1FD6kJjHUrk+39xun"                # password for
FileDaemon
}
```

can be replaced with the following:

```
$ vi playbooks/templates/backup_bareos_fd.conf.j2
Client {
  Name = bareos-fd
  Description = "Client resource of the Director itself."
  Address = localhost
  Password = "{{ bareos_fd_dir_password }}"
}
```

The template files generally have the .j2 suffix to indicate the Jinja2 template engine. We would store that password value in our Ansible Vault–encrypted file, like we did the database password. The template module syntax is similar to the copy module. For more information on templating, please see http://docs. ansible.com/ansible/template_module.html.

There are other ways we can add values into files as well. We can search and replace lines and replace blocks of marked text in a file and more. More information on the different types of file modules can be found here: http://docs.ansible.com/ansible/list_of_files_modules.html.

```
  - name: create backup directory
    file: path=/data/backups/FileStorage state=directory owner=bareos group=bareos mode=0750
```

Next we create the directory to store our backups using the file module. This directory path is on the target host, and the state can be absent to remove the file or directory, file to create a file, link to create a symlink, directory to create a directory, touch to create an empty file, and hard for creating hardlinks.

Lastly we have our handler. As we said, this will run at the end of the block of tasks in the playbook.

```
  handlers:
  - name: mariadb_restart
    service: name=mariadb state=restarted
```

So now if we run our playbook and we have a package change for our database, our database will automatically be restarted at the end of the playbook. You could add handlers for the Bareos component services as well.

■ **Caution** With databases, automatically upgrading and restarting your database version may not be a sensible thing to do as package version updates can cause unpredictable behavior in your databases, which can be disastrous!

Running the Playbook

Running the playbook is fairly easy from this point. Ansible uses the `ansible-playbook` command to execute plays. It has similar command options to the `ansible` command. Let's take a look at them now; see Table 19-2.

Table 19-2. *ansible-playbook Options*

`-i`	Path to the inventory file.
`--ask-become-pass`	Prompt for the remote host password for escalation of privileges.
`--list-hosts`	Shows you the hosts that your playbook will be acting upon.
`--list-tags`	Lists tags that are available in your playbook.
`--list-tasks`	Shows tasks that will be executed in your playbook.
`--module-path=`	Adds a different module path.
`-v -vv -vvv`	Increases verbosity for debugging.
`--syntax-check`	Validates that the playbook syntax is correct.
`--user`	Remote user to sign in as.
`--private-key=`	Private SSH key of user.
`--connection=`	Choose the connection type (`paramiko`, `ssh`, `winrm`, `local`); defaults to smart.
`--extra-vars=`	You can add key/value pairs to the playbook at runtime as well as pass in any files containing variables (including `ansible-vault` files).
`--start-at-task=`	Start at this task.
`--step`	Step through each task asking for confirmation before proceeding to the next.
`--tags`	Run only tasks with these tags.
`--skip-tags`	Don't run these tagged tasks.

To make sure we are targeting the right hosts when we execute this playbook, let's issue the following:

```
$ sudo ansible-playbook --list-hosts -b playbooks/backup.yml
ERROR! Decryption failed
```

We have issued the --list-hosts, but we have a decryption failed message. That is because we have the encrypted Ansible Vault and we could not read it. Let's add the prompt to add to the password.

```
$ sudo ansible-playbook --list-hosts --ask-vault-pass -b playbooks/backup.yml
Vault password:

playbook: playbooks/backup.yml

  play #1 (backup.example.com):            TAGS: []
    pattern: [u'backup.example.com']
    hosts (1):
      backup.example.com
```

This should come as no surprise as we are targeting this host in the host: section of our playbook. If we were using a group or a regular expression to define our host, this listing would be more immediately useful.

There is still one thing we need to do before we can run our playbook command, and this is not obvious. We have created our database secrets in a group vars directory called dbs, which means that the backup.example.com host must be a member of that host group. If we don't add it, we will see an error like this when we run our playbook.

```
TASK [create db user bareos] ************************************************
fatal: [backup.example.com]: FAILED! => {"failed": true, "msg": "ERROR! 'backup_database_
password' is undefined"}
```

So, we will add backup.example.com to the [dbs] host group in the /etc/ansible/hosts file.

```
[dbs]
db.example.com ansible_user=vagrant
backup.example.com
```

A host can be part of more than one group, and this will enable Ansible to see the vars for that host group. Now we are ready to run the playbook.

```
$ sudo ansible-playbook  --ask-vault-pass -b playbooks/backup.yml
Vault password:

PLAY **********************************************************************

TASK [setup] **************************************************************
ok: [backup.example.com]

TASK [install epel] ******************************************************
changed: [backup.example.com]

TASK [install pip] *******************************************************
changed: [backup.example.com] => (item=[u'python-pip', u'python-devel'])

TASK [add bareos] ********************************************************
changed: [backup.example.com]
```

```
TASK [install mariadb] ********************************************************
changed: [backup.example.com] => (item=[u'mariadb-devel', u'mariadb-server'])

TASK [install pre-reqs] ********************************************************
changed: [backup.example.com]

TASK [start db service] ********************************************************
changed: [backup.example.com]

TASK [install bareos] *********************************************************
changed: [backup.example.com] => (item=[u'bareos-client', u'bareos-director', u'bareos-
storage', u'bareos-storage-glusterfs', u'bareos-bconsole', u'bareos-filedaemon'])

TASK [create db] *************************************************************
changed: [backup.example.com]

TASK [create db user bareos] **************************************************
changed: [backup.example.com]

TASK [install bareos-database-mysql CentOS] ***********************************
changed: [backup.example.com]

TASK [add bareos-dir.conf] ****************************************************
changed: [backup.example.com]

TASK [add bareos-sd.conf] *****************************************************
changed: [backup.example.com]

TASK [add bareos-fd.conf] *****************************************************
changed: [backup.example.com]

TASK [add bconsole.conf] ******************************************************
changed: [backup.example.com]

TASK [create backup directory] ***********************************************
ok: [backup.example.com]

PLAY RECAP ******************************************************************
backup.example.com          : ok=2    changed=14   unreachable=0    failed=0
```

We have successfully run our playbook. When a task executes and makes a change to your system, it will be changed and be added to the final recap line. Where there was no need to execute the task, it will be ok and added to the recap line. If there are no failed tasks, then we consider this a success.

Serverspec Testing

We can now automate the building of our hosts, but how do we know if we make a change to one of our tasks that it doesn't unintentionally break some other important configuration? If we have some basic compliance requirements, how do we know that we are still meeting those obligations with each new build? Well, just like normal code, we can write tests that give us assurance that the hosts we build meet the defined requirements specified in our tests.

Both Ansible and Puppet lend themselves to being tested. We are going to show you how to use a tool called ServerSpec to help your testing, but you can use other testing frameworks in any of the scripting languages to help test your code. In fact, you can use Test Driven Development (TDD) practices to first write your tests that define success and failure scenarios and then write your Ansible or Puppet code to pass those tests.

Serverspec is written in Ruby and uses the RSpec framework run the tests. While we will not attempt to explain RSpec in any depth, you can visit a number of tutorial sites online. The main RSpec web site is here: http://rspec.info/.

If you don't like to install Ruby and RSpec, you can use this alternative Python-based framework, which is designed to be the Python equivalent of Serverspec; see https://testinfra.readthedocs.io/en/latest/. If you were using Ansible, then this might be the better option for you. We are going to test both Puppet and Ansible side by side, so we will choose Serverspec.

Installing Serverspec

In this testing scenario, we have checked out a particular Git repository that will have our configuration management files we want to test. We are going to use Vagrant to help bring up and test how our configurations are applied to our hosts. We use Serverspec to start our Vagrant hosts if they are not started, apply our provisioning instructions, and then test the results of those instructions.

■ **Note**   We explained Git and how to set up Vagrant in Chapter 3, so now would be a good time to revisit that chapter if you have forgotten.

Let's assume we have a Git repository already created, and we will clone to our local system.

```
$ git clone git@some.git.hosting:/ouruser/ourrepo.git
$ cd ourrepo
```

In this checkout, we already have a Vagrantfile that contains the following:

```
$ vi Vagrantfile
Vagrant.configure(2) do |config|
  config.vm.provider "virtualbox" do |vb|
    vb.memory = "1024"
  end

  config.vm.define "ansible" do |xenial|
    xenial.vm.box = "ubuntu/xenial64"
    xenial.vm.hostname = "ansible"
    xenial.vm.provision :shell do |shell|
      shell.path = "bootscript.sh"
    end
    xenial.vm.provision :ansible do |ansible|
      ansible.playbook = 'ansible/playbooks/ansible.yml'
    end
  end
```

```
  config.vm.define "puppet" do |centos|
    centos.vm.box = "centos/7"
    centos.vm.hostname = "puppet"
    centos.vm.provision :shell do |shell|
      shell.path = "bootscript.sh"
    end
    centos.vm.provision "puppet"
  end
end
```

This Vagrantfile will allow us to run up a Xenial Ubuntu host and a CentOS 7 host. The Xenial host will apply an Ansible playbook while the CentOS host will run a Puppet apply. We will create the provisioning files shortly. We will then test that both hosts have the same configuration, which will be a HTTPD server listening on port 80.

■ **Tip**   Remember that using Vagrant is a great way to share your configuration environments because you can share the same code to build your hosts.

Now let's talk about Serverspec. Serverspec is available as a Ruby gem. You can use another Ruby gem called Bundler (http://bundler.io/) to keep track of your installed gems for a particular application in a file called a Gemfile. We are going to use that to install our required gems as we go along. This also helps us pin particular version of gems to our git commits and helps us track changes to the gem release versions we are using.

```
$ sudo yum install -y ruby rubygems && gem install bundler --no-ri --no-rdoc
```

Here we are using a CentOS host and install the ruby and rubygems packages and then install into the local account the gem bundler (without the associated docs and help for a faster install).

With the Bundler gem installed, we will now create a gem file with the following in our repository directory like so:

```
$ vi Gemfile
source 'https://rubygems.org'

gem 'serverspec'
```

Here we have added the Serverspec gem to the gemfile. The source statement is where we will be downloading the gem from, which is the public rubygems.org server where people publish their Ruby gems.

Now we can use the bundle command to install the gem locally.

```
$ bundle install --path vendor/cache
Fetching gem metadata from https://rubygems.org/.......
Fetching version metadata from https://rubygems.org/.
Resolving dependencies...
Installing diff-lcs 1.2.5
Installing multi_json 1.12.1
Installing net-ssh 3.2.0
...
```

This will install the serverspec gem and any serverspec gem requirements. We are now ready to initialize serverspec for our currently checked-out repository, which is the equivalent of running a setup script. We do that with the serverspec-init command.

```
$ serverspec-init
Select OS type:

  1) UN*X
  2) Windows

Select number: 1
```

We are asked what type of OS we are going to test; here we choose 1) UN*X.

```
Select a backend type:


  1) SSH
  2) Exec (local)

Select number: 1
```

We can now choose how we are going to access the host: either run serverspec commands locally or use SSH to sign into a host and run commands from inside that host. We are going to use SSH, so choose 1.

```
Vagrant instance y/n: y
Auto-configure Vagrant from Vagrantfile? y/n: y
0) ansible
1) puppet
Choose a VM from the Vagrantfile: 0
 + spec/
 + spec/ansible/
 + spec/ansible/sample_spec.rb
 + spec/spec_helper.rb
```

Serverspec has detected the Vagrantfile and now wants to know whether we want to configure one of those hosts automatically for us. Choosing either puppet or ansible is fine here, so we will use the copy command to add the other.

We have now set up Serverspec. There is a spec directory that has been created, and Serverspec is managed via the spec/spec_helper.rb file. Serverspec will look for a directory in the spec directory that matches a host declared in the Vagrantfile and run any tests it finds in those directories that end in *_spec.rb. So, we can now copy the spec/ansible directory to spec/puppet, and now both hosts will be tested.

```
$ cp -r spec/ansible spec/puppet
```

If we take a look at the sample_spec.rb file, it will show us our Serverspec tests.

```
require 'spec_helper'


describe package('httpd'), :if => os[:family] == 'redhat' do
  it { should be_installed }
end

describe package('apache2'), :if => os[:family] == 'ubuntu' do
  it { should be_installed }
end

describe service('httpd'), :if => os[:family] == 'redhat' do
  it { should be_enabled }
  it { should be_running }
end

describe service('apache2'), :if => os[:family] == 'ubuntu' do
  it { should be_enabled }
  it { should be_running }
end

describe service('org.apache.httpd'), :if => os[:family] == 'darwin' do
  it { should be_enabled }
  it { should be_running }
end

describe port(80) do
  it { should be_listening }
end
```

The _spec.rb file should be easily read, which is one of the design goals of RSpec to make testing clear. The first line is Ruby; the require is similar to a Python import statement and is just making the spec_helper available to us.

The next lines read like this. We want to describe a package called httpd. If we are on a redhat family host, that package should be installed. Now you can read the others, and they are similar and describe what we expect to find when we run Serverspec. Serverspec will take these plain descriptions and handle how it will validate our tests.

We will remove the second last test describing a Darwin family operating system (Mac OS), but the rest of the tests suit our purpose well.

Running Tests

Let's start by running our tests; we can then see the work we need to do to get our tests to pass. We do this using some tools that came when we installed Serverspec.

```
$ rake spec:ansible

Package "apache2"
  should be installed (FAILED - 1)

Service "apache2"
  should be enabled (FAILED - 2)
  should be running (FAILED - 3)

Port "80"
  should be listening (FAILED - 4)
```

To run our tests, we are going to execute what's called a rake task. rake is a Ruby version of the make utility; you can see more about it here: https://github.com/ruby/rake. The task we are going to run is called spec:ansible, and that will fire up the Ansible Vagrant host and then run the Serverspec tests.

You can see why the tests failed in the Failures: section.

```
Failures:

  1) Package "httpd" should be installed
     On host `puppet'
     Failure/Error: it { should be_installed }
       expected Package "httpd" to be installed
       sudo -p 'Password: ' /bin/sh -c rpm\ -q\ httpd
       package httpd is not installed

     # ./spec/puppet/sample_spec.rb:4:in `block (2 levels) in <top (required)>'
```

You can see that Serverspec tried to run the rpm -q httpd command but could not find httpd installed. This is as expected as we haven't installed it yet. We are now going to write the Ansible code to install it and have it provisioned on our Vagrant host.

```
$ vi ansible/playbooks/ansible.yml
---
- hosts: all
  gather_facts: true
  become: true
  tasks:
  - name: install apache2
    apt: name=apache2 state=latest
```

We will do the same for Puppet now too.

```
$ vi manifests/site.pp
class httpd {

  package {'httpd': ensure => 'latest' }

}

include httpd
```

We are going to provision our hosts now using the vagrant provision command. Let's run the Serverspec test again.

```
$ rake spec
Package "apache2"
  should be installed

Service "apache2"
  should be enabled
  should be running

Port "80"
  should be listening

Finished in 0.06987 seconds (files took 11.03 seconds to load)
4 examples, 0 failures
...
Package "httpd"
  should be installed

Service "httpd"
  should be enabled (FAILED - 1)
  should be running (FAILED - 2)

Port "80"
  should be listening (FAILED - 3)
```

Running rake spec will run the tests over any of the hosts in our spec/ folder. Our tests for the Ansible host is already all green. That is because on Ubuntu when you install service packages they can be started automatically. With CentOS, they won't do this until they are told. Let's make the CentOS host green.

```
$ vi manifests/site.pp
class httpd {

  package {'httpd': ensure => 'latest' }
  service { 'httpd': enable => true, ensure => true }

}

include httpd
```

Running the provision and the rake spec again, and we can now see we are green in both Ansible and Puppet.

```
Package "apache2"
  should be installed

Service "apache2"
  should be enabled
  should be running

Port "80"
  should be listening

Finished in 0.06992 seconds (files took 8.41 seconds to load)
4 examples, 0 failures

-----
Package "httpd"
  should be installed

Service "httpd"
  should be enabled
  should be running

Port "80"
  should be listening

Finished in 0.11897 seconds (files took 7.98 seconds to load)
4 examples, 0 failures
```

There are many more tests that you can run, and these were very basic, but we now get the idea how helpful this can be when you are making lots of changes to systems. You should now hook these tests up to your Jenkins or CI testing infrastructure and get it to run prior to any commit to your master VCS branch.

There is a tutorial for Serverspec here: http://serverspec.org/tutorial.html.

You can see more resource types to test here: http://serverspec.org/resource_types.html.

Summary

In this chapter, we introduced you to some simple provisioning tools that make the process of building and installing your hosts quick and easy. You learned how to do the following:

- Install and configure Cobbler

- Automatically boot a host with a chosen operating system

- Install a chosen operating system and automatically answer the installation questions

We also introduced a configuration management tool, Puppet, that will help you consistently and accurately manage your environment. You learned how to do the following:

- Install Puppet

- Configure Puppet

- Use Puppet to manage the configuration of your hosts

- Use the more advanced features of Puppet

- Install and configure Ansible

- Run Ansible playbooks

- Install and run Serverspec to test your configurations

Index

© Dennis Matotek, James Turnbull and Peter Lieverdink 2017

D. Matotek et al., *Pro Linux System Administration*, DOI 10.1007/978-1-4842-2008-5

Get the eBook for only $4.99!

Why limit yourself?

Now you can take the weightless companion with you wherever you go and access your content on your PC, phone, tablet, or reader.

Since you've purchased this print book, we are happy to offer you the eBook for just $4.99.

Convenient and fully searchable, the PDF version enables you to easily find and copy code—or perform examples by quickly toggling between instructions and applications.

To learn more, go to http://www.apress.com/us/shop/companion or contact support@apress.com.